T0134766

Lecture Notes in Computer Science　11219

Commenced Publication in 1973
Founding and Former Series Editors:
Gerhard Goos, Juris Hartmanis, and Jan van Leeuwen

More information about this series at http://www.springer.com/series/7412

Vittorio Ferrari · Martial Hebert
Cristian Sminchisescu · Yair Weiss (Eds.)

Computer Vision – ECCV 2018

15th European Conference
Munich, Germany, September 8–14, 2018
Proceedings, Part XV

 Springer

Editors
Vittorio Ferrari
Google Research
Zurich
Switzerland

Martial Hebert
Carnegie Mellon University
Pittsburgh, PA
USA

Cristian Sminchisescu
Google Research
Zurich
Switzerland

Yair Weiss
Hebrew University of Jerusalem
Jerusalem
Israel

ISSN 0302-9743   ISSN 1611-3349   (electronic)
Lecture Notes in Computer Science
ISBN 978-3-030-01266-3   ISBN 978-3-030-01267-0   (eBook)
https://doi.org/10.1007/978-3-030-01267-0

Library of Congress Control Number: 2018955489

LNCS Sublibrary: SL6 – Image Processing, Computer Vision, Pattern Recognition, and Graphics

This Springer imprint is published by the registered company Springer Nature Switzerland AG
The registered company address is: Gewerbestrasse 11, 6330 Cham, Switzerland

Foreword

It was our great pleasure to host the European Conference on Computer Vision 2018 in Munich, Germany. This constituted by far the largest ECCV event ever. With close to 2,900 registered participants and another 600 on the waiting list one month before the conference, participation more than doubled since the last ECCV in Amsterdam. We believe that this is due to a dramatic growth of the computer vision community combined with the popularity of Munich as a major European hub of culture, science, and industry. The conference took place in the heart of Munich in the concert hall Gasteig with workshops and tutorials held at the downtown campus of the Technical University of Munich.

One of the major innovations for ECCV 2018 was the free perpetual availability of all conference and workshop papers, which is often referred to as open access. We note that this is not precisely the same use of the term as in the Budapest declaration. Since 2013, CVPR and ICCV have had their papers hosted by the Computer Vision Foundation (CVF), in parallel with the IEEE Xplore version. This has proved highly beneficial to the computer vision community.

We are delighted to announce that for ECCV 2018 a very similar arrangement was put in place with the cooperation of Springer. In particular, the author's final version will be freely available in perpetuity on a CVF page, while SpringerLink will continue to host a version with further improvements, such as activating reference links and including video. We believe that this will give readers the best of both worlds; researchers who are focused on the technical content will have a freely available version in an easily accessible place, while subscribers to SpringerLink will continue to have the additional benefits that this provides. We thank Alfred Hofmann from Springer for helping to negotiate this agreement, which we expect will continue for future versions of ECCV.

September 2018

Horst Bischof
Daniel Cremers
Bernt Schiele
Ramin Zabih

Organization

General Chairs

Horst Bischof   Graz University of Technology, Austria
Daniel Cremers   Technical University of Munich, Germany
Bernt Schiele   Saarland University, Max Planck Institute for Informatics, Germany
Ramin Zabih   CornellNYCTech, USA

Program Committee Co-chairs

Vittorio Ferrari   University of Edinburgh, UK
Martial Hebert   Carnegie Mellon University, USA
Cristian Sminchisescu   Lund University, Sweden
Yair Weiss   Hebrew University, Israel

Local Arrangements Chairs

Björn Menze   Technical University of Munich, Germany
Matthias Niessner   Technical University of Munich, Germany

Workshop Chairs

Stefan Roth   TU Darmstadt, Germany
Laura Leal-Taixé   Technical University of Munich, Germany

Tutorial Chairs

Michael Bronstein   Università della Svizzera Italiana, Switzerland
Laura Leal-Taixé   Technical University of Munich, Germany

Website Chair

Friedrich Fraundorfer   Graz University of Technology, Austria

Demo Chairs

Federico Tombari   Technical University of Munich, Germany
Joerg Stueckler   Technical University of Munich, Germany

Publicity Chair

Giovanni Maria   University of Catania, Italy
  Farinella

Industrial Liaison Chairs

Florent Perronnin   Naver Labs, France
Yunchao Gong   Snap, USA
Helmut Grabner   Logitech, Switzerland

Finance Chair

Gerard Medioni   Amazon, University of Southern California, USA

Publication Chairs

Albert Ali Salah   Boğaziçi University, Turkey
Hamdi Dibeklioğlu   Bilkent University, Turkey

Area Chairs

Kalle Åström   Lund University, Sweden
Zeynep Akata   University of Amsterdam, The Netherlands
Joao Barreto   University of Coimbra, Portugal
Ronen Basri   Weizmann Institute of Science, Israel
Dhruv Batra   Georgia Tech and Facebook AI Research, USA
Serge Belongie   Cornell University, USA
Rodrigo Benenson   Google, Switzerland
Hakan Bilen   University of Edinburgh, UK
Matthew Blaschko   KU Leuven, Belgium
Edmond Boyer   Inria, France
Gabriel Brostow   University College London, UK
Thomas Brox   University of Freiburg, Germany
Marcus Brubaker   York University, Canada
Barbara Caputo   Politecnico di Torino and the Italian Institute
                        of Technology, Italy
Tim Cootes   University of Manchester, UK
Trevor Darrell   University of California, Berkeley, USA
Larry Davis   University of Maryland at College Park, USA
Andrew Davison   Imperial College London, UK
Fernando de la Torre Carnegie Mellon University, USA
Irfan Essa   GeorgiaTech, USA
Ali Farhadi   University of Washington, USA
Paolo Favaro   University of Bern, Switzerland
Michael Felsberg   Linköping University, Sweden

Sanja Fidler	University of Toronto, Canada
Andrew Fitzgibbon	Microsoft, Cambridge, UK
David Forsyth	University of Illinois at Urbana-Champaign, USA
Charless Fowlkes	University of California, Irvine, USA
Bill Freeman	MIT, USA
Mario Fritz	MPII, Germany
Jürgen Gall	University of Bonn, Germany
Dariu Gavrila	TU Delft, The Netherlands
Andreas Geiger	MPI-IS and University of Tübingen, Germany
Theo Gevers	University of Amsterdam, The Netherlands
Ross Girshick	Facebook AI Research, USA
Kristen Grauman	Facebook AI Research and UT Austin, USA
Abhinav Gupta	Carnegie Mellon University, USA
Kaiming He	Facebook AI Research, USA
Martial Hebert	Carnegie Mellon University, USA
Anders Heyden	Lund University, Sweden
Timothy Hospedales	University of Edinburgh, UK
Michal Irani	Weizmann Institute of Science, Israel
Phillip Isola	University of California, Berkeley, USA
Hervé Jégou	Facebook AI Research, France
David Jacobs	University of Maryland, College Park, USA
Allan Jepson	University of Toronto, Canada
Jiaya Jia	Chinese University of Hong Kong, SAR China
Fredrik Kahl	Chalmers University, USA
Hedvig Kjellström	KTH Royal Institute of Technology, Sweden
Iasonas Kokkinos	University College London and Facebook, UK
Vladlen Koltun	Intel Labs, USA
Philipp Krähenbühl	UT Austin, USA
M. Pawan Kumar	University of Oxford, UK
Kyros Kutulakos	University of Toronto, Canada
In Kweon	KAIST, South Korea
Ivan Laptev	Inria, France
Svetlana Lazebnik	University of Illinois at Urbana-Champaign, USA
Laura Leal-Taixé	Technical University of Munich, Germany
Erik Learned-Miller	University of Massachusetts, Amherst, USA
Kyoung Mu Lee	Seoul National University, South Korea
Bastian Leibe	RWTH Aachen University, Germany
Aleš Leonardis	University of Birmingham, UK
Vincent Lepetit	University of Bordeaux, France and Graz University of Technology, Austria
Fuxin Li	Oregon State University, USA
Dahua Lin	Chinese University of Hong Kong, SAR China
Jim Little	University of British Columbia, Canada
Ce Liu	Google, USA
Chen Change Loy	Nanyang Technological University, Singapore
Jiri Matas	Czech Technical University in Prague, Czechia

Yasuyuki Matsushita	Osaka University, Japan
Dimitris Metaxas	Rutgers University, USA
Greg Mori	Simon Fraser University, Canada
Vittorio Murino	Istituto Italiano di Tecnologia, Italy
Richard Newcombe	Oculus Research, USA
Minh Hoai Nguyen	Stony Brook University, USA
Sebastian Nowozin	Microsoft Research Cambridge, UK
Aude Oliva	MIT, USA
Bjorn Ommer	Heidelberg University, Germany
Tomas Pajdla	Czech Technical University in Prague, Czechia
Maja Pantic	Imperial College London and Samsung AI Research Centre Cambridge, UK
Caroline Pantofaru	Google, USA
Devi Parikh	Georgia Tech and Facebook AI Research, USA
Sylvain Paris	Adobe Research, USA
Vladimir Pavlovic	Rutgers University, USA
Marcello Pelillo	University of Venice, Italy
Patrick Pérez	Valeo, France
Robert Pless	George Washington University, USA
Thomas Pock	Graz University of Technology, Austria
Jean Ponce	Inria, France
Gerard Pons-Moll	MPII, Saarland Informatics Campus, Germany
Long Quan	Hong Kong University of Science and Technology, SAR China
Stefan Roth	TU Darmstadt, Germany
Carsten Rother	University of Heidelberg, Germany
Bryan Russell	Adobe Research, USA
Kate Saenko	Boston University, USA
Mathieu Salzmann	EPFL, Switzerland
Dimitris Samaras	Stony Brook University, USA
Yoichi Sato	University of Tokyo, Japan
Silvio Savarese	Stanford University, USA
Konrad Schindler	ETH Zurich, Switzerland
Cordelia Schmid	Inria, France and Google, France
Nicu Sebe	University of Trento, Italy
Fei Sha	University of Southern California, USA
Greg Shakhnarovich	TTI Chicago, USA
Jianbo Shi	University of Pennsylvania, USA
Abhinav Shrivastava	UMD and Google, USA
Yan Shuicheng	National University of Singapore, Singapore
Leonid Sigal	University of British Columbia, Canada
Josef Sivic	Czech Technical University in Prague, Czechia
Arnold Smeulders	University of Amsterdam, The Netherlands
Deqing Sun	NVIDIA, USA
Antonio Torralba	MIT, USA
Zhuowen Tu	University of California, San Diego, USA

Tinne Tuytelaars	KU Leuven, Belgium
Jasper Uijlings	Google, Switzerland
Joost van de Weijer	Computer Vision Center, Spain
Nuno Vasconcelos	University of California, San Diego, USA
Andrea Vedaldi	University of Oxford, UK
Olga Veksler	University of Western Ontario, Canada
Jakob Verbeek	Inria, France
Rene Vidal	Johns Hopkins University, USA
Daphna Weinshall	Hebrew University, Israel
Chris Williams	University of Edinburgh, UK
Lior Wolf	Tel Aviv University, Israel
Ming-Hsuan Yang	University of California at Merced, USA
Todd Zickler	Harvard University, USA
Andrew Zisserman	University of Oxford, UK

Technical Program Committee

Hassan Abu Alhaija	Peter Anderson	Arunava Banerjee
Radhakrishna Achanta	Juan Andrade-Cetto	Atsuhiko Banno
Hanno Ackermann	Mykhaylo Andriluka	Aayush Bansal
Ehsan Adeli	Anelia Angelova	Yingze Bao
Lourdes Agapito	Michel Antunes	Md Jawadul Bappy
Aishwarya Agrawal	Pablo Arbelaez	Pierre Baqué
Antonio Agudo	Vasileios Argyriou	Dániel Baráth
Eirikur Agustsson	Chetan Arora	Adrian Barbu
Karim Ahmed	Federica Arrigoni	Kobus Barnard
Byeongjoo Ahn	Vassilis Athitsos	Nick Barnes
Unaiza Ahsan	Mathieu Aubry	Francisco Barranco
Emre Akbaş	Shai Avidan	Adrien Bartoli
Eren Aksoy	Yannis Avrithis	E. Bayro-Corrochano
Yağız Aksoy	Samaneh Azadi	Paul Beardlsey
Alexandre Alahi	Hossein Azizpour	Vasileios Belagiannis
Jean-Baptiste Alayrac	Artem Babenko	Sean Bell
Samuel Albanie	Timur Bagautdinov	Ismail Ben
Cenek Albl	Andrew Bagdanov	Boulbaba Ben Amor
Saad Ali	Hessam Bagherinezhad	Gil Ben-Artzi
Rahaf Aljundi	Yuval Bahat	Ohad Ben-Shahar
Jose M. Alvarez	Min Bai	Abhijit Bendale
Humam Alwassel	Qinxun Bai	Rodrigo Benenson
Toshiyuki Amano	Song Bai	Fabian Benitez-Quiroz
Mitsuru Ambai	Xiang Bai	Fethallah Benmansour
Mohamed Amer	Peter Bajcsy	Ryad Benosman
Senjian An	Amr Bakry	Filippo Bergamasco
Cosmin Ancuti	Kavita Bala	David Bermudez

Jesus Bermudez-Cameo
Leonard Berrada
Gedas Bertasius
Ross Beveridge
Lucas Beyer
Bir Bhanu
S. Bhattacharya
Binod Bhattarai
Arnav Bhavsar
Simone Bianco
Adel Bibi
Pia Bideau
Josef Bigun
Arijit Biswas
Soma Biswas
Marten Bjoerkman
Volker Blanz
Vishnu Boddeti
Piotr Bojanowski
Terrance Boult
Yuri Boykov
Hakan Boyraz
Eric Brachmann
Samarth Brahmbhatt
Mathieu Bredif
Francois Bremond
Michael Brown
Luc Brun
Shyamal Buch
Pradeep Buddharaju
Aurelie Bugeau
Rudy Bunel
Xavier Burgos Artizzu
Darius Burschka
Andrei Bursuc
Zoya Bylinskii
Fabian Caba
Daniel Cabrini Hauagge
Cesar Cadena Lerma
Holger Caesar
Jianfei Cai
Junjie Cai
Zhaowei Cai
Simone Calderara
Neill Campbell
Octavia Camps

Xun Cao
Yanshuai Cao
Joao Carreira
Dan Casas
Daniel Castro
Jan Cech
M. Emre Celebi
Duygu Ceylan
Menglei Chai
Ayan Chakrabarti
Rudrasis Chakraborty
Shayok Chakraborty
Tat-Jen Cham
Antonin Chambolle
Antoni Chan
Sharat Chandran
Hyun Sung Chang
Ju Yong Chang
Xiaojun Chang
Soravit Changpinyo
Wei-Lun Chao
Yu-Wei Chao
Visesh Chari
Rizwan Chaudhry
Siddhartha Chaudhuri
Rama Chellappa
Chao Chen
Chen Chen
Cheng Chen
Chu-Song Chen
Guang Chen
Hsin-I Chen
Hwann-Tzong Chen
Kai Chen
Kan Chen
Kevin Chen
Liang-Chieh Chen
Lin Chen
Qifeng Chen
Ting Chen
Wei Chen
Xi Chen
Xilin Chen
Xinlei Chen
Yingcong Chen
Yixin Chen

Erkang Cheng
Jingchun Cheng
Ming-Ming Cheng
Wen-Huang Cheng
Yuan Cheng
Anoop Cherian
Liang-Tien Chia
Naoki Chiba
Shao-Yi Chien
Han-Pang Chiu
Wei-Chen Chiu
Nam Ik Cho
Sunghyun Cho
TaeEun Choe
Jongmoo Choi
Christopher Choy
Wen-Sheng Chu
Yung-Yu Chuang
Ondrej Chum
Joon Son Chung
Gökberk Cinbis
James Clark
Andrea Cohen
Forrester Cole
Toby Collins
John Collomosse
Camille Couprie
David Crandall
Marco Cristani
Canton Cristian
James Crowley
Yin Cui
Zhaopeng Cui
Bo Dai
Jifeng Dai
Qieyun Dai
Shengyang Dai
Yuchao Dai
Carlo Dal Mutto
Dima Damen
Zachary Daniels
Kostas Daniilidis
Donald Dansereau
Mohamed Daoudi
Abhishek Das
Samyak Datta

Achal Dave
Shalini De Mello
Teofilo deCampos
Joseph DeGol
Koichiro Deguchi
Alessio Del Bue
Stefanie Demirci
Jia Deng
Zhiwei Deng
Joachim Denzler
Konstantinos Derpanis
Aditya Deshpande
Alban Desmaison
Frédéric Devernay
Abhinav Dhall
Michel Dhome
Hamdi Dibeklioğlu
Mert Dikmen
Cosimo Distante
Ajay Divakaran
Mandar Dixit
Carl Doersch
Piotr Dollar
Bo Dong
Chao Dong
Huang Dong
Jian Dong
Jiangxin Dong
Weisheng Dong
Simon Donné
Gianfranco Doretto
Alexey Dosovitskiy
Matthijs Douze
Bruce Draper
Bertram Drost
Liang Du
Shichuan Du
Gregory Dudek
Zoran Duric
Pınar Duygulu
Hazım Ekenel
Tarek El-Gaaly
Ehsan Elhamifar
Mohamed Elhoseiny
Sabu Emmanuel
Ian Endres

Aykut Erdem
Erkut Erdem
Hugo Jair Escalante
Sergio Escalera
Victor Escorcia
Francisco Estrada
Davide Eynard
Bin Fan
Jialue Fan
Quanfu Fan
Chen Fang
Tian Fang
Yi Fang
Hany Farid
Giovanni Farinella
Ryan Farrell
Alireza Fathi
Christoph Feichtenhofer
Wenxin Feng
Martin Fergie
Cornelia Fermuller
Basura Fernando
Michael Firman
Bob Fisher
John Fisher
Mathew Fisher
Boris Flach
Matt Flagg
Francois Fleuret
David Fofi
Ruth Fong
Gian Luca Foresti
Per-Erik Forssén
David Fouhey
Katerina Fragkiadaki
Victor Fragoso
Jan-Michael Frahm
Jean-Sebastien Franco
Ohad Fried
Simone Frintrop
Huazhu Fu
Yun Fu
Olac Fuentes
Christopher Funk
Thomas Funkhouser
Brian Funt

Ryo Furukawa
Yasutaka Furukawa
Andrea Fusiello
Fatma Güney
Raghudeep Gadde
Silvano Galliani
Orazio Gallo
Chuang Gan
Bin-Bin Gao
Jin Gao
Junbin Gao
Ruohan Gao
Shenghua Gao
Animesh Garg
Ravi Garg
Erik Gartner
Simone Gasparin
Jochen Gast
Leon A. Gatys
Stratis Gavves
Liuhao Ge
Timnit Gebru
James Gee
Peter Gehler
Xin Geng
Guido Gerig
David Geronimo
Bernard Ghanem
Michael Gharbi
Golnaz Ghiasi
Spyros Gidaris
Andrew Gilbert
Rohit Girdhar
Ioannis Gkioulekas
Georgia Gkioxari
Guy Godin
Roland Goecke
Michael Goesele
Nuno Goncalves
Boqing Gong
Minglun Gong
Yunchao Gong
Abel Gonzalez-Garcia
Daniel Gordon
Paulo Gotardo
Stephen Gould

Venu Govindu
Helmut Grabner
Petr Gronat
Steve Gu
Josechu Guerrero
Anupam Guha
Jean-Yves Guillemaut
Alp Güler
Erhan Gündoğdu
Guodong Guo
Xinqing Guo
Ankush Gupta
Mohit Gupta
Saurabh Gupta
Tanmay Gupta
Abner Guzman Rivera
Timo Hackel
Sunil Hadap
Christian Haene
Ralf Haeusler
Levente Hajder
David Hall
Peter Hall
Stefan Haller
Ghassan Hamarneh
Fred Hamprecht
Onur Hamsici
Bohyung Han
Junwei Han
Xufeng Han
Yahong Han
Ankur Handa
Albert Haque
Tatsuya Harada
Mehrtash Harandi
Bharath Hariharan
Mahmudul Hasan
Tal Hassner
Kenji Hata
Soren Hauberg
Michal Havlena
Zeeshan Hayder
Junfeng He
Lei He
Varsha Hedau
Felix Heide

Wolfgang Heidrich
Janne Heikkila
Jared Heinly
Mattias Heinrich
Lisa Anne Hendricks
Dan Hendrycks
Stephane Herbin
Alexander Hermans
Luis Herranz
Aaron Hertzmann
Adrian Hilton
Michael Hirsch
Steven Hoi
Seunghoon Hong
Wei Hong
Anthony Hoogs
Radu Horaud
Yedid Hoshen
Omid Hosseini Jafari
Kuang-Jui Hsu
Winston Hsu
Yinlin Hu
Zhe Hu
Gang Hua
Chen Huang
De-An Huang
Dong Huang
Gary Huang
Heng Huang
Jia-Bin Huang
Qixing Huang
Rui Huang
Sheng Huang
Weilin Huang
Xiaolei Huang
Xinyu Huang
Zhiwu Huang
Tak-Wai Hui
Wei-Chih Hung
Junhwa Hur
Mohamed Hussein
Wonjun Hwang
Anders Hyden
Satoshi Ikehata
Nazlı Ikizler-Cinbis
Viorela Ila

Evren Imre
Eldar Insafutdinov
Go Irie
Hossam Isack
Ahmet Işçen
Daisuke Iwai
Hamid Izadinia
Nathan Jacobs
Suyog Jain
Varun Jampani
C. V. Jawahar
Dinesh Jayaraman
Sadeep Jayasumana
Laszlo Jeni
Hueihan Jhuang
Dinghuang Ji
Hui Ji
Qiang Ji
Fan Jia
Kui Jia
Xu Jia
Huaizu Jiang
Jiayan Jiang
Nianjuan Jiang
Tingting Jiang
Xiaoyi Jiang
Yu-Gang Jiang
Long Jin
Suo Jinli
Justin Johnson
Nebojsa Jojic
Michael Jones
Hanbyul Joo
Jungseock Joo
Ajjen Joshi
Amin Jourabloo
Frederic Jurie
Achuta Kadambi
Samuel Kadoury
Ioannis Kakadiaris
Zdenek Kalal
Yannis Kalantidis
Sinan Kalkan
Vicky Kalogeiton
Sunkavalli Kalyan
J.-K. Kamarainen

Shih-Yao Lin
Tsung-Yi Lin
Weiyao Lin
Yen-Yu Lin
Haibin Ling
Or Litany
Roee Litman
Anan Liu
Changsong Liu
Chen Liu
Ding Liu
Dong Liu
Feng Liu
Guangcan Liu
Luoqi Liu
Miaomiao Liu
Nian Liu
Risheng Liu
Shu Liu
Shuaicheng Liu
Sifei Liu
Tyng-Luh Liu
Wanquan Liu
Weiwei Liu
Xialei Liu
Xiaoming Liu
Yebin Liu
Yiming Liu
Ziwei Liu
Zongyi Liu
Liliana Lo Presti
Edgar Lobaton
Chengjiang Long
Mingsheng Long
Roberto Lopez-Sastre
Amy Loufti
Brian Lovell
Canyi Lu
Cewu Lu
Feng Lu
Huchuan Lu
Jiajun Lu
Jiasen Lu
Jiwen Lu
Yang Lu
Yujuan Lu

Simon Lucey
Jian-Hao Luo
Jiebo Luo
Pablo Márquez-Neila
Matthias Müller
Chao Ma
Chih-Yao Ma
Lin Ma
Shugao Ma
Wei-Chiu Ma
Zhanyu Ma
Oisin Mac Aodha
Will Maddern
Ludovic Magerand
Marcus Magnor
Vijay Mahadevan
Mohammad Mahoor
Michael Maire
Subhransu Maji
Ameesh Makadia
Atsuto Maki
Yasushi Makihara
Mateusz Malinowski
Tomasz Malisiewicz
Arun Mallya
Roberto Manduchi
Junhua Mao
Dmitrii Marin
Joe Marino
Kenneth Marino
Elisabeta Marinoiu
Ricardo Martin
Aleix Martinez
Julieta Martinez
Aaron Maschinot
Jonathan Masci
Bogdan Matei
Diana Mateus
Stefan Mathe
Kevin Matzen
Bruce Maxwell
Steve Maybank
Walterio Mayol-Cuevas
Mason McGill
Stephen Mckenna
Roey Mechrez

Christopher Mei
Heydi Mendez-Vazquez
Deyu Meng
Thomas Mensink
Bjoern Menze
Domingo Mery
Qiguang Miao
Tomer Michaeli
Antoine Miech
Ondrej Miksik
Anton Milan
Gregor Miller
Cai Minjie
Majid Mirmehdi
Ishan Misra
Niloy Mitra
Anurag Mittal
Nirbhay Modhe
Davide Modolo
Pritish Mohapatra
Pascal Monasse
Mathew Monfort
Taesup Moon
Sandino Morales
Vlad Morariu
Philippos Mordohai
Francesc Moreno
Henrique Morimitsu
Yael Moses
Ben-Ezra Moshe
Roozbeh Mottaghi
Yadong Mu
Lopamudra Mukherjee
Mario Munich
Ana Murillo
Damien Muselet
Armin Mustafa
Siva Karthik Mustikovela
Moin Nabi
Sobhan Naderi
Hajime Nagahara
Varun Nagaraja
Tushar Nagarajan
Arsha Nagrani
Nikhil Naik
Atsushi Nakazawa

P. J. Narayanan
Charlie Nash
Lakshmanan Nataraj
Fabian Nater
Lukáš Neumann
Natalia Neverova
Alejandro Newell
Phuc Nguyen
Xiaohan Nie
David Nilsson
Ko Nishino
Zhenxing Niu
Shohei Nobuhara
Klas Nordberg
Mohammed Norouzi
David Novotny
Ifeoma Nwogu
Matthew O'Toole
Guillaume Obozinski
Jean-Marc Odobez
Eyal Ofek
Ferda Ofli
Tae-Hyun Oh
Iason Oikonomidis
Takeshi Oishi
Takahiro Okabe
Takayuki Okatani
Vlad Olaru
Michael Opitz
Jose Oramas
Vicente Ordonez
Ivan Oseledets
Aljosa Osep
Magnus Oskarsson
Martin R. Oswald
Wanli Ouyang
Andrew Owens
Mustafa Özuysal
Jinshan Pan
Xingang Pan
Rameswar Panda
Sharath Pankanti
Julien Pansiot
Nicolas Papadakis
George Papandreou
N. Papanikolopoulos

Hyun Soo Park
In Kyu Park
Jaesik Park
Omkar Parkhi
Alvaro Parra Bustos
C. Alejandro Parraga
Vishal Patel
Deepak Pathak
Ioannis Patras
Viorica Patraucean
Genevieve Patterson
Kim Pedersen
Robert Peharz
Selen Pehlivan
Xi Peng
Bojan Pepik
Talita Perciano
Federico Pernici
Adrian Peter
Stavros Petridis
Vladimir Petrovic
Henning Petzka
Tomas Pfister
Trung Pham
Justus Piater
Massimo Piccardi
Sudeep Pillai
Pedro Pinheiro
Lerrel Pinto
Bernardo Pires
Aleksis Pirinen
Fiora Pirri
Leonid Pischulin
Tobias Ploetz
Bryan Plummer
Yair Poleg
Jean Ponce
Gerard Pons-Moll
Jordi Pont-Tuset
Alin Popa
Fatih Porikli
Horst Possegger
Viraj Prabhu
Andrea Prati
Maria Priisalu
Véronique Prinet

Victor Prisacariu
Jan Prokaj
Nicolas Pugeault
Luis Puig
Ali Punjani
Senthil Purushwalkam
Guido Pusiol
Guo-Jun Qi
Xiaojuan Qi
Hongwei Qin
Shi Qiu
Faisal Qureshi
Matthias Rüther
Petia Radeva
Umer Rafi
Rahul Raguram
Swaminathan Rahul
Varun Ramakrishna
Kandan Ramakrishnan
Ravi Ramamoorthi
Vignesh Ramanathan
Vasili Ramanishka
R. Ramasamy Selvaraju
Rene Ranftl
Carolina Raposo
Nikhil Rasiwasia
Nalini Ratha
Sai Ravela
Avinash Ravichandran
Ramin Raziperchikolaei
Sylvestre-Alvise Rebuffi
Adria Recasens
Joe Redmon
Timo Rehfeld
Michal Reinstein
Konstantinos Rematas
Haibing Ren
Shaoqing Ren
Wenqi Ren
Zhile Ren
Hamid Rezatofighi
Nicholas Rhinehart
Helge Rhodin
Elisa Ricci
Eitan Richardson
Stephan Richter

Qing Sun
Zhaohui Sun
David Suter
Eran Swears
Raza Syed Hussain
T. Syeda-Mahmood
Christian Szegedy
Duy-Nguyen Ta
Tolga Taşdizen
Hemant Tagare
Yuichi Taguchi
Ying Tai
Yu-Wing Tai
Jun Takamatsu
Hugues Talbot
Toru Tamak
Robert Tamburo
Chaowei Tan
Meng Tang
Peng Tang
Siyu Tang
Wei Tang
Junli Tao
Ran Tao
Xin Tao
Makarand Tapaswi
Jean-Philippe Tarel
Maxim Tatarchenko
Bugra Tekin
Demetri Terzopoulos
Christian Theobalt
Diego Thomas
Rajat Thomas
Qi Tian
Xinmei Tian
YingLi Tian
Yonghong Tian
Yonglong Tian
Joseph Tighe
Radu Timofte
Massimo Tistarelli
Sinisa Todorovic
Pavel Tokmakov
Giorgos Tolias
Federico Tombari
Tatiana Tommasi

Chetan Tonde
Xin Tong
Akihiko Torii
Andrea Torsello
Florian Trammer
Du Tran
Quoc-Huy Tran
Rudolph Triebel
Alejandro Troccoli
Leonardo Trujillo
Tomasz Trzcinski
Sam Tsai
Yi-Hsuan Tsai
Hung-Yu Tseng
Vagia Tsiminaki
Aggeliki Tsoli
Wei-Chih Tu
Shubham Tulsiani
Fred Tung
Tony Tung
Matt Turek
Oncel Tuzel
Georgios Tzimiropoulos
Ilkay Ulusoy
Osman Ulusoy
Dmitry Ulyanov
Paul Upchurch
Ben Usman
Evgeniya Ustinova
Himanshu Vajaria
Alexander Vakhitov
Jack Valmadre
Ernest Valveny
Jan van Gemert
Grant Van Horn
Jagannadan Varadarajan
Gul Varol
Sebastiano Vascon
Francisco Vasconcelos
Mayank Vatsa
Javier Vazquez-Corral
Ramakrishna Vedantam
Ashok Veeraraghavan
Andreas Veit
Raviteja Vemulapalli
Jonathan Ventura

Matthias Vestner
Minh Vo
Christoph Vogel
Michele Volpi
Carl Vondrick
Sven Wachsmuth
Toshikazu Wada
Michael Waechter
Catherine Wah
Jacob Walker
Jun Wan
Boyu Wang
Chen Wang
Chunyu Wang
De Wang
Fang Wang
Hongxing Wang
Hua Wang
Jiang Wang
Jingdong Wang
Jinglu Wang
Jue Wang
Le Wang
Lei Wang
Lezi Wang
Liang Wang
Lichao Wang
Lijun Wang
Limin Wang
Liwei Wang
Naiyan Wang
Oliver Wang
Qi Wang
Ruiping Wang
Shenlong Wang
Shu Wang
Song Wang
Tao Wang
Xiaofang Wang
Xiaolong Wang
Xinchao Wang
Xinggang Wang
Xintao Wang
Yang Wang
Yu-Chiang Frank Wang
Yu-Xiong Wang

Zhaowen Wang
Zhe Wang
Anne Wannenwetsch
Simon Warfield
Scott Wehrwein
Donglai Wei
Ping Wei
Shih-En Wei
Xiu-Shen Wei
Yichen Wei
Xie Weidi
Philippe Weinzaepfel
Longyin Wen
Eric Wengrowski
Tomas Werner
Michael Wilber
Rick Wildes
Olivia Wiles
Kyle Wilson
David Wipf
Kwan-Yee Wong
Daniel Worrall
John Wright
Baoyuan Wu
Chao-Yuan Wu
Jiajun Wu
Jianxin Wu
Tianfu Wu
Xiaodong Wu
Xiaohe Wu
Xinxiao Wu
Yang Wu
Yi Wu
Ying Wu
Yuxin Wu
Zheng Wu
Stefanie Wuhrer
Yin Xia
Tao Xiang
Yu Xiang
Lei Xiao
Tong Xiao
Yang Xiao
Cihang Xie
Dan Xie
Jianwen Xie

Jin Xie
Lingxi Xie
Pengtao Xie
Saining Xie
Wenxuan Xie
Yuchen Xie
Bo Xin
Junliang Xing
Peng Xingchao
Bo Xiong
Fei Xiong
Xuehan Xiong
Yuanjun Xiong
Chenliang Xu
Danfei Xu
Huijuan Xu
Jia Xu
Weipeng Xu
Xiangyu Xu
Yan Xu
Yuanlu Xu
Jia Xue
Tianfan Xue
Erdem Yörük
Abhay Yadav
Deshraj Yadav
Payman Yadollahpour
Yasushi Yagi
Toshihiko Yamasaki
Fei Yan
Hang Yan
Junchi Yan
Junjie Yan
Sijie Yan
Keiji Yanai
Bin Yang
Chih-Yuan Yang
Dong Yang
Herb Yang
Jianchao Yang
Jianwei Yang
Jiaolong Yang
Jie Yang
Jimei Yang
Jufeng Yang
Linjie Yang

Michael Ying Yang
Ming Yang
Ruiduo Yang
Ruigang Yang
Shuo Yang
Wei Yang
Xiaodong Yang
Yanchao Yang
Yi Yang
Angela Yao
Bangpeng Yao
Cong Yao
Jian Yao
Ting Yao
Julian Yarkony
Mark Yatskar
Jinwei Ye
Mao Ye
Mei-Chen Yeh
Raymond Yeh
Serena Yeung
Kwang Moo Yi
Shuai Yi
Alper Yılmaz
Lijun Yin
Xi Yin
Zhaozheng Yin
Xianghua Ying
Ryo Yonetani
Donghyun Yoo
Ju Hong Yoon
Kuk-Jin Yoon
Chong You
Shaodi You
Aron Yu
Fisher Yu
Gang Yu
Jingyi Yu
Ke Yu
Licheng Yu
Pei Yu
Qian Yu
Rong Yu
Shoou-I Yu
Stella Yu
Xiang Yu

Yang Yu
Zhiding Yu
Ganzhao Yuan
Jing Yuan
Junsong Yuan
Lu Yuan
Stefanos Zafeiriou
Sergey Zagoruyko
Amir Zamir
K. Zampogiannis
Andrei Zanfir
Mihai Zanfir
Pablo Zegers
Eyasu Zemene
Andy Zeng
Xingyu Zeng
Yun Zeng
De-Chuan Zhan
Cheng Zhang
Dong Zhang
Guofeng Zhang
Han Zhang
Hang Zhang
Hanwang Zhang
Jian Zhang
Jianguo Zhang
Jianming Zhang
Jiawei Zhang
Junping Zhang
Lei Zhang
Linguang Zhang
Ning Zhang
Qing Zhang

Quanshi Zhang
Richard Zhang
Runze Zhang
Shanshan Zhang
Shiliang Zhang
Shu Zhang
Ting Zhang
Xiangyu Zhang
Xiaofan Zhang
Xu Zhang
Yimin Zhang
Yinda Zhang
Yongqiang Zhang
Yuting Zhang
Zhanpeng Zhang
Ziyu Zhang
Bin Zhao
Chen Zhao
Hang Zhao
Hengshuang Zhao
Qijun Zhao
Rui Zhao
Yue Zhao
Enliang Zheng
Liang Zheng
Stephan Zheng
Wei-Shi Zheng
Wenming Zheng
Yin Zheng
Yinqiang Zheng
Yuanjie Zheng
Guangyu Zhong
Bolei Zhou

Guang-Tong Zhou
Huiyu Zhou
Jiahuan Zhou
S. Kevin Zhou
Tinghui Zhou
Wengang Zhou
Xiaowei Zhou
Xingyi Zhou
Yin Zhou
Zihan Zhou
Fan Zhu
Guangming Zhu
Ji Zhu
Jiejie Zhu
Jun-Yan Zhu
Shizhan Zhu
Siyu Zhu
Xiangxin Zhu
Xiatian Zhu
Yan Zhu
Yingying Zhu
Yixin Zhu
Yuke Zhu
Zhenyao Zhu
Liansheng Zhuang
Zeeshan Zia
Karel Zimmermann
Daniel Zoran
Danping Zou
Qi Zou
Silvia Zuffi
Wangmeng Zuo
Xinxin Zuo

Contents – Part XV

Poster Session

CNN-PS: CNN-Based Photometric Stereo for General Non-convex Surfaces

Satoshi Ikehata[✉]

National Institute of Informatics, Tokyo, Japan
sikehata@nii.ac.jp

Abstract. Most conventional photometric stereo algorithms inversely solve a BRDF-based image formation model. However, the actual imaging process is often far more complex due to the global light transport on the non-convex surfaces. This paper presents a photometric stereo network that directly learns relationships between the photometric stereo input and surface normals of a scene. For handling unordered, arbitrary number of input images, we merge all the input data to the intermediate representation called *observation map* that has a fixed shape, is able to be fed into a CNN. To improve both training and prediction, we take into account the rotational pseudo-invariance of the observation map that is derived from the isotropic constraint. For training the network, we create a synthetic photometric stereo dataset that is generated by a physics-based renderer, therefore the global light transport is considered. Our experimental results on both synthetic and real datasets show that our method outperforms conventional BRDF-based photometric stereo algorithms especially when scenes are highly non-convex.

Keywords: Photometric stereo · Convolutional neural networks

1 Introduction

In 3-D computer vision problems, the input data is often *unstructured* (*i.e.*, the number of input images is varying and the images are unordered). A good example is the multi-view stereo problem where the scene geometry is recovered from unstructured multi-view images. Due to this unstructuredness, 3-D reconstruction from multiple images less relied on the supervised learning-based algorithms except for some structured problems such as binocular stereopsis [1] and two-view SfM [2] whose number of input images is always fixed. However, recent advances in deep convolutional neural network (CNN) have motivated researchers to address unstructured 3-D computer vision problems with deep neural networks. For instance, a recent work from Kar *et al.* [3] presented an

---

This work was supported by JSPS KAKENHI Grant Number JP17H07324.

Electronic supplementary material The online version of this chapter (https://doi.org/10.1007/978-3-030-01267-0_1) contains supplementary material, which is available to authorized users.

end-to-end learned system for the multi-view stereopsis while Kim *et al.* [4] presented a learning-based surface reflectance estimation from multiple RGB-D images. Either work intelligently merged all the unstructured input to a structured, intermediate representation (*i.e.*, 3-D feature grid [3] and 2-D hemispherical image [4]).

Photometric stereo is another 3-D computer vision problem whose input is unstructured, where surface normals of a scene are recovered from appearance variations under different illuminations. Photometric stereo algorithms typically solved an inverse problem of the pointwise image formation model which was based on the Bidirectional Reflectance Distribution Function (BRDF). While effective, a BRDF-based image formation model generally cannot account the global illumination effects such as shadows and inter-reflections, which are often problematic to recover non-convex surfaces. Some algorithms attempted the robust outlier rejection to suppress the non-Lambertian effects [5–8], however the estimation failed when the non-Lambertian observation was dominant. This limitation inevitably occurs due to the fact that multiple interactions of light and a surface are difficult to be modeled in a mathematically tractable form.

To tackle this issue, this paper presents an end-to-end CNN-based photometric stereo algorithm that learns the relationships between surface normals and their appearances without physically modeling the image formation process. For better scalability, our approach is still pixelwise and rather inherit from conventional robust approaches [5–8], which means that we learn the network that automatically "neglects" the global illumination effects and estimate the surface normal from "inliers" in the observation. To achieve this goal, we will train our network on as much as possible synthetic patterns of the input that is "corrupted" by global effects. Images are rendered with different complex objects under the diverse material and illumination condition.

Our challenge is to apply the deep neural network to the photometric stereo problem whose input is unstructured. In similar with recent works [3,4], we merge all the photometric stereo data to an intermediate representation called *observation map* that has a fixed shape, therefore is naturally fed to a standard CNN. As many photometric stereo algorithms were, our work is also primarily concerned with isotropic materials, whose reflections are invariant under rotation about the surface normal. We will show that this isotropy can be taken advantages of in a form of the *rotational pseudo-invariance* of the observation map for both augmenting the input data and reducing the prediction errors. To train the network, we create a synthetic photometric stereo dataset (*CyclesPS*) by leveraging the physics-based Cycles renderer [9] to simulate the complex global light transport. For covering diverse real-world materials, we adopt the Disney's principled BSDF [10] that was proposed for artists to render various scenes by controlling small number of parameters.

We evaluate our algorithm on the DiLiGenT Photometric Stereo Dataset [11] which is a real benchmark dataset containing images and calibrated lightings. We compare our method against conventional photometric stereo algorithms [5–8,12–21] and show that our end-to-end learning-based algorithm most successfully recovers the non-convex, non-Lambertian surfaces among all the algorithms concerned.

The summary of contributions is following:

(1) We firstly propose a supervised CNN-based calibrated photometric stereo algorithm that takes unstructured images and lighting information as input.
(2) We present a synthetic photometric stereo dataset (*CyclesPS*) with a careful injection of the global illumination effects such as cast shadows, inter-reflections.
(3) Our extensive evaluation shows that our method performs best on the DiLi-GenT benchmark dataset [11] among various conventional algorithms especially when the surfaces are highly non-convex and non-Lambertian.

Henceforth we rely on the classical assumptions on the photometric stereo problem (*i.e.*, fixed, linear orthographic camera and known directional lighting).

2 Related Work

Diverse appearances of real world objects can be encoded by a BRDF ρ, which relates the observed intensity I_j to the associated surface normal $n \in \mathbb{R}^3$, the j-th incoming lighting direction $l_j \in \mathbb{R}^3$, its intensity $L_j \in \mathbb{R}$, and the outgoing viewing direction $v \in \mathbb{R}^3$ via

$$I_j = L_j \rho(n, l_j, v) \max(n^\top l_j, 0) + \epsilon_j, \tag{1}$$

where $\max(n^\top l_j, 0)$ accounts for attached shadows and ϵ_j is an additive error to the model. Equation (1) is generally called *image formation model*. Most photometric stereo algorithms assumed the specific shape of ρ and recovered the surface normals of a scene by inversely solving Eq. (1) from a collection of observations under m different lighting conditions ($j \in 1, \cdots, m$). All the effects that are not represented by a BRDF (image noises, cast shadows, inter-reflections and so on) are typically put together in ϵ_j. Note that when the BRDF is Lambertian and the additive error is removed, it is simplified to the traditional Lambertian image formation model [12].

Since Woodham firstly introduced the Lambertian photometric stereo algorithm, the extension of its work to non-Lambertian scenes has been a problems of significant interest. Photometric stereo approaches to dealing with non-Lambertian effects are mainly categorized into four classes: (a) robust approach, (b) reflectance modeling with non-Lambertian BRDF, (c) example-based reflectance modeling and (d) learning-based approach.

Many photometric stereo algorithms recover surface normals of a scene via a simple diffuse reflectance modeling (*e.g.*, Lambertian) while treating other effects as outliers. For instance, Wu *et al.* [5] have proposed a rank-minimization based approach to decompose images into the low-rank Lambertian image and non-Lambertian sparse corruptions. Ikehata *et al.* extended their method by constraining the rank-3 Lambertian structure [6] (or the general diffuse structure [7]) for better computational stability. Recently, Queau *et al.* [8] have presented a robust variational approach for inaccurate lighting as well as various non-Lambertian corruptions. While effective, a drawback of this approach is that if it were not for dense diffuse inliers, the estimation fails.

Despite their computational complexity, various algorithms arrange the parametric or non-parametric models of non-Lambertian BRDF. In recent years, there has been an emphasis on representing a material with a small number of fundamental BRDF. Goldman *et al.* [22] have approximated each fundamental BRDF by the Ward model [23] and Alldrin *et al.* [13] later extended it to non-parametric representation. Since the high-dimensional ill-posed problem may cause the instability of the estimation, Shi *et al.* [18] presented a compact biquadratic representation of isotropic BRDF. On the other hand, Ikehata *et al.* [17] introduced the sum-of-lobes isotropic reflectance model [24] to account all frequencies in isotropic observations. For improving the efficiency of the optimization, Shen *et al.* [25] presented a kernel regression approach, which can be transformed to an eigen decomposition problem. This approach works well as far as a resultant image formation model is correct without model outliers.

A few amount of photometric stereo algorithms are grouped into the *example-based* approach, which takes advantages of the surface reflectance of objects with known shape, captured under the same illumination environment with the target scene. The earliest example-based approach [26] requires a reference object whose material is exactly same with that of target object. Hertzmann *et al.* [27] have eased this restriction to handle uncalibrated scenes and spatially varying materials by assuming that materials can be expressed as a small number of basis materials. Recently, Hui *et al.* [20] presented an example-based method without a physical reference object by taking advantages of virtual spheres rendered with various materials. While effective, this approach also suffers from model outliers and has a drawback that the lighting configuration of the reference scene must be taken over at the target scene.

Machine learning techniques have been applied in a few very recent photometric stereo works [19,21]. Santo *et al.* [19] presented a supervised learning-based photometric stereo method using a neural network that takes as input a normalized vector where each element corresponds to an observation under specific illumination. A surface normal is predicted by feeding the vector to one dropout layer and adjacent six dense layers. While effective, this method has limitation that lightings remain the same between training and test phases, making it inapplicable to the unstructured input. One another work by Taniai and Maehara [21] presented an unsupervised learning framework where surface normals and BRDFs are predicted by the network trained by minimizing reconstruction loss between observed and synthesized images with a rendering equation. While their network is invariant to the number and permutation of the images, the rendering equation is still based on a point-wise BRDF and intolerant to the model outliers. Furthermore, they reported slow running time (*i.e.*, 1 h to do 1000 SGD iterations for each scene) due to its self-supervision manner.

In summary, there is still a constant struggle in the design of the photometric stereo algorithm among its complexity, efficiency, stability and robustness. Our goal is to solve this dilemma. Our end-to-end learning-based algorithm builds upon the deep CNN trained on synthetic datasets, abandoning the modeling of complicated image formation process. Our network accepts the unstructured input (*i.e.*, our network is invariant to both number and order of input images) and works for various real-world scenes where non-Lambertian reflections are intermingled with global illumination effects.

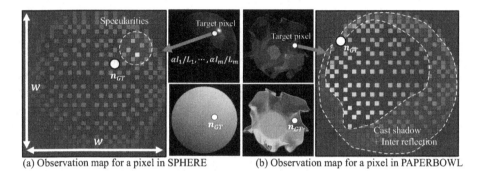

(a) Observation map for a pixel in SPHERE   (b) Observation map for a pixel in PAPERBOWL

Fig. 1. We project pairs of images and lightings to a fixed-size observation map based on the objective mapping of a light direction from a hemisphere to the 2-D coordinate system perpendicular to the viewing axis. This figure shows observation maps for (a) a point on a smooth convex surface and (b) a point on a rough non-convex surface. We also projected the true surface normal at the point onto the same coordinate system of the observation map for reference.

3   Proposed Method

Our goal is to recover surface normals of a scene of (a) spatially-varying isotropic materials and with (b) global illumination effects (*e.g.*, shadows and interreflections) (c) where the scene is illuminated by unknown number of lights. To achieve this goal, we propose a CNN architecture for the calibrated photometric stereo problem which is invariant to both the number and order of input images. The tolerance to global illumination effects is learned from the synthetic images of non-convex scenes rendered with the physics-based renderer.

3.1   2-D Observation Map for Unstructured Photometric Stereo Input

We firstly present the *observation map* which is generated by a pixelwise hemispherical projection of observations based on known lighting directions. Since a lighting direction is a vector spanned on a unit hemisphere, there is a objective mapping from $l_j \triangleq [l_x^j \ l_y^j \ l_z^j]^\top \in \mathbb{R}^3$ to $[l_x^j \ l_y^j]^\top \in \mathbb{R}^2$ (s.t., $l_x^2 + l_y^2 + l_z^2 = 1$) by projecting a vector onto the x-y coordinate system which is perpendicular to a viewing direction (*i.e.*, $\boldsymbol{v} = [0\ 0\ 1]$).[1] Then we define an observation map $O \in \mathbb{R}^{w \times w}$ as

$$O_{\text{int}(w(l_x+1)/2),\text{int}(w(l_y+1)/2)} = \alpha I_j / L_j \ \forall\, j \in 1, \cdots, m, \tag{2}$$

where "int" is an operator to round a floating value to an integer and α is a scaling factor to normalize data (*i.e.*, we simply use $\alpha = \max L_j / I_j$). Once all the observations and lightings are stored in the observation map, we take it as an input of the CNN. Despite its simplicity, this representation has three major benefits. First, its shape is independent of the number and size of input images. Second, the projection of observations is order-independent (*i.e.*, the observation map does not change when swapping i-th and j-th images). Third, it is unnecessary to explicitly feed the lighting information into the network.

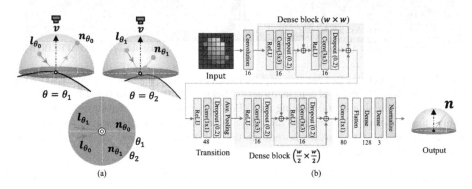

Fig. 2. (a) Isotropy guarantees that the appearance of a surface from $\boldsymbol{v}$ is invariant of the rotation of $\boldsymbol{l}$ and $\boldsymbol{n}$ around the view axis. (b) Our network architecture is a variation of DenseNet [28] that outputs a normalized surface normal from a 32×32 observation map. Numbers of the filter are presented below each layer.

Figure 1 illustrates examples of the observation map of two objects namely SPHERE and PAPERBOWL, one is purely convex and the other is highly non-convex. Figure 1(a) indicates that the target point could be on the convex surface since the values of the observation map gradually decrease to zero as the light direction is going apart from the true surface normal ($\boldsymbol{n}_{GT}$). The local concentration of large intensity values also indicates the narrow specularity on the smooth surface. On the other hand, the abrupt change of values in Fig. 1(b) evidences the presence of cast shadows or inter-reflections on the non-convex surface. Since there is no local concentration of intensity values, the surface is likely to be rough. In this way, an observation map reasonably encodes the geometry, material and behavior of the light at around a surface point.

---

[1] We preliminarily tried the projection on the spherical coordinate system (θ, ϕ), but the performance was worse than one on the standard x-y coordinate system.

3.2   Rotation Pseudo-invariance for the Isotropy Constraint

An observation map O is sparse in a general photometric stereo setup (*e.g.*, assuming that $w = 32$ and we have 100 images as input, the ratio of non-zero entries in O is about 10%). The missing data is generally considered problematic as CNN input and often interpolated [4]. However, we empirically found that smoothly interpolating missing entries degrades the performance since an observation map is often non-smooth and zero values have an important meaning (*i.e.*, shadows). Therefore we alternatively try to improve the performance by taking into account the isotropy of the material.

Many real-world materials exhibit identically same appearance when the surface is rotated along a surface normal. The presence of this behavior is referred to as isotropy [29,30]. Isotropic BRDFs are parameterized in terms of three values instead of four [31] as

$$\rho = f(\boldsymbol{n}^\top \boldsymbol{l}, \boldsymbol{n}^\top \boldsymbol{v}, \boldsymbol{l}^\top \boldsymbol{v}), \tag{3}$$

where f is an arbitrary reflectance function.[2] Combining Eq. (3) with Eq. (1), we get following image formation model.

$$I = L f(\boldsymbol{n}^\top \boldsymbol{l}, \boldsymbol{n}^\top \boldsymbol{v}, \boldsymbol{l}^\top \boldsymbol{v}) \max{(\boldsymbol{n}^\top \boldsymbol{l}, 0)}. \tag{4}$$

Note that lighting index and model error are omitted for brevity. Let's consider the rotation of surface normal $\boldsymbol{n}$ and lighting direction $\boldsymbol{l}$ around the z-axis (*i.e.*, viewing axis) as $\boldsymbol{n}' = [(R[n_x\ n_y]^\top)^\top\ n_z]^\top, \boldsymbol{l}' = [(R[l_x\ l_y]^\top)^\top\ l_z]^\top$ where $\boldsymbol{n} \triangleq [n_x\ n_y\ n_z]^\top$ and $R \in SO(2)$ is an arbitrary rotation matrix. Then,

$$\boldsymbol{n}'^\top \boldsymbol{l}' = [(R[n_x\ n_y]^\top)^\top\ n_z][(R[l_x\ l_y]^\top)^\top\ l_z]^\top \tag{5}$$
$$= [n_x\ n_y] R^\top R [l_x\ l_y]^\top + n_z l_z = \boldsymbol{n}^\top \boldsymbol{l},$$

$$\boldsymbol{n}'^\top \boldsymbol{v}' = [(R[n_x\ n_y]^\top)^\top\ n_z][0\ 0\ 1]^\top = n_z = \boldsymbol{n}^\top \boldsymbol{v}, \tag{6}$$

$$\boldsymbol{l}'^\top \boldsymbol{v}' = [(R[l_x\ l_y]^\top)^\top\ l_z][0\ 0\ 1]^\top = l_z = \boldsymbol{l}^\top \boldsymbol{v}. \tag{7}$$

Feeding them into Eq. (4) gives following equation,

$$I = L f(\boldsymbol{n}'^\top \boldsymbol{l}', \boldsymbol{n}'^\top \boldsymbol{v}, \boldsymbol{l}'^\top \boldsymbol{v}) \max{(\boldsymbol{n}'^\top \boldsymbol{l}', 0)} \tag{8}$$
$$= L f(\boldsymbol{n}^\top \boldsymbol{l}, \boldsymbol{n}^\top \boldsymbol{v}, \boldsymbol{l}^\top \boldsymbol{v}) \max{(\boldsymbol{n}^\top \boldsymbol{l}, 0)}.$$

Therefore, the rotation of lighting and surface normal around z-axis does not change the appearance as illustrated in Fig. 2(a). Note that this theorem holds even for the indirect illumination in non-convex scenes by rotating all the geometry and environment illumination around the viewing axis. This result is important for our CNN-based algorithm. We suppose that a neural network is a mapping function $g : x \mapsto g(x)$ that maps x (*i.e.*, a set of images and lightings) to $g(x)$ (*i.e.*, a surface normal) and r is a rotation operator of lighting/normal at the same angle around z-axis. From Eq. (8), we get $r(g(x)) = g(r(x))$. We call this

---

[2] Note that there are other parameterizations of an isotropic BRDF [32].

relationship as *rotational pseudo-invariance* (the standard rotation invariance is $g(x) = g(r(x))$). Note that this rotational pseudo-invariance is also applied on the observation map since the rotation of lightings around the viewing axis results in the rotation of the observation map around the z-axis[3].

We constrain the network with the rotational pseudo-invariance in the similar manner that the rotation invariance is achieved. Within the CNN framework, two approaches are generally adopted to encode the rotation invariance. One is applying rotations to the input image [33] and the other is applying rotations to the convolution kernels [34]. We adopt the first strategy due to its simplicity. Concretely, we augment the training set with many rotated versions of lightings and surface normal, which allows the network to learn the invariance without explicitly enforcing it. In our implementation, we rotate the vectors at 10 regular intervals from 0 to 360.

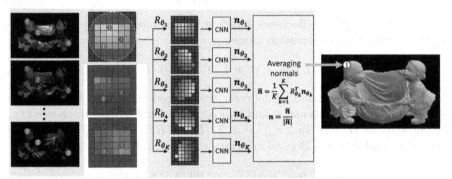

Input images   2-D Observation maps   Surface normal prediction via CNN   Recovered surface normal map

Fig. 3. The illustration of the prediction module. For each surface point, we generate K observation maps taking into account the rotational pseudo-invariance. Each observation map is fed into the network and all the output normals are averaged.

3.3   Architecture Details

In this section, we describe the framework of training and prediction. Given images and lightings, we produce observation maps followed by Eq. (2). Data is augmented to achieve the rotational pseudo-invariance by rotating both lighting and surface normal vectors around the viewing axis. Note that a color image is converted to a gray-scale image. The size of the observation map (w) should be chosen carefully. As w increases, the observation map becomes sparser. On the other hand, the smaller observation map has less representability. Considering this trade-off, we empirically found that $w = 32$ is a reasonable choice (we tried

---

[3] Strictly speaking, we rotate the lighting directions instead of the observation map itself. Therefore, we do not need to suffer from the boundary issue unlike the standard rotational data augmentation.

$w = 8, 16, 32, 64$ and $w = 32$ showed the best performance when the number of images is less than one thousand).

A variation of densely connected convolutional neural network (DenseNet [28]) architecture is used to estimate a surface normal from an observation map. The network architecture is shown in Fig. 2(b). The network includes two 2-layer dense blocks, each consists of one activation layer (relu), one convolution layer (3×3) and a dropout layer (20% drop) with a concatenation from the previous layers. Between two dense blocks, there is a transition layer to change feature-map sizes via convolution and pooling. We do not insert a batch normalization layer that was found to degrade the performance in our experiments. After the dense blocks, the network has two dense layers followed by one normalization layer which convert a feature to an unit vector. The network is trained with a simple mean squared loss between predicted and ground truth surface normals. The loss function is minimized using Adam solver [35]. We should note that since our input data size is relatively small (*i.e.*, $32 \times 32 \times 1$), the choice of the network architecture is not a critical component in our framework.[4]

The prediction module is illustrated in Fig. 3. Given observation maps, we predict surface normals based on the trained network. Since it is practically impossible to train the perfect rotational pseudo-invariant network, estimated surface normals for differently rotated observation maps were not identical (typically the difference of angular errors between every two different rotations was less than 10%–20% of their average). For further emphasizing the rotational pseudo-invariance, we again augment the input data by rotating lighting vectors at a certain angle $\theta \in \theta_1, \cdots \theta_K$ and then merge the outputs into one. Suppose the surface normal ($\boldsymbol{n}_\theta$) is a prediction from the input data rotated by R_θ, then we simply average the inversely rotated surface normals as follows,

$$\bar{\boldsymbol{n}} = \frac{1}{K} \sum_{k=1}^{K} R_{\theta_k}^\top \boldsymbol{n}_{\theta_k},$$ (9)

$$\boldsymbol{n} = \bar{\boldsymbol{n}}/\|\bar{\boldsymbol{n}}\|.$$

3.4   Training Dataset (*CyclesPS* Dataset)

In this section, we present our *CyclesPS* training dataset. *DiLiGenT* [11], the largest real photometric stereo dataset contains only ten scenes with fixed lighting configuration. Some works [17–19] attempted to synthesize images with MERL BRDF database [29], however only one hundred measured BRDFs cannot cover the tremendous real-world materials. Therefore, we decided to create our own training dataset that has diverse materials, geometries and illumination.

For rendering scenes, we collected high quality 3-D models under royalty free license from the internet.[5] We carefully chose fifteen models for training and

---

[4] We compared architectures of AlexNet, VGG-NET and densenet as well as much simpler architectures with only two or three convolutoinal layers and the dense layer(s). Among the architectures we tested, the current architecture was slightly better.

[5] References to each 3-D model are included in supplementary.

three models for test whose surface geometry is sufficiently complex to cover the diverse surface normal distribution. Note that we empirically found 3-D models in ShapeNet [36] which was used in a previous work [4] are generally too simple (*e.g.*, models are often low-polygonal, mostly planar) to train the network.

Parameter	Value
baseColor	0.0 to 1.0
metallic	0.0 (Diffuse, Specular) or 1.0 (Metallic)
specular	0.0 to 1.0 (Diffuse, Metallic) or 0.0 to 4.0 (Specular)
roughness	0.0 to 1.0 (Diffuse, Specular) or 0.3 to 0.7 (Metallic)
sheen	0.0 to 1.0
sheen tint	0.0 to 1.0
IOR	$2/(1 - \sqrt{0.08 * specular}) - 1$

(a)   (b)

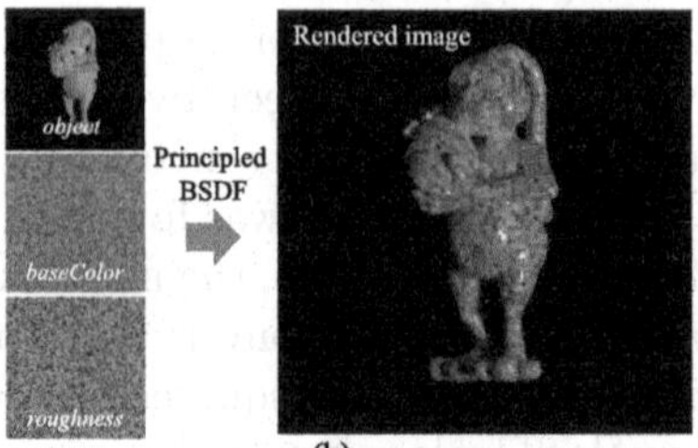

Fig. 4. (a) The range of each parameter in the principled BSDF [10] is restricted by three different material configurations (Diffuse, Specular, Metallic). (b) The material parameters are passed to the renderer in the form of a 2-D texture map.

The representation of the reflectance is also important to make the network robust to wide varieties of real-world materials. Due to its representability, we choose Disney's principled BSDF [10] which integrates five different BRDFs controlled by eleven parameters (*baseColor, subsurface, metallic, specular, specularTint, roughness, anisotropic, sheen, sheenTint, clearcoat, clearcoatGloss*). Since our target is isotropic materials without subsurface scattering, we neglect parameters such as *subsurface* and *anisotropic*. We also neglect *specularTint* that artistically colorizes the specularity and *clearcort* and *clearcoatGloss* that does not strongly affect the rendering results. While principled BSDF is effective, we found that there are some unrealistic combinations of parameters that we want to skip (*e.g.*, metallic = 1 and roughness = 0, or metallic = 0.5). For avoiding those unrealistic parameters, we divide the entire parameter sets into three categories, (a) Diffuse, (b) Specular and (c) Metallic. We generate three datasets individually and evenly merge them when training the network. The value of each parameter is randomly selected within specific ranges for each parameter (see Fig. 4(a)). To realize spatially varying materials, we divide the object region in the rendered image into P (*i.e.*, 5000 for the training data) superpixels and use the same set of parameters at pixels within a superpixel (See Fig. 4(b)).

For simulating complex light transport, we use *Cycles* [9] renderer bundled in Blender [37]. The orthographic camera and the directional light are specified. For each rendering, we choose a set of an object, BSDF parameter maps (one for each parameter), and lighting configuration (*i.e.*, Once roughly 1300 lights are uniformly distributed on the hemisphere, small random noises are added to each light). Once images were rendered, we create *CyclesPS* dataset by generating observation maps pixelwisely. For making the network robust to the test data of any number of images, observation maps are generated from a pixelwisely different number of images. Concretely, when generating an observation map, we pick a random subset of images whose number is within 50 to 1300 and whose corresponding elevation angle of the light direction is more than a random threshold value within 20–90° degrees.[6] The training process takes 10 epochs for 150 image sets (*i.e.*, 15 objects × 10 rotations for the rotational pseudo-invariance). Each image set contains around 50000 samples (*i.e.*, number of pixels in the object mask).

4 Experimental Results

We evaluate our method on synthetic and real datasets. All experiments were performed on a machine with 3×GeForce GTX 1080 Ti and 64 GB RAM. For training and prediction, we use Keras library [38] with Tensorflow background and use default learning parameters. The training process took around 3 h.

4.1 Datasets

We evaluated our method on three datasets, two are synthetic and one is real.

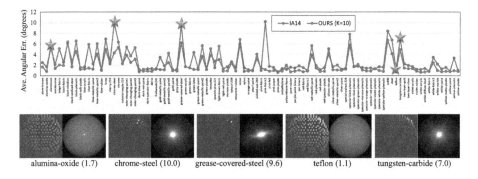

Fig. 5. Evaluation on the *MERLSphere* dataset. A sphere is rendered with 100 measured BRDF in MERL BRDF database [29]. Our CNN-based method was compared against a model-based algorithm (IA14 [7]) based on the mean angular errors of predicted surface normals in degree. We also showed some examples of rendered images and observation maps for further analysis (See Sect. 4.2).

MERLSphere is a synthetic dataset where images are rendered with one hundred isotropic BRDFs in MERL database [29] from diffuse to metallic. We generated 32-bit HDR images of a sphere (256 × 256) with a ground truth surface normal map and a foreground mask. There is no cast shadow and inter-reflection.

CyclesPSTest is a synthetic dataset of three objects, SPHERE, TURTLE and PAPERBOWL. TURTLE and PAPERBOWL are non-convex objects where

---

[6] The minimum number of images is 50 for avoiding too sparse observation map and we only picked the lights whose elevation angles were more than 20° since it is practically less possible that the scene is illuminated from the side.

the inter-reflection and cast shadow appear on rendered images. This dataset was generated in the same manner with the *CyclesPS* training dataset except that the number of superpixels in the parameter map was 100 and the material condition was either Specular or Metallic (Note that objects and parameter maps in *CyclesPSTest* are NOT in *CyclesPS*). Each data contains 16-bit integer images with a resolution of 512 × 512 under 17 or 305 known uniform lightings.

DiLiGenT [11] is a public benchmark dataset of 10 real objects of general reflectance. Each data provides 16-bit integer images with a resolution of 612 × 512 from 96 different known lighting directions. The ground truth surface normals for the orthographic projection and the single-view setup are also provided.

4.2   Evaluation on *MERLSphere* Dataset

We compared our method (with $K = 10$ in Eq. (9)) against one of the state-of-the-art isotropic photometric stereo algorithms (IA14 [17][7]) on the *MERLSphere*

Table 1. Evaluation on the *CyclesPSTest* dataset. Here m is the number of input images in each dataset and $\{S, M\}$ are types of material *i.e.*, Specular (S) or Metallic (M) (See Fig. 4 for details). For each cell, we show the average angular errors in degrees

OBJECT	m=17						m=305					
	SPHERE (S)	SPHERE (M)	TURTLE (S)	TURTLE (M)	PAPERBOWL (S)	PAPERBOWL (M)	SPHERE (S)	SPHERE (M)	TURTLE (S)	TURTLE (M)	PAPERBOWL (S)	PAPERBOWL (M)
OURS (K=1)	4.9	11.9	12.9	20.2	22.2	36.8	1.6	2.0	4.2	6.5	6.8	11.1
OURS (K=10)	3.3	9.0	9.9	17.8	20.1	34.2	0.9	1.4	3.3	5.7	6.0	9.5
IA14 [17]	2.7	41.0	13.4	39.1	37.2	43.1	2.8	50.7	16.5	39.0	41.7	42.0
IW12 [6]	1.6	31.0	9.0	35.1	27.7	42.0	1.6	41.7	9.3	37.8	27.6	39.6
IW14 [7]	1.4	23.1	10.5	28.4	36.9	44.2	1.2	20.5	10.2	25.9	37.4	39.5
ST14 [18]	4.4	36.3	12.0	40.6	31.4	41.1	1.0	19.0	19.9	25.5	51.0	50.3
BASELINE[12]	4.6	35.4	12.3	39.7	29.4	39.3	5.0	44.5	12.6	40.2	28.8	37.0

Table 2. Evaluation on the *DiLiGenT* dataset. We show the angular errors averaged within each object and over all the objects. (*) Our method discarded first 20 images in BEAR since they are corrupted (We explain about this issue in the supplementary)

	BALL	BEAR	BUDDHA	CAT	COW	GOBLET	HARVEST	POT1	POT2	READING	AVE. ERR	RANK
OURS (K=10)	2.2	4.1*	7.9	4.6	8.0	7.3	14.0	5.4	6.0	12.6	7.2	1
OURS (K=1)	2.7	4.5*	8.6	5.0	8.2	7.1	14.2	5.9	6.3	13.0	7.6	2
HS17 [20]	1.3	5.6	8.5	4.9	8.2	7.6	15.8	5.2	6.4	12.1	7.6	2
TM18 [21]	1.5	5.8	10.4	5.4	6.3	11.5	22.6	6.1	7.8	11.0	8.8	4
IW14 [7]	2.0	4.8	8.4	5.4	13.3	8.7	18.9	6.9	10.2	12.0	9.0	5
SS17 [20]	2.0	6.3	12.7	6.5	8.0	11.3	16.9	7.1	7.9	15.5	9.4	6
ST14 [18]	1.7	6.1	10.6	6.1	13.9	10.1	25.4	6.5	8.8	13.6	10.3	7
SH17 [25]	2.2	5.3	9.3	5.6	16.8	10.5	24.6	7.3	8.4	13.0	10.3	7
IA14 [17]	3.3	7.1	10.5	6.7	13.1	9.7	26.0	6.6	8.8	14.2	10.6	9
GC10 [14]	3.2	6.6	14.9	8.2	9.6	14.2	27.8	8.5	7.9	19.1	12.0	10
BASELINE [12]	4.1	8.4	14.9	8.4	25.6	18.5	30.6	8.9	14.7	19.8	15.4	-

---

[7] We used the authors' implementation of [17] with $N_1 = 2, N_2 = 4$ and turning on the retro-reflection handling. Attached shadows were removed by a simple thresholding. Note that our method takes into account all the input information unlike [17].

dataset. Without global illumination effects, we simply evaluate the ability of our network in representing wide varieties of materials compared to the sum-of-lobes BRDF [24] introduced in IA14. The results are illustrated in Fig. 5. We observed that our CNN-based algorithm performs comparably well, though not better than IA14, for most of materials, which indicates that Disney's principled BSDF [10] covers various real-world materials. We should note that as was commented in [10], some of very shiny materials, particularly the metals (e.g., chrome-steel and tungsten-carbide), exhibited asymmetric highlights suggestive of lens flare or perhaps anisotropic surface scratches. Since our network was trained on purely isotropic materials, they inevitably degrade the performance.

4.3   Evaluation on *CyclesPSTest* Dataset

To evaluate the ability of our method in recovering non-convex surfaces, we tested our method on *CyclesPSTest*. Our method was compared against two robust algorithms IW12 [6] and IW14 [7][8], two model-based algorithms ST14 [18][9] and IA14 [17] and BASELINE [12]. When running algorithms except for ours, we discarded samples whose intensity values were less than 655 in a 16-bit integer image for the shadow removal. In this experiment, we also studied the effects of number of images and rotational merging in the prediction.[10] Concretely, we tested our method on 17 or 305 images with $K = 1$ and $K = 10$

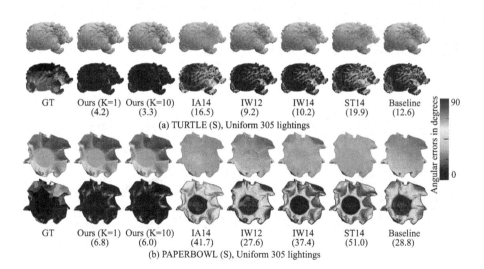

(a) TURTLE (S), Uniform 305 lightings

| GT | Ours (K=1) (4.2) | Ours (K=10) (3.3) | IA14 (16.5) | IW12 (9.2) | IW14 (10.2) | ST14 (19.9) | Baseline (12.6) |

(b) PAPERBOWL (S), Uniform 305 lightings

| GT | Ours (K=1) (6.8) | Ours (K=10) (6.0) | IA14 (41.7) | IW12 (27.6) | IW14 (37.4) | ST14 (51.0) | Baseline (28.8) |

Fig. 6. Recovered surface normals and error maps for (a) TURTLE and (b) PAPER-BOWL of Specular material. Images were rendered under uniform 305 lightings

---

[8]   We used authors' implementation and set parameters of [6] as $\lambda = 0, \sigma = 1.0^{-6}$ and parameters of [7] as $\lambda = 0, p = 3, \sigma_a = 1.0$.

[9]   We used our implementation of [18] and set $T_{low} = 0.25$.

[10]   We still augment data by rotations in the training step.

in Eq. (9). We show the results in Table 1 and Fig. 6. We observed that all the algorithms worked well on the convex specular SPHERE dataset. However, when surfaces were non-convex, all the algorithms except ours failed in the estimation due to strong cast shadow and inter-reflections. It is interesting to see that even the robust algorithms (IA12 [6] and IA14 [7]) could not deal with the global effects as outliers. We also observed that the rotational averaging based on the rotational pseudo-invariance definitely improved the accuracy, though not very much.

4.4   Evaluation on *DiLiGenT* Dataset

Finally, we present a side-by-side comparison on the *DiLiGenT* dataset [11]. We collected existing benchmark results for the calibrated photometric stereo algorithms [5–8, 12–21]. Note that we compared the mean angular errors of [5, 12–18] reported in [11], ones reported in their own works [19–21] and ones from our experiment using authors' implementation [6–8].[11] The results are illustrated in Table 2. Due to the space limit, we only show the top-10 algorithms[12] w.r.t the overall mean angular, and BASELINE [12]. We observed that our method

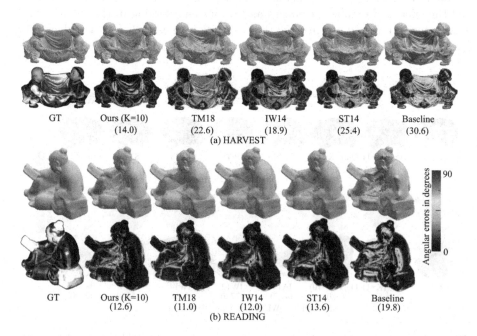

Fig. 7. Recovered surface normals and error maps for (a) HARVEST and (b) READING in the *DiLiGenT* dataset

---

[11] As for [8], we used the default setting of their package except that we gave the camera intrinsics provided by [11] and changed the noise variance to zero.

[12] Please find the full comparison in our supplementary.

achieved the smallest errors averaged over 10 objects, best scores for 6 of 10 objects. It is valuable to note that other top-ranked algorithms [20,21] are time-consuming since HS17 [20] requires the dictionary learning for every different light configuration and TM18 [21] needs the unsupervised training for every estimation while our inference time is less than five seconds (when $K = 1$) for each dataset on CPU. Taking a close look at each object, Fig. 7 provides some important insights. HARVEST is the most non-convex scene in *DiLiGenT* and other state-of-the art algorithms (TM18 [21], IW14 [7], ST14 [18]) failed in the estimation of normals inside the "bag" due to strong shadow and inter-reflections. Our CNN-based method estimated much more reasonable surface normals there thanks to the network trained based on the carefully created *CyclesPS* dataset. On the other hand, our method did not work best (though not bad) for READING which is another non-convex scene. Our analysis indicated that this is because of the inter-reflection of *high-intensity narrow specularities* that were rarely observed in our training dataset (Narrow specularities appear only when *roughness* in the principled BSDF is near zero).

5   Conclusion

In this paper, we have presented a CNN-based photometric stereo method which works for various kind of isotropic scenes with global illumination effects. By projecting photometric images and lighting information onto the observation map, unstructured information is naturally fed into the CNN. Our detailed experimental results have shown the state-of-the-art performance of our method for both synthetic and real data especially when the surface is non-convex. To make better training set for handling narrow inter-reflections is our future direction.

References

1. Kendall, A., et al.: End-to-end learning of geometry and context for deep stereo regression. In: Proceedings of ICCV (2017)
2. Vijayanarasimhan, S., Ricco, S., Schmid, C., Sukthankar, R., Fragkiadaki, K.: Sfm-net: learning of structure and motion from video (2017). arXiv preprint arXiv:1704.07804
3. Kar, A., Häne, C., Malik, J.: Learning multi-view stereo machine. In: Proceedings of NIPS (2017)
4. Kim, K., Gu, J., Tyree, S., Molchanov, P., Niessner, M., Kautz, J.: A lightweight approach for on-the-fly reflectance estimation. In: Proceedings of ICCV (2017)
5. Wu, L., Ganesh, A., Shi, B., Matsushita, Y., Wang, Y., Ma, Y.: Robust photometric stereo via low-rank matrix completion and recovery. In: Kimmel, R., Klette, R., Sugimoto, A. (eds.) ACCV 2010. LNCS, vol. 6494, pp. 703–717. Springer, Heidelberg (2011). https://doi.org/10.1007/978-3-642-19318-7_55
6. Ikehata, S., Wipf, D., Matsushita, Y., Aizawa, K.: Robust photometric stereo using sparse regression. In: Proceedings of CVPR (2012)
7. Ikehata, S., Wipf, D., Matsushita, Y., Aizawa, K.: Photometric stereo using sparse bayesian regression for general diffuse surfaces. IEEE Trans. Pattern Anal. Mach. Intell. **36**(9), 1816–1831 (2014)

8. Quau, Y., Wu, T., Lauze, F., Durou, J.D., Cremers, D.: A non-convex variational approach to photometric stereo under inaccurate lighting. In: Proceedings of CVPR (2017)
9. Cycles. https://www.cycles-renderer.org/
10. Burley, B.: Physically-based shading at disney, part of practical physically based shading in film and game production. In: SIGGRAPH 2012 Course Notes (2012)
11. Shi, B., Mo, Z., Wu, Z., Duan, D., Yeung, S.K., Tan, P.: A benchmark dataset and evaluation for non-lambertian and uncalibrated photometric stereo. IEEE Trans. Pattern Anal. Mach. Intell. (2018, to appear)
12. Woodham, P.: Photometric method for determining surface orientation from multiple images. Opt. Engg **19**(1), 139–144 (1980)
13. Alldrin, N., Zickler, T., Kriegman, D.: Photometric stereo with non-parametric and spatially-varying reflectance. In: Proceedings of CVPR (2008)
14. Goldman, D.B., Curless, B., Hertzmann, A., Seitz, S.M.: Shape and spatially-varying brdfs from photometric stereo. IEEE Trans. Pattern Anal. Mach. Intell. **32**(6), 1060–1071 (2010)
15. Higo, T., Matsushita, Y., Ikeuchi, K.: Consensus photometric stereo. In: Proceedings of CVPR (2010)
16. Shi, B., Tan, P., Matsushita, Y., Ikeuchi, K.: Elevation angle from reflectance monotonicity: photometric stereo for general isotropic reflectances. In: Fitzgibbon, A., Lazebnik, S., Perona, P., Sato, Y., Schmid, C. (eds.) ECCV 2012. LNCS, vol. 7574, pp. 455–468. Springer, Heidelberg (2012). https://doi.org/10.1007/978-3-642-33712-3_33
17. Ikehata, S., Aizawa, K.: Photometric stereo using constrained bivariate regression for general isotropic surfaces. In: Proceedings of CVPR (2014)
18. Shi, B., Tan, P., Matsushita, Y., Ikeuchi, K.: Bi-polynomial modeling of low-frequency reflectances. IEEE Trans. Pattern Anal. Mach. Intell. **36**(6), 1078–1091 (2014)
19. Santo, H., Samejima, M., Sugano, Y., Shi, B., Matsushita, Y.: Deep photometric stereo network. In: International Workshop on Physics Based Vision meets Deep Learning (PBDL) in Conjunction with IEEE International Conference on Computer Vision (ICCV) (2017)
20. Hui, Z., Sankaranarayanan, A.C.: Shape and spatially-varying reflectance estimation from virtual exemplars. IEEE Trans. Pattern Anal. Mach. Intell. **39**(10), 2060–2073 (2017)
21. Taniai, T., Maehara, T.: Neural inverse rendering for general reflectance photometric stereo. In: Proceedings of ICML (2018)
22. Goldman, D., Curless, B., Hertzmann, A., Seitz, S.: Shape and spatially-varying brdfs from photometric stereo. In: Proceedings of ICCV (2005)
23. Ward, G.: Measuring and modeling anisotropic reflection. Comput. Graph. **26**(2), 265–272 (1992)
24. Chandraker, M., Ramamoorthi, R.: What an image reveals about material reflectance. In: Proceedings of ICCV (2011)
25. Shen, H.L., Han, T.Q., Li, C.: Efficient photometric stereo using kernel regression. IEEE Trans. Image Process. **26**(1), 439–451 (2017)
26. Silver, W.M.: Determining shape and reflectance using multiple images. Master's thesis, MIT (1980)
27. Hertzmann, A., Seitz, S.: Example-based photometric stereo: shape reconstruction with general, varying brdfs. IEEE Trans. Pattern Anal. Mach. Intell. **27**(8), 1254–1264 (2005)

28. Huang, G., Liu, Z., van der Maaten, L., Weinberger, K.Q.: Densely connected convolutional networks. In: Proceedings of CVPR (2017)
29. Matusik, W., Pfister, H., Brand, M., McMillan, L.: A data-driven reflectance model. ACM Trans. Graph. **22**(3), 759–769 (2003)
30. Alldrin, N., Kriegman, D.: Toward reconstructing surfaces with arbitrary isotropic reflectance: a stratified photometric stereo approach. In: Proceedings of ICCV (2007)
31. Stark, M., Arvo, J., Smits, B.: Barycentric parameterizations for isotropic brdfs. IEEE Trans. Vis. Comput. Graph. **11**(2), 126–138 (2011)
32. Montes, R., Urena, C.: An overview of brdf models. Technical report, LSI-2012-001 en Digibug Coleccion: TIC167 - Articulos (2012)
33. Simard, P.Y., Steinkraus, D., Platt, J.C.: Best practices for convolutional neural networks applied to visual document analysis. In: Proceedings of ICDAR (2003)
34. Schmidt, U., Roth, S.: Learning rotation-aware features: from invariant priors to equivariant descriptors. In: Proceedings of CVPR (2012)
35. Kingma, D., Ba, J.: Adam: a method for stochastic optimization. In: proceedings of ICLR (2014)
36. Chang, A.X., et al.: ShapeNet: an information-rich 3D model repository. Technical report, Stanford University, Princeton University, Toyota Technological Institute at Chicago (2015). arXiv:1512.03012 [cs.GR]
37. Blender. https://www.cycles-renderer.org/
38. Chollet, F., et al.: Keras (2015). https://github.com/keras-team/keras

Dynamic Conditional Networks
for Few-Shot Learning

Fang Zhao[1], Jian Zhao[1,2]([⊠]), Shuicheng Yan[1,3], and Jiashi Feng[1]

[1] National University of Singapore, Singapore, Singapore
{elezhf,eleyans,elefjia}@nus.edu.sg
[2] National University of Defense Technology, Hunan, China
[3] Qihoo 360 AI Institute, Beijing, China
zhaojian90@u.nus.edu
https://zhaoj9014.github.io/

Abstract. This paper proposes a novel Dynamic Conditional Convolutional Network (DCCN) to handle conditional few-shot learning, i.e, only a few training samples are available for each condition. DCCN consists of dual subnets: DyConvNet contains a dynamic convolutional layer with a bank of basis filters; CondiNet predicts a set of adaptive weights from conditional inputs to linearly combine the basis filters. In this manner, a specific convolutional kernel can be dynamically obtained for each conditional input. The filter bank is shared between all conditions thus only a low-dimension weight vector needs to be learned. This significantly facilitates the parameter learning across different conditions when training data are limited. We evaluate DCCN on four tasks which can be formulated as conditional model learning, including specific object counting, multi-modal image classification, phrase grounding and identity based face generation. Extensive experiments demonstrate the superiority of the proposed model in the conditional few-shot learning setting.

Keywords: Conditional model · Few-shot learning · Deep learning Dynamic convolution · Filter bank

1 Introduction

A conditional model is a significant machine learning framework which can be exploited in many tasks, such as multi-modal learning and conditional generative models. It usually contains two inputs. One is interest of task, and the other one is conditional input and provides additional information of specific situation. Recently deep conditional models have attracted much attention since deep neural networks have achieved unprecedented advances in many important fields, such as computer vision [13,15], natural language processing [19,37] and speech recognition [1,26]. However, they generally suffer performance decline in

---

F. Zhao and J. Zhao—equal contribution.

© Springer Nature Switzerland AG 2018
V. Ferrari et al. (Eds.): ECCV 2018, LNCS 11219, pp. 20–36, 2018.
https://doi.org/10.1007/978-3-030-01267-0_2

the challenging **conditional few-shot learning** scenario, where training samples for each condition are limited due to the high dimension of the condition space although the total number of training samples can be large.

Deep learning based methods typically require a huge amount of labelled data for training as well as specialized computational platform and optimization strategies to achieve satisfactory performance. Their performance usually drops severely for learning problems with small training sample size due to severe over-fitting issues. In contrast, humans, even children can grasp a new concept (*e.g.*, a "giraffe") remarkably fast, "sample efficiently" and generalize to novel cases reasonably from just a short exposure to few examples (*e.g.*, pictures in a book) [4,20]. This phenomenon motivates the research on the problem of *few-shot learning*, *i.e.*, the task to learn a new concept on the fly, from a few or even a single annotated example for each category [3,36].

Few-shot learning is of great significance both academically and industrially, since (1) models excelling at this task would help alleviate expensive and labour-intensive data collection and labeling as they would not require massive labelled training data to achieve reasonable performance; (2) the target data in practice usually have a large number of different categories but very few examples per category. For instance, when operating in natural environments, robots are supposed to recognize many unfamiliar objects after seeing only few examples for each [17]. The ability of generalizing in such scenarios would be beneficial to modeling the practical data distribution more effectively.

In this paper, we mainly focus on improving two kinds of models in the conditional few-shot learning scenario, *i.e.*, the discriminative one and the generative one. The discriminative models often resort to hand-crafted features with huge human-engineering efforts and then adopt metric learning algorithms or data-driven deep learning solutions from ample labelled data. However, such data-driven methods are too computationally complex to meet practical applications. Moreover, massive labelled training data covering all underlying variations are usually expensive and unavailable. The generative models often leverage data generative models, *e.g.*, Generative Adversarial Networks (GANs) [10], Conditional Generative Adversarial Networks (Conditional-GANs) [24], Boundary Equilibrium Generative Adversarial Networks (BE-GANs) [2], *etc.*, for synthesizing auxiliary training data for data augmentation. However, among current generative methods, the quality of synthesized data is still far from being satisfactory to perform practical analysis tasks. ·

In order to address the challenging and realistic conditional few-shot learning problems, we explore a novel approach to learn a deep conditional model from a few labeled examples of each condition, which can generalize well to other cases of the same condition. The conditions could be based on category labels, on some part of data, or even on data from different modalities. Moreover, to enable on-the-fly computation with high efficiency, we embody this conditional few-shot learning problem into learning dual subnets jointly in an end-to-end way. One subnet is called DyConNet, which contains a **Dy**namic **Conv**olutional layer with a bank of trainable basis filters. Given any **Condi**tional input, the other subnet, called CondiNet, predicts a set of adaptive weights to linearly combine the basis filters. In this manner, a specific convolutional kernel can be dynamically obtained for each conditional input, as illustrated in Fig. 1. During optimization, the filter bank is shared between all conditionals thus only a low-dimension weight vector needs to be leaned for each condition, which significantly compensates the limited information in few-shot setting and facilitates the sample-efficient parameter learning across conditions. We term this model as **Dynamic Conditional Convolutional Network** (DCCN). We evaluate DCCN on four distinct tasks, all of which can be formulated as conditional model learning, including specific object counting, multi-modal image classification, phrase grounding and identity based face generation. The proposed DCCN outperforms other discriminative and generative conditional models for all the tasks.

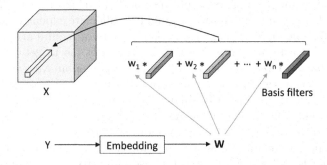

Fig. 1. Dynamic convolutional layer of DyConvNet. It has a filter bank consisting of several basis filters. A set of adaptive weights $\mathbf{W} = \{w_1, w_2, \cdots, w_n\}$ is predicted by the embedding of CondiNet from conditional inputs Y to perform the linear combination on the basis filters, which produces the convolution filters applied on feature maps X

Our contributions in this paper are summarized as follows. (1) We present a novel and effective deep architecture, which contains a **Dynamic Conv**olutional sub**Net** (DyConvNet) and a **Condi**tional sub**Net** (CondiNet) that jointly perform learning to learn in an end-to-end way. This deep architecture provides a unified framework for efficient conditional few-shot learning. (2) The dynamic convolution is achieved through linearly combining the basis filters of the filter bank in the DyConvNet with a set of adaptive weights predicted by the CondiNet from conditional inputs, which is different from existing conditional learning approaches that combine the two inputs through direct concatenation. (3) Our architecture is general and works well for multiple distinct conditional model learning tasks. The source codes as well as the trained models of our deep architecture will be made available to the community.

2 Related Works

Our work is related to several others in the literature. However, we believe to be the first to look at methods that can learn the parameters of deep conditional models in the few-shot setting.

Since its inception, few-shot learning has been widely studied in the context of generative approaches. The real annotated data covering all variations are expensive to achieve, even impossible, thus synthesizing realistic data is beneficial for more efficiently training deep models for few-shot learning, by augmenting the number of samples with desired variations and avoiding costly annotation work [39,40]. Successful generation from limited labelled training samples usually requires carefully tuned inductive biases using additional available information due to the high dimensionality of the feature space [14]. Such additional information can be accessed through various ways. For instance, (1) more samples of categories of interest can be obtained from huge amount of unlabelled data as in semi-supervised learning [6,42]; (2) the available labelled training data can be augmented using simple transformations, such as jittering, noise injection, *etc.*, as commonly used in deep learning [7,8,18]; (3) samples from other relevant categories can be utilized through transfer learning to assist parameter learning [21]; (4) new virtual samples can be synthesized, either rendered explicitly with GAN-based techniques [2,10,24] or created implicitly through compositional representations [25,41]. Recently, Mehrotra *et al.* [23] argued that having a learnable and more expressive similarity objective is an essential missing component, and proposed a network design inspired by deep residual networks that allows the efficient computation of this more expressive pairwise similarity objective. These approaches can significantly advance the performance of few-shot learning if a generative model that accounts for the underlying data distribution is known. However, such a model is usually unavilable and the generation of additional real or synthesized samples often requires substantial efforts.

A different trend of approaches to few-shot learning is to learn a discriminative embedding space, which is typically done with a siamese network [5]. Given an exemplar of a novel category, recognition is performed in the embedding space by a simple rule such as nearest-neighbor. Training is usually performed by classifying pairs according to distance [9], or by enforcing a distance ranking with a triplet loss [27]. A variant is to combine embeddings using the outer-product, which yields a bilinear classification rule [22]. Built on the advances made by the siamese architecture, Vinyals *et al.* [33] employed ideas from metric learning based on deep neural features and from recent advances that augment neural networks with external memories. They proposed a framework which learns a network that maps a small labelled support set and an unlabelled example to its label, obviating the need for fine-tuning to adapt to new class types. Ravi and Larochelle [31] proposed an Long Short Term Memory (LSTM) based meta-learner model to learn the exact optimization algorithm used to train another learner neural network classifier in the few-shot regime. The parametrization of their model allows it to learn appropriate parameter updates specifically for the scenario where a set amount of updates will be made, while also learning a general initialization of the learner (classifier) network that allows for quick convergence of training. However, these methods did not consider conditional model learning and are usually computational expensive for effectively and efficiently solving the few-shot learning problems.

Compared with previous attempts, our proposed method is conceptually simple yet powerful for conditional few-shot learning, which allows learning all parameters from scratch, generalizing across different tasks, and can be seen as a network that effectively "learns to learn". Detailed comparisons with gernerative and discriminative counterparts on various tasks are provided in Sect. 4.

3   Dynamic Conditional Parameter Prediction

Despite the recent success of deep neural networks, it remains challenging to accommodate such models to an extremely large number of categories with limited samples for each, as in the scenario of few-shot learning. Many works to date have mainly focused on learning one-to-one mappings from input to output. However, many interesting problems are more naturally considered as a probabilistic one-to-many mapping. For instance, in the case of image labelling, there may be many different tags that could appropriately be applied to a given image, and different data annotators may use different terms to describe the same image. One way to help address the issue is to leverage additional information from other modalities and to use a conditional model, taking as input small samples and conditional variables, and the one-to-many mapping is instantiated as a conditional predictive distribution.

Since we consider few-shot learning in a conditional modeling task, we start with formulating the standard conditional model learning. It aims to find the parameter W that minimizes the loss $\mathcal{L}$ of a predictor function $h(X|Y;W)$, averaged over N samples x_i and corresponding conditions y_i:

$$\min_{W} \frac{1}{N} \sum_{i=1}^{N} \mathcal{L}(h(x_i|y_i;W)), \tag{1}$$

where the model can be a discriminative one to learn a classifier or a generative one to learn a conditional distribution over X and Y.

In the case when the dimension of the condition space is too high, the training samples are still scarce for each conditional state even though there are massive training data in total, and the goal is to learn W from small samples with the condition y of interest, called conditional few-shot learning. The main challenge in conditional few-shot learning is to find a mechanism to incorporate domain-specific information into the network. Another challenge, which is of practical importance in applications of few-shot learning, is to enhance efficiency of optimization for Eq. (1).

We propose to address both challenges by learning the parameter W of the predictor from small samples with the conditions y using a meta-learning process, i.e., a non-iterative feed-forward function φ (meta learner) that maps $(y;W')$ to an optimal W of the predictor (base learner). We parameterize this function using a neural network model and we call it a CondiNet. The CondiNet output depends on the condition y which is a representative of the condition of interest, and contains parameter W' of its own. We train the CondiNet as follows such that it can produce suitable W for different tasks. We optimize the CondiNet using the following objective function. The feed-forward CondiNet evaluation is much faster than solving the optimization problem of Eq. (1).

$$\min_{\varphi} \frac{1}{N} \sum_{i=1}^{N} \mathcal{L}(h(x_i; \varphi(y_i; W'))). \tag{2}$$

Importantly, the parameters of the original W of Eq. (1) now adapt dynamically to each conditional input y. Note that the training scheme is reminiscent of that of siamese networks [5] which also employ dual subnets. However, siamese networks adopt the same network architecture with shared weights, and compute the inner-product of their outputs to produce a similarity score:

$$\min_{W} \frac{1}{N} \sum_{i=1}^{N} \mathcal{L}(\langle h(x_i; W), h(y_i; W)\rangle). \tag{3}$$

There are two key differences with our model: (1) we treat $h(\cdot)$ and $\varphi(\cdot)$ asymmetrically, which results in a different objective function; (2) more importantly, the output of $\varphi(y; W')$ is used to parametrize convolutional layers that determine the intermediate representations in the network $h(\cdot)$ dynamically. This is significantly different from siamese networks [5] and bilinear networks [22], as well as traditional conditional networks [24] based on the conditional probability $p(X|Y; W)$.

Now, we explain the implementation of the CondiNet $\varphi(\cdot)$ and the main predictor $h(\cdot)$ formally. Given an input tensor $x \in \mathbb{R}^{p \times q \times c}$, weights $W \in \mathbb{R}^{k \times k \times c \times d}$ (where k is the kernel size), and biases $b \in \mathbb{R}^d$, the output $f \in \mathbb{R}^{p' \times q' \times d}$ of a convolutional layer is given by

$$f = W * x + b, \tag{4}$$

where $*$ denotes convolution operation, and the biases b are applied to each of the d channels.

We propose to formulate the weights and biases as functions of y, $W(y)$ and $b(y)$, to represent the dynamic conditional parameters given the conditional input $y \in \mathbb{R}$:

$$f = W(y) * x + b(y). \tag{5}$$

While Eq. (5) seems to be a straightforward drop-in replacement for convolutional layers, careful analysis reveals that it scales extremely poorly. The main reason is the typically high dimensionality of the output space of the CondiNet $\varphi(\cdot) : \mathbb{R} \to \mathbb{R}^{k \times k \times c \times d}$. Since k is usually small and so is k^2, for a comparable number of input and output channels in a convolutional layer ($c \simeq d$), the output space of the CondiNet grows quadratically with the number of channels. Overfitting issues, memory and time costs make learning such a regressor difficult in few-shot learning settings.

In order to address the above-mentioned issue when learning a conditional model in few shot, we herein propose a simple yet effective method to reduce the output space by considering a decomposition as below (we drop the bias term b for simplification),

$$f = \sum_{i=1}^{n} (w'_i(y) \cdot w_i) * x, \tag{6}$$

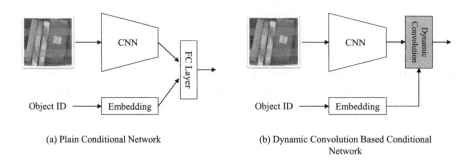

(a) Plain Conditional Network   (b) Dynamic Convolution Based Conditional Network

Fig. 2. Flow charts of object counting based on specific object ID

where $w \in \mathbb{R}^{k \times k \times c \times d}$, $w'(y) \in \mathbb{R}$, the product $(w'_i(y) \cdot w_i)$ can be seen as a decomposed representation of convolutional kernels, to linearly combine the adaptive weights w'_i predicted by the CondiNet $\varphi(\cdot)$ and the basis filters w_i of a filter bank, and n denotes the number of basis filters.

The filter bank is shared between all conditional states and only the weights of basis filters are specific for each conditional state. Both w and w' contain trainable parameters, but they are modest in size compared to the case discussed in Eq. (5). Importantly, the CondiNet $\varphi(\cdot)$ now only needs to predict a set of adaptive weights, so its output space grows linearly with the number of basis filters in the filter bank (i.e., $\varphi(\cdot) : \mathbb{R} \to \mathbb{R}^n$). Since the resulted convolutional kernel $(w'_i \cdot w_i)$ in Eq. (6) is dynamically changed, depending on the prediction of the CondiNet $\varphi(\cdot)$ and the filter bank of the main predictor $h(\cdot)$, we construct $h(\cdot)$ as another subnet — DyConvNet. The dual subnets operate cooperatively for jointly learning parameters of a deep conditional model with conventional chain rules and **B**ack **P**ropagation (BP) algorithms in few shot.

4   Experiments

We evaluate our model on four conditional few-shot learning problems to verify the effectiveness of dynamically combining the basis filters, including specific object counting, multi-modal image classification, phrase grounding and identity based face generation.

4.1   Specific Object Counting

The specific object counting task is from Amazon Bin Image Dataset (ABID) Challenge, which is to predict the quantity of the object in a bin, given an image and the target category. When the maximal quantity of an object in a bin is set to a constant (here is 5), we formulate this task as a conditional classification model by viewing the object category as a conditional input. As shown in Fig. 2(b), one network is used to extract image features, and the other network is used to embed the object ID. Finally, our dynamic conditional layer is used to combine the last layers of the two networks to output the quantity of the object. Here we use a plain conditional network (Fig. 2(a)) as a baseline, i.e., directly concatenating the last layers and substituting our dynamic conditional layer with a fully-connected layer.

Table 1. Accuracies of object quantity verification and identification on the Amazon Bin Image dataset

Methods	Dynamic			Plain
	4-D	8-D	16-D	
Identification	76.60%	**76.81%**	75.66%	74.48%
Verification	85.39%	**85.48%**	84.81%	84.87%

Dataset and Evaluation Metric. We evaluate our model on two subtasks, i.e., object quantity verification and identification. The former is to verify whether the given object quantity is correct for a bin image. The latter is to directly count the objects in a bin image. The dataset contains 535,234 bin images and is divided into two subsets, 481,711 images for training and the remaining images for test. For the object quantity verification, we test on triplets of image, object ID and quantity. The accuracy is used to measure the performance of both the tasks.

Architecture and Training. Similar with the model architecture settings provided by the dataset website, we use the ResNet-34 network to extract image features. The embedding dimension of the object ID in the plain conditional network is 512. The dimension of the dynamic conditional layer is set to 4, 8 and 16 respectively to investigate effects of using different numbers of basis filters. All images are resized into 224×224 for convenient training and comparison. Because it is actually a classification task, the Softmax loss is adopted to optimize the entire network. We train for 30 epochs. The initial learning rate is 0.1 and it is dropped by a factor of 10 every 10 epochs.

Results and Analysis. Table 1 reports accuracies of our method under various dimensions of the dynamic convolutional layer and the plain conditional network. One can see that our network using 8-D dynamic layer achieves the best accuracy. The plain conditional network performs not well because the set of object IDs is too large and each ID is only associated with few training examples (one example for most IDs). It is hard to learn a conditional network for each ID when the embedding dimension is too high, and the network coditional output would not be discriminative enough if the embedding dimension is low. In contrast, the proposed DCCN makes different IDs share a filter bank. Only a low-dimension vector is needed to learn to combine the set of filters as a convolutional kernel. Through applying this kernel on the top layer of the feature network, the spatially local correlation of image and object ID can be learned to make the conditional output more discriminative for different IDs. Note that as the dimension of dynamic layer continuously increases, such as 16, the performance decreases instead due to overfitting.

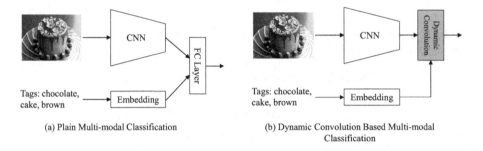

(a) Plain Multi-modal Classification

(b) Dynamic Convolution Based Multi-modal Classification

Fig. 3. Flow charts of multi-modal image classification

4.2   Multi-modal Image Classification

Multi-modal classification can be formulated as a typical conditional model consisting of two networks. Figure 3(a) shows a general framework of multi-modal classification. The inputs of the two network are an image and text describing the image, respectively. The texts are usually transformed into bag-of-words vectors at first. The outputs of the networks are then combined into a feature vector through a fully connected layer. We use this plain conditional network as a baseline. Fig. 3(b) illustrates the proposed dynamic convolution used for multi-modal classification, where we substitute the fully connected layer with the dynamic conditional layer.

Dataset and Evaluation Metric. We evaluate our model on the MIRFlickr-25K dataset [16] which consists of 25,000 images downloaded from the social website Flickr. Each image associates with some of 20,000 tags. 38 class labels including various scenes and objects, such as sunset, car and bird, are used to annotate these images and an image may belong to multiple class labels. We randomly sample 20,000 images for training and the rest for testing. The multi-label classification performance is measured by the Intersection over Union (IoU) in the multi-label setting, which is defined as the number of correctly predicted labels divided by the union of predicted and ground-truth labels.

Architecture and Training. The base network for both the baseline and our method is the ResNet-34 network. The embedding dimension of the text in the baseline is 512. We set the dimensions of the dynamic conditional layer to 32, 64 and 128 respectively. To deal with the multiple labels in one image, here we adopt the cross entropy loss to learn the conditional networks. The training epoch is 90. Beginning with 0.1, the learning rate is dropped by a factor of 10 every 30 epochs.

Table 2. IoU of multi-modal multi-label classification on the MIR-Flickr25K dataset

Methods		Dynamic		Plain
	32-D	64-D	128-D	
Tags 5k	0.6517	**0.6553**	0.6520	0.6489
10k	0.6513	**0.6606**	0.6560	0.6516
20k	0.6549	**0.6577**	0.6543	0.6490

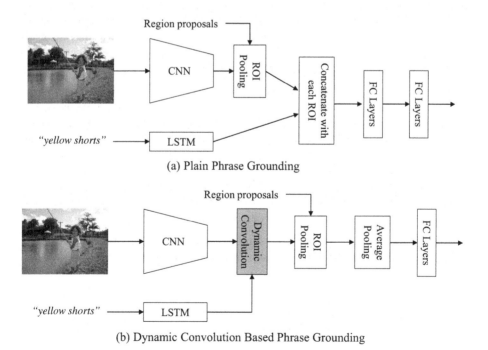

(a) Plain Phrase Grounding

(b) Dynamic Convolution Based Phrase Grounding

Fig. 4. Flow charts of phrase grounding

Results and Analysis. Table 2 reports the results of different methods on the MIR-Flickr25K dataset. It can be observed that when the dimension of the dynamic layer is 64, our dynamic conditional network outperforms the baseline under the condition of various numbers of tags. We argue that although the total training images are sufficient, there are only a few ones for each tag. That is to say, it is still a few-shot learning for each tag. Thus the dynamic layer which reduces the parameters of the conditional network is able to address the problem of overfitting effectively for this kind of few-shot conditional learning, and the filter bank shared by tags can be learned easily by using all training images.

4.3   Phrase Grounding

The task of phrase grounding is to localize objects or scenes described by text phrases in images [29,32]. This task can also be modeled as a conditional model. A typical framework of phrase grounding is illustrated in Fig. 4(a). One convolutional neural network is used to produce a spatial feature map of an input image, and Long Short-Term Memory network (LSTM) [11] is used to embed an input phrase into a vector with fixed length. Then the features of a set of region proposals (i.e., Edge Boxes [43]) are extracted by applying the ROI pooling on the spatial feature map. Finally, the proposal features are concatenated with the phrase vector respectively to compute correlation scores by two fully connected layers. Figure 4(b) shows the proposed dynamic convolution based phrase grounding. We firstly use the dynamic conditional layer to combine the phrase vector with the image feature map to obtain a correlative feature map. Then the ROI pooling is applied to obtain the correlative feature map for each region proposal, which is fed into the average pooling and a fully connected layer sequentially to compute the correlation score.

Dataset and Evaluation Metric. The Flickr30k Entities dataset [30] is used to evaluate our model for phrase grounding, which is an extension of the Flickr30K dataset [38]. It consists of 31,000 images and their captions which are associated with 276,000 manually annotated bounding boxes. We use 2,000 images for testing and the remaining images for training. Following [30], if a single phrase (*e.g.*, rainbow flags) has multiple ground truth bounding boxes, the union of the boxes is used to represent the phrase. If the IoU of an image region predicted for a phrase and the ground truth bounding box is larger than 0.5, the predicted region is deemed correct for the phrase.

Architecture and Training. The same with [32], we adopt the VGG-16 network to extract the image feature map, which is pretrained on the PascalVOC

Table 3. Accuracy (IoU > 0.5) of phrase grounding on the Flickr30k Entities dataset

Methods	Dynamic			SMPL	NonlinearSP	GroundeR
	8-D	16-D	32-D			
Accuracy	50.18	**50.65**	50.52	42.08	43.89	47.81

Table 4. Accuracy (IoU > 0.5) of phrase grounding for various phrase types on the Flickr30k Entities dataset

Methods	People	Clothing	Body parts	Animals	Vehicles	Instruments	Scene	Other
SMPL	57.89	34.61	15.87	55.98	52.25	23.46	34.22	26.23
GroundeR	61.00	38.12	10.33	62.55	**68.75**	36.42	**58.18**	29.08
Dynamic	**67.37**	**38.12**	**18.22**	**69.93**	56.04	**37.57**	54.05	**32.59**

dataset for object detection and then is fixed when training the entire conditional model. Both the numbers of the hidden and input units of LSTM are 512. The dimension of the dynamic layer is set to 8, 16 and 32, respectively. 100 region proposals generated by Edge Boxes are used as candidate bounding boxes. We employ the Softmax loss to learn the model to maximize the correlation score of the input phrase with the correct region proposal. We train for 90 epochs. The initial learning rate is 0.01 and every 30 epochs it is dropped by a factor of 10.

Results and Analysis. Table 3 reports the accuracy of phrase grounding for different methods under the condition of IoU > 0.5 on the Flickr30k Entities dataset. One can see that our dynamic conditional network achieves the best accuracy compared with the state-of-the-art methods when the dimension of the dynamic layer is 16. NonlinearSP [34] and GroundR [32] have similar frameworks with Fig. 4(a), i.e., using fully connected layers to combine the features of the image region and phrase. SMPL [35] utilizes a bipartite matching to compute their correlation score. However, all of these methods do not consider that only a few training images are available for each phrase although there are a large number of training images in this dataset. In this sense, this task can be viewed as a conditional few-shot learning problem which can be solved better by our dynamic conditional layer. Table 4 reports the accuracy of phrase grounding for different types of phrases. Our method has better performance than other methods for most phrase types.

Although there are some phrase grounding methods which have better performance than our method, e.g., RtP [28] and SPC+PPC [29], we argue that these methods employ additional cues to improve correlation learning of image region and phrase, such as region-phrase compatibility, candidate position and size. Actually, our model is mostly like a proof-of-concept and applied on the task of phrase grounding to verify its effectiveness on the conditional few-shot learning. It is orthogonal to many technical improvements found in the phrase grounding literature.

4.4 Identity Based Face Generation

The proposed DCCN can also be used to improve conditional generative models. Here we test DCCN on the task of identity based face generation. Figure 5(a) shows a general framework based on conditional generative adversarial nets (GAN) [24], which consists of a generative model G and a discriminative model

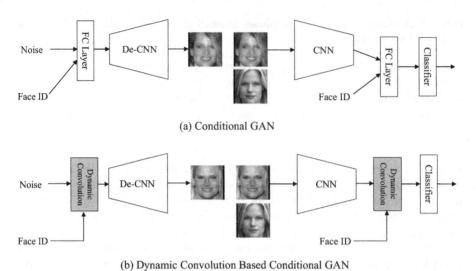

(a) Conditional GAN

(b) Dynamic Convolution Based Conditional GAN

Fig. 5. Flow charts of identity based face generation

D. In G, the prior input noise and the face ID are combined through a fully connected layer to obtain a joint hidden representation. Then the representation is fed into a deconvolutional neural network to generate a face image of the input ID. In D, a convolutional neural network is employed to extract the features of the faces generated by G and the real faces. Then the feature and the embedding vector of the face ID are concatenated and fed into a classifier, which judges whether the face is real or not for this ID. The proposed dynamic convolution based conditional GAN is illustrated in Fig. 5(b). We use the dynamic conditional layer to integrate the face ID with the noise in D and the image feature in G, respectively.

Dataset and Evaluation Metric. We evaluate our model on the MS-Celeb-1M dataset [12] which contains about 10M face images for 100 K subjects. For the training set, we randomly sample 100 subjects and 10 face images for each subject to simulate the conditional few-shot setting. In testing, given a generated face image, a pretrained face recognition model is used to predict which one of the 100 subjects it belongs to. 50 images are generated for each subject. The precision-coverage (PC) curve and the cumulative match characteristic (CMC) curve are used to measure the performance of face identification.

Architecture and Training. We use five-layer fully convolutional and deconvolutional network in the generative and discriminative models, respectively. To learn the conditional GAN, we optimize the generative model G and the discriminative model D alternatively. D is trained to minimize the classification loss under the condition of the input ID, and G is trained to maximize the loss under the same condition, i.e., G trying to generate face images which can confuse G.

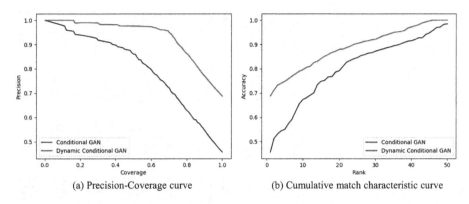

(a) Precision-Coverage curve   (b) Cumulative match characteristic curve

Fig. 6. Precision-Coverage and cumulative match characteristic curves of face identification for identity based face generation.

Results and Analysis. Figure 6 illustrates the PR and CMC curves of the face identification for generated face images. Table 5 reports the precision when Coverage = 0.99 and 0.95 and the accuracies of rank 1 and 5. It can be observed that dynamic conditional GAN achieves better performance than the plain conditional GAN in terms of all the metrics. The dynamic layer can effectively incorporate the information of conditional input through sharing filter bank across conditions when limited training data are available for each condition. Some examples of generated faces are shown in Fig. 7. Each row of faces corresponds to one subject. The faces generated by the dynamic conditional GAN are obviously more similar with the real face of the subject.

Table 5. Accuracy and Precision@Coverage of face identification for generated faces

Methods	Accuracy		Pricison@Coverage	
	Rank 1	Rank 5	P@C = 0.99	P@C = 0.95
Plain	0.457	0.550	0.05	0.18
Dynamic	**0.688**	**0.748**	**0.21**	**0.71**

5   Conclusion

This paper addressed the problem of conditional few-shot learning. A Dynamic Conditional Convolutional Network is presented to incorporate conditional input in a deep model when only a few training samples are available for each condition. In this model, a set of adaptive weights from conditional inputs is predicted to linearly combine the basis filters of a filter bank shared by all conditions. Then a dynamic convolutional kernel can be obtained according to different

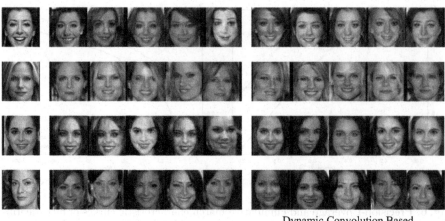

Conditional GAN

Dynamic Convolution Based
Conditional GAN

Fig. 7. Examples of identity based face generation

conditional inputs. Finally the dynamic kernel is applied on the top layer of the other network to provide conditional output. Qualitative and quantitative experiments on four tasks demonstrate that the proposed model achieves better performance compared with other conditional learning models.

Acknowledgments. Jian Zhao was partially supported by China Scholarship Council (CSC) grant 201503170248. Jiashi Feng was partially supported by NUS IDS R-263-000-C67-646, ECRA R-263-000-C87-133 and MOE Tier-II R-263-000-D17-112.

References

1. Amodei, D., et al.: Deep speech 2: end-to-end speech recognition in English and mandarin. In: International Conference on Machine Learning, pp. 173–182 (2016)
2. Berthelot, D., Schumm, T., Metz, L.: Began: boundary equilibrium generative adversarial networks. arXiv preprint arXiv:1703.10717 (2017)
3. Bertinetto, L., Henriques, J.F., Valmadre, J., Torr, P., Vedaldi, A.: Learning feedforward one-shot learners. In: Advances in Neural Information Processing Systems, pp. 523–531 (2016)
4. Bloom, P.: How Children Learn the Meanings of Words. The MIT Press (2000)
5. Bromley, J., Guyon, I., LeCun, Y., Säckinger, E., Shah, R.: Signature verification using a "siamese" time delay neural network. In: Advances in Neural Information Processing Systems, pp. 737–744 (1994)
6. Chapelle, O., Scholkopf, B., Zien, A.: Semi-supervised learning (chapelle, o. et al., eds. 2006)[book reviews]. IEEE Trans. Neural Netw. **20**(3), 542–542 (2009)
7. Chatfield, K., Simonyan, K., Vedaldi, A., Zisserman, A.: Return of the devil in the details: delving deep into convolutional nets. arXiv preprint arXiv:1405.3531 (2014)

8. Dosovitskiy, A., Springenberg, J.T., Riedmiller, M., Brox, T.: Discriminative unsupervised feature learning with convolutional neural networks. In: Advances in Neural Information Processing Systems, pp. 766–774 (2014)

9. Fan, H., Cao, Z., Jiang, Y., Yin, Q., Doudou, C.: Learning deep face representation. arXiv preprint arXiv:1403.2802 (2014)

10. Goodfellow, I., et al.: Generative adversarial nets. In: Advances in neural information processing systems, pp. 2672–2680 (2014)

11. Guadarrama, S., et al.: Long short-term memory. Neural Comput. (1997)

12. Guo, Y., Zhang, L., Hu, Y., He, X., Gao, J.: MS-Celeb-1M: a dataset and benchmark for large-scale face recognition. In: Leibe, B., Matas, J., Sebe, N., Welling, M. (eds.) ECCV 2016. LNCS, vol. 9907, pp. 87–102. Springer, Cham (2016). https://doi.org/10.1007/978-3-319-46487-9_6

13. He, K., Zhang, X., Ren, S., Sun, J.: Deep residual learning for image recognition. In: Proceedings of the IEEE Conference on Computer Vision and Pattern Recognition, pp. 770–778 (2016)

14. Hertz, T., Hillel, A.B., Weinshall, D.: Learning a kernel function for classification with small training samples. In: Proceedings of the International Conference on Machine Learning, pp. 401–408. ACM (2006)

15. Huang, G., Liu, Z., Weinberger, K.Q., van der Maaten, L.: Densely connected convolutional networks. arXiv preprint arXiv:1608.06993 (2016)

16. Huiskes, M.J., Lew, M.S.: The MIR flickr retrieval evaluation. In: Proceedings of the ACM International Conference on Multimedia Information Retrieval (2008)

17. Krause, E.A., Zillich, M., Williams, T.E., Scheutz, M.: Learning to recognize novel objects in one shot through human-robot interactions in natural language dialogues (2014)

18. Krizhevsky, A., Sutskever, I., Hinton, G.E.: Imagenet classification with deep convolutional neural networks. In: Advances in Neural Information Processing Systems, pp. 1097–1105 (2012)

19. Kumar, A., et al.: Ask me anything: dynamic memory networks for natural language processing. In: International Conference on Machine Learning, pp. 1378–1387 (2016)

20. Lake, B.M., Salakhutdinov, R.R., Tenenbaum, J.: One-shot learning by inverting a compositional causal process. In: Advances in Neural Information Processing Systems, pp. 2526–2534 (2013)

21. Lim, J.J., Salakhutdinov, R.R., Torralba, A.: Transfer learning by borrowing examples for multiclass object detection. In: Advances in Neural Information Processing Systems, pp. 118–126 (2011)

22. Lin, T.Y., RoyChowdhury, A., Maji, S.: Bilinear CNN models for fine-grained visual recognition. In: Proceedings of the IEEE International Conference on Computer Vision, pp. 1449–1457 (2015)

23. Mehrotra, A., Dukkipati, A.: Generative adversarial residual pairwise networks for one shot learning. arXiv preprint arXiv:1703.08033 (2017)

24. Mirza, M., Osindero, S.: Conditional generative adversarial nets. arXiv preprint arXiv:1411.1784 (2014)

25. Movshovitz-Attias, Y., Yu, Q., Stumpe, M.C., Shet, V., Arnoud, S., Yatziv, L.: Ontological supervision for fine grained classification of street view storefronts. In: Proceedings of the IEEE Conference on Computer Vision and Pattern Recognition, pp. 1693–1702 (2015)

26. Oord, A.v.d., et al.: Wavenet: a generative model for raw audio. arXiv preprint arXiv:1609.03499 (2016)

27. Parkhi, O.M., Vedaldi, A., Zisserman, A., et al.: Deep face recognition
28. Plummer, B.A., Wang, L., Cervantes, C.M., Caicedo, J.C., Hockenmaier, J., Lazebnik, S.: Flickr30k entities: collecting region-to-phrase correspondences for richer imageto-sentence models. Int. J. Comput. Vis. **123**(1), 74–93 (2017)
29. Plummer1, B.A., Mallya, A., Cervantes, C.M., Hockenmaier, J., Lazebnik., S.: Phrase localization and visual relationship detection with comprehensive image-language cues. In: Proceedings of the IEEE International Conference on Computer Vision (2017)
30. Plummer1, B.A., Wang, L., Cervantes, C.M., Caicedo, J.C.: Flickr30k entities: collecting region-to-phrase correspondences for richer image-to-sentence models. In: Proceedings of the IEEE International Conference on Computer Vision (2015)
31. Ravi, S., Larochelle, H.: Optimization as a model for few-shot learning (2016)
32. Rohrbach, A., Rohrbach, M., Hu, R., Darrell, T., Schiele, B.: Grounding of textual phrases in images by reconstruction. In: Leibe, B., Matas, J., Sebe, N., Welling, M. (eds.) ECCV 2016. LNCS, vol. 9905, pp. 817–834. Springer, Cham (2016). https://doi.org/10.1007/978-3-319-46448-0_49
33. Vinyals, O., Blundell, C., Lillicrap, T., Wierstra, D., et al.: Matching networks for one shot learning. In: Advances in Neural Information Processing Systems, pp. 3630–3638 (2016)
34. Wang, L., Li, Y., Lazebnik, S.: Earning deep structure preserving image-text embeddings. In: Proceedings of the IEEE Conference on Computer Vision and Pattern Recognition (2016)
35. Wang, M., Azab, M., Kojima, N., Mihalcea, R., Deng, J.: Structured matching for phrase localization. In: Leibe, B., Matas, J., Sebe, N., Welling, M. (eds.) ECCV 2016. LNCS, vol. 9912, pp. 696–711. Springer, Cham (2016). https://doi.org/10.1007/978-3-319-46484-8_42
36. Wang, Y.-X., Hebert, M.: Learning to learn: model regression networks for easy small sample learning. In: Leibe, B., Matas, J., Sebe, N., Welling, M. (eds.) ECCV 2016. LNCS, vol. 9910, pp. 616–634. Springer, Cham (2016). https://doi.org/10.1007/978-3-319-46466-4_37
37. Wu, Y., et al.: Google's neural machine translation system: bridging the gap between human and machine translation. arXiv preprint arXiv:1609.08144 (2016)
38. Young, P., Lai, A., Hodosh, M., Hockenmaier, J.: From image descriptions to visual denotations: new similarity metrics for semantic inference over event descriptions. Trans. Assoc. Comput. Linguist. (2014)
39. Zhang, Z., Song, Y., Qi, H.: Age progression/regression by conditional adversarial autoencoder. In: Proceedings of the IEEE Conference on Computer Vision and Pattern Recognition (2017)
40. Zhao, J., Xiong, L., Jayashree, K., et al.: Dual-agent GANs for photorealistic and identity preserving profile face synthesis. In: Advances in Neural Information Processing Systems, pp. 66–76 (2017)
41. Zhu, X., Vondrick, C., Fowlkes, C.C., Ramanan, D.: Do we need more training data? Int. J. Comput. Vis. **119**(1), 76–92 (2016)
42. Zhu, X.: Semi-supervised learning literature survey (2005)
43. Zitnick, C.L., Dollár, P.: Edge boxes: locating object proposals from edges. In: Fleet, D., Pajdla, T., Schiele, B., Tuytelaars, T. (eds.) ECCV 2014. LNCS, vol. 8693, pp. 391–405. Springer, Cham (2014). https://doi.org/10.1007/978-3-319-10602-1_26

Deep Factorised Inverse-Sketching

Kaiyue Pang[1]([⊠]), Da Li[1], Jifei Song[1], Yi-Zhe Song[1], Tao Xiang[1],
and Timothy M. Hospedales[1,2]

[1] SketchX, Queen Mary University of London, London, UK
{kaiyue.pang,da.li,yizhe.song,j.song,t.xiang}@qmul.ac.uk
[2] The University of Edinburgh, Edinburgh, UK
t.hospedales@ed.ac.uk

Abstract. Modelling human free-hand sketches has become topical
recently, driven by practical applications such as fine-grained sketch
based image retrieval (FG-SBIR). Sketches are clearly related to photo
edge-maps, but a human free-hand sketch of a photo is not simply a
clean rendering of that photo's edge map. Instead there is a fundamental process of abstraction and iconic rendering, where overall geometry is
warped and salient details are selectively included. In this paper we study
this sketching process and attempt to invert it. We model this inversion
by translating iconic free-hand sketches to contours that resemble more
geometrically realistic projections of object boundaries, and separately
factorise out the salient added details. This factorised re-representation
makes it easier to match a free-hand sketch to a photo instance of an
object. Specifically, we propose a novel unsupervised image style transfer
model based on enforcing a cyclic embedding consistency constraint. A
deep FG-SBIR model is then formulated to accommodate complementary discriminative detail from each factorised sketch for better matching
with the corresponding photo. Our method is evaluated both qualitatively and quantitatively to demonstrate its superiority over a number
of state-of-the-art alternatives for style transfer and FG-SBIR.

1 Introduction

Free-hand sketch is the simplest form of human visual rendering. Albeit with
varying degrees of skill, it comes naturally to humans at young ages, and has
been used for millennia. Today it provides a convenient tool for communication,
and a promising input modality for visual retrieval. Prior sketch studies focus
on sketch recognition [4] or sketch-based image retrieval (SBIR). SBIR methods
can be further grouped into category-level [5] and instance-level fine-grained
SBIR (FG-SBIR) [43]. This dichotomy corresponds to how a sketch is created
– based on a category-name or a (real or mental) picture of a specific object
instance. These produce different granularities of visual cues (e.g., prototypical
vs. specific object detail). As argued in [43], it is fine-grained sketches of specific
object instances that bring practical benefit for image retrieval over the standard
text modality.

© Springer Nature Switzerland AG 2018
V. Ferrari et al. (Eds.): ECCV 2018, LNCS 11219, pp. 37–54, 2018.
https://doi.org/10.1007/978-3-030-01267-0_3

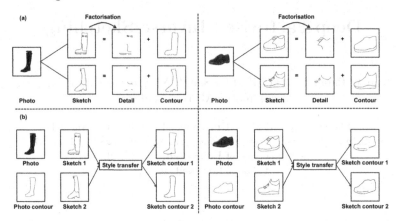

Fig. 1. (a) A free-hand object instance sketch consists of two parts: iconic contour and object details. (b) Given a sketch, our style transfer model restyles it into distortion-free contour. The synthesised contours of different sketches of the same object instance resembles each other as well as the corresponding photo contour.

Modelling fine-grained object sketches and matching them with corresponding photo images containing the same object instances is extremely challenging. This is because photos are exact perspective projections of a real world scene or object, while free-hand sketches are iconic abstractions with different geometry, and selected choice of included detail. Moreover, sketches are drawn by people of different backgrounds, drawing abilities and styles, and different subjective perspectives about the salience of details to include. Thus two people can draw very different sketches of the same object as shown in Fig. 1(a) photo→sketch.

A closer inspection of the human sketching process reveals that it includes two components. As shown in [21], a sketcher typically first deploys long strokes to draw iconic object contours, followed by shorter strokes to depict visual details (e.g., shoes laces or buckles in Fig. 1(a)). Both the iconic contour and object details are important for recognising the object instance and matching a sketch with its corresponding photo. The contour is informative about object subcategory (e.g., a boot or trainer), while the details distinguish instances within the subcategory – modelling both are thus necessary. However, they have very different characteristics demanding different treatments. The overall geometry of the sketch contour experiences large and user-specific distortion compared to the true edge contour of the photo (compare sketch contour in Fig. 1(a) with photo object contour in Fig. 1(b)). Photo edge contours are an exact perspective projection of the object boundary; and free-hand sketches are typically an orthogonal projection at best, and usually much more distorted than that – if only because humans seem unable to draw long smooth lines without distortion [6]. In contrast, distortion is less of an issue for shorter strokes in the object detail part. But choice and amount of details varies by artist (e.g., buckles in Fig. 1(a)).

In this paper, for the first time, we propose to model human sketches by inverting the sketching process. That is, instead of modelling the forward sketching pass (i.e., from photo/recollection to sketch), we study the inverse problem of translating sketches into visual representations that closely resemble the perspective geometry of photos. We further argue that this inversion problem is best tackled on two levels by separately factorising out object contours and the salient sketching details. Such factorisation is important for both modelling sketches and matching them with photos. This is due to the differences mentioned above: sketch contours are consistently present but suffer from large distortions, while details are less distorted but more inconsistent in their presence and abstraction level. Both parts can thus only be modelled effectively when they are factorised.

We tackle the first level of inverse-sketching by proposing a novel deep image synthesis model for style transfer. It takes a sketch as input, restyles the sketch into natural contours resembling the more geometrically realistic contours extracted from photo images, while removing object details (see Fig. 1(b)). This stylisation task is extremely difficult because (a) Collecting a large quantity of sketch-photo pairs is infeasible so the model needs to be trained in an unsupervised manner. (b) There is no pixel-to-pixel correspondence between the distorted sketch contour and realistic photo contour, making models that rely on direct pixel correspondence such as [14] unsuitable. To overcome these problems, we introduce a new cyclic embedding consistency in the proposed unsupervised image synthesis model. It forces the sketch and unpaired photo contours to share some support in a common low-dimensional semantic embedding space.

We next complete the inversion in a discriminative model designed for matching sketches with photos. It importantly utilises the synthesised contours to factor out object details to better assist with sketch-photo matching. Specifically, given a training set of sketches, their synthesised geometrically-realistic contours, and corresponding photo images, we develop a new FG-SBIR model that extracts factorised feature representations corresponding to the contour and detail parts respectively before fusing them to match against the photo. The model is a deep Siamese neural network with four branches. The sketch and its synthesised contours have their own branches respectively. A decorrelation loss is applied to ensure the two branch's representations are complementary and non-overlapping (i.e., factorised). The two features are then fused and subject to triplet matching loss with the features extracted from the positive and negative photo branches to make them discriminative.

The contributions of this work are as follows: (1) For the first time, the problem of factorised inverse-sketching is defined and identified as a key for both sketch modelling and sketch-photo matching. (2) A novel unsupervised sketch style transfer model is proposed to translate a human sketch into a geometrically-realistic contour. (3) We further develop a new FG-SBIR model which extracts an object detail representation to complement the synthesised contour for effective matching against photos.

2   Related Work

Sketch modelling: There are several lines of research aiming to deal with abstract sketches so that either sketch recognition or SBIR can be performed.

The most best studied is invariant representation engineering or learning. These either aim to hand-engineer features that are invariant to abstract sketch vs concrete photo domain [3,5,13], or learn a domain invariant representation given supervision of sketch-photo categories [12,23,37] and sketch-photo pairs [35,43]. More recent works have attempted to leverage insights from the human sketching process. [2,45] recognised the importance of stroke ordering, and [45] introduced ordered stroke deformation as a data augmentation strategy to generate more training sketches for sketch recognition task. The most explicit model of sketching to our knowledge is the stroke removal work considered in [30]. It abstracts sketches by proposing reinforcement learning (RL) of a stroke removal policy that estimates which strokes can be safely removed without affecting recognisability. It evaluates on FG-SBIR and uses the proposed RL-based framework to generate abstract variants of training sketches for data augmentation. Compared to [30,45], both of which perform within-domain abstraction (i.e., sketch to abstracted sketch), our approach presents a fundamental shift in that it models the inverse-sketching process (i.e., sketch to photo contour) therefore directly solving for the sketch-photo domain gap, without the need for data augmentation. Finally, we note that no prior work has taken our step of modelling sketches by factorisation into contour and detail parts.

Neural image synthesis: Recent advances in neural image synthesis have led to a number of practical applications, including image stylisation [7,15,22,26], single image super-resolution [19], video frame prediction [28], image manipulation [18,47] and conditional image generation [29,31,33,40,46]. The models most relevant to our style transfer model are deep image-to-image translation models [14,16,24,41,48], particularly the unsupervised ones [16,24,41,48]. The goal is to translate an image from one domain to another with a deep encoder-decoder architecture. In order to deal with the large domain gap between a sketch containing both distorted sketch contour and details and a distortion-free contour extracted from photo edges, our model has a novel component, that is, instead of the cyclic visual consistency deployed in [16,24,41,48], we enforce cyclic embedding constraint, a softer version for better synthesis quality. Both qualitative and quantitative results show that our model outperforms existing models.

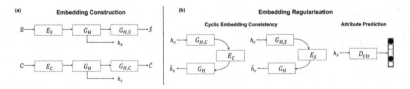

Fig. 2. Schematic of our sketch style transfer model with cyclic embedding consistency. (a) Embedding space construction. (b) Embedding regularisation through cyclic embedding consistency and an attribute prediction task.

Fine-grained SBIR: In the context of image retrieval, sketches provide a convenient modality for providing fine-grained visual query descriptions — a sketch speaks for a 'hundred' words. FG-SBIR was first proposed in [20], which employed a deformable part-based model (DPM) representation and graph matching. It is further tackled by deep models [35,39,43] which aim to learn an embedding space where sketch and photo can be compared directly – typically using a three-branch Siamese network with a triplet ranking loss. More recently, FG-SBIR was addressed from an image synthesis perspective [32] as well as an explicit photo to vector sketch synthesis perspective [38]. The latter study used a CNN-RNN generative sketcher and used the resulting synthetic sketches for data augmentation. Our FG-SBIR model is also a Siamese joint embedding model. However, it differs in that it employs our synthesised distortion-free contours both as a bridge to narrow the domain gap between sketch and photo, and a means for factorising out the detail parts of the sketch. We show that our model is superior to all existing models on the largest FG-SBIR dataset.

3   Sketch Stylisation with Cyclic Embedding Consistency

Problem definition: Suppose we have a set of free-hand sketches S drawn by amateurs based on their mental recollection of object instances [43] and a set of photo object contours C sparsely extracted from photos using an off-the-shelf edge detection model [49], with empirical distribution $s \sim p_{data}(S)$ and $c \sim p_{data}(C)$ respectively. They are theme aligned but otherwise *unpaired* and *non-overlapped* meaning they can contain different sets of object instances. This makes training data collection much easier. Our objective is to learn an unsupervised deep style transfer model, which inverts the style of a sketch to a cleanly rendered object contour with more realistic geometry, and user-specific details removed (see Fig. 1(b)).

3.1   Model Formulation

Our model aims to transfer images in a source domain (original human sketches) to a target domain (photo contours). It consists of two encoder-decoders, $\{E_S, G_S\}$ and $\{E_C, G_C\}$, which map an image from the source (target) domain to the target (source) domain and produce an image whose style is indistinguishable from that in the target (source) domain. Once learned, we can use $\{E_S, G_C\}$ to transfer the style of S into that of C, i.e., distortion-free and geometrically realistic contours. Note that under the unsupervised (unpaired) setting, such a mapping is highly under-constrained – there are infinitely many mappings $\{E_S, G_C\}$ that will induce the same distribution over contours c. This issue calls for adding more structural constraints into the loop, to ensure s and c lie on some shared embedding space for effective style transfer and instance identity preserving between the two. To this end, the decoder G_S (G_C) is decomposed into two subnetworks: a shared embedding space construction subnet G_H, and an unshared embedding decoder $G_{H,S}$ ($G_{H,C}$), i.e., $G_S \equiv G_H \circ G_{H,S}, G_C \equiv G_H \circ G_{H,C}$ (see Fig. 2(a)).

Embedding space construction: We construct our embedding space similarly to [24, 25]: The G_H projects the outputs of the encoders into a shared embedding space. We thus have $h_s = G_H(E_S(s)), h_c = G_H(E_C(c))$. The projections in the embedding space are then used as inputs by the decoder to perform reconstruction: $\hat{s} = G_{H,S}(h_s), \hat{c} = G_{H,C}(h_c)$.

Embedding regularisation: As illustrated in Fig. 2(b), the embedding space is learned with two regularisations: (i) Cyclic embedding consistency: this exploits the property that the learned style transfer should be 'embedding consistent', that is, given a translated image, we can arrive at the same spot in the shared embedding space with its original input. This regularisation is formulated as $h_s = G_H(E_S(s)) \rightarrow G_{H,C}(G_H(E_S(s))) \rightarrow G_H(E_C(G_{H,C}(G_H(E_S(s))))) \approx h_s$, and $h_c = G_H(E_C(c)) \rightarrow G_{H,S}(G_H(E_C(c))) \rightarrow G_H(E_S(G_{H,S}(G_H(E_C(c))))) \approx h_c$ for the two domains respectively. This is different from the cyclic visual consistency used by existing unsupervised image-to-image translation models [24, 25, 48], by which the input image is reconstructed by translating back the translated input image. The proposed cyclic embedding consistency is much 'softer' compared to the cyclic visual consistency since the reconstruction is performed in the embedding space rather than at the per-pixel level in the image space. It is thus more capable of coping with domain discrepancies caused by the large pixel-level mis-alignments due to contour distortion and the missing of details inside the contours. (ii) Attribute prediction: to cope with the large variations of sketch appearance when the same object instance is drawn by different sketchers (see Fig. 1(a)), we add an attribute prediction task to the embedding subnet so that the embedding space needs to preserve all the information required to predict a set of semantic attributes.

Adversarial training: Finally, as in most existing deep image synthesis models, we introduce a discriminative network to perform adversarial training [8]: the discriminator is trained to be unable to distinguish generated contours from sketch inputs and the photo contours extracted from object photos.

3.2   Model Architecture

Encoder: Most existing unsupervised image-to-image translation models design a specific encoder architecture and train the encoder from scratch. We found that this works poorly for sketches due to lack of training data and the large appearance variations mentioned earlier. We therefore adopt a fixed VGG encoder pretrained on ImageNet. As shown in Fig. 3, the encoder consists of five convolutional layers before each of the five max-pooling operations of a pre-trained VGG-16 network, namely *conv1_2*, *conv2_2*, *conv3_3*, *conv4_3* and *conv5_3*. Note that adopting a pretrained encoder means that now we have $E_S = E_C$.

Decoder: The two subnets of the decoder: G_H and $G_{H,S}$ ($G_{H,C}$) use a residual design. Specifically, for convolutional feature map extracted at each spatial resolution, we start with $1 * 1$ conv, upsample it by a factor of 2 with bilinear interpolation and then add the output of the corresponding encoder layer. It

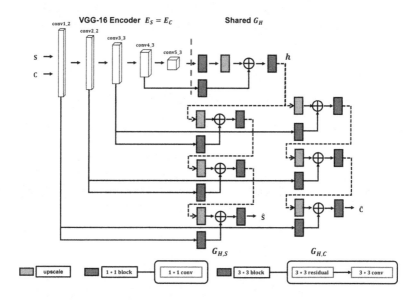

Fig. 3. A schematic of our specifically-designed encoder-decoder.

is further followed by a $3 * 3$ residual and $3 * 3$ conv for transformation learning and adjusting appropriate channel numbers for the next resolution. Note that shortcut connections between the encoder and decoder corresponding layers are also established in the residual form. As illustrated in Fig. 3, the shared embedding construction subnet G_H is composed of one such block while the unshared embedding decoders $G_{H,S}$ ($G_{H,C}$) have three. For more details of the encoder/decoder and discriminator architecture, please see Sect. 5.1.

3.3 Learning Objectives

Embedding consistency loss: Given s (c), and its cross-domain synthesised image $G_C(E_S(s))$ ($G_S(E_C(c))$), they should arrive back to the same location in the embedding space. We enforce this by minimising the Euclidean distance between them in the embedding space:

$$\mathcal{L}_{embed} = \mathbb{E}_{s \sim S, c \sim C}[||G_H(E_S(s)) - G_H(E_C(G_C(E_S(s))))||_2 \\ + ||G_H(E_C(c)) - G_H(E_S(G_S(E_C(c))))||_2]. \tag{1}$$

Self-reconstruction loss: Given s (c), and its reconstructed result $G_S(E_S(s))$ ($G_C(E_C(c))$), they should be visually close. We thus have

$$\mathcal{L}_{recons} = \mathbb{E}_{s \sim S, c \sim C}[||s - G_S(E_S(s))||_1 + ||c - G_C(E_C(c))||_1]. \tag{2}$$

Self-reconstruction loss: Given s (c), and its reconstructed result $G_S(E_S(s))$ ($G_C(E_C(c))$), they should be visually close. We thus have

$$\mathcal{L}_{recons} = \mathbb{E}_{s \sim S, c \sim C}[||s - G_S(E_S(s))||_1 + ||c - G_C(E_C(c))||_1]. \tag{3}$$

Attribute prediction loss: Given a sketch s and its semantic attribute vector a, we hope its embedding $G_H(E_S(s))$ can be used to predict the attributes a. To realise this, we introduce an auxiliary one-layer subnet D_{cls} on top of the embedding space h and minimise the classification errors:

$$\mathcal{L}_{cls} = \mathbb{E}_{s,a \sim S}[-\log D_{cls}(a|G_H(E_S(s)))]. \tag{4}$$

Domain-adversarial loss: Given s (c) and its cross-domain synthesised image $G_C(E_S(s))$ $(G_S(E_C(c)))$, the synthesised image should be indistinguishable to a target domain image c (s) using the adversarially-learned discriminator, denoted D_C (D_S). To stabilise training and improve the quality of the synthesised images, we adopt the least square generative adversarial network (LSGAN) [27] with gradient penalty [9]. The domain-adversarial loss is defined as:

$$
\begin{aligned}
\mathcal{L}_{adv_g} &= \mathbb{E}_{s \sim S}[||D_C(G_C(E_S(s))) - 1||_2] \\
&\quad + \mathbb{E}_{c \sim C}[||D_S(G_S(E_C(c))) - 1||_2] \\
\mathcal{L}_{adv_{ds}} &= \mathbb{E}_{s \sim S}[||D_S(s) - 1||_2] + \mathbb{E}_{c \sim C}[||D_S(G_S(E_C(c)))||_2] \\
&\quad - \lambda_{gp} \mathbb{E}_{\tilde{s}}[(||\nabla_{\tilde{s}} D_S(\tilde{s})||_2 - 1)^2] \\
\mathcal{L}_{adv_{dc}} &= \mathbb{E}_{c \sim C}[||D_C(c) - 1||_2] + \mathbb{E}_{s \sim S}[||D_C(G_C(E_S(s)))||_2] \\
&\quad - \lambda_{gp} \mathbb{E}_{\tilde{c}}[(||\nabla_{\tilde{c}} D_C(\tilde{c})||_2 - 1)^2]
\end{aligned}
\tag{5}
$$

where $\tilde{s}, \tilde{c}$ are sampled uniformly along a straight line between their corresponding domain pair of real and generated images. We set weighting factor $\lambda_{gp} = 10$.

Full learning objectives: Our full model is trained alternatively as with a standard conditional GAN framework, with the following joint optimisation:

$$
\begin{aligned}
&\underset{D_S, D_C}{\arg\min} \lambda_{adv} L_{adv_{ds}} + \lambda_{adv} L_{adv_{dc}} \\
&\underset{E_S, E_C, G_S, G_C, D_{cls}}{\arg\min} \lambda_{embed} L_{embed} + \lambda_{recons} L_{recons} + \lambda_{adv} L_{adv_g} + \lambda_{cls} L_{cls}
\end{aligned}
\tag{6}
$$

where $\lambda_{adv}, \lambda_{embed}, \lambda_{recons}, \lambda_{cls}$ are hyperparameters that control the relative importance of each loss. In this work, we set $\lambda_{adv} = 10, \lambda_{embed} = 100, \lambda_{recons} = 100$ and $\lambda_{cls} = 1$ to keep the losses in roughly the same value range.

4   Discriminative Factorisation for FG-SBIR

The sketch style transfer model in Sect. 3.1 addresses the first level of inverse-sketching by translating a sketch into a geometrically realistic contour. Specifically, for a given sketch s, we can synthesise its distortion-free sketch contour s_c as $G_C(E_S(s))$. However, the model is not trained to synthesise the sketch details inside the contour – this is harder because sketch details exhibit more subjective abstraction yet less distorted. In this section, we show that for learning a discriminative FG-SBIR model, such a partial factorisation is enough: we can take s and s_c and extract complementary detail features from s_c to complete the inversion process.

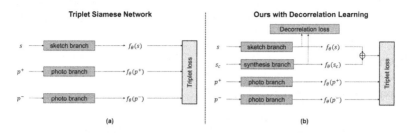

Fig. 4. (a) Existing three-branch Siamese Network [35,43] vs. (b) our four-branch network with decorrelation loss.

Problem definition: For a given query sketch s and a set of N candidate photos $\{p_i\}_{i=1}^N \in P$, FG-SBIR aims to find a specific photo containing the same instance as the query sketch. This can be solved by learning a joint sketch-photo embedding using a CNN f_θ [35,43]. In this space, the visual similarity between a sketch s and a photo p can be measured simply as $D(s,p) = ||f_\theta(s) - f_\theta(p)||_2^2$.

Enforcing factorisation via de-correlation loss: In our approach, clean and accurate contour features are already provided in s_c via our style transfer network defined previously. Now we aim to extract detail-related features from s. To this end we introduce a decorrelation loss between $f_\theta(s)$ and $f_\theta(s_c)$:

$$L_{decorr} = ||\overline{f_\theta(s)}^T \overline{f_\theta(s_c)}||_F^2, \tag{7}$$

where $\overline{f_\theta(s)}$ and $\overline{f_\theta(s_c)}$ are obtained by normalising $f_\theta(s)$ and $f_\theta(s_c)$ with zero-mean and unit-variance respectively, and $||.||_F^2$ is the squared Frobenius norm. This ensures that $f_\theta(s)$ encodes detail-related features in order to meet the decorrelation constraint with complementary contour encoding $f_\theta(s_c)$.

Model design: Existing deep FG-SBIR models [32,43] adopt a three-branch Siamese network architecture, shown in Fig. 4(a). Given an anchor sketch s and a positive photo p^+ containing the same object instance and a negative photo p^-, the outputs of the three branches are subject to a triplet ranking loss to align the sketch and photo in the discriminative joint embedding space learned by f_θ. To exploit our contour and detail representation, we use a four-branch Siamese network with inputs s, s_c, p^+, p^- respectively (Fig. 4(b)). The extracted features from s and s_c are then fused before being compared with those extracted from p^+ and p^-. The fusion is denoted as $f_\theta(s) \oplus f_\theta(s_c)$, where $\oplus$ is the element-wise addition[1]. The triplet ranking loss is then formulated as:

$$L_{tri} = \max(0, \Delta + D(f_\theta(s) \oplus f_\theta(s_c), f_\theta(p^+)) - D(f_\theta(s) \oplus f_\theta(s_c), f_\theta(p^-))) \tag{8}$$

where Δ is a hyperparameter representing the margin between the query-to-positive and query-to-negative distances. Our final objective for discriminatively training SBIR becomes:

$$\min_\theta \sum_{t \in T} L_{tri} + \lambda_{decorr} L_{decorr} \tag{9}$$

---

[1] Other fusion strategies have been tried and found to be inferior.

we set $\Delta = 0.1, \lambda_{decorr} = 1$ in our experiments so two losses have equal weights.

5   Experiments

5.1   Experimental Settings

Dataset and preprocessing: We use the public QMUL-Shoe-V2 [44] dataset, the largest single-category paired sketch-photo dataset to date, to train and evaluate both our sketch style transfer model and FG-SBIR model. It contains 6648 sketches and 2000 photos. We follow its standard train/test split with 5982 and 1800 sketch-photo pairs respectively. Each shoe photo is annotated with 37 part-based semantic attributes. We remove four decoration-related ones ('frontal', 'lateral', 'others' and 'no decoration'), which are contour-irrelevant and keep the rest. Since our style transfer model is unsupervised and does not require paired training examples, we use a large shoe photo dataset UT-Zap50K dataset [42] as the target photo domain. This consists of 50,025 shoe photos which are disjoint with the QMUL-Shoe-V2 dataset. For training the style transfer model, we scale and centre the sketches and photo contours to 64×64 size, while for FG-SBIR model, the inputs of all four branches are resized to 256×256.

Photo contour extraction: We obtain the contour c from a photo p as follows: (i) extracting edge probability map e using [49] followed by non-max suppression; (ii) e is binarised by keeping the edge pixels with edge probabilities smaller than x, where x is dynamically determined so that when e contains many non-zero edge pixel detections, x should be small to eliminate the noisy ones, e.g., texture. This is achieved by formulating $x = e_{sort}(l_{sort} \times \min(\alpha e^{-\beta \times r}, 0.9))$, where e_{sort} is the edge pixels detected in e sorted in the ascending order, l_{sort} is the length of e_{sort}, and r is the ratio between detected and total pixels. We set $\alpha = 0.08, \beta = 0.12$ in our experiments. Examples of photos and their extracted contours can be seen in the last two columns of Fig. 5.

Implementation details: We implement both models in Tensorflow with a single NVIDIA 1080Ti GPU. For the **style transfer task**: as illustrated in Fig. 3, we denote $k * k$ conv as a $k \times k$ Convolution-BatchNorm-ReLU layer with stride 1 and $k * k$ residual as a residual block that contains two $k * k$ conv blocks with reflection padding to reduce artifacts. Upscale operation is performed with bilinear up-sampling. We do not use BatchNorm and replace ReLU activation with Tanh for the last output layer. Our discriminator has the same architecture as in [14], but with BatchNorm replaced with LayerNorm [1] since gradient penalty is introduced. The number of discriminator iterations per generator update is set as 1. We trained for $50k$ iterations with a batch size of 64. For the **FG-SBIR task**: we fine-tune ImageNet-pretrained ResNet-50 [10] to obtain f_θ with the final classification layer removed. Same with [43], we enforce l_2 normalisation on f_θ for stable triplet learning. We train for $60k$ iterations with a triplet batch size of 16. For both tasks, the Adam [17] optimiser is used, where we set $\beta_1 = 0.5$ and $\beta_2 = 0.9$ with an initial learning rate of 0.0001 respectively.

Competitors: For style transfer, four competitors are compared. **Pix2pix** [14] is a supervised image-to-image translation model. It assumes that visual connections can be directly established between sketch and contour pairs with l_1 translation loss and adversarial training. Note that we can only use the QMUL-Shoe-V2 train split for training Pix2pix, rather than UT-Zap50K, since sketch-photo pairs are required. **UNIT** [24] is the latest variant of the popular unsupervised CycleGAN [16,41,48]. Similar to our model, it also has a shared embedding construction subnet. Unlike our model, there is no attribute prediction regularisation and visual consistency instead of embedding consistency is enforced. **UNIT-vgg:** for fair comparison, we substitute the learned-from-scratch encoder in UNIT to our fixed VGG-encoder, and introduce the same self-residual architecture in the decoder. **Ours-attr**: This is a variant of our model without the attribute prediction task for embedding regularisation. For FG-SBIR, competitors include: **Sketchy** [35] is a three-branch Heterogeneous triplet network. For fair comparison, the same ResNet50 is used as the base network. **Vanilla-triplet** [43] differs from Sketchy in that a Siamese architecture is adopted. It is vanilla as the model is trained without any synthetic augmentation. **DA-triplet**[38] is the state-of-the-art model, which uses synthetic sketches from photos as a means of data augmentation to pretrain the Vanilla-triplet network and fine-tune it with real human sketches. **Ours-decorr** is a variant of our model, obtained by discarding the decorrelation loss.

5.2   Results on Style Transfer

Qualitative results: Figure 5 shows example synthesised sketches using the various models. It shows clearly that our method is able to invert the sketching process by effectively factorising out any details inside the object contour and restyling the remaining contour parts with smooth strokes and more realistic perspective geometry. In contrast, the supervised model Pix2pix failed completely due to sparse training data and the assumption of pixel-to-pixel alignment across the two domains. The unsupervised UNIT model is able to remove the details, but struggles to emulate the style of the object photo contours featured with smooth and continuous strokes. Using a fixed VGG-16 as encoder (UNIT-vgg) alleviates the problem but introduces the new problem of keeping the detail part. These results suggest that the visual cycle consistency constraint used in UNIT is too strong a constraint on the embedding subnet, leaving it with little freedom to perform both the detail removal and contour restyling tasks. As an ablation, we compare ours-attr with ours-full and observe that the attribute prediction task does provide a useful regularisation to the embedding subnet to make the synthesised contour more smooth and less fragmented. Our model is far from being perfect. Figure 6 shows some failure cases. Most failure cases are caused by the sketcher unsuccessfully attempting to depict objects with rich texture by an overcomplicated sketch. This suggests that our model is mostly focused on the

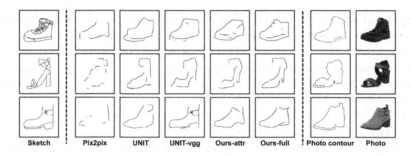

Fig. 5. Different competitors for translating sketching abstraction at contour-level. Illustrations shown here have never been seen by its corresponding model during training.

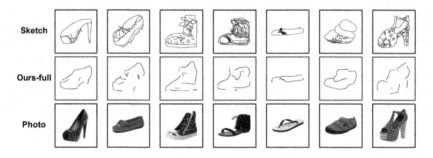

Fig. 6. Typical failure of our model when sketching style is too abstract or complex.

shape cues contained in sketches and confused by the sudden presence of large amounts of texture cues.

Quantitative results: Quantitative evaluation of image synthesis models remains an open problem. Consequently, most studies either run human perceptual studies or explore computational metrics attempting to predict human perceptual similarity judgements [11,34]. We perform both quantitative evaluations.

Computational evaluation: In this evaluation, we seek a metric based on the insight that if the synthesised sketches are realistic and free of distortion,

Table 1. Comparative retrieval results using the synthetic sketches obtained using different models.

	Chance	Pix2pix [43]	UNIT [24]	UNIT-vgg	Ours-attr	Ours-full
acc@1	0.50%	3.60%	4.50%	4.95%	6.46%	**8.26%**
acc@5	2.50%	10.51%	15.02%	17.87%	22.22%	**23.27%**
acc@10	5.00%	17.87%	26.28%	29.88%	31.38%	**35.14%**

they should be useful for retrieving photos containing the same objects, despite the fact that the details inside the contours may have been removed. We thus retrain the FG-SBIR model of [43] on the QMUL-Shoe-V2 training split and used the sketches synthesised using different style transfer models to retrieve photos in QMUL-Shoe-V2 test split. The results in Table 1 show that our full model outperforms all competitors. The performance gap over the chance suggests that despite lack of detail, our synthetic sketches still capture instance-discriminative visual cues. The superior results to the competitors indicate the usefulness of cyclic embedding consistency and attribute prediction regularisation.

Human perceptual study: We further evaluate our model via a human subjective study. We recruit N $(N = 10)$ workers and ask each of them to perform the same pairwise A/B test based on the 50 randomly-selected sketches from QMUL-Shoe-V2 test split. Specifically, each worker undertakes two trials, where three images are given at once, i.e., a sketch and two restyled version of the sketch using two compared models. The worker is then asked to choose one synthesised sketch based on two criteria: (i) correspondence (measured as r_c): which image keeps more key visual traits of the original sketches, i.e., more instance-level identifiable; (ii) naturalness (measured as r_n): which image looks more like a contour extracted from a shoe photo. The left-right order and the image order are randomised to ensure unbiased comparisons. We denote each of the $2N$ ratings for each synthetic sketch under one comparative test as c_i and n_i respectively, and compute the correspondence measure $r_c = \sum_{i=1}^{N} c_i$, and naturalness measure $r_n = \sum_{i=1}^{N} n_i$. We then average them to obtain one score based on a weighting: $r_{avr} = \frac{1}{N}(w_c r_c + w_n r_n)$. Intuitively, w_c should be greater than w_n because ultimately we care more about how the synthesised sketches help FG-SBIR. In Table 2, we list in each cell the percentage of trials where our full model is preferred over the other competitors. Under different weighting

Table 2. Pairwise comparison results of human perceptual study. Each cell lists the percentage where our full model is preferred over the other method. Chance is at 50%.

(w_c, w_n)	UNIT vs. Ours-full	UNIT-vgg vs. Ours-full	Ours-attr vs. Ours-full
(0.9, 0.1)	88.0%	72.0%	62.0%
(0.8, 0.2)	88.0%	70.0%	64.0%
(0.7, 0.3)	88.0%	70.0%	64.0%
(0.6, 0.4)	86.0%	68.0%	62.0%
(0.5, 0.5)	84.0%	70.0%	64.0%

Table 3. Comparative results on QMUL-Shoe-V2. Retrieval accuracy at rank 1 (acc@1).

Sketchy [35]	Vanilla-triplet [43]	DA-triplet [38]	Ours-decorr	Ours-full
21.62%	33.48%	33.78%	33.93%	**35.89%**

combinations, the superiority of our design is consistent (>50%), drawing the same conclusion as our computational evaluation. In particular, compared with prior state-of-the-art, UNIT, our full model is preferred by humans nearly 90% of the time.

5.3   Results on FG-SBIR

Quantitative: In Table 3, we compare the proposed FG-SBIR model (Ours-full) with three state-of-the-art alternatives (Sketchy, Vanilla-triplet and DA-triplet) and a variant of our model (Ours-decorr). The following observations can be made: (i) Compared with the three existing models, our full model yields 14.27%, 2.41% and 2.11% acc@1 improvements respectively. Given that the three competitors have exactly the same base network in each network branch, and the same model complexity as our model, this demonstrates the effectiveness of our complementary detail representation from contour-detail factorisation. (ii) Without the decorrelation loss, Ours-decorr produces similar accuracy as the two baselines and is clearly inferior to Ours-full. This is not surprising – without forcing the original sketch (s) branch to extract something different from the sketch contour (s_c) branch (i.e., details), the fused features will be dominated by the s branch as s contains much richer information. The four-branch model thus degenerates to a three-branch model.

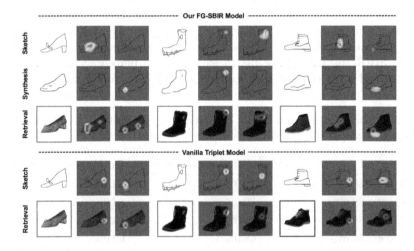

Fig. 7. We highlight supporting regions for the top 2 most discriminative feature dimensions of two compared models. Green and red borders on the photos indicate correct and incorrect retrieval, respectively.

Visualisation: We carry out model visualisation to demonstrate that $f_\theta(s)$ and $f_\theta(s_c)$ indeed capture different and complementary features that are useful for FG-SBIR, and give some insights on why such a factorisation helps. To this end, we use Grad-Cam [36] to highlight where in the image the discriminative features are extracted using our model. Specifically, the two non-zero dimensions of $f_\theta(s) \oplus f_\theta(s_c)$ that contribute the most similarity for the retrieval are selected and their gradients are propagated back along the s and s_c branches as well as the photo branch to locate the support regions. The top half of Fig. 7 shows clearly that (i) the top discriminative features are often a mixture of contour and detail as suggested by the highlighted regions on the photo images; and (ii) the corresponding regions are accurately located in s and s_c; importantly the contour features activate mostly in s_c and detail features in s. This validates that factorisation indeed takes place. In contrast, the bottom half of Fig. 7 shows that using the vanilla-triplet model without the factorisation, the model appears to be overly focused on the details, ignoring the fact that the contour part also contains useful information for matching object instances. This leads to failure cases (red box) and explains the inferior performance of vanilla-triplet.

6   Conclusion

We have for the first time proposed a framework for inverting the iconic rendering process in human free-hand sketch, and for contour-detail factorisation. Given a sketch, our deep style transfer model learns to factorise out the details inside the object contour and invert the remaining contours to match more geometrically realistic contours extracted from photos. We subsequently develop a sketch-photo joint embedding which completes the inversion process by extracting distinct complementary detail features for FG-SBIR. We demonstrated empirically that our style transfer model is more effective compared to existing models thanks to a novel cyclic embedding consistency constraint. We also achieve state-of-the-art FG-SBIR results by exploiting our sketch inversion and factorisation.

References

1. Ba, J.L., Kiros, J.R., Hinton, G.E.: Layer normalization. arXiv preprint arXiv:1607.06450 (2016)
2. Berger, I., Shamir, A., Mahler, M., Carter, E., Hodgins, J.: Style and abstraction in portrait sketching. TOG (2013)
3. Bui, T., Collomosse, J.: Scalable sketch-based image retrieval using color gradient features. In: ICCV Workshops (2015)
4. Eitz, M., Hays, J., Alexa, M.: How do humans sketch objects? SIGGRAPH (2012)

5. Eitz, M., Hildebrand, K., Boubekeur, T., Alexa, M.: Sketch-based image retrieval: benchmark and bag-of-features descriptors. TVCG (2011)
6. Flash, T., Hogan, N.: The coordination of arm movements: an experimentally confirmed mathematical model. J. Neurosci. (1985)
7. Gatys, L.A., Ecker, A.S., Bethge, M.: Image style transfer using convolutional neural networks. In: CVPR (2016)
8. Goodfellow, I., Pouget-Abadie, J., Mirza, M., Xu, B., Warde-Farley, D., Ozair, S., Courville, A., Bengio, Y.: Generative adversarial nets. In: NIPS (2014)
9. Gulrajani, I., Ahmed, F., Arjovsky, M., Dumoulin, V., Courville, A.C.: Improved training of wasserstein gans. In: NIPS (2017)
10. He, K., Zhang, X., Ren, S., Sun, J.: Deep residual learning for image recognition. In: CVPR (2016)
11. Heusel, M., Ramsauer, H., Unterthiner, T., Nessler, B., Hochreiter, S.: Gans trained by a two time-scale update rule converge to a local nash equilibrium. In: NIPS (2017)
12. Hu, C., Li, D., Song, Y.Z., Xiang, T., Hospedales, T.: Sketch-a-classifier: sketch-based photo classifier generation. In: CVPR (2018)
13. Hu, R., Collomosse, J.: A performance evaluation of gradient field hog descriptor for sketch based image retrieval. CVIU (2013)
14. Isola, P., Zhu, J.Y., Zhou, T., Efros, A.A.: Image-to-image translation with conditional adversarial networks. In: CVPR (2017)
15. Johnson, J., Alahi, A., Fei-Fei, L.: Perceptual losses for real-time style transfer and super-resolution. In: ECCV (2016)
16. Kim, T., Cha, M., Kim, H., Lee, J., Kim, J.: Learning to discover cross-domain relations with generative adversarial networks. In: ICML (2017)
17. Kingma, D., Ba, J.: Adam: a method for stochastic optimization. arXiv preprint arXiv:1412.6980 (2014)
18. Korshunova, I., Shi, W., Dambre, J., Theis, L.: Fast face-swap using convolutional neural networks. In: ICCV (2017)
19. Ledig, C., Theis, L., Huszár, F., Caballero, J., Cunningham, A., Acosta, A., Aitken, A., Tejani, A., Totz, J., Wang, Z., et al.: Photo-realistic single image super-resolution using a generative adversarial network. In: CVPR (2017)
20. Li, Y., Hospedales, T.M., Song, Y.Z., Gong, S.: Fine-grained sketch-based image retrieval by matching deformable part models. In: BMVC (2014)
21. Li, Y., Song, Y.Z., Hospedales, T.M., Gong, S.: Free-hand sketch synthesis with deformable stroke models. IJCV (2017)
22. Liao, J., Yao, Y., Yuan, L., Hua, G., Kang, S.B.: Visual attribute transfer through deep image analogy. SIGGRAPH (2017)
23. Liu, L., Shen, F., Shen, Y., Liu, X., Shao, L.: Deep sketch hashing: fast free-hand sketch-based image retrieval. In: CVPR (2017)
24. Liu, M.Y., Breuel, T., Kautz, J.: Unsupervised image-to-image translation networks. In: NIPS (2017)
25. Liu, M.Y., Tuzel, O.: Coupled generative adversarial networks. In: NIPS (2016)

26. Luan, F., Paris, S., Shechtman, E., Bala, K.: Deep photo style transfer. In: CVPR (2017)
27. Mao, X., Li, Q., Xie, H., Lau, R.Y., Wang, Z., Smolley, S.P.: Least squares generative adversarial networks. In: ICCV (2017)
28. Mathieu, M., Couprie, C., LeCun, Y.: Deep multi-scale video prediction beyond mean square error. In: ICLR (2016)
29. Mirza, M., Osindero, S.: Conditional generative adversarial nets. arXiv preprint arXiv:1411.1784 (2014)
30. Muhammad, U., Yang, Y., Song, Y.Z., Xiang, T., Hospedales, T.M.: Learning deep sketch abstraction. In: CVPR (2018)
31. Odena, A., Olah, C., Shlens, J.: Conditional image synthesis with auxiliary classifier gans. In: ICML (2017)
32. Pang, K., Song, Y.Z., Xiang, T., Hospedales, T.M.: Cross-domain generative learning for fine-grained sketch-based image retrieval. In: BMVC (2017)
33. Reed, S., Akata, Z., Yan, X., Logeswaran, L., Schiele, B., Lee, H.: Generative adversarial text to image synthesis. In: ICML (2016)
34. Salimans, T., Goodfellow, I., Zaremba, W., Cheung, V., Radford, A., Chen, X.: Improved techniques for training gans. In: NIPS (2016)
35. Sangkloy, P., Burnell, N., Ham, C., Hays, J.: The sketchy database: learning to retrieve badly drawn bunnies. SIGGRAPH (2016)
36. Selvaraju, R.R., Cogswell, M., Das, A., Vedantam, R., Parikh, D., Batra, D.: Grad-CAM: visual explanations from deep networks via gradient-based localization. In: ICCV (2017)
37. Shen, Y., Liu, L., Shen, F., Shao, L.: Zero-shot sketch-image hashing. In: CVPR (2018)
38. Song, J., Pang, K., Song, Y.Z., Xiang, T., Hospedales, T.M.: Learning to sketch with shortcut cycle consistency. In: CVPR (2018)
39. Song, J., Qian, Y., Song, Y.Z., Xiang, T., Hospedales, T.: Deep spatial-semantic attention for fine-grained sketch-based image retrieval. In: ICCV (2017)
40. Yan, X., Yang, J., Sohn, K., Lee, H.: Attribute2image: conditional image generation from visual attributes. In: ECCV (2016)
41. Yi, Z., Zhang, H., Tan, P., Gong, M.: DualGAN: Unsupervised dual learning for image-to-image translation. In: ICCV (2017)
42. Yu, A., Grauman, K.: Fine-grained visual comparisons with local learning. In: CVPR (2014)
43. Yu, Q., Liu, F., Song, Y.Z., Xiang, T., Hospedales, T.M., Loy, C.C.: Sketch me that shoe. In: CVPR (2016)
44. Yu, Q., Song, Y.Z., Xiang, T., Hospedales, T.M.: SketchX! - Shoe/Chair fine-grained SBIR dataset. http://sketchx.eecs.qmul.ac.uk (2017)
45. Yu, Q., Yang, Y., Liu, F., Song, Y.Z., Xiang, T., Hospedales, T.M.: Sketch-a-net: a deep neural network that beats humans. IJCV (2017)
46. Zhang, H., Xu, T., Li, H., Zhang, S., Huang, X., Wang, X., Metaxas, D.: Stack-gan: text to photo-realistic image synthesis with stacked generative adversarial networks. In: ICCV (2017)

47. Zhu, J.Y., Krähenbühl, P., Shechtman, E., Efros, A.A.: Generative visual manipulation on the natural image manifold. In: ECCV (2016)
48. Zhu, J.Y., Park, T., Isola, P., Efros, A.A.: Unpaired image-to-image translation using cycle-consistent adversarial networks. In: ICCV (2017)
49. Zitnick, C.L., Dollár, P.: Edge boxes: locating object proposals from edges. In: ECCV (2014)

Look Deeper into Depth: Monocular Depth Estimation with Semantic Booster and Attention-Driven Loss

Jianbo Jiao[1,2]([✉]) [iD], Ying Cao[1], Yibing Song[3], and Rynson Lau[1]

[1] City University of Hong Kong, Kowloon, Hong Kong SAR
jianbjiao2-c@my.cityu.edu.hk, caoying59@gmail.com,
dynamicstevenson@gmail.com
[2] University of Illinois at Urbana-Champaign, Urbana, USA
[3] Tencent AI Lab, Shenzhen, China
rynson.lau@cityu.edu.hk

Abstract. Monocular depth estimation benefits greatly from learning based techniques. By studying the training data, we observe that the per-pixel depth values in existing datasets typically exhibit a long-tailed distribution. However, most previous approaches treat all the regions in the training data equally regardless of the imbalanced depth distribution, which restricts the model performance particularly on distant depth regions. In this paper, we investigate the long tail property and delve deeper into the distant depth regions (*i.e.* the tail part) to propose an attention-driven loss for the network supervision. In addition, to better leverage the semantic information for monocular depth estimation, we propose a synergy network to automatically learn the information sharing strategies between the two tasks. With the proposed attention-driven loss and synergy network, the depth estimation and semantic labeling tasks can be mutually improved. Experiments on the challenging indoor dataset show that the proposed approach achieves state-of-the-art performance on both monocular depth estimation and semantic labeling tasks.

Keywords: Monocular depth · Semantic labeling · Attention loss

1 Introduction

Depth acquisition has been actively studied over the past decades with widespread applications in 3D modeling, scene understanding, depth-aware image synthesis, *etc.* However, traditional hardware or software based approaches are restricted by either environment or multi-view observations assumption. To overcome these limitations, there is a growing interest in predicting depth from a single image.

Monocular depth prediction is an ill-posed problem and inherently ambiguous. However, humans can well perceive depth from a single image, given that sufficient samples (*e.g.* the appearances of nearby/distant objects) have

ⓒ Springer Nature Switzerland AG 2018
V. Ferrari et al. (Eds.): ECCV 2018, LNCS 11219, pp. 55–71, 2018.
https://doi.org/10.1007/978-3-030-01267-0_4

been learned over lifetimes. With the success of deep learning techniques and available training data, the performance of monocular depth estimation has been greatly improved [5,53]. While existing methods measure depth estimation accuracy by vanilla loss functions (*e.g.* ℓ_1 or ℓ_2), they assume that all regions in the scene contribute equally without considering the depth data statistics. We have empirically found that the depth values in the indoor/outdoor scenes vary greatly across different regions and exhibit a long tail distribution (see Fig. 1). This is an inherent property of the nature that mainly caused by the perspective-effect during the depth acquisition process. Given such imbalanced data, loss functions that treat all regions equally will be dominated by the samples with small depth, leading the models to be "short-sighted" and not effective to predict the depth of distant regions.

Moreover, complement to the learned prior knowledge like perspective, semantic understanding of the scene (*e.g.* sky is faraway, wall is vertical) essentially benefits depth estimation. For example, knowing a cylinder-like object to be a pencil or a pole can help estimate its depth. Furthermore, depth information is also helpful to differentiate semantic labels, especially for different objects with similar appearances [4,11,41]. Estimating depth and semantics can thus be mutually beneficial. Unfortunately, there is a lack of strategy to efficiently propagate and share information across the two tasks.

In this work, we propose to address the above two challenges by presenting a deep network to predict depth as well as semantic labels from a single still image. A novel attention-driven loss with depth-aware objective is proposed to supervise the network training, which alleviates the data bias issue and guides the model to *look deeper* into the scene. In addition, in our synergy network architecture, we propose an information propagation strategy that performs in a dynamic routing fashion to better incorporate semantics into depth estimation. The strategy is achieved by a lateral sharing unit and a semi-dense skip-up connection, which allow information to propagate through internal representations across and within both tasks. Experimental results on the challenging indoor dataset show that, with the proposed loss and knowledge sharing strategy, the performance of monocular depth estimation is significantly improved and reaching state-of-the-art. Our contributions are summarized as follows:

- We propose a novel attention-driven loss to better supervise the network training on existing datasets with long tail distributions. It helps improve depth prediction performance especially for distant regions.
- We present a synergy network architecture that better propagates semantic information to depth prediction, via a proposed information propagation strategy for both inter- and intra-task knowledge sharing.
- Extensive experiments demonstrate the effectiveness of our method with state-of-the-art performance on both depth and semantics prediction tasks.

2   Related Work

Depth from Single Image. Early works on monocular depth estimation mainly leverage hand-crafted features. Saxena *et al.* [44] predict the monocular depth by a linear model on an over-segmented input image. Hoiem *et al.* [17] further group the superpixels into geometric meaningful labels and construct a 3D model accordingly. Later on, with large-scale RGB-D data available, data-driven approaches [21,22,27,28,30,35,43] become feasible. Eigen *et al.* [4,5] construct a multi-scale deep convolutional neural network (CNN) to produce dense depth maps. Some methods [24,29,34,51–53,56] try to increase the accuracy by including Conditional Random Fields (CRFs). Despite notable improvements, the model complexity increases as well. Other works [1,57] predict depth by exploring ordinal relationships. Data imbalance is reported in [28,43] while not explicitly addressed. Some other works [6,9,26,55] propose to supervise the network by a reconstruction loss from the other stereo or temporal view. While requiring no depth supervision, rectification and alignment are usually necessary, and they rely on multi-view images during training. Although remarkable performance has been achieved, the long tail property of depth data distribution has not yet been well-explored.

Depth with Semantics. As depth and semantic labels share context information, some methods [3,4,11,42,46] take depth map as a guidance to improve the semantic segmentation performance. In [46], Silberman *et al.* propose the NYU RGBD dataset and use the combination of RGB and depth to improve the segmentation. Based on this dataset, some methods [3,11] take RGBD as input to perform semantic segmentation. Eigen and Fergus [4] design a deep CNN that takes RGB, depth, surface normal as input to predict the semantic labels. Owing to the power of CNN models, other methods [41,49,50] are proposed to better leverage depth for semantic labeling recently. While great performance has been demonstrated, the ground truth depth is indispensable for the labeling task. On the other hand, prior information encoded in the semantic labels can be leveraged to assist depth prediction. Instead of directly mapping from color image to depth, Liu *et al.* [33] first perform a semantic segmentation on the scene and then use the labels to guide depth prediction, in a sequential manner.

Joint Representation Sharing. Some recent works attempt to investigate the representation sharing between different tasks [16,19,20,27,38,39,51]. Ladicky *et al.* [27] propose a semantic depth classifier and analyze perspective geometry for image manipulation, whereas they rely on hand-crafted features locally. In [12], a traditional framework is presented for joint segmentation and 3D reconstruction. Wang *et al.* [51] use a CNN following by a hierarchical CRF to jointly predict semantic labels and depth. However, they only modify the last layer for prediction and rely on superpixels and CRF. A concurrent work [23] proposes a weighting strategy for multi-task losses. Misra *et al.* [38] propose a cross-stitch (CS) network for multi-task learning. While performs better than baselines, it may suffer from propagation interruption if the combination weights degenerates into 0. The two-parallel-CNN design also increases the number of parameters and learning complexity. Another sharing approach [18] applying dense connections between each layer in a CNN is proposed for recognition tasks. The fully-dense connections share all the information but increase memory consumption as well.

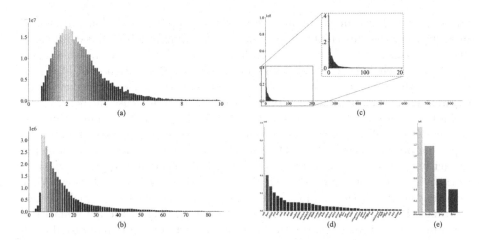

Fig. 1. Long tail distributed datasets on depth and semantic labels. Vertical axes indicate the number of pixels. (a) shows the depth value (horizontal axis, in meter) distribution of the NYUD v2 dataset [46], and (b) shows the distribution of the KITTI dataset [7]. (c) gives the semantic label distribution (label index as horizontal axis) of the NYUD v2, while (d, e) are the distributions of the mapped 40 [10] and 4 [46] categories from the 800+ categories in (c). Imbalanced long-tailed distribution can be observed in these datasets, even for semantic labels mapped to only four categories.

In our work, we jointly train semantic labeling and depth estimation in an end-to-end fashion, without complicated pre- or post-processing. We also propose to capture better synergy representations between the two tasks. Furthermore, we investigate the long-tail data distribution in existing datasets and propose an attention-driven loss to better supervise the network training.

3   Depth-Aware Synergy Network

3.1   Depth-Aware Objective

Most state-of-the-art monocular depth estimation methods make use of CNNs to enable accurate depth prediction. In these frameworks, the depth prediction is formulated as a regression problem, where ℓ_1 or ℓ_2 loss is usually used to minimize the pixel-wise distance between the predicted and ground truth depth maps based on the training data. When estimating monocular depth, we observe that a long tail distribution resides in both indoor (NYUD v2 [46]) and outdoor (KITTI [7]) depth datasets. As shown in Fig. 1(a), (b), the number of samples/pixels per depth value falls dramatically after a particular depth, with only a small depth range dominating a large number of pixels. This data imbalance problem shares similarity with that in object detection [32,45] but differs in nature. It is because the inherent natural property of perspective effect from the imaging process leads to the uneven distribution of depth pixels, which can not be eliminated by simply increasing training data. As a result, training deep models on such datasets using the loss functions that treat all pixels equally as in previous works can be problematic. The easy samples with small depth pixel values can easily overwhelm the training while hard samples with large depth pixel values have very limited contribution, leading the models tend to predict smaller depth values.

Based on the above observations, we propose to guide the network to pay more attentions to the distant depth regions during training and adaptively adjust the backpropagation flow accordingly. The proposed depth-aware objective is formulated as:

$$L_{DA} = \frac{1}{N} \sum_{i=1}^{N} (\alpha_D + \lambda_D) \cdot \ell(d_i, d_i^{GT}), \tag{1}$$

where i is the pixel index, N is the number of pixels in the depth map. d_i and d_i^{GT} are the predicted depth value and ground truth value respectively. $\ell(\cdot)$ is a distance metric can be ℓ_1, ℓ_2, etc. α_D is a depth-aware attention term that guides the network to focus more on distant hard depth regions to reduce the data distribution bias. Therefore, the gradients during backpropagation weight more on minority distant regions with respect to vast nearby regions. In this way, α_D should be positively correlated to the depth and can be defined as a linear function with respect to the ground truth depth.

To avoid gradient vanishing at the beginning of training and avoid cutting off of learning for nearby regions, a regularization term λ_D is introduced along with the attention term as:

$$\lambda_D = 1 - \frac{\min(\log(d_i), \log(d_i^{GT}))}{\max(\log(d_i), \log(d_i^{GT}))}, \tag{2}$$

which describes the learning state during training. If the network at current state predicts pixel i close to the ground truth, the regularization term λ_D approaches 0. When the network does not accurately predicts the value, λ_D approaches 1. As a result, even for very near $(\alpha_D \to 0)$ regions that are not accurately predicted, the gradients can still be backpropagated, which approaches the original ℓ loss function. In this way, Eq. 2 ensures the stableness during training. Our depth-aware objective guides the network to adaptively focus on different regions and automatically adjusts the strength/attention for each training sample, thus ensures the optimization direction of the model to be comparatively balanced. In sum, while L_{DA} preserves the focus on nearby pixel samples, it enables the network to put more attentions on the distant ones during training.

3.2 Network Architecture

The proposed synergy network is a multi-task deep CNN that mainly consists of four parts: the depth prediction sub-network, semantic labeling sub-network, knowledge sharing unit/connection, and the attention-driven loss. An overview architecture is shown in Fig. 2. The input RGB image is passed through a backbone encoder (*e.g.* VGG [47], ResNet [14]) to convert the color space into a high-dimension feature space. Following the backbone are two sub-networks

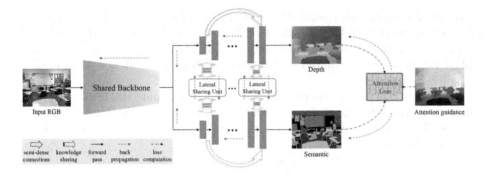

Fig. 2. Overview of the proposed network architecture. A single RGB image is fed into the shared backbone encoder network (purple), and then decoupled to the depth prediction (grey) and semantic labeling (pink) sub-networks. Knowledge between the two sub-networks is shared through lateral sharing units (details in Fig. 3 left) for both inference and backpropagation, together with internal sharing by semi-dense up-skip connections (Fig. 3 right). The training is supervised by an attention loss (Sect. 3.3). (Color figure online)

reconstructing the depth and semantic labels from the shared high-dimension feature. Knowledge sharing between these two tasks is achieved by a Lateral Sharing Unit (LSU), which is proposed to automatically learn the propagation flow during the training process and results in an optimum structure at test time. Besides, knowledge sharing is also performed internally at each sub-network through the proposed semi-dense up-skip connections (SUC). Finally, the whole training process is supervised by an attention-driven loss which consists of the proposed depth-aware and other attention-based loss terms.

Lateral Sharing Unit. We empirically explore different information sharing structures, which reveals that different multi-task networks result in diverse performance and the knowledge sharing strategy is hard to tune manually. In our synergy network, we propose a bi-directional *Lateral Sharing Unit* (LSU) to automatically learn the sharing strategy in a dynamic routing fashion. Information sharing is achieved for both forward pass and backpropagation. Between every two up-conv layers in the network, we add such LSU to share residual knowledge/representations from the other task, in addition to the intra-task propagation. Different from hand-tuned structures, our LSU is able to acquire additional fractional sharing from inter and intra-task layers. Specifically, the structure of LSU is illustrated in Fig. 3 left, which provides fully-sharing routes

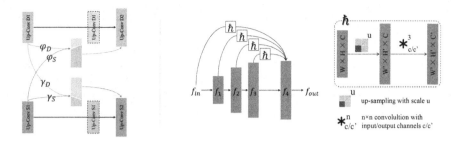

Fig. 3. Left: Structure of the proposed lateral sharing unit at every two consecutive up-conv layers D1 and D2, with identity mappings (black links). **Right:** Structure of the proposed semi-dense up-skip connections; dotted lines indicate up-skip connections, with operator $\hbar$ (bilinear up-sampling with convolution) shown on the right.

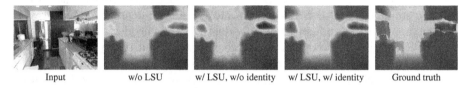

| Input | w/o LSU | w/ LSU, w/o identity | w/ LSU, w/ identity | Ground truth |

Fig. 4. Illustration on the effectiveness of LSU. All depth maps are with the same scale.

between the two tasks. Suppose the feature maps generated by current up-conv layers are D1 and S1. Then the feature representation for sharing can be formed as,

$$\begin{cases} LSU_{D2} = D1 + (\varphi_D \cdot D1 + \varphi_S \cdot S1) \\ LSU_{S2} = S1 + (\gamma_D \cdot D1 + \gamma_S \cdot S1) \end{cases}, \tag{3}$$

where φ_D, γ_D are the weighted parameters for feature D1, and φ_S, γ_S for feature S1. The sharing representations LSU_{D2} and LSU_{S2} are propagated to the subsequent up-conv layers. Note all the parameters in LSU are learnt during training, resulting in dynamic sharing route between every two up-conv layers. Although all LSUs share same internal structure, their parameters are not tied, allowing for a more flexible sharing. We propose to add identity mappings in addition to the combined sharing. With identity mappings, the intra-task information propagation is ensured, avoiding the risk of "propagation interruption" or feature pollution. Such residual-like structure (identity connection [15] associated with the residual sharing) also benefits efficient backpropagation of gradients. In addition, our LSU is applied between consecutive up-conv layers, instead of the encoding backbone. In this way, much fewer combination parameters and network parameters need to learn. An example illustrates the effectiveness of our LSU is shown in Fig. 4. We can see that when incorporating LSU, semantics is propagated to the depth thus improve its accuracy (the top-right cabinet). Whereas if without the identity mapping, artifacts may also be introduced by the semantic propagation (bottom-right cabinet). With identity mapping, less artifacts and higher accuracy can be achieved (the fourth column).

Semi-dense Up-skip Connections. In order to perform better intra-task knowledge sharing and preserve long-term memory, we introduce the *Semi-dense Up-skip Connections* (SUCs) between up-conv layers, as shown in Fig. 2 and detailed in Fig. 3 right. Denote f_{in} and f_{out} as the input and output features of the decoder, the output features of each up-conv layer as f_i. In addition to the short-term memory from preceding single up-conv layer, we add skip connections to propagate long-term memory. Therefore, our SUC is formulated as,

$$f_{out} = \hbar(f_{in}) + \sum_{i=1}^{n} \hbar(f_i), \tag{4}$$

where n is the number of up-conv layers ($n = 4$ in our work), and $\hbar$ denotes an up-resize operation in order to match the size of feature in the last up-conv layer. We also tried the concatenation of features which performs slightly worse than the summation. Our SUC is performed in a semi-dense manner between adjacent up-conv layers, instead of fully-dense in the encoder. In this way, the memory consumption is reduced to a large extent without performance sacrifice according to our experiment. In addition, with long- short-term connections the features from different up-conv steps are able to fuse in a coarse-to-fine multi-scale fashion, which incorporates both global and local information.

3.3 Attention-Driven Loss

Depth-Aware Loss. As defined in Sect. 3.1, during training, we use depth-aware loss term (Eq. 1) to supervise the depth prediction task. Specially, we set the attention term $\alpha_D = d^{GTn}$ where d^{GTn} is the normalized ground truth depth (attention guidance in Fig. 2) over whole range. The distance metric ℓ is set as reverse smooth L_1-norm [8,28] due to its robustness.

Joint Gradient Loss. In order to better preserve details on local structure and surface regions, we propose to set constraints on gradients and introduce the gradient loss layers with kernels set as the Sobel detector in both horizontal (∇_h) and vertical (∇_v) directions,

$$L_g(d, d^{GT}) = \frac{1}{N} \sum_{i=1}^{N} \left| \nabla_h d_i - \nabla_h d_i^{GT} \right| + \left| \nabla_v d_i - \nabla_v d_i^{GT} \right|. \tag{5}$$

In addition, the semantic information is also taken into consideration as a joint gradient loss term, by substituting the semantic segmentation result s for d^{GT} as: $L_g(d, s)$. Then the joint gradient loss term is formulated as $L_{JG} = L_g(d, d^{GT}) + L_g(d, s)$.

Semantic Focal Loss. As shown in Fig. 1 (c–e), the category distribution also belongs to a long-tailed one, even mapping to much fewer number (*e.g.* 40 or 4) of categories. Such imbalanced distribution not only influences the semantic labeling task but also impacts the depth prediction through LSUs and back-propagation. Inspired by the Focal Loss [32] proposed for object detection, we propose to guide the network to pay more attention to the hard tailed categories and set the loss term as,

$$L_{semF}(l, l^{GT}) = -\frac{1}{N} \sum_{i=1}^{N} \sum_{k=1}^{K} l_{i,k}^{GT} \alpha_k (1 - l_{i,k})^\gamma \log(l_{i,k}), \qquad (6)$$

where l_i is the label prediction at pixel i and k is the category index. α_k and γ are the balancing weight and focusing parameter to modulate the loss attention.

| Input | Depth attention | Backbone attention | Semantic attention |

Fig. 5. Network attention visualization. Given an input RGB image, the spatial attention of the network is shown as an overlay to the input.

The above loss terms/layers consist the proposed attention-driven loss as in Fig. 2, which is defined as,

$$L_{attention} = L_{DA} + L_{JG} + L_{semF}. \qquad (7)$$

3.4   Attention Visualization

In order to better illustrate the proposed attention-driven loss, we visualize the learned attention of the network, *i.e.* which region the network focuses more on. Following [54], here we use the spatial attention map to show the network attention. The attention maps of the network on monocular depth estimation in shown in Fig. 5 (second column) as heat-map, where red indicates high values. Note that the attention map here is different from the attention guidance in Fig. 2, although they share the similar high-level meaning. Here the attention map is represented by the aggregation of the feature activations from the first up-conv layer. In addition to the depth estimation, the attention maps of the shared backbone and semantic labeling are also presented for a thorough understanding of the network attention distribution in Fig. 5.

From the visualization we can see the network mainly focuses on distant regions when performing monocular depth estimation. On the other hand, the shared backbone focuses on a larger region around the distant area, indicating a more general attention on the whole scene while still driven by the distance. For the attention of semantic labeling, besides the dominant categories, some "tailed" categories also receive high attention, *e.g.* television, books, bag, *etc.* The above attention visualization results provide a better understanding of the network focus and validate the mechanism of the proposed attention-driven approach.

4   Experiments

In this section, we evaluate the proposed approach on monocular depth estimation, and compare to state-of-the-art methods. Performance on semantic labeling is also presented to show the benefits of knowledge sharing.

4.1   Experimental Setup

Dataset and Evaluation Metrics. We use the NYU Depth v2 (NYUD2) dataset [46] for our evaluation, which consists of 464 different indoor scenes with 894 different object categories (distributions shown in Fig. 1). We follow the standard train/test split with 795 aligned (RGB, depth) pairs for training, and 654 pairs for testing, as adopted in [35,53,56]. Besides, each of the standard splits images is manually annotated with semantic labels. In our experiment, we map the semantic labels into 4 and 40 categories, according to [46] and [10], respectively. We perform data augmentation on the training samples by random in-plane rotation ($[-5°, +5°]$), translation, horizontal flips, color (multiply with RGB value $\in [0.8, 1.2]^3$) and contrast (multiply with value $\in [0.5, 2.0]$) shift.

We quantitatively evaluate the performance of monocular depth prediction using the metrics of: mean absolute relative error (rel), mean $\log_{10}$ error ($\log 10$), root mean squared error (rms), rms(log), and the accuracy under threshold ($\delta < 1.25^i, i = 1, 2, 3$), following previous works [4,9,28,51].

Implementation Details. We implement our proposed deep model on a single Nvidia Tesla K80 GPU, using the PyTorch [40] framework. In our final model, the ResNet-50 [14] pre-trained on ImageNet is taken as our shared backbone network, by removing the last classification layers. The structure of decoder layers are set following state-of-the-art designs [28,53]. All the other parameters in the depth decoder, semantic decoder, SUCs, and LSUs are randomly initialized by the strategy in [13] and trained from scratch. We train our model with a batch size of 12 using the Adam solver [25] with parameters $(\beta_1, \beta_2, \epsilon) = (0.9, 0.999, 10^{-8})$. α, γ are set with reference to [32]. The images are first down-sampled to half size with invalid borders cropped, and at the end up-sampled to the original size using techniques similar to previous works [4,30,35]. We first freeze the semantic branch with all the LSUs, and train the rest model for depth prediction with a learning rate of 10^{-3}. Then freeze the depth branch and train the rest with learning rate of 10^{-5} on backbone and 10^{-3} on semantic branch. Finally, the whole model is trained end-to-end with initial learning rate 10^{-4} for backbone and 10^{-2} for others. The learning rate is decreased by 10 times every 20 epochs.

4.2   Experimental Results

Architecture Analysis. We first compare different settings of the network architecture: depth-only branch, *i.e.* ResNet with up-convs; with the SUC; with our proposed depth-aware loss (L_{DA}); adding semantic branch with and without LSUs. To better illustrate the effectiveness of the proposed knowledge sharing strategy, we also include the CS structure [38] (substitutes LSU) for comparison. Our final method with the attention-driven loss is compared to these baselines. In this analysis the semantic labels are mapped to 4 categories. The comparison results are shown in Table 1, where we can see the performance is continuously improved by incorporating each term. Specifically, after introducing the proposed depth-aware loss, performance among all the metrics are improved by a large margin. We note the CS structure do benefits representation sharing while our LSU performs slightly better. The synergy boosting from semantic labeling task also benefits a lot to the depth estimation. To summarize, the attention-driven loss contributes most to the performance, with secondary contributions of knowledge sharing from semantic labeling.

Table 1. Architecture analysis. Results are shown on NYUD2 dataset with 4-category mapped as semantic labeling task

Method	Lower is better				Higher is better		
	rel	log10	rms	rms (log)	$\delta < 1.25$	$\delta < 1.25^2$	$\delta < 1.25^3$
depth	0.157	0.062	0.642	0.208	0.763	0.943	0.985
+SUC	0.147	0.057	0.572	0.192	0.797	0.951	0.987
+SUC+L_{DA}	0.126	0.050	0.416	0.154	0.868	0.973	0.993
+SUC+L_{DA}+sem.	0.112	0.045	0.367	0.140	0.896	0.978	0.994
+SUC+L_{DA}+sem.+CS	0.110	0.044	0.363	0.138	0.898	0.979	0.995
+SUC+L_{DA}+sem.+LSU	0.105	0.042	0.351	0.133	0.906	0.980	0.995
Proposed	0.100	0.040	0.333	0.127	0.915	0.983	0.996

Table 2. Analysis on robustness to data "tail". Study performed on NYUD2 with 4-category mapped semantic labels

Depth range	Lower is better				Higher is better		
	rel	log10	rms	rms (log)	$\delta < 1.25$	$\delta < 1.25^2$	$\delta < 1.25^3$
$\leq 4\,$m	0.105	0.042	0.300	0.130	0.908	0.981	0.995
$\leq 6\,$m	0.101	0.041	0.326	0.127	0.915	0.983	0.996
$\leq 8\,$m	0.100	0.040	0.326	0.127	0.915	0.983	0.996
All	0.100	0.040	0.333	0.127	0.915	0.983	0.996

Robustness to "Tail". In order to validate the robustness of the proposed approach to long-tailed data, we perform an ablation study on the tailed part of the data. Specifically, we divide the depth range of the test data into four parts by cutting corresponding tails by 2 m for each (*i.e.*, $\leq$4 m, 6 m, 8 m, 10 m). Then we evaluate our method on these depth ranges as shown in Table 2. From the table we can see that even our attention-driven loss supervises the network to focus more on distant depth, it performs well on shorter-tailed data and consistently among different ranges, which indicates the proposed attention loss is able to adaptively vary according to the data distribution. In addition, our method also achieves state of the art even on nearby depth.

Table 3. Comparison with state-of-the-art methods on NYUD2 dataset. The last two rows show the proposed approach with 4 and 40 semantic categories, respectively

Method	Lower is better				Higher is better		
	rel	log10	rms	rms (log)	$\delta < 1.25$	$\delta < 1.25^2$	$\delta < 1.25^3$
Karsch *et al.* [21]	0.349	0.131	1.214	-	0.447	0.745	0.897
Ladicky *et al.* [27]	-	-	-	-	0.542	0.829	0.941
Liu *et al.* [36]	0.335	0.127	1.06	-	-	-	-
Zhuo *et al.* [56]	0.305	0.122	1.04	-	0.525	0.838	0.962
Li *et al.* [29]	0.232	0.094	0.821	-	0.621	0.886	0.968
Liu *et al.* [34]	0.230	0.095	0.824	-	0.614	0.883	0.975
Eigen *et al.* [5]	0.215	-	0.907	0.285	0.611	0.887	0.971
Roy and Todorovic [43]	0.187	0.078	0.744	-	-	-	-
Eigen and Fergus [4]	0.158	-	0.641	0.214	0.769	0.950	0.988
Laina *et al.* [28]	0.127	0.055	0.573	0.195	0.811	0.953	0.988
Xu *et al.* [53]	0.121	0.052	0.586	-	0.811	0.954	0.987
Li *et al.* [30]	0.143	0.063	0.635	-	0.788	0.958	0.991
Wang *et al.* [51]	0.220	0.094	0.745	0.262	0.605	0.890	0.970
Mousavian *et al.* [39]	0.200	-	0.816	0.314	0.568	0.856	0.956
Jafari *et al.* [19]	0.157	0.068	0.673	0.216	0.762	0.948	0.988
Laina *et al.* [28]+sem.	0.122	0.052	0.525	0.184	0.813	0.958	0.989
Proposed-4c	*0.100*	**0.040**	*0.333*	*0.127*	*0.915*	**0.983**	**0.996**
Proposed-40c	**0.098**	**0.040**	**0.329**	**0.125**	**0.917**	**0.983**	**0.996**

Comparison with State-of-the-Art. We also compare other state-of-the-art methods with the proposed approach. Here we directly use the reported results in their original papers. The comparison results on NYUD2 is shown in Table 3. For our approach, we consider two sharing settings with the semantic labeling task: sharing information from 4 mapped categories, and 40 mapped categories, as shown in the last two rows. From the results in Table 3 we can see, our approach performs favorably against other state-of-the-art methods. Note that [19,39,51] also utilize the semantic labeling information in a joint prediction manner, which perform not as well as ours. We also include a state-of-the-art method [28] accompanied a semantic labeling branch for better understanding of the semantic booster. The improvement over [28] favorably validates the effectiveness of adding semantic task, while information sharing is still underexplored. Another observation is that using more categories benefits the depth prediction, since it provides more semantic information of the objects in the scene.

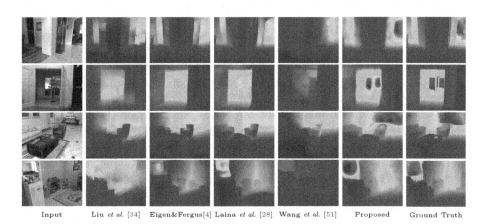

Input   Liu *et al.* [34]   Eigen&Fergus[4] Laina *et al.* [28] Wang *et al.* [51]   Proposed   Ground Truth

Fig. 6. Qualitative results on the NYUD2 dataset. Our method predicts more accurate depth compared to other state-of-the-art methods, especially on distant regions. Depth maps are in the same range with ground truth. Warm color indicates large depth.

Table 4. Evaluation of semantic labeling on the NYUD2-40

Method	Input	Pix. acc.	Mean acc.	IoU
FCN [37]	RGB-D	65.4	46.1	34.0
Eigen & Fergus [4]	RGB-D	65.6	45.1	34.1
Mousavian *et al.* [39]	RGB	68.6	52.3	39.2
RefineNet [31]	RGB	73.6	58.9	46.5
3DGNN [41]	RGB-D	-	55.7	43.1
Baseline	RGB	69.0	50.5	39.9
Without depth	RGB	75.7	55.7	48.9
Proposed	RGB	**81.1**	**62.2**	**50.9**

In addition to the quantitative comparison, some qualitative results are also presented in Fig. 6. All the depth maps are shown in the same range with the ground truth for better comparison. As we can see in the figure, the proposed method predicts more accurate depth values compared to other methods. For instance, the large-depth (red) regions in these examples, and the wall region in the last example. Furthermore, semantic prior also benefits the depth prediction, $e.g.$ the floor mat in the last example should have similar depth to the floor instead of floating. This again validates the effectiveness of the proposed approach, which focuses more on hard distant depth and object semantic meaning.

Semantic Labeling. Although the semantic labeling task is incorporated to perform knowledge sharing and boost the depth prediction task, the proposed network infers a semantic segmentation map as well. Here we evaluate whether the depth prediction task benefits semantic labeling, by three metrics in percentage (%): pixel accuracy, mean accuracy, Intersection over Union (IoU). We set the model without depth branch and L_{semF} as a baseline, and the model with L_{semF} (without depth) for comparison. Other semantic segmentation methods are also included for comparison (with their reported performance). The results on NYUD2 dataset with mapped 40 categories are shown in Table 4. As the table shows, our inferred semantic result achieves state-of-the-art performance as well. We note that without the depth information, our model still performs favorably against [4] and [37] which take RGB-D as input. This validates the effectiveness of the proposed SUC and L_{semF} to some extent. We also compare with [19,51] which mapped the raw data to 5 categories, different from the standard 4-category. After fine-tuning our 4-category model on their data, we achieve a result of (87.11, 66.77) on (pix.acc., IoU), with respect to (70.29, 44.20) from [51] and (73.04, 54.27) from [19].

Fig. 7. Results on SUN. Some regions (white boxes) are difficult even to capture GT.

Generalization Analysis. In addition to the NYUD2 dataset, we further explore the generalization ability of our model to other indoor and outdoor scenes. Performance on another indoor dataset SUN-RGBD [48] is shown in Fig. 7, where *Ours* are predicted by our original model without finetuning on SUN. The results show that even SUN differs from NYU in data distribution, our model could predict plausible results. For outdoor scenes, we fine-tune the indoor model on 200 standard training images (with sparse depth and semantic labels) from the KITTI dataset [7]. The performance is (RMSE, RMSElog, $\delta < 1.25, \delta < 1.25^2, \delta < 1.25^3$) = (5.110, 0.215, 0.843, 0.950, 0.981), following the evaluation setups in [9,26]. We also evaluate on the Cityscapes dataset [2], following the setups in [23]. The (Mean Error, RMSE) on the converted disparity is (2.11, 4.92), in comparison to (2.92, 5.88) for [23]. The above evaluations reveal that despite the difference in distribution and scene structures, our model is shown to have the generalization ability to other datasets.

5 Conclusions

We have introduced an attention-driven learning approach for monocular depth estimation, which also predicts corresponding accurate semantic labels. In order to predict accurate depth information for the whole scene, we delve into the *deeper* part of the scene and propose a novel attention-driven loss that supervises the training in an attention-driven manner. We have also presented a sharing strategy with LSU and SUC, to better propagate both inter- and intra-task knowledge. Experimental results on NYUD2 dataset showed that the proposed method performs favorably against state-of-the-arts, especially on hard distant regions. We have also shown the generality of our model to other datasets/scenes.

Acknowledgments. This work is partially supported by the Hong Kong PhD Fellowship Scheme (HKPFS) from the RGC of Hong Kong.

References

1. Chen, W., Fu, Z., Yang, D., Deng, J.: Single-image depth perception in the wild. In: NIPS (2016)
2. Cordts, M., et al.: The cityscapes dataset for semantic urban scene understanding. In: CVPR (2016)
3. Couprie, C., Farabet, C., Najman, L., LeCun, Y.: Indoor semantic segmentation using depth information (2013). arXiv preprint arXiv:1301.3572
4. Eigen, D., Fergus, R.: Predicting depth, surface normals and semantic labels with a common multi-scale convolutional architecture. In: ICCV (2015)
5. Eigen, D., Puhrsch, C., Fergus, R.: Depth map prediction from a single image using a multi-scale deep network. In: NIPS (2014)
6. Garg, R., Carneiro, G., Reid, I.: Unsupervised cnn for single view depth estimation: geometry to the rescue. In: ECCV (2016)
7. Geiger, A., Lenz, P., Urtasun, R.: Are we ready for autonomous driving? The kitti vision benchmark suite. In: CVPR (2012)
8. Girshick, R.: Fast r-cnn. In: ICCV (2015)
9. Godard, C., Mac Aodha, O., Brostow, G.J.: Unsupervised monocular depth estimation with left-right consistency. In: CVPR (2017)
10. Gupta, S., Arbelaez, P., Malik, J.: Perceptual organization and recognition of indoor scenes from rgb-d images. In: CVPR (2013)
11. Gupta, S., Girshick, R., Arbeláez, P., Malik, J.: Learning rich features from rgb-d images for object detection and segmentation. In: ECCV (2014)
12. Hane, C., Zach, C., Cohen, A., Angst, R., Pollefeys, M.: Joint 3d scene reconstruction and class segmentation. In: CVPR (2013)
13. He, K., Zhang, X., Ren, S., Sun, J.: Delving deep into rectifiers: surpassing human-level performance on imagenet classification. In: ICCV (2015)

14. He, K., Zhang, X., Ren, S., Sun, J.: Deep residual learning for image recognition. In: CVPR (2016)
15. He, K., Zhang, X., Ren, S., Sun, J.: Identity mappings in deep residual networks. In: ECCV (2016)
16. He, S., Jiao, J., Zhang, X., Han, G., Lau, R.W.: Delving into salient object subitizing and detections. In: ICCV (2017)
17. Hoiem, D., Efros, A.A., Hebert, M.: Automatic photo pop-up. ACM TOG **24**(3), 577–584 (2005)
18. Huang, G., Liu, Z., van der Maaten, L., Weinberger, K.Q.: Densely connected convolutional networks. In: CVPR (2017)
19. Jafari, O.H., Groth, O., Kirillov, A., Yang, M.Y., Rother, C.: Analyzing modular cnn architectures for joint depth prediction and semantic segmentation. In: ICRA (2017)
20. Jiao, J., Yang, Q., He, S., Gu, S., Zhang, L., Lau, R.W.: Joint image denoising and disparity estimation via stereo structure pca and noise-tolerant cost. IJCV **124**(2), 204–222 (2017)
21. Karsch, K., Liu, C., Kang, S.B.: Depth transfer: depth extraction from video using non-parametric sampling. IEEE TPAMI **36**(11), 2144–2158 (2014)
22. Kendall, A., Gal, Y.: What uncertainties do we need in bayesian deep learning for computer vision? In: NIPS (2017)
23. Kendall, A., Gal, Y., Cipolla, R.: Multi-task learning using uncertainty to weigh losses for scene geometry and semantics. In: CVPR (2018)
24. Kim, S., Park, K., Sohn, K., Lin, S.: Unified depth prediction and intrinsic image decomposition from a single image via joint convolutional neural fields. In: ECCV (2016)
25. Kingma, D., Ba, J.: Adam: a method for stochastic optimization (2014). arXiv preprint arXiv:1412.6980
26. Kuznietsov, Y., Stückler, J., Leibe, B.: Semi-supervised deep learning for monocular depth map prediction. In: CVPR (2017)
27. Ladicky, L., Shi, J., Pollefeys, M.: Pulling things out of perspective. In: CVPR (2014)
28. Laina, I., Rupprecht, C., Belagiannis, V., Tombari, F., Navab, N.: Deeper depth prediction with fully convolutional residual networks. In: 3D Vision (3DV) (2016)
29. Li, B., Shen, C., Dai, Y., van den Hengel, A., He, M.: Depth and surface normal estimation from monocular images using regression on deep features and hierarchical crfs. In: CVPR (2015)
30. Li, J., Klein, R., Yao, A.: A two-streamed network for estimating fine-scaled depth maps from single rgb images. In: ICCV (2017)
31. Lin, G., Milan, A., Shen, C., Reid, I.: Refinenet: multi-path refinement networks for high-resolution semantic segmentation. In: CVPR (2017)
32. Lin, T.Y., Goyal, P., Girshick, R., He, K., Dollár, P.: Focal loss for dense object detection. In: ICCV (2017)
33. Liu, B., Gould, S., Koller, D.: Single image depth estimation from predicted semantic labels. In: CVPR (2010)
34. Liu, F., Shen, C., Lin, G.: Deep convolutional neural fields for depth estimation from a single image. In: CVPR (2015)
35. Liu, F., Shen, C., Lin, G., Reid, I.: Learning depth from single monocular images using deep convolutional neural fields. IEEE TPAMI **38**(10), 2024–2039 (2016)
36. Liu, M., Salzmann, M., He, X.: Discrete-continuous depth estimation from a single image. In: CVPR (2014)

37. Long, J., Shelhamer, E., Darrell, T.: Fully convolutional networks for semantic segmentation. In: CVPR (2015)
38. Misra, I., Shrivastava, A., Gupta, A., Hebert, M.: Cross-stitch networks for multi-task learning. In: CVPR (2016)
39. Mousavian, A., Pirsiavash, H., Košecká, J.: Joint semantic segmentation and depth estimation with deep convolutional networks. In: 3D Vision (3DV) (2016)
40. Paszke, A., et al.: Automatic differentiation in pytorch (2017)
41. Qi, X., Liao, R., Jia, J., Fidler, S., Urtasun, R.: 3d graph neural networks for rgbd semantic segmentation. In: ICCV (2017)
42. Ren, X., Bo, L., Fox, D.: Rgb-(d) scene labeling: features and algorithms. In: CVPR (2012)
43. Roy, A., Todorovic, S.: Monocular depth estimation using neural regression forest. In: CVPR (2016)
44. Saxena, A., Sun, M., Ng, A.Y.: Make3d: learning 3d scene structure from a single still image. IEEE TPAMI **31**(5), 824–840 (2009)
45. Shrivastava, A., Gupta, A., Girshick, R.: Training region-based object detectors with online hard example mining. In: CVPR (2016)
46. Silberman, N., Hoiem, D., Kohli, P., Fergus, R.: Indoor segmentation and support inference from RGBD images. In: Fitzgibbon, A., Lazebnik, S., Perona, P., Sato, Y., Schmid, C. (eds.) ECCV 2012. LNCS, vol. 7576, pp. 746–760. Springer, Heidelberg (2012). https://doi.org/10.1007/978-3-642-33715-4_54
47. Simonyan, K., Zisserman, A.: Very deep convolutional networks for large-scale image recognition (2014). arXiv preprint arXiv:1409.1556
48. Song, S., Lichtenberg, S.P., Xiao, J.: Sun rgb-d: a rgb-d scene understanding benchmark suite. In: CVPR (2015)
49. Song, S., Yu, F., Zeng, A., Chang, A.X., Savva, M., Funkhouser, T.: Semantic scene completion from a single depth image. In: CVPR (2017)
50. Del Giorno, A., Bagnell, J.A., Hebert, M.: A discriminative framework for anomaly detection in large videos. In: Leibe, B., Matas, J., Sebe, N., Welling, M. (eds.) ECCV 2016. LNCS, vol. 9909, pp. 334–349. Springer, Cham (2016). https://doi.org/10.1007/978-3-319-46454-1_21
51. Wang, P., Shen, X., Lin, Z., Cohen, S., Price, B., Yuille, A.L.: Towards unified depth and semantic prediction from a single image. In: CVPR (2015)
52. Wang, P., Shen, X., Russell, B., Cohen, S., Price, B., Yuille, A.L.: Surge: surface regularized geometry estimation from a single image. In: NIPS (2016)
53. Xu, D., Ricci, E., Ouyang, W., Wang, X., Sebe, N.: Multi-scale continuous crfs as sequential deep networks for monocular depth estimation. In: CVPR (2017)
54. Zagoruyko, S., Komodakis, N.: Paying more attention to attention: improving the performance of convolutional neural networks via attention transfer. In: ICLR (2017)
55. Zhou, T., Brown, M., Snavely, N., Lowe, D.G.: Unsupervised learning of depth and ego-motion from video. In: CVPR (2017)
56. Zhuo, W., Salzmann, M., He, X., Liu, M.: Indoor scene structure analysis for single image depth estimation. In: CVPR (2015)
57. Zoran, D., Isola, P., Krishnan, D., Freeman, W.T.: Learning ordinal relationships for mid-level vision. In: ICCV (2015)

Summarizing First-Person Videos from Third Persons' Points of Views

Hsuan-I Ho[1], Wei-Chen Chiu[2], and Yu-Chiang Frank Wang[1(✉)]

[1] Department of Electrical Engineering, National Taiwan University, Taiwan,
Republic of China
{b01901029,ycwang}@ntu.edu.tw
[2] Department of Computer Science, National Chiao Tung University, Taiwan,
Republic of China
walon@cs.nctu.edu.tw

Abstract. Video highlight or summarization is among interesting topics in computer vision, which benefits a variety of applications like viewing, searching, or storage. However, most existing studies rely on training data of third-person videos, which cannot easily generalize to highlight the first-person ones. With the goal of deriving an effective model to summarize first-person videos, we propose a novel deep neural network architecture for describing and discriminating vital spatiotemporal information across videos with different points of view. Our proposed model is realized in a semi-supervised setting, in which fully annotated third-person videos, unlabeled first-person videos, and a small number of annotated first-person ones are presented during training. In our experiments, qualitative and quantitative evaluations on both benchmarks and our collected first-person video datasets are presented.

Keywords: Video summarization · First-person vision
Transfer learning · Metric learning

1 Introduction

Wearable and head-mounted cameras have changed the way how people record and browse videos. These devices enable users to capture life-logging videos without intentionally focus on particular subjects. Thus, the resulting first-person videos (or egocentric videos) would exhibit very unique content and properties when comparing to those of third-person ones. As pointed out by Molino *et al.* [18], the lack of sufficient structural information and repetitive content for first-person videos would limit viewing quality. Therefore, it is desirable to be able to highlight or summarize such videos for improving user viewing experiences.

Electronic supplementary material The online version of this chapter (https://doi.org/10.1007/978-3-030-01267-0_5) contains supplementary material, which is available to authorized users.

© Springer Nature Switzerland AG 2018
V. Ferrari et al. (Eds.): ECCV 2018, LNCS 11219, pp. 72–89, 2018.
https://doi.org/10.1007/978-3-030-01267-0_5

With the goal of encapsulating informative segments from videos, video summarization aims at identifying the highlight video segments. Existing approaches for video summarization either select the most representative video segments [8,16] or detect particular or pre-defined visual structures or objects as summarized outputs [13–15]. With the recent development of deep learning, a recent work [28] successfully utilized deep neural networks for first-person video summarization, by using a pre-collected and annotated first-person video dataset.

Nevertheless, it is difficult to collect a large amount of fully annotated first-person video data (note that the dataset in [28] is not publicly available). To address such limitations, the technique of transfer learning becomes an alternative solution. To be more precise, it is possible for one to learn from annotated third-person videos and aim at transferring the learned model to summarize the first-person ones. However, since significant differences of visual appearance can be expected between third and first-person videos, how to apply and adapt existing third-person video summarization approaches would be a challenging task. Moreover, a satisfying first-person video summary should consist of segments important to both the recorder and the viewer. Without observing any annotated first-person video revealing such information, it would be difficult to learn an effective model for solving the corresponding task.

Existing transfer learning works have been focusing on alleviating the domain shift (or dataset bias) across data domains [19]. With the recent success of deep learning, architectures of deep neural networks have also been utilized to solve similar problems [21]. Recent deep learning based video summarization approaches like [11,17,30] did not explicitly address this issue. To advance transfer learning for first-person video summarization, one could utilize fully annotated third-person videos plus a number of annotated first-person videos for training their models. In order to increase the training set size of first-person videos without label information, one could further extend the above supervised domain adaptation setting to a more challenging yet practical semi-supervised one. That is, additional unlabeled first-person videos can be also presented during training. As a result, one not only requires to alleviate the domain (viewpoint) bias between first and third-person videos, how to learn deep neural networks in a semi-supervised setting needs to be also addressed.

In this paper, we propose a deep learning framework which performs cross-domain feature embedding and transfers highlight information across video domains. More specifically, our network architecture jointly performs domain adaptation (across third-and first-person videos) in a semi-supervised setting. That is, in addition to third-person videos with fully annotated highlight scores, first-person videos are also presented during training, while only a small portion of them are with ground-truth scores. Moreover, we further integrate a sequence-to-sequence model based on recurrent neural networks (RNN), which allows the exploitation of long-term temporal information for improved summarization.

In summary, our contributions are threefold: (1) By reducing the semantic gap between third and first-person videos, our proposed network transfers informative spatiotemporal features across video domains to perform first-person video summarization; (2) our network is able to handle unlabeled data during adaptation, which not only allows our model to be trained in a semi-supervised setting, possible overfitting due to a small amount of annotated first-person video data can be also alleviated; (3) in addition to the use of SumMe [7] dataset, we collect a larger-scale first-person video dataset for further evaluation, which is now available.[1]

2   Related Works

First-Person Video Summarization. Summarizing first-person videos has attracted the computer vision community in recent years [2,4,18]. Most existing approaches follow a basic workflow consisting of (1) visual feature extraction and (2) keyframe selection or scene segmentation, while the latter is typically subject to pre-defined criteria. For example, Lee *et al.* [13,14] select video frames containing important subjects and objects alongside visual diversity, while Bettadapura *et al.* [3] look for artistic properties in vacation-related videos. Lin *et al.* [15] train a context-specific highlight detector for each type of egocentric videos, which enables online summarization and solves the problem of data storage. Xu *et al.* [27] exploit gaze information to predict the attention given to video segments, resulting summarization that reflects the recorder preferences. However, the above methods are mainly applied to specific video contexts (e.g., daily live or cooking videos). Although a recent work by Yao *et al.* [28] learns an associated ranking function via deep metric learning to score video segments of 15 categories, it requires an enormous number of fully-annotated first-person videos (over 50 h) for training. This is why a semi-supervised transfer learning framework (as ours) for video summarization is practically preferable, with the goal of leveraging information across video domains for improved summarization.

Deep Learning for Video Summarization. Some recent deep-learning based methods approach video summarization by solving a sequence-to-sequence problem, in which the video frames are encoded by Recurrent Neural Network (RNN) schemes. For example, Zhang *et al.* [30] propose a summarization model based on a bidirectional Long Short Term Memory (biLSTM) framework, which is trained on videos with annotated importance scores for keyframe selection. They additionally apply determinantal point process (DPP) to enhance the diversity of the chosen keyframes. Ji *et al.* [11] further extend such biLSTM models by integrating the attention mechanism. Their model considers temporal information in finer granularity when decoding the feature vectors of video segments generated by biLSTM.

Although supervised approaches exhibit promising video summarization results, existing datasets (with ground-truth data) for video summarization [7,23] are generally with smaller scales. For learning effective summarization

---

[1] The dataset and code is available on: https://github.com/azuxmioy/fpvsum.

models, it would be desirable to have a large number of labeled videos for training purposes. Several works thus attempt to utilize various techniques in order to address this issue. For example, Panda et al. [20] collect weakly annotated videos from YouTube 8M [1] and train their summarization model with auxiliary labels of activity classes; Sun et al. [24] train their highlight classifiers by utilizing a collection of YouTube videos that have been edited as positive training data, while the negative ones are retrieved from raw videos. Alternatively, Gygli et al. [9] present summarization models by collecting massive training pairs mined from GIF image websites. By advancing sequential generative adversarial networks, Mahasseni et al. [17] perform video summarization by predicting video keyframe distribution.

Nevertheless, the above approaches generally focus on summarizing third-person videos, or those with mixed type of videos [7,23] (i.e., no distinction between third and first-person ones). As noted above, highlighting first-person videos would be particularly challenging due to significant changes in visual content and appearances (plus, due to the lack of a sufficient amount of annotated training data). This is the reason why we choose to address first-person video summarization in a semi-supervised setting, and propose deep transfer learning techniques for solving this problem.

Datasets for Video Summarization. Finally, we summarize the characteristics of existing datasets for both first-person and third-person video summarization in Table 1. UT Ego [13] annotates the keyframes including important objects and people in daily lives videos. VideoSet [29] provides extra textual labels for videos in UT Ego [13] and Disneyworld [6], including tools for summarization evaluation. EgoSum+gaze [27] consists of shot-level annotations obtained from camera wearers together with their gaze information. However, the context of the above first-person datasets are very limited (e.g., daily lives, cooking, etc. activities). Moreover, it is difficult for viewers to obtain frame-level importance scores due to their long duration and redundancy.

Yao et al. [28] first propose a large-scale dataset including frame-level annotations for various sports videos mined from YouTube. In contrast to two widely used dataset SumMe [7] and TvSum [23], most first-person videos mined from YouTube are either over-edited or overlong, which can result in very different viewpoints across videos, plus frame discontinuity and annotation biases within the dataset. It is worth noting that, most first-person datasets for video summarization are not publicly available, this is the reason why one of our major contributions is to collect and release a first-person video dataset including viewer-friendly videos and unbiased importance scores for research purposes.

3   Proposed Framework

For the sake of completeness, we first explain the notations in this paper. We have an annotated video collection including a set of third-person videos $V^T = \{V_1^T, ..., V_M^T\}$ and few first-person videos $V^F = \{V_1^F, ..., V_N^F\}$, where M and N

Table 1. Comparisons of existing video summarization datasets.

Dataset	Type	Length	# of videos	Annotation/Score	Description
UT Ego [13]	1st-person	17 h	4	Video frames which contain important people and objects	- Videos of daily activities in a uncontrolled setting
VideoSet [29]	1st-person	>60 h	13	Textual description for each 5-seconds video segment	- Provide textual labels for UT Ego [13] and Disney-World [6] - **Not publicly available**
EgoSum+gaze [27]	1st-person	>15 h	21	~ 15 events selected by 5 camera wearers	- Daily lives videos together with gaze data - **Not publicly available**
Yao et al. [28]	1st-person	>100 h	600	Fully annotated frame-level scores from 12 annotators	- 15 categories of GoPro sports videos mined from YouTube - **Not publicly available**
SumMe [7]	3rd-person 1st-person	50 min 14 min	20 5	Fully annotated frame-level scores from at least 15 annotators	- Raw user videos containing interesting events
TvSum [23]	3rd-person	3 h 30 min	50	Fully annotated frame-level scores from 20 annotators	- 50 YouTube videos in 10 categories from the TRECVid MED task
Proposed	1st-person	7 h 56 min	98	Fully annotated frame-level scores from at least 10 annotators	- 14 categories of GoPro viewer-friendly videos selected from YouTube

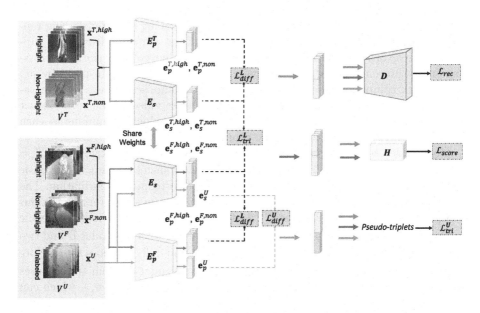

Fig. 1. Our first-person video summarization framework via semi-supervised domain adaptation. Note that fully annotated third-person videos V^T, unlabeled first-person videos V^U, plus a number of annotated first-person ones V^F are presented during training. We have $\mathbf{x}$, $\mathbf{e}_s$, and $\mathbf{e}_p$ denote the input, *shared* and *private* features, respectively.

denote the numbers of third-and first-person videos respectively (where typically $M > N$). Their corresponding annotations (i.e., importance scores) at the frame-level are $S^T = \{S_1^T, ..., S_M^T\}$ and $S^F = \{S_1^F, ..., S_N^F\}$. In addition, we have another set of first-person videos $V^U = \{V_1^U, ..., V_K^U\}$ without any annotation of importance scores, with the number of videos $K \gg N$. The goal of our work is to bridge the semantic gap across V^T, V^F and V^U, so that the learned model can be applied for first-person video summarization.

The architecture of our proposed method is shown in Fig. 1, which consists of network components for cross-domain feature embedding and summarization. The highlights of our method include: (1) our domain separation architecture learns shared and private features across video domains, while adapting cross-domain highlight information for summarization; (2) a self-learning scheme for leveraging unlabeled first-person video data, so that our model can be trained in a semi-supervised setting; and (3) our highlight detection network for exploiting long-term temporal information to improve final summarization. Details of our framework will be described in the following subsections.

3.1 Cross-Domain Feature Embedding

To adapt information across video domains for highlighting a particular video domain of interest, the first stage of our proposed network performs cross-domain feature embedding. More specifically, we aim at retrieving and transferring representative highlight information across third and first-person videos, while suppressing irrelevant features in each domain. This is achieved by performing cross-domain feature embedding via a domain separation structure. Inspired by [5], our network component for domain separation decomposes feature representations into of two subspaces: a *shared* subspace across video domains to extract domain-invariant information, and *private* subspaces which are unique to each domain for describing domain-specific properties.

Given video segments with fixed-length, i.e., $X^T = \{\mathbf{x}_1^T, ..., \mathbf{x}_m^T\}$ and $X^F = \{\mathbf{x}_1^F, ..., \mathbf{x}_n^F\}$ from V^T and V^F, respectively, we view such segments as the basic elements in our framework for capturing video spatiotemporal information. The shared encoder E_s in Fig. 1 encodes $\mathbf{x}^T, \mathbf{x}^F$ into domain-invariant representations $\mathbf{e}_s^T, \mathbf{e}_s^F$, while the private encoders E_p^T and E_p^F embed them into domain-specific features $\mathbf{e}_p^T$ and $\mathbf{e}_p^F$. These encoders are jointly learned with a decoder D and two explicit loss functions: the reconstruction loss $\mathcal{L}_{rec}^L$ and difference loss $\mathcal{L}_{diff}^L$. Note that, $\mathcal{L}_{rec}^L$ encourages the reconstruction of $\mathbf{x}$ by decoder D from the features concatenating shared and private representations $\mathbf{e} = \text{concat}(\mathbf{e}_s, \mathbf{e}_p)$, which can be written as:

$$\mathcal{L}_{rec}^L = \sum_{i \in \{F,T\}} \left\| f_D(\mathbf{e}^i) - \mathbf{x}^i \right\|_2^2. \tag{1}$$

As for the difference loss $\mathcal{L}_{diff}^L$, it is imposed on the orthogonality between $\mathbf{e}_s$ and $\mathbf{e}_p$, and thus enforces E_s and E_p to capture different aspects of information (shared and private ones) from $\mathbf{x}$. Thus, $\mathcal{L}_{diff}^L$ is defined as:

$$\mathcal{L}_{diff}^L = \left\| \mathbf{E}_p^{T\top} \mathbf{E}_s^T \right\|_F^2 + \left\| \mathbf{E}_p^{F\top} \mathbf{E}_s^F \right\|_F^2, \tag{2}$$

where $\mathbf{E}_p^T$ and $\mathbf{E}_s^T$ are the matrices consisted of private and shared features of the third-person video segments in a batch. Likewise, $\mathbf{E}_p^F$ and $\mathbf{E}_s^F$ denote the matrices for the corresponding first-person embedded features. Exploiting the above domain separation architecture allows us to mitigate domain differences via shared feature embedding across video domains, and meanwhile retains sufficient domain-specific characteristic in the private subspaces for each domain.

Despite the above use of domain separation components for suppressing feature differences across video domains, there is *no* guarantee the shared encoder E_s captures the semantics of highlight information from input videos. Hence, we further advance deep metric learning with the triplet network [10,22] for improved feature embedding. This not only allows us to better describe videos over third and first-person views but also reflects and shares highlight information across video domains for later summarization purposes.

To achieve the above goal, we divide the cross-domain videos in shared features with ground-truth score annotation into highlight and non-highlight subsets: $\{\mathbf{e}_s^{T,high}, \mathbf{e}_s^{T,non}\}$ and $\{\mathbf{e}_s^{F,high}, \mathbf{e}_s^{F,non}\}$, where $\mathbf{e}_s^{T,high}$ and $\mathbf{e}_s^{T,non}$ relate to the highlight and non-highlight third-person video subsets, respectively. Similarly, we have first-person video subsets $\{\mathbf{e}_s^{F,high}, \mathbf{e}_s^{F,non}\}$. To jointly eliminate video domain differences and adapt highlight information across domains, the triplets are built from a set of features $\{e_s^{T,high}, e_s^{T,non}, e_s^{F,high}, e_s^{F,non}\}$ to include feature pairs extracted from within and across-domain video data. Take $\{e_s^{T,high}, e_s^{T,non}, e_s^{F,high}\}$ as examples, the corresponding triplet loss is calculated as:

$$\mathcal{L}_{tri}^L = max\left\{0, \mathcal{M} - \mathcal{D}_{cos}(e_s^{T,high}, e_s^{T,non}) + \mathcal{D}_{cos}(e_s^{F,high}, e_s^{T,high})\right\}, \quad (3)$$

where $\mathcal{D}_{cos}(e, e') = 1 - \frac{e \cdot e'}{\|e\|_2 \|e'\|_2}$ returns the distance between the embedding features, and $\mathcal{M}$ denotes the margin for metric learning. Note that such losses are calculated for all triplets from within and cross-video data.

3.2 Self-learning with Unlabeled First-Person Videos

The feature embedding network described in Sect. 3.1 allows us to identify domain-invariant and domain-specific features across video domains. However, since the number of labeled first-person videos is generally much smaller than that of third-person ones, it would be desirable to further exploit unlabeled first-person ones, so that possible overfitting can be alleviated.

In our proposed network, we thus introduce a *self-learning* component for addressing this task. As illustrated in Fig. 1, unlabeled segments of first-person videos pass through the embedding network, resulting in feature vectors e_p^U, e_s^U. The reconstruction loss $\mathcal{L}_{rec}^U$ and difference loss $\mathcal{L}_{diff}^U$, which are identical to $\mathcal{L}_{rec}^L$ and $\mathcal{L}_{diff}^L$ respectively but applied for unlabeled e^U and $\mathbf{E}^U$, are also used in training:

$$\mathcal{L}_{rec}^U = \left\| f_D(e^U) - \mathbf{x}^U \right\|_2^2, \mathcal{L}_{diff}^U = \left\| \mathbf{E}_p^{U\top} \mathbf{E}_s^U \right\|_F^2. \quad (4)$$

To further utilize unlabeled first-person videos together with the annotated cross-domain data for improved cross-domain feature embedding, we extend the above learning scheme by generating pseudo triplets, which allows us to finetune the above cross-domain embedding network. To be more precise, in a subset built upon samples from $\{e^T, e^F\}$, the farthest and nearest features with respect to each reference $e^U = \text{concat}(e_s^U, e_p^U)$ would be viewed as the negative pair e^- and positive pair e^+ for e^U, thus forming pseudo triplets. Therefore, without observing ground-truth annotation scores, the loss of such a pseudo triplet $\mathcal{L}_{tri}^U$ can be calculated for each unlabeled first-person video:

$$\mathcal{L}_{tri}^U = max\left\{0, \mathcal{M} - \mathcal{D}_{cos}(e^U, e^-) + \mathcal{D}_{cos}(e^U, e^+)\right\}. \quad (5)$$

With the above self-learning strategy, we are now able to jointly exploit both supervised and unlabeled video data during training, so that network components E_p^F, E_s and D can be updated accordingly.

3.3 From Segment to Sequence Based Highlight Detection

From the above subsections, we see that the first stage of our network performs feature embedding across video domains in a semi-supervised setting, while both representation and discriminative highlight information are preserved in the feature space. Since the focus of our network is to perform first-person video summarization, we finally introduce a highlight detection network. As depicted in Fig. 1, this would additionally enforce the resulting joint features of first-person videos to exhibit sufficient highlight information.

With our use of highlight and non-highlight scores, the introduced highlight detection network serves as a binary classifier, which distinguishes between the associated video segments accordingly. Thus, we do not consider ranking loss as [9,24,28] did. Instead, following [17], we apply classification loss for our highlight detection model.

To detail this highlight detection process, we have concatenated features $\{\mathbf{e}_1, ..., \mathbf{e}_B\}$ as inputs to the highlight detection network H for predicting the importance scores $\hat{\mathbf{s}}_i = f_H(\mathbf{e}_i)$. Note that $\mathbf{e}_i = \text{concat}(\mathbf{e}_{p,i}, \mathbf{e}_{s,i})$, and B as the number of instances in each batch. The scoring loss between the predicted and ground-truth scores is calculated as:

$$\mathcal{L}_{score} = -\frac{1}{B} \sum_{i=1}^{B} \mathbf{y}_i \cdot \log(\hat{\mathbf{s}}_i), \tag{6}$$

where each ground-truth scores s_i are converted to 2-D one-hot vectors $\mathbf{y}_i = (0,1) \vee (1,0)$, and the network H returns a 2-D softmax prediction $\hat{\mathbf{s}}_i$ instead of an 1-D scalar $\hat{s}_i$.

To extend the above segment-based video highlight detection into sequence-based prediction, we further extend the proposed network architecture to a sequence level, i.e., the feature output of the embedding network is now served as the input to a recurrent neural network (RNN). As suggested in [11,17,30], integration with such RNN-based components allows one to observe long-term dependency between segments within a video sequence. While recent RNN-based models can be easily applied and integrated into our framework (e.g., LSTM-based models [30], adversarial LSTM networks [17], and attention-based encoder-decoder networks [11]), we particularly take the video summarization LSTM (vsLSTM) in [30] for our use. We note that vsLSTM consists of a bidirectional LSTM (biLSTM) cell followed by a single-hidden-layer MLP. The biLSTM cell takes a sequence of concatenated features $\mathcal{E} = \{\mathbf{e}_1, ..., \mathbf{e}_t\}$ as inputs and returns both forward hidden states $\mathbf{h}^{forward} = \{\overrightarrow{\mathbf{h}}_1, ..., \overrightarrow{\mathbf{h}}_t\}$ and backward hidden states $\mathbf{h}^{backward} = \{\overleftarrow{\mathbf{h}}_1, ..., \overleftarrow{\mathbf{h}}_t\}$. These observed hidden states would exploit and preserve semantic information across time periods. Upon the introduction of LSTM-based models, a single-hidden-layer MLP can be directly deployed for predicting the importance scores $\hat{\mathbf{s}} = \{\hat{\mathbf{s}}_1, ..., \hat{\mathbf{s}}_t\}$ with inputs $\mathbf{h}^{forward}, \mathbf{h}^{backward}$, and $\mathcal{E}$. As a result, the scoring loss for updating vsLSTM can be calculated via (6).

3.4   Learning of Our Network

It is worth noting that, our proposed network allows end-to-end training, which updates the parameters for each component by calculating the following loss:

$$\mathcal{L}_{total} = \mathcal{L}_{tri} + \alpha \cdot \mathcal{L}_{rec} + \beta \cdot \mathcal{L}_{diff} + \gamma \cdot \mathcal{L}_{score}, \tag{7}$$

where α, β, γ are hyperparameters that control the interaction of overall loss. Except for $\mathcal{L}_{score}$ which relies on video data with ground-truth scores, the remaining losses are calculated and summed over labeled and unlabeled data.

As for the learning of sequence-based highlight detection network, a two-stage training scheme is implemented. That is, we first train the feature embedding network using video segment pairs as shown in Fig. 1 (i.e., segment-based highlight detection network), followed by jointly training of RNN and the resulting network using consecutive video segments as inputs.

4   Experiments

4.1   Datasets

We now describe the datasets (including the one we collect) for experiments. Two publicly available datasets with full annotations, **SumMe** [7] and **TVSum** [23], are recently used to evaluate the performance of video summarization task. Both cover a variety of video contexts for summarization purposes. **SumMe** consists of 25 user videos with a length varying from 1 to 6 min, in which the annotations of frame-level importance scores are provided. Within this dataset, there are five first-person videos, "Base jumping, Bike Polo, Scuba, Valparaiso Downhill, Uncut Evening Flight", which are applied as test data for quantitative evaluation and comparisons. On the other hand, **TVSum** consists of 50 third-person videos collected from YouTube, and each of them is annotated with frame-level importance scores. The videos in this dataset are viewed as the third-person labeled data for our training purposes.

Nevertheless, the number of first-person videos in SumMe is far from sufficient for training effective deep learning models for summarization. Thus, following the procedure of [28], we additionally create a new first-person dataset containing various categories of first-person videos from YouTube along with corresponding frame-level importance scores.

During the collection of the first-person videos, we found that a large number of such videos on YouTube are not raw videos but edited ones, consisting of obvious frame discontinuity (selected/edited by users), transitions of point-of-view, and unrelated contents. Thus, they cannot be directly applied and added to the data collection for training/testing. Another observation is about the annotation collection. We observe that most annotators would lose concentration on assigning scores for long videos. Therefore, we collect a first-person video summarization dataset **FPVSum** with a total number of 98 videos. Excluding the edited or discontinuous videos, our collected video data are from 14 categories with varying lengths (over 7 h in total). For each category, about 35% of the video sequences are annotated with ground-truth scores by at least 10 users, while the remaining are viewed as the unlabeled ones.

Complete discussions and comparisons of the datasets considered are listed in Table 2. We note that, when evaluating the performance of first-person video summarization, only our proposed model can be realized in a semi-supervised setting, while existing baseline and state-of-the-art approaches cannot handle unlabeled first-person videos during training.

4.2   Experimental Setup

Evaluation Metrics. We follow the criteria used in [17,30] for video summarization evaluation, with the length of video summaries less than 15% of the total length of the original video. Let $\mathcal{A}$ be the set of generated summaries, and $\mathcal{B}$ is the set of video segments selected by user-annotated importance scores, the resulting precision $\mathcal{P}$ and recall $\mathcal{R}$ are defined as:

$$\mathcal{P} = \frac{\text{total overlap duration of } \mathcal{A} \text{ and } \mathcal{B}}{\text{total duration of } \mathcal{A}}, \tag{8}$$

$$\mathcal{R} = \frac{\text{total overlap duration of } \mathcal{A} \text{ and } \mathcal{B}}{\text{total duration of } \mathcal{B}}. \tag{9}$$

Thus, the F-measure is computed as $\mathcal{F} = 2 \times \mathcal{P} \times \mathcal{R}/(\mathcal{P} + \mathcal{R}) \times 100\%$. In addition, we further calculate the area-under-curve (AUC) values based on the resulting precision-recall curves, which allow us to perform detailed comparisons with respect to different lengths of summaries.

Methods of Interest. We compare our work with four baselines (noted as **Random, Uniform, DSN** [5] and **C3D** [26]) and two state-of-the-art supervised video summarization models: **TDCNN** [28] and **vsLSTM** [30]. We first describe sequentially how the four baselines are obtained.

- **Random:** 15% of segments from each test video are randomly sampled as the highlight.
- **Uniform:** Instead of random sampling, 15% of segments from each test video are equidistantly selected as the highlight.
- **DSN:** The direct use of domain separation networks (DSN) [5] for performing cross-view video summarization.
- **C3D:** We extract C3D [26] pre-trained features for each video segment. A highlight classifier taking C3D features as the inputs is trained by the classification loss (6). The segments with top 15% prediction scores in each video are selected as the highlight outputs.

As for the two state-of-the-art methods, their original objectives and experimental settings are different from our semi-supervised one. Thus, we cannot directly report and compare their performances. Instead, we implement their works with the following settings for fair comparisons.

- **TDCNN:** Although [28] originally designs a two-stream network that exploits two visual features (i.e., AlexNet [12] and C3D) in their model, we compare TDCNN (C3D) only in our experiments for the sake of fairness. We train a temporal highlight detection network which is built upon a 6-layers fully connected Siamese network and outputs importance

Table 2. Descriptions and properties of video datasets considered in the experiments

Dataset	Video type	Total length	# of videos	Usage	Annotations
SumMe	1st-person	14 min	5	Testing	Yes
	3rd-person	50 min	20	Training (V^T)	Yes
TvSum	3rd-person	210 min	50	Training (V^T)	Yes
FPVSum	1st-person labeled	162 min	56	25% Training (V^F) 55% Training (V^U) 20% Testing	Yes
	1st-person unlabeled	314 min	42	Training (V^U)	None

scores. The loss function for the TDCNN classifier is defined as $\mathcal{L}_{pair} = max\left\{0, 1 - s(\mathbf{x}^{high}) + s(\mathbf{x}^{non})\right\}$, where $s(\mathbf{x}^{high})$ and $s(\mathbf{x}^{non})$ are the scores of highlight and non-highlight segments. The positive and negative pairs of training data for learning the Siamese network of TDCNN classifier is produced by following the same criteria described in Sect. 3.1.

- **vsLSTM**: As shown in [30], it is implemented as an architecture of stacking a video feature extractor, a biLSTM with 256 hidden units, and a single-hidden-layer MLP, where the parameters of vsLSTM are learned by using the mean squared loss. Note that the original GoogLeNet [25] feature extractor is now replaced by the same C3D architecture. We further experiments another variant of vsLSTM using classification loss as (6), which is utilized in [17].

Both TDCNN and vsLSTM models are trained with V^T and V^F, and the resulting summaries are selected from segments with top 15% scores. In addition, we implement another two variants of our approach for controlled experiments:

- **Ours w/o V^U**: We train our model in Fig. 1 with supervised training data V^T and V^F only, i.e., a fully-supervised version without observing unlabeled first-person videos.
- **Ours (non-sequential)**: Instead of RNN, we apply a 2-layer fully connected network as the highlight detection network in Fig. 1. Note that this variant is applicable to both fully-supervised and semi-supervised settings.

Table 3. Performance evaluation and comparisons on first-person video summarization in terms of F-measures and AUC values. Note that only Ours utilizes unlabeled first-person videos during training, while vsLSTM+ replaces its original MSE loss by our classification loss.

Method		F-measure		AUC value	
		SumMe	FPVSum	SumMe	FPVSum
Baseline	Random	16.312	15.071	–	–
	Uniform	15.053	15.670	–	–
	DSN [5]	22.658	19.345	0.2075	0.1662
	C3D [26]	26.945	19.595	0.2091	0.1938
Non-sequential	TDCNN [28]	28.623	31.174	0.2340	0.2658
	Ours w/o V^U	35.272	37.098	0.2489	0.2904
	Ours	**38.649**	**38.409**	**0.2733**	**0.2962**
Seuqential	vsLSTM [30]	29.850	19.901	–	–
	vsLSTM+	31.468	26.204	0.2421	0.2266
	Ours w/o V^U	35.980	37.366	–	–
	Ours	**41.991**	**38.572**	**0.3165**	**0.3120**

4.3   Quantitative Evaluation

Comparisons. Table 3 summarizes the quantitative results of our framework, baselines, and the state-of-the-art video summarization algorithms. When comparing non-sequential based methods (including baselines), our model produced favorable results due to learning of cross-domain feature embedding and exploitation of unlabeled training data V^U. Recent approaches of C3D and TDCNN were not able to achieve comparable results due to their lack of ability in learning from data across video domains. We also observe that the direct use of DSN to summarize videos across data domains without exploiting any cross-domain label information could not yield satisfactory performances.

We note that the use of our proposed model without observing unlabeled first-person video training data (i.e., **Ours w/o** V^U in Table 3) still performed against the above state-of-the-art methods. This again verifies the effectiveness of our cross-domain embedding framework. As shown in Table 3, the full version of our method achieved the best performance, which was above those reported by recent recurrent models of vsLSTMs. This is due to the fact that vsLSTM only takes C3D features as inputs, and is not designed to deal with cross-domain video data.

Table 4. Analysis of our network design and settings. Note that Ours† indicates our model without using any private encoders, Ours$_{\text{ranking}}$/Ours$_{\text{MSE}}$ denote the uses of ranking and MSE losses as the scoring loss in our model, Ours* is the version excluding the pseudo triplet loss $\mathcal{L}_{tri}^U$, and Ours** represents the version without observing unlabeld data V^U.

Method	Cross-domain embedding		Scoring losses		Unlabeled videos		
	TDCNN [28]	Ours†	Ours$_{\text{ranking}}$	Ours$_{\text{MSE}}$	Ours*	Ours**	Ours
SumMe	28.623	29.754	28.435	29.078	34.252	35.272	**38.649**
FPVSum	31.174	31.020	34.007	36.046	35.485	37.098	**38.409**

Analysis of Our Network Design. We now perform controlled experiments using variants of our model in the non-sequential setting. As noted in Table 4, Ours† denotes our model using only shared encoder to describe cross-domain data, and Ours$_{\text{ranking}}$/Ours$_{\text{MSE}}$ are the ones using the associated losses, which were suggested in [9,28,30]. Finally, Ours* represents our model without enforcing the pseudo triplet loss in (5), while Ours** indicates the supervised version of our model (i.e., without observing any unlabeled first-person videos). From the results listed in Table 4, it is clear that our full model achieved the best performance performed. Thus, our model design and integration of the above components are desirable for cross-domain video summarization.

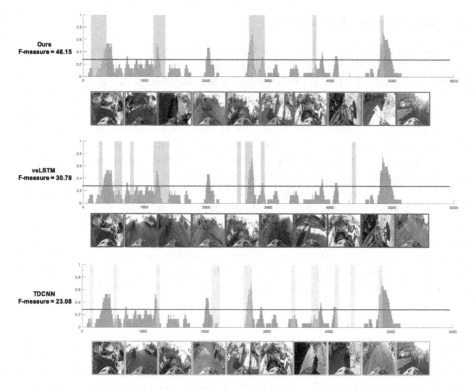

Fig. 2. Example summarization results of video "Valparaiso Downhill" from SumMe. The ground-truth annotation scores are shown in blue, while the predicted summaries from our model, vsLSTM, and TDCNN are shown in green, red and yellow, respectively. Note that the red horizontal line indicates the threshold which splits the scores into highlight and non-highlight ones. Note that our method produces desirable results by detecting movements such as "jumping" and "going downstairs". In contrast, others fail to capture the moments with a large number of false predictions.

4.4   Example Visualization Results

Figure 2 shows example summarization results of a challenging first-person test video "Valparaiso Downhill" in SumMe dataset (with ground-truth scores provided). This video is 3-minute long recorded by a camera mounted on a helmet. It is a typical first-person video since the video content reflects the motion of the recorder (i.e., the bike rider) and no specific objects are intentionally focused. The blue bars in Fig. 2 indicate frame-level ground-truth scores annotated by users. The interval colored in green, red and yellow correspond to summaries generated by our model, vsLSTM, and TDCNN, respectively. The red horizontal lines represent the threshold for splitting highlight and non-highlight parts, as described in Sect. 3.1.

It is worth noting that, there are two particular actions, "jumping" and "going downstairs", in this video. These two action types are very unique and closely related to first-person videos, and thus are generally not present in third-person videos like those in SumMe and TvSum dataset. We see that, while both TDCNN and vsLSTM failed to predict such highlight moments, our model was able to produce satisfactory summarization outputs due to the exploitation of information across annotated third and first-person videos (including unlabeled ones).

5   Conclusions

In this paper, we proposed a novel deep learning architecture of first-person video summarization. Our network uniquely integrates modules of cross-domain feature embedding and highlight detection in a recurrent framework, which allows the extraction and adaptation of spatiotemporal discriminative highlight information across video domains. Moreover, to alleviate possible overfitting due to a small amount of labeled first-person video data during training, the introduced self-learning scheme further allows us to exploit information observed from unlabeled first-person videos (i.e., a semi-supervised setting). In addition to evaluation of benchmark datasets, we additionally collect a new first-person video dataset. Quantitative and qualitative experimental results confirmed the effectiveness and robustness of our proposed model for first-person video summarization.

Acknowledgments. This work was supported in part by the Ministry of Science and Technology of Taiwan under grants MOST 107-2636-E-009-001 and 107-2634-F-002-010.

References

1. Abu-El-Haija, S., Kothari, N., Lee, J., Natsev, P., Toderici, G., Varadarajan, B., Vijayanarasimhan, S.: Youtube-8m: A large-scale video classification benchmark. arXiv:1609.08675 (2016)
2. Betancourt, A., Morerio, P., Regazzoni, C.S., Rauterberg, M.: The evolution of first person vision methods: a survey. IEEE Trans. Circuits Syst. Video Technol. (TCSVT) **25**(5), 744–760 (2015)
3. Bettadapura, V., Castro, D., Essa, I.: Discovering picturesque highlights from egocentric vacation videos. In: Proceedings of the IEEE Winter Conference on Applications of Computer Vision (WACV) (2016)
4. Bolanos, M., Dimiccoli, M., Radeva, P.: Toward storytelling from visual lifelogging: an overview. IEEE Trans. Hum.-Mach. Syst. (THMS) **47**(1), 77–90 (2017)
5. Bousmalis, K., Trigeorgis, G., Silberman, N., Krishnan, D., Erhan, D.: Domain separation networks. In: Advances in Neural Information Processing Systems (NIPS) (2016)
6. Fathi, A., Hodgins, J.K., Rehg, J.M.: Social interactions: a first-person perspective. In: Proceedings of the IEEE Conference on Computer Vision and Pattern Recognition (CVPR) (2012)

7. Gygli, M., Grabner, H., Riemenschneider, H., Van Gool, L.: Creating summaries from user videos. In: Proceedings of the European Conference on Computer Vision (ECCV) (2014)
8. Gygli, M., Grabner, H., Van Gool, L.: Video summarization by learning submodular mixtures of objectives. In: Proceedings of the IEEE Conference on Computer Vision and Pattern Recognition (CVPR) (2015)
9. Gygli, M., Song, Y., Cao, L.: Video2gif: Automatic generation of animated gifs from video. In: Proceedings of the IEEE Conference on Computer Vision and Pattern Recognition (CVPR) (2016)
10. Hoffer, E., Ailon, N.: Deep metric learning using triplet network. In: International Workshop on Similarity-Based Pattern Recognition (2015)
11. Ji, Z., Xiong, K., Pang, Y., Li, X.: Video summarization with attention-based encoder-decoder networks. arXiv:1708.09545 (2017)
12. Krizhevsky, A., Sutskever, I., Hinton, G.E.: Imagenet classification with deep convolutional neural networks. In: Advances in Neural Information Processing Systems (NIPS) (2012)
13. Lee, Y.J., Ghosh, J., Grauman, K.: Discovering important people and objects for egocentric video summarization. In: Proceedings of the IEEE Conference on Computer Vision and Pattern Recognition (CVPR) (2012)
14. Lee, Y.J., Grauman, K.: Predicting important objects for egocentric video summarization. Int. J. Comput. Vis. (IJCV) 114(1), 38–55 (2015)
15. Lin, Y.L., Morariu, V.I., Hsu, W.: Summarizing while recording: Context-based highlight detection for egocentric videos. In: Proceedings of the IEEE International Conference on Computer Vision Workshops (2015)
16. Lu, Z., Grauman, K.: Story-driven summarization for egocentric video. In: Proceedings of the IEEE Conference on Computer Vision and Pattern Recognition (CVPR) (2013)
17. Mahasseni, B., Lam, M., Todorovic, S.: Unsupervised video summarization with adversarial lstm networks. In: Proceedings of the IEEE Conference on Computer Vision and Pattern Recognition (CVPR) (2017)
18. del Molino, A.G., Tan, C., Lim, J.H., Tan, A.H.: Summarization of egocentric videos: a comprehensive survey. IEEE Trans. Hum.-Mach. Syst. 47(1), 65–76 (2017)
19. Pan, S.J., Yang, Q.: A survey on transfer learning. IEEE Trans. Knowl. Data Eng. (TKDE) 22(10), 1345–1359 (2010)
20. Panda, R., Das, A., Wu, Z., Ernst, J., Roy-Chowdhury, A.K.: Weakly supervised summarization of web videos. In: Proceedings of the IEEE International Conference on Computer Vision (ICCV) (2017)
21. Patel, V.M., Gopalan, R., Li, R., Chellappa, R.: Visual domain adaptation: a survey of recent advances. IEEE Signal Process. Mag. 32(3), 53–69 (2015)
22. Sermanet, P., Lynch, C., Chebotar, Y., Hsu, J., Jang, E., Schaal, S., Levine, S.: Time-contrastive networks: self-supervised learning from video. In: Proceedings of the IEEE International Conference on Robotics and Automation (ICRA) (2018). http://arxiv.org/abs/1704.06888
23. Song, Y., Vallmitjana, J., Stent, A., Jaimes, A.: Tvsum: summarizing web videos using titles. In: Proceedings of the IEEE Conference on Computer Vision and Pattern Recognition (CVPR) (2015)
24. Sun, M., Farhadi, A., Seitz, S.: Ranking domain-specific highlights by analyzing edited videos. In: Proceedings of the European Conference on Computer Vision (ECCV) (2014)

25. Szegedy, C., Liu, W., Jia, Y., Sermanet, P., Reed, S., Anguelov, D., Erhan, D., Vanhoucke, V., Rabinovich, A.: Going deeper with convolutions. In: Proceedings of the IEEE Conference on Computer Vision and Pattern Recognition (CVPR) (2015)
26. Tran, D., Bourdev, L., Fergus, R., Torresani, L., Paluri, M.: Learning spatiotemporal features with 3d convolutional networks. In: Proceedings of the IEEE International Conference on Computer Vision (ICCV) (2015)
27. Xu, J., Mukherjee, L., Li, Y., Warner, J., Rehg, J.M., Singh, V.: Gaze-enabled egocentric video summarization via constrained submodular maximization. In: Proceedings of the IEEE Conference on Computer Vision and Pattern Recognition (CVPR) (2015)
28. Yao, T., Mei, T., Rui, Y.: Highlight detection with pairwise deep ranking for first-person video summarization. In: Proceedings of the IEEE Conference on Computer Vision and Pattern Recognition (CVPR) (2016)
29. Yeung, S., Fathi, A., Fei-Fei, L.: Videoset: video summary evaluation through text. arXiv:1406.5824 (2014)
30. Zhang, K., Chao, W.L., Sha, F., Grauman, K.: Video summarization with long short-term memory. In: Proceedings of the European Conference on Computer Vision (ECCV) (2016)

Learning Single-View 3D Reconstruction with Limited Pose Supervision

Guandao Yang[1]([✉]), Yin Cui[1,2], Serge Belongie[1,2], and Bharath Hariharan[1]

[1] Department of Computer Science, Cornell University, Ithaca, USA
gy46@cornell.edu
[2] Cornell Tech, New York, USA

Abstract. It is expensive to label images with 3D structure or precise camera pose. Yet, this is precisely the kind of annotation required to train single-view 3D reconstruction models. In contrast, unlabeled images or images with just category labels are easy to acquire, but few current models can use this weak supervision. We present a unified framework that can combine both types of supervision: a small amount of camera pose annotations are used to enforce pose-invariance and view-point consistency, and unlabeled images combined with an adversarial loss are used to enforce the realism of rendered, generated models. We use this unified framework to measure the impact of each form of supervision in three paradigms: semi-supervised, multi-task, and transfer learning. We show that with a combination of these ideas, we can train single-view reconstruction models that improve up to 7 points in performance (AP) when using only 1% pose annotated training data.

Keywords: Single-image 3D-reconstruction · Few-shot learning
GANs

1 Introduction

The ability to understand 3D structure from single images is a hallmark of the human visual system and a crucial step in visual reasoning and interaction. Of course, a single image by itself does not have enough information to allow 3D reconstruction, and a machine vision system must rely on some prior over shape: all cars have wheels, for example. The crucial question is how a machine vision system can acquire such priors.

One possibility is to leverage datasets of 3D shapes [4], but obtaining such a dataset for a wide variety of categories requires either 3D modeling expertise or 3D scanning tools and is therefore expensive. Another option, extensively explored recently [21,27], is to show the machine many different views of a multitude of objects from calibrated cameras. The machine can then use photometric

Electronic supplementary material The online version of this chapter (https://doi.org/10.1007/978-3-030-01267-0_6) contains supplementary material, which is available to authorized users.

consistency between rendered views of hypothesized shape and the corresponding view of the real object as a learning signal. Although more tractable than collecting 3D models, this approach is still very expensive in practice: one needs to either physically acquire *thousands* of objects and place them on a turntable, or ask human annotators to annotate images in the wild with both the camera parameters and the precise *instance* that the image depicts. The assumption that *multiple, calibrated* views of *thousands* of objects are available is also biologically implausible: a human infant must physically interact with objects to acquire such training data, but most humans can understand airplane shape very easily despite having played with very few airplanes.

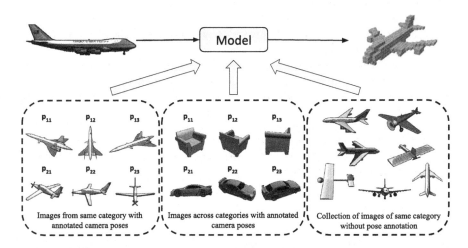

Fig. 1. We propose a unified framework for single-view 3D reconstruction. Our model can be trained with different types of data, including pose-annotated images from the same object category or across multiple categories, and unlabeled images.

Our goal in this paper is to learn effective single-view 3D reconstruction models when calibrated multi-view images are available for very few objects. To do so we look at two additional sources of information. First, what if we had a large collection of images of a category but without any annotation of the precise instance or pose? Such a dataset is easy to acquire by simply downloading images of this category from the web (Fig. 1, lower right). While it might be hard to extract 3D information from such images, they can capture the distribution of the visual appearance of objects from this category. Second, we look at annotations from other semantic classes (Fig. 1, lower middle). These other classes might not tell us about the nuances of a particular class, but they can still help delineate what *shapes in general* look like. For example, most shapes are compact, smooth, tend to be convex, etc.

This paper presents a framework that can effectively use all these sources of information. First, we design a unified model architecture and loss functions that combine pose supervision with weaker supervision from unlabeled images. Then, we use our model and training framework to evaluate and compare many training paradigms and forms of supervision to come up with the best way of using a small number of pose annotations effectively. In particular, we show that:

1. Images without instance or pose annotations are indeed useful and can provide significant gains in performance (up to 5 points in AP). At the same time a little bit of pose supervision (<50 objects) gives a large gain (>20 points AP) when compared to not using pose information at all.
2. Category-agnostic priors obtained by pooling training data across classes work just as well as, but not better than, category-specific priors trained on each class individually.
3. *Fine-tuning* category-agnostic models for a novel semantic class using a small amount (i.e. only 1%) of pose supervision significantly improves performance (up to 7 points in AP).
4. When faced with a novel category with nothing but a tiny set of pose-annotated images, a category-agnostic model trained on pooled data and fine-tuned on the category of interest outperforms a baseline trained on only the novel category by an enormous margin (up to 20 points in AP).

In summary, our results convincingly show large accuracy gains to be accrued from combining multiple sources of data (unlabeled or labeled from different classes) with a single unified model.

2   Related Work

Despite many successes in reconstructing 3D scenes from multiple images [1,22], doing it on a single image remains challenging. Classic work on single-image 3D reconstruction relies on having access to images labeled with the 3D structure [19]. This is also true for many recent deep learning approaches [5,6,8,18, 24]. To get away from this need for precise 3D models, some work leverages keypoint and silhouette annotations [12,23]. More recent approaches assume multiple views with calibrated cameras for training [10,17,21,27], and design training loss functions that leverage photometric consistency and/or enforce invariance to pose. Among these, our encoder-decoder architecture is similar to the one proposed in PTN [27], but our model is trained end-to-end and is additionally able to leverage unlabeled images to deal with limited supervision. In terms of the required supervision, Tulsiani et al. [20] remove the requirement for *pose* annotations but still require images to be annotated with the *instance* they correspond to. PrGAN [7] reduces the supervision requirement further by *only* using unlabeled images. As we show in this paper, this makes the problem needlessly challenging, while adding small amounts of pose supervision leads to large accuracy gains.

Recovering 3D structure from a single image requires strong priors about shape, and another line of work has focused on better capturing the manifold of shape. Classic work has used low-dimensional parametric models [3,12]. More recently, the rediscovery of convolutional networks has led to a resurgence in interest in deep generative models. Wu et al. [26] used deep belief nets to model 3D shapes while Rezende et al. [17] consider variants of variational autoencoders. Generative adversarial networks or GANs [9] can also be used to build generative models of shapes [25]. The challenge is to train them *without* 3D data: Gadelha et al. [7] show that this is indeed possible. While we use an adversarial loss as they suggest, our generator is trained jointly with an encoder end-to-end on a combination of pose-supervised and unlabeled images.

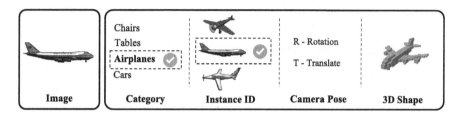

Fig. 2. Different forms of training annotations for single-view 3D reconstruction. Note that some annotations (e.g. category) are cheaper to obtain than others (e.g. 3D shapes); and conversely some offer a better training signal than others.

3   Training Paradigms

For single-view 3D reconstruction, we consider four types of annotations for an image as illustrated in Fig. 2. Our goal is to minimize the need for the more expensive annotations (instance ID, camera pose and 3D shape). Towards this end, we look at three different training paradigms.

3.1   Semi-supervised Single-Category

In this setting, we assume all images are from a single category. Noting the fact that camera pose and model-instance annotations are difficult to collect in the wild, we restrict to a semi-supervised setting where only some of the images are labeled with camera pose and most of them are unlabeled. Formally, we are given a dataset of images annotated with both camera pose and the instance ID: $\mathcal{X}_l = \{(\mathbf{x}_{ij}, \mathbf{p}_{ij}, i)\}_{i,j}$, where $\mathbf{x}_{ij}$ represents the j-th image of the i-th instance when projected with camera pose $\mathbf{p}_{ij}$. We also have a dataset without any annotation: $\mathcal{X}_u = \{\mathbf{x}_i\}_i$. The goal is to use $\mathcal{X}_l$ and $\mathcal{X}_u$ to learn a category-specific model for single image 3D reconstruction.

3.2   Semi-supervised Multi-category

An alternative to building a separate model for each category is to build a category-agnostic model. This allows one to combine training data across multiple categories, and even use training images that do not have any category labels. Thus, instead of a separate labeled training set $\mathcal{X}_l^c$ for each category c, here we only assume a combined dataset $\mathcal{X}_l^{multi} = \mathcal{X}_l^{c_1} \cup \mathcal{X}_l^{c_2} \cup \cdots \cup \mathcal{X}_l^{c_n}$. Similarly, we assume access to an unlabeled set of images $\mathcal{X}_u^{multi}$ (now without category labels). Note that this multi-category setting is harder than the single-category since it introduces cross-category confusion, but it also allows the model to learn category-agnostic shape information across different categories.

3.3   Few-Shot Transfer Learning

Collecting a large dataset that can cover all categories we would ever encounter is infeasible. Therefore, we also need a way to adapt a pre-trained model to a new category. This strategy can also be used for adapting a *category-agnostic* model to a specific category. We assume that for this adaptation, a dataset $\mathcal{X}_l^{(new)}$ containing a very small number of images with pose and instance annotations (<100) are available for the category of interest. We also assume that the semi-supervised multi-category dataset described above is available as a pre-training dataset: $\mathcal{X}_l^{pre} = \mathcal{X}_l^{multi}$ and $\mathcal{X}_u^{pre} = \mathcal{X}_u^{multi}$.

4   A Unified Framework

We need a model and a training framework that can utilize both images with pose and instance annotations, and images without any labels. The former set of images can be used to enforce the consistency of the predicted 3D shape across views, as well as the similarity between the rendered 3D shape and the corresponding view of the real object. The latter set of images can only provide constraints on the realism of the generated shapes. To capture all these constraints, we propose a unified model architecture with three main components:

1. An **Encoder** E that takes an image (silhouette) as input and produces a latent representation of shape.
2. A **Generator** G that takes a latent representation of shape as input and produces a voxel grid.
3. A **Discriminator** D that tries to distinguish between rendered views of the voxel output by the generator and views of the real objects.

In addition, we make use of a "projector" module P that takes a voxel and a viewpoint as input, and it renders the voxel from the inputted viewpoint. We use a differentiable projector similar to the one in PrGAN [7]. We extend it to perspective projection. P has no trainable parameters.

The training process alternates between an iteration on images labeled with pose and instance, and an iteration on unlabeled images. The two sets of iterations use different loss functions but update the same model.

4.1   Training on Pose-Annotated Images

In each pass on the annotated images, the encoder is provided with pairs of images x_{i1}, x_{i2} of the same 3D object i taken from different camera poses $\mathbf{p}_1$ and $\mathbf{p}_2$. The encoder E embeds each image into latent vectors $\mathbf{z}_1$, $\mathbf{z}_2$. The generator (decoder) G is tasked with predicting the 3D voxel grid from $\mathbf{z}_1$ and $\mathbf{z}_2$.

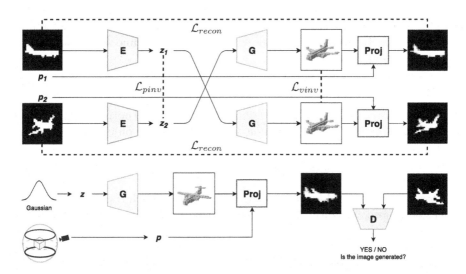

Fig. 3. Overview of the proposed model architecture. An encoder E and a generator G with pose consistency (on the top) learn from images with pose supervision, and a discriminator D (on the bottom) helps G to learn from unlabeled images. Notice that two encoders E and three generator G in the diagram all share parameters, respectively.

The 3D voxel grid produced by the generator should be: (1) a good reconstruction of the object and (2) invariant to the pose of the input image [27]. This requires that the latent shape representation also be invariant to the camera pose of the input image. To ensure the pose invariance of the learned latent representation $\mathbf{z}_1$, the predicted 3D voxel from $\mathbf{z}_1$ should be able to reconstruct the second input image when projected to the second viewpoint $\mathbf{p}_2$, and vice versa.

With these intuitions in mind, we explore the following three losses.

Reconstruction Loss: The predicted 3D model, when projected with a certain camera pose, should be consistent with the ground truth image projected from that camera pose. More specifically, let $(\mathbf{x}_1, \mathbf{p}_1)$ and $(\mathbf{x}_2, \mathbf{p}_2)$ be two pairs of image-pose pair sampled from a 3D-model, then the voxel reconstructed from $E(\mathbf{x}_1)$ should produce the same image as $\mathbf{x}_2$ if projected from camera pose $\mathbf{p}_2$. Same for the other view. Let $P(\mathbf{v}, \mathbf{p})$ represent the image generated by projecting voxel $\mathbf{v}$ using camera pose $\mathbf{p}$. We define the reconstruction loss to address this consistency requirement as:

$$\mathcal{L}_{recon} = \|P(G(E(\mathbf{x}_2)), \mathbf{p}_1) - \mathbf{x}_1\|_{1+2} + \|P(G(E(\mathbf{x}_1)), \mathbf{p}_2) - \mathbf{x}_2\|_{1+2} \qquad (1)$$

where $\|\cdot\|_{1+2} = \|\cdot\|_1 + \|\cdot\|_2$ is the summation of ℓ_1 and ℓ_2 reconstruction losses. Such reconstruction loss has been used in prior work [27]. We add ℓ_1 loss since ℓ_1 loss could better cope with sparse vectors such as silhouette images.

Pose-Invariance Loss on Representations: Given two randomly sampled views of an object, the encoder E should be able to embed their latent representations close by, irrespective of pose. Therefore, we define a *pose-invariance* loss on the latent representations:

$$\mathcal{L}_{pinv} = \|E(\mathbf{x}_1) - E(\mathbf{x}_2)\|_2 \qquad (2)$$

Pose-Invariance Loss on Voxels: Similarly, the 3D voxel output reconstructed by the generator G from two different views of the same object should be the same. Thus, we introduce a *voxel-based* pose invariance loss:

$$\mathcal{L}_{vinv} = \|G(E(\mathbf{x}_1)) - G(E(\mathbf{x}_2))\|_1 \qquad (3)$$

Losses are illustrated by the dashed lines in Fig. 3. Each training step on the images with pose annotations tries to minimize the combined supervised loss:

$$\mathcal{L}_{supervised} = \mathcal{L}_{recon} + \alpha \mathcal{L}_{pinv} + \beta \mathcal{L}_{vinv} \qquad (4)$$

where α and β are weights for $\mathcal{L}_{pinv}$ and $\mathcal{L}_{vinv}$, respectively. We use $\alpha = \beta = 0.1$ in all of our experiments.

4.2   Training on Unlabeled Images

In order to learn from unlabeled images, we use an adversarial loss, as illustrated in the bottom of Fig. 3. The intuition is to let the generator G learn to *generate* 3D voxel grids. When projected from a random viewpoint, the 3D voxel grid should be able to produce an image that is indistinguishable from a real image. Another advantage of an adversarial loss is regularization, as in the McRecon approach [10]. Specifically, we first sample a vector $\mathbf{z} \sim \mathcal{N}(0, I)$ and a viewpoint $\mathbf{p}$ uniformly sampled from the range of camera poses observed in the training set. Then the generator G will take the latent vector $\mathbf{z}$ and reconstruct a 3D shape. This 3D shape will be projected to an image using the random pose $\mathbf{p}$. No matter which camera pose we project, the projected image should look like an image sampled from the dataset. We update the generator and discriminator by using an adversarial loss similar to the one used by PrGAN [7]:

$$\mathcal{L}_D = \mathbb{E}_{\mathbf{z},\mathbf{p}}[\log(1 - D(P(G(\mathbf{z}), \mathbf{p})))] + \mathbb{E}_{\mathbf{x} \sim \mathcal{X}}[\log D(\mathbf{x})] \qquad (5)$$
$$\mathcal{L}_G = -\mathbb{E}_{\mathbf{z},\mathbf{p}}[\log D(P(G(\mathbf{z}), \mathbf{p}))] \qquad (6)$$

Note that instead of normally distributed $\mathbf{z}$ vectors, one could also use the encoder output on sampled training images. However, encouraging G to produce meaningful shapes even on noise input might force G to capture shape priors.

4.3   Implementation Details

The detailed architectures of encoder, generator and discriminator are illustrated in Fig. 4. In the projector (not shown in Fig. 4), we first rotate the voxelized 3D model by its center and then use perspective projection to produce the image according to the camera pose. The whole model is trained end-to-end by alternating between iterations on pose-annotated and unlabeled images. We use Adam optimizer [13] with learning rates of 10^{-3}, 10^{-4}, and 10^{-4} for encoder, generator, and discriminator respectively. While training using the adversarial loss, we used the gradient penalty introduced by DRAGAN [14] to improve training stability. Codes are available at https://github.com/stevenygd/3d-recon.

5   Experiments

5.1   Dataset

We use voxelized $32 \times 32 \times 32$ 3D shapes from the ShapeNetCore [4] dataset. We look at 10 categories: `airplanes`, `cars`, `chairs`, `displays`, `phones`, `speakers`, `tables`, `benches`, `vessels`, and `cabinets`. For each category, we use ShapeNet's default split for training, validation, and test. While generating the training images, we first rotate the voxelized 3D model around its center using a rotation vector $\mathbf{r} = [r_x, r_y, r_z]$, where $r_x \in [-20°, 40°]$ and $r_y \in [0°, 360°]$ are uniformly sampled rotation angles of Altitude and Azimuth; we always set $r_z = 0$. We then project the rotated 3D voxel into a binary mask as the image for training, validation, and testing, where the rotation vector $\mathbf{r}$ is the camera pose. For each 3D shape, we generate 5 masks from different camera poses. During the

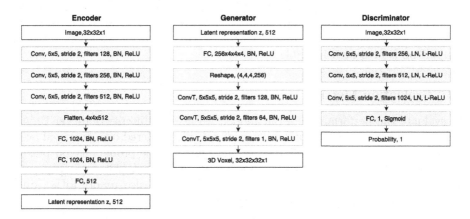

Fig. 4. Model Architectures of encoder, generator and discriminator. `Conv`: Convolution, `BN`: Batch Normalization [11], `LN`: Layer Normalization [2], `L-ReLU`: leaky ReLU with slope of 0.2 [15], `ConvT`: Transposed Convolution that is often used in generation tasks [16,25]. `FC, k`: Fully-Connected layers with k outputs. The discriminator outputs a probability that the image is generated.

experiments, we also want to restrict the amount of pose supervision. A model is trained with $r\%$ of pose supervision if $r\%$ of model instances are annotated with poses. We will explore 100%, 50%, 10%, and 1% of pose annotations in different settings. All training images, no matter whether they have pose annotations or not, are used as unlabeled images in all settings.

Table 1. Comparison between synthetic datasets used in prior work and ours. The key difference is the amount of pose annotations available during training. We experiment with multiple settings.

Dataset properties	MVC [20]	McRecon [10]	PTN [27]	Ours
Input image	64 × 64/RGB	127 × 127/RGB	64 × 64/RGB	32 × 32/Grayscale
Supervision image	64 × 64/Mask	127 × 127/Mask	32 × 32/Mask	32 × 32/Mask
Supervision level	2D	2D + U3D	2D	2D
Pose annotations	100%	100%	100%	**0–100%**
#views per image	5	Unavailable	8–24	5
Pose selection	Random	Random	Fixed discrete	Random

Note that our data settings are different from prior work, and indeed the settings in prior works differ from each other. We use input images with the lowest resolution (32 × 32) and no color cues (grayscale) compared to the synthetic dataset from Tulsiani *et al.* [20], McRecon [10], and PTN [27]. We use fewer viewpoints than PTN [27], and our viewpoints are sampled randomly, making it a more difficult task. Our data setting only provides 2D supervision with camera pose, which is different from McRecon [10] that also used unlabeled 3D supervision (U3D). The precise data setting is orthogonal to our focus, which is on combining pose supervision and unlabeled images. As such, we select the setting with less information provided when compared to prior works. A detailed comparison is presented in Table 1.

5.2 Evaluation Metrics

To evaluate the performance of our model, we use the Intersection-over-Union (IoU) between the ground truth voxel grid and the predicted one, averaged over all objects. Computing the IoU requires thresholding the probability output of voxels from the generator. As suggested by Tulsiani *et al.* [20], we sweep over thresholds and report the maximum average IoU. We also report $IoU_{0.4}$ and $IoU_{0.5}$ for comparison with previous work, and the Average Precision (AP).

5.3 Semi-supervised Single-Category

We use 6 categories: `airplanes`, `benches`, `cars`, `chairs`, `sofas`, and `tables` for single-category experiments under semi-supervised setting. In this setting, we train a separate model for each category. We experiment with varying amounts of pose supervision from 0% to 100%.

Comparison with Prior Work: We first compare with prior work that uses full pose/instance supervision. We train our models with 50% of the images annotated with instance and pose. The models are trained for 20,000 iterations with early stopping (i.e., keeping the model with the best performance in validation set). Performance comparisons are shown in Table 2. The performance of our model is comparable with prior work across multiple metrics. The results suggest that while using only 50% of pose supervisions, our model outperforms McRecon [10] and MVC [20], but it performs worse than PTN [27] in terms of $IoU_{0.5}$. However, note that due to differences in the setting across different approaches, the numbers are not exactly commensurate.

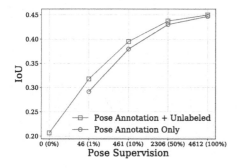 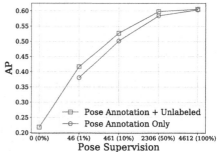

Fig. 5. Comparison between three variations of our models trained with: (1) combined pose-annotated and unlabeled images, (2) pose-annotated images only, and (3) unlabeled images only. Our model is able to leverage both data with pose annotation and unlabeled data. Unlabeled data is especially helpful in the case of limited supervision.

Table 2. Comparison between our model and prior work on single-view 3D reconstruction. All models are trained with images from a single category. Our model's performance is comparable with prior models while using only 50% pose supervision.

Category	MVC [20]	McRecon [10]		PTN [27]	Ours (50% pose annotations)			
	IoU	AP	$IoU_{0.4}$	$IoU_{0.5}$	IoU	AP	$IoU_{0.4}$	$IoU_{0.5}$
airplanes	0.55	0.59	0.37	–	**0.57**	**0.75**	**0.56**	0.57
benches	–	0.39	0.30	–	0.36	**0.48**	**0.35**	0.35
cars	0.75	0.82	0.56	–	**0.78**	**0.92**	**0.77**	0.77
chairs	0.42	0.48	0.35	**0.49**	**0.44**	**0.60**	**0.43**	0.42
sofas	–	0.56	0.38	–	0.54	**0.69**	**0.53**	0.52
tables	–	0.46	0.35	–	0.44	**0.63**	**0.43**	0.42

Are unlabeled images useful? We next ask if using unlabeled images and an adversarial loss to provide additional supervision and regularization is useful. We compare three models: (1) a model trained with both pose-annotated and unlabeled images; (2) a model trained on just the pose-annotated images; and (3) a model trained on only the unlabeled images. In the third case, since the model doesn't have data to train the encoder, we adopt the training scheme of PrGAN [7] by first training the generator G and discriminator D together as a GAN, and then using the generator to train an encoder E once the GAN training is done. We compare these models on the chair category with different amounts of pose supervision. Results are presented in Fig. 5.

First, compared to the purely unsupervised approach (0 pose supervision), when only 1% of the data has pose annotations (45 models, 225 images), performance increases significantly. This suggests that pose supervision is necessary, and that our model could successfully leverage such supervision to make better predictions. Second, the model that combines pose annotations with unlabeled images outperforms the one that uses only pose-annotated images. The lesser the pose annotation available, the larger the gain, indicating that an adversarial loss on unlabeled images is useful especially in the case when pose supervisions and viewpoints are limited ($\leq 10\%$). Third, given enough pose supervision (50% or even 100%), the performance gap between the pose-supervision-only model and the combined model is greatly reduced. This suggests that when there are enough images with pose annotations, leveraging unlabeled data is unnecessary.

5.4   Semi-supervised Multi-category

We next experiment with a *category-agnostic* model on combined training data from 7 categories: airplanes, cars, chairs, displays, phones, speakers, and tables. This experiment is also conducted with different amount of pose annotations. Results are reported in Table 3.

In general, using more pose supervision yields better performance of category-agnostic model. With the same amount of pose supervision (50%) for each category, the category-agnostic model achieves similar performance compared with the category-specific models. This suggests that the model is able to remedy the removal of category information by learning a category-agnostic representation.

5.5   Few-Shot Transfer Learning

What happens when a new class comes along that the system has not seen before? In this case, the model should be able to *transfer* the knowledge it has acquired and adapt it to the new class with very limited annotated training data.

To evaluate if this is possible, we use the category-agnostic model, pre-trained on the dataset described in Sect. 5.4, and adapt it to three *unseen* categories: benches, vessels, and cabinets. For each of the novel categories, only 1% of the pose-annotated data is provided. As a result, each novel category usually has about 13 3D-shapes or about 65 pose-annotated images.

Table 3. Performance of category-agnostic models under different amount of pose supervision. Using same amount of supervision (50%), the performance of category-agnostic model is on par with its category-specific counterpart, indicating that we don't need category supervision.

Test categories	Pose supervision and problem setting									
	50% single		100% multi		50% multi		10% multi		1% multi	
	IoU	AP	IoU	AP	IoU	AP	IoU	AP	IoU	AP
Airplanes	0.57	0.75	0.58	0.76	0.57	0.73	0.54	0.75	0.49	0.63
Cars	0.78	0.92	0.79	0.93	0.78	0.93	0.78	0.93	0.71	0.81
Chairs	0.44	0.60	0.45	0.57	0.44	0.57	0.41	0.54	0.31	0.39
Displays	0.44	0.61	0.43	0.59	0.43	0.58	0.36	0.49	0.26	0.32
Phones	0.55	0.69	0.55	0.72	0.56	0.73	0.50	0.64	0.42	0.52
Speakers	0.58	0.73	0.59	0.74	0.59	0.73	0.55	0.69	0.45	0.58
Tables	0.44	0.63	0.46	0.63	0.45	0.61	0.40	0.54	0.29	0.39
Mean	0.54	0.70	0.55	0.71	0.55	0.70	0.51	0.65	0.42	0.52

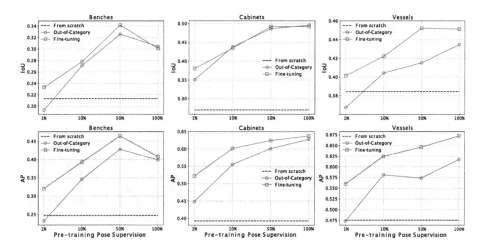

Fig. 6. Few-shot transfer learning on novel categories. Each column represents the performance on a novel category (IoU in top row and AP in bottom row). Notice that the horizontal axis shows the amount of pose annotated supervision in *pre-training*.

We compare three models in this experiment. **From scratch**: a model trained from scratch on the given novel category without using any pre-training; **Out-of-Category** [27]: the pre-trained category-agnostic model directly applied on the novel classes without any additional training; and **Fine-tuning**: a pre-trained category-agnostic model fine-tuned on the given novel category. The fine-tuning is done by fixing the encoder and training the generator only using pose-annotated images for a few iterations. We used the same training strat-

Table 4. Comparing different training strategies on `chairs` with 1% pose annotations. Fine-tuning a category-agnostic model on the target category works the best.

	S, P	S, U	S, P+U	M	FT
IoU	0.2913	0.2065	0.3175	0.3104	**0.3250**
AP	0.3800	0.2180	0.4162	0.3859	**0.4247**

egy as mentioned in Sect. 4.3 for all three models. In this experiment, we varies the amount of pose annotations used for pre-training. The results are shown in Fig. 6.

First, we observe that fine-tuning a pre-trained model for a novel category performs much better than training from scratch without pre-training. This suggests that transferring the knowledge learned from a pre-trained model is essential for few-shot learning on new categories. Second, compared with the out-of-category baseline, fine-tuning improves the performance a lot upon directly using the pre-trained model, especially in the case of limited pose supervision. This indicates that our model is able to quickly adapt to a novel category with few training examples via fine-tuning.

5.6   How Best to Use Limited Annotation?

We now have all the ingredients necessary to answer the question: given a very small number of pose annotations, what is the best way to train a single-view 3D reconstruction model?

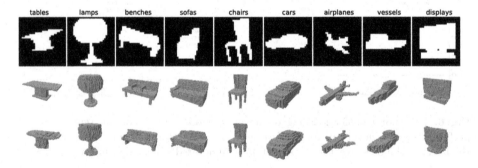

Fig. 7. 3D shape generation on the validation set. The top row shows input images (32 × 32 grayscale). The corresponding ground truth voxels and generated ones are presented in the middle row and bottom row, respectively. The models are trained with semi-supervised single-category setting with 50% pose supervision.

Table 4 compares multiple training strategies on `chairs`: using just the pose-annotated images of `chairs` (**S, P**), using just unlabeled images of `chairs` (**S, U**), using both pose-annotated and unlabeled images of `chairs` (**S, P+U**),

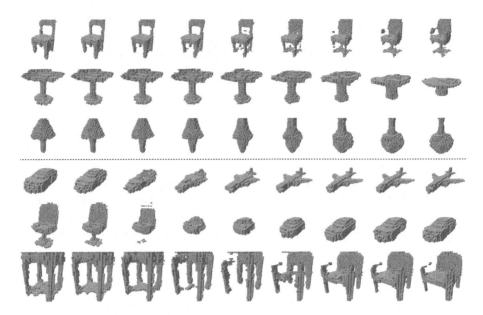

Fig. 8. Interpolation within-category (top 3 rows) and cross-category (bottom 3 rows). Given the latent vector of the left most shape $\mathbf{z}_1$ and the right-most shape $\mathbf{z}_2$, intermediate shapes correspond to $G(\mathbf{z}_1 + \alpha(\mathbf{z}_2 - \mathbf{z}_1))$, where $\alpha \in [0, 1]$.

Fig. 9. Latent space arithmetic.

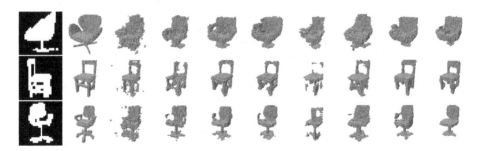

Fig. 10. Shape predictions from models with different amount of pose supervisions. From left to right: input image, ground truth voxel, and then shapes from models presented in Fig. 5. P: training with pose annotation; S: training with unlabeled data. The percentage indicates the amount of pose annotation.

combining multiple categories to train a category-agnostic model (**M**), and fine-tuning a category-agnostic model for `chairs` (**FT**). The fine-tuned model works best, indicating that it is best to combine both pose-annotated and unlabeled images, to leverage multiple categories and to retain category-specificity.

5.7   Qualitative Results

Figure 7 shows some qualitative results from our category-specific model trained with 50% pose annotations. In addition to single-image 3D reconstruction, our model learns a meaningful representation of shape, as shown by the ability to do interpolation and arithmetic in the latent space (Figs. 8 and 9).

The qualitative impact of reducing annotations is shown in Fig. 10. When the amount of supervision is reduced, one sees a significant amount of noise in the 3D reconstructions, which seems to reduce when unlabeled images are included.

6   Conclusions

In conclusion, we propose a unified and end-to-end model to use both images labeled with camera pose and unlabeled images as supervision for single view 3D reconstruction, and evaluate different training strategies when annotations are limited. Our experiments show that one can train a single-view reconstruction model with few pose annotations when leveraging unlabeled data. Future work will include confirming and extending these results on more practical settings with high resolution RGB images and arbitrary camera locations.

References

1. Agarwal, S.: Building rome in a day. Commun. ACM **54**(10), 105–112 (2011)
2. Ba, J.L., Kiros, J.R., Hinton, G.E.: Layer normalization. arXiv preprint arXiv:1607.06450 (2016)
3. Blanz, V., Vetter, T.: A morphable model for the synthesis of 3D faces. In: Proceedings of the 26th Annual Conference on Computer Graphics and Interactive Techniques. ACM Press/Addison-Wesley Publishing Co. (1999)
4. Chang, A.X., et al.: ShapeNet: an information-rich 3D model repository. Technical report arXiv:1512.03012 [cs.GR], Stanford University – Princeton University – Toyota Technological Institute at Chicago (2015)
5. Choy, C.B., Xu, D., Gwak, J.Y., Chen, K., Savarese, S.: 3D-R2N2: a unified approach for single and multi-view 3D object reconstruction. In: Leibe, B., Matas, J., Sebe, N., Welling, M. (eds.) ECCV 2016. LNCS, vol. 9912, pp. 628–644. Springer, Cham (2016). https://doi.org/10.1007/978-3-319-46484-8_38
6. Fan, H., Su, H., Guibas, L.J.: A point set generation network for 3D object reconstruction from a single image. In: CVPR, vol. 2, p. 6 (2017)
7. Gadelha, M., Maji, S., Wang, R.: 3D shape induction from 2D views of multiple objects. In: 3DV (2017)

8. Girdhar, R., Fouhey, D.F., Rodriguez, M., Gupta, A.: Learning a predictable and generative vector representation for objects. In: Leibe, B., Matas, J., Sebe, N., Welling, M. (eds.) ECCV 2016. LNCS, vol. 9910, pp. 484–499. Springer, Cham (2016). https://doi.org/10.1007/978-3-319-46466-4_29

9. Goodfellow, I., et al.: Generative adversarial nets. In: NIPS (2014)

10. Gwak, J., Choy, C.B., Garg, A., Chandraker, M., Savarese, S.: Weakly supervised generative adversarial networks for 3D reconstruction. In: 3DV (2017)

11. Ioffe, S., Szegedy, C.: Batch normalization: accelerating deep network training by reducing internal covariate shift. In: ICML (2015)

12. Kar, A., Tulsiani, S., Carreira, J., Malik, J.: Category-specific object reconstruction from a single image. In: CVPR (2015)

13. Kingma, D.P., Ba, J.: Adam: a method for stochastic optimization. In: ICLR (2015)

14. Kodali, N., Hays, J., Abernethy, J., Kira, Z.: On convergence and stability of GANs (2018)

15. Maas, A.L., Hannun, A.Y., Ng, A.Y.: Rectifier nonlinearities improve neural network acoustic models. In: ICML (2013)

16. Radford, A., Metz, L., Chintala, S.: Unsupervised representation learning with deep convolutional generative adversarial networks. In: ICLR (2016)

17. Rezende, D.J., Eslami, S.A., Mohamed, S., Battaglia, P., Jaderberg, M., Heess, N.: Unsupervised learning of 3D structure from images. In: NIPS (2016)

18. Rock, J., Gupta, T., Thorsen, J., Gwak, J., Shin, D., Hoiem, D.: Completing 3D object shape from one depth image. In: CVPR (2015)

19. Saxena, A., Sun, M., Ng, A.Y.: Make3D: learning 3D scene structure from a single still image. In: PAMI (2009)

20. Tulsiani, S., Efros, A.A., Malik, J.: Multi-view consistency as supervisory signal for learning shape and pose prediction. In: CVPR (2018)

21. Tulsiani, S., Zhou, T., Efros, A.A., Malik, J.: Multi-view supervision for single-view reconstruction via differentiable ray consistency. In: CVPR (2017)

22. Ullman, S.: The interpretation of structure from motion. Proc. R. Soc. Lond. B. **203**(1153), 405–426 (1979)

23. Vicente, S., Carreira, J., Agapito, L., Batista, J.: Reconstructing PASCAL VOC. In: CVPR (2014)

24. Wu, J., et al.: Single image 3D interpreter network. In: Leibe, B., Matas, J., Sebe, N., Welling, M. (eds.) ECCV 2016. LNCS, vol. 9910, pp. 365–382. Springer, Cham (2016). https://doi.org/10.1007/978-3-319-46466-4_22

25. Wu, J., Zhang, C., Xue, T., Freeman, W.T., Tenenbaum, J.B.: Learning a probabilistic latent space of object shapes via 3D generative-adversarial modeling. In: NIPS (2016)

26. Wu, Z., et al.: 3D shapenets: a deep representation for volumetric shapes. In: CVPR (2015)

27. Yan, X., Yang, J., Yumer, E., Guo, Y., Lee, H.: Perspective transformer nets: learning single-view 3D object reconstruction without 3D supervision. In: NIPS (2016)

Weakly- and Semi-supervised Panoptic Segmentation

Qizhu Li, Anurag Arnab$^{(\boxtimes)}$, and Philip H.S. Torr

University of Oxford, Oxford, UK
{liqizhu,aarnab,phst}@robots.ox.ac.uk

Abstract. We present a weakly supervised model that jointly performs both semantic- and instance-segmentation – a particularly relevant problem given the substantial cost of obtaining pixel-perfect annotation for these tasks. In contrast to many popular instance segmentation approaches based on object detectors, our method does not predict any overlapping instances. Moreover, we are able to segment both "thing" and "stuff" classes, and thus explain all the pixels in the image. "Thing" classes are weakly-supervised with bounding boxes, and "stuff" with image-level tags. We obtain state-of-the-art results on Pascal VOC, for both full and weak supervision (which achieves about 95% of fully-supervised performance). Furthermore, we present the first weakly-supervised results on Cityscapes for both semantic- and instance-segmentation. Finally, we use our weakly supervised framework to analyse the relationship between annotation quality and predictive performance, which is of interest to dataset creators.

Keywords: Weak supervision · Instance segmentation
Semantic segmentation · Scene understanding

1 Introduction

Convolutional Neural Networks (CNNs) excel at a wide array of image recognition tasks [1–3]. However, their ability to learn effective representations of images requires large amounts of labelled training data [4,5]. Annotating training data is a particular bottleneck in the case of segmentation, where labelling each pixel in the image by hand is particularly time-consuming. This is illustrated by the Cityscapes dataset where finely annotating a single image took "more than 1.5 h on average" [6]. In this paper, we address the problems of semantic- and instance-segmentation using only weak annotations in the form of bounding boxes and image-level tags. Bounding boxes take only 7 s to draw

---

Q. Li and A. Arnab—Equal first authorship.

Electronic supplementary material The online version of this chapter (https://doi.org/10.1007/978-3-030-01267-0_7) contains supplementary material, which is available to authorized users.

V. Ferrari et al. (Eds.): ECCV 2018, LNCS 11219, pp. 106–124, 2018.
https://doi.org/10.1007/978-3-030-01267-0_7

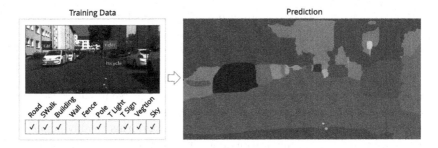

Fig. 1. We propose a method to train an instance segmentation network from weak annotations in the form of bounding-boxes and image-level tags. Our network can explain both "thing" and "stuff" classes in the image, and does not produce overlapping instances as common detector-based approaches [22–24].

using the labelling method of [7], and image-level tags an average of 1 s per class [8]. Using only these weak annotations would correspond to a reduction factor of 30 in labelling a Cityscapes image which emphasises the importance of cost-effective, weak annotation strategies.

Our work differs from prior art on weakly-supervised segmentation [9–13] in two primary ways: Firstly, our model jointly produces semantic- and instance-segmentations of the image, whereas the aforementioned works only output instance-agnostic semantic segmentations. Secondly, we consider the segmentation of both "thing" and "stuff" classes [14,15], in contrast to most existing work in both semantic- and instance-segmentation which only consider "things".

We define the problem of instance segmentation as labelling every pixel in an image with both its object class and an instance identifier [16,17]. It is thus an extension of semantic segmentation, which only assigns each pixel an object class label. "Thing" classes (such as "person" and "car") are countable and are also studied extensively in object detection [18,19]. This is because their finite extent makes it possible to annotate tight, well-defined bounding boxes around them. "Stuff" classes (such as "sky" and "vegetation"), on the other hand, are amorphous regions of homogeneous or repetitive textures [14]. As these classes have ambiguous boundaries and no well-defined shape they are not appropriate to annotate with bounding boxes [20]. Since "stuff" classes are not countable, we assume that all pixels of a stuff category belong to the same, single instance. Recently, this task of jointly segmenting "things" and "stuff" at an instance-level has also been named "Panoptic Segmentation" by [21].

Note that many popular instance segmentation algorithms which are based on object detection architectures [22–26] are not suitable for this task, as also noted by [21]. These methods output a ranked list of proposed instances, where the different proposals are allowed to overlap each other as each proposal is processed independently of the other. Consequently, these architectures are not suitable where each pixel in the image has to be explained, and assigned a unique label of either a "thing" or "stuff" class as shown in Fig. 1. This is in contrast to other instance segmentation methods such as [16,27–30].

In this work, we use weak bounding box annotations for "thing" classes, and image-level tags for "stuff" classes. Whilst there are many previous works on semantic segmentation from image-level labels, the best performing ones [10,31–33] used a saliency prior. The salient parts of an image are "thing" classes in popular saliency datasets [34–36] and this prior therefore does not help at all in segmenting "stuff" as in our case. We also consider the "semi-supervised" case where we have a mixture of weak- and fully-labelled annotations.

To our knowledge, this is the first work which performs weakly-supervised, non-overlapping instance segmentation, allowing our model to explain all "thing" and "stuff" pixels in the image (Fig. 1). Furthermore, our model jointly produces semantic- and instance-segmentations of the image, which to our knowledge is the first time such a model has been trained in a weakly-supervised manner. Moreover, to our knowledge, this is the first work to perform either weakly supervised semantic- or instance-segmentation on the Cityscapes dataset. On Pascal VOC, our method achieves about 95% of fully-supervised accuracy on both semantic- and instance-segmentation. Furthermore, we surpass the state-of-the-art on fully-supervised instance segmentation as well. Finally, we use our weakly- and semi-supervised framework to examine how model performance varies with the number of examples in the training set and the annotation quality of each example, with the aim of helping dataset creators better understand the trade-offs they face in this context.

2   Related Work

Instance segmentation is a popular area of scene understanding research. Most top-performing algorithms modify object detection networks to output a ranked list of segments instead of boxes [22–26,37]. However, all of these methods process each instance independently and thus overlapping instances are produced – one pixel can be assigned to multiple instances simultaneously. Additionally, object detection based architectures are not suitable for labelling "stuff" classes which cannot be described well by bounding boxes [20]. These limitations, common to all of these methods, have also recently been raised by Kirillov et al. [21]. We observe, however, that there are other instance segmentation approaches based on initial semantic segmentation networks [16,27–29] which do not produce overlapping instances and can naturally handle "stuff" classes. Our proposed approach extends methods of this type to work with weaker supervision.

Although prior work on weakly-supervised instance segmentation is limited, there are many previous papers on weak semantic segmentation, which is also relevant to our task. Early work in weakly-supervised semantic segmentation considered cases where images were only partially labelled using methods based on Conditional Random Fields (CRFs) [38,39]. Subsequently, many approaches have achieved high accuracy using only image-level labels [9,10,40,41], bounding boxes [11,12,42], scribbles [20] and points [13]. A popular paradigm for these works is "self-training" [43]: a model is trained in a fully-supervised manner by generating the necessary ground truth with the model itself in an iterative,

Expectation-Maximisation (EM)-like procedure [11,12,20,41]. Such approaches are sensitive to the initial, approximate ground truth which is used to bootstrap training of the model. To this end, Khoreva *et al.* [42] showed how, given bounding box annotations, carefully chosen unsupervised foreground-background and segmentation-proposal algorithms could be used to generate high-quality approximate ground truth such that iterative updates to it were not required thereafter.

Our work builds on the "self-training" approach to perform instance segmentation. To our knowledge, only Khoreva *et al.* [42] have published results on weakly-supervised instance segmentation. However, the model used by [42] was not competitive with the existing instance segmentation literature in a fully-supervised setting. Moreover, [42] only considered bounding-box supervision, whilst we consider image-level labels as well. Recent work by [44] modifies Mask-RCNN [22] to train it using fully-labelled examples of some classes, and only bounding box annotations of others. Our proposed method can also be used in a semi-supervised scenario (with a mixture of fully- and weakly-labelled training examples), but unlike [44], our approach works with only weak supervision as well. Furthermore, in contrast to [42,44], our method does not produce overlapping instances, handles "stuff" classes and can thus explain every pixel in an image as shown in Fig. 1.

3 Proposed Approach

We first describe how we generate approximate ground truth data to train semantic- and instance-segmentation models with in Sect. 3.1 through 3.4. Thereafter, in Sect. 3.5, we discuss the network architecture that we use.

3.1 Training with Weaker Supervision

In a fully-supervised setting, semantic segmentation models are typically trained by performing multinomial logistic regression independently for each pixel in the image. The loss function, the cross entropy between the ground-truth distribution and the prediction, can be written as

$$L = -\sum_{i \in \Omega} \log p(l_i|\mathbf{I}) \tag{1}$$

where l_i is the ground-truth label at pixel i, $p(l_i|\mathbf{I})$ is the probability (obtained from a softmax activation) predicted by the neural network for the correct label at pixel i of image $\mathbf{I}$ and Ω is the set of pixels in the image.

In the weakly-supervised scenarios considered in this paper, we do not have reliable annotations for all pixels in Ω. Following recent work [9,13,41,42], we use our weak supervision and image priors to approximate the ground-truth for a subset $\Omega' \subset \Omega$ of the pixels in the image. We then train our network using the estimated labels of this smaller subset of pixels. Section 3.2 describes how we estimate Ω' and the corresponding labels for images with only bounding-box annotations, and Sect. 3.3 for image-level tags.

Our approach to approximating the ground truth is based on the principle of only assigning labels to pixels which we are confident about, and marking the remaining set of pixels, $\Omega \setminus \Omega'$, as "ignore" regions over which the loss is not computed. This is motivated by Bansal *et al.* [45] who observed that sampling only 4% of the pixels in the image for computing the loss during fully-supervised training yielded about the same results as sampling all pixels, as traditionally done. This supported their hypothesis that most of the training data for a pixel-level task is statistically correlated within an image, and that randomly sampling a much smaller set of pixels is sufficient. Moreover, [46,47] showed improved results by respectively sampling only 6% and 12% of the hardest pixels, instead of all of them, in fully-supervised training.

3.2   Approximate Ground Truth from Bounding Box Annotations

We use GrabCut [48] (a classic foreground segmentation technique given a bounding-box prior) and MCG [50] (a segment-proposal algorithm) to obtain a foreground mask from a bounding-box annotation, following [42]. To achieve high precision in this approximate labelling, a pixel is only assigned to the object class represented by the bounding box if both GrabCut and MCG agree (Fig. 2).

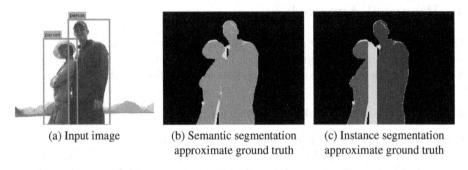

| (a) Input image | (b) Semantic segmentation approximate ground truth | (c) Instance segmentation approximate ground truth |

Fig. 2. An example of generating approximate ground truth from bounding box annotations for an image (a). A pixel is labelled the with the bounding-box label if it belongs to the foreground masks of both GrabCut [48] and MCG [49] (b). Approximate instance segmentation ground truth is generated using the fact that each bounding box corresponds to an instance (c). Grey regions are "ignore" labels over which the loss is not computed due to ambiguities in label assignment.

Note that the final stage of MCG uses a random forest trained with pixel-level supervision on Pascal VOC to rank all the proposed segments. We do not perform this ranking step, and obtain a foreground mask from MCG by selecting the proposal that has the highest Intersection over Union (IoU) with the bounding box annotation.

This approach is used to obtain labels for both semantic- and instance-segmentation as shown in Fig. 2. As each bounding box corresponds to an instance, the foreground for each box is the annotation for that instance. If the foreground of two bounding boxes of the same class overlap, the region is marked as "ignore" as we do not have enough information to attribute it to either instance.

3.3   Approximate Ground-Truth from Image-Level Annotations

When only image-level tags are available, we leverage the fact that CNNs trained for image classification still have localisation information present in their convolutional layers [51]. Consequently, when presented with a dataset of only images and their tags, we first train a network to perform multi-label classification. Thereafter, we extract weak localisation cues for all the object classes that are present in the image (according to the image-level tags). These localisation heatmaps (as shown in Fig. 3) are thresholded to obtain the approximate ground-truth for a particular class. It is possible for localisation heatmaps for different classes to overlap. In this case, thresholded heatmaps occupying a smaller area are given precedence. We found this rule, like [9], to be effective in preventing small or thin objects from being missed.

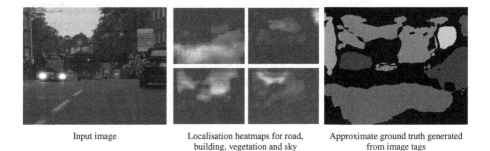

| Input image | Localisation heatmaps for road, building, vegetation and sky | Approximate ground truth generated from image tags |

Fig. 3. Approximate ground truth generated from image-level tags using weak localisation cues from a multi-label classification network. Cluttered scenes from Cityscapes with full "stuff" annotations makes weak localisation more challenging than Pascal VOC and ImageNet that only have "things" labels. Black regions are labelled "ignore". Colours follow Cityscapes convention.

Though this approach is independent of the weak localisation method used, we used Grad-CAM [52]. Grad-CAM is agnostic to the network architecture unlike CAM [51] and also achieves better performance than Excitation BP [53] on the ImageNet localisation task [4].

We cannot differentiate different instances of the same class from only image tags as the number of instances is unknown. This form of weak supervision is thus appropriate for "stuff" classes which cannot have multiple instances. Note that saliency priors, used by many works such as [10,31,32] on Pascal VOC, are not suitable for "stuff" classes as popular saliency datasets [34–36] only consider "things" to be salient.

3.4   Iterative Ground Truth Approximation

The ground truth approximated in Sects. 3.2 and 3.3 can be used to train a network from random initialisation. However, the ground truth can subsequently be iteratively refined by using the outputs of the network on the training set as the new approximate ground truth as shown in Fig 4. The network's output is also post-processed with DenseCRF [54] using the parameters of Deeplab [55] (as also done by [9,42]) to improve the predictions at boundaries. Moreover, any pixel labelled a "thing" class that is outside the bounding-box of the "thing" class is set to "ignore" as we are certain that a pixel for a thing class cannot be outside its bounding box. For a dataset such as Pascal VOC, we can set these pixels to be "background" rather than "ignore". This is because "background" is the only "stuff" class in the dataset.

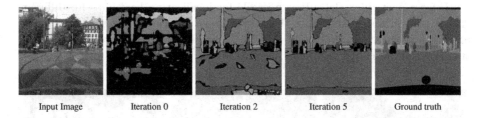

| Input Image | Iteration 0 | Iteration 2 | Iteration 5 | Ground truth |

Fig. 4. By using the output of the trained network, the initial approximate ground truth produced according to Sects. 3.2 and 3.3 (Iteration 0) can be improved. Black regions are "ignore" labels over which the loss is not computed in training. Note for instance segmentation, permutations of instance labels of the same class are equivalent.

3.5   Network Architecture

Using the approximate ground truth generation method described in this section, we can train a variety of segmentation models. Moreover, we can trivially combine this with full human-annotations to operate in a semi-supervised setting. We use the architecture of Arnab *et al.* [16] as it produces both semantic- and instance-segmentations, and can be trained end-to-end, given object detections. This network consists of a semantic segmentation subnetwork, followed by an instance subnetwork which partitions the initial semantic segmentation into an instance segmentation with the aid of object detections, as shown in Fig. 5.

We denote the output of the first module, which can be any semantic segmentation network, as $\mathbf{Q}$ where $Q_i(l)$ is the probability of pixel i of being assigned semantic label l. The instance subnetwork has two inputs – $\mathbf{Q}$ and a set of object detections for the image. There are D detections, each of the form (l_d, s_d, B_d) where l_d is the detected class label, $s_d \in [0, 1]$ the score and B_d the set of pixels lying within the bounding box of the dth detection. This model assumes that each object detection represents a possible instance, and it assigns every pixel in the initial semantic segmentation an instance label using a Conditional Random Field (CRF). This is done by defining a multinomial random variable, X_i, at

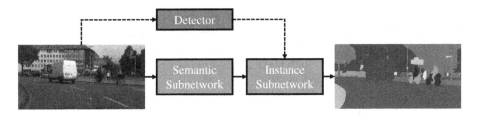

Fig. 5. Overview of the network architecture. An initial semantic segmentation is partitioned into an instance segmentation, using the output of an object detector as a cue. Dashed lines indicate paths which are not backpropagated through during training.

each of the N pixels in the image, with $\mathbf{X} = [X_1, X_2 \ldots, X_N]^\top$. This variable takes on a label from the set $\{1, \ldots, D\}$ where D is the number of detections. This formulation ensures that each pixel can only be assigned one label. The energy of the assignment $\mathbf{x}$ to all instance variables $\mathbf{X}$ is then defined as

$$E(\mathbf{X} = \mathbf{x}) = -\sum_{i}^{N} \ln\left(w_1 \psi_{Box}(x_i) + w_2 \psi_{Global}(x_i) + \epsilon\right) + \sum_{i<j}^{N} \psi_{Pairwise}(x_i, x_j).$$

$$(2)$$

The first unary term, the box term, encourages a pixel to be assigned to the instance represented by a detection if it falls within its bounding box,

$$\psi_{Box}(X_i = k) = \begin{cases} s_k Q_i(l_k) & \text{if } i \in B_k \\ 0 & \text{otherwise.} \end{cases} \tag{3}$$

Note that this term is robust to false-positive detections [16] since it is low if the semantic segmentation at pixel i, $Q_i(l_k)$ does not agree with the detected label, l_k. The global term,

$$\psi_{Global}(X_i = k) = Q_i(l_k), \tag{4}$$

is independent of bounding boxes and can thus overcome errors in mislocalised bounding boxes not covering the whole instance. Finally, the pairwise term is the common densely-connected Gaussian and bilateral filter [54] encouraging appearance and spatial consistency.

In contrast to [16], we also consider stuff classes (which object detectors are not trained for), by simply adding "dummy" detections covering the whole image with a score of 1 for all stuff classes in the dataset. This allows our network to jointly segment all "things" and "stuff" classes at an instance level. As mentioned before, the box and global unary terms are not affected by false-positive detections arising from detections for classes that do not correspond to the initial semantic segmentation $\mathbf{Q}$. The Maximum-a-Posteriori (MAP) estimate of the CRF is the final labelling, and this is obtained by using mean-field inference, which is formulated as a differentiable, recurrent network [56,57].

We first train the semantic segmentation subnetwork using a standard cross-entropy loss with the approximate ground truth described in Sects. 3.2 and 3.3.

Thereafter, we append the instance subnetwork and finetune the entire network end-to-end. For the instance subnetwork, the loss function must take into account that different permutations of the same instance labelling are equivalent. As a result, the ground truth is "matched" to the prediction before the cross-entropy loss is computed as described in [16].

4 Experimental Evaluation

4.1 Experimental Set-Up

Datasets and Weak Supervision. We evaluate on two standard segmentation datasets, Pascal VOC [18] and Cityscapes [6]. Our weakly- and fully-supervised experiments are trained with the same images, but in the former case, pixel-level ground truth is approximated as described in Sect. 3.1 through 3.4.

Pascal VOC has 20 "thing" classes annotated, for which we use bounding box supervision. There is a single "background" class for all other object classes. Following common practice on this dataset, we utilise additional images from the SBD dataset [58] to obtain a training set of 10582 images. In some of our experiments, we also use 54000 images from Microsoft COCO [19] only for the initial pretraining of the semantic subnetwork. We evaluate on the validation set, of 1449 images, as the evaluation server is not available for instance segmentation.

Cityscapes has 8 "thing" classes, for which we use bounding box annotations, and 11 "stuff" class labels for which we use image-level tags. We train our initial semantic segmentation model with the images for which 19998 coarse and 2975 fine annotations are available. Thereafter, we train our instance segmentation network using the 2975 images with fine annotations available as these have instance ground truth labelled. Details of the multi-label classification network we trained in order to obtain weak localisation cues from image-level tags (Sect. 3.3) are described in the supplementary. When using Grad-CAM, the original authors originally used a threshold of 15% of the maximum value for weak localisation on ImageNet. However, we increased the threshold to 50% to obtain higher precision on this more cluttered dataset.

Network Training. Our underlying segmentation network is a reimplementation of PSPNet [59]. For fair comparison to our weakly-supervised model, we train a fully-supervised model ourselves, using the same training hyperparameters (detailed in the supplementary) instead of using the authors' public, fully-supervised model. The original PSPNet implementation [59] used a large batch size synchronised over 16 GPUs, as larger batch sizes give better estimates of batch statistics used for batch normalisation [59,60]. In contrast, our experiments are performed on a single GPU with a batch size of one 521×521 image crop. As a small batch size gives noisy estimates of batch statistics, our batch statistics are "frozen" to the values from the ImageNet-pretrained model as common practice [61,62]. Our instance subnetwork requires object detections, and we train Faster-RCNN [3] for this task. All our networks use a ResNet-101 [1] backbone.

Evaluation Metrics. We use the AP^r metric [37], commonly used in evaluating instance segmentation. It extends the AP, a ranking metric used in object detection [18], to segmentation where a predicted instance is considered correct if its Intersection over Union (IoU) with the ground truth instance is more than a certain threshold. We also report the AP^r_{vol} which is the mean AP^r across a range of IoU thresholds. Following the literature, we use a range of 0.1 to 0.9 in increments of 0.1 on VOC, and 0.5 to 0.95 in increments of 0.05 on Cityscapes.

However, as noted by several authors [16,21,27,63], the AP^r is a ranking metric that does not penalise methods which predict more instances than there actually are in the image as long as they are ranked correctly. Moreover, as it considers each instance independently, it does not penalise overlapping instances. As a result, we also report the Panoptic Quality (PQ) recently proposed by [21],

$$
PQ = \underbrace{\frac{\sum_{(p,g)\in TP} \mathrm{IoU}(p,g)}{|TP|}}_{\text{Segmentation Quality (SQ)}} \times \underbrace{\frac{|TP|}{|TP| + \frac{1}{2}|FP| + \frac{1}{2}|FN|}}_{\text{Detection Quality (DQ)}}, \tag{5}
$$

where p and g are the predicted and ground truth segments, and TP, FP and FN respectively denote the set of true positives, false positives and false negatives.

4.2   Results on Pascal VOC

Tables 1 and 2 show the state-of-art results of our method for semantic- and instance-segmentation respectively. For both semantic- and instance-segmentation, our weakly supervised model obtains about 95% of the performance of its fully-supervised counterpart, emphasising that accurate models can be learned from only bounding box annotations, which are significantly quicker and cheaper to obtain than pixelwise annotations. Table 2 also shows that our weakly-supervised model outperforms some recent fully supervised instance segmentation methods such as [17,65]. Moreover, our fully-supervised instance segmentation model outperforms all previous work on this dataset. The main difference of our model to [16] is that our network is based on the PSPNet architecture using ResNet-101, whilst [16] used the network of [66] based on VGG [2].

We can obtain semantic segmentations from the output of our semantic subnetwork, or from the final instance segmentation (as we produce non-overlapping instances) by taking the union of all instances which have the same semantic label. We find that the IoU obtained from the final instance segmentation, and the initial pretrained semantic subnetwork to be very similar, and report the latter in Table 1. Further qualitative and quantitative results, including success and failure cases, are included in the supplement.

End-to-End Training of Instance Subnetwork. Our instance subnetwork can be trained in a piecewise fashion, or the entire network including the semantic subnetwork can be trained end-to-end. End-to-end training was shown to obtain higher performance by [16] for full supervision. We also observe this effect for weak supervision from bounding box annotations. A weakly supervised model,

Table 1. Comparison of semantic segmentation performance to recent methods using only weak, bounding-box supervision on Pascal VOC. Note that [11,12] use the less accurate VGG network, whilst we and [42] use ResNet-101. "FS%" denotes the percentage of fully-supervised performance.

Method	Validation set			Test set		
	IoU (weak)	IoU (full)	FS%	IoU (weak)	IoU (full)	FS%
Without COCO annotations						
BoxSup [12]	62.0	63.8	**97.2**	64.6	–	–
Deeplab WSSL [11]	60.6	67.6	89.6	62.2	70.3	88.5
SDI [42]	69.4	74.5	93.2	–	–	–
Ours	**74.3**	**77.3**	96.1	**75.5**	**78.6**	**96.3**
With COCO annotations						
SDI [42]	74.2	77.7	95.5	–	–	–
Ours	**75.7**	**79.0**	**95.8**	**76.7**	**79.4**	**96.6**

trained with COCO annotations improves from an AP^r_{vol} of 53.3 to 55.5. When not using COCO for training the initial semantic subnetwork, a slightly higher increase by 3.9 from 51.7 is observed. This emphasises that our training strategy (Sect. 3.1) is effective for both semantic- and instance-segmentation.

Iterative Training. The approximate ground truth used to train our model can also be generated in an iterative manner, as discussed in Sect. 3.4. However, as the results from a single iteration (Tables 1 and 2) are already very close to fully-supervised performance, this offers negligible benefit. Iterative training is, however, crucial for obtaining good results on Cityscapes as discussed in Sect. 4.3.

Semi-supervision. We also consider the case where we have a combination of weak and full annotations. As shown in Table 3, we consider all combinations of weak- and full-supervision of the training data from Pascal VOC and COCO. Table 3 shows that training with fully-supervised data from COCO and weakly-supervised data from VOC performs about the same as weak supervision from both datasets for both semantic- and instance-segmentation. Furthermore, training with fully annotated VOC data and weakly labelled COCO data obtains similar results to full supervision from both datasets. We have qualitatively observed that the annotations in Pascal VOC are of higher quality than those of Microsoft COCO (random samples from both datasets are shown in the supplementary). And this intuition is evident in the fact that there is not much difference between training with weak or full annotations from COCO. This suggests that in the case of segmentation, per-pixel labelling of additional images is not particularly useful if they are not labelled to a high standard, and that labelling fewer images at a higher quality (Pascal VOC) is more beneficial than labelling many images at a lower quality (COCO). This is because Table 3 demonstrates how both semantic- and instance-segmentation networks can be trained to achieve

Table 2. Comparison of instance segmentation performance to recent (fully- and weakly-supervised) methods on the VOC 2012 validation set.

Method	AP^r					AP^r_{vol}	PQ
	0.5	0.6	0.7	0.8	0.9		
Weakly supervised without COCO							
SDI [42]	44.8	–	–	–	–	–	–
Ours	**60.5**	**55.2**	**47.8**	**37.6**	**21.6**	**55.6**	**59.0**
Fully supervised without COCO							
SDS [37]	43.8	34.5	21.3	8.7	0.9	–	–
Chen *et al.* [64]	46.3	38.2	27.0	13.5	2.6	–	–
PFN [65]	58.7	51.3	42.5	31.2	15.7	52.3	–
Ours (fully supervised)	**63.6**	**59.5**	**53.8**	**44.7**	**30.2**	**59.2**	**62.7**
Weakly supervised with COCO							
SDI [42]	46.4	–	–	–	–	–	–
Ours	**60.9**	**55.9**	**48.0**	**37.2**	**21.7**	**55.5**	**59.5**
Fully supervised with COCO							
Arnab *et al.* [17]	58.3	52.4	45.4	34.9	20.1	53.1	–
MPA [26]	62.1	56.6	47.4	36.1	18.5	56.5	–
Arnab *et al.* [16]	61.7	55.5	48.6	39.5	25.1	57.5	–
SGN [30]	61.4	55.9	49.9	42.1	26.9	–	–
Ours (fully supervised)	**63.9**	**59.3**	**54.3**	**45.4**	**30.2**	**59.5**	**63.1**

similar performance by using only bounding box labels instead of low-quality segmentation masks. The average annotation time can be considered a proxy for segmentation quality. While a COCO instance took an average of 79 s to segment [19], this figure is not mentioned for Pascal VOC [18,67].

4.3 Results on Cityscapes

Tables 4 and 5 present, what to our knowledge is, the first weakly supervised results for either semantic or instance segmentation on Cityscapes. Table 4 shows that, as expected for semantic segmentation, our weakly supervised model performs better, relative to the fully-supervised model, for "thing" classes compared to "stuff" classes. This is because we have more informative bounding box labels for "things", compared to only image-level tags for "stuff". For semantic segmentation, we obtain about 97% of fully-supervised performance for "things" (similar to our results on Pascal VOC) and 83% for "stuff". Note that we evaluate images at a single-scale, and higher absolute scores could be obtained by multi-scale ensembling [59,61].

For instance-level segmentation, the fully-supervised ratios for the PQ are similar to the IoU ratio for semantic segmentation. In Table 5, we report the AP^r_{vol} and PQ for both thing and stuff classes, assuming that there is only one

Table 3. Semantic- and instance-segmentation performance on Pascal VOC with varying levels of supervision from the Pascal and COCO datasets. The former is measured by the IoU, and latter by the AP^r_{vol} and PQ.

Dataset		IoU	AP^r_{vol}	PQ
VOC	COCO			
Weak	Weak	75.7	55.5	59.5
Weak	Full	75.8	56.1	59.8
Full	Weak	77.5	58.9	62.7
Full	Full	79.0	59.5	63.1

Table 4. Semantic segmentation performance on the Cityscapes validation set. We use more informative, bounding-box annotations for "thing" classes, and this is evident from the higher IoU than on "stuff" classes for which we only have image-level tags.

Method	IoU (weak)	IoU (full)	FS%
Ours (thing classes)	68.2	70.4	96.9
Ours (stuff classes)	60.2	72.4	83.1
Ours (overall)	63.6	71.6	88.8

instance of a "stuff" class in the image if it is present. Here, the AP^r_{vol} for "stuff" classes is higher than that for "things". This is because there can only be one instance of a "stuff" class, which makes instances easier to detect, particularly for classes such as "road" which typically occupy a large portion of the image. The Cityscapes evaluation server, and previous work on this dataset, only report the AP^r_{vol} for "thing" classes. As a result, we report results for "stuff" classes only on the validation set. Table 5 also compares our results to existing work which produces non-overlapping instances on this dataset, and shows that both our fully- and weakly-supervised models are competitive with recently published work on this dataset. We also include the results of our fully-supervised model, initialised from the public PSPNet model [59] released by the authors, and show that this is competitive with the state-of-art [30] among methods producing non-overlapping segmentations (note that [30] also uses the same PSPNet model). Figure 7 shows some predictions of our weakly supervised model; further results are in the supplementary.

Iterative Training. Iteratively refining our approximate ground truth during training, as described in Sect. 3.4, greatly improves our performance on both semantic- and instance-segmentation as shown in Fig. 6. We trained the network for 150 000 iterations before regenerating the approximate ground truth using the network's own output on the training set. Unlike on Pascal VOC, iterative training is necessary to obtain good performance on Cityscapes as the approximate ground truth generated on the first iteration is not sufficient to obtain high accuracy. This was expected for "stuff" classes, since we began from

Table 5. Instance-level segmentation results on Cityscapes. On the validation set, we report results for both "thing" (th.) and "stuff" (st.) classes. The online server, which evaluates the test set, only computes the AP^r for "thing" classes. We compare to other fully-supervised methods which produce non-overlapping instances. To our knowledge, no published work has evaluated on both "thing" and "stuff" classes. Our fully supervised model, initialised from the public PSPNet model [59] is equivalent to our previous work [16], and competitive with the state-of-art. Note that we cannot use the public PSPNet pretrained model in a weakly-supervised setting.

Method	Validation						Test
	AP^r_{vol} th.	AP^r_{vol} st.	AP^r_{vol} all	PQ th.	PQ st.	PQ all	AP th.
Ours (weak, ImageNet init.)	17.0	33.1	26.3	35.8	43.9	40.5	12.8
Ours (full, ImageNet init.)	24.3	42.6	34.9	39.6	52.9	47.3	18.8
Ours (full, PSPNet init.) [16]	28.6	52.6	42.5	42.5	62.1	53.8	23.4
Pixel Encoding [68]	9.9	–	–	–	–	–	8.9
RecAttend [69]	–	–	–	–	–	–	9.5
InstanceCut [29]	–	–	–	–	–	–	13.0
DWT [27]	21.2	–	–	–	–	–	19.4
SGN [30]	29.2	–	–	–	–	–	25.0

weak localisation cues derived from the image-level tags. However, as shown in Fig. 6, "thing" classes also improved substantially with iterative training, unlike on Pascal VOC where there was no difference. Compared to VOC, Cityscapes is a more cluttered dataset, and has large scale variations as the distance of an object from the car-mounted camera changes. These dataset differences may explain why the image priors employed by the methods we used (GrabCut [48] and MCG [49]) to obtain approximate ground truth annotations from bounding boxes are less effective. Furthermore, in contrast to Pascal VOC, Cityscapes has frequent co-occurrences of the same objects in many different images, making it more challenging for weakly supervised methods.

Effect of Ranking Methods on the AP^r. The AP^r metric is a ranking metric derived from object detection. It thus requires predicted instances to be scored such that they are ranked in the correct relative order. As our network uses object detections as an additional input and each detection represents a possible instance, we set the score of a predicted instance to be equal to the object detection score. For the case of stuff classes, which object detectors are not trained for, we use a constant detection score of 1 as described in Sect. 3.5. An alternative to using a constant score for "stuff" classes is to take the mean of the softmax-probability of all pixels within the segmentation mask. Table 6 shows that this latter method improves the AP^r for stuff classes. For "things", ranking with the detection score performs better and comes closer to oracle performance which is the maximum AP^r that could be obtained with the predicted instances.

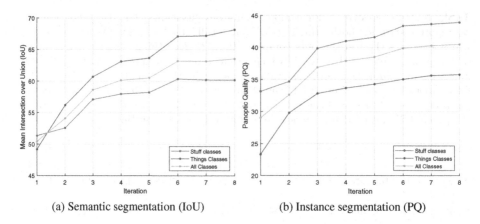

(a) Semantic segmentation (IoU)   (b) Instance segmentation (PQ)

Fig. 6. Iteratively refining our approximate ground truth during training improves both semantic and instance segmentation on the Cityscapes validation set.

Table 6. The effect of different instance ranking methods on the AP_{vol}^r of our weakly supervised model computed on the Cityscapes validation set.

Ranking Method	AP_{vol}^r th.	AP_{vol}^r st.	PQ all
Detection score	17.0	26.7	40.5
Mean seg. confidence	14.6	33.1	40.5
Oracle	21.6	37.0	40.5

Fig. 7. Example results on Cityscapes of our weakly supervised model.

Changing the score of a segmented instance does not change the quality of the actual segmentation, but does impact the AP^r greatly as shown in Table 6. The PQ, which does not use scores, is unaffected by different ranking methods, and this suggests that it is a better metric for evaluating non-overlapping instance segmentation where each pixel in the image is explained.

5   Conclusion and Future Work

We have presented, to our knowledge, the first weakly-supervised method that jointly produces non-overlapping instance and semantic segmentation for both "thing" and "stuff" classes. Using only bounding boxes, we are able to achieve 95% of state-of-art fully-supervised performance on Pascal VOC. On Cityscapes, we use image-level annotations for "stuff" classes and obtain 88.8% of fully-supervised performance for semantic segmentation and 85.6% for instance segmentation (measured with the PQ). Crucially, the weak annotations we use incur only about 3% of the time of full labelling. As annotating pixel-level segmentation is time consuming, there is a dilemma between labelling few images with high quality or many images with low quality. Our semi-supervised experiment suggests that the latter is not an effective use of annotation budgets as similar performance can be obtained from only bounding-box annotations.

Future work is to perform instance segmentation using only image-level tags and the number of instances of each object present in the image as supervision. This will require a network architecture that does not use object detections as an additional input.

Acknowledgements. This work was supported by Huawei Technologies Co., Ltd., the EPSRC, Clarendon Fund, ERC grant ERC-2012-AdG 321162-HELIOS, EPRSRC grant Seebibyte EP/M013774/1 and EPSRC/MURI grant EP/N019474/1.

References

1. He, K., Zhang, X., Ren, S., Sun, J.: Deep residual learning for image recognition. In: CVPR (2016)
2. Simonyan, K., Zisserman, A.: Very deep convolutional networks for large-scale image recognition. In: ICLR (2015)
3. Ren, S., He, K., Girshick, R., Sun, J.: Faster R-CNN: towards real-time object detection with region proposal networks. In: NIPS (2015)
4. Russakovsky, O., et al.: Imagenet large scale visual recognition challenge. IJCV (2015)
5. Sun, C., Shrivastava, A., Singh, S., Gupta, A.: Revisiting unreasonable effectiveness of data in deep learning era. In: ICCV, pp. 843–852. IEEE (2017)
6. Cordts, M., et al.: The cityscapes dataset for semantic urban scene understanding. In: CVPR (2016)
7. Papadopoulos, D.P., Uijlings, J.R., Keller, F., Ferrari, V.: Extreme clicking for efficient object annotation. In: ICCV, pp. 4940–4949. IEEE (2017)
8. Papadopoulos, D.P., Clarke, A.D.F., Keller, F., Ferrari, V.: Training object class detectors from eye tracking data. In: Fleet, D., Pajdla, T., Schiele, B., Tuytelaars, T. (eds.) ECCV 2014. LNCS, vol. 8693, pp. 361–376. Springer, Cham (2014). https://doi.org/10.1007/978-3-319-10602-1_24
9. Kolesnikov, A., Lampert, C.H.: Seed, expand and constrain: three principles for weakly-supervised image segmentation. In: Leibe, B., Matas, J., Sebe, N., Welling, M. (eds.) ECCV 2016. LNCS, vol. 9908, pp. 695–711. Springer, Cham (2016). https://doi.org/10.1007/978-3-319-46493-0_42
10. Wei, Y., Feng, J., Liang, X., Cheng, M.M., Zhao, Y., Yan, S.: Object region mining with adversarial erasing: a simple classification to semantic segmentation approach. In: CVPR (2017)
11. Papandreou, G., Chen, L., Murphy, K., Yuille, A.L.: Weakly- and semi-supervised learning of a DCNN for semantic image segmentation. In: ICCV (2015)

12. Dai, J., He, K., Sun, J.: Boxsup: exploiting bounding boxes to supervise convolutional networks for semantic segmentation. In: ICCV (2015)
13. Bearman, A., Russakovsky, O., Ferrari, V., Fei-Fei, L.: What's the point: semantic segmentation with point supervision. In: Leibe, B., Matas, J., Sebe, N., Welling, M. (eds.) ECCV 2016. LNCS, vol. 9911, pp. 549–565. Springer, Cham (2016). https://doi.org/10.1007/978-3-319-46478-7_34
14. Forsyth, D.A., et al.: Finding pictures of objects in large collections of images. In: Ponce, J., Zisserman, A., Hebert, M. (eds.) ORCV 1996. LNCS, vol. 1144, pp. 335–360. Springer, Heidelberg (1996). https://doi.org/10.1007/3-540-61750-7_36
15. Adelson, E.H.: On seeing stuff: the perception of materials by humans and machines. In: Human Vision and Electronic Imaging VI, vol. 4299, pp. 1–13. International Society for Optics and Photonics (2001)
16. Arnab, A., Torr, P.H.S.: Pixelwise instance segmentation with a dynamically instantiated network. In: CVPR (2017)
17. Arnab, A., Torr, P.H.S.: Bottom-up instance segmentation using deep higher-order CRFs. In: BMVC (2016)
18. Everingham, M., Van Gool, L., Williams, C.K., Winn, J., Zisserman, A.: The pascal visual object classes (voc) challenge. IJCV (2010)
19. Lin, T.-Y., et al.: Microsoft COCO: common objects in context. In: Fleet, D., Pajdla, T., Schiele, B., Tuytelaars, T. (eds.) ECCV 2014. LNCS, vol. 8693, pp. 740–755. Springer, Cham (2014). https://doi.org/10.1007/978-3-319-10602-1_48
20. Lin, D., Dai, J., Jia, J., He, K., Sun, J.: Scribblesup: scribble-supervised convolutional networks for semantic segmentation. In: CVPR, pp. 3159–3167 (2016)
21. Kirillov, A., He, K., Girshick, R., Rother, C., Dollár, P.: Panoptic segmentation. arXiv preprint arXiv:1801.00868 (2018)
22. He, K., Gkioxari, G., Dollár, P., Girshick, R.: Mask R-CNN. In: ICCV (2017)
23. Dai, J., He, K., Sun, J.: Instance-aware semantic segmentation via multi-task network cascades. In: CVPR (2016)
24. Li, Y., Qi, H., Dai, J., Ji, X., Wei, Y.: Fully convolutional instance-aware semantic segmentation. In: CVPR (2017)
25. Liu, S., Qi, L., Qin, H., Shi, J., Jia, J.: Path aggregation network for instance segmentation. arXiv preprint arXiv:1803.01534 (2018)
26. Liu, S., Qi, X., Shi, J., Zhang, H., Jia, J.: Multi-scale patch aggregation (MPA) for simultaneous detection and segmentation. In: CVPR (2016)
27. Bai, M., Urtasun, R.: Deep watershed transform for instance segmentation. In: CVPR, pp. 2858–2866. IEEE (2017)
28. De Brabandere, B., Neven, D., Van Gool, L.: Semantic instance segmentation with a discriminative loss function. In: CVPR Workshop (2017)
29. Kirillov, A., Levinkov, E., Andres, B., Savchynskyy, B., Rother, C.: Instancecut: from edges to instances with multicut. In: CVPR (2017)
30. Liu, S., Jia, J., Fidler, S., Urtasun, R.: SGN: sequential grouping networks for instance segmentation. In: ICCV (2017)
31. Wei, Y., Liang, X., Chen, Y., Shen, X., Cheng, M.M., Feng, J., Zhao, Y., Yan, S.: STC: a simple to complex framework for weakly-supervised semantic segmentation. PAMI **39**(11), 2314–2320 (2017)
32. Oh, S.J., Benenson, R., Khoreva, A., Akata, Z., Fritz, M., Schiele, B.: Exploiting saliency for object segmentation from image level labels. In: CVPR (2017)
33. Chaudhry, A., Dokania, P.K., Torr, P.H.: Discovering class-specific pixels for weakly-supervised semantic segmentation. In: BMVC (2017)
34. Cheng, M.M., Mitra, N.J., Huang, X., Torr, P.H., Hu, S.M.: Global contrast based salient region detection. PAMI **37**(3), 569–582 (2015)

35. Yang, C., Zhang, L., Lu, H., Ruan, X., Yang, M.H.: Saliency detection via graph-based manifold ranking. In: CVPR, pp. 3166–3173. IEEE (2013)
36. Shi, J., Yan, Q., Xu, L., Jia, J.: Hierarchical image saliency detection on extended CSSD. PAMI **38**(4), 717–729 (2016)
37. Hariharan, B., Arbeláez, P., Girshick, R., Malik, J.: Simultaneous detection and segmentation. In: Fleet, D., Pajdla, T., Schiele, B., Tuytelaars, T. (eds.) ECCV 2014. LNCS, vol. 8695, pp. 297–312. Springer, Cham (2014). https://doi.org/10.1007/978-3-319-10584-0_20
38. Verbeek, J.J., Triggs, B.: Scene segmentation with CRFs learned from partially labeled images. In: NIPS, pp. 1553–1560 (2008)
39. He, X., Zemel, R.S.: Learning hybrid models for image annotation with partially labeled data. In: NIPS, pp. 625–632 (2009)
40. Pinheiro, P.O., Collobert, R.: From image-level to pixel-level labeling with convolutional networks. In: CVPR (2015)
41. Pathak, D., Krahenbuhl, P., Darrell, T.: Constrained convolutional neural networks for weakly supervised segmentation. In: ICCV (2015)
42. Khoreva, A., Benenson, R., Hosang, J., Hein, M., Schiele, B.: Simple does it: weakly supervised instance and semantic segmentation. In: CVPR (2017)
43. Scudder, H.: Probability of error of some adaptive pattern-recognition machines. IEEE Trans. Inf. Theory **11**(3), 363–371 (1965)
44. Hu, R., Dollár, P., He, K., Darrell, T., Girshick, R.: Learning to segment every thing. arXiv preprint arXiv:1711.10370 (2017)
45. Bansal, A., Chen, X., Russell, B., Gupta, A., Ramanan, D.: Pixelnet: representation of the pixels, by the pixels, and for the pixels. arXiv preprint arXiv:1702.06506 (2017)
46. Pohlen, T., Hermans, A., Mathias, M., Leibe, B.: Full-resolution residual networks for semantic segmentation in street scenes. In: CVPR (2017)
47. Li, Q., Arnab, A., Torr, P.H.: Holistic, instance-level human parsing. In: BMVC (2017)
48. Rother, C., Kolmogorov, V., Blake, A.: Grabcut: interactive foreground extraction using iterated graph cuts. ACM TOG (2004)
49. Arbelaez, P., Pont-Tuset, J., Barron, J., Marques, F., Malik, J.: Multiscale combinatorial grouping. In: CVPR (2014)
50. Pont-Tuset, J., Arbelaez, P., Barron, J.T., Marques, F., Malik, J.: Multiscale combinatorial grouping for image segmentation and object proposal generation. PAMI **39**(1), 128–140 (2017)
51. Zhou, B., Khosla, A., Lapedriza, A., Oliva, A., Torralba, A.: Learning deep features for discriminative localization. In: CVPR, pp. 2921–2929. IEEE (2016)
52. Selvaraju, R.R., Cogswell, M., Das, A., Vedantam, R., Parikh, D., Batra, D.: Grad-CAM: visual explanations from deep networks via gradient-based localization. In: ICCV (2017)
53. Zhang, J., Lin, Z., Brandt, J., Shen, X., Sclaroff, S.: Top-down neural attention by excitation backprop. In: Leibe, B., Matas, J., Sebe, N., Welling, M. (eds.) ECCV 2016. LNCS, vol. 9908, pp. 543–559. Springer, Cham (2016). https://doi.org/10.1007/978-3-319-46493-0_33
54. Krähenbühl, P., Koltun, V.: Efficient inference in fully connected CRFs with Gaussian edge potentials. In: NIPS (2011)
55. Chen, L.C., Papandreou, G., Kokkinos, I., Murphy, K., Yuille, A.L.: Semantic image segmentation with deep convolutional nets and fully connected CRFs. ICLR (2015)

56. Zheng, S., et al.: Conditional random fields as recurrent neural networks. In: ICCV (2015)
57. Arnab, A., et al.: Conditional random fields meet deep neural networks for semantic segmentation: combining probabilistic graphical models with deep learning for structured prediction. IEEE Signal Proc. Mag. 35(1), 37–52 (2018)
58. Hariharan, B., Arbeláez, P., Bourdev, L., Maji, S., Malik, J.: Semantic contours from inverse detectors. In: ICCV (2011)
59. Zhao, H., Shi, J., Qi, X., Wang, X., Jia, J.: Pyramid scene parsing network. In: CVPR (2017)
60. Chen, L.C., Papandreou, G., Schroff, F., Adam, H.: Rethinking atrous convolution for semantic image segmentation. arXiv preprint arXiv:1706.05587 (2017)
61. Chen, L.C., Papandreou, G., Kokkinos, I., Murphy, K., Yuille, A.L.: Deeplab: semantic image segmentation with deep convolutional nets, atrous convolution, and fully connected CRFs. arXiv preprint arXiv:1606.00915v2 (2016)
62. Huang, J., et al.: Speed/accuracy trade-offs for modern convolutional object detectors. In: CVPR (2017)
63. Yang, Y., Hallman, S., Ramanan, D., Fowlkes, C.C.: Layered object models for image segmentation. PAMI (2012)
64. Chen, Y.T., Liu, X., Yang, M.H.: Multi-instance object segmentation with occlusion handling. In: CVPR (2015)
65. Liang, X., Wei, Y., Shen, X., Yang, J., Lin, L., Yan, S.: Proposal-free network for instance-level object segmentation. arXiv preprint arXiv:1509.02636 (2015)
66. Arnab, A., Jayasumana, S., Zheng, S., Torr, P.H.S.: Higher order conditional random fields in deep neural networks. In: Leibe, B., Matas, J., Sebe, N., Welling, M. (eds.) ECCV 2016. LNCS, vol. 9906, pp. 524–540. Springer, Cham (2016). https://doi.org/10.1007/978-3-319-46475-6_33
67. Everingham, M., Eslami, S.A., Van Gool, L., Williams, C.K., Winn, J., Zisserman, A.: The pascal visual object classes challenge: a retrospective. IJCV 111(1) (2015)
68. Uhrig, J., Cordts, M., Franke, U., Brox, T.: Pixel-level encoding and depth layering for instance-level semantic labeling. In: Rosenhahn, B., Andres, B. (eds.) GCPR 2016. LNCS, vol. 9796, pp. 14–25. Springer, Cham (2016). https://doi.org/10.1007/978-3-319-45886-1_2
69. Ren, M., Zemel, R.S.: End-to-end instance segmentation with recurrent attention. In: CVPR (2017)

Making Deep Heatmaps Robust to Partial Occlusions for 3D Object Pose Estimation

Markus Oberweger[1]([envelope]) [iD], Mahdi Rad[1] [iD], and Vincent Lepetit[2,1]

[1] Institute for Computer Graphics and Vision, Graz University of Technology,
Graz, Austria
{oberweger,rad,lepetit}@icg.tugraz.at
[2] Laboratoire Bordelais de Recherche en Informatique, Université de Bordeaux,
Bordeaux, France

Abstract. We introduce a novel method for robust and accurate 3D object pose estimation from a single color image under large occlusions. Following recent approaches, we first predict the 2D projections of 3D points related to the target object and then compute the 3D pose from these correspondences using a geometric method. Unfortunately, as the results of our experiments show, predicting these 2D projections using a regular CNN or a Convolutional Pose Machine is highly sensitive to partial occlusions, even when these methods are trained with partially occluded examples. Our solution is to predict heatmaps from multiple small patches independently and to accumulate the results to obtain accurate and robust predictions. Training subsequently becomes challenging because patches with similar appearances but different positions on the object correspond to different heatmaps. However, we provide a simple yet effective solution to deal with such ambiguities. We show that our approach outperforms existing methods on two challenging datasets: The Occluded LineMOD dataset and the YCB-Video dataset, both exhibiting cluttered scenes with highly occluded objects.

Keywords: 3D object pose estimation · Heatmaps · Occlusions

1 Introduction

3D object pose estimation from images is an old but currently highly researched topic, mostly due to the advent of Deep Learning-based approaches and the possibility of using large datasets for training such methods. 3D object pose estimation from RGB-D already has provided compelling results [1–4], and the accuracy of methods that only require RGB images recently led to huge progress in the field [2–8]. In particular, one way to obtain an accurate pose is to rely on

---

Electronic supplementary material The online version of this chapter (https://doi.org/10.1007/978-3-030-01267-0_8) contains supplementary material, which is available to authorized users.

V. Ferrari et al. (Eds.): ECCV 2018, LNCS 11219, pp. 125–141, 2018.
https://doi.org/10.1007/978-3-030-01267-0_8

a Deep Network to initially predict the 2D projections of some chosen 3D points and then compute the 3D pose of the object using a PnP method [9]. Such an approach has been shown to be more accurate than the approach of directly predicting the pose used in [5–7], and, therefore, we used the former approach in the research described in this paper.

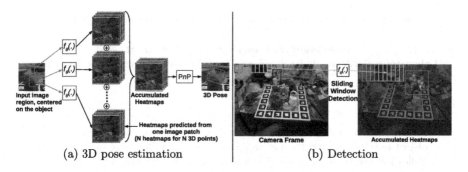

(a) 3D pose estimation   (b) Detection

Fig. 1. Overview of our method. (a) Given an image region centered on the target object, we sample image patches from which we predict heatmaps for the 2D projections of the corners of the object's 3D bounding box. This prediction is done by a Deep Network $f_\theta(\cdot)$. We aggregate the heatmaps and extract the global maxima for each heatmap, from which we compute the 3D object pose using a PnP algorithm. *We show that $f_\theta(\cdot)$ can be trained simply and efficiently despite the ambiguities that may arise when using small patches as input.* (b) To obtain the image region centered on the object, we apply the predictor in a sliding window fashion and accumulate the heatmaps for the full camera frame. We keep the image region with the largest values after accumulation.

However, while Deep Learning methods allow researchers to predict the pose of fully visible objects, they suffer significantly from occlusions, which are very common in practice: Parts of the target object can be hidden by other objects or by a hand interacting with the object. A common *ad hoc* solution is to train the network with occluded objects in the training data. As the results of our experiments presented in this paper show, the presence of large occlusions and unknown occluders still decrease the accuracy of the predicted pose.

Instead of using the entire image of the target object as input to the network, we consider image patches, as illustrated in Fig. 1, since at least some of these are not corrupted by the occluder. Using an image patch as input, our approach learns to predict heatmaps over the 2D projections of 3D points related to the target object. By combining the heatmaps predicted from many patches, we obtain an accurate 3D pose even if some patches actually lie on the occluder or the background instead of on the object.

When moving to an image patch as input, the prediction becomes multimodal. This is shown in Fig. 2: Some patches may appear on different parts of the target object but look similar. These patches are ambiguous, as they can correspond to different predictions. In such a case, we would like to predict heatmaps with multiple local maxima, one for each possible prediction. The main challenge is that the ambiguities are difficult to identify: This would require us to identify the patches that have similar appearances, from all the possible viewpoints and at all the possible positions on the object.

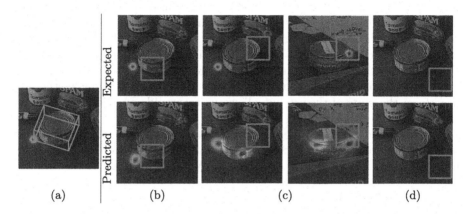

(a)   (b)   (c)   (d)

Fig. 2. Predicting heatmaps from image patches. In this example, we consider predicting the projection of the 3D corner highlighted in (a) for the *tuna fish can* object of the YCB-Video dataset [3]. The red boxes show the input patch of the predicted heatmap. (b) shows a patch from which the projection can be predicted unambiguously. (c) shows two patches that are located in two different positions on the can (notice that the can is flipped and rotated between the two images) while having a similar appearance. In presence of such patches, it is only possible to predict a distribution over the possible locations for the projection. (d) shows a patch on the background, from which we predict a uniform heatmap as it does not provide additional information. See text for details.

The authors of [10] faced a similar problem in the context of 2D object detection when aiming to localize semantic parts from feature vectors of a convolutional layer computed by a CNN. As we discuss in Sect. 2, the method they proposed is complex both for training and inference, and also inaccurate. The solution we propose is much simpler yet efficient: We train a network to predict heatmaps corresponding to a single solution for training image patches using a least-squares loss function. Thanks to the properties of the least-squares loss, this makes the network naturally predict the *average* of the possible heatmap solutions for a given patch. This is exactly what we want, because it is the best information we can obtain from a single patch even if the information remains ambiguous. We then follow an ensemble approach and take the average of the heatmaps predicted for many patches, which allows us to resolve the ambiguities that arise with individual patches. We finally extract the global maximum from this average as the final 2D location.

Our main contribution is, therefore, a simple method that can be used to accurately predict the 3D pose of an object under partial occlusion. We also considered applying Transfer Learning to exploit additional synthetic training data and improve performances. However, as we show, if the input to a network contains an occluder, the occlusion significantly influences the network output even when the network has been trained with occlusion examples and simply adding more training data does not help. In our case, some of the input patches used by our method will not contain occluders, and Transfer Learning becomes useful. In practice, we use the Feature Mapping described in [11], which can be used to map the image features extracted from real images to corresponding image features for synthetic images. This step is not needed for our method to outperform the state-of-the-art but allows us to provide an additional performance boost.

In the remainder of this paper, we first discuss related work, then present our approach, and finally evaluate it and compare it to the state-of-the-art methods on the Occluded LineMOD [12] and the YCB-Video [3] datasets.

2 Related Work

The literature on 3D object pose estimation is extremely large. After the popularity of edge-based [13] and keypoint-based methods [14] waned, Machine Learning and Deep Learning became popular in recent years for addressing this problem [2–8,15]. Here, we will mostly focus on recent work based on RGB images. In the Evaluation section, we compare our method to recent methods [3–5,7].

[4,8] proposed a cascade of modules, whereby the first module is used to localize the target objects, and the second module, to regress the object surface 3D coordinates. These coordinates then are used to predict the object pose through hypotheses sampling with a pre-emptive RANSAC [9]. Most importantly, we do not directly predict 3D points but average 2D heatmaps. Predicting 3D points for corresponding 2D points seems to be much more difficult than predicting 2D points for 3D points, as discussed in [3]. Also, surface coordinates are not adapted to deal with symmetric objects. In [5] the target object was also first detected, then the 2D projections of the corners of the object's 3D bounding boxes were predicted and, finally, the 3D object pose from their 3D correspondences was estimated using a PnP algorithm. [7] integrated this idea into a recent object detector [16] to predict 2D projections of the corners of the 3D bounding boxes, instead of a 2D bounding box. Similarly, in [6], 2D keypoints were predicted in the form of a set of heatmaps as we do in this work. However, it uses the entire image as input and, thus, performs poorly on occlusions. It also requires training images annotated with keypoint locations, while we use virtual 3D points. In [17], 2D keypoint detection was also relied upon. The authors considered partially occluded objects for inferring the 3D object location from these keypoints. However, their inference adopted a complex model fitting and required the target objects to co-occur in near-regular configuration.

In [2], the SSD architecture [18] was extended to estimate the objects' 2D locations and 3D rotations. In a next step, the authors used these predictions together with pre-computed information to estimate the object's 3D pose. However, this required a refinement step to get an accurate pose, which was influenced by occlusions. The objects were segmented in [3], and an estimate of their 3D poses was made by predicting the translation and a quaternion for the rotation, refined by ICP. Segmenting objects makes their approach robust to occlusions to some extent, however, it requires the use of a highly complex model. In [15], object parts were considered to handle partial occlusion by predicting a set of 2D-3D correspondences from each of these parts. However, the parts had to be manually picked, and it is not clear which parts can represent objects such as those we evaluate in this paper.

As mentioned in the introduction, our method is related to that described in [10]. In the context of 2D object detection, semantic parts are localized as in [10] from neighboring feature vectors using a spatial offset map. The offset maps are accumulated in a training phase. However, they need to be able to identify which feature vectors support a semantic part from these maps, and complex statistical measures are used to identify such vectors. Our method is significantly simpler, as the mapping between the input patches and the 2D projections does not have to be established explicitly.

The authors of [19] already evaluated CNNs trained on occlusions in the context of 2D object detection and recognition and proposed modifying training to penalize large spatial filters support. This yields better performance; however, this does not fully cancel out the influence of occlusions. Some recent work also describes explicitly how to handle occlusions for 3D pose estimation when dealing with 3D or RGB-D data: Like us, [20] relied on a voting scheme to increase robustness to occlusions; [21] first segmented and identified the objects from an RGB-D image. They then performed an extensive randomized search over possible object poses by considering physical simulation of the configuration. In [22], holistic and local patches were combined for object pose estimation, using a codebook for local patches and applying a nearest-neighbor search to find similar poses, as in [23,24]. In contrast to these methods, we use only color images.

Our method is also related to ensemble methods and, in particular, the Hough Forests [25], which are based on regression trees. Hough Forests also predict 2D locations from multiple patches and are multimodal. Multimodal prediction is easy to perform with trees, as the multiple solutions can be stored in the tree leaves. With our method, we aim to combine the ability of Hough Forests for multimodal predictions and the learning power of Deep Learning. [26] already reformulated a Hough Forest as a CNN by predicting classification and regression for patches of the input image. However, this method required to handle the detection separately, and each patch regressed a single vector, which was not multimodal and required clustering of the predicted vectors. In this paper, we show that carrying out a multimodal prediction with Deep Networks to address our problem is, in fact, simple.

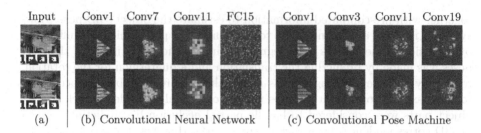

| Input | Conv1 Conv7 Conv11 FC15 | Conv1 Conv3 Conv11 Conv19 |

(a) | (b) Convolutional Neural Network | (c) Convolutional Pose Machine

Fig. 3. Effect of occlusions on the feature maps of Deep Networks. (a) Input image without (top) and with (bottom) partial occlusion. (b-Top) Sums of absolute differences between the feature maps with and without occlusions for a CNN trained without occlusions. (b-Bottom) Same when the network is trained with occlusion examples. (c) Same for a Convolutional Pose Machine. The influence of the occlusion increases with the layers' depths, as receptive fields are larger in the deeper layers than in the first layers, even when the method is trained with occlusion examples. For more details we refer to the supplementary material.

3   Influence of Occlusions on Deep Networks

In this section, we describe how we evaluate how much a partial occlusion influences a Deep Network, whether it is a standard Convolutional Neural Network (CNN) or a Convolutional Pose Machine (CPM) [27]. Specifically, a CPM is a carefully designed CNN that predicts dense heatmaps by sequentially refining results from previous stages. The input features are concatenated to intermediary heatmaps in order to learn spatial dependencies.

For this experiment, depicted in Fig. 3, we use an image centered on an object as input to a network—here, the *Cat* object from the Occluded LineMOD dataset [12]. We then compare the layer activations in the absence of occlusion, and when the object is occluded by an artificial object (here, a striped triangle). We consider two networks: A standard CNN trained to predict the 2D projections of 3D points as a vector [5], and a CPM [27] with 3 stages trained to predict a heatmap for each of the same 2D projections. For the 3D points, we use the corners of the 3D bounding box of the object.

As can be seen in Fig. 3, the occlusion induces changes in the activations of all the layers of both networks. For a standard CNN, the occlusion spreads to more than 20% in the last feature map, and, beyond the first fully-connected layer, more than 45% of all activations are changed. In this case, all the predictions for the 2D projections, occluded or not, are inaccurate. A similar effect can be observed for CPMs: Here, the altered activations are more specifically localized to the occluded region due to the convolutions, with more than 29% of the activations changed in the last feature map. In this case, the predictions of the 2D projections are inaccurate when the 3D points are occluded. When the 3D points are not occluded, the predicted projections are sometimes correct, because the influence of the occluder spreads less with a CPM than with a standard CNN.

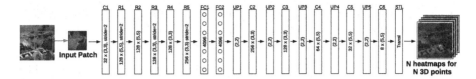

Fig. 4. Network architecture for $f_\theta(\cdot)$. C denotes a convolutional layer with the number of filters and the filter size inscribed; FC, a fully-connected layer with the number of neurons; UP, an unpooling layer [28]; R, a residual module [29] with the number of filters and filter size; and STL, a Spatial Transformation Layer [30] used for translation. All layers have ReLU activations, and the output of the last layer is linear.

4   Minimizing the Effect of Occlusions

In this section, we first describe our training procedure given an input image region centered on the object, then the run-time inference of the pose. Finally, we explain how we identify the input image region in practice.

4.1   Training

Datasets for 3D pose estimation typically provide training images annotated with the objects' poses and the 3D models of the objects. From this data, we generate our training set $\{(I^{(i)}, \{\mathbf{p}_j^{(i)}\}_j, M^{(i)})\}_i$, where $I^{(i)}$ is the i-th training image; $\mathbf{p}_j^{(i)}$, the 2D projection of the j-th 3D corner; and $M^{(i)}$, the 2D mask of the object in image $I^{(i)}$. This mask can be obtained by projecting the 3D object model into the image using the object's pose.

The Unambiguous Case. Let us first ignore the fact that some image patches can be ambiguous and that the learning problem is actually multimodal. We train a network $f_\theta(\cdot)$ to predict a heatmap for each projection $\mathbf{p}_j$. The architecture we use for this network is shown in Fig. 4. $f_\theta(\cdot)$ takes an input patch of size $32 \times 32px$, and predicts a set of heatmaps of size $128 \times 128px$, and we train it by minimizing:

$$\min_\theta \sum_i \sum_{u,v} \|\mathcal{H}^{(i)} - \text{Transl}(f_\theta(\mathcal{P}(I^{(i)}, u, v)), -u, -v)\|^2 , \tag{1}$$

where:

- $\mathcal{P}(I^{(i)}, u, v)$ is an image patch centered on location (u, v) in image $I^{(i)}$;
- $\mathcal{H}^{(i)}$ is the set of expected heatmaps for $\mathcal{P}(I^{(i)}, u, v)$. It contains one heatmap for each 2D projection $\mathbf{p}_j^{(i)}$. We describe how $\mathcal{H}^{(i)}$ is defined in detail below;
- $f_\theta(\mathcal{P})$ returns a set of heatmaps, one for each 2D projection $\mathbf{p}_j^{(i)}$.
- $\text{Transl}(H, -u, -v)$ translates the predicted heatmaps H by $(-u, -v)$. $f_\theta(\cdot)$ learns to predict the heatmaps with respect to the patch center (u, v), and

this translation is required to correctly align the predicted heatmaps together. Such a translation can be efficiently implemented using a Spatial Transformation Layer [30], which makes the network trainable end-to-end.

The sum $\sum_{(u,v)}$ is over 2D locations randomly sampled from the image. The heatmaps in $\mathcal{H}^{(i)}$ are defined as a Gaussian distribution with a small standard deviation (we use $\sigma = 4px$ in practice) and centered on the expected 2D projections $\mathbf{p}_j^{(i)}$ when patch $\mathcal{P}(I^{(i)}, u, v)$ overlaps the object mask $M^{(i)}$. The top row of Fig. 2 shows examples of such heatmaps.

When the patch does not overlap the object mask, the heatmaps in $\mathcal{H}^{(i)}$ are defined as a uniform distribution of value $\frac{1}{W \cdot H}$, where $W \times H$ is the heatmap's resolution, since there is no information in the patch to predict the 2D projections. In addition, we use patches sampled from the ImageNet dataset [31] and train the network to predict uniform heatmaps as well for these patches. Considering these patches (outside the object's mask or from ImageNet) during training allows us to correctly handle patches appearing in the background or on the occluders and significantly reduces the number of false positives observed at run-time.

The Multimodal Case. Let us now consider the real problem, where the prediction is multimodal: Two image patches such as the ones shown in Fig. 2(c) can be similar but extracted from different training images and, therefore, correspond to different expected heatmaps. In other words, in our training set, we can have values for samples i, i' and locations (u, v) and (u', v') such that $\mathcal{P}(I^{(i)}, u, v) \approx \mathcal{P}(I^{(i')}, u', v')$ and $\mathcal{H}^{(i)} \neq \mathcal{H}^{(i')}$.

It may seem as though, in this case, training given by Eq. (1) would fail or need to be modified. *In fact,* Eq. (1) *remains valid.* This is because we use the least-squares loss function: For image patches with similar appearances that correspond to different possible heatmaps, $f_\theta(\cdot)$ will learn to predict the average of these heatmaps, which is exactly what we want. The bottom row of Fig. 2 shows such heatmaps. At run-time, because we will combine the contribution of multiple image patches, we will be able to resolve the ambiguities.

4.2   Run-Time Inference

At run-time, given an input image I, we extract patches from randomly selected locations from the input image and feed them into the predictor $f_\theta(\cdot)$. To combine the contributions of the different patches, we use a simple ensemble approach and average the predicted heatmaps for each 2D projection. We take the locations of the global maxima after averaging them as the final predictions for the 2D projections.

More formally, the final prediction $\widetilde{\mathbf{p}}_j$ for the 2D projection $\mathbf{p}_j$ is the location of the global maximum of $\sum_{u,v} \mathrm{Transl}(f_\theta(\mathcal{P}(I, u, v)), -u, -v)[j]$, the sum of the heatmaps predicted for the j-th projection, translated such that these heatmaps align correctly. The sum is performed over randomly sampled patches. An evaluation of the effect of the number of samples is provided in the supplementary material. To compute the pose, we use a PnP estimation with RANSAC [9] on the correspondences between the corners of the object's 3D bounding box and the $\widetilde{\mathbf{p}_j}$ locations.

4.3 Two-Step Procedure

In practice, we first estimate the 2D location of the object of interest, using the same method as in the previous subsection, but instead of sampling random locations, we apply the network $f_\theta(\cdot)$ in a sliding window fashion, as illustrated in Fig. 1 (b). For each image location, we compute a score by summing up the heatmap values over a bounding box of size 128×128 and over the 8 corners for each object, which is done efficiently using integral images. We apply Gaussian smoothing and thresholding to the resulting score map. We use the centers-of-mass of the regions after thresholding as the centers of the input image I. Finally, we use this image as input to the method described in the previous subsection. We use a fixed size for this region as our method is robust to scale changes.

5 Evaluation

In this section, we evaluate our method and compare it to the state-of-the-art. For this, we use two datasets: The Occluded LineMOD dataset [12], and the YCB-Video dataset [3]. Both datasets contain challenging sequences with partially occluded objects and cluttered backgrounds. In the following, we first provide the implementation details, the evaluation metrics used and then present the results of evaluation of the two datasets, including the results of an ablative analysis of our method.

5.1 Implementation Details

Training Data: The training data consist of real and synthetic images with annotated 3D poses and object masks, as was also the case in [3]. To render the synthetic objects, we use the models that are provided with the datasets. We crop the objects of interest from the training images and paste them onto random backgrounds [32] sampled from ImageNet [31] to achieve invariance to different backgrounds. We augment the dataset with small affine perturbations in HSV color space.

Network Training: The network is optimized using ADAM [33] with default parameters and using a minibatch size of 64, a learning rate of 0.001, and 100k iterations. We train one network per object starting from a random initialization.

Symmetric Objects: We adapt the heatmap generation to symmetric objects present in the two datasets. For rotationally symmetric objects, *e.g.*, cylindrical shapes, we only predict a single position around the rotation axis. For mirror-symmetric objects, we only train on half the range of the symmetry axis, as was performed in [5].

Feature Mapping: Optionally, we apply the Feature Mapping method as described in [11] to compensate for a lack of real training data. We apply the mapping between the FC1 and FC2 layers shown in Fig. 4. The mapping network uses the same architecture as described in [11], but the weight for the feature loss is significantly lower (10^{-5}).

5.2   Evaluation Metrics

We consider the most common metrics. The 2D Reprojection error [8] computes the distances between the projections of the 3D model points when projected using the ground truth pose, and when using the predicted pose. The ADD metric [34] calculates the average distance in 3D between the model points, after applying the ground truth pose and the predicted pose. For symmetric objects, the 3D distances are calculated between the closest 3D points, denoted as the ADI metric. Below, we refer to these two metrics as AD{D|I} and use the one appropriate to the object. The exact formulas for these metrics are provided in the supplementary material.

5.3   Occluded LineMOD Dataset

The Occluded LineMOD dataset [12] consists of a sequence of 1215 frames, each frame labeled with the 3D poses of 8 objects as well as object masks. The objects show severe occlusions, which makes pose estimation extremely challenging. The sequences were captured using an RGB-D camera with $640 \times 480px$ images, however, we use *only the color images* for our method and all results reported.

For training the heatmap predictors, we use the LineMOD dataset [34] that contains the same objects as the Occluded LineMOD dataset. This protocol is commonly used for the dataset [3–5,7], since the Occluded LineMOD dataset only contains testing sequences. Figure 5 shows some of the qualitative results obtained. We give an extensive quantitative evaluation in the following section.

Fig. 5. Some qualitative results on the Occluded LineMOD dataset [12]. We show the 3D bounding boxes of the objects projected onto the color image. Ground truth poses are shown in green, and our predictions are shown in blue. More results are provided in the supplementary material.

Quantitative Results. Figure 6 shows the fraction of frames where the 2D Reprojection error is smaller than a given threshold, for each of the 8 objects from the dataset. A larger area under the curve denotes better results. We compare these results to those obtained from the use of several recent methods that also work only with color images, namely, BB8 [5], PoseCNN [3], Jafari et al. [4], and Tekin et al. [7]. Note that the method described in [5] uses ground truth detection, whereas ours does not. Our method performs significantly more accurately on all sequences. Notably, we also provide results for the *Eggbox* object, which, so far, was not considered since it was too difficult to learn for [4, 5, 7].

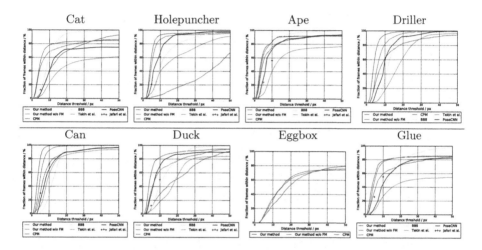

Fig. 6. Evaluation on the Occluded LineMOD dataset [12] using color images only. We plot the fraction of frames for which the 2D Reprojection error is smaller than the threshold on the horizontal axis. Our method provides results that significantly outperform those reported by previous work. "w/o FM" denotes without Feature Mapping.

Adding Feature Mapping [11] improves the 2D Reprojection error for a threshold of $5px$ by 17% on average. We also tried Feature Mapping for the approach of [5], but it did not improve the results because the occlusions influence the feature maps too greatly when the network input contains occluders, as already discussed in the introduction.

Further quantitative results are given in Table 1, where we provide the percentage of frames for which the ADD or ADI metric is smaller than 10% of the object diameter, as [3] reported such results on the Occluded LineMOD dataset. This is considered a highly challenging metric. We also give the percentage of frames that have a 2D Reprojection error of less than $5px$. Our method significantly outperforms all other methods on these metrics by a large margin.

Table 1. Comparison on the Occluded LineMOD dataset [12] with color images only. We provide the percentage of frames for which the AD{D|I} error is smaller than 10% of the object diameter, and for which the 2D Reprojection error is smaller than 5px. Objects marked with a * are considered to be symmetric.

Method	AD{D|I}-10%									2D Reprojection Error-5px								
	Ape	Can	Cat	Driller	Duck	Eggbox*	Glue*	Holepun.	Average	Ape	Can	Cat	Driller	Duck	Eggbox*	Glue*	Holepun.	Average
PoseCNN [3]	9.6	45.2	0.93	41.4	19.6	22.0	38.5	22.1	24.9	34.6	15.1	10.4	7.40	31.8	1.90	13.8	23.1	17.2
Tekin et al. [7]	–	–	–	–	–	–	–	–	–	7.01	11.2	3.62	1.40	5.07	–	6.53	8.26	6.16
BB8 [5]	–	–	–	–	–	–	–	–	–	28.5	1.20	9.60	0.00	6.80	–	4.70	2.40	7.60
Jafari et al. [4]	–	–	–	–	–	–	–	–	–	24.2	30.2	12.3	–	12.1	–	25.9	20.6	20.8
CPM [27]	12.5	25.6	1.43	23.8	6.99	18.3	15.0	0.74	13.0	55.4	30.6	15.7	27.9	26.6	7.97	18.5	1.81	23.1
Our method w/o FM	16.5	42.5	2.82	47.1	11.0	24.7	39.5	21.9	25.8	64.7	53.0	47.9	35.1	36.1	10.3	44.9	52.9	43.1
Our method	17.6	53.9	3.31	62.4	19.2	25.9	39.6	21.3	30.4	69.6	82.6	65.1	73.8	61.4	13.1	54.9	66.4	60.9

The Effect of Seeing Occlusions During Training. We evaluate the importance of knowing the occluder in advance. [3,5,7] assumed that the occluder is another object from the LineMOD dataset and only used occlusions from these objects during training. However, in practice, this assumption does not hold, since the occluder can be an arbitrary object. Therefore, we investigated how the performance was affected by the use of occlusions during training.

We compare our results (without Feature Mapping) to two state-of-the-art approaches: our reimplementations of BB8 [5] and CPM [27]. To avoid bias introduced by the limited amount of training data in the Occluded LineMOD dataset [12], we consider synthetic images both for training and for testing here.

We investigate three different training schemes: (a) No occlusions used for training; (b) random occlusions by simple geometric shapes; (c) random occlusions with the same objects from the dataset, as described in [4,5,7]. We compare the different training schemes in Fig. 7. Training without occlusions clearly result in worse performance for BB8 and CPM, whereas our method is significantly more robust. Adding random geometric occlusions during training slightly increases the performance of BB8 and CPM, since the networks learn invariance to occlusions, however, mainly for these specific occlusions, whereas our approach maintains the accuracy compared to training without occlusions. Using occluders from the dataset gives the best results, since the networks learn to ignore specific features from these occluders. This, however, is only possible when the occluders are known in advance, which is not necessarily the case in practice.

Patch Size and Number of Patches. We evaluated the influence of the patch size on the predicted pose accuracy. There is a range of sizes (25px to 40px) for which the performances stay very close to those presented in Table 1. Small patches seem to lack discriminative power, the 2D Reprojection metric gets 19% worse with 8px patches, and large patches are sensitive to occlusions, which leads to a decrease in the 2D Reprojection metric of 5% for 128px patches.

In the supplementary material, we provide a detail study of the influence of the number of patches on the predicted pose accuracy. The main conclusions are that the accuracy starts to flatten when more than 64 patches are used, and that — if a preprocessing algorithm could be used to provide a segmentation mask — we could reduce the number of patches to achieve the same level of accuracy.

Runtime. We implemented our method in Python on an Intel i7 with 3.2 GHz and 64GB of RAM, using an nVidia GTX 980 Ti graphics card. Pose estimation is $100ms$ for 64 patches, and detection takes $150ms$ on a 640×480 camera frame. Predicting the heatmaps for a single patch takes $4ms$, and the total runtime could, thus, be significantly reduced by processing the individual patches in parallel.

5.4 YCB-Video Dataset

The recently proposed YCB-Video dataset [3] consists of 92 video sequences, where 12 sequences are used for testing and the remaining 80 sequences for

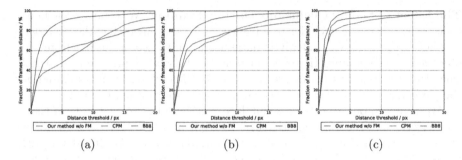

(a)   (b)   (c)

Fig. 7. Evaluation of synthetic renderings of scenes from the Occluded LineMOD dataset (see text) using the 2D Reprojection error. (a) Training without occlusions; (b) training with random geometric occlusions; and (c) training with occluding objects from the LineMOD dataset [34]. Knowing the occluders in advance significantly improves the performances of BB8 [5] and CPM [27], however, this knowledge is often not available in practice. Our method does not require this knowledge.

training. In addition, the dataset contains 80k synthetically rendered images, which can be used for training as well. There are 21 objects in the dataset, which are taken from the YCB dataset [35] and are publicly available for purchase. The dataset is captured with two different RGB-D sensors, each providing 640×480 images, but we only use the color images. The test images are extremely challenging due to the presence of significant image noise and different illumination levels. Each image is annotated with the 3D object poses, as well as the objects' masks. Figure 8 shows some qualitative results. We give an extensive quantitative evaluation in the following section.

Quantitative Results. We provide the 2D Reprojection error and the AD{D|I} metrics averaged over all the objects in Table 2. In [3], the area under the accuracy-threshold curve was used as a metric, which we also provide.[1] Again, our approach results in better performance according to these metrics.

Fig. 8. Qualitative results on the YCB-Video dataset [3]. The green bounding boxes correspond to the ground truth poses, the blue ones to our estimated poses. More results are provided in the supplementary material.

---

[1] The metrics are calculated from the results provided by the authors at their website.

Table 2. Comparison on the YCB-Video dataset [3]. We refer to the supplementary material for the object-specific numbers and additional plots. Our method clearly outperforms the baseline.

Method	PoseCNN [3]			Our method w/o FM			Our method		
	AUC	AD{D|I}-10%	2D Repr-5px	AUC	AD{D|I}-10%	2D Repr-5px	AUC	AD{D|I}-10%	2D Repr-5px
Average	61.0	21.3	3.72	61.4	33.6	23.1	**72.8**	**53.1**	**39.4**

6 Discussion and Conclusion

In this paper, we introduced a novel method for 3D object pose estimation that is inherently robust to partial occlusions of the object. To do this, we considered only small image patches as input and merged their contributions. Because we chose to compute the pose by initially predicting the 2D projections of 3D points related to the object, the prediction can be performed in the form of 2D heatmaps. Since heatmaps are closely related to density functions, they can be conveniently applied to capture the ambiguities that arise when using small image patches as input. We showed that training a network to predict the heatmaps in the presence of such ambiguities is much simpler than it may sound. This resulted in a simple pipeline, which outperformed much more complex methods on two challenging datasets.

Our approach can be extended in different ways. The heatmaps could be merged in a way that is more robust to erroneous values than simple averaging. The pose could be estimated by considering the best local maxima rather than only the global maxima. Sampling only patches intersecting with the object mask, which could be predicted by a segmentation method, would limit the influence of occluders and background in the accumulated heatmaps even more. Predicting the heatmaps could be performed in parallel.

Acknowledgment. This work was funded by the Christian Doppler Laboratory for Semantic 3D Computer Vision. We would like to thank Yu Xiang for providing additional results.

References

1. Krull, A., Brachmann, E., Michel, F., Yang, M.Y., Gumhold, S., Rother, C.: Learning analysis-by-synthesis for 6D pose estimation in RGB-D images. In: International Conference on Computer Vision (2015)
2. Kehl, W., Manhardt, F., Tombari, F., Ilic, S., Navab, N.: SSD-6D: making RGB-based 3D detection and 6D pose estimation great again. In: International Conference on Computer Vision (2017)
3. Xiang, Y., Schmidt, T., Narayanan, V., Fox, D.: PoseCNN: a convolutional neural network for 6D object pose estimation in cluttered scenes. In: Robotics: Science and Systems Conference (2018)

4. Jafari, O.H., Mustikovela, S.K., Pertsch, K., Brachmann, E., Rother, C.: iPose: instance-aware 6D pose estimation of partly occluded objects. CoRR abs/1712.01924 (2017)
5. Rad, M., Lepetit, V.: BB8: a scalable, accurate, robust to partial occlusion method for predicting the 3D poses of challenging objects without using depth. In: International Conference on Computer Vision (2017)
6. Pavlakos, G., Zhou, X., Chan, A., Derpanis, K.G., Daniilidis, K.: 6-DoF object pose from semantic Keypoints. In: International Conference on Intelligent Robots and Systems (2018)
7. Tekin, B., Sinha, S.N., Fua, P.: Real-time seamless single shot 6D object pose prediction. In: Conference on Computer Vision and Pattern Recognition (2018)
8. Brachmann, E., Michel, F., Krull, A., Yang, M.M., Gumhold, S., Rother, C.: Uncertainty-Driven 6D pose estimation of objects and scenes from a single RGB image. In: Conference on Computer Vision and Pattern Recognition (2016)
9. Hartley, R., Zisserman, A.: Multiple View Geometry in Computer Vision. Cambridge University Press, New York (2000)
10. Wang, J., Xie, Q., Zhang, Z., Zhu, J., Xie, L., Yuille, A.L.: Detecting semantic parts on partially occluded objects. In: British Machine Vision Conference (2017)
11. Rad, M., Oberweger, M., Lepetit, V.: Feature mapping for learning fast and accurate 3D pose inference from synthetic images. In: Conference on Computer Vision and Pattern Recognition (2018)
12. Brachmann, E., Krull, A., Michel, F., Gumhold, S., Shotton, J., Rother, C.: Learning 6D object pose estimation using 3D object coordinates. In: European Conference on Computer Vision (2014)
13. Harris, C., Stennett, C.: RAPID-a video rate object tracker. In: British Machine Vision Conference (1990)
14. Lowe, D.: Distinctive image features from scale-invariant keypoints. Int. J. Comput. Vis. **20**(2), 91–110 (2004)
15. Crivellaro, A., Rad, M., Verdie, Y., Yi, K., Fua, P., Lepetit, V.: Robust 3D object tracking from monocular images using stable parts. IEEE Trans. Pattern Anal. Mach. Intell. **40**, 1465–1479 (2017)
16. Redmon, J., Divvala, S., Girshick, R., Farhadi, A.: You only look once: unified, real-time object detection. In: Conference on Computer Vision and Pattern Recognition (2016)
17. Hueting, M., Reddy, P., Kim, V., Carr, N., Yumer, E., Mitra, N.: SeeThrough: finding chairs in heavily occluded indoor scene images. CoRR abs/1710.10473 (2017)
18. Liu, W. et al.: SSD: single shot multibox detector. In: European Conference on Computer Vision (2016)
19. Osherov, E., Lindenbaum, M.: Increasing CNN robustness to occlusions by reducing filter support. In: International Conference on Computer Vision (2017)
20. Buch, A.G., Kiforenko, L., Kraft, D.: Rotational subgroup voting and pose clustering for robust 3D object recognition. In: International Conference on Computer Vision (2017)
21. Mitash, C., Boularias, A., Bekris, K.E.: Improving 6D pose estimation of objects in clutter via physics-aware monte carlo tree search. In: International Conference on Robotics and Automation (2018)
22. Zhang, H., Cao, Q.: Combined holistic and local patches for recovering 6D object pose. In: International Conference on Computer Vision Workshops (2017)
23. Doumanoglou, A., Balntas, V., Kouskouridas, R., Kim, T.: Siamese regression networks with efficient mid-level feature extraction for 3D object pose estimation. CoRR abs/1607.02257 (2016)

24. Kehl, W., Milletari, F., Tombari, F., Ilic, S., Navab, N.: Deep Learning of local RGB-D patches for 3D object detection and 6D pose estimation. In: European Conference on Computer Vision (2016)
25. Gall, J., Lempitsky, V.: Class-specific hough forests for object detection. In: Conference on Computer Vision and Pattern Recognition (2009)
26. Riegler, G., Ferstl, D., Rüther, M., Bischof, H.: Hough networks for head pose estimation and facial feature localization. In: British Machine Vision Conference (2014)
27. Wei, S.E., Ramakrishna, V., Kanade, T., Sheikh, Y.: Convolutional pose machines. In: Conference on Computer Vision and Pattern Recognition (2016)
28. Zeiler, M., Krishnan, D., Taylor, G., Fergus, R.: Deconvolutional networks. In: Conference on Computer Vision and Pattern Recognition (2010)
29. He, K., Zhang, X., Ren, S., Sun, J.: Deep residual learning for image recognition. In: Conference on Computer Vision and Pattern Recognition (2016)
30. Jaderberg, M., Simonyan, K., Zisserman, A., Kavukcuoglu, K.: Spatial transformer networks. In: Advances in Neural Information Processing Systems (2015)
31. Deng, J., Dong, W., Socher, R., Li, L.J., Li, K., Fei-Fei, L.: ImageNet: a large-scale hierarchical image database. In: Conference on Computer Vision and Pattern Recognition (2009)
32. Dwibedi, D., Misra, I., Hebert, M.: Cut, paste and learn: surprisingly easy synthesis for instance detection. In: International Conference on Computer Vision (2017)
33. Kingma, D.P., Ba, J.: Adam: a method for stochastic optimization. In: International Conference on Machine Learning (2015)
34. Hinterstoisser, S. et al.: Model based training, detection and pose estimation of texture-less 3D objects in heavily cluttered scenes. In: Asian Conference on Computer Vision (2012)
35. Calli, B., et al.: Yale-CMU-Berkeley dataset for robotic manipulation research. Int. J. Robot. Res. **36**, 261–268 (2017)

Deep Co-Training for Semi-Supervised Image Recognition

Siyuan Qiao[1(✉)], Wei Shen[1,2], Zhishuai Zhang[1], Bo Wang[3], and Alan Yuille[1]

[1] Johns Hopkins University, Baltimore, USA
siyuan.qiao@jhu.edu
[2] Shanghai University, Shanghai, China
[3] Hikvision Research Institute, Hangzhou, China

Abstract. In this paper, we study the problem of semi-supervised image recognition, which is to learn classifiers using both labeled and unlabeled images. We present Deep Co-Training, a deep learning based method inspired by the Co-Training framework. The original Co-Training learns two classifiers on two *views* which are data from *different* sources that describe *the same* instances. To extend this concept to deep learning, Deep Co-Training trains multiple deep neural networks to be the different views and exploits adversarial examples to encourage view difference, in order to prevent the networks from collapsing into each other. As a result, the co-trained networks provide different and complementary information about the data, which is necessary for the Co-Training framework to achieve good results. We test our method on SVHN, CIFAR-10/100 and ImageNet datasets, and our method outperforms the previous state-of-the-art methods by a large margin.

Keywords: Co-Training · Deep networks · Semi-supervised learning

1 Introduction

Deep neural networks achieve the state-of-art performances in many tasks [1–17]. However, training networks requires large-scale labeled datasets [18,19] which are usually difficult to collect. Given the massive amounts of unlabeled natural images, the idea to use datasets without human annotations becomes very appealing [20]. In this paper, we study the semi-supervised image recognition problem, the task of which is to use the unlabeled images in addition to the labeled images to build better classifiers. Formally, we are provided with an image dataset $\mathcal{D} = \mathcal{S} \cup \mathcal{U}$ where images in $\mathcal{S}$ are labeled and images in $\mathcal{U}$ are not. The task is to build classifiers on the categories $\mathcal{C}$ in $\mathcal{S}$ using the data in $\mathcal{D}$ [21–23]. The test data contains only the categories that appear in $\mathcal{S}$. The problem of learning models on supervised datasets has been extensively studied, and the state-of-the-art methods are deep convolutional networks [1,2]. The core problem is how to use the unlabeled $\mathcal{U}$ to help learning on $\mathcal{S}$.

© Springer Nature Switzerland AG 2018
V. Ferrari et al. (Eds.): ECCV 2018, LNCS 11219, pp. 142–159, 2018.
https://doi.org/10.1007/978-3-030-01267-0_9

The method proposed in this paper is inspired by the Co-Training framework [24], which is an award-winning method for semi-supervised learning. It assumes that each data x in $\mathcal{D}$ has two *views*, *i.e.* x is given as $x = (v_1, v_2)$, and each view v_i is sufficient for learning an effective model. For example, the views can have different data sources [24] or different representations [25–27]. Let $\mathcal{X}$ be the distribution that $\mathcal{D}$ is drawn from. Co-Training assumes that f_1 and f_2 trained on view v_1 and v_2 respectively have consistent predictions on $\mathcal{X}$, *i.e.*,

$$f(x) = f_1(v_1) = f_2(v_2), \quad \forall x = (v_1, v_2) \sim \mathcal{X} \text{(Co-Training Assumption)} \quad (1)$$

Based on this assumption, Co-Training proposes a dual-view self-training algorithm: it first learns a separate classifier for each view on $\mathcal{S}$, and then the predictions of the two classifiers on $\mathcal{U}$ are gradually added to $\mathcal{S}$ to continue the training. Blum and Mitchell [24] further show that under an additional assumption that the two views of each instance are conditionally independent given the category, Co-Training has PAC-like guarantees on semi-supervised learning.

Given the superior performances of deep neural networks on supervised image recognition, we are interested in extending the Co-Training framework to apply deep learning to semi-supervised image recognition. A naive implementation is to train two neural networks simultaneously on $\mathcal{D}$ by modeling Eq. 1. But this method suffers from a critical drawback: there is no guarantee that the views provided by the two networks give different and complementary information about each data point. Yet Co-Training is beneficial only if the two views are different, ideally conditionally independent given the category; after all, there is no point in training two identical networks. Moreover, the Co-Training assumption encourages the two models to make similar predictions on both $\mathcal{S}$ and $\mathcal{U}$, which can even lead to collapsed neural networks, as we will show by experiments in Sect. 3. Therefore, in order to extend the Co-Training framework to take the advantages of deep learning, it is necessary to have a force that pushes networks away to balance the Co-Training assumption that pulls them together.

The force we add to the Co-Training Assumption is *View Difference Constraint* formulated by Eq. 2, which encourages the networks to be different

$$\exists \mathcal{X}' : \ f_1(v_1) \neq f_2(v_2), \ \forall x = (v_1, v_2) \sim \mathcal{X}' \text{(View Difference Constraint)} \quad (2)$$

The challenge is to find a proper and sufficient $\mathcal{X}'$ that is compatible with Eq. 1 (*e.g.* $\mathcal{X}' \cap \mathcal{X} = \varnothing$) and our tasks. We construct $\mathcal{X}'$ by adversarial examples [28].

In this paper, we present Deep Co-Training (DCT) for semi-supervised image recognition, which extends the Co-Training framework without the drawback discussed above. Specifically, we model the Co-Training assumption by minimizing the expected Jensen-Shannon divergence between the predictions of the two networks on $\mathcal{U}$. To avoid the neural networks from collapsing into each other, we impose the view difference constraint by training each network to be resistant to the adversarial examples [28,29] of the other. The result of the training is that each network can keep its predictions unaffected on the examples that the other network fails on. In other words, the two networks provide different and complementary information about the data because they are trained not to make errors at the same time on the adversarial examples for them. To summarize, the main contribution of DCT is a differentiable modeling that takes into account both the Co-Training assumption and the view difference constraint. It is a end-to-end solution which minimizes a loss function defined on the dataset $\mathcal{S}$ and $\mathcal{U}$. Naturally, we extend the dual-view DCT to a scalable multi-view DCT. We test our method on four datasets, SVHN [30], CIFAR10/100 [31] and ImageNet [18], and DCT outperforms the previous state-of-the-arts by a large margin.

2   Deep Co-Training

In this section, we present our model of Deep Co-Training (DCT) and naturally extend dual-view DCT to multi-view DCT.

2.1   Co-Training Assumption in DCT

We start with the dual-view case where we are interested in co-training two deep neural networks for image recognition. Following the notations in Sect. 1, we use $\mathcal{S}$ and $\mathcal{U}$ to denote the labeled and the unlabeled dataset. Let $\mathcal{D} = \mathcal{S} \cup \mathcal{U}$ denote all the provided data. Let $v_1(x)$ and $v_2(x)$ denote the two views of data x. In this paper, $v_1(x)$ and $v_2(x)$ are convolutional representations of x before the final fully-connected layer $f_i(\cdot)$ that classifies $v_i(x)$ to one of the categories in $\mathcal{S}$. On the supervised dataset $\mathcal{S}$, we use the standard cross entropy loss

$$\mathcal{L}_{\sup}(x, y) = H\Big(y, f_1\big(v_1(x)\big)\Big) + H\Big(y, f_2\big(v_2(x)\big)\Big) \tag{3}$$

for any data (x, y) in $\mathcal{S}$ where y is the label for x and $H(p, q)$ is the cross entropy between distribution p and q.

Next, we model the Co-Training assumption. Co-Training assumes that on the distribution $\mathcal{X}$ where x is drawn from, $f_1(v_1(x))$ and $f_2(v_2(x))$ agree on their predictions. In other words, we want networks $p_1(x) = f_1(v_1(x))$ and $p_2(x) = f_2(v_2(x))$ to have close predictions on $\mathcal{U}$. Therefore, we use a natural measure of similarity, the Jensen-Shannon divergence between $p_1(x)$ and $p_2(x)$, $i.e.$,

$$\mathcal{L}_{\cot}(x) = H\Big(\frac{1}{2}\big(p_1(x) + p_2(x)\big)\Big) - \frac{1}{2}\Big(H\big(p_1(x)\big) + H\big(p_2(x)\big)\Big) \tag{4}$$

where $x \in \mathcal{U}$ and $H(p)$ is the entropy of p. Training neural networks based on the Co-Training assumption minimizes the expected loss $\mathbb{E}[\mathcal{L}_{\cot}]$ on the unlabeled set $\mathcal{U}$. As for the labeled set $\mathcal{S}$, minimizing loss $\mathcal{L}_{\sup}$ already encourages them to have close predictions on $\mathcal{S}$ since they are trained with labels; therefore, minimizing $\mathcal{L}_{\cot}$ on $\mathcal{S}$ is unnecessary, and we only implement it on $\mathcal{U}$ ($i.e.$ not on $\mathcal{S}$).

2.2   View Difference Constraint in DCT

The key condition of Co-Training to be successful is that the two views are different and provide complementary information about each data x. But minimizing

Eqs. 3 and 4 only encourages the neural networks to output the same predictions on $\mathcal{D} = \mathcal{S} \cup \mathcal{U}$. Therefore, it is necessary to encourage the networks to be different and complementary. To achieve this, we create another set of images $\mathcal{D}'$ where $p_1(x) \neq p_2(x)$, $\forall x \in \mathcal{D}'$, which we will generate by adversarial examples [28, 29].

Since Co-Training assumes that $p_1(x) = p_2(x)$, $\forall x \in \mathcal{D}$, we know that $\mathcal{D} \cap \mathcal{D}' = \varnothing$. But $\mathcal{D}$ is all the data we have; therefore, $\mathcal{D}'$ must be built up by a generative method. On the other hand, suppose that $p_1(x)$ and $p_2(x)$ can achieve very high accuracy on naturally obtained data (e.g. $\mathcal{D}$), assuming $p_1(x) \neq p_2(x)$, $\forall x \in \mathcal{D}'$ also implies that $\mathcal{D}'$ should be constructed by a generative method.

We consider a simple form of generative method $g(x)$ which takes data x from $\mathcal{D}$ to build $\mathcal{D}'$, i.e. $\mathcal{D}' = \{g(x) \mid x \in \mathcal{D}\}$. For any $x \in \mathcal{D}$, we want $g(x) - x$ to be small so that $g(x)$ also looks like a natural image. But when $g(x) - x$ is small, it is very possible that $p_1(g(x)) = p_1(x)$ and $p_2(g(x)) = p_2(x)$. Since Co-Training assumes $p_1(x) = p_2(x)$, $\forall x \in \mathcal{D}$ and we want $p_1(g(x)) \neq p_2(g(x))$, when $p_1(g(x)) = p_1(x)$, it follows that $p_2(g(x)) \neq p_2(x)$. These considerations imply that $g(x)$ is an adversarial example [28] of p_2 that fools the network p_2 but not the network p_1. Therefore, in order to prevent the deep networks from collapsing into each other, we propose to train the network p_1 (or p_2) to be resistant to the adversarial examples $g_2(x)$ of p_2 (or $g_1(x)$ of p_1) by minimizing the cross entropy between $p_2(x)$ and $p_1(g_2(x))$ (or between $p_1(x)$ and $p_2(g_1(x))$), i.e.,

$$\mathcal{L}_{\text{dif}}(x) = H\Big(p_1(x), p_2\big(g_1(x)\big)\Big) + H\Big(p_2(x), p_1\big(g_2(x)\big)\Big) \tag{5}$$

Using artificially created examples in image recognition has been studied. They can serve as regularization techniques to smooth outputs [32], or create negative examples to tighten decision boundaries [23, 33]. Now, they are used to make networks different. To summarize the Co-Training with the view difference constraint in a sentence, we want the models to have *the same* predictions on $\mathcal{D}$ but make *different* errors when they are exposed to adversarial attacks. By minimizing Eq. 5 on $\mathcal{D}$, we encourage the models to generate complementary representations, each is resistant to the adversarial examples of the other.

2.3   Training DCT

In Deep Co-Training, the objective function is of the form

$$\mathcal{L} = \mathbb{E}_{(x,y) \in \mathcal{S}} \mathcal{L}_{\text{sup}}(x, y) + \lambda_{\text{cot}} \mathbb{E}_{x \in \mathcal{U}} \mathcal{L}_{\text{cot}}(x) + \lambda_{\text{dif}} \mathbb{E}_{x \in \mathcal{D}} \mathcal{L}_{\text{dif}}(x) \tag{6}$$

which linearly combines Eqs. 3, 4 and 5 with hyperparameters λ_{cot} and λ_{dif}. We present one iteration of the training loop in Algorithm 1. The full training procedure repeats the computations in Algorithm 1 for many iterations and epochs using gradient descent with decreasing learning rates.

Note that in each iteration of the training loop of DCT, the two neural networks receive different supervised data. This is to increase the difference between them by providing them with supervised data in different time orders. Consider that the data of the two networks are provided by two data streams s

and $\bar{s}$. Each data d from s and $\bar{d}$ from $\bar{s}$ are of the form $[d_s, d_u]$, where d_s and d_u denote a batch of supervised data and unsupervised data, respectively. We call $(s, \bar{s})$ a *bundle of data streams* if their d_u are the same and the sizes of d_s are the same. Algorithm 1 uses a bundle of data streams to provide data to the two networks. The idea of using bundles of data streams is important for scalable multi-view Deep Co-Training, which we will present in the following subsections.

Algorithm 1. One Iteration of the Training Loop of Deep Co-Training

---

1 **Data Sampling** Sample data batch $b_1 = (x_{b_1}, y_{b_1})$ for p_1 and $b_2 = (x_{b_2}, y_{b_2})$ for p_2 from $\mathcal{S}$ s.t. $|b_1| = |b_2| = b$. Sample data batch $b_u = (x_u)$ from $\mathcal{U}$.

2 **Create Adversarial Examples** Compute the adversarial examples $g_1(x)$ of p_1 for all $x \in x_{b_1} \cup x_u$ and $g_2(x)$ of p_2 for all $x \in x_{b_2} \cup x_u$ using FGSM [28].

3 $\mathcal{L}_{\text{sup}} = \frac{1}{b} \left[\sum_{(x,y) \in b_1} H(y, p_1(x)) + \sum_{(x,y) \in b_2} H(y, p_2(x)) \right]$

4 $\mathcal{L}_{\text{cot}} = \frac{1}{|b_u|} \sum_{x \in b_u} \left[H\left(\frac{1}{2} (p_1(x) + p_2(x)) \right) - \frac{1}{2} \left(H(p_1(x)) + H(p_2(x)) \right) \right]$

5 $\mathcal{L}_{\text{dif}} = \frac{1}{b + |b_u|} \left[\sum_{x \in x_1 \cup x_u} H(p_1(x), p_2(g_1(x))) + \sum_{x \in x_2 \cup x_u} H(p_2(x), p_1(g_2(x))) \right]$

6 $\mathcal{L} = \mathcal{L}_{\text{sup}} + \lambda_{\text{cot}} \mathcal{L}_{\text{cot}} + \lambda_{\text{dif}} \mathcal{L}_{\text{dif}}$

7 **Update** Compute the gradients with respect to $\mathcal{L}$ by backpropagation and update the parameters of p_1 and p_2 using gradient descent.

2.4   Multi-View DCT

In the previous subsection, we introduced our model of dual-view Deep Co-Training. But dual-view is only a special case of multi-view learning, and multi-view co-training has also been studied for other problems [34,35]. In this subsection, we present a scalable method for multi-view Deep Co-Training. Here, the scalability means that the hyperparameters λ_{cot} and λ_{dif} in Eq. 6 that work for dual-view DCT are also suitable for increased numbers of views. Recall that in the previous subsections, we propose a concept called a bundle of data streams $s = (s, \bar{s})$ which provides data to the two neural networks in the dual-view setting. Here, we will use multiple data stream bundles to provide data to different views so that the dual-view DCT can be adapted to the multi-view settings.

Specifically, we consider n views $v_i(\cdot)$, $i = 1, .., n$ in the multi-view DCT. We assume that n is a even number for simplicity of presenting the multi-view algorithm. Next, we build $n/2$ independent data stream bundles $B = ((s_1, \bar{s_1}), ..., (s_{n/2}, \bar{s_{n/2}}))$. Let $B_i(t)$ denote the training data that bundle B_i provides at iteration t. Let $\mathcal{L}(v_i, v_j, B_k(t))$ denote the loss $\mathcal{L}$ in Step 6 of Algorithm 1 when dual training v_i and v_j using data $B_k(t)$. Then, at each iteration t, we consider the training scheme implied by the following loss function

$$\mathcal{L}_{\text{fake } n\text{-view}}(t) = \sum_{i=1}^{n/2} \mathcal{L}(v_{2i-1}, v_{2i}, B_i(t)) \tag{7}$$

We call this *fake multi-view DCT* because Eq. 7 can be considered as $n/2$ independent dual-view DCTs. Next, we adapt Eq. 7 to the *real multi-view DCT*. In our multi-view DCT, at each iteration t, we consider an index list l randomly shuffled from $\{1, 2, .., n\}$. Then, we use the following training loss function

$$\mathcal{L}_{n\text{-view}}(t) = \sum_{i=1}^{n/2} \mathcal{L}(v_{l_{2i-1}}, v_{l_{2i}}, B_i(t)) \tag{8}$$

Compared with Eqs. 7, 8 randomly chooses a pair of views to train for each data stream bundle at each iteration. The benefits of this modeling are multifold. Firstly, Eq. 8 is converted from $n/2$ independent dual-view trainings; therefore, the hyperparameters for the dual-view setting are also suitable for multi-view settings. Thus, we can save our efforts in tuning parameters for different number of views. Secondly, because of the relationship between Eqs. 7 and 8, we can directly compare the training dynamics between different number of views. Thirdly, compared with computing the expected loss on all the possible pairs and data at each iteration, this modeling is also computationally efficient.

2.5 Implementation Details

To fairly compare with the previous state-of-the-art methods, we use the training and evaluation framework of Laine and Aila [22]. We port their implementation to PyTorch for easy multi-GPU support. Our multi-view implementation will automatically spread the models to different devices for the maximal utilizations. For SVHN and CIFAR, we use a network architecture similar to [22]: we only change their weight normalization and mean-only batch normalization layers [36] to the natively supported batch normalization layers [37]. This change results in performances a little worse than but close to those reported in their paper. [22] thus is the most natural baseline. For ImageNet, we use a small model ResNet-18 [1] for fast experiments. In the following, we introduce the datasets SVHN, CIFAR and ImageNet, and how we train our models on them.

SVHN The Street View House Numbers (SVHN) dataset [30] contains real-world images of house numbers, each of which is of size 32×32. The label for each image is the centermost digit. Therefore, this is a classification problem with 10 categories. Following Laine and Aila [22], we only use 1000 images out of 73257 official training images as the supervised part $\mathcal{S}$ to learn the models and the full test set of 26032 images for testing. The rest 73257 - 1000 images are considered as the unsupervised part $\mathcal{U}$. We train our method with the standard data augmentation, and our method significantly outperforms the previous state-of-the-art methods. Here, the data augmentation is only the random translation by at most 2 pixels. We do not use any other types of data augmentations.

CIFAR CIFAR [31] has two image datasets, CIFAR-10 and CIFAR-100. Both of them contain color natural images of size 32×32, while CIFAR-10 includes 10 categories and CIFAR-100 contains 100 categories. Both of them have 50000 images for training and 10000 images for testing. Following Laine and Aila [22], for CIFAR-10, we only use 4000 images out of 50000 training images as the supervised part S and the rest 46000 images are used as the unsupervised part $\mathcal{U}$. As for CIFAR-100, we use 10000 images out of 50000 training images as the supervised part S and the rest 40000 images as the unsupervised part $\mathcal{U}$. We use the full 10000 test images for evaluation for both CIFAR-10 and CIFAR-100. We train our methods with the standard data augmentation, which is the combination of random horizontal flip and translation by at most 2 pixels.

ImageNet The ImageNet dataset contains about 1.3 million natural color images for training and 50000 images for validation. The dataset includes 1000 categories, each of which typically has 1300 images for training and 50 for evaluation. Following the prior work that reported results on ImageNet [21,38,39], we uniformly choose 10% data from 1.3 million training images as supervised S and the rest as unsupervised $\mathcal{U}$. We report the single center crop error rates on the validation set. We train our models with data augmentation, which includes random resized crop to 224×224 and random horizontal flip. We do not use other advanced augmentation techniques such as color jittering or PCA lighting [4].

For SVHN and CIFAR, following [22], we use a warmup scheme for the hyperparameters λ_{cot} and λ_{dif}. Specifically, we warmup them in the first 80 epochs such that $\lambda = \lambda_{\max} \cdot \exp(-5(1 - T/80)^2)$ when the epoch $T \le 80$, and $\lambda_{\max}$ after that. For SVHN and CIFAR, we set $\lambda_{\text{cot,max}} = 10$. For SVHN and CIFAR-10, $\lambda_{\text{dif,max}} = 0.5$, and for CIFAR-100 $\lambda_{\text{dif,max}} = 1.0$. For training, we train the networks using stochastic gradient descent with momentum 0.9 and weight decay 0.0001. The total number of training epochs is 600 and we use a cosine learning rate schedule $lr = 0.05 \times (1.0 + \cos((T - 1) \times \pi/600))$ at epoch T [40]. The batch size is set to 100 for SVHN, CIFAR-10 and CIFAR-100.

For ImageNet, we choose a different training scheme. Before using any data from $\mathcal{U}$, we first train two ResNet-18 individually with different initializations and training sequences on only the labeled data S. Following ResNet [1], we train the models using stochastic gradient descent with momentum 0.9, weight decay 0.0001 and batch size 256 for 600 epochs, the time of which is the same as training 60 epochs with full supervision. The learning rate is initialized as 0.1 and multiplied by 0.1 at the 301st epoch. Then, we take the two pre-trained models to our unsupervised training loops. This time, we directly set λ to the maximum values $\lambda = \lambda_{\max}$ because the previous 600 epochs have already warmed up the models. Here, $\lambda_{\text{cot,max}} = 1$ and $\lambda_{\text{dif,max}} = 0.1$. In the unsupervised loops, we use a cosine learning rate $lr = 0.005 \times (1.0 + \cos((T - 1) \times \pi/20))$ and we train the networks for 20 epochs on both $\mathcal{U}$ and S. The batch size is set to 128.

To make the loss $\mathcal{L}$ stable across different training iterations, we require that each data stream provides data batches whose proportions of the supervised data are close to the ratio of the size of S to the size of $\mathcal{D}$. To achieve this, we evenly divide the supervised and the unsupervised data to build each data batch in the data streams. As a result, the difference of the numbers of the supervised images between any two batches is no greater than 1.

3   Results

In this section, we will present the experimental results on four datasets, *i.e.* SVHN [30], CIFAR-10, CIFAR-100 [31] and ImageNet [18].

3.1   SVHN and CIFAR-10

SVHN and CIFAR-10 are the datasets that the previous state-of-the-art methods for semi-supervised image recognition mostly focus on. Therefore, we first present the performances of our method and show the comparisons with the previous state-of-the-art methods on these two datasets. Next, we will also provide ablation studies on the two datasets for better understandings of the dynamics and characteristics of dual-view and multi-view Deep Co-Training.

Table 1. Error rates on SVHN (1000 labeled) and CIFAR-10 (4000 labeled) benchmarks. Note that we report the averages of the single model error rates without ensembling them for the fairness of comparisons. We use architectures that are similar to that of Π Model [22]. "–" means that the original papers did not report the corresponding error rates. We report means and standard deviations from 5 runs.

Method	SVHN	CIFAR-10
GAN [41]	8.11 ± 1.30	18.63 ± 2.32
Stochastic Transformations [21]	–	11.29 ± 0.24
Π Model [22]	4.82 ± 0.17	12.36 ± 0.31
Temporal Ensembling [22]	4.42 ± 0.16	12.16 ± 0.24
Mean Teacher [39]	3.95 ± 0.19	12.31 ± 0.28
Bad GAN [23]	4.25 ± 0.03	14.41 ± 0.30
VAT [32]	3.86	10.55
Deep Co-Training with 2 Views	3.61 ± 0.15	9.03 ± 0.18
Deep Co-Training with 4 Views	3.38 ± 0.05	8.54 ± 0.12
Deep Co-Training with 8 Views	3.29 ± 0.03	8.35 ± 0.06

Table 1 compares our method Deep Co-Training with the previous state-of-the-arts on SVHN and CIFAR-10 datasets. To make sure these methods are fairly compared, we do not ensemble the models of our method even through there are multiple well-trained models after the entire training procedure. Instead, we only report the average performances of those models. Compared with other state-of-the-art methods, Deep Co-Training achieves significant performance improvements when 2, 4 or 8 views are used. As we will discuss in Sect. 4, all the methods listed in Table 1 require implicit or explicit computations of multiple models, *e.g.* GAN [41] has a discriminative and a generative network, Bad GAN [23] adds another encoder network based on GAN, and Mean Teacher [39] has an additional EMA model. Therefore, the dual-view Deep Co-Training does not require more computations in terms of the total number of the networks.

Another trend we observe is that although 4-view DCT gives significant improvements over 2-view DCT, we do not see similar improvements when we increase the number of the views to 8. For this observation, we speculate that this is because compared with 2-views, 4-views can use the majority vote rule when we encourage them to have close predictions on $\mathcal{U}$. When we increase the number of views to 8, although it is expected to perform better, the advantages over 4-views are not that strong compared with that of 4-views over 2-views. But 8-view DCT converges faster than 4-view DCT, which is even faster than dual-view DCT. The training dynamics of DCT with different numbers of views will be presented in the later subsections. We first provide our results on CIFAR-100 and ImageNet datasets in the next subsection.

Table 2. Error rates on CIFAR-100 with 10000 images labeled. Note that other methods listed in Table 1 have not published results on CIFAR-100. The performances of our method are the averages of single model error rates of the networks without ensembling them for the fairness of comparisons. We use architectures that are similar to that of Π Model [22]. "–" means that the original papers did not report the corresponding error rates. CIFAR-100+ and CIFAR-100 indicate that the models are trained with and without data augmentation, respectively. Our results are reported from 5 runs.

Method	CIFAR-100	CIFAR-100+
Π Model [22]	43.43 ± 0.54	39.19 ± 0.36
Temporal Ensembling [22]	–	38.65 ± 0.51
Dual-View Deep Co-Training	$\mathbf{38.77 \pm 0.28}$	$\mathbf{34.63 \pm 0.14}$

3.2   CIFAR-100 and ImageNet

Compared with SVHN and CIFAR-10, CIFAR-100 and ImageNet are considered harder benchmarks [22] for the semi-supervised image recognition problem because their numbers of categories are 100 and 1000, respectively, greater than 10 categories in SVHN and CIFAR-10. Here, we provide our results on these two datasets. Table 2 compares our method with the previous state-of-the-art methods that report the performances on CIFAR-100 dataset, *i.e.* Π Model and Temporal Ensembling [22]. Dual-view Deep Co-Training even without data augmentation achieves similar performances with the previous state-of-the-arts that use data augmentation. When our method also uses data augmentation, the error rate drops significantly from 38.65 to 34.63. These results demonstrate the effectiveness of the proposed Deep Co-Training when the number of categories and the difficulty of the datasets increase.

Next, we show our results on ImageNet with 1000 categories and 10% labeled in Table 3. Our method has better performances than the supervised-only but is still behind the accuracy when 100% supervision is used. When compared with the previous state-of-the-art methods, however, DCT shows significant improvements on both the Top-1 and Top-5 error rates. Here, the performances of [21]

Table 3. Error rates on the validation set of ImageNet benchmark with 10% images labeled. The image size of our method in training and testing is 224×224.

Method	Architecture	# Param	Top-1	Top-5
Stochastic Transformations [21]	AlexNet	61.1M	–	39.84
VAE [38] with 10% Supervised	Customized	30.6M	51.59	35.24
Mean Teacher [39]	ResNet-18	11.6M	49.07	23.59
100% Supervised	ResNet-18	11.6M	30.43	10.76
10% Supervised	ResNet-18	11.6M	52.23	27.54
Dual-View Deep Co-Training	ResNet-18	11.6M	**46.50**	**22.73**

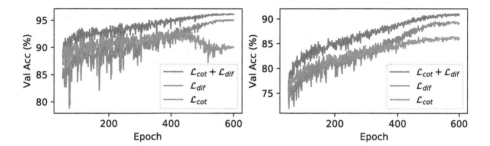

Fig. 1. Ablation study on $\mathcal{L}_{\mathrm{cot}}$ and $\mathcal{L}_{\mathrm{dif}}$. The left plot is the training dynamics of dual-view Deep Co-Training on SVHN dataset, and the right is on CIFAR-10 dataset. "λ_{cot}","λ_{dif}" represent the loss functions are used alone while "$\lambda_{\mathrm{cot}} + \lambda_{\mathrm{dif}}$" correspond to the weighted sum loss used in Deep Co-Training. In all the cases, $\mathcal{L}_{\mathrm{sup}}$ is used.

and [38] are quoted from their papers, and the performance of Mean Teacher [39] with ResNet-18 [1] is from running their official implementation on GitHub. When using the same architecture, DCT outperforms Mean Teacher by $\sim 2.6\%$ for Top-1 error rate, and $\sim 0.9\%$ for Top-5 error rate. Compared with [21] and [38] that use networks with more parameters and larger input size 256×256, Deep Co-Training also achieves lower error rates.

3.3   Ablation Study

In this subsection, we will provide several ablation studies for better understandings of our proposed Deep Co-Training method.

On $\mathcal{L}_{\mathrm{cot}}$ and $\mathcal{L}_{\mathrm{dif}}$ Recall that the loss function used in Deep Co-Training has three parts, the supervision loss $\mathcal{L}_{\mathrm{sup}}$, the co-training loss $\mathcal{L}_{\mathrm{cot}}$ and the view difference constraint $\mathcal{L}_{\mathrm{dif}}$. It is of interest to study the changes when the loss function $\mathcal{L}_{\mathrm{cot}}$ and $\mathcal{L}_{\mathrm{dif}}$ are used alone in addition to $\mathcal{L}_{\mathrm{sup}}$ in $\mathcal{L}$. Figure 1 shows the plots of the training dynamics of Deep Co-Training when different loss functions are used on SVHN and CIFAR-10 dataset. In both plots, the blue lines represent the loss function that we use in practice in training DCT, the green lines represent only the co-training loss $\mathcal{L}_{cot}$ and $\mathcal{L}_{sup}$ are applied, and the orange lines represent only the the view difference constraint $\mathcal{L}_{dif}$ and $\mathcal{L}_{sup}$ are used. From Fig. 1, we can see that the Co-Training assumption ($\mathcal{L}_{cot}$) performs better at the beginning, but soon is overtaken by $\mathcal{L}_{dif}$. $\mathcal{L}_{cot}$ even falls into an extreme case in the SVHN dataset where its validation accuracy drops suddenly around the 400-th epoch. For this phenomenon, we speculate that this is because the networks have collapsed into each other, which motivates us to investigate the dynamics of loss $\mathcal{L}_{dif}$. If our speculation is correct, there will also be abnormalities in loss $\mathcal{L}_{dif}$ around that epoch, which indeed we show in the next subsection. Moreover, this also supports our argument at the beginning of the paper that a force to push models away is necessary for co-training multiple neural networks for semi-supervised learning. Another phenomenon we observe is that $\mathcal{L}_{dif}$ alone can achieve reasonable results. This is because when the adversarial algorithm fails to fool the networks, $\mathcal{L}_{dif}$ will degenrate to $\mathcal{L}_{cot}$. In other words, $\mathcal{L}_{dif}$ in practice combines the Co-Training assumption and View Difference Constraint, depending on the success rate of the adversarial algorithm.

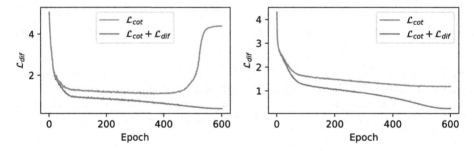

Fig. 2. Ablation study on the view difference. The left plot is $\mathcal{L}_{dif}$ on SVHN dataset, and the right plot shows $\mathcal{L}_{dif}$ on CIFAR-10. Without minimizing $\mathcal{L}_{dif}$, $\mathcal{L}_{dif}$ is usually big in "$\mathcal{L}_{cot}$", indicating that the two models are making similar errors. In the SVHN dataset, the two models start to collapse into each other after around the 400-th epoch because we observe a sudden increase of $\mathcal{L}_{dif}$. This corresponds to the sudden drop in the left plot of Fig. 1, which shows the relation between view difference and accuracy.

On the View Difference This is a sanity check on whether in dual-view training, two models tend to collapse into each other when we only model the Co-Training assumption, and if $\mathcal{L}_{dif}$ can push them away during training. To study this, we plot $\mathcal{L}_{dif}$ when it is minimized as in the Deep Co-Training and when it is not minimized, *i.e.* $\lambda_{dif} = 0$. Figure 2 shows the plots of $\mathcal{L}_{dif}$ for SVHN dataset and CIFAR dataset, which correspond to the validation accuracies shown in Fig. 1. It is clear that when $\mathcal{L}_{dif}$ is not minimized as in the "$\mathcal{L}_{cot}$" case, $\mathcal{L}_{dif}$ is far greater than 0, indicating that each model is vulnerable to the adversarial examples of the other. Like the extreme case we observe in Fig. 1 for SVHN dataset (left) around the 400-th epoch, we also see a sudden increase of $\mathcal{L}_{dif}$ here in Fig. 2 for SVHN at the similar epochs. This means that every

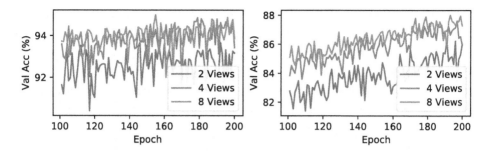

Fig. 3. Training dynamics of Deep Co-Training with different numbers of views on SVHN dataset (left) and CIFAR-10 (right). The plots focus on the epochs from 100 to 200 where the differences are clearest. We observe a faster convergence speed when the number of views increases, but the improvements become smaller when the numbers of views increase from 4 to 8 compared with that from 2 to 4.

adversarial example of one model fools the other model, *i.e.* they collapse into each other. The collapse directly causes a significant drop of the validation accuracy in the left of Fig. 1. These experimental results demonstrate the positive correlation between the view difference and the validation error. It also shows that the models in the dual-view training tend to collapse into each other when no force is applied to push them away. Finally, these results also support the effectiveness of our proposed $\mathcal{L}_{\text{dif}}$ as a loss function to increase the difference between the models.

On the Number of Views We have provided the performances of Deep Co-Training with different numbers of views for SVHN and CIFAR-10 datasets in Table 1, where we show that increasing the number of the views from 2 to 4 improves the performances of each individual model. But we also observe that the improvement becomes smaller when we further increase the number of views to 8. In Fig. 3, we show the training dynamics of Deep Co-Training when different numbers of views are trained simultaneously.

As shown in Fig. 3, we observe a faster convergence speed when we increase the number of views to train simultaneously. We focus on the epochs from 100 to 200 where the differences between different numbers of views are clearest. The performances of different views are directly comparable because of the scalability of the proposed multi-view Deep Co-Training. Like the improvements of 8 views over 4 views on the final validation accuracy, the improvements of the convergence speed also decrease compared with that of 4 views over 2 views.

4 Discussions

In this section, we discuss the relationship between Deep Co-Training and the previous methods. We also present perspectives alternative to the Co-Training framework for discussing Deep Co-Training.

4.1   Related Work

Deep Co-Training is also inspired by the recent advances in semi-supervised image recognition techniques [21,22,32,42,43] which train deep neural networks $f(\cdot)$ to be resistant to noises $\epsilon(z)$, *i.e.* $f(x) = f(x + \epsilon(z))$. We notice that their computations in one iteration require double feedforwardings and backpropagations, one for $f(x)$ and one for $f(x + \epsilon(z))$. We ask the question: what would happen if we train two individual models as doing so requires the same amount of computations? We soon realized that training two models and encouraging them to have close predictions is related to the Co-Training framework [24], which has good theoretical results, provided that the two models are conditional independent given the category. However, training models with only the Co-Training assumption is not sufficient for getting good performances because the models tend to collapse into each other, which is against the view difference between different models which is necessary for the Co-Training framework.

As stated in Sect. 2.2, we need a generative method to generate images on which two models predict differently. Generative Adversarial Networks (GANs) [23,41,44] are popular generative models for vision problems, and have also been used for semi-supervised image recognition. A problem of GANs is that they will introduce new networks to the Co-Training framework for generating images, which also need to be learned. Compared with GANs, Introspective Generative Models [33,45] can generate images from discriminative models in a lightweight manner, which bears some similarities with the adversarial examples [28]. The generative methods that use discriminative models also include DeepDream [46], Neural Artistic Style [47], *etc*. We use adversarial examples in our Deep Co-Training for its natural applicability to avoiding models from collapsing into each other by training each model with the adversarial examples of the others.

Before the work discussed above, semi-supervised learning in general has already been widely studied. For example, the mutual-exclusivity loss used in [21] and the entropy minimization used in [32] resemble soft implementations of the self-training technique [48,49], one of the earliest approaches for semi-supervised classification tasks. [20] provides a good survey for the semi-supervised learning methods in general.

4.2   Alternative Perspectives

In this subsection, we discuss the proposed Deep Co-Training method from several perspectives alternative to the Co-Training framework.

Model Ensemble Ensembling multiple independently trained models to get a more accurate and stable classifier is a widely used technique to achieve higher performances [50]. This is also applicable to deep neural networks [51,52]. In other words, this suggests that when multiple networks with the same architecture are initialized differently and trained using data sequences in different time orders, they can achieve similar performances but in a complementary way [53]. In multi-view Deep Co-Training, we also train multiple models in parallel, but not independently, and our evaluation is done by taking one of them as the final classifier instead of averaging their predicted probabilities. Deep Co-Training in effect is searching for an initialization-free and data-order-free solution.

Multi-Agent Learning After the literature review of the most recent semi-supervised learning methods for image recognition, we find that almost all of them are within the multi-agent learning framework [54]. To name a few, GAN-based methods at least have a discriminative network and a generative network. Bad GAN [23] adds an encoder network based on GAN. The agents in GANs are interacting in an adversarial way. As we stated in Sect. 2.1, the methods that train deep networks to be resistant to noises also have the interacting behaviors as what two individual models would have, *i.e.* double feedforwardings and backpropagations. The agents in these methods are interacting in a cooperative way. Deep Co-Training explicitly models the cooperative multi-agent learning, which trains multiple agents from the supervised data and cooperative interactions between different agents. In the multi-agent learning framework, $\mathcal{L}_{\text{dif}}$ can be understood as learning from the errors of the others, and the loss function Eq. 8 resembles the simulation of interactions within a crowd of agents.

Knowledge Distillation One characteristic of Deep Co-Training is that the models not only learn from the supervised data, but also learn from the predictions of the other models. This is reminiscent to knowledge distillation [55] where student models learn from teacher models instead of the supervisions from the datasets. In Deep Co-Training, all the models are students and learn from not only the predictions of the other student models but also the errors they make.

5   Conclusion

In this paper, we present Deep Co-Training, a method for semi-supervised image recognition. It extends the Co-Training framework, which assumes that the data has two complementary views, based on which two effective classifiers can be built and are assumed to have close predictions on the unlabeled images. Motivated by the recent successes of deep neural networks in supervised image recognition, we extend the Co-Training framework to apply deep networks to the task of semi-supervised image recognition. In our experiments, we notice that the models are easy to collapse into each other, which violates the requirement of the view difference in the Co-Training framework. To prevent the models from collapsing, we use adversarial examples as the generative method to generate data on which the views have different predictions. The experiments show that this additional force that pushes models away is helpful for training and improves accuracies significantly compared with the Co-Training-only modeling.

Since Co-Training is a special case of multi-view learning, we also naturally extend the dual-view DCT to a scalable multi-view Deep Co-Training method where the hyperparameters for two views are also suitable for increased numbers of views. We test our proposed Deep Co-Training on the SVHN, CIFAR-10/100 and ImageNet datasets which are the benchmarks that the previous state-of-the-art methods are tested on. Our method outperforms them by a large margin.

Acknowledgments. We thank Wanyu Huang, Huiyu Wang, Chenxi Liu, Lingxi Xie and Yingda Xia for their insightful comments and suggestions. We gratefully acknowledge funding supports from NSF award CCF-1317376 and ONR N00014-15-1-2356. This work was also supported in part by the National Natural Science Foundation of China under Grant 61672336.

References

1. He, K., Zhang, X., Ren, S., Sun, J.: Deep residual learning for image recognition. In: IEEE Conference on Computer Vision and Pattern Recognition, CVPR (2016)
2. Huang, G., Liu, Z., Weinberger, K.Q.: Densely connected convolutional networks. In: IEEE Conference on Computer Vision and Pattern Recognition, CVPR (2017)
3. Qiao, S., Shen, W., Qiu, W., Liu, C., Yuille, A.L.: Scalenet: guiding object proposal generation in supermarkets and beyond. In: 2017 IEEE International Conference on Computer Vision, ICCV 2017, Venice, Italy, October 22–29 (2017)
4. Krizhevsky, A., Sutskever, I., Hinton, G.E.: Imagenet classification with deep convolutional neural networks. In: Pereira, F., Burges, C.J.C., Bottou, L., Weinberger, K.Q. (eds.) Advances in Neural Information Processing Systems, vol. 25, pp. 1097–1105 (2012)
5. Qiao, S., Liu, C., Shen, W., Yuille, A.L.: Few-shot image recognition by predicting parameters from activations. In: IEEE Conference on Computer Vision and Pattern Recognition, CVPR (2018)
6. Simonyan, K., Zisserman, A.: Very deep convolutional networks for large-scale image recognition. CoRR abs/1409.1556 (2014)
7. Szegedy, C. et al.: Going deeper with convolutions. In: Computer Vision and Pattern Recognition (CVPR) (2015)
8. Wang, Y. et al.: SORT: second-order response transform for visual recognition. In: IEEE International Conference on Computer Vision (2017)
9. Zeiler, M.D., Fergus, R.: Visualizing and understanding convolutional networks. CoRR abs/1311.2901 (2013)
10. Qiao, S., Zhang, Z., Shen, W., Wang, B., Yuille, A.L.: Gradually updated neural networks for large-scale image recognition. In: International Conference on Machine Learning (ICML) (2018)
11. Chen, L., Papandreou, G., Kokkinos, I., Murphy, K., Yuille, A.L.: Semantic image segmentation with deep convolutional nets and fully connected crfs. In: International Conference on Learning Representations (2015)
12. Girshick, R.B., Donahue, J., Darrell, T., Malik, J.: Rich feature hierarchies for accurate object detection and semantic segmentation. In: 2014 IEEE Conference on Computer Vision and Pattern Recognition, CVPR 2014 (2014)
13. Long, J., Shelhamer, E., Darrell, T.: Fully convolutional networks for semantic segmentation. In: IEEE Conference on Computer Vision and Pattern Recognition, CVPR 2015, Boston, MA, USA, June 7–12, 2015 (2015)
14. Ren, S., He, K., Girshick, R.B., Sun, J.: Faster R-CNN: towards real-time object detection with region proposal networks. In: Advances in Neural Information Processing Systems 28: Annual Conference on Neural Information Processing Systems 2015, December 7–12, 2015, Montreal, Quebec, Canada (2015)
15. Zhang, Z., Qiao, S., Xie, C., Shen, W., Wang, B., Yuille, A.L.: Single-shot object detection with enriched semantics. In: IEEE Conference on Computer Vision and Pattern Recognition, CVPR (2018)

16. Qiu, W. et al: Unrealcv: Virtual worlds for computer vision. In: ACM Multimedia Open Source Software Competition (2017)
17. Wang, Y., Xie, L., Qiao, S., Zhang, Y., Zhang, W., Yuille, A.L.: Multi-scale spatially-asymmetric recalibration for image classification. CoRR abs/1804.00787 (2018)
18. Russakovsky, O., et al.: ImageNet large scale visual recognition challenge. Int. J. Comput. Vis. (IJCV) **115**(3), 211–252 (2015)
19. Lin, T. et al.: Microsoft COCO: common objects in context. CoRR abs/1405.0312 (2014)
20. Zhu, X.: Semi-supervised learning literature survey. Technical report, Computer Science, University of Wisconsin-Madison (2006)
21. Sajjadi, M., Javanmardi, M., Tasdizen, T.: Regularization with stochastic transformations and perturbations for deep semi-supervised learning. In: Advances in Neural Information Processing Systems 29: Annual Conference on Neural Information Processing Systems 2016, December 5–10, 2016, Barcelona, Spain, pp. 1163–1171 (2016)
22. Laine, S., Aila, T.: Temporal ensembling for semi-supervised learning. In: International Conference on Learning Representations, ICLR, 2017 (2017)
23. Dai, Z., Yang, Z., Yang, F., Cohen, W.W., Salakhutdinov, R.: Good semi-supervised learning that requires a bad GAN. In: Advances in Neural Information Processing Systems 30: Annual Conference on Neural Information Processing Systems 2017, 4–9 December 2017, Long Beach, CA, USA, pp. 6513–6523 (2017)
24. Blum, A., Mitchell, T.M.: Combining labeled and unlabeled data with co-training. In: Proceedings of the Eleventh Annual Conference on Computational Learning Theory, COLT 1998, Madison, Wisconsin, USA, July 24–26, 1998, pp. 92–100 (1998)
25. Nigam, K., Ghani, R.: Analyzing the effectiveness and applicability of co-training. In: Proceedings of the 2000 ACM CIKM International Conference on Information and Knowledge Management, McLean, VA, USA, November 6–11, 2000, pp. 86–93 (2000)
26. Bai, X., Wang, B., Yao, C., Liu, W., Tu, Z.: Co-transduction for shape retrieval. IEEE Trans. Image Process. **21**(5), 2747–2757 (2012)
27. Xia, R., Wang, C., Dai, X., Li, T.: Co-training for semi-supervised sentiment classification based on dual-view bags-of-words representation. In: Proceedings of the 53rd Annual Meeting of the Association for Computational Linguistics and the 7th International Joint Conference on Natural Language Processing of the Asian Federation of Natural Language Processing, ACL 2015, July 26–31, 2015, Beijing, China, Volume 1: Long Papers, pp. 1054–1063 (2015)
28. Goodfellow, I., Shlens, J., Szegedy, C.: Explaining and harnessing adversarial examples. In: International Conference on Learning Representations, ICLR, 2015 (2015)
29. Xie, C., Wang, J., Zhang, Z., Zhou, Y., Xie, L., Yuille, A.L.: Adversarial examples for semantic segmentation and object detection. In: IEEE International Conference on Computer Vision, ICCV 2017, Venice, Italy, October 22–29, 2017, pp. 1378–1387 (2017)
30. Netzer, Y., Wang, T., Coates, A., Bissacco, A., Wu, B., Ng, A.Y.: Reading digits in natural images with unsupervised feature learning. In: NIPS Workshop on Deep Learning and Unsupervised Feature Learning 2011 (2011)
31. Krizhevsky, A., Hinton, G.: Learning multiple layers of features from tiny images. Master's thesis, Department of Computer Science, University of Toronto (2009)

32. Miyato, T., Maeda, S., Koyama, M., Ishii, S.: Virtual adversarial training: a regularization method for supervised and semi-supervised learning. CoRR abs/1704.03976 (2017)

33. Jin, L., Lazarow, J., Tu, Z.: Introspective classification with convolutional nets. In: Advances in Neural Information Processing Systems 30: Annual Conference on Neural Information Processing Systems 2017, 4–9 December 2017, Long Beach, CA, USA, pp. 823–833 (2017)

34. Zhou, Z.H., Li, M.: Tri-training: exploiting unlabeled data using three classifiers. IEEE Trans. Knowl. Data Eng. **17**(11), 1529–1541 (2005)

35. Xu, C., Tao, D., Xu, C.: A survey on multi-view learning. CoRR abs/1304.5634 (2013)

36. Salimans, T., Kingma, D.P.: Weight normalization: a simple reparameterization to accelerate training of deep neural networks. In: Advances in Neural Information Processing Systems 29: Annual Conference on Neural Information Processing Systems 2016, December 5–10, 2016, Barcelona, Spain, p. 901 (2016)

37. Ioffe, S., Szegedy, C.: Batch normalization: accelerating deep network training by reducing internal covariate shift. In: Proceedings of the 32nd International Conference on Machine Learning, ICML (2015)

38. Pu, Y., Gan, Z., Henao, R., Yuan, X., Li, C., Stevens, A., Carin, L.: Variational autoencoder for deep learning of images, labels and captions. In: Advances in Neural Information Processing Systems 29: Annual Conference on Neural Information Processing Systems 2016, December 5–10, 2016, Barcelona, Spain, pp. 2352–2360 (2016)

39. Tarvainen, A., Valpola, H.: Mean teachers are better role models: weight-averaged consistency targets improve semi-supervised deep learning results. In: Advances in Neural Information Processing Systems 30: Annual Conference on Neural Information Processing Systems 2017, 4–9 December 2017, Long Beach, CA, USA, pp. 1195–1204 (2017)

40. Loshchilov, I., Hutter, F.: Sgdr: stochastic gradient descent with warm restarts. arXiv preprint arXiv:1608.03983 (2016)

41. Salimans, T., Goodfellow, I.J., Zaremba, W., Cheung, V., Radford, A., Chen, X.: Improved techniques for training gans. In: Advances in Neural Information Processing Systems 29: Annual Conference on Neural Information Processing Systems 2016, December 5–10, 2016, Barcelona, Spain, pp. 2226–2234 (2016)

42. Bachman, P., Alsharif, O., Precup, D.: Learning with pseudo-ensembles. In: Advances in Neural Information Processing Systems 27: Annual Conference on Neural Information Processing Systems 2014, December 8–13 2014, Montreal, Quebec, Canada, pp. 3365–3373 (2014)

43. Rasmus, A., Berglund, M., Honkala, M., Valpola, H., Raiko, T.: Semi-supervised learning with ladder networks. In: Advances in Neural Information Processing Systems 28: Annual Conference on Neural Information Processing Systems 2015, December 7–12, 2015, Montreal, Quebec, Canada, pp. 3546–3554 (2015)

44. Arjovsky, M., Chintala, S., Bottou, L.: Wasserstein GAN. CoRR abs/1701.07875 (2017)

45. Tu, Z.: Learning generative models via discriminative approaches. In: 2007 IEEE Conference on Computer Vision and Pattern Recognition, pp. 1–8, June 2007

46. Mordvintsev, A., Olah, C., Tyka, M.: Deepdream - a code example for visualizing neural networks. Google Res. (2015)

47. Gatys, L.A., Ecker, A.S., Bethge, M.: A neural algorithm of artistic style. CoRR abs/1508.06576 (2015)

48. Iii, H.J.S.: Probability of error of some adaptive pattern-recognition machines. IEEE Trans. Inf. Theor. **11**(3), 363–371 (1965)
49. Fralick, S.C.: Learning to recognize patterns without a teacher. IEEE Trans. Inf. Theor. **13**(1), 57–64 (1967)
50. Breiman, L.: Bagging predictors. Mach. Learn. **24**(2), 123–140 (1996)
51. Zhou, Z., Wu, J., Tang, W.: Ensembling neural networks: Many could be better than all. Artif. Intell. **137**(1–2), 239–263 (2002)
52. Zhou, Z.H.: Ensemble Methods: Foundations and Algorithms. Chapman & Hall/CRC Press, New York (2012)
53. Breiman, L.: Statistical modeling: the two cultures (with comments and a rejoinder by the author). Statist. Sci. **16**(3), 199–231 (2001)
54. Panait, L., Luke, S.: Cooperative multi-agent learning: the state of the art. Auton. Agents Multi-Agent Syst. **11**, 387–434 (2005)
55. Hinton, G.E., Vinyals, O., Dean, J.: Distilling the knowledge in a neural network. CoRR abs/1503.02531 (2015)

Visual Coreference Resolution in Visual Dialog Using Neural Module Networks

Satwik Kottur[1,2](✉), José M. F. Moura[2], Devi Parikh[1,3], Dhruv Batra[1,3], and Marcus Rohrbach[1]

[1] Facebook AI Research, Menlo Park, USA
[2] Carnegie Mellon University, Pittsburgh, USA
skottur@andrew.cmu.edu
[3] Georgia Institute of Technology, Atlanta, USA

Abstract. Visual dialog entails answering a series of questions grounded in an image, using dialog history as context. In addition to the challenges found in visual question answering (VQA), which can be seen as one-round dialog, visual dialog encompasses several more. We focus on one such problem called *visual coreference resolution* that involves determining which words, typically noun phrases and pronouns, *co-refer* to the same entity/object instance in an image. This is crucial, especially for pronouns (e.g., '*it*'), as the dialog agent must first link it to a previous coreference (e.g., '*boat*'), and only then can rely on the visual grounding of the coreference '*boat*' to reason about the pronoun '*it*'. Prior work (in visual dialog) models visual coreference resolution either (a) implicitly via a memory network over history, or (b) at a coarse level for the entire question; and not explicitly at a phrase level of granularity. In this work, we propose a neural module network architecture for visual dialog by introducing two novel modules—**Refer** and **Exclude**—that perform explicit, grounded, coreference resolution at a finer word level. We demonstrate the effectiveness of our model on MNIST Dialog, a visually simple yet coreference-wise complex dataset, by achieving near perfect accuracy, and on VisDial, a large and challenging visual dialog dataset on real images, where our model outperforms other approaches, and is more interpretable, grounded, and consistent qualitatively.

1 Introduction

The task of Visual Dialog [11,40] involves building agents that 'see' (i.e.understand an image) and 'talk' (i.e.communicate this understanding in a dialog). Specifically, it requires an agent to answer a sequence of questions about an image, requiring it to reason about both the image and the past dialog history. For instance, in Fig. 1, to answer '*What color is it?*', the agent needs to

---

Work partially done as an intern at Facebook AI Research.

Electronic supplementary material The online version of this chapter (https://doi.org/10.1007/978-3-030-01267-0_10) contains supplementary material, which is available to authorized users.

© Springer Nature Switzerland AG 2018
V. Ferrari et al. (Eds.): ECCV 2018, LNCS 11219, pp. 160–178, 2018.
https://doi.org/10.1007/978-3-030-01267-0_10

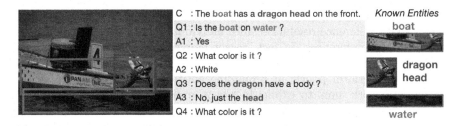

Fig. 1. Our model begins by grounding entities in the caption (C), *boat* (brown) and *dragon head* (green), and stores them in a pool for future coreference resolution in the dialog (right). When asked *'Q1: Is the boat on water?'*, it identifies that the *boat* (known entity) and *water* (unknown entity) are crucial to answer the question. It then grounds the novel entity *water* in the image (blue), but resolves *boat* by referring back to the pool and reusing the available grounding from the caption, before proceeding with further reasoning. Thus, our model explicitly resolves coreferences in visual dialog.

reason about the history to know what *'it'* refers to and the image to find out the color. This generalization of visual question answering (VQA) [6] to dialog takes a step closer to real-world applications (aiding visually impaired users, intelligent home assistants, natural language interfaces for robots) but simultaneously introduces new modeling challenges at the intersection of vision and language. The particular challenge we focus on in this paper is that of *visual coreference resolution* in visual dialog. Specifically, we introduce a new model that performs explicit visual coreference resolution and interpretable entity tracking in visual dialog.

It has long been understood [16,31,44,46] that humans use *coreferences*, different phrases and short-hands such as pronouns, to refer to the same entity or referent in a single text. In the context of visually grounded dialog, we are interested in referents which are in the image, e.g. an object or person. All phrases in the dialog which refer to the same entity or referent in the image are called visual coreferences. Such coreferences can be noun phrases such as *'a dragon head'*, *'the head'*, or pronouns such as *'it'* (Fig. 1). Especially when trying to answer a question that contains an anaphora, for instance the pronoun *'it'*, which refers to its full form (the antecedent) *'a dragon head'*, it is necessary to *resolve* the coreference on the language side and ground it to the underlying visual referent. More specifically, to answer the question *'What color is it?'* in Fig. 1, the model must correctly identify which object *'it'* refers to, in the given context. Notice that a word or phrase can refer to different entities in different contexts, as is the case with *'it'* in this example. Our approach to explicitly resolve visual coreferences is inspired from the functionality of variables or memory in a computer program. In the same spirit as how one can refer back to the contents of variables at a later time in a program without explicitly re-computing them, we propose a model which can refer back to entities from previous rounds of dialog and reuse the associated information; and in this way resolve coreferences.

Prior work on VQA [2,13,28] has (understandably) largely ignored the problem of visual coreference resolution since individual questions asked in isolation rarely contain coreferences. In fact, recent empirical studies [1,15,20,47] suggest that today's vision and language models seem to be exploiting dataset-level statistics and perform poorly at grounding entities into the correct pixels. In contrast, our work aims to explicitly reason over past dialog interactions by referring back to previous references. This allows for increased interpretability of the model. As the dialog progresses (Fig. 1), we can inspect the pool of entities known to the model, and also visualize which entity a particular phrase in the question has been resolved to. Moreover, our explicit entity tracking model has benefits even in cases that may not strictly speaking require coreference resolution. For instance, by explicitly referring *'dragon'* in Q3 (Fig. 1) back to a known entity, the model is consistent with itself and (correctly) grounds the phrase in the image. We believe such consistency in model outputs is a strongly desirable property as we move towards human-machine interaction in dialog systems.

Our main technical contribution is a neural module network architecture for visual dialog. Specifically, we propose two novel modules—`Refer` and `Exclude`—that perform explicit, grounded, coreference resolution in visual dialog. In addition, we propose a novel way to handle captions using neural module networks at a word-level granularity finer than a traditional sentence-level encoding. We show quantitative benefits of these modules on a reasoning-wise complicated but visually simple MNIST dialog dataset [37], where achieve near perfect accuracy. On the visually challenging VisDial dataset [11], our model not only outperforms other approaches but also is more interpretable by construction and enables word-level coreference resolution. Furthermore, we qualitatively show that our model is (a) more interpretable (a user can inspect which entities were detected and tracked as the dialog progresses, and which ones were referred to for answering a specific question), (b) more grounded (where the model looked to answer a question in the dialog), (c) more consistent (same entities are considered across rounds of dialog).

2   Related Work

We discuss: (a) existing approaches to visual dialog, (b) related tasks such as visual grounding and coreference resolution, and (c) neural module networks.

Visual Dialog. Though the origins of visual dialog can be traced back to [14,43], it was largely formalized by [11,40] who collected human annotated datasets for the same. Specifically, [11] paired annotators to collect free-form natural-language questions and answers, where the questioner was instructed to ask questions to help them imagine the hidden scene (image) better. On the other hand, dialogs from [40] are more goal driven and contain yes/no questions directed towards identifying a secret object in the image. The respective follow up works used reinforcement learning techniques to solve this problem [12,39]. Other approaches to visual dialog include transferring knowledge from a discriminatively trained model to a generative dialog model [27], using attention networks to solve visual coreferences [37], and more recently, a probabilistic treatment of dialogs using conditional variational autoencoders [30]. Amongst these, [37] is the closest to this work, while [27,30] are complementary. To solve visual coreferences, [37] relies on global visual attentions used to answer previous questions. They store these attention maps in a memory against keys based on textual representations of the entire question and answer, along with the history. In contrast, operating at a finer word-level granularity within each question, our model can resolve different phrases of a question, and ground them to different parts of the image, a core component in correctly understanding and grounding coreferences. E.g., *'A man and woman in a car. Q: Is he or she driving?'*, which requires resolving *'he'* and *'she'* individually to answer the question.

Grounding Language in Images and Video. Most works in this area focus on the specific task of localizing a textual referential expression in the image [19, 22, 29, 32, 35, 41, 46] or video [5, 24, 34, 45]. Similar to these works, one component of our model aims to localize words and phrases in the image. However, the key difference is that if the phrase being grounded is an anaphora (e.g., *'it'*, *'he'*, *'she'*, etc.), our model first resolves it explicitly to a known entity, and then grounds it by borrowing the referent's visual grounding.

Coreference Resolution. The linguistic community defines coreference resolution as the task of clustering phrases, such as noun phrases and pronouns, which refer to the same entity in the world (see, for example, [8]). The task of visual coreference resolution links the coreferences to an entity in the visual data. For example, [33] links character mentions in TV show descriptions with their occurrence in the video, while [22] links text phrases to objects in a 3D scene. Different from these works, we predict a program for a given natural language question about an image, which then tries to resolve any existing coreferences, to then answer the question. An orthogonal direction is to generate language while jointly grounding and resolving coreferences – e.g., [36] explore this for movie descriptions. While out of scope for this work, it is an interesting direction for future work in visual dialog, especially when generating questions.

Neural Module Networks. [4] are an elegant class of models where an instance-specific architecture is composed from neural 'modules' (or building blocks) that are shared across instances. The high-level idea is inspired by 'options' or sub-tasks in hierarchical RL. They have been shown to be successful for visual question answering in real images and linguistic databases [3] and for more complex reasoning tasks in synthetic datasets [18,21]. For this, [18,21] learn program prediction and module parameters jointly, end-to-end. Within this context, our work generalizes the formulation in [18] from VQA to visual dialog by introducing a novel module to perform explicit visual coreference resolution.

3   Approach

Recall that visual dialog [11] involves answering a question Q_t at the current round t, given an image I, and the dialog history (including the image

caption) $H = (\underbrace{C}_{H_0}, \underbrace{(Q_1, A_1)}_{H_1}, \cdots, \underbrace{(Q_{t-1}, A_{t-1})}_{H_{t-1}})$, by ranking a list of 100 candidate answers $\mathcal{A}_t = \{A_t^{(1)}, \cdots, A_t^{(100)}\}$. As a key component for building better
visual dialog agents, our model explicitly resolves visual coreferences in the current question, if any.

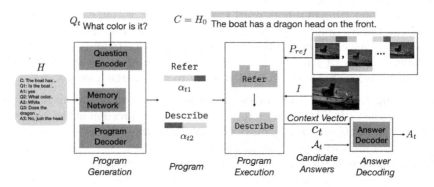

Fig. 2. Overview of our model architecture. The question Q_t (orange bar) is encoded along with the history H through a memory augmented question encoder, using which a program (`Refer Describe`) is decoded. For each module in the program, an attention α_{ti} over Q_t is also predicted, used to compute the text feature x_{txt}. For Q_t, attention is over 'it' for `Refer` and 'What color' for `Describe`, respectively (orange bars with red attention). `Refer` module uses the coreference pool P_{ref}, a dictionary of all previously seen entities with their visual groundings, resolves 'it', and borrows the referent's visual grounding (*boat* in this case). Finally, `Describe` extracts the 'color' to produce c_t used by a final decoder to pick the answer A_t from the candidate pool $\mathcal{A}_t$.

Towards this end, our model first identifies relevant words or phrases in the current question that refer to entities in the image (typically objects and attributes). The model also predicts whether each of these has been mentioned in the dialog so far. Next, if these are novel entities (unseen in the dialog history), they are localized in the image before proceeding, and for seen entities, the model predicts the (first) relevant coreference in the conversation history, and retrieves its corresponding visual grounding. Therefore, as rounds of dialog progress, the model collects unique entities and their corresponding visual groundings, and uses this *reference pool* to resolve any coreferences in subsequent questions.

Our model has three broad components: (a) *Program Generation* (Sect. 3.3), where a reasoning pathway, as dictated by a *program*, is predicted for the current question Q_t, (b) *Program Execution* (Sect. 3.4), where the predicted program is executed by dynamically connecting neural modules [3,4,18] to produce a *context* vector summarizing the semantic information required to answer Q_t from the context (I, H), and lastly, (c) *Answer Decoding* (Sect. 3.4), where the context vector c_t is used to obtain the final answer $\hat{A}_t$. We begin with a general characterization of neural modules used for VQA in Sect. 3.1 and then discuss our novel modules for coreference resolution (Sect. 3.2) with details of the reference pool. After describing the inner working of the modules, we explain each of the above three components of our model.

3.1 Neural Modules for Visual Question Answering

The main technical foundation of our model is the neural module network (NMN) [4]. In this section, we briefly recap NMNs and more specifically, the attentional modules from [18]. In the next section, we discuss novel modules we propose to handle additional challenges in visual dialog.

For a module m, let x_{vis} and x_{txt} be the input image and text embeddings, respectively. In particular, the image embeddings x_{vis} are spatial activation maps of the image I from a convolutional neural network. The text embedding x_{txt} is computed as a weighted sum of embeddings of words in the question Q_t using the soft attention weights α predicted by a program generator for module m (more details in Sect. 3.3). Further, let $\{a_i\}$ be the set of n_m single-channel spatial maps corresponding to the spatial image embeddings, where n_m is the number of attention inputs to m. Denoting the module parameters with θ_m, a neural module m is essentially a parametric function $y = f_m(x_{vis}, x_{txt}, \{a_i\}_{i=1}^{n_m}; \theta_m)$. The output from the module y can either be a spatial image attention map (denoted by a) or a context vector (denoted by c), depending on the module. The output spatial attention map a feeds into next level modules while a context vector c is used to obtain the final answer A_t. The upper part of Table 1 lists modules we adopt from prior work, with their functional forms. We shortly summarize their behavior. A `Find` module localizes objects or attributes by producing an attention over the image. The `Relocate` module takes in an input image attention and performs necessary spatial relocations to handle relationships like *'next to'*, *'in front of'*, *'beside'*, etc.. Intersection or union of attention maps can be obtained using `And` and `Or`, respectively. Finally, `Describe`, `Exist`, and `Count` input an attention map to produce the context vector by describing an attribute, checking for existence, or counting, respectively, in the given input attention map. As noted in [18], these modules are designed and named for a potential 'atomic' functionality. However, we do not enforce this explicitly and let the modules discover their expected behavior by training in an end-to-end manner.

3.2 Neural Modules for Coreference Resolution

We now introduce novel components and modules to handle visual dialog.

Reference Pool (P_{ref}). The role of the reference pool is to keep track of entities seen so far in the dialog. Thus, we design P_{ref} to be a dictionary of key-value pairs (x_{txt}, a) for all the `Find` modules instantiated while answering previous questions $(Q_i)_{i=1}^{t-1}$. Recall that `Find` localizes objects/attributes specified by x_{txt}, and thus by storing each output attention map y, we now have access to all the

Table 1. Neural modules used in our work for visual dialog, along with their inputs, outputs, and function formulations. The upper portion contains modules from prior work used for visual question answering, while the bottom portion lists our novel modules designed to handle additional challenges in visual dialog.

Name	Inputs	Output	Function
Neural modules for VQA [18]			
Find	x_{vis}, x_{txt}	attention	$y = \text{conv}_2(\text{conv}_1(x_{vis} \odot W x_{txt}))$
Relocate	a, x_{vis}, x_{txt}	attention	$\tilde{y} = W_1\text{sum}(a \odot x_{vis})$
			$y = \text{conv}_2(\text{conv}_1(x_{vis}) \odot \tilde{y} \odot W_2 x_{txt})$
And	a_1, a_2	attention	$y = \min\{a_1, a_2\}$
Or	a_1, a_2	attention	$y = \max\{a_1, a_2\}$
Exist	a, x_{vis}, x_{txt}	context	$y = W^T \text{vec}(a)$
Describe	a, x_{vis}, x_{txt}	context	$y = W_1^T(W_2\text{sum}(a \odot x_{vis}) \odot W_3 x_{txt})$
Count	a, x_{vis}, x_{txt}	context	$y = W_1^T([\text{vec}(a), \max\{a\}, \min\{a\}])$
Neural modules for coreference resolution (Ours)			
Not	a	attention	$y = \text{norm}_{L_1}(1 - a)$
Refer	x_{txt}, P_{ref}	attention	(see text for details, (3))
Exclude	a, x_{vis}, x_{txt}	attention	$y = \text{And}[\text{Find}[x_{vis}, x_{txt}], \text{Not}[a]]$

entities mentioned so far in the dialog with their corresponding visual groundings. Interestingly, even though x_{txt} and y are intermediate outputs from our model, both are easily interpretable, making our reference pool a *semantic dictionary*. To the best of our knowledge, our model is the first to attempt explicit, interpretable coreference resolution in visual dialog. While [37] maintains a dictionary similar to P_{ref}, they do not consider word/entity level coreferences nor do their keys lend similar interpretability as ours. With $P_{ref} = \{(x_p^{(i)}, a_p^{(i)})\}_i$ as input to Refer, we can now resolve references in Q_t.

Refer Module. This novel module is responsible for resolving references in the question Q_t and ground them in the conversation history H. To enable grounding in dialog history, we generalize the above formulation to give the module access to a pool of references P_{ref} of previously identified entities. Specifically, Refer only takes the text embedding x_{txt} and the reference pool P_{ref} as inputs, and resolves the entity represented by x_{txt} in the form of a soft attention α over Q_t. in this section after introducing P_{ref}. For the example shown in Fig. 2, α for Refer attends to '*it*', indicating the phrase it is trying to resolve.

At a high level, Refer treats x_{txt} as a 'query' and retrieves the most likely match from P_{ref} as measured by some similarity with respect to keys $\{x_p^{(i)}\}_i$ in P_{ref}. The associated image attention map of the best match is used as the visual grounding for the phrase that needed resolution (i.e. '*it*'). More concretely, we first learn a *scoring network* which when given a query x_{txt} and a possible candidate $x_p^{(i)}$, returns a scalar value s_i indicating how likely these text features refer to the same entity (1). To enable Refer to consider the sequential nature of dialog when assessing a potential candidate, we additionally provide $\Delta_i t$, a measure of the 'distance' of a candidate $x_p^{(i)}$ from x_{txt} in the dialog history, as input to the scoring network. $\Delta_i t$ is formulated as the absolute difference between the round of x_{txt} (current round t) and the round when $x_p^{(i)}$ was first mentioned. Collecting these scores from all the candidates, we apply a softmax function to compute contributions $\tilde{s}_i$ from each entity in the pool (2). Finally, we weigh the corresponding attention maps via these contributions to obtain the visual grounding a_{out} for x_{txt} (3).

$$s_i = \text{MLP}([x_{txt}, x_p^{(i)}, \Delta_i t]) \tag{1}$$

$$\tilde{s}_i = \text{Softmax}(s_i) \tag{2}$$

$$a_{out} = \sum_{i=1}^{|P_{ref}|} \tilde{s}_i a_p^{(i)} \tag{3}$$

Not Module. Designed to focus on regions of the image **not** attended by the input attention map a, it outputs $y = \text{norm}_{L_1}(1-a)$, where $\text{norm}_{L_1}(.)$ normalizes the entries to sum to one. This module is used in Exclude, described next.

Exclude Module. To handle questions like *'What other red things are present?'*, which seek other objects/attributes in the image than those specified by an input attention map a, we introduce yet another novel module – Exclude. It is constructed using Find, Not, and And modules as $y = \text{And}[\text{Find}[x_{txt}, x_{vis}],$ $\text{Not}[a]]$, where x_{txt} is the text feature input to the Exclude module, for example, *'red things'*. More explicitly, Find first localizes all objects instances/attributes in the image. Next, we focus on regions of the image other than those specified by a using Not$[a]$. Finally, the above two outputs are combined via And to obtain the output y of the Exclude module.

3.3   Program Generation

A *program* specifies the network layout for the neural modules for a given question Q_t. Following [18], it is serialized through the reverse polish notation (RPN) [9]. This serialization helps us convert a hard, structured prediction problem into a more tractable sequence prediction problem. In other words, we need a program predictor to output a series of module tokens in order, such that a valid layout can be retrieved from it. There are two primary design considerations for our predictor. First, in addition to the program, our predictor must also output a soft attention α_{ti}, over the question Q_t, for every module m_i in the program. This attention is responsible for the *correct* module instantiation in the current context. For example, to answer the question *'What color is the cat sitting next to the dog?'*, a Find module instance attending to *'cat'* qualitatively serves a different purpose than one attending to *'dog'*. This is implemented by using the attention over Q_t to compute the text embedding x_{txt} that is directly fed as an input to the module during execution. Second, to decide whether an entity in

Q_t has been seen before in the conversation, it must be able to 'peek' into the history H. Note that this is unique to our current problem and does not exist in [18]. To this effect, we propose a novel augmentation of attentional recurrent neural networks [7] with memory [42] to address both the requirements (Fig. 2).

The program generation proceeds as follows. First, each of the words in Q_t are embedded to give $\{w_{ti}\}_{i=1}^T$, where T denotes the number of tokens in Q_t. We then use a *question encoder*, a multi-layer LSTM, to process w_{ti}'s, resulting in a sequence of hidden states $\{\hat{w}_{ti}\}_{i=1}^T$ (4). Notice that the last hidden state h_T is the question encoding, which we denote with q_t. Next, each piece of history $(H_i)_{i=0}^{t-1}$ is processed in a similar way by a *history encoder*, which is a multi-layer LSTM akin to the question encoder. This produces encodings $(h_i)_{i=0}^{t-1}$ (5) that serve as memory units to help the program predictor 'peek' into the conversation history. Using the question encoding q_t, we attend over the history encodings $(h_i)_{i=0}^{t-1}$, and obtain the history vector $\hat{h}_t$ (6). The history-agnostic question encoding q_t is then fused with the history vector $\hat{h}_t$ via a fully connected layer to give a history-aware question encoding $\hat{q}_t$ (7), which is fed into the *program decoder*.

Question Encoder

$$\{\hat{w}_{ti}\} = \mathrm{LSTM}(\{w_{ti}\}) \tag{4}$$
$$q_t = \hat{w}_{tT}$$

History Memory

$$\hat{h}_i = \mathrm{LSTM}(h_i) \tag{5}$$
$$\beta_{ti} = \mathrm{Softmax}(q_t^T \hat{h}_i)$$
$$\hat{h}_t = \sum_{i=0}^{t-1} \beta_{ti}\hat{h}_i \tag{6}$$
$$\hat{q}_t = \mathrm{MLP}([q_t, \hat{h}_t]) \tag{7}$$

Program Decoder

$$\tilde{u}_{ti}^{(j)} = \mathrm{Linear}([\hat{w}_{tj}, d_{ti}])$$
$$u_{ti}^{(j)} = v^T \tanh(\tilde{u}_{ti}^{(j)})$$
$$\alpha_{ti}^{(j)} = \mathrm{Softmax}(u_{ti}^{(j)})$$
$$e_{ti} = \sum_{j=1}^{T} \alpha_{ti}^{(j)} \hat{w}_{tj} \tag{8}$$
$$\tilde{e}_{ti} = \mathrm{MLP}([e_{ti}, d_{ti}]) \tag{9}$$
$$p(m_i | \{m_k\}_{k=1}^{i-1}, Q_t, H) = \mathrm{Softmax}(\tilde{e}_{ti}) \tag{10}$$

The decoder is another multi-layer LSTM network (with hidden states $\{d_{ti}\}$) which, at every time step i, produces a soft attention map α_{ti} over the input sequence (Q_t) [7]. This soft attention map for each module is used to compute the corresponding text embedding, $x_{txt} = \sum_j \alpha_{ti}^{(j)} w_{tj}$. Finally, to predict a module token m_i at time step i, a weighted sum of encoder hidden states e_{ti} (8) and the history-aware question vector $\hat{q}_t$ are combined via another fully-connected layer (9), followed by a softmax to give a distribution $P(m_i | \{m_k\}_{k=1}^{i-1}, Q_t, H)$ over the module tokens (10). During training, we minimize the cross-entropy loss $\mathcal{L}_Q^{prog}$ between this predicted distribution and the ground truth program tokens. Fig. 2 outlines the schematics of our program generator.

Modules on Captions. As the image caption C is also a part of the dialog (history H_0 at round 0), it is desirable to track entities from C via the coreference pool P_{ref}. To this effect, we propose a novel extension of neural module networks to captions by using an auxiliary task that checks the alignment of a (caption, image) pair. First, we learn to predict a program from C, different from those generated from Q_t, by minimizing the negative log-likelihood $\mathcal{L}_C^{prog}$, akin to $\mathcal{L}_Q^{prog}$, of the ground truth caption program. Next, we execute the caption program on two images $I^+ = I$ and I^- (a random image from the dataset), to produce caption context vectors c_C^+ and c_C^-, respectively. Note that c_C^+ and c_C^- are different from the context vector c_t produced from execution of the question program. Finally, we learn a binary classifier on top to output classes $+1/-1$ for c_C^+ and c_C^-, respectively, by minimizing the binary cross entropy loss $\mathcal{L}_C^{aux}$. The intuition behind the auxiliary task is: to rightly classify aligned (C, I^+) from misaligned (C, I^-), the modules will need to localize and focus on salient entities in the caption. These entities (specifically, outputs from Find in the caption program) are then collected in P_{ref} for explicit coreference resolution on Q_t.

Entities in Answers. Using an analogous argument as above, answers from the previous rounds $\{A_i\}_{i=1}^{t-1}$ could have entities necessary to resolve coreferences in Q_t. For example, '*Q: What is the boy holding? A: A ball. Q: What color is it?*' requires resolving 'it' with the 'ball' mentioned in the earlier answer. To achieve this, at the end of round $t-1$, we encode $H_{t-1} = (Q_{t-1}, A_{t-1})$ as h_t^{ref} using a multi-layer LSTM, obtain the last image attention map a fed to the last module in the program that produced the context vector c_t, and add (h^{ref}, a) as an additional candidate to the reference pool P_{ref}. Notice that h^{ref} contains the information about the answer A_{t-1} in the context of the question Q_{t-1}, while a denotes the image attention which was the last crucial step in arriving at A_{t-1} in the earlier round. In resolving coreferences in Q_t, if any, all the answers from previous rounds now become potential candidates by virtue of being in P_{ref}.

3.4   Other Model Components

Program Execution. This component takes the generated program and associated text features x_{txt} for each participating module, and executes it. To do so, we first deserialize the given program from its RPN to a hierarchical module layout. Next, we arrange the modules dynamically according to the layout, giving us the network to answer Q_t. At this point, the network is a simple feed-forward neural network, where we start the computation from the leaf modules and feed outputs activations from modules at one layer as inputs into modules at the next layer (see Fig. 2). Finally, we feed a context vector c_t produced from the last module into the next answer decoding component.

Answer Decoding. This is the last component of our model that uses the context vector c_t to score answers from a pool of candidates $\mathcal{A}_t$, based on their correctness. The answer decoder: (a) encodes each candidate $A_t^{(i)} \in \mathcal{A}_t$ with a multi-layer LSTM to obtain $o_t^{(i)}$, (b) computes a score via a dot product with the context vector, i.e., $c_t^T o_t^{(i)}$, and (c) applies a softmax activation to get a distribution over the candidates. During training, we minimize the negative log-likelihood $\mathcal{L}_A^{dec}$ of the ground truth answer A_t^{gt}. At test time, the candidate with the maximum score is picked as $\mathcal{A}_t$. Using nomenclature from [11], this is a *discriminative* decoder. Note that our approach is not limited to a discriminative decoder, but can also be used with a *generative* decoder (see supplement).

Training Details. Our model components have fully differentiable operations within them. Thus, to train our model, we combine the supervised loss terms from both program generation $\{\mathcal{L}_Q^{prog}, \mathcal{L}_C^{prog}, \mathcal{L}_C^{aux}\}$ and answer decoding $\{\mathcal{L}_A^{dec}\}$, and minimize the sum total loss $\mathcal{L}^{total}$.

4   Experiments

We first show results on the synthetic MNIST Dialog dataset [37], designed to contain complex coreferences across rounds while being relatively easy textually and visually. It is important to resolve these coreferences accurately in order to do well on this dataset, thus stress testing our model. We then experiment with a large visual dialog dataset on real images, VisDial [11], which offers both linguistic and perceptual challenge in resolving visual coreferences and grounding them in the image. Implementation details are in the supplement.

4.1   MNIST Dialog Dataset

Dataset. The dialogs in the MNIST dialog dataset [37] are grounded in images composed from a 4×4 grid of MNIST digits [23]. Digits in the grid have four attributes—digit class $(0 - 9)$, color, stroke, and background color. Each dialog has 10 question-answer pairs, where the questions are generated through language templates, and the answers are single words. Further, the questions are designed to query attributes of target digit(s), count digits with similar attributes, etc., all of which need tracking of the target digits(s) by resolving references across dialog rounds. Thus, coreference resolution plays a crucial part in the reasoning required to answer the question, making the MNIST dataset both interesting and challenging (Fig. 3). The dataset contains $30k$ training, $10k$ validation, and $10k$ test images, with three 10-round dialogs for each image.

Models and Baselines. Taking advantage of single-word answers in this dataset, we simplify our answer decoder to be a N-way classifier, where N is

Table 2. Answer accuracy on MNIST Dialog dataset. Higher the better. Our CorefNMN outperforms all other models with a near perfect accuracy on test set.

Model	Acc.
I [37]	20.2
Q [37]	36.6
AMEM\Seq [37]	89.2
AMEM [37]	96.4
NMN [18]	23.8
CorefNMN\Seq	88.7
CorefNMN	**99.3**

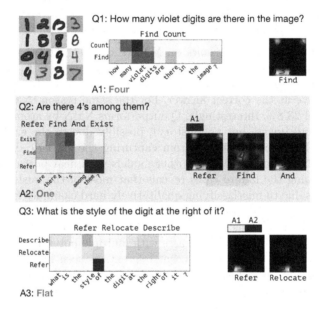

Fig. 3. Illustration of explicit coreference resolution reasoning of our model on the MNIST dialog dataset. For each question, a program and corresponding attentions (α's) over question words (hot matrix on the left) is predicted. A layout is unpacked from the program, and modules are connected to form a feed-forward network used to answer the question, shown in green to indicate correctness. We also visualize output attention maps (right) from each participating module. Specifically, in Q1 and Q2, Find localizes all violet digits and 4's, respectively (indicated by the corresponding α). In Q2, Refer resolves *'them'* and borrows the visual grounding from previous question.

the number of possible answers. Specifically, the context vector c_t now passes through a fully connected layer of size N, followed by softmax activations to give us a distribution over possible answer classes. At training time, we minimize the cross-entropy $\mathcal{L}_A^{dec}$ of the predicted answer distribution with the ground truth answer, at every round. Note that single-word answers also simplify evaluation as answer accuracy can now be used to compare different models. We further simplify our model by removing the memory augmentation to the program generator, i.e., $\hat{q}_t = q_t$ (7), and denote it as CorefNMN. In addition to the full model, we also evaluate an ablation, CorefNMN\Seq, without $\Delta_i t$ that additionally captured sequential nature of dialog (see `Refer` description). We compete against the explicit reasoning model (NMN) [18] and a comprehensive set of baselines AMEM, image-only (I), and question-only (Q), all from [37].

Supervision. In addition to the ground truth answer, we also need program supervision for questions to learn the program generation. For each of the 5 'types' of questions, we manually create one program which we apply as supervision for all questions of the corresponding type. The type of question is provided with the question. Note that our model needs program supervision only while training, and uses predictions from program generator at test time.

Results. Table 2 shows the results on MNIST dataset. The following are the key observations: (a) The text-only Q (36.6%) and image-only I (20.2%) do not perform well, perhaps as expected as MNIST Dialog needs resolving strong coreferences to arrive at the correct answer. For the same reason, NMN [18] has a low accuracy of 23.8%. Interestingly, Q outperforms NMN by around 13% (both use question and image, but not history), possibly due to the explicit reasoning nature of NMN prohibiting it from capturing the statistic dataset priors. (b) Our CorefNMN outperforms all other models with near perfect accuracy of 99.3%. Examining the failure cases reveals that most of the mistakes made by CorefNMN was due to misclassifying qualitatively hard examples from the original MNIST dataset. (c) Factoring the sequential nature of the dialog additionally in the model is beneficial, as indicated by the 10.6% improvement in CorefNMN, and 7.2% in AMEM. Intuitively, phrases with multiple potential referents, more often than not, refer to the most recent referent, as seen in Fig. 1, where *'it'* has to be resolved to the closest referent in history. Figure 3 shows a qualitative example.

4.2 VisDial Dataset

Dataset. The VisDial dataset [11] is a crowd-sourced dialog dataset on COCO images [25], with free-form answers. The publicly available VisDial v0.9 contains 10-round dialogs on around $83k$ training images, and $40k$ validation images. VisDial was collected from pairs of human workers, by instructing one of them to ask questions in a live chat interface to help them imagine the scene better. Thus, the dialogs contain a lot of coreferences in natural language, which need to be resolved to answer the questions accurately.

Models and Baselines. In addition to the CorefNMN model described in Sect. 3, we also consider ablations without the memory network augmented program generator (CorefNMN\Mem) or the auxiliary loss $\mathcal{L}_C^{aux}$ to train modules on captions (CorefNMN\$\mathcal{L}_C^{aux}$), and without both (CorefNMN\Mem\$\mathcal{L}_C^{aux}$).

As strong baselines, we consider: (a) neural module network without history [18] with answer generation, (b) the best *discriminative* model based on memory networks MN-QIH-D from [11], (c) history-conditioned image attentive encoder (HCIAE-D-MLE) [26], and (d) Attention-based visual coreference model (AMEM+SEQ-QI) [37]. We use ImageNet pretrained VGG-16 [38] to extract x_{vis}, and also ResNet-152 [17] for CorefNMN. Further comparisons are in supplement.

Evaluation. Evaluation in visual dialog is via retrieval of the ground truth answer A_t^{gt} from a pool of 100 candidate answers $\mathcal{A}_t = \{A_t^{(1)}, \cdots A_t^{(100)}\}$. These candidates are ranked based the discriminative decoder scores. We report Recall@k for $k = \{1, 5, 10\}$, mean rank, and mean reciprocal rank (MRR), as suggested by [11], on the set of $40k$ validation images (there is not test available for v0.9).

Supervision. In addition to the ground truth answer A_t^{gt} at each round, our model gets program supervision for Q_t, to train the program generator. We automatically obtain (weak) program supervision from a language parser on questions (and captions) [19] and supervision to predict for `Refer` from an off-the-shelf text coreference resolution tool[1], based on [10]. For questions that are a part of coreference chain, we replace `Find` with `Refer` in the parser supervised program. Our model predicts everything from the questions at test time.

Results. We summarize our observations from Table 3 below: (a) Our CorefNMN outperforms all other approaches across all the metrics, highlighting the importance of explicitly resolving coreferences for visual dialog. Specifically, our R@k $(k = 1, 2, 5)$ is at least 1 point higher than the best prior work

Table 3. Retrieval performance on the validation set of VisDial dataset [11] (discriminative models) using VGG [38] features (except last row). Higher the better for mean reciprocal rank (MRR) and recall@k (R@1, R@5, R@10), while lower the better for mean rank. Our CorefNMN model outperforms all other models across all metrics.

Model	MRR	R@1	R@5	R@10	Mean
MN-QIH-D [11]	0.597	45.55	76.22	85.37	5.46
HCIAE-D-MLE [27]	0.614	47.73	77.50	86.35	5.15
AMEM+SEQ-QI [37]	0.623	48.53	78.66	87.43	4.86
NMN[18]	0.616	48.24	77.54	86.75	4.98
CorefNMN\Mem	0.618	48.56	77.76	86.95	4.92
CorefNMN\$\mathcal{L}_C^{aux}$	**0.636**	**50.49**	79.56	88.30	4.60
CorefNMN\Mem\$\mathcal{L}_C^{aux}$	0.617	48.47	77.54	86.77	4.99
CorefNMN	**0.636**	50.24	**79.81**	**88.51**	**4.53**
CorefNMN(ResNet-152)	0.641	50.92	80.18	88.81	4.45

---

[1] https://github.com/huggingface/neuralcoref

(AMEM+SEQ-QI), and almost 2 points higher than NMN. (b) Removing memory augmentation (CorefNMN\Mem) hurts performance uniformly over all metrics, as the model is unable to peek into history to decide when to resolve coreferences via the `Refer` module. Modules on captions seems to have varied effect on the full model, with decrease in R@1, but marginal increase or no effect in other metrics. (c) Fig. 4 illustrates the interpretable and grounded nature of our model.

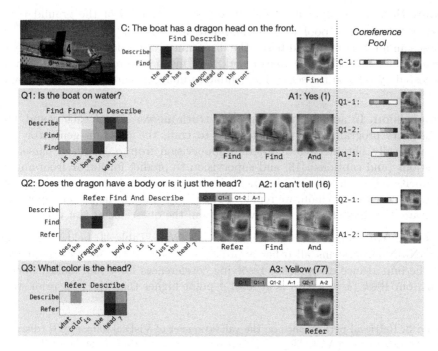

Fig. 4. Example to demonstrate explicit coreference resolution by our CorefNMN model. It begins by grounding *'dragon head'* from the caption C (shown on top), and saves it in the coreference pool P_{ref} (right). At this point however, it does not consider the entity *'boat'* important, and misses it. Next, to answer Q1, it localizes *'boat'* and *'water'*, both of which are 'unseen', and rightly answers with *Yes*. The ground truth rank (1 for Q1) is shown in the brackets. Additionally, it also registers these two entities in P_{ref} for coreference resolution in future dialog. For Q2, it refers the phrase *'the head'* to the referent registered as C-1, indicated by attention on the bar above `Refer`.

5   Conclusions

We introduced a novel model[2] for visual dialog based on neural module networks that provides an introspective reasoning about visual coreferences. It

---

[2] Code: https://github.com/facebookresearch/corefnmn/

explicitly links coreferences and grounds them in the image at a word-level, rather than implicitly or at a sentence-level, as in prior visual dialog work. Our CorefNMN outperforms prior work on both the MNIST dialog dataset (close to perfect accuracy), and on VisDial dataset, while being more interpretable, grounded, and consistent by construction.

Acknowledgment. This work was supported in part by NSF, AFRL, DARPA, Siemens, Google, Amazon, ONR YIPs and ONR Grants N00014-16-1-{2713,2793}, N000141210903. The views and conclusions contained herein are those of the authors and should not be interpreted as necessarily representing the official policies or endorsements, either expressed or implied, of the U.S. Government, or any sponsor.

References

1. Agrawal, A., Batra, D., Parikh, D.: Analyzing the behavior of visual question answering models. In: Proceedings of the Conference on Empirical Methods in Natural Language Processing (EMNLP) (2016)
2. Anderson, P. et al.: Bottom-up and top-down attention for image captioning and vqa. In: Proceedings of the IEEE Conference on Computer Vision and Pattern Recognition (CVPR) (2018)
3. Andreas, J., Rohrbach, M., Darrell, T., Klein, D.: Learning to compose neural networks for question answering (2016)
4. Andreas, J., Rohrbach, M., Darrell, T., Klein, D.: Neural module networks. In: Proceedings of the IEEE Conference on Computer Vision and Pattern Recognition (CVPR) (2016)
5. Hendricks, L.A., Wang, O., Shechtman, E., Sivic, J., Darrell, T., Russell, B.: Localizing moments in video with natural language. In: Proceedings of the IEEE International Conference on Computer Vision (ICCV) (2017)
6. Antol, S. et al.: Vqa: Visual question answering. In: Proceedings of the IEEE International Conference on Computer Vision (ICCV) (2015)
7. Bahdanau, D., Cho, K., Bengio, Y.: Neural machine translation by jointly learning to align and translate. In: Proceedings of the International Conference on Learning Representations (ICLR) (2015)
8. Bergsma, S., Lin, D.: Bootstrapping path-based pronoun resolution. In: Proceedings of the Annual Meeting of the Association for Computational Linguistics (ACL). Association for Computational Linguistics (2006)
9. Burks, A.W., Warren, D.W., Wright, J.B.: An analysis of a logical machine using parenthesis-free notation. Math. Tables Other Aids Comput. 8(46), 53–57 (1954). http://www.jstor.org/stable/2001990
10. Clark, K., Manning, C.D.: Deep reinforcement learning for mention-ranking coreference models. In: Proceedings of the Conference on Empirical Methods in Natural Language Processing (EMNLP) (2016)
11. Das, A. et al.: Visual dialog. In: CVPR (2017)
12. Das, A., Kottur, S., Moura, J.M., Lee, S., Batra, D.: Learning cooperative visual dialog agents with deep reinforcement learning. arXiv preprint arXiv:1703.06585 (2017)
13. Fukui, A., Park, D.H., Yang, D., Rohrbach, A., Darrell, T., Rohrbach, M.: Multimodal compact bilinear pooling for visual question answering and visual grounding. In: Proceedings of the Conference on Empirical Methods in Natural Language Processing (EMNLP) (2016)

14. Geman, D., Geman, S., Hallonquist, N., Younes, L.: Visual Turing Test for computer vision systems. In: Proceedings of the National Academy of Sciences (2015)
15. Goyal, Y., Khot, T., Summers-Stay, D., Batra, D., Parikh, D.: Making the v in vqa matter: elevating the role of image understanding in visual question answering. In: Proceedings of the IEEE Conference on Computer Vision and Pattern Recognition (CVPR) (2017)
16. Grice, H.P.: Logic and conversation. In: Cole, P., Morgan, J.L. (eds.) Syntax and Semantics: Vol. 3: Speech Acts, pp. 41–58. Academic Press, New York (1975). http://www.ucl.ac.uk/ls/studypacks/Grice-Logic.pdf
17. He, K., Zhang, X., Ren, S., Sun, J.: Deep residual learning for image recognition. In: Proceedings of the IEEE Conference on Computer Vision and Pattern Recognition (CVPR) (2016)
18. Hu, R., Andreas, J., Rohrbach, M., Darrell, T., Saenko, K.: Learning to reason: End-to-end module networks for visual question answering. In: Proceedings of the IEEE International Conference on Computer Vision (ICCV) (2017)
19. Hu, R., Xu, H., Rohrbach, M., Feng, J., Saenko, K., Darrell, T.: Natural language object retrieval. In: Proceedings of the IEEE Conference on Computer Vision and Pattern Recognition (CVPR) (2016)
20. Johnson, J., Hariharan, B., van der Maaten, L., Fei-Fei, L., Zitnick, C.L., Girshick, R.: Clevr: a diagnostic dataset for compositional language and elementary visual reasoning. In: Proceedings of the IEEE Conference on Computer Vision and Pattern Recognition (CVPR). IEEE (2017)
21. Johnson, J. et al.: Inferring and executing programs for visual reasoning. In: Proceedings of the IEEE International Conference on Computer Vision (ICCV) (2017)
22. Kong, C., Lin, D., Bansal, M., Urtasun, R., Fidler, S.: What are you talking about? text-to-image coreference. In: Proceedings of the IEEE Conference on Computer Vision and Pattern Recognition (CVPR) (2014)
23. LeCun, Y., Cortes, C.: MNIST handwritten digit database (2010). http://yann.lecun.com/exdb/mnist/
24. Lin, D., Fidler, S., Kong, C., Urtasun, R.: Visual semantic search: Retrieving videos via complex textual queries. In: Proceedings of the IEEE Conference on Computer Vision and Pattern Recognition (CVPR) (2014)
25. Lin, T.Y., et al.: Microsoft COCO: common objects in context. In: Proceedings of the European Conference on Computer Vision (ECCV) (2014)
26. Lu, J., Kannan, A., Yang, J., Parikh, D., Batra, D.: Best of both worlds: transferring knowledge from discriminative learning to a generative visual dialog model. In: Advances in Neural Information Processing Systems (NIPS) (2017)
27. Lu, J., Yang, J., Batra, D., Parikh, D.: Hierarchical question-image co-attention for visual question answering. In: Advances in Neural Information Processing Systems (NIPS) (2016)
28. Malinowski, M., Rohrbach, M., Fritz, M.: Ask your neurons: a neural-based approach to answering questions about images. In: Proceedings of the IEEE International Conference on Computer Vision (ICCV) (2015)
29. Mao, J., Huang, J., Toshev, A., Camburu, O., Yuille, A., Murphy, K.: Generation and comprehension of unambiguous object descriptions. In: Proceedings of the IEEE Conference on Computer Vision and Pattern Recognition (CVPR) (2016)
30. Massiceti, D., Siddharth, N., Dokania, P.K., Torr, P.H.S.: Flipdial: A generative model for two-way visual dialogue (2018)

31. Mitchell, M., van Deemter, K., Reiter, E.: Generating expressions that refer to visible objects. In: Proceedings of the 2013 Conference of the North American Chapter of the Association for Computational Linguistics: Human Language Technologies, pp. 1174–1184. Association for Computational Linguistics, Atlanta, Georgia, June 2013. http://www.aclweb.org/anthology/N13-1137

32. Plummer, B., Wang, L., Cervantes, C., Caicedo, J., Hockenmaier, J., Lazebnik, S.: Flickr30k entities: collecting region-to-phrase correspondences for richer image-to-sentence models. In: Proceedings of the IEEE International Conference on Computer Vision (ICCV) (2015)

33. Ramanathan, V., Joulin, A., Liang, P., Fei-Fei, L.: Linking people in videos with "their" names using coreference resolution. In: Proceedings of the European Conference on Computer Vision (ECCV) (2014)

34. Regneri, M., Rohrbach, M., Wetzel, D., Thater, S., Schiele, B., Pinkal, M.: Grounding action descriptions in videos. Trans. Assoc. Comput. Linguist. (TACL) 1, 25–36 (2013)

35. Rohrbach, A., Rohrbach, M., Hu, R., Darrell, T., Schiele, B.: Grounding of textual phrases in images by reconstruction. In: Proceedings of the European Conference on Computer Vision (ECCV) (2016)

36. Rohrbach, A., Rohrbach, M., Tang, S., Oh, S.J., Schiele, B.: Generating descriptions with grounded and co-referenced people. In: Proceedings of the IEEE Conference on Computer Vision and Pattern Recognition (CVPR) (2017)

37. Seo, P.H., Lehrmann, A., Han, B., Sigal, L.: Visual reference resolution using attention memory for visual dialog. In: Advances in Neural Information Processing Systems (NIPS) (2017)

38. Simonyan, K., Zisserman, A.: Very deep convolutional networks for large-scale image recognition. In: Proceedings of the International Conference on Learning Representations (ICLR) (2015)

39. Strub, F., de Vries, H., Mary, J., Piot, B., Courville, A.C., Pietquin, O.: End-to-end optimization of goal-driven and visually grounded dialogue systems. In: Proceedings of the International Joint Conference on Artificial Intelligence (IJCAI) (2017)

40. de Vries, H., Strub, F., Chandar, S., Pietquin, O., Larochelle, H., Courville, A.C.: Guesswhat?! visual object discovery through multi-modal dialogue. In: Proceedings of the IEEE Conference on Computer Vision and Pattern Recognition (CVPR) (2017)

41. Wang, L., Li, Y., Lazebnik, S.: Learning deep structure-preserving image-text embeddings. In: Proceedings of the IEEE Conference on Computer Vision and Pattern Recognition (CVPR) (2016)

42. Weston, J., Chopra, S., Bordes, A.: Memory networks. In: Proceedings of the International Conference on Learning Representations (ICLR) (2015)

43. Winograd, T.: Procedures as a representation for data in a computer program for understanding natural language. Technical report, DTIC Document (1971)

44. Winograd, T.: Understanding Natural Language. Academic Press Inc., Orlando, FL, USA (1972)

45. Yu, H., Siskind, J.M.: Grounded language learning from videos described with sentences. In: Proceedings of the Annual Meeting of the Association for Computational Linguistics (ACL) (2013)

46. Yu, L., Poirson, P., Yang, S., Berg, A.C., Berg, T.L.: Modeling context in referring expressions. In: Proceedings of the European Conference on Computer Vision (ECCV) (2016)
47. Zhang, P., Goyal, Y., Summers-Stay, D., Batra, D., Parikh, D.: Yin and Yang: balancing and answering binary visual questions. In: Proceedings of the IEEE Conference on Computer Vision and Pattern Recognition (CVPR) (2016)

Learning Blind Video Temporal Consistency

Wei-Sheng Lai[1]([✉]), Jia-Bin Huang[2], Oliver Wang[3], Eli Shechtman[3], Ersin Yumer[4], and Ming-Hsuan Yang[1,5]

[1] UC Merced, Merced, USA
wlai24@ucmerced.edu
[2] Virginia Tech, Blacksburg, USA
[3] Adobe Research, Seattle, USA
[4] Argo AI, Mountain View, USA
[5] Google Cloud AI, Sunnyvale, USA

Abstract. Applying image processing algorithms independently to each frame of a video often leads to undesired inconsistent results over time. Developing temporally consistent video-based extensions, however, requires domain knowledge for individual tasks and is unable to generalize to other applications. In this paper, we present an efficient approach based on a deep recurrent network for enforcing temporal consistency in a video. Our method takes the original and per-frame processed videos as inputs to produce a temporally consistent video. Consequently, our approach is agnostic to specific image processing algorithms applied to the original video. We train the proposed network by minimizing both short-term and long-term temporal losses as well as a perceptual loss to strike a balance between temporal coherence and perceptual similarity with the processed frames. At test time, our model does not require computing optical flow and thus achieves real-time speed even for high-resolution videos. We show that our single model can handle multiple and unseen tasks, including but not limited to artistic style transfer, enhancement, colorization, image-to-image translation and intrinsic image decomposition. Extensive objective evaluation and subject study demonstrate that the proposed approach performs favorably against the state-of-the-art methods on various types of videos.

1 Introduction

Recent advances of deep convolutional neural networks (CNNs) have led to the development of many powerful image processing techniques including, image filtering [30,37], enhancement [10,24,38], style transfer [17,23,29], colorization [19,41], and general image-to-image translation tasks [21,27,43]. However,

---

Electronic supplementary material The online version of this chapter (https://doi.org/10.1007/978-3-030-01267-0_11) contains supplementary material, which is available to authorized users.

V. Ferrari et al. (Eds.): ECCV 2018, LNCS 11219, pp. 179–195, 2018.
https://doi.org/10.1007/978-3-030-01267-0_11

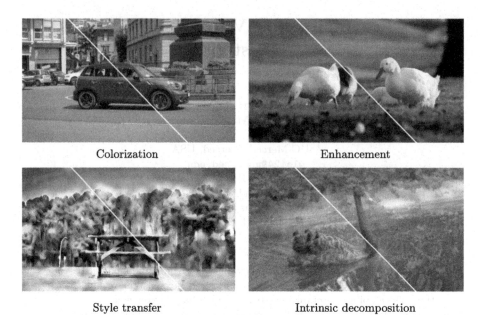

Colorization   Enhancement

Style transfer   Intrinsic decomposition

Fig. 1. Applications of the proposed method. Our algorithm takes per-frame processed videos with serious temporal flickering as inputs (lower-left) and generates temporally stable videos (upper-right) while maintaining perceptual similarity to the processed frames. Our method is blind to the specific image processing algorithm applied to input videos and runs at a high frame-rate. This figure contains *animated videos* (see supplementary material).

extending these CNN-based methods to video is non-trivial due to memory and computational constraints, and the availability of training datasets. Applying image-based algorithms independently to each video frame typically leads to temporal flickering due to the instability of global optimization algorithms or highly non-linear deep networks. One approach for achieving temporally coherent results is to explicitly embed flow-based temporal consistency loss in the design and training of the networks. However, such an approach suffers from two drawbacks. First, it requires domain knowledge to re-design the algorithm [1,16], re-train a deep model [12,15], and video datasets for training. Second, due to the dependency of flow computation at test time, these approaches tend to be slow.

Bonneel et al. [6] propose a general approach to achieve temporal coherent results that is *blind* to specific image processing algorithms. The method takes the original video and the per-frame processed video as inputs and solves a gradient-domain optimization problem to minimize the temporal warping error between consecutive frames. Although the results of Bonneel et al. [6] are temporally stable, their algorithm highly depends on the quality of dense correspondence (e.g., optical flow or PatchMatch [2]) and may fail when a severe occlusion occurs. Yao et al. [39] further extend the method of Bonneel et al. [6] to account for occlusion by selecting a set of key-frames. However, the computational cost increases linearly with the number of key-frames, and thus their approach cannot be efficiently applied to long video sequences. Furthermore, both approaches assume that the gradients of the original video are similar to the gradients of the processed video, which restricts them from handling tasks that may generate new contents (e.g., stylization).

In this work, we formulate the problem of video temporal consistency as a learning task. We propose to learn a deep recurrent network that takes the input and processed videos and generates temporally stable output videos. We minimize the short-term and long-term temporal losses between output frames and impose a perceptual loss from the pre-trained VGG network [34] to maintain the perceptual similarity between the output and processed frames. In addition, we embed a convolutional LSTM (ConvLSTM) [36] layer to capture the spatial-temporal correlation of natural videos. Our network processes video frames sequentially and can be applied to videos with arbitrary lengths. Furthermore, our model does not require computing optical flow at *test* time and thus can process videos at real-time rates (400+ FPS on 1280×720 videos).

As existing video datasets typically contain low-quality frames, we collect a high-quality video dataset with 80 videos for training and 20 videos for evaluation. We train our model on a wide range of applications, including colorization, image enhancement, and artistic style transfer, and demonstrate that a *single* trained model generalizes well to *unseen* applications (e.g., intrinsic image decomposition, image-to-image translation, see Fig. 1). We evaluate the quality of the output videos using temporal warping error and a learned perceptual metric [42]. We show that the proposed method strikes a good balance between maintaining the temporal stability and perceptual similarity. Furthermore, we conduct a user study to evaluate the subjective preference between the proposed method and state-of-the-art approaches.

We make the following contributions in this work:

1. We present an efficient solution to remove temporal flickering in videos via learning a deep network with a ConvLSTM module. Our method does not require pre-computed optical flow or frame correspondences at *test* time and thus can process videos in real-time.
2. We propose to minimize the short-term and long-term temporal loss for improving the temporal stability and adopt a perceptual loss to maintain the perceptual similarity.
3. We provide a *single* model for handling multiple applications, including but not limited to colorization, enhancement, artistic style transfer, image-to-image translation and intrinsic image decomposition. Extensive subject and objective evaluations demonstrate that the proposed algorithm performs favorably against existing approaches on various types of videos.

Table 1. Comparison of blind temporal consistency methods. Both the methods of Bonneel et al. [6] and Yao et al. [39] require dense correspondences from optical flow or PatchMatch [2], while the proposed method does not explicitly rely on these correspondences at test time. The algorithm of Yao et al. [39] involves a key-frame selection from the entire video and thus cannot generate output in an online manner.

	Bonneel et al. [6]	Yao et al. [39]	Ours
Content constraint	Gradient	Local affine	Perceptual loss
Short-term temporal constraint	✓	–	✓
Long-term temporal constraint	–	✓	✓
Require dense correspondences (at test time)	✓	✓	–
Online processing	✓	–	✓

2   Related Work

We address the temporal consistency problem on a wide range of applications, including automatic white balancing [14], harmonization [4], dehazing [13], image enhancement [10], style transfer [17,23,29], colorization [19,41], image-to-image translation [21,43], and intrinsic image decomposition [3]. A complete review of these applications is beyond the scope of this paper. In the following, we discuss task-specific and task-independent approaches that enforce temporal consistency on videos.

Task-Specific Approaches. A common solution to embed the temporal consistency constraint is to use optical flow to propagate information between frames, e.g., colorization [28] and intrinsic decomposition [40]. However, estimating optical flow is computationally expensive and thus is impractical to apply on high-resolution and long sequences. Temporal filtering is an efficient approach to extend image-based algorithms to videos, e.g., tone-mapping [1], color transfer [5], and visual saliency [25] to generate temporally consistent results. Nevertheless, these approaches assume a specific filter formulation and cannot be generalized to other applications.

Recently, several approaches have been proposed to improve the temporal stability of CNN-based image style transfer. Huang et al. [15] and Gupta et al. [12] train feed-forward networks by jointly minimizing content, style and temporal warping losses. These methods, however, are limited to the specific styles used during training. Chen et al. [7] learn flow and mask networks to adaptively blend the intermediate features of the pre-trained style network. While the architecture design is independent of the style network, it requires the access to intermediate features and cannot be applied to non-differentiable tasks. In contrast, the proposed model is entirely blind to specific algorithms applied to the input frames and thus is applicable to optimization-based techniques, CNN-based algorithms, and combinations of Photoshop filters.

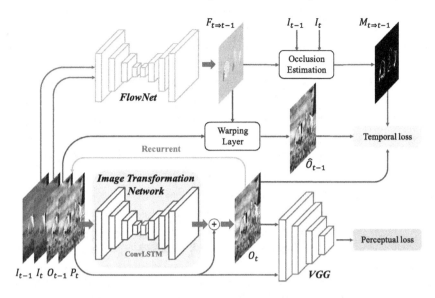

Fig. 2. Overview of the proposed method. We train an image transformation network that takes I_{t-1}, I_t, O_{t-1} and processed frame P_t as inputs and generates the output frame O_t which is temporally consistent with the output frame at the previous time step O_{t-1}. The output O_t at the current time step then becomes the input at the next time step. We train the image transformation network with the VGG perceptual loss and the short-term and long-term temporal losses.

Task-Independent Approaches. Several methods have been proposed to improve temporal consistency for multiple tasks. Lang et al. [25] approximate global optimization of a class of energy formulation (e.g., colorization, optical flow estimation) via temporal edge-aware filtering. In [9], Dong et al. propose a segmentation-based algorithm and assume that the image transformation is spatially and temporally consistent. More general approaches assume gradient similarity [6] or local affine transformation [39] between the input and the processed frames. These methods, however, cannot handle more complicated tasks (e.g., artistic style transfer). In contrast, we use the VGG perceptual loss [23] to impose high-level perceptual similarity between the output and processed frames. We list the feature-by-feature comparisons between Bonneel et al. [6], Yao et al. [39] and the proposed method in Table 1.

3 Learning Temporal Consistency

In this section, we describe the proposed recurrent network and the design of the loss functions for enforcing temporal consistency on videos.

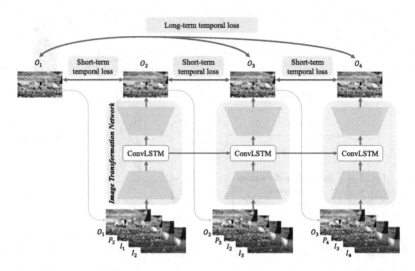

Fig. 3. Temporal losses. We adopt the short-term temporal loss on neighbor frames and long-term temporal loss between the first and all the output frames.

3.1 Recurrent Network

Figure 2 shows an overview of the proposed recurrent network. Our model takes as input the original (unprocessed) video $\{I_t | t = 1 \cdots T\}$ and per-frame processed videos $\{P_t | t = 1 \cdots T\}$, and produces temporally consistent output videos $\{O_t | t = 1 \cdots T\}$. In order to efficiently process videos with arbitrary length, we develop an image transformation network as a *recurrent convolutional network* to generate output frames in an online manner (i.e., sequentially from $t = 1$ to T). Specifically, we set the first output frame $O_1 = P_1$. In each time step, the network learns to generate an output frame O_t that is temporally consistent with respect to O_{t-1}. The current output frame is then fed as the input at the next time step. To capture the spatial-temporal correlation of videos, we integrate a ConvLSTM layer [36] into our image transformation network. We discuss the detailed design of our image transformation network in Sect. 3.3.

3.2 Loss Functions

Our goal is to reduce the temporal inconsistency in the output video while maintaining the perceptual similarity with the processed frames. Therefore, we propose to train our model with (1) a perceptual content loss between the output frame and the processed frame and (2) short-term and long-term temporal losses between output frames.

Content Perceptual Loss. We compute the similarity between O_t and P_t using the perceptual loss from a pre-trained VGG classification network [34], which is commonly adopted in several applications (e.g., style transfer [23], super-resolution [26], and image inpainting [31]) and has been shown to correspond well to human perception [42]. The perceptual loss is defined as:

$$\mathcal{L}_p = \sum_{t=2}^{T} \sum_{i=1}^{N} \sum_{l} \left\| \phi_l(O_t^{(i)}) - \phi_l(P_t^{(i)}) \right\|_1, \tag{1}$$

where $O_t^{(i)}$ represents a vector $\in R^3$ with RGB pixel values of the output O at time t, N is the total number of pixels in a frame, and $\phi_l(\cdot)$ denotes the feature activation at the l-th layer of the VGG-19 network ϕ. We choose the 4-th layer (i.e., relu4-3) to compute the perceptual loss.

Short-Term Temporal Loss. We formulate the temporal loss as the warping error between the output frames:

$$\mathcal{L}_{st} = \sum_{t=2}^{T} \sum_{i=1}^{N} M_{t \Rightarrow t-1}^{(i)} \left\| O_t^{(i)} - \hat{O}_{t-1}^{(i)} \right\|_1, \tag{2}$$

where $\hat{O}_{t-1}$ is the frame O_{t-1} warped by the optical flow $F_{t \Rightarrow t-1}$, and $M_{t \Rightarrow t-1} = \exp(-\alpha \| I_t - \hat{I}_{t-1} \|_2^2)$ is the visibility mask calculated from the warping error between input frames I_t and warped input frame $\hat{I}_{t-1}$. The optical flow $F_{t \Rightarrow t-1}$ is the backward flow between I_{t-1} and I_t. We use the FlowNet2 [20] to efficiently compute flow on-the-fly during training. We use the bilinear sampling layer [22] to warp frames and empirically set $\alpha = 50$ (with pixel range between $[0, 1]$).

Long-Term Temporal Loss. While the short-term temporal loss Eq. 2 enforces the temporal consistency between consecutive frames, there is no guarantee for long-term (e.g., more than 5 frames) coherence. A straightforward method to enforce long-term temporal consistency is to apply the temporal loss on *all* pairs of output frames. However, such a strategy requires significant computational costs (e.g., optical flow estimation) during training. Furthermore, computing temporal loss between two intermediate outputs is not meaningful before the network converges.

Instead, we propose to impose long-term temporal losses between the *first* output frame and all of the output frames:

$$\mathcal{L}_{lt} = \sum_{t=2}^{T} \sum_{i=1}^{N} M_{t \Rightarrow 1}^{(i)} \left\| O_t^{(i)} - \hat{O}_1^{(i)} \right\|_1. \tag{3}$$

We illustrate an unrolled version of our recurrent network as well as the short-term and long-term losses in Fig. 3. During the training, we enforce the long-term temporal coherence over a maximum of 10 frames ($T = 10$).

Overall Loss. The overall loss function for training our image transformation network is defined as:

$$\mathcal{L} = \lambda_p \mathcal{L}_p + \lambda_{st} \mathcal{L}_{st} + \lambda_{lt} \mathcal{L}_{lt}, \tag{4}$$

where λ_p, λ_{st} and λ_{lt} are the weights for the content perceptual loss, short-term and long-term losses, respectively.

3.3   Image Transformation Network

The input of our image transformation network is the concatenation of the currently processed frame P_t, previous output frame O_{t-1} as well as the current and previous unprocessed frames I_t, I_{t-1}. As the output frame typically looks similar to the currently processed frame, we train the network to predict the *residuals* instead of actual pixel values, i.e., $O_t = P_t + \mathcal{F}(P_t)$, where $\mathcal{F}$ denotes the image transformation network. Our image transformation network consists of two strided convolutional layers, B residual blocks, one ConvLSTM layer, and two transposed convolutional layers.

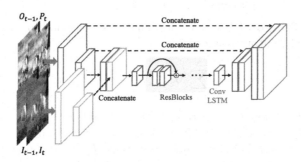

Fig. 4. Architecture of our image transformation network. We split the input into two streams to avoid transferring low-level information from the input frames to output.

We add skip connections from the encoder to the decoder to improve the reconstruction quality. However, for some applications, the processed frames may have a dramatically different appearance than the input frames (e.g., style transfer or intrinsic image decomposition). We observe that the skip connections may transfer low-level information (e.g., color) to the output frames and produce visual artifacts. Therefore, we divide the input into two streams: one for the processed frames P_t and O_{t-1}, and the other stream for input frames I_t and I_{t-1}. As illustrated in Fig. 4, the skip connections only add skip connections from the processed frames to avoid transferring the low-level information from the input frames. We provide all the implementation details in the supplementary material.

4   Experimental Results

In this section, we first describe the employed datasets for training and testing, followed by the applications of the proposed method and the metrics for evaluating the temporal stability and perceptual similarity. We then analyze the effect of each loss term in balancing the temporal coherence and perceptual similarity, conduct quantitative and subjective comparisons with existing approaches, and finally discuss the limitations of our method. The source code and datasets are publicly available at http://vllab.ucmerced.edu/wlai24/video_consistency.

4.1 Datasets

We use the DAVIS-2017 dataset [32], which is designed for video segmentation and contains a variety of moving objects and motion types. The DAVIS dataset has 60 videos for training and 30 videos for validation. However, the lengths of the videos in the DAVIS dataset are usually short (less than 3 s) with 4,209 training frames in total. Therefore, we collect additional 100 high-quality videos from Videvo.net [35], where 80 videos are used for training and 20 videos for testing. We scale the height of video frames to 480 and keep the aspect ratio. We use both the DAVIS and VIDEVO training sets, which contains a total of 25,735 frames, to train our network.

4.2 Applications

As we do not make any assumptions on the underlying image-based algorithms, our method is applicable for handling a wide variety of applications.

Artistic Style Transfer. The tasks of image style transfer have been shown to be sensitive to minor changes in content images due to the non-convexity of the Gram matrix matching objective [12]. We apply our method to the results from the state-of-the-art style transfer approaches [23,29].

Colorization. Single image colorization aims to hallucinate plausible colors from a given grayscale input image. Recent algorithms [19,41] learn deep CNNs from millions of natural images. When applying colorization methods to a video frame-by-frame, those approaches typically produce low-frequency flickering.

Image Enhancement. Gharbi et al. [10] train deep networks to learn the user-created action scripts of Adobe Photoshop for enhancing images. Their models produce high-frequency flickering on most of the videos.

Intrinsic Image Decomposition. Intrinsic image decomposition aims to decompose an image into a reflectance and a shading layer. The problem is highly ill-posed due to the scale ambiguity. We apply the approach of Bell et al. [3] to our test videos. As expected, the image-based algorithm produces serious temporal flickering artifacts when applied to each frame in the video independently.

Image-to-Image Translation. In recent years, the image-to-image translation tasks attract considerable attention due to the success of the Generative Adversarial Networks (GAN) [11]. The CycleGAN model [43] aims to learn mappings from one image domain to another domain without using paired training data. When the transformations generate a new texture on images (e.g., photo $\rightarrow$ painting, horse $\rightarrow$ zebra) or the mapping contains multiple plausible solutions (e.g., gray $\rightarrow$ RGB), the resulting videos inevitably suffer from temporal flickering artifacts.

The above algorithms are general and can be applied to any type of videos. When applied, they produce temporal flickering artifacts on most videos in our test sets. We use the WCT [29] style transfer algorithm with three style images, one of the enhancement models of Gharbi et al. [10], the colorization method of

Zhang et al. [41] and the shading layer of Bell et al. [3] as our training tasks, with the rest of the tasks being used for testing purposes. We demonstrate that the proposed method learns a *single* model for multiple applications and also generalizes to *unseen* tasks.

4.3   Evaluation Metrics

Our goal is to generate a temporally smooth video while maintaining the perceptual similarity with the per-frame processed video. We use the following metrics to measure the temporal stability and perceptual similarity on the output videos.

Temporal Stability. We measure the temporal stability of a video based on the flow warping error between two frames:

$$E_{\text{warp}}(V_t, V_{t+1}) = \frac{1}{\sum_{i=1}^{N} M_t^{(i)}} \sum_{i=1}^{N} M_t^{(i)} \| V_t^{(i)} - \hat{V}_{t+1}^{(i)} \|_2^2, \tag{5}$$

where $\hat{V}_{t+1}$ is the warped frame V_{t+1} and $M_t \in \{0, 1\}$ is a non-occlusion mask indicating non-occluded regions. We use the occlusion detection method in [33] to estimate the mask M_t. The warping error of a video is calculated as:

$$E_{\text{warp}}(V) = \frac{1}{T-1} \sum_{t=1}^{T-1} E_{\text{warp}}(V_t, V_{t+1}), \tag{6}$$

which is the average warping error over the entire sequence.

Perceptual Similarity. Recently, the features of the pre-trained VGG network [34] have been shown effective as a training loss to generate realistic images in several vision tasks [8,26,31]. Zhang et al. [42] further propose a perceptual metric by calibrating the deep features of ImageNet classification networks. We adopt the calibrated model of the SqueezeNet [18] (denote as $\mathcal{G}$) to measure the perceptual distance of the processed video P and output video O:

$$D_{\text{perceptual}}(P, O) = \frac{1}{T-1} \sum_{t=2}^{T} \mathcal{G}(O_t, P_t). \tag{7}$$

We note that the first frame is fixed as a reference in both Bonneel et al. [6] and our algorithm. Therefore, we exclude the first frame from computing the perceptual distance in Eq. 7.

4.4   Analysis and Discussions

An extremely blurred video may have high temporal stability but with low perceptual similarity; in contrast, the processed video itself has perfect perceptual similarity but is temporally unstable. Due to the trade-off between the temporal stability and perceptual similarity, it is important to balance these two properties and produce visually pleasing results.

To understand the relationship between the temporal and content losses, we train models with the several combinations of λ_p and λ_t $(= \lambda_{st} = \lambda_{lt})$. We use one of the styles (i.e., udnie) from the fast neural style transfer method [23] for evaluation. We show the quantitative evaluation on the DAVIS test set in Fig. 5. We observe that the ratio $r = \lambda_t/\lambda_p$ plays an important role in balancing the temporal stability and perceptual similarity. When the ratio $r < 10$, the perceptual loss dominates the optimization of the network, and the temporal flickering remains in the output videos. When the ratio $r > 10$, the output videos become overly blurred and therefore have a large perceptual distance to the processed videos. When λ_t is sufficiently large (i.e., $\lambda_t \geq 100$), the setting $r = 10$ strikes a good balance to reduce temporal flickering while maintaining small perceptual distance. Our results find similar observation on other applications as well.

λ_t	λ_p	$r = \frac{\lambda_t}{\lambda_p}$	E_{warp}	$D_{\mathrm{perceptual}}$
10	0.01	1000	0.0279	0.1744
10	0.1	100	0.0265	0.1354
10	1	10	0.0615	0.0071
10	10	1	0.0621	0.0072
100	1	100	0.0277	0.1324
100	10	10	0.0442	0.0170
100	100	1	0.0621	0.0072
1000	1	1000	0.0262	0.1848
1000	10	100	0.0275	0.1341
1000	100	10	0.0453	0.0158
1000	1000	1	0.0621	0.0072

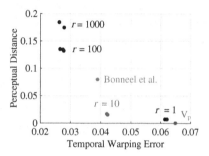

Fig. 5. Analysis of parameters. (Left) When λ_t is large enough, choosing $r = 10$ (shown in red) achieves a good balance between reducing temporal warping error as well as perceptual distance. (Right) The trade off between perceptual similarity and temporal warping with different ratios r, as compared to Bonneel et al. [6], and the original processed video, V_p.

(a) Original frames   (b) Processed frames   (c) Bonneel et al. [6]   (d) Ours

Fig. 6. Visual comparisons on style transfer. We compare the proposed method with Bonneel et al. [6] on smoothing the results of WCT [29]. Our approach maintains the stylized effect of processed video and reduce the temporal flickering.

4.5   Comparison with State-of-the-Art Methods

We evaluate the temporal warping error Eq. 6 and perceptual distance Eq. 7 on the two video test sets. We compare the proposed method with Bonneel et al. [6] on 16 applications: 2 styles of Johnson et al. [23], 6 styles of WCT [29], 2 enhancement models of Gharbi et al. [10], reflectance and shading layers of Bell et al. [3], 2 photo-to-painting models of CycleGAN [43] and 2 colorization algorithms [19,41]. We provide the average temporal warping error and perceptual distance in Tables 2 and 3, respectively. In general, our results achieves lower perceptual distance while maintains comparable temporal warping error with the results of Bonneel et al. [6].

We show visual comparisons with Bonneel et al. [6] in Figs. 6 and 7. Although the method of Bonneel et al. [6] produces temporally stable results, the assumption of identical gradients in the processed and original video leads to overly smoothed contents, for example from stylization effects. Furthermore, when the occlusion occurs in a large region, their method fails due to the lack of a long-term temporal constraint. In contrast, the proposed method dramatically reduces the temporal flickering while maintaining the perceptual similarity with the

Table 2. Quantitative evaluation on temporal warping error. The "Trained" column indicates the applications used for training our model. Our method achieves a similarly reduced temporal warping error as Bonneel et al. [6], which is significantly less than the original processed video (V_p).

Task	Trained	DAVIS			VIDEVO		
		V_p	[6]	Ours	V_p	[6]	Ours
WCT [29]/antimono	✓	0.054	**0.031**	0.035	0.025	0.014	**0.013**
WCT [29]/asheville		0.088	**0.047**	0.055	0.045	0.025	**0.023**
WCT [29]/candy	✓	0.069	**0.037**	0.045	0.034	**0.018**	**0.018**
WCT [29]/feathers		0.052	**0.029**	**0.029**	0.027	0.016	**0.012**
WCT [29]/sketch	✓	0.046	0.028	**0.023**	0.022	0.015	**0.009**
WCT [29]/wave		0.049	0.030	**0.027**	0.026	0.015	**0.011**
Fast-neural-style [23]/princess		0.073	0.048	**0.047**	0.039	0.023	**0.021**
Fast-neural-style [23]/udnie		0.065	**0.039**	0.042	0.028	0.017	**0.015**
DBL [10]/expertA	✓	0.039	0.035	**0.028**	0.018	0.016	**0.010**
DBL [10]/expertB		0.034	0.031	**0.025**	0.015	0.014	**0.008**
Intrinsic [3]/reflectance		0.024	0.020	**0.015**	0.012	0.008	**0.005**
Intrinsic [3]/shading	✓	0.016	0.012	**0.009**	0.008	0.006	**0.003**
CycleGAN [43]/photo2ukiyoe		0.037	0.030	**0.026**	0.019	0.016	**0.010**
CycleGAN [43]/photo2vangogh		0.040	0.032	**0.029**	0.021	0.017	**0.013**
Colorization [41]	✓	0.030	0.028	**0.024**	0.012	0.011	**0.008**
Colorization [19]		0.030	0.028	**0.023**	0.012	0.011	**0.008**
Average		0.047	0.032	**0.030**	0.023	0.015	**0.012**

Table 3. Quantitative evaluation on perceptual distance. Our method has lower perceptual distance than Bonneel et al. [6].

Task	Trained	DAVIS		VIDEVO	
		[6]	Ours	[6]	Ours
WCT [29]/antimono	✓	0.098	**0.019**	0.106	**0.016**
WCT [29]/asheville		0.090	**0.019**	0.098	**0.015**
WCT [29]/candy	✓	0.133	**0.023**	0.139	**0.018**
WCT [29]/feathers		0.093	**0.016**	0.100	**0.011**
WCT [29]/sketch	✓	0.042	**0.021**	0.046	**0.014**
WCT [29]/wave		0.065	**0.015**	0.072	**0.013**
Fast-neural-style [23]/princess		0.143	**0.029**	0.165	**0.018**
Fast-neural-style [23]/udnie		0.070	**0.017**	0.076	**0.014**
DBL [10]/expertA	✓	0.026	**0.011**	0.033	**0.007**
DBL [10]/expertB		0.023	**0.011**	0.030	**0.007**
Intrinsic [3]/reflectance		0.044	**0.013**	0.056	**0.008**
Intrinsic [3]/shading	✓	0.029	**0.017**	0.032	**0.009**
CycleGAN [43]/photo2ukiyoe		0.042	**0.012**	0.054	**0.007**
CycleGAN [43]/photo2vangogh		0.067	**0.016**	0.079	**0.011**
Colorization [41]	✓	0.062	**0.013**	0.055	**0.009**
Colorization [19]		0.033	**0.011**	0.034	**0.008**
Average		0.088	**0.017**	0.073	**0.012**

processed videos. We note that our approach is not limited to the above applications but can also be applied to tasks such as automatic white balancing [14], image harmonization [4] and image dehazing [13]. Due to the space limit, we provide more results and videos on our project website.

4.6   Subjective Evaluation

We conduct a user study to measure user preference on the quality of videos. We adopt the pairwise comparison, i.e., we ask participants to choose from a pair of videos. In each test, we provide the original and processed videos as references and show two results (Bonneel et al. [6] and ours) for comparisons. We randomize the presenting order of the result videos in each test. In addition, we ask participants to provide the reasons that they prefer the selected video from the following options: (1) The video is less flickering. (2) The video preserves the effect of the processed video well.

We evaluate all 50 test videos with the 10 test applications that were held out during training. We ask each user to compare 20 video pairs and obtain results from a total of 60 subjects. Fig. 8(a) shows the percentage of obtained votes, where our approach is preferred on all 5 applications. In Fig. 8(b), we show the reasons when a method is selected. The results of Bonneel et al. [6] are selected due to temporal stability, while users prefer our results as we preserve the effect of the processed video well. The observation in the user study basically follows the quantitative evaluation in Sect. 4.5.

4.7   Execution Time

We evaluate the execution time of the proposed method and Bonneel et al. [6] on a machine with a 3.4 GHz Intel i7 CPU (64G RAM) and an Nvidia Titan X GPU. As the proposed method does not require computing optical flow at test time, the execution speed achieves 418 FPS on GPU for videos with a resolution of 1280×720. In contrast, the speed of Bonneel et al. [6] is 0.25 FPS on CPU.

4.8   Limitations and Discussion

Our approach is not able to handle applications that generate entirely different image content on each frame, e.g., image completion [31] or synthesis [8]. Extending those methods to videos would require incorporating strong video

(a) Original frames   (b) Processed frames   (c) Bonneel et al. [6]   (d) Ours

Fig. 7. Visual comparisons on colorization. We compare the proposed method with Bonneel et al. [6] on smoothing the results of image colorization [19]. The method of Bonneel et al. [6] cannot preserve the colorized effect when occlusion occurs.

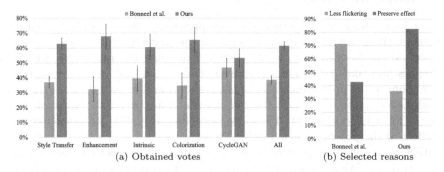

(a) Obtained votes   (b) Selected reasons

Fig. 8. Subjective evaluation. On average, our method is preferred by 62% users. The error bars show the 95% confidence interval.

priors or temporal constraints, most likely into the design of the specific algorithms themselves.

In addition, in the way the task is formulated there is always a trade-off between being temporally coherent or perceptually similar to the processed video. Depending on the specific effect applied, there will be cases where flicker (temporal instability) is preferable to blur, and vice versa. In our current method, the user can choose a model based on their preference for flicker or blur, but an interesting area for future work would be to investigate perceptual models for what is considered acceptable flicker and acceptable blur. Nonetheless, we use the same trained model (same parameters) for all our results and showed clear viewer preference over prior methods for blind temporal stability.

5   Conclusions

In this work, we propose a deep recurrent neural network to reduce the temporal flickering problem in per-frame processed videos. We optimize both short-term and long-term temporal loss as well as a perceptual loss to reduce temporal instability while preserving the perceptual similarity to the processed videos. Our approach is agnostic to the underlying image-based algorithms applied to the video and generalize to a wide range of unseen applications. We demonstrate that the proposed algorithm performs favorably against existing blind temporal consistency method on a diverse set of applications and various types of videos.

Acknowledgments. This work is supported in part by the NSF CAREER Grant #1149783, NSF Grant No. # 1755785, and gifts from Adobe and Nvidia.

References

1. Aydin, T.O., Stefanoski, N., Croci, S., Gross, M., Smolic, A.: Temporally coherent local tone mapping of HDR video. ACM TOG (2014)
2. Barnes, C., Shechtman, E., Finkelstein, A., Goldman, D.B.: PatchMatch: a randomized correspondence algorithm for structural image editing. ACM TOG (2009)
3. Bell, S., Bala, K., Snavely, N.: Intrinsic images in the wild. ACM TOG (2014)
4. Bonneel, N., Rabin, J., Peyré, G., Pfister, H.: Sliced and radon wasserstein barycenters of measures. J. Math. Imaging Vis. **1**(51), 22–45 (2015)
5. Bonneel, N., Sunkavalli, K., Paris, S., Pfister, H.: Example-based video color grading. ACM TOG (2013)
6. Bonneel, N., Tompkin, J., Sunkavalli, K., Sun, D., Paris, S., Pfister, H.: Blind video temporal consistency. ACM TOG (2015)
7. Chen, D., Liao, J., Yuan, L., Yu, N., Hua, G.: Coherent online video style transfer. In: ICCV (2017)
8. Chen, Q., Koltun, V.: Photographic image synthesis with cascaded refinement networks. In: ICCV (2017)
9. Dong, X., Bonev, B., Zhu, Y., Yuille, A.L.: Region-based temporally consistent video post-processing. In: CVPR (2015)
10. Gharbi, M., Chen, J., Barron, J.T., Hasinoff, S.W., Durand, F.: Deep bilateral learning for real-time image enhancement. ACM TOG (2017)

11. Goodfellow, I. et al.: Generative adversarial nets. In: NIPS (2014)
12. Gupta, A., Johnson, J., Alahi, A., Fei-Fei, L.: Characterizing and improving stability in neural style transfer. In: ICCV (2017)
13. He, K., Sun, J., Tang, X.: Single image haze removal using dark channel prior. In: TPAMI (2011)
14. Hsu, E., Mertens, T., Paris, S., Avidan, S., Durand, F.: Light mixture estimation for spatially varying white balance. ACM TOG (2008)
15. Huang, H. et al.: Real-time neural style transfer for videos. In: CVPR (2017)
16. Huang, J.B., Kang, S.B., Ahuja, N., Kopf, J.: Temporally coherent completion of dynamic video. ACM TOG (2016)
17. Huang, X., Belongie, S.: Arbitrary style transfer in real-time with adaptive instance normalization. In: ICCV (2017)
18. Iandola, F.N., Han, S., Moskewicz, M.W., Ashraf, K., Dally, W.J., Keutzer, K.: Squeezenet: Alexnet-level accuracy with 50x fewer parameters and < 0.5 mb model size (2016)
19. Iizuka, S., Simo-Serra, E., Ishikawa, H.: Let there be color!: joint end-to-end learning of global and local image priors for automatic image colorization with simultaneous classification. ACM TOG (2016)
20. Ilg, E., Mayer, N., Saikia, T., Keuper, M., Dosovitskiy, A., Brox, T.: Flownet 2.0: evolution of optical flow estimation with deep networks. In: CVPR (2017)
21. Isola, P., Zhu, J.Y., Zhou, T., Efros, A.A.: Image-to-image translation with conditional adversarial networks. In: CVPR (2017)
22. Jaderberg, M., Simonyan, K., Zisserman, A., Kavukcuoglu, K.: Spatial transformer networks. In: NIPS (2015)
23. Johnson, J., Alahi, A., Fei-Fei, L.: Perceptual losses for real-time style transfer and super-resolution. In: ECCV (2016)
24. Lai, W.S., Huang, J.B., Ahuja, N., Yang, M.H.: Deep laplacian pyramid networks for fast and accurate super-resolution. In: CVPR (2017)
25. Lang, M., Wang, O., Aydin, T.O., Smolic, A., Gross, M.H.: Practical temporal consistency for image-based graphics applications. ACM TOG (2012)
26. Ledig, C. et al.: Photo-realistic single image super-resolution using a generative adversarial network. In: CVPR (2017)
27. Lee, H.Y., Tseng, H.Y., Huang, J.B., Singh, M.K.S., Yang, M.H.: Diverse image-to-image translation via disentangled representation. In: ECCV (2018)
28. Levin, A., Lischinski, D., Weiss, Y.: Colorization using optimization. ACM TOG (2004)
29. Li, Y., Fang, C., Yang, J., Wang, Z., Lu, X., Yang, M.H.: Universal style transfer via feature transforms. In: NIPS (2017)
30. Li, Y., Huang, J.B., Narendra, A., Yang, M.H.: Deep joint image filtering. In: ECCV (2016)
31. Pathak, D., Krahenbuhl, P., Donahue, J., Darrell, T., Efros, A.A.: context encoders: feature learning by inpainting. In: CVPR (2016)
32. Perazzi, F., Pont-Tuset, J., McWilliams, B., Van Gool, L., Gross, M., Sorkine-Hornung, A.: A benchmark dataset and evaluation methodology for video object segmentation. In: CVPR (2016)
33. Ruder, M., Dosovitskiy, A., Brox, T.: Artistic style transfer for videos. In: German Conference on Pattern Recognition (2016)
34. Simonyan, K., Zisserman, A.: Very deep convolutional networks for large-scale image recognition. In: ICLR (2015)
35. Videvo. https://www.videvo.net/

36. Xingjian, S., Chen, Z., Wang, H., Yeung, D.Y., Wong, W.K., Woo, W.C.: Convolutional LSTM network: a machine learning approach for precipitation nowcasting. In: NIPS (2015)

37. Xu, L., Ren, J., Yan, Q., Liao, R., Jia, J.: Deep edge-aware filters. In: ICML (2015)

38. Yan, Z., Zhang, H., Wang, B., Paris, S., Yu, Y.: Automatic photo adjustment using deep neural networks. ACM TOG (2016)

39. Yao, C.H., Chang, C.Y., Chien, S.Y.: Occlusion-aware video temporal consistency. In: ACM MM (2017)

40. Ye, G., Garces, E., Liu, Y., Dai, Q., Gutierrez, D.: Intrinsic video and applications. ACM TOG (2014)

41. Zhang, R., Isola, P., Efros, A.A.: Colorful image colorization. In: ECCV (2016)

42. Zhang, R., Isola, P., Efros, A.A., Shechtman, E., Wang, O.: The unreasonable effectiveness of deep features as a perceptual metric. In: CVPR (2018)

43. Zhu, J.Y., Park, T., Isola, P., Efros, A.A.: Unpaired image-to-image translation using cycle-consistent adversarial networks. In: ICCV (2017)

Salient Objects in Clutter: Bringing Salient Object Detection to the Foreground

Deng-Ping Fan[1], Ming-Ming Cheng[1($\boxtimes$)], Jiang-Jiang Liu[1],
Shang-Hua Gao[1], Qibin Hou[1], and Ali Borji[2]

[1] College of Computer Science, Nankai University, Tianjin, China
cmm@nankai.edu.cn
[2] CRCV, University of Central Florida, Orlando, Florida, US
http://mmcheng.net/SOCBenchmark/

Abstract. We provide a comprehensive evaluation of salient object detection (SOD) models. Our analysis identifies a serious design bias of existing SOD datasets which assumes that each image contains at least one clearly outstanding salient object in low clutter. The design bias has led to a saturated high performance for state-of-the-art SOD models when evaluated on existing datasets. The models, however, still perform far from being satisfactory when applied to real-world daily scenes. Based on our analyses, we first identify 7 crucial aspects that a comprehensive and balanced dataset should fulfill. Then, we propose a new high quality dataset and update the previous saliency benchmark. Specifically, our **SOC** (Salient Objects in Clutter) dataset, includes images with salient and non-salient objects from daily object categories. Beyond object category annotations, each salient image is accompanied by attributes that reflect common challenges in real-world scenes. Finally, we report attribute-based performance assessment on our dataset.

Keywords: Salient object detection · Saliency benchmark
Dataset · Attribute

1 Introduction

This paper considers the task of salient object detection (SOD). Visual saliency mimics the ability of the human visual system to select a certain subset of the visual scene. SOD aims to detect the most attention-grabbing objects in a scene and then extract pixel-accurate silhouettes of the objects. The merit of SOD lies in it applications in many other computer vision tasks including: visual tracking [4], image retrieval [14,16], computer graphics [9], content aware image resizing [45], and weakly supervised semantic segmentation [18,39,40].

Our work is motivated by two observations. First, existing SOD datasets [2,5,10,11,23,26,29,32,43,44] are flawed either in the data collection procedure or quality of the data. Specifically, most datasets assume that an image contains

© Springer Nature Switzerland AG 2018
V. Ferrari et al. (Eds.): ECCV 2018, LNCS 11219, pp. 196–212, 2018.
https://doi.org/10.1007/978-3-030-01267-0_12

Fig. 1. Sample images from our new dataset including *non-salient* object images (first row) and salient object images (rows 2 to 4). For salient object images, instance-level ground truth map (different color), object attributes (Attr) and category labels are provided. Please refer to the supplemental material for more illustrations of our dataset.

at least one salient object, and thus discard images that do not contain salient objects. We call this *data selection bias*. Moreover, existing datasets mostly contain images with a single object or several objects (often a person) in low clutter. These datasets do not adequately reflect the complexity of images in the real world where scenes usually contain multiple objects amidst lots of clutter. As a result, all top performing models trained on the existing datasets have nearly saturated the performance (*e.g.*, > 0.9 *F-measure* over most current datasets) but unsatisfactory performance on realistic scenes (*e.g.*, < 0.45 *F-measure* in Table 3). Because current models may be biased towards ideal conditions, their effectiveness may be impaired once they are applied to real world scenes. To solve this problem, it is important to introduce a dataset that reaches closer to realistic conditions.

Second, only the overall performance of the models can be analyzed over existing datasets. None of the datasets contains various attributes that reflect challenges in real-world scenes. Having attributes helps (1) gain a deeper insight into the SOD problem, (2) investigate the pros and cons of the SOD models, and (3) objectively assess the model performances over different perspectives, which might be diverse for different applications.

Considering the above two issues, we make two contributions. Our main contribution is the collection of a new high quality SOD dataset, named the **SOC**, Salient Objects in Clutter. To date, SOC is the largest instance-level SOD dataset and contains 6,000 images from more than 80 common categories.

It differs from existing datasets in three aspects: (1) salient objects have category annotation which can be used for new research such as weakly supervised SOD tasks, (2) the inclusion of non-salient images which make this dataset closer to the real-world scenes and more challenging than the existing ones, and (3) salient objects have attributes reflecting specific situations faced in the real-wold such as *motion blur, occlusion and cluttered background*. As a consequence, our SOC dataset narrows the **gap** between existing datasets and the real-world scenes and provides a more realistic benchmark (see Fig. 1).

In addition, we provide a comprehensive evaluation of several state-of-the-art convolutional neural networks (CNNs) based models [8,15,17,23,24,28,31,36, 38,48–51]. To evaluate the models, we introduce three metrics that measure the region similarity of the detection, the pixel-wise accuracy of the segmentation, and the structure similarity of the result. Furthermore, we give an attribute-based performance evaluation. These attributes allow a deeper understanding of the models and point out promising directions for further research.

We believe that our dataset and benchmark can be very influential for future SOD research in particular for application-oriented model development. The entire dataset and analyzing tools will be released freely to the public.

2   Related Works

In this section, we briefly discuss existing datasets designed for SOD tasks, especially in the aspects including annotation type, the number of salient objects per image, number of images, and image quality. We also review the CNNs based SOD models.

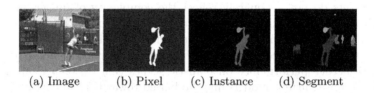

(a) Image   (b) Pixel   (c) Instance   (d) Segment

Fig. 2. Previous SOD datasets only annotate the image by drawing (b) pixel-accurate silhouettes of salient objects. Different from (d) MS COCO object segmentation dataset [27] (Objects are not necessarily being *salient*), our work focuses on (c) segmenting *salient object instances*.

2.1   Datasets

Early datasets are either limited in the number of images or in their coarse annotation of salient objects. For example, the salient objects in datasets **MSRA-A** [29] and **MSRA-B** [29] are roughly annotated in the form of bounding boxes. **ASD** [1] and **MSRA10K** [11] mostly contain only one salient object in each image, while the **SED2** [2] dataset contains two objects in a single image but contains only 100 images. To improve the quality of datasets, researchers in recent years started to collect datasets with multiple objects in relatively complex and cluttered backgrounds. These datasets include **DUT-OMRON** [44], **ECSSD** [43], **Judd-A** [5], and **PASCAL-S** [26]. These datasets have been improved in terms of annotation quality and the number of images, compared to their predecessors. Datasets **HKU-IS** [23], **XPIE** [41], and **DUTS** [37] resolved the shortcomings by collecting large amounts of pixel-wise labeled images (Fig. 2b) with more than one salient object in images. However, they ignored the non-salient objects and did not offer instance-level (Fig. 2c) salient objects annotation. Beyond these, researchers of [19] collected about 6k *simple background images* (most of them are pure texture images) to account for the non-salient scenes. This dataset is not sufficient to reflect real scenes as the real-world scenes are more complicated. The **ILSO** [22] dataset contains instance-level salient objects annotation but has boundaries roughly labeled as shown in Fig. 5a.

To sum up, as discussed above, existing datasets mostly focus on images with clear salient objects in simple backgrounds. Taking into account the aforementioned limitations of existing datasets, a more realistic dataset which contains realistic scenes with non-salient objects, textures "in the wild", and salient objects with attributes, is needed for future investigations in this field. Such a dataset can offer deep insights into weaknesses and strengths of SOD models.

2.2 Models

We divide the state-of-the-art deep models for SOD based on the number of tasks.

Single-task models have the single goal of detecting the salient objects in images. In **LEGS** [36], local information and global contrast were separately captured by two different deep CNNs, and were then fused to generate a saliency map. In [51], Zhao *et al.* presented a multi-context deep learning framework (**MC**) for SOD. Li *et al.* [23] (**MDF**) proposed to use multi-scale features extracted from a deep CNNs to derive a saliency map. Li *et al.* [24] presented a deep contrast network (**DCL**), which not only considered the pixel-wise information but also fused the segment-level guidance into the network. Lee *et al.* [15] (**ELD**) considered both high-level features extracted from CNNs and hand-crafted features. Liu *et al.* [28] (**DHS**) designed a two-stage network, in which a coarse downscaled prediction map was produced. It is then followed by another network to refine the details and upsample the prediction map hierarchically and progressively. Long *et al.* [30] proposed a fully convolutional network (**FCN**) to make dense pixel prediction problem feasible for end-to-end training. **RFCN** [38] used a recurrent FCN to incorporate the coarse predictions as saliency priors and refined the generated predictions in a stage-wise manner. The **DISC** [8] framework was proposed for fine-grained image saliency computing. Two stacked CNNs were utilized to obtain coarse-level and fine-grained saliency maps, respectively. **IMC** [48] integrated saliency cues at different levels

Table 1. CNNs based SOD models. We divided these models into single-task (S-T) and multi-task (M-T). *Training Set:* MB is the MSRA-B dataset [29]. MK is the MSRA-10K [11] dataset. ImageNet dataset refers to [34]. D is the DUT-OMRON [44] dataset. H is the HKU-IS [23] dataset. P is the PASCAL-S [26] dataset. P2010 is the PASCAL VOC 2010 semantic segmentation dataset [12]. *Base Model:* VGGNet, ResNet-101, AlexNet, GoogleNet are base models. *FCN:* whether model uses the fully convolutional network. *Sp:* whether model uses superpixels. *Proposal:* whether model uses the object proposal. *Edge:* whether model uses the edge or contour information

	No	Model	Year	Pub	#Training	*Training set*	*Base model*	FCN	Sp	*Proposal*	*Edge*
S-T	1	**LEGS** [36]	2015	CVPR	3,340	MB + P	–	×	×	✓	×
	2	**MC** [51]	2015	CVPR	8,000	MK	GoogLeNet	×	✓	×	×
	3	**MDF** [23]	2015	CVPR	2,500	MB	–	×	✓	×	✓
	4	**DCL** [24]	2016	CVPR	2,500	MB	VGGNet	✓	✓	×	×
	5	**ELD** [15]	2016	CVPR	9,000	MK	VGGNet	×	✓	×	×
	6	**DHS** [28]	2016	CVPR	9,500	MK+D	VGGNet	×	×	×	×
	7	**RFCN** [38]	2016	ECCV	10,103	P2010	–	✓	✓	×	✓
	8	**DISC** [8]	2016	TNNLS	9,000	MK	–	×	✓	×	×
	9	**IMC** [48]	2017	WACV	6,000	MK	ResNet-101	✓	✓	×	×
	10	**DSS** [17]	2017	CVPR	2,500	MB	VGGNet	✓	×	×	✓
	11	**NLDF** [31]	2017	CVPR	2,500	MB	VGGNet	✓	×	×	×
	12	**AMU** [49]	2017	ICCV	10,000	MK	VGGNet	✓	×	×	✓
	13	**UCF** [50]	2017	ICCV	10,000	MK	–	✓	×	×	×
M-T	1	**DS** [25]	2016	TIP	10,000	MK	VGGNet	✓	✓	×	×
	2	**WSS** [37]	2017	CVPR	456K	ImageNet	VGGNet	✓	✓	×	×
	3	**MSR** [22]	2017	CVPR	5,000	MB + H	VGGNet	✓	×	✓	✓

through FCN. It could efficiently exploit both learned semantic cues and higher-order region statistics for edge-accurate SOD. Recently, a deep architecture [17] with short connections (**DSS**) was proposed. Hou *et al.* added connections from high-level features to low-level features based on the HED [42] architecture, achieving good performance. **NLDF** [31] integrated local and global features and added a boundary loss term into standard cross entropy loss to train an end-to-end network. **AMU** [49] was a generic aggregating multi-level convolutional feature framework. It integrated coarse semantics and fine detailed feature maps into multiple resolutions. Then it adaptively learned to combine these feature maps at each resolution and predicted saliency maps with the combined features. **UCF** [50] was proposed to improve the robustness and accuracy of saliency detection. They introduced a reformulated dropout after specific convolutional layers to construct an uncertain ensemble of internal feature units. Also, they proposed reformulated dropout after an effective hybrid up-sampling method to reduce the checkerboard artifacts of deconvolution operators in the decoder network.

Multi-task models at present include three methods, **DS**, **WSS**, and **MSR**. The **DS** [25] model set up a multi-task learning scheme for exploring the intrinsic correlations between saliency detection and semantic image segmentation, which shared the information in FCN layers to generate effective features for object perception. Recently, Wang *et al.* [37] proposed a model named **WSS** which developed a weakly supervised learning method using image-level tags for saliency detection. First, they jointly trained Foreground Inference Net (FIN) and FCN for image categorization. Then, they used FIN fine-tuned with iterative CRF to enforce spatial label consistency to predict the saliency map. **MSR** [22] was designed for both salient region detection and salient object contour detection, integrated with multi-scale combinatorial grouping and a MAP-based [47] subset optimization framework. Using three refined VGG network streams with shared parameters and a learned attentional model for fusing results at different scales, the authors were able to achieve good results.

We benchmark a large set of the state-of-the-art CNNs based models (see Table 1) on our proposed dataset, highlighting the current issues and pointing out future research directions.

3   The Proposed Dataset

In this section, we present our new challenging SOC dataset designed to reflect the real-world scenes in detail. Sample images from SOC are shown in Fig. 1. Moreover, statistics regarding the categories and the attributes of SOC are shown in Figs. 4a and 6, respectively. Based on the strengths and weaknesses of the existing datasets, we identify seven crucial aspects that a comprehensive and balanced dataset should fulfill.

(1) Presence of Non-Salient Objects. Almost all of the existing SOD datasets make the assumption that an image contains at least one salient object and discard the images that do not contain salient objects. However, this assumption is an ideal setting which leads to *data selection bias*. In a realistic setting, images do not always contain salient objects. For example, some amorphous background images such as sky, grass and texture contain no salient objects at all [6]. The non-salient objects or background "stuff" may occupy the entire scene, and hence heavily constrain possible locations for a salient object. Xia *et al.* [41] proposed a state-of-the-art SOD model by judging what is or what is not a salient object, indicating that the non-salient object is crucial for reasoning about the salient object. This suggests that the non-salient objects deserve equal attention as the salient objects in SOD. Incorporating a number of images containing non-salient objects makes the dataset closer to real-world scenes, while becoming more challenging. Thus, we define the *"non-salient objects"* as images without salient objects or images with "stuff" categories. As suggested in [6,41], the "stuff" categories including (a) densely distributed similar objects, (b) fuzzy shape, and (c) region without semantics, which are illustrated in Fig. 3a–c, respectively.

Based on the characteristics of non-salient objects, we collected 783 texture images from the DTD [21] dataset. To enrich the diversity, 2217 images including aurora, sky, crowds, store and many other kinds of realistic scenes were gathered from the Internet and other datasets [26,27,32,35]. We believe that incorporating enough non-salient objects would open up a promising direction for future works.

(a)   (b)   (c)

Fig. 3. Some examples of non-salient objects.

(2) Number and Category of Images. A considerably large amount of images is essential to capture the diversity and abundance of real-world scenes. Moreover, with large amounts of data, SOD models can avoid over-fitting and enhance generalization. To this end, we gathered 6,000 images from more than 80 categories, containing 3,000 images with salient objects and 3,000 images without salient objects. We divide our dataset into training set, validation set and test set in the ratio of 6:2:2. To ensure fairness, the test set is not published, but with the *on-line testing* provided on our website[1]. Figure 4a shows the number of salient objects for each category. It shows that the "person" category accounts for a large proportion, which is reasonable as people usually appear in daily scenes along with other objects.

(3) Global/Local Color Contrast of Salient Objects. As described in [26], the term "salient" is related to the global/local contrast of the foreground and background. It is essential to check whether the salient objects are easy to detect. For each object, we compute RGB color histograms for foreground and background separately. Then, χ^2 distance is utilized to measure the distance between the two histograms. The global and local color contrast distribution are shown in Fig. 4b and c, respectively. In comparison to ILSO, our SOC has more proportion of objects with low global color contrast and local color contrast.

(4) Locations of Salient Objects. *Center bias* has been identified as one of the most significant biases of saliency detection datasets [3,20,26]. Figure 4d illustrates a set of images and their overlay map. As can be seen, although salient objects are located in different positions, the overlay map still shows that somehow this set of images is center biased. Previous benchmarks often adopt this incorrect way to analyze the location distribution of salient objects. To avoid this misleading phenomenon, we plot the statistics of two quantities r_o and r_m in Fig. 4e, where r_o and r_m denote how far an object center and the farthest (margin) point in an object are from the image center, respectively. Both r_o and r_m are divided by half image diagonal length for normalization so that $r_o, r_m \in [0, 1]$. From these statistics, we can observe that salient objects in our dataset do not suffer from center bias.

(5) Size of Salient Objects. The size of an instance-level salient object is defined as the proportion of pixels in the image [26]. As shown in Fig. 4(g), the

---

[1] http://dpfan.net/SOCBenchmark/.

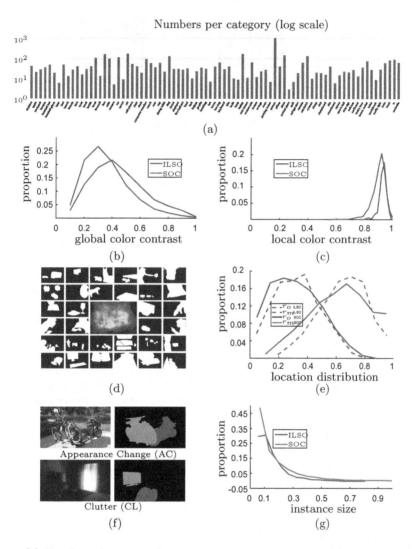

Fig. 4. (a) Number of annotated instances per category in our SOC dataset. (b, c) The statistics of global color contrast and local color contrast, respectively. (d) A set of saliency maps from our dataset and their overlay map. (e) Location distribution of the salient objects in SOC. (f) Attribute visual examples. (g) The distribution of instance sizes for the SOC and ILSO [22].

size of salient objects in our SOC varies in a broader range, compared with the only existing instance-level ILSO [22] dataset. Also, medium-sized objects in SOC have a higher proportion.

(6) High-Quality Salient Object Labeling. As also noticed in [17], training on the ECSSD dataset (1,000) allows to achieve better results than other

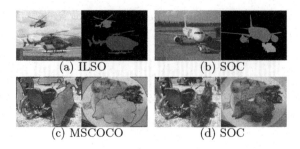

(a) ILSO   (b) SOC

(c) MSCOCO   (d) SOC

Fig. 5. Compared with the recent new (a) instance-level ILSO dataset [22] which is labeled with discontinue coarse boundaries, (c) MSCOCO dataset [27] which is labeled with polygons, our (b, d) SOC dataset is labeled with smooth fine boundaries.

Table 2. The list of salient object image attributes and the corresponding description. By observing the characteristics of the existing datasets, we summarize these attributes. Some visual examples can be found in Figs. 1 and 4f. For more examples, please refer to the supplementary materials

Attr	Description
AC	***Appearance Change.*** The obvious illumination change in the object region
BO	***Big Object.*** The ratio between the object area and the image area is larger than 0.5
CL	***Clutter.*** The foreground and background regions around the object have similar color. We labeled images that their global color contrast value is larger than 0.2, local color contrast value is smaller than 0.9 with clutter images (see Sect. 3)
HO	***Heterogeneous Object.*** Objects composed of visually distinctive/dissimilar parts
MB	***Motion Blur.*** Objects have fuzzy boundaries due to shake of the camera or motion
OC	***Occlusion.*** Objects are partially or fully occluded
OV	***Out-of-View.*** Part of object is clipped by image boundaries
SC	***Shape Complexity.*** Objects have complex boundaries such as thin parts (*e.g.*, the foot of animal) and holes
SO	***Small Object.*** The ratio between the object area and the image area is smaller than 0.1

datasets (*e.g.*, MSRA10K, with 10,000 images). Besides the scale, dataset quality is also an important factor. To obtain a large amount of high quality images, we randomly select images from the MSCOCO dataset [27], which is a large-scale real-world dataset whose objects are labeled with polygons (*i.e.*, coarse labeling). High-quality labels also play a critical role in improving the accuracy of SOD models [1]. Toward this end, we relabel the dataset with pixel-wise annotations. Similar to famous SOD task oriented benchmark datasets [1, 2, 11, 19, 22, 23, 29, 32, 37, 41, 43], we did not use the eye tracker device. We have taken a number of steps to provide the high-quality of the annotations. These steps include two stages: **In the bounding boxes (bboxes) stage**, (i) we ask 5 viewers to annotate objects with bboxes that they think are salient in each image. (ii) keep the images which majority ($\geq$ 3) viewers annotated the same (the IOU of the bbox $>$ 0.8) object. After the first stage, we have 3,000 salient object images annotated with bboxes. **In the second stage**, we further manually label the accurate silhouettes of the salient objects according to the bboxes. Note that we have 10 volunteers involved in the whole steps for cross-check the quality of annotations. In the end, we keep 3,000 images with high-quality, instance-level labeled salient objects. As shown in Fig. 5b, d, the boundaries of our object labels are precise, sharp and smooth. During the annotation process, we also add some new categories (*e.g.*, *computer monitor, hat, pillow*) that are not labeled in the MSCOCO dataset [27].

(7) Salient Objects with Attributes. Having attributes information regarding the images in a dataset helps objectively assess the performance of models over different types of parameters and variations. It also allows the inspection of model failures. To this end, we define a set of attributes to represent specific situations faced in the real-wold scenes such as *motion blur*, *occlusion* and *cluttered background* (summarized in Table 2). Note that one image can be annotated with multiple attributes as these attributes are not exclusive.

Inspired by [33], we present the distribution of attributes over the dataset as shown in Fig. 6 Left. Type *SO* has the largest proportion due to accurate instance-level (*e.g.*, tennis racket in Fig. 2) annotation. Type *HO* accounts for a large proportion, because the real-world scenes are composed of different constituent materials. *Motion blur* is more common in video frames than still images, but it also occurs in still images sometimes. Thus, type *MB* takes a relatively small proportion in our dataset. Since a realistic image usually contains multiple attributes, we show the dominant dependencies among attributes based on the frequency of occurrences in the Fig. 6 Right. For example, a scene containing

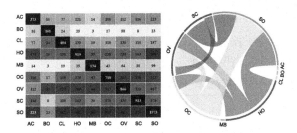

Fig. 6. Left: Attributes distribution over the salient object images in our SOC dataset. Each number in the grids indicates the image number of occurrences. Right: The *dominant dependencies* among attributes base on the frequency of occurrences. Larger width of a link indicates higher probability of an attribute to other ones.

lots of heterogeneous objects is likely to have a large number of objects blocking each other and forming complex spatial structures. Thus, type *HO* has a strong dependency with type *OC, OV*, and *SO*.

4   Benchmarking Models

In this section, we present the evaluation results of the sixteen SOD models on our SOC dataset. Nearly all representative CNNs based SOD models are evaluated. However, since the codes of some models are not publicly available, we do not consider them here. In addition, most models are not optimized for non-salient objects detection. Thus, to be fair, we only use the test set of our SOC dataset to evaluate SOD models. We describe the evaluation metrics in Sect. 4.1. Overall model performance on SOC dataset is presented in Sect. 4.2 and summarized in Table 3, while the attribute level performance (*e.g.*, performance of the appearance changes) is discussed in Sect. 4.3 and summarized in Table 4. The evaluation scripts are publicly available, and on-line evaluation test is provided on our website.

4.1   Evaluation Metrics

In a supervised evaluation framework, given a predicted map M generated by a SOD model and a ground truth mask G, the evaluation metrics are expected to tell which model generates the best result. Here, we use three different evaluation metrics to evaluate SOD models on our SOC dataset.

Pixel-wise Accuracy ε. The region similarity evaluation measure does not consider the true negative saliency assignments. As a remedy, we also compute the normalized ([0,1]) mean absolute error (MAE) between M and G, defined as:

$$\varepsilon = \frac{1}{W \times H} \sum_{x=1}^{W} \sum_{y=1}^{H} ||M(x,y) - G(x,y)||, \tag{1}$$

where W and H are the width and height of images, respectively.

Region Similarity F. To measure how well the regions of the two maps match, we use the *F-measure*, defined as:

$$F = \frac{(1 + \beta^2) Precision \times Recall}{\beta^2 Precision + Recall}, \tag{2}$$

where $\beta^2 = 0.3$ is suggested by [1] to trade-off the *recall* and *precision*. However, the black (all-zero matrix) ground truth is not well defined in *F-measure* when calculating *recall* and *precision*. Under this circumstances, different foreground maps get the same result 0, which is apparently unreasonable. Thus, *F-measure* is not suitable for measuring the results of non-salient object detection.

However, both metrics of ε and F are based on pixel-wise errors and often ignore the structural similarities. Behavioral vision studies have shown that the human visual system is highly sensitive to structures in scenes [13]. In many applications, it is desired that the results of the SOD model retain the structure of objects.

Structure Similarity S. *S-measure* proposed by Fan *et al.* [13] evaluates the structural similarity, by considering both regions and objects. Therefore, we additionally use *S-measure* to evaluate the structural similarity between M and G. Note that the next overall performance we evaluated and analyzed are based on the *S-measure*.

4.2   Metric Statistics

To obtain an overall result, we average the scores of the evaluation metrics η ($\eta \in \{F, \varepsilon, S\}$), denoted by:

$$M_\eta(D) = \frac{1}{|D|} \sum_{I \in D} \bar{\eta}(I_i), \tag{3}$$

where $\bar{\eta}(I_i)$ is the evaluation score of the image I_i within the image dataset D.

Table 3. The performance of SOD models under three metrics. F stands for region similarity, ε is the mean absolute error, and S is the structure similarity. ↑ stand for the higher the number the better, and vice versa for ↓. The evaluation results are calculated according to Eq. (3) over our SOC dataset. $S_{all}, F_{all}, \varepsilon_{all}$ indicate the overall performance using the metric of S, F, ε, respectively. **Bold** for the best.

Type	Single-task													Multi-task		
	LEGS	MC	MDF	DCL	AMU	RFCN	DHS	ELD	DISC	IMC	UCF	DSS	NLDF	DS	WSS	MSR
	[36]	[51]	[23]	[24]	[24]	[38]	[28]	[15]	[8]	[48]	[50]	[17]	[31]	[25]	[37]	[22]
F_{all} ↑	.276	.291	.307	.339	.341	**.435**	.360	.317	.288	.352	.333	.341	.352	.347	.327	**.380**
S_{all} ↑	.677	.757	.736	.771	.737	.814	.804	.776	.737	.664	.657	.807	**.818**	.779	.785	**.819**
ε_{all} ↓	.230	.138	.150	.157	.185	.113	.118	.135	.173	.269	.282	.111	**.104**	.155	.133	.113

Single-task: For the single-task models, the best performing model on the entire SOC dataset (S_{all} in Table 3) is NLDF [31] ($M_S = 0.818$), followed by RFCN [38] ($M_S = 0.814$). MDF [23] and AMU [49] use edge cues to promote the saliency map but fail to achieve the ideal goal. Aiming at using the local region information of images, MC [51], MDF [23], ELD [15], and DISC [8] try to use superpixel methods to segment images into regions and then extract features from these regions, which is complex and time-consuming. To further improve the performance, UCF [50], DSS [17], NLDF [31], and AMU [49] utilize the FCN to improve the performance of SOD (S_{sal} in Table 4). Some other methods such as DCL [24] and IMC [48] try to combine superpixels with FCN to build a powerful model. Furthermore, RFCN [38] combines two related cues including edges and superpixels into FCN to obtain the good performance ($M_F = 0.435$, $M_S = 0.814$) over the overall dataset.

Multi-task: Different from models mentioned above, MSR [22] detects the instance-level salient objects using three closely related steps: estimating saliency maps, detecting salient object contours, and identifying salient object instances. It creates a multi-scale saliency refinement network that results in the highest performance (S_{all}). Other two multi-task models DS [25] and WSS [37] utilize the segmentation and classification results simultaneously to generate the saliency maps, obtaining a moderate performance. It is worth mentioning that although WSS is a weakly supervised multi-task model, it still achieves comparable performance to other single-task, fully supervised models. So, the weakly-supervised and multi-task based models can be promising future directions.

4.3 Attributes-Based Evaluation

We assign the salient images with attributes as discussed in Sect. 3 and Table 2. Each attribute stands for a challenging problem faced in the real-world scenes. The attributes allow us to identify groups of images with a dominant feature (*e.g.*, presence of clutter), which is crucial to illustrate the performance of SOD models and to relate SOD to application-oriented tasks. For example, sketch2photo application [7] prefers models with good performance on big objects, which can be identified by attributes-based performance evaluation methods.

Results. In Table 4, we show the performance on subsets of our dataset characterized by a particular attribute. Due to space limitation, in the following parts, we only select some representative attributes for further analysis. More details can be found in the supplementary material.

Big Object (BO) scenes often occur when objects are in a close distance with the camera, in which circumstances the tiny text or patterns would always be seen clearly. In this case, the models which prefer to focus on local information will be mislead seriously, leading to a considerable (*e.g.*, 28.9% loss for DSS [17], 20.8% loss for MC [51] and 23.8% loss for RFCN [38]) loss of performance.

However, the performance of IMC [48] model goes up for a slight margin of 3.2% instead. After taking a deeper look of the pipeline of this model, we came up a reasonable explanation. IMC uses a coarse predicted map to express semantics and utilizes over-segmented images to supplement the structural information, achieving a satisfying result on type *BO*. However, over-segmented images cannot make up the missing details, causing 4.6% degradation of performance on the type of *SO*.

Small Object (SO) is tricky for all SOD models. All models encounter performance degradation (*e.g.*, from DSS [17] −0.3% to LEGS [36] −5.6%), because *SOs* are easily ignored during down-sampling of CNNs. DSS [17] is the only model that has a slight decrease of performance on type *SO*, while it has the biggest (28.9%) loss of performance on type *BO*. MDF [23] uses multi-scale superpixels as the input of network, so it retains the details of small objects well. However, due to the limited size of superpixels, MDF can not efficiently sense the global semantics, causing a big failure on type *BO*.

Table 4. Attributes-based performance on our SOC salient objects sub-dataset. For each model, the score corresponds to the average structure similarity M_S (in Sect. 4.1) over all datasets with that specific attribute (*e.g.*, CL). The higher the score the better the performance. **Bold** for the best. The average salient-object performance S_{sal} is presented in the first row using the structure similarity S. The symbol of $^+$ and $^-$ indicates *increase* and *decrease* compared to the average (S_{sal}) result, respectively

	Single-task													Multi-task		
Attr	LEGS	MC	MDF	DCL	AMU	RFCN	DHS	ELD	DISC	IMC	UCF	DSS	NLDF	DS	WSS	MSR
	[36]	[51]	[23]	[24]	[24]	[38]	[28]	[15]	[8]	[48]	[50]	[17]	[31]	[25]	[37]	[22]
S_{sal}	.607	.619	.610	.705	.705	.709	**.728**	.664	.629	.679	.678	.698	.714	.719	.676	**.748**
AC	.625	.631	.614	.734	.736	.744	**.745**	.673	.644	.702	.714	.726	.737	.764	.691	**.789**
BO	.509	.490	.461$^-$	.610	.569	.540	.590	.576	.517	**.701**$^+$	.636	.496$^-$	.568	.685	.566	.667
CL	.620	.635	.566	.699	.708	.714	**.743**	.658	.635	.696	.704	.677$^-$	.713	.729	.678	**.756**
HO	.666	.666	.648	.745	.755	.759	**.766**	.706	.681	.715	.744	.748	.755	.756	.707	**.777**
MB	.543$^-$	.603	.615	.693	.706	.715	**.722**	.639	.600	.689	.682	.695	.685	.711	.641	**.757**
OC	.609	.617	.608	.708$^+$	**.725**$^+$	.711	.716	.658	.630	.672	.701$^+$	.689	.709	.725$^+$	.672	**.740**
OV	.548	.584	.568	.699	**.708**$^+$	.687	.706	.637	.573	.693$^+$	.685$^+$	.665	.688	.722$^+$	.624	**.743**
SC	.608	.620	.669$^+$	.738	.731	.735	**.763**	.688	.653	.690	.722$^+$	.746$^+$	.745	.724	.677	**.773**
SO	.573$^-$	.601	.621	.691	.685	.698	**.713**	.644	.614	.648$^-$	.650	.696$^-$	.703	.696	.659	**.730**

Occlusions (OC) scenes in which objects are partly obscured. Thus, it requires SOD models to capture global semantics to make up for the incomplete information of objects. To do so, DS [25] & AMU [49] made use of the multi-scale features in the down-sample progress to generate a fused saliency map; UCF [50] proposed an uncertain learning mechanism to learn uncertain convolutional features. All these methods try to get saliency maps containing both global and local features. Unsurprisingly, these methods have achieved pretty good results on type *OC*. Based on the above analyses, we also find that these three models perform very well on the scenes requiring more semantic information like type *AC*, *OV* and *CL*.

Heterogeneous Object (HO) is a common attribute in nature scenes. The performance of different models on type *HO* gets some improvement to their average performances respectively, all fluctuating from 3.9% to 9.7%. We suspect this is because type *HO* accounts for a significant proportion of all datasets, objectively making models more fitting to this attribute. This result in some degree confirms our statistics in Fig. 6.

5   Discussion and Conclusion

To our best knowledge, this work presents the currently largest scale performance evaluation of CNNs based salient object detection models. Our analysis points out a serious *data selection bias* in existing SOD datasets. This design bias has lead to state-of-the-art SOD algorithms almost achieve saturated high performance when evaluated on existing datasets, but are still far from being satisfactory when applied to real-world daily scenes. Based on our analysis, we first identify 7 important aspects that a comprehensive and balanced dataset should fulfill. We firstly introduces a high quality SOD dataset, **SOC**. It contains salient objects from daily life in their natural environments which reaches closer to realistic settings. The SOC dataset will evolve and grow over time and will enable research possibilities in multiple directions, *e.g.*, salient object subitizing [46], instance level salient object detection [22], weakly supervised based salient object detection [37], *etc.* Then, a set of attributes (*e.g.*, *Appearance Change*) is proposed in the attempt to obtain a deeper insight into the SOD problem, investigate the pros and cons of the SOD algorithms, and objectively assess the model performances over different perspectives/requirements. Finally, we report attribute-based performance assessment on our SOC dataset. The results open up promising future directions for model development and comparison.

Acknowledgments. This research was supported by NSFC (NO. 61620106008, 61572264), the national youth talent support program, Tianjin Natural Science Foundation for Distinguished Young Scholars (NO. 17JCJQJC43700), Huawei Innovation Research Program.

References

1. Achanta, R., Hemami, S., Estrada, F., Susstrunk, S.: Frequency-tuned Salient Region Detection. In: CVPR, pp. 1597–1604. IEEE (2009)
2. Alpert, S., Galun, M., Basri, R., Brandt, A.: Image segmentation by probabilistic bottom-up aggregation and cue integration. In: CVPR, pp. 1–8. IEEE (2007)
3. Borji, A., Cheng, M.M., Jiang, H., Li, J.: Salient object detection: a benchmark. IEEE Trans. Image Process. **24**(12), 5706–5722 (2015)
4. Borji, A., Itti, L.: State-of-the-art in visual attention modeling. IEEE Trans. Pattern Anal. Mach. Intell. **35**(1), 185–207 (2013)
5. Borji, A., Sihite, D.N., Itti, L.: Salient object detection: a benchmark. In: Fitzgibbon, A., Lazebnik, S., Perona, P., Sato, Y., Schmid, C. (eds.) ECCV 2012. LNCS, pp. 414–429. Springer, Heidelberg (2012). https://doi.org/10.1007/978-3-642-33709-3_30
6. Caesar, H., Uijlings, J., Ferrari, V.: COCO-stuff: thing and stuff classes in context. In: CVPR. IEEE (2018)
7. Chen, T., Cheng, M.M., Tan, P., Shamir, A., Hu, S.M.: Sketch2photo: internet image montage. ACM Trans. Graph. (TOG) **28**(5), 124 (2009)
8. Chen, T., Lin, L., Liu, L., Luo, X., Li, X.: DISC: deep image saliency computing via progressive representation learning. IEEE Trans. Neural Netw. Learn. Syst. **27**(6), 1135–1149 (2016)
9. Cheng, M.M., Hou, Q.B., Zhang, S.H., Rosin, P.L.: Intelligent visual media processing: when graphics meets vision. J. Comput. Sci. Technol. **32**(1), 110–121 (2017)
10. Cheng, M.M., Mitra, N.J., Huang, X., Hu, S.M.: Salientshape: group saliency in image collections. Vis. Comput. **30**(4), 443–453 (2014)

11. Cheng, M.M., Mitra, N.J., Huang, X., Torr, P.H.S., Hu, S.M.: Global contrast based salient region detection. IEEE Trans. Pattern Anal. Mach. Intell. **37**(3), 569–582 (2015)

12. Everingham, M., Van Gool, L., Williams, C.K.I., Winn, J., Zisserman, A.: The PASCAL Visual Object Classes Challenge 2010 (VOC 2010) Results. https:// www.researchgate.net/profile/Luc_Van_Gool/publication/277292831_The_2005_ pascal_visual_object_classes_challenge/links/57224cf108aef9c00b7c7efb.pdf

13. Fan, D.P., Cheng, M.M., Liu, Y., Li, T., Borji, A.: Structure-measure: a new way to evaluate foreground maps. In: ICCV, pp. 4548–4557. IEEE (2017)

14. Fan, D.P., Gong, C., Cao, Y., Ren, B., Cheng, M.M., Borji, A.: Enhanced-alignment measure for binary foreground map evaluation. In: International Joint Conference on Artificial Intelligence (IJCAI), pp. 698–704 (2018)

15. Gayoung, L., Yu-Wing, T., Junmo, K.: Deep saliency with encoded low level distance map and high level features. In: CVPR, IEEE (2016)

16. He, J. et al.: Mobile product search with bag of hash bits and boundary reranking. In: CVPR, pp. 3005–3012. IEEE (2012)

17. Hou, Q., Cheng, M.M., Hu, X., Borji, A., Tu, Z., Torr, P.: Deeply supervised salient object detection with short connections. IEEE TPAMI (2018). https://doi.org/10. 1109/TPAMI.2018.2815688

18. Hou, Q., Dokania, P.K., Massiceti, D., Wei, Y., Cheng, M.M., Torr, P.H.S.: Bottom-up top-down cues for weakly supervised semantic segmentation. In: EMMCVPR. IEEE (2017)

19. Jiang, H., Cheng, M.M., Li, S.J., Borji, A., Wang, J.: Joint salient object detection and existence prediction. Front. Comput. Sci., 1–11 (2017)

20. Judd, T., Durand, F., Torralba, A.: A benchmark of computational models of saliency to predict human fixations. In: MIT Technical Report (2012)

21. Lazebnik, S., Schmid, C., Ponce, J.: A sparse texture representation using local affine regions. IEEE TPAMI **27**(8), 1265–1278 (2005)

22. Li, G., Xie, Y., Lin, L., Yu, Y.: Instance-level salient object segmentation. In: CVPR, pp. 247–256. IEEE (2017)

23. Li, G., Yu, Y.: Visual saliency based on multiscale deep features. In: CVPR, pp. 5455–5463. IEEE (2015)

24. Li, G., Yu, Y.: Deep contrast learning for salient object detection. In: CVPR, pp. 478–487. IEEE (2016)

25. Li, X., Zhao, L., Wei, L., Yang, M.H., Wu, F., Zhuang, Y., Ling, H., Wang, J.: DeepSaliency: multi-task deep neural network model for salient object detection. IEEE TIP **25**(8), 3919–3930 (2016)

26. Li, Y., Hou, X., Koch, C., Rehg, J.M., Yuille, A.L.: The secrets of salient object segmentation. In: CVPR, pp. 280–287. IEEE (2014)

27. Lin, T.-Y. et al.: Microsoft COCO: common objects in context. In: Fleet, D., Pajdla, T., Schiele, B., Tuytelaars, T. (eds.) ECCV 2014. LNCS, vol. 8693, pp. 740–755. Springer, Cham (2014). https://doi.org/10.1007/978-3-319-10602-1_48

28. Liu, N., Han, J.: DHSNet: deep hierarchical saliency network for salient object detection. In: CVPR, pp. 678–686. IEEE (2016)

29. Liu, T., Sun, J., Zheng, N., Tang, X., Shum, H.Y.: Learning to detect a salient object. In: CVPR, pp. 1–8. IEEE (2007)

30. Long, J., Shelhamer, E., Darrell, T.: Fully convolutional networks for semantic segmentation. In: CVPR, pp. 3431–3440. IEEE (2015)

31. Luo, Z., Mishra, A.K., Achkar, A., Eichel, J.A., Li, S., Jodoin, P.M.: Non-local deep features for salient object detection. In: CVPR, vol. 2, p. 7 (2017)

32. Martin, D., Fowlkes, C., Tal, D., Malik, J.: A database of human segmented natural images and its application to evaluating segmentation algorithms and measuring ecological statistics. In: ICCV, vol. 2, pp. 416–423. IEEE (2001)

33. Perazzi, F., Pont-Tuset, J., McWilliams, B., Van Gool, L., Gross, M., Sorkine-Hornung, A.: A benchmark dataset and evaluation methodology for video object segmentation. In: CVPR, pp. 724–732. IEEE (2016)

34. Russakovsky, O. et al.: Imagenet large scale visual recognition challenge. IJCV **115**(3), 211–252 (2015)

35. Wang, J., Jiang, H., Yuan, Z., Cheng, M.M., Hu, X., Zheng, N.: Salient object detection: a discriminative regional feature integration approach. IJCV **123**(2), 251–268 (2017)

36. Wang, L., Lu, H., Ruan, X., Yang, M.H.: Deep networks for saliency detection via local estimation and global search. In: CVPR, pp. 3183–3192. IEEE (2015)

37. Wang, L. et al.: Learning to detect salient objects with image-level supervision. In: CVPR, pp. 136–145. IEEE (2017)

38. Wang, L., Wang, L., Lu, H., Zhang, P., Ruan, X.: Saliency detection with recurrent fully convolutional networks. In: Leibe, B., Matas, J., Sebe, N., Welling, M. (eds.) ECCV 2016. LNCS, vol. 9908, pp. 825–841. Springer, Cham (2016). https://doi.org/10.1007/978-3-319-46493-0_50

39. Wei, Y., Feng, J., Liang, X., Cheng, M.M., Zhao, Y., Yan, S.: Object region mining with adversarial erasing: a simple classification to semantic segmentation approach. In: CVPR. IEEE (2017)

40. Wei, Y.: STC: A simple to complex framework for weakly-supervised semantic segmentation. IEEE TPAMI **39**(11), 2314–2320 (2017)

41. Xia, C., Li, J., Chen, X., Zheng, A., Zhang, Y.: What is and what is not a salient object? Learning salient object detector by ensembling linear exemplar regressors. In: CVPR. IEEE (2017)

42. Xie, S., Tu, Z.: Holistically-nested edge detection. In: ICCV, pp. 1395–1403. IEEE (2015)

43. Yan, Q., Xu, L., Shi, J., Jia, J.: Hierarchical saliency detection. In: CVPR, pp. 1155–1162. IEEE (2013)

44. Yang, C., Zhang, L., Lu, H., Ruan, X., Yang, M.H.: Saliency detection via graph-based manifold ranking. In: CVPR, pp. 3166–3173. IEEE (2013)

45. Zhang, G.X., Cheng, M.M., Hu, S.M., Martin, R.R.: A shape-preserving approach to image resizing. Comput. Graph. Forum **28**(7), 1897–1906 (2009)

46. Zhang, J. et al.: Salient object subitizing. In: CVPR, pp. 4045–4054. IEEE (2015)

47. Zhang, J., Sclaroff, S., Lin, Z., Shen, X., Price, B., Mech, R.: Unconstrained salient object detection via proposal subset optimization. In: CVPR, pp. 5733–5742. IEEE (2016)

48. Zhang, J., Dai, Y., Porikli, F.: Deep salient object detection by integrating multi-level cues. In: Winter Conference on Applications of Computer Vision (WACV), pp. 1–10. IEEE (2017)

49. Zhang, P., Wang, D., Lu, H., Wang, H., Ruan, X.: Amulet: aggregating multi-level convolutional features for salient object detection. In: ICCV, pp. 202–211 (2017)

50. Zhang, P., Wang, D., Lu, H., Wang, H., Yin, B.: Learning uncertain convolutional features for accurate saliency detection. In: ICCV, pp. 212–221 (2017)

51. Zhao, R., Ouyang, W., Li, H., Wang, X.: Saliency detection by multi-context deep learning. In: CVPR, pp. 1265–1274. IEEE (2015)

Gray-Box Adversarial Training

B. S. Vivek$^{(\boxtimes)}$ (iD), Konda Reddy Mopuri (iD), and R. Venkatesh Babu (iD)

Indian Institute of Science, Bangalore, India
svivek@iisc.ac.in, kondamopuri@iisc.ac.in, venky@iisc.ac.in

Abstract. Adversarial samples are perturbed inputs crafted to mislead the machine learning systems. A training mechanism, called adversarial training, which presents adversarial samples along with clean samples has been introduced to learn robust models. In order to scale adversarial training for large datasets, these perturbations can only be crafted using fast and simple methods (e.g., gradient ascent). However, it is shown that adversarial training converges to a degenerate minimum, where the model appears to be robust by generating weaker adversaries. As a result, the models are vulnerable to simple black-box attacks.

In this paper we, (i) demonstrate the shortcomings of existing evaluation policy, (ii) introduce novel variants of white-box and black-box attacks, dubbed "gray-box adversarial attacks" based on which we propose novel evaluation method to assess the robustness of the learned models, and (iii) propose a novel variant of adversarial training, named "Gray-box Adversarial Training" that uses intermediate versions of the models to seed the adversaries. Experimental evaluation demonstrates that the models trained using our method exhibit better robustness compared to both undefended and adversarially trained models.

Keywords: Adversarial perturbations
Attacks on machine learning models · Adversarial training
Robust machine learning models

1 Introduction

Machine learning models are observed [1,2,4,7,17,20] to be susceptible to *adversarial examples*: samples perturbed with mild but structured noise to manipulate model's output. Further, Szegedy *et al.* [20] demonstrated that adversarial samples are transferable across multiple models, i.e., samples crafted to mislead one model often fool other models also. This will enable to launch simple black-box attacks [12,18] on the models deployed in real world. These methods to generate

Electronic supplementary material The online version of this chapter (https://doi.org/10.1007/978-3-030-01267-0_13) contains supplementary material, which is available to authorized users.

© Springer Nature Switzerland AG 2018
V. Ferrari et al. (Eds.): ECCV 2018, LNCS 11219, pp. 213–228, 2018.
https://doi.org/10.1007/978-3-030-01267-0_13

adversarial samples, generally known as *adversaries*, range from simple gradient ascent [4] to complex optimization procedures (e.g., [14]).

Augmenting the training data with adversarial samples, known as *Adversarial Training (AT)* [4,20] has been introduced as a simple defense mechanism against these attacks. In the adversarial training regime, models are trained with mini-batches comprising of both clean and adversarial samples, typically obtained from the same model. It is shown by Madry *et al.* [13] that adversarial training helps to learn models robust to white-box attacks, provided the perturbations computed during the training closely maximize the model's loss. However, in order to scale adversarial training for large datasets, the perturbations can only be crafted with fast and simple methods such as single-step FGSM [4,9], an attack based on linearization of the model's loss. Tramèr *et al.* [21] demonstrated that adversarial training with single-step attacks leads to a degenerate minimum where linear approximation of model's loss is not reliable. They revealed that the model's decision surface exhibits sharp curvature near the data points which leads to overfitting in adversarially trained models. Thus, (i) adversarially trained models using single-step attacks remain susceptible to simple attacks, and (ii) perturbations crafted on undefended models transfer and form black-box attacks.

Tramèr *et al.* [21] proposed to decouple the adversary generation process from the model parameters and to increase the diversity of the perturbations shown to the model during training. Their training mechanism, called *Ensemble Adversarial Training (EAT)*, incorporates perturbations from multiple (e.g., N different) pre-trained models. They showed that EAT enables to learn models with increased robustness against black-box attacks.

However, EAT has severe drawbacks in presenting diverse perturbations during the training. Since they augment the white-box perturbations (from the model being learned) with black-box perturbations from an ensemble of different pre-trained models, it is required to train those models before we start learning a robust model. Therefore, the computational cost increases linearly with the population of the ensemble. Because of this, the experiments presented in [21] have a maximum of 4 members in the ensemble. Though it is argued that diverse set of perturbations is important to learn robust models, EAT fails to efficiently bring diversity to the table.

Unlike EAT, we demonstrate that it is feasible to efficiently generate diverse set of perturbations and augment the white-box perturbations. Further, utilizing these additional perturbations we learn models that are significantly robust compared to those learned with vanilla and ensemble adversarial training (EAT). The major contributions of this work can be listed as follows:

- We bring out an important observation that the pseudo robustness of an adversarially trained model is due to the limitations in the existing evaluation procedure.
- We introduce a novel evaluation procedure via robustness plots (3.2) and a derived metric "Worst-case Performance (A_w)" that can assess the susceptibility of the learned models. For that, we present variants of the white-box

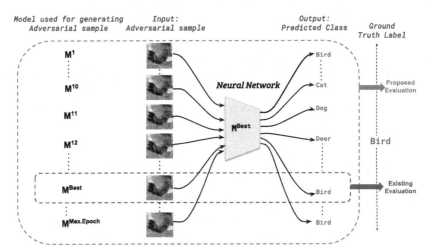

Fig. 1. Overview of existing and proposed evaluation methods for testing the robustness of *adversarially trained network* against adversarial attacks. For existing evaluation, *best model's* robustness against adversarial attack is tested by obtaining it's prediction on adversarial samples generated by itself. Whereas, for the proposed evaluation method adversarial samples are not only generated by *best model* but also by the intermediate models obtained while training.

and black-box attacks, termed "Gray-box adversarial attacks" that can be launched by temporally evolving intermediate models. Given the efficiency to generate and the ability to examine the robustness, we strongly recommend the community to consider robustness plots and "Worst-case Performance" as standard bench-marking for evaluating the models.
- Harnessing the above observations, we propose a novel variant of adversarial training, termed "Gray-box Adversarial Training" that uses our gray-box perturbations in order to learn robust models.

The paper is organized as follows: Sect. 2 introduces the notation followed in the subsequent sections of the paper, Sect. 3 presents the drawbacks in the current robustness evaluation methods for deep networks and proposes improved procedure, Sect. 4 hosts the experiments and results, Sect. 5 discusses existing works that are relevant, and Sect. 6 concludes the paper.

2 Notations and Terminology

In this section we define the notations followed throughout this paper:

- x : clean image from the dataset.
- x^* : a potential adversarial image corresponding to the image x.
- y_{true} : ground truth label corresponding to the image x.

- y_{pred} : prediction of the neural network for the input image x.
- ϵ : defines the strength of perturbation added to the clean image.
- θ : parameters of the neural network.
- J : loss function used to train the neural network.
- $\nabla_x J$: gradient of the loss J with respect to image x.
- *Best Model* (M^{Best}): Model corresponding to least validation loss, typically obtained at the end of the training.
- M_t^i : represents model at *ith* epoch of training, obtained when network M is trained using method 't'.

3   Gray-Box Adversarial Attacks

3.1   Limitations of Existing Evaluation Method

Existing ways of evaluating an adversarially trained network consists of evaluating the best model's accuracy on adversarial samples generated by itself. This way of evaluating the networks gives false inference about their robustness against adversarial attacks. This assumes (though explicitly not mentioned) that robustness to the adversarial samples generated by the best model extends to the adversarial samples generated by the intermediate models evolved during the training, crafted via linear approximation of the loss (e.g., FGSM [4]). Clearly, this is not true, as shown by our robustness plots (see Fig. 2). We show this by obtaining robustness plot which captures accuracy of best-model not only on adversarial samples generated by itself but also on adversarial samples generated by the intermediate models, which are obtained during training. Based on the above facts we propose two new ways of evaluating adversarially trained network, shown in Table 1.

3.2   Robustness Plot and Worst-Case Performance

We propose a new way of evaluating the robustness of a network, which is a plot of recognition accuracy of the best model M^{Best} on adversarial samples of different perturbation strengths ϵ, generated by multiple intermediate models that are obtained during training. That is, performance of the model under investigation is evaluated against the adversaries of different perturbation strengths ϵ, generated by checkpoints or models saved during training. Based on the source of these *saved models* which seed adversarial samples, we differentiate robustness plot into two categories.

- If the saved models and the best model are obtained from the same network and also they both have the same training procedure, then we name such *robustness plot* as *Extended White-box robustness plot*. Further, we name the attacks as "*Extended White-box adversarial attacks*".
- Else, if the network trained or the training procedure used are different, then we call such robustness plot as *Extended Black-box robustness plot* and such attacks as "*Extended Black-box adversarial attacks*".

In general, we call these attacks as *Gray-box adversarial attacks*. We believe it is intuitive to call the proposed attacks as "Extensions" to existing white and black box attacks. White-box attack means the attacker has full access to the target model: architecture, parameters, training data and procedure. Typically, source model that creates adversaries is same as the target model under attack. Whereas, "extended white-box" attack means, some aspects of the setup are known while some are not. Specifically, the architecture and the training procedure of the source and target model are same while the model parameters differ. Similarly, black-box attack means the scenario where the attacker has no information about the target such as architecture, parameters, training procedure, etc. Generally, the source model would be a fully trained model that has different architecture (and hence parameters) compared to the target model. However, the "extended black-box" attack mean, the source model can be a partially trained model having different network architecture. Note that it is not very different compared to the existing black-box attack except the source model can now be a partially trained model. We jointly call these two extended attacks as "Gray-box Adversarial Attacks". Table 1 lists the definitions of both the existing and our extended attacks with the notation we introduced earlier in the paper.

Table 1. List of the adversarial attacks. Note that the subscript denotes the training procedure how the model is trained, superscript denotes the training epoch at which the model is considered. M^i denotes intermediate model and M^{Best} denotes the best model.

Source	Target	Name of the attack
$M_{Adv.}^{Best}$	$M_{Adv.}^{Best}$	White-box attack
X_{normal}^{Best}	$M_{Adv.}^{Best}$	Black-box attack
$M_{Adv.}^{i}$, $i = 1, \ldots, \text{MaxEpoch}$	$M_{Adv.}^{Best}$	Extended White-box attack
$X_{Normal/Adv.}^{i}$, $i = 1, \ldots, \text{MaxEpoch}$	$M_{Adv.}^{Best}$	Extended Black-box attack

Worst-Case Performance (A_w): We introduce a metric derived from the proposed robustness plot to infer the susceptibility of the trained model quantitatively in terms of its weakest performance. We name it "Worst-case Performance (A_w)" of the model, which is the least recognition accuracy achieved for a given attack strength (ϵ). Ideally, for a robust model the value of A_w should be high (close to its performance on clean samples).

3.3 Which Attack to Use for Adversarial Training, FGSM, FGSM-LL or FGSM-Rand?

Kurakin *et al.* [9] suggested to use FGSM-LL or FGSM-Rand variants for adversarial training, in order to reduce the effect of *label leaking* [9]. *Label leaking* effect is observed in adversarially trained networks, where the accuracy of the model on the adversarial samples of higher perturbation is greater than that on the adversarial samples of lower perturbation. It is necessary for adversarial training to include stronger attacks in the training process in order to make the model robust. We empirically show (in Sect. 4.2 and Fig. 3) that FGSM is stronger attack compared to FGSM-LL and FGSM-Rand through robustness plots with the three different attacks for a normally trained network.

In addition, for models (of same architecture) adversarially trained using FGSM, FGSM-LL and FGSM-Rand attacks respectively, FGSM attack causes more damage compared to other two attacks. We show (in Sect. 4.2 and Fig. 4) this by obtaining robustness plots with FGSM, FGSM-LL, and FGSM-Rand attacks respectively, for all three variants of adversarial training methods. Based on these observations we use FGSM for all our experiments.

3.4   Gray-Box Adversarial Training

Based on the observations presented in Sect. 3.1, we propose *Gray-box Adversarial Training* in Algorithm 1 to alleviate the drawbacks of existing adversarial training. During training, for every iteration, we replace a portion of clean samples in the mini-batch with its corresponding adversarial samples which are generated not only by the current state of the network but also by one of the saved intermediate models. We use "drop in training loss" as a criterion for saving these intermediate models during training i.e., for every D drop in the training loss we save the model and this process of saving the models continues until training loss reaches minimum prefixed value EL (End Loss).

The intuition behind using "drop in training loss" as a criterion for saving the intermediate models is that, models substantially apart in the training (evolution) process can source different set of adversaries. Having variety of adversarial samples to participate in the adversarial training procedure makes the model robust [21]. As training progresses, network representations evolve and loss decreases from the initial value. Thus, we use the "drop in training loss" as a useful index to pick source models that can potentially generate different adversaries. We represent this quantity as D in the proposed algorithm.

Ideally we would like to have an ensemble of as many different source models as possible. However, bigger ensembles would pose additional challenges such as computational, memory overheads and slow down the training process. Therefore, D has to be picked depending on the trade-off between performance and overhead. Note that too small value of D will include highly correlated models in the ensemble. Also, towards later stages of the training, model evolves very slowly and representations would not change significantly. So, after some time into the training, we stop augmenting the ensemble of source models. For this we define a parameter denoted as EL (End Loss) which is a threshold on the loss that defines when to stop saving the intermediate models. During the training process, once the loss falls below EL, we stop saving of intermediate models and prevent augmenting the ensemble with redundant models.

Further, in the best case we would like to pick different saved model for every iteration during our Gray-box Adversarial Training. However, this creates bottleneck because loading a saved model at each iteration is time consuming. In order to reduce this additional overhead, we pick a saved model and use this

---

Algorithm 1: Gray-box adversarial training of network N

Input:

      m = Size of the training minibatch

      k = No. of adversarial images in minibatch generated using current state of the network N

      p = No. of adversarial images in minibatch generated using ith state of the network N

      $MaxItertion$ = Maximum training iterations

      Number of clean samples in minibatch = $m - k - p$

      Hyper-parameters EL, D and T

1 **Initialization**

  Randomly initialize network **N**

  /*Set containing the iterations at which seed models are saved*/

  $AdvBag =\{\}$

  $AdvPtr=0$ */*Pointer to elements in set 'AdvBag'*/*

  $i=0$ */*Refers to initial state of the network*/*

  Initialize $LossSetPoint$ with initial training loss

  $iteration = 0$

2 **while** $iteration \neq MaxItertion$ **do**

3   Read minibatch $B = \{x^1, \ldots, x^m\}$ from training set

4   Generate 'k' adversarial examples $\{x_{adv}^1, \ldots, x_{adv}^k\}$ from corresponding clean samples $\{x^1, \ldots, x^k\}$ using current state of the network N

5   Generate 'p' adversarial examples $\{x_{adv}^{k+1}, \ldots, x_{adv}^{k+p}\}$ from corresponding clean samples $\{x^{k+1}, \ldots, x^{k+p}\}$ using ith state of the network N

6   Make new minibatch $B^* = \{x_{adv}^1, \ldots, x_{adv}^k, x_{adv}^{k+1}, \ldots, x_{adv}^{k+p}, x^{k+p+1}, \ldots, x^m\}$

7   */*forward pass, compute loss, backward pass, and update parameters*/*

8   Do one training step of Network N using minibatch B^*

9   */*moving average loss computed over 10 iterations*/*

      $LossCurrentValue = MovingAverage(loss)$

10   */*Logic for saving seed model */*

11   **if** $(LossSetPoint - LossCurrentValue) \geq D$ and $LossSetPoint \geq EL$ **then**

12         $AdvBag.add(iteration)$

13   SaveModel($N^{iteration}$)

14         $LossSetPoint = LossCurrentValue$

15   **end**

16   */*Logic for picking saved seed model*/*

17   **if** $(iteration \% T) == 0$ and $len(AdvBank) \neq 0$ **then**

18         $i = AdvBank[AdvPtr]$

19         $AdvPtr = (AdvPtr + 1)\% len(AdvBank)$

20   **end**

21     $iteration = iteration + 1$

22 **end**

---

for T consecutive iterations after which we pick another saved model in a round-robin fashion. In total, we have three hyper-parameters namely, D, EL, and T, and we show the effect of these hyper-parameters in Sect. 4.3.

4 Experiments

In our experiments we show results on CIFAR-100, CIFAR-10 [8], and MNIST [10] dataset. We work with WideResNet-28-10 [22] for CIFAR-100, ResNet-18 [6] for CIFAR-10 and LeNet [11] for MNIST dataset, all these networks achieve near state of the art performance on the respective dataset. These networks are trained for 100 epochs (25 epochs for LeNet) using SGD with momentum, and models are saved at the end of each epoch. For learning rate scheduling, step-policy is used. We pre-process images to be in [0, 1] range, and random crop and horizontal flip are performed for data-augmentation (except for MNIST). Experiments and results on MNIST dataset are shown in supplementary document.

4.1 Limitations of Existing Evaluation Method

In this subsection, we present the relevant experiments to understand the issues present in the existing evaluation method as discussed in Sect. 3.1. We adversarially train, WideResNet-28-10 and ResNet-18 on CIFAR-100 and CIFAR-10 datasets respectively and while training, FGSM is used for adversarial sample generation process. After training, we obtain their corresponding Extended White-box robustness plot using FGSM attack. Figure 2 shows the obtained Extended White-box robustness plot. It can be observed that adversarially trained networks are not robust to the adversaries generated by the intermediate models, which the existing way of evaluation fails to capture. It also infers that the implicit assumption of best model's robustness to adversaries generated by the intermediate models is false. We also reiterate the fact that existing adversarial training formulation does not make the network robust but makes them to generate weaker adversaries.

4.2 Which Attack to use for Adversarial Training, FGSM, FGSM-LL or FGSM-Rand?

We perform normal training of WideResNet-28-10 on CIFAR-100 dataset and obtain its corresponding Extended White-box robustness plots using FGSM, FGSM-LL, and FGSM-Rand attacks respectively. Figure 3 shows the obtained plots. It is clear that FGSM attack (column-1) produces stronger attacks compared to FGSM-LL (column-2) and FGSM-Rand (column-3) attacks. That is, drop in the model's accuracy is more for FGSM attack.

Additionally, we adversarially train the above network using FGSM, FGSM-LL and FGSM-Rand respectively for adversarial sample generation process. After training, we obtain robustness plots with FGSM, FGSM-LL and FGSM-Rand attacks respectively. Figure 4 shows the obtained Extended White-box robustness plots for all the three versions of adversarial training. It is observed that the model is more susceptible to FGSM attack (column-1) compared to other two attacks. Similar trends are observed for networks trained on CIFAR-10 and MNIST datasets and corresponding results are shown in supplementary document.

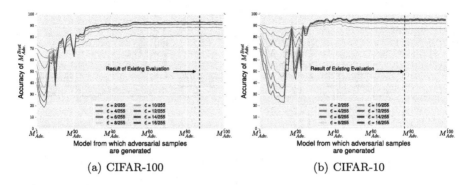

(a) CIFAR-100   (b) CIFAR-10

Fig. 2. Extended White-box robustness plots with FGSM attack, obtained for (a) WideResNet-28-10 adversarially trained on CIFAR-100 dataset, (b) ResNet-18 adversarially trained on CIFAR-10 dataset. Note that the classification accuracy of the best model (M_{Adv}^{Best}) is poor for the attacks generated by early models (towards origin) as opposed to that by the later models.

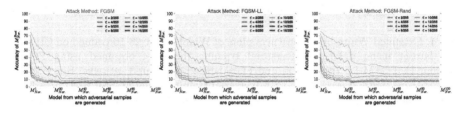

Fig. 3. Extended White-box robustness plots of WideResNet-28-10 normally trained on CIFAR-100 dataset, obtained using FGSM (column-1), FGSM-LL (column-2) and FGSM-Rand (column-3) attacks. Note that for a wide range of perturbations, FGSM attack causes more dip in the accuracy

4.3 Gray-Box Adversarial Training

We train WideResNet-28-10 and Resent-18 on CIFAR-100 and CIFAR-10 datasets respectively, using the proposed Gray-box Adversarial Training (GAT) algorithm. In order to create strong adversaries, we chose FGSM to generate adversarial samples. We use the same set of hyper-parameters $D = 0.2$, $EL = 0.5$, and $T = (1/4th$ of an epoch), for all the networks trained. Specifically, we save intermediate models for every 0.2 drop (D) in the training loss till the loss falls below 0.5 (EL). Also, each of the saved models are sampled from the ensemble, generates adversarial samples for 1/4th of an epoch. After training, we obtain Extended White-box robustness plots and Extended Black-box robustness plots for networks trained with the Gray-box adversarial training (Algorithm 1) and for adversarially trained networks. Figure 5 shows the

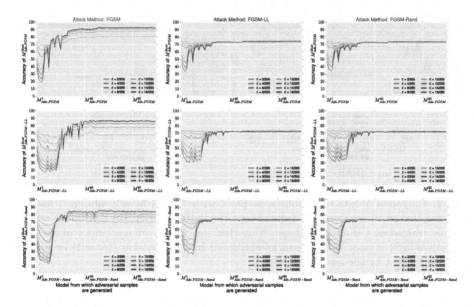

Fig. 4. Extended White-box robustness plots of WideResNet-28-10 trained on CIFAR-100 dataset using different adversarial training methods, obtained using FGSM (column-1), FGSM-LL (column-2) and FGSM-Rand (column-3) attacks. Rows represents training method used, Row-1 : Adversarial training using FGSM, Row-2 : Adversarial training using FGSM-LL and Row-3 : Adversarial training using FGSM-Rand.

obtained robustness plots, it is observed from the plots that in the proposed gray-box adversarial training (row-2) there are no deep valleys in the robustness plots, whereas for the networks trained using existing adversarially training method (row-1) exhibits deep valley in the robustness plots. Table 2 presents the *worst-case accuracy* A_w of the models trained using different training methods. Note that A_w is significantly better for the proposed *GAT* compared to the model trained with *AT* and *EAT* for a wide range of attack strength (ϵ).

Effect of Hyper-parameters: In order to study the effect of hyper parameters, we train ResNet-18 on CIFAR-10 dataset using Gray-box adversarial training for different hyper-parameter settings. Extended White-box robustness plots are obtained for each setting with two of them fixed and the other being varied. The hyper-parameter D defines the value of "drop in training loss" for which intermediate models are saved to generate adversarial samples. Figure 6a shows the effect of varying D from 0.2 to 0.4. It is observed that for higher values of D, the depth and the width of the valley increases. This is because choosing higher values of D might miss saving of models that are potential sources for generating stronger adversarial samples, and also choosing very low values of D will results in saving large number of models that are redundant and may not be useful. The hyper-parameter EL decides when to stop saving of intermediate seed models.

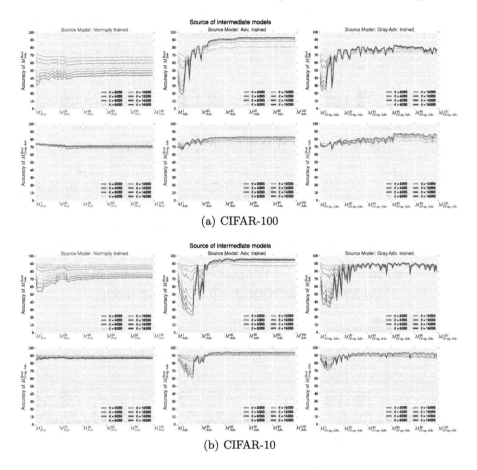

(a) CIFAR-100

(b) CIFAR-10

Fig. 5. Robustness plots obtained using FGSM attack for (a)WideResNet-28-10 trained on CIFAR-100 and (b) ResNet-18 trained on CIFAR-10. Rows represents the training method, Row-1:Model trained adversarially using FGSM and Row-2:Model trained using Gray-box adversarial training. Adversarial samples are generated by intermediate models of Column-1:Normal training, Column-2: Adversarial training using FGSM, Column-3:Gray-box adversarial training

Figure 6b shows the effect of EL for fixed values of D and T. We observe that as EL increases the width of the valley increases since higher values of EL prevents saving of potential models. Finally, the hyper-parameter T decides the duration for which a member of ensemble is used after getting sampled from the ensemble to generate adversarial samples. Figure 6c shows the effect of varying T from $1/4th$ epoch to $3/4th$ epoch. Note that T has minimal effect on the robustness plot within that range.

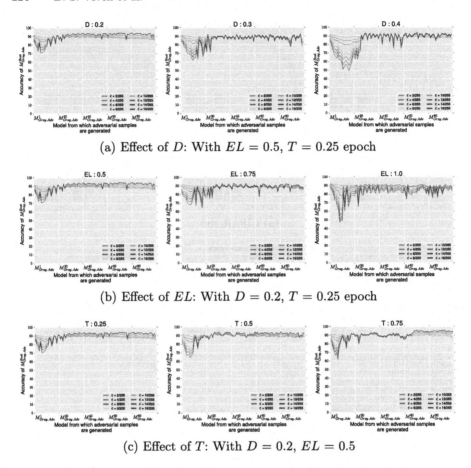

(a) Effect of D: With $EL = 0.5$, $T = 0.25$ epoch

(b) Effect of EL: With $D = 0.2$, $T = 0.25$ epoch

(c) Effect of T: With $D = 0.2$, $EL = 0.5$

Fig. 6. Extended White-box robustness plots of ResNet-18 trained on CIFAR-10 dataset using Gray-box adversarial training (Algorithm 1), for different hyper-parameters settings. Effects of hyper-parameters are shown in (a) Effect of D, (b) Effect of EL and (c) Effect of T (measured in fraction of an epoch).

4.4   Ensemble Adversarial Training

In this subsection, we compare our Gray-box Adversarial Training against Ensemble Adversarial Training [21]. We work with the networks on CIFAR-100 and CIFAR-10 datasets. Ensemble adversarial training uses fixed set of pre-trained models for generating adversarial samples along with the current state of the network. For each iteration during training, the source model for generating adversaries is picked at random among the current and ensemble models. Table 3 shows the setup used for ensemble adversarial training, which contains network to be trained, pre-trained source models used for generating adversarial samples and the held-out model used for black-box attack. Figure 7 shows the Extended White-box robustness plots for the networks trained using ensemble adversar-

Table 2. Worst case accuracy of models trained on (a) CIFAR-100 and (b) CIFAR-10, using different training methods. For ensemble adversarial training (EAT) refer to Sect. 4.4. A, B and C refers to the ensemble used in EAT.

(a) CIFAR-100						(b) CIFAR-10					
Training Method		A_w for various ϵ				Training Method		A_w for various ϵ			
		2/255	4/255	8/255	16/255			2/255	4/255	8/255	16/255
Normal		20.81	11.58	7.09	4.8	Normal		38.15	20.84	12.2	9.34
AT		70.04	62.34	44.04	18.58	Adversarial		87.08	79.25	56.09	22.87
EAT	A	65.39	55.55	36.8	15.2	EAT	A	83.27	73.4	53.96	31.01
	B	65.45	54.63	35.65	14.26		B	82.56	72.35	56.11	34.84
	C	65.71	56.05	37.43	15.98		C	82.64	73.84	55.19	32.33
GAT(ours)		**70.84**	**66.5**	**65.43**	**67.41**	GAT(ours)		**89.46**	**85.89**	**79.28**	**60.81**

Table 3. Setup for ensemble adversarial training

	Network to be trained	Pre-trained models	Held-out model
CIFAR-100	WideResNet-28-10(Ensemble-A)	Resnet-50, ResNet-34	WideResNet-28-10
	WideResNet-28-10(Ensemble-B)	WideResNet-28-10, ResNet-50	ResNet-34
	WideResNet-28-10(Ensemble-C)	WideResNet-28-10, ResNet-34	ResNet-50
CIFAR-10	ResNet-34(Ensemble-A)	ResNet-34, ResNet-18	VGG-16
	ResNet-34(Ensemble-B)	ResNet-34, VGG-16	ResNet-18
	ResNet-34(Ensemble-C)	ResNet-18, VGG-16	ResNet-34

ial training algorithm. Note the presence of deep and wide valleys in the plot. Whereas, the Extended White-box robustness plots for the models trained using the Gray-box adversarial training shown in Fig. 5 (row:2, column:3), do not have deep and wide valley. Also, because of the space restrictions, Extended Black-box robustness plots for the above trained networks using ensemble adversarial training algorithm are shown in supplementary document.

5   Related Works

Following the findings of Szegedy *et al.* [20], various attack methods (e.g. [3,4,14–16]) and various defense techniques (e.g. [4,5,13,19,21]) have been proposed. On the defense side, adversarial training shows promising results. In order to scale adversarial training [9] to large datasets, single-step attack methods (use 1st order approximation of model's loss to generate attack) are used while training. Goodfellow *et al.* [4] observed that adversarially trained models, incurs higher loss on transferred samples than on the white-box single-step attacks. Further, Kurakin [9] observed that adversarially trained models were susceptible to adversarial samples generated using multi-step methods under white-box setting. This paradoxical behaviour is explained by Tramèr *et al.* [21] through the inaccuracy of linear approximation of the model's loss function in the vicinity of the data samples. Madry et al. [13] showed that adversarially trained model can become robust against white-box attacks, if adversaries added during training closely maximizes the model's loss. However, such methods are hard to scale to difficult tasks such as ILSVRC [9]. Tramèr *et al.* [21] showed that having diversity

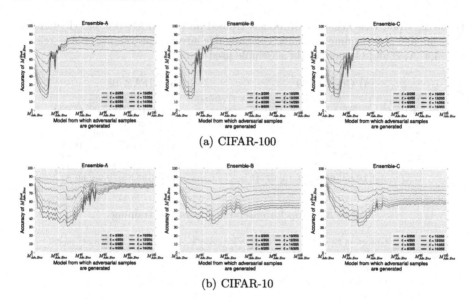

Fig. 7. Extended White-box robustness plots of models trained using ensemble adversarial training algorithm. (a) models trained on CIFAR-100 dataset and (b) models trained on CIFAR-10 dataset

in the adversarial samples presented during the training can alleviate the effect of gradient masking. However, it is inefficient to have an ensemble of different pre-trained models to seed the adversarial samples. Apart from highlighting the flaws in the existing evaluation and proposing better evaluation method, we propose efficient way of generating diverse adversarial samples for learning robust models.

6   Conclusions

Presence of adversarial samples indicates the vulnerability of the machine learning models. Learning robust models and measuring their susceptibility against adversarial attacks are need of the day. In this paper, we demonstrated important gaps in the existing evaluation method for testing the robustness of a model against adversarial attacks. Also, we proposed a novel evaluation method called "Robustness plots" and a derived metric "Worst-case performance (A_w)". From the proposed evaluation method, it is observed that the existing adversarial training methods which use first order approximation of loss function for generating samples, do not make the model robust. Instead, they make the model to generate weaker adversaries. Finally, the proposed "Gray-box Adversarial Training (GAT)" which harnesses the presence of stronger adversaries during training, achieves better robustness against adversarial attacks compared to the existing adversarial training methods (that follow single step adversarial generation process).

References

1. Biggio, B., et al.: Evasion attacks against machine learning at test time. In: Joint European Conference on Machine Learning and Knowledge Discovery in Databases, pp. 387–402 (2013)
2. Biggio, B., Fumera, G., Roli, F.: Pattern recognition systems under attack: design issues and research challenges. Int. J. Pattern Recogn. Artif. Intell. **28**(07) (2014)
3. Carlini, N., Wagner, D.A.: Towards evaluating the robustness of neural networks. In: 2017 IEEE Symposium on Security and Privacy, SP 2017, San Jose, CA, USA, pp. 39–57 (22–26 May 2017)
4. Goodfellow, I.J., Shlens, J., Szegedy, C.: Explaining and harnessing adversarial examples. In: International Conference on Learning Representations (ICLR) (2015)
5. Guo, C., Rana, M., Cisse, M., van der Maaten, L.: Countering adversarial images using input transformations. In: International Conference on Learning Representations (ICLR) (2018)
6. He, K., Zhang, X., Ren, S., Sun, J.: Deep residual learning for image recognition. In: Proceedings of the IEEE Computer Vision and Pattern Recognition (CVPR), pp. 770–778 (2016)
7. Huang, L., Joseph, A.D., Nelson, B., Rubinstein, B.I., Tygar, J.D.: Adversarial machine learning. In: Proceedings of the 4th ACM Workshop on Security and Artificial Intelligence. AISec 2011 (2011)
8. Krizhevsky, A.: Learning multiple layers of features from tiny images. Technical report, University of Toronto (2009)
9. Kurakin, A., Goodfellow, I.J., Bengio, S.: Adversarial machine learning at scale. In: International Conference on Learning Representations (ICLR) (2017)
10. LeCun, Y.: The mnist database of handwritten digits. http://yann.lecun.com/exdb/mnist/
11. LeCun, Y., et al.: Lenet-5, convolutional neural networks. http://yann.lecun.com/exdb/lenet/
12. Liu, Y., Chen, X., Liu, C., Song, D.: Delving into transferable adversarial examples and black-box attacks. In: International Conference on Learning Representations (ICLR) (2017)
13. Madry, A., Makelov, A., Schmidt, L., Dimitris, T., Vladu, A.: Towards deep learning models resistant to adversarial attacks. In: International Conference on Learning Representations (ICLR) (2018)
14. Moosavi-Dezfooli, S.M., Fawzi, A., Frossard, P.: Deepfool: a simple and accurate method to fool deep neural networks. In: Proceedings of the IEEE Conference on Computer Vision and Pattern Recognition (CVPR), pp. 2574–2582 (2016)
15. Mopuri, K.R., Garg, U., Babu, R.V.: Fast feature fool: a data independent approach to universal adversarial perturbations. In: Proceedings of the British Machine Vision Conference (BMVC) (2017)
16. Mopuri, K.R., Ojha, U., Garg, U., Babu, R.V.: NAG: Network for adversary generation. In: Proceedings of the IEEE Computer Vision and Pattern Recognition (CVPR) (2018)
17. Papernot, N., McDaniel, P., Jha, S., Fredrikson, M., Celik, Z.B., Swami, A.: The limitations of deep learning in adversarial settings. In: 2016 IEEE European Symposium on Security and Privacy (EuroS&P), pp. 372–387. IEEE (2016)
18. Papernot, N., McDaniel, P.D., Goodfellow, I.J., Jha, S., Celik, Z.B., Swami, A.: Practical black-box attacks against deep learning systems using adversarial examples. In: Asia Conference on Computer and Communications Security (ASIACCS) (2017)

19. Samangouei, P., Kabkab, M., Chellappa, R.: Defense-GAN: protecting classifiers against adversarial attacks using generative models. In: International Conference on Learning Representations (ICLR) (2018)
20. Szegedy, C., et al. : Intriguing properties of neural networks. In: International Conference on Learning Representations (ICLR) (2014)
21. Tramèr, F., Kurakin, A., Papernot, N., Boneh, D., McDaniel, P.: Ensemble adversarial training: attacks and defenses. In: International Conference on Learning Representations (ICLR) (2018)
22. Zagoruyko, S., Komodakis, N.: Wide residual networks. In: Richard C., Wilson, E.R.H., Smith, W.A.P. (eds.) Proceedings of the British Machine Vision Conference (BMVC), pp. 87.1–87.12. BMVA Press (Sept 2016)

Visual Question Answering as a Meta Learning Task

Damien Teney$^{(\boxtimes)}$ and Anton van den Hengel

Australian Institute for Machine Learning, University of Adelaide,
Adelaide, Australia
{damien.teney,anton.vandenhengel}@adelaide.edu.au

Abstract. The predominant approach to Visual Question Answering (VQA) demands that the model represents within its weights all of the information required to answer any question about any image. Learning this information from any real training set seems unlikely, and representing it in a reasonable number of weights doubly so. We propose instead to approach VQA as a meta learning task, thus separating the question answering method from the information required. At test time, the method is provided with a support set of example questions/answers, over which it reasons to resolve the given question. The support set is not fixed and can be extended without retraining, thereby expanding the capabilities of the model. To exploit this dynamically provided information, we adapt a state-of-the-art VQA model with two techniques from the recent meta learning literature, namely prototypical networks and meta networks. Experiments demonstrate the capability of the system to learn to produce completely novel answers (*i.e.* never seen during training) from examples provided at test time. In comparison to the existing state of the art, the proposed method produces qualitatively distinct results with higher recall of rare answers, and a better sample efficiency that allows training with little initial data. More importantly, it represents an important step towards vision-and-language methods that can learn and reason on-the-fly.

The task of Visual Question Answering (VQA) demands that an agent correctly answer a previously unseen question about a previously unseen image. The fact that neither the question nor the image is specified until test time means that the agent must embody most of the achievements of Computer Vision and Natural Language Processing, and many of those of Artificial Intelligence.

VQA is typically framed in a purely supervised learning setting. A large training set of example questions, images, and their correct answers is used to train a method to map a question and image to scores over a predetermined, fixed vocabulary of possible answers using the maximum likelihood [39]. This approach has inherent scalability issues, as it attempts to represent all world

Electronic supplementary material The online version of this chapter (https://doi.org/10.1007/978-3-030-01267-0_14) contains supplementary material, which is available to authorized users.

© Springer Nature Switzerland AG 2018
V. Ferrari et al. (Eds.): ECCV 2018, LNCS 11219, pp. 229–245, 2018.
https://doi.org/10.1007/978-3-030-01267-0_14

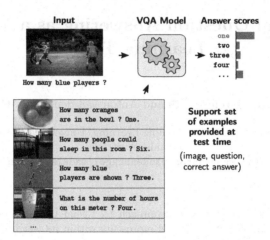

Fig. 1. This paper considers visual question answering in a meta learning setting. The model is initially trained on a small set of questions/answers, and is provided with a, possibly large, additional *support set* of examples at test time. The model must *learn to learn*, or to exploit the additional data on-the-fly, without the need for retraining the model. Notably, performance improves as additional and more relevant examples are included.

knowledge within the finite set of parameters of a model such as deep neural network. Consequently, a trained VQA system can only be expected to produce correct answers to questions from a very similar distribution to those in the training set. Extending the model knowledge or expanding its domain coverage is only possible by retraining it from scratch, which is computationally costly, at best. This approach is thus fundamentally incapable of fulfilling the ultimate promise of VQA, which is answering general questions about general images.

As a solution to these issues we propose a meta-learning approach to the problem. The meta learning approach implies that the model *learns to learn*, *i.e.* it learns to use a set of examples provided at test time to answer the given question (Fig. 1). Those examples are questions and images, each with their correct answer, such as might form part of the training set in a traditional setting. They are referred to here as the *support set*. Importantly, the support set is not fixed. Note also that the support set may be large, and that the majority of its elements may have no relevance to the current question. It is provided to the model at test time, and can be expanded with additional examples to increase the capabilities of the model. The model we propose 'learns to learn' in that it is able to identify and exploit the relevant examples within a potentially large support set dynamically, at test time. Providing the model with more information thus does not require retraining, and the ability to exploit such a support set greatly improves the practicality and scalability of the system. Indeed, it is ultimately desirable for a practical VQA system to be adaptable to new domains and to continuously improve as more data becomes available. That vision is a long term objective and this work takes only a small step in that direction.

There is significant practical interest to the meta-learning approach to VQA. It can ultimately allow the following scenarios, which are well outside the reach of traditional approaches:

- models using constantly expanding support (*e.g.* from knowledge bases, surveillance imagery, medical data, *etc.*.) with no need for constant retraining;
- models using support data too large to be captured within the weights of the model *e.g.* from web searches;
- models trained and distributed without encapsulating sensitive data, for privacy or security reasons; after training the model on sanitized data, it is provided **at test time only** with the sensitive information.

Our central technical contribution is to adapt a state-of-the-art VQA model [34] to the meta learning setting. The resulting model is a deep neural network that uses sets of dynamic parameters – also known as fast weights – determined at test time depending on the provided support set. The dynamic parameters allow to modify adaptively the computations performed by the network and adapt its behaviour depending on the support set. We perform a detailed study to evaluate the effectiveness of those techniques under various regimes of training and support set sizes. Those experiments are based on the VQA v2 benchmark, for which we propose data splits appropriate to study a meta learning setting.

A completely new capability demonstrated by the resulting system is to learn to produce completely novel answers (*i.e.* answers not seen during training). Those new answers are only demonstrated by instances of the support set provided at test time. In addition to these new capabilities, the system exhibits a qualitatively distinct behaviour to existing VQA systems in its improved handling of rare answers. Since datasets for VQA exhibit a heavy class imbalance, with a small number of answers being much more frequent than most others, models optimized for current benchmarks are prone to fall back on frequent "safe" answers. In contrast, the proposed model is inherently less likely to fall victim to dataset biases, and exhibits a higher recall over rare answers. The proposed model does *not* surpass existing methods on the common aggregate accuracy metric, as is to be expected given that it does not overfit to the dataset bias, but it nonetheless exhibits desirable traits overall.

The contributions of this paper are summarized as follows.

1. We re-frame VQA as a meta learning task, in which the model is provided a test time with a support set of supervised examples (questions and images with their correct answers).
2. We describe a neural network architecture and training procedure able to leverage the meta learning scenario. The model is based on a state-of-the-art VQA system and takes inspiration in techniques from the recent meta learning literature, namely prototypical networks [33] and meta networks [24].
3. We provide an experimental evaluation of the proposed model in different regimes of training and support set sizes and across variations in design choices.

4. Our results demonstrate the unique capability of the model to produce novel answers, *i.e.* answers never seen during training, by learning from support instances, an improved recall of rare answers, and a better sample efficiency than existing models.

1   Related Work

Visual Question Answering Visual question answering has gathered significant interest from the computer vision community [6], as it constitutes a practical setting to evaluate deep visual understanding. In addition to visual parsing, VQA requires the comprehension of a text question, and combined reasoning over vision and language, sometimes on the basis of external or common-sense knowledge. See [39] for a recent survey of methods and datasets.

VQA is always approached in a supervised setting, using large datasets [6, 15,22,44] of human-proposed questions with their correct answers to train a machine learning model. The *VQA-real* and *VQA v2* datasets [6,15] have served as popular benchmarks by which to evaluate and compare methods. Despite the large scale of those datasets, *e.g.* more than 650,000 questions in *VQA v2*, several limitations have been recognized. These relate to the dataset bias (*i.e.* the non-uniform, long-tailed distribution of answers) and the question-conditioned bias (making answers easy to guess given a question without the image). For example, the answer *Yes* is particularly prominent in [6] compared to *no*, and questions starting with *How many* can be answered correctly with the answer *two* more than 30% of the time [15]. These issues plague development in the field by encouraging methods which fare well on common questions and concepts, rather than on rare answers or more complicated questions. The aggregate accuracy metric used to compare methods is thus a poor indication of method capabilities for visual understanding. Improvements to datasets have been introduced [1,15,43], including the *VQA v2*, but they only partially solve the evaluation problems. An increased interest has appeared in the handling of rare words and answers [29,35]. The model proposed in this paper is inherently less prone to incorporate dataset biases than existing methods, and shows superior performance for handling rare answers. It accomplishes this by keeping a memory made up of explicit representations of training and support instances.

VQA with Additional Data In the classical supervised setting, a fixed set of questions and answers is used to train a model once and for all. With few exceptions, the performance of such a model is fixed as it cannot use additional information at test time. Among those exceptions, [38,40] use an external knowledge base to gather non-visual information related to the input question. In [35], the authors use visual information from web searches in the form of exemplar images of question words, and better handle rare and novel words appearing in questions as a result. In [34], the same authors use similar images from web searches to obtain visual representations of candidate answers.

Those methods use ad-hoc engineered techniques to incorporate external knowledge in the VQA model. In comparison, this paper presents a much more general approach. We expands the model knowledge with data provided in the form of additional supervised examples (questions and images with their correct answer). A demonstration of the broader generality of our framework over the works above is its ability to produce novel answers, *i.e.* never observed during initial training and learned only from test-time examples.

Recent works on text-based question answering have investigated the retrieval of external information with reinforcement learning [8,25,26]. Those works are tangentially related and complementary to the approach explored in this paper.

Meta Learning and Few Shot Learning The term *meta learning* broadly refers to methods that *learn to learn*, *i.e.* that train models to make better use of training data. It applies to approaches including the learning of gradient descent-like algorithms such as [5,13,17,30] for faster training or fine-tuning of neural networks, and the learning of models that can be directly fed training examples at test time [7,33,36]. The method we propose falls into the latter category. Most works on meta learning are motivated by the challenge of one-shot and few-shot visual recognition, where the task is to classify an image into categories defined by a few examples each. Our meta learning setting for VQA bears many similarities. VQA is treated as a classification task, and we are provided, at test time, with examples that illustrate the possible answers – possibly a small number per answer. Most few-shot learning methods are, however, not directly applicable to our setting, due to the large number of classes (*i.e.* possible answers), the heavy class imbalance, and the need to integrate into an architecture suitable to VQA. For example, recent works such as [36] propose efficient training procedures that are only suitable for a small number of classes.

Our model uses a set of memories within a neural network to store the activations computed over the support set. Similarly, Kaiser *et al.* [19] store past activations to remember "rare events", which was notably evaluated on machine translation. Our model also uses network layers parametrized by dynamic weights, also known as fast weights. Those are determined at test time depending on the actual input to the network. Dynamic parameters have a long history in neural networks [32] and have been used previously for few-shot recognition [7] and for VQA [27]. One of the memories within our network stores the gradient of the loss with respect to static weights of the network, which is similar to the Meta Networks model proposed by Munkhdalai *et al.* [24]. Finally, our output stage produces scores over possible answers by similarity to prototypes representing the output classes (answers). This follows a similar idea to the Prototypical Networks [33].

Continuum Learning An important outcome of framing VQA in a meta learning setting is to develop models capable of improving as more data becomes available. This touches the fields of incremental [12,31] and continuum learning [2,23,42]. Those works focus on the fine-tuning of a network with new training data, output classes and/or tasks. In comparison, our model does not modify itself over time and cannot experience negative domain shift or catastrophic forgetting, which are a central concern of continuum learning [21]. Our approach is rather to use such additional data on-the-fly, at test time, *i.e.* without an iterative retraining. An important motivation for our framework is its potential to apply to support data of a different nature than question/answer examples. We consider this to be an important direction for future work. This would allow to leverage general, non VQA-specific data, *e.g.* from knowledge bases or web searches.

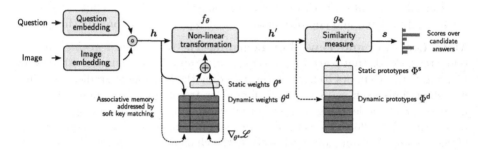

Fig. 2. Overview of the proposed model. We obtain an embedding the input question and image following [34] and our contributions concern the mapping of this embedding to scores over a set of candidate answers. First, a **non-linear transformation** (implemented as a gated hyperbolic tangent layer) is parametrized by static and dynamic weights. Static ones are learned like traditional weights by gradient descent, while dynamic ones are determined based on the actual input and a memory of candidate dynamic weights filled by processing the support set. Second, a **similarity measure** compares the resulting feature vector to a set of prototypes, each representing a specific candidate answer. Static prototypes are learned like traditional weights, while dynamic prototypes are determined by processing the support set. Dashed lines indicate data flow during the processing of the support set. See Sect. 3 for details.

2   VQA in a Meta Learning Setting

The traditional approach to VQA is in a supervised setting described as follows. A model is trained to map an input question Q and image I to scores over candidate answers [39]. The model is trained to maximize the likelihood of correct answers over a training set $\mathcal{T}$ of triplets $(Q, I, \hat{s})$, where $\hat{s} \in [0, 1]^A$ represents the vector of ground truth scores of the predefined set of A possible answers. At test time, the model is evaluated on another triplet $(Q', I', \hat{s}')$ from an evaluation or test set $\mathcal{E}$. The model predicts scores s' over the set of candidate answers, which can be compared to the ground truth $\hat{s}'$ for evaluation purposes.

We extend the formulation above to a meta learning setting by introducing an additional *support set* $\mathcal{S}$ of similar triplets $(Q'', I'', \hat{s}'')$. These are provided to the model at test time. At a minimum, we define the support set to include the training examples themselves, *i.e.* $\mathcal{S} = \mathcal{T}$, but more interestingly, the support set can include novel examples $\mathcal{S}'$ provided at test time. They constitute additional data to learn from, such that $\mathcal{S} = \mathcal{T} \cup \mathcal{S}'$. The triplets $(Q, I, \hat{s})$ in the support set can also include novel answers, never seen in the training set. In that case, the ground truth score vectors $\hat{s}$ of the other elements in the support are simply padded with zeros to match the larger size A' of the extended set of answers.

The following sections describe a deep neural network that can take advantage of the support set at test time. To leverage the information contained in the support set, the model must learn to utilize these examples on-the-fly at test time, without retraining of the whole model.

3   Proposed Model

The proposed model (Fig. 2) is a deep neural network that extends the state-of-art VQA system of Teney *et al.* [34]. Their system implements the joint embedding approach common to most modern VQA models [18,20,39,41], which is followed by a multi-label classifier over candidate answers. Conceptually, we separate the architecture into (1) the embedding part that encodes the input question and image, and (2) the classifier part that handles the reasoning and actual question answering[1]. The contributions of this paper address only the second part. Our contributions are orthogonal to developments on the embedding part, which could also benefit *e.g.* from advanced attention mechanisms or other computer vision techniques [3,37,39]. We follow the implementation of [34] for the embedding part. For concreteness, let us mention that the question embedding uses *GloVe* word vectors [28] and a Recurrent Gated Unit (GRU [10]). The image embedding uses features from a CNN (Convolutional Neural Network) with bottom-up attention [3] and question-guided attention over those features. See [34] for details.

For the remainder of this paper, we abstract the embedding to modules that produce respectively the question and image vectors q and $v \in \mathbb{R}^D$. They are combined with a Hadamard (element-wise) product into $h = q \circ v$, which forms the input to the classifier on which we now focus on. The role of the classifier is to map h to a vector of scores $s \in [0,1]^A$ over the candidate answers. We propose a definition of the classifier that generalizes the implementation of traditional models such as [34]. The input to the classifier $h \in \mathbb{R}^D$ is first passed through a non-linear transformation $f_\theta : \mathbb{R}^D \to \mathbb{R}^D$, then through a mapping to scores over the set of candidate answers $g_\Phi : \mathbb{R}^D \to [0,1]^A$. This produces a vector of predicted scores $s = g_\Phi(f_\theta(h))$. In traditional models, the two functions correspond to a stack of non-linear layers for f_θ, and a linear layer followed by a softmax or sigmoid for g_Φ. We now show how to extend f_θ and g_Φ to take advantage of the meta learning setting.

3.1   Non-linear Transformation

The $f_\theta(\cdot)$ role of the non-linear transformation $f_\theta(h)$ is to map the embedding of the question/image h to a representation suitable for the following (typically

---

[1] The separation of the network into an embedding and a classifier parts is conceptual. The division is arbitrarily placed after the fusion of the question and image embeddings. Computational requirements aside, the concept of dynamic parameters is in principle applicable to earlier layers as in [7].

linear) classifier. This transformation can be implemented in a neural network with any type of non-linear layers. Our contributions are agnostic to this implementation choice. We follow [34] and use a gated hyperbolic tangent layer [11], defined as

$$f_\theta(h) \;=\; \sigma(Wh + b) \circ \tanh(W'h + b') \tag{1}$$

where σ is the logistic activation function, $W, W' \in \mathbb{R}^{D \times D}$ are learned weights, $b, b' \in \mathbb{R}^D$ are learned biases, and $\circ$ is the Hadamard (element-wise) product. We define the parameters θ as the concatenation of the vectorized weights and biases, $i.e.$ $\theta = [W_:; W'_:; b; b']$, where colons denote the vectorization of matrices. The vector θ thus contains all weights and biases used by the non-linear transformation. A traditional model would learn the weights θ by backpropagation and gradient descent on the training set, and they would be held static during test time. We propose instead to adaptively adjust the weights at test time, depending on the input h and the available support set. Concretely, we use a combination of static parameters θ^s learned in the traditional manner, and dynamic ones θ^d determined at test time. They are combined as $\theta = \theta^s + w\theta^d$, with $w \in \mathbb{R}^D$ a vector of learned weights. The dynamic weights can therefore be seen as an adjustment made to the static ones depending on the input h.

A set of candidate dynamic weights are maintained in an associative memory $\mathcal{M}$. This memory is a large set (as large as the support set, see Sect. 3.2) of key/value pairs $\mathcal{M} = \{(\tilde{h}_i, \tilde{\theta}_i^d)\}_{i \in 1 \ldots |\mathcal{S}|}$. The interpretation for $\tilde{\theta}_i^d$ is of dynamic weights suited to an input similar to $\tilde{h}_i$. Therefore, at test time, we retrieve appropriate dynamic weights θ^d by soft key matching:

$$\theta^d \;=\; \sum_i \tilde{\theta}_i^d \; softmax_i\big(d_{\mathsf{cos}}(h, \tilde{h}_i)\big) \tag{2}$$

where $d_{\mathsf{cos}}(\cdot, \cdot)$ is the cosine similarity function. We therefore retrieve a weighted sum, in which the similarity of h with the memory keys $\tilde{h}_i$ serves to weight the memory values $\tilde{\theta}_i^d$. In practice and for computational reasons, the softmax function cuts off after the top k largest values, with k in the order of a thousand elements (see Sect. 4). We detail in Sect. 3.2 how the memory is filled by processing the support set. Note that the above formulation can be made equivalent to the original model in [34] by using only static weights ($\theta = \theta^s$). This serves as a baseline in our experiments (see Sect. 4).

Mapping to Candidate Answers $g_\Phi(\,\cdot\,)$ The function $g_\Phi(h)$ maps the output of the non-linear transformation to a vector of scores $s \in [0,1]^A$ over the set of candidate answers. It is traditionally implemented as a simple affine or linear transformation ($i.e.$ a matrix multiplication). We generalize the definition of $g_\Phi(h)$ by interpreting it as a similarity measure between its input h and prototypes $\Phi = \{\phi_i^a\}_{i,a}$ representing the possible answers. In traditional models, each prototype corresponds to one row of the weight matrix. Our general formulation allows one or several prototypes per possible answer a as $\{\phi_i^a\}_{i=1}^{N^a}$ (where a is an index over candidate answers and i

indexes the N_a support examples having a as a correct answer). Intuitively, the prototypes represent the typical expected feature vector when a is a correct answer. The score for a is therefore obtained as the similarity between the provided $\boldsymbol{h}'$ and the corresponding prototypes of a. When multiple prototypes are available, the similarities are averaged. Concretely, we define

$$g_\Phi^a(\boldsymbol{h}') \;=\; \sigma\Big(\frac{1}{N^a}\sum_{i=1}^{N^a} d(\boldsymbol{h}', \boldsymbol{\phi}_i^a) + b''\Big) \tag{3}$$

where $d(\cdot, \cdot)$ is a similarity measure, σ is a sigmoid (logistic) activation function to map the similarities to $[0, 1]$, and b'' is a learned bias term. The traditional models that use a matrix multiplication [18,34,35] correspond to $g_\Phi(\cdot)$ that uses a dot product as the similarity function. In comparison, our definition generalizes to multiple prototypes per answer and to different similarity measures. Our experiments evaluate the dot product and the weighted L-p norm of vector differences:

$$d_{\mathsf{dot}}(\boldsymbol{h}, \boldsymbol{\theta}) \;=\; \boldsymbol{h}^\mathsf{T} \boldsymbol{\theta} \tag{4}$$

$$d_{\mathsf{L1}}(\boldsymbol{h}, \boldsymbol{\theta}) \;=\; \boldsymbol{w}'''^\mathsf{T} |\boldsymbol{h} - \boldsymbol{\theta}| \tag{5}$$

$$d_{\mathsf{L2}}(\boldsymbol{h}, \boldsymbol{\theta}) \;=\; \boldsymbol{w}'''^\mathsf{T} (\boldsymbol{h} - \boldsymbol{\theta})^2 \tag{6}$$

where $\boldsymbol{w}''' \in \mathbb{R}^D$ is a vector of learned weights applied coordinate-wise.

Our model uses two sets of prototypes, the static Φ^s and the dynamic Φ^d. The static ones are learned during training as traditional weights by backpropagation and gradient descent, and held fixed at test time. The dynamic ones are determined at test time by processing the provided support set (see Sect. 3.2). Thereafter, all prototypes $\Phi = \Phi^\mathsf{s} \cup \Phi^\mathsf{d}$ are used indistinctively. Note that our formulation of $g_\Phi(\cdot)$ can be made equivalent to the original model of [34] by using only static prototypes ($\Phi = \Phi^\mathsf{d}$) and the dot-product similarity measure $d_{\mathsf{dot}}(\cdot, \cdot)$. This will serve as a baseline in our experiments (Sect. 4).

Finally, the output of the network is attached to a cross-entropy loss $\mathscr{L}(\boldsymbol{s}, \hat{\boldsymbol{s}})$ between the predicted and ground truth for training the model end-to-end [34].

3.2   Processing of Support Set

Both functions $f_\theta(\cdot)$ and $g_\Phi(\cdot)$ defined above use dynamic parameters that are dependent on the support set. Our model processes the entire support set in a forward and backward pass through the network as described below. This step is to be carried out once at test time, prior to making predictions on any instance of the test set. At training time, it is repeated before every epoch to account for the evolving static parameters of the network as training progresses (see the algorithm in the supplementary material).

We pass all elements of the support set $\mathcal{S}$ through the network in mini-batches for both a forward and backward pass. The evaluation of $f_\theta(\cdot)$ and $g_\Phi(\cdot)$ use *only static weights and prototypes, i.e.* $\boldsymbol{\theta} = \boldsymbol{\theta}^\mathsf{s}$ and $\phi = \phi^\mathsf{s}$. To fill the memory $\mathcal{M}$, we collect, for every element of the support set, its feature vector h and the gradient $\nabla_{\theta^s}\mathcal{L}$ of the final loss relative to the static weights θ. This effectively captures the adjustments that would be made by a gradient descent algorithm to those weights for that particular example. The pair $(h, \nabla_{\theta^s}\mathcal{L})$ is added to the memory $\mathcal{M}$, which thus holds $|\mathcal{S}|$ elements at the end of the process.

To determine the set of dynamic prototypes ϕ^d, we collect the feature vectors $h' = f_\theta(h)$ over all instances of the support set. We then compute their average over instances having the same correct answer. Concretely, the dynamic prototype for answer a is obtained as $\phi^a = \frac{1}{N^a}\sum_{i:\hat{s}_i^a=1}^{N^a} h'_i$.

During training, we must balance the need for data to train the static parameters of the network, and the need for an "example" support set, such that the network can learn to use novel data. If the network is provided with a fixed, constant support set, it will overfit to that input and be unable to make use of novel examples at test time. Our training procedure uses all available data as the training set $\mathcal{T}$, and we form a different support set $\mathcal{S}$ at each training epoch as a random subset of $\mathcal{T}$. The procedure is summarized in the algorithm provided in the supplementary material. Note that in practice, it is parallelized to process instances in mini-batches rather than individually.

4   Experiments

We perform a series of experiments to evaluate (1) how effectively the proposed model and its different components can use the support set, (2) how useful novel support instances are for VQA, (3) whether the model learns different aspects of a dataset from classical VQA methods trained in the classical setting.

Datasets The *VQA v2* dataset [15] serves as the principal current benchmark for VQA. The heavy class imbalance among answers makes it very difficult to draw meaningful conclusions or perform a qualitative evaluation, however. We additionally propose a series of experiments on a subset referred to as *VQA-Numbers*. It includes all questions marked in *VQA v2* as a "number" question, which are further cleaned up to remove answers appearing less than 1,000 times in the training set, and to remove questions that do not have an unambiguous answer (we keep only those with ground truth scores containing a single element equal to 1.0). Questions from the original validation set of *VQA v2* are used for evaluation, and the original training set (45,965 questions after clean up) is used for training, support, and validation. The precise data splits will be available publicly. Most importantly, the resulting set of candidate answers corresponds to the seven numbers from 0 to 6. See details in the supplementary material.

Metrics The standard metric for evaluation on *VQA v2* is the accuracy defined, using the notations of Sect. 2, as $\frac{1}{|\mathscr{E}|}\sum_i \hat{s}_i^{a_i^\star}$ with ground truth scores $\hat{s}_i$ and $a_i^\star$ the answer of highest predicted score, $argmax_a s_i^a$. We also define the recall of an answer a as $\sum_i s_i^{a^\star}/\sum_i \hat{s}_i^a$. We look at the recall averaged (uniformly) over all possible answers to better reflect performance across a variety of answers, rather than on the most common ones.

Table 1. On *VQA-Numbers*, ablative evaluation, trained and evaluated on all answers. See discussion in Sect. 4.1.

	Average answer recall
(1a) Chance	14.28
(1b) State-of-the-art model [34], equivalent to: 1 static prototype per answer, dot prod. similarity, no dynamic param	29.72
(2b) 1 Static prot./ans., L1 similarity	29.97
(2c) 1 Static prot./ans., L2 similarity	27.80
(2d) 2 Static prot./ans., dot prod. similarity	30.28
(2e) 2 Static prot./ans., L1 similarity	28.34
(2f) 2 Static prot./ans., L2 similarity	31.48
(3a) Dynamic Weights (+2f)	31.81
(3b) **Proposed: dynamic weights and prototypes** (+2f)	**32.32**

Implementation Our implementation is based on the code provided by the authors of [34]. Details non-specific to our contributions can be found there. We initialize all parameters, in particular static weights and static prototypes as if they were those of a linear layer in a traditional architecture, following Glorot and Bengio [14]. During training, the support set is subsampled (Sect. 3.2) to yield a set of 1,000 elements. We use, per answer, one or two static prototypes, and zero or one dynamic prototype (as noted in the experiments). All experiments use an embedding dimension $D=128$ and a mini-batches of 256 instances. Experiments with *VQA v2* use a set of candidate answers capped to a minimum number of training occurrences of 16, giving 1,960 possible answers [34]. Past works have shown that small differences in implementation can have noticeable impact on performance. Therefore, to ensure fair comparisons, we repeated all evaluations of the baseline [34] with our code and preprocessing. Results are therefore not directly comparable with those reported in [34]. In particular, we do not use the *Visual Genome* dataset [22] for training.

4.1   VQA-Numbers

Ablative Evaluation We first evaluate the components of the proposed model in comparison to the state-of-the-art of [34] which serves as a baseline, being equivalent to our model with 1 static prototype per answer, the dot product similarity, and no dynamic parameters. We train and evaluate on all 7 answers. To provide the baseline with a fair chance[2], we train all models with standard supersampling [9,16], *i.e.* selecting training examples with equal probability with respect to their correct answer. In these experiments, the support set is equal to the training set.

As reported in Table 1, the proposed dynamic weights improve over the baseline, and the dynamic prototypes bring an additional improvement. We compare

---

[2] The *VQA-Numbers* data is still heavily imbalanced, "1" and "2" making up almost 60% of correct answers in equal parts.

different choices for the similarity function. Interestingly, swapping the dot product in the baseline for an L2 distance has a negative impact. When using two static prototypes however, the L2 distances proves superior to the L1 or to the dot product. This is consistent with [33] where a prototypes network also performed best with an L2 distance.

Additional Support Set and Novel Answers We now evaluate the ability of the model to exploit support data never seen until test time (see Fig. 3). We train the same models designed for 7 candidate answers, but only provide them with training data for a subset of them. The proposed model is additionally provided with a complete support set, covering all 7 answers. Each reported result is averaged over 10 runs. The set of k answers excluded from training is randomized across runs but identical to all models for a given k.

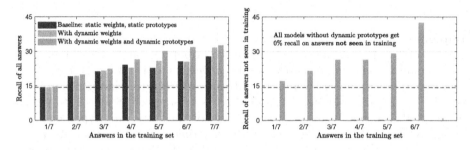

Fig. 3. On *VQA-Numbers*, performance of the proposed model and ablations, with training data for subsets of the 7 answers. (Left) Performance on all answers. (Right) Performance on answers not seen in training. Only the model with dynamic prototypes makes this setting possible. Remarkably, a model trained on two answers (2/7) maintains a capacity to learn about all others. Chance baseline shown as horizontal dashes.

The proposed model proves superior than the baseline and all other ablations (Fig. 3, top). The dynamic prototypes are particularly beneficial. With very little training data, the use of dynamic weights is less effective and sometimes even detrimental. We hypothesize that the model may then suffer from overfitting due to the additional learned parameters. When evaluated on novel answers (not seen during training and only present in the test-time support set), the dynamic prototypes provide a remarkable ability to learn those from the support set alone (Fig. 3, bottom). Their efficacy is particularly strong when only a single novel answer has to be learned. Remarkably, a model trained on only two answers maintains some capacity to learn about all others (average recall of 17.05%, versus the chance baseline of 14.28%). Note that we cannot claim the ability of the model to count to those novel numbers, but at the very least it is able to associate those answers with particular images/questions (possibly utilizing question-conditioned biases).

4.2   VQA v2

We performed experiments on the complete *VQA v2* dataset. We report results of different ablations, trained with 50% or 100% of the official training set, evaluated on the validation set as in [34]. The proposed model uses the remaining of the official training set as additional support data at test time. The complexity and varying quality of this dataset do not lead to clear-cut conclusions from the standard accuracy metric (see Table 2). The answer recall leads to more consistent observations that align with those made on *VQA-Numbers*. Both dynamic weights and dynamic parameters provide a consistent advantage (Fig. 4). Each technique is beneficial in isolation, but their combination performs generally best. Individually, the dynamic prototypes appear more impactful than the dynamic weights. Note that our experiments on *VQA v2* aimed at quantifying the effect of the contributions in the meta learning setting, and we did not seek to maximize absolute performance in the traditional benchmark setting.

To obtain a better insight into the predictions of the model, we examine the individual recall of possible answers. We compare the values with those obtained by the baseline. The difference (Fig. 5) indicates which of the two models provides the best predictions for every answer. We observe a qualitatively

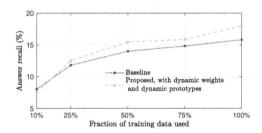

Fig. 4. On *VQA v2*, performance using varying amounts of training data. See Sect. 4.2.

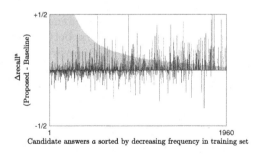

Fig. 5. On *VQA v2*, difference in answer recall between the proposed model (Table 2, last row, last column) and the baseline (Table 2, first row, last column). Each blue bar corresponds to one of the candidate answers, sorted decreasing number of occurrences in the training set (gray background, units not displayed). The two models show qualitatively different behaviour: the baseline is effective with frequent answers, but the proposed model fares better (mostly positive values) in the long tail of rare answers.

Table 2. On *VQA v2*, evaluation of the proposed model and ablations (question accuracy/answer recall). The full proposed model exhibits qualitatively different strengths than the classical approach [34], producing a generally higher recall (averaged over possible answers) and lower accuracy (averaged over questions). In these experiments, the objective for a "perfect" metalearning model would be to match the performance of the baseline trained with 100% of data (row 1, right column), while using less training data and the remaining as support (last row, left column).

	Trained on 50%	Trained on 100%
Baseline [34]	**57.6**/14.0	59.8/15.8
Proposed model		
With dynamic weights, no dynamic prototypes	**57.6**/14.1	**60.0**/16.3
No dynamic weights, **with** dynamic prototypes	**57.6**/15.2	59.7/**18.0**
Same, no static prototypes, only dyn. ones	57.2/3.6	58.6/4.29
With dyn. weights and dyn. prototypes	57.5/**15.5**	59.9/**18.0**

different behaviour between the models. While the baseline is most effective with frequent answers, the proposed model fares better (mostly positive values) in the long tail of rare answers. This corroborates previous discussions on dataset biases [15,18,43] which classical models are prone to overfit to. The proposed model is inherently more robust to such behaviour.

5   Conclusions and Future Work

We have devised a new approach to VQA through framing it as a meta learning task. This approach enables us to provide the model with supervised data at test time, thereby allowing the model to adapt or improve as more data is made available. We believe this view could lead to the development of scalable VQA systems better suited to practical applications. We proposed a deep learning model that takes advantage of the meta learning scenario, and demonstrated a range of benefits: improved recall of rare answers, better sample efficiency, and a unique capability of to learn to produce novel answers, *i.e.* those never seen during training, and learned only from support instances.

The learning-to-learn approach we propose here enables a far greater separation of the questions answering method from the information used in the process than has previously been possible. Our contention is that this separation is essential if vision-and-language methods are to move beyond benchmarks to tackle real problems, because embedding all of the information a method needs to answer real questions in the model weights is impractical.

Even though the proposed model is able to use novel support data, the experiments showed room for improvement, since a model trained initially from the same amount of data still shows superior performance. Practical considerations should also be addressed to apply this model to a larger scale, in particular for handling the memory of dynamic weights that currently grows linearly with the support set. Clustering schemes could be envisioned to reduce its size [33] and hashing methods [4, 19] could improve the efficiency of the content-based retrieval.

Generally, the handling of additional data at test time opens the door to VQA systems that interact with other sources of information. While the proposed model was demonstrated with a support set of questions/answers, the principles extend to any type of data obtained at test time *e.g.* from knowledge bases or web searches. This would drastically enhance the scalability of VQA systems.

References

1. Agrawal, A., Kembhavi, A., Batra, D., Parikh, D.: C-vqa: a compositional split of the visual question answering (vqa) v1. 0 dataset. arXiv preprint arXiv:1704.08243 (2017)
2. Aljundi, R., Chakravarty, P., Tuytelaars, T.: Expert gate: Lifelong learning with a network of experts. arXiv preprint arXiv:1611.06194 (2016)
3. Anderson, P. et al.: Bottom-up and top-down attention for image captioning and vqa. arXiv preprint arXiv:1707.07998 (2017)
4. Andoni, A., Indyk, P.: Near-optimal hashing algorithms for approximate nearest neighbor in high dimensions. In: 47th Annual IEEE Symposium on Foundations of Computer Science, 2006. FOCS 2006, pp. 459–468. IEEE (2006)
5. Andrychowicz, M. et al.: Learning to learn by gradient descent by gradient descent. In: Advances in Neural Information Processing Systems, pp. 3981–3989 (2016)
6. Antol, S. et al.: VQA: visual question answering. In: Proceedings IEEE International Conference Computer Vision (2015)
7. Bertinetto, L., Henriques, J.F., Valmadre, J., Torr, P.H.S., Vedaldi, A.: Learning feed-forward one-shot learners. In: NIPS, pp. 523–531 (2016)
8. Buck, C. et al.: Ask the right questions: Active question reformulation with reinforcement learning. arXiv preprint arXiv:1705.07830 (2017)
9. Buda, M., Maki, A., Mazurowski, M.A.: A systematic study of the class imbalance problem in convolutional neural networks. arXiv preprint arXiv:1710.05381 (2017)
10. Cho, K., van Merrienboer, B., Gulcehre, C., Bougares, F., Schwenk, H., Bengio, Y.: Learning phrase representations using RNN encoder-decoder for statistical machine translation. In: Proceedings Conference Empirical Methods in Natural Language Processing (2014)
11. Dauphin, Y.N., Fan, A., Auli, M., Grangier, D.: Language modeling with gated convolutional networks. arXiv preprint arXiv:1612.08083 (2016)
12. Fernando, C. et al.: Pathnet: Evolution channels gradient descent in super neural networks. arXiv preprint arXiv:1701.08734 (2017)
13. Finn, C., Abbeel, P., Levine, S.: Model-agnostic meta-learning for fast adaptation of deep networks. arXiv preprint arXiv:1703.03400 (2017)
14. Glorot, X., Bengio, Y.: Understanding the difficulty of training deep feedforward neural networks. In: Proceedings International Conference Artificial Intell. & Stat, pp. 249–256 (2010)
15. Goyal, Y., Khot, T., Summers-Stay, D., Batra, D., Parikh, D.: Making the V in VQA matter: elevating the role of image understanding in Visual Question Answering. arXiv preprint arXiv:1612.00837 (2016)

16. Guo, H., Li, Y., Shang, J., Mingyun, G., Yuanyue, H., Bing, G.: Learning from class-imbalanced data: Review of methods and applications. Expert Syst. Appl. **73**, 220–239 (2017)

17. Hochreiter, Sepp, Younger, A.Steven, Conwell, Peter R.: Learning to learn using gradient descent. In: Dorffner, Georg, Bischof, Horst, Hornik, Kurt (eds.) ICANN 2001. LNCS, vol. 2130, pp. 87–94. Springer, Heidelberg (2001). https://doi.org/10.1007/3-540-44668-0_13

18. Jabri, A., Joulin, A., van der Maaten, L.: Revisiting visual question answering baselines (2016)

19. Kaiser, L., Nachum, O., Roy, A., Bengio, S.: Learning to remember rare events (2017)

20. Kazemi, V., Elqursh, A.: Show, ask, attend, and answer: a strong baseline for visual question answering. arXiv preprint arXiv:1704.03162 (2017)

21. Kirkpatrick, J. et al.: Overcoming catastrophic forgetting in neural networks. arXiv preprint arXiv:1612.00796 (2016)

22. Krishna, R. et al.: Visual genome: Connecting language and vision using crowd-sourced dense image annotations. arXiv preprint arXiv:1602.07332 (2016)

23. Lopez-Paz, D., Ranzato, M.: Gradient episodic memory for continuum learning. arXiv preprint arXiv:1706.08840 (2017)

24. Munkhdalai, T., Yu, H.: Meta networks. In: International Conference on Machine Learning (ICML), pp. 2554–2563 (2017)

25. Narasimhan, K., Yala, A., Barzilay, R.: Improving information extraction by acquiring external evidence with reinforcement learning. arXiv preprint arXiv:1603.07954 (2016)

26. Nogueira, R., Cho, K.: Task-oriented query reformulation with reinforcement learning. arXiv preprint arXiv:1704.04572 (2017)

27. Noh, H., Seo, P.H., Han, B.: Image question answering using convolutional neural network with dynamic parameter prediction. In: Proceedings IEEE Conference on Computer Vision and Pattern Recognition (2016)

28. Pennington, J., Socher, R., Manning, C.: Glove: global vectors for word representation. In: Conference on Empirical Methods in Natural Language Processing (2014)

29. Ramakrishnan, S.K., Pal, A., Sharma, G., Mittal, A.: An empirical evaluation of visual question answering for novel objects. arXiv preprint arXiv:1704.02516 (2017)

30. Ravi, S., Larochelle, H.: Optimization as a model for few-shot learning (2017)

31. Rebuffi, S., Kolesnikov, A., Lampert, C.H.: icarl: Incremental classifier and representation learning. arXiv preprint arXiv:1611.07725 (2016)

32. Schmidhuber, J.: Learning to control fast-weight memories: an alternative to dynamic recurrent networks. Learning **4**(1), 131–139 (2008)

33. Snell, J., Swersky, K., Zemel, R.S.: Prototypical networks for few-shot learning. arXiv preprint arXiv:1703.05175 (2017)

34. Teney, D., Anderson, P., He, X., van den Hengel, A.: Tips and tricks for visual question answering: Learnings from the 2017 challenge. arXiv preprint arXiv:1708.02711 (2017)

35. Teney, D., van den Hengel, A.: Zero-shot visual question answering (2016)

36. Triantafillou, E., Zemel, R., Urtasun, R.: Few-shot learning through an information retrieval lens. arXiv preprint arXiv:1707.02610 (2017)

37. Wang, P., Wu, Q., Shen, C., van den Hengel, A.: The VQA-Machine: learning how to use existing vision algorithms to answer new questions. arXiv preprint arXiv:1612.05386 (2016)

38. Wang, P., Wu, Q., Shen, C., van den Hengel, A., Dick, A.: Explicit knowledge-based reasoning for visual question answering. arXiv preprint arXiv:1511.02570 (2015)
39. Wu, Q., Teney, D., Wang, P., Shen, C., Dick, A., van den Hengel, A.: Visual question answering: a survey of methods and datasets. Comput. Vis. Image Underst. (2017)
40. Wu, Q., Wang, P., Shen, C., Dick, A., Hengel, A.v.d.: Ask me anything: free-form visual question answering based on knowledge from external sources. In: Conference on Computer Vision and Pattern Recognition (2016)
41. Yang, Z., He, X., Gao, J., Deng, L., Smola, A.: Stacked attention networks for image question answering. In: Conference on Computer Vision and Pattern Recognition (2016)
42. Yoon, J., Yang, E., Lee, J., ju Hwang, S.: Lifelong learning with dynamically expandable networks. arXiv preprint arXiv:1708.01547 (2017)
43. Zhang, P., Goyal, Y., Summers-Stay, D., Batra, D., Parikh, D.: Yin and yang: balancing and answering binary visual questions. In: Conference on Computer Vision and Pattern Recognition (2016)
44. Zhu, Y., Groth, O., Bernstein, M., Fei-Fei, L.: Visual7W: grounded question answering in images. In: Proceedings IEEE Conference on Computer Vision and Pattern Recognition (2016)

On Offline Evaluation of Vision-Based Driving Models

Felipe Codevilla[1], Antonio M. López[1], Vladlen Koltun[2],
and Alexey Dosovitskiy[3(✉)]

[1] Computer Vision Center, Universitat Autònoma de Barcelona, Barcelona, Spain
fcodevilla@cvc.uab.es
[2] Intel Labs, Santa Clara, USA
[3] Intel Labs, Munich, Germany
adosovitskiy@gmail.com

Abstract. Autonomous driving models should ideally be evaluated by deploying them on a fleet of physical vehicles in the real world. Unfortunately, this approach is not practical for the vast majority of researchers. An attractive alternative is to evaluate models offline, on a pre-collected validation dataset with ground truth annotation. In this paper, we investigate the relation between various online and offline metrics for evaluation of autonomous driving models. We find that offline prediction error is not necessarily correlated with driving quality, and two models with identical prediction error can differ dramatically in their driving performance. We show that the correlation of offline evaluation with driving quality can be significantly improved by selecting an appropriate validation dataset and suitable offline metrics.

Keywords: Autonomous driving · Deep learning

1 Introduction

Camera-based autonomous driving can be viewed as a computer vision problem. It requires analyzing the input video stream and estimating certain high-level quantities, such as the desired future trajectory of the vehicle or the raw control signal to be executed. Standard methodology in computer vision is to evaluate an algorithm by collecting a dataset with ground-truth annotation and evaluating the results produced by the algorithm against this ground truth (Fig. 1(a)). However, driving, in contrast with most computer vision tasks, is inherently active. That is, it involves interaction with the world and other agents. The end goal is to drive well: safely, comfortably, and in accordance with traffic rules. An ultimate evaluation would involve deploying a fleet of vehicles in the real world and executing the model on these (Fig. 1(b)). The logistical difficulties

Electronic supplementary material The online version of this chapter (https:// doi.org/10.1007/978-3-030-01267-0_15) contains supplementary material, which is available to authorized users.

V. Ferrari et al. (Eds.): ECCV 2018, LNCS 11219, pp. 246–262, 2018.
https://doi.org/10.1007/978-3-030-01267-0_15

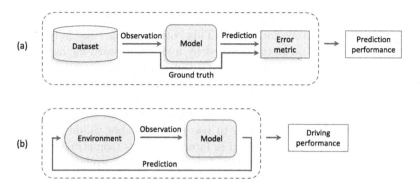

Fig. 1. Two approaches to evaluation of a sensorimotor control model. Top: offline (passive) evaluation on a fixed dataset with ground-truth annotation. Bottom: online (active) evaluation with an environment in the loop.

associated with such an evaluation lead to the question: Is it possible to evaluate a driving model without actually letting it drive, but rather following the offline dataset-centric methodology?

One successful approach to evaluation of driving systems is via decomposition. It stems from the modular approach to driving where separate subsystems deal with subproblems, such as environment perception, mapping, and vehicle control. The perception stack provides high-level understanding of the scene in terms of semantics, 3D layout, and motion. These lead to standard computer vision tasks, such as object detection, semantic segmentation, depth estimation, 3D reconstruction, or optical flow estimation, which can be evaluated offline on benchmark datasets [5,10,19]. This approach has been extremely fruitful, but it only applies to modular driving systems.

Recent deep learning approaches [1,27] aim to replace modular pipelines by end-to-end learning from images to control commands. The decomposed evaluation does not apply to models of this type. End-to-end methods are commonly evaluated by collecting a large dataset of expert driving [27] and measuring the average prediction error of the model on the dataset. This offline evaluation is convenient and is consistent with standard practice in computer vision, but how much information does it provide about the actual driving performance of the models?

In this paper, we empirically investigate the relation between (offline) prediction accuracy and (online) driving quality. We train a diverse set of models for urban driving in realistic simulation [6] and correlate their driving performance with various metrics of offline prediction accuracy. By doing so, we aim to find offline evaluation procedures that can be executed on a static dataset, but at the same time correlate well with driving quality. We empirically discover best practices both in terms of selection of a validation dataset and the design of an error metric. Additionally, we investigate the performance of several models on the real-world Berkeley DeepDrive Video (BDDV) urban driving dataset [27].

Our key finding is that offline prediction accuracy and actual driving quality are surprisingly weakly correlated. This correlation is especially low when prediction is evaluated on data collected by a single forward-facing camera on expert driving trajectories – the setup used in most existing works. A network with very low prediction error can be catastrophically bad at actual driving. Conversely, a model with relatively high prediction error may drive well.

We found two general approaches to increasing this poor correlation between prediction and driving. The first is to use more suitable validation data. We found that prediction error measured in lateral cameras (sometimes mounted to collect additional images for imitation learning) better correlates with driving performance than prediction in the forward-facing camera alone. The second approach is to design offline metrics that depart from simple mean squared error (MSE). We propose offline metrics that correlate with driving performance more than 60% better than MSE.

2   Related Work

Vision-based autonomous driving tasks have traditionally been evaluated on dedicated annotated real-world datasets. For instance, KITTI [10] is a comprehensive benchmarking suite with annotations for stereo depth estimation, odometry, optical flow estimation, object detection, semantic segmentation, instance segmentation, 3D bounding box prediction, etc. The Cityscapes dataset [5] provides annotations for semantic and instance segmentation. The BDDV dataset [27] includes semantic segmentation annotation. For some tasks, ground truth data acquisition is challenging or nearly impossible in the physical world (for instance, for optical flow estimation). This motivates the use of simulated data for training and evaluating vision models, as in the SYNTHIA [22], Virtual KITTI [9], and GTA5 datasets [20], and the VIPER benchmark [19]. These datasets and benchmarks are valuable for assessing the performance of different components of a vision pipeline, but they do not allow evaluation of a full driving system.

Recently, increased interest in end-to-end learning for driving has led to the emergence of datasets and benchmarks for the task of direct control signal prediction from observations (typically images). To collect such a dataset, a vehicle is equipped with one or several cameras and additional sensors recording the coordinates, velocity, sometimes the control signal being executed, etc. The Udacity dataset [25] contains recordings of lane following in highway and urban scenarios. The CommaAI dataset [23] includes 7 h of highway driving. The Oxford RobotCar Dataset [16] includes over 1000 km of driving recoded under varying weather, lighting, and traffic conditions. The BDDV dataset [27] is the largest publicly available urban driving dataset to date, with 10,000 h of driving recorded from forward-facing cameras together with smartphone sensor data such as GPS, IMU, gyroscope, and magnetometer readings. These datasets provide useful training data for end-to-end driving systems. However, due to their static nature (passive pre-recorded data rather than a living environment), they do not support evaluation of the actual driving performance of the learned models.

Online evaluation of driving models is technically challenging. In the physical world, tests are typically restricted to controlled simple environments [4,13] and qualitative results [1,18]. Large-scale real-world evaluations are impractical for the vast majority of researchers. One alternative is simulation. Due of its logistical feasibility, simulation have been commonly employed for driving research, especially in the context of machine learning. The TORCS simulator [26] focuses on racing, and has been applied to evaluating road following [3]. Rich active environments provided by computer games have been used for training and evaluation of driving models [7]; however, the available information and the controllability of the environment are typically limited in commercial games. The recent CARLA driving simulator [6] allows evaluating driving policies in living towns, populated with vehicles and pedestrians, under different weather and illumination conditions. In this work we use CARLA to perform an extensive study of offline performance metrics for driving.

Although the analysis we perform is applicable to any vision-based driving pipeline (including ones that comprise separate perception [2,12,21,24,28] and control modules [17]), in this paper we focus on end-to-end trained models. This line of work dates back to the ALVINN model of Pomerleau [18], capable of road following in simple environments. More recently, LeCun et al. [15] demonstrated collision avoidance with an end-to-end trained deep network. Chen et al. [3] learn road following in the TORCS simulator, by introducing an intermediate representation of "affordances" rather than going directly from pixels to actions. Bojarski et al. [1] train deep convolutional networks for lane following on a large real-world dataset and deploy the system on a physical vehicle. Fernando et al. [8] use neural memory networks combining visual inputs and steering wheel trajectories to perform long-term planning, and use the CommaAI dataset to validate the method. Hubschneider et al. [11] incorporate turning signals as additional inputs to their DriveNet. Codevilla et al. [4] propose conditional imitation learning, which allows imitation learning to scale to complex environments such as urban driving by conditioning action prediction on high-level navigation commands. The growing interest in end-to-end learning for driving motivates our investigation of the associated evaluation metrics.

3 Methodology

We aim to analyze the relation between offline prediction performance and online driving quality. To this end, we train models using conditional imitation learning [4] in a simulated urban environment [6]. We then evaluate the driving quality on goal-directed navigation and correlate the results with multiple offline prediction-based metrics. We now describe the methods used to train and evaluate the models.

3.1 Conditional Imitation Learning

For training the models we use conditional imitation learning – a variant of imitation learning that allows providing high-level commands to a model. When coupled with a high-level topological planner, the method can scale to complex navigation tasks such as driving in an urban environment. We briefly review the approach here and refer the reader to Codevilla et al. [4] for further details.

We start by collecting a training dataset of tuples $\{\langle \mathbf{o}_i, \mathbf{c}_i, \mathbf{a}_i \rangle\}$, each including an observation $\mathbf{o}_i$, a command $\mathbf{c}_i$, and an action $\mathbf{a}_i$. The observation $\mathbf{o}_i$ is an image recorded by a camera mounted on a vehicle. The command $\mathbf{c}_i$ is a high-level navigation instruction, such as "turn left at the next intersection". We use four commands – continue, straight, left, and right – encoded as one-hot vectors. Finally, $\mathbf{a}_i$ is a vector representing the action executed by the driver. It can be raw control signal – steering angle, throttle, and brake – or a more abstract action representation, such as a waypoint representing the intended trajectory of the vehicle. We focus on predicting the steering angle in this work.

Given the dataset, we train a convolutional network F with learnable parameters $\boldsymbol{\theta}$ to perform command-conditional action prediction, by minimizing the average prediction loss:

$$\boldsymbol{\theta}^* = \arg\min_{\boldsymbol{\theta}} \sum_i \ell(F(\mathbf{o}_i, \mathbf{c}_i, \boldsymbol{\theta}), \mathbf{a}_i), \tag{1}$$

where ℓ is a per-sample loss. We experiment with several architectures of the network F, all based on the branched model of Codevilla et al. [4]. Training techniques and network architectures are reviewed in more detail in Sect. 3.2. Further details of training are provided in the supplement.

3.2   Training

Data Collection. We collect a training dataset by executing an automated navigation expert in the simulated environment. The expert makes use of privileged information about the environment, including the exact map of the environment and the exact positions of the ego-car, all other vehicles, and pedestrians. The expert keeps a constant speed of 35 km/h when driving straight and reduces the speed when making turns. We record the images from three cameras: a forward-facing one and two lateral cameras facing 30 degrees left and right. In 10% of the data we inject noise in the driving policy to generate examples of recovery from perturbations. In total we record 80 h of driving data.

Action Representation. The most straightforward approach to end-to-end learning for driving is to output the raw control command, such as the steering angle, directly [1,4]. We use this representation in most of our experiments. The action is then a vector $\mathbf{a} \in \mathbb{R}^3$, consisting of the steering angle, the throttle value, and the brake value. To simplify the analysis and preserve compatibility with prior work [1,27], we only predict the steering angle with a deep network. We use throttle and brake values provided by the expert policy described above.

Loss Function. In most of our experiments we follow standard practice [1,4] and use mean squared error (MSE) as a per-sample loss:

$$\ell(F(\mathbf{o}_i, \mathbf{c}_i, \boldsymbol{\theta}), \mathbf{a}_i) = \|F(\mathbf{o}_i, \mathbf{c}_i, \boldsymbol{\theta}) - \mathbf{a}_i\|^2. \tag{2}$$

We have also experimented with the L1 loss. In most experiments we balance the data during training. We do this by dividing the data into 8 bins based on the ground-truth steering angle and sampling an equal number of datapoints from each bin in every mini-batch. As a result, the loss being optimized is not the average MSE over the dataset, but its weighted version with higher weight given to large steering angles.

Regularization. Even when evaluating in the environment used for collecting the training data, a driving policy needs to generalize to previously unseen views of this environment. Generalization is therefore crucial for a successful driving policy. We use dropout and data augmentation as regularization measures when training the networks.

Dropout ratio is 0.2 in convolutional layers and 0.5 in fully-connected layers. For each image to be presented to the network, we apply a random subset of a set of transformations with randomly sampled magnitudes. Transformations include contrast change, brightness, and tone, as well as the addition of Gaussian blur, Gaussian noise, salt-and-pepper noise, and region dropout (masking out a random set of rectangles in the image, each rectangle taking roughly 1% of image area). In order to ensure good convergence, we found it helpful to gradually increase the data augmentation magnitude in proportion to the training step. Further details are provided in the supplement.

Model Architecture. We experiment with a feedforward convolutional network, which takes as input the current observation as well as an additional vector of measurements (in our experiments the only measurement is the current speed of the vehicle). This network implements a purely reactive driving policy, since by construction it cannot make use of temporal context. We experiment with three variants of this model. The architecture used by Codevilla et al. [4], with 8 convolutional layers, is denoted as "standard". We also experiment with a deeper architecture with 12 convolutional layers and a shallower architecture with 4 convolutional layers.

3.3 Performance Metrics

Offline Error Metrics. Assume we are given a validation set $\mathcal{V}$ of tuples $\langle \mathbf{o}_i, \mathbf{c}_i, \mathbf{a}_i, v_i \rangle$, indexed by $i \in V$. Each tuple includes an observation, an input command, a ground-truth action vector, and the speed of the vehicle. We assume the validation set consists of one or more temporally ordered driving sequences. (For simplicity in what follows we assume it is a single sequence, but generalization to multiple sequences is trivial.) Denote the action predicted by the model by $\widehat{\mathbf{a}}_i = F(\mathbf{o}_i, \mathbf{c}_i, \boldsymbol{\theta})$. In our experiments, $\mathbf{a}_i$ and $\widehat{\mathbf{a}}_i$ will be scalars, representing the steering angle. Speed is also a scalar (in m/s).

Table 1 lists offline metrics we evaluate in this paper. The first two metrics are standard: mean squared error (which is typically the training loss) and absolute error. Absolute error gives relatively less weight to large mistakes than MSE.

The higher the speed of the car, the larger the impact a control mistake can have. To quantify this intuition, we evaluate speed-weighted absolute error. This

Table 1. Offline metrics used in the evaluation. δ is the Kronecker delta function, θ is the Heaviside step function, Q is a quantization function (see text for details), $|V|$ is the number of samples in the validation dataset.

Metric name	Parameters	Metric definition
Squared error	–	$\frac{1}{|V|} \sum_{i \in V} \|\mathbf{a}_i - \widehat{\mathbf{a}}_i\|^2$
Absolute error	–	$\frac{1}{|V|} \sum_{i \in V} \|\mathbf{a}_i - \widehat{\mathbf{a}}_i\|_1$
Speed-weighted absolute error	–	$\frac{1}{|V|} \sum_{i \in V} \|\mathbf{a}_i - \widehat{\mathbf{a}}_i\|_1 v_i$
Cumulative speed-weighted absolute error	T	$\frac{1}{|V|} \sum_{i \in V} \left\| \sum_{t=0}^{T} (\mathbf{a}_{i+t} - \widehat{\mathbf{a}}_{i+t}) v_{i+t} \right\|_1$
Quantized classification error	σ	$\frac{1}{|V|} \sum_{i \in V} (1 - \delta\,(Q(\mathbf{a}_i, \sigma), Q(\widehat{\mathbf{a}}_i, \sigma)))$
Thresholded relative error	α	$\frac{1}{|V|} \sum_{i \in V} \theta\,(\|\widehat{\mathbf{a}}_i - \mathbf{a}_i\| - \alpha \|\mathbf{a}_i\|)$

metric approximately measures how quickly the vehicle is diverging from the ground-truth trajectory, that is, the projection of the velocity vector onto the direction orthogonal to the heading direction.

We derive the next metric by accumulating speed-weighted errors over time. The intuition is that the average prediction error may not be characteristic of the driving quality, since it does not take into account the temporal correlations in the errors. Temporally uncorrelated noise may lead to slight oscillations around the expert trajectory, but can still result in successful driving. In contrast, a consistent bias in one direction for a prolonged period of time inevitably leads to a crash. We therefore accumulate the speed-weighted difference between the ground-truth action and the prediction over T time steps. This measure is a rough approximation of the divergence of the vehicle from the desired trajectory over T time steps.

Another intuition is that small noise may be irrelevant for the driving performance, and what matters is getting the general direction right. Similar to Xu et al. [27], we quantize the predicted actions and evaluate the classification error. For quantization, we explicitly make use of the fact that the actions are scalars (although a similar strategy can be applied to higher-dimensional actions). Given a threshold value σ, the quantization function $Q(x, \sigma)$ returns -1 if $x < -\sigma$, 0 if $-\sigma \le x < \sigma$, and 1 if $x \ge \sigma$. For steering angle, these values correspond to going left, going straight, and going right. Given the quantized predictions and the ground truth, we compute the classification error.

Finally, the last metric is based on quantization and relative errors. Instead of quantizing with a fixed threshold as in the previous metric, here the threshold is adaptive, proportional to the ground truth steering signal. The idea is that for large action values, small discrepancies with the ground truth are not as important as for small action values. Therefore, we count the fraction of samples for which $\|\widehat{\mathbf{a}}_i - \mathbf{a}_i\| \ge \alpha \|\mathbf{a}_i\|$.

Online Performance Metrics. We measure the driving quality using three metrics. The first one is the success rate, or simply the fraction of successfully completed navigation trials. The second is the average fraction of distance traveled towards the goal per episode (this value can be negative is the agent moves away form the goal). The third metric measures the average number of kilometers traveled between two infractions. (Examples of infractions are collisions, driving on the sidewalk, or driving on the opposite lane.)

4   Experiments

We perform an extensive study of the relation between online and offline performance of driving models. Since conducting such experiments in the real world would be impractical, the bulk of the experiments are performed in the CARLA simulator [6]. We start by training a diverse set of driving models with varying architecture, training data, regularization, and other parameters. We then correlate online driving quality metrics with offline prediction-based metrics, aiming to find offline metrics that are most predictive of online driving performance. Finally, we perform an additional analysis on the real-world BDDV dataset. Supplementary materials can be found on the project page: https://sites.google.com/view/evaluatedrivingmodels.

4.1   Experimental Setup

Simulation. We use the CARLA simulator to evaluate the performance of driving models in an urban environment. We follow the testing protocol of Codevilla et al. [4] and Dosovitskiy et al. [6]. We evaluate goal-directed navigation with dynamic obstacles. One evaluation includes 25 goal-directed navigation trials.

CARLA provides two towns (Town 1 and Town 2) and configurable weather and lighting conditions. We make use of this capability to evaluate generalization of driving methods. We use Town 1 in 4 weathers (Clear Noon, Heavy Rain Noon, Clear Sunset and Clear After Rain) for training data collection, and we use two test conditions: Town 1 in clear noon weather and Town 2 in Soft Rain Sunset weather. The first condition is present in the training data; yet, note that the specific images observed when evaluating the policies have almost certainly not been seen during training. Therefore even this condition requires generalization. The other condition – Town 2 and soft rain sunset weather – is completely new and requires strong generalization.

For validation we use 2 h of driving data with action noise and 2 h of data without action noise, in each of the conditions. With three cameras and a frame rate of 10 frames per second, one hour of data amounts to $108,000$ validation images.

Real-World Data. For real-world tests we use the validation set of the BDDV dataset [27], containing 1816 dashboard camera videos. We computed the offline metrics over the entire dataset using the pre-trained models and the data filtering procedures provided by Xu et al. [27].

Network Training and Evaluation. All models were trained using the Adam optimizer [14] with minibatches of 120 samples and an initial learning rate of 10^{-4}. We reduce the learning rate by a factor of 2 every $50K$ iterations. All models were trained up to 500 K iterations. In order to track the evolution of models during the course of training, for each model we perform both online and offline evaluation after the following numbers of training mini-batches: 2 K, 4 K, 8 K, 16 K, 32 K, 64 K, 100 K, 200 K, 300 K, 400 K, and 500 K.

4.2   Evaluated Models

We train a total of 45 models. The parameters we vary can be broadly separated into three categories: properties of the training data, of the model architecture, and of the training procedure. We vary the amount and the distribution of the training data. The amount varies between 0.2 h and 80 h of driving. The distribution is one of the following four: all data collected from three cameras and with noise added to the control, only data from the central camera, only data without noise, and data from the central camera without noise. The model architecture variations amount to varying the depth between 4 and 12 layers. The variations in the training process are the use of data balancing, the loss function, and the regularization applied (dropout and the level of data augmentation). A complete list of parameters varied during the evaluation is provided in the supplement.

4.3   Correlation Between Offline and Online Metrics

We start by studying the correlation between online and offline performance metrics on the whole set of evaluated models. We represent the results by scatter plots and correlation coefficients. To generate a scatter plot, we select two metrics and plot each evaluated model as a circle, with the coordinates of the center of the circle equal to the values of these two metrics, and the radius of the circle proportional to the training iteration the model was evaluated at. To quantify the correlations, we use the standard sample Pearson correlation coefficient, computed over all points in the plot. In the figures below, we plot results in generalization conditions (Town 2, unseen weather). We focus our analysis on the well-performing models, by discarding the 50% worst models according to the offline metric. Results in training conditions, as well as scatter plots with all models, are shown in the supplement.

The Effect of Validation Data. We first plot the (offline) average steering MSE versus the (online) success rate in goal-directed navigation, for different offline validation datasets. We vary the number of cameras used for validation (just a forward-facing camera or three cameras including two lateral ones) and the presence of action noise in the validation set. This experiment is inspired by the fact that the 3-camera setup and the addition of noise have been advocated for training end-to-end driving models [1,4,6,27].

The results are shown in Fig. 2. The most striking observation is that the correlation between offline prediction and online performance is weak. For the basic setup – central camera and no action noise – the absolute value of the correlation coefficient is only 0.39. The addition of action noise improves the correlation to 0.54. Evaluating on data from three cameras brings the correlation up to 0.77. This shows that a successful policy must not only predict the actions of an expert on the expert's trajectories, but also for observations away from the expert's trajectories. Proper validation data should therefore include examples of recovery from perturbations.

Offline Metrics. Offline validation data from three cameras or with action noise may not always be available. Therefore, we now aim to find offline metrics that are predictive of driving quality even when evaluated in the basic setup with a single forward-facing camera and no action noise.

Figure 3 shows scatter plots of offline metrics described in Sect. 3.3, versus the navigation success rate. MSE is the least correlated with the driving success rate: the absolute value of the correlation coefficient is only 0.39. Absolute steering error is more strongly correlated, at 0.61. Surprisingly, weighting the error by speed or accumulating the error over multiple subsequent steps does not improve the correlation. Finally, quantized classification error and thresholded relative error are also more strongly correlated, with the absolute value of the correlation coefficient equal to 0.65 and 0.64, respectively.

Online Metrics. So far we have looked at the relation between offline metrics and a single online metric – success rate. Is success rate fully representative of actual driving quality? Here we compare the success rate with two other online metrics: average fraction of distance traveled towards the goal and average number of kilometers traveled between two infractions.

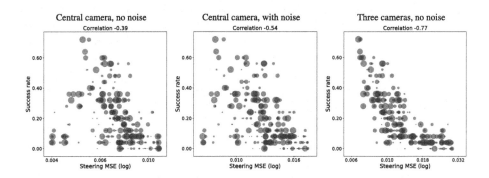

Fig. 2. Scatter plots of goal-directed navigation success rate vs. steering MSE when evaluated on data from different distributions. We evaluate the models in the generalization condition (Town 2) and we plot the 50% best-performing models according to the offline metric. Sizes of the circles denote the training iterations at which the models were evaluated. We additionally show the sample Pearson correlation coefficient for each plot. Note how the error on the basic dataset (single camera, no action noise) is the least informative of the driving performance.

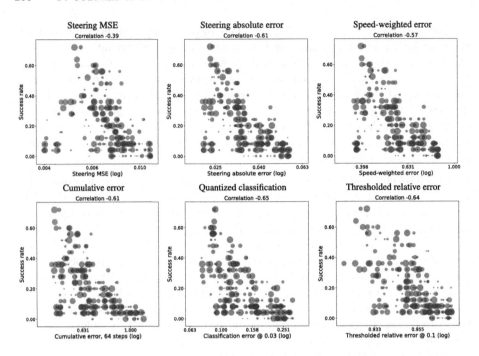

Fig. 3. Scatter plots of goal-directed navigation success rate vs. different offline metrics. We evaluate the models in the generalization condition (Town 2) and we plot the 50% best-performing models according to the offline metric. Note how correlation is generally weak, especially for mean squred error (MSE).

Figure 4 shows pairwise scatter plots of these three online metrics. Success rate and average completion are strongly correlated, with a correlation coefficient of 0.8. The number of kilometers traveled between two infractions is similarly correlated with the success rate (0.77), but much less correlated with the average completion (0.44). We conclude that online metrics are not perfectly correlated and it is therefore advisable to measure several online metrics when evaluating driving models. Success rate is well correlated with the other two metrics, which justifies its use as the main online metric in our analysis.

Case Study. We have seen that even the best-correlated offline and online metrics have a correlation coefficient of only 0.65. Aiming to understand the reason for this remaining discrepancy, here we take a closer look at two models which achieve similar prediction accuracy, but drastically different driving quality. The first model was trained with the MSE loss and forward-facing camera only. The second model used the L1 loss and three cameras. We refer to these models as Model 1 and Model 2, respectively.

Figure 5 (top left) shows the ground truth steering signal over time (blue), as well as the predictions of the models (red and green, respectively). There is no obvious qualitative difference in the predictions of the models: both often

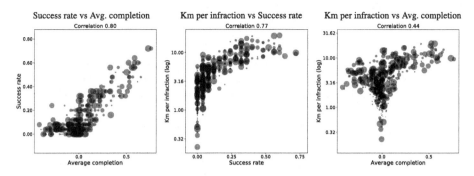

Fig. 4. Scatter plots of online driving quality metrics versus each other. The metrics are: success rate, average fraction of distance to the goal covered (average completion), and average distance (in km) driven between two infractions. Success rate is strongly correlated with the other two metrics, which justifies its use as the main online metric in our analysis.

deviate from the ground truth. One difference is a large error in the steering signal predicted by Model 1 in a turn, as shown in Fig. 5 (top right). Such a short-term discrepancy can lead to a crash, and it is difficult to detect based on average prediction error. The advanced offline metrics evaluated above are designed to be better at capturing such mistakes.

Figure 5 (bottom) shows several trajectories driven by both models. Model 1 is able to drive straight for some period of time, but eventually crashes in every single trial, typically because of wrong timing or direction of a turn. In contrast, Model 2 drives well and successfully completes most trials. This example illustrates the difficulty of using offline metrics for predicting online driving behavior.

4.4   Real-World Data

Evaluation of real-world urban driving is logistically complicated, therefore we restrict the experiments on real-world data to an offline evaluation. We use the BDDV dataset and the trained models provided by [27]. The models are trained to perform 4-way classification (accelerate, brake, left, right), and we measure their classification accuracy. We evaluate on the validation set of BDDV.

The offline metrics we presented above are designed for continuous values and cannot be directly applied to classification-based models. Yet, some of them can be adapted to this discrete setting. Table 2 shows the average accuracy, as well as several additional metrics. First, we provide a breakdown of classification accuracy by subsets of the data corresponding to different ground truth labels. The prediction error in the turns is most informative, yielding the largest separation between the best and the worst models. Second, we try weighting the errors with the ground-truth speed. We measure the resulting metric for the full validation dataset, as well as for turns only. These metrics reduce the gap between the feedforward and the LSTM models.

4.5   Detailed Evaluation of Models

Scatter plots presented in the previous sections indicate general tendencies, but not the performance of specific models. Here we provide a more detailed evaluation of several driving models, with a focus on several parameters: the amount of training data, its distribution, the regularization being used, the network architecture, and the loss function. We evaluate two offline metrics – MSE and the

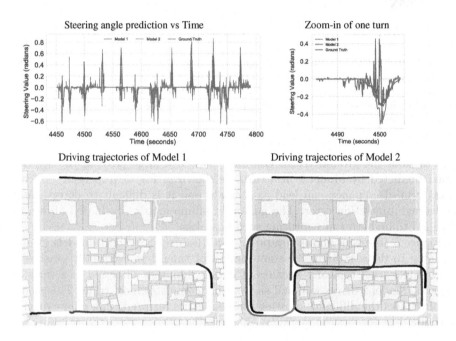

Fig. 5. Detailed evaluation of two driving models with similar offline prediction quality, but very different driving behavior. Top left: Ground-truth steering signal (blue) and predictions of two models (red and green) over time. Top right: a zoomed fragment of the steering time series, showing a large mistake made by Model 1 (red). Bottom: Several trajectories driven by the models in Town 1. Same scenarios indicated with the same color in both plots. Note how the driving performance of the models is dramatically different: Model 1 crashes in every trial, while Model 2 can drive successfully.

Table 2. Detailed accuracy evaluations on the BDDV dataset. We report the 4-way classification accuracy (in %) for various data subsets and varying speed.

Model	Average accuracy				Weighted with speed	
	All data	Straight	Stop	Turns	All data	Turns
Feedforward	78.0	90.0	72.0	32.4	80.7	27.7
CNN + LSTM	81.8	90.2	78.1	49.3	83.0	43.2
FCN + LSTM	83.3	90.4	80.7	50.7	83.6	44.4

Table 3. Detailed evaluation of models in CARLA. "TRE" stands for thresholded relative error, "Success rate" for the driving success rate. For MSE and TRE lower is better, for the success rate higher is better. We mark with bold the best result in each section. We highlight in green the cases where the best model according to an offline metric is also the best at driving, separately for each section and each town. Both MSE and TRE are not necessarily correlated with driving performance, but generally TRE is more predictive of driving quality, correctly identifying 10 best-driving models out of 12, compared to 6 out of 12 for MSE.

Parameter	Value	MSE		TRE @ 0.1		Success rate	
		Town 1	Town 2	Town 1	Town 2	Town 1	Town 2
Amount of training data	0.2 h	0.0086	0.0481	0.970	0.985	0.44	0.00
	1 h	0.0025	0.0217	0.945	0.972	0.44	0.04
	5 h	**0.0005**	**0.0093**	0.928	0.961	0.60	**0.08**
	25 h	0.0007	0.0166	**0.926**	**0.958**	0.76	0.04
Type of training data	1 cam., no noise	0.0007	**0.0066**	**0.922**	0.947	**0.84**	0.04
	1 cam., noise	0.0009	0.0077	0.926	**0.946**	0.80	**0.20**
	3 cam., no noise	**0.0004**	0.0086	0.928	0.953	**0.84**	0.08
	3 cam., noise	0.0007	0.0166	0.926	0.958	0.76	0.04
Data balancing	No balancing	0.0012	**0.0065**	0.907	**0.924**	0.88	0.36
	With balancing	**0.0011**	0.0066	**0.891**	0.930	**0.92**	**0.56**
Regularization	None	0.0014	0.0092	**0.911**	0.953	**0.92**	0.08
	Mild dropout	0.0010	0.0074	0.921	0.953	0.84	0.20
	High dropout	**0.0007**	0.0166	0.926	0.958	0.76	0.04
	High drop., data aug.	0.0013	**0.0051**	0.919	**0.931**	0.88	**0.36**
Network architecture	Shallow	**0.0005**	0.0111	0.936	0.963	0.68	0.12
	Standard	0.0007	0.0166	**0.926**	0.958	**0.76**	0.04
	Deep	0.0011	**0.0072**	0.928	**0.949**	0.76	**0.24**
Loss function	L2	**0.0010**	0.0074	0.921	0.953	0.84	0.20
	L1	0.0012	**0.0061**	**0.891**	**0.944**	**0.96**	**0.52**

thresholded relative error (TRE) – as well as the goal-directed navigation success rate. For TRE we use the parameter $\alpha = 0.1$.

The results are shown in Table 3. In each section of the table all parameters are fixed, except for the parameter of interest. (Parameters may vary between sections.) Driving performance is sensitive to all the variations. Larger amount of training data generally leads to better driving. Training with one or three cameras has a surprisingly minor effect. Data balancing helps in both towns. Regularization helps generalization to the previously unseen town and weather. Deeper networks generally perform better. Finally, the L1 loss leads to better driving than the usual MSE loss. This last result is in agreement with Fig. 3, which shows that absolute error is better correlated with the driving quality than MSE.

Next, for each of the 6 parameters and each of the 2 towns we check if the best model chosen based on the offline metrics is also the best in terms of the driving quality. This simulates a realistic parameter tuning scenario a practitioner might face. We find that TRE is more predictive of the driving performance than MSE, correctly identifying the best-driving model in 10 cases out of 12, compared to 6 out of 12 for MSE. This demonstrates that TRE, although far from being perfectly correlated with the online driving quality, is much more indicative of well-driving models than MSE.

5   Conclusion

We investigated the performance of offline versus online evaluation metrics for autonomous driving. We have shown that the MSE prediction error of expert actions is not a good metric for evaluating the performance of autonomous driving systems, since it is very weakly correlated with actual driving quality. We explore two avenues for improving the offline metrics: modifying the validation data and modifying the metrics themselves. Both paths lead to improved correlation with driving quality.

Our work takes a step towards understanding the evaluation of driving models, but it has several limitations that can be addressed in future work. First, the evaluation is almost entirely based on simulated data. We believe that the general conclusion about weak correlation of online and offline metrics is likely to transfer to the real world; however, it is not clear if the details of our correlation analysis will hold in the real world. Performing a similar study with physical vehicles operating in rich real-world environments would therefore be very valuable. Second, we focus on the correlation coefficient as the measure of relation between two quantities. Correlation coefficient estimates the connection between two variables to some degree, but a finer-grained analysis may be needed provide a more complete understanding of the dependencies between online and offline metrics. Third, even the best offline metric we found is far from being perfectly correlated with actual driving quality. Designing offline performance metrics that are more strongly correlated with driving performance remains an important challenge.

Acknowledgements. Antonio M. López and Felipe Codevilla acknowledge the Spanish project TIN2017-88709-R (Ministerio de Economia, Industria y Competitividad), the Generalitat de Catalunya CERCA Program and its ACCIO agency. Felipe Codevilla was supported in part by FI grant 2017FI-B1-00162.

References

1. Bojarski, M. et al.: End to end learning for self-driving cars. arXiv:1604.07316 (2016)
2. Bresson, G., Alsayed, Z., Yu, L., Glaser, S.: Simultaneous localization and mapping: a survey of current trends in autonomous driving. IEEE Trans. Intell. Veh. (2017)
3. Chen, C., Seff, A., Kornhauser, A.L., Xiao, J.: DeepDriving: learning affordance for direct perception in autonomous driving. In: International Conference on Computer Vision (ICCV) (2015)
4. Codevilla, F., Müller, M., López, A., Koltun, V., Dosovitskiy, A.: End-to-end driving via conditional imitation learning. In: International Conference on Robotics and Automation (ICRA) (2018)

5. Cordts, M. et al.: The Cityscapes dataset for semantic urban scene understanding. In: Computer Vision and Pattern Recognition (CVPR) (2016)
6. Dosovitskiy, A., Ros, G., Codevilla, F., López, A., Koltun, V.: CARLA: an open urban driving simulator. In: Conference on Robot Learning (CoRL) (2017)
7. Ebrahimi, S., Rohrbach, A., Darrell, T.: Gradient-free policy architecture search and adaptation. In: Conference on Robot Learning (CoRL) (2017)
8. Fernando, T., Denman, S., Sridharan, S., Fookes, C.: Going deeper: autonomous steering with neural memory networks. In: International Conference on Computer Vision (ICCV) Workshops (2017)
9. Gaidon, A., Wang, Q., Cabon, Y., Vig, E.: Virtual worlds as proxy for multi-object tracking analysis. In: Computer Vision and Pattern Recognition (CVPR) (2016)
10. Geiger, A., Lenz, P., Urtasun, R.: Are we ready for autonomous driving? The KITTI vision benchmark suite. In: Computer Vision and Pattern Recognition (CVPR) (2012)
11. Hubschneider, C., Bauer, A., Weber, M., Zollner, J.M.: Adding navigation to the equation: turning decisions for end-to-end vehicle control. In: Intelligent Transportation Systems Conference (ITSC) Workshops (2017)
12. Jin, X. et al.: Predicting scene parsing and motion dynamics in the future. In: Neural Information Processing Systems (NIPS) (2017)
13. Kahn, G., Villaflor, A., Pong, V., Abbeel, P., Levine, S.: Uncertainty-aware reinforcement learning for collision avoidance. arXiv:1702.01182 (2017)
14. Kingma, D.P., Ba, J.: Adam: a method for stochastic optimization. In: International Conference on Learning Representation (ICLR) (2015)
15. LeCun, Y., Muller, U., Ben, J., Cosatto, E., Flepp, B.: Off-road obstacle avoidance through end-to-end learning. In: Neural Information Processing Systems (NIPS) (2005)
16. Maddern, W., Pascoe, G., Linegar, C., Newman, P.: 1 Year, 1000 km: the Oxford RobotCar dataset. Int. J. Robot. Res. (IJRR) (2017)
17. Paden, B., Cáp, M., Yong, S.Z., Yershov, D.S., Frazzoli, E.: A survey of motion planning and control techniques for self-driving urban vehicles. IEEE Trans. Intell. Veh. (2016)
18. Pomerleau, D.: ALVINN: an autonomous land vehicle in a neural network. In: Neural Information Processing Systems (NIPS) (1988)
19. Richter, S.R., Hayder, Z., Koltun, V.: Playing for benchmarks. In: International Conference on Computer Vision (ICCV) (2017)
20. Richter, S.R., Vineet, V., Roth, S., Koltun, V.: Playing for data: Ground truth from computer games. In: European Conference on Computer Vision (ECCV) (2016)
21. Ros, G., Ramos, S., Granados, M., Bakhtiary, A., Vázquez, D., López, A.M.: Vision-based offline-online perception paradigm for autonomous driving. In: Winter Conference on Applications of Computer Vision (WACV) (2015)
22. Ros, G., Sellart, L., Materzynska, J., Vázquez, D., López, A.M.: The SYNTHIA dataset: a large collection of synthetic images for semantic segmentation of urban scenes. In: Computer Vision and Pattern Recognition (CVPR) (2016)
23. Santana, E., Hotz, G.: Learning a driving simulator. arXiv:1608.01230 (2016)
24. Schneider, L. et al.: Semantic stixels: depth is not enough. In: Intelligent Vehicles Symposium (IV) (2016)
25. Udacity: https://github.com/udacity/self-driving-car

26. Wymann, B., Espié, E., Guionneau, C., Dimitrakakis, C., Coulom, R., Sumner, A.:
    TORCS, The Open Racing Car Simulator. http://www.torcs.org
27. Xu, H., Gao, Y., Yu, F., Darrell, T.: End-to-end learning of driving models from
    large-scale video datasets. In: Computer Vision and Pattern Recognition (CVPR)
    (2017)
28. Zhu, Z., Liang, D., Zhang, S., Huang, X., Li, B., Hu, S.: Traffic-sign detection and
    classification in the wild. In: Computer Vision and Pattern Recognition (CVPR)
    (2016)

Visual Psychophysics for Making Face Recognition Algorithms More Explainable

Brandon RichardWebster[1]([⊠]) [iD], So Yon Kwon[2], Christopher Clarizio[1], Samuel E. Anthony[2,3], and Walter J. Scheirer[1]

[1] University of Notre Dame, Notre Dame, IN 46556, USA
brichar1@nd.edu
[2] Perceptive Automata, Inc., Somerville, USA
[3] Harvard University, Cambridge, MA 02138, USA

Abstract. Scientific fields that are interested in faces have developed their own sets of concepts and procedures for understanding how a target model system (be it a person or algorithm) perceives a face under varying conditions. In computer vision, this has largely been in the form of dataset evaluation for recognition tasks where summary statistics are used to measure progress. While aggregate performance has continued to improve, understanding individual causes of failure has been difficult, as it is not always clear why a particular face fails to be recognized, or why an impostor is recognized by an algorithm. Importantly, other fields studying vision have addressed this via the use of visual psychophysics: the controlled manipulation of stimuli and careful study of the responses they evoke in a model system. In this paper, we suggest that visual psychophysics is a viable methodology for making face recognition algorithms more explainable. A comprehensive set of procedures is developed for assessing face recognition algorithm behavior, which is then deployed over state-of-the-art convolutional neural networks and more basic, yet still widely used, shallow and handcrafted feature-based approaches.

Keywords: Face recognition · Biometrics · Explainable AI Visual psychophysics · Biometric menagerie

1 Introduction

With much fanfare, Apple unveiled its Face ID product for the iPhone X in the Fall of 2017 at what was supposed to be a highly scripted event for the media. Touted as one of the most sophisticated facial recognition capabilities available to consumers, Face ID was designed to tolerate the wide range of user behaviors and environmental conditions that can be expected in a mobile biometrics setting. Remarkably, during the on-stage demo, Face ID failed [1]. Immediate

Electronic supplementary material The online version of this chapter (https://doi.org/10.1007/978-3-030-01267-0_16) contains supplementary material, which is available to authorized users.

© Springer Nature Switzerland AG 2018
V. Ferrari et al. (Eds.): ECCV 2018, LNCS 11219, pp. 263–281, 2018.
https://doi.org/10.1007/978-3-030-01267-0_16

speculation, especially from those with some familiarity with biometrics, centered around the possibility of a false negative, where an enrolled user failed to be recognized. After all, it was very dark on stage, with a harsh spotlight on the presenter, whose appearance was a bit more polished than usual—all variables that conceivably were not in the training set that the deep learning-based model behind Face ID was trained on. Apple, for its part, released a statement claiming that it was too many imposter authentication attempts before the demo that caused the problem [2]. Of course, that did little to satisfy the skeptics.

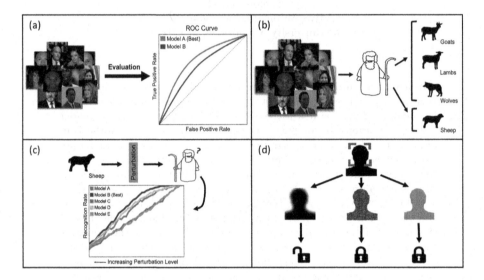

Fig. 1. Visual Pyschophysics [3–5] helps us explain algorithm behavior in a way that traditional dataset evaluation (a) cannot. Our proposed methodology introduces a theoretical mapping between elements of psychopysical testing and the biometric menagerie paradigm [6], where a shepherd function first isolates cooperative users ("sheep") from all others (b). From a perfect matching scenario, the images of the sheep are incrementally perturbed using a chosen image transformation, and item-response curves are plotted so that points of failure can be identified (c). The results can then be used to explain why matching works for some input images, but not others (d).

This controversy highlights a critical difficulty now facing the computer vision community: what is the true source of a problem when the object of study is a black box? While Apple may have access to the internals of its phones, ordinary users do not. But even with direct access to an algorithm, we can't always get what we want when it comes to an understanding of the conditions that lead to failure [7,8]. Given the fact that face recognition is one of the most common user-facing applications in computer vision, the ability to diagnose problems and validate claims about algorithm design and performance is desirable from the perspective of both the researcher and administrator charged with operating such systems. This is exactly why we want AI for face recognition to be *explainable*. In this paper, we look at a new methodology for doing this with any face recognition algorithm that takes an image as input. But first, let us consider the way we currently use evaluation procedures to try to understand their output.

The development cycle of face recognition algorithms relies on large-scale datasets. Progress is measured in a dataset context via summary statistics (*e.g.*, false positive rate, true positive rate, identification rate) computed over an evaluation set or n folds partitioned [9] from the evaluation set and expressed as a ROC or CMC curve (Fig. 1, Panel a). Such datasets have become even more important with the rise of machine learning, where both large training and evaluation sets are needed. For face verification (1:1 matching), there are a number of datasets that brought performance up to usable levels in controlled settings with cooperative subjects [10–14]. More recently, web-scale data [15–21] has been used to investigate more difficult recognition settings including face identification (1:N matching) and challenging impostor settings. There is a continuing push for larger datasets, which does not always address the problems observed in the algorithms trained over them. While aggregate performance has continued to improve, understanding individual causes of failure remains difficult, as it is not always clear why a particular face fails to be recognized, or why an impostor is recognized by an algorithm when considering a summary statistic.

Importantly, other fields studying vision have addressed this via the use of visual psychophysics: the controlled manipulation of stimuli and careful study of the responses they evoke in a model system [3–5]. In particular, the field of psychology has developed specific concepts and procedures related to visual psychophysics for the study of the human face and how it is perceived [22–25]. Instead of inferring performance from summary statistics expressed as curves like ROC or CMC, visual psychophysics allows us to view performance over a comprehensive range of conditions, permitting an experimenter to pinpoint the exact condition that results in failure. The gold standard for face recognition experimentation with people is the Cambridge Face Memory Test [23], which uses progressively degraded variations of faces to impede recognition. It has led to landmark studies on prosopagnosia (the inability to recognize a face) [26], super recognizers (people with an uncanny ability to recognize faces) [27], and face recognition ability and heritability [28]. Similarly, visual psychophysics has been used to study the role of holistic features in recognition by swapping parts to break the recognition ability [22]. More recent work has moved into the realm of photo-realistic 3D face synthesis, where changes in face perception can be studied by varying aspects of facial anatomy [24] and the age of the face used as a stimulus [25]. Given the breadth of its applicability, psychophysics also turns out to be an extremely powerful regime for explaining the behavior of algorithms.

We already see visual psychophysics becoming an alternate way of studying algorithm behavior in other areas of computer vision such as object recognition [29], face detection [30], and reinforcement learning [31]. However, no work has been undertaken yet in the area of face recognition. In this paper, we propose to address this by building a bridge from vision science to biometrics. Working from a recently established framework for conducting psychophysics experiments on computer vision algorithms [29] and infusing it with the proper methods from visual psychophysics for the study of face recognition in people, we fill in the missing pieces for automatic face recognition. Specifically, this involves a theoretical mapping between elements of psychopysical testing and the biometric menagerie paradigm [6], where cooperative users ("sheep") are isolated (Fig. 1, Panel b), and incremental perturbations degrade their performance (Fig. 1, Panel c). Results gathered from psychophysics experiments making use of highly controlled procedurally generated stimuli can then inform the way we should use a face recognition algorithm by explaining its failure modes (Fig. 1, Panel d).

2   Related Work

Explainable AI. An increasing emphasis on artificial neural networks in AI has resulted in a corresponding uptick in interest in explaining how trained models work. With respect to representations, Zeiler and Fergus [32] suggested that a multi-layer deconvolutional network can be used to project feature activations of a target convolutional network (CNN) back to pixel-space, thus allowing a researcher to reverse engineer the stimuli that excite the feature-maps at any layer in the CNN. Subsequent work by Mahendran and Vedaldi [33] generalized the understanding of representations via the analysis of the representation itself coupled with a natural image prior. With respect to decision making, Ribeiro et al. [8] have introduced a framework for approximating any classifier with an explicitly interpretable model. In a different, but related tactic, Fong and Vedaldi [34] use image perturbations to localize image regions relevant to classification. Image perturbations will form an important part of our methodology, described below in Sect. 3. A number of alternative regimes have also been proposed, including a sampling-based strategy that can be applied to face recognition algorithms [35], sampling coupled with reinforcement learning [7], and a comprehensive probabilistic programming framework [36]. What we propose in this paper is not meant to be a replacement for any existing method for explaining an AI model, and can work in concert with any of the above methods.

Psychophysics for Computer Vision. The application of psychophysics to computer vision has largely been an outgrowth of interdisciplinary work between brain scientists and computer scientists looking to build explanatory models that are consistent with observed behavior in animals and people. A recent example of this is the work of Rajalingham et al. [37], which compares the recognition behavior of monkeys, people and CNNs, noting that CNNs do not account for the image-level behavioral patterns of primates. Other have carried out studies using just humans as a reference point, with similar conclusions [38–41]. With respect to approaches designed specifically to perform psychophysics on computer vision algorithms, a flexible framework is PsyPhy, introduced by RichardWebster et al. [29]. PysPhy facilitates a psychophysical analysis for object recognition through the use of item-response theory. We build from that work to support a related item-response analysis for face recognition. Outside of research to explain the mechanisms of AI algorithms, other work in computer vision has sought to infuse psychophysical measurements into machine learning models [30, 42]. Data in several of these studies has relied on the popular crowd-sourced psychophysics website TestMyBrain.org [43]. In this work, we make use of a similar human-testing platform for comparison experiments.

Methods from Psychology Applied to Biometrics. While there is growing interest in what psychology can teach computer vision at large, the biometrics community was early to adopt some of its methods. Sinha et al. [44] outlined 19 findings from human vision that have important consequences for automatic face recognition. Several of these findings have served as direct inspiration for the adoption of CNNs for face recognition. A significant outgrowth of NIST-run face recognition evaluations has been a series of human vs. computer performance tests [45–49]. Even though these studies have not made use of psychophysics, they still shed new light on face recognition capabilities. In some cases such as changes in illumination [45, 46], good quality images [47], and matching frontal faces in still images [48], algorithms have been shown to be superior. However, one should keep in mind that these are controlled (or mostly controlled) verification settings, where images were intentionally acquired to reflect operational matching scenarios. In other cases, especially with more naturalistic data and video matching scenarios [48, 49], humans are shown to be superior. Studies such as these have established human perception as a measureable baseline for evaluating face recognition algorithms. We also look at human vs. algorithm performance as a baseline in this paper.

Biometrics and Perturbed Inputs. Many studies have sought to simulate real-world conditions that reduce matching performance. This has often taken the form of perturbations applied to the pixels on a face image—the primary form of transformation we will consider for our psychophysics experiments. Karahan et al. [50] and Grm et al. [51] have studied the impact of incrementally perturbing face images for transformations like Gaussian blur, noise, occlusion, contrast and color balance. In order to compensate for Gaussian blur, Ding and Tao [52] perturb sequences of face images for the purpose of learning blur-insensitive features within a CNN model. These experimental studies share an underlying motivation with this work, but are qualitatively and quantitatively different from the item-response-based approach we describe.

3 Psychophysics for Face Recognition Algorithms

In the *M-alternative forced-choice match-to-sample* (*M*-AFC) psychophysics procedure in psychology [5], a *sample* stimulus (*e.g.*, visual, auditory, or tactile) is used to elicit a perceptual response from a subject. The subject is then given a refractory period to allow their response to return to neutral. Once their response returns to neutral, the subject is presented with an *alternate* stimulus and given, if needed, another refractory period. This process is then repeated for a total of *M* unique alternate stimuli. Finally, the subject is *forced* to choose one of the alternate stimuli that best *matched* the sample stimulus. This is where the procedure name *M*-alternative forced-choice match-to-sample comes from. By carefully linking sample or alternate stimuli to a single condition at a specific stimulus level, a scientist running the experiment can measure mean or median accuracy achieved at each of the observed stimulus levels across all subjects. Together, these stimulus levels and their aggregated accuracy yield an interpretable item-response curve [3] (see Fig. 1, Panel c for an example).

RichardWebster et al. [29] introduced a technique using the M-AFC method to produce item-response curves for general object classification models that involves procedurally rendering objects. The process consists of two steps: (1) the identification of a preferred view and (2) the generation of an item-response curve. A preferred view is an extension of a canonical view [53], the theory that humans naturally prefer similar inter-class object orientations when asked for the best orientation which maximizes discriminability. The preferred view serves as the initial orientation of the procedurally rendered objects, allowing transformations such as rotation or scaling to guarantee a degradation of model performance. When item-response curves are generated, a modified M-AFC procedure is invoked that maps the alternate choices to the output of a classifier. However, instead of explicitly presenting alternate choices, the alternate choices are implicitly the learned classes of the classifier. Thus accuracy is computed by how frequently the correct class was chosen.

Although psychophysics for face recognition uses the same foundational M-AFC match-to-sample concepts, in practice it is very different than the psychophysics procedure for general object recognition. To begin with, an individual trial of the M-AFC procedure described above for human subjects is identical to the face identification procedure of biometrics. A face is acquired, and the system is queried to determine the identity of the face by matching the acquired image to enrolled faces within the system. Thus, a single M-AFC match-to-sample trial is equivalent to 1:N identification in biometrics. However, one difference between an algorithm performing 1:N matching and a human performing the same task is the need to set a threshold for the decision of "match" or "non-match" in the case of the algorithm (to reject match instances with insufficiently high scores).

Like any good scientific method, a method from psychophysics attempts to isolate a single variable to observe the effect it has on the rest of the system. In psychophysics experiments for face recognition, we call the isolated variable the perturbation level, which represents the degree of transformation applied with a perturbation function directly to an identity or to the image containing an identity. Thus, the first step in performing psychophysics for face recognition systems is to remove identities from an initial dataset that consistently cause false matches or false non-matches—errors that are already inherent within the matching process and would be a confound to studying the effect of the transformation. Doddington et al. [54] formally grouped users interacting with a biometric system into four classes whimsically named after farm animals, which together are called the *biometric menagerie* [6,55]. The biometric menagerie consists of *goats* (identities that are difficult to match), *lambs* (identities that are easily impersonated), *wolves* (identities that impersonate easily), and finally *sheep* (identities that match well to themselves but poorly to others). Since we

---

Algorithm 1. $H(\Upsilon, I)$: a "herding" function to isolate Doddington et al.'s [54] sheep from the goats, lambs, and wolves

---

Input: Υ, a "shepherd" function for a face recognition algorithm
Input: I, a set of input identities from a dataset
1: $S \leftarrow \Upsilon(I, I)$ ▷ similarity matrix
2: $S \leftarrow \frac{(S + S^\intercal)}{2}$ ▷ enforce symmetry
3: $t_h \leftarrow$ optimize loss function λ with TPE   ▷ Hyperopt [56–58]
4: $I_h \leftarrow \lambda(S, t_h)$ ▷ the "sheep" identities produced by λ
Output: t_h, the optimal threshold to produce I_h
Output: I_h, the "sheep" identities isolated by the optimal threshold t_h

---

want to remove all identities that lead to errors, we must remove the wolves, goats, and lambs. We call this the "herding" process.

The herding function, H (Algorithm 1), takes a set of input identities from an initial dataset, I, and a "shepherd" function, Υ, as input, and determines which identities Υ considers sheep. The Υ function is a wrapper function to a face recognition algorithm, f, and accepts two sets of identities: I_p the probe set and I_g the gallery set. It returns a standard similarity matrix where I_p is row-wise and I_g is column-wise. An example shepherd function can be seen in Algorithm 2. During the herding step, the input set I is split into I_p and I_g, which are used as input to Υ. The herding function itself is quite simple: it obtains a similarity matrix from the shepherd function, forces matrix symmetry, and then optimizes the loss function, λ (Algorithm 3), for 250 iterations with Hyperopt's implementation of the Tree-structured Parzen Estimator (TPE) hyperparameter optimizer [56–58]. More complicated is the loss function λ that the herding function uses.

λ takes as input a similarity matrix, S, and a threshold, t. The first step, thresholding the matrix, is standard in biometrics applications. However, the next step is not. The thresholded matrix is then XORed with an identity matrix, $\mathcal{I}$, to isolate all of the false match and false non-match pairs of identities ($\mathcal{I}$ represents the correct true matches). This new matrix can be considered an adjacency matrix, G, where all of the edges represent the false matches and false non-matches and each vertex is an identity.

The next step is to selectively remove vertices/identities until no edges remain while also removing as small a number of identities as possible. A strategy inspired by graph cuts allows us to sort the vertices by degree, remove the vertex with the highest degree from G, and repeat until no edges in G remain (see Supp. Algorithm 1 for the exact description[1]). At the end, G will be a completely disconnected graph, where no remaining identity will cause a false match or false non-match with any other remaining identity. By definition, all of the remaining identities are sheep. The returned loss value is the number of identities removed, where the function favors a lower false match rate, *i.e.*, higher thresholds are

---

[1] Supp. mat. available at http://www.bjrichardwebster.com/papers/menagerie/supp.

Algorithm 2. $\Upsilon_f(I_p, I_g)$: a "shepherd" function that produces a similarity matrix for the face recognition function f

---

Input: f, a face recognition function that produces a feature representation
Input: I_p, a set of probe identities
Input: I_g, a set of gallery identities
  1: $R_p \leftarrow i \in I_p : f(i)$ ▷ feature representation for each identity
  2: $R_g \leftarrow i \in I_g : f(i)$
  3: $S \leftarrow r_p \in R_p, r_g \in R_g : \mathrm{dist}(r_p, r_g)$ ▷ matrix of distances
  4: $S \leftarrow \mathrm{normalize}(S)$ ▷ normalize distances to standard similarity matrix
Output: S, the similarity matrix

Algorithm 3. $\lambda(S, t)$: a loss function that favors more *sheep*, and favors a lower false match rate (FMR) over false non-match rate (FNMR)

Input: S, similarity matrix
Input: t, a threshold
  1: $M \leftarrow S \geq t$
  2: $M \leftarrow M \oplus \mathcal{I}$ ▷ isolate FM and FNM pairs
  3: $G = (V, E)$ from M ▷ adjacency list
  4: $\nu \leftarrow |V|$
  5: **while** $|E| > 0$ **do**   ▷ remove goats, lambs, and wolves
  6:      $v_r \leftarrow \mathrm{argmax}_{v \in V} \deg(v)$
  7:      **remove** v_r from V ▷ remove the vertex and connected edges from G
  8: **end while**
  9: $l \leftarrow \nu - |V|$ ▷ number of goats, lambs, and wolves removed
10: $l \leftarrow l + (1 - 0.99999 * t)$ ▷ favor lower FMR over FNMR
Output: l, the loss value

---

favored. After λ is optimized, the optimal threshold t_h and sheep identities I_h are returned.

The sheep identities I_h and the threshold t_h serve as two of the inputs to the item-response point generator function Φ (Algorithm 4). Φ generates a point on an item-response curve that represents the rank one match rate for a specific perturbation function, T, and its respective perturbation level. The perturbation function takes an image and a perturbation level as input, applies some transformation to the image, and returns the transformed image. In the context of the biometric menagerie, this function is analogous to "perturbing" a sheep (dying the wool, shearing the wool, etc.) and asking its shepherd if it can properly identify the sheep. Thus Φ also takes Υ as a parameter. Φ uses T to perturb each input identity in I_h to create the set of perturbed probe identities for 1:N identification. The remaining steps of Φ are standard to face recognition systems operating in the identification mode: obtain similarity matrix from probe to gallery pairs, threshold the matrix, and calculate the match rate. The return value of the Φ function is an x, y coordinate pair $\{s, \alpha\}$ for one item-response point, where s represents the perturbation level and α is the match rate.

Algorithm 4. $\Phi_T(\Upsilon, I_h, t_h, \delta)$: an item-response point generation function for any image transformation function $T(i, \delta)$

Input: Υ, a "shepherd" function for a facial recognition model
Input: I_h, the "sheep" identities for the found threshold t_h
Input: t_h, the optimal threshold to produce I_h
Input: δ, the stimulus level
1: $I_h' \leftarrow i \in I_h : T(i, \delta)$ ▷ perturb identities to create probes
2: $S \leftarrow \Upsilon(I_h', I_h)$ ▷ similarity matrix
3: $M \leftarrow S \geq t_h$
4: $\alpha \leftarrow \frac{|M \wedge \mathcal{I}|}{|I_h|}$ ▷ obtain match rate using identity matrix $\mathcal{I}$
Output: $\{s, \alpha\}$, an x, y coordinate pair (stimulus level, match rate)

Algorithm 5. $\mathcal{C}_T(\Upsilon, I_h, t_h, n, b_l, bu)$: an item-response curve generation function for any type of "shepherd" function

Input: Υ, a "shepherd" function for a facial recognition model
Input: t_h, the optimal threshold to produce I_h
Input: I_h, the "sheep" identities for the found threshold t_h
Input: n, the number of stimulus levels
Input: b_l and b_u, the lower and upper bound values of the stimulus levels
1: **Let** Δ be n log-spaced stimulus levels from b_l to b_u
2: $k \leftarrow \bigcup_{\delta \in \Delta} \{\Phi_T(\Upsilon, I_h, t_h, \delta)\}$
Output: k, the item-response curve

A shepherd's behavior for a set of sheep identities can be represented with an item-response curve (a collection of points obtained from Φ), which is an interpretable representation of the shepherd's behavior in response to perturbation. For biometric identification, the x-axis is a series of values that represent a perturbation level from the original sheep identities and the y-axis is the match rate. To produce the item-response curves, the function $\mathcal{C}$ (Algorithm 5) is called once for each transformation type. $\mathcal{C}$ repeatedly calls a point generated with Φ (Algorithm 4) to create one point for each stimulus level from the least amount of perturbation, b_l, to the most, b_u (b_l are the non-transformed sheep identities). The parameter n is the number of stimulus levels to be used to produce the points on the match-response curve and are typically log-spaced to give finer precision near the non-transformed sheep identities. The final parameter w is the number of identities examined at each stimulus level where $w \in [1, |I_h|]$.

4   Experiments

Experiments were designed with four distinct objectives in mind: (1) to survey the performance of deep CNNs and other alternative models from the literature; (2) to look more closely at a surprising finding in order to explain the observed model behavior; (3) to study networks with stochastic outputs, which are prevalent in Bayesian analysis; and (4) to compare human vs. algorithm performance.

For all experiments, we made use of the following face recognition algorithms: VGG-Face [59], FaceNet [60], OpenFace [61], a simple three-layer CNN trained via high-throughput search of random weights [62] (labeled "slmsimple" below), and OpenBR 1.1.0 [63], which makes use of handcrafted features. For each of the networks, the final feature layer was used with normalized cosine similarity as the similarity metric[2]. All used models were used as-is from their corresponding authors, with no additional fine-tuning. A complete set of plots for all experiments can be found in the supplemental material.

Data Generation. The following transformations were applied to 2D images from the LFW dataset [64]: Gaussian blur, linear occlusion, salt & pepper noise, Gaussian noise, brown noise, pink noise, brightness, contrast, and sharpness. Note that we intentionally chose LFW because state-of-the-art algorithms have reached ceiling performance on it. The psychophysics testing regime makes it far more difficult for the algorithms, depending on the chosen transformation. Each face recognition algorithm was asked to "herd" 1000 initial images before item-response curve generation. All algorithms except OpenBR recognized all the initial images as sheep (see Supp. Sect. 2 for a breakdown). For each transformation, we generated 200 different log-spaced stimulus levels, using each algorithm's choice of sheep, to create a corresponding item-response curve. In all, this resulted in ~5.5 *million* unique images and ~13.7 *billion* image comparisons.

Inspired by earlier work in psychology [24, 25, 65] making use of the FaceGen software package [66], we used it to apply transformations related to emotion and expression. A complete list can be found in the supplemental material. Each face algorithm selected sheep from 220 initial images (all face textures provided by FaceGen, mapped to its "average" 3D "zero" model) for item-response curve generation. All chose 206 sheep, with a nearly identical selection by each (see Supp. Sect. 3 for a complete list). 50 stimulus levels were rendered for each image, resulting in ~400,000 unique 3D images and ~17.5 *billion* image comparisons.

Identification with 2D Images. Given recent results on datasets, one would expect that the deep CNNs (FaceNet, OpenFace, and VGG-Face) would be the best performers on an M-AFC task, following by the shallower network (slmsimple), and then the approach that makes use of handcrafted features (OpenBR). Surprisingly, this is not what we observed for any of the experiments (Figs. 2 and 4; Supp. Figs. 1–2). Overall, VGG-Face is the best performing network, as it is able to withstand the perturbations to a greater degree than the rest of the algorithms. At some points (*e.g.*, left-hand side of Fig. 2) the perturbations have absolutely no effect on VGG-Face, while severely degrading the performance of other algorithms, signifying strong learned invariance.

Remarkably, the non-deep learning approach OpenBR is not the worst performing algorithm. It turned out to outperform several of the deep networks in most experiments. This is the kind of finding that would not be apparent from a CMC or ROC curve calculated from a dataset, where OpenBR is easily outperformed by many algorithms across many datasets [63, 67]. Why does

---

[2] Source code is available at www.bjrichardwebster.com/papers/menagerie/code.

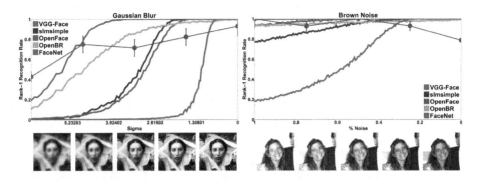

Fig. 2. A selection of item-response curves for the M-AFC task using data from the LFW dataset [64]. Each experiment used five different face recognition algorithms [59–63]. A perfect curve would be a flat line at the top of the plot. The images at the bottom of each curve show how the perturbations increase from right to left, starting with no perturbation (*i.e.*, the original image) for all conditions. The red dots indicate mean human performance for a selected stimulus level; error bars are standard error. Curves are normalized so chance is 0 on the y-axis. All plots are best viewed in color.

this occur? These results indicate that it's not always possible to rely on large amounts of training data to learn strongly invariant features—a task that can be different from learning representations that perform well on a chosen dataset. The design of the algorithm is also consequential: OpenBR's choice of LBP [68] and SIFT [69] leads to better performance than FaceNet and OpenFace, which each learned features over hundreds of thousands of faces images.

Identification with 3D Images. Computer graphics allows us to generate images for which all parameters are known—something not achievable with 2D data. One such parameter, expression, has been widely studied [70–72], but not in the highly incremental manner we propose here. Where exactly do algorithms break for specific expression changes? We can find this out by controlling the face with graphics (Figs. 3 and 4; Supp. Figs. 3–4). For instance, for the bodily function of blinking (Fig. 3) VGG-Face and slmsimple are the best, while this very small change to the visual appearance of the face causes a significant degradation of matching performance in the three other algorithms. OpenFace and FaceNet once again have trouble learning invariance from their training data. This trend holds over several expressions and emotions (Supp. Figs. 3–4).

OpenFace vs. FaceNet. It is often difficult to assess the claims made by the developers of machine-learning-based algorithms. During the course of our experimentation, we discovered an interesting discrepancy between two networks, FaceNet [60] and OpenFace [61], which both reported to be implementations of Google's FaceNet algorithm [20]. While it is good for end-users that deep learning has, in a sense, become "plug-and-play," there is also some concern surrounding this. It is not always clear if a re-implementation of an algorithm matches the original specification. Psychophysics can help us find this out. Across all experiments, FaceNet demonstrates very weak invariance properties compared to OpenFace (Figs. 3–4; Supp. Figs. 3–4), and fails well before the other algorithms

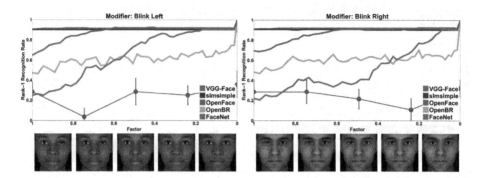

Fig. 3. A selection of item-response curves for the M-AFC task using rendered 3D face models as stimuli [66]. Curves are normalized so chance is 0. Here we see that three of the algorithms are drastically affected by the simple bodily function of blinking, while two others are not impacted at all. As in Fig. 2, VGG-Face is once again the best performing algorithm, but remarkably, we see that the three-layer CNN trained via a random search for weights (labeled "slmsimple") works just as well.

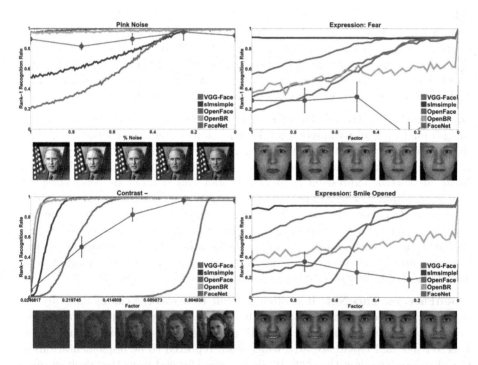

Fig. 4. Two of the algorithms we evaluated, FaceNet [60] and OpenFace [61], both reported to be an implementation of Google's FaceNet [20] algorithm. Curiously, we found major disagreement between them in almost all of our experiments. Note the gaps between their respective curves in the above plot. This performance gap was not evident when analyzing their reported accuracy performance on LFW.

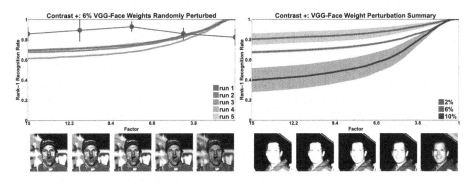

Fig. 5. Weight perturbations for stochastic model output can be combined with stimulus perturbations for a stronger reliability assessment. (Left) Five independent model runs where 6% of the weights have been perturbed, with input stimuli reflecting increasing contrast. (Right) Curves represent the average of five runs for three different levels of weight perturbation from 2% to 10%. Shaded regions are standard error.

in most cases. From these results, we can conclude that use of this particular implementation of Google's FaceNet should be avoided. But why is it so different from OpenFace, and what would be causing it to fail, in spite of it reporting superior accuracy on LFW (0.992 for FaceNet vs. 0.9292 for OpenFace)?

One can find three key differences in the code and data—after being prompted to look there by the psychophysics experiments. (1) OpenFace uses 500k training images by combining CASIA-WebFace [17] and FaceScrub [73]; FaceNet uses a subset of MS-Celeb-1M [74] where difficult images that contain partial occlusion, silhouettes, etc. *have been removed* as a function of facial landmark detection. This is likely the weakest link, as the network does not have an opportunity to learn invariance to these conditions. (2) OpenFace uses the exact architecture described by Schroff et al. [20], while FaceNet opts for Inception ResNet v1 [75]. (3) FaceNet uses a Multi-Task CNN [76] for facial landmark detection and alignment, while OpenFace uses dlib [77]—which FaceNet intentionally avoids due to its lower yield of faces for the training set. FaceNet may have hit upon the right combination of network elements for LFW, but it does not generalize like the original work, which OpenFace is more faithful to.

Weight Perturbation Coupled with Stimulus Perturbation. The procedure of applying perturbations directly to the weights of a neural network has an interpretation of Bayesian inference over the weights, and leads to stochastic output [78,79]. This is potentially important for face recognition because it gives us another measure of model reliability. To look at the effect of CNN weight perturbations coupled with stimulus perturbations, we use VGG-Face as a case study. A percentage of its weights are replaced with a random value from the normal distribution, $\mathcal{N}(0,1)$, targeting all layers. From Fig. 5, we can see that both perturbation types have an impact. Under a regime that perturbs just 6% of the weights (left-hand side of Fig. 5), we can gain a sense that VGG-Face is stable across models with respect to its performance when processing increasing levels of contrast. However, too much weight perturbation increases the variance, leading to undesirable behavior on the perturbed input. On the right-hand side of Fig. 5, each curve represents the average of five runs when perturbing between 2% and 10% of the weights. Perturbing 10% of the weights breaks the invariant features of VGG-Face and induces more variance between models. Similar effects for other transformations can be seen in Supp. Figs. 5–6.

Human Comparisons. As discussed in Sect. 2, there is a rich literature within biometrics comparing human and algorithm performance. However, thus far, such studies have not made use of any procedures from visual psychophysics. Here we fill this gap. To obtain human data points for Figs. 2–5 (the red dots in the plots), we conducted a study with 14 participants. The task the participants performed largely followed the standard M-AFC protocol described above: a participant is briefly shown an image, it is hidden from sight, and then they are shown three images and directed to choose the image that is most similar to the first one. Each participant performed the task three times for each perturbation level. Each set of images within a task was chosen carefully to keep human performance from being perfect. For both 2D and 3D images, the images were divided by gender such that participants could not match solely by it [80]. For 3D images, the data was also divided by ethnicity such that it could not be the sole criterion to match by [81]. To interrupt iconic memory [82], after each sample image is shown, a scrambled inverse frequency function was applied to the image to produce colored noise, and shown for 500ms prior to the alternate choices. 2D images were shown for 50ms and 3D images for 200ms. Humans struggled to identify faces in the 3D context where different identities are closer in visual appearance, but excelled in the 2D context where there was greater separation between identities. The plots for Gaussian blur (Fig. 2) and Decreasing Contrast (Fig. 4) hint at behavioral consistency between AI and humans in these cases.

5   Conclusion

Given the model capacity of today's deep neural network-based algorithms, there is an enormous burden to explain what is learned and how that translates into algorithm behavior. Psychophysics allows us to do this in a straightforward manner when methods from psychology are adapted to conform to the typical procedures of biometric matching, as we have shown. Companies launching new products incorporating face recognition can potentially prevent (or at least mitigate) embarrassing incidents like Apple's botched demo of FaceID by matching the operational setting of an algorithm to a useable input space. And even if a company provides an explanation for a product's failure, anyone can directly interrogate it via a psychophysics experiment to find out if those claims are true. To facilitate this, all source code and data associated with this paper will be released upon publication. With the recent uptick in psychophysics work for computer vision [29, 30, 37–40, 42], we expect to see new face recognition algorithms start to use these data to improve their performance.

Acknowledgments. Funding was provided under IARPA contract #D16PC00002, NSF DGE #1313583, and NSF SBIR Award #IIP-1738479. Hardware support was generously provided by the NVIDIA Corporation, and made available by the National Science Foundation (NSF) through grant #CNS-1629914.

References

1. Apple Inc: IPHONE X FACE ID FAIL (2017). https://www.youtube.com/watch? v=m7xmCCTVS7Q. Accessed 1 Mar 2018
2. Hern, A.: Apple: Face ID didn't fail at iPhone X launch, our staff did. The Guardian, 14 Sep 2017
3. Embretson, S.E., Reise, S.P.: Item Response Theory for Psychologists. Lawrence Erlbaum Associates, Inc., Mahwah (2000)
4. Lu, Z.L., Dosher, B.: Visual Psychophysics: From Laboratory to Theory. MIT Press (2013)
5. Kingdom, F., Prins, N.: Psychophysics: A Practical Introduction. Academic Press (2016)
6. Yager, N., Dunstone, T.: The biometric menagerie. IEEE Trans. Pattern Anal. Mach. Intell. **32**(2), 220–230 (2010)
7. Hendricks, L.A., Akata, Z., Rohrbach, M., Donahue, J., Schiele, B., Darrell, T.: Generating visual explanations. In: Leibe, B., Matas, J., Sebe, N., Welling, M. (eds.) ECCV 2016. LNCS, vol. 9908, pp. 3–19. Springer, Cham (2016). https:// doi.org/10.1007/978-3-319-46493-0_1
8. Ribeiro, M.T., Singh, S., Guestrin, C.: Why should I trust you?: explaining the predictions of any classifier. In: ACM KDD (2016)
9. Haralick, R.M.: Performance characterization in computer vision. In: Hogg, D., Boyle, R. (eds.) BMVC 1992, pp. 1–8. Springer, London (1992). https://doi.org/ 10.1007/978-1-4471-3201-1_1
10. Phillips, P.J., Moon, H., Rizvi, S.A., Rauss, P.J.: The FERET evaluation methodology for face-recognition algorithms. IEEE Trans. Pattern Anal. Mach. Intell. **22**(10), 1090–1104 (2000)
11. Phillips, P.J., et al.: Overview of the face recognition grand challenge. In: IEEE CVPR (2005)
12. Phillips, P.J., et al.: Overview of the multiple biometrics grand challenge. In: Tistarelli, M., Nixon, M.S. (eds.) ICB 2009. LNCS, vol. 5558, pp. 705–714. Springer, Heidelberg (2009). https://doi.org/10.1007/978-3-642-01793-3_72
13. Beveridge, J.R., et al.: The challenge of face recognition from digital point-and-shoot cameras. In: IEEE BTAS (2013)
14. Phillips, P.J., et al.: An introduction to the good, the bad, & the ugly face recognition challenge problem. In: IEEE FG (2011)
15. Kemelmacher-Shlizerman, I., Seitz, S.M., Miller, D., Brossard, E.: The megaface benchmark: 1 million faces for recognition at scale. In: IEEE CVPR (2016)
16. Klare, B.F., et al.: Pushing the frontiers of unconstrained face detection and recognition: IARPA Janus Benchmark A. In: IEEE CVPR (2015)
17. Yi, D., Lei, Z., Liao, S., Li, S.Z.: Learning face representation from scratch (2014). arXiv preprint arXiv:1411.7923
18. Ortiz, E.G., Becker, B.C.: Face recognition for web-scale datasets. Comput. Vis. Image Underst. **118**, 153–170 (2014)

19. Bhattarai, B., Sharma, G., Jurie, F., Pérez, P.: Some faces are more equal than others: hierarchical organization for accurate and efficient large-scale identity-based face retrieval. In: Agapito, L., Bronstein, M.M., Rother, C. (eds.) ECCV 2014. LNCS, vol. 8926, pp. 160–172. Springer, Cham (2015). https://doi.org/10.1007/978-3-319-16181-5_12

20. Schroff, F., Kalenichenko, D., Philbin, J.: Facenet: a unified embedding for face recognition and clustering. In: IEEE CVPR (2015)

21. Wang, D., Otto, C., Jain, A.K.: Face search at scale. IEEE Trans. Pattern Anal. Mach. Intell. **39**(6), 1122–1136 (2017)

22. Tanaka, J.W., Farah, M.J.: Parts and wholes in face recognition. Q. J. Exp. Psychol. **46**(2), 225–245 (1993)

23. Duchaine, B., Nakayama, K.: The Cambridge face memory test: results for neurologically intact individuals and an investigation of its validity using inverted face stimuli and prosopagnosic participants. Neuropsychologia **44**(4), 576–585 (2006)

24. Oosterhof, N.N., Todorov, A.: The functional basis of face evaluation. Proc. Natl. Acad. Sci. **105**(32), 11087–11092 (2008)

25. Germine, L.T., Duchaine, B., Nakayama, K.: Where cognitive development and aging meet: face learning ability peaks after age 30. Cognition **118**(2), 201–210 (2011)

26. Duchaine, B., Germine, L., Nakayama, K.: Family resemblance: ten family members with prosopagnosia and within-class object agnosia. Cogn. Neuropsychol. **24**(4), 419–430 (2007)

27. Russell, R., Duchaine, B., Nakayama, K.: Super-recognizers: people with extraordinary face recognition ability. Psychon. Bull. Rev. **16**(2), 252–257 (2009)

28. Wilmer, J.B., et al.: Human face recognition ability is specific and highly heritable. Proc. Natl. Acad. Sci. **107**(11), 5238–5241 (2010)

29. RichardWebster, B., Anthony, S., Scheirer, W.: Psyphy: a psychophysics driven evaluation framework for visual recognition. IEEE Trans. Pattern Anal. Mach. Intell. 1–1 (2018). Preprint

30. Scheirer, W.J., Anthony, S.E., Nakayama, K., Cox, D.D.: Perceptual annotation: Measuring human vision to improve computer vision. IEEE Trans. Pattern Anal. Mach. Intell. **36**(8), 1679–1686 (2014)

31. Leibo, J.Z., et al.: Psychlab: a psychology laboratory for deep reinforcement learning agents (2018). arXiv preprint arXiv:1801.08116

32. Zeiler, M.D., Fergus, R.: Visualizing and understanding convolutional networks. In: Fleet, D., Pajdla, T., Schiele, B., Tuytelaars, T. (eds.) ECCV 2014. LNCS, vol. 8689, pp. 818–833. Springer, Cham (2014). https://doi.org/10.1007/978-3-319-10590-1_53

33. Mahendran, A., Vedaldi, A.: Understanding deep image representations by inverting them. In: IEEE CVPR (2015)

34. Fong, R.C., Vedaldi, A.: Interpretable explanations of black boxes by meaningful perturbation. In: IEEE ICCV (2017)

35. Turner, R.: A model explanation system. In: 2016 IEEE 26th International Workshop on Machine Learning for Signal Processing (MLSP) (2016)

36. Lake, B.M., Salakhutdinov, R., Tenenbaum, J.B.: Human-level concept learning through probabilistic program induction. Science **350**(6266), 1332–1338 (2015)

37. Rajalingham, R., Issa, E.B., Bashivan, P., Kar, K., Schmidt, K., DiCarlo, J.J.: Large-scale, high-resolution comparison of the core visual object recognition behavior of humans, monkeys, and state-of-the-art deep artificial neural networks, 240614 (2018). bioRxiv

38. Gerhard, H.E., Wichmann, F.A., Bethge, M.: How sensitive is the human visual system to the local statistics of natural images? PLoS Comput. Biol. **9**(1), e1002873 (2013)
39. Eberhardt, S., Cader, J., Serre, T.: How deep is the feature analysis underlying rapid visual categorization? In: NIPS (2016)
40. Geirhos, R., Janssen, D.H.J., Schütt, H.H., Rauber, J., Bethge, M., Wichmann, F.A.: Comparing deep neural networks against humans: object recognition when the signal gets weaker (2017). arXiv preprint arXiv:1706.06969
41. Heath, M., Sarkar, S., Sanocki, T., Bowyer, K.: Comparison of edge detectors: a methodology and initial study. In: 1996 IEEE Computer Society Conference on Computer Vision and Pattern Recognition. Proceedings CVPR 1996, pp. 143–148. IEEE (1996)
42. McCurie, M., Beletti, F., Parzianello, L., Westendorp, A., Anthony, S.E., Scheirer, W.J.: Predicting first impressions with deep learning. In: IEEE FG (2017)
43. Germine, L., Nakayama, K., Duchaine, B.C., Chabris, C.F., Chatterjee, G., Wilmer, J.B.: Is the web as good as the lab? Comparable performance from web and lab in cognitive/perceptual experiments. Psychon. Bull. Rev. **19**(5), 847–857 (2012)
44. Sinha, P., Balas, B., Ostrovsky, Y., Russell, R.: Face recognition by humans: nineteen results all computer vision researchers should know about. Proc. IEEE **94**(11), 1948–1962 (2006)
45. O'Toole, A.J., Phillips, P.J., Jiang, F., Ayyad, J., Penard, N., Abdi, H.: Face recognition algorithms surpass humans matching faces over changes in illumination. IEEE Trans. Pattern Anal. Mach. Intell. **29**(9), 1642–1646 (2007)
46. O'Toole, A.J., Phillips, P.J., Narvekar, A.: Humans versus algorithms: comparisons from the face recognition vendor test 2006. In: IEEE FG (2008)
47. O'Toole, A.J., An, X., Dunlop, J., Natu, V., Phillips, P.J.: Comparing face recognition algorithms to humans on challenging tasks. ACM Trans. Appl. Percept. (TAP) **9**(4), 16 (2012)
48. Phillips, P.J., O'Toole, A.J.: Comparison of human and computer performance across face recognition experiments. Image Vis. Comput. **32**(1), 74–85 (2014)
49. Phillips, P.J., Hill, M.Q., Swindle, J.A., O'Toole, A.J.: Human and algorithm performance on the PaSC face recognition challenge. In: IEEE BTAS (2015)
50. Karahan, S., Yildirum, M.K., Kirtac, K., Rende, F.S., Butun, G., Ekenel, H.K.: How image degradations affect deep CNN-based face recognition? In: International Conference of the Biometrics Special Interest Group (BIOSIG) (2016)
51. Grm, K., Struc, V., Artiges, A., Caron, M., Ekenel, H.K.: Strengths and weaknesses of deep learning models for face recognition against image degradations. IET Biom. **7**(1), 81–89 (2018)
52. Ding, C., Tao, D.: Trunk-branch ensemble convolutional neural networks for video-based face recognition. IEEE Trans. Pattern Anal. Mach. Intell. (2017, to appear)
53. Blanz, V., Tarr, M.J., Bülthoff, H.H.: What object attributes determine canonical views? Perception **28**(5), 575–599 (1999)
54. Doddington, G., Liggett, W., Martin, A., Przybocki, M., Reynolds, D.: Sheep, goats, lambs and wolves: a statistical analysis of speaker performance in the NIST 1998 speaker recognition evaluation. Technical report, National Institute of Standards and Technology (1998)
55. Teli, M.N., Beveridge, J.R., Phillips, P.J., Givens, G.H., Bolme, D.S., Draper, B.A.: Biometric zoos: theory and experimental evidence. In: IEEE/IAPR IJCB (2011)
56. Bergstra, J.S., Bardenet, R., Bengio, Y., Kégl, B.: Algorithms for hyper-parameter optimization. In: NIPS (2011)

57. Bergstra, J., Yamins, D., Cox, D.D.: Hyperopt: a python library for optimizing the hyperparameters of machine learning algorithms. In: 12th Python in Science Conference (2013)

58. Bergstra, J., Komer, B., Eliasmith, C., Yamins, D., Cox, D.D.: Hyperopt: a python library for model selection and hyperparameter optimization. Comput. Sci. Discov. 8(1), 014008 (2015)

59. Parkhi, O.M., Vedaldi, A., Zisserman, A., et al.: Deep face recognition. In: BMVC, vol. 1, p. 6 (2015)

60. Sandberg, D.: Face recognition using tensorflow (2017). https://github.com/davidsandberg/facenet. Accessed 1 Mar 2018

61. Amos, B., Ludwiczuk, B., Satyanarayanan, M.: Openface: a general-purpose face recognition library with mobile applications. Technical report, CMU-CS-16-118, CMU School of Computer Science (2016)

62. Cox, D.D., Pinto, N.: Beyond simple features: a large-scale feature search approach to unconstrained face recognition. In: IEEE FG (2011)

63. Klontz, J.C., Klare, B.F., Klum, S., Jain, A.K., Burge, M.J.: Open source biometric recognition. In: IEEE BTAS (2013)

64. Huang, G.B., Ramesh, M., Berg, T., Learned-Miller, E.: Labeled faces in the wild: a database for studying face recognition in unconstrained environments. Technical report, 07-49, University of Massachusetts, Amherst (2007)

65. Yildirim, I., Kulkarni, T.D., Freiwald, W.A., Tenenbaum, J.B.: Efficient and robust analysis-by-synthesis in vision: a computational framework, behavioral tests, and modeling neuronal representations. In: Annual Conference of the Cognitive Science Society (2015)

66. Singular Inversions: Facegen (2017). https://facegen.com/. Accessed 1 Mar 2018

67. Amos, B.: Openface 0.2.0: higher accuracy and halved execution time (2016). http://bamos.github.io/2016/01/19/openface-0.2.0/. Accessed 1 Mar 2018

68. Ahonen, T., Hadid, A., Pietikainen, M.: Face description with local binary patterns: application to face recognition. IEEE Trans. Pattern Anal. Mach. Intell. 28(12), 2037-2041 (2006)

69. Lowe, D.G.: Object recognition from local scale-invariant features. In: IEEE ICCV (1999)

70. Sim, T., Baker, S., Bsat, M.: The CMU pose, illumination, and expression (PIE) database. In: IEEE FG (2002)

71. Gross, R., Matthews, I., Cohn, J., Kanade, T., Baker, S.: Multi-PIE. Image Vis. Comput. 28(5), 807-813 (2010)

72. Dutta, A., Veldhuis, R., Spreeuwers, L.: A Bayesian model for predicting face recognition performance using image quality. In: IEEE/IAPR IJCB (2014)

73. Ng, H.W., Winkler, S.: A data-driven approach to cleaning large face datasets. In: IEEE ICIP (2014)

74. Guo, Y., Zhang, L., Hu, Y., He, X., Gao, J.: MS-Celeb-1M: a dataset and benchmark for large-scale face recognition. In: Leibe, B., Matas, J., Sebe, N., Welling, M. (eds.) ECCV 2016. LNCS, vol. 9907, pp. 87-102. Springer, Cham (2016). https://doi.org/10.1007/978-3-319-46487-9_6

75. Szegedy, C., Ioffe, S., Vanhoucke, V., Alemi, A.A.: Inception-v4, inception-resnet and the impact of residual connections on learning. In: AAAI (2017)

76. Zhang, K., Zhang, Z., Li, Z., Qiao, Y.: Joint face detection and alignment using multitask cascaded convolutional networks. IEEE Signal Process. Lett. 23(10), 1499-1503 (2016)

77. King, D.E.: Dlib-ml: a machine learning toolkit. J. Mach. Learn. Res. 10, 1755-1758 (2009)

78. Graves, A.: Practical variational inference for neural networks. In: NIPS (2011)
79. Goodfellow, I., Bengio, Y., Courville, A., Bengio, Y.: Deep learning, vol. 1. MIT Press Cambridge (2016)
80. O'Toole, A.J., Deffenbacher, K.A., Valentin, D., McKee, K., Huff, D., Abdi, H.: The perception of face gender: the role of stimulus structure in recognition and classification. Mem. Cogn. **26**(1), 146–160 (1998)
81. Webster, M.A., MacLeod, D.I.: Visual adaptation and face perception. Philos. Trans. R. Soc. Lond. B Biol. Sci. **366**(1571), 1702–1725 (2011)
82. Dick, A.O.: Iconic memory and its relation to perceptual processing and other memory mechanisms. Percept. Psychophys. **16**(3), 575–596 (1974)

Conditional Prior Networks for Optical Flow

Yanchao Yang[(✉)] and Stefano Soatto

UCLA Vision Lab, University of California, Los Angeles, CA 90095, USA
{yanchao.yang,soatto}@cs.ucla.edu

Abstract. Classical computation of optical flow involves generic priors (regularizers) that capture rudimentary statistics of images, but not long-range correlations or semantics. On the other hand, fully supervised methods learn the regularity in the annotated data, without explicit regularization and with the risk of overfitting. We seek to learn richer priors on the set of possible flows that are statistically compatible with *an* image. Once the prior is learned in a supervised fashion, one can easily learn the full map to infer optical flow directly from *two or more* images, without any need for (additional) supervision. We introduce a novel architecture, called Conditional Prior Network (CPN), and show how to train it to yield a conditional prior. When used in conjunction with a simple optical flow architecture, the CPN beats all variational methods and all unsupervised learning-based ones using the same data term. It performs comparably to fully supervised ones, that however are fine-tuned to a particular dataset. Our method, on the other hand, performs well even when transferred between datasets. Code is available at: https://github.com/YanchaoYang/Conditional-Prior-Networks.

1 Introduction

Consider Fig. 1: A given image (left) could give rise to many different optical flows (OF) [18] depending on what another image of the same scene looks like: It could show a car moving to the right (top), or the same apparently moving to the left due to camera motion to the right (middle), or it could be an artificial motion because the scene was a picture portraying the car, rather than the actual physical scene. A single image biases, but does not constrain, the set of possible flows the underlying scene can generate. We wish to leverage the information an image contains about possible compatible flows to learn better priors than those implied by generic regularizers. Note that all three flows in Fig. 1 are equally valid under a generic prior (piecewise smoothness), but not under a natural prior (cars moving in the scene).

Electronic supplementary material The online version of this chapter (https://doi.org/10.1007/978-3-030-01267-0_17) contains supplementary material, which is available to authorized users.

© Springer Nature Switzerland AG 2018
V. Ferrari et al. (Eds.): ECCV 2018, LNCS 11219, pp. 282–298, 2018.
https://doi.org/10.1007/978-3-030-01267-0_17

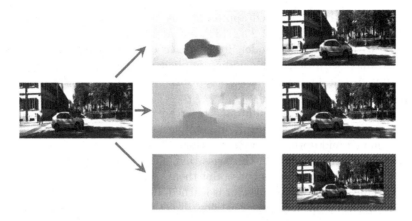

Fig. 1. A single image biases, but does not constrain, the set of optical flows that can be generated from it, depending on whether the camera was static but objects were moving (top), or the camera was moving (center), or the scene was flat (bottom) and moving on a plane in an un-natural scenario. Flow fields here are generated by our CPNFlow

A regularizer is a criterion that, when added to a data fitting term, constrains the solution of an inverse problem. These two criteria (data term and regularizer) are usually formalized as an energy function, which is minimized to, ideally, find a unique global optimum.[1]

1.1 Our Approach in Context

In classical (variational) OF, the regularizer captures very rudimentary low-order statistics [4,5,9,29,37], for instance the high kurtosis of the gradient distribution. This does not help with the scenario in Fig. 1. There has been a recent surge of (supervised) learning-based approaches to OF [15,19,32], that do not have explicit regularization nor do they use geometric reprojection error as a criterion for data fit. Instead, a map is learned from pairs of images to flows, where regularization is implicit in the function class [13],[2] in the training procedure [11] (e.g. noise of stochastic gradient descent – SGD), and in the datasets used for training (e.g. Sintel [10], Flying Chair [15]).

Our method does not attempt to learn geometric optics anew, even though black-box approaches are the top performers in several benchmarks. Instead, we seek to learn richer priors on the set of possible flows that are statistically compatible with an image (Fig. 1).

---

[1] We use the terms regularizer, prior, model, or assumption, interchangeably and broadly to include any restriction on the solution space, or bias on the solution, imposed without full knowledge of the data. In OF, the full data is (at least) two images.

[2] In theory, deep neural networks are universal approximants, but there is a considerable amount of engineering in the architectures to capture suitable inductive biases.

Unsupervised learning-based approaches use the same or similar loss functions as variational methods [2, 20, 27, 33], including priors, but restrict the function class to a parametric model, for instance convolutional neural networks (CNNs) trained with SGD, thus adding implicit regularization [11]. Again, the priors only encode first-order statistics, which fail to capture the phenomena in Fig. 1.

We advocate learning a conditional prior, or regularizer, from data, but do so once and forall, and then use it in conjunction with any data fitting term, with any model and optimization one wishes.

What we learn is a prior in the sense that it imposes a bias on the possible solutions, but it does not alone constraint them, which happens only in conjunction with a data term. Once the prior is learned, in a supervised fashion, one can also learn the full map to infer optical flow directly from data, without any need for (additional) supervision. In this sense, our method is *"semi-unsupervised"*: Once *we* learn the prior, *anyone* can train an optical flow architecture entirely unsupervised. The key idea here is to learn a prior for the set of optical flows that are statistically compatible with *a single image*. Once done, we train a relatively simple network *in an unsupervised fashion* to map *pairs of images* to optical flows, where the loss function used for training includes explicit regularization in the form of the conditional prior, added to the reprojection error.

Despite a relatively simple architecture and low computational complexity, our method beats all variational ones and all unsupervised learning-based ones. It is on par or slightly below a few fully supervised ones, that however are fine-tuned to a particular dataset, and are extremely onerous to train. More importantly, available fully supervised methods perform best *on the dataset on which they are trained.* Our method, on the other hand, performs well even when the prior is trained on one dataset and used on a different one. For instance, a fully-supervised method trained on Flying Chair beats our method on Flying Chair, but underperforms it on KITTI and vice-versa (Table 1). Ours is consistently among the top in all datasets. More importantly, our method is complementary, and can be used in conjunction with more sophisticated networks and data terms.

1.2   Formalization

Let $I_1, I_2 \in \mathbb{R}_+^{H \times W \times 3}$ be two consecutive images and $f : \mathbb{R}^2 \to \mathbb{R}^2$ the flow, implicitly defined in the co-visible region by $I_1 = I_2 \circ f + n$ where $n \sim P_n$ is some distribution. The posterior $P(f|I_1, I_2) \propto P_n(I_1 - I_2 \circ f)$ can be decomposed as

$$\log P(f|I_1, I_2) = \log P(I_2|I_1, f) + \log P(f|I_1) - \log P(I_2|I_1)$$
$$\approx \log P(I_2|I_1, f) + \log P(f|I_1) \quad (1)$$

We call the first term (data) **prediction error**, and the second **conditional prior**. It is a prior in the sense that, given I_1 alone, many flows can have high likelihood for a suitable I_2. However, it is informed by I_1 in the sense of capturing image-dependent regularities such as flow discontinuities often occurring at *object* *boundaries*, which may or may not correspond to generic image discontinuities. A special case of this model assumes a Gaussian likelihood (ℓ^2 prediction error) and an ad-hoc prior of the form

$$E(f, I_1, I_2) = \int (I_1(x) - I_2(x + f(x)))^2 dx + \int \alpha(x, I_1) \|\nabla f(x)\|^2 dx \quad (2)$$

where α is a scalar function that incorporates our belief in an irradiance boundary of I_1 corresponding to an object boundary.[3] This type of conditional prior has several limitations: First, in the absence of *semantic context*, it is not possible to differentiate occluding boundaries (where f can be discontinuous) from material boundaries (irradiance discontinuities), or illumination boundaries (cast shadows) where f is smooth. Second, the image I_1 only informs the flow *locally*, through its gradient, and does not capture global regularities. Figure 2 shows that flow fails to propagate into homogeneous region. This can be mitigated by using a fully connected CRF [36] but at a heavy computational cost.

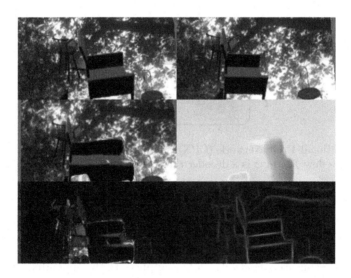

Fig. 2. First row: two images I_1, I_2 from the Flying Chair dataset; Second row: warped image $I_2 \circ \hat{f}$ (left) using the flow (right) estimated by minimizing Eq. (2); Third row: residual $n = \|I_1 - I_2 \circ f\|$ (left) compared to the edge strength of I_1 (right). Note the flow estimated at the right side of the chair fails to propagate into the homogeneous region where the image gradient is close to zero.

Our goal can be formalized as *learning the conditional prior* $P(f|I_1)$ in a manner that exploits the semantic context of the scene[4] and captures the global

---

[3] When α is constant, we get an even more special case, the original Horn & Schunk model where the prior is also Gaussian and unconditional (independent of I_1).

[4] The word "semantic" is often used to refer to *identities* and *relations* among discrete entities (objects). What matters in our case is the *geometric and topological relations*

statistics of I_1. We will do so by leveraging the power of deep convolutional neural networks trained end-to-end, to enable which we need to design differentiable models, which we do next.

2   Method

To learn a conditional prior we need to specify the inference criterion (loss function), which we do in Sect. 2.2 and the class of functions (architecture), with respect to which the loss is minimized end-to-end. We introduce our choice of architecture next, and the optimization in Sect. 2.3.

2.1   Conditional Prior Network (CPN)

We construct the conditional prior from a modified autoencoder trained to reconstruct a flow f that is compatible with the given (single) image I. We call this a Conditional Prior Network (CPN) shown in Fig. 3.

Fig. 3. Conditional Prior Network (CPN) architecture for learning $P(f|I)$: ψ is an encoder of the flow f, and φ is a decoder that has full access to the image I.

In a CPN, ψ encodes only the flow f, then φ takes the image I and the output of ψ to generate a reconstruction of f, $\hat{f} = \varphi(I, \psi(f))$. Both ψ and φ are realized by pure convolutional layers with subsampling (striding) by two to create a bottleneck. Note that φ is a U-shape net [15] with skip connections, at whose center a concatenation with $\psi(f)$ is applied. In the appendix, we articulate the reasons for our choice of architecture, and argue that it is better than an ordinary autoencoder that encodes both f and I in one branch. This is connected to the choice of loss function and how it is trained, which we discuss next.

2.2   Loss Function

We are given a dataset D sampled from the joint distribution $D = \{(f_j, I_j)\}_{j=1}^n \sim P(f, I)$, with n samples. We propose approximating $P(f|I)$ with a CPN as follows

$$Q_{w_\varphi, w_\psi}(f|I) = \exp\left(-\|\varphi(I, \psi(f)) - f\|^2\right) \propto P(f|I) \qquad (3)$$

that may result in occluding boundaries on the image plane. The name of an object does not matter to that end, so we ignore identities and do not require object labels.

where w_φ, w_ψ are the parameters of φ and ψ respectively. Given I, for every flow f, the above returns a positive value whose log, after training, is equal to the negative squared autoencoding loss. To determine the parameters that yield an approximation of $P(f|I)$, we should solve the following optimization problem

$$w_\varphi^*, w_\psi^* = \arg \min_{w_\varphi, w_\psi} \mathbb{E}_{I \sim P(I)} \mathbb{KL}(P(f|I) \| Q_{w_\varphi, w_\psi}(f|I)) \tag{4}$$

where the expectation is with respect to all possible images I, and $\mathbb{KL}$ is the Kullback-Leibler divergence between $P(f|I)$ and the CPN $Q_{w_\varphi, w_\psi}(f|I)$. In the appendix we show that the above is equivalent to:

$$w_\varphi^*, w_\psi^* = \arg \max_{w_\varphi, w_\psi} \int_I \int_f P(f, I) \log[Q_{w_\varphi, w_\psi}(f|I)] df dI$$

$$= \arg \min_{w_\varphi, w_\psi} \int_I \int_f P(f, I) \| \varphi_{w_\varphi}(I, \psi_{w_\psi}(f)) - f \|^2 df dI \tag{5}$$

which is equivalent to minimizing the empirical autoencoding loss since the ground truth flow is quantized, $\sum_{j=1}^{n} \| \hat{f}_j - f_j \|^2$. If the encoder had no bottleneck (sufficient information capacity), it could overfit by returning $\hat{f} = \varphi_{w_\varphi}(I, \psi_{w_\psi}(f)) = f$, rendering the conditional prior $Q_{w_\varphi, w_\psi}(f|I)$ uninformative (constant). Consistent with recent developments in the theory of Deep Learning [1], sketched in the appendix, we introduce an information regularizer (bottleneck) on the encoder ψ leading to the **CPN training loss**

$$w_\varphi^*, w_\psi^* = \arg \min_{w_\varphi, w_\psi} \mathbb{E}_{I \sim P(I)} \mathbb{KL}(P(f|I) \| Q_{w_\varphi, w_\psi}(f|I)) + \beta \boldsymbol{I}(f, \psi_{w_\psi}(f)) \tag{6}$$

where $\beta > 0$ modulates complexity (information capacity) and fidelity (data fit), and $\boldsymbol{I}(f, \psi_{w_\psi}(f))$ is the mutual information between the flow f and its representation (code) $\psi_{w_\psi}(f)$. When β is large, the encoder is lossy, thus preventing $Q_{w_\varphi, w_\psi}(f|I)$ from being uninformative.[5]

2.3 Training a CPN

While the first term in Eq. (6) can simply be the empirical autoencoding loss, the second term can be realized in many ways, e.g., an ℓ^2 or ℓ^1 penalty on the parameters w_ψ. Here we directly increase the bottleneck β by decreasing the coding length ℓ_ψ of ψ. Hence the training procedure of the proposed CPN can be summarized as follows:

1. Initialize the coding length of the encoder ℓ_ψ with a large number ($\beta = 0$).
2. Train the encoder-decoder ψ, φ jointly by minimizing $e = \frac{1}{n} \sum_{j=1}^{n} \| \hat{f}_j - f_j \|^2$ until convergence. The error at convergence is denoted as e^*.
3. If $e^* > \lambda$, training done.[6]
   Otherwise, decrease ℓ_ψ, (increase β), and goto step 2.

---

[5] The decoder φ imposes no architectural bottleneck due to skip connections.
[6] In our experiments, $\lambda = 0.5$.

It would be time consuming to train for every single coding length ℓ_ψ. We only iteratively train for the integer powers, $2^k, k \leq 10$.

Inference: suppose the optimal parameters obtained from the training procedure are w_ψ^*, w_φ^*, then for any given pair (f, I), we can use $Q_{w_\varphi^*, w_\psi^*}(f|I)$ as the conditional prior up to a constant. In the next section we add a data discrepancy term to the (log) prior to obtain an energy functional for learning direct mapping from images to optical flows.

2.4 Semi-unsupervised Learning Optical Flow

Unlike a generative model such as a variational autoencoder [22], where sampling is required in order to evaluate the probability of a given observation, here (f, I) is directly mapped to a scalar using Eq. (3), thus differentiable w.r.t f, and suitable for training a new network to predict optical flow given images I_1, I_2, by minimizing the following compound loss:

$$E(f|I_1, I_2) = \int_{\Omega \backslash O} \rho(I_1(x) - I_2(x + f(x)))dx - \alpha \log[Q_{w_\varphi^*, w_\psi^*}(f|I_1)]$$

$$= \int_{\Omega \backslash O} \rho(I_1(x) - I_2(x + f(x)))dx + \alpha \|\varphi^*(I_1, \psi^*(f)) - f\|^2 \quad (7)$$

with $\alpha > 0$, $Q_{w_\varphi^*, w_\psi^*}$ our learned conditional prior, and $\rho(x) = (x^2 + 0.001^2)^\eta$ the generalized Charbonnier penalty function [8]. Note that the integration in the data term is on the co-visible area, i.e. the image domain Ω minus the occluded area O, which can be set to empty for simplicity or modeled using the forward-backward consistency as done in [27] with a penalty on O to prevent trivial solutions. In the following section, we describe our implementation and report results and comparisons on several benchmarks.

3 Experiments

3.1 Network Details

CPN: we adapt the FlowNetS network structure proposed in [15] to be the decoder φ, and the contraction part of FlowNetS to be the encoder ψ in our CPN respectively. Both parts are shrunk versions of the original FlowNetS with a factor of 1/4; altogether our CPN has 2.8M parameters, which is an order of magnitude less than the 38M parameters in FlowNetS. As we mentioned before, the bottleneck in Eq. (6) is controlled by the coding length ℓ_ψ of the encoder ψ, here we make the definition of ℓ_ψ explicit, which is the number of the convolutional kernels in the last layer of the encoder. In our experiments, $\ell_\psi = 128$ always satisfies the stopping criterion described in Sect. 2.3, which ends up with a reduction rate 0.015 in the dimension of the flow f.

CPNFlow: we term our flow prediction network CPNFlow. The network used on all benchmarks for comparison is the original FlowNetS with no modifications, letting us focus on the effects of different loss terms. The total number of parameters is 38 M. FlowNetS is the most basic network structure for learning optical flow [15], *i.e.*, only convolutional layers with striding for dimension reduction, however, when trained with loss Eq. (7) that contains the learned conditional prior (CPN), it achieves better performance than the more complex network structure FlowNetC [15], or even stack of FlowNetS and FlowNetC. Please refer to Sect. 3.4 for details and quantitative comparisons.

3.2 Datasets for Training

Flying Chairs is a synthesized dataset proposed in [15], by superimposing images of chairs on background images from Flickr. Randomly sampled 2-D affine transformations are applied to both chairs and background images. Thus there are independently moving objects together with background motion. The whole dataset contains about $22\,$k 512×384 image pairs with ground truth flows. **MPI-Sintel** [10] is collected from an animation that made to be realistic. It contains scenes with natural illumination, objects moving fast, and articulated motion. Final and clean versions of the dataset are provided. The final version contains motion blur and fog effects. The training set contains only $1,041$ pairs of images, much smaller compared to Flying Chairs.
KITTI 2012 [16] and 2015 [28] are the largest real-world datasets containing ground truth optical flows collected in a driving scenario. The ground truth flows are obtained from simultaneously recorded video and 3-D laser scans, together with some manual corrections. Even though the multi-view extended version contains roughly 15k image pairs, ground truth flows exist for only 394 pairs of image, which makes fully supervised training of optical flow prediction from scratch under this scenario infeasible. However, it provides a base for unsupervised learning of optical flow, and a stage to show the benefit of semi-unsupervised optical flow learning, that utilizes both the conditional prior (CPN) learned from the synthetic dataset, and the virtually unlimited amount of real world videos.

3.3 Training Details

We use Adam [21] as the optimizer with its default parameters in all our experiments. We train our conditional prior network (CPN) using Flying Chairs dataset due to its large amount of synthesized ground truth flows. The initial learning rate is 1.0e-4, and is halved every 100 k steps until the maximum 600 k training steps. The batch size is 8, and the autoencoding loss after training is around 0.6.

There are two versions of our CPNFlow, i.e. CPNFlow-C and CPNFlow-K. Both employ the FlowNetS structure, and they differ in the training set on which Eq. (7) is minimized. CPNFlow-C is trained on Flying Chairs dataset, similarly CPNFlow-K is trained on KITTI dataset with the multi-view extension. The consideration here is: when trained on Flying Chairs dataset, the conditional prior network (CPN) is supposed to only capture the statistics of the affine transformations (a) CPNFlow-C is to test whether our learned prior works properly or not. If it works, (b) CPNFlow-K tests how the learned prior generalizes to real world scenarios. Both CPNFlow-C and CPNFlow-K have the same training schedule with the initial learning rate 1.0e-4, which is halved every 100 k steps until the maximum 400 k steps.[7] Note that in [33], layer-wise loss adjustment is used during training to simulate coarse-to-fine estimation, however, we will not adopt this training technique to avoid repeatedly interrupting the training process. In a similar spirit, we will not do network stacking as in [19,27], which increases both the training complexity and the network size.

In terms of data augmentation, we apply the same augmentation method as in [15] whenever our network is trained on Flying Chairs dataset with a cropping of 384 × 448. When trained on KITTI, resized to 384 × 512, only vertical flipping, horizontal flipping and image order switching are applied. The batch size used for training on Flying Chairs is 8 and on KITTI is 4.

3.4   Benchmark Results

Table 1 summarizes our evaluation on all benchmarks mentioned above, together with quantitative comparisons to the state-of-the-art methods from different categories: Fully supervised, variational, and unsupervised learning methods. Since CPNFlow has the same network structure as FlowNetS, and both CPNFlow-C and FlowNetS are trained on Flying Chairs dataset, the comparison between CPNFlow-C and FlowNetS shows that even if CPNFlow-C is trained without knowing the correspondences between pairs of image and the ground truth flows, it can still achieve similar performance compared to the fully supervised ones on the synthetic dataset MPI-Sintel. When both are applied to KITTI, CPNFlow-C achieves 11.2% and 21.6% improvement over FlowNetS and FlowNetC respectively on KITTI 2012 Train, hence CPNFlow generalizes better to out of domain data.

One might notice that FlowNet2 [19] consistently achieves the highest score on MPI-Sintel and KITTI Train, however, it has a totally different network structure where several FlownetS [15] and FlowNetC [15] are stacked together, and it is trained in a sequential manner, and on additional datasets, e.g. FlyingThings3D [26] and a new dataset designed for small displacement [19], thus not directly comparable to CPNFlow. However, when we simply apply the learned conditional prior to train our CPNFlow on KITTI using Eq. (7), the final network CPNFlow-K surpasses FlowNet2 by 8% on KITTI 2012 Train, yet the training procedure of CPNFlow is much simpler, and there is no need to switch between datasets nor between different modules of the network.

Since the emergence of unsupervised training of optical flow [20], there has not been a single method that beats the variational methods, as shown in Table 1, even if both variational methods and unsupervised learning methods are minimizing the same type of loss function. One reason might be that when we implement the variational methods, we could apply some "secret" operations as mentioned in [34], e.g. median filtering, such that implicit regularization is triggered. Extra data term can also be added to bias the optimization, as in [7],

---

[7] $\alpha = 0.1, \eta = 0.25$ for CPNFlow-C, and $\alpha = 0.045, \eta = 0.38$ for CPNFlow-K.

Table 1. Quantitative evaluation and comparison to the state-of-the-art optical flow estimation methods coming from three different categories. Sup: Fully supervised, Var: Variational methods, and Unsup: Unsupervised learning methods. The performance measure is the end-point-error (EPE), except for the last column where percentage of erroneous pixels is used. The best performer in each category is highlighted in bold, and the number in parentheses is fine-tuned on the tested dataset. For more detailed comparisons on KITTI test sets, please refer to the online benchmark website: http://www.cvlibs.net/datasets/kitti/eval_flow.php

	Methods	Chairs test	Sintel Train		Sintel Test		KITTI Train		KITTI Test	
			Clean	Final	Clean	Final	2012	2015	2012	2015
Sup	FlowNetS [15]	2.71	4.50	5.45	7.42	8.43	8.26	——	**9.1**	——
	FlowNetC [15]	**2.19**	4.31	5.87	7.28	8.81	9.35	——	——	——
	SPyNet [32]	2.63	4.12	5.57	6.69	8.43	9.12	——	10.1	——
	FlowNet2 [19]	——	**2.02**	**3.14**	**3.96**	**6.02**	**4.09**	10.06	——	——
Var	Classic-NL [34]	——	6.03	7.99	7.96	9.15	——	——	16.4	——
	LDOF [7]	**3.47**	**4.29**	6.42	**7.56**	**9.12**	13.7	——	12.4	——
	HornSchunck [35]	——	7.23	8.38	8.73	9.61	——	——	**11.7**	41.8%
	DIS-Fast [24]	——	5.61	**6.31**	9.35	10.13	**11.01**	**21.2**	14.4	——
Unsup	DSTFlow [33]	5.11	6.93	7.82	10.40	11.11	16.98	24.30	——	——
	DSTFlow-ft [33]	5.11	(6.16)	(6.81)	10.41	11.27	10.43	16.79	12.4	39%
	BackToBasic [20]	5.30	——	——	——	——	11.30	——	**9.9**	——
	UnFlowC [27]	——	——	——	——	——	7.11	14.17	——	——
	UnFlowC-oc [27]	——	——	8.64	——	——	3.78	8.80	——	——
	UnFlowCSS-oc [27]	——	——	7.91	**9.37**	10.22	**3.29**	**8.10**	——	——
	DenseNetF [40]	**4.73**	——	——	——	10.07	——	——	11.6	——
	CPNFlow-C	**3.81**	**4.87**	**5.95**	**7.66**	**8.58**	7.33	14.61	——	——
	CPNFlow-K	4.37	6.46	7.12	——	——	3.76	9.63	4.7	30.8%
	CPNFlow-K-o	——	7.01	7.52	——	——	**3.11**	**7.82**	**3.6**	**30.4%**

sparse matches are used as a data term to deal with large displacements. However, when combined with our learned conditional prior, even the simplest data term would help unsupervisedly train a network that outperforms the state-of-the-art variational optical flow methods. As shown in Table 1 our CPNFlow consistently achieves similar or better performance than LDOF [7], especially on KITTI 2012 Train, the improvement is at least 40%.

Compared to unsupervised optical flow learning, the advantage of our learned conditional prior becomes obvious. Although DenseNetF [40] and UnFlowC [27] employ more powerful network structures than FlowNetS, their EPEs on MPI-Sintel Test are still 1.5 higher than our CPNFlow. Note that in [27], several versions of result are reported, e.g. UnFlowC: trained with brightness data term and second order smoothness term, UnFlowC-oc: census transform based data term together with occlusion modeling and bidirectional flow consistency penalty, and UnFlowCSS-oc: a stack of one FlowNetC and two FlowNetS's sequentially trained using the same loss as in UnFlowC-oc. Our CPNFlow-K outperforms UnFlowC by 47% on KITTI 2012 Train and 32% on KITTI 2015 Train. When occlusion reasoning is effective in Eq. (7) as done in [27], our CPNFlow-K-o outperforms UnFlowC-oc by 17.7% on KITTI 2012 Train, 11.1% on KITTI 2015 Train, and 12.9% on Sintel Train Final, even without a more robust census trans-

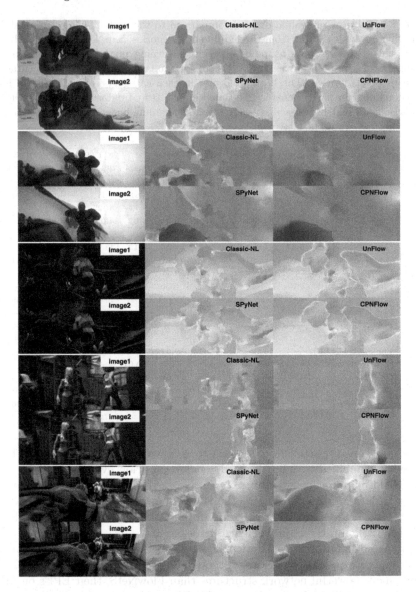

Fig. 4. Visual comparison on MPI-Sintel. Variational: CLassic-NL [34], Supervised: SPyNet [32], Unsupervised: UnFlowC [27] and our CPNFlow-C.

form based data term and flow consistency penalty, which demonstrate the effectiveness of our learned conditional prior across different data terms. Note that our CPNFlow-K-o even outperforms UnFlowCSS-oc, which is far more complex in training and network architecture.

Figures 4, 5, 6 show the visual comparisons on MPI-Sintel, KITTI 2012 and KITTI 2015 respectively. Note that our CPNFlow is generally much smoother,

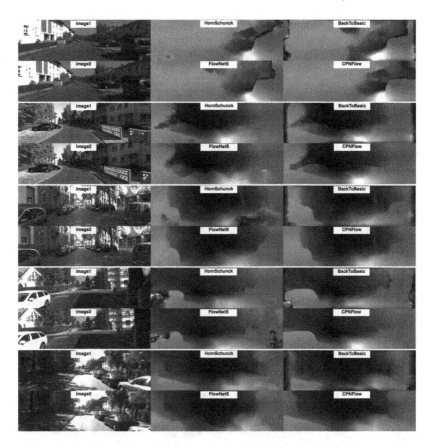

Fig. 5. Visual comparison on KITTI 2012. Variational: HornSchunck [35], Supervised: FlowNetS [15], Unsupervised: BackToBasic [20] and our CPNFlow-K.

and at the same time sharper at object boundaries, e.g. the girl in the 3rd, 4th rows and the dragon in the 5th row in Fig. 4. This demonstrates that our conditional prior network (CPN) is capable of learning high level (semantic) regularities imposed by object entities. In Fig. 5, we can also observe that discontinuities in the flow fields align well with object boundaries, for example the cars in all pairs. This, again, demonstrates that our learned conditional prior is able to generalize to different scenarios. The error of the estimated flows is also displayed in Fig. 6.

4   Discussion and Related Work

Generic priors capturing rudimentary statistics to regularize optical flow have been used for decades, starting with Horn and Schunk's ℓ^2 norm of the gradient, to ℓ^1, Total Variation, etc. We seek to design or learn image-dependent priors that capture long-range correlation and semantics.

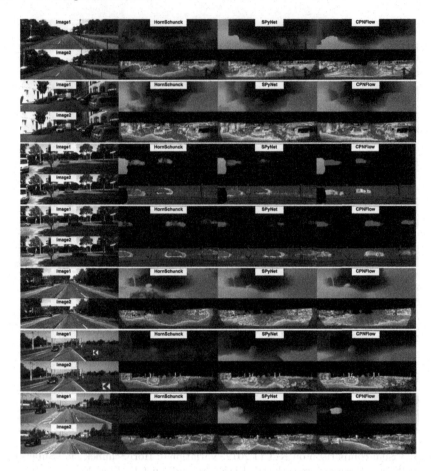

Fig. 6. Visual comparison on KITTI 2015. Variational: HornSchunck [35], Supervised: SPyNet [32] and our CPNFlow-K. The 2nd row in each pair shows the end-point-error of the estimated flow, red is high and blue is low.

Image-dependent priors of the form Eq. (2) include [6,12,14,23,30,31,37], whereas most recent methods learn optical flow end-to-end, without explicitly isolating the likelihood and prior terms, for instance [15,19,32] are the top performing on MPI-Sintel. Some methods even cast optical flow as dense or semi-dense feature matching [3,25,38,39] in order to deal with large displacements, while the regularity is merely imposed by forward-backward matching consistency (see references therein for a detailed review of related literature).

It would be tempting to use a GAN [17] to learn the prior distribution of interest. A GAN can be thought of as a method to learn a map g such that its push-forward g_* maps two distributions, one known μ, and one we can sample from, p, so $\hat{g} = \arg\min \mathbb{KL}(g_*\mu \| p)$. It does so via an adversarial process such that a generative model G will capture the data distribution p_{data}. If we sample from the generative model G, we will have samples that are equivalently sampled from p_{data}, in order to evaluate $p_{data}(x)$ of a sample x, we can not circumvent the sampling step, thus making the method unsuitable for our purpose where we want a differentiable scalar function.

Our work entails constructing an autoencoder of the flow, so it naturally relates to [22]. Similarly, evaluating the probability of a test example is intractable, even if we can approximately evaluate the lower bound of the probability of a data point, which again can not be computed in closed form due to the expectation over the noise.

Optical flow learning algorithms typically rely on synthesized datasets, due to the extreme difficulty in obtaining ground truth flows for realistic videos. Recently, unsupervised optical flow learning methods have flourished, making use of vast amount of unlabeled videos. Although unsupervised optical flow learning methods are able to learn from unlimited amount of data, when compared to variational methods, their performance usually falls behind, even when a similar loss is employed. A phenomenon observed is that almost all unsupervised optical flow learning methods use the Horn-Schunck type surrogate losses. And there is debate on which feature to use for the data term, *e.g.*, the raw photometric value or the edge response, or on the prior/regularizer term, *e.g.* , penalizing the first order gradient of the flow or the second order, or on how to weight the prior term in a pixel-wise manner. Surrogate losses are getting more and more complex. Instead of focusing on the data term, we ask what should be the best form for the prior term. Our answer is that structural consistency between an image and the flow, as well as high-order statistics, such as semantic consistency, are important. We show that when combined with the raw photometric warping error, this kind of prior serves as a better regularizer than all the other hand-designed ones. We show its effectiveness on several contemporary optical flow benchmarks, also thanks to its ability to leverage existing limited supervised (synthetic) datasets and unlimited real world videos.

Acknowledgments. Research supported by ONR N00014-17-1-2072 and ARO W911NF-15-1-0564/66731-CS.

References

1. Achille, A., Soatto, S.: Emergence of invariance and disentangling in deep representations. J. Mach. Learn. Res. (JMLR), in press. (Also in Proceedings of the ICML Workshop on Principled Approaches to Deep Learning; arXiv:1706.01350, May 30, 2017)
2. Ahmadi, A., Patras, I.: Unsupervised convolutional neural networks for motion estimation. In: 2016 IEEE International Conference on Image Processing (ICIP), pp. 1629–1633. IEEE (2016)
3. Bailer, C., Taetz, B., Stricker, D.: Flow fields: Dense correspondence fields for highly accurate large displacement optical flow estimation. In: Proceedings of the IEEE International Conference on Computer Vision, pp. 4015–4023 (2015)

4. Baker, S., Scharstein, D., Lewis, J., Roth, S., Black, M.J., Szeliski, R.: A database and evaluation methodology for optical flow. Int. J. Comput. Vis. **92**(1), 1–31 (2011)

5. Black, M.J., Anandan, P.: A framework for the robust estimation of optical flow. In: Proceedings of the Fourth International Conference on Computer Vision, pp. 231–236. IEEE (1993)

6. Brox, T., Bruhn, A., Papenberg, N., Weickert, J.: High accuracy optical flow estimation based on a theory for warping. In: Pajdla, T., Matas, J. (eds.) ECCV 2004. LNCS, vol. 3024, pp. 25–36. Springer, Heidelberg (2004). https://doi.org/10.1007/978-3-540-24673-2_3

7. Brox, T., Malik, J.: Large displacement optical flow: descriptor matching in variational motion estimation. IEEE Trans. Pattern Anal. Mach. Intell. **33**(3), 500–513 (2011)

8. Bruhn, A., Weickert, J.: Towards ultimate motion estimation: Combining highest accuracy with real-time performance. In: Tenth IEEE International Conference on Computer Vision, ICCV, vol. 1, pp. 749–755. IEEE (2005)

9. Bruhn, A., Weickert, J., Schnörr, C.: Lucas/kanade meets horn/schunck: combining local and global optic flow methods. Int. J. Comput. Vis. **61**(3), 211–231 (2005)

10. Butler, D.J., Wulff, J., Stanley, G.B., Black, M.J.: A naturalistic open source movie for optical flow evaluation. In: Fitzgibbon, A., Lazebnik, S., Perona, P., Sato, Y., Schmid, C. (eds.) ECCV 2012. LNCS, vol. 7577, pp. 611–625. Springer, Heidelberg (2012). https://doi.org/10.1007/978-3-642-33783-3_44

11. Chaudhari, P., Soatto, S.: Stochastic gradient descent performs variational inference, converges to limit cycles for deep networks (2017). arXiv preprint arXiv:1710.11029

12. Chen, Q., Koltun, V.: Full flow: Optical flow estimation by global optimization over regular grids. In: Proceedings of the IEEE Conference on Computer Vision and Pattern Recognition, pp. 4706–4714 (2016)

13. Cohen, N., Shashua, A.: Inductive bias of deep convolutional networks through pooling geometry (2016). arXiv preprint arXiv:1605.06743

14. Deriche, R., Kornprobst, P., Aubert, G.: Optical-flow estimation while preserving its discontinuities: a variational approach. In: Li, S.Z., Mital, D.P., Teoh, E.K., Wang, H. (eds.) ACCV 1995. LNCS, vol. 1035, pp. 69–80. Springer, Heidelberg (1996). https://doi.org/10.1007/3-540-60793-5_63

15. Dosovitskiy, A., Fischer, P., Ilg, E., Hausser, P., Hazirbas, C., Golkov, V., et al.: Learning optical flow with convolutional networks. In: Proceedings of the IEEE International Conference on Computer Vision, pp. 2758–2766 (2015)

16. Geiger, A., Lenz, P., Urtasun, R.: Are we ready for autonomous driving? The kitti vision benchmark suite. In: 2012 IEEE Conference on Computer Vision and Pattern Recognition (CVPR), pp. 3354–3361. IEEE (2012)

17. Goodfellow, I., Pouget-Abadie, J., Mirza, M., Xu, B., Warde-Farley, D., Ozair, S., et al.: Generative adversarial nets. In: Advances in neural information processing systems, pp. 2672–2680 (2014)

18. Horn, B.K., Schunck, B.G.: Determining optical flow. Artif. Intell. **17**(1–3), 185–203 (1981)

19. Ilg, E., Mayer, N., Saikia, T., Keuper, M., Dosovitskiy, A., Brox, T.: Flownet 2.0: Evolution of optical flow estimation with deep networks. In: Proceedings of the IEEE Conference on Computer Vision and Pattern Recognition, pp. 2462–2470 (2017)

20. Jason, J.Y., Harley, A.W., Derpanis, K.G.: Back to basics: unsupervised learning of optical flow via brightness constancy and motion smoothness. In: European Conference on Computer Vision, pp. 3–10. Springer (2016)
21. Kingma, D.P., Ba, J.: Adam: A method for stochastic optimization (2014). arXiv preprint arXiv:1412.6980
22. Kingma, D.P., Welling, M.: Auto-encoding variational bayes (2013). arXiv preprint arXiv:1312.6114
23. Krähenbühl, P., Koltun, V.: Efficient nonlocal regularization for optical flow. In: Fitzgibbon, A., Lazebnik, S., Perona, P., Sato, Y., Schmid, C. (eds.) ECCV 2012. LNCS, vol. 7572, pp. 356–369. Springer, Heidelberg (2012). https://doi.org/10.1007/978-3-642-33718-5_26
24. Kroeger, T., Timofte, R., Dai, D., Van Gool, L.: Fast optical flow using dense inverse search. In: Leibe, B., Matas, J., Sebe, N., Welling, M. (eds.) ECCV 2016. LNCS, vol. 9908, pp. 471–488. Springer, Cham (2016). https://doi.org/10.1007/978-3-319-46493-0_29
25. Liu, C., Yuen, J., Torralba, A., Sivic, J., Freeman, W.T.: SIFT flow: dense correspondence across different scenes. In: Forsyth, D., Torr, P., Zisserman, A. (eds.) ECCV 2008. LNCS, vol. 5304, pp. 28–42. Springer, Heidelberg (2008). https://doi.org/10.1007/978-3-540-88690-7_3
26. Mayer, N., Ilg, E., Hausser, P., Fischer, P., Cremers, D., Dosovitskiy, A., et al.: A large dataset to train convolutional networks for disparity, optical flow, and scene flow estimation. In: Proceedings of the IEEE Conference on Computer Vision and Pattern Recognition, pp. 4040–4048 (2016)
27. Meister, S., Hur, J., Roth, S.: UnFlow: unsupervised learning of optical flow with a bidirectional census loss. In: AAAI. New Orleans, Louisiana (Feb 2018)
28. Menze, M., Geiger, A.: Object scene flow for autonomous vehicles. In: Conference on Computer Vision and Pattern Recognition (CVPR) (2015)
29. Papenberg, N., Bruhn, A., Brox, T., Didas, S., Weickert, J.: Highly accurate optic flow computation with theoretically justified warping. Int. J. Comput. Vis. 67(2), 141–158 (2006)
30. Proesmans, M., Van Gool, L., Pauwels, E., Oosterlinck, A.: Determination of optical flow and its discontinuities using non-linear diffusion. In: Eklundh, J.-O. (ed.) ECCV 1994. LNCS, vol. 801, pp. 294–304. Springer, Heidelberg (1994). https://doi.org/10.1007/BFb0028362
31. Ranftl, R., Bredies, K., Pock, T.: Non-local total generalized variation for optical flow estimation. In: Fleet, D., Pajdla, T., Schiele, B., Tuytelaars, T. (eds.) ECCV 2014. LNCS, vol. 8689, pp. 439–454. Springer, Cham (2014). https://doi.org/10.1007/978-3-319-10590-1_29
32. Ranjan, A., Black, M.J.: Optical flow estimation using a spatial pyramid network. In: Proceedings of the IEEE Conference on Computer Vision and Pattern Recognition, pp. 4161–4170 (2017)
33. Ren, Z., Yan, J., Ni, B., Liu, B., Yang, X., Zha, H.: Unsupervised deep learning for optical flow estimation. In: Thirty-First AAAI Conference on Artificial Intelligence (2017)
34. Sun, D., Roth, S., Black, M.J.: Secrets of optical flow estimation and their principles. In: 2010 IEEE Conference on Computer Vision and Pattern Recognition (CVPR), pp. 2432–2439. IEEE (2010)
35. Sun, D., Roth, S., Black, M.J.: A quantitative analysis of current practices in optical flow estimation and the principles behind them. Int. J. Comput. Vis. 106(2), 115–137 (2014)

36. Sutton, C., McCallum, A.: An introduction to conditional random fields. Found. Trends® Mach. Learn. **4**(4), 267–373 (2012)
37. Xu, L., Jia, J., Matsushita, Y.: Motion detail preserving optical flow estimation. IEEE Trans. Pattern Anal. Mach. Intell. **34**(9), 1744–1757 (2012)
38. Yang, Y., Lu, Z., Sundaramoorthi, G., et al.: Coarse-to-fine region selection and matching. In: 2015 IEEE Conference on Computer Vision and Pattern Recognition (CVPR), pp. 5051–5059. IEEE (2015)
39. Yang, Y., Soatto, S.: S2f: Slow-to-fast interpolator flow. In: 2017 IEEE Conference on Computer Vision and Pattern Recognition (CVPR), pp. 3767–3776. IEEE (2017)
40. Zhu, Y., Newsam, S.: Densenet for dense flow (2017). arXiv preprint arXiv:1707.06316

Robust Optical Flow in Rainy Scenes

Ruoteng Li[1(✉)], Robby T. Tan[1,2], and Loong-Fah Cheong[1]

[1] National University of Singapore, Singapore, Singapore
liruoteng@gmail.com
[2] Yale-NUS College, Singapore, Singapore

Abstract. Optical flow estimation in rainy scenes is challenging due to degradation caused by rain streaks and rain accumulation, where the latter refers to the poor visibility of remote scenes due to intense rainfall. To resolve the problem, we introduce a residue channel, a single channel (gray) image that is free from rain, and its colored version, a colored-residue image. We propose to utilize these two rain-free images in computing optical flow. To deal with the loss of contrast and the attendant sensitivity to noise, we decompose each of the input images into a piecewise-smooth structure layer and a high-frequency fine-detail texture layer. We combine the colored-residue images and structure layers in a unified objective function, so that the estimation of optical flow can be more robust. Results on both synthetic and real images show that our algorithm outperforms existing methods on different types of rain sequences. To our knowledge, this is the first optical flow method specifically dealing with rain. We also provide an optical flow dataset consisting of both synthetic and real rain images.

Keywords: Optical flow · Rain · Decomposition · Residue channel

1 Introduction

Optical flow methods have been developed for many decades [7,16,22,32,35,37] and achieved significant results in terms of accuracy and robustness[1,17,29,31, 39,42]. They are shown to generally work when applied to outdoor scenes in clear daylight, but tend to be erroneous in bad weather. In particular, of all the bad weather conditions, rain has the most marked detrimental impact on performance [28]. To our knowledge, no methods have been proposed to handle optical flow estimation in rainy scenes. Addressing this problem is important,

This work is supported by the DIRP Grant R-263-000-C46-232. R.T. Tan's research is supported in part by Yale-NUS College Start-Up Grant.

Electronic supplementary material The online version of this chapter (https:// doi.org/10.1007/978-3-030-01267-0_18) contains supplementary material, which is available to authorized users.

V. Ferrari et al. (Eds.): ECCV 2018, LNCS 11219, pp. 299–317, 2018.
https://doi.org/10.1007/978-3-030-01267-0_18

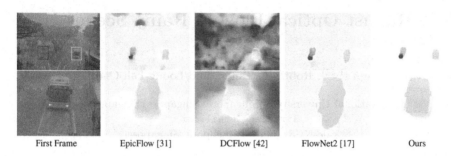

First Frame   EpicFlow [31]   DCFlow [42]   FlowNet2 [17]   Ours

Fig. 1. Optical flow estimation from heavy rain images with a static background and a few moving vehicles. **Top**: Purple and yellow colors indicate upward and downward motions, respectively. **Bottom**: Focusing on the estimated flow of the downward moving vehicle. Our estimation is more robust to rain than those of existing methods. Note, the rain streaks and rain accumulation can be observed by zooming in the input images.

since more and more vision systems are deployed in outdoor scenes, and rain is an inevitable natural phenomenon or even an everyday occurrence in some regions of the world. In this paper, we develop an optical flow algorithm that can handle heavy rain with apparent rain streaks and a fog-like rain accumulation effect.

The challenge of estimating optical flow in rainy scenes can be categorized into two problems. One problem refers to rain streaks, which due to their dynamic nature, appear in different locations from frame to frame, thus causing violation to the brightness constancy constraint (BCC) and the gradient constancy constraint (GCC). The other problem refers to rain-streak accumulation, where rain streaks are accumulated along the line of sight in such a way that we can no longer see the individual streaks (visually similar to fog). Images affected by the rain accumulation generally suffer from low contrast and weakened background information. Under torrential downpour, the second problem is severe enough to warrant a special mechanism to come to grips with the issue.

A direct solution is to apply a deraining method, either a video based (e.g., [3, 14]) or single-image based deraining method (e.g. [19,23,46]), before optical flow computation. However, most of the video-based deraining methods are designed only for rain streaks removal and assume static background, whereas the existing single-image based deraining methods process each frame independently, and therefore consistency across frames cannot be guaranteed. Moreover, most of the deraining methods introduce artifacts, such as blur around rain streak regions, high frequency texture loss, image color change, etc. These artifacts are also inconsistent in their appearance throughout an image sequence, thus rendering the BCC and GCC invalid.

To achieve our goal, there are several key ideas in our method. First, we introduce a residue channel, a gray image that is free from both rain streaks and rain accumulation. This rain free can be generated after ensuring that the rain-streak and rain-accumulation terms in our model are achromatic (colorless). The residue channel, however, can cause some color boundaries to disappear, making the optical flow computation deprived of this important information. To resolve this, we then introduce a colored-residue image, which is the colored version of the residue channel and thus is also free from rain streak and accumulation. Yet, there is another problem with both the residue channel and the colored-residue image, namely, when the background is achromatic or the rain accumulation is considerably thick, then the affected regions become dark due to the subtraction operation in the residue image formation, depriving the optical flow estimation of any intensity variation information in the achromatic channel. Generally, images of rainy scenes already suffer from low contrast; this is further compounded by the residue operation such that the signal-to-noise ratio is further suppressed, reaching the nadir in the aforementioned dark regions.

To handle the resultant noise sensitivity, our solution is to perform a structure-texture decomposition on each of the input images and use the extracted structure layers to provide a further regularizing influence on the optical flow estimation. The underlying rationales are twofold: (1) The structure-texture decomposition acts as a denoiser, moving noise, rain streaks, and fine textures in the scene to the texture layer. While the structure layer necessarily loses out some fine texture information, it provides a stabilizing influence on the detailed flow information coming from the colored-residue image. (2) For the regions in the colored-residue image that are dark, the information coming from the structure layer is all that we have; even though it is admittedly lacking in details and might be somewhat inaccurate (since in dealing with rain, the structure layer extraction does not make use of the underlying physics of the rain formation process). Finally, by combining the colored-residue images and structure layers in one objective function, we make sure that the structure-texture variational denoising is done in a way consistent across images (critical for optical flow estimation), and the decomposition can also benefit from the redundancy coming from the multiple frames. As a result, we can compute the flow from rain images robustly.

Particularly with respect to optical flow computation in rainy scenes, our contributions are: (1) Introducing the residue channel and colored-residue image that are both free from rain streaks and rain accumulation, (2) proposing an objective function and its optimization mechanism that combine the colored-residue images and piecewise-smooth structure layers, (3) providing a real rain optical flow benchmark containing both synthesized motion (660 sequences) and real motion (100 sequences) to the public. Note that, in this paper we do not address raindrops attached to the camera lens. We assume that the camera is well protected from raindrops (e.g. placing the camera under a shelter, or using a special hardware like Spintec, which can deflect rain from the camera).

2 Related Work

Optical flow algorithms that are robust to noise and outliers have been studied for a long time (e.g., [4,5,33,38]). While these techniques may be able to handle a moderate amount of corruptions such as those brought about by a drizzle

[21, 26, 40, 44], they are unlikely to prevail against the heavy corruptions caused by a torrential downpour. Compounding these issues is the loss of contrast caused by rain accumulation, it causes both the BCC and GCC to be highly susceptible to noise.

One of the popular practices in optical flow estimation is to perform structure-texture decomposition. [34, 36] and then use the texture layer for optical flow computation. However, for rainy scenes, rain streaks and significant noise will appear in the texture layer and compromise the utility of the texture layer for flow estimation. Our method relies more on the structure rather than the texture layer. Yang et al. [45] propose a double-layer decomposition framework for estimating optical flow of reflective surfaces. The method decomposes transmission (foreground) layer and reflection (background) layer, and then computes the optical flow of each layer, assuming both layers follow the sparse gradient distribution of natural images. However, this algorithm cannot be applied to rain images, since the assumption does not hold for rain streaks and accumulation. Our proposed colored-residue image belongs to the class of color space transformation methods such as [25] to render invariance against perturbation. However, the well-known HSV and $r\phi\theta$ color space approaches do not result in measures that are invariant under rain, and hence cannot be directly applied to rain images.

It is beyond the scope of this paper to offer a comprehensive review of the immense optical flow literature, but the emerging deep learning approach certainly deserves a mention. A few deep learning methods (e.g., [10, 11, 17, 29]) are proposed to estimate flow, but these methods are meant for optical flow estimation under clear scenes. Moreover, these methods are heavily optimized over a lot of training data with ground truths. Unfortunately, obtaining the optical flow ground-truths for rainy scenes is considerably intractable. In contrast, our method leverages on the physics of the image formation process. Theoretically, our rain streak formation model and the residue channel idea are applicable to snow and sleet too; our approach thus offers a much more parsimonious solution to a range of problems posed by different weather phenomena.

3   Residue Channel

3.1   Rain Streak Image Formation

The appearance of rain streaks is the result of raindrop movement during the camera exposure[12]. If we assume the exposure time is T and the elapsed time while a raindrop is passing through a pixel $\mathbf{x}$ is τ, the intensity captured by the CCD sensor can be described as a linear combination of the raindrop's time-average radiance $\bar{E}_{rs}$ and the background radiance E_{bg}:

$$E(\mathbf{x}) = \tau \bar{E}_{rs}(\mathbf{x}) + (T - \tau)E_{bg}(\mathbf{x}), \tag{1}$$

where $\bar{E}_{rs} = \frac{1}{\tau} \int_0^\tau E_{rs} dt$, $0 \leqslant \tau \leqslant T$. E_{rs} is the radiance of the raindrop at a particular time. The value of E_{rs} is determined by the raindrop's specular and internal reflections, in addition to the refracted light, where their proportions depends on the direction of the light rays relative to the raindrop, the camera viewing direction, and the shape of the raindrop [15].

Most cameras have spectral sensitivities (a.k.a. camera RGB filters) to produce coloured images. Considering this, we express the colored-image intensity of a rain-streak image as:

$$\tilde{\mathbf{I}}(\mathbf{x}) = \tau \int_{\Omega} \bar{E}_{rs}(\mathbf{x}, \lambda) q_c(\lambda) d\lambda + (T - \tau) \int_{\Omega} E_{bg}(\mathbf{x}, \lambda) q_c(\lambda) d\lambda, \qquad (2)$$

where $\tilde{\mathbf{I}} = (\tilde{I}_r, \tilde{I}_g, \tilde{I}_b)^T$ is the color vector representing the colored intensity, λ is the light wavelength, q_c is the camera-spectral-sensitivity distribution function, with index c indicates the RGB color channel. Ω is the range of wavelengths that can be captured by the camera sensitivities. As shown in the appendix, we can express the model as:

$$\tilde{\mathbf{I}}(\mathbf{x}) = \tau \rho_{rs}(\mathbf{x}) L \boldsymbol{\sigma} + (T - \tau) B \boldsymbol{\pi}, \qquad (3)$$

where $\mathbf{L} = (L_r, L_g, L_b)^T$ is the color vector of the light brightness, and $\mathbf{B} = (B_r, B_g, B_b)^T$ is the color vector of the background reflection. $L = L_r + L_b + L_g$ and $B = B_r + B_b + B_g$. We define $\boldsymbol{\sigma} = \mathbf{L}/L$ and $\boldsymbol{\pi} = \mathbf{B}/B$, the chromacities of $\mathbf{L}$ and $\mathbf{B}$, respectively. ρ_{rs} is composed of refraction, specular reflection, and internal reflection coefficients of a raindrop [13]. We assume that ρ_{rs} is independent from wavelength, implying a raindrop is achromatic (colorless). In the model (Eq. (3)), the first term is the rain-streak term, and the second term is the background term.

3.2   Residue Channel Computation

In our method, to generate the residue channel that is free from rain streaks, we need to cancel the light chromaticity, $\boldsymbol{\sigma}$, in the rain streak term in Eq. (3). For this, we employ any existing color constancy algorithm (e.g. [9]) to estimate $\boldsymbol{\sigma}$, and then apply the following normalization step to the input image:

$$\mathbf{I}(\mathbf{x}) = \frac{\tilde{\mathbf{I}}(\mathbf{x})}{\boldsymbol{\sigma}} = I_{rs}(\mathbf{x})\mathbf{i} + \mathbf{I}_{bg}(\mathbf{x}), \qquad (4)$$

where $\mathbf{i} = (1, 1, 1)^T$, $I_{rs} = \tau \rho_{rs} L$, and $\mathbf{I}_{bg} = (T - \tau)\mathbf{B}/\boldsymbol{\sigma}$. The vector division is done element wise. Note, when we normalize the image, we do not only cancel the light chromaticity, but also the color effect of the spectral sensitivities.

Therefore, based on the last equation, given a rain image $\mathbf{I}$, we define our residue-channel as:

$$I_{res}(\mathbf{x}) = I^M(\mathbf{x}) - I^m(\mathbf{x}), \qquad (5)$$

where $I^M(\mathbf{x}) = \max\{I_r(\mathbf{x}), I_g(\mathbf{x}), I_b(\mathbf{x})\}$, and $I^m(\mathbf{x}) = \min\{I_r(\mathbf{x}), I_g(\mathbf{x}), I_b(\mathbf{x})\}$. We call I_{res} the *residue channel* of image $\mathbf{I}$, and it is free from rain streaks. Figure 2 shows some examples of the residue channel. The reason why residue channel can be free from rain streaks is because the rain-streak term in Eq. (4) is achromatic, whose values are cancelled when applying Eq. (5).

To generate the residue channel, we theoretically need to apply color constancy so that the rain-streak term can be achromatic. However, in our experiments, we also noticed that even without applying color constancy, the residue channel can still work. This is because in most cases, the appearance of rain streaks is already achromatic, which is due to the dominant gray atmospheric light generated by a cloudy sky (see the discussion in the supplementary material).

Fig. 2. Top: Images captured in rain scenes with rain streaks and rain accumulation. **Middle**: Residue channels of the corresponding rain images. **Bottom**: The colored residue images of the corresponding rain images. The rain streaks are significantly reduced in the residue channel and colored-residue images, though some regions become dark due to achromatic background and rain accumulation. Note, we increase the intensity of the dark regions for visualization purpose.

3.3   Colored Residue Image

Since the residue channel is a single channel map, it has no color information. To obtain a colored residue image, we need to transform the original rain image into the YCbCr domain:

$$C_b = 128 - (37.945/256)I_r - (74.494/256)I_g + (112.439/256)I_b, \qquad (6)$$
$$C_r = 128 - (112.439/256)I_r - (94.154/256)I_g - (18.285/256)I_b.$$

In C_b and C_r, the achromatic value of the rain-streak term is cancelled out, since the sum of the coefficients in the definition equals to zero, and thus the two are independent from rain streaks. For Y channel, however, we do not use it in our computation, since it is still affected by rain streaks. Instead, we replace it using the residue channel (from Eq. 5), which is free from rain streaks. Having obtained the values of all image intensities in the I_{res}CbCr domain, we tranform them back to the RGB domain, in order to obtain the colored residue image as shown in Fig. 2.

One drawback of both the residue channel and colored-residue image is that when the background is achromatic (i.e., white, gray or black), the generated background becomes dark. This is because the background term in Eq. (4) becomes achromatic, instead of a colored vector; and thus, it is cancelled out along with the rain-streak term.

3.4   Residue Image and Rain Accumulation

Rain images typically have severe rain accumulation particularly in the heavy rain. For each pixel, the intensity contributed by the rain is the accumulation of all the raindrops along the line of sight from the camera to the background object. Considering that rain accumulation is so dense that each individual streaks cannot be observed, we thus model the rain accumulation appearance similar to that of fog:

$$E(\mathbf{x}) = (1 - \alpha_t(\mathbf{x})) L + \alpha_t(\mathbf{x}) E_{bg}(\mathbf{x}), \tag{7}$$

where $\alpha_t(\mathbf{x})$ is the transmission, whose value depends on the rain droplet's attenuation factor and the distance between the camera and the background along the line of sight. This model has been successfully used in a few rain removal methods (e.g. [19,46]).

Similar to the discussion in Sect. 3.1, by taking into consideration the camera spectral sensitivities, the colored image intensity of the rain accumulation and background can be expressed as: $\tilde{\mathbf{I}}(\mathbf{x}) = (1 - \alpha_t(\mathbf{x}))\mathbf{L} + \alpha_t(\mathbf{x})\mathbf{B}(\mathbf{x})$. Moreover, if we incorporate the rain streak model into the rain accumulation and background, then we can express all the terms into one equation:

$$\tilde{\mathbf{I}}(\mathbf{x}) = \tau\rho_{rs}(\mathbf{x})\mathbf{L} + (T - \tau)\left[(1 - \alpha_t(\mathbf{x}))\mathbf{L} + \alpha_t(\mathbf{x})\mathbf{B}(\mathbf{x})\right]. \tag{8}$$

By employing a color constancy method (i.e., [9]), we can estimate the light chromaticity, $\boldsymbol{\sigma}$, and use it to cancel the light chromaticity in the image:

$$\mathbf{I}(\mathbf{x}) = I_{rs}(\mathbf{x})\mathbf{i} + I_{ra}(\mathbf{x})\mathbf{i} + \mathbf{I}'_{bg}(\mathbf{x}), \tag{9}$$

where $I_{ra} = (T - \tau)(1 - \alpha_t)L$. $\mathbf{I}'_{bg} = \alpha_t(T - \tau)\mathbf{B}/\boldsymbol{\sigma}$.

Therefore, in this all-inclusive model, Eq. (9), we have three terms: the rain-streak term (the first term), rain accumulation term (the second term), and the background term (the third term). When we see an individual streak in the input image, it is modelled by the rain streak term; however, for those rain streaks that are accumulated such that individual streaks are not distinguishable, then they are modelled by the second term.

If we apply the residue channel (Eq. (5)) or the colored-residue image to our rain model of Eq. (9), both rain streaks and rain accumulation will be removed from the images, since the rain-streak and rain-accumulation terms are both achromatic. This implies, our residue channel and colored-residue image are also free from rain accumulation. However, it comes with a price. First, for achromatic background regions, the residue channel becomes dark, since all the three terms in Eq. (9) are achromatic. Second, when rain accumulation is considerably thick, the background term is significantly suppressed, and as a result, the residue channel and image also become relatively dark, depending on the thickness of the rain accumulation. Nevertheless, in this paper, our goal is not to generate visually pleasing rain-free images, but to create an optical flow algorithm that is robust to rain. Thus, despite the presence of these dark regions, we shall see that residue channel and colored-residue image are useful tools to achieve our goal. In the subsequent section, we will discuss how to utilize the residue channel and colored-residue image to estimate optical flow robustly.

4   Decomposition Framework

In the classic variational framework, the optical flow objective function is expressed as:

$$\mathcal{L}_1(\mathbf{u}) = \sum_{\mathbf{x}} \{\Phi_D[I_1(\mathbf{x}) - I_2(\mathbf{x} + \mathbf{u})] + \lambda_s \Phi_S(\nabla \mathbf{u}(\mathbf{x}))\}, \tag{10}$$

where I_1, I_2 are the gray versions of $\mathbf{I}_1, \mathbf{I}_2$, respectively. $\mathbf{u}$ is the flow vector with λ_s as a regularization parameter and Φ_D and Φ_S are the data and spatial penalty functions. However, as we have discussed, these I_1 and I_2 are affected by rain, and thus the BCC and GCC do not hold. The simplest idea to compute optical flow would be to use the colored-residue images as input to any modern optical flow algorithm. Unfortunately, while the colored-residue image is free from rain streaks and rain accumulation, it suffers from low contrast and the dark region effect. Hence, in our objective function, we incorporate both the colored-residue image and the input image. Our idea is that when encountering dark regions in the residue channel, we turn to the input image for computing the flow; otherwise we use the colored-residue image. Based on this, we change our objective function:

$$\begin{aligned}\mathcal{L}_2(\mathbf{u}) = \sum_{\mathbf{x}} \{&(1 - w(\mathbf{x}))\Phi_D[I_1(\mathbf{x}) - I_2(\mathbf{x} + \mathbf{u})] \\ &+ w(\mathbf{x})\Phi_D[R_1(\mathbf{x}) - R_2(\mathbf{x} + \mathbf{u})] \\ &+ \lambda_s \Phi_S(\nabla \mathbf{u})\},\end{aligned} \tag{11}$$

where R_1, R_2 are the gray versions of the two colored-residue images of the two input rain frames, respectively.

Employing the input images in the objective function, however, adds some complexity. Since, besides affected by rain, raw rain images in fact have a fair amount of noise, which is not surprising since they are usually taken under dim conditions. Those who are well-versed with the art of optical flow estimation will know that this situation of low contrast and substantial noise is a sure recipe for trouble. To address the problem, our idea is to employ the structure/texture image decomposition [43] to the input images and use the structure layer extracted to provide a coarse and complementary source of flow information. While the flow information from the structure layer may be lacking in details (since the detailed textures are discarded), it is less influenced by noise. It also serves to fill in the missing information in the dark regions of the colored-residue image. Formally, the observed rain image $\mathbf{I}$ can be modeled as a linear combination of the piecewise-smooth structure layer $\mathbf{J}$ and the fine-detail texture layer $\mathbf{K}$, namely: $\mathbf{I} = \mathbf{J} + \mathbf{K}$, where the piecewise-smooth structure layer describes the principal regions of the image and the texture layer contains the fine-detailed background textures, rain streaks, and any other possible noises. The decomposition can be done by: $\min_{\mathbf{J}} \parallel \mathbf{I} - \mathbf{J} \parallel^2 + \lambda \parallel \nabla \mathbf{J} \parallel_0$, where $\nabla = (\partial x, \partial y)^T$, and λ is the weighting factor. We use the $L0$-norm, since, being a discrete counting metric, it can deliver sharper edges and has better ability to preserve large gradients [43]. Putting all the above ideas together, we have the following unified objective function:

$$
\begin{aligned}
\mathcal{L}_F(\mathbf{u}, J_1, J_2) = \sum_{\mathbf{x}} \{ & \lambda_d \{ (1 - w(\mathbf{x})) \Phi_D[J_1(\mathbf{x}) - J_2(\mathbf{x} + \mathbf{u})] \\
& + w(\mathbf{x}) \Phi_D[R_1(\mathbf{x}) - R_2(\mathbf{x} + \mathbf{u})] \} + \lambda_s \Phi_S(\nabla \mathbf{u}(\mathbf{x})) \\
& + \alpha(||I_1(\mathbf{x}) - J_1(\mathbf{x})||^2 + ||I_2(\mathbf{x}) - J_2(\mathbf{x})||^2) \\
& + \beta(||\nabla J_1(\mathbf{x})||_0 + ||\nabla J_2(\mathbf{x})||_0) \},
\end{aligned}
\tag{12}
$$

where J_1, J_2 are the gray versions of the structure images of the two frames respectively.

Parameter w is the tunable weighting factor that mediates the relative contribution of the structure layer and the colored-residue image for flow computation (first and second lines of Eq. (12) respectively). It weighs more on using the colored-residue image when the residual channel is not dark. We define $w(\mathbf{x}) = \gamma I_{res}(\mathbf{x})$, where γ is a scaling factor such that there is always some contribution from the structure images. The structure-texture decomposition (third and fourth lines of Eq. (12)) is carried out jointly with the optical flow estimation, so that the denoising can be done in a consistent way across both frames, and that the decomposition can benefit from the redundancy of multiple frames. λ_s is the smoothness parameter for the flow $\mathbf{u}$. β is the parameter controlling the gradient threshold. The higher the β, the fewer boundaries in the piecewise-smooth background layer. Φ_D and Φ_S are the 'Charbonnier' penalty function for the data term and smoothness term.[1]

---

[1] Regarding the colored-residue images in our objective function, one may wonder the purpose of generating it, if in the end we use the gray version R_1, R_2 of it. The reason is that when two objects have different colors, there are some cases where their residue channel values are identical, and thus when the objects are adjacent to each other, their color boundaries disappear, and as a result optical flow is deprived of this important information. However, if we use the gray version of the colored-residue images, we can retain the boundary information. Fig. 3 shows an example of this.

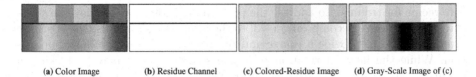

(a) Color Image   (b) Residue Channel   (c) Colored-Residue Image   (d) Gray-Scale Image of (c)

Fig. 3. (a) A color palette and spectrum. **(b)** The residue channel of (a). (Single channel map) **(c)** The colored-residue image of (a). **(d)** The gray scaled version of colored-residue image (c)

Algorithm 1

1: **Input:** Image sequence I_1, I_2, parameters λ_s, α, β, convergence criteria ϵ
2: **Initialization:**   Assign $J_1^{(0)} \leftarrow I_1, J_2^{(0)} \leftarrow I_2$, and initial flow $\mathbf{u}^0 \leftarrow J_1^{(0)}, J_2^{(0)}$,
   R_1, R_2
3: **repeat**   (Start from i=0)
4:    Compute $J_1^{(i+1)} \leftarrow \{J_2^{(i)}, I_1, \mathbf{u}^{(i)}\}, J_2^{(i+1)} \leftarrow \{J_1^{(i)}, I_2, \mathbf{u}^{(i)}\}$ (Subtask 1)
5:    Estimate Flow $\{\mathbf{u}^{(i+1)} \leftarrow J_1^{(i+1)}, J_2^{(i+1)}, R_1, R_2\}$.   (Subtask 2)
6: **until** $\|\mathbf{u}^{i+1} - \mathbf{u}^i\| < \epsilon$
7: **Output:** Estimated flow field $\mathbf{u}^{(M)}$

---

5   Optimization

First, we generate the residue channel maps (R_1, R_2) from the input image and then initialize $J_1 = I_1, J_2 = I_2$, and $\mathbf{u}$ by solving Eq. (13) following the method of [7]. To optimize our objective function, we alternatingly solve the following subtasks until convergence:

Subtask 1: Layer Separation. Given the current optical flow $\mathbf{u}$, we compute the piecewise-smooth background layer J_1, and J_2 separately:

$$J_1^* = \arg\min_{J_1} \sum_{\mathbf{x}} \{\lambda_d \Phi_D[J_1(\mathbf{x}) - J_2(\mathbf{x} + \mathbf{u})] + \alpha|I_1(\mathbf{x}) - J_1(\mathbf{x})|^2 + \beta|\nabla J_1(\mathbf{x})|_0\}$$

$$J_2^* = \arg\min_{J_2} \sum_{\mathbf{x}} \{\lambda_d \Phi_D[J_1(\mathbf{x}) - J_2(\mathbf{x} + \mathbf{u})] + \alpha|I_2(\mathbf{x}) - J_2(\mathbf{x})|^2 + \beta|\nabla J_2(\mathbf{x})|_0\}$$

The objective functions are not convex due to the $L0$-norm terms, unlike the standard structure-texture decomposition. To resolve this problem, we adopt the alternating optimization strategy from [43], by introducing two auxiliary variables to decouple the unsmooth gradient term and the smooth quadratic terms.

Subtask 2: Optical Flow Computation. Given current piecewise-smooth background layers (J_1, J_2), we estimate the optical flow vector $\mathbf{u}$ following the method of [7]:

$$\mathbf{u}^* = \arg\min_{\mathbf{u}} \sum_{\mathbf{x}} \{\lambda_d((1 - w(\mathbf{x}))\Phi_D[J_1(\mathbf{x}) - J_2(\mathbf{x} + \mathbf{u})]$$
$$+ w(\mathbf{x})\Phi_D[R_1(\mathbf{x}) - R_2(\mathbf{x} + \mathbf{u})]) + \lambda_s \Phi_S(\nabla \mathbf{u}(\mathbf{x}))\} \tag{13}$$

Although there is no guarantee for convergence to this non-convex problem, with initialization as proposed above, this algorithm performs well in practice. In our experiments, we run our algorithm on hundreds of different rain scenes and it showed good convergence. A video of is attached in supplementary material to demonstrate the stability, robustness and the convergence of the proposed method.

6   Experiments

Ablation Study. To study how the colored-residue image and structure layer complement each other, we conduct the following ablation experiments using a dataset [27] rendered with rain. We compare the performance of our algorithm with a few baseline methods.

First, we evaluate the performance of the colored-residue image alone by subjecting it to increasingly dense rain streaks and increasing levels of rain accumulation along with the additive white Gaussian noise (Fig. 4 the top two rows). The optical flow results are shown on the top row of Fig. 4a, b. As can be seen, while the colored-residue image is effective in dealing with rain streaks, it is negatively affected by the low contrast brought by the rain accumulation. This is where the structure layer (or the decomposition) comes in. Second, we evaluate the performance of the structure layer alone similarly by subjecting it to increasingly dense rain streaks and increasing levels of rain accumulation. From the result in the top row of Fig. 4c., the structure alone does not achieve good

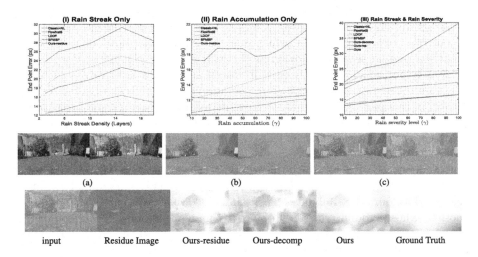

Fig. 4. Ablation study. Top two rows: Input images and the performance graph of the proposed method on the driving dataset rendered with (a) rain streaks alone, (b) rain accumulation alone, (c) combining rain streaks and rain accumulation. Bottom row: Input and optical flow qualitative results using the colored-residue image alone (ours-residue), structure layer alone (ours-decomp), and combined (ours).

performance, since rain streaks in the original input can have rather strong gradients and remain in the structure layer. However, when combined the colored-residue image and structure layer, the performance improves, showing a graceful degradation of performance as rain increases (also in Fig. 4c). More results of our ablation study including on real images are available in the supplementary material. The bottom row of Fig. 4 shows the qualitative results of using the colored-residue only, the structure layer only, and our combination.

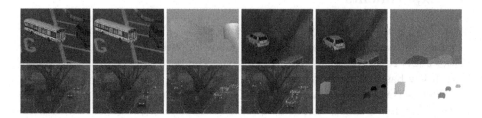

Fig. 5. Top: Two examples from the Flying Vehicles with Rain (FVR-660). From left to right are the generated image pair, and the color coded flow field ground truth. **Bottom**: An example of NUS-100 dataset. From left to right are the input image pair, the annotated labels for objects with motion, the horizontal component of the flow, and the flow ground truth.

Evaluation Datasets. To obtain optical flow ground-truths for real images is considerably difficult, however it is even more difficult for rain scenes. Baker et al. [2] obtain ground-truth data of only a couple of real image pairs using a controlled experiment setup, which does not work under outdoor rain. Using a LIDAR system to obtain flow ground truths is also problematic, since layers of densely accumulated raindrops will absorb and reflect laser rays, which can lead to missing data points and wrong measurements in the echo-backed results. Hence, in this paper, for quantitative evaluations, we use a few different strategies. First, we generate synthetic rain by following the rain model dGarg:2006 on Middlebury [2], Sintel[8] and KITTI [24] optical flow datasets. Second, we combine real rain images with synthesized object motions, creating a new hybrid dataset named FVR-660, which the ground-truths are known. There are in total 660 sequences in this dataset. The top row of Fig. 5 shows some examples. Third, we introduce our NUS-100 dataset containing 100 sequences of real rain and real motion, whose ground truth is obtained by human annotation. An example is shown in the bottom row of Fig. 5. The details of FVR-660 and NUS-100 dataset generation are included in the supplementary material.[2]

---

[2] FVR-600 and NUS-100 datasets are available at : https://liruoteng.github.io/RobustOpticalFlowProject

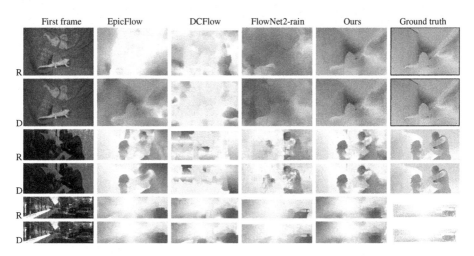

| First frame | EpicFlow | DCFlow | FlowNet2-rain | Ours | Ground truth |

Fig. 6. Method comparisons on Middlebury, MPI Sintel, and KITTI datasets, which are all rendered with rain. The first column "R" and "D" represent synthesized rain sequences and the same sequences after [46]'s deraining method. (**Best zoomed in on screen**).

Synthetic Rain Results. Using our synthetic data, we compare our algorithm with a few conventional methods, i.e. Classic+NL [33], LDOF [6], and SP-MBP [18], EpicFlow [30], as well as recent deep learning methods such as FlowNet2 [17], DCFlow [41] and FlowNet [11], specifically the FlowNetS variant. For a fair comparison, we utilize the recent deraining method [46] as a preprocessing step for these methods. The quantitative results are shown in columns 1 to 3 of Table 1. The qualitative results of these comparisons are shown in Fig. 6. In the figure, the original synthesized rain image is denoted with 'R', and the image produced by the deraining operation is denoted with 'D'. FlowNet2 [17] and FlowNetS [11] are not originally trained using rain images, and thus may not perform well under rain conditions. Hence, we render the Flying Chair dataset [11] with synthetic rain streaks using the same rain streak model as the test dataset. We then fine-tune FlowNetS and FlowNet2 end-to-end on this dataset and pick the best performed model for evaluation. The fine-tuned models are denoted as FlowNetS-rain and FlowNet2-rain respectively.

Real Rain Results. To verify the effectiveness of our algorithm, we perform a sanity check on the estimated flow for static real-rain image pairs as shown in Fig. 7. Since this is a static scene under heavy rain, the true optical flow for the background should be zero everywhere. From the figure (the top row), one can see that the baseline methods produce erroneous flow due to the motion of the rain. In comparison, the result of our algorithm shows a significantly cleaner result. The average magnitude of our flow field is 0.000195 pixel, which is essentially zero flow. Moreover, the plots in the bottom row also show that during the iteration process, the optical flow estimation improves. This means

Table 1. A comparison of our algorithm with several top-performing methods on synthesized rain datasets. "De-rain" indicates the results of each method performed on the sequences after Yang et al.'s [46] de-rain method

Method	Middlebury			Sintel			KITTI2012			FVR-660		NUS-100	
	Rain	De-rain	Clean	Rain	De-rain	Clean	Rain	De-rain	Clean	Rain	De-rain	Rain	De-rain
Classic+NL-fast [33]	0.90	0.60	**0.22**	7.97	6.79	4.94	9.17	9.14	3.84	2.17	2.19	0.49	0.53
LDOF [6]	0.90	0.66	0.45	10.68	6.70	4.29	10.17	9.90	5.05	2.93	2.98	0.68	0.60
SP-MBP [18]	0.93	0.60	1.92	12.32	7.06	3.56	15.71	15.94	6.01	5.37	5.50	0.50	0.55
EpicFlow [30]	1.57	0.48	0.35	14.92	7.03	2.46	6.94	6.78	1.44	4.52	4.44	0.35	0.36
DCFlow [41]	1.62	0.68	0.35	10.68	6.70	2.28	10.17	6.70	**1.04**	46.71	30.69	0.30	0.30
FlowNetS [11]	2.58	1.54	1.09	7.40	6.85	4.50	17.43	18.73	4.27	2.18	2.55	0.53	0.55
FlowNetS-Rain	1.45	1.42	1.28	6.90	5.82	4.65	6.84	6.91	5.68	2.85	3.79	0.63	0.65
FlowNet2 [17]	0.79	0.58	0.40	7.68	8.56	**2.13**	7.23	8.64	2.22	5.73	6.07	0.28	0.30
FlowNet2-Rain	1.24	1.11	0.32	7.54	6.30	5.22	8.01	8.13	6.70	2.21	2.18	0.42	0.43
Ours	**0.30**	**0.332**	0.32	**5.46**	**5.06**	4.71	**6.65**	**6.67**	4.05	**1.76**	**1.81**	**0.22**	**0.19**

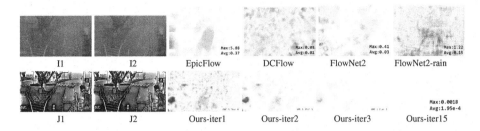

Fig. 7. Static Scene Analysis. **I1,I2** are captured rainy image pair of a static scene. **J1, J2** are the corresponding piecewise-smooth layers of **I1, I2** respectively. Flow map produced by competing algorithms are shown in top row. Flow map produced by our method at different optimization stages are shown in bottom row.

that the structure layer does provide complementary information to the colored-residue image.

We also compare the baseline methods with our algorithm on the FVR-660 dataset for quantitative evaluation (column 5 of Table 1) and qualitative evaluation (Fig. 8). For this evaluation, the deraining preprocessing [46] is applied to the existing methods. As one can see from Fig. 8, the results of the baseline methods contain obvious erroneous flow due to the presence of rain streaks. The state-of-the-art deraining method does not generalize well on different rain types, hence rain streaks are not removed clearly and some deraining artifacts may also be introduced. Finally, we compare our algorithm with baseline methods on the manually annotated real rainy sequences in the NUS-100 dataset. The quantitative result is included in column 6 of Table 1 and qualitative results are shown in Fig. 9.

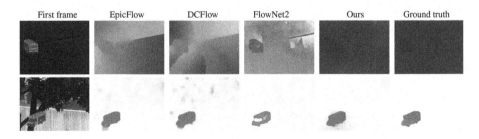

Fig. 8. Method comparison on Flying Vehicle with Rain (FVR-660) dataset. (**Best viewed on screen**).

Input Image	EpicFlow	DCFlow	FlowNet2	Ours	Ground Truth

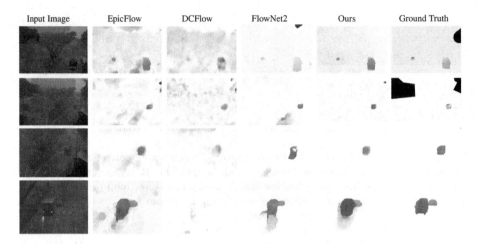

Fig. 9. Method comparison on real rainy scenes with different severity level. The last column is annotated ground truth using [20]. The black region in Ground Truth indicates invalid region, which is not counted in flow evaluation. (**Best zoomed in on screen**).

7   Conclusion

We have introduced a robust algorithm for optical flow in rainy scenes. To our knowledge, it is the first time an optical flow algorithm is specifically designed to deal with rain. Through this work, we make a few contributions. We introduced the residue channel and colored-residue image that are both free from rain streaks and rain accumulation. We proposed an integrated framework to deal with rain that combine the residue channel, colored-residue image, and piecewise-smooth structure layer extraction. We provide a rain optical flow benchmark containing both synthesized motion and real motion to the public.

References

1. Bailer, C., Taetz, B., Stricker, D.: Flow fields: Dense correspondence fields for highly accurate large displacement optical flow estimation (2015). arXiv:CoRRabs/1508.05151
2. Baker, S., Scharstein, D., Lewis, J.P., Roth, S., Black, M.J., Szeliski, R.: A database and evaluation methodology for optical flow. Int. J. Comput. Vis. **92**(1), 1–31 (2011)
3. Barnum, P., Kanade, T., Narasimhan, S.: Spatio-temporal frequency analysis for removing rain and snow from videos. In: Proceedings of the First International Workshop on Photometric Analysis For Computer Vision-PACV, pp. 8–p. INRIA (2007)
4. Barron, J.L., Fleet, D.J., Beauchemin, S.S.: Performance of optical flow techniques. Int. J. Comput. Vis. **12**(1), 43–77 (1994). https://doi.org/10.1007/BF01420984

5. Black, M.J., Anandan, P.: The robust estimation of multiple motions. Comput. Vis. Image Underst. **63**(1), 75–104 (1996). https://doi.org/10.1006/cviu.1996.0006

6. Brox, T., Malik, J.: Large displacement optical flow: descriptor matching in variational motion estimation. IEEE Trans. Pattern Anal. Mach. Intell. **33**(3), 500–513 (2011). http://lmb.informatik.uni-freiburg.de//Publications/2011/Bro11a

7. Bruhn, A., Weickert, J., Schnörr, C.: Lucas/kanade meets horn/schunck: combining local and global optic flow methods. Int. J. Comput. Vis. **61**(3), 211–231 (2005). https://doi.org/10.1023/B:VISI.0000045324.43199.43

8. Butler, D.J., Wulff, J., Stanley, G.B., Black, M.J.: A naturalistic open source movie for optical flow evaluation. In: Fitzgibbon, A., Lazebnik, S., Perona, P., Sato, Y., Schmid, C. (eds.) ECCV 2012. LNCS, vol. 7577, pp. 611–625. Springer, Heidelberg (2012). https://doi.org/10.1007/978-3-642-33783-3_44

9. Cheng, D., Prasad, D.K., Brown, M.S.: Illuminant estimation for color constancy: Why spatial-domain methods work and the role of the color distribution. JOSA A **31**(5), 1049–1058 (2014)

10. Choy, C.B., Gwak, J., Savarese, S., Chandraker, M.: Universal correspondence network. In: Advances in Neural Information Processing Systems, vol. 29 (2016)

11. Dosovitskiy, A., Fischer, P., Ilg, E., Golkov, V., Husser, P., Hazrba, C., Golkov, V., Smagt, P., Cremers, D., Brox, T.: Flownet: Learning optical flow with convolutional networks. In: IEEE International Conference on Computer Vision (ICCV) (2015)

12. Garg, K., Nayar, S.K.: Vision and rain. Int. J. Comput. Vis. **75**(1), 3–27 (2007)

13. Garg, K., Nayar, S.K.: Photometric model of a rain drop. Tech. rep. (2003)

14. Garg, K., Nayar, S.K.: Detection and removal of rain from videos. In: 2004 Proceedings of the 2004 IEEE Computer Society Conference on Computer Vision and Pattern Recognition, CVPR, vol. 1, pp. I–I. IEEE (2004)

15. Garg, K., Nayar, S.K.: Photorealistic rendering of rain streaks. ACM Trans. Graph. **25**(3), 996–1002 (2006). https://doi.org/10.1145/1141911.1141985

16. Horn, B.K.P., Schunck, B.G.: Determining optical flow. Artif. Intell. **17**, 185–203 (1981)

17. Ilg, E., Mayer, N., Saikia, T., Keuper, M., Dosovitskiy, A., Brox, T.: Flownet 2.0: Evolution of optical flow estimation with deep networks (2016). arXiv:CoRRabs/1612.01925

18. Li, Y., Min, D., Brown, M.S., Do, M.N., Lu, J.: Spm-bp: Sped-up patchmatch belief propagation for continuous mrfs. In: 2015 IEEE International Conference on Computer Vision (ICCV), pp. 4006–4014 (Dec 2015). https://doi.org/10.1109/ICCV.2015.456

19. Li, Y., Tan, R.T., Guo, X., Lu, J., Brown, M.S.: Rain streak removal using layer priors. In: The IEEE Conference on Computer Vision and Pattern Recognition (CVPR) (June 2016)

20. Liu, C., Freeman, W.T., Adelson, E.H., Weiss, Y.: Human-assisted motion annotation. In: 2008 IEEE Conference on Computer Vision and Pattern Recognition, pp. 1–8 (June 2008). https://doi.org/10.1109/CVPR.2008.4587845

21. Liu, C., Yuen, J., Torralba, A.: Sift flow: Dense correspondence across scenes and its applications. IEEE Trans. Pattern Anal. Mach. Intell. **33**(5), 978–994 (2011). https://doi.org/10.1109/TPAMI.2010.147

22. Lucas, B.D., Kanade, T.: An iterative image registration technique with an application to stereo vision. In: Proceedings of the 7th International Joint Conference on Artificial Intelligence, vol. 2, pp. 674–679. IJCAI1981, Morgan Kaufmann Publishers Inc., San Francisco, CA, USA (1981). http://dl.acm.org/citation.cfm?id=1623264.1623280

23. Luo, Y., Xu, Y., Ji, H.: Removing rain from a single image via discriminative sparse coding. In: 2015 IEEE International Conference on Computer Vision (ICCV), pp. 3397–3405 (Dec 2015). https://doi.org/10.1109/ICCV.2015.388

24. Menze, M., Geiger, A.: Object scene flow for autonomous vehicles. In: Conference on Computer Vision and Pattern Recognition (CVPR) (2015)

25. Mileva, Y., Bruhn, A., Weickert, J.: Illumination-Robust Variational Optical Flow with Photometric Invariants, pp. 152–162. Springer, Berlin, Heidelberg (2007). https://doi.org/10.1007/978-3-540-74936-3_16

26. Mohamed, M.A., Rashwan, H.A., Mertsching, B., Garca, M.A., Puig, D.: Illumination-robust optical flow using a local directional pattern. IEEE Trans. Circuits Syst. Video Technol. **24**(9), 1499–1508 (2014). https://doi.org/10.1109/TCSVT.2014.2308628

27. Mayer, N., Ilg, E., Häusser, P.,Fischer, P., Cremers, D., Dosovitskiy, A., Brox, T.: A large dataset to train convolutional networks for disparity, optical flow, and scene flow estimation. In: IEEE International Conference on Computer Vision and Pattern Recognition (CVPR) (2016). http://lmb.informatik.uni-freiburg.de/Publications/2016/MIFDB16, arXiv:1512.02134

28. R. Richter, S., Hayder, Z., Koltun, V.: Playing for benchmarks (Sept 2017)

29. Ranjan, A., Black, M.J.: Optical flow estimation using a spatial pyramid network (2016). arXiv:1611.00850

30. Revaud, J., Weinzaepfel, P., Harchaoui, Z., Schmid, C.: Epicflow: edge-preserving interpolation of correspondences for optical flow. Comput. Vis. Pattern Recognit. (2015)

31. Revaud, J., Weinzaepfel, P., Harchaoui, Z., Schmid, C.: Deepmatching: hierarchical deformable dense matching. Int. J. Comput. Vis. **120**(3), 300–323 (2016)

32. Scharstein, D., Szeliski, R., Zabih, R.: A taxonomy and evaluation of dense two-frame stereo correspondence algorithms. In: Proceedings IEEE Workshop on Stereo and Multi-Baseline Vision (SMBV 2001), pp. 131–140 (2001). https://doi.org/10.1109/SMBV.2001.988771

33. Sun, D., Roth, S., Black, M.J.: Secrets of optical flow estimation and their principles. In: IEEE Conference on Computer Vision and Pattern Recognition (CVPR), pp. 2432–2439. IEEE (June 2010)

34. Szeliski, R., Avidan, S., Anandan, P.: Layer extraction from multiple images containing reflections and transparency. In: Proceedings IEEE Conference on Computer Vision and Pattern Recognition. CVPR 2000 (Cat. No.PR00662), vol. 1, pp. 246–253 (2000). https://doi.org/10.1109/CVPR.2000.855826

35. Szeliski, R.: Image alignment and stitching: a tutorial. Found. Trends. Comput. Graph. Vis. **2**(1), 1–104 (2006). https://doi.org/10.1561/0600000009

36. Trobin, W., Pock, T., Cremers, D., Bischof, H.: An unbiased second-order prior for high-accuracy motion estimation. In: 2008 Proceedings of the Pattern Recognition, 30th DAGM Symposium, Munich, Germany, vol. 10–13, pp. 396–405 (June 2008). https://doi.org/10.1007/978-3-540-69321-5_40

37. Wedel, A., Pock, T., Zach, C., Bischof, H., Cremers, D.: An improved algorithm for tv-l1 optical flow. In: Cremers, D., Rosenhahn, B., Yuille, A.L., Schmidt, F.R. (eds.) Statistical and Geometrical Approaches to Visual Motion Analysis, pp. 23–45. Springer, Berlin, Heidelberg (2009)

38. Wedel, A., Pock, T., Zach, C., Bischof, H., Cremers, D.: Statistical and geometrical approaches to visual motion analysis. chap. In: An Improved Algorithm for TV-L1 Optical Flow, pp. 23–45. Springer, Berlin (2009). https://doi.org/10.1007/978-3-642-03061-1_2

39. Weinzaepfel, P., Revaud, J., Harchaoui, Z., Schmid, C.: DeepFlow: Large displacement optical flow with deep matching. In: IEEE Intenational Conference on Computer Vision (ICCV). Sydney, Australia (Dec 2013). http://hal.inria.fr/hal-00873592

40. Xiao, J., Cheng, H., Sawhney, H., Rao, C., Isnardi, M.: Bilateral filtering-based optical flow estimation with occlusion detection. In: Leonardis, A., Bischof, H., Pinz, A. (eds.) ECCV 2006. LNCS, vol. 3951, pp. 211–224. Springer, Heidelberg (2006). https://doi.org/10.1007/11744023_17

41. Xu, J., Ranftl, R., Koltun, V.: Accurate optical flow via direct cost volume processing. In: CVPR (2017)

42. Xu, J., Ranftl, R., Koltun, V.: Accurate optical flow via direct cost volume processing (2017). arxiv:CoRR abs/1704.07325

43. Xu, L., Lu, C., Xu, Y., Jia, J.: Image smoothing via l0 gradient minimization. ACM Trans. Graph. (SIGGRAPH Asia) (2011)

44. Yang, H., Lin, W.Y., Lu, J.: Daisy filter flow: A generalized discrete approach to dense correspondences. In: 2014 IEEE Conference on Computer Vision and Pattern Recognition. pp. 3406–3413, June 2014. https://doi.org/10.1109/CVPR.2014.435

45. Yang, J., Li, H., Dai, Y., Tan, R.T.: Robust optical flow estimation of double-layer images under transparency or reflection. In: 2016 IEEE Conference on Computer Vision and Pattern Recognition (CVPR). pp. 1410–1419 June 2016. https://doi.org/10.1109/CVPR.2016.157

46. Yang, W., Tan, R.T., Feng, J., Liu, J., Guo, Z., Yan, S.: Joint rain detection and removal via iterative region dependent multi-task learning (2016), arXiv:abs/1609.07769

Rethinking Spatiotemporal Feature Learning: Speed-Accuracy Trade-offs in Video Classification

Saining Xie[1,2], Chen Sun[1(✉)], Jonathan Huang[1], Zhuowen Tu[1,2], and Kevin Murphy[1]

[1] Google Research, Mountain View, USA
chensun@google.com
[2] University of California San Diego, San Diego, USA

Abstract. Despite the steady progress in video analysis led by the adoption of convolutional neural networks (CNNs), the relative improvement has been less drastic as that in 2D static image classification. Three main challenges exist including spatial (image) feature representation, temporal information representation, and model/computation complexity. It was recently shown by Carreira and Zisserman that 3D CNNs, inflated from 2D networks and pretrained on ImageNet, could be a promising way for spatial and temporal representation learning. However, as for model/computation complexity, 3D CNNs are much more expensive than 2D CNNs and prone to overfit. We seek a balance between speed and accuracy by building an effective and efficient video classification system through systematic exploration of critical network design choices. In particular, we show that it is possible to replace many of the 3D convolutions by low-cost 2D convolutions. Rather surprisingly, best result (in both speed and accuracy) is achieved when replacing the 3D convolutions at the bottom of the network, suggesting that temporal representation learning on high-level "semantic" features is more useful. Our conclusion generalizes to datasets with very different properties. When combined with several other cost-effective designs including separable spatial/temporal convolution and feature gating, our system results in an effective video classification system that that produces very competitive results on several action classification benchmarks (Kinetics, Something-something, UCF101 and HMDB), as well as two action detection (localization) benchmarks (JHMDB and UCF101-24).

1 Introduction

The resurgence of convolutional neural networks (CNNs) has led to a wave of unprecedented advances for image classification using end-to-end hierarchical feature learning architectures [1–4]. The task of video classification, however, has not enjoyed the same level of performance jump as in image classification. In the past, one limitation was the lack of large-scale labeled video datasets.

© Springer Nature Switzerland AG 2018
V. Ferrari et al. (Eds.): ECCV 2018, LNCS 11219, pp. 318–335, 2018.
https://doi.org/10.1007/978-3-030-01267-0_19

However, the recent creation of Sports-1M [5], Kinetics [6], Something-something [7], ActivityNet [8], Charades [9], etc. has partially removed that impediment.

Now we face more fundamental challenges. In particular, we have three main barriers to overcome: (1) how best to represent spatial information (i.e., recognizing the appearances of objects); (2) how best to represent temporal information (i.e., recognizing context, correlation and causation through time); and (3) how best to tradeoff model complexity with speed, both at training and testing time.

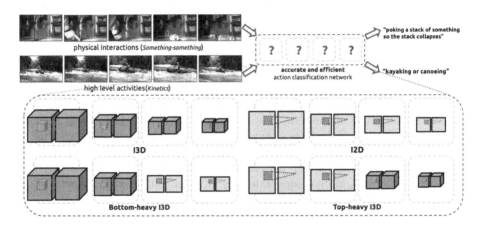

Fig. 1. Our goal is to classify videos into different categories, as shown in the top row. We focus on two qualitatively different kinds of datasets: Something-something which requires recognizing low-level physical interactions, and Kinetics, which requires recognizing high-level activities. The main question we seek to answer is what kind of network architecture to use. We consider 4 main variants: I2D, which is a 2D CNN, operating on multiple frames; I3D, which is a 3D CNN, convolving over space and time; Bottom-Heavy I3D, which uses 3D in the lower layers, and 2D in the higher layers; and Top-Heavy I3D, which uses 2D in the lower (larger) layers, and 3D in the upper layers.

In this paper, we study these three questions by considering various kinds of 3D CNNs. Our starting point is the state of the art approach, due to Carreira and Zisserman [10], known as "I3D" (since it "inflates" the 2D convolutional filters of the "Inception" network [2] to 3D). Despite giving good performance, this model is very computationally expensive. This prompts several questions, which we seek to address in this paper:

- Do we even need 3D convolution? If so, what layers should we make 3D, and what layers can be 2D? Does this depend on the nature of the dataset and task?
- Is it important that we convolve jointly over time and space, or would it suffice to convolve over these dimensions independently?
- How can we use answers to the above questions to improve on prior methods in terms of accuracy, speed and memory footprint?

To answer the first question, we apply "network surgery" to obtain several variants of the I3D architecture. In one family of variants, which we call Bottom-Heavy-I3D, we retain 3D temporal convolutions at the lowest layers of the network (the ones closest to the pixels), and use 2D convolutions for the higher layers. In the other family of variants, which we call Top-Heavy-I3D, we do the opposite, and retain 3D temporal convolutions at the top layers, and use 2D for the lower layers (see Fig. 1). We then investigate how to trade between accuracy and speed by varying the number of layers that are "deflated" (converted to 2D) in this way. We find that the Top-Heavy-I3D models are faster, which is not surprising, since they only apply 3D to the abstract feature maps, which are smaller than the low level feature maps due to spatial pooling. However, we also find that Top-Heavy-I3D models are often more accurate, which is surprising since they ignore low-level motion cues.

To answer the second question (about separating space and time), we consider replacing 3D convolutions with spatial and temporal separable 3D convolutions, i.e., we replace filters of the form $k_t \times k \times k$ by $1 \times k \times k$ followed by $k_t \times 1 \times 1$, where k_t is the width of the filter in time, and k is the height/width of the filter in space. We call the resulting model S3D, which stands for "separable 3D CNN". S3D obviously has many fewer parameters than models that use standard 3D convolution, and it is more computationally efficient. Surprisingly, we also show that it also has better accuracy than the original I3D model.

Finally, to answer the third question (about putting things together for an efficient and accurate video classification system), we combine what we have learned in answering the above two questions with a spatio-temporal gating mechanism to design a new model architecture which we call S3D-G. We show that this model gives significant gains in accuracy over baseline methods on a variety of challenging video classification datasets, such as Kinetics, Something-something, UCF-101 and HMDB, and also outperforms many other methods on other video recognition tasks, such as action localization on JHMDB.

2   Related work

2D CNNs have achieved state of the art results for image classification, so, not surprisingly, there have been many recent attempts to extend these successes to video classification. The Inception 3D (I3D) architecture [10] proposed by Carreira and Zisserman is one of the current state-of-the-art models. There are three key ingredients for its success: first, they "inflate" all the 2D convolution filters used by the Inception V1 architecture [2] into 3D convolutions, and carefully choose the temporal kernel size in the earlier layers. Second, they initialize the inflated model weights by duplicating weights that were pre-trained on ImageNet classification over the temporal dimension. Finally, they train the network on the large-scale Kinetics dataset [6].

Unfortunately, 3D CNNs are computationally expensive, so there has been recent interest in more efficient variants. In concurrent work, [11] has recently proposed a variety of models based on top of the ResNet architecture [4]. In particular, they consider models that use 3D convolution in either the bottom or top layers, and 2D in the rest; they call these "mixed convolutional" models. This is similar to our top-heavy and bottom-heavy models. They conclude that bottom heavy networks are more accurate, which contradicts our finding. However, the differences they find between top heavy and bottom heavy are fairly small, and are conflated with changes in computational complexity. By studying the entire speed-accuracy tradeoff curve (of Inception variants), we show that there are clear benefits to using a top-heavy design for a given computational budget (see Sect. 4.2).

Another way to save computation is to replace 3D convolutions with separable convolutions, in which we first convolve spatially in 2D, and then convolve temporally in 1D. We call the resulting model S3D. This factorization is similar in spirit to the depth-wise separable convolutions used in [12–14], except that we apply the idea to the temporal dimension instead of the feature dimension. This idea has been used in a variety of recent papers, including [11] (who call it "R(2+1)D"), [15] (who call it "Pseudo-3D network"), [16] (who call it "factorized spatio-temporal convolutional networks"), etc. We use the same method, but combine it with both top-heavy and bottom-heavy designs, which is a combination that leads to a very efficient video classification system. We show that the gains from separable convolution are complementary to the gains from using a top-heavy design (see Sect. 4.4).

An efficient way to improve accuracy is to use feature gating, which captures dependencies between feature channels with a simple but effective multiplicative transformation. This can be viewed as an efficient approximation to second-order pooling as shown in [17]. Feature gating has been used for many tasks, such as machine translation [18], VQA [19], reinforcement learning [20], image classification [21,22], and action recognition [23]. We consider a variant of the above techniques in which we place the feature gating module after each of the temporal convolutions in an S3D network, and show that this results in substantial gains in accuracy (see Sect. 4.6).

Another way to improve accuracy (at somewhat higher cost) is to use precomputed optical flow features. This idea was successfully used in [24], who proposed a two-stream architecture where one CNN stream handles raw RGB input, and the other handles precomputed optical flow. Since then, many video classification methods follow the same multi-stream 2D CNN design, and have made improvements in terms of new representations [25,26], different backbone architecture [17,27–29], fusion of the streams [30–33] and exploiting richer temporal structures [34–36]. We will study the benefits of using optical flow in Sect. 5.1.

3   Experiment Setup

3.1   Datasets

In this paper, we consider two large video action classification datasets. The first one is Kinetics [6], which is a large dataset collected from YouTube, containing 400 action classes and 240 K training examples. Each example is temporally trimmed to be around 10 seconds. Since the full Kinetics dataset is quite large, we have created a smaller dataset that we call Mini-Kinetics-200.[1] Mini-Kinetics-200 consists of the 200 categories with most training examples; for each category, we randomly sample 400 examples from the training set, and 25 examples from the validation set, resulting in 80 K training examples and 5 K validation examples in total. The splits are publicly released to enable future comparisons. We also report some results on the original Kinetics dataset, which we will call Kinetics-Full for clarity.

The second main dataset is Something-something [7]. It consists of 110 k videos of 174 different low-level actions, each lasting between 2 to 6 s. In contrast to Kinetics, this dataset requires making fine-grained low-level distinctions, such as between "Pushing something from left to right" and "Pushing something from right to left". It is therefore an interesting question whether the same principles will hold and the same architectures will work well on both datasets.

We also consider two smaller action classification datasets to test the transferability of our model, which we discuss in Sect. 5.2, as well as two action detection datasets, which we discuss in Sect. 5.3.

3.2   Model Training

Our training procedure largely follows [10]. During training, we densely sample 64 frames from a video and resize input frames to 256×256 and then take random crops of size 224×224. During evaluation, we use all frames and take 224×224 center crops from the resized frames. Our models are implemented with TensorFlow and optimized with a vanilla synchronous SGD algorithm with momentum of 0.9 and on 56 GPUs, batch size is set to 6 per GPU. For Mini-Kinetics-200, we train our model for 80 k steps with an initial learning rate of 0.1. We decay the learning rate at step 60k to 0.01, and step 70 k to 0.001. Since Something-something is a smaller dataset, we reduce the number of GPUs to 16 and train at learning rate of 0.1 for 10 k steps.

3.3   Measuring Speed and Accuracy

We report top-1 and top-5 accuracy. To measure the computational efficiency of our models, we report theoretical FLOPS based on a single input video sequence of 64 frames and spatial size 224×224. We pad the total number of frames to 250 for Mini-Kinetics-200 and 64 for Something-something when evaluating.

---

[1] The original "Mini-Kinetics" dataset used in [6] contains videos that are no longer available. We created the new Mini-Kinetics-200 dataset in collaboration with the original authors.

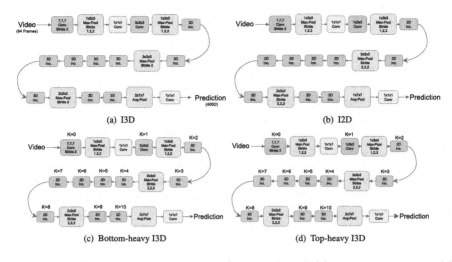

Fig. 2. Network architecture details for (a) I3D, (b) I2D, (c) Bottom-Heavy and (d) Top-Heavy variants. K indexes the spatio-temporal convolutional layers. The "2D Inc." and "3D Inc." blocks refer to 2D and 3D inception blocks, defined in Fig. 3.

4   Network Surgery

In this section, we report the results of various "network surgery" experiments, where we vary different aspects of the I3D model to study the effects on speed and accuracy (Fig. 2).

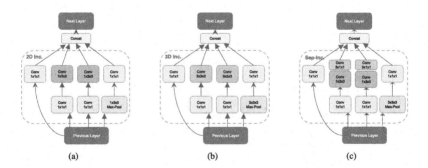

Fig. 3. (a) 2D Inception block; (b) 3D Inception block; (c) 3D temporal separable Inception block used in S3D networks.

4.1   Replacing *all* 3D Convolutions with 2D

In this section, we seek to determine how much value 3D convolution brings, motivated by the surprising success of 2D CNN approaches to video classification (see e.g., [36]). We do this by replacing every 3D filter in the I3D model with a 2D filter. This yields what we will refer to as the I2D model.[2]

Theoretically, the I2D network should be invariant to the temporal reversal of the input frames, since it is not capable of incorporating global signals. To verify this, we train I2D and the original I3D model on the Kinetics-Full and Something-something datasets with normal frame order, and apply the trained models on validation data in which the frames are in normal order and reversed temporal order. The results of the experiment are shown in Table 1. We see that I2D has the same performance on both versions during testing, as is to be expected. However, we notice an interesting difference between the Kinetics dataset and the Something-something dataset. In the former case, the performance of I3D is indifferent to the "arrow of time" [37], whereas in the latter case, reversing the order hurts performance. We believe this is because Something-something dataset requires fine-grained distinctions between visually similar action categories.

Table 1. Top-1 accuracy on Kinetics-Full and Something-something datasets. We train on frames in normal order, and then test on frames in normal order or reverse order. Not surprisingly, 2D CNNs do not care about the order of the frames. For 3D CNNs on Kinetics-Fullthe results are the same on normal and reverse order, indicating that capturing the "arrow of time" is not important on this dataset. However, on Something-something the exact order does matter.

	Kinetics-Full		Something-something	
Model	Normal (%)	Reversed (%)	Normal (%)	Reversed (%)
I3D	71.1	71.1	45.8	15.2
I2D	67.0	67.2	34.4	35.2

4.2 Replacing *some* 3D Convolutions with 2D

Although we have seen that 3D convolution can boost accuracy compared to 2D convolution, it is computationally very expensive. In this section, we investigate the consequences of only replacing some of the 3D convolutions with 2D. Specifically, starting with an I2D model, we gradually inflate 2D convolutions into 3D, from low-level to high-level layers in the network, to create what we call the Bottom-Heavy-I3D model. We also consider the opposite process, in which we inflate the top layers of the model to 3D, but keep the lower layers 2D; we call such models Top-Heavy-I3D models.

---

[2] To reduce the memory and time requirements, and to keep the training protocol identical to I3D (in terms of the number of clips we use for training in each batch, etc), we retain two max-pooling layers with temporal stride 2 between Inception modules. Hence, strictly speaking, I2D is not a pure 2D model. However, it is very similar to a single-frame 2D classification model.

We train and evaluate the Bottom-Heavy-I3D and Top-Heavy-I3D models on Mini-Kinetics-200 and Something-something, and show the results in Fig. 4. We see that the solid blue lines (top heavy I3D) are much better than the dotted blue lines (bottom heavy I3D) under the same FLOPS, which indicates that top heavy models are faster and more accurate. The speed increase is expected, since in a top-heavy model, the feature maps are reduced in size using spatial pooling before being convolved in 3D. For fixed computation budget, Top-Heavy-I3D is often significantly more accurate than Bottom-Heavy-I3D. This suggests that 3D convolutions are more capable and useful to model temporal patterns amongst high level features that are rich in semantics.

4.3   Analysis of Weight Distribution of Learned Filters

To verify the above intuition, we examined the weights of an I3D model which was trained on Kinetics-Full. Fig. 5 shows the distribution of these weights across 4 layers of our model, from low-level to high-level. In particular, each boxplot shows the distribution of $W_l(t, :, :, :)$ for temporal offset t and layer l. We use $t = 0$ to indicate no offset in time, i.e., the center in the temporal kernel. At initialization, all the filters started with the same set of (2D convolution) weights (derived from an Inception model pre-trained on Imagenet) for each value of $t \in \{-1, 0, 1\}$. After training, we see that the temporally offset filters (i.e., for $t \neq 0$) have a weight distribution that is still closely centered on zero in the lower layers (see left panel), whereas the variance of the distribution increases in higher layers (see right panel). This suggests once again that the higher level temporal patterns are more useful for the Kinetics action classification task.

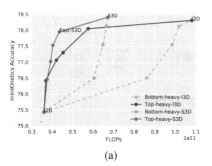
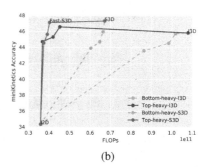

(a)   (b)

Fig. 4. Accuracy vs number of FLOPS needed to perform inference on 64 RGB frames. Left: Mini-Kinetics-200 dataset. Right: Something-something dataset. Solid lines denote top-heavy models, dotted lines denote bottom-heavy models. Orange denotes spatial and temporal separable 3D convolutions, blue denotes full 3D convolutions.

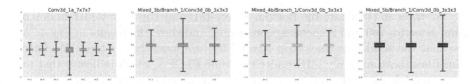

Fig. 5. Statistics of convolutional filter weights of an I3D model trained on Kinetics-Full. Each boxplot shows the distribution of $W_l(t, :, :, :)$ for temporal offset t, with $t = 0$ being in the middle. Results for different layers l are shown in different panels, with lowest layers on the left. All filters with different temporal offset are initialized with the same set of weights. Low-level filters essentially ignore the temporal dimension, unlike higher level filters, where the weights distributed nicely across different temporal offsets.

4.4 Separating Temporal Convolution from Spatial Convolutions

In this section, we study the effect of replacing standard 3D convolution with a factored version which disentangles this operation into a temporal part and a spatial part. In more detail, our method is to replace each 3D convolution with two consecutive convolution layers: one 2D convolution layer to learn spatial features, followed by a 1D convolution layer purely on the temporal axis. This can be implemented by running two 3D convolutions, where the first (spatial) convolution has filter shape $[1, k, k]$ and the second (temporal) convolution has filter shape $[k, 1, 1]$. By applying this factorization to I3D, we obtain a model which we refer to as S3D. For a detailed illustration of the architecture, please refer to Fig. 6.[3]

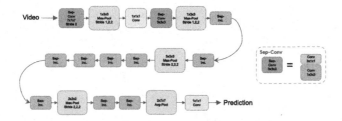

Fig. 6. An illustration of the S3D model. Dark red boxes are temporal separable convolutions (sep-conv), and pink boxes are temporal separable inception blocks, shown in Fig. 3c.

---

[3] There are 4 branches in an Inception block, but only two of them have 3x3 convolutions (the other two being pointwise 1x1 convolutions), as shown in Fig. 3. As such, when I3D inflates the convolutions to 3D, only some of the features contain temporal information. However, by using separable temporal convolution, we can add temporal information to all 4 branches. This improves the performance from 78.4% to 78.9% on Mini-Kinetics-200. In the following sections, whenever we refer to an S3D model, we mean S3D with such configuration.

Table 2 compares the results of S3D and I3D on Kinetics-Full. Table 3 shows that S3D also outperforms I3D on the Something-something dataset. The results show that, despite a substantial compression in model size (12.06M parameters for I3D reduced to 8.77M for S3D), and a large speed-up (107.9 GFLOPS for I3D reduced to 66.38 GFLOPS for S3D), the separable model is even more accurate (top-1 accuracy improved from 71.1% to 72.2% for Kinetics-Full, and from 45.8% to 47.3% for Something-something). We believe the gain in accuracy is because the spatio-temporal factorization reduces overfitting, in a way without sacrificing the expressiveness of the representation, as we find that simply reducing the parameters of the network does not help with the performance.

Note that we can apply this separable transformation to any place where 3D convolution is used; thus this idea is orthogonal to the question of which layers should contain 3D convolution, which we discussed in Sect. 4.1. We denote the separable version of the Bottom-Heavy-I3D models by Bottom-Heavy-S3D, and the separable version of the Top-Heavy-I3D models by Top-Heavy-S3D, thus giving us 4 families of models.

We plot the speed vs accuracy of these models in Fig. 4. We see that separable top-heavy models offer the best speed-accuracy trade-off. In particular, the model in which we keep the top 2 layers as separable 3D convolutions, and make the rest 2D convolutions, seems to be a kind of "sweet spot". We call this model "Fast-S3D", since it is is 2.5 times more efficient than I3D (43.47 vs 107.9 GFLOPS), and yet has comparable accuracy (78.0% vs 78.4% on Mini-Kinetics-200).

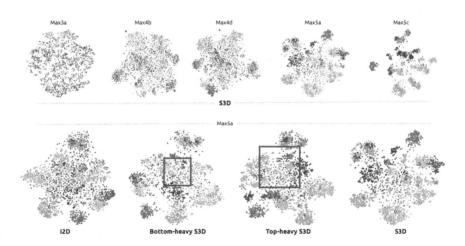

Fig. 7. tSNE projection of activation maps derived from images in the Something-something dataset. Colors and numbers represent the 10 action groups defined in [7]. The top row shows increasing semantic separation as we move to higher layers of S3D. The bottom row shows activations at level Max5a for 4 different models. We see that Top-Heavy-S3D has better semantic separation than Bottom-Heavy-S3D, especially for visually similar categories inside the red box.

4.5   tSNE Analysis of the Features

Here we explore the spatiotemporal representations learned by different levels of the S3D model on the Something-something dataset, using the tool of tSNE projection [38]. The behavior of the I3D models is very similar. Instead of using samples from all 174 categories, we use a smaller vocabulary, namely the "10 action groups" defined in [7].[4] We sample 2,200 data points from the validation set. In Fig. 7, the top row shows representations learned by a S3D model, at levels from Max3a to Max5c. The class separation becomed increasingly clearer at higher levels.

The bottom row shows representations learned at a certain feature level (Max5a), but across different models including I2D, Bottom-Heavy-S3D and Top-Heavy-S3D (both have a 2D-3D transition point at Max4b layer), as well as a full S3D model. Comparing the bottom-heavy and top-heavy models, for subtle actions such as "3: Picking", "4: Putting" and "5: Poking" something, representations learned with a top-heavy model are more discriminative than that in a bottom-heavy model, thus leading to better class separations with the tSNE projection (highlighted with the red box). A top-heavy model can learn features that are as good as those learned with a full 3D model, and significantly better than those from the 2D model, without much sacrifice in processing speed. This observation further supports our hypothesis that temporal information modeling is most effective at top levels in the feature hierarchy for action classification tasks.

Table 2. Effect of separable convolution and feature gating on the Kinetics-Full validation set using RGB features.

Model	Top-1 (%)	Top-5 (%)	Params (M)	FLOPS (G)
I3D	71.1	89.3	12.06	107.89
S3D	72.2	90.6	8.77	66.38
S3D-G	**74.7**	**93.4**	11.56	71.38

4.6   Spatio-Temporal Feature Gating

In this section we further improve the accuracy of our model by using feature gating. We start by considering the context feature gating mechanism first used for video classification in [23]. They consider an unstructured input feature vector

---

[4] The labels are as follows. 0: Dropping [something], 1: Moving [something] from right to left, 2: Moving [something] from left to right, 3: Picking [something], 4:Putting [something], 5: Poking [something], 6: Tearing [something], 7: Pouring [something], 8: Holding [something], 9: Showing [something].

Table 3. Effect of separable convolution and feature gating on the Something-something validation and test sets using RGB features.

Model	Backbone	Val Top-1 (%)	Val Top-5 (%)	Test Top-1 (%)
Pre-3D CNN + Avg [7]	VGG-16	-	-	11.5
Multi-scale TRN [39]	Inception	34.4	63.2	33.6
I2D	Inception	34.4	69.0	-
I3D	Inception	45.8	76.5	-
S3D	Inception	47.3	78.1	-
S3D-G	Inception	**48.2**	**78.7**	**42.0**

$x \in \mathcal{R}^n$ (usually learned at final embedding layers close to the logit output), and produce an output feature vector $y \in \mathcal{R}^n$ as follows:

$$y = \sigma(Wx + b) \odot x$$

where $\odot$ represents elementwise multiplication, $W \in \mathcal{R}^{n \times n}$ is a weight matrix, and $b \in \mathcal{R}^n$ is the bias term. This mechanism allows the model to upweight certain dimensions of x if the context model $\sigma(Wx + b)$ predicts that they are important, and to downweight irrelevant dimensions; this can be thought of as a "self-attention" mechanism.

We now extend this to feature tensors, with spatio-temporal structure. Let $X \in \mathcal{R}^{T \times W \times H \times D}$ be the input tensor, and let Y be an output tensor of the same shape. We replace the matrix product Wx with $W\text{pool}(X)$, where the pooling operation averages the dimensions of X across space and time. (We found that this worked better than just averaging across space or just across time.) We then compute $Y = \sigma(W\text{pool}(X) + b) \odot X$, where $\odot$ represents multiplication across the feature (channel) dimension, (i.e., we replicate the attention map $\sigma(W\text{pool}(X) + b)$ across space and time).

We can plug this gating module into any layer of the network. We experimented with several options, and got the best results by applying it directly after each of the $[k, 1, 1]$ temporal convolutions in the S3D network. We call the final model (S3D with gating) S3D-G. We see from Table 2 that this results in a healthy gain in accuracy compared to S3D on the Kinetics-Full dataset (72.2% top-1 to 74.7%) at a very modest cost increase (66.38 GFLOPS to 71.38). Table 3 shows that S3D-G also outperforms S3D and I3D on Something-something. We also significantly outperform the current state of the art method, which is the Multi-scale TRN of [39], improving top-1 accuracy from 33.6% to 42.0%.

5   Generalization to Other Modalities, Data and Tasks

In this section, we evaluate the generality and robustness of the proposed S3D-G architecture by conducting transfer learning experiments on different input modalities, video datasets, and tasks.

5.1   Using Optical Flow Features

We first verify if S3D-G also works with optical flow inputs. For these experiments, we follow the standard setup as described in [10] and extract optical
flow features with the TV-L1 approach [40]. We truncate the flow magnitude at
$[-20, 20]$ and store them as encoded JPEG files. Other experiment settings are
the same as the RGB experiments. From Table 4, we can see that the improvement of S3D-G over I3D is consistent with the gain we saw with RGB inputs,
bringing the performance up from 63.91% to 68.00%. By ensembling the two
streams of RGB and flow, we obtain a performance of 77.22%, which is a 3%
boost over the I3D network when trained on the same data. We note that even
though we focus on the speed-accuracy trade-offs in action classification network
design, the performance is competitive compared with recent Kinetics Challenge
winners and concurrent works; notably [41,42] use heavier backbone architectures (e.g. ResNet 101 has 8.5x more FLOPS than our S3D-G architecture)

Table 4. Benefits of using optical flow. We report results on the Kinetics-Full validation
set. We report I3D performance based on our implementation, as [10] only report results
on the held-out test set (where they get a top-1 accuracy of 74.2% using RGB+flow
and ImNet pretraining).

Model	Inputs	Backbone	Pre-train	Top-1 (%)	Top-5 (%)
NL I3D [42]	RGB	ResNet-101	ImNet	**77.7**	**93.3**
SAN [41]	RGB+Flow+Audio	Inception-ResNet-v2	ImNet	**77.7**	**93.2**
TSN [36]	RGB+Flow	Inception	ImNet	73.9	91.1
ARTNet [43]	RGB+Flow	ResNet-18	ImNet	72.4	90.4
R(2+1)D [11]	RGB+Flow	ResNet-34	Sports-1M	75.4	91.9
I3D	Flow	Inception	ImNet	63.9	85.0
I3D	RGB	Inception	ImNet	71.1	89.3
I3D	RGB+Flow	Inception	ImNet	74.1	91.6
S3D-G	Flow	Inception	ImNet	68.0	87.6
S3D-G	RGB	Inception	ImNet	74.7	**93.4**
S3D-G	RGB+Flow	Inception	ImNet	**77.2**	93.0

5.2   Fine-Tuning on Other Video Classification Datasets

Next we conduct transfer learning experiments from Kinetics to other video
classification datasets, namely HMDB-51 [44] and UCF-101 [45]. HMDB-51 contains around 7,000 videos spanning over 51 categories, while UCF-101 has 13,320
videos spanning over 101 categories. Both datasets consist of short video clips
that are temporally trimmed, and contain 3 training and validation splits. We
follow the standard setup as used in previous work and report average accuracy
across all splits.

For our transfer learning experiments, we use the same setup as training on
Kinetics, but change the number of GPUs to 8 and lower the learning rate to

0.01 for 6 K steps, and 0.001 for another 2K steps. For simplicity, we only use RGB (no optical flow).

Table 5 shows the results of this experiment. On UCF-101, our proposed S3D-G architecture, which only uses Kinetics for pretraining, outperforms I3D, and matches R(2+1)D, both of which use largescale datasets (Kinetics and Sports-1M) for pretraining. On HMDB-51, we outperform all previous methods published to date.

Table 5. Results of various methods on action classification on the UCF-101 and HMDB-51 datasets. All numbers are computed as the average accuracy across three splits.

Model	Inputs	Pre-train	UCF-101	HMDB-51
P3D [15]	RGB	Sports-1M	88.6	-
C3D [46]	RGB	Sports-1M	82.3	51.6
Res3D [47]	RGB	Sports-1M	85.8	54.9
ARTNet w/ TSN [43]	RGB	Kinetics	94.3	70.9
I3D [10]	RGB	ImNet+Kinetics	95.6	74.8
R(2+1)D [11]	RGB	Kinetics	**96.8**	74.5
S3D-G	RGB	ImNet+Kinetics	**96.8**	**75.9**

5.3 Spatio-Temporal Action Detection in Video

Finally, we demonstrate the effectiveness of S3D-G on action detection tasks, where the inputs are video frames, and the outputs are bounding boxes associated with action labels on the frames. Similar to the framework proposed in [48], we use the Faster-RCNN [49] object detection algorithm to jointly perform person localization and action recognition. We use the same approach as described in [50] to incorporate temporal context information via 3D networks. To be more specific, the model uses a 2D ResNet-50 [4] network that takes the annotated keyframe (frame with box annotations) as input, and extract features for region proposal generation on the keyframe. We then use a 3D network (such as I3D or S3D-G) that takes the frames surrounding the keyframe as input, and extract feature maps which are then pooled for bounding box classification. The 2D region proposal network (RPN) and 3D action classification network are jointly trained end-to-end. Note that we extend the ROIPooling operation to handle 3D feature maps by simply pooling at the same spatial locations over all time steps.

We report performance on two widely adopted video action detection datasets: JHDMB [51] and UCF-101-24 [45]. JHMDB dataset is a subset of HMDB-51, it consists of 928 videos for 21 action categories, and each video clip contains 15–40 frames. UCF-101-24 is a subset of UCF-101 with 24 labels and

3207 videos; we use the cleaned bounding box annotations from [52]. We report performance using the standard frame-AP metric defined in [53], which is computed as the average precision of action detection over all individual frames, at the intersection-over-union (IoU) threshold of 0.5. As commonly used by previous work, we report average performance over three splits of JHMDB and the first split for UCF-101-24.

Our implementation is based on the TensorFlow Object Detection API [54]. We train Faster-RCNN with asynchronous SGD on 11 GPUs for 600 K iterations. We fix the input resolution to be 320×400 pixels. For both training and validation, we fix the size of temporal context to 20 frames. All the other model parameters are set based on the recommended values from [54]. The ResNet-50 networks are initialized with ImageNet pre-trained models, and I3D and S3D-Gare pre-trained from Kinetics. We extract 3D feature maps from the "*Mixed 4e*" layer which has a spatial stride of 16.

Table 6 shows the comparison between I3D, S3D-G, and other state-of-the-art methods. We can see that both 3D networks outperform previous architectures by large margins, while S3D-G is consistently better than I3D.

Table 6. Results of various methods on action detection in JHMDB and UCF101. We report frame-mAP at IoU threshold of 0.5 on JHMDB (all splits) and UCF-101-24 (split 1) datasets.

Model	Inputs	JHMDB	UCF-101
Gkioxari and Malik [53]	RGB+Flow	36.2	-
Weinzaepfel *et al.* [55]	RGB+Flow	45.8	35.8
Peng and Schmid [48]	RGB+Flow	58.5	65.7
Kalogeiton *et al.* [56]	RGB+Flow	65.7	69.5
Faster RCNN + I3D [50]	RGB+Flow	73.2	76.3
Faster RCNN + S3D-G	RGB+Flow	**75.2**	**78.8**

6   Conclusion

We show that we can significantly improve on the previous state of the art 3D CNN video classification model, known as I3D, in terms of efficiency, by combining 3 key ideas: a top-heavy model design, temporally separable convolution, and spatio-temporal feature gating. Our modifications are simple and can be applied to other architectures. We hope this will boost performance on a variety of video understanding tasks.

Acknowledgment. We would like to thank the authors of [6] for the help on the Kinetics dataset and the baseline experiments, especially Joao Carreira for many constructive discussions. We also want to thank Abhinav Shrivastava, Jitendra Malik, and Rahul Sukthankar for valuable feedbacks. S.X. is supported by Google. Z.T. is supported by NSF IIS-1618477 and NSF IIS-1717431.

References

1. Krizhevsky, A., Sutskever, I., Hinton, G.E.: Imagenet classification with deep convolutional neural networks. In: NIPS (2012)
2. Szegedy, C., et al.: Going deeper with convolutions. In: CVPR (2015)
3. Simonyan, K., Zisserman, A.: Very deep convolutional networks for large-scale image recognition. In: ICLR (2015)
4. He, K., Zhang, X., Ren, S., Sun, J.: Deep residual learning for image recognition. In: CVPR (2016)
5. Karpathy, A., Toderici, G., Shetty, S., Leung, T., Sukthankar, R., Fei-Fei, L.: Large-scale video classification with convolutional neural networks. In: CVPR (2014)
6. Kay, W., et al.: The kinetics human action video dataset. In: CVPR (2017)
7. Goyal, R., et al.: The something something video database for learning and evaluating visual common sense. In: ICCV (2017)
8. Caba Heilbron, F., Escorcia, V., Ghanem, B., Niebles, J.C.: ActivityNet: A large-scale video benchmark for human activity understanding. In: CVPR (2015)
9. Sigurdsson, G.A., Varol, G., Wang, X., Farhadi, A., Laptev, I., Gupta, A.: Hollywood in homes: crowdsourcing data collection for activity understanding. In: ECCV (2016)
10. Carreira, J., Zisserman, A.: Quo vadis, action recognition? A new model and the kinetics dataset. In: CVPR (2017)
11. Tran, D., Wang, H., Torresani, L., Ray, J., LeCun, Y., Paluri, M.: A closer look at spatiotemporal convolutions for action recognition. In: CVPR (2018)
12. Chollet, F.: Xception: Deep learning with depthwise separable convolutions. In: CVPR (2017)
13. Howard, A.G., et al.: MobileNets: efficient convolutional neural networks for mobile vision applications (2017). arXiv:1704.04861
14. Xie, S., Girshick, R., Dollár, P., Tu, Z., He, K.: Aggregated residual transformations for deep neural networks. In: CVPR (2017)
15. Qiu, Z., Yao, T., Mei, T.: Learning spatio-temporal representation with pseudo-3D residual networks. In: ICCV (2017)
16. Sun, L., Jia, K., Yeung, D.Y., Shi, B.E.: Human action recognition using factorized spatio-temporal convolutional networks. In: ICCV (2015)
17. Girdhar, R., Ramanan, D.: Attentional pooling for action recognition. In: NIPS (2017)
18. Dauphin, Y.N., Fan, A., Auli, M., Grangier, D.: Language modeling with gated convolutional networks. In: ICML (2017)
19. Perez, E., Strub, F., de Vries, H., Dumoulin, V., Courville, A.: Film: visual reasoning with a general conditioning layer. In: AAAI (2018)
20. Elfwing, S., Uchibe, E., Doya, K.: Sigmoid-weighted linear units for neural network function approximation in reinforcement learning. Neural Netw. (2018)
21. Ramachandran, P., Zoph, B., Le, Q.V.: Swish: a self-gated activation function (2017). arXiv:1710.05941

22. Hu, J., Shen, L., Sun, G.: Squeeze-and-excitation networks. In: CVPR (2018)
23. Miech, A., Laptev, I., Sivic, J.: Learnable pooling with context gating for video classification (2017). arXiv:1706.06905
24. Simonyan, K., Zisserman, A.: Two-stream convolutional networks for action recognition in videos. In: INIPS (2014)
25. Bilen, H., Fernando, B., Gavves, E., Vedaldi, A., Gould, S.: Dynamic image networks for action recognition. In: CVPR (2016)
26. Bilen, H., Fernando, B., Gavves, E., Vedaldi, A.: Action recognition with dynamic image networks. IEEE PAMI (2017)
27. Feichtenhofer, C., Pinz, A., Wildes, R.P.: Temporal residual networks for dynamic scene recognition. In: CVPR (2017)
28. Wang, L., Xiong, Y., Wang, Z., Qiao, Y.: Towards good practices for very deep two-stream convnets (2015). arXiv:1507.02159
29. Ng, J.Y., Hausknecht, M.J., Vijayanarasimhan, S., Vinyals, O., Monga, R., Toderici, G.: Beyond short snippets: deep networks for video classification. In: CVPR (2015)
30. Feichtenhofer, C., Pinz, A., Zisserman, A.: Convolutional two-stream network fusion for video action recognition. In: CVPR (2016)
31. Feichtenhofer, C., Pinz, A., Wildes, R.: Spatiotemporal multiplier networks for video action recognition. In: CVPR (2017)
32. Feichtenhofer, C., Pinz, A., Wildes, R.P.: Spatiotemporal residual networks for video action recognition. In: NIPS (2016)
33. Zolfaghari, M., Oliveira, G.L., Sedaghat, N., Brox, T.: Chained multi-stream networks exploiting pose, motion, and appearance for action classification and detection. In: ICCV (2017)
34. Donahue, J., et al.: Long-term recurrent convolutional networks for visual recognition and description. In CVPR (2015)
35. Wang, X., Farhadi, A., Gupta, A.: Actions transformations. In: CVPR (2016)
36. Wang, L., Xiong, Y., Wang, Z., Qiao, Y., Lin, D., Tang, X., Van Gool, L.: Temporal segment networks: Towards good practices for deep action recognition. In: ECCV (2016)
37. Pickup, L.C., et al.: Seeing the arrow of time. In: CVPR (2014)
38. Maaten, L.V.D., Hinton, G.: Visualizing data using t-SNE. JMLR (2008)
39. Zhou, B., Andonian, A., Torralba, A.: Temporal relational reasoning in videos (2017). arXiv:1711.08496
40. Zach, C., Pock, T., Bischof, H.: A duality based approach for realtime tv-l1 optical flow. Pattern Recognit. (2007)
41. Bian, Y., et al.: Revisiting the effectiveness of off-the-shelf temporal modeling approaches for large-scale video classification (2017). arXiv:1708.03805
42. Wang, X., Girshick, R., Gupta, A., He, K.: Non-local neural networks. In: CVPR (2018)
43. Wang, L., Li, W., Li, W., Gool, L.V.: Appearance-and-relation networks for video classification. In: CVPR (2018)
44. Kuehne, H., Jhuang, H., Garrote, E., Poggio, T., Serre, T.: HMDB: A large video database for human motion recognition. In: ICCV (2011)
45. Soomro, K., Zamir, A., Shah, M.: UCF101: a dataset of 101 human actions classes from videos in the wild. Technical Report CRCV-TR-12-01 (2012)
46. Tran, D., Bourdev, L.D., Fergus, R., Torresani, L., Paluri, M.: C3D: Generic features for video analysis (2014). arXiv:1412.0767
47. Tran, D., Ray, J., Shou, Z., Chang, S., Paluri, M.: Convnet architecture search for spatiotemporal feature learning (2017). arXiv:1708.05038

48. Peng, X., Schmid, C.: Multi-region two-stream R-CNN for action detection. In: Leibe, B., Matas, J., Sebe, N., Welling, M. (eds.) ECCV 2016. LNCS, vol. 9908, pp. 744–759. Springer, Cham (2016). https://doi.org/10.1007/978-3-319-46493-0_45

49. Ren, S., He, K., Girshick, R., Sun, J.: Faster R-CNN: Towards real-time object detection with region proposal networks. In: NIPS (2015)

50. Gu, C., et al.: AVA: A video dataset of spatio-temporally localized atomic visual actions. In: CVPR (2018)

51. Jhuang, H., Gall, J., Zuffi, S., Schmid, C., Black, M.: Towards understanding action recognition. In: ICCV (2013)

52. Saha, S., Sing, G., Cuzzolin, F.: AMTnet: Action-micro-tube regression by end-to-end trainable deep architecture. In: ICCV (2017)

53. Gkioxari, G., Malik, J.: Finding action tubes. In: CVPR (2015)

54. Huang, J., et al.: Speed/accuracy trade-offs for modern convolutional object detectors. In: CVPR (2017)

55. Weinzaepfel, P., Harchaoui, Z., Schmid, C.: Learning to track for spatio-temporal action localization. In: ICCV (2015)

56. Kalogeiton, V., Weinzaepfel, P., Ferrari, V., Schmid, C.: Action tubelet detector for spatio-temporal action localization. In: ICCV (2017)

Variational Wasserstein Clustering

Liang Mi[1(✉)], Wen Zhang[1], Xianfeng Gu[2], and Yalin Wang[1]

[1] Arizona State University, Tempe, USA
{liangmi,wzhan139}@asu.edu
ylwang@asu.edu
[2] Stony Brook University, Stony Brook, USA
gu@cs.stonybrook.edu

Abstract. We propose a new clustering method based on optimal transportation. We discuss the connection between optimal transportation and k-means clustering, solve optimal transportation with the variational principle, and investigate the use of power diagrams as transportation plans for aggregating arbitrary domains into a fixed number of clusters. We drive cluster centroids through the target domain while maintaining the minimum clustering energy by adjusting the power diagram. Thus, we simultaneously pursue clustering and the Wasserstein distance between the centroids and the target domain, resulting in a measure-preserving mapping. We demonstrate the use of our method in domain adaptation, remeshing, and learning representations on synthetic and real data.

Keywords: Clustering · Discrete distribution · K-means
Measure preserving · Optimal transportation · Wasserstein distance

1 Introduction

Aggregating distributional data into clusters has ubiquitous applications in computer vision and machine learning. A continuous example is unsupervised image categorization and retrieval where similar images reside close to each other in the image space or the descriptor space and they are clustered together and form a specific category. A discrete example is document or speech analysis where words and sentences that have similar meanings are often grouped together. k-means [1,2] is one of the most famous clustering algorithms, which aims to partition empirical observations into k clusters in which each observation has the closest distance to the *mean* of its own cluster. It was originally developed for solving quantization problems in signal processing and in early 2000s researchers have discovered its connection to another classic problem optimal transportation which seeks a transportation plan that minimizes the transportation cost between probability measures [3].

The optimal transportation (OT) problem has received great attention since its very birth. Numerous applications such as color transfer and shape retrieval have benefited from solving OT between probability distributions. Furthermore,

© Springer Nature Switzerland AG 2018
V. Ferrari et al. (Eds.): ECCV 2018, LNCS 11219, pp. 336–352, 2018.
https://doi.org/10.1007/978-3-030-01267-0_20

by regarding the minimum transportation cost – *the Wasserstein distance* – as a metric, researchers have been able to compute the barycenter [4] of multiple distributions, e.g. [5,6], for various applications. Most researchers regard OT as finding the optimal coupling of the two probabilities and thus each sample can be mapped to multiple places. It is often called Kantorovich's OT. Along with this direction, several works have shown their high performances in clustering distributional data via optimal transportation, e.g. [6–8]. On the other hand, some researchers regard OT as a measure-preserving mapping between distributions and thus a sample cannot be split. It is called Monge-Brenier's OT.

In this paper, we propose a clustering method from Monge-Brenier's approach. Our method is based on Gu *et al.* [9] who provided a variational solution to Monge-Brenier OT problem. We call it *variational optimal transportation* and name our method *variational Wasserstein clustering*. We leverage the connection between the *Wasserstein distance* and the clustering error function, and simultaneously pursue the Wasserstein distance and the k-means clustering by using a power Voronoi diagram. Given the empirical observations of a target probability distribution, we start from a sparse discrete measure as the initial condition of the centroids and alternatively update the partition and update the centroids while maintaining an optimal transportation plan. From a computational point of view, our method is solving a special case of the *Wasserstein barycenter* problem [4,5] when the target is a univariate measure. Such a problem is also called the *Wasserstein means* problem [8]. We demonstrate the applications of our method to three different tasks – domain adaptation, remeshing, and representation learning. In domain adaptation on synthetic data, we achieve competitive results with D2 [7] and JDOT [10], two methods from Kantorovich's OT. The advantages of our approach over those based on Kantorovich's formulation are that (1) it is a local diffeomorphism; (2) it does not require pre-calculated pairwise distances; and (3) it avoids searching in the product space and thus dramatically reduces the number of parameters.

The rest of the paper is organized as follows. In Sects. 2 and 3, we provide the related work and preliminaries on optimal transportation and k-means clustering. In Sect. 4, we present the variational principle for solving optimal transportation. In Sect. 5, we introduce our formulation of the k-means clustering problem under variational Wasserstein distances. In Sect. 6, we show the experiments and results from our method on different tasks. Finally, we conclude our work in Sect. 7 with future directions.

2   Related Work

2.1   Optimal Transportation

The optimal transportation (OT) problem was originally raised by Monge [11] in the 18th century, which sought a transportation plan for matching distributional data with the minimum cost. In 1941, Kantorovich [12] introduced a relaxed version and proved its existence and uniqueness. Kantorovich also provided an optimization approach based on linear programming, which has become the dominant direction. Traditional ways of solving the Kantorovich's OT problem rely on pre-defined pairwise transportation costs between measure points, e.g. [13], while recently researchers have developed fast approximations that incorporate computing the costs within their frameworks, e.g. [6].

Meanwhile, another line of research followed Monge's OT and had a breakthrough in 1987 when Brenier [14] discovered the intrinsic connection between optimal transportation and convex geometry. Following Brenier's theory, Mérigot [15], Gu *et al.* [9], and Lévy [16] developed their solutions to Monge's OT problem. Mérigot and Lévy's OT formulations are non-convex and they leverage damped Newton and quasi-Newton respectively to solve them. Gu *et al.* proposed a convex formulation of OT particularly for convex domains where pure Newton's method works and then provided a variational method to solve it.

2.2 Wasserstein Metrics

The Wasserstein distance is the minimum cost induced by the optimal transportation plan. It satisfies all metric axioms and thus is often borrowed for measuring the similarity between probability distributions. The transportation cost generally comes from the product of the geodesic distance between two sample points and their measures. We refer to p–Wasserstein distances to specify the exponent p when calculating the geodesic [17]. The 1–Wasserstein distance or earth mover's distance (EMD) has received great attention in image and shape comparison [18,19]. Along with the rising of deep learning in numerous areas, 1–Wasserstein distances have been adopted in many ways for designing loss functions for its superiority over other measures [20–23]. The 2–Wasserstein distance, although requiring more computation, are also popular in image and geometry processing thanks to its geometric properties such as barycenters [4,6]. In this paper, we focus on 2–Wasserstein distances.

2.3 K-Means Clustering

The K-means clustering method goes back to Lloyd [1] and Forgy [2]. Its connections to the 1, 2-Wasserstein metrics were leveraged in [8] and [24], respectively. The essential idea is to use a sparse discrete point set to cluster denser or continuous distributional data with respect to the Wasserstein distance between the original data and the sparse representation, which is equivalent to finding a Wasserstein barycenter of a single distribution [5]. A few other works have also contributed to this problem by proposing fast optimization methods, e.g. [7].

In this paper, we approach the k-means problem from the perspective of optimal transportation in the variational principle. Because we leverage power Voronoi diagrams to compute optimal transportation, we simultaneously pursue the Wasserstein distance and k-means clustering. We compare our method with others through empirical experiments and demonstrate its applications in different fields of computer vision and machine learning research.

3   Preliminaries

We first introduce the optimal transportation (OT) problem and then show its connection to k-means clustering. We use X and Y to represent two Borel probability measures and M their compact embedding space.

3.1   Optimal Transportation

Suppose $\mathcal{P}(M)$ is the space of all Borel probability measures on M. Without losing generality, suppose $X(x,\mu)$ and $Y(y,\nu)$ are two such measures, i.e. X, $Y \in \mathcal{P}(M)$. Then, we have $1 = \int_M \mu(x)dx = \int_M \nu(y)dy$, with the supports $\Omega_X = \{x\} = \{m \in M \mid \mu(m) > 0\}$ and $\Omega_Y = \{y\} = \{m \in M \mid \nu(m) > 0\}$. We call a mapping $T : X(x,\mu) \to Y(y,\nu)$ a measure-preserving one if the measure of any subset B of Y is equal to the measure of the origin of B in X, which means $\mu(T^{-1}(B)) = \nu(B), \forall B \subset Y$.

We can regard T as the *coupling* $\pi(x,y)$ of the two measures, each being a corresponding *marginal* $\mu = \pi(\cdot, y)$, $\nu = \pi(x, \cdot)$. Then, all the couplings are the probability measures in the product space, $\pi \in \prod(M \times M)$. Given a transportation cost $c : M \times M \to \mathbb{R}^+$—usually the geodesic distance to the power of p, $c(x, y) = d(x, y)^p$—the problem of optimal transportation is to find the mapping $\pi_{opt} : x \to y$ that minimizes the total cost,

$$W_p(\mu, \nu) \overset{\text{def}}{=} \left(\inf_{\pi \in \prod(\mu, \nu)} \int_{M \times M} c(x, y)d\pi(x, y) \right)^{1/p}, \tag{1}$$

where p indicates the power. We call the minimum total cost the $p-Wasserstein$ *distance*. Since we address Monge's OT in which mass cannot be split, we have the restriction that $d\pi(x, y) = d\pi_T(x, y) \equiv d\mu(x)\delta[y = T(x)]$, inferring that

$$\pi_{T\,opt} = T_{opt} = \arg\min_T \int_M c(x, T(x))d\mu(x). \tag{2}$$

In this paper, we follow Eq. (2). The details of the optimal transportation problem and the properties of the Wasserstein distance can be found in [23,25]. For simplicity, we use π to denote the optimal transportation map.

3.2   K-Means Clustering

Given the empirical observations $\{(x_i, \mu_i)\}$ of a probability distribution $X(x, \mu)$, the k-means clustering problem seeks to assign a cluster centroid (or prototype) $y_j = y(x_i)$ with label $j = 1, ..., k$ to each empirical sample x_i in such a way that the error function (3) reaches its minimum and meanwhile the measure of each cluster is preserved, i.e. $\nu_j = \sum_{y_j = y(x_i)} \mu_i$. It is equivalent to finding a partition $V = \{(V_j, y_j)\}$ of the embedding space M. If M is convex, then so is V_j.

$$\arg\min_y \sum_{x_i} \mu_i d(x_i, y(x_i))^p \equiv \arg\min_V \sum_{j=1}^K \sum_{x_i \in V_j} \mu_i d(x_i, y(V_j))^p. \tag{3}$$

Such a clustering problem (3), when ν is fixed, is equivalent to Monge's OT problem (2) when the support of y is sparse and not fixed because π and V induce each other, i.e. $\pi \Leftrightarrow V$. Therefore, the solution to Eq. (3) comes from the optimization in the search space $\mathcal{P}(\pi, y)$. Note that when ν is not fixed such a problem becomes *the Wasserstein barycenter* problem as finding a minimum in $\mathcal{P}(\pi, y, \nu)$, studied in [4,5,7].

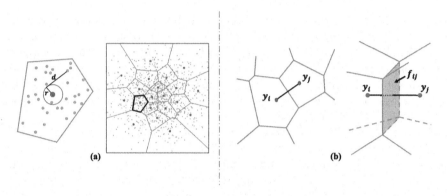

(a)   (b)

Fig. 1. (a) Power Voronoi diagram. Red dots are centroids of the Voronoi cells, or clusters. The Power distances has an offset depending on the weight of the cell. (b) Intersection of adjacent cells in 2D and 3D for computing Hessian. (Color figure online)

4 Variational Optimal Transportation

We present the variational principle for solving the optimal transportation problem. Given a metric space M, a Borel probability measure $X(x, \mu)$, and its compact support $\Omega = supp\ \mu = \{x \in M \mid \mu(x) > 0\}$, we consider a sparsely supported point set with Dirac measure $Y(y, \nu) = \{(y_j, \nu_j > 0)\}$, $j = 1, ..., k$. (Strictly speaking, the empirical measure $X(x, \mu)$ is also a set of Dirac measures but in this paper we refer to X as the empirical measure and Y as the Dirac measure for clarity.) Our goal is to find an optimal transportation plan or map (OT-map), $\pi : x \rightarrow y$, with the *push-forward* measure $\pi_{\#}\mu = \nu$. This is *semi-discrete OT*.

We introduce a vector $\boldsymbol{h} = (h_1, ..., h_k)^T$, a hyperplane on M, $\gamma_j(\boldsymbol{h}) : \langle m, y_j \rangle + h_j = 0$, and a piecewise linear function:

$$\theta_h(x) = \max\{\langle x, y_j \rangle + h_j\}, \ j = 1, ..., k.$$

Theorem 1. *(Alexandrov [26]) Suppose Ω is a compact convex polytope with non-empty interior in $\mathbb{R}^n$ and $y_1, ..., y_k \subset \mathbb{R}^n$ are k distinct points and $\nu_1, ..., \nu_k > 0$ so that $\sum_{j=1}^k \nu_j = vol(\Omega)$. There exists a unique vector $\boldsymbol{h} = (h_1, ..., h_k)^T \in \mathbb{R}^k$ up to a translation factor $(c, ..., c)^T$ such that the piecewise linear convex function $\theta_h(x) = \max\{\langle x, y_j \rangle + h_j\}$ satisfies $vol(x \in \Omega \mid \nabla \theta_h(x) = y_j) = \nu_j$.*

Algorithm 1: Variational optimal transportation

Function `Variational-OT`$(X(x, \mu),\ Y(y, v),\ \epsilon)$

  $\boldsymbol{h} \leftarrow \boldsymbol{0}$.

  repeat

      Update power diagram V with $(y, \boldsymbol{h})$.

      Compute cell weight $w(\boldsymbol{h}) = \{\sum_{m \in V_j} \mu(m)\}$.

      Compute gradient $\nabla E(\boldsymbol{h})$ and Hessian H using Eqs. (5) and (6).

      $\boldsymbol{h} \leftarrow \boldsymbol{h} - \lambda H^{-1} \nabla E(\boldsymbol{h})$. // Update the minimizer $\boldsymbol{h}$ according to (7)

  until $|\nabla E(\boldsymbol{h})| < \epsilon$.

  return $V, \boldsymbol{h}$.

end

Furthermore, Brenier [14] proved that the gradient map $\nabla\theta$ provides the solution to Monge's OT problem, that is, $\nabla\theta_h$ minimizes the transportation cost $\int_\Omega \|x - \theta_h(x)\|^2$. Therefore, given X and Y, $\boldsymbol{h}$ by itself induces OT.

From [27], we know that a convex subdivision associated to a piecewise-linear convex function $u_h(x)$ on $\mathbb{R}^n$ equals a *power Voronoi diagram*, or *power diagram*. A typical power diagram on $M \subset \mathbb{R}^n$ can be represented as:

$$V_j \overset{\text{def}}{=} \{m \in M \mid \|m - y_j\|^2 - r_j^2 \leqslant \|m - y_i\|^2 - r_i^2\},\ \forall j \neq i.$$

Then, a simple calculation gives us

$$m \cdot y_j - \frac{1}{2}(y_j \cdot y_j + r_j^2) \leqslant m \cdot y_i - \frac{1}{2}(y_i \cdot y_i + r_i^2),$$

where $m \cdot y_j = \langle m, y_j \rangle$ and w_j represents the offset of the *power distance* as shown in Fig. 1a. On the other hand, the graph of the hyperplane $\pi_j(\boldsymbol{h})$ is

$$U_i \overset{\text{def}}{=} \{m \in M \mid \langle m, y_j \rangle - h_j \geqslant \langle m, y_i \rangle - h_i\},\ \forall j \neq i.$$

Thus, we obtain the numerical representation $h_j = -\frac{|y_j|^2 - r_j^2}{2}$.

We substitute $M(m)$ with the measure $X(x)$. In our formulation, Brenier's gradient map $\nabla\theta_h : V_j(\boldsymbol{h}) \to y_j$ "transports" each $V_j(\boldsymbol{h})$ to a specific point y_j. The total mass of $V_j(\boldsymbol{h})$ is denoted as: $w_j(\boldsymbol{h}) = \sum_{x \in V_j(\boldsymbol{h})} \mu(x)$.

Now, we introduce an energy function

$$E(\boldsymbol{h}) \overset{\text{def}}{=} \int_\Omega \theta_h(x)\mu(x)dx - \sum_{j=1}^{k} \nu_i h_j$$

$$\equiv \int^h \sum_{j=1}^{k} w_j(\xi)d\xi - \sum_{j=1}^{k} \nu_i h_j. \tag{4}$$

E is differentiable w.r.t. $\boldsymbol{h}$ [9]. Its gradient and Hessian are then given by

---

Algorithm 2: Iterative measure-preserving mapping

Function `Iterative-Measure-Preserving-Mapping`$(X(x,\mu), Y(y,\nu))$

   repeat

      $V(\boldsymbol{h}) \leftarrow$ Variational-OT(x, μ, y, ν). // 1. Update Voronoi partition

      $y_j \leftarrow \sum_{x \in V_j} \mu_i x_i / \sum_{x \in V_j} \mu_i$. // 2. Update y

   until y converges.

   return y, V.

end

$$\nabla E(\boldsymbol{h}) = (w_1(\boldsymbol{h}) - \nu_1, ..., w_k(\boldsymbol{h}) - \nu_k)^T, \tag{5}$$

$$H = \frac{\partial^2 E(\boldsymbol{h})}{\partial h_i \partial h_j} = \begin{cases} \sum_l \frac{\int_{f_{il}} \mu(x)dx}{\|y_l - y_i\|}, & i = j, \ \forall l, s.t. \ f_{il} \neq \emptyset, \\ -\frac{\int_{f_{ij}} \mu(x)dx}{\|y_j - y_i\|}, & i \neq j, \ f_{ij} \neq \emptyset, \\ 0, & i \neq j, \ f_{ij} = \emptyset, \end{cases} \tag{6}$$

where $\| \cdot \|$ is the $L1$–norm and $\int_{f_{ij}} \mu(x)dx = \text{vol}(f_{ij})$ is the volume of the intersection f_{ij} between two adjacent cells. Figure 1b illustrates the geometric relation. The Hessian H is positive semi-definite with only constant functions spanned by a vector $(1, ..., 1)^T$ in its null space. Thus, E is strictly convex in $\boldsymbol{h}$. By Newton's method, we solve a linear system,

$$H\delta\boldsymbol{h} = \nabla E(\boldsymbol{h}), \tag{7}$$

and update $\boldsymbol{h}^{(t+1)} \leftarrow \boldsymbol{h}^{(t)} + \delta\boldsymbol{h}^{(t)}$. The energy E (4) is motivated by Theorem 1 which seeks a solution to $vol(x \in \Omega \mid \nabla\theta_h(x) = y_j) = \nu_j$. Move the right-hand side to left and take the integral over $\boldsymbol{h}$ then it becomes E (4). Thus, minimizing (4) when the gradient approaches $\boldsymbol{0}$ gives the solution. We show the complete algorithm for obtaining the OT-Map $\pi : X \rightarrow Y$ in Algorithm 1.

5   Variational Wasserstein Clustering

We now introduce in detail our method to solve clustering problems through variational optimal transportation. We name it *variational Wasserstein clustering* (VWC). We focus on the semi-discrete clustering problem which is to find a set of discrete sparse centroids to best represent a continuous probability measure, or its discrete empirical representation. Suppose M is a metric space and we embody in it an empirical measure $X(x, \mu)$. Our goal is to find such a sparse measure $Y(y, \nu)$ that minimizes Eq. (3).

We begin with an assumption that the distributional data are embedded in the same Euclidean space $M = \mathbb{R}^n$, i.e. $X, Y \in \mathcal{P}(M)$. We observe that if ν is fixed then Eqs. (2) and (3) are mathematically equivalent. Thus, the computational approaches to these problems could also coincide. Because the

---

Algorithm 3: Variational Wasserstein clustering

Input : Empirical measures $X_M(x, \mu)$ and $Y_N(y, \nu)$
Output: Measure-preserving Map $\pi : X \to Y$ represented as (y, V).
begin

    $\nu \leftarrow$ Sampling-known-distribution. // Initialization.
    Harmonic-mapping: $M, N \to \mathbb{R}^n$ or $\mathbb{D}^n$. // Unify domains.
    $y, V \leftarrow$ Iterative-Measure-Preserving-Mapping(x, μ, y, ν).

end
return y, V.

---

space is convex, each cluster is eventually a Voronoi cell and the resulting partition $V = \{(V_j, y_j)\}$ is actually a power Voronoi diagram where we have $\|x - y_j\|^2 - r_j^2 \leq \|x - y_i\|^2 - r_i^2$, $x \in V_j$, $\forall j \neq i$ and r is associated with the total mass of each cell. Such a diagram is also the solution to Monge's OT problem between X and Y. From the previous section, we know that if X and Y are fixed the power diagram is entirely determined by the minimizer $\boldsymbol{h}$. Thus, assuming ν is fixed and y is allowed to move freely in M, we reformulate Eq. (3) to

$$f(\boldsymbol{h}, y) = \sum_{j=1}^{K} \sum_{x_i \in V_j(\boldsymbol{h})} \mu_i \|x_i - y_j\|^2, \tag{8}$$

where every V_j is a power Voronoi cell.

The solution to Eq. (8) can be achieved by iteratively updating $\boldsymbol{h}$ and y. While we can use Algorithm 1 to compute $\boldsymbol{h}$, updating y can follow the rule:

$$y_j^{(t+1)} \leftarrow \sum \mu_i x_i^{(t)} \Big/ \sum \mu_i, \ x_i^{(t)} \in V_j. \tag{9}$$

Since the first step preserves the measure and the second step updates the measure, we call such a mapping an *iterative measure-preserving mapping*. Our algorithm repeatedly updates the partition of the space by variational-OT and computes the new centroids until convergence, as shown in Algorithm 2. Furthermore, because each step reduces the total cost (8), we have the following propositions.

Proposition 1. *Algorithm 2 monotonically minimizes the object function (8).*

Proof. It is sufficient for us to show that for any $t \geq 0$, we have

$$f(\boldsymbol{h}^{(t+1)}, y^{(t+1)}) \leq f(\boldsymbol{h}^{(t)}, y^{(t)}). \tag{10}$$

The above inequality is indeed true since $f(\boldsymbol{h}^{(t+1)}, y^{(t)}) \leq f(\boldsymbol{h}^{(t)}, y^{(t)})$ according to the convexity of our OT formulation, and $f(\boldsymbol{h}^{(t+1)}, y^{(t+1)}) \leq f(\boldsymbol{h}^{(t+1)}, y^{(t)})$ for the updating process itself minimizes the mean squared error. $\qquad\square$

Corollary 1. *Algorithm 2 converges in a finite number of iterations.*

Proof. We borrow the proof for k-means. Given N empirical samples and a fixed number k, there are k^N ways of clustering. At each iteration, Algorithm 2 produces a new clustering rule only based on the previous one. The new rule induces a lower cost if it is different than the previous one, or the same cost if it is the same as the previous one. Since the domain is a finite set, the iteration must eventually enter a cycle whose length cannot be greater than 1 because otherwise it violates the fact of the monotonically declining cost. Therefore, the cycle has the length of 1 in which case the Algorithm 2 converges in a finite number of iterations. □

Corollary 2. *Algorithm 2 produces a unique (local) solution to Eq. (8).*

Proof. The initial condition, y the centroid positions, is determined. Each step of Algorithm 2 yields a unique outcome, whether updating $\boldsymbol{h}$ by variational OT or updating y by weighted averaging. Thus, Algorithm 2 produces a unique outcome. □

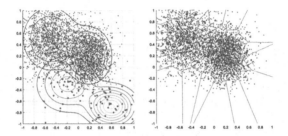

Fig. 2. Given the source domain (red dots) and target domain (grey dots), the distribution of the source samples are driven into the target domain and form a power Voronoi diagram. (Color figure online)

Now, we introduce the concept of variational Wasserstein clustering. For a subset $M \subset \mathbb{R}^n$, let $\mathcal{P}(M)$ be the space of all Borel probability measures. Suppose $X(x, \mu) \in \mathcal{P}(M)$ is an existing one and we are to aggregate it into k clusters represented by another measure $Y(y, \nu) \in \mathcal{P}(M)$ and assignment $y_j = \pi(x)$, $j = 1, ..., k$. Thus, we have $\pi \in \mathcal{P}(M \times M)$. Given ν fixed, our goal is to find such a combination of Y and π that minimize the object function:

$$Y_{y,\nu} = \underset{\substack{Y \in P(M) \\ \pi \in P(M \times M)}}{argmin} \sum_{j=1}^{k} \sum_{y_j = \pi(x_i)} \mu_i \|x_i - y_j\|^2, \ s.t. \ \nu_j = \sum_{y_j = \pi(x_i)} \mu_i. \tag{11}$$

Equation (11) is not convex w.r.t. y as discussed in [5]. We thus solve it by iteratively updating π and y. When updating π, since y is fixed, Eq. (11) becomes

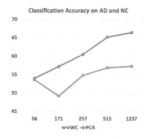

Fig. 3. Classification accuracies of VWC and PCA on AD and NC w.r.t. number of centroids.

an optimal transportation problem. Therefore, solving Eq. (11) is equivalent to approaching the infimum of the 2-Wasserstein distance between X and Y:

$$\inf_{\substack{Y \in P(M) \\ \pi \in P(M \times M)}} \sum_{j=1}^{k} \sum_{y_j = \pi(x_i)} \mu_i \|x_i - y_j\|^2 = \inf_{Y \in P(M)} W_2^2(X, Y). \tag{12}$$

Assuming the domain is convex, we can apply iterative measure-preserving mapping (Algorithm 2) to obtain y and h which induces π. In case that X and Y are not in the same domain i.e. $Y(y, \nu) \in P(N)$, $N \subset \mathbb{R}^n$, $N \neq M$, or the domain is not necessarily convex, we leverage *harmonic mapping* [28,29] to map them to a convex canonical space. We wrap up our complete algorithm in Algorithm 3. Figure 2 illustrates a clustering result. Given a source Gaussian mixture (red dots) and a target Gaussian mixture (grey dots), we cluster the target domain with the source samples. Every sample has the same mass in each domain for simplicity. Thus, we obtain an unweighted Voronoi diagram. In the next section, we will show examples that involve different mass. We implement our algorithm in C/C++ and adopt Voro++ [30] to compute Voronoi diagrams. The code is available at https://github.com/icemiliang/vot.

6   Applications

While the k-means clustering problem is ubiquitous in numerous tasks in computer vision and machine learning, we present the use of our method in approaching domain adaptation, remeshing, and representation learning.

6.1   Domain Adaptation on Synthetic Data

Domain adaptation plays a fundamental role in knowledge transfer and has benefited many different fields such as scene understanding and image style transfer. Several works have coped with domain adaptation by transforming distributions in order to close their gap with respect to a measure. In recent years, Courty *et al.* [31] took the first steps in applying optimal transportation to domain adaptation. Here we revisit this idea and provide our own solution to *unsupervised many-to-one domain adaptation* based on variational Wasserstein clustering.

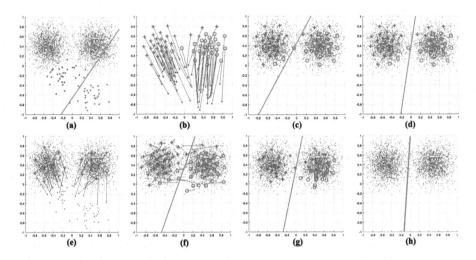

Fig. 4. SVM RBF boundaries for domain adaptation. (a) Target domain in gray dots and source domain of two classes in red and blue dots; (b) Mapping of centroids by using VWC; (c,d) Boundaries from VWC with linear and RBF kernels; (e) k-means++ [32] fails to produce a model; (f) After recentering source and target domains, k-means++ yields acceptable boundary; (g) D2 [7]; (h) JDOT [10], final centroids not available. (Color figure online)

Consider a two-class classification problem in the 2D Euclidean space. The source domain consists of two independent Gaussian distributions sampled by red and blue dots as shown in Fig. 4a. Each class has 30 samples. The target domain has two other independent Gaussian distributions with different means and variances, each having 1500 samples. They are represented by denser gray dots to emulate the source domain after an unknown transformation.

We adopt support vector machine (SVM) with linear and radial basis function (RBF) kernels for classification. The kernel scale for RBF is 5. One can notice that directly applying the RBF classifier learned from the source domain to the target domain provides a poor classification result (59.80%). While Fig. 4b shows the final positions of the samples from the source domain by VWC, (c) and (d) show the decision boundaries from SVMs with a linear kernel and an RBF kernel, respectively. In (e) and (f) we show the results from the classic k-means++ method [32]. In (e) k-means++ fails to cluster the unlabeled samples into the original source domain and produces an extremely biased model that has 50% of accuracy. Only after we recenter the source and the target domains yields k-means++ better results as shown in (f).

For more comparison, we test two other methods – D2 [7] and JDOT [10]. The final source positions from D2 are shown in (g). Because D2 solves the general barycenter problem and also updates the weights of the source samples, it converges as soon as it can find them some positions when the weights can also satisfy the minimum clustering loss. Thus, in (g), most of the source samples dive into the right, closer density, leaving those moving to the left with larger weights. We show the decision boundary obtained from JDOT [10] in (h). JDOT does not update the centroids, so we only show its decision boundary. In this experiment, both our method for Monge's OT and the methods [7,10] for Kantorovich's OT can effectively transfer knowledge between different domains, while the traditional method [32] can only work after a prior knowledge between the two domains, e.g. a linear offset. Detailed performance is reported in Table 1.

Table 1. Classification accuracy for domain adaptation on synthetic data

	k-means++ [32][a]	k-means++[b]		D2 [7]		JDOT [10]		VWC	
Kernel	Linear/RBF	Linear	RBF	Linear	RBF	Linear	RBF	Linear	RBF
Acc.	50.00	97.88	99.12	95.85	99.25	99.03	99.23	98.56	99.31
Sen.	100.00	98.13	98.93	99.80	99.07	98.13	99.60	98.00	99.07
Spe.	0.00	97.53	99.27	91.73	99.40	99.93	98.87	99.07	99.53

[a]Extremely biased model labeling all samples with same class;
[b]After recenterd

6.2 Deforming Triangle Meshes

Triangle meshes is a dominant approximation of surfaces. Refining triangle meshes to best represent surfaces have been studied for decades, including [33–35]. Given limited storage, we prefer to use denser and smaller triangles to represent the areas with relatively complicated geometry and sparser and larger triangles for flat regions. We follow this direction and propose to use our method to solve this problem. The idea is to drive the vertices toward high-curvature regions.

We consider a surface $\mathbb{S}^2$ approximated by a triangle mesh $T_{\mathbb{S}^2}(v)$. To drive the vertices to high-curvature positions, our general idea is to reduce the areas of the triangles in there and increase them in those locations of low curvature, producing a new triangulation $T'_{\mathbb{S}^2}(v)$ on the surface. To avoid computing the geodesic on the surface, we first map the surface to a *unit disk* $\phi : \mathbb{S}^2 \to \mathbb{D}^2 \subset \mathbb{R}^2$ and equip it with the Euclidean metric. We drop the superscripts 2 for simplicity. To clarify notations, we use $T_{\mathbb{S}}(v)$ to represent the original triangulation on surface $\mathbb{S}$; $T_{\mathbb{D}}(v)$ to represent its counterpart on $\mathbb{D}$ after harmonic mapping; $T'_{\mathbb{D}}(v)$ for the target triangulation on $\mathbb{D}$ and $T'_{\mathbb{S}}(v)$ on $\mathbb{S}$. Figure 5a and b illustrate the

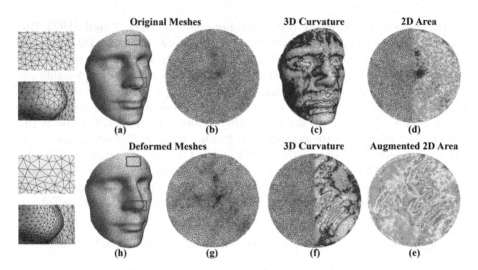

Fig. 5. Redistribute triangulation based on curvature. Original mesh (a) is mapped to a unit disk (b). Mean curvature on the 3D mesh (c) is copied to the disk (f). Design an "augmented" measure μ (e) on the disk by incorporating curvature C into 2D vertex area A (d), e.g. $\mu = 0.4A + 0.6C$. A vertex y with a large curvature C, in order to maintain its original measure A, will shrink its own cluster. As a result vertices collapse in high-curvature regions (g). Mesh will be pulled back to 3D (h) by inverse mapping.

triangulation before and after the harmonic mapping. Our goal is to rearrange the triangulation on $\mathbb{D}$ and then the following composition gives the desired triangulation on the surface:

$$T_{\mathbb{S}}(v) \xrightarrow{\phi} T_{\mathbb{D}}(v) \xrightarrow{\pi} T'_{\mathbb{D}}(v) \xrightarrow{\phi^{-1}} T'_{\mathbb{S}}(v).$$

π is where we apply our method.

Suppose we have an original triangulation $T_{sub,\mathbb{S}}(v)$ and an initial downsampled version $T_{\mathbb{S}}(v)$ and we map them to $T_{sub,\mathbb{D}}(v)$ and $T_{\mathbb{D}}(v)$, respectively. The vertex area $A_{\mathbb{D}} : v \rightarrow a$ on $\mathbb{D}$ is the source (Dirac) measure. We compute the (square root of absolute) mean curvature $C_{sub,\mathbb{S}} : v_{sub} \rightarrow c_{sub}$ on $\mathbb{S}$ and the area $A_{sub,\mathbb{D}} : v_{sub} \rightarrow a_{sub}$ on $\mathbb{D}$. After normalizing a and c, a weighted summation gives us the target measure, $\mu_{sub,\mathbb{D}} = (1 - \lambda) \, a_{sub,\mathbb{D}} + \lambda \, c_{sub,\mathbb{D}}$. We start from the source measure (v, a) and cluster the target measure (v_{sub}, μ_{sub}). The intuition is the following. If $\lambda = 0$, $\mu_{i,sub} = a_{i,sub}$ everywhere, then a simple unweighted Voronoi diagram which is the dual of $T_{\mathbb{D}}(v)$ would satisfy Eq. (12). As λ increases, the clusters $V_j(v_j, a_j)$ in the high-curvature $(c_{sub,\mathbb{D}})$ locations will require smaller areas $(a_{sub,\mathbb{D}})$ to satisfy $a_j = \sum_{v_{i,sub} \in V_j} \mu_{i,sub}$.

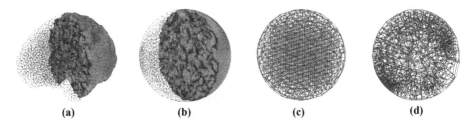

(a) **(b)** **(c)** **(d)**

Fig. 6. Brain images are projected to tetrahedral meshes (a) that are generated from brain surfaces. Meshes are deformed into unit balls (b) via harmonic mapping. A sparse uniform distribution inside the ball (c) is initialized and shown with the initial Voronoi diagram. We start from (c) as the initial centroids and cluster (b) as the empirical measure by using our proposed method. (d) shows the resulting centroids and diagram.

We apply our method on a human face for validation and show the result in Fig. 5. On the left half, we show the comparison before and after the remeshing. The tip of the nose has more triangles due to the high curvature while the forehead becomes sparser because it is relatively flatter. The right half of Fig. 5 shows different measures that we compute for moving the vertices. (c) shows the mean curvature on the 3D surface. We map the triangulation with the curvature onto the planar disk space (f). (d) illustrates the vertex area of the planar triangulation and (e) is the weighted combination of 3D curvature and 2D area. Finally, we regard area (d) as the source domain and the "augmented" area (e) as the target domain and apply our method to obtain the new arrangement (g) of the vertices on the disk space. After that, we pull it back to the 3D surface (h). As a result, vertices are attracted into high-curvature regions. Note the boundaries of the deformed meshes (g,h) have changed after the clustering. We could restrict the boundary vertices to move *on* the unit circle if necessary. Rebuilding a Delaunay triangulation from the new vertices is also an optional step after.

6.3 Learning Representations of Brain Images

Millions of voxels contained in a 3D brain image bring efficiency issues for computer-aided diagnoses. A good learning technique can extract a better representation of the original data in the sense that it reduces the dimensionality and/or enhances important information for further processes. In this section, we address learning representations of brain images from a perspective of Wasserstein clustering and verify our algorithm on magnetic resonance imaging (MRI).

In the high level, given a brain image $X(x, \mu)$ where x represents the voxels and μ their intensities, we aim to cluster it with a known sparse distribution $Y(y, \nu)$. We consider that each brain image is a submanifold in the 3D Euclidean space, $M \subset \mathbb{R}^3$. To prepare the data, for each image, we first remove the skull and extract the surface of the brain volume by using Freesurfer [36], and use Tetgen [37] to create a tetrahedral mesh from the surface. Then, we project the image onto the tetrahedral mesh by finding the nearest neighbors and perform harmonic mapping to deform it into a *unit ball* as shown in Fig. 6a and b.

Now, following Algorithm 3, we set a discrete uniform distribution sparsely supported in the unit ball, $Y(y, \nu) \sim U_{\mathbb{D}^3}(-1, 1)$ as shown in Fig. 6c. Starting from this, we learn such a new y that the representation mapping $\pi : x \to y$ has the minimum cost (12). Thus, we can think of this process as a non-parametric mapping from the input to a latent space $\mathcal{P}(y)$ of dimension $k \times n \ll |x|$ where k is the number of clusters and n specifies the dimension of the original embedding space, e.g. 3 for brain images. Figure 6d shows the resulting centroids and the corresponding power diagram. We compare our method with principle component analysis (PCA) to show its capacity in dimensionality reduction. We apply both methods on 100 MRI images with 50 of them labeled Alzheimer's disease (AD) and 50 labeled normal control (NC). After obtaining the low-dimensional features, we directly apply a linear SVM classifier on them for 5-fold cross-validation. The plots in Fig. 3 show the superiority of our method. It is well known that people with AD suffer brain atrophy resulting in a group-wise shift in the images [38]. The result shows the potential of VWC in embedding the brain image in low-dimensional spaces. We could further incorporate prior knowledge such as regions-of-interest into VWC by hand-engineering initial centroids.

7   Discussion

Optimal transportation has gained increasing popularity in recent years thanks to its robustness and scalability in many areas. In this paper, we have discussed its connection to k-means clustering. Built upon variational optimal transportation, we have proposed a clustering technique by solving iterative measure-preserving mapping and demonstrated its applications to domain adaptation, remeshing, and learning representations.

One limitation of our method at this point is computing a high-dimensional Voronoi diagram. It requires complicated geometry processing which causes efficiency and memory issues. A workaround of this problem is to use gradient descent for variational optimal transportation because the only thing we need from the diagram is the intersections of adjacent convex hulls for computing the Hessian. The assignment of each empirical observation obtained from the diagram can be alternatively determined by nearest search algorithms. This is beyond the scope of this paper but it could lead to more real-world applications.

The use of our method for remeshing could be extended to the general feature redistribution problem on a compact 2–manifold. Future work could also include adding regularization to the centroid updating process to expand its applicability to specific tasks in computer vision and machine learning. The extension of our formulation of Wasserstein means to barycenters is worth further study.

Acknowledgments. The research is partially supported by National Institutes of Health (R21AG043760, RF1AG051710, and R01EB025032), and National Science Foundation (DMS-1413417 and IIS-1421165).

References

1. Lloyd, S.: Least squares quantization in pcm. IEEE Trans. Inf. Theory **28**(2), 129–137 (1982)
2. Forgy, E.W.: Cluster analysis of multivariate data: efficiency versus interpretability of classifications. Biometrics **21**, 768–769 (1965)
3. Graf, S., Luschgy, H.: Foundations of Quantization for Probability Distributions. LNM, vol. 1730. Springer, Heidelberg (2000). https://doi.org/10.1007/BFb0103945
4. Agueh, M., Carlier, G.: Barycenters in the Wasserstein space. SIAM J. Math. Anal. **43**(2), 904–924 (2011)
5. Cuturi, M., Doucet, A.: Fast computation of wasserstein barycenters. In: International Conference on Machine Learning, pp. 685–693 (2014)
6. Solomon, J., et al.: Convolutional wasserstein distances: efficient optimal transportation on geometric domains. ACM Trans. Graph. (TOG) **34**(4), 66 (2015)
7. Ye, J., Wu, P., Wang, J.Z., Li, J.: Fast discrete distribution clustering using Wasserstein barycenter with sparse support. IEEE Trans. Signal Process. **65**(9), 2317–2332 (2017)
8. Ho, N., Nguyen, X., Yurochkin, M., Bui, H.H., Huynh, V., Phung, D.: Multilevel clustering via Wasserstein means (2017). arXiv preprint arXiv:1706.03883
9. Gu, X., Luo, F., Sun, J., Yau, S.T.: Variational principles for minkowski type problems, discrete optimal transport, and discrete monge-ampere equations (2013). arXiv preprint arXiv:1302.5472
10. Courty, N., Flamary, R., Habrard, A., Rakotomamonjy, A.: Joint distribution optimal transportation for domain adaptation. In: Advances in Neural Information Processing Systems, pp. 3733–3742 (2017)
11. Monge, G.: Mémoire sur la théorie des déblais et des remblais. Histoire de l'Académie Royale des Sciences de Paris (1781)
12. Kantorovich, L.V.: On the translocation of masses. Dokl. Akad. Nauk SSSR. **37**, 199–201 (1942)
13. Cuturi, M.: Sinkhorn distances: lightspeed computation of optimal transport. In: Advances in neural information processing systems, pp. 2292–2300 (2013)
14. Brenier, Y.: Polar factorization and monotone rearrangement of vector-valued functions. Commun. Pure Appl. Math. **44**(4), 375–417 (1991)
15. Mérigot, Q.: A multiscale approach to optimal transport. In: Computer Graphics Forum, vol. 30, pp. 1583–1592. Wiley Online Library (2011)
16. Lévy, B.: A numerical algorithm for l2 semi-discrete optimal transport in 3d. ESAIM Math. Model. Numer. Anal. **49**(6), 1693–1715 (2015)
17. Givens, C.R., Shortt, R.M.: A class of wasserstein metrics for probability distributions. Mich. Math. J. **31**(2), 231–240 (1984)
18. Rubner, Y., Tomasi, C., Guibas, L.J.: The earth mover's distance as a metric for image retrieval. Int. J. Comput. Vis. **40**(2), 99–121 (2000)
19. Ling, H., Okada, K.: An efficient earth mover's distance algorithm for robust histogram comparison. IEEE Trans. Pattern Anal. Mach. Intell. **29**(5), 840–853 (2007)
20. Lee, K., Xu, W., Fan, F., Tu, Z.: Wasserstein introspective neural networks. In: The IEEE Conference on Computer Vision and Pattern Recognition (CVPR), June 2018
21. Arjovsky, M., Chintala, S., Bottou, L.: Wasserstein generative adversarial networks. In: International Conference on Machine Learning, pp. 214–223 (2017)
22. Frogner, C., Zhang, C., Mobahi, H., Araya, M., Poggio, T.A.: Learning with a Wasserstein loss. In: Advances in Neural Information Processing Systems, pp. 2053–2061 (2015)

23. Gibbs, A.L., Su, F.E.: On choosing and bounding probability metrics. Int. Stat. Rev. **70**(3), 419–435 (2002)
24. Applegate, D., Dasu, T., Krishnan, S., Urbanek, S.: Unsupervised clustering of multidimensional distributions using earth mover distance. In: Proceedings of the 17th ACM SIGKDD International Conference on Knowledge Discovery and Data Mining, pp. 636–644. ACM (2011)
25. Villani, C.: Topics in Optimal Transportation, no. 58. American Mathematical Society (2003)
26. Alexandrov, A.D.: Convex Polyhedra. Springer Science & Business Media (2005)
27. Aurenhammer, F.: Power diagrams: properties, algorithms and applications. SIAM J. Comput. **16**(1), 78–96 (1987)
28. Gu, X.D., Yau, S.T.: Computational Conformal Geometry. International Press Somerville, Mass, USA (2008)
29. Wang, Y., Gu, X., Chan, T.F., Thompson, P.M., Yau, S.T.: Volumetric harmonic brain mapping. In: 2004 IEEE International Symposium on Biomedical Imaging: Nano to Macro, pp. 1275–1278. IEEE (2004)
30. Rycroft, C.: Voro++: a three-dimensional Voronoi cell library in c++ (2009)
31. Courty, N., Flamary, R., Tuia, D.: Domain adaptation with regularized optimal transport. In: Calders, T., Esposito, F., Hüllermeier, E., Meo, R. (eds.) ECML PKDD 2014. LNCS (LNAI), vol. 8724, pp. 274–289. Springer, Heidelberg (2014). https://doi.org/10.1007/978-3-662-44848-9_18
32. Arthur, D., Vassilvitskii, S.: k-means++: the advantages of careful seeding. In: Proceedings of the Eighteenth Annual ACM-SIAM Symposium on Discrete Algorithms. Society for Industrial and Applied Mathematics, pp. 1027–1035 (2007)
33. Shewchuk, J.R.: Delaunay refinement algorithms for triangular mesh generation. Comput. Geom. **22**(1–3), 21–74 (2002)
34. Fabri, A., Pion, S.: Cgal: the computational geometry algorithms library. In: Proceedings of the 17th ACM SIGSPATIAL International Conference on Advances in Geographic Information Systems, pp. 538–539. ACM (2009)
35. Goes, F.d., Memari, P., Mullen, P., Desbrun, M.: Weighted triangulations for geometry processing. ACM Trans. Graph. (TOG) **33**(3), 28 (2014)
36. Fischl, B.: Freesurfer. Neuroimage **62**(2), 774–781 (2012)
37. Si, H., TetGen, A.: A Quality Tetrahedral Mesh Generator and Three-dimensional Delaunay Triangulator, p. 81. Weierstrass Institute for Applied Analysis and Stochastic, Berlin, Germany (2006)
38. Fox, N.C., Freeborough, P.A.: Brain atrophy progression measured from registered serial mri: validation and application to alzheimer's disease. J. Magn. Reson. Imaging **7**(6), 1069–1075 (1997)

Show, Tell and Discriminate: Image Captioning by Self-retrieval with Partially Labeled Data

Xihui Liu[1], Hongsheng Li[1(✉)], Jing Shao[2], Dapeng Chen[1],
and Xiaogang Wang[1]

[1] The Chinese University of Hong Kong, Hong Kong, China
{hsli,xgwang}@ee.cuhk.edu.hk, xihui-liu@link.cuhk.edu.hk,
dpchen@cuhk.edu.hk
[2] SenseTime Research, Hong Kong, China
shaojing@sensetime.com

Abstract. The aim of image captioning is to generate captions by machine to describe image contents. Despite many efforts, generating discriminative captions for images remains non-trivial. Most traditional approaches imitate the language structure patterns, thus tend to fall into a stereotype of replicating frequent phrases or sentences and neglect unique aspects of each image. In this work, we propose an image captioning framework with a self-retrieval module as training guidance, which encourages generating discriminative captions. It brings unique advantages: (1) the self-retrieval guidance can act as a metric and an evaluator of caption discriminativeness to assure the quality of generated captions. (2) The correspondence between generated captions and images are naturally incorporated in the generation process without human annotations, and hence our approach could utilize a large amount of unlabeled images to boost captioning performance with no additional annotations. We demonstrate the effectiveness of the proposed retrieval-guided method on COCO and Flickr30k captioning datasets, and show its superior captioning performance with more discriminative captions.

Keywords: Image captioning · Language and vision
Text-image retrieval

1 Introduction

Image captioning, generating natural language description for a given image, is a crucial task that has drawn remarkable attention in the field of vision and language [2,5,14,21,22,26,35,41,43,47,49]. However, results by existing image captioning methods tend to be generic and templated. For example, in Fig. 1, although for humans there are non-neglectable differences between the first and second images, the captioning model gives identical ambiguous descriptions "A vase with flowers sitting on a table", while the ground-truth captions contain

© Springer Nature Switzerland AG 2018
V. Ferrari et al. (Eds.): ECCV 2018, LNCS 11219, pp. 353–369, 2018.
https://doi.org/10.1007/978-3-030-01267-0_21

Conventional: A vase with flowers sitting on a table.

GT: A vase filled with flowers and lemons on a table.

Conventional: A vase with flowers sitting on a table.

GT: Creative centerpiece floral arrangement at an outdoor table.

Conventional: A bird is sitting on top of a bird feeder.

Most similar GT in training: A bird is on top of a bird feeder.

Fig. 1. Examples of generated captions by conventional captioning models. The generated captions are templated and generic.

details and clearly show the differences between those images. Moreover, about fifty percent of the captions generated by conventional captioning methods are exactly the same as ground-truth captions from the training set, indicating that the captioning models only learn a stereotype of sentences and phrases in the training set, and have limited ability of generating discriminative captions. The image on the right part of Fig. 1 shows that although the bird is standing on a mirror, the captioning model generates the caption "A bird is sitting on top of a bird feeder", as a result of replicating patterns appeared in the training set.

Existing studies working on the aforementioned problems either used Generative Adversarial Networks (GAN) to generate human-like descriptions [8,36], or focused on enlarging the diversity of generated captions [40,42,44]. Those methods improve the diversity of generated captions but sacrifice overall performance on standard evaluation criteria. Another work [38] generates discriminative captions for an image in context of other semantically similar images by an inference technique on both target images and distractor images, which cannot be applied to generic captioning where distractor images are not provided.

In this study, we wish to show that with the innovative model design, both the discriminativeness and fidelity can be effectively improved for caption generation. It is achieved by involving a self-retrieval module to train a captioning module, motivated from two aspects: (1) the discriminativeness of a caption can be evaluated by how well it can distinguish its corresponding image from other images. This criterion can be introduced as a guidance for training, and thus encourages discriminative captions. (2) Image captioning and text-to-image retrieval can be viewed as dual tasks. Image captioning generates a description of a given image, while text-to-image retrieval retrieves back the image based on the generated caption. Specifically, the model consists of a **Captioning Module** and a **Self-retrieval Module**. The captioning module generates captions based on given images, while the self-retrieval module conducts text-to-image retrieval, trying to retrieve corresponding images based on the generated captions. It acts as an evaluator to measure the quality of captions and encourages the model to generate discriminative captions. Since generating each word of a caption contains non-differentiable operations, we take the negative retrieval loss as self-retrieval reward and adopt REINFORCE algorithm to compute gradients.

Such retrieval-guided captioning framework can not only guarantee the discriminativeness of captions, but also readily obtain benefits from additional unlabeled images, since a caption naturally corresponds to the image it is generated from, and do not need laborious annotations. In detail, for unlabeled images, only self-retrieval module is used to calculate reward, while for labeled images, both the ground-truth captions and self-retrieval module are used to calculate reward and optimize the captioning model. Mining moderately hard negative samples from unlabeled data further boost both the fidelity and discriminativeness of image captioning.

We test our approach on two image captioning datasets, COCO [6] and Flickr30k [51], in fully-supervised and semi-supervised settings. Our approach achieves state-of-the-art performance and additional unlabeled data could further boost the captioning performance. Analysis of captions generated by our model shows that the generated captions are more discriminative and achieve higher self-retrieval performance than conventional methods.

2 Related Work

Image captioning methods can be divided into three categories [49]. **Template-based methods** [20,29,48] generate captions based on language templates. **Search-based methods** [11,13] search for the most semantically similar captions from a sentence pool. Recent works mainly focus on **language-based methods** with an encoder-decoder framework [7,14–17,28,41,43,46,47], where a convolutional neural network (CNN) encodes images into visual features, and an Long Short Term Memory network (LSTM) decodes features into sentences [41]. It has been shown that attention mechanisms [5,26,31,47] and high-level attributes and concepts [14,16,49,50] can help with image captioning.

Maximum Likelihood Estimation (MLE) was adopted for training by many previous works. It maximizes the conditional likelihood of the next word conditioned on previous words. However, it leads to the exposure bias problem [33], and the training objective does not match evaluation metrics. Training image captioning models by reinforcement learning techniques [37] solves those problems [24,34,35] and significantly improves captioning performance.

A problem of current image captioning models is that they tend to replicate phrases and sentences seen in the training set, and most generated captions follow certain templated patterns. Many recent works aim at increasing diversity of generated captions [40,42,44]. Generative adversarial networks (GAN) can be incorporated into captioning models to generate diverse and human-like captions [8,36]. Dai *et al.* [9] proposed a contrastive learning technique to generate distinctive captions while maintaining the overall quality of generated captions. Vedantam *et al.* [38] introduced an inference technique to produce discriminative context-aware image captions using generic context-agnostic training data, but with a different problem setting from ours. It requires context information, *i.e.*, a distractor class or a distractor image, for inference, which is not easy to obtain in generic image captioning applications.

In this work, we improve discriminativeness of captions by using a self-retrieval module to explicitly encourage generating discriminative captions during training. Based on the intuition that a discriminative caption should be able to successfully retrieve back the image corresponding to itself, the self-retrieval module performs text-to-image retrieval with the generated captions, serving

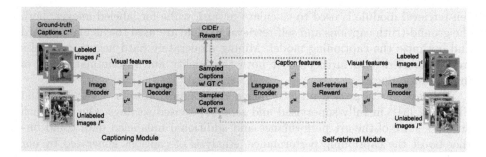

Fig. 2. Overall Framework of our proposed method. The captioning module (left) and the self-retrieval module (right) shares the same image encoder. Dotted lines mean that the reward for each sampled caption is back-propagated by REINFORCE algorithm. The captioning performance is improved by training the captioning module with text-to-image self-retrieval reward. Unlabeled images are naturally handled by our framework

as an evaluator of the captioning module. The retrieval reward for generated captions is back-propagated by REINFORCE algorithm. Our model can also be trained with partially labeled data to boost the performance. A concurrent work [27] by Luo *et al.* also uses a discriminability objective similar to that of ours to generate discriminative captions. However, our work differs from it in utilizing unlabeled image data and mining moderately hard negative samples to further encourage discriminative captions.

3 Methodology

Given an image I, the goal of image captioning is to generate a caption $C = \{w_1, w_2, \ldots, w_T\}$, where w_i denotes the ith word, and we denote the ground-truth captions by $C^* = \{w_1^*, w_2^*, \ldots, w_T^*\}$.

The overall framework, as shown in Fig. 2, comprises of a captioning module and a self-retrieval module. The captioning module generates captions for given images. A Convolutional Neural Network (CNN) encodes images to visual features, and then a Long Short Term Memory network (LSTM) decodes a sequence of words based on the visual features. The self-retrieval module is our key contribution, which is able to boost the performance of the captioning module with only partially labeled images. It first evaluates the similarities between generated captions with their corresponding input images and other distractor images. If the captioning module is able to generate discriminative enough descriptions, the similarity between the corresponding generated-caption-image pairs should be higher than those of non-corresponding pairs. Such constraint is modeled as a text-to-image retrieval loss and is back-propagated to the improve the captioning module by REINFORCE algorithm.

3.1 Image Captioning with Self-retrieval Reward

Captioning Module. The captioning module, aiming at generating captions for given images, is composed of a CNN image encoder $E_i(I)$ and an LSTM language decoder $D_c(v)$. The image encoder E_i encodes an image I to obtain its visual features v, and the language decoder D_c decodes the visual features v to generate a caption C that describes the contents of the image,

$$v = E_i(I), \quad C = D_c(v). \tag{1}$$

For conventional training by maximum-likelihood estimation (MLE), given the ground-truth caption words up to time step $t-1$, $\{w_1^*, \ldots, w_{t-1}^*\}$, the model is trained to maximize the likelihood of w_t^*, the ground-truth word of time step t. Specifically, the LSTM outputs probability distribution of the word at time step t, given the visual features and ground-truth words up to time step $t-1$, and is optimized with the cross-entropy loss,

$$L_{CE}(\theta) = -\sum_{t=1}^{T} \log(p_\theta(w_t^*|v, w_1^*, \ldots, w_{t-1}^*)), \tag{2}$$

where θ represents learnable weights of the captioning model.

For inference, since the ground-truth captions are not available, the model outputs the distribution of each word conditioned on previous generated words and visual features, $p_\theta(w_t|v, w_1, \ldots, w_{t-1})$. The word at each time step t is chosen based on the probability distribution of each word by greedy decoding or beam search.

Self-retrieval Module. A captioning model trained by MLE training often tends to imitate the word-by-word patterns in the training set. A common problem of conventional captioning models is that many captions are templated and generic descriptions (*e.g.* "A woman is standing on a beach"). Reinforcement learning with evaluation metrics (such as CIDEr) as reward [24, 35] allows the captioning model to explore more possibilities in the sample space and gives a better supervision signal compared to MLE. However, the constraint that different images should not generate the same generic captions is still not taken into account explicitly. Intuitively, a good caption with rich details, such as "A woman in a blue dress is walking on the beach with a black dog", should be able to distinguish the corresponding image in context of other distractor images. To encourage such discriminative captions, we introduce the self-retrieval module to enforce the constraint that the generated captions should match its corresponding images better than other images.

We therefore model the self-retrieval module to conduct text-to-image retrieval with the generated caption as a query. Since retrieving images from the whole dataset for each generated caption is time-consuming and infeasible during each training iteration, we consider text-to-image matching in each mini-batch. We first encode images and captions into features in the same embedding space a CNN encoder E_i and a Gated Recurrent Unit (GRU) encoder E_c for captions,

$$v = E_i(I), \quad c = E_c(C), \tag{3}$$

where I and C denote images and captions, and v and c denote visual features and caption features, respectively. Then the similarities between the embedded image features and caption features are calculated. The similarities between the features of a caption c_i and the features of the jth image v_j is denoted as $s(c_i, v_j)$. For a mini-batch of images $\{I_1, I_2, \ldots, I_n\}$ and a generated caption C_i of the ith image, we adopt the triplet ranking loss with hardest negatives (*VSE++* [12]) for text-to-image retrieval,

$$L_{ret}(C_i, \{I_1, I_2, \ldots, I_n\}) = \max_{j \neq i}[m - s(c_i, v_i) + s(c_i, v_j)]_+, \tag{4}$$

where $[x]_+ = \max(x, 0)$. For a query caption C_i, we compare the similarity between the positive feature pair $\{c_i, v_i\}$ with the negative pairs $\{c_i, v_j\}$, where $j \neq i$. This loss forces the similarity of the positive pair to be higher than the similarity of the hardest negative pair by a margin m. We also explore other retrieval loss formulations in Sect. 4.4.

The self-retrieval module acts as a discriminativeness evaluator of the captioning module, which encourages a caption generated from a given image by the captioning module to be the best matching to the given image among a batch of distractor images.

Back-Propagation by REINFORCE Algorithm. For each input image, since self-retrieval is performed based on the complete generated caption, and sampling a word from a probability distribution is non-differentiable, we cannot back-propagate the self-retrieval loss to the captioning module directly. Therefore, REINFORCE algorithm is adopted to back-propagate the self-retrieval loss to the captioning module.

For image captioning with reinforcement learning, the LSTM acts as an "agent", and the previous generated words and image features are "environment". The parameters θ define the policy p_θ and at each step the model chooses an "action", which is the prediction of the next word based on the policy and the environment. Denote $C^s = \{w_1^s, \ldots, w_T^s\}$ as the caption sampled from the predicted word distribution. Each sampled sentence receives a "reward" $r(C^s)$, which indicates its quality. Mathematically, the goal of training is to minimize the negative expected reward of the sampled captions,

$$L_{RL}(\theta) = -\mathbb{E}_{C^s \sim p_\theta}[r(C^s)]. \tag{5}$$

Since calculating the expectation of reward over the policy distribution is intractable, we estimate it by Monte Carlo sampling based on the policy p_θ. To avoid differentiating $r(C^s)$ with respect to θ, we calculate the gradient of the expected reward by REINFORCE algorithm [45],

$$\nabla_\theta L_{RL}(\theta) = -\mathbb{E}_{C^s \sim p_\theta}[r(C^s)\nabla_\theta \log p_\theta(C^s)]. \tag{6}$$

To reduce the variance of the gradient estimation, we subtract the reward with a baseline b, without changing the expected gradient [37]. b is chosen as the reward of greedy decoding captions [35].

$$\nabla_\theta L_{RL}(\theta) = -\mathbb{E}_{C^s \sim p_\theta}[(r(C^s) - b)\nabla_\theta \log p_\theta(C^s)]. \tag{7}$$

For calculation simplicity, the expectation is approximated by a single Monte-Carlo sample from p_θ,

$$\nabla_\theta L_{RL}(\theta) \approx -(r(C^s) - b)\nabla_\theta \log p_\theta(C^s). \tag{8}$$

In our model, for each sampled caption C_i^s, we formulate the reward as a weighted summation of its CIDEr score and the self-retrieval reward, which is the negative caption-to-image retrieval loss.

$$r(C_i^s) = r_{cider}(C_i^s) + \alpha \cdot r_{ret}(C_i^s, \{I_1, \ldots, I_n\}), \tag{9}$$

where $r_{cider}(C_i^s)$ denotes the CIDEr score of C_i^s, $r_{ret} = -L_{ret}$ is the self-retrieval reward, and α is the weight to balance the rewards. The CIDEr reward ensures that the generated captions are similar to the annotations, and the self-retrieval reward encourages the captions to be discriminative. By introducing this reward function, we can optimize the sentence-level reward through sampled captions.

3.2   Improving Captioning with Partially Labeled Images

Training with Partially Labeled Data. The self-retrieval module compares a generated caption with its corresponding image and other distractor images in the mini-batch. As the caption-image correspondence is incorporated naturally in caption generation, *i.e.*, a caption with the image it is generated from automatically form a positive caption-image pair, and with other images form negative pairs, our proposed self-retrieval reward does not require ground-truth captions. So our framework can generalize to semi-supervised setting, where a portion of images do not have ground-truth captions. Thus more training data can be involved in training without extra annotations.

We mix labeled data and unlabeled data with a fixed proportion in each mini-batch. Denote the labeled images in a mini-batch as $\{I_1^l, I_2^l, \ldots, I_{n_l}^l\}$, and their generated captions as $\{C_1^l, C_2^l, \ldots, C_{n_l}^l\}$. Denote unlabeled images in the same mini-batch as $\{I_1^u, I_2^u, \ldots, I_{n_u}^u\}$ and the corresponding generated captions as $\{C_1^u, C_2^u, \ldots, C_{n_u}^u\}$. The reward for labeled data is the composed of the CIDEr reward and self-retrieval reward computed in the mini-batch for each generated caption,

$$r(C_i^l) = r_{cider}(C_i^l) + \alpha \cdot r_{ret}(C_i^l, \{I_1^l, \ldots, I_{n_l}^l\} \cup \{I_1^u, \ldots, I_{n_u}^u\}). \tag{10}$$

The retrieval reward r_{ret} compares the similarity between a caption and the corresponding image, with those of all other labeled and unlabeled images in the mini-batch, to reflect how well the generated caption can discriminate its corresponding image from other distractor images.

As CIDEr reward cannot be computed without ground-truth captions, the reward for unlabeled data is only the retrieval reward computed in the mini-batch,

$$r(C_i^u) = \alpha \cdot r_{ret}(C_i^u, \{I_1^l, \ldots, I_{n_l}^l\} \cup \{I_1^u, \ldots, I_{n_u}^u\}). \tag{11}$$

In this way, the unlabeled data could also be used in training without captioning annotations, to further boost the captioning performance.

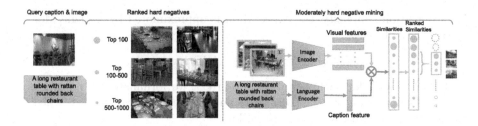

Fig. 3. Moderately hard negative mining. The left part shows a ground-truth caption and its top hard negatives mined from unlabeled images. The right part shows the process of moderately hard negative mining. The circles of different sizes stand for the similarities between each image and the query caption.

Moderately Hard Negative Mining in Unlabeled Images. As described before, the self-retrieval reward is calculated based on the similarity between positive (corresponding) caption-image pairs and negative (non-corresponding) pairs. The training goal is to maximize the similarities of positive pairs and minimize those of negative pairs. To further encourage discriminative captions, we introduce hard negative caption-image pairs in each mini-batch. For example, in Fig. 1, although the first two images are similar, humans are not likely to describe them in the same way. We would like to encourage captions that can distinguish the second image from the first one (*e.g.*, "Creative centerpiece floral arrangement at an outdoor table"), instead of a generic description (*e.g.*, "A vase sitting on a table").

However, an important observation is that choosing the hardest negatives may impede training. This is because images and captions do not always follow strictly one-to-one mapping. In the left part of Fig. 3, we show a ground-truth caption and its hard negatives mined from unlabeled images. The top negative images from the unlabeled dataset often match well with the ground-truth captions from the labeled dataset. For example, when the query caption is "A long restaurant table with rattan rounded back chairs", some of the retrieved top images can also match the caption well. So directly taking the hardest negative pairs is not optimal. Therefore, we propose to use *moderately hard negatives* of the generated captions instead of the hardest negatives.

We show moderately hard negative mining in the right part of Fig. 3. We encode a ground-truth caption C^* from the labeled dataset into features c^* and all unlabeled images $\{I_1^u, \ldots, I_{n_u}^u\}$ into features $\{v_1^u, \ldots, v_{n_u}^u\}$. The similarities $\{s(c^*, v_1^u), \ldots, s(c^*, v_{n_u}^u)\}$ between the caption and each unlabeled image are derived by the retrieval model. Then we rank the unlabeled images by the similarities between each image and the query caption C^* in a descending order. Then the indexes of moderately hard negatives are randomly sampled from a given range $[h_{min}, h_{max}]$. The sampled hard negatives from unlabeled images and the captions' corresponding images from the labeled dataset together form a mini-batch.

By moderately hard negative mining, we select proper samples for training, encouraging the captioning model to generate captions that could discriminate the corresponding image from other distractor images.

3.3 Training Strategy

We first train the text-to-image self-retrieval module with all training images and corresponding captions in the labeled dataset. The captioning module shares the image encoder with the self-retrieval module. When training the captioning module, the retrieval module and CNN image encoder are fixed.

For captioning module, we first pre-train it with cross-entropy loss, to provide a stable initial point, and reduce the sample space for reinforcement learning. The captioning module is then trained by REINFORCE algorithm with CIDEr reward and self-retrieval reward with either fully labeled data or partially labeled data. The CIDEr reward guarantees the generated captions to be similar to ground-truth captions, while the self-retrieval reward encourages the generated captions to be discriminative. For labeled data, the reward is the weighted sum of CIDEr reward and self-retrieval reward (Eq. (10)), and for unlabeled data, the reward is only the self-retrieval reward (Eq. (11)). The unlabeled data in each mini-batch is chosen by moderately hard negative mining from unlabeled data. Implementation details can be found in Sect. 4.2.

4 Experiments

4.1 Datasets and Evaluation Criteria

We perform experiments on COCO and Flickr30k captioning datasets. For fair comparison, we adopt the widely used Karpathy split [17] for COCO dataset, which uses 5,000 images for validation, 5,000 for testing, and the rest 82,783 for training. For data preprocessing, we first convert all characters into lower case and remove the punctuations. Then we replace words that occur less than 6 times with an 'UNK' token. The captions are truncated to be no more than 16 words during training. When training with partially labeled data, we use the officially released COCO unlabeled images as additional data without annotations. The widely used BLEU [30], METEOR [10], ROUGE-L [23], CIDEr-D [39] and SPICE [1] scores are adopted for evaluation.

4.2 Implementation Details

Self-retrieval Module. For the self-retrieval module, each word is embedded into a 300-dimensional vector and inputted to the GRU language encoder, which encodes a sentence into 1024-dimensional features. The image encoder is a ResNet-101 model, which encodes an image into 2048-dimensional visual features. Both the encoded image features and sentence features are projected to the joint embedding space of dimension 1024. The similarity between image features and sentence features is the inner product between the normalized feature vectors. We follow the training strategy in [12].

Captioning Module. The captioning module shares the same image encoder with the self-retrieval module. The self-retrieval module and image encoder are fixed when training the captioning module. We take the $2048 \times 7 \times 7$ features before the average pooling layer from ResNet-101 as the visual features. For the language decoder, we adopt a topdown attention LSTM and a language LSTM, following the Top-Down attention model in [2]. We do not use Up-Down model in the same paper, because it involves an object detection model and requires external data and annotations from Visual Genome [19] for training.

The captioning module is trained with Adam [18] optimizer. The model is first pre-trained by cross-entropy loss, and then trained by REINFORCE. Restart technique [25] is used improve the model convergence. We use scheduled sampling [3] and increase the probability of feeding back a sample of the word posterior by 0.05 every 5 epochs, until the feedback probability reaches 0.25. We set the weight of self-retrieval reward α to 1. For training with partially labeled data, the proportion of labeled and unlabeled images in a mini-batch is 1:1.

Inference. For inference, we use beam search with beam size 5 to generate captions. Specifically, we select the top 5 sentences with the highest probability at each time step, and consider them as the candidates based on which to generate the next word. We do not use model ensemble in our experiments.

4.3   Results

Quantitative results. We compare our captioning model performance with existing methods on COCO and Flickr30k datasets in Tables 1 and 2. The models are all pre-trained by cross-entropy loss and then trained with REINFORCE algorithm. The baseline model is the captioning module only trained with only CIDEr reward. The SR-FL model is our proposed framework trained with fully labeled data, with both CIDEr and self-retrieval rewards. The SR-PL model is our framework trained with partially labeled data (all labeled data and additional unlabeled data), with both rewards for labeled images and only self-retrieval reward for unlabeled images. It is shown from the results that the baseline model without self-retrieval module is already a strong baseline. Incorporating the self-retrieval module with fully-labeled data (SR-FL) improves most metrics by large margins. Training with additional unlabeled data (SR-PL) further enhances the performance. The results validate that discriminativeness is crucial to caption quality, and enforcing this constraint by self-retrieval module leads to better captions.

Qualitative Results. Figure 4 shows some examples of our generated captions and ground-truth captions. Both the baseline model and our model with self-retrieval reward can generate captions relevant to the images. However, it is easy to observe that our model can generate more discriminative captions, while the baseline model generates generic and templated captions. For example, the first and the second images in the first row share slightly different contents. The baseline model fails to describe their differences and generates identical captions "A vase with flowers sitting on a table". But our model captures the

Table 1. Single-model performance by our proposed method and state-of-the-art methods on COCO standard Karpathy test split.

Methods	CIDEr	SPICE	BLEU-1	BLEU-2	BLEU-3	BLEU-4	METEOR	ROUGE-L
Hard-attention [47]	-	-	71.8	50.4	35.7	25.0	23.0	-
Soft-attention [47]	-	-	70.7	49.2	34.4	24.3	23.9	-
VAE [32]	90.0	-	72.0	52.0	37.0	28.0	24.0	-
ATT-FCN [50]	-	-	70.9	53.7	40.2	30.4	24.3	-
Att-CNN+RNN [46]	94.0	-	74.0	56.0	42.0	31.0	26.0	-
SCN-LSTM [14]	101.2	-	72.8	56.6	43.3	33.0	25.7	-
Adaptive [26]	108.5	-	74.2	58.0	43.9	33.2	26.6	-
SCA-CNN [5]	95.2	-	71.9	54.8	41.1	31.1	25.0	53.1
SCST-Att2all [35]	114.0	-	-	-	-	34.2	26.7	55.7
LSTM-A [49]	100.2	18.6	73.4	56.7	43.0	32.6	25.4	54.0
DRL [34]	93.7	-	71.3	53.9	40.3	30.4	25.1	52.5
Skeleton Key [43]	106.9	-	74.2	57.7	44.0	33.6	26.8	55.2
CNNL+RHN [16]	98.9	-	72.3	55.3	41.3	30.6	25.2	-
TD-M-ATT [4]	111.6	-	76.5	60.3	45.6	34.0	26.3	55.5
ATTN+C+D(1) [27]	114.25	**21.05**	-	-	-	**36.14**	27.38	**57.29**
Ours-baseline	112.7	20.0	79.7	62.2	47.1	35.0	26.7	56.4
Ours-SR-FL	114.6	20.5	79.8	62.3	47.1	34.9	27.1	56.6
Ours-SR-PL	**117.1**	21.0	**80.1**	**63.1**	**48.0**	35.8	**27.4**	57.0

Table 2. Single-model performance by our proposed method and state-of-the-art methods on Flickr30k.

Methods	CIDEr	SPICE	BLEU-1	BLEU-2	BLEU-3	BLEU-4	METEOR	ROUGE-L
Hard-attention [47]	-	-	66.9	43.9	29.6	19.9	18.5	-
Soft-attention [47]	-	-	66.7	43.4	28.8	19.1	18.5	-
VAE [32]	-	-	72.0	53.0	38.0	25.0	-	-
ATT-FCN [50]	-	-	64.7	46.0	32.4	23.0	18.9	-
Att-CNN+RNN [46]	-	-	73.0	55.0	40.0	28.0	-	-
SCN-LSTM [14]	-	-	73.5	53.0	37.7	25.7	21.0	-
Adaptive [26]	53.1	-	67.7	49.4	35.4	25.1	20.4	-
SCA-CNN [5]	-	-	66.2	46.8	32.5	22.3	19.5	-
CNNL+RHN [16]	61.8	15.0	**73.8**	**56.3**	**41.9**	**30.7**	21.6	-
Ours-baseline	57.1	14.2	72.8	53.4	38.0	27.1	20.7	48.5
Ours-SR-FL	61.7	15.3	72.0	53.4	38.5	27.8	21.5	49.4
Ours-SR-PL	**65.0**	**15.8**	72.9	54.5	40.1	29.3	**21.8**	**49.9**

distinction, and expresses with sufficient descriptive details "red flowers", "white vase" and "in a garden" that help to distinguish those images. The captions for the last images in both rows show that the baseline model falls into a stereotype and generates templated captions, because of a large number of similar phrases in the training set. However, captions generated by our model alleviates this problem, and generates accurate descriptions for the images.

Fig. 4. Qualitative results by baseline model and our proposed model.

Table 3. Ablation study results on COCO.

Experiment settings		CIDEr	SPICE	BLEU-3	BLEU-4	METEOR	ROUGE-L
Baseline		112.7	20.0	47.1	35.0	26.7	56.4
Retrieval loss	VSE++	**117.1**	**21.0**	**48.0**	**35.8**	**27.4**	**57.0**
	VSE0	116.9	20.9	47.7	35.7	**27.4**	56.8
	Softmax	114.5	20.5	46.8	34.6	27.1	56.5
Weight of self-retrieval reward α	0	112.7	20.0	47.1	35.0	26.7	56.4
	1	**117.1**	**21.0**	**48.0**	**35.8**	**27.4**	**57.0**
	4	113.7	20.5	46.5	34.3	27.0	56.5
Ratio between labeled and unlabeled	1:2	115.4	20.5	46.8	34.7	27.2	56.6
	1:1	**117.1**	**21.0**	**48.0**	**35.8**	**27.4**	**57.0**
	2:1	115.0	20.5	46.8	34.7	27.2	56.7
Hard negative index range	No hard mining	114.6	20.7	46.7	34.6	27.3	56.7
	Top 100	114.1	20.3	46.6	34.5	27.0	56.4
	Top 100–1000	**117.1**	**21.0**	**48.0**	**35.8**	**27.4**	**57.0**

4.4 Ablation Study

Formulation of Self-retrieval Loss. As described in Sect. 3.1, the self-retrieval module requires a self-retrieval loss to measure the discriminativeness of the generated captions. Besides *VSE++* loss (Eq. (4)), we explore triplet ranking loss without hard negatives, denoted by *VSE0*,

$$L_{ret}(C_i, \{I_1, I_2, \ldots, I_n\}) = \sum_{j \neq i} [m - s(c_i, v_i) + s(c_i, v_j)]_+, \qquad (12)$$

and softmax classification loss, denoted by *softmax*,

$$L_{ret}(C_i, \{I_1, I_2, \ldots, I_n\}) = -\log \frac{\exp\left(s(c_i, v_i)/T\right)}{\sum_{j=1}^{n} \exp\left(s(c_i, v_j)/T\right)}, \qquad (13)$$

where T is the temperature parameter that normalizes the caption-image similarity to a proper range. We show the results trained by the three loss formulations in Table 3.[1] All of those loss formulations lead to better performance compared to the baseline model, demonstrating the effectiveness of our proposed self-retrieval module. Among them, $vse++$ loss performs slightly better, which is consistent with the conclusion in [12] that $vse++$ loss leads to better visual-semantic embeddings.

Balance Between Self-retrieval Reward and CIDEr Reward. During training by REINFORCE algorithm, the total reward is formulated as the weighted summation of CIDEr reward and self-retrieval reward, as shown in Eq. (10). To determine how much each of them should contribute to training, we investigate how the weight between them should be set. As shown in Table 3, we investigate $\{0, 1, 4\}$ for the weight of self-retrieval reward α, and the results indicate that $\alpha = 1$ leads to the best performance. Too much emphasis on self-retrieval reward will harm the model performance, because it fails to optimize the evaluation metric CIDEr. This shows that both CIDEr and our proposed self-retrieval reward are crucial and their contributions need to be balanced properly.

Proportion of Labeled and Unlabeled Data. When training with partially labeled data, we use a fixed proportion between labeled and unlabeled images. We experiment on the proportion of forming a mini-batch with labeled and unlabeled data. We try three proportions, 1:2, 1:1 and 2:1, with the same self-retrieval reward weight $\alpha = 1$. The results in Table 3 show that the proportion of 1:1 leads to the best performance.

Moderately Hard Negative Mining. In Sect. 3.2, we introduce how to mine semantically similar images from unlabeled data to provide moderately hard negatives for training. We analyze the contribution of moderately hard negative mining in Table 3. Firstly, the performance gain is relatively low without hard negative mining, demonstrating the effectiveness of this operation. Secondly, after ranking unlabeled images based on the similarity between the given ground-truth caption and unlabeled images in the descending order, the index range $[h_{min}, h_{max}]$ of selecting hard negatives also impacts results. There are cases that an unlabeled image is very similar to an image in the training set, and a caption may naturally correspond to several images. Therefore, selecting the hardest negatives is very likely to confuse the model. In our experiments, we found that setting the hard negative index range $[h_{min}, h_{max}]$ to $[100, 1000]$ for the ranked unlabeled images is optimal.

4.5 Discriminativeness of Generated Captions

Retrieval Performance by Generated Captions. Since the self-retrieval module encourages discriminative captions, we conduct an experiment to retrieve images with the generated captions as queries, to validate that captions generated by our model are indeed more discriminative than those generated by the model without self-retrieval module. Different from the self-retrieval study in [9],

---

[1] For the reported results in all experiments and ablation study, we tuned hyperparameters on the validation set and directly used validations best point to report results on the test set.

Table 4. Text-to-image retrieval performance, and uniqueness and novelty of generated captions by different methods on COCO.

Methods	Generated-caption-to-image retrieval			Uniqueness and novelty evaluation	
	recall@1	recall@5	recall@10	Unique captions	Novel captions
Skeleton key [43]	-	–	-	66.96%	52.24%
Ours-baseline	27.5	59.3	74.0	61.56%	51.38%
Ours-SR-PL	**33.0**	**66.4**	**80.1**	**72.34%**	**61.52%**

which uses the conditional probabilities of generated captions given images to obtain a ranked list of images, we perform self-retrieval by our self-retrieval module. More precisely, we rank the images based on the similarities between the images and a generated query sentence calculated by our retrieval module. We compute the recall of the corresponding image that appears in the top-k ranked images. The retrieval performance is an indicator of the discriminativeness of generated captions. In Table 4, we report retrieval results on COCO Karpathy test split. It can be clearly seen that the our model improves the retrieval performance by a large margin.

Uniqueness and Novelty Evaluation. A common problem for captioning models is that they have limited ability of generating captions that have not been seen in the training set, and generates identical sentences for similar images [11]. This demonstrates that the language decoder is simply repeating the sequence patterns it observed in the training set. Although our approach is not directly designed to improve diversity or encourage novel captions, we argue that by encouraging discriminative captions, we can improve the model's ability to generate unique and novel captions. Following the measurements in [43], we evaluate the percentage of unique captions (captions that are unique in all generated captions) and novel captions (captions that have not been seen in training) on COCO Karpathy test split. It is shown in Table 4 that our framework significantly improves uniqueness and novelty of the generated captions.

5   Conclusions

In this work, we address the problem that captions generated by conventional approaches tend to be templated and generic. We present a framework that explicitly improves discriminativeness of captions via training with self-retrieval reward. The framework is composed of a captioning module and a novel self-retrieval module, which boosts discriminativeness of generated captions. The self-retrieval reward is back-propagated to the captioning module by REINFORCE algorithm. Results show that we obtain more discriminative captions by this framework, and achieve state-of-the-art performance on two widely used image captioning datasets.

Acknowledgement. This work is supported by SenseTime Group Limited, the General Research Fund sponsored by the Research Grants Council of Hong Kong (Nos. CUHK14213616, CUHK14206114, CUHK14205615, CUHK14203015, CUHK14239816,

CUHK419412, CUHK14207814, CUHK14208417, CUHK14202217), the Hong Kong Innovation and Technology Support Program (No.ITS/121/15FX).

References

1. Anderson, P., Fernando, B., Johnson, M., Gould, S.: SPICE: semantic propositional image caption evaluation. In: Leibe, B., Matas, J., Sebe, N., Welling, M. (eds.) ECCV 2016. LNCS, vol. 9909, pp. 382–398. Springer, Cham (2016). https://doi.org/10.1007/978-3-319-46454-1_24

2. Anderson, P., et al.: Bottom-up and top-down attention for image captioning and VQA (2017). arXiv:1707.07998

3. Bengio, S., Vinyals, O., Jaitly, N., Shazeer, N.: Scheduled sampling for sequence prediction with recurrent neural networks. In: Advances in Neural Information Processing Systems, pp. 1171–1179 (2015)

4. Chen, H., Ding, G., Zhao, S., Han, J.: Temporal-difference learning with sampling baseline for image captioning (2017)

5. Chen, L., Zhang, H., Xiao, J., Nie, L., Shao, J., Liu, W., Chua, T.S.: Sca-cnn: spatial and channel-wise attention in convolutional networks for image captioning. In: Proceedings of the IEEE Conference on Computer Vision and Pattern Recognition, pp. 5659–5667 (2017)

6. Chen, X., et al.: Microsoft coco captions: data collection and evaluation server (2015). arXiv:1504.00325

7. Chen, X., Lawrence Zitnick, C.: Mind's eye: a recurrent visual representation for image caption generation. In: Proceedings of the IEEE Conference on Computer Vision and Pattern Recognition, pp. 2422–2431 (2015)

8. Dai, B., Fidler, S., Urtasun, R., Lin, D.: Towards diverse and natural image descriptions via a conditional gan. In: Proceedings of the IEEE Conference on Computer Vision and Pattern Recognition, pp. 2970–2979 (2017)

9. Dai, B., Lin, D.: Contrastive learning for image captioning. In: Advances in Neural Information Processing Systems, pp. 898–907 (2017)

10. Denkowski, M., Lavie, A.: Meteor universal: language specific translation evaluation for any target language. In: Proceedings of the Ninth Workshop on Statistical Machine Translation, pp. 376–380 (2014)

11. Devlin, J., Cheng, H., Fang, H., Gupta, S., Deng, L., He, X., Zweig, G., Mitchell, M.: Language models for image captioning: the quirks and what works (2015). arXiv:1505.01809

12. Faghri, F., Fleet, D.J., Kiros, J.R., Fidler, S.: VSE++: improved visual-semantic embeddings (2017). arXiv:1707.05612

13. Farhadi, A., Hejrati, M., Sadeghi, M.A., Young, P., Rashtchian, C., Hockenmaier, J., Forsyth, D.: Every picture tells a story: generating sentences from images. In: Daniilidis, K., Maragos, P., Paragios, N. (eds.) ECCV 2010. LNCS, vol. 6314, pp. 15–29. Springer, Heidelberg (2010). https://doi.org/10.1007/978-3-642-15561-1_2

14. Gan, Z., Gan, C., He, X., Pu, Y., Tran, K., Gao, J., Carin, L., Deng, L.: Semantic compositional networks for visual captioning. In: Proceedings of the IEEE Conference on Computer Vision and Pattern Recognition, vol. 2 (2017)

15. Gu, J., Cai, J., Wang, G., Chen, T.: Stack-captioning: coarse-to-fine learning for image captioning (2017). arXiv:1709.03376

16. Gu, J., Wang, G., Cai, J., Chen, T.: An empirical study of language cnn for image captioning. In: Proceedings of the International Conference on Computer Vision (ICCV) (2017)

17. Karpathy, A., Fei-Fei, L.: Deep visual-semantic alignments for generating image descriptions. In: Proceedings of the IEEE Conference on Computer Vision and Pattern Recognition, pp. 3128–3137 (2015)
18. Kingma, D.P., Ba, J.: Adam: a method for stochastic optimization (2014). arXiv:1412.6980
19. Krishna, R., Zhu, Y., Groth, O., Johnson, J., Hata, K., Kravitz, J., Chen, S., Kalantidis, Y., Li, L.J., Shamma, D.A.: Visual genome: connecting language and vision using crowdsourced dense image annotations. Int. J. Comput. Vis. **123**(1), 32–73 (2017)
20. Krishna, R., Zhu, Y., Groth, O., Johnson, J., Hata, K., Kravitz, J., Chen, S., Kalantidis, Y., Li, L.J., Shamma, D.A.: Visual genome: connecting language and vision using crowdsourced dense image annotations. Int. J. Comput. Vis. **123**(1), 32–73 (2017)
21. Li, Y., Ouyang, W., Zhou, B., Cui, Y., Shi, J., Wang, X.: Factorizable net: an efficient subgraph-based framework for scene graph generation (2018)
22. Li, Y., Ouyang, W., Zhou, B., Wang, K., Wang, X.: Scene graph generation from objects, phrases and region captions. In: ICCV (2017)
23. Lin, C.Y.: Rouge: a package for automatic evaluation of summaries. In: Text Summarization Branches Out (2004)
24. Liu, S., Zhu, Z., Ye, N., Guadarrama, S., Murphy, K.: Improved image captioning via policy gradient optimization of spider. In: Proceedings of the IEEE Conference on Computer Vision and Pattern Recognition, pp. 873–881 (2017)
25. Loshchilov, I., Hutter, F.: Sgdr: Stochastic gradient descent with warm restarts (2016). arXiv:1608.03983
26. Lu, J., Xiong, C., Parikh, D., Socher, R.: Knowing when to look: Adaptive attention via a visual sentinel for image captioning. In: Proceedings of the IEEE Conference on Computer Vision and Pattern Recognition (CVPR), vol. 6 (2017)
27. Luo, R., Price, B., Cohen, S., Shakhnarovich, G.: Discriminability objective for training descriptive captions. In: Proceedings of the IEEE Conference on Computer Vision and Pattern Recognition, pp. 6964–6974 (2018)
28. Mao, J., Xu, W., Yang, Y., Wang, J., Huang, Z., Yuille, A.: Deep captioning with multimodal recurrent neural networks (m-rnn) (2014). arXiv:1412.6632
29. Mitchell, M., Han, X., Dodge, J., Mensch, A., Goyal, A., Berg, A., Yamaguchi, K., Berg, T., Stratos, K., Daumé III, H.: Midge: Generating image descriptions from computer vision detections. In: Proceedings of the 13th Conference of the European Chapter of the Association for Computational Linguistics, pp. 747–756. Association for Computational Linguistics (2012)
30. Papineni, K., Roukos, S., Ward, T., Zhu, W.J.: Bleu: a method for automatic evaluation of machine translation. In: Proceedings of the 40th Annual Meeting on Association for Computational Linguistics, pp. 311–318. Association for Computational Linguistics (2002)
31. Pedersoli, M., Lucas, T., Schmid, C., Verbeek, J.: Areas of attention for image captioning. In: ICCV-International Conference on Computer Vision (2017)
32. Pu, Y., Gan, Z., Henao, R., Yuan, X., Li, C., Stevens, A., Carin, L.: Variational autoencoder for deep learning of images, labels and captions. In: Advances in neural Information Processing Systems, pp. 2352–2360 (2016)
33. Ranzato, M., Chopra, S., Auli, M., Zaremba, W.: Sequence level training with recurrent neural networks (2015). arXiv:1511.06732
34. Ren, Z., Wang, X., Zhang, N., Lv, X., Li, L.J.: Deep reinforcement learning-based image captioning with embedding reward. In: 2017 IEEE Conference on Computer Vision and Pattern Recognition (CVPR), pp. 1151–1159. IEEE (2017)

35. Rennie, S.J., Marcheret, E., Mroueh, Y., Ross, J., Goel, V.: Self-critical sequence training for image captioning. In: Proceedings of the IEEE Conference on Computer Vision and Pattern Recognition, pp. 7008–7024 (2017)
36. Shetty, R., Rohrbach, M., Hendricks, L.A., Fritz, M., Schiele, B.: Speaking the same language: Matching machine to human captions by adversarial training. In: Proceedings of the IEEE International Conference on Computer Vision (ICCV) (2017)
37. Sutton, R.S., Barto, A.G.: Reinforcement Learning: An Introduction, vol. 1. MIT Press, Cambridge (1998)
38. Vedantam, R., Bengio, S., Murphy, K., Parikh, D., Chechik, G.: Context-aware captions from context-agnostic supervision. In: Computer Vision and Pattern Recognition (CVPR), vol. 3 (2017)
39. Vedantam, R., Lawrence Zitnick, C., Parikh, D.: Cider: Consensus-based image description evaluation. In: Proceedings of the IEEE Conference on Computer Vision and Pattern Recognition, pp. 4566–4575 (2015)
40. Vijayakumar, A.K., Cogswell, M., Selvaraju, R.R., Sun, Q., Lee, S., Crandall, D., Batra, D.: Diverse beam search: decoding diverse solutions from neural sequence models (2016). arXiv:1610.02424
41. Vinyals, O., Toshev, A., Bengio, S., Erhan, D.: Show and tell: a neural image caption generator. In: 2015 IEEE Conference on Computer Vision and Pattern Recognition (CVPR), pp. 3156–3164. IEEE (2015)
42. Wang, L., Schwing, A., Lazebnik, S.: Diverse and accurate image description using a variational auto-encoder with an additive gaussian encoding space. In: Advances in Neural Information Processing Systems, pp. 5758–5768 (2017)
43. Wang, Y., Lin, Z., Shen, X., Cohen, S., Cottrell, G.W.: Skeleton key: image captioning by skeleton-attribute decomposition. In: Proceedings of the IEEE Conference on Computer Vision and Pattern Recognition, pp. 7272–7281 (2017)
44. Wang, Z., Wu, F., Lu, W., Xiao, J., Li, X., Zhang, Z., Zhuang, Y.: Diverse image captioning via grouptalk. In: IJCAI, pp. 2957–2964 (2016)
45. Williams, R.J.: Simple statistical gradient-following algorithms for connectionist reinforcement learning. Mach. Learn. 8(3–4), 229–256 (1992)
46. Wu, Q., Shen, C., Liu, L., Dick, A., van den Hengel, A.: What value do explicit high level concepts have in vision to language problems? In: Proceedings of the IEEE Conference on Computer Vision and Pattern Recognition, pp. 203–212 (2016)
47. Xu, K., Ba, J., Kiros, R., Cho, K., Courville, A., Salakhudinov, R., Zemel, R., Bengio, Y.: Show, attend and tell: Neural image caption generation with visual attention. In: International Conference on Machine Learning, pp. 2048–2057 (2015)
48. Yang, Y., Teo, C.L., Daumé III, H., Aloimonos, Y.: Corpus-guided sentence generation of natural images. In: Proceedings of the Conference on Empirical Methods in Natural Language Processing, pp. 444–454. Association for Computational Linguistics (2011)
49. Yao, T., Pan, Y., Li, Y., Qiu, Z., Mei, T.: Boosting image captioning with attributes. In: Proceedings of the IEEE Conference on Computer Vision and Pattern Recognition, pp. 4894–4902 (2017)
50. You, Q., Jin, H., Wang, Z., Fang, C., Luo, J.: Image captioning with semantic attention. In: Proceedings of the IEEE Conference on Computer Vision and Pattern Recognition, pp. 4651–4659 (2016)
51. Young, P., Lai, A., Hodosh, M., Hockenmaier, J.: From image descriptions to visual denotations: new similarity metrics for semantic inference over event descriptions. Trans. Assoc. Comput. Linguist. 2, 67–78 (2014)

Contour Knowledge Transfer for Salient Object Detection

Xin Li[1], Fan Yang[1(✉)], Hong Cheng[1], Wei Liu[1], and Dinggang Shen[2]

[1] University of Electronic Science and Technology of China, Chengdu 611731, China
xinli_uestc@hotmail.com, fanyang_uestc@hotmail.com, hcheng@uestc.edu.cn
[2] Department of Radiology and BRIC, University of North Carolina at Chapel Hill,
Chapel Hill, NC 27599, USA
dgshen@med.unc.edu

Abstract. In recent years, deep Convolutional Neural Networks (CNNs) have broken all records in salient object detection. However, training such a deep model requires a large amount of manual annotations. Our goal is to overcome this limitation by automatically converting an existing deep contour detection model into a salient object detection model without using any manual salient object masks. For this purpose, we have created a deep network architecture, namely Contour-to-Saliency Network (C2S-Net), by grafting a new branch onto a well-trained contour detection network. Therefore, our C2S-Net has two branches for performing two different tasks: (1) predicting contours with the original contour branch, and (2) estimating per-pixel saliency score of each image with the newly-added saliency branch. To bridge the gap between these two tasks, we further propose a contour-to-saliency transferring method to automatically generate salient object masks which can be used to train the saliency branch from outputs of the contour branch. Finally, we introduce a novel alternating training pipeline to gradually update the network parameters. In this scheme, the contour branch generates saliency masks for training the saliency branch, while the saliency branch, in turn, feeds back saliency knowledge in the form of saliency-aware contour labels, for fine-tuning the contour branch. The proposed method achieves state-of-the-art performance on five well-known benchmarks, outperforming existing fully supervised methods while also maintaining high efficiency.

Keywords: Saliency detection · Deep learning · Transfer learning

1 Introduction

Salient object detection, which aims at locating the most visually conspicuous object(s) in natural images, is critically important to computer vision. It can be used in a variety of tasks such as human pose estimation [5], semantic segmentation [11], image/video captioning [24], and dense semantic correspondences [33].

Both authors contribute equally to this work. Code and pre-trained models are available at https://github.com/lixin666/C2SNet.

© Springer Nature Switzerland AG 2018
V. Ferrari et al. (Eds.): ECCV 2018, LNCS 11219, pp. 370–385, 2018.
https://doi.org/10.1007/978-3-030-01267-0_22

Over the past decades, the techniques of salient object detection have evolved dramatically. Traditional methods [3,4,19] only use low-level features and cues for identifying salient regions in an image, leading to their inability to summarize high-level semantic knowledge. Therefore, these methods are unsuitable for handling images with complex scenes. Recently, fully-supervised approaches [8,9,20,23] based on deep Convolutional Neural Networks (CNNs) have greatly improved the performance of salient object detection. The success of these methods depends mostly on a huge number of training images containing manually annotated salient objects. Unfortunately, in salient object detection, annotations are provided in the form of pixel-wise masks. Annotating a large-scale training dataset requires tremendous cost and effort.

To eliminate the need for time-consuming image annotation, we propose to facilitate feature learning in salient object detection by borrowing knowledge from an existing contour detection model. Although salient object detection and contour extraction seem inherently different, they are actually related to each other. On one hand, contours provide useful priors or cues for identifying salient regions in an image. For example, salient regions are often surrounded by contours. On the other hand, saliency knowledge helps remove background clutter, and thus improves contour detection results. Therefore, it is reasonable to transfer knowledge between these two involved domains [15–17].

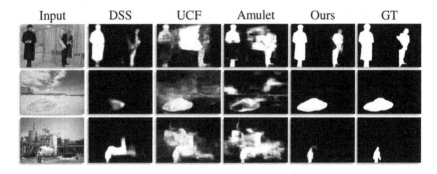

Fig. 1. Saliency maps produced by currently best deep saliency models (DSS [8], UCF [37], and Amulet [36]) and ours. Different from these fully supervised methods, our method requires *no groundtruth salient object mask* for training deep CNNs.

Our goal is to convert a trained contour detection model (CEDN) [34] into a saliency detection model *without* using any manually labeled salient object masks. With this goal, we first graft a new branch onto the existing CEDN to form a multi-task network architecture, i.e., Contour-to-Saliency Network (C2S-Net). Then, we employ the well-trained contour branch to generate contour maps for all images and use a novel contour-to-saliency transferring method to produce the corresponding saliency masks. The newly-added branch is trained under the strong supervision of these automatically generated saliency masks.

After that, the trained branch in turn transfers the learned saliency knowledge, in the form of saliency-aware contour labels, to the contour branch. In this way, the original contour branch learns to detect the contours of only the most attention-grabbing object(s). The interaction between the original branch and newly-added branch is iterated in order to increase accuracy. Although the generated salient object masks and saliency-aware contour labels may contain errors in the beginning, they gradually become more reliable after several iterations. More importantly, the well-trained CEDN undergoes essential changes through the alternating training procedure between the two branches (i.e., Contour-to-Saliency procedure and Saliency-to-Contour procedure), becoming a powerful saliency detection model, where one branch focuses on salient object contour detection and the other branch predicts saliency score of each pixel.

Despite not using manually annotated salient object labels for training, our proposed method is capable of generating a reliable saliency map for each input (See Fig. 1). The experiments show that our proposed method yields higher accuracy than the existing fully-supervised deep models. Furthermore, it takes only 0.03 s to perform each image, which is much faster than most existing methods.

In summary, this paper makes the following three major contributions:

- We present a new idea and solution for salient object detection by automatically converting a well-trained contour detection model into a saliency detection model, *without* requiring any groudtruth salient object labels.
- We propose a novel Contour-to-Saliency Network (C2S-Net) based on the well-trained contour detection network. In this architecture, the same feature encoder is used by both the original contour branch and the newly-added saliency branch. We also introduce cross-domain connections to enable the saliency branch to fully encode contour knowledge during the learning process.
- We introduce a simple yet effective contour-to-saliency transferring method to bridge the gap between contours and salient object regions. Therefore, the results generated by the well-trained contour branch can be used to generate reliable saliency masks for training the saliency branch. In addition, we propose a novel alternating training pipeline to update the network parameters of our C2S-Net.

2   Related Work

Salient object detection has evolved quickly over the past two decades. Earlier methods [3,4,19] rely on low-level features and cues such as intensity, color, and texture. Although these methods can produce accurate saliency maps in most simple cases, they are unable to deal with complex images due to the lack of semantic knowledge.

In recent years, fully-supervised CNNs have demonstrated highly accurate performance in salient object detection tasks. These methods can be categorized into two groups: region-based methods and pixel-wise saliency prediction methods. Region-based methods predict saliency score in a region-wise manner. Zhao *et al.* [38] integrate both global and local context into a multi-context CNN framework for saliency detection. In [13], a multi-layer fully connected network is proposed for estimating the saliency score of each super pixel. Wang *et al.* [27] proposed the integration of both local estimation and global search for patch-wise saliency score estimation. All these methods treat image patches as independent units, and thus they may result in spatial information loss and redundant computations. To overcome these drawbacks, pixel-wise saliency prediction methods directly map an input image to the corresponding saliency map by using a trained deep Fully Convolutional Network (FCN). Li *et al.* [18] proposed the use of a multi-task fully-convolutional neural network for salient object detection. Wang *et al.* [29] proposed a recurrent FCN to encode saliency prior knowledge for salient object detection. In [8], Hou *et al.* introduce short connections into the Holistically-nested Edge Detector (HED) network architecture [30] so as to solve scale-space problems in salient object detection. Li *et al.* [20] developed a multi-scale cascade network, which can encode multi-scale context information and thus produce a better result. In general, these fully-supervised CNN-based methods can achieve good performance even when handling complex scenes. However, training deep CNN models requires a large amount of pixel-level annotations, which have to be created manually in a time-consuming and expensive way.

Notable previous attempts at detecting salient object(s), while using no saliency mask for training, are Weakly Supervised Saliency (WSS) [28] and Supervision by Fusion (SBF) [36] methods. WSS takes advantage of image-level tags to generate pixel-wise annotations for training a deep saliency model. SBF trains the desirable deep saliency model by automatically generating reliable supervisory signals from the fusion process of weak saliency models. However, due to the lack of detailed object shape information, these methods perform far worse in challenging cases compared to fully-supervised methods. Compared with the methods proposed in [28,36], our method can achieve much higher accuracy. This is because our solution obviates the need for image-level tags in training, and thus the accuracy can be increased by using a much larger number of training images from any class (not limited to predefined categories). Furthermore, the contour knowledge is successfully transferred for salient region detection. This enables the deep CNN network to learn detailed object shape information and improve the overall performance. To the best of our knowledge, the idea of transferring contour knowledge for salient object detection has not been investigated before.

3 Approach

3.1 Overview

This paper tackles the problem of borrowing contour knowledge for salient object detection without the need of labeled data. Given an existing contour detection network (CEDN) [34], our objective is to convert this already well-trained model

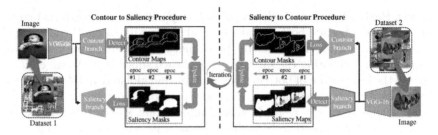

Fig. 2. The proposed alternating training pipeline. Our training algorithm is composed of two procedures: **a** contour-to-saliency procedure and **b** saliency-to-contour procedure. In the contour-to-saliency procedure, we use the generated saliency masks to train the newly-added saliency branch. In the saliency-to-contour procedure, the generated saliency-aware contours are used to fine-tune the original contour branch.

into an accurate deep saliency detection model without using any manually labeled saliency mask.

First, we propose a novel Contour-to-Saliency Network by grafting a new branch onto the existing CEDN. In this architecture, the original contour branch and the newly-added saliency branch share the same feature extractor (or encoder). The feature extractor and contour branch are initialized using CEDN, and the saliency branch is randomly initialized. Therefore, our C2S-Net has the ability to naturally detect contours of the input image after parameter initialization.

Then, we train the saliency branch and update the parameters of the contour branch on two different unlabeled image sets through a novel alternating training pipeline. The training algorithm is composed of two procedures: (1) contour-to-saliency procedure and (2) saliency-to-contour procedure. In the contour-to-saliency procedure, the contour branch is first used to detect contours in each image. Next, a novel contour-to-saliency transfer method is utilized to generate salient object masks based on the detected contours. These generated masks are used to simulate strong supervision over the saliency branch. In the saliency-to-contour procedure, we employ the opposite process to update the parameters of the contour branch. Alternating the two procedures above enables the saliency branch to progressively derive semantically strong features for salient object detection, and the contour branch learns to identify only the contours of salient regions. Figure 2 illustrates the main steps of the alternating training pipeline. In the following sections, we will give a detailed description of C2S-Net, contour-to-saliency transfer method, and our alternating training pipeline.

3.2 Contour-to-Saliency Network

Architecture. Figure 3 illustrates the detailed configuration of our Contour-to-Saliency Network (C2S-Net). Our C2S-Net is rooted in a fully Convolutional Encoder-Decoder Network (CEDN) [34] originally designed for contour detection. We update the network by grafting a new decoder for saliency detection

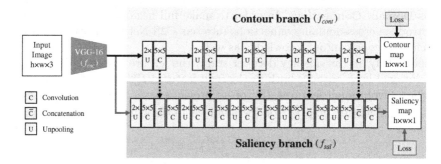

Fig. 3. The two-branch C2S-Net roots in the CEDN [34] for salient object detection. With cross-domain connections (the dashed line), the saliency branch is naturally capable of consolidating both saliency and contour knowledge.

onto the original encoder. By doing this, our C2S-Net is made of three major components: encoder (f_{enc}), contour decoder (f_{cont}) and saliency decoder (f_{sal}). In our network, the encoder extracts high-level feature representations from an input image, the contour decoder identifies contours of the salient region, and the saliency decoder estimates the saliency score of each pixel.

Encoder. The encoder takes an image $\mathcal{I}_i$ as its input, and outputs a feature map $\mathcal{F}_i$. Following CEDN, we employ VGG-16 [26] for feature extractor part (encoder f_{enc}) with the last two layers removed.

Contour Decoder. The contour decoder is built upon the feature extractor, and it takes a feature map $\mathcal{F}_i$, and produces a saliency-aware contour map $C(\mathcal{F}_i, \theta_c)$ where θ_c denotes the model parameter of contour branch. The training of contour decoder can be treated as a per-pixel regression problem to the ground-truth contour labels, by minimizing the following objective function:

$$\min_{\theta_c} \sum_i e_{cont}(\mathcal{L}_{cont}(\mathcal{I}_i), C(\mathcal{F}_i; \theta_c)), \tag{1}$$

where $\mathcal{L}_{cont}(\mathcal{I}_i)$ denotes the ground-truth contour labels of the i-th example, and $e_{cont}(\mathcal{L}_{cont}(\mathcal{I}_i), C(\mathcal{F}_i; \theta_c))$ is the per-pixel loss function.

Saliency Decoder. The saliency decoder f_{sal} share the same encoder f_{enc} with the contour decoder f_{enc}. Similarly, it takes the feature map $\mathcal{F}_i$ as input and produces a single-channel saliency map $S(\mathcal{F}_i, \theta_s)$, where θ_s is the model parameter of saliency decoder. Because salient object detection is a more difficult task than contour detection, we add another convolutional layer in each saliency decoder group. The objective of the saliency branch is to minimize the per-pixel error between the ground-truths and estimated saliency maps. Formally, the objective function can be written as:

$$\min_{\theta_s} \sum_i e_{sal}(\mathcal{L}_{sal}(\mathcal{I}_i), S(\mathcal{F}_i; \theta_s)), \tag{2}$$

where $\mathcal{L}_{sal}(\mathcal{I}_i)$ is the ground-truth salient object mask of the i-th image, and $e_{sal}(\mathcal{L}_{sal}(\mathcal{I}_i), C(\mathcal{F}_i; \theta_s))$ is the per-pixel loss of $S(\mathcal{F}_i; \theta_s))$ with respect to $\mathcal{L}_{sal}(\mathcal{I}_i)$.

Cross-Domain Connections. In order to make full use of contour information, we introduce cross-domain connections into our C2S-Net to enable the saliency branch to encode contour knowledge as well.

Specifically, in the saliency decoder stage, the feature learning of the second convolutional layer encodes both the learned features $f_{s_i}^{cont}$ from contour branch and the convolutional features $f_{s_i}^{sal}$ of its previous layer. Therefore, the second convolutional feature map $\tilde{f}_{s_i}^{sal}$ on the i-th level in the saliency branch is formally written as:

$$\tilde{f}_{s_i}^{sal} = \sigma(cat(f_{s_i}^{cont}, f_{s_i}^{sal}) \otimes w_{s_i}^{sal} + b_{s_i}^{sal}), \tag{3}$$

where $w_{s_i}^{sal}$ and $b_{s_i}^{sal}$ are convolutional filters and biases for the i-th decoder stage in the saliency branch, respectively. $\otimes$ represents convolution operation, and $cat(\cdot)$ is used to concatenate the two learned feature maps of different tasks. RELU serves as the non-linear function $\sigma(\cdot)$.

Our C2S-Net use pixel-level saliency-aware contour labels $\mathcal{L}_{cont}$ and saliency masks $\mathcal{L}_{sal}$ as supervision. Unlike the fully supervised methods, in this paper, these labels are automatically generated, rather than manually annotated. This is achieved by a novel transferring method, which will be introduced in the following section.

3.3   Contour-to-Saliency Transfer

Since our C2S-Net is rooted in a well-trained contour detection network [34], its contour branch is able to identity contours after parameter initialization. The detected contours provide important cues for salient object detection. As observed by many previous works [6,7], salient objects are usually well-surrounded by contours or edges. Therefore, we can leverage this important cue to bridge the gap between object contours and salient object regions.

With detected contour maps in a large collection of unlabeled images, our goal is to utilize them to generate corresponding salient object masks, so as to simulate strong human supervision over saliency branch training. First, we adopt Multiscale Combinatorial Grouping (MCG) [1] to generate some proposal candidate masks $\mathcal{C}$ *from our detected contours* in each image. Then, different from [2], we design an objective function to pick out only a very few masks $\mathcal{B}$ from $\mathcal{C}$ that are most likely to cover the entire salient regions to form the salient object mask $\mathcal{L}_{sal}$ for each image. Formally, our objective function is defined as:

$$\max_{\mathcal{B}}\{S(\mathcal{B}) - \alpha \cdot O(\mathcal{B}) - \kappa \cdot N(\mathcal{B})\} \tag{4}$$
$$s.t. \quad \mathcal{B} \subseteq \mathcal{C}$$

where $S(\cdot)$ is the data term that encourages the selection of region proposals with a higher saliency score. $O(\cdot)$ denotes the overlap term which penalizes intersection between selected region proposals. $N(\cdot)$ is number term which penalizes the number of selected region masks. α and κ are the weights of overlap term and number term, respectively. By maximizing the objective function above, we can

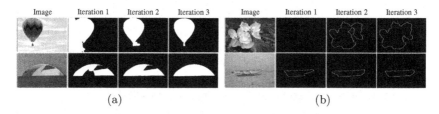

(a)   (b)

Fig. 4. Update of contour labels and saliency masks. Here we show the generated **a** saliency masks and **b** contour labels in Iter #1, Iter #2 and Iter #3. These updated labels and masks will be used as the supervision for the next iteration.

determine a small number of region proposals whose union serves as the salient object mask $\mathcal{L}_{sal}$ used for training.

To be more specific, a binary variable c_i is used to indicate the selection of proposal b_i from all candidate masks $\mathcal{C}$. If b_i is selected, we set $c_i = 1$ otherwise $c_i = 0$. Therefore, we rewrite Eq. 4 as follows:

$$\max\{\sum_{b_i \subseteq C} S_i c_i - \alpha \cdot \sum_{\substack{b_i, b_j \in C \\ i \neq j}} K(b_i, b_j) c_i c_j - \kappa \cdot \sum_{b_i \subseteq C} c_i\} \tag{5}$$
$$s.t. \quad c_i, c_j = 0 \quad or \quad 1$$

Here, $K(b_i, b_j)$ is the Intersection-over-Union (IoU) score between two different region masks b_i and b_j. S_i denotes the score reflecting the likelihood of region mask b_i to be a salient region mask. According to [6,7], a region that is better surrounded by contours is more likely to be a salient region. In addition, the saliency map obtained in the previous stage provides useful prior knowledge. Therefore, we also use it to estimate the saliency score of a given region mask. Formally, the saliency score of each region proposal can be formally written as:

$$S_i = K(cnt(b_i), C^{e_r}) + \gamma \cdot K(b_i, S^{e_r}) \tag{6}$$

where $cnt(b_i)$ denotes a function that extracts contour map from a given region mask b_i. This is simply achieved through computing the gradient on the binary region mask b_i. C^{e_r} and S^{e_r} denote the detected contour and saliency map after the r-th training epoch, respectively. As the parameters of saliency branch are randomly initialized and our network cannot generate saliency maps at the very beginning, we set the combination weight $\gamma = 0$ in the first epoch, and $\gamma = 1$ in the following epoches.

Optimization. Seeking the solution to Eq. 5 is a NP-hard problem. Here, we adopt a greedy algorithm described in [35] to address this problem efficiently.

3.4 Alternating Training

Our C2S-Net has three important components: encoder f_{enc}, contour decoder f_{cont} and newly-added saliency decoder f_{sal}. We initialize parameters of both

f_{enc} and f_{cont} by parameter values of the existing well-trained contour detection model (CEDN) [34], and initialize parameters of f_{sal} randomly from the normal distribution. To avoid the poor local optimum problem, we use two different sets of unlabeled images ($\mathcal{M}$ and $\mathcal{N}$) to interactively train the saliency branch and contour branch. During the training time, the network parameters are optimized by back-propagation and stochastic gradient descent (SGD).

We iteratively perform contour-to-saliency procedure and saliency-to-contour procedure, fixing one set of network parameters while solving for the other set. Specifically, in the contour-to-saliency procedure, by fixing the encoder parameters θ_e and the contour decoder parameters θ_c, we generate contour map of each image on the unlabeled set $\mathcal{M}$ by using the initialized C2S-Net in the first time-step (and the updated C2S-Net in each following time-step). After that, we use the proposed contour-to-saliency transfer method to produce salient object masks $\mathcal{L}_{sal}$ as training samples for updating the saliency decoder parameters θ_s. In this procedure, we also measure confidence score of every generated contour map by $\frac{C(\mathcal{F}_i, \theta_c) \geq 0.9}{C(\mathcal{F}_i, \theta_c) \geq 0.1}$, and choose contour maps whose scores are larger than a pre-defined threshold ($\vartheta = 0.15$) so as to filter out unreliable contour maps. In the saliency-to-contour procedure, we fix the network parameters θ_e and θ_s , and use the learned C2S-Net to generate both contour maps and saliency maps. These generated results are then utilized to produce salient object masks on unlabeled set $\mathcal{N}$ using Eq. 5. We adopt $cnt(\cdot)$ in Eq. 6 to generate saliency-aware contour labels $\mathcal{L}_{cont}$, and use these generated labels to update the contour decoder parameters θ_c. For each round of iteration, we update the network parameters to improve the quality of estimated labels for the next round.

Our alternating training pipeline successfully takes advantage of the complementary benefits of two related domains. On one hand, the contour branch is able to learn saliency knowledge, and thus it can focus more on the contours of those attention-grabbing objects. More importantly, the training samples generated by saliency branch are not limited to a small number of predefined categories. Therefore, the contour branch can learn saliency properties from a large set of images to detect contours of "unseen" objects. On the other hand, the saliency branch learns detailed object shape information so that it can produce saliency maps with clear boundaries. As shown in Fig. 4, the estimated salient object masks and contour maps become more and more reliable, and then provide useful information for network training.

4   Experiments

4.1   Experimental Setup

Dataset. The training set contains $10K$ images from MSRA10K (ignoring labels), and another $20K$ unlabelled images collected from the Web as additional training data. These images contain one or multiple object(s) and cluttered backgrounds, and are not overlapped with any test image. We randomly divide the training set into two subsets, $\mathcal{M}$ and $\mathcal{N}$, to train contour branch and saliency branch of our C2S-Net, respectively. In addition, we augment each subset through horizontal flipping.

For the performance evaluation, we utilize five most challenging benchmarks including ECSSD [31], PASCAL-S [21], DUT-OMRON [32], HKU-IS [13] and DUTS-TE [28].

Implementation. Our C2S-Net is implemented based on the public code of CEDN [34], which was based on Caffe toolbox [10]. The network parameters of encoder and contour decoder are initialized by the CEDN model. The parameters of saliency decoder are initialized randomly. We set $\alpha = 0.5$ and $\kappa = 0.25$ in Eq. 4.

During training, we adopt the "poly" learning rate policy, where the learning rate is automatically scaled by $(1 - \frac{iter}{max_{iter}})^p$. We set the initial learning rate to 10^{-6}, and p to 0.9. The maximum number of iterations is set based on the number of training data ($max_{iter} = N \times 3$, where N denotes the number of training data). The mini-batch size is set to 5. At each training round, we update network parameters by fine-tuning the model trained from the previous round. In addition, as discussed in Sect. 3.4, at each training round, we first solve for parameters of one branch while fixing the parameters of the other, and then perform the opposite procedure.

During testing, the input RGB image is forwarded through our C2S-Net to generate a saliency map with the same size as the output. Unlike other methods, we *do not* need to adopt any pre-processing or post-processing steps, e.g., DenseCRF, for further improving the detected results.

Evaluation Metrics. We use four evaluation metrics to evaluate the performance of our method: Precision-Recall curves (PR), F-measure (F_β), weighted F-measure (F_β^w), and Mean Absolute Error (MAE). The F-measure is computed by $F_\beta = (1 + \beta^2)\frac{Precision \times Recall}{\beta^2 Precision + Recall}$, where β^2 is set to 0.3 to emphasize precision. We also adopt the weighted F-measure [25] to assess the performance of our method, which is defined as $F_\beta^w = (1 + \beta^2)\frac{Precision^w \times Recall^w}{\beta^2 Precision^w + Recall^w}$. MAE is defined as the average pixel-wise absolute difference between the ground-truth mask and estimated saliency map. All these universally-agreed evaluation metrics have been widely adopted by previous works.

4.2 Ablation Analysis

In this section, we conduct ablation studies on ECSSD dataset by comparing the weighted F-measure (F_β^w) and MAE to verify impact of each component in the framework. Details of the results are summarized in Table 1.

Impact of Cross-Domain Connections. We evaluate the performance differences of the proposed C2S-Net with and without cross-domain connections (CDC). For a fair comparison, we train both models using the same training images (i.e., $5K$ images randomly selected from MSRA10K with pixel-wise ground truths), and the same training parameters which are described in Sect. 4.1. The experiments show that our C2S-Net with CDC can improve the F_β^w by 2.4%, and significantly lower the MAE score by 21.3%. Compared with

Table 1. Analysis of the proposed method. Our results are obtained on ECSSD. "CDC" denotes the cross domain connections that used in our C2S-Net. "AVG-P" means the two-stage strategy, "WTA" denotes the "winner-take-all" strategy, and "CTS" refers to the contour-to-saliency transferring method used in this paper. "SCJ" denotes that we optimize the parameters of two branches jointly, and "$AT_{(i)}$" means that i-th alternating training iterations are used to update network parameters. "† " denotes the model used in this paper for comparing with fully supervised models. Weighted F-measure (F_β^w): the higher the better; MAE: the lower the better

Method	data/annotations	F_β^w	MAE
C2S-Net	5K w/ masks	0.793	0.103
C2S-Net + CDC	5K w/ masks	0.812	0.081
C2S-Net + CDC + AVG-P	5K w/o masks	0.665	0.121
C2S-Net + CDC + WTA	5K w/o masks	0.732	0.112
C2S-Net + CDC + CTS	5K w/o masks	0.743	0.093
C2S-Net + CDC + CTS + SCJ	10K w/o masks	0.759	0.088
C2S-Net + CDC + CTS + $AT_{(1)}$	10K w/o masks	0.778	0.080
C2S-Net + CDC + CTS + $AT_{(3)}$	10K w/o masks	0.837	0.059
C2S-Net + CDC + CTS + $AT_{(5)}$	10K w/o masks	0.838	0.059
C2S-Net + CDC + CTS + $AT_{(3)}$	20K w/o masks	0.849	0.056
† C2S-Net + CDC + CTS + $AT_{(3)}$	30K w/o masks	0.852	0.054

only sharing the same encoder, our CDC enables the proposed model to better explore the intrinsic correlations between saliency detection and contour detection, and results in a better performance.

Effectiveness of Contour-to-Saliency Transferring. Automatically generating a reliable salient object mask for each image, based on generated proposal candidate masks C (about 500 proposals), is a challenging task. Here, we take three different approaches to generate saliency masks for training our model. One approach is the two-stage strategy, the second is the "winner-take-all" strategy, and the third is our contour-to-saliency transferring strategy. These approaches are respectively referred to as AVG-P, WTA, and CTS. Specifically, for AVG-P, we first simply take an average of all proposals (generated from detected contours) to form a saliency map for each image, and then use SalCut [3] to produce its salient object mask. As for WTA, all generated proposals are re-scored according to Eq. 6 and only the proposal with the highest score is picked out to serve as salient object mask for each image. As for our CTS, we use the method described in Sect. 3.3 to produce salient object masks for all images. We also use the same $5K$ images from MSRA10K as the training set, but we ignore all of the manual masks. The third, fourth and fifth lines of Table 1 show the corresponding results of using AVG-P, WTA and CTS to generate saliency masks for training our C2S-Net, respectively. Clearly, the proposed CTS enables our C2S-Net to achieve much better performance than other strategies.

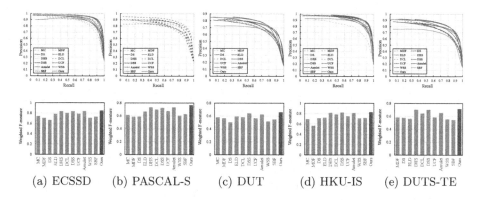

|(a) ECSSD|(b) PASCAL-S|(c) DUT|(d) HKU-IS|(e) DUTS-TE|

Fig. 5. From top to bottom, Precision-recall (PR) curves and *weighted* F-measure of our method and other state-of-the-art approaches are shown, respectively.

Impact of Alternating Training. To verify the effectiveness of our alternating training (AT) approach, we use another $5K$ unlabeled images, the remaining images of MSRA10K, to serve as the training set of contour branch. The experiments show that our alternating training approach (AT) can largely boost the performance of our C2S-Net. After the first iteration, our model achieves competitive performance as fully-supervised approaches ($F_\beta^w = 0.778$, and $MAE = 0.080$). Our C2S-Net with three AT iterations achieves much better performance according to F_β^w (0.837) and MAE score (0.059). We observe that the performance of our model with five AT iterations ($F_\beta^w = 0.838$, and $MAE = 0.059$) is just slightly better than that of model with three AT iterations. This is because the estimated saliency masks and contour maps have already become reliable enough after three AT iterations. Considering the training time and model's performance, we believe that three AT iterations should be a good choice.

In addition, to show the superiority of our alternating training scheme, we use the same $10K$ images with estimated labels (including both saliency and contour labels) to train our C2S-Net. One loss is for contour branch and another loss is for saliency branch. We optimize the parameters of two branches jointly, and denote this training strategy as SCJ in Table 1. According to our experiments, when given the same amount of training data, our alternating training strategy can achieve much better performance.

Impact of Data Size. According to our reported results (Table 1), the models performance on ECSSD improves as the training data expands. This indicates that data size is a big influencing factor for saliency model's performance. Feeding more training samples to the deep CNN models can lead to better performance.

Table 2. Quantitative comparisons with 10 leading CNN-Based methods on five widely-used benchmarks. The top three results are shown in Red, Blue, and Green, respectively. F_β: the higher the better; MAE: the lower the better

Methods	ECSSD		PASCAL-S		DUT		HKU-IS		DUTS-TE	
	F_β	MAE	F_β	MAE	F_β	MAE	F_β	MAE	F_β	MAE
SBF [37]	0.852	0.880	0.765	0.130	0.685	0.108	0.842	0.075	0.698	0.107
WSS [29]	0.856	0.103	0.770	0.139	0.689	0.110	0.860	0.079	0.737	0.100
Ours(10K)	0.896	0.059	0.835	0.086	0.733	0.079	0.883	0.051	0.790	0.066
MC [39]	0.822	0.107	0.721	0.147	0.703	0.088	0.781	0.098	-	-
MDF [14]	0.832	0.105	0.759	0.142	0.694	0.092	0.860	0.129	0.768	0.099
DS [19]	0.882	0.122	0.757	0.172	0.716	0.120	0.866	0.079	0.776	0.090
ELD [12]	0.869	0.098	0.777	0.121	0.720	0.091	0.767	0.071	0.758	0.097
DHS [23]	0.902	0.061	0.820	0.092	-	-	0.892	0.052	0.812	0.065
DCL [15]	0.887	0.072	0.798	0.109	0.718	0.094	0.879	0.059	0.771	0.079
DSS [8]	0.903	0.062	0.821	0.101	0.761	0.074	0.899	0.051	0.813	0.064
UCF [38]	0.910	0.078	0.819	0.127	0.735	0.132	0.885	0.074	0.771	0.117
Amulet [37]	0.915	0.059	0.828	0.100	0.743	0.098	0.895	0.052	0.778	0.085
Ours(30K)	0.910	0.054	0.846	0.081	0.757	0.071	0.896	0.048	0.807	0.062

4.3   Comparison to Other Methods

We compare the proposed method with nine top-ranked fully deep supervised saliency detection models including MC [38], MDF [13], DS [18], ELD [12], DHS [22], DCL [14], DSS [8], UCF [37], and Amulet [36], one weakly supervised deep saliency model WSS [28], and one unsupervised deep saliency model SBF [36]. In all experiments, we use the models provided by original authors.

Quantitative Comparison. In order to obtain a fair comparison with existing weakly supervised and unsupervised deep models, we first use the same training set as in SBF [36] (MSRA10K without masks), and test over all of the evaluation datasets using the same model. As shown in Table 2, our model (with $10K$ training images) consistently outperforms the existing weakly supervised and unsupervised deep saliency models with a large margin, and compares favorably with the top-ranked fully supervised deep models.

One of the advantages of our method is that it can use a large amount of unlabeled data for training, while the existing fully supervised methods are constrained by the amount of labeled data. Here, we use additional 20K unlabelled images collected from the Web (30K in total) to train our model, and compare it with all top-ranked fully deep supervised models. As shown in Table 2 and Fig. 5, our method can largely outperform other leading methods in nearly all evaluation metrics across all the datasets. Specifically, on ECSSD, PASCAL-S, DUT-OMRON, HKU-IS, and DUTS-TE, our method decreases the lowest MAE score by 8.5%, 11.9%, 4.1%, 5.9% and 3.1%, respectively. This indicates that our method can produce more confident results and generate more reliable saliency maps that are close to the ground truth. In terms of F-measure and PR curves, our method consistently ranks among the top three on all datasets (see Table 2 and Fig. 5). In addition, as shown in Fig. 5, we improve the current best weighted F-measure (F_{β}^{w}) by 1.2%, 4.4%, 2.7%, 0.1% and 0.2% on ECSSD, PASCAL-S, DUT-OMRON, HKU-IS, and DUTS-TE, respectively. In general, the experimental results convincingly demonstrate the effectiveness of our method. It also should be noted that our method requires *no manual salient object label* for training the network while other top-ranked deep models are trained with pixel-wise annotations. As our method can benefit from unlimited number of unlabeled images, it has full potential for further performance improvement.

Qualitative Comparison. Figure 6 provides a qualitative comparison between our method and other approaches. It can be seen that our method can consistently and accurately highlight the salient objects in different challenging cases. Because the contour knowledge has been encoded by our C2S-Net, our model can always better preserve object contours than other comparison methods.

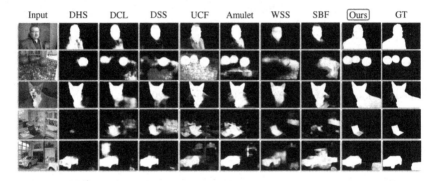

Fig. 6. Qualitative comparisons of our method and the state-of-the-art approaches. The ground truth (GT) is shown in the last column.

Table 3. Comparison of running times.

Method	MC	MDF	DS	ELD	DHS	DCL	DSS	UCF	Amulet	WSS	SBF	**Ours**
Times(s)	2.38	8.04	0.73	0.59	0.06	1.17	0.05	0.11	0.06	0.02	0.03	0.03

Speed Performance. Lastly, we show the speed performance of our method and other approaches in Table 3. The evaluation is conducted with an NVIDIA GTX 1080ti GPU with 11G RAM. Our method takes only 0.03 second to produce a saliency map for a 400×300 input image.

5 Conclusions

In this paper, we propose a novel method to borrow contour knowledge for salient object detection. We first build a C2S-Net by grafting a new branch onto a well-trained object contour detection network. To bridge the gap between contours and salient object regions, we propose a novel transferring method that can automatically generate a saliency mask for each image from its contour map. These generated masks are then used to train the saliency branch of C2S-Net. Finally, we use a novel alternating training pipeline to further improve the performance of our C2S-Net. Extensive experiments on five datasets show that our method surpasses the current top saliency detection approaches.

Acknowledgments. This research was funded in part by the National Key R&D Program of China (2017YFB1302300), the National Nature Science Foundation of China (U1613223), and the Open Research Subject of Comprehensive Health Management Center of Xihua University (JKGL2018-029).

References

1. Arbelez, P., Pont-Tuset, J., Barron, J., Marques, F., Malik, J.: Multiscale combinatorial grouping. In: CVPR, pp. 328–335 (2014)
2. Bertasius, G., Shi, J., Torresani, L.: Semantic segmentation with boundary neural fields. In: The IEEE Conference on Computer Vision and Pattern Recognition (CVPR), June 2016
3. Cheng, M.M., Mitra, N.J., Huang, X., Torr, P.H., Hu, S.M.: Global contrast based salient region detection. TPAMI **37**(3), 569–582 (2015)
4. Cheng, M.M., Warrell, J., Lin, W.Y., Zheng, S., Vineet, V., Crook, N.: Efficient salient region detection with soft image abstraction. In: ICCV, pp. 1529–1536 (2013)
5. Chu, X., Yang, W., Ouyang, W., Ma, C., Yuille, A.L., Wang, X.: Multi-context attention for human pose estimation. In: CVPR, July 2017
6. Deng, Q., Luo, Y.: Edge-based method for detecting salient objects. Opt. Eng. **50**(5), 301–301 (2011)
7. Du, S., Chen, S.: Salient object detection via random forest. IEEE SPL **21**(1), 51–54 (2013)
8. Hou, Q., Cheng, M.M., Hu, X., Borji, A., Tu, Z., Torr, P.H.S.: Deeply supervised salient object detection with short connections. In: CVPR, July 2017
9. Hu, P., Shuai, B., Liu, J., Wang, G.: Deep level sets for salient object detection. In: CVPR, July 2017
10. Jia, Y., Shelhamer, E., Donahue, J., Karayev, S., Long, J., Girshick, R., Guadarrama, S., Darrell, T.: Caffe: Convolutional architecture for fast feature embedding. In: ACM MM, pp. 675–678 (2014)
11. Jin, B., Ortiz Segovia, M.V., Susstrunk, S.: Webly supervised semantic segmentation. In: CVPR, July 2017
12. Lee, G., Tai, Y.W., Kim, J.: Deep saliency with encoded low level distance map and high level features. In: CVPR (2016)
13. Li, G., Yu, Y.: Visual saliency based on multiscale deep features. In: CVPR, pp. 5455–5463 (2015)
14. Li, G., Yu, Y.: Deep contrast learning for salient object detection. In: CVPR, pp. 478–487 (2016)
15. Li, J., Lu, K., Huang, Z., Zhu, L., Shen, H.T.: Transfer independently together: a generalized framework for domain adaptation. IEEE Trans. Cybern. (2018). https://doi.org/10.1109/TCYB.2018.2820174

16. Li, J., Wu, Y., Zhao, J., Lu, K.: Low-rank discriminant embedding for multiview learning. IEEE Trans. Cybern. **47**(11), 3516–3529 (2017)
17. Li, J., Zhao, J., Lu, K.: Joint feature selection and structure preservation for domain adaptation. In: IJCAI, pp. 1697–1703 (2016)
18. Li, X., Zhao, L., Wei, L., Yang, M.H., Wu, F., Zhuang, Y., Ling, H., Wang, J.: Deepsaliency: multi-task deep neural network model for salient object detection. TIP **25**(8), 3919–3930 (2016)
19. Li, X., Yang, F., Chen, L., Cai, H.: Saliency transfer: an example-based method for salient object detection. In: IJCAI, pp. 3411–3417 (2016)
20. Li, X., Yang, F., Cheng, H., Chen, J., Guo, Y., Chen, L.: Multi-scale cascade network for salient object detection. In: ACM MM, Oct 2017
21. Li, Y., Hou, X., Koch, C., Rehg, J.M., Yuille, A.L.: The secrets of salient object segmentation. In: CVPR, pp. 280–287 (2014)
22. Liu, N., Han, J.: Dhsnet: Deep hierarchical saliency network for salient object detection. In: CVPR, pp. 678–686 (2016)
23. Luo, Z., Mishra, A., Achkar, A., Eichel, J., Li, S., Jodoin, P.M.: Non-local deep features for salient object detection. In: CVPR, July 2017
24. Ramanishka, V., Das, A., Zhang, J., Saenko, K.: Top-down visual saliency guided by captions. In: CVPR, July 2017
25. Ran, M., Zelnikmanor, L., Tal, A.: How to evaluate foreground maps. In: Computer Vision and Pattern Recognition, pp. 248–255 (2014)
26. Simonyan, K., Zisserman, A.: Very deep convolutional networks for large-scale image recognition. In: ICLR (2015)
27. Wang, L., Lu, H., Ruan, X., Yang, M.H.: Deep networks for saliency detection via local estimation and global search. In: CVPR, pp. 3183–3192 (2015)
28. Wang, L., Lu, H., Wang, Y., Feng, M., Wang, D., Yin, B., Ruan, X.: Learning to detect salient objects with image-level supervision. In: CVPR, July 2017
29. Wang, L., Wang, L., Lu, H., Zhang, P., Ruan, X.: Saliency detection with recurrent fully convolutional networks. In: ECCV, pp. 825–841. Springer (2016)
30. Xie, S., Tu, Z.: Holistically-nested edge detection. In: ICCV, pp. 1395–1403 (2015)
31. Xie, Y., Lu, H., Yang, M.H.: Bayesian saliency via low and mid level cues. TIP **22**(5), 1689–1698 (2013)
32. Yang, C., Zhang, L., Lu, H., Xiang, R., Yang, M.H.: Saliency detection via graph-based manifold ranking. In: CVPR, pp. 3166–3173 (2013)
33. Yang, F., Li, X., Cheng, H., Li, J., Chen, L.: Object-aware dense semantic correspondence. In: CVPR, July 2017
34. Yang, J., Price, B., Cohen, S., Lee, H., Yang, M.H.: Object contour detection with a fully convolutional encoder-decoder network. In: CVPR, June 2016
35. Zhang, J., Sclaroff, S., Lin, Z., Shen, X., Price, B., Mech, R.: Unconstrained salient object detection via proposal subset optimization. In: CVPR, pp. 5733–5742 (2016)
36. Zhang, P., Wang, D., Lu, H., Wang, H., Ruan, X.: Amulet: Aggregating multi-level convolutional features for salient object detection. In: ICCV (2017)
37. Zhang, P., Wang, D., Lu, H., Wang, H., Yin, B.: Learning uncertain convolutional features for accurate saliency detection. In: ICCV, Oct 2017
38. Zhao, R., Ouyang, W., Li, H., Wang, X.: Saliency detection by multi-context deep learning. In: CVPR, pp. 1265–1274 (2015)

Learning Category-Specific Mesh Reconstruction from Image Collections

Angjoo Kanazawa$^{(\boxtimes)}$, Shubham Tulsiani, Alexei A. Efros, and Jitendra Malik

University of California, Berkeley, USA
{kanazawa,shubhtuls,efros,malik}@eecs.berkeley.edu

Abstract. We present a learning framework for recovering the 3D shape, camera, and texture of an object from a single image. The shape is represented as a deformable 3D mesh model of an object category where a shape is parameterized by a learned mean shape and per-instance predicted deformation. Our approach allows leveraging an annotated image collection for training, where the deformable model and the 3D prediction mechanism are learned without relying on ground-truth 3D or multi-view supervision. Our representation enables us to go beyond existing 3D prediction approaches by incorporating texture inference as prediction of an image in a canonical appearance space. Additionally, we show that semantic keypoints can be easily associated with the predicted shapes. We present qualitative and quantitative results of our approach on CUB and PASCAL3D datasets and show that we can learn to predict diverse shapes and textures across objects using only annotated image collections. The project website can be found at https://akanazawa.github.io/cmr/.

1 Introduction

Consider the image of the bird in Fig. 1. Even though this flat two-dimensional picture printed on a page may be the first time we are seeing this particular bird, we can infer its rough 3D shape, understand the camera pose, and even guess what it would look like from another view. We can do this because all the previously seen birds have enabled us to develop a mental model of what birds are like, and this knowledge helps us to recover the 3D structure of this novel instance.

In this work, we present a computational model that can similarly learn to infer a 3D representation given just a single image. As illustrated in Fig. 1, the learning only relies on an annotated 2D image collection of a given object category, comprising of foreground masks and semantic keypoin t labels. Our training procedure, depicted in Fig. 2, forces a common prediction model to

---

A. Kanazawa and S. Tulsiani—Procrastinated equally on this work.

Electronic supplementary material The online version of this chapter (https://doi.org/10.1007/978-3-030-01267-0_23) contains supplementary material, which is available to authorized users.

explain all the image evidences across many examples of an object category. This allows us to learn a meaningful 3D structure despite only using a single-view per training instance, without relying on any ground-truth 3D data for learning.

Fig. 1. Given an annotated image collection of an object category, we learn a predictor f that can map a novel image I to its 3D shape, camera pose, and texture.

At inference, given a single unannotated image of a novel instance, our learned model allows us to infer the shape, camera pose, and texture of the underlying object. We represent the shape as a 3D mesh in a canonical frame, where the predicted camera transforms the mesh from this canonical space to the image coordinates. The particular shape of each instance is instantiated by deforming a learned category-specific mean shape with instance-specific predicted deformations. The use of this shared 3D space affords numerous advantages as it implicitly enforces correspondences across 3D representations of different instances. As we detail in Sect. 2, this allows us to formulate the task of inferring mesh texture of different objects as that of predicting pixel values in a common texture representation. Furthermore, we can also easily associate semantic keypoints with the predicted 3D shapes.

Our shape representation is an instantiation of deformable models, the history of which can be traced back to Thompson [29], who in turn was inspired by the work of Dürer [6]. Thompson observed that shapes of objects of the same category may be aligned through geometrical transformations. Cootes and Taylor [5] operationalized this idea to learn a class-specific model of deformation for 2D images. Pioneering work of Blanz and Vetter [2] extended these ideas to 3D shapes to model the space of faces. These techniques have since been applied to model human bodies [1,19], hands [17,27], and more recently on quadruped animals [40]. Unfortunately, all of these approaches require a large collection of 3D data to learn the model, preventing their application to categories where such data collection is impractical. In contrast, our approach is able to learn using only an annotated image collection.

Sharing our motivation for relaxing the requirement of 3D data to learn morphable models, some related approaches have examined the use of similarly annotated image collections. Cashman and Fitzgibbon [3] use keypoint correspondences and segmentation masks to learn a morphable model of dolphins from images. Kar *et al.* [15] extend this approach to general rigid object categories. Both approaches follow a *fitting-based* inference procedure, which relies on mask (and optionally keypoint) annotations at test-time and is computationally inefficient. We instead follow a *prediction-based* inference approach, and learn a parametrized predictor which can directly infer the 3D structure from an unannotated image. Moreover, unlike these approaches, we also address the task of texture prediction which cannot be easily incorporated with these methods.

While deformable models have been a common representation for 3D inference, the recent advent of deep learning based prediction approaches has resulted in a plethora of alternate representations being explored using varying forms of supervision. Relying on ground-truth 3D supervision (using synthetic data), some approaches have examined learning voxel [4,8,33,39], point cloud [7] or octree [10,26] prediction. While some learning based methods do pursue mesh prediction [14,18,24,35], they also rely on 3D supervision which is only available for restricted classes or in a synthetic setting. Reducing the supervision to multi-view masks [9,21,30,34] or depth images [30] has been explored for voxel prediction, but the requirement of multiple views per instance is still restrictive. While these approaches show promising results, they rely on stronger supervision (ground-truth 3D or multi-view) compared to our approach.

In the context of these previous approaches, the proposed approach differs primarily in three aspects:

- *Shape representation and inference method.* We combine the benefits of the classically used deformable mesh representations with those of a learning based prediction mechanism. The use of a deformable mesh based representation affords several advantages such as memory efficiency, surface-level reasoning and correspondence association. Using a learned prediction model allows efficient inference from a single unannotated image
- *Learning from an image collection.* Unlike recent CNN based 3D prediction methods which require either ground-truth 3D or multi-view supervision, we only rely on an annotated image collection, with only one available view per training instance, to learn our prediction model.
- *Ability to infer texture.* There is little past work on predicting the 3D shape and the texture of objects from a single image. Recent *prediction-based* learning methods use representations that are not amenable to textures (*e.g.* voxels). The classical deformable model *fitting-based* approaches cannot easily incorporate texture for generic objects. An exception is texture inference on human faces [2,22,23,28], but these approaches require a large-set of 3D ground truth data with high quality texture maps. Our approach enables us to pursue the task of texture inference from image collections alone, and we address the related technical challenges regarding its incorporation in a learning framework.

2   Approach

We aim to learn a predictor f_θ (parameterized as a CNN) that can infer the 3D structure of the underlying object instance from a single image I. The prediction $f_\theta(I)$ is comprised of the 3D shape of the object in a canonical frame, the associated texture, as well as the camera pose. The shape representation we pursue in this work is of the form of a 3D mesh. This representation affords several advantages over alternates like probabilistic volumetric grids *e.g.* amenability to texturing, correspondence inference, surface level reasoning and interpretability.

The overview of the proposed framework is illustrated in Fig. 2. The input image is passed through an encoder to a latent representation that is shared by three modules that estimate the camera pose, shape deformation, and texture parameters. The deformation is added to the learned category-level mean shape to obtain the final predicted shape. The objective of the network is to minimize the corresponding losses when the shape is rendered onto the image. We train a separate model for each object category.

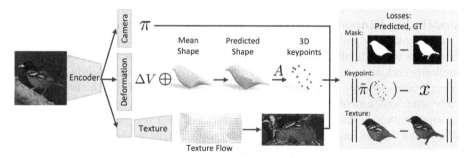

Fig. 2. Overview of the proposed framework. An image I is passed through a convolutional encoder to a latent representation that is shared by modules that estimate the camera pose, deformation and texture parameters. Deformation is an offset to the learned mean shape, which when added yield instance specific shapes in a canonical coordinate frame. We also learn correspondences between the mesh vertices and the semantic keypoints. Texture is parameterized as an UV image, which we predict through texture flow (see Sect. 2.3). The objective is to minimize the distance between the rendered mask, keypoints and textured rendering with the corresponding ground truth annotations. We do not require ground truth 3D shapes or multi-view cues for training.

We first present the representations predicted by our model in Sect. 2.1, and then describe the learning procedure in Sect. 2.2. We initially present our framework for predicting shape and camera pose, and then describe how the model is extended to predict the associated texture in Sect. 2.3.

2.1   Inferred 3D Representation

Given an image I of an instance, we predict $f_\theta(I) \equiv (M, \pi)$, a mesh M and camera pose π to capture the 3D structure of the underlying object. In addition to these directly predicted aspects, we also learn the association between the mesh vertices and the category-level semantic keypoints. We describe the details of the inferred representations below.

Shape Parametrization. We represent the shape as a 3D mesh $M \equiv (V, F)$, defined by vertices $V \in \mathbb{R}^{|V| \times 3}$ and faces F. We assume a fixed and pre-determined mesh connectivity, and use the faces F corresponding to a spherical mesh. The vertex positions V are instantiated using (learned) instance-independent mean vertex locations $\bar{V}$ and instance-dependent predicted deformations Δ_V, which when added, yield instance vertex locations $V = \bar{V} + \Delta_V$. Intuitively, the mean shape $\bar{V}$ can be considered as a learnt bias term for the predicted shape V.

Camera Projection. We model the camera with weak-perspective projection and predict, from the input image I, the scale $s \in \mathbb{R}$, translation $\mathbf{t} \in \mathbb{R}^2$, and rotation (captured by quaternion $\mathbf{q} \in \mathbb{R}^4$). We use $\pi(P)$ to denote the projection of a set of 3D points P onto the image coordinates via the weak-perspective projection defined by $\pi \equiv (s, \mathbf{t}, \mathbf{q})$.

Associating Semantic Correspondences. As we represent the shape using a category-specific mesh in the canonical frame, the regularities across instances encourage semantically consistent vertex positions across instances, thereby implicitly endowing semantics to these vertices. We can use this insight and learn to explicitly associate semantic keypoints *e.g.*, beak, legs *etc.* with the mesh via a keypoint assignment matrix $A \in \mathcal{R}_+^{|K| \times |\bar{V}|}$ s.t. $\sum_v A_{k,v} = 1$. Here, each row A_k represents a probability distribution over the mesh vertices of corresponding to keypoint k, and can be understood as approximating a one-hot vector of vertex selection for each keypoint. As we describe later in our learning formulation, we encourage each A_k to be a peaked distribution. Given the vertex positions V, we can infer the location v_k for the kth keypoint as $v_k = \sum_v A_{k,v} v$. More concisely, the keypoint locations induced by vertices V can be obtained as $A \cdot V$. We initialize the keypoint assignment matrix A uniformly, but over the course of training it learns to better associate semantic keypoints with appropriate mesh vertices.

In summary, given an image I of an instance, we predict the corresponding camera π and the shape deformation Δ_V as $(\pi, \Delta_V) = f(I)$. In addition, *we also learn* (across the dataset), instance-independent parameters $\{\bar{V}, A\}$. As described above, these category-level (learned) parameters, in conjunction with the instances-specific predictions, allow us to recover the mesh vertex locations V and coordinates of semantic keypoints $A \cdot V$.

2.2   Learning from an Image Collection

We present an approach to train f_θ without relying on strong supervision in the form of ground truth 3D shapes or multi-view images of an object instance. Instead, we guide the learning from an image collection annotated with sparse keypoints and segmentation masks. Such a setting is more natural and easily obtained, particularly for animate and deformable objects such as birds or animals. It is extremely difficult to obtain scans, or even multiple views of the same instance for these classes, but relatively easier to acquire a single image for numerous instances.

Given the annotated image collection, we train f_θ by formulating an objective function that consists of instance specific losses and priors. The instance-specific energy terms ensure that the predicted 3D structure is consistent with the available evidence (masks and keypoints) and the priors encourage generic desired properties *e.g.* smoothness. As we learn a common prediction model f_θ across many instances, the common structure across the category allows us to learn meaningful 3D prediction despite only having a single-view per instance.

Training Data. We assume an annotated training set $\{(I_i, S_i, x_i)\}_{i=1}^N$ for each object category, where I_i is the image, S_i is the instance segmentation, and $x_i \in \mathbb{R}^{2 \times K}$ is the set of K keypoint locations. As previously leveraged by [15,31], applying structure-from-motion to the annotated keypoint locations additionally allows us to obtain a rough estimate of the weak-perspective camera $\tilde{\pi}_i$ for each training instance. This results in an augmented training set $\{(I_i, S_i, x_i, \tilde{\pi}_i)\}_{i=1}^N$, which we use for training our predictor f_θ.

Instance Specific Losses. We ensure that the predicted 3D structure matches the available annotations. Using the semantic correspondences associated to the mesh via the keypoint assignment matrix A, we formulate a keypoint reprojection loss. This term encourages the predicted 3D keypoints to match the annotated 2D keypoints when projected onto the image:

$$L_{\texttt{reproj}} = \sum_i ||x_i - \tilde{\pi}_i(AV_i)||_2. \tag{1}$$

Similarly, we enforce that the predicted 3D mesh, when rendered in the image coordinates, is consistent with the annotated foreground mask: $L_{\texttt{mask}} = \sum_i ||S_i - \mathcal{R}(V_i, F, \tilde{\pi}_i)||_2$. Here, $\mathcal{R}(V, F, \pi)$ denotes a rendering of the segmentation mask image corresponding to the 3D mesh $M = (V, F)$ when rendered through camera π. In all of our experiments, we use Neural Mesh Renderer [16] to provide a differentiable implementation of $\mathcal{R}(\cdot)$.

We also train the predicted camera pose to match the corresponding estimate obtained via structure-from-motion using a regression loss $L_{\texttt{cam}} = \sum_i ||\tilde{\pi}_i - \pi_i||_2$. We found it advantageous to use the structure-from-motion camera $\tilde{\pi}_i$, and not the predicted camera π_i, to define $L_{\texttt{mask}}$ and $L_{\texttt{reproj}}$ losses. This is because during training, in particular the initial stages when the predictions are often incorrect, an error in the predicted camera can lead to high errors despite accurate shape, and possibly adversely affect learning.

Priors. In addition to the data-dependent losses which ensure that the predictions match the evidence, we leverage generic priors to encourage additional properties. The prior terms that we use are:

Smoothness. In the natural world, shapes tend to have a smooth surface and we would like our recovered 3D shapes to behave similarly. An advantage of using a mesh representation is that it naturally affords reasoning at the surface level. In particular, enforcing smooth surface has been extensively studied by the Computer Graphics community [20,25]. Following the literature, we formulate surface smoothness as minimization of the mean curvature. On meshes, this is captured by the norm of the graph Laplacian, and can be concisely written as $L_{\texttt{smooth}} = ||LV||_2$, where L is the discrete Laplace-Beltrami operator. We construct L once using the connectivity of the mesh and this can be expressed as a simple linear operator on vertex locations. See appendix for details.

Deformation Regularization. In keeping with a common practice across deformable model approaches [2,3,15], we find it beneficial to regularize the deformations as it discourages arbitrarily large deformations and helps learn a meaningful mean shape. The corresponding energy term is expressed as $L_{\texttt{def}} = ||\Delta_V||_2$.

Keypoint Association. As discussed in Sect. 2.1, we encourage the keypoint assignment matrix A to be a peaked distribution as it should intuitively correspond to a one-hot vector. We therefore minimize the average entropy over all keypoints: $L_{\texttt{vert2kp}} = \frac{1}{|K|} \sum_k \sum_v -A_{k,v} \log A_{k,v}$.

In summary, the overall objective for shape and camera is

$$L = L_{\texttt{reproj}} + L_{\texttt{mask}} + L_{\texttt{cam}} + L_{\texttt{smooth}} + L_{\texttt{def}} + L_{\texttt{vert2kp}}. \qquad (2)$$

Symmetry Constraints. Almost all common object categories, including the ones we consider, exhibit reflectional symmetry. To exploit this structure, we constrain the predicted shape and deformations to be mirror-symmetric. As our mesh topology corresponds to that of a sphere, we identify symmetric vertex pairs in the initial topology. Given these pairs, we only learn/predict parameters for one vertex in each pair for the mean shape $\bar{V}$ and deformations Δ_V. See appendix for details.

Initialization and Implementation Details. While our mesh topology corresponds to a sphere, following previous fitting based deformable model approaches [15], we observe that a better initialization of the mean vertex positions $\bar{V}$ speeds up learning. We compute the convex hull of the mean keypoint locations obtained during structure-from-motion and initialize the mean vertex locations to lie on this convex hull – the procedure is described in more detail in the appendix. As the different energy terms in Eq. (2) have naturally different magnitudes, we weight them accordingly to normalize their contribution.

2.3   Incorporating Texture Prediction

In our formulation, all recovered shapes share a common underlying 3D mesh structure – each shape is a deformation of the mean shape. We can leverage this property to reduce texturing of a particular instance to predicting the texture of the mean shape. Our mean shape is isomorphic to a sphere, whose texture can be represented as an image I^{uv}, the values of which get mapped onto the surface via a fixed UV mapping (akin to unrolling a globe into a flat map) [13]. Therefore, we formulate the task of texture prediction as that of inferring the pixel values of I^{uv}. This image can be thought of as a canonical appearance space of the object category. For example, a particular triangle on the predicted shape always maps to a particular region in I^{uv}, irrespective of how it was deformed. This is illustrated in Fig. 3. In this texture parameterization, each pixel in the UV image has a consistent

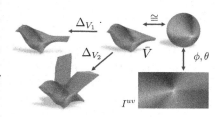

Fig. 3. Illustration of the UV mapping. We illustrate how a texture image I^{uv} can induce a corresponding texture on the predicted meshes. A point on a sphere can be mapped onto the image I^{uv} via using spherical coordinates. As our mean shape has the same mesh geometry (vertex connectivity) as a sphere we can transfer this mapping onto the mean shape. The different predicted shapes, in turn, are simply deformations of the mean shape and can use the same mapping.

semantic meaning, thereby making it easier for the prediction model to leverage common patterns such as correlation between the bird back and the body color.

We incorporate texture prediction module into our framework by setting up a decoder that upconvolves the latent representation to the spatial dimension of I^{uv}. While directly regressing the pixel values of I^{uv} is a feasible approach, this often results in blurry images. Instead, we take inspiration from [38] and formulate this task as that of predicting the appearance flow. Instead of regressing the pixel values of I^{uv}, the texture module outputs where to copy the color of the pixel from the original input image. This prediction mechanism, depicted in Fig. 4, easily allows our predicted texture to retain the details present in the input image. We refer to this output as 'texture flow' $\mathcal{F} \in \mathbb{R}^{H_{uv} \times W_{uv} \times 2}$, where H_{uv}, W_{uv} are the height and width of I^{uv}, and $\mathcal{F}(u, v)$ indicates the (x, y) coordinates of the input image to sample the pixel value from. This allows us to generate the UV image $I^{uv} = G(I; \mathcal{F})$ by bilinear sampling G of the original input image I according to the predicted flow $\mathcal{F}$. This is illustrated in Fig. 4.

Now we formulate our texture loss, which encourages the rendered texture image to match the foreground image:

$$L_{\texttt{texture}} = \sum_i \text{dist}(S_i \odot I_i, S_i \odot \mathcal{R}(V_i, F, \tilde{\pi}_i, I^{uv})). \tag{3}$$

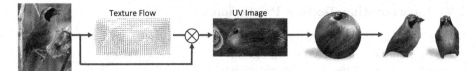

Fig. 4. Illustration of texture flow. We predict a texture flow $\mathcal{F}$ that is used to bilinearly sample the input image I to generate the texture image I^{uv}. We can use this predicted UV image I^{uv} to then texture the instance mesh via the UV mapping procedure illustrated in Fig. 3.

$\mathcal{R}(V_i, F, \tilde{\pi}_i, I_i^{uv})$ is the rendering of the 3D mesh with texture defined by I^{uv}. We use the perceptual metric of Zhang *et al.* [37] as the distance metric.

The loss function above provides supervisory signals to regions of I^{uv} corresponding to the foreground portion of the image, but not to other regions of I^{uv} corresponding to parts that are not directly visible in the image. While the common patterns across the dataset *e.g.* similar colors for bird body and back can still allow meaningful prediction, we find it helpful to add a further loss that encourages the texture flow to select pixels only from the foreground region in the image. This can be simply expressed by sampling the distance transform field of the foreground mask $\mathcal{D}_S$ (where for all points x in the foreground, $\mathcal{D}_S(x) = 0$) according to $\mathcal{F}$ and summing the resulting image:

$$L_{\mathrm{dt}} = \sum_i \sum_{u,v} G(\mathcal{D}_{S_i}; \mathcal{F}_i)(u, v). \tag{4}$$

In contrast to inferring the full texture map, directly sampling the actual pixel values that the predicted mesh projects onto creates holes and leaking of the background texture at the boundaries. Similarly to the shape parametrization, we also explicitly encode symmetry in our I^{uv} prediction, where symmetric faces gets mapped on to the same UV coordinate in I^{uv}. Additionally, we only back-propagate gradients from L_{texture} to the predicted texture (and not the predicted shape) since bilinear sampling often results in high-frequency gradients that destabilize shape learning. Our shape prediction is therefore learned only using the objective in Eq. (2), and the losses L_{texture} and L_{dt} can be viewed as encouraging prediction of correct texture 'on top' of the learned shape.

3   Experiments

We demonstrate the ability of our presented approach to learn single-view inference of shape, texture and camera pose using only a category-level annotated image collection. As a running example, we consider the 'bird' object category as it represents a challenging scenario that has not been addressed via previous approaches. We first present, in Sect. 3.1, our experimental setup, describing the annotated image collection and CNN architecture used.

As ground-truth 3D is not available for benchmarking, we present extensive qualitative results in Sect. 3.2, demonstrating that we learn to predict meaningful shapes and textures across birds. We also show we capture the shape deformation space of the category and that the implicit correspondences in the deformable model allow us to have applications like texture transfer across instances.

We also present some quantitative results to provide evidence for the accuracy of our shape and camera estimates in Sect. 3.3. While there has been little work for reconstructing categories like birds, some approaches have examined the task of learning shape prediction using an annotated image collection for some rigid classes. In Sect. 3.4 we present our method's results on some additional representative categories, and show that our method performs comparably, if not better than the previously proposed alternates while having several additional advantages *e.g.* learning semantic keypoints and texture prediction.

3.1 Experimental Setup

Dataset. We use the CUB-200-2011 dataset [32], which has 6000 training and test images of 200 species of birds. Each image is annotated with the bounding box, visibility indicator and locations of 14 semantic keypoints, and the ground truth foreground mask. We filter out nearly 300 images where the visible number of keypoints are less than or equal to 6, since these typically correspond to truncated close shots. We divide the test set in half to create a validation set, which we use for hyper-parameter tuning.

Network Architecture. A schematic of the various modules of our prediction network is depicted in Fig. 2. The encoder consists of an ImageNet pretrained ResNet-18 [12], followed by a convolutional layer that downsamples the spatial and the channel dimensions by half. This is vectorized to form a 4096-D vector, which is sent to two fully-connected layers to get to the shared latent space of size 200. The deformation and the camera prediction components are linear layers on top of this latent space. The texture flow component consists of 5 upconvolution layers where the final output is passed through a $tanh$ function to keep the flow in a normalized $[-1, 1]$ space. We use the neural mesh renderer [16] so all rendering procedures are differentiable. All images are cropped using the instance bounding box and resized such that the maximum image dimension is 256. We augment the training data on the fly by jittering the scale and translation of the bounding box and with image mirroring. Our mesh geometry corresponds to that of a perfectly symmetric sphere with 642 vertices and 1280 faces.

3.2 Qualitative Results

We visualize the results and application of our learned predictor using the CUB dataset. We show various reconstructions corresponding to different input images, visualize some of the deformation modes learned, and show that the common deformable model parametrization allows us to transfer the texture of one instance onto another.

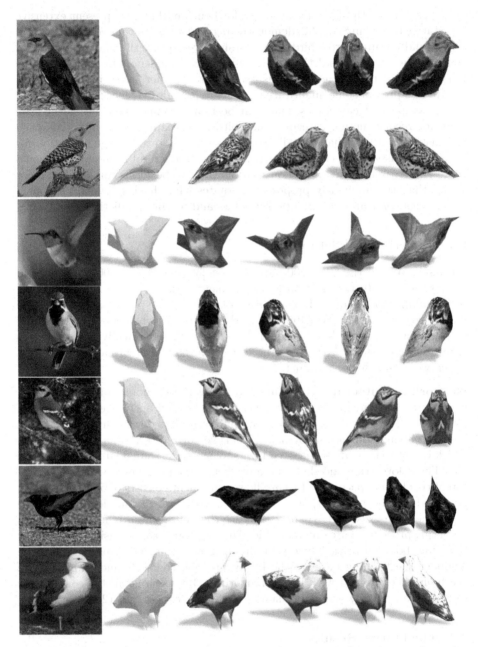

Fig. 5. Sample results. We show predictions of our approach on images from the test set. For each input image on the left, we visualize (in order): the predicted 3D shape and texture viewed from the predicted camera, and textured shape from three novel viewpoints. See the appendix for additional randomly selected results and video at https://akanazawa.github.io/cmr/.

Single-View 3D Reconstruction. We show sample reconstruction results on images from the CUB test set in Fig. 5. We show the predicted shape and texture from the inferred camera viewpoint, as well as from novel views. Please see appendix for additional randomly selected samples and videos showing the results from 360 views.

We observe that our learned model can accurately predict the shape, estimate the camera and also infer meaningful texture from the corresponding input image. Our predicted 3D shape captures the overall shape (fat or thin birds), and even some finer details *e.g.* beaks or large deformations *e.g.* flying birds. Additionally, our learned pose and texture prediction are accurate and realistic across different instances. We observe that the error modes corresponds to not predicting rare poses, and inability to incorporate asymmetric articulation. However, we feel that these predictions learned using only an annotated image collection are encouraging.

Learned Shape Space. The presented approach represents the shape of an instance via a category-level learned mean shape and a per-instance predicted deformation Δ_V. To gain insight into the common modes of deformation captured via our predictor, obtained the principal deformation modes by computing PCA on the predicted deformations across all instances in the training set.

We visualize in Fig. 6 our mean shape deformed in directions corresponding three common deformation modes. We note that these plausibly correspond to some of the natural factors of variation in the 3D structure across birds *e.g.* fat or thin birds, opening of wings, deformation of tails and legs.

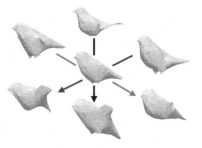

Fig. 6. Learned deformation modes. We visualize the space of learned shapes by depicting the mean shape (centre) and three common modes of deformation as obtained by PCA on the predicted deformations across the dataset.

Texture Transfer. Recall that the textures of different instance in our formulation are captured in a canonical appearance space in the form of a predicted 'texture image' I_{uv}. This parametrization allows us to easily modify the surface appearance, and in particular transfer texture across instances.

We show some results in Fig. 7 where we sample pairs of instances, and transfer the texture from one image onto the predicted shape of the other. We can achieve this by simply using the predicted texture image corresponding to the first when rendering the predicted 3D for the other. We note that even though the two views might be different, since the underlying 'texture image' space is consistent, the transferred texture is also semantically consistent *e.g.* the colors corresponding to the one bird's body are transferred onto the other bird's body.

Fig. 7. Texture Transfer Results. Our representation allows us to easily transfer the predicted texture across instances using the canonical appearance image (see text for details). We visualize sample results of texture transfer across different pairs of birds. For each pair, we show (left): the input image, (middle): the predicted textured mesh from the predicted viewpoint, and (right): the predicted mesh textured using the predicted texture of the other bird.

3.3   Quantitative Evaluation

We attempt to indirectly measure the quality of our recovered reconstructions on the CUB dataset. As there is no ground-truth 3D available for benchmarking, we instead evaluate the mask reprojection accuracy. For each test instance in the CUB dataset, we obtain a mask prediction via rendering the predicted 3D shape from the predicted camera viewpoint. We then compute the intersection over union (IoU) of this predicted mask with the annotated ground-truth mask. Note that to correctly predict the foreground mask, we need both, accurate shape and accurate camera.

Our results are plotted in Fig. 8. We compare the accuracy our full shape prediction (using learned mean shape $\bar{V}$ and predicted deformation Δ_V) against only using the learned mean shape to obtain the predicted mask. We observe that the predicted deformations result in improvements, indicating that we are able to capture the specifics of the shape of different instances. Additionally, we also report the performance using the camera obtained via structure from motion (which uses ground-truth annotated keypoints) instead of using the predicted camera. We note that comparable results in the two settings demonstrate the accuracy of our learned camera estimation. Lastly, we can also measure our

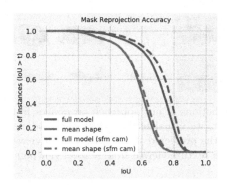

Fig. 8. Mask reprojection accuracy evaluation on CUB. We plot the fraction of test instances with IoU between the predicted and ground-truth mask higher than different thresholds (higher is better) and compare the predictions using the full model against only using the learned mean shape. We report the reprojection accuracy using predicted cameras and cameras obtained via structure-from-motion based on keypoint annotation.

Table 1. Reconstruction evaluation using PASCAL 3D+. We report the mean intersection over union (IoU) on PASCAL 3D+ to benchmark the obtained 3D reconstructions (higher is better). We compare to previous deformable model fitting-based [15] and volumetric prediction [30] approaches that use similar image collection supervision. Note that our approach can additionally predict texture and semantics

Method	Aeroplane	Car
CSDM [15]	0.40	0.60
DRC [30]	0.42	0.67
Ours	0.46	0.64

keypoint reprojection accuracy using the percentage of correct keypoints (PCK) metric [36]. We similarly observe that our full predicted shape performs (slightly) better than only relying on the category-level mean shape – by obtaining a PCK (at normalized distance threshold 0.1) of 0.81 compared to 0.80. The improvement over the mean shape is less prominent in this scenario as most of the semantic keypoints defined are on the torso and therefore typically undergo only small deformations.

3.4 Evaluation on Other Object Classes

While our primary results focus on predicting the 3D shape and texture of birds using the CUB dataset, we note that some previous approaches have examined the task of shape inference/prediction using a similar annotated image collection as supervision. While these previous methods do not infer texture, we can compare our shape predictions against those obtained by these techniques.

We compare to previous deformable model fitting-based [15] and volumetric prediction [30] methods using the PASCAL 3D+ dataset and examine the car and aeroplane categories. Both of these approaches can leverage the annotation we have available *i.e.* segmentation masks and keypoints to learn 3D shape inference (although [30] requires annotated cameras instead of keypoints). Similar to [30], we use PASCAL VOC and Imagenet images with available keypoint annotations from PASCAL3D+ to train our model, and use an off-the shelf segmentation algorithm [11] to obtain foreground masks for the ImageNet subset.

Fig. 9. Pascal 3D+ results. We show predictions of our approach on images from the test set. For each input image on the left, we visualize (in order): the predicted 3D shape viewed from the predicted camera, the predicted shape with texture viewed from the predicted camera, and the shape with texture viewed from a novel viewpoint.

We report the mean IoU evaluation on the test set in Table 1 and observe that we perform comparably, if not better than these alternate methods. We also note that our approach yields additional outputs *e.g.* texture, that these methods do not. We visualize some predictions in Fig. 9. While our predicted shapes are often reasonable, the textures have more errors due to shiny regions (*e.g.* for cars) or smaller amount of training data (*e.g.* for aeroplanes).

4   Discussion

We have presented a framework for learning single-view prediction of a textured 3D mesh using an image collection as supervision. While our results represent an encouraging step, we have by no means solved the problem in the general case, and a number of interesting challenges and possible directions remain. Our formulation addresses shape change and articulation via a similar shape deformation mechanism, and it may be beneficial to extend our deformable shape model to explicitly allow articulation. Additionally, while we presented a method to synthesize texture via copying image pixels, a more sophisticated mechanism that allows both, copying image content and synthesizing novel aspects might be desirable. Finally, even though we can learn using only a single-view per training instance, our approach may be equally applicable, and might yield perhaps even better results, for the scenario where multiple views per training instance are available. However, on the other end of the supervision spectrum, it would be desirable to relax the need of annotation even further, and investigate learning similar prediction models using unannotated image collections.

Acknowledgments. We thank David Fouhey for the creative title suggestions and members of the BAIR community for helpful discussions and comments. This work was supported in part by Intel/NSF VEC award IIS-1539099, NSF Award IIS-1212798, and BAIR sponsors.

References

1. Anguelov, D., Srinivasan, P., Koller, D., Thrun, S., Rodgers, J., Davis, J.: SCAPE: shape completion and animation of people. ACM Trans. Graph. (TOG) (Proceedings of ACM SIGGRAPH) (2005)

2. Blanz, V., Vetter, T.: A morphable model for the synthesis of 3D faces. In: ACM SIGGRAPH (1999)
3. Cashman, T.J., Fitzgibbon, A.W.: What shape are dolphins? Building 3D morphable models from 2D images. TPAMI **5**(1), 232–244 (2013)
4. Choy, C.B., Xu, D., Gwak, J., Chen, K., Savarese, S.: 3D–R2N2: a unified approach for single and multi-view 3D object reconstruction. In: ECCV (2016)
5. Cootes, T.F., Taylor, C.J.: Active shape modelssmart snakes. In: BMVC (1992)
6. Dürer, A.: Four Books on Human Proportion. Formschneyder (1528)
7. Fan, H., Su, H., Guibas, L.J.: A point set generation network for 3D object reconstruction from a single image. In: CVPR (2017)
8. Girdhar, R., Fouhey, D., Rodriguez, M., Gupta, A.: Learning a predictable and generative vector representation for objects. In: ECCV (2016)
9. Gwak, J., Choy, C.B., Garg, A., Chandraker, M., Savarese, S.: Weakly supervised 3D reconstruction with adversarial constraint. In: 3DV (2017)
10. Häne, C., Tulsiani, S., Malik, J.: Hierarchical surface prediction for 3d object reconstruction. In: 3DV (2017)
11. He, K., Gkioxari, G., Dollár, P., Girshick, R.: Mask R-CNN. In: ICCV (2017)
12. He, K., Zhang, X., Ren, S., Sun, J.: Identity mappings in deep residual networks. In: ECCV (2016)
13. Hughes, J.F., Foley, J.D.: Computer graphics: principles and practice. Pearson Education (2014)
14. Kanazawa, A., Black, M.J., Jacobs, D.W., Malik, J.: End-to-end recovery of human shape and pose. In: CVPR (2018)
15. Kar, A., Tulsiani, S., Carreira, J., Malik, J.: Category-specific object reconstruction from a single image. In: CVPR (2015)
16. Kato, H., Ushiku, Y., Harada, T.: Neural 3D mesh renderer. In: CVPR (2018)
17. Khamis, S., Taylor, J., Shotton, J., Keskin, C., Izadi, S., Fitzgibbon, A.: Learning an efficient model of hand shape variation from depth images. In: CVPR (2015)
18. Laine, S., Karras, T., Aila, T., Herva, A., Saito, S., Yu, R., Li, H., Lehtinen, J.: Production-level facial performance capture using deep convolutional neural networks. In: Proceedings of the ACM SIGGRAPH/Eurographics Symposium on Computer Animation (2017)
19. Loper, M., Mahmood, N., Romero, J., Pons-Moll, G., Black, M.J.: SMPL: A skinned multi-person linear model. ACM Trans. Graph. (Proceedings SIGGRAPH Asia) (2015)
20. Pinkall, U., Polthier, K.: Computing discrete minimal surfaces and their conjugates. Exp. Math. (1993)
21. Rezende, D.J., Eslami, S.A., Mohamed, S., Battaglia, P., Jaderberg, M., Heess, N.: Unsupervised learning of 3D structure from images. In: NIPS (2016)
22. Saito, S., Wei, L., Hu, L., Nagano, K., Li, H.: Photorealistic facial texture inference using deep neural networks. In: CVPR (2017)
23. Sela, M., Richardson, E., Kimmel, R.: Unrestricted facial geometry reconstruction using image-to-image translation. In: ICCV (2017)
24. Sinha, A., Unmesh, A., Huang, Q., Ramani, K.: Surfnet: Generating 3d shape surfaces using deep residual networks. In: CVPR (2017)
25. Sorkine, O., Cohen-Or, D., Lipman, Y., Alexa, M., Rössl, C., Seidel, H.P.: Laplacian surface editing. In: Proceedings of the 2004 Eurographics/ACM SIGGRAPH Symposium on Geometry Processing, pp. 175–184. ACM (2004)
26. Tatarchenko, M., Dosovitskiy, A., Brox, T.: Octree generating networks: efficient convolutional architectures for high-resolution 3D outputs. In: ICCV (2017)

27. Taylor, J., Stebbing, R., Ramakrishna, V., Keskin, C., Shotton, J., Izadi, S., Hertzmann, A., Fitzgibbon, A.: User-specific hand modeling from monocular depth sequences. In: CVPR (2014)
28. Tewari, A., Zollhöfer, M., Kim, H., Garrido, P., Bernard, F., Pérez, P., Theobalt, C.: Mofa: model-based deep convolutional face autoencoder for unsupervised monocular reconstruction. In: ICCV (2017)
29. Thompson, D.: On Growth and Form. Cambridge Univ, Press (1917)
30. Tulsiani, S., Zhou, T., Efros, A.A., Malik, J.: Multi-view supervision for single-view reconstruction via differentiable ray consistency. In: CVPR (2017)
31. Vicente, S., Carreira, J., Agapito, L., Batista, J.: Reconstructing PASCAL VOC. In: CVPR (2014)
32. Wah, C., Branson, S., Welinder, P., Perona, P., Belongie, S.: The Caltech-UCSD Birds-200-2011 Dataset. Tech. Rep. CNS-TR-2011-001, California Institute of Technology (2011)
33. Wu, J., Wang, Y., Xue, T., Sun, X., Freeman, W.T., Tenenbaum, J.B.: MarrNet: 3D Shape Reconstruction via 2.5D Sketches. In: NIPS (2017)
34. Yan, X., Yang, J., Yumer, E., Guo, Y., Lee, H.: Perspective transformer nets: learning single-view 3D object reconstruction without 3D supervision. In: NIPS (2016)
35. Yang, B., Rosa, S., Markham, A., Trigoni, N., Wen, H.: 3D object dense reconstruction from a single depth view. arXiv preprint arXiv:1802.00411 (2018)
36. Yang, Y., Ramanan, D.: Articulated pose estimation with flexible mixtures-of-parts. In: CVPR (2011)
37. Zhang, R., Isola, P., Efros, A.A., Shechtman, E., Wang, O.: The unreasonable effectiveness of deep networks as a perceptual metric. In: CVPR (2018)
38. Zhou, T., Tulsiani, S., Sun, W., Malik, J., Efros, A.A.: View synthesis by appearance flow. In: ECCV (2016)
39. Zhu, R., Kiani, H., Wang, C., Lucey, S.: Rethinking reprojection: closing the loop for pose-aware shape reconstruction from a single image. In: ICCV (2017)
40. Zuffi, S., Kanazawa, A., Jacobs, D., Black, M.J.: 3D menagerie: modeling the 3D shape and pose of animals. In: CVPR (2017)

Learning to Forecast and Refine Residual Motion for Image-to-Video Generation

Long Zhao[1(✉)], Xi Peng[2], Yu Tian[1], Mubbasir Kapadia[1],
and Dimitris Metaxas[1]

[1] Rutgers University, Piscataway, USA
{lz311,yt219,mk1353,dnm}@cs.rutgers.edu
[2] Binghamton University, Binghamton, USA
xpeng@binghamton.edu

Abstract. We consider the problem of image-to-video translation, where an input image is translated into an output video containing motions of a single object. Recent methods for such problems typically train transformation networks to generate future frames conditioned on the structure sequence. Parallel work has shown that short high-quality motions can be generated by spatiotemporal generative networks that leverage temporal knowledge from the training data. We combine the benefits of both approaches and propose a two-stage generation framework where videos are generated from structures and then refined by temporal signals. To model motions more efficiently, we train networks to learn residual motion between the current and future frames, which avoids learning motion-irrelevant details. We conduct extensive experiments on two image-to-video translation tasks: facial expression retargeting and human pose forecasting. Superior results over the state-of-the-art methods on both tasks demonstrate the effectiveness of our approach.

Keywords: Video generation · Motion forecasting · Residual learning

1 Introduction

Recently, Generative Adversarial Networks (GANs) [7] have attracted a lot of research interests, as they can be utilized to synthesize realistic-looking images or videos for various vision applications [15,16,39,44,46,47]. Compared with image generation, synthesizing videos is more challenging, since the networks need to learn the appearance of objects as well as their motion models. In this paper, we study a form of classic problems in video generation that can be framed as image-to-video translation tasks, where a system receives one or more images as the input and translates it into a video containing realistic motions of a *single* object. Examples include facial expression retargeting [13,21,34], future prediction [37,38,40], and human pose forecasting[1] [5,6,39].

---

[1] The project website is publicly available at https://garyzhao.github.io/FRGAN.

© Springer Nature Switzerland AG 2018
V. Ferrari et al. (Eds.): ECCV 2018, LNCS 11219, pp. 403–419, 2018.
https://doi.org/10.1007/978-3-030-01267-0_24

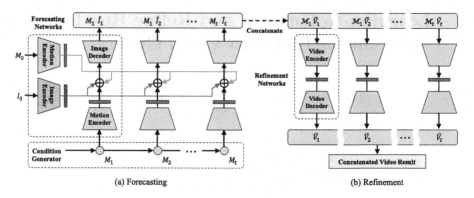

(a) Forecasting   (b) Refinement

Fig. 1. Method overview. Videos are (a) generated from conditions and then (b) refined. Our framework consists of three components: a condition generator, motion forecasting networks and refinement networks. Each part is explained in the corresponding section.

One approach for the long-term future generation [39, 41] is to train a transformation network that translates the input image into each future frame separately conditioned by a sequence of structures. It suggests that it is beneficial to incorporate high-level structures during the generative process. In parallel, recent work [11, 31, 36, 37, 40] has shown that temporal visual features are important for video modeling. Such an approach produces temporally coherent motions with the help of spatiotemporal generative networks but is poor at long-term conditional motion generation since no high-level guidance is provided.

In this paper, we combine the benefits of these two methods. Our approach includes two motion transformation networks as shown in Fig. 1, where the entire video is synthesized in a generation and then refinement manner. In the generation stage, the *motion forecasting networks* observe a single frame from the input and generate all future frames individually, which are conditioned by the structure sequence predicted by a *motion condition generator*. This stage aims to generate a coarse video where the spatial structures of the motions are preserved. In the refinement stage, spatiotemporal *motion refinement networks* are used for refining the output from the previous stage. It performs the generation guided by temporal signals, which targets at producing temporally coherent motions.

For more effective motion modeling, two transformation networks are trained in the *residual space*. Rather than learning the mapping from the structural conditions to motions directly, we force the networks to learn the differences between motions occurring in the current and future frames. The intuition is that learning only the residual motion avoids the redundant motion-irrelevant information, such as static backgrounds, which remains unchanged during the transformation. Moreover, we introduce a novel network architecture using *dense connections* for decoders. It encourages reusing spatially different features and thus yields realistic-looking results.

We experiment on two tasks: facial expression retargeting and human pose forecasting. Success in either task requires reasoning realistic spatial structures as well as temporal semantics of the motions. Strong performances on both tasks demonstrate the effectiveness of our approach. In summary, our work makes the following *contributions*:

- We devise a novel two-stage generation framework for image-to-video translation, where the future frames are generated according to the spatial structure sequence and then refined with temporal signals;
- We investigate learning residual motion for video generation, which focuses on the motion-specific knowledge and avoids learning redundant or irrelevant details from the inputs;
- Dense connections between layers of decoders are introduced to encourage spatially different feature reuse during the generation process, which yields more realistic-looking results;
- We conduct extensive experimental validation on standard datasets which both quantitatively and subjectively compares our method with the state-of-the-arts to demonstrate the effectiveness of the proposed algorithm.

2   Related Work

Deep learning techniques have improved the accuracy of various vision systems [23,24,32,33]. Especially, a lot of generative problems [8,25,26,35] have been solved by GANs [7]. However, traditional frameworks fail to handle complicated tasks, e.g., to generate fine-grained images or videos with large motion changes. Recent approaches [16,42,43] prove that coarse-to-fine strategy can handle these cases. Our model also employs this strategy for video generation.

Xiong et al. [42] proposed an algorithm to generate video in two stages, but there are important differences between their work and ours. First, [42] is proposed for time-lapse videos while we can generate general videos. Second, we make use of structure conditions to guide the generation in the first stage but [42] models this stage with 3D convolutional networks. Finally, we can make long-term predictions while [42] only generates videos with fixed length.

Video Generation. Recent methods [17,38,39,41] solve image-to-video generation problem by training transformation networks that translate the input image into each future frame separately, together with a generator predicting the structure sequence which conditions the future frames. However, due to the absence of pixel-level temporal knowledge during the training process, motion artifacts can be observed from the results of these methods.

Other approaches explore learning temporal visual features from video with spatiotemporal networks. Ji et al. [11] showed how 3D convolutional networks could be applied to human action recognition. Tran et al. [36] employed spatiotemporal 3D convolutions to model features encoded in videos. Vondrick et al. [40] built a model to generate scene dynamics with 3D generative adversarial networks. Our method differs from the two-stream model of [40] in two aspects. First, our residual motion map disentangles motion from the input: the generated frame is conditioned on the current and future motion structures. Second, we can control object motions in future frames efficiently by using structure conditions. Therefore, our method can be applied to motion manipulation problems.

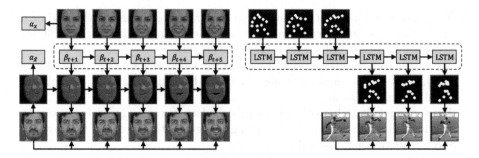

Fig. 2. Illustration of our motion condition generators designed for two tasks. *Left*: For facial expression retargeting, 3D Morphable Model [4] is utilized as domain knowledge to produce expression conditional sequence. *Right*: For human pose forecasting, the pose is represented by the 2D positions of joints. The LSTM [6] observes a sequence of human pose inputs and predicts the next several timesteps.

Dense Connections. Recent studies [9,10] used dense connections for image classification. They have proven that dense connections for encoders strengthen feature propagation and also encourage feature reuse. Instead, we introduce dense connections for decoders. Compared with multi-scale feature fusion in [14] where feature maps are only concatenated to the last layer of the network, our dense connections upsample and concatenate feature maps with different scales to all intermediate layers. Our approach is more efficient at feature re-use when utilized for generation, which yields sharper and more realistic-looking results.

3   Method

As shown in Fig. 1, our framework consists of three components: a motion condition generator G_C, an image-to-image transformation network G_M for forecasting motion conditioned by G_C to each future frame individually, and a video-to-video transformation network G_R which aims to refine the video clips concatenated from the output of G_M. G_C is a task-specific generator that produces a sequence of structures to condition the motion of each future frame. Two discriminators are utilized for adversarial learning, where D_I differentiates real frames from generated ones and D_V is employed for video clips. In the following sections, we explain how each component is designed respectively.

3.1   Motion Condition Generators

In this section, we illustrate how the motion condition generators G_C are implemented for two image-to-video translation tasks: facial expression retargeting

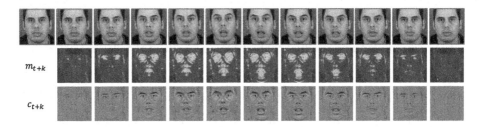

m_{t+k}

c_{t+k}

Fig. 3. Illustration of our residual formulation. We disentangle the motion differences between the input and future frames into a residual motion map m_{t+k} and a residual content map c_{t+k}. Compared with the difference map directly computed from them, our formulation makes the learning task much easier.

and human pose forecasting. One superiority of G_C is that domain-specific knowledge can be leveraged to help the prediction of motion structures.

Facial Expression Retargeting. As shown in Fig. 2, we utilize 3D Morphable Model (3DMM) [4] to model the sequence of expression motions. Given a video containing expression changes of an actor x, it can be parameterized with α_x and $(\beta_t, \beta_{t+1}, \dots, \beta_{t+k})$ using 3DMM, where α_x represents the facial identity and β_t is the expression coefficients in the frame t. In order to retarget the sequence of expressions to another actor $\hat{x}$, we compute the facial identity vector $\alpha_{\hat{x}}$ and combine it with $(\beta_t, \beta_{t+1}, \dots, \beta_{t+k})$ to reconstruct a new sequence of 3D face models with corresponding facial expressions. The conditional motion maps are the normal maps calculated from the 3D models respectively.

Human Pose Forecasting. We follow [39] to implement an LSTM architecture [6] as the human pose predictor. The human pose of each frame is represented by the 2D coordinate positions of joints. The LSTM observes consecutive pose inputs to identify the type of motion, and then predicts the pose for the next period of time. An example is shown in Fig. 2. Note that the motion map is calculated by mapping the output 2D coordinates from the LSTM to heatmaps and concatenating them on depth.

3.2 Motion Forecasting Networks

Starting from the frame I_t at time t, our network synthesizes the future frame I_{t+k} by predicting the residual motion between them. Previous work [16,28] implemented this idea by letting the network estimate a difference map between the input and output, which can be denoted as:

$$I_{t+k} = I_t + G_M(I_t|M_t, M_{t+k}), \tag{1}$$

where M_t is the motion map which conditions I_t. However, this straightforward formulation easily fails when employed to handle videos including large motions, since learning to generate a combination of residual changes from both dynamic and static contents in a single map is quite difficult. Therefore, we introduce an enhanced formulation where the transformation is disentangled into a residual motion map m_{t+k} and a residual content map c_{t+k} with the following definition:

$$I_{t+k} = \underbrace{m_{t+k} \odot c_{t+k}}_{\text{residual motion}} + \underbrace{(1 - m_{t+k}) \odot I_t}_{\text{static content}}, \tag{2}$$

where both m_{t+k} and c_{t+k} are predicted by G_M, and $\odot$ is element-wise multiplication. Intuitively, $m_{t+k} \in [0, 1]$ can be viewed as a spatial mask that highlights where the motion occurs. c_{t+k} is the content of the residual motions. By summing the residual motion with the static content, we can obtain the final result. Note that as visualized in Fig. 3, m_{t+k} forces G_M to reuse the static part from the input and concentrate on inferring dynamic motions.

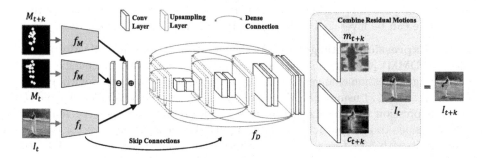

Fig. 4. Architecture of our motion forecasting network G_M. The network observes the input frame I_t with its corresponding motion map M_t, and the motion map of the future frame M_{t+k}. Through analogy learning, the network estimates the *residual motion* between the current frame I_t and future frame I_{t+k}. Note that the *dashed* layers upsample the inputs and connect them to the subsequent dense blocks.

Architecture. Figure 4 shows the architecture of G_M, which is inspired by the visual-structure analogy learning [27]. The future frame I_{t+k} can be generated by transferring the structure differences from M_t to M_{t+k} to the input frame I_t. We use a motion encoder f_M, an image encoder f_I and a residual content decoder f_D to model this concept. And the residual motion is learned by:

$$\Delta(I_{t+k}, I_t) = f_D(f_M(M_{t+k}) - f_M(M_t) + f_I(I_t)). \tag{3}$$

Intuitively, f_M aims to identify key motion features from the motion map containing high-level structural information; f_I learns to map the appearance model of the input into an embedding space, where the motion feature transformations can be easily imposed to generate the residual motion; f_D learns to decode the embedding. Note that we add skip connections [20] between f_I and f_D, which makes it easier for f_D to reuse features of static objects learned from f_I.

Huang et al. [9,10] introduce dense connections to enhance feature propagation and reuse in the network. We argue that this is an appealing property for motion transformation networks as well, since in most cases the output frame shares similar high-level structure with the input frame. Especially, dense connections make it easy for the network to reuse features of different spatial positions when large motions are involved in the image. The decoder of our network thus consists of multiple *dense connections*, each of which connects different dense blocks. A dense block contains two 3×3 convolutional layers. The output of a dense block is connected to the first convolutional layers located in *all* subsequent blocks in the network. As dense blocks have different feature resolutions, we upsample feature maps with lower resolutions when we use them as inputs into higher resolution layers.

Training Details. Given a video clip, we train our network to perform random jumps in time to learn forecasting motion changes. To be specific, for every iteration at training time, we sample a frame I_t and its corresponding motion map M_t given by G_C at time t, and then force it to generate frame I_{t+k} given motion map M_{t+k}. Note that in order to let our network perform learning in the entire residual motion space, k is also randomly defined for each iteration. On the other hand, learning with jumps in time can prevent the network from falling into suboptimal parameters as well [39]. Our network is trained to minimize the following objective function:

$$\mathcal{L}_{G_M} = \mathcal{L}_{rec}(I_{t+k}, \tilde{I}_{t+k}) + \mathcal{L}_r(m_{t+k}) + \mathcal{L}_{gen}. \tag{4}$$

$\mathcal{L}_{rec}$ is the reconstruction loss defined in the image space which measures the pixel-wise differences between the predicted and target frames:

$$\mathcal{L}_{rec}(I_{t+k}, \tilde{I}_{t+k}) = \|I_{t+k} - \tilde{I}_{t+k}\|_1, \tag{5}$$

where $\tilde{I}_{t+k}$ denotes the frame predicted by G_M. The reconstruction loss intuitively offers guidance for our network in making a rough prediction that preserves most content information of the target image. More importantly, it leads the result to share similar structure information with the input image. $\mathcal{L}_r$ is an L-1 norm regularization term defined as:

$$\mathcal{L}_r(m_{t+k}) = \|m_{t+k}\|_1, \tag{6}$$

where m_{t+k} is the residual motion map predicted by G_M. It forces the predicted motion changes to be sparse, since dynamic motions always occur in local positions of each frame while the static parts (e.g., background objects) should be unchanged. $\mathcal{L}_{gen}$ is the adversarial loss that enables our model to generate realistic frames and reduce blurs, and it is defined as:

$$\mathcal{L}_{gen} = -D_I([\tilde{I}_{t+k}, M_{t+k}]), \tag{7}$$

where D_I is the discriminator for images in adversarial learning. We concatenate the output of G_M and motion map M_{t+k} as the input of D_I and make the discriminator conditioned on the motion [18].

Note that we follow WGAN [3,8] to train D_I to measure the Wasserstein distance between distributions of the real images and results generated from G_M. During the optimization of D_I, the following loss function is minimized:

$$\mathcal{L}_{D_I} = D_I([\tilde{I}_{t+k}, M_{t+k}]) - D_I([I_{t+k}, M_{t+k}]) + \lambda \cdot \mathcal{L}_{gp}, \tag{8}$$

$$\mathcal{L}_{gp} = (\|\nabla_{[\hat{I}_{t+k}, M_{t+k}]} D_I([\hat{I}_{t+k}, M_{t+k}])\|_2 - 1)^2, \tag{9}$$

where λ is experimentally set to 10. $\mathcal{L}_{gp}$ is the gradient penalty term proposed by [8] where $\hat{I}_{t+k}$ is sampled from the interpolation of I_{t+k} and $\tilde{I}_{t+k}$, and we extend it to be conditioned on the motion M_{t+k} as well. The adversarial loss in combination with the rest of loss terms allows our network to generate high-quality frames given the motion conditions.

3.3   Motion Refinement Networks

Let $\tilde{V}_t = [\tilde{I}_{t+1}, \tilde{I}_{t+2}, \ldots, \tilde{I}_{t+K}]$ be the video clip with length K temporally concatenated from the outputs of G_M. The goal of the motion refinement network G_R is to refine $\hat{V}_t$ to be more temporally coherent, which is achieved by performing pixel-level refinement with the help of spatiotemporal generative networks. We extends Eq. 2 by adding one additional temporal dimension to let G_R estimate the residual between the real video clip V_t and $\hat{V}_t$, which is defined as:

$$V_t = m_t \odot c_t + (1 - m_t) \odot \tilde{V}_t, \tag{10}$$

where m_t is a spatiotemporal mask which selects either to be refined for each pixel location and timestep, while c_t produces a spatiotemporal cuboid which stands for the refined motion content masked by m_t.

Architecture. Our motion refinement network roughly follows the architectural guidelines of [40]. As shown in Fig. 5, we do not use pooling layers, instead strided and fractionally strided convolutions are utilized for in-network downsampling and upsampling. We also add skip connections to encourage feature reuse. Note that we concatenate the frames with their corresponding conditional motion maps as the inputs to guide the refinement.

Training Details. The key requirement for G_R is that the refined video should be temporal coherent in motion while preserving the annotation information from the input. To this end, we propose to train the network by minimizing a combination of three losses which is similar to Eq. 4:

$$\mathcal{L}_{G_R} = \mathcal{L}_{rec}(V_t, \bar{V}_t) + \mathcal{L}_r(m_t) + \bar{\mathcal{L}}_{gen}, \tag{11}$$

where $\bar{V}_t$ is the output of G_R. $\mathcal{L}_{rec}$ and $\mathcal{L}_r$ share the same definition with Eqs. 5 and 6 respectively. $\mathcal{L}_{rec}$ is the reconstruction loss that aims at refining the synthesized video towards the ground truth with minimal error. Compared with the self-regularization loss proposed by [29], we argue that the sparse regularization term $\mathcal{L}_r$ is also efficient to preserve the annotation information (e.g., the facial

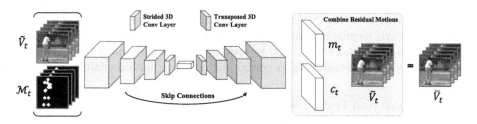

Fig. 5. Architecture of our motion refinement network G_R. The network receives temporally concatenated frames generated by G_M together with their corresponding conditional motion map as the input and aims to refine the video clip to be more temporally coherent. It performs learning in the residual motion space as well.

identity and the type of pose) during the refinement, since it force the network to only modify the essential pixels. $\bar{\mathcal{L}}_{gen}$ is the adversarial loss:

$$\bar{\mathcal{L}}_{gen} = -D_V([\bar{V}_t, \mathcal{M}_t]) - \frac{1}{K} \sum_{i=1}^{K} D_I([\bar{I}_{t+i}, M_{t+i}]), \qquad (12)$$

where $\mathcal{M}_t = [M_{t+1}, M_{t+2}, \ldots, M_{t+K}]$ is the temporally concatenated condition motion maps, and $\bar{I}_{t+i}$ is the i-th frame of $\bar{V}_t$. In the adversarial learning term $\bar{\mathcal{L}}_{gen}$, both D_I and D_V play the role to judge whether the input is a real video clip or not, providing criticisms to G_R. The image discriminator D_I criticizes G_R based on individual frames, which is trained to determine if each frame is sampled from a real video clip. At the same time, D_V provides criticisms to G_R based on the whole video clip, which takes a fixed length video clip as the input and judges if a video clip is sampled from a real video as well as evaluates the motions contained. As suggested by [37], although D_V alone should be sufficient, D_I significantly improves the convergence and the final results of G_R.

We follow the same strategy as introduced in Eq. 8 to optimize D_I. Note that in each iteration, one pair of real and generated frames is randomly sampled from V_t and $\bar{V}_t$ to train D_I. On the other hand, training D_V is also based on the WGAN framework, where we extend it to spatiotemporal inputs. Therefore, D_V is optimized by minimizing the following loss function:

$$\mathcal{L}_{D_V} = D_V([\bar{V}_t, \mathcal{M}_t]) - D_V([V_t, \mathcal{M}_t]) + \lambda \cdot \mathcal{L}_{gp}, \qquad (13)$$

$$\mathcal{L}_{gp} = (\|\nabla_{[\hat{V}_t, \mathcal{M}_t]} D_V([\hat{V}_t, \mathcal{M}_t])\|_2 - 1)^2, \qquad (14)$$

where $\hat{V}_t$ is sampled from the interpolation of V_t and $\bar{V}_t$. Note that G_R, D_I and D_V are trained alternatively. To be specific, we update D_I and D_V in one step while fixing G_R; in the alternating step, we fix D_I and D_V while updating G_R.

4 Experiments

We perform experiments on two image-to-video translation tasks: facial expression retargeting and human pose forecasting. For facial expression retargeting, we demonstrate that our method is able to combine domain-specific knowledge, such as 3DMM, to generate realistic-looking results. For human pose forecasting, experimental results show that our method yields high-quality videos when applied for video generation tasks containing complex motion changes.

4.1 Settings and Databases

To train our networks, we use Adam [12] for optimization with a learning rate of 0.0001 and momentums of 0.0 and 0.9. We first train the forecasting networks, and then train the refinement networks using the generated coarse frames. The batch size is set to 32 for all networks. Due to space constraints, we ask the reader to refer to the project website for the details of the network designs.

We use the *MUG Facial Expression Database* [1] to evaluate our approach on facial expression retargeting. This dataset is composed of 86 subjects (35 women and 51 men). We crop the face regions with regards to the landmark ground truth and scale them to 96×96. To train our networks, we use only the sequences representing one of the six facial expressions: anger, fear, disgust, happiness, sadness, and surprise. We evenly split the database into three groups according to the subjects. Two groups are used for training G_M and G_R respectively, and the results are evaluated on the last one. The 3D Basel Face Model [22] serves as the morphable model to fit the facial identities and expressions for the condition generator G_C. We use [48] to compute the 3DMM parameters for each frame. Note that we train G_R to refine the video clips every 32 frames.

The *Penn Action Dataset* [45] consists of 2326 video sequences of 15 different human actions, which is used for evaluating our method on human pose forecasting. For each action sequence in the dataset, 13 human joint annotations are provided as the ground truth. To remove very noisy joint ground-truth in the dataset, we follow the setting of [39] to sub-sample the actions. Therefore, 8 actions including baseball pitch, baseball swing, clean and jerk, golf swing, jumping jacks, jump rope, tennis forehand, and tennis serve are used for training our networks. We crop video frames based on temporal tubes to remove as much background as possible while ensuring the human actions are in all frames, and then scale each cropped frame to 64×64. We evenly split the standard dataset into three sets. G_M and G_R are trained in the first two sets respectively, while we evaluate our models in the last set. We employ the same strategy as [39] to train the LSTM pose generator. It is trained to observe 10 inputs and predict 32 steps. Note that G_R is trained to refine the video clips with the length of 16.

4.2 Evaluation on Facial Expression Retargeting

We compare our method to MCNet [38], MoCoGAN [37] and Villegas et al. [39] on the MUG Database. For each facial expression, we randomly select one video as the reference, and retarget it to all the subjects in the testing set with different methods. Each method only observes the input frame of the target subject, and performs the generation based on it. Our method and [39] share the same 3DMM-based condition generator as introduced in Sect. 3.1.

Quantitative Comparison. The quality of a generated video are measured by the Average Content Distance (ACD) as introduced in [37]. For each generated video, we make use of OpenFace [2], which outperforms human performance in the face recognition task, to measure the video quality. OpenFace produces a feature vector for each frame, and then the ACD is calculated by measuring the L-2 distance of these vectors. We introduce two variants of the ACD in this experiment. The ACD-I is the average distance between each generated frame and the original input frame. It aims to judge if the facial identity is well-preserved in the generated video. The ACD-C is the average pairwise distance of the per-frame feature vectors in the generated video. It measures the content consistency of the generated video.

Fig. 6. Examples of facial expression retargeting using our algorithm on the MUG Database [1]. We show two expressions as an illustration: (a) happiness and (b) surprise. The reference video and the input target images are highlighted in *green*, while the generated frames are highlighted in *red*. The results are sampled every 8 frames.

Table 1. Video generation quality comparison on the MUG Dataset [1]. We also compute the ACD-* score for the training set, which is the reference

Methods	ACD-I	ACD-C
MCNet [38]	0.545	0.322
Villegas et al. [39]	0.683	0.130
MoCoGAN [37]	0.291	0.205
Ours	**0.184**	**0.107**
Reference	0.109	0.098

Table 2. Average user preference score (the average number of times, a user prefers our result to the competing one) on the MUG Dataset [1]. Our results own higher preference scores compared with the others

Methods	Preference (%)
Ours/MCNet [38]	**84.2**/15.8
Ours/Villegas et al. [39]	**74.6**/25.4
Ours/MoCoGAN [37]	**62.5**/37.5

Table 1 summarizes the comparison results. From the table, we find that our method achieves ACD-* scores both lower than 0.2, which is substantially better than the baselines. One interesting observation is that [39] has the worst ACD-I but its ACD-C is the second best. We argue that this is due to the high-level information offered by our 3DMM-based condition generator, which plays a vital role for producing content consistency results. Our method outperforms other state-of-the-arts, since we utilize both domain knowledge (3DMM) and temporal signals for video generation. We show that it is greatly beneficial to incorporate both factors into the generative process.

We also conduct a user study to quantitatively compare these methods. For each method, we randomly select 10 videos for each expression. We then randomly pair the videos generated by ours with the videos from one of the competing methods to form 54 questions. For each question, 3 users are asked to select the video which is more realistic. To be fair, the videos from different methods are shown in random orders. We report the average user preference scores (the average number of times, a user prefers our result to the competing one) in Table 2. We find that the users consider the videos generated by ours more realistic most of the time. This is consistent with the ACD results in Table 1, in which our method substantially outperforms the baselines.

Visual Results. In Fig. 6, we show the visual results (the expressions of happiness and surprise) generated by our method. We observe that our method is able to generate realistic motions while the facial identities are well-preserved. We hypothesize that the domain knowledge (3DMM) employed serves as a good prior which improves the generation. More visual results of different expressions and subjects are given on the project website.

4.3 Evaluation on Human Pose Forecasting

We compare our approach with VGAN [40], Mathieu et al. [17] and Villegas et al. [39] on the Penn Action Dataset. We produce the results of their models according to their papers or reference codes. For fair comparison, we generate videos with 32 generated frames using each method, and evaluate them starting from the first frame. Note that we train an individual VGAN for different action categories with randomly picked video clips from the dataset, while one network among all categories are trained for every other method. Both [39] and our method perform the generation based on the pre-trained LSTM provided by [39], and we train [39] through the same strategy of our motion forecasting network G_M.

Implementation. Following the settings of [39], we engage the feature similarity loss term $\mathcal{L}_{feat}$ for our motion forecasting network G_M to capture the appearance (C_1) and structure (C_2) of the human action. This loss term is added to Eq. 4, which is defined as:

$$\mathcal{L}_{feat} = \|C_1(I_{t+k}) - C_1(\tilde{I}_{t+k})\|_2^2 + \|C_2(I_{t+k}) - C_2(\tilde{I}_{t+k})\|_2^2, \tag{15}$$

where we use the last convolutional layer of the VGG16 Network [30] as C_1, and the last layer of the Hourglass Network [19] as C_2. Note that we compute the bounding box according to the group truth to crop the human of interest for each frame, and then scale it to 224×224 as the input of the VGG16.

Results. We evaluate the predictions using Peak Signal-to-Noise Ratio (PSNR) and Mean Square Error (MSE). Both metrics perform pixel-level analysis between the ground truth frames and the generated videos. We also report the results of our method and [39] using the condition motion maps computed from the ground truth joints (GT). The results are shown in Fig. 7 and Table 3 respectively. From these two scores, we discover that the proposed method achieves better quantitative results which demonstrates the effectiveness of our algorithm.

Figure 8 shows visual comparison of our method with [39]. We can find that the predicted future of our method is closer to the ground-true future. To be speclfic, our method yields more consistent motions and keeps human appearances as well. Due to space constraints, we ask the reader to refer to the project website for more side by side visual results.

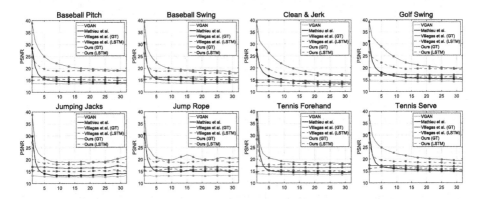

Fig. 7. Comparison of state-of-the-arts using Peak Signal-to-Noise Ratio (PSNR) on different human action categories from the Penn Action Dataset [45].

Table 3. Comparison of state-of-the-art algorithms on the Penn Action Database [45]. A smaller MSE score means better performance

Methods	MSE	MSE (GT)
VGAN [40]	0.047	–
Mathieu et al. [17]	0.041	–
Villegas et al. [39]	0.030	0.025
Ours	**0.023**	**0.011**

Table 4. Quantitative results of ablation study. We report the ACD-* scores on the MUG Database [1] and MSE scores on the Penn Action Dataset [45]

Settings	ACD-I	ACD-C	MSE
G_M ~~(Dense)~~, ~~G_R~~	0.459	0.155	0.027
G_M (Dense), ~~G_R~~	0.252	0.140	0.014
G_M (Dense), G_R	**0.184**	**0.107**	**0.011**

4.4 Ablation Study

Our method consists of three main modules: residual learning, dense connections for the decoder and the two-stage generation schema. Without residual learning, our network decays to [39]. As shown in Sects. 4.2 and 4.3, ours outperforms [39]

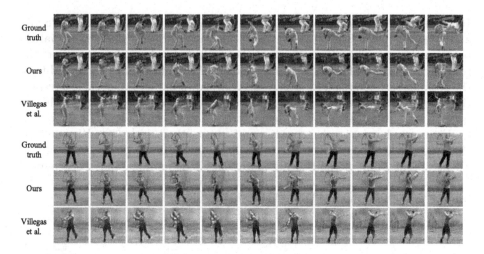

Fig. 8. Visual comparison of our method with Villegas et al. [39] on the Penn Action Dataset [45]. Examples are sampled from the action of baseball (*top*) and tennis (*bottom*) respectively. The results are taken every 5 frames.

which demonstrates the effectiveness of residual learning. To verify the rest modules, we train one partial variant of G_M, where the dense connections are not employed in the decoder f_D. Then we evaluate three different settings of our method on both tasks: G_M without dense connections, using only G_M for generation and our full model. Note that in order to get rid of the influence from the LSTM, we report the results using the conditional motion maps calculated from the ground truth on the Penn Action Dataset. Results are shown in Table 4. Our approach with more modules performs better than those with less components, which suggests the effectiveness of each part of our algorithm.

5   Conclusions

In this paper, we combine the benefits of high-level structural conditions and spatiotemporal generative networks for image-to-video translation by synthesizing videos in a generation and then refinement manner. We have applied this method to facial expression retargeting where we show that our method is able to engage domain knowledge for realistic video generation, and to human pose forecasting where we demonstrate that our method achieves higher performance than state-of-the-arts when generating videos involving large motion changes. We also incorporate residual learning and dense connections to produce high-quality results. In the future, we plan to further explore the use of our framework for other image or video generation tasks.

Acknowledgment. This work is partly supported by the Air Force Office of Scientific Research (AFOSR) under the Dynamic Data-Driven Application Systems Program, NSF 1763523, 1747778, 1733843 and 1703883 Awards. Mubbasir Kapadia has been funded in part by NSF IIS-1703883, NSF S&AS-1723869, and DARPA SocialSim-W911NF-17-C-0098.

References

1. Aifanti, N., Papachristou, C., Delopoulos, A.: The MUG facial expression database. In: International Workshop on Image Analysis for Multimedia Interactive Services (WIAMIS) (2010)

2. Amos, B., Ludwiczuk, B., Satyanarayanan, M.: OpenFace: a general-purpose face recognition library with mobile applications. Technical report, CMU-CS-16-118, CMU School of Computer Science (2016)

3. Arjovsky, M., Chintala, S., Bottou, L.: Wasserstein generative adversarial networks. In: International Conference on Machine Learning (ICML) (2017)

4. Blanz, V., Vetter, T.: Face recognition based on fitting a 3D morphable model. IEEE Trans. Pattern Anal. Mach. Intell. (TPAMI) **25**(9), 1063–1074 (2003)

5. Chao, Y.W., Yang, J., Price, B., Cohen, S., Deng, J.: Forecasting human dynamics from static images. In: IEEE Conference on Computer Vision and Pattern Recognition (CVPR) (2017)

6. Fragkiadaki, K., Levine, S., Felsen, P., Malik, J.: Recurrent network models for human dynamics. In: IEEE International Conference on Computer Vision (ICCV), pp. 4346–4354 (2015)

7. Goodfellow, I. et al.: Generative adversarial nets. In: Annual Conference on Neural Information Processing Systems (NIPS), pp. 2672–2680 (2014)

8. Gulrajani, I., Ahmed, F., Arjovsky, M., Dumoulin, V., Courville, A.: Improved training of wasserstein GANs. In: Annual Conference on Neural Information Processing Systems (NIPS) (2017)

9. Huang, G., Liu, S., van der Maaten, L., Weinberger, K.Q.: Condensenet: an efficient densenet using learned group convolutions. In: IEEE Conference on Computer Vision and Pattern Recognition (CVPR) (2018)

10. Huang, G., Liu, Z., van der Maaten, L., Weinberger, K.Q.: Densely connected convolutional networks. In: IEEE Conference on Computer Vision and Pattern Recognition (CVPR) (2017)

11. Ji, S., Xu, W., Yang, M., Yu, K.: 3D convolutional neural networks for human action recognition. IEEE Trans. Pattern Anal. Mach. Intell. (TPAMI) **35**(1), 221–231 (2013)

12. Kingma, D.P., Ba, J.: Adam: a method for stochastic optimization. In: International Conference on Learning Representations (ICLR) (2014)

13. Laine, S. et al.: Production-level facial performance capture using deep convolutional neural networks. In: Proceedings of the ACM SIGGRAPH/Eurographics Symposium on Computer Animation (2017)

14. Liu, Z., Yeh, R.A., Tang, X., Liu, Y., Agarwala, A.: Video frame synthesis using deep voxel flow. In: IEEE International Conference on Computer Vision (ICCV) (2017)

15. Lu, J., Issaranon, T., Forsyth, D.: SafetyNet: detecting and rejecting adversarial examples robustly. In: IEEE International Conference on Computer Vision (ICCV) (2017)

16. Ma, L., Jia, X., Sun, Q., Schiele, B., Tuytelaars, T., Van Gool, L.: Pose guided person image generation. In: Annual Conference on Neural Information Processing Systems (NIPS), pp. 405–415 (2017)
17. Mathieu, M., Couprie, C., LeCun, Y.: Deep multi-scale video prediction beyond mean square error. In: International Conference on Learning Representations (ICLR) (2016)
18. Mirza, M., Osindero, S.: Conditional generative adversarial nets. arXiv preprint arXiv:1411.1784 (2014)
19. Newell, A., Yang, K., Deng, J.: Stacked hourglass networks for human pose estimation. In: Leibe, B., Matas, J., Sebe, N., Welling, M. (eds.) ECCV 2016. LNCS, vol. 9912, pp. 483–499. Springer, Cham (2016). https://doi.org/10.1007/978-3-319-46484-8_29
20. Ronneberger, O., Fischer, P., Brox, T.: U-Net: convolutional networks for biomedical image segmentation. In: Navab, N., Hornegger, J., Wells, W.M., Frangi, A.F. (eds.) MICCAI 2015. LNCS, vol. 9351, pp. 234–241. Springer, Cham (2015). https://doi.org/10.1007/978-3-319-24574-4_28
21. Olszewski, K. et al.: Realistic dynamic facial textures from a single image using GANs. In: IEEE International Conference on Computer Vision (ICCV) (2017)
22. Paysan, P., Knothe, R., Amberg, B., Romdhani, S., Vetter, T.: A 3D face model for pose and illumination invariant face recognition. In: IEEE International Conference on Advanced Video and Signal based Surveillance (AVSS) for Security, Safety and Monitoring in Smart Environments (2009)
23. Peng, X., Feris, R.S., Wang, X., Metaxas, D.N.: A recurrent encoder-decoder network for sequential face alignment. In: European Conference on Computer Vision (ECCV), pp. 38–56 (2016)
24. Peng, X., Huang, J., Hu, Q., Zhang, S., Elgammal, A., Metaxas, D.: From circle to 3-sphere: head pose estimation by instance parameterization. Comput. Vis. Image Underst. (CVIU) **136**, 92–102 (2015)
25. Peng, X., Tang, Z., Yang, F., Feris, R.S., Metaxas, D.: Jointly optimize data augmentation and network training: Adversarial data augmentation in human pose estimation. In: IEEE Conference on Computer Vision and Pattern Recognition (CVPR), pp. 2226–2234 (2018)
26. Perarnau, G., van de Weijer, J., Raducanu, B., Álvarez, J.M.: Invertible conditional GANs for image editing. In: NIPS Workshop on Adversarial Training (2016)
27. Reed, S.E., Zhang, Y., Zhang, Y., Lee, H.: Deep visual analogy-making. In: Annual Conference on Neural Information Processing Systems (NIPS) (2015)
28. Shen, W., Liu, R.: Learning residual images for face attribute manipulation. In: IEEE Conference on Computer Vision and Pattern Recognition (CVPR) (2017)
29. Shrivastava, A., Pfister, T., Tuzel, O., Susskind, J., Wang, W., Webb, R.: Learning from simulated and unsupervised images through adversarial training. In: IEEE Conference on Computer Vision and Pattern Recognition (CVPR) (2017)
30. Simonyan, K., Zisserman, A.: Very deep convolutional networks for large-scale image recognition. In: International Conference on Learning Representations (ICLR) (2015)
31. Simonyan, K., Zisserman, A.: Two-stream convolutional networks for action recognition in videos. In: Annual Conference on Neural Information Processing Systems (NIPS), pp. 568–576 (2014)
32. Tang, Z., Peng, X., Geng, S., Wu, L., Zhang, S., Metaxas, D.N.: Quantized densely connected U-Nets for efficient landmark localization. In: European Conference on Computer Vision (ECCV) (2018)

33. Tang, Z., Peng, X., Geng, S., Zhu, Y., Metaxas, D.: CU-Net: coupled U-Nets. In: British Machine Vision Conference (BMVC) (2018)
34. Thies, J., Zollhöfer, M., Stamminger, M., Theobalt, C., Nießner, M.: Face2Face: real-time face capture and reenactment of RGB videos. In: IEEE Conference on Computer Vision and Pattern Recognition (CVPR) (2016)
35. Tian, Y., Peng, X., Zhao, L., Zhang, S., Metaxas, D.N.: CR-GAN: learning complete representations for multi-view generation. In: International Joint Conference on Artificial Intelligence (IJCAI), pp. 942–948 (2018)
36. Tran, D., Bourdev, L., Fergus, R., Torresani, L., Paluri, M.: Learning spatiotemporal features with 3D convolutional networks. In: IEEE International Conference on Computer Vision (ICCV), pp. 4489–4497 (2015)
37. Tulyakov, S., Liu, M.Y., Yang, X., Kautz, J.: MoCoGAN: decomposing motion and content for video generation. In: IEEE Conference on Computer Vision and Pattern Recognition (CVPR) (2018)
38. Villegas, R., Yang, J., Hong, S., Lin, X., Lee, H.: Decomposing motion and content for natural video sequence prediction. In: International Conference on Learning Representations (ICLR) (2017)
39. Villegas, R., Yang, J., Zou, Y., Sohn, S., Lin, X., Lee, H.: Learning to generate long-term future via hierarchical prediction. In: International Conference on Machine Learning (ICML) (2017)
40. Vondrick, C., Pirsiavash, H., Torralba, A.: Generating videos with scene dynamics. In: Annual Conference on Neural Information Processing Systems (NIPS) (2016)
41. Xingjian, S., Chen, Z., Wang, H., Yeung, D.Y., Wong, W.K., Woo, W.c.: Convolutional LSTM network: A machine learning approach for precipitation nowcasting. In: Annual Conference on Neural Information Processing Systems (NIPS), pp. 802–810 (2015)
42. Xiong, W., Luo, W., Ma, L., Liu, W., Luo, J.: Learning to generate time-lapse videos using multi-stage dynamic generative adversarial networks. In: IEEE Conference on Computer Vision and Pattern Recognition (CVPR) (2018)
43. Zhang, H. et al.: StackGAN: text to photo-realistic image synthesis with stacked generative adversarial networks. In: IEEE International Conference on Computer Vision (ICCV) (2017)
44. Zhang, H., Sindagi, V., Patel, V.M.: Image de-raining using a conditional generative adversarial network. arXiv preprint arXiv:1701.05957 (2017)
45. Zhang, W., Zhu, M., Derpanis, K.: From Actemes to action: a strongly-supervised representation for detailed action understanding. In: IEEE International Conference on Computer Vision (ICCV) (2013)
46. Zhang, Z., Xie, Y., Yang, L.: Photographic text-to-image synthesis with a hierarchically-nested adversarial network. In: IEEE Conference on Computer Vision and Pattern Recognition (CVPR) (2018)
47. Zhang, Z., Yang, L., Zheng, Y.: Translating and segmenting multimodal medical volumes with cycle-and shapeconsistency generative adversarial network. In: IEEE Conference on Computer Vision and Pattern Recognition (CVPR) (2018)
48. Zhu, X., Lei, Z., Liu, X., Shi, H., Li, S.: Face alignment across large poses: A 3D solution. In: IEEE Conference on Computer Vision and Pattern Recognition (CVPR) (2016)

Teaching Machines to Understand Baseball Games: Large-Scale Baseball Video Database for Multiple Video Understanding Tasks

Minho Shim⬤, Young Hwi Kim⬤, Kyungmin Kim⬤, and Seon Joo Kim$^{(\boxtimes)}$⬤

Yonsei University, Seoul, South Korea
{minhoshim,younghwikim,kyungminkim,seonjookim}@yonsei.ac.kr

Abstract. A major obstacle in teaching machines to understand videos is the lack of training data, as creating temporal annotations for long videos requires a huge amount of human effort. To this end, we introduce a new large-scale baseball video dataset called the BBDB, which is produced semi-automatically by using play-by-play texts available online. The BBDB contains 4200+hr of baseball game videos with 400k+ temporally annotated activity segments. The new dataset has several major challenging factors compared to other datasets: (1) the dataset contains a large number of visually similar segments with different labels. (2) It can be used for many video understanding tasks including video recognition, localization, text-video alignment, video highlight generation, and data imbalance problem. To observe the potential of the BBDB, we conducted extensive experiments by running many different types of video understanding algorithms on our new dataset. The database is available at https://sites.google.com/site/eccv2018bbdb/.

Keywords: Video understanding · Large-scale video dataset
Action recognition · Temporal localization

1 Introduction

As from the old saying "Seeing is believing," paintings, photos, and videos are all produced to deliver what humans see. The ultimate goal of computer vision is to make machines to understand those visual media, and due to the rapid progress in the deep learning technology, we have now reached a point where we can teach a machine to understand a single image fairly well.

Among the visual media, videos are the most comprehensive media that most resembles how we as humans perceive the visual world. However, making machines to understand videos is still very challenging due to the additional temporal dimension. Videos include varying length of events and separating between

---

M. Shim, Y. H. Kim and K. Kim—Equal contribution

V. Ferrari et al. (Eds.): ECCV 2018, LNCS 11219, pp. 420–437, 2018.
https://doi.org/10.1007/978-3-030-01267-0_25

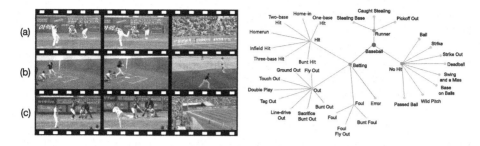

Fig. 1. *(left)* Understanding baseball videos: (a), (b), and (c) show a few samples from homerun, infield hit, and foul sequence, respectively. It is simply not enough to recognize a few frames or a discrete set of actions like hitting or running, to fully understand a baseball game or in general any video. *(right)* Semantic class hierarchy based on the baseball rule.

different classes of similar actions require better understanding of the motion. For example, classifying between walking and swimming may be relatively easy as the classification can rely solely on the visual features. For such a problem, just one single image may be enough to carry out the classification task. However, separating between similar activities like walking and running requires good motion features on top of the visual features. In addition, inferring the temporal progression of an event is another factor that needs to be accounted in video recognition. By looking at a man running, a system cannot easily determine whether it will end up with a vault or a long jump.

The goal of this paper is to introduce a new large-scale video database to promote the research in video understanding. Many video datasets have been introduced already [1, 3, 7, 14–16, 21, 22, 24–26, 28, 33, 34, 37, 41, 42, 52]. However, most of the existing databases fall short when trying to learn the minute difference between similar actions. The class labels in the existing database are quite distinct such as vacuuming floor, cleaning toilet, and cleaning windows. While they provide good data to learn good visual and motion features for video analysis, we are more interested in providing data with much more similarity.

Thus we present a new large-scale video dataset called the BBDB (stands for **B**ase-**b**all **D**ata**b**ase). BBDB contains 4,200+ hours (more than 500 million frames) of baseball game videos with 400k+ temporally annotated activity segments. The temporal boundaries have been annotated by making use of the play-by-play texts available online with minimal human validation, reducing the huge amount of human labor necessary for the labeling process. We categorize the actions in baseball games into 30 classes that include strike pitch, ball pitch, single/double/triple hits, homerun, etc (Fig. 1). What sets our database apart from the previous datasets is the visual and the motion similarities between the classes. A strike pitch and a ball pitch are visually similar and differentiating between the two can be difficult even for humans.

Our dataset can be used to solve other interesting problems in computer vision in addition to video recognition and localization. Class-imbalance is inherently imposed in our dataset; e.g.home-run is rare compared to strike and ball.

Learning with imbalanced class sizes is a very important problem in machine learning that have yet been looked at in depth. Our dataset provides a natural opportunity to tackle this imbalance problem. We have also collected corresponding highlights for each game in the dataset. This could be used for video highlight generation research.

2   Related Work

Database. Numerous video databases have been introduced to boost up the capability of video understanding models. Datasets for the action recognition [15,22,25,42] have been widely used, but those benchmarks provide temporally trimmed video around the action, limiting the practical use for various video understanding tasks.

Sports-1M [21] and YouTube-8M [1] introduce untrimmed video datasets, providing more complete data for realistic video understanding. KTH [34], THUMOS'15 [14], ActivityNet [3], and Charades [37] provide untrimmed videos with temporal locations, but most classes are visually distinct so that inferring an action class may depend on a few frames rather than understanding the whole sequence. Also, [3,14] contain only a small number of action instances per video; 1.1 and 1.41 annotations on average, respectively. MultiTHUMOS [52] is an extended version of THUMOS with the goal of providing multi-labeled annotation. While the dataset includes fine-grained classes such as basketball dunk, dribble, and guard, the number of videos of those classes is 420 on average, which still falls short of training a deep neural network for understanding visually similar classes. Relevant datasets [26,33] capturing fine-grained human actions exist, but those datasets consist of relatively short videos. Meanwhile, [7,16,41] provide useful benchmarks for the video summarization tasks. These datasets ask annotators to score units of video clips depending on annotators' criteria of importance. The labeling process requires many annotators per video, resulting in small size dataset.

Our large-scale video dataset BBDB provides more than 4,200 h of videos. Out of 30 activity classes in our dataset, 23 classes have more than 1000 video clips and the other 7 classes also have more than 400 clips on average. Furthermore, an average length of the untrimmed videos in our dataset is 3.6 h, making our benchmark more challenging as the models have to understand longer sequence of events. Each video is accompanied by its corresponding highlight video, and therefore our database can be used for the video summarization or highlight generation as well. Finally, our dataset is collected through a semi-automatic process with minimal human effort, so it is easy to scale up the size of the dataset.

Action Recognition. Before the deep learning era, handcrafted motion features like the improved dense trajectories [48] were widely used to extract appearance and motion features. One popular approach to learn spatio-temporal representation is to exploit 3D convolution. In the early stage, [20,45,46] applied simple 3D convolution network on action recognition. Recently, deeper 3D ConvNets [4,17,32,47] are proposed showing the state-of-the-art performance by inflating the well-known 2D networks (e.g.ResNet) into 3D. Another branch of video representation learning is the two-stream method [39] consisting of two complementary networks, appearance and motion network. Variations of the two-stream [10–12] were also introduced, exploring various ways of fusing the two streams. Aforementioned methods leverage only a fixed length of frames and a video level representation is obtained by computing the average score of segments. To model long-term temporal information, [9,29,44] employed RNN on top of the CNN and more sophisticated schemes such as TSN [50] have been proposed to watch the entire video during training.

Handling Imbalanced Dataset. Real data are imbalanced by nature. We see people walking all the time but rarely see a person back-flipping. Being able to deal with this problem of imbalance in the number of data per class is an important problem in machine learning [18], but it has yet been explored extensively. Classic approaches include heuristic sampling or adjusting cost functions to reflect the frequency of classes [5,23]. One could also use the focal loss [27] that has been proposed recently, which adjusts the cross entropy loss based on whether a class is well classified or not.

Temporal Action Localization. Temporal action localization is the problem of extracting target video segments in untrimmed videos. The basic approach for this problem [13,49] is to divide clips by a sliding window, extract features from the clips, and pass it to a classifier. Various deep learning based solutions [36, 53,54] have also been introduced to solve this problem. The precision of the temporal action localization task is still low compared to other tasks. It has been pointed out that the main reason for the lack of precision is the lack of data, due to the difficulty of annotating the dataset [54].

Text-Video Alignment. Collecting dense annotations of action is costly and time-consuming. Several approaches were proposed to learn temporal localization in a weakly supervised manner. The goal is to label each frame with the corresponding action label, given only the sequence of actions without exact time stamps. An extended CTC framework [19] was proposed to evaluate all the possible alignments, enforced to be consistent with inter-frame visual similarities. Another approach [2] formulated the problem as a convex relaxation on discriminative clustering under ordering constraints.

3 Baseball Database

The goal of our Baseball Database (BBDB) is to provide a challenging benchmark for higher level understanding of videos. Previous datasets have focused on literal human actions such as running, and jumping. Only a few datasets have elaborate labels on videos; e.g.dense detailed labels [37,52], or dense caption [24]. When a sports game is analyzed with a visual recognition system trained on those simple actions, retrieved sequences of human actions will not be comprehensive enough to understand the game. This is because a sports game is a series of events, which can only be explained by a combination of action, sequential, and semantic information.

Constructing a large video dataset is challenging, especially when tasks require annotated temporal boundaries. Labeling videos involves tremendous amount of human effort, such that automating such process is one of the goals of an action detection algorithm. Labels of BBDB are collected in a semi-automatic manner making use of the play-by-play broadcasts available online. With this strategy, we could dramatically reduce human labor and create precise temporal annotations.

Among different video domains, baseball has a number of advantages over others. First, baseball has less anomalies due to its clear-cut rules and abundant statistics. This is why the play-by-play texts from the broadcasters can be utilized to generate precise segment locations. The rules are also crucial in the validation step, to analyze whether a system correctly understood the events and the underlying rules; e.g.strike-out can only come after two strike counts. Second, thousands of new games are played every year, so the database can be easily expanded over time with minimal costs. Finally, baseball, as one of the most popular sports, has a lot of practical applications as well as high demand for automatic analysis tools.

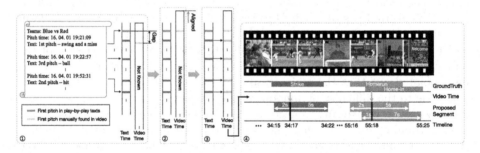

Fig. 2. Illustration of how BBDB has been collected. Left-top scroll is an example of play-by-play texts. ① From the texts, extract date and time of every pitch in a sorted order. In the video, manually find the first pitching moment. ② Using the obtained gap, align the first pitch of the video with the first pitch of the ordered text times. ③ Since text time and video time are aligned, all pitch times can be transferred from text time to video time. ④ The temporal boundaries are set with the pitch times and predetermined length of each action.

3.1   Database Collection

Nowadays, full videos of baseball games can be found in online video archives, accompanied by play-by-play texts. Those text broadcasts (Fig. 2) include broad information about each game like the participating teams and players, and most importantly, every game activities and time stamps of pitches. With the provided pitch times, which are in absolute time with date, we can semi-automatically align the game video with the texts by just manually calculating the relative difference between the first pitch in the video and the text broadcast. Then, action segments can be extracted from videos based on pitch times and predetermined length of each action.

To make sure that the labels collected with our method are correct, we incorporate a review process for each game by checking the correctness of last few segments and their labels. If the gap is consistent throughout the game, the last segment will have correct boundaries. This is why annotators only need to check a few of last segments in each game. If there exists an inconsistency on the label (time annotation) of the last segment, the whole game is discarded in our database to ensure that none of the incorrect labels get included in the dataset.

To evaluate the semi-automatic labeling, we compared the semi-automatically labeled data with human annotation on 20 games. The details are explained in Sect. 4. On average, annotating 3 h of video takes around 4 h while our semi-automatic method takes about 5 min per game. This is because of the difficulty in temporally annotating untrimmed videos; after observing an event, an annotator has to seek back to find the starting or ending point of the event. Repeating this process causes the labeling to take more time than the video's duration. However, our collection method only requires to find a gap, and to easily validate by observing a few last segments.

3.2 Properties

The BBDB is a challenging dataset for two key properties: (1) the dataset contains a large number of visually similar segments with different labels, that have evidently distinguishable differences. In baseball, strike and ball are basically the same pitching action. However, the last position of the ball, referee's movement, and on-screen graphics are distinctive cues. To solve this problem, a system must be more than just a action-category classifier, by taking more temporal information and semantics into account. (2) The number of segment instances for each class is imbalanced. Since thousands of baseball games are used for the dataset, this imbalance is naturally imposed and statistically meaningful.

Videos. The initial version of BBDB contains 1,172 full baseball game videos. It is split into three sets; training set with 703 videos, validation set with 234 videos, and test set with 235 videos. In total, the dataset contains 4,254 h of baseball. Each video is either 480p or 720p, and it is mostly in 30 fps, with a few 60 fps videos. Game duration ranges from 120 min to 350 min.

Highlights. Beside full game videos, we have also collected highlight videos that corresponds to each game in the dataset. Automatic generation of sports highlight is easier to evaluate compared to highlights of general user created videos, since sports highlight has less ambiguity about 'what is important' criteria. Even though those highlights are still cherry-picked by human experts, rare events like homerun or double-play are definitely more important than the others. BBDB can also serve as a good highlight database, providing a challenge of creating highlights not only through visual understanding but also by understanding storylines.

Table 1. Comparison with other recognition, temporal localization (detection), and summarization video datasets. Our BBDB has peculiarities dedicated for new challenges of video analytics. † denotes the number of temporally annotated instances, available only for databases with detection tasks. ‡Database with large #instances/#videos ratio can be used as sequential alignment database, since text-video alignment is trained without temporal boundary annotations. Values are referenced from each dataset or [24] otherwise.

Dataset	#instances†/ #videos	Avg.Len.	Untrimmed	Detection	Sequence‡	Summary
UCF101 [42]	/13 k	7 s	–	–	–	–
HMDB51 [25]	/7 k	3 s	–	–	–	–
Sth-Sth-V2 [15]	/220 k	4 s	–	–	–	–
Kinetics [22]	/306 k	10 s	–	–	–	–
SumMe [16]	/25	240 s	–	–	–	✓
TvSum [41]	/50	150 s	–	–	–	✓
VSUMM [7]	/100	180 s	–	–	–	✓
Hollywood2 [28]	/4 k	20 s	✓	–	–	–
Sports-1M [21]	/1.1 M	300 s	✓	–	–	–
Youtube-8M [1]	/8.3 M	230 s	✓	–	–	–
KTH [34]	2.4 k/600	20 s	✓	✓	–	–
THUMOS'15 [14]	23.1 k/21 k	4 s	✓	✓	△	–
MultiTHUMOS [52]	39 k/400	270 s	✓	✓	△	–
ActivityNet [3]	28 k/20 k	180 s	✓	✓	△	–
Charades [37]	67 k/9.8 k	30 s	✓	✓	✓	–
MPII cooking [33]	5.6 k/44	600 s	✓	✓	✓	–
TUM Breakfast [26]	11 k/2 k	140 s	✓	✓	✓	–
BBDB (ours)	**405 k/1 k**	**13,000 s**	✓	✓	✓	✓

Annotations. The BBDB contains 404,964 annotated segments over 30 baseball activities. This is 345 activity instances per video on average. Labeled classes are not written as discrete human actions, but as baseball activities e.g.strike, ball, and homerun. Derived annotations comprise lexicon of labels. The lexicon has a tree structure to help semantically subdivide labels into groups (Fig. 1). The structure can be utilized to deal with disproportion of the number of instances per action class, as well as the visual similarity between two or more activities over the temporal domain.

Comparisons. For a brief comparison with other datasets, refer to Table 1. The BBDB has unparallel number of temporally annotated segments, with long full game videos. This enables the dataset to be used not only for temporal localization tasks ('Detection' in the table), but also for the text-video alignment. The alignment task does not use the temporal boundaries of the segments but the order of segments. So higher $\frac{\#instances}{\#videos}$ ratio gives more sequential information useful for the alignment task. Additionally, the BBDB has incomparable number of videos to be used for summarization or highlight generation task compared to other video summarization datasets.

Currently, we utilize a set of words as labels to evaluate the dataset. Those labels can be easily extended to sophisticated captions by making use of rich information in the play-by-play texts. The texts even contain information about rosters, number of inning, whether a player is on the first base or not, and so on. Ultimately, automatic commentary system can be established with those captions.

4 Database Evaluation

To validate our semi-automatically collected dataset, we evaluated the dataset against manually annotated videos. We randomly selected 20 baseball games in the dataset, and manually annotated about 7,000 temporal boundaries (7 k is already comparable to other localization datasets).

Results of the comparison between the semi-automatic and the manual labels are shown in Table 2. For IoU threshold ≤0.5, the semi-automatic label shows very accurate results. While the accuracy drops for thresholds over 0.5, it is still quite accurate considering that the state-of-the-art methods do not reach even 30 on these measures. In addition, a high IoU threshold is a very strict measure that is sensitive to fine difference in boundaries. On the class *strike*, for example, the semi-automatic labeling makes a segment between one second before starting pitch and one second after the catcher throws back to catcher. However, human annotators have their own standard for making segments, e.g. between right after starting pitch and right before the catcher throws back. These minor differences in the boundaries do not affect the ultimate goal of our vision task, since all of them are visually correct. Note that labeling the data with many annotators will inherently have difference as exact start and finish time can be different from person to person. Compared to manual labeling, the semi-automatic labels will have more consistency. Therefore, we conclude that the semi-automatic labeling is accurate enough with its own standard for making boundaries.

Table 2. Precision of semi-automatic labeling against human labeling on the BBDB. IoU threshold ranges from 0.3 to 0.7.

IoU threshold	0.3	0.4	0.5	0.6	0.7
BBDB	98.8	97.0	93.5	75.6	60.1

5 Video Understanding Algorithms

We evaluate several video understanding methods using our dataset. We first explain the methods in this section.

5.1 Action Recognition

IDT+FV. Dense trajectories [48] features include local descriptors like histogram of oriented gradients (HOG), optical flow (HOF), and motion boundary histogram (MBH). Albeit computationally expensive, Fisher vector [31] encoding of those descriptors has been used for video classification, and showed better results compared to their contemporary bag-of-words features. We used HOG, HOF, MBH descriptors and followed the configuration of feature encoding in [48]. Due to storage limitation and feasibility, all videos are set to 3 fps and frames are resized with fixed height of 240 pixels, while width is resized maintaining aspect ratio. The extracted IDT from training set is about 17TB even after resizing and reducing fps. Then, we trained 1-vs-rest SVM classifiers over Fisher vectors of all annotated segments of the training set. The classifiers are trained with Stochastic Gradient Descent (SGD) since the training data is over 10 TB and cannot fit into memory.

Single Frame. We utilize the 16-layer VGG model [40] to see how a single frame based video classification and frame-level detection works. This network is originally trained on ImageNet [8] for image classification, so it provides comparisons with other systems that takes temporal changes into account. We fine-tuned the model on frames from training set segments over 30 classes.

Optical Flow Stacking. In action recognition, a flow of movement can be an important cue. This method only utilizes the optical flow information so that we can see how motion impacts the classification performance. First, we extract optical flows from clips for every 5 frame and normalize it to [0, 255], which allows storing the optical flow as an image. Then, the optical flow network is trained on a stack of 10 optical flow frames. We utilize ResNet-50 model to train motion stream network.

Two-Stream. Appearance and movement are complementary. Two-stream method utilizes both appearance and optical flow, so we can see how well two information bring together a synergy. The network designs for extracting the spatial and the temporal features are the same as Single frame and Optical flow stacking. For aggregating the results of the two networks, we average the softmax output and obtain the final result.

CNN+GRU. One of the useful tool to utilize the temporal information is recurrent neural network (RNN). In action recognition task, combinations of CNN and RNN [9] are widely used. We used 5 CNN layers to extract spatial features for each frame, and those features are fed into a RNN layer to make temporal features. We select the gated recurrent unit (GRU) [6] for its efficiency. The extracted temporal features are used as the input to a fully-connected layer and the softmax layer for the classification.

C3D. C3D is a 3D convolution network architecture in the early stage of 3D ConvNet. C3D consists of 8 convolution of $3 \times 3 \times 3$ kernels, 5 max-pooling, and 2 fully-connected layers. Its input is 16 sequential frames so that the model directly learns spatio-temporal representations within 16 frames. We train C3D from scratch not from the pre-trained weights on Sport-1M, since all the clips point to 'Baseball' class at the very first stage leading the network to stay in a local minima.

I3D. I3D was first introduced in [4]. Unlike previous 3D ConvNets, I3D inflates not only 2D kernels into 3D, but also the 2D weight values pre-trained on ImageNet into 3D. Specifically, each $t \times k \times k$ 3D kernel is initialized by pre-trained $k \times k$ weights repeating t times along the time dimension and rescaling by $1/t$. We follow the 3D network architecture used in [51].

5.2   Handling Class Imbalance

To address the class imbalance in our dataset (Fig. 5), we ran experiments with five methods. All following experiments is based on the CNN+GRU model in Sect. 5.1, with variations in data selection, class structure, and the loss function.

Naïve Training. As the baseline of this experiment, we kept the dataset untouched and trained using CNN+GRU model.

Oversampling. Due to the highly imbalanced distribution among classes, we first randomly pick a class, and then retrieve a video in that class. This allows the model to learn each video class with equal chance. We set this method as our default setting, applying to all the action recognition experiments except Naïve training mentioned above.

Hierarchical Classification. We can hierarchically divide 30 classes as shown in Fig. 1. The distribution of the subsets are relatively balanced compared to that of the whole set. Following the hierarchy of the dataset, we trained the first level 3-class classifier, the batting-level 4-class classifier, and the last subset classifier.

Class Weight Adjustment. When a distribution among the classes is known, an additional weight can be imposed to loss values. Following [43], we tried setting a weight for each class according to the ratio of total number of samples and the number of samples from the class.

Focal Loss [27]. To prevent the cross entropy being overwhelmed [27] by severe class imbalance, we tried another approach by adding the focal loss balancing factor so the network focuses more on poorly classified examples:

$$\mathcal{FL} = -\sum_{i=1}^{c} (1 - p_i)^{\gamma} y_i \log(p_i) \tag{1}$$

where c, i denotes the number of classes and class indices respectively, $y_i \in \{0, 1\}$ specifies the ground-truth class, and p_i denotes class prediction probabilities. The parameter γ controls the rate at which well-classified examples are downweighted.

5.3   Temporal Localization

A temporal localization task is to predict the start and end points of events as well as the corresponding class of each event. There are various designs of methods to localize segments. One way is to first propose candidate segments and then to classify those segments. The main drawback of this approach is losing the preciseness on the temporal domain. Another method is to evaluate every frame before grouping neighboring frames with high predicted probabilities. In this case, grouping can be exceedingly heuristic and maintaining temporal information around each frame becomes the main challenge.

We use Single frame model trained in Sect. 5.1 to evaluate the temporal localization task. We also evaluate using Convolutional-De-Convolutional (CDC) filter [35]. Most of settings are the same as [35], but without using pre-trained weights from Sports-1M dataset [21] for the same reason as C3D in Sect. 5.1. Using those two models, every frame in full game videos in the test set is fed into the models to produce class probabilities. Then, we use the sliding window approach [30] with window sizes of 5, 6, $\cdots$, 15, and 16 s, sliding with a stride of 1/3 second over the predicted probabilities. The detected windows are non-maximum suppressed based on each window's maximum class probability, to remove any overlapping detection. All videos are set to 3 fps before evaluation for equal comparison.

5.4   Text-Video Alignment

In this task, we apply the method of ordering constrained discriminative clustering (OCDC) [2] on our dataset. The method uses the idea of discriminative clustering with an order of actions as the constraint. OCDC solves alignment problem by jointly learning a classifier per each action. A loss function for discriminative clustering is a square loss function and we use a linear classifier to make the objective function quadratic. This allows us to apply a convex relaxation of our problem using Frank-Wolf Algorithm. We use HOF descriptor encoded by Fisher vector as frame-level representation.

6   Experimental Results

6.1   Action Recognition

In this section, we evaluate the action recognition methods with our BBDB dataset. Each clipped segments in the test set is evaluated to produce prediction probabilities, or confidence scores in the case of the SVM classifier. All clips are sorted with the scores to compute the average precision (AP), then the APs are averaged with the number of classes to compute mean AP (mAP). Table 3 shows mAP of each method.

Exploiting both the appearance and the motion information shows better performance than using only one of them. C3D shows slightly lower performance compared to the Two-stream network, but I3D outperforms Two-stream, which reveals the importance of network depth, initialization method, and temporal resolution. CNN+GRU with maximum sequence length of $l = 256$ shows a large performance improvement compared to other methods.

Table 3. Evaluations of technical approaches applied to BBDB. l denotes the maximum sequence length of GRU, and Jac stands for Jaccard measure.

Method	mAP	Input # frames	
Action recognition (Oversampling)		Training	Testing
IDT + FV [48]	23.6	1 rgb	25 rgb
Single frame [40]	35.0	1 rgb	25 rgb
Optical flow stacking [39]	36.9	10 flow	250 flow
Two-stream [39]	42.3	1 rgb, 10 flow	25 rgb, 250 flow
C3D [46]	40.2	16 rgb	160 rgb
I3D [4]	44.2	32 rgb	320 rgb
CNN+GRU [9] ($l = 64$)	36.2	$\leq$64 rgb	$\leq$64 rgb
CNN+GRU ($l = 128$)	52.8	$\leq$128 rgb	$\leq$128 rgb
CNN+GRU ($l = 256$)	**62.8**	$\leq$256 rgb	$\leq$256rgb
Handling Imbalance ($l = 256$)			
CNN+GRU (Naïve)	67.0		
CNN+GRU (Oversampling)	62.8		
CNN+GRU (Hierarchical)	50.4		
CNN+GRU+FL [27] ($\gamma = 2$)	61.6		
CNN+GRU (Weight Adjustment)	55.3		
Per-frame Labeling		Training	Testing
Single frame	9.25	1 rgb	1 rgb
CDC [35]	**23.3**	32 rgb	32 rgb
Text-Video Alignment	Jac		
OCDC [2]	7.0		

Our experimental results are different from other works, where it has been shown that Two-stream or a 3D Convolution based networks usually work better than the CNN+GRU. We believe this is due to the difference in the nature of the dataset. Due to the visual similarity among the classes in our dataset, the classifier should take fine-grained features, e.g. trajectory of the ball, runner's direction, or referee's actions. CNN-based models take a limited number of frames as input during training, which is too short to express longer sequences. However, the RNN structure takes the whole frames of the segment as input, so it is able to consider the fine-grained motion information better. In the same context, GRUs with shorter sequence length of $l = 64, 128$ show worse performances.

We also observed the relationship among the classes (Fig. 6). Ball and strike classes are the most confusing part, even though those classes have a lot of training examples. It shows that distinguishing a ball from a strike is challenging. There are more classes that are easily confused, but most extreme cases include

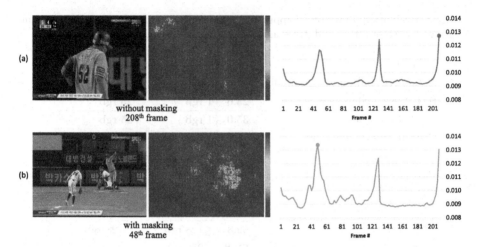

Fig. 3. Saliency on the class *foul* with corresponding video frame: saliency of CNN+GRU trained (a) without masking, (b) with on-screen socreboard masking. 48th and 208th frame are the most responsible moments for the *foul* clip with and without masking, respectively (marked as dots on the line graphs).

tag out, error, and bunt out/hit classes. In a baseball game, these situations may occur simultaneously with other situations leading to the confusion.

6.2 Saliency Analysis

As an attempt to understand what the neural net is looking at when recognizing actions, we provide further analysis through the saliency map [38]. Instead of computing the saliency map in the spatial domain as is done in [38], we extend the idea to the temporal domain to see where and when the network focuses to recognize actions.

A saliency result for CNN+GRU is shown in Fig. 3(a). From the results, it is clear that the network is relying heavily on the scoreboard to make a decision. So the network learned to cheat as the easiest and the most accurate way to classify a strike or a ball event is to actually look at the scoreboard rather than the motions.

To prevent the network from cheating, we trained the network with the scoreboard masked out. A saliency results with the scoreboard masked is shown in Fig. 3(b). After masking, the network focuses more on the motions to recognize actions. With the score board masked out, the accuracy for recognizing the *ball* event went down from 0.908 to 0.719, and the *strike* event from 0.720 to 0.394. For the events on which the scoreboard does not provide additional information, the accuracy was similar with the masking.

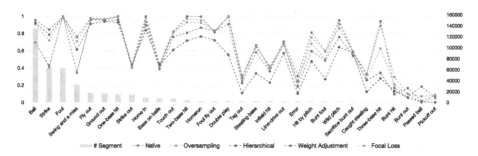

Fig. 4. APs (left axis) of classes computed with imbalance handling approaches; Naïve, Oversampling, Hierarchical classification, and Focal loss. Bars indicate the number of segments for each class (right axis). Points connected with dashed lines show AP for each class, and the dashed lines are drawn for illustration to easily seek between points. Focal loss has achieved better performance than oversampling in small-quantity classes, by improving 3.9% on average over 19 classes. However, it lost significant performance over 3 large-quantity classes by 29.2%.

6.3   Handling Class Imbalance

For handling the class imbalance, APs for every class are shown in Fig. 4 since mAPs in Table 3 can be misleading when understanding and comparing the imbalance handling methods. Oversampling failed to address the imbalance, getting worse AP in every class compared to the naïvely trained network. The gap was bigger in classes with very large and small number of samples like strike, and passed-ball. We suppose this is because the severe imbalance between classes gave the network less chance to learn the visual similarities between difficult classes like ball and strike.

Hierarchical classification showed the worst results among imbalance handling approaches. The irreversible property of the hierarchical structure mainly affected the performance. For instance, if *hit by pitch* is classified into runner or batting category, it loses any chance of being detected as *hit by pitch*. The results also present that the top classifiers could not distinguish the semantic differences of the topmost categories.

The network trained with the focal loss is based on the default oversampling technique, and it showed improvements throughout most of classes with less samples. Improvement was 3.9% on average, over 19 classes with less samples. However, the focal loss actually failed to discriminate visually similar classes like ball, strike, and swing-and-miss; losing 29.2% on average over 3 classes with large number of samples. We can infer the focusing factor $(1 - p_i)^\gamma$ kept the network from learning difficult classes by cutting down the loss. We also tried different γ values of 0.5, 1, 2, and 5 but they showed little differences.

Class weight adjustment shows the second worst performance. This is expected since setting weight according to the number of classes is a more pre-hoc way of tuning loss values, compared to focal loss that balances the loss while training.

6.4 Temporal Localization

Table 4 shows temporal activity localization mAP. The proposed temporal boundary is counted as true, when the boundary's Intersection-over-Union (IoU) with ground truth is bigger than the threshold. Compared with the Single frame model, the CDC shows better performance both in per-frame labeling (Table 3) and temporal localization tasks.

6.5 Text-Video Alignment

We apply OCDC on parts of the test set to show the expandability of BBDB on Text-Video Alignment. It is meaningful only on benchmarks where the number of instances per videos is large. Since representations of one simple video is too large, we divide fullgames by the end of the innings. Even with the shortened videos, OCDC results in 7.0 by Jaccard measure, which is a relatively low accuracy over the result on a subset of Hollywood2 dataset [2], which is around 45.

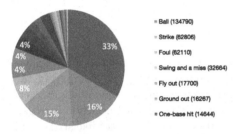

Fig. 5. Distribution of 30 classes in BBDB.

Table 4. Temporal localization mAP on BBDB. IoU threshold ranges from 0.3 to 0.7.

IoU threshold	0.3	0.4	0.5	0.6	0.7
Single frame	9.96	7.86	3.44	2.48	1.62
CDC [35]	**26.1**	**22.2**	**11.3**	**9.54**	**6.07**

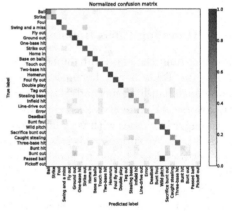

Fig. 6. Confusion matrix for CNN+GRU result. Ball and strike classes are confused each other. Tag out, error, bunt out/hit and those not having enough train data do not work correctly.

7 Conclusion

We have introduced our very large-scale BBDB with annotation made with minimal human labor. BBDB can be applied to video understanding tasks like action recognition, temporal action localization, text-video alignment, video highlight generation, and data imbalance problem. BBDB has a great deal of visual and motion similarity between the classes, and the class distribution follows natural statistics. We plan to develop novel video understanding algorithms using our BBDB and extend it to other video domains.

Acknowledgment. This work was supported by Samsung Research Funding Center of Samsung Electronics under Project Number SRFC-IT1701-01.

References

1. Abu-El-Haija, S. et al.: Youtube-8m: a large-scale video classification benchmark. CoRR abs/1609.08675 (2016)
2. Bojanowski, P., et al.: Weakly supervised action labeling in videos under ordering constraints. In: Fleet, D., Pajdla, T., Schiele, B., Tuytelaars, T. (eds.) ECCV 2014. LNCS, vol. 8693, pp. 628–643. Springer, Cham (2014). https://doi.org/10.1007/978-3-319-10602-1_41
3. Caba Heilbron, F., Escorcia, V., Ghanem, B., Carlos Niebles, J.: Activitynet: a large-scale video benchmark for human activity understanding. In: CVPR (2015)
4. Carreira, J., Zisserman, A.: Quo vadis, action recognition? A new model and the kinetics dataset. In: CVPR (2017)
5. Chawla, N.V., Japkowicz, N., Kotcz, A.: Editorial: special issue on learning from imbalanced data sets. SIGKDD Explor. Newsl. **6**(1), 1–6 (2004)
6. Chung, J., Gulcehre, C., Cho, K., Bengio, Y.: Empirical evaluation of gated recurrent neural networks on sequence modeling. In: NIPS Deep Learning and Representation Learning Workshop (2014)
7. De Avila, S.E.F., Lopes, A.P.B., da Luz Jr, A., de Albuquerque Araújo, A.: VSUMM: a mechanism designed to produce static video summaries and a novel evaluation method. Pattern Recogn. Lett. **32**(1), 56–68 (2011)
8. Deng, J., Dong, W., Socher, R., Li, L.J., Li, K., Fei-Fei, L.: ImageNet: a large-scale hierarchical image database. In: CVPR (2009)
9. Donahue, J., Hendricks, L.A. et al.: Long-term recurrent convolutional networks for visual recognition and description. In: CVPR (2015)
10. Feichtenhofer, C., Pinz, A., Wildes, R.P.: Spatiotemporal residual networks for video action recognition. In: NIPS (2016)
11. Feichtenhofer, C., Pinz, A., Wildes, R.P.: Spatiotemporal multiplier networks for video action recognition. In: CVPR (2017)
12. Feichtenhofer, C., Pinz, A., Zisserman, A.: Convolutional two-stream network fusion for video action recognition. In: CVPR (2016)
13. Gaidon, A., Harchaoui, Z., Schmid, C.: Actom sequence models for efficient action detection. In: CVPR (2011)
14. Gorban, A. et al.: THUMOS challenge: action recognition with a large number of classes. http://www.thumos.info/ (2015)
15. Goyal, R. et al.: The 'something something' video database for learning and evaluating visual common sense. In: ICCV (2017)
16. Gygli, M., Grabner, H., Riemenschneider, H., Van Gool, L.: Creating summaries from user videos. In: Fleet, D., Pajdla, T., Schiele, B., Tuytelaars, T. (eds.) ECCV 2014. LNCS, vol. 8695, pp. 505–520. Springer, Cham (2014). https://doi.org/10.1007/978-3-319-10584-0_33
17. Hara, K., Kataoka, H., Satoh, Y.: Can spatiotemporal 3D CNNs retrace the history of 2D CNNs and ImageNet? In: CVPR (2018)
18. He, H., Garcia, E.A.: Learning from imbalanced data. IEEE Trans. Knowl. Data Eng. **21**(9), 1263–1284 (2009)

19. Huang, D.-A., Fei-Fei, L., Niebles, J.C.: Connectionist temporal modeling for weakly supervised action labeling. In: Leibe, B., Matas, J., Sebe, N., Welling, M. (eds.) ECCV 2016. LNCS, vol. 9908, pp. 137–153. Springer, Cham (2016). https://doi.org/10.1007/978-3-319-46493-0_9

20. Ji, S., Xu, W., Yang, M., Yu, K.: 3d convolutional neural networks for human action recognition. PAMI **35**(1), 221–231 (2013)

21. Karpathy, A., Toderici, G., Shetty, S., Leung, T., Sukthankar, R., Li, F.: Large-scale video classification with convolutional neural networks. In: CVPR (2014)

22. Kay, W. et al.: The kinetics human action video dataset. CoRR abs/1705.06950 (2017)

23. Krawczyk, B.: Learning from imbalanced data: open challenges and future directions. Prog. Artif. Intell. **5**(4), 221–232 (2016)

24. Krishna, R., Hata, K., Ren, F., Fei-Fei, L., Niebles, J.C.: Dense-captioning events in videos. In: ICCV (2017)

25. Kuehne, H., Jhuang, H., Garrote, E., Poggio, T., Serre, T.: HMDB: a large video database for human motion recognition. In: ICCV (2011)

26. Kuehne, H., Arslan, A., Serre, T.: The language of actions: Recovering the syntax and semantics of goal-directed human activities. In: CVPR (2014)

27. Lin, T.Y., Goyal, P., Girshick, R., He, K., Dollár, P.: Focal loss for dense object detection. In: ICCV (2017)

28. Marszałek, M., Laptev, I., Schmid, C.: Actions in context. In: CVPR (2009)

29. Ng, J.Y.H., Hausknecht, M.J., Vijayanarasimhan, S., Vinyals, O., Monga, R., Toderici, G.: Beyond short snippets: deep networks for video classification. In: CVPR (2015)

30. Oneata, D., Verbeek, J., Schmid, C.: The lear submission at thumos 2014. In: ECCV THUMOS Workshop (2014)

31. Perronnin, F., Sánchez, J., Mensink, T.: Improving the fisher kernel for large-scale image classification. In: Daniilidis, K., Maragos, P., Paragios, N. (eds.) ECCV 2010. LNCS, vol. 6314, pp. 143–156. Springer, Heidelberg (2010). https://doi.org/10.1007/978-3-642-15561-1_11

32. Qiu, Z., Yao, T., Mei, T.: Learning spatio-temporal representation with pseudo-3d residual networks. In: ICCV (2017)

33. Rohrbach, M., Amin, S., Andriluka, M., Schiele, B.: A database for fine grained activity detection of cooking activities. In: CVPR (2012)

34. Schuldt, C., Laptev, I., Caputo, B.: Recognizing human actions: a local svm approach. In: ICPR (2004)

35. Shou, Z., Chan, J., Zareian, A., Miyazawa, K., Chang, S.F.: CDC: Convolutional-de-convolutional networks for precise temporal action localization in untrimmed videos. In: CVPR (2017)

36. Shou, Z., Wang, D., Chang, S.F.: Temporal action localization in untrimmed videos via multi-stage cnns. In: CVPR (2016)

37. Sigurdsson, G.A., Varol, G., Wang, X., Farhadi, A., Laptev, I., Gupta, A.: Hollywood in homes: crowdsourcing data collection for activity understanding. In: Leibe, B., Matas, J., Sebe, N., Welling, M. (eds.) ECCV 2016. LNCS, vol. 9905, pp. 510–526. Springer, Cham (2016). https://doi.org/10.1007/978-3-319-46448-0_31

38. Simonyan, K., Vedaldi, A., Zisserman, A.: Deep inside convolutional networks: visualising image classification models and saliency maps. In: ICLR Workshop (2014)

39. Simonyan, K., Zisserman, A.: Two-stream convolutional networks for action recognition in videos. In: NIPS (2014)

40. Simonyan, K., Zisserman, A.: Very deep convolutional networks for large-scale image recognition. In: ICLR (2015)
41. Song, Y., Vallmitjana, J., Stent, A., Jaimes, A.: Tvsum: Summarizing web videos using titles. In: CVPR (2015)
42. Soomro, K., Roshan Zamir, A., Shah, M.: UCF101: A dataset of 101 human actions classes from videos in the wild. In: CRCV-TR-12-01 (2012)
43. Sozykin, K., Protasov, S., Khan, A., Hussain, R., Lee, J.: Multi-label class-imbalanced action recognition in hockey videos via 3d convolutional neural networks. In: IEEE/ACIS SNPD (2018)
44. Sun, L., Jia, K., Chen, K., Yeung, D., Shi, B.E., Savarese, S.: Lattice long short-term memory for human action recognition. In: ECCV (2017)
45. Taylor, G.W., Fergus, R., LeCun, Y., Bregler, C.: Convolutional learning of spatio-temporal features. In: Daniilidis, K., Maragos, P., Paragios, N. (eds.) ECCV 2010. LNCS, vol. 6316, pp. 140–153. Springer, Heidelberg (2010). https://doi.org/10.1007/978-3-642-15567-3_11
46. Tran, D., Bourdev, L., Fergus, R., Torresani, L., Paluri, M.: Learning spatiotemporal features with 3d convolutional networks. In: ICCV (2015)
47. Tran, D., Ray, J., Shou, Z., Chang, S., Paluri, M.: Convnet architecture search for spatiotemporal feature learning. CoRR abs/1708.05038 (2017)
48. Wang, H., Schmid, C.: Action Recognition with improved trajectories. In: ICCV (2013)
49. Wang, L., Qiao, Y., Tang, X.: Action recognition and detection by combining motion and appearance features. In: ECCV THUMOS Workshop (2014)
50. Wang, L., Xiong, Y., Wang, Z., Qiao, Y., Lin, D., Tang, X., Van Gool, L.: Temporal segment networks: towards good practices for deep action recognition. In: Leibe, B., Matas, J., Sebe, N., Welling, M. (eds.) ECCV 2016. LNCS, vol. 9912, pp. 20–36. Springer, Cham (2016). https://doi.org/10.1007/978-3-319-46484-8_2
51. Wang, X., Girshick, R., Gupta, A., He, K.: Non-local neural networks. In: CVPR (2018)
52. Yeung, S., Russakovsky, O., Jin, N., Andriluka, M., Mori, G., Fei-Fei, L.: Every moment counts: dense detailed labeling of actions in complex videos. IJCV **126**(2), 375–389 (2018)
53. Yeung, S., Russakovsky, O., Mori, G., Fei-Fei, L.: End-to-end learning of action detection from frame glimpses in videos. In: CVPR (2016)
54. Yuan, J., Ni, B., Yang, X., Kassim, A.A.: Temporal action localization with pyramid of score distribution features. In: CVPR (2016)

SketchyScene: Richly-Annotated Scene Sketches

Changqing Zou[1], Qian Yu[2], Ruofei Du[1], Haoran Mo[3], Yi-Zhe Song[2],
Tao Xiang[2], Chengying Gao[3], Baoquan Chen[4(✉)], and Hao Zhang[5]

[1] University of Maryland, College Park, US
[2] Queen Mary University of London, London, UK
[3] Sun Yat-sen University, Guangzhou, China
[4] Shandong University, Jinan, China
baoquan@sdu.edu.cn
[5] Simon Fraser University, Burnaby, Canada

Abstract. We contribute the first large-scale dataset of *scene sketches*,
SKETCHYSCENE, with the goal of advancing research on sketch understanding at both the object and scene level. The dataset is created
through a novel and carefully designed *crowdsourcing* pipeline, enabling
users to efficiently generate large quantities of realistic and diverse scene
sketches. SKETCHYSCENE contains more than 29,000 scene-level sketches,
7,000+ pairs of scene templates and photos, and 11,000+ object sketches.
All objects in the scene sketches have ground-truth semantic and instance
masks. The dataset is also highly scalable and extensible, easily allowing augmenting and/or changing scene composition. We demonstrate
the potential impact of SKETCHYSCENE by training new computational
models for semantic segmentation of scene sketches and showing how
the new dataset enables several applications including image retrieval,
sketch colorization, editing, and captioning, etc. The dataset and code
can be found at https://github.com/SketchyScene/SketchyScene.

Keywords: Sketch dataset · Scene sketch · Sketch segmentation

1 Introduction

In the age of data-driven computing, large-scale datasets have become a driving force for improving and differentiating the performance, robustness, and
generality of machine learning algorithms. In recent years, the computer vision
community have embraced a number of large and richly annotated datasets
for images (e.g., ImageNET [8] and Microsoft COCO [15]), 3D objects (e.g.,
ShapeNET [2,31] and PointNET [17]), and scene environments (e.g., SUN [32]
and the NYU database [22]). Among the various representations of visual forms,

Electronic supplementary material The online version of this chapter (https://
doi.org/10.1007/978-3-030-01267-0_26) contains supplementary material, which is
available to authorized users.

© Springer Nature Switzerland AG 2018
V. Ferrari et al. (Eds.): ECCV 2018, LNCS 11219, pp. 438–454, 2018.
https://doi.org/10.1007/978-3-030-01267-0_26

hand-drawn sketches occupy a special place since, unlike most others, they come from human creation. Humans are intimately familiar with sketches as an art form and sketching is arguably the most compact, intuitive, and frequently adopted mechanism to visually express and communicate our impression and ideas.

Fig. 1. A scene sketch from our dataset SKETCHYSCENE that is user-generated based on the reference image shown, a segmentation result (middle) obtained by a method trained on SKETCHYSCENE, and a typical application: sketch captioning.

Significant progress has been made on sketch understanding and sketch-based modeling in computer vision and graphics recently [7, 9, 11, 14, 20, 23–25, 30, 35, 39]. Several large-scale sketch datasets [9, 10, 19] have also been constructed and utilized along the way. Nevertheless, these datasets have all been formed by *object* sketches and the sketch analysis and processing tasks have mostly been at the stroke or object level. Extending both to the *scene* level is a natural progression towards a deeper and richer reasoning about sketched visual forms. The ensuing analysis and data synthesis problems become more challenging since a sketched scene may contain numerous objects interacting in a complex manner. While scene understanding is one of the hallmark tasks of computer vision, the problem of understanding scene sketches have not been well studied.

In this paper, we introduce the first large-scale dataset of *scene sketches*, which we refer to as SKETCHYSCENE, to facilitate sketch understanding and processing at both the object and scene level. Obviously, converting images to edge maps [33] does not work since the results are characteristically different from hand-drawn sketches. Automatically composing existing object sketches based on predefined layout templates and fitting the object sketches into stock photos are both challenging problems that are unlikely to yield a large quantity of realistic outcomes (see Fig. 2(b)). In our work, we resort to *crowdsourcing* and design a novel and intuitive interface to reduce burden placed on the users and improve their productivity. Instead of asking the users to draw entire scene sketches from scratch, which can be tedious and intimidating, we provide object sketches so that the scene sketches can be created via simple interactive operations such as drag-n-dropping and scaling the object sketches. To ensure diversity

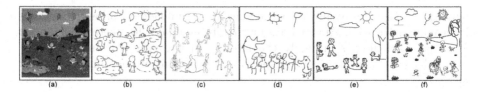

Fig. 2. (a) reference image; (b) response of edge detector; (c) synthesized scene using object sketches from Sketchy and TU-Berlin (using the same pipeline as (f)); (d) non-artist's drawing with the hint of a short description; (e) artist's drawing with the hint of reference image; (f) synthesized scene using our system. Processes of (c)–(f) take 6, 8, 18, and 5 min, respectively.

and realism of the scene sketches, we provide reference images to guide/inspire the users during their sketch generation. With a user-friendly interface, partici-pants can create high-quality scene sketches efficiently. On the other hand, the scene sketches synthesized this way are by and large *sketchy sketches* [9,19] and they do not quite resemble ones produced by professional artists.

SKETCHYSCENE contains both object- and scene-level data, accompanied with rich annotations. In total, the dataset has more than *29,000 scene sketches* and more than *11,000 object sketches* belonging to 45 common categories. In addition, more than *7,000 pairs of scene sketch templates and reference photos* and more than *200,000 labeled instances* are provided. Note that, *all* objects in the scene sketches have ground-truth semantic and instance masks. More importantly, SKETCHYSCENE is *flexible* and *extensible* due to its object-oriented synthesis mechanism. Object sketches in a sketch scene template can be switched in/out using available instances in SKETCHYSCENE to enrich the dataset.

We demonstrate the potential impact of SKETCHYSCENE through experi-ments. Foremost, the dataset provides a springboard to investigate an assort-ment of problems related to scene sketches (a quick Google Image Search on "scene sketches" returns millions of results). In our work, we investigate seman-tic segmentation of scene sketches for the first time. To this end, we evaluated the advanced natural image segmentation model, DeepLab-v2 [3], exploring the effect of different factors and providing informative insights. We also demon-strate several applications enabled by the new dataset, including sketch-based scene image retrieval, sketch colorization, editing, and captioning.

2   Related Work

2.1   Large-Scale Sketch Datasets

There has been a surge of large-scale sketch datasets in recent years, mainly driven by applications such as sketch recognition/synthesis [9,10] and SBIR [19,36]. Yet the field remains relatively under-developed with existing datasets mainly facilitating object-level analysis of sketches. This is a direct result of the non-ubiquitous nature of human sketches data – they have to be carefully crowd-sourced other than automatically crawled for free (as for photos).

TU-Berlin [9] is the first such large-scale crowd-sourced sketch dataset which was primarily designed for sketch recognition. It consist of 20,000 sketches spanning over 250 categories. The more recent QuickDraw[10] dataset is much larger, with 50 million sketches across 345 categories. Albeit being large enough to facilitate stroke-level analysis[6], sketches sourced in these datasets were produced by sketching towards a semantic concept (e.g., "cat", "house"), without a reference photo or mental recollection of natural scene/objects. This greatly limits the level of visual detail and variations depicted, therefore making them unfitting for fine-grained matching and scene-level parsing. For example, faces are almost all in their frontal view, and depicted as a smiley in QuickDraw.

The concurrent work of [36] and [19] progressed the field further by collecting object instance sketches for FG-SBIR. QMUL database [36] consists of 716 sketch-photo pairs across two object categories (shoe and chair), with reference photos crawled from on-line shopping websites. Sketchy [19] contains 75,471 sketches and 12,500 corresponding photos across a much wider selection of categories (125 in total). Object instance sketches are produced by asking crowd-sourcers to depict their mental recollection of a reference photo. In comparison with concept sketches [9,10], they by and large exhibit more object details and have matching poses with the reference photos. However, a common drawback for both, for the purpose this project, lies with their limited pose selection and object configurations. QMUL sketches exhibit only one object pose (side view) under a single object configuration. Scene sketches albeit exhibits more object poses and configurations, are still restricted since their reference photos mainly consists of single objects centered on relatively plain backgrounds (thus depicts no object interactions). This drawback essentially renders them both unsuitable for our task of scene sketch parsing, where complex mutual object interactions dictate high degree of object pose and configuration variations, as well as subtle details. For example, within a picnic scene depicted in Figure 1, people appear in different poses and configurations with subtle eye contacts among each other. Fig. 2(c) shows a composition result using sketches from Sketchy and TU-Berlin.

SKETCHYSCENE is the first large-scale dataset specifically designed for scene-level sketch understanding. It differs from all aforementioned datasets in that it goes beyond single object sketch understanding to tackle scene sketch, and purposefully includes an assorted selection of object sketches with diverse poses, configurations and object details to accommodate the complex scene-level object interactions. Although the existing dataset Abstract Scenes [38] serves a similar motivation for understanding high-level semantic information in visual data, they focus on abstract scenes composed using clip arts, which include much more visual cues such as color and texture. In addition, their scenes are restricted in describing interactions between two characters and a handful of objects, while the scene contents and mutual object interactions in SKETCHYSCENE are a lot more diverse.

2.2   Sketch Understanding

Sketch recognition is perhaps the most studied problem in sketch understanding. Since the release of TU-Berlin dataset [9], many works have been proposed and recognition performance had long passed human-level [37]. Existing algorithms can be roughly classified into two categories: (1) those using hand-crafted features [9,20], and (2) those learning deep feature representation [10,37], where the latter generally outperforms the former by a clear margin. Other stream of work had delved into parsing object-level sketches into their semantic parts. [26] proposes an entropy descent stroke merging algorithm for both part-level and object-level sketch segmentation. Huang et al. [13] leverages a repository of 3D template models composed of semantically labeled components to derive part-level structures. Schneider and Tuytelaars [21] performs sketch segmentation by looking at salient geometrical features (such as T junctions and X junctions) under a CRF framework. Instead of studying single object recognition or part-level sketch segmentation, this work conducts exploratory study for scene-level parsing of sketches, by proposing the first large-scale scene sketch dataset.

2.3   Scene Sketch Based Applications

While no prior work aimed at parsing sketches at scene-level, some interesting applications had been proposed that utilize scene sketches as input. Sketch2Photo [5] is a system which combines sketching and photo montage for realistic image synthesis, where Sketch2Cartoon [29] is a similar system that works on cartoon images. Similarly, assuming objects have been segmented in a sketchy scene, Xu et al. [34] proposed a system named sketch2scene which automatically generates 3D scenes by aligning retrieved 3D shapes to segmented objects in 2D sketch scenes. Sketch2Tag [27] is a SBIR system where scene items are automatically recognized and used as a text query to improve retrieval performance. Without exception, all aforementioned applications involve manual tagging and/or segmentation of sense sketches. In this work, we provide means of automatic segmentation of scene sketches, and demonstrate the potential of the proposed dataset by proposing a few novel applications.

3   SKETCHYSCENE Dataset

A scene sketch dataset should reflect the scenes with sufficient diversity, in terms of their configurations, object interactions and subtle appearance details, where sketch should also contain multiple objects of different categories. Besides, the volume of a dataset is important, especially in the context of deep learning. However, as previously discussed, building such dataset based on existing datasets is infeasible, while collecting data from humans can be expensive and time-consuming, therefore an efficient and effective data collection pipeline is required.

   The easiest solution is to ask people to draw a scene directly with provided objects or scene labels as hints (i.e., the strategy used in [9]). Unfortunately, this method has proven to be infeasible in our case: (1) Most people are not trained artists. As a result, they struggled to draw complex objects present in a scene, especially when they are in different poses and object configurations (see Fig. 2(d)); (2) although different people have different drawing styles, people

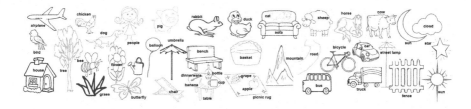

Fig. 3. Representative object sketches of SKETCHYSCENE.

tend to draw a specific scene layout. For example, given the hint *"several people are playing on the ground, sun, tree, cloud, balloon and dog"*, people always draw the objects along a horizontal line. That makes the collected scene sketches monotonous in layout and sparse in visual feature. (3) Importantly, this solution is unscalable – it takes average person around 8 min to finish a scene sketch of reasonable quality, where costing 18 min for a professional (see Fig. 2(e)). This will prohibit us from collecting a large-scale dataset.

A new data collection strategy is thus devised which is to synthesize a sketchy scene by composing provided object components under the guidance of a reference image. The whole process includes three steps.

Step1: Data Preparation. We selected 45 categories for our dataset, including objects and stuff classes. Specifically, we first considered several common scenes (e.g., garden, farm, dinning room, and park) and extracted 100 objects/stuff classes from them as raw candidates. Then we defined three super-classes, i.e. Weather, Object, and Field (Environment), and assigned the candidates into each super-class. Finally, we selected 45 from them by considering their combinations and commonness in real life.

Instead of asking workers to draw each object, we provided them with plenty of object sketches (each object candidate is also refer to a "component") as candidates. In order to have enough variations in the object appearance in terms of pose and appearance, we searched and downloaded around 1,500 components for each category. Then we employed 5 experienced workers to manually sort out the sketches containing single component or cutout individual component from sketches having multiple components. For some categories with few searched components (<20) like "umbrella", components were augmented through manual drawing. We totally collected 11,316 components for all 44 categories (excluding "road", which are all hand-drawing, and "others"). These components of each category are split into three sets: training (5468), validation (2362), and test (3486). Representative components of the 45 categories are shown in Fig. 3.

In order to guarantee the diversity of the scene layout in our dataset, we additionally collected a set of cartoon photos as reference images. Through sampling the class label(s) from each of our predefined super-classes, e.g., sun (Weather), rabbit (Object), mountain (Environment), we generated 1,800 query items [1]. And around 300 cartoon photos were retrieved for each query items. After remov-

---

[1] We add another label "cartoon" to each query in order to retrieve cartoon photos

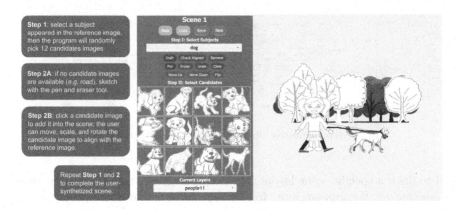

Fig. 4. Interface and work flow of *USketch* for crowdsourcing the dataset. See areas of function buttons (upper left), component display (lower left), and canvas (right).

ing the repeated ones manually, there are 7,264 reference images (4730 images are unique). These reference images are also split into three sets for training (5,616), validation (535), and test (1,113).

Step2: Scene Sketch Synthesis. To boost the efficiency of human creators, we devised a customary, web-based application for sketch scene synthesis. About 80 workers were employed to create scene sketches. Figure 4 shows the interface of the application (named "USketch").

As explained before, we facilitated the creation of the sketchy scene images by allowing the worker to drag, rotate, scale, and deform the component sketch with the guidance of the reference image. The process is detailed in Fig. 4. It's worth noting that (1) we provided different sets of component sketches (even the same category) to different workers, to implicitly control the diversity of object sketches. Otherwise, workers tend to select the first several samples from the candidate pool; (2) We required the workers to produce as various occlusions as possible during the scene synthesis. This is to simulate the real scenarios and facilitate the research in segmentation. Our server recorded the transformation and semantic labels of each scene item of resulting sketchy scenes.

At this step, we collected one scene sketch based on each reference image, using the components from the corresponding component repository. We therefore obtained 7,264 unique scene sketches. These unique scene sketches are further used as scene templates to generate more scene sketches.

Step3: Annotation and Data Augmentation. The reference image is designed to help the worker to compose the scene and enrich the layouts of the scene sketches. However, the objects in a reference image is not necessarily included in our dataset, i.e., 45 categories. In order to facilitate the future research by providing more accurate annotations, we required workers to annotate the alignment status of each object instance.

Given there are plenty of components in our dataset, an efficient data augmentation strategy is to replace the object sketch with the rest components from

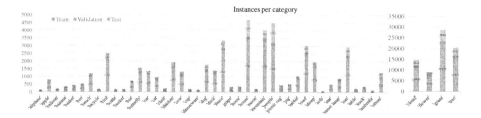

Fig. 5. Object instance frequency for each category.

Fig. 6. From left to right: reference image, synthesized sketchy scene ("L" is used to mark the category alignment), ground-truth of semantic and instance segmentation.

the same category. Specifically, we automatically generated another 20 scene sketches for each worker-generated scene, and asked the worker to select the 4 most reasonable scenes for each scene template of Step2. Finally, we got 29K+ sketchy scene images after data augmentation.

Dataset Statistics and Analysis. To summarize, we totally obtain:

1. 7,264 unique scene templates created by human. Each scene template contains at least 3 object instances, where the maximum number of object instances is 94. On average there are 16 instances, 6 object classes, and 7 occluded instances per template. The maximum number of occluded instances is 66. Figure. 5 shows the distribution of object frequencies.
2. 29,056 scene sketches after data augmentation (Step 3);
3. 11,316 object sketches belonging to 44 categories. These components can be used for object-level sketch research tasks;
4. 4730 unique reference cartoon style images which have pairwise object correspondence to the scene sketches;
5. All sketches have 100% accurate semantic-level and instance-level segmentation annotation (as shown in Fig. 6).

Extensibility. With the scene templates and sketch components provided in the dataset, SKETCHYSCENE can be further augmented. (1) People can segment each sketch component to get the part-level or stroke-level information; (2) The sketch components can be replaced by sketches from other resources to generate scene sketches with more varied styles.

4   Sketch Scene Segmentation

SKETCHYSCENE can be used to study various computer vision problems. In this section, we focus on semantic segmentation of scene sketches by modifying an existing image segmentation model. Performance is evaluated on SKETCHYSCENE to help us identify future research directions.

Problem Definition. In semantic segmentation, each pixel needs to be classified into one of the candidate classes. Specifically, there is a label space $L = \{l_1, l_2, ..., l_K\}$, K refers to the number of object of stuff classes. Each sketch scene image $s = \{p_1, p_2, ..., p_N\} \in \mathbb{R}^{H \times W}$ contains $N = W \times H$ pixels. A model trained for semantic segmentation is required to assign a label to each pixel[2]. So far the definition of sketch scene segmentation is identical to that of photo image segmentation. However, different from photos, a sketch only consists of black lines (pixel intensity value equals to 0) and white background (pixel value equals to 255). Given the fact that only black pixels convey semantic information, we define the semantic segmentation in sketchy scenes as predicting a class label for each pixel whose value is 0. Taking the second image of Fig. 6 as an example, when segmenting trees, house, sun and cloud, all black pixels on the line segments (including contours and the lines within the contours) should be classified while the rest white pixels are treated as background.

Challenges. Segmenting a sketchy scene is challenging due to the sparsity of visual feature. First of all, a sketch scene image is dominated by white pixels. In SKETCHYSCENE, the background ratio is 87.83%. The rest pixels belong to K foreground classes. The classes are thus very imbalanced. Second, segmenting occluded objects becomes much harder. In photos, an object instance often contain uniform color or texture. Such cues do not exist in a sketch scene image.

4.1   Formulation

We employ a state-of-the-art semantic segmentation model developed for photo images, DeepLab-v2 [3], which is customized for segmenting scene sketches. DeepLab-v2 has three key features, including atrous convolution, spatial pyramid spatial pooling (ASPP), and utilizing fully-connected CRF as post-processing. It is a FCN-based [16] model, i.e., adapting a classification model for segmentation by replacing the final fully connected layer(s) with fully convolutional layer(s). For each input sketch, the output is a $K \times h \times w$ tensor, K represents the number of class while $h \times w$ are the output segmentation dimension. A common per-pixel softmax cross-entropy is used during training.

Among the three features, fully-connected CRF, or denseCRF, is widely used in segmentation as a post-process. However, there are large blank areas in scene sketches which should be treated differently. We show that directly applying DeepLab-v2 to model the sketches results in inferior performance, and denseCRF further degrades the coarse segmentation results (see Sect. 4.2).

---

[2] In this study, we consider a sketch s as a bitmap image.

Based on the characteristics of sketchy scenes, we propose to ignore the background class during modeling. This is because (1) the ratio of background pixels is much higher than the non-background pixels, which may introduce bias into the model; (2) the background information is provided in the input image and we can filter them out easily by treating the input as a mask after segmentation. Specifically, in our implementation, the background pixels do not contribute to the loss during training. During the inference, these background pixels are assigned a non-background class label, followed by a denseCRF for refinement. Finally, the background pixels are filtered out by the input image.

4.2 Experiments

We conducted all the experiments on SKETCHYSCENE, using the set of 7,264 unique scene sketch templates which are split into training (5,616), validation (535), and test (1,113). Microsoft COCO is employed to verify the effectiveness of pre-training.

Implementation Details. We use Tensorflow and ResNet101 as the base network. The initial learning rate is set to 0.0001 and mini-batch size to 1. We set the maximum training iterations as 100 K and the optimiser is Adam. We keep the data as their original size (750*750), without applying any data augmentation on the input as we are not targeting optimal performance. We use deconvolution to scale the prediction to the same size as the ground truth mask. For denseCRF, we set the hyper parameters $\sigma_\alpha, \sigma_\beta, \sigma_\gamma$ to 7, 3, and 3, respectively.

Competitors. We compare four existing models for segmenting natural photos: FCN-8s[4], SegNet[1], DeepLab-v2[3] and DeepLab-v3[16]. FCN-8s is the first deep segmentation model adapted from deep classification. It further combines coarse and fine features from different layers to boost performance. SegNet employs an encoder-decoder architecture which modifies the upsampling process to generate a more accurate segmentation result. DeepLab-v2 employs atrous convolution and denseCRF for segmentation, as explained in Sect. 4. Compared with DeepLab-v2, DeepLab-v3 incorporates global information and batch normalization, achieving comparable performance as DeepLab-v2 without employing denseCRF for refinement. In our experiment, FCN-8s and SegNet use VGG-16 while both DeepLab-v2 and v3 use ResNet101 as the base network. For fair comparison, we apply the same data processing strategy in all four models.

Evaluation Metrics. Four metrics are used to evaluate each model: Overall accuracy (OVAcc) indicates the ratio of correctly classified pixels; Mean accuracy (MeanAcc) computes the ratio of the correctly classified pixels over all classes; Mean Intersection over Union (MIoU), a commonly used metric for segmentation, computes the ratio between the intersection and union of two sets, averaged over all classes; FWIoU improves MIoU slightly by adding a class weight.

Comparison. Table 1 compares the performance of different baseline models on the new task. Clearly, both DeepLab-v2 and DeepLab-v3 perform much better than FCN and SegNet. However, DeepLab-v3 yielded similar performance as DeepLab-v2, indicating that contextual information does not have much effect for the task. This can be explained by the sparsity of sketchy scenes, and the fact that the structures in a sketch are more diverse than those in natural photos. Thus contextual information is less important than that in natural images.

Table 1. Comparison of DeepLab-v2 and other baselines (%)

Model	OVAcc		MeanAcc		MIoU		FWIoU	
	Val	Test	Val	Test	Val	Test	Val	Test
FCN-8s	83.38	73.78	62.82	57.80	45.26	39.16	73.63	60.16
SegNet	84.61	78.61	58.29	54.05	42.56	38.32	76.28	67.91
DeepLab-v3	92.71	88.07	82.83	**76.40**	73.03	**63.69**	86.71	79.19
DeepLab-v2(final)	**92.94**	**88.38**	**84.95**	75.92	**73.49**	63.10	**87.10**	**79.76**

Table 2. Comparison of including/excluding background (%)

Model	OVAcc		MeanAcc		MIoU		FWIoU	
	Val	Test	Val	Test	Val	Test	Val	Test
With BG (train&test)	**95.38**	**94.22**	42.48	34.56	38.34	30.05	**91.29**	**89.34**
With BG (train)	90.21	86.41	73.54	66.49	61.50	52.58	82.67	77.09
w/o BG (final)	92.94	88.38	**84.95**	**75.92**	**73.49**	**63.10**	87.10	79.76

Table 3. Comparison of pre-training strategy (%)

Model	OVAcc		MeanAcc		MIoU		FWIoU	
	Val	Test	Val	Test	Val	Test	Val	Test
Variant-1	**93.07**	**88.67**	82.23	74.97	71.41	62.12	**87.42**	**80.19**
Variant-2	91.22	87.08	76.91	71.70	65.41	57.81	84.36	78.01
Variant-3	91.47	86.44	79.17	72.24	67.91	58.54	84.80	77.18
Pre-ImageNet (final)	92.94	88.38	**84.95**	**75.92**	**73.49**	**63.10**	87.10	79.76

Qualitative Results. Figure 7 shows several segmentation results generated by DeepLab-v2 (each class is highlighted by a different colour). Although the results are encouraging, there is still large space to improve. In particular, the failure are mainly caused by two reasons: (1) The intra-class variation is large while sketch itself is significantly deformed. For example, in the bottom image of the fourth column of Fig. 7, the "sheep" (highlighted in purple) is classified as a "dog" (highlighted in green); (2) occlusions between different object instances

Fig. 7. Visualizations of our segmentation results. Left: 6 examples with good segmentation results; right: two failure cases.

or instances being spatially too close. As shown in the top image of the fourth column, "cat", "human" and "sofa" are clustered together, making the pixels in the junction part classified wrongly. Since sketches are sparse in visual cues and we only utilize pixel-level information, it would thus be helpful to integrate object-level information. Note that the second problem is more challenging and sketch-specific. In photo images, pixels on the contours are typically ignored. However, they are the only pixels of interest in the new task. Therefore, some sketch-specific model design need to be introduced. For examples, some perceptual grouping principles [18] can be introduced to remedy this problem. See more segmentation results in the Supplementary Material.

Effect of Background. As discussed earlier, the large area of background is the key problem to be solved for sketchy scene segmentation. We propose to ignore the background class during model training. When considering the background class, it mainly affects two processes, modeling by deep network and refinement by denseCRF. So we decoupled them and conducted the following experiments: (1) **withBG (train&test)**: considering the background during training the deep model and applying denseCRF for refinement, and (2) **withBG (train)**: only consider the background during training but ignore this class for refinement, i.e., when generating the coarse segmentation, the model assigns the background class pixels a non-background class label and then feed it to denseCRF. Table 2 compares the performance. We can make the following observations: (1) The performance measured in both Mean Accuracy and MIoU have a significant improvement when excluding background as a class. The Overall Accuracy and FWIoU drop since the accuracy on "background" class is much higher than other classes; (2) The processing of background mainly affects the performance of denseCRF. This is as expected because it infers the label for each pixel by considering the neighbor pixels, thus the classes which have large ratio in the images tend to spread out. Some qualitative results are shown in Fig. 8. From the images shown in the second column, we can see with the refinement of denseCRF, lots of pixels are merged into "background". The last image shows the result following our proposed data processing.

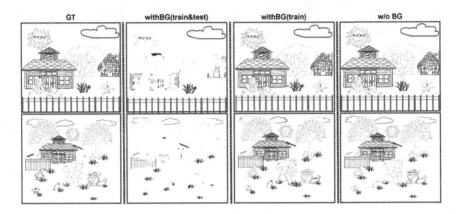

Fig. 8. Comparing segmentation results when including/excluding background (BG).

Effect of Pre-training. Our final model is pre-trained on ImageNet and fine-tuned on SKETCHYSCENE. In this experiment, we implemented three pre-training variants: (1) **Variant-1**: Based on the ImageNet pre-trained model, we further pre-trained on the large-scale natural image segmentation dataset, i.e., Microsoft COCO, then fine-tuned on SKETCHYSCENE. (2) **Variant-2**: Instead of pre-training on the natural images, we trained the model on edge maps extracted from the COCO dataset. In this variant, the mask of each object is region-based, i.e., with inner region pixels. (3) **Variant-3**: To simulate the target task, we further remove the inner region pixels of the mask used in Variant-2. That is, the mask covers the edges only, which is more similar to our final task. Table 3 shows: (1) pre-training on COCO does not help. This is probably due to the large domain gap between the sketch and the natural photo. (2) Pre-training on edge maps (no matter what kind of mask they use) does not bring benefits either. Again this is due to the domain gap: different from sketches, edge maps contain lots of noise. (3) Variant-3 outperforms Variant-2, which is as expected since Variant-3 is more similar to our final task.

5   Other Applications Using SKETCHYSCENE

In this section, we propose several interesting applications which are enabled by our SKETCHYSCENE dataset.

Image Retrieval. Here we demonstrate an application of scene-level SBIR, which complements conventional SBIR [12,19,36] by using scene-level sketches to retrieve images. Considering the objects presented in the sketches of

SKETCHYSCENE are not 100% aligned with the reference images (as explained in Sect. 3), we selected sketch-photo pairs whose semantic-IoU are higher than 0.5 (2,472 pairs for training and validation while 252 for testing). Here semantic-IoU refers to the category-level overlap between the scene sketch and reference image. We develop a triplet ranking network similar to [36] by changing the base network to InceptionV3 [28], and adding a sigmoid cross-entropy loss as the auxiliary loss (this is to utilize the object category information to learn a more domain-invarint feature). We report accuracy at rank1 (acc.@1) and rank10 (acc.@10) inline with other SBIR papers. Overall, we obtain 32.13% on acc.@1 and 69.48% on acc.@10. Fig. 9 offers an example qualitative retrieval results.

Fig. 9. Retrieval results. The corresponding reference image is highlighted by red box.

Sketch Captioning and Editing. Here we demonstrate two simple applications, namely sketch captioning and sketch editing (illustrated in Fig. 10(b) and (c), respectively). The assumption is, based on the segmentation results, with extra annotations like image description, an image captioning model can be developed based on SKETCHYSCENE. Furthermore, people can edit a specific object using the instance-level annotations. As shown in Fig. 10(c), the "chicken" can be changed to a "duck" while the other objects are kept the same. Both of these two applications could be useful for children education.

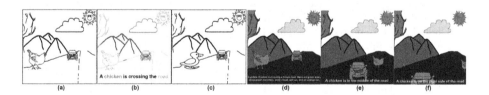

Fig. 10. Applications: captioning (b), editing (c), colorization (d), and dynamic scene synthesis (d-f).

Sketch Colorization. Here we show the potential of using our dataset to achieve automatic sketch colorization, when combined with the recognition and segmentation engine developed in Sect. 4.2. In Fig. 10(d), we show a colorization result by assigning different colors to different segmented objects, taking into account of their semantic labels (e.g., the sun is red).

Dynamic Scene Synthesis. Finally, we demonstrate a more advanced application, dynamic sketch scene synthesis. We achieve this by manipulating our scene templates to construct a series of frames which are then colorized coherently across all frames. Fig. 10(d)–(f) depicts an example, "chicken road crossing".

6   Conclusion, Discussion, and Future Work

In this paper, we introduce the first large-scale dataset of scene sketches, termed SKETCHYSCENE. It consists of a total of 29,056 scene sketches, generated using 7,264 scene templates and 11,316 object sketches. Each object in the scene is further augmented with semantic labels and instance-level masks. The dataset was collected following a modular data collection process, which makes it highly extensible and scalable. We have shown the main challenges and informative insights of adapting multiple image-based segmentation models to scene sketch data. There are several promising future directions to further enhance our scene sketch dataset, including adding scene-level annotations and text captions to enable applications such as text-based scene generation.

Acknowledgment. This work was partially supported by the China National 973 Program (2015CB352501), NSFC-ISF(61561146397), NSERC 611370, and the China Scholarship Council (CSC).

References

1. Badrinarayanan, V., Kendall, A., Cipolla, R.: Segnet: a deep convolutional encoder-decoder architecture for image segmentation. TPAMI **39**(12), 2481–2495 (2017)
2. Chang, A.X. et al.: ShapeNet: An information-rich 3D model repository. CoRR, abs/1512.03012 (2015)
3. Chen, L.C., Papandreou, G., Kokkinos, I., Murphy, K., Yuille, A.L.: Deeplab: semantic image segmentation with deep convolutional nets, atrous convolution, and fully connected crfs. arXiv:1606.00915 (2016)
4. Chen, L.C., Papandreou, G., Schroff, F., Adam, H.: Rethinking atrous convolution for semantic image segmentation. arXiv preprint arXiv:1706.05587 (2017)
5. Chen, T., Cheng, M., Tan, P., Shamir, A., Hu, S.: Sketch2photo: internet image montage. ACM Trans. Graph. **28**(5), 124:1–124:10 (2009)
6. Chen, Y., Tu, S., Yi, Y., Xu, L.: Sketch-pix2seq: a model to generate sketches of multiple categories. arXiv preprint arXiv:1709.04121 (2017)
7. Dekel, T., Gan, C., Krishnan, D., Liu, C., Freeman, W.T.: Smart, sparse contours to represent and edit images. arXiv preprint arXiv:1712.08232 (2017)
8. Deng, J., Dong, W., Socher, R., Li, L.J., Li, K., Fei-Fei, L.: Imagenet: a large-scale hierarchical image database. In: CVPR (2009)
9. Eitz, M., Hays, J., Alexa, M.: How do humans sketch objects? ACM Trans. Graph. **31**(4), 44:1–44:10 (2012)
10. Ha, D., Eck, D.: A neural representation of sketch drawings. arXiv preprint arXiv:1704.03477 (2017)
11. Hu, C., Li, D., Song, Y.Z., Xiang, T., Hospedales, T.M.: Sketch-a-classifier: sketch-based photo classifier generation. In: CVPR (2018)

12. Hu, R., Collomosse, J.: A performance evaluation of gradient field hog descriptor for sketch based image retrieval. CVIU **117**(7), 790–806 (2013)
13. Huang, Z., Fu, H., Lau, R.W.H.: Data-driven segmentation and labeling of freehand sketches. ACM Trans. Graph. **33**(6), 175:1–175:10 (2014)
14. Li, L., Huang, Z., Zou, C., Tai, C., Lau, R.W.H., Zhang, H., Tan, P., Fu, H.: Model-driven sketch reconstruction with structure-oriented retrieval. In: SIGGRAPH ASIA, Technical Briefs (2016)
15. Lin, T.-Y., et al.: Microsoft COCO: common objects in context. In: Fleet, D., Pajdla, T., Schiele, B., Tuytelaars, T. (eds.) ECCV 2014. LNCS, vol. 8693, pp. 740–755. Springer, Cham (2014). https://doi.org/10.1007/978-3-319-10602-1_48
16. Long, J., Shelhamer, E., Darrell, T.: Fully convolutional networks for semantic segmentation. In: CVPR (2015)
17. Qi, C.R., Su, H., Mo, K., Guibas, L.J.: Pointnet: Deep learning on point sets for 3d classification and segmentation. In: CVPR (2017)
18. Qi, Y. et al.: Making better use of edges via perceptual grouping. In: CVPR (2015)
19. Sangkloy, P., Burnell, N., Ham, C., Hays, J.: The sketchy database: learning to retrieve badly drawn bunnies. In: SIGGRAPH (2016)
20. Schneider, R.G., Tuytelaars, T.: Sketch classification and classification-driven analysis using fisher vectors. ACM Trans. Graph. **33**(6), 174:1–174:9 (2014)
21. Schneider, R.G., Tuytelaars, T.: Example-based sketch segmentation and labeling using crfs. ACM Trans. Graph. **35**(5), 151:1–151:9 (2016)
22. Silberman, N., Hoiem, D., Kohli, P., Fergus, R.: Indoor segmentation and support inference from RGBD images. In: Fitzgibbon, A., Lazebnik, S., Perona, P., Sato, Y., Schmid, C. (eds.) ECCV 2012. LNCS, vol. 7576, pp. 746–760. Springer, Heidelberg (2012). https://doi.org/10.1007/978-3-642-33715-4_54
23. Song, J., Pang, K., Song, Y.Z., Xiang, T., Hospedales, T.M.: Learning to sketch with shortcut cycle consistency. In: CVPR (2018)
24. Song, J., Yu, Q.: Deep spatial-semantic attention for fine-grained sketch-based image retrieval. In: ICCV (2017)
25. Su, Q., Bai, X., Fu, H., Tai, C., Wang, J.: Live sketch: Video-driven dynamic deformation of static drawings. In: CHI (2018)
26. Sun, Z., Wang, C., Zhang, L., Zhang, L.: Free hand-drawn sketch segmentation. In: Fitzgibbon, A., Lazebnik, S., Perona, P., Sato, Y., Schmid, C. (eds.) ECCV 2012. LNCS, vol. 7572, pp. 626–639. Springer, Heidelberg (2012). https://doi.org/10.1007/978-3-642-33718-5_45
27. Sun, Z., Wang, C., Zhang, L., Zhang, L.: Sketch2tag: automatic hand-drawn sketch recognition. In: ACM Multimedia, pp. 1255–1256 (2012)
28. Szegedy, C., Vanhoucke, V., Ioffe, S., Shlens, J., Wojna, Z.: Rethinking the inception architecture for computer vision. In: CVPR (2016)
29. Wang, C., Zhang, J., Yang, B., Zhang, L.: Sketch2cartoon: Composing cartoon images by sketching. In: ACM Multimedia, pp. 789–790 (2011)
30. Wang, F., Kang, L., Li, Y.: Sketch-based 3d shape retrieval using convolutional neural networks. In: CVPR (2015)
31. Wu, Z. et al.: 3d shapenets: A deep representation for volumetric shapes. In: CVPR (2015)
32. Xiao, J., Hays, J., Ehinger, K.A., Oliva, A., Torralba, A.: SUN database: Large-scale scene recognition from abbey to zoo. In: CVPR (2010)
33. Xie, S., Tu, Z.: Holistically-nested edge detection. In: ICCV (2015)
34. Xu, K., Chen, K., Fu, H., Sun, W., Hu, S.: Sketch2scene: sketch-based co-retrieval and co-placement of 3d models. ACM Trans. Graph. **32**(4), 123:1–123:15 (2013)

35. Xu, P. et al.: Sketchmate: Deep hashing for million-scale human sketch retrieval. In: CVPR (2018)
36. Yu, Q., Liu, F., SonG, Y.Z., Xiang, T., Hospedales, T., Loy, C.C.: Sketch me that shoe. In: CVPR (2016)
37. Yu, Q., Yang, Y., Liu, F., Song, Y., Xiang, T., Hospedales, T.M.: Sketch-a-net: a deep neural network that beats humans. IJCV **122**(3), 411–425 (2017)
38. Zitnick, C.L., Parikh, D.: Bringing semantics into focus using visual abstraction. In: CVPR (2013)
39. Zou, C., Yang, H., Liu, J.: Separation of line drawings based on split faces for 3d object reconstruction. In: CVPR (2014)

Learn-to-Score: Efficient 3D Scene Exploration by Predicting View Utility

Benjamin Hepp[1,2(✉)], Debadeepta Dey[2], Sudipta N. Sinha[2], Ashish Kapoor[2], Neel Joshi[2], and Otmar Hilliges[1]

[1] ETH Zurich, Zurich, Switzerland
benjamin.hepp@inf.ethz.ch
[2] Microsoft Research, Redmond, USA

Abstract. Camera equipped drones are nowadays being used to explore large scenes and reconstruct detailed 3D maps. When free space in the scene is approximately known, an offline planner can generate optimal plans to efficiently explore the scene. However, for exploring unknown scenes, the planner must predict and maximize usefulness of where to go on the fly. Traditionally, this has been achieved using handcrafted utility functions. We propose to learn a better utility function that predicts the usefulness of future viewpoints. Our learned utility function is based on a 3D convolutional neural network. This network takes as input a novel volumetric scene representation that implicitly captures previously visited viewpoints and generalizes to new scenes. We evaluate our method on several large 3D models of urban scenes using simulated depth cameras. We show that our method outperforms existing utility measures in terms of reconstruction performance and is robust to sensor noise.

Keywords: 3D reconstruction · Exploration · Active vision · 3D CNN

1 Introduction

Quadrotors, drones, and other robotic cameras are becoming increasingly powerful, inexpensive and are being used for a range of tasks in computer vision and robotics applications such as autonomous navigation, mapping, 3D reconstruction, reconnaissance, and grasping and manipulation. For these applications, modeling the surrounding space and determining which areas are occupied is of key importance.

Recently, several approaches for robotic scanning of indoor [37] and outdoor [20,31] scenes have been proposed. Such approaches need to reason about whether voxels are free, occupied, or unknown space to ensure safety of the robot and to achieve good coverage w.r.t. their objective function (e.g. coverage of the 3D surfaces [31]). Model-based approaches require approximate information

Electronic supplementary material The online version of this chapter (https:// doi.org/10.1007/978-3-030-01267-0_27) contains supplementary material, which is available to authorized users.

V. Ferrari et al. (Eds.): ECCV 2018, LNCS 11219, pp. 455–472, 2018.
https://doi.org/10.1007/978-3-030-01267-0_27

about free space and occupied space, which is typically acquired or input manually. This prevents such approaches from being fully autonomous or deployed in entirely unknown scenes [35]. Model-free approaches can be applied in unknown environments [8,19,24,27]. Irrespective of the type of approach used, all algorithms require a utility function that predicts how useful a new measurement (i.e. depth image) would be. Based on this utility function a planner reasons about the sequence of viewpoints to include in the motion plan. This utility function is often a hand-crafted heuristic and hence it is difficult to incorporate prior information about the expected distributions of 3D geometry in certain scenes.

We propose to devise a better utility function using a data-driven approach. The desired target values for our utility function stem from an oracle with access to ground truth data. Our learned utility function implicitly captures knowledge about building and geometry distributions from approporiate training data and is capable of predicting the utility of new viewpoints given only the current occupancy map. To this end we train a 3D ConvNet on a novel multi-scale voxel representation of an underlying occupancy map, which encodes the current model of the environment. We then demonstrate that the learned utility function can be utilized to efficiently explore unknown environments.

The input to our network relies only on occupancy and hence abstracts away the capture method (i.e. stereo, IR depth camera, etc.). While our training data consists of perfect simulated depth images we demonstrate in our experiments that our learned model can be used with imperfect sensor data at test time, such as simulated noisy depth cameras or stereo data. The approach is not limited to environments with a fixed extent and generalizes to new scenes that are substantially different from ones in the training data. Our approach outperforms existing methods, that use heuristic-based utility functions [8,24,35] and is more than 10× faster to compute than the methods from [8,24].

2   Related Work

Exploration and mapping are well studied problems. We first discuss theoretical results and then describe approaches in the active vision domain and finally work in 3D vision.

Submodular sensor placement: In the case of a priori known environments and a given set of measurement locations, much work is dedicated to submodular objective functions for coverage [11,29]. Submodularity is a mathematical property enabling approximation guarantees on the solution using greedy methods. While work exists on dynamic environments where the utility of future measurements can change upon performing a measurement [16,22], these methods are usually difficult to scale to large state and observation spaces, which we considered in this paper as they are common in computer vision applications.

Next-best-view and exploration: In the next-best-view setting, the set of measurement locations is often fixed a priori as in the submodular coverage work described above. The work in this area is usually concerned with defining good heuristic utility functions and approximating the coverage task to make it computationally feasible [3,10,12,27,36]. A number of heuristics is explicitly compared in [8,24], and a subset of these is computed and used as a feature vector by Choudhury et al. [4] to imitate an approximately optimal strategy with ground-truth access.

Based on an a priori fixed set of camera poses and a binary input mask of already visited poses Devrim et al. [9] use reinforcement learning to regress a scalar parameter used in the selection algorithm for the next view. In contrast to our work the approach is concerned with a priori known, fixed environments and camera poses making it suitable for inspection planning.

In active vision, a large body of work is concerned with exploration through only partially known scenes. Frontier-based algorithms [38] are used for autonomous mapping and exploration of the environment using stereo [13], RGB-D, or monocular cameras [32]. Heng et al. [19] propose a method which alternates between exploration and optimizing coverage for 3D reconstruction.

All of the approaches discussed above either define or are based on heuristics to decide on the utility of the next measurement or require prior knowledge of environment and possible camera poses. Instead of hand-crafting a utility function our work is concerned with learning such a function that can outperform existing hand-crafted functions and is computationally cheaper to evaluate. Additionally, our approach does not need a priori knowledge of the map.

3D convolutional neural networks: A large body of work in computer vision is concerned with processing of 3D input and output data using convolutional neural networks. In some cases this data stems from RGB-D images such as in Song et al. [33] where the goal is to detect objects. In other contexts, volumetric input in the form of binary occupancy labels or signed distance functions are used for diverse tasks such as shape classification and semantic voxel labeling [6, 30], surface completion [7], hand pose estimation [14], or feature learning [40]. These works are concerned with passive tasks on uniform input grids of fixed dimensions, containing the object or surface of interest. This prevents reasoning across large distances or requires one to reduce the level of detail of the input.

Different representations of occupancy grids have been proposed to mitigate the trade-off of large uniform input dimensions and level of detail [30]. However, in the context of our work the occupancy map is often not very sparse as it is generated by casting rays into a tri-state map and updating continuous values which results in very few homogeneous regions which would benefit from the formulation by Riegler et al. [30]. Also related to our work are approaches to multi-view reconstruction [5] where the output is predicted based on a sequence of input images. In contrast to our work Liu et al. [28] reconstruct small objects in a fixed size volume whereas we are concerned with large city scenes containing several buildings.

3   Problem Setting and Overview

Our work is concerned with the automatic exploration of an a priori unknown 3D world with the ultimate goal of reconstructing the surfaces of the scene in an efficient manner. In this setting, illustrated in Fig. 1, an algorithm has to make decisions about the next viewpoint based only on the current map information. In Fig. 1 the camera is surrounded by some space, already known to be free (white) and part of the surface has been observed (blue). The next viewpoint is restricted to the known free space, whereas moving into unknown space (light green) could lead to collisions. The main difficulty stems from the fact that the algorithm needs to predict how much unknown surface can be discovered from a new viewpoint. Much work has been dedicated to developing and studying various heuristics to compute a score that quantifies the expected value of possible viewpoints [8, 24].

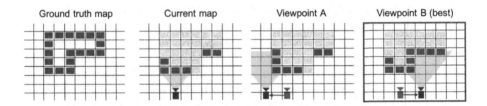

Fig. 1. The exploration task (here depicted in 2D for clarity) is to discover occupied surface voxels (shown here in blue). Voxels are initially unknown (shown here in light green) and get discovered by taking a measurement, e.g., shooting rays from the camera into the scene. Voxels that are not surface voxels will be discovered as free voxels (shown here in white). Each possible viewpoint has a corresponding utility value depending on how much it contributes to our knowledge of the surface (shown here in dark green). To decide which viewpoint we should go to next, an ideal utility score function would tell us the expected utility of viewpoints before performing them. This function can then be used in a planing algorithm to visit a sequence of viewpoints with the highest expected utility.

We propose a data-driven approach where we use supervised learning to find a utility function that imitates an oracle. The oracle has access to the ground truth map and can compute the true utility score. For this task we introduce a map representation consisting of multi-scale sub-volumes extracted around the camera's position. For all possible viewpoints this data is fed into a 3D ConvNet at training time together with the oracle's score as a target value. Intuitively, the model learns to predict the likelihood of seeing additional surface voxels for any given pose, given the current occupancy map. However, we do not explicitly model this likelihood but instead provide only the oracle's score to the learner. We experimentally show that our formulation generalizes well to new scenes with different object shape and distribution and can handle input resulting from noisy sensor measurements.

We follow related work [8,9,24] and evaluate our method on simulated but high-fidelity environments. This allows for evaluation of the utility function and reduces the influence of environmental factors and specific robotic platforms. Our environments contain realistic models of urban areas in terms of size and distribution of buildings. Furthermore it is important to note that our technique only takes occupancy information as input and does not directly interface with raw sensor data. In addition we test our approach on real data from outdoor and indoor scenes to demonstrate that our method is not limited to synthetic environments.

4   Predicting View Utility

We first formally define our task and the desired utility function and then introduce our method for learning and evaluating this function.

4.1   World Model

We model the world as a uniform voxel grid V with resolution r. A map M is a tuple $M = (M^o, M^u)$ of functions $M^o : V \to [0, 1]$, $M^u : V \to [0, 1]$ that map each voxel $v \in V$ to an occupancy value $M^o(v)$ describing the fraction of the voxel's volume that is occupied and an associated uncertainty value $M^u(v)$, i.e. 1 for total uncertainty and 0 for no uncertainty. Maps change over time so we denote the map at time t as M_t.

After moving to a viewpoint $\mathbf{p}$ the camera acquires a new measurement in the form of a depth image and the map M is updated. We denote the updated map as $M|_{\mathbf{p}}$. The uncertainty is updated according to

$$M^u|_{\mathbf{p}}(v) = \exp(-\eta)M^u(v)   , \tag{1}$$

where $\eta \in \mathbb{R}_{>0}$ describes the amount of information added by a single measurement. This is a simple but effective measure providing a diminishing information gain of repeated measurements. Note that $M^u|_{\mathbf{p}}(v) \leq M^u(v)$ so uncertainty decreases with additional measurements. As is typical in occupancy mapping [23,34] we update the voxel occupancies $M^o(v)$ according to a beam-based inverse sensor model. Please see Sect. 4.4 for details on initialization of the map.

4.2   Oracle Utility Function

To select viewpoints, we need a utility function that assigns scores to all possible viewpoints at any time. We first introduce an oracle utility function with access to the ground truth (set of true surface voxels) during evaluation. It returns the desired true utility measure. We will then learn to imitate the oracle without access to ground truth.

We characterize a good viewpoint as one that discovers a large amount of surface voxels. Let $ObsSurf(M)$ be the total number of observed surface voxels in map M weighted by their associated certainty value:

$$ObsSurf(M) = \sum_{v \in Surf} (1 - M^u(v)) \quad , \tag{2}$$

where $Surf \subseteq V$ is the set of ground truth surface voxels, i.e. all voxels that intersect the surface. Note that $ObsSurf(M)$ increases monotonically with additional measurements because the certainty of voxels can only increase according to Eq. (1).

The decrease in uncertainty of surface voxels with a new measurement defines the oracle's utility score. We express this score as a function of the current map M and the camera pose $\mathbf{p}$:

$$
\begin{aligned}
s(M, \mathbf{p}) &= ObsSurf(M|_{\mathbf{p}}) - ObsSurf(M) \\
&= \sum_{v \in Surf} (-M^u|_{\mathbf{p}}(v) + M^u(v)) = \sum_{v \in Surf} (1 - \exp(-\eta)) M^u(v) \geq 0 \quad .
\end{aligned}
\tag{3}
$$

4.3   Learning the Utility Function

Computing the utility score introduced in Eq. 3 for any viewpoint requires access to the ground truth map. Our goal is to predict $s(M, \mathbf{p})$ without access to this data so we can formulate a regression problem that computes score values given occupancy maps as input.

Multi-scale map representation   We propose to make predictions directly based on the occupancy map, rather than based on a temporal sequence of raw inputs. This occupancy map encodes our knowledge of already observed surfaces and free space and ultimately can be used to build up a map for both navigation and 3D reconstruction.

For use in a 3D ConvNet the map has to be represented with fixed dimensionalities. Here a trade-off between memory consumption, computational cost, reach and resolution arises. For example, extracting a small high resolution grid around the camera would constrain information to a small spatial extent whereas a grid with large spatial extent would either lead to rapid increase in memory consumption and computational cost or would lead to drastic reduction in resolution.

To mitigate this issue we introduce a multi-scale representation by sampling the occupancy map at multiple scales as depicted in Fig. 2. For each scale $l \in \{1, \ldots, L\}$ we extract values on a 3D grid of size $D_x \times D_y \times D_z$ and resolution $2^l r$ (orange points in Fig. 2). On scale l the map values are given by averaging the 2^l closest voxels (gray rectangles in Fig. 2). This can be done efficiently by representing the map as an octree. The 3D grids are translated and rotated

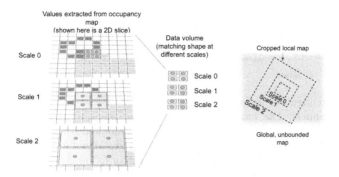

Fig. 2. Local multi-scale representation of an occupancy map. For clarity of presentation we shows the 2D case for a grid of size 2×2. The occupancy map is sampled with 3D grids at multiple scales centered around the camera position. Sample points on different scales are shown in orange and their extent in gray.

according to the measurement pose $\mathbf{p}$ and we use tri-linear interpolation of the map values to compute the values on the grid. This representation allows us to capture both coarse parts of the map that are far away from the camera but still keep finer detail in its direct surroundings. Furthermore, it provides an efficient data representation of fixed size, suitable for training of a 3D ConvNet. We denote the multi-scale representation by $x(M, \mathbf{p}) \in \mathbb{R}^{D_x \times D_y \times D_z \times 2L}$. Note that the factor 2 stems from extracting the occupancy and the uncertainty value on each scale.

ConvNet Architecture We now describe our proposed model architecture used to learn the desired utility function $f : \mathbb{R}^{D_x \times D_y \times D_z \times 2L} \to \mathbb{R}$. The general architecture is shown in Fig. 3 and consists of a number N_c of convolutional blocks followed by two fully connected layers with ReLu activations. Each convolutional block contains a series of N_u units where a unit is made up of a 3D convolution, followed by Batch-Norm, followed by ReLu activation. Each 3D convolution increases the number of feature maps by N_f. After each block the spatial dimensions are downscaled by a factor of 2 using 3D max-pooling. The first fully connected layer has N_{h1} hidden units and the second one has N_{h2} hidden units. Note that we do not separate the input data at different scales so that the network can learn to combine data on different scales. More details on the exact architecture are provided in Sect. 5.1 and an evaluation of different variants is provided in Supplementary Material.

We use a weight-regularized $L2$ loss

$$\mathcal{L}(X, Y; \theta) = \sum_{i=1}^{N} \| f(X_i) - Y_i \|_2^2 + \lambda \| \theta \|_2^2 \quad , \tag{4}$$

where θ are the model parameters, λ is the regularization factor and (X_i, Y_i) for $i \in \{1, \ldots, N\}$ are the samples of input and target from our dataset.

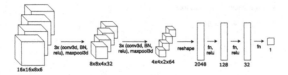

Fig. 3. Our architecture for an input size of $16 \times 16 \times 8$ with $L = 3$ scales resulting in $2L = 6$ channels. The model consists of blocks (made up of multiple units each performing 3D convolution, batch-norm and ReLu) followed by downscaling using 3D max-pooling. This pattern is performed until we arrive at a data volume with spatial dimension $4 \times 4 \times 2$. This is reshaped into a single vector followed by two fully connected layers with ReLu activation and a final linear layer predicting a scalar score value.

4.4   3D Scene Exploration

To evaluate the effectiveness of our utility function, we implement a next-best-view (NBV) planning approach, to sequentially explore a 3D scene. Here we provide details of our world model and our methods for execution of episodes for the data generation phase and at test time.

We assume exploration of the world occurs in episodes. To initialize a new episode, the camera pose at time t_0 is chosen randomly in free space such that no collision occurs and the camera can move to each neighboring viewpoint without collision. A collision occurs if a bounding box of size $(1\,m,\ 1\,m,\ 1\,m)$ centered at the camera pose intersects with any occupied or unknown voxel. Initially, all voxels $v \in V$ are initialized to be unknown, i.e. $M_{t_0}^u(v) = 1, M_{t_0}^o(v) = v^{o,prior}\ \forall v \in V$, where $v^{o,prior}$ is a prior assumption on the occupancy and we use $v^{o,prior} = 0.5$ throughout this work. To enable initial movement of the camera we clear (i.e. set to free space) a bounding box of $(6\,m)^3$ around the initial camera position.

At each time step t, we evaluate each potential viewpoint with our utility function, and move to the viewpoint $\mathbf{p}^*(t)$ that gives the best expected reward according to:

$$\mathbf{p}^*(t) = argmax_{\mathbf{p} \in P(t)} u(M_t, \mathbf{p}) \quad , \tag{5}$$

where $P(t)$ is the set of potential viewpoints and $u(\cdot)$ is the utility function in use.

At the start of each episode the set of potential viewpoints only contains the initial viewpoint. At each time step the set $P(t)$ is extended by those neighbors of the current viewpoint that do not lead to a collision. We ignore potential viewpoints if they have already been observed twice. Each viewpoint has 9 neighbors, 6 of them being positive and negative translations of $2.5\,m$ along each axis of the camera frame, 2 rotations of $25°$, clock-wise and counter-clockwise along the yaw axis, and a full turnaround of $180°$ along the yaw axis. We keep pitch and roll angles fixed throughout.

After moving to a new viewpoint, the camera takes a measurement in the form of a depth image and the map is updated (see Supplementary Material for details on the camera parameters and the map update). Note that we use ground truth depth when generating training data but later demonstrate that we can use noisy depth images and even stereo depth at test time.

Note that we assume that the utility function is submodular. While this is true for the oracle utility it is not necessarily the case for other utility functions (i.e. our learned model). Nevertheless, this assumption allows us to perform lazy evaluations of the utility function [26] (see Supplementary Material for details).

4.5   Dataset

To learn the utility function $f(x)$, approximating the oracle (see Eq. 3) we require labeled training data. Our data should capture large urban environments with a variety of structures typical for human-made environments. To this end we chose models from the *3D Street View* dataset [39]. These models feature realistic building distributions and geometries from different cities. Additionally, we chose a large scene from a photo-realistic game engine (https://www.unrealengine. com) containing small buildings in a suburban environment, including trees, smaller vegetation and power lines. All environments are shown in Fig. 4. Note that we only use data from *Washington2* to train our model. While *Washington1* and *Paris* are similar in terms of building height the building distribution and geometry is clearly different. A particular challenge is posed by the *SanFrancisco* scene which includes tall buildings never seen before in *Washington2*. Similarly, the buildings and vegetation in the *Neighborhood* scene are unlike anything seen in the training data.

We generate samples by running episodes with $r = 0.4$ m until time $t_e = 200$ and selecting the best viewpoint **p** according to the oracle's score at each time step. For each step t we store tuples of input $x(M, \mathbf{p})$ and target value from the oracle $s(M, \mathbf{p})$ for each neighboring viewpoint.

Fig. 4. Normal rendering of environments. From left to right: *Washington2, Washington1, Paris, SanFrancisco, Neighborhood*.

Note that we record samples for each possible neighbor of the current viewpoint (instead of only the best selected viewpoint). This is necessary as our predictor will have to provide approximate scores for arbitrary viewpoints at test time. We record a total of approximately 1,000,000 samples and perform a 80/20 split into training and validation set. To encourage future comparison we will release our code for generating the data and evaluation.

5   Experiments

We describe our ConvNet architecture and then show different evaluations of our method.

5.1   ConvNet Architectures and Training

We evaluated different ConvNet variants by varying N_c, N_u and N_f. We also tried modifications such as using residual units [17,18]. We report these results in the supplementary material. Here we report results on the best performing model with input size $16 \times 16 \times 8$ ($N_c = 2$, $N_u = 4$, $N_f = 8$, $L = 3$, $N_{h1} = 128$, $N_{h2} = 32$), denoted as **Ours** in the rest of the section. Training of the model is done with ADAM using a mini-batch size of 128, regularization $\lambda = 10^{-4}$, $\alpha = 10^{-4}$ and the values suggested by Kingma *et al.* [25] for the other parameters. Dropout with a rate of 0.5 is used after fully-connected layers during training. Network parameters are initialized according to Glorot *et al.* [15] (corrected for ReLu activations). We use early stopping when over-fitting on test data is observed.

5.2   Evaluation

Our evaluation consists of three parts. First we evaluate our model on datasets generated as described in Sect. 4.5 and report spearman's rho to show the rank correlation of predicted scores and ground truth scores. Following this, we compare our models with previously proposed utility functions from [8,24,35]. We use the open-source implementation provided by [8,24] and report results on their best performing methods on our scenes, *ProximityCount* and *AverageEntropy*. We also compare with a frontier-based function measuring the number of unobserved voxels visible from a viewpoint as in [2,19]. For this comparison we use simulated noise-free depth images for all methods. Finally, we evaluate our models with depth images perturbed by noise and depth images produced by stereo matching in a photo-realistic rendering engine.

To demonstrate the generalization capability of our models we use four test scenes (column 2–5 in Fig. 4) that show different building distribution and geometry than the scene used to collect training data. We also perform the experiments on the training scenes where the exploration remains difficult due to random start poses and possible ambiguity in the incomplete occupancy maps.

To compute score and efficiency values, we run 50 episodes with $r = 0.4\,\mathrm{m}$ until $t_e = 200$ for each method and compute the sample mean and standard deviation at each time step. To enable a fair comparison, we select a random start position for each episode in advance and use the same start positions for each method.

In order to report a single metric of performance for comparison we compute the area under the curve of observed surface versus time (see plots in Fig. 5):

$$\mathit{eff} = \sum_{t=0}^{t_e} \mathit{ObsSurf}(M_t) \quad . \tag{6}$$

We call this metric *Efficiency* as it gives a higher score to a method that discovers surface early on.

5.3   Model Performance on Different Datasets

Here we evaluate the performance of our model on data collected from different scenes as described in Sect. 4.5. The model was trained on the training set of *Washington2* and we report Spearman's rho as well as the loss value from Eq. (4) in Table 1.

Table 1. Spearman's rho and loss values for our model on the different datasets. Despite the different building distribution and geometry of the test scenes (i.e. all scenes but *Washington2*) compared to training data Spearman's rho value shows a high rank correlation with the oracle score. This is even the case for the *Neighborhood* scene which features building shapes and trees unlike any in the training data.

	Evaluation on different datasets					
	Washington2 train	*Washington2* test	*Washington1*	*Paris*	*SanFrancisco*	*Neighborhood*
Spearman's rho	0.88	0.87	0.83	0.69	0.73	0.48
Loss value	0.25	0.28	0.43	0.63	0.60	0.93

The Spearman's rho shows a clear rank correlation even for the *Neighborhood* scene which features building distribution and geometry significantly different from *Washington2* which was used to generate training data. Interestingly, the model shows a high rank correlation for the *SanFrancisco* scene which features tall buildings and thus requires our model to generalize to different occupancy map distributions at high viewpoints.

5.4   Comparison with Baselines

In Table 2 we compare the performance of our models against related hand-crafted utility functions [8,24,35]. Our method consistently outperforms the existing functions in terms of the efficiency measure, and as shown in Table 3, is faster to compute than other methods.

We also show plots of observed surface voxels vs. time for our model, the oracle with access to ground truth and baseline methods in Fig. 5. Note that the scenes shown have not been used to generate any training data. The results show that our method performs better compared to the baseline methods at all time steps. Additionally the behavior of our method is consistent over all scenes while the performance of the baselines varies from scene to scene. The progression of reconstructed 3D models is shown by the renderings of the occupancy map at different times.

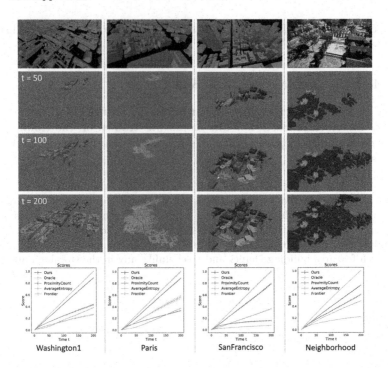

Fig. 5. Results on all test scenes. Top row: Visualization of the underlying mesh model. Row 2–4: Reconstructed 3D models at different time steps. Shown are only occupied voxels and the color coding indicates the voxel position along the z-axis. Bottom row: Plot of observed surface voxels vs. time for all methods, the oracle with access to ground truth and the baseline methods. Our method performs the best and approaches the oracle's performance. Best viewed in color and zoomed in. Larger versions in Supplementary Material.

5.5   Noisy Input Sensor

While all our training is done on simulated data using ground truth depth images our intermediate state representation as an occupancy map makes our models robust to the noise characteristics of the input sensor. Here we evaluate the performance of our models at test time with depth images perturbed by noise of different magnitude. Additionally we test our models with depth images computed from a virtual stereo camera. To this end we utilize a photorealistic game engine to synthesize RGB stereo pairs and compute depth maps with semi-global matching.

Episodes were run with noisy depth images and the viewpoint sequence was recorded. We replayed the same viewpoint sequences and used ground truth depth images to build up an occupancy map and measure the efficiency. Resulting *Efficiency* values are listed in Table 4. One can see that our method is robust to different noise levels. More importantly, even with depth images from the

Table 2. Comparison of *Efficiency* metric. Our method achieves a higher value than the other utility functions on all scenes showing that our learned models can generalize to other scenes. Note that the model is trained only on data recorded from *Washington2*. *Efficiency* values are normalized with respect to the oracle for easier comparison.

	Evaluation on different scenes				
	Washington2	*Washington1*	*Paris*	*SanFrancisco*	*Neighborhood*
Frontier	0.40	0.29	0.57	0.09	0.27
AverageEntropy [24]	0.26	0.36	0.32	0.30	0.50
ProximityCount [24]	0.52	0.47	0.37	0.23	0.60
Ours	**0.91**	**0.88**	**0.87**	**0.77**	**0.74**
Oracle (GT access)	1.00	1.00	1.00	1.00	1.00

Table 3. Comparison of computation time per step. Our method is as fast as a simple raycast in the *Frontier* method and more than $10\times$ faster than *ProximityCount* and *AverageEntropy*.

	Computation time per step			
	Frontier	ProximityCount	AverageEntropy	Ours
Time in s	0.61	5.89	8.35	**0.57**

Table 4. Comparison of our method using noisy depth images. *Efficiency* values are normalized to the noise-free case. For the noise cases 40% of pixels in each depth image were dropped and each remaining pixel was perturbed by normal noise ($\sigma = 0.1$ m for low, $\sigma = 0.2$ m for medium, $\sigma = 0.5$ m for high, $\sigma = 1.0$ m for very high). In the case of stereo matching we used a photo realistic rendering engine to generate stereo images with a baseline of 0.5 m. A disparity and depth image was computed using semi global matching [21]. Note that all values have a standard deviation of ≈ 0.03.

Evaluation using noisy depth images (normalized)					
Noise	None	Low	Medium	High	Very high	Stereo
eff	1.00	0.99	1.01	0.99	1.02	0.99

virtual stereo camera, resulting in realistic perturbations of the depth images (see Supplementary Material), our method does not degrade.

5.6   Additional Results on Real Data

To show that our method is general and also works with real scenes we conducted additional experiments on high-fidelity 3D reconstructions of buildings and on the 2D-3D-S indoor dataset [1] that was acquired with a Matterports[1] camera. Result are shown in Table 5, Figs. 6 and 7. For the outdoor case we trained our model on the church (Fig. 6a) and evaluated on the historic building (Fig. 6c). Despite the differences of both buildings in terms of geometry and scale (the historic building is about $2x$ smaller in each dimension) our model is able to generalize. For the indoor case we trained on *Area1* and evaluated on *Area5b* of the 2D-3D-S indoor dataset [1]. Both experiments demonstrate that our method also works with real detailed scenes.

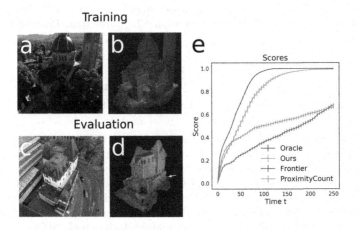

Fig. 6. Shown are example explorations on *real* outdoor data – (a) Picture of church scene. (b) Occupancy map of the church scene (training data) (200 steps). (c) Picture of historic building scene. (d) Occupancy map of the historic building scene (evaluation) (100 steps). (e) Performance plot for the historic building scene. Color coding of observed voxels: High uncertainty (red) and low uncertainty (cyan).

6   Discussion and Conclusions

We presented an approach for efficient exploration of unknown 3D environments by predicting the utility of new views using a 3D ConvNet. We input a novel multi-scale voxel representation of an underlying occupancy map, which represents the current model of the environment. Pairs of input and target utility score are obtained from an oracle that has access to ground truth information. Importantly, our model is able to generalize to scenes other than the training data and the underlying occupancy map enables robustness to noisy sensor input such

---

[1] https://matterport.com/.

Table 5. Comparison of *Efficiency* metric on the additional real data. Our method achieves a higher value than the other utility functions on both ourdoor and indoor scenes. Note that in both cases the model was trained on data recorded from a single scene that was different from the evaluation scene. *Efficiency* values are normalized with respect to the oracle for easier comparison.

	Evaluation on additional real data			
	Frontier	ProximityCount [24]	**Ours**	Oracle (GT access)
Outdoor	0.46	0.58	**0.90**	1.00
Indoor	0.44	0.52	**0.78**	1.00

as depth images from a stereo camera. Experiments indicate that our approach improves upon previous methods in terms of reconstruction efficiency.

Limitations of our method include dependence on the surface voxel distribution in the training data. In future work, it would be interesting to see how the method performs on vastly different geometries such as rock formations and other natural landscapes. Similarly, our model is bound to the map resolution and mapping parameters used in the training data.

Another limitation is the underlying assumption on a static scene. A dynamic object such as a human walking in front of the camera would lead to occupied voxels that do not correspond to a static object. While these voxels can change their state from occupied to free after additional observations if the human walked away the intermediate occupancy map can lead to utility predictions that are not desired. A possible solution to address this problem is to identify and segment dynamic objects in the depth maps before integrating them into the occupancy map.

Our work suggests several directions for future work. We used our learned utility function to implement a greedy next-best-view algorithm; however, our utility function could be used to develop more sophisticated policies that look multiple steps ahead. In addition, our approach could be extended to be used in

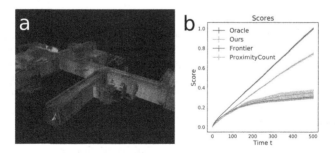

Fig. 7. Shown are example explorations on *real* indoor data – (a) Occupancy map of S3Dis Area5b (400 steps). (b) Performance plot for S3Dis Area5b (training on Area1). Color coding of observed voxels: High uncertainty (red) and low uncertainty (cyan).

a generative way to predict future states of the 3D occupancy map or to predict 2D depth maps for unobserved views. This could be used for model completion or hole-filling which has numerous applications in computer vision and robotics.

References

1. Armeni, I., Sax, S., Zamir, A.R., Savarese, S.: Joint 2d–3d-semantic data for indoor scene understanding, Preprint arXiv:1702.01105 (2017)
2. Bircher, A., Kamel, M., Alexis, K., Oleynikova, H., Siegwart, R.: Receding horizon "next-best-view" planner for 3d exploration. In: 2016 IEEE International Conference on Robotics and Automation (ICRA), pp. 1462–1468. IEEE (2016)
3. Chen, S., Li, Y., Kwok, N.M.: Active vision in robotic systems: a survey of recent developments. Int. J. Robot. Res. **30**(11), 1343–1377 (2011)
4. Choudhury, S., Kapoor, A., Ranade, G., Scherer, S., Dey, D.: Adaptive information gathering via imitation learning. Robotics Science and Systems (2017)
5. Choy, C.B., Xu, D., Gwak, J., Chen, K., Savarese, S.: 3D-R2N2: a unified approach for single and multi-view 3d object reconstruction. In: Leibe, B., Matas, J., Sebe, N., Welling, M. (eds.) ECCV 2016. LNCS, vol. 9912, pp. 628–644. Springer, Cham (2016). https://doi.org/10.1007/978-3-319-46484-8_38
6. Dai, A., Chang, A.X., Savva, M., Halber, M., Funkhouser, T., Nießner, M.: Scannet: richly-annotated 3d reconstructions of indoor scenes. http://arxiv.org/abs/1702.04405 (2017)
7. Dai, A., Qi, C.R., Nießner, M.: Shape completion using 3d-encoder-predictor cnns and shape synthesis. http://arxiv.org/abs/1612.00101 (2016)
8. Delmerico, J., Isler, S., Sabzevari, R., Scaramuzza, D.: A comparison of volumetric information gain metrics for active 3d object reconstruction. Autonomous Robots pp. 1–12 (2017)
9. Devrim Kaba, M., Gokhan Uzunbas, M., Nam Lim, S.: A reinforcement learning approach to the view planning problem. In: Proceedings of the IEEE Conference on Computer Vision and Pattern Recognition, pp. 6933–6941 (2017)
10. Dunn, E., Frahm, J.M.: Next best view planning for active model improvement. In: BMVC, pp. 1–11 (2009)
11. Feige, U.: A threshold of ln n for approximating set cover. JACM (1998)
12. Forster, C., Pizzoli, M., Scaramuzza, D.: Appearance-based active, monocular, dense reconstruction for micro aerial vehicles. In: Robotics: Science and Systems (RSS) (2014)
13. Fraundorfer, F., Heng, L., Honegger, D., Lee, G.H., Meier, L., Tanskanen, P., Pollefeys, M.: Vision-based autonomous mapping and exploration using a quadrotor mav. In: 2012 IEEE/RSJ International Conference on Intelligent Robots and Systems (IROS), pp. 4557–4564. IEEE (2012)
14. Ge, L., Liang, H., Yuan, J., Thalmann, D.: 3d convolutional neural networks for efficient and robust hand pose estimation from single depth images. In: Proceedings of the IEEE Conference on Computer Vision and Pattern Recognition, pp. 1991–2000 (2017)
15. Glorot, X., Bengio, Y.: Understanding the difficulty of training deep feedforward neural networks. In: Proceedings of the Thirteenth International Conference on Artificial Intelligence and Statistics, pp. 249–256 (2010)
16. Golovin, D., Krause, A.: Adaptive submodularity: Theory and applications in active learning and stochastic optimization. JAIR (2011). https://arxiv.org/pdf/1003.3967v4.pdf

17. He, K., Zhang, X., Ren, S., Sun, J.: Deep residual learning for image recognition. In: The IEEE Conference on Computer Vision and Pattern Recognition (CVPR) (June 2016)

18. He, K., Zhang, X., Ren, S., Sun, J.: Identity mappings in deep residual networks. In: Leibe, B., Matas, J., Sebe, N., Welling, M. (eds.) ECCV 2016. LNCS, vol. 9908, pp. 630–645. Springer, Cham (2016). https://doi.org/10.1007/978-3-319-46493-0_38

19. Heng, L., Gotovos, A., Krause, A., Pollefeys, M.: Efficient visual exploration and coverage with a micro aerial vehicle in unknown environments. In: ICRA (2015). http://ieeexplore.ieee.org/document/7139309/

20. Hepp, B., Nießner, M., Hilliges, O.: Plan3d: Viewpoint and trajectory optimization for aerial multi-view stereo reconstruction, Preprint arXiv:1705.09314 (2017)

21. Hirschmuller, H.: Stereo processing by semiglobal matching and mutual information. IEEE Trans. Pattern Anal. Mach. Intell. **30**(2), 328–341 (2008)

22. Hollinger, G.A., Englot, B., Hover, F.S., Mitra, U., Sukhatme, G.S.: Active planning for underwater inspection and the benefit of adaptivity. IJRR (2012). http://journals.sagepub.com/doi/abs/10.1177/0278364912467485

23. Hornung, A., Wurm, K.M., Bennewitz, M., Stachniss, C., Burgard, W.: OctoMap: an efficient probabilistic 3D mapping framework based on octrees. Autonomous Robots (2013). 10.1007/s10514-012-9321-0, software available at http://octomap.github.com

24. Isler, S., Sabzevari, R., Delmerico, J., Scaramuzza, D.: An Information Gain Formulation for Active Volumetric 3D Reconstruction. In: ICRA (2016). http://ieeexplore.ieee.org/document/7487527/

25. Kingma, D., Ba, J.: Adam: a method for stochastic optimization, Preprint arXiv:1412.6980 (2014)

26. Krause, A., Golovin, D.: Submodular function maximization. In: Tractability: Practical Approaches to Hard Problems (2012). https://las.inf.ethz.ch/files/krause12survey.pdf

27. Kriegel, S., Rink, C., Bodenmüller, T., Suppa, M.: Efficient next-best-scan planning for autonomous 3d surface reconstruction of unknown objects. J. Real-Time Image Proces. **10**(4), 611–631 (2015)

28. Liu, F., Shen, C., Lin, G.: Deep convolutional neural fields for depth estimation from a single image. In: Proceedings of the IEEE Conference on Computer Vision and Pattern Recognition, pp. 5162–5170 (2015)

29. Nemhauser, G.L., Wolsey, L.A., Fisher, M.L.: An analysis of approximations for maximizing submodular set functionsi. Math. Program. **14**(1), 265–294 (1978)

30. Riegler, G., Ulusoy, A.O., Geiger, A.: Octnet: Learning deep 3d representations at high resolutions. In: Conference on Computer Vision and Pattern Recognition (CVPR) (2017)

31. Roberts, M., Dey, D., Truong, A., Sinha, S., Shah, S., Kapoor, A., Hanrahan, P., Joshi, N.: Submodular trajectory optimization for aerial 3d scanning. In: International Conference on Computer Vision (ICCV) (2017)

32. Shen, S., Michael, N., Kumar, V.: Autonomous multi-floor indoor navigation with a computationally constrained mav. In: 2011 IEEE International Conference on Robotics and Automation (ICRA), pp. 20–25. IEEE (2011)

33. Song, S., Xiao, J.: Deep sliding shapes for amodal 3d object detection in rgb-d images. In: Proceedings of the IEEE Conference on Computer Vision and Pattern Recognition, pp. 808–816 (2016)

34. Thrun, S., Burgard, W., Fox, D.: Probabilistic Robotics. MIT Press, Cambridge (2005)

35. Vasquez-Gomez, J.I., Sucar, L.E., Murrieta-Cid, R., Lopez-Damian, E.: Volumetric next-best-view planning for 3d object reconstruction with positioning error. Int. J. Adv. Robot. Syst. **11**(10), 159 (2014)
36. Wenhardt, S., Deutsch, B., Angelopoulou, E., Niemann, H.: Active visual object reconstruction using d-, e-, and t-optimal next best views. In: 2007 IEEE Conference on Computer Vision and Pattern Recognition, pp. 1–7. IEEE (2007)
37. Xu, K., Zheng, L., Yan, Z., Yan, G., Zhang, E., Nießner, M., Deussen, O., Cohen-Or, D., Huang, H.: Autonomous reconstruction of unknown indoor scenes guided by time-varying tensor fields. ACM Trans. Gr. (TOG) **36**, 202 (2017)
38. Yamauchi, B.: A frontier-based approach for autonomous exploration. In: 1997 IEEE International Symposium on Computational Intelligence in Robotics and Automation, CIRA'97, pp. 146–151. IEEE (1997)
39. Zamir, A.R., Wekel, T., Agrawal, P., Wei, C., Malik, Jitendra, Savarese, Silvio: Generic 3D representation via pose estimation and matching. In: Leibe, B., Matas, J., Sebe, N., Welling, M. (eds.) ECCV 2016. LNCS, vol. 9907, pp. 535–553. Springer, Cham (2016). https://doi.org/10.1007/978-3-319-46487-9_33
40. Zeng, A., Song, S., Nießner, M., Fisher, M., Xiao, J., Funkhouser, T.: 3dmatch: Learning local geometric descriptors from rgb-d reconstructions. In: CVPR (2017)

Revisiting RCNN: On Awakening the Classification Power of Faster RCNN

Bowen Cheng[1], Yunchao Wei[1(✉)], Honghui Shi[2], Rogerio Feris[2],
Jinjun Xiong[2], and Thomas Huang[1]

[1] University of Illinois at Urbana-Champaign, Champaign, IL, USA
{bcheng9,yunchao,t-huang1}@illinois.edu
[2] IBM T.J. Watson Research Center, Ossining, NY, USA
Honghui.Shi@ibm.com, {rsferis,jinjun}@us.ibm.com

Abstract. Recent region-based object detectors are usually built with separate classification and localization branches on top of shared feature extraction networks. In this paper, we analyze failure cases of state-of-the-art detectors and observe that most *hard false positives* result from classification instead of localization. We conjecture that: (1) Shared feature representation is not optimal due to the mismatched goals of feature learning for classification and localization; (2) multi-task learning helps, yet optimization of the multi-task loss may result in sub-optimal for individual tasks; (3) large receptive field for different scales leads to redundant context information for small objects. We demonstrate the potential of detector classification power by a simple, effective, and widely-applicable *Decoupled Classification Refinement* (DCR) network. DCR samples hard false positives from the base classifier in Faster RCNN and trains a RCNN-styled strong classifier. Experiments show new state-of-the-art results on PASCAL VOC and COCO without any bells and whistles.

Keywords: Object detection

1 Introduction

Region-based approaches with convolutional neural networks (CNNs) [2,10,11, 17–20,27,31,33] have achieved great success in object detection. Such detectors are usually built with separate classification and localization branches on top of shared feature extraction networks, and trained with multi-task loss. In particular, Faster RCNN [27] learns one of the first end-to-end two-stage detector with remarkable efficiency and accuracy. Many follow-up works, such as R-FCN [3], Feature Pyramid Networks (FPN) [21], Deformable ConvNets (DCN) [4], have been leading popular detection benchmark in PASCAL VOC [6] and COCO [23] datasets in terms of accuracy. Yet, few work has been proposed to study what is the full potential of the classification power in Faster RCNN styled detectors.

Electronic supplementary material The online version of this chapter (https://doi.org/10.1007/978-3-030-01267-0_28) contains supplementary material, which is available to authorized users.

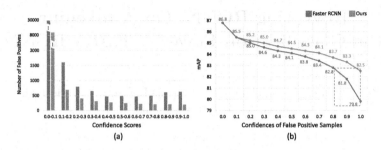

Fig. 1. (a) Comparison of the number of false positives in different ranges. (b) Comparison of the mAP gains by progressively removing false positives; from right to left, the detector is performing better as false positives are removed according to their confidence scores.

To answer this question, in this paper, we begin with investigating the key factors affecting the performance of Faster RCNN. As shown in Fig. 1(a), we conduct object detection on PASCAL VOC 2007 using Faster RCNN and count the number of false positive detections in different confidence score intervals (blue). Although only a small percentage of all false positives are predicted with high confidence scores, these samples lead to a significant performance drop in mean average precision (mAP). In particular, we perform an analysis of potential gains in mAP using Faster RCNN: As illustrated in Fig. 1(b), given the detection results from Faster RCNN and a confidence score threshold, we assume that all false positives with predicted confidence score above that threshold were classified correctly and we report the correspondent hypothesized mAP. It is evident that by correcting all false positives, Faster RCNN could, hypothetically, have achieved 86.8% in mAP instead of 79.8%. Moreover, even if we only eliminate false positives with high confidences, as indicated in the red box, we can still improve the detection performance significantly by 3.0% mAP, which is a desired yet hard-to-obtain boost for modern object detection systems.

The above observation motivates our work to alleviate the burden of false positives and improve the classification power of Faster RCNN based detectors. By scrutinizing the false positives produced by Faster RCNN, we conjecture that such errors are mainly due to three reasons: (1) Shared feature representation for both classification and localization may not be optimal for region proposal classification, the mismatched goals in feature learning lead to the reduced classification power of Faster RCNN; (2) Multi-task learning in general helps to improve the performance of object detectors as shown in Fast RCNN [10] and Faster RCNN, but the joint optimization also leads to possible sub-optimal to balance the goals of multiple tasks and could not directly utilize the full potential on individual tasks; (3) Receptive fields in deep CNNs such as ResNet-101 [15] are large, the whole image are usually fully covered for any given region proposals. Such large receptive fields could lead to inferior classification capacity by introducing redundant context information for small objects.

Following the above argument, we propose a simple yet effective approach, named Decoupled Classification Refinement (DCR), to eliminate high-scored false positives and improve the region proposal classification results. DCR decouples the classification and localization tasks in Faster RCNN styled detectors. It takes input from a base classifier, *e.g.* the Faster RCNN, and refine the classification results using a RCNN-styled network. DCR samples *hard false positives*, namely the false positives with high confidence scores, from the base classifier, and then trains a stronger correctional classifier for the classification refinement. Designedly, we do not share any parameters between the Faster RCNN and our DCR module, so that the DCR module can not only utilize the multi-task learning improved results from region proposal networks (RPN) and bounding box regression tasks, but also better optimize the newly introduced module to address the challenging classification cases.

We conduct extensive experiments based on different Faster RCNN styled detectors (*i.e.* Faster RCNN, Deformable ConvNets, FPN) and benchmarks (*i.e.* PASCAL VOC 2007 & 2012, COCO) to demonstrate the effectiveness of our proposed simple solution in enhancing the detection performance by alleviating hard false positives. As shown in Fig. 1(a), our approach can significantly reduce the number of hard false positives and boost the detection performance by 2.7% in mAP on PASCAL VOC 2007 over a strong baseline as indicated in Fig. 1(b). All of our experiment results demonstrate that our proposed DCR module can provide consistent improvements over various detection baselines, as shown in Fig. 2. Our contributions are threefold:

1. We analyze the error modes of region-based object detectors and formulate the hypotheses that might cause these failure cases.
2. We propose a set of design principles to improve the classification power of Faster RCNN styled object detectors along with the DCR module based on the proposed design principles.
3. Our DCR module consistently brings significant performance boost to strong object detectors on popular benchmarks. In particular, following common practice (ResNet-101 as backbone), we achieve mAP of 84.0% and 81.2% on the classic PASCAL VOC 2007 and 2012, respectively, and 43.1% on the more challenging COCO2015 *test-dev*, which are the new state-of-the-art.

2   Related Work

Object Detection. Recent CNN based object detectors can generally be categorized into two-stage and single stage. One of the first two-stage detector is RCNN [11], where selective search [29] is used to generate a set of region proposals for object candidates, then a deep neural network to extract feature vector of each region followed by SVM classifiers. SPPNet [14] improves the efficiency of RCNN by sharing feature extraction stage and use spatial pyramid pooling to extract fixed length feature for each proposal. Fast RCNN [10] improves over SPPNet by introducing an differentiable ROI Pooling operation

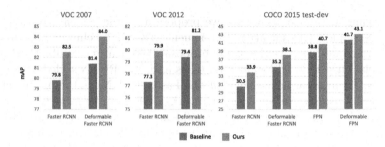

Fig. 2. Comparison of our approach and baseline in terms of different Faster RCNN series and benchmarks.

to train the network end-to-end. Faster RCNN [27] embeds the region proposal step into a Region Proposal Network (RPN) that further reduce the proposal generation time. R-FCN [3] proposed a position sensitive ROI Pooling (PSROI Pooling) that can share computation among classification branch and bounding box regression branch. Deformable ConvNets (DCN) [4] further add deformable convolutions and deformable ROI Pooling operations, that use learned offsets to adjust position of each sampling bin in naive convolutions and ROI Pooling, to Faster RCNN. Feature Pyramid Networks (FPN) [21] add a top-down path with lateral connections to build a pyramid of features with different resolutions and attach detection heads to each level of the feature pyramid for making prediction. Finer feature maps are more useful for detecting small objects and thus a significant boost in small object detection is observed with FPN. Most of the current state-of-the-art object detectors are two-stage detectors based of Faster RCNN, because two-stage object detectors produce more accurate results and are easier to optimize. However, two-stage detectors are slow in speed and require very large input sizes due to the ROI Pooling operation. Aimed at achieving real time object detectors, one-stage method, such as OverFeat [28], SSD [9,24] and YOLO [25,26], predict object classes and locations directly. Though single stage methods are much faster than two-stage methods, their results are inferior and they need more extra data and extensive data augmentation to get better results. Our paper follows the method of two-stage detectors [10,11,27], but with a main focus on analyzing reasons why detectors make mistakes.

Classifier Cascade. The method of classifier cascade commonly trains a stage classifier using misclassified examples from a previous classifier. This has been used a lot for object detection in the past. The Viola Jones Algorithm [30] for face detection used a hard cascades by Adaboost [8], where a strong region classifier is built with cascade of many weak classifier focusing attentions on different features and if any of the weak classifier rejects the window, there will be no more process. Soft cascades [1] improved [30] built each weak classifier based on the output of all previous classifiers. Deformable Part Model (DPM) [7] used a cascade of parts method where a root filter on coarse feature covering the entire object is combined with some part filters on fine feature with greater

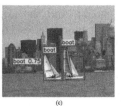

(a)   (b)   (c)

Fig. 3. Demonstration of hard false positives. Results are generate by Faster RCNN with 2 fully connected layer (2fc) as detector head [21,27], red boxes are ground truth, green boxes are hard false positives with scores higher than 0.3; (a) boxes covering only part of objects with high confidences; (b) incorrect classification due to similar objects; (c) misclassified backgrounds.

localization accuracy. More recently, Li et al. [16] proposed the Convolutional Neural Network Cascade for fast face detection. Our paper proposed a method similar to the classifier cascade idea, however, they are different in the following aspects. The classifier cascade aims at producing an efficient classifier (mainly in speed) by cascade weak but fast classifiers and the weak classifiers are used to reject examples. In comparison, our method aims at improving the overall system accuracy, where exactly two strong classifiers are cascaded and they work together to make more accurate predictions. More recently, Cascade RCNN [2] proposes training object detector in a cascade manner with gradually increased IoU threshold to assign ground truth labels to align the testing metric, ie. average mAP with IOU 0.5:0.05:0.95.

3   Problems with Faster RCNN

Faster RCNN produces 3 typical types of hard false positives, as shown in Fig. 3: (1) The classification is correct but the overlap between the predicted box and ground truth has low IoU, *e.g.* < 0.5 in Fig. 3(a). This type of false negative boxes usually cover the most discriminative part and have enough information to predict the correct classes due to translation invariance. (2) Incorrect classification for predicted boxes but the IoU with ground truth are large enough, *e.g.* in Fig. 3(b). It happens mainly because some classes share similar discriminative parts and the predicted box does not align well with the true object and happens to cover only the discriminative parts of confusion. Another reason is that the classifier used in the detector is not strong enough to distinguish between two similar classes. (3) the detection is a "confident" background, meaning that there is no intersection or small intersection with ground truth box but classifier's confidence score is large, *e.g.* in Fig. 3(c). Most of the background pattern in this case is similar to its predicted class and the classifier is too weak to distinguish. Another reason for this case is that the receptive field is fixed and it is too large for some box that it covers the actual object in its receptive field. In Fig. 3(c), the misclassified background is close to a ground truth box (the left boat), and the large receptive field (covers more than 1000 pixels in ResNet-101) might "sees" too much object features to make the wrong prediction. Given above analysis, we can conclude that the hard false positives are mainly caused by the suboptimal classifier embedded in the detector. The reasons may be that: (1) feature sharing between classification and localization, (2) optimizing the sum of classification loss and localization loss, and (3) detector's receptive field does not change according to the size of objects.

Problem with Feature Sharing. Detector backbones are usually adapted from image classification model and pre-trained on large image classification dataset. These backbones are original designed to learn scale invariant features for classification. Scale invariance is achieved by adding sub-sampling layers, *e.g.* max pooling, and data augmentation, *e.g.* random crop. Detectors place a classification branch and localization branch on top of the same backbone, however, classification needs **translation invariant** feature whereas localization needs **translation covariant** feature. During fine-tuning, the localization branch will force the backbone to gradually learn translation covariant feature, which might potentially down-grade the performance of classifier.

Problem with Optimization. Faster RCNN series are built with a feature extractor as backbone and two task-specified branches for classifying regions and the other for localizing correct locations. Denote loss functions for classification and localization as L_{cls} and L_{bbox}, respectively. Then, the optimization of Faster RCNN series is to address a Multi-Task Learning (MTL) problem by minimizing the sum of two loss functions: $L_{detection} = L_{cls} + L_{bbox}$. However, the optimization might converge to a compromising suboptimal of two tasks by simultaneously considering the sum of two losses, instead of each of them.

Originally, such a MTL manner is found to be effective and observed improvement over state-wise learning in Fast(er) RCNN works. However, MTL for object detection is not studied under the recent powerful classification backbones, *e.g.* ResNets. Concretely, we hypothesize that MTL may work well based on a weak backbone (*e.g.* AlexNet or VGG16). As the backbone is getting stronger, the powerful classification capacity within the backbone may not be fully exploited and MTL becomes the bottleneck.

Problem with Receptive Field. Deep convolutional neural networks have fixed receptive fields. For image classification, inputs are usually cropped and resized to have fixed sizes, *e.g.* 224 × 224, and network is designed to have a receptive field little larger than the input region. However, since contexts are cropped and objects with different scales are resized, the "effective receptive field" is covering the whole object.

Unlike image classification task where a single large object is in the center of a image, objects in detection task have various sizes over arbitrary locations.

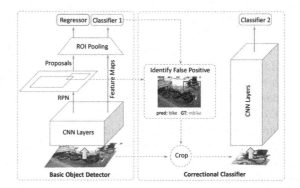

Fig. 4. Left: base detector (*e.g.* Faster RCNN). Right: our proposed Decoupled Classification Refinement (DCR) module.

In Faster RCNN, the ROI pooling is introduced to crop object from 2-D convolutional feature maps to a 1-D fixed size representation for the following classification, which results in fixed receptive field (*i.e.* the network is attending to a fixed-size window of the input image). In such a case, objects have various sizes and the fixed receptive field will introduce different amount of context. For a small object, the context might be too large for the network to focus on the object whereas for a large object, the receptive field might be too small that the network is looking at part of the object. Although some works introduce multi-scale features by aggregating features with different receptive field, the number of sizes is still too small comparing with the number various sizes of objects.

4   Revisiting RCNN for Improving Faster RCNN

In this section, we look back closely into the classic RCNN [11] method, and give an in-depth analysis of why RCNN can be used as a "complement" to improve Faster RCNN. Based on our findings, we provide a simple yet effective decoupled classification refinement module, that can be easily added to any current state-of-the-art object detectors to provide performance improvements.

4.1   Learning from RCNN Design

We train a modified RCNN with ResNet-50 as backbone and Faster RCNN predictions as region proposals. We find that with RCNN along, the detection result is deteriorated by more than 30% (from 79.8% to 44.7%)! Since RCNN does not modify box coordinate, the inferior result means worse classification. We find that many boxes having small intersections with an object are classified as that object instead of the background which Faster RCNN predicts. Based on this finding, we hypothesize that the drawback of RCNN is mainly root from that classification model is pre-trained without awaring object location. Since ResNet-50 is trained on ImageNet in multi-crop manner, no matter how much the intersection of the crop to the object is, classifier is encouraged to predict that class. This leads to the classifier in RCNN being "too strong" for proposal classification, and this is why RCNN needs a carefully tuned sampling strategy, *i.e.* a ratio of 1:3 of fg to bg. Straightforwardly, we are interested whether RCNN is "strong" enough to correct hard negatives. We make a minor modification to multiply RCNN classification score with Faster RCNN classification score and observe a boost of 1.9% (from 79.8% to 81.7%)! Thus, we consider that RCNN can be seen as a compliment of Faster RCNN in the following sense: the classifier of Faster RCNN is weaker but aware of object location whereas the classifier of RCNN is unaware of object location but stronger. Based on our findings, we propose the following three principals to design a better object detector.

Decoupled Features. Current detectors still place classification head and localization head on the same backbone, hence we propose that classification head and localization head should not share parameter (as the analysis given in Sect. 3), resulted in a decoupled feature using pattern by RCNN.

Decoupled Optimization. RCNN also decouples the optimization for object proposal and classification. In this paper, we make a small change in optimization. We propose a novel two-stage training where, instead of optimizing the sum of classification and localization loss, we optimize the concatenation of classification and localization loss, $L_{detection} = [L_{cls} + L_{bbox}, L_{cls}]$, where each entry is being optimized independently in two steps.

Adaptive Receptive Field. The most important advantage of RCNN is that its receptive field always covers the whole ROI, *i.e.* the receptive field size adjusts according to the size of the object by cropping and resizing each proposal to a fixed size. We agree that context information may be important for precise detection, however, we conjuncture that different amount of context introduced by fixed receptive filed might cause different performance to different sizes of objects. It leads to our last proposed principal that a detector should an adaptive receptive field that can change according to the size of objects it attends to. In this principal, the context introduced for each object should be proportional to its size, but how to decide the amount of context still remains an open question to be studied in the future. Another advantage of adaptive receptive field is that its features are well aligned to objects. Current detectors make predictions at high-level, coarse feature maps usually having a large stride, *e.g.* a stride of 16 or 32 is used in Faster RCNN, due to sub-sampling operations. The sub-sampling introduces unaligned features, *e.g.* one cell shift on a feature map of stride 32 leads to 32 pixels shift on the image, and defects the predictions. With adaptive receptive field, the detector always attends to the entire object resulting in an aligned feature to make predictions. RCNN gives us a simple way to achieve adaptive receptive field, but how to find a more efficient way to do so remains an interesting problem needs studying.

4.2 Decoupled Classification Refinement (DCR)

Following these principals, we propose a DCR module that can be easily augmented to Faster RCNN as well as any object detector to build a stronger detector. The overall pipeline is shown in Fig. 4. The left part and the right part are the original Faster RCNN and our proposed DCR module, respectively. In particular, DCR mainly consists a crop-resize layer and a strong classifier. The crop-resize layer takes two inputs, the original image and boxes produced by Faster RCNN, crops boxes on the original image and feeds them to the strong classifier after resizing them to a predefined size. Region scores of DCR module (Classifier 2) is aggregated with region scores of Faster RCNN (Classifier 1) by element-wise product to form the final score of each region. The two parts are trained separately in this paper and the scores are only combined during test time.

The DCR module does not share any feature with the detector backbone in order to preserve the quality of classification-aimed translation invariance feature. Furthermore, there is no error propagation between DCR module and the base detector, thus the optimization of one loss does not affect the other. This in turn results in a decoupled pattern where the base detector is focused more on localization whereas the DCR module focuses more on classification. DCR module introduces adaptive receptive field by resizing boxes to a predefined size. Noticed that this processing is very similar to moving an ROI Pooling from final feature maps to the image, however, it is quite different than doing ROI Pooling on feature maps. Even though the final output feature map sizes are the same, features from ROI Pooling sees larger region because objects embedded in an image has richer context. We truncated the context by cropping objects directly on the image and the network cannot see context outside object regions.

4.3 Training

Since there is no error propagates from the DCR module to Faster RCNN, we train our object detector in a two-step manner. First, we train Faster RCNN to converge. Then, we train our DCR module on mini-batches sampled from hard false positives of Faster RCNN. Parameters of DCR module are pre-trained by ImageNet dataset [5]. We follow the image-centric method [10] to sample N images with a total mini-batch size of R boxes, $i.e.$ R/N boxes per image. We use $N = 1$ and $R = 32$ throughout experiments. We use a different sampling heuristic that we sample not only foreground and background boxes but also hard false positive **uniformly**. Because we do not want to apply any prior knowledge to impose unnecessary bias on classifier. However, we observed that boxes from the same image have little variance. Thus, we fix Batch Normalization layer with ImageNet training set statistics. The newly added linear classifier (fully connected layer) is set with 10 times of the base learning rate since we want to preserve translation invariance features learned on the ImageNet dataset.

Table 1. Ablation studies results. Evaluate on PASCAL VOC2007 test set. Baseline is Faster RCNN with ResNet-101 as backbone. DCR module uses ResNet-50. (a) Ablation study on sampling heuristics. (b) Ablation study on threshold for defining hard false positives. (c) Ablation study on sampling size. (d) Ablation study on ROI scale and test time (measured in seconds/image). (e) Ablation study on depth of DCR module and test time (measured in seconds/image). (f) DCR module with difference base detectors. Faster denotes Faster RCNN and DCN denotes Deformable Faster RCNN, both use ResNet-101 as backbone. (g) Comparison of Faster RCNN with same size as Faster RCNN + DCR.

Sample method	mAP	FP Score	mAP	Sample size	mAP	ROI scale	mAP	Test Time
Baseline	79.8	Baseline	79.8	Baseline	79.8	Baseline	79.8	0.0855
Random	81.8	0.20	82.2	8 Boxes	82.0	56 × 56	80.6	0.0525
FP Only	81.4	0.25	81.9	16 Boxes	82.1	112 × 112	82.0	0.1454
FP+FG	81.6	0.30	**82.3**	32 Boxes	**82.3**	224 × 224	**82.3**	0.5481
FP+BG	80.3	0.35	82.2	64 Boxes	82.1	320 × 320	82.0	1.0465
FP+FG+BG	**82.3**	0.40	82.0					
RCNN-like	81.7							
(a)		(b)		(c)			(d)	

DCR Depth	mAP	Test Time	Base detector	mAP	Model capacity		mAP
Baseline	79.8	0.0855	Faster	79.8	Faster w/ Res101		79.8
18	81.4	0.1941	Faster+DCR	82.3	Faster w/ Res152		80.3
34	81.9	0.3144	DCN	81.4	Faster Ensemble		81.1
50	82.3	0.5481	DCN+DCR	83.2	Faster w/ Res101+DCR-50		82.3
101	82.3	0.9570					
152	**82.5**	1.3900					
(e)			(f)		(g)		

5 Experiments

5.1 Implementation Details

We train base detectors, *e.g.* Faster RCNN, following their original implementations. We use default settings in Sect. 4.3 for DCR module, we use ROI size 224 × 224 and use a threshold of 0.3 to identify hard false positives. Our DCR module is first pre-trained on ILSVRC 2012 [5]. In fine-tuning, we set the initial learning rate to 0.0001 *w.r.t.* one GPU and weight decay of 0.0001. We follow linear scaling rule in [12] for data parallelism on multiple GPUs and use 4 GPUs for PASCAL VOC and 8 GPUs for COCO. Synchronized SGD with momentum 0.9 is used as optimizer. No data augmentation except horizontal flip is used.

5.2 Ablation Studies on PASCAL VOC

We comprehensively evaluate our method on the PASCAL VOC detection benchmark [6]. We use the union of VOC 2007 trainval and VOC 2012 trainval as well as their horizontal flip as training data and evaluate results on the VOC 2007 test set. We primarily evaluate the detection mAP with IoU 0.5 (mAP@0.5). Unless otherwise stated, all ablation studies are performed with ResNet-50 as classifier for our DCR module.

Ablation Study on Sampling Heuristic. We compare results with different sampling heuristic in training DCR module:

- random sample: a minibatch of ROIs are randomly sampled for each image
- hard false positive only: a minibatch of ROIs that are hard postives are sampled for each image
- hard false positive and background: a minibatch of ROIs that are either hard postives or background are sampled for each image
- hard false positive and foreground: a minibatch of ROIs that are either hard postives or foreground are sampled for each image
- hard false positive, background and foreground: the difference with random sample heuristic is that we ignore easy false positives during training.
- RCNN-like: we follow the Fast RCNN's sampling heuristic, we sample two images per GPU and 64 ROIs per image with fg:bg = 1:3.

Results are shown in Table 1(a). We find that the result is insensitive to sampling heuristic. Even with random sampling, an improvement of 2.0% in mAP is achieved. With only hard false positive, the DCR achieves an improvement of 1.6% already. Adding foreground examples only further gains a 0.2% increase. Adding background examples to false negatives harms the performance by a large margin of 1.1%. We hypothesize that this is because comparing to false positives, background examples dominating in most images results in a classifier bias to predicting background. This finding demonstrate the importance of hard negative in DCR training. Unlike RCNN-like detectors, we do not make any assumption of the distribution of hard false positives, foregrounds and backgrounds. To balance the training of classifier, we simply uniformly sample from the union set of hard false positives, foregrounds and backgrounds. This uniform sample heuristic gives the largest gain of 2.5% mAP. We also compare our training with RCNN-like training. Training with RCNN-like sampling heuristic with fg:bg = 1:3 only gains a margin of 1.9%.

Ablation Study on Other Hyperparameters. We compare results with different threshold for defining hard false positive: [0.2, 0.25, 0.3, 0.35, 0.4]. Results are shown in Table 1(b). We find that the results are quite insensitive to threshold of hard false positives and we argue that this is due to our robust uniform sampling heuristic. With hard false positive threshold of 0.3, the performance is the best with a gain of 2.5%. We also compare the influence of size of sampled RoIs during training: [8, 16, 32, 64]. Results are shown in Table 1 (c). Surprisingly, the difference of best and worst performance is only 0.3%, meaning our method is highly insensitive to the sampling size. With smaller sample size, the training is more efficient without severe drop in performance.

Speed and Accuracy Trade-Off. There are in general two ways to reduce inference speed, one is to reduce the size of input and the other one is to reduce the depth of the network. We compare 4 input sizes: 56×56, 112×112, 224×224, 320×320 as well as 5 depth choices: 18, 34, 50, 101, 152 and their speed. Results are shown in Table 1(d) and (e). The test speed is linearly related to the area of input image size and there is a severe drop in accuracy if the image size is too small, *e.g.* 56 × 56. For the depth of classifier, deeper model results in more accurate predictions but also more test time. We also notice that the accuracy is correlated with the classification accuracy of classification model, which can be used as a guideline for selecting DCR module.

Generalization to More Advanced Object Detectors. We evaluate the DCR module on Faster RCNN and advanced Deformable Convolution Nets (DCN) [4]. Results are shown in Table 1(f). Although DCN is already among one of the most accurate detectors, its classifier still produces hard false positives and our proposed DCR module is effective in eliminating those hard false positives.

Where is the Gain Coming from? One interesting question is where the accuracy gain comes from. Since we add a large convolutional network on top of the object detector, does the gain simply comes from more parameters? Or, is DCR an ensemble of two detectors? To answer this question, we compare the results of Faster RCNN with ResNet-152 as backbone (denoted Faster-152) and Faster RCNN with ResNet-101 backbone + DCR-50 (denoted Faster-101+DCR-50) and results are shown in Table 1(g). Since the DCR module is simply a classifier, the two network have approximately the same number of parameters. However, we only observe a marginal gain of 0.5% with Faster-152 while our Faster-101+DCR-50 has a much larger gain of 2.5%. To show DCR is not simply then ensemble to two Faster RCNNs, we further ensemble Faster RCNN with ResNet-101 and ResNet-152 and the result is 81.1% which is still 1.1% worse than our Faster-101+DCR-50 model. This means that the capacity does not merely come from more parameters or ensemble of two detectors.

5.3   PASCAL VOC Results

VOC 2007 We use a union of VOC2007 trainval and VOC2012 trainval for training and we test on VOC2007 test. We use the default training setting and ResNet-152 as classifier for the DCR module. We train our model for 7 epochs and reduce learning rate by $\frac{1}{10}$ after 4.83 epochs. Results are shown in Table 2. Notice that based on DCN as base detector, our single DCR module achieves the new state-of-the-art result of 84.0% without using extra data (*e.g.* COCO data), multi scale training/testing, ensemble or other post processing tricks.

VOC 2012 We use a union of VOC2007 trainvaltest and VOC2012 trainval for training and we test on VOC2012 test. We use the same training setting of VOC2007. Results are shown in Table 3. Our model DCN-DCR is the first to achieve over 81.0% on the VOC2012 test set. The new state-of-the-art 81.2% is achieved using only single model, without any post processing tricks.

Table 2. PASCAL VOC2007 test detection results.

Method	mAP	aero	bike	bird	boat	bottle	bus	car	cat	chair	cow	table	dog	horse	mbike	person	plant	sheep	sofa	train	tv
Faster [15]	76.4	79.8	80.7	76.2	68.3	55.9	85.1	85.3	89.8	56.7	87.8	69.4	88.3	88.9	80.9	78.4	41.7	78.6	79.8	85.3	72.0
R-FCN [3]	80.5	79.9	87.2	81.5	72.0	69.8	86.8	88.5	**89.8**	67.0	88.1	74.5	89.8	**90.6**	79.9	81.2	53.7	81.8	81.5	85.9	79.9
SSD [9,24]	80.6	84.3	87.6	**82.6**	71.6	59.0	88.2	88.1	89.3	64.4	85.6	76.2	88.5	88.9	**87.5**	83.0	53.6	83.9	82.2	87.2	81.3
DSSD [9]	81.5	86.6	86.2	**82.6**	74.9	62.5	89.0	88.7	88.8	65.2	87.0	**78.7**	88.2	89.0	**87.5**	83.7	51.1	86.3	81.6	85.7	83.7
Faster (2fc)	79.8	79.6	87.5	79.5	72.8	66.7	88.5	88.0	88.9	64.5	84.8	71.9	88.7	88.2	84.8	79.8	53.8	80.3	81.4	**87.9**	78.5
Faster-Ours (2fc)	82.5	80.5	**89.2**	80.2	75.1	74.8	79.8	89.4	89.7	70.1	88.9	76.0	89.5	89.9	86.9	80.4	57.4	86.2	83.5	87.2	**85.3**
DCN (2fc)	81.4	83.9	85.4	80.1	75.9	68.8	88.4	88.6	89.2	68.0	87.2	75.5	89.5	89.0	86.3	84.8	54.1	85.2	82.6	86.2	80.3
DCN-Ours (2fc)	**84.0**	**89.3**	88.7	80.5	**77.7**	**76.3**	**90.1**	**89.6**	**89.8**	**72.9**	**89.2**	77.8	**90.1**	90.0	**87.5**	**87.2**	**58.6**	**88.2**	**84.3**	87.5	85.0

Table 3. PASCAL VOC2012 **test** detection results.

Method	mAP	aero	bike	bird	boat	bottle	bus	car	cat	chair	cow	table	dog	horse	mbike	person	plant	sheep	sofa	train	tv
Faster [15]	73.8	86.5	81.6	77.2	58.0	51.0	78.6	76.6	93.2	48.6	80.4	59.0	92.1	85.3	84.8	80.7	48.1	77.3	66.5	84.7	65.6
R-FCN [3]	77.6	86.9	83.4	81.5	63.8	62.4	81.6	81.1	93.1	58.0	83.8	60.8	92.7	86.0	84.6	84.4	59.0	80.8	68.6	86.1	72.9
SSD [9,24]	79.4	90.7	**87.3**	78.3	66.3	56.5	84.1	83.7	94.2	62.9	84.5	**66.3**	92.9	**88.6**	87.9	85.7	55.1	83.6	**74.3**	88.2	76.8
DSSD [9]	80.0	**92.1**	86.6	80.3	68.7	58.2	84.3	**85.0**	**94.6**	63.3	85.9	65.6	93.0	88.5	87.8	86.4	57.4	85.2	73.4	87.8	76.8
Faster (2fc)	77.3	87.3	82.6	78.8	66.8	59.8	82.5	80.3	92.6	58.8	82.3	61.4	91.3	86.3	84.3	84.6	57.3	80.9	68.3	87.5	71.4
Faster-Ours (2fc)	79.9	89.1	84.6	81.6	70.9	66.1	**84.4**	83.8	93.7	61.5	85.2	63.0	92.8	87.1	86.4	86.3	62.9	84.1	69.6	87.8	**76.9**
DCN (2fc)	79.4	87.9	86.2	81.6	71.1	62.1	83.1	83.0	94.2	61.0	84.5	63.9	93.1	87.9	87.2	86.1	60.4	84.0	70.5	**89.0**	72.1
DCN-Ours (2fc)	**81.2**	89.6	86.7	**83.8**	**72.8**	**68.4**	83.7	85.0	94.5	**64.1**	**86.6**	66.1	**94.3**	88.5	**88.5**	**87.2**	**63.7**	**85.6**	71.4	88.1	76.1

5.4   COCO Results

All experiments on COCO follow the default settings and use ResNet-152 for DCR module. We train our model for 8 epochs on the COCO dataset and reduce the learning rate by $\frac{1}{10}$ after 5.33 epochs. We report results on two different partition of COCO dataset. One partition is training on the union set of COCO2014 train and COCO2014 val35k together with 115k images and evaluate results on the COCO2014 minival with 5k images held out from the COCO2014 val. The other partition is training on the standard COCO2014 trainval with 120k images and evaluate on the COCO2015 test-dev. We use Faster RCNN [27], Feature Pyramid Networks (FPN) [21] and the Deformable ConvNets [4] as base detectors.

COCO Minival. Results are shown in Table 4. Our DCR module improves Faster RCNN by 3.1% from 30.0% to 33.1% in COCO AP metric. Faster RCNN with DCN is improved by 2.8% from 34.4% to 37.2% and FPN is improved by 2.0% from 38.2% to 40.2%. Notice that FPN+DCN is the base detector by top-3 teams in the COCO2017 detection challenge, but there is still an improvement of 1.2% from 41.4% to 42.6%. This observation shows that currently there is no perfect detector that does not produce hard false positives.

COCO Test-dev. Results are shown in Table 5. The trend is similar to that on the COCO minival, with Faster RCNN improved from 30.5% to 33.9%, Faster

Table 4. COCO2014 `minival` detection results.

Method	Backbone	AP	AP_{50}	AP_{75}	AP_S	AP_M	AP_L
Faster (2fc)	ResNet-101	30.0	50.9	30.9	9.9	33.0	49.1
Faster-Ours (2fc)	ResNet-101 + ResNet-152	33.1	56.3	34.2	13.8	36.2	51.5
DCN (2fc)	ResNet-101	34.4	53.8	37.2	14.4	37.7	53.1
DCN-Ours (2fc)	ResNet-101 + ResNet-152	37.2	58.6	39.9	17.3	41.2	55.5
FPN	ResNet-101	38.2	61.1	41.9	21.8	42.3	50.3
FPN-Ours	ResNet-101 + ResNet-152	40.2	63.8	44.0	24.3	43.9	52.6
FPN-DCN	ResNet-101	41.4	63.5	45.3	24.4	45.0	55.1
FPN-DCN-Ours	ResNet-101 + ResNet-152	**42.6**	**65.3**	**46.5**	**26.4**	**46.1**	**56.4**

Table 5. COCO2015 `test-dev` detection results.

Method	Backbone	AP	AP_{50}	AP_{75}	AP_S	AP_M	AP_L
SSD [9, 24]	ResNet-101-SSD	31.2	50.4	33.3	10.2	34.5	49.8
DSSD513 [9]	ResNet-101-DSSD	36.2	59.1	39.0	18.2	39.0	48.2
Mask RCNN [13]	ResNeXt-101-FPN [32]	39.8	62.3	43.4	22.1	43.2	51.2
RetinaNet [22]	ResNeXt-101-FPN	40.8	61.1	44.1	24.1	44.2	51.2
Faster (2fc)	ResNet-101	30.5	52.2	31.8	9.7	32.3	48.3
Faster-Ours (2fc)	ResNet-101 + ResNet-152	33.9	57.9	35.3	14.0	36.1	50.8
DCN (2fc)	ResNet-101	35.2	55.1	38.2	14.6	37.4	52.6
DCN-Ours (2fc)	ResNet-101 + ResNet-152	38.1	59.7	41.1	17.9	41.2	54.7
FPN	ResNet-101	38.8	61.7	42.6	21.9	42.1	49.7
FPN-Ours	ResNet-101 + ResNet-152	40.7	64.4	44.6	24.3	43.7	51.9
FPN-DCN	ResNet-101	41.7	64.0	45.9	23.7	44.7	53.4
FPN-DCN-Ours	ResNet-101 + ResNet-152	**43.1**	**66.1**	**47.3**	**25.8**	**45.9**	**55.3**

B. Cheng et al.

RCNN+DCN improved from 35.2% to 38.1%, FPN improved from 38.8% to 40.7% and FPN+DCN improved from 41.7% to 43.1%. We also compare our results with recent state-of-the-arts reported in publications and our best model achieves state-of-the-art result on COCO2015 test-dev with ResNet as backbone.

6 Conclusion

In this paper, we analyze error modes of state-of-the-art region-based object detectors and study their potentials in accuracy improvement. We hypothesize that good object detectors should be designed following three principles: decoupled features, decoupled optimization and adaptive receptive field. Based on these principles, we propose a simple, effective and widely-applicable DCR module that achieves new state-of-the-art. In the future, we will further study what architecture makes a good object detector, adaptive feature representation in multi-task learning, and efficiency improvement of our DCR module.

Acknowledgements. This work is in part supported by IBM-ILLINOIS Center for Cognitive Computing Systems Research (C3SR) - a research collaboration as part of the IBM AI Horizons Network; and by the Intelligence Advanced Research Projects Activity (IARPA) via Department of Interior/Interior Business Center (DOI/IBC) contract number D17PC00341. The U.S. Government is authorized to reproduce and distribute reprints for Governmental purposes notwithstanding any copyright annotation thereon. Disclaimer: The views and conclusions contained herein are those of the authors and should not be interpreted as necessarily representing the official policies or endorsements, either expressed or implied, of IARPA, DOI/IBC, or the U.S. Government. We thank Jiashi Feng for helpful discussions.

References

1. Bourdev, L., Brandt, J.: Robust object detection via soft cascade. In: IEEE CVPR, vol. 2, pp. 236–243 (2005)
2. Cai, Z., Vasconcelos, N.: Cascade R-CNN: delving into high quality object detection. In: IEEE CVPR, June 2018
3. Dai, J., Li, Y., He, K., Sun, J.: R-FCN: object detection via region-based fully convolutional networks. In: NIPS, pp. 379–387 (2016)
4. Dai, J., et al.: Deformable convolutional networks. In: IEEE ICCV, pp. 764–773 (2017)
5. Deng, J., Dong, W., Socher, R., Li, L.J., Li, K., Fei-Fei, L.: Imagenet: a large-scale hierarchical image database. In: IEEE CVPR, pp. 248–255 (2009)
6. Everingham, M., Van Gool, L., Williams, C.K.I., Winn, J., Zisserman, A.: The pascal visual object classes (VOC) challenge. IJCV **88**(2), 303–338 (2010)
7. Felzenszwalb, P.F., Girshick, R.B., McAllester, D., Ramanan, D.: Object detection with discriminatively trained part-based models. IEEE TPAMI **32**(9), 1627–1645 (2010)
8. Freund, Y., Schapire, R.E.: A decision-theoretic generalization of on-line learning and an application to boosting. J. Comput. Syst. Sci. **55**(1), 119–139 (1997)

9. Fu, C.Y., Liu, W., Ranga, A., Tyagi, A., Berg, A.C.: DSSD: deconvolutional single shot detector. arXiv preprint arXiv:1701.06659 (2017)

10. Girshick, R.: Fast R-CNN. In: IEEE ICCV, pp. 1440–1448 (2015)

11. Girshick, R., Donahue, J., Darrell, T., Malik, J.: Rich feature hierarchies for accurate object detection and semantic segmentation. In: IEEE CVPR, pp. 580–587 (2014)

12. Goyal, P., et al.: Accurate, large minibatch SGD: training imagenet in 1 hour. arXiv preprint arXiv:1706.02677 (2017)

13. He, K., Gkioxari, G., Dollár, P., Girshick, R.: Mask R-CNN. In: IEEE ICCV, pp. 2980–2988 (2017)

14. He, K., Zhang, X., Ren, S., Sun, J.: Spatial pyramid pooling in deep convolutional networks for visual recognition. In: Fleet, D., Pajdla, T., Schiele, B., Tuytelaars, T. (eds.) ECCV 2014. LNCS, vol. 8691, pp. 346–361. Springer, Cham (2014). https://doi.org/10.1007/978-3-319-10578-9_23

15. He, K., Zhang, X., Ren, S., Sun, J.: Deep residual learning for image recognition. In: IEEE CVPR, pp. 770–778 (2016)

16. Li, H., Lin, Z., Shen, X., Brandt, J., Hua, G.: A convolutional neural network cascade for face detection. In: IEEE CVPR, pp. 5325–5334 (2015)

17. Li, J., et al.: Multistage object detection with group recursive learning. IEEE Trans. Multimed. **20**(7), 1645–1655 (2018)

18. Li, J., Liang, X., Wei, Y., Xu, T., Feng, J., Yan, S.: Perceptual generative adversarial networks for small object detection. In: IEEE CVPR (2017)

19. Li, J., et al.: Attentive contexts for object detection. IEEE Trans. Multimed. **19**(5), 944–954 (2017)

20. Liang, X., Liu, S., Wei, Y., Liu, L., Lin, L., Yan, S.: Towards computational baby learning: a weakly-supervised approach for object detection. In: IEEE ICCV, pp. 999–1007 (2015)

21. Lin, T.Y., Dollár, P., Girshick, R., He, K., Hariharan, B., Belongie, S.: Feature pyramid networks for object detection. In: IEEE CVPR, vol. 1, p. 4 (2017)

22. Lin, T.Y., Goyal, P., Girshick, R., He, K., Dollar, P.: Focal loss for dense object detection. In: IEEE ICCV, pp. 2980–2988 (2017)

23. Lin, T.-Y., Maire, M., Belongie, S., Hays, J., Perona, P., Ramanan, D., Dollár, P., Zitnick, C.L.: Microsoft COCO: common objects in context. In: Fleet, D., Pajdla, T., Schiele, B., Tuytelaars, T. (eds.) ECCV 2014. LNCS, vol. 8693, pp. 740–755. Springer, Cham (2014). https://doi.org/10.1007/978-3-319-10602-1_48

24. Liu, W., Anguelov, D., Erhan, D., Szegedy, C., Reed, S., Fu, C.-Y., Berg, A.C.: SSD: single shot multibox detector. In: Leibe, B., Matas, J., Sebe, N., Welling, M. (eds.) ECCV 2016. LNCS, vol. 9905, pp. 21–37. Springer, Cham (2016). https://doi.org/10.1007/978-3-319-46448-0_2

25. Redmon, J., Divvala, S., Girshick, R., Farhadi, A.: You only look once: unified, real-time object detection. In: IEEE CVPR, pp. 779–788 (2016)

26. Redmon, J., Farhadi, A.: YOLO9000: better, faster, stronger. In: IEEE CVPR, pp. 6517–6525 (2017)

27. Ren, S., He, K., Girshick, R., Sun, J.: Faster R-CNN: towards real-time object detection with region proposal networks. In: NIPS, pp. 91–99 (2015)

28. Sermanet, P., Eigen, D., Zhang, X., Mathieu, M., Fergus, R., LeCun, Y.: Overfeat: integrated recognition, localization and detection using convolutional networks. arXiv preprint arXiv:1312.6229 (2013)

29. Uijlings, J.R., Van De Sande, K.E., Gevers, T., Smeulders, A.W.: Selective search for object recognition. IJCV **104**(2), 154–171 (2013)

30. Viola, P., Jones, M.J.: Robust real-time face detection. IJCV **57**(2), 137–154 (2004)
31. Wei, Y., et al.: TS2C: tight box mining with surrounding segmentation context for weakly supervised object detection. In: ECCV (2018)
32. Xie, S., Girshick, R., Dollár, P., Tu, Z., He, K.: Aggregated residual transformations for deep neural networks. In: IEEE CVPR, pp. 5987–5995 (2017)
33. Xu, H., Lv, X., Wang, X., Ren, Z., Chellappa, R.: Deep regionlets for object detection. arXiv preprint arXiv:1712.02408 (2017)

Semi-supervised Generative Adversarial Hashing for Image Retrieval

Guan'an Wang[1,3], Qinghao Hu[2,3], Jian Cheng[2,3,4],
and Zengguang Hou[1,3,4(✉)]

[1] The State Key Laboratory for Management and Control of Complex Systems,
Institute of Automation, Chinese Academy of Sciences, Beijing, China
{wangguanan2015,zengguang.hou}@ia.ac.cn
[2] National Laboratory of Pattern Recognition, Institute of Automation, Chinese
Academy of Sciences, Beijing, China
{qinghao.hu,jcheng}@nlpr.ia.ac.cn
[3] University of Chinese Academy of Sciences, Beijing, China
[4] Center for Excellence in Brain Science and Intelligence Technology, Beijing, China

Abstract. With explosive growth of image and video data on the Internet, hashing technique has been extensively studied for large-scale visual search. Benefiting from the advance of deep learning, deep hashing methods have achieved promising performance. However, those deep hashing models are usually trained with supervised information, which is rare and expensive in practice, especially class labels. In this paper, inspired by the idea of generative models and the minimax two-player game, we propose a novel semi-supervised generative adversarial hashing (SSGAH) approach. Firstly, we unify a generative model, a discriminative model and a deep hashing model in a framework for making use of triplet-wise information and unlabeled data. Secondly, we design novel structure of the generative model and the discriminative model to learn the distribution of triplet-wise information in a semi-supervised way. In addition, we propose a semi-supervised ranking loss and an adversary ranking loss to learn binary codes which preserve semantic similarity for both labeled data and unlabeled data. Finally, by optimizing the whole model in an adversary training way, the learned binary codes can capture better semantic information of all data. Extensive empirical evaluations on two widely-used benchmark datasets show that our proposed approach significantly outperforms state-of-the-art hashing methods.

Keywords: Information retrieval · Hashing · Deep learning · GANs

1 Introduction

With explosive growth of image and video data on the Internet, large-scale image retrieval task has attracted more and more attention in recent years. One of traditional methods applied to this task is Nearest Neighbor Search (NNS), where the first k images with the smallest distance between the query one are returned

© Springer Nature Switzerland AG 2018
V. Ferrari et al. (Eds.): ECCV 2018, LNCS 11219, pp. 491–507, 2018.
https://doi.org/10.1007/978-3-030-01267-0_29

as results. However, for large-scale images with high-dimensional feature, NNS is extremely expensive in terms of space and time. Hashing technique [25,26] is a popular Approximate Nearest Neighbor Search due to its both computation efficiency and high retrieval accuracy by calculating the Hamming distance between binary codes.

Hashing methods can be mainly grouped into traditional hashing methods and deep hashing methods. In traditional hashing methods, images are firstly represented with the hand-crafted visual descriptors (e.g. SIFT [15], GIST [20], HOG [3]), and then hash functions and quantization algorithm are separately learned to encode the features into binary codes. Based on whether the supervised information is adopted, traditional methods can be categorized into unsupervised hashing models (LSH [4], SH [29], ITQ [10], AGH [14]) and supervised hashing models (SSH [27], BRE[8], MLH [18], KSH [13], SDH [24]). Deep hashing methods (CNNH [30], NINH [9], DPSH [12], DHN [35], DSDH[11]) simultaneously learn feature representation and hash functions based on deep networks and usually are trained with supervised information. Due to its powerful ability of feature representation and nonlinear mapping, deep hashing methods have shown their better performance than traditional ones.

Although encouraging performance reported in the models above, obtaining labeled data is expensive. Contrarily, unlabeled data is always enough and free. Thus, semi-supervised hashing method is a good solution where a small amount of labeled data and lots of unlabeled data are utilized to learn better binary codes. Semi-supervised Hashing (SSH) [27] is proposed to minimize the empirical error over labeled data and maximize the information entropy of binary codes over both labeled and unlabeled data. However, SSH is implemented without deep networks, which leads to unsatisfying performance compared with deep hashing methods. Deep Semantic Hashing with GANs (DSH-GANs) [21] minimizes the empirical error over synthetic data generated conditioned on class labels based on deep architecture. However, class labels are more difficult and expensive to obtain than triplet-wise labels [9]. Semi-supervised Deep Hashing (SSDH) [34] and Deep Hashing with a Bipartite Graph (BGDH) use graph structure to model unlableled data. However, constructing the graph model of large-scale data is extremely expensive in terms of time and space, and using batch data instead may lead to a suboptimal result.

To solve the problem above, we propose a novel semi-supervised generative adversarial hashing (SSGAH), which utilizes a generative model to model unlabeled data and uses triplet-wise labels as supervised information. Specifically, our SSGAH includes a generative model, a discriminative model and a deep hashing model, where all three models are optimized together in an adversarial framework. The generative model can well learn the triplet-wise information in a semi-supervised way. Benefiting from both adversary learning and the generative model, the deep hashing model is able to learn binary codes which not only preserve semantic similarity but also capture the meaningful triplet-wise information. Main contributions of our proposed approach are outlined as below:

(1) We propose a novel semi-supervised generative adversarial hashing (SSGAH) approach to make full use of triplet-wise information and unlabeled data. Our approach unifies generative, discriminative and deep hashing models in an adversarial framework, where the generative and discriminative models are carefully designed for capturing the distribution of triplet-wise information in a semi-supervised way, all of which contribute to semantic preserving binary codes.

(2) We propose novel semi-supervised ranking loss and adversary ranking loss to learn better binary codes that capturing semantic information of both labeled and unlabeled data. For semi-supervised ranking loss, we propose to preserve relative similarity of real and synthetic samples. For adversary ranking loss, we propose to make the deep hashing model and generative model improve each other in a two-player minimax game.

(3) Extensive evaluations on two widely-used datasets demonstrate that our SSGAH approach significantly outperforms the state-of-the-art methods, and component analysis verifies the effectiveness of each part of our model.

2   Related Work

Traditional Hashing Methods. Conditioning whether labeled data is used in training process, traditional hashing methods can be divided into unsupervised and supervised ones. Unsupervised hashing methods employ unlabeled data even no data. Local Sensitive Hashing (LSH) [4] uses random linear projections to map similar samples to nearby binary codes. Spectral Hashing (SH) [29] tries to keep hash functions balanced and uncorrelated. Iterative Quantization (ITQ) [10] proposes an alternating minimization algorithm to minimize the quantization error. Anchor Graph Hashing (AGH) [14] preserves the neighborhood structures by anchor graphs. Supervised hashing methods utilize labeled information to improve binary codes. Semi-supervised Hashing (SSH) [27] minimizes the empirical error and maximizes information entropy. Binary Reconstruction Embedding (BRE) [8] minimizes the reconstruction error between original distances and reconstructed distances in the Hamming space. Minimal Loss Hashing (MLH) [18] minimizes loss between the learned Hamming distance and quantization error. Supervised Hashing with Kernels (KSH) [13] utilizes the equivalence between optimizing codes inner products and Hamming distance. Supervised Discrete hashing (SDH) [24] integrates hash codes generation and classifier training.

Deep Hashing Methods. Recently, deep learning has shown its powerful ability in various domains including classification, object detection, semantic segmentation and so on. Inspired by powerful feature representation learning of deep networks, many hashing methods based on deep networks have been proposed. Most deep hashing methods are trained in a supervised way. Convolutional Neural Network Hashing (CNNH) [30] firstly learns binary codes by similarity matrix decomposition, then utilizes convolutional neural networks to simultaneously learn good feature representation and hash functions guided by those binary codes. Network in Network Hashing (NINH) [9] straightly learns feature representation and hash functions for binary codes which preserve relative similarity of raw samples in an end-to-end manner. Deep Pairwise-Supervised Hashing (DPSH) [12] performs simultaneous feature learning and binary codes learning with pair-wise labels. Deep Hashing Network (DHN) [35] simultaneously optimizes pair-wise cross entropy loss and pair-wise quantization loss to remit quantization error. Deep Supervised Discrete Hashing (DSDH) [11] straightly optimize binary codes without relaxation by proposing a iterative optimization algorithm. Supervised Semantics-preserving Deep Hashing [32] constructs hash functions as a latent layer in a deep network and trains the model over classification error. Semi-supervised Deep Hashing (SSDH) [34] and BGDH [31] minimizes empirical error on labeled data and exploits unlabeled data through a graph construction method. Different from SSDH and BGDH, which use the graph to model unlabeled data and is time and space consuming, our approach utilizes generative models to learn unlabeled data. DSH-GANs [21] utilizes class labels to train AC-GANs [19] for synthetic images, and then use those synthetic images to train a deep hashing model. Different from DSH-GANs, our approach utilizes triplet-labels which are more common, and specifically designs a GANs model which can be well learned with limited supervised information. What's more, we import adversarial learning between the generative model and the deep hashing model for better binary codes, while DSH-GANs not.

Generative Models. The generative model is a kind of important model in machine learning, which can understand data by learning its distribution. Goodfellow proposes an efficient yet straightforward framework for estimating generative models named Generative Adversarial Networks (GANs) [5] by making a generative model and a discriminative model play a two-player minimax game. Conditional Generative Adversarial Networks (cGANs) [17] extends GANs to its conditional version by using class labels to limit the generator and the discriminator. Different from existed generative models, the generative model in our approach is particularly designed for triplet-wise information and unlabeled data.

3   Semi-supervised Generative Adversarial Hashing

Given a dataset $\mathcal{X}$ that is composed of unlabeled data $\mathcal{X}^u = \{x_i^u | i = 1, \ldots, m\}$ in form of individual images and labeled data $\mathcal{X}^l = \{(x^q, x^p, x^n)_i | i = 1, \ldots, n\}$ with triplet-wise information where the query image x^q is more similar to positive one x^p than to negative one x^n , our primal goal is to learn a mapping function $\mathcal{B}(\cdot)$ which encodes the input image $x \subset \mathcal{X}$ into k-bit binary codes $\mathcal{B}(x) \in \{0,1\}^k$, while preserves relative semantic similarity of images in the dataset $\mathcal{X}$.

As shown in Fig. 1, our SSGAH approach consists of a generative model G, a discriminative model D and a deep hashing model H. The generative model is to learn the distribution of triplet-wise information in a semi-supervised way and generates synthetic triplets $\{(x, x_{syn}^q, x_{syn}^n)_i | i = 1, 2, \cdots, m+n\}$, where the real

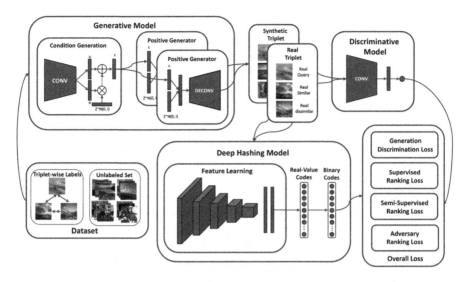

Fig. 1. Overview of our proposed SSGAH approach, where the curves indicate the data flow and the straight lines indicate the fully connected layers. Our model consists of a generative model, a discriminative model and a deep hashing model. The generative model is to capture the distribution of triplet-wise information and unlabeled data, the discriminative model is to distinguish the real triplets from synthetic ones, the deep hashing model is to learn binary codes which not only preserve semantic similarity but also can identificate small difference between real and synthetic images. The whole model is trained in an adversary way.

image x is more similar to the synthetic image x_{syn}^q than to another synthetic one x_{syn}^n. The discriminative model is to distinguish the real triplets from synthetic ones. The deep hashing model is to learn binary codes which preserve semantic similarity on the whole dataset. All three models are trained together in an adversary way.

3.1 Model Architecture Structure

Generative and Discriminative Models. The goals of our generative and discriminative models are to learn the distribution of unlabeled data $\mathcal{X}^u = \{x_i^u | i = 1, 2, \ldots, n\}$ and labeled data $\mathcal{X}^l = \{(x^q, x^p, x^n)_i | i = 1, 2, \ldots, n\}$, and then synthesize realistic meaningful triplets. Specifically, given a real sample $x \in \{\mathcal{X}^u, \mathcal{X}^l\}$, a synthetic triplet $(x, x_{syn}^p, x_{syn}^n)$ should be generated, where x is more similar to the positive synthetic one x_{syn}^p than to negative synthetic one x_{syn}^n, and both synthetic ones are realistic. Compared with common conditionally image generation tasks, several difficulties exist in ours. Firstly, in common tasks, their conditions are low-dimensional and meaningful (e.g. class labels) [17,19], or their real and synthetic images share similar structure [6,33]. In our task, the conditions are raw images which are high-dimensional and noisy, and our synthetic images share only semantic information with raw ones, neither structure nor texture. What's more, our labeled data is limited.

To mitigate the problem above, we propose novel generative and discriminative models, whose architecture are shown in Fig. 1. Firstly, to filter the noise and produce meaningful conditions, images are feed into a stack of convolutional layers followed by a fully connected layer to extract short, meaningful features ν. Secondly, in order to ease the lack of labeled data, the final conditions are randomly sampled from an independent Gaussian distribution $\mathcal{N}(\mu(\nu), \Sigma(\nu))$, where the mean $\mu(\nu)$ and diagonal covariance matrix $\Sigma(\nu)$ are learned from the ν. What's more, for better understanding of the semantic relationship of triplets, we improve the discriminative model to distinguish real triplets (x, x^p, x^n) from synthetic ones $(x, x^p_{syn}, x^n_{syn})$, and design extra triplets (x, x^n, x^p) as negative samples beside synthetic triplets.

The architecture of the two models are shown in Fig. 1. Firstly, a condition vector c is generated through the condition generation module given an real image. Secondly, a random vector z sampled from standard normal distribution concatenated with the generated condition is feed into the positive generator G_p and the negative generator G_n to generate triplets $(x, x^p_{syn}, x^n_{syn})$ where the x is more similar to x^p_{syn} than to x^n_{syn}. Then, the discriminative model determines the probability that input triplets are real. Finally, the generative model and the discriminative model can be optimized by playing a two-player minimax game with value function $\mathcal{L}_{GD}$.

$$
\min_{G} \max_{D} \mathcal{L}_{GD} = E_{(x^q, x^p, x^n) \in \mathcal{X}^l} \{ log D(x^q, x^p, x^n) + log[1 - D(x^q, x^n, x^p)] \}
$$
$$
+ E_{x \in \{ \mathcal{X}^u, \mathcal{X}^l \}} \{ log[1 - D(x, G_p(x), G_n(x))] \}
$$
$$
+ D_{KL}(\mathcal{N}(\mu(\nu), \Sigma(\nu)) \parallel \mathcal{N}(0, I))
$$
$$
\tag{1}
$$

where $D(\cdot, \cdot, \cdot)$ is the probability that input triplet is from labeled data $\mathcal{X}^l$, $G_p(x)$ and $G_n(x)$ is the synthetic images generated by the two generators, D_{KL} is a regularization term which means the Kullback-Leibler divergence between standard Gaussian distribution and conditioning Gaussian distribution.

Deep Hashing Model. For easy comparison with other hashing algorithms, we adopt AlexNet [7] as our basic network. AlexNet contains 5 convolutional layers ($conv1 - conv5$) with max-pooling operations followed by 2 fully connected layers ($fc6 - fc7$) and an output layer. In the convolutional layers, units are organized into feature maps and are connected locally to patches in the outputs of the previous layer. The fully connected layers ($fc6 - fc7$) are activated by rectified linear units (Relu) for faster training.

AlexNet is designed particularly for multi-class classification task, so the amount of units in the output layer is equal to class amounts. To adapt AlexNet to our deep hashing architecture, we replace the output layer with a fully connected layer f_h and activate it by a sigmoid function, through which the high dimensional feature of the $fc7$ layer can be projected to k-bits hash real-value in $[0, 1]$. The formulation is in Eq. (2), where $f(x)$ is the feature representation in $fc7$ layer of AlexNet, W^h and b^h denote weights and bias in hash layer f_h, σ is sigmoid function. Since the output of the neural network is continuous, we transfer the $\mathcal{H}(x) \in [0, 1]^k$ to binary codes $\mathcal{B}(x) \in \{0, 1\}^k$ with Eq. (3)

$$\mathcal{H}(x) = \sigma(f(x)W^h + b^h) \tag{2}$$

$$\mathcal{B}(x) = (sgn(\mathcal{H}(x) - 0.5) + 1)/2 \tag{3}$$

3.2   Objective Function

Existing deep hashing methods usually design the objective function to preserve the relative semantic similarity of samples in labeled data, but ignore the unlabeled data. To address the problem, we propose novel semi-supervised ranking loss and adversary ranking loss to exploit the relative similarity of samples in both triplet-wise label and unlabeled data. By jointly minimizing the supervised ranking loss, semi-supervised ranking loss, as well as adversary ranking loss, the learned binary codes can better capture semantic information of all data.

Supervised Ranking Term. For most existing hashing methods, class labels [32], pair-wise labels [30], and triplet-wise labels [9] are most frequently used as supervised information. Among the three kinds of labels, class labels contain the most accurate information, followed by pair-wise ones and triplet-wise ones. In contrast, the most easily available labels are triplet-wise labels, followed by pair-wise ones and class ones [9]. Considering easy acquirement in practice, we choose triplet-wise labels as our supervised information. Specially, given labeled data $\mathcal{X}_s = \{(x_i^q, x_i^p, x_i^n)|i = 1, \ldots, n\}$, the supervised ranking loss can be formulated in Eq. (4), where $|| \cdot ||_H$ denotes Hamming distance, $\mathcal{B}(x)$ is the binary codes of x, and m_{sr} is the margin between match pairs and the mismatch pairs.

$$
\begin{aligned}
\min_{H} \hat{\mathcal{L}}_{sr} &= \sum_{i=1}^{n} \hat{\mathcal{L}}_{triplet}(m_{sr}, (x^q, x^p, x^n)_i) \\
&= \sum_{i=1}^{n} max(0, m_{sr} - (||\mathcal{B}(x^q) - \mathcal{B}(x^n)||_H - ||\mathcal{B}(x^q) - \mathcal{B}(x^p)||_H)_i)
\end{aligned}
\tag{4}
$$

Semi-supervised Ranking Term. Training the deep hashing model solely based on supervised information usually leads to an unsatisfying result for that limited labeled data can't accurately reflect similarity relation of samples in unlabeled data. In order to address the problem, we propose to leverage Generative Adversarial Networks (GANs) to learn distribution of real data, which is composed of limited labeled data and lots of unlabeled data, and in return synthetic samples generated by GANs are used to train the deep hashing model to learn better feature representation and more discriminative binary codes.

Accordingly, we propose a novel semi-supervised ranking loss. On the one hand, to learn more discriminative binary codes, we use a synthetic sample x_{syn}^p which is similar with the query one x^q in a real triplet or a synthetic sample x_{syn}^n which is dissimilar with x^q to replace corresponding real one. Through this method, labeled data can be augmented without losing supervision information. On the other hand, for better utilizing the unlabeled data, given an unlabeled sample, we generate a synthetic triplet where the given real sample is more similar to a synthetic positive sample than to a synthetic negative one.

Specifically, given a real triplet (x^q, x^p, x^n), we can get synthetic triplets (x^q, x^p_{syn}, x^n) and (x^q, x^p, x^n_{syn}), where x^p_{syn} and x^n_{syn} are generated by positive generator G_p and negative generator G_n respectively conditioned on real sample x^q and random noise z. For a real unlabeled sample $x^u \in \mathcal{X}_u$, similar procedure can be performed to generate a synthetic triplet $(x^u, x^p_{syn}, x^n_{syn})$. Hence the semi-supervised ranking term can be defined in Eq. (5), where $\hat{\mathcal{L}}_{triplet}(\cdot, (\cdot, \cdot, \cdot))$ is defined in Eq. (4).

$$
\begin{aligned}
\min_{H} \hat{\mathcal{L}}_{ssr} = &\sum_{i=1}^{n} [\hat{\mathcal{L}}_{triplet}(m_{ssr}, (x^q, x^p_{syn}, x^n)_i) + \hat{\mathcal{L}}_{triplet}(m_{ssr}, (x^q, x^p, x^n_{syn})_i)] \\
&+ \sum_{i=1}^{m} \hat{\mathcal{L}}_{triplet}(m_{ssr}, (x^u, x^p_{syn}, x^n_{syn})_i)
\end{aligned}
\tag{5}
$$

Adversary Ranking Term. Wang et al. [28] has shown simultaneously learning a generative retrieval model and a discriminative retrieval model in an adversary way is able to improve both models and achieve a better performance than separately training them. Inspired by the idea, we also introduce the idea of minimax two-player game between the generative and deep hashing models and propose a novel adversary ranking loss. Specifically, in the minimax two-player game, the deep hashing model try to learn binary codes that can identificate small difference between (x, x^p) and (x, x^p_{syn}), and the generative model is to make the binary codes of x, x^p and x^p_{syn} distinguishable. Given real triplets $\{(x^q, x^p, x^n)_i | i = 1, 2, \ldots, n\}$ and corresponding synthetic triplets $\{(x^q, x^p_{syn}, x^n_{syn})_i | i = 1, 2, \ldots, n\}$, the minimax two-player game can be formulated in Eq. (6), where $\hat{\mathcal{L}}_{triplet}(\cdot, (\cdot, \cdot, \cdot))$ is defined in Eq. (4).

$$
\min_{H} \max_{G} \hat{\mathcal{L}}_{ar} = \sum_{i=1}^{n} \hat{\mathcal{L}}_{triplet}(m_{ar}, (x^q, x^p, x^p_{syn}))
\tag{6}
$$

3.3   Overall Objective Function and Adversary Learning

The overall objective function of our semi-supervised generative adversarial hashing approach integrates loss in Eq. (1), supervised ranking loss in Eq. (4), semi-supervised ranking loss in Eq. (5) and adversary ranking loss in Eq. (6). Hence, the overall objective function $\hat{\mathcal{L}}$ can be formulated in Eq. (7).

$$
\min_{G} \max_{D, H} \hat{\mathcal{L}} = \mathcal{L}_{GD} - \hat{\mathcal{L}}_{sr} - \hat{\mathcal{L}}_{ssr} - \hat{\mathcal{L}}_{ar}
\tag{7}
$$

Considering the the mapping function $\mathcal{B}(\cdot)$ is discrete and Hamming distance $||\cdot||_H$ is not differentiable, natural relaxation are utilized on Eq. (7) by changing the integer constraint to a range constraint and replacing Hamming distance with Euclidean Distance $||\cdot||_2$. Using the supervised ranking term as an example, relaxed term $\mathcal{L}_{sr}$ is in Eq. (8).

$$
\begin{aligned}
\mathcal{L}_{sr} &= \sum_{i=1}^{n} \mathcal{L}_{triplet}(m_{sr}, (x^q, x^p, x^n)_i) \\
&= \sum_{i=1}^{n} max(0, m_{sr} - (||\mathcal{H}(x^q) - \mathcal{H}(x^n)||_2^2 - ||\mathcal{H}(x^q) - \mathcal{H}(x^p)||_2^2)_i)
\end{aligned}
\tag{8}
$$

Then, the relaxed semi-supervised ranking loss $\mathcal{L}_{ssr}$ and adversary ranking loss $\mathcal{L}_{ar}$ and be derived similarly. Finally, we apply mini-batch gradient descent, in conjunction with back propagation [16] to network training in Eq. (9).

$$
\min_{G} \max_{D,H} \mathcal{L} = \mathcal{L}_{GD} - \mathcal{L}_{sr} - \mathcal{L}_{ssr} - \mathcal{L}_{ar}
\tag{9}
$$

3.4 Image Retrieval

After the optimization of SSGAH, one can compute binary codes of a new image and find its similar images. Firstly, a query image x is fed into the deep hashing model and real-value codes $\mathcal{H}(x)$ can be obtained through Eq. (2). Secondly, binary codes $\mathcal{B}(x)$ can be calculated by quantization process via Eq. (3). Finally, the retrieval list of images is produced by sorting the Hamming distances of binary codes between the query image and images in search pool.

4   Experiment

4.1 Dataset

We conduct our experiments on two widely-used datasets, namely CIFAR-10 and NUS-WIDE. CIFAR-10 is a small image dataset including 60,000 32×32 color images in 10 categories with 6000 images per class. NUS-WIDE [2] contains nearly 270,000 images collected from Flickr associated with one or multiple labels in 91 semantic concepts. For NUS-WIDE, we follow [9] to use the images associated with the 21 most frequent concepts, where each of these concepts associates with at least 5,000 images.

Following [9,30], we randomly sample 100 images per class to construct query set, and the others are as the base set. In training process, we randomly sample 500 images per class from the base set as labeled data, and the others are as unlabeled data. Triplets are generated from the labeled set conditioned on corresponding labels. Specifically, (x^q, x^p, x^n) are constructed where x^q shares at least one label with x^p and no label with x^n.

4.2 Evaluation Protocol and Baseline Methods

We adopt mean Average Precision (mAP) to measure the performance of hashing methods, and mAP on the NUS-WIDE dataset is calculated with the top 5,000 returned neighbors. Based on the evaluation protocol, we compare our SSGAH with nine state-of-the-art hashing methods, including four traditional hashing methods LSH [4], SH [29], ITQ [10], SDH [24], two supervised deep hashing methods CNNH [30], NINH [9], and three semi-supervised deep hashing methods DSH-GANs [21], SSDH [34] and BGDH [31].

Following the settings in [9], hand-crafted features for traditional hashing methods are presented by 512-dimensional GIST [20] features in the CIFAR-10 dataset and by 500-dimensional bag-of-words features in the NUS-WIDE dataset. Besides, for a fair comparison between traditional and deep hashing methods, we also construct traditional methods on features extracted from the $fc7$ layer of AlexNet which is pre-trained on ImageNet. For deep hashing methods, we adopt raw pixels as input.

4.3   Implementation Details

We implement our SSGAH based on the open-source Tensorflow [1] framework. The generative and discriminative models are implemented and optimized under the guidance of DCGANs [22]. Specifically, we use fractional-strided convolutions and ReLU activation for the generative model, strided convolutions and Leaky ReLU activation for the discriminative model, and both models utilize batch normalization and are optimized by ADAM with learning rate 0.0002 and β_1

Table 1. Mean Average Precision (mAP) scores for different methods on two datasets. The best mAP scores are emphasized in boldface. Note that the mAP scores on NUS-WIDE dataset is calculated based on the top 5,000 returned neighbors.

Methods	CIFAR-10				NUS-WIDE			
	12bits	24bits	32bits	48bits	12bits	24bits	32bits	48bits
SSGAH(*Ours*)	**0.819**	**0.837**	**0.847**	**0.855**	**0.835**	**0.847**	**0.859**	**0.865**
BGDH	0.805	0.824	0.826	0.833	0.803	0.818	0.822	0.828
SSDH	0.801	0.813	0.812	0.814	0.773	0.779	0.778	0.778
DSH-GANs	0.745	0.789	0.793	0.811	0.807	0.820	0.831	0.834
NINH	0.535	0.552	0.566	0.558	0.581	0.674	0.697	0.713
CNNH	0.439	0.476	0.472	0.489	0.611	0.618	0.625	0.608
SDH+CNN	0.363	0.528	0.529	0.542	0.520	0.507	0.591	0.610
ITQ+CNN	0.212	0.230	0.234	0.240	0.728	0.707	0.689	0.661
SH+CNN	0.158	0.157	0.154	0.151	0.620	0.611	0.620	0.591
LSH+CNN	0.134	0.157	0.173	0.185	0.438	0.586	0.571	0.507
SDH	0.255	0.330	0.344	0.360	0.414	0.465	0.451	0.454
ITQ	0.162	0.169	0.172	0.175	0.452	0.468	0.472	0.477
SH	0.124	0.125	0.125	0.126	0.433	0.426	0.426	0.423
LSH	0.116	0.121	0.124	0.131	0.404	0.421	0.426	0.441

0.5. The hyper-parameters m_{sr}, m_{ssr}, m_{ar} are set $\frac{k}{4}$, $\frac{k}{8}$ and 1 respectively via cross validation, where k is code length. The deep hashing model is optimized by stochastic gradient descent with learning rate 0.0001 and momentum 0.9. The mini-batch size of images is 64. For faster convergence, we firstly train the generative and discriminative models under the Eq. (1), and then optimize the whole model under the Eq. (9).

4.4 Experiment Results and Analysis

The mAP scores of hashing methods on CIFAR-10 and NUS-WIDE datasets with different code length k are shown in Table 1. From Table 1 we can see that our proposed SSGAH substantially outperforms the other methods. Specifically, the performance of traditional hashing method with hand-crafted features is poor, where SDH achieves only 36.0% on CIFAR-10 datasets, and ITQ achieves only 47.7% on the NUS-WIDE dataset. Traditional methods with CNN features achieve better performance, which shows that features learned from deep neural networks capture more semantic information.

Among deep methods except ours, the best performance on the two datasets are achieved by BGDH [31] and DSH-GANs [21] with 83.3% and 83.4% respectively. The semi-supervised methods (BGDH, SSDH, DSH-GANs) outperforms the supervised ones (NINH, CNNH), which demonstrates that unlabeled data indeed improves the performance of binary codes. Finally, our SSGAH approach outperforms all methods on two datasets by 2.2% and 3.1% and achieves 85.5% and 86.5% correspondingly.

Note that the two graph-based models BGDH and SSDH achieve good performance on CIFAR-10, but a common performance on NUS-WIDE, DSH-GANs obtains an opposite result, and our SSGAH achieves the best performance on both datasets. The reason may be that compared with complex multi-label images on NUS-WIDE, a graph is easier to capture the structure of simple images

Table 2. Mean Average Precision (mAP) scores under retrieval of unseen classes on two datasets. The best mAP scores are emphasized in boldface. Following settings in [34], mAP scores are calculated based on all returned images.

Methods	CIFAR-10				NUS-WIDE			
	12bits	24bits	32bits	48bits	12bits	24bits	32bits	48bits
SSGAH(*Ours*)	**0.309**	**0.323**	**0.341**	**0.339**	**0.539**	**0.553**	**0.565**	**0.579**
SSDH	0.285	0.291	0.311	0.325	0.510	0.533	0.549	0.551
NINH	0.241	0.249	0.253	0.272	0.484	0.483	0.485	0.487
DRSCH	0.219	0.223	0.242	0.251	0.457	0.464	0.469	0.460
CNNH	0.210	0.225	0.227	0.231	0.445	0.463	0.471	0.477
SDH+CNN	0.185	0.193	0.199	0.213	0.471	0.490	0.489	0.507
ITQ+CNN	0.157	0.165	0.189	0.201	0.488	0.493	0.508	0.503
SH+CNN	0.134	0.127	0.126	0.124	0.416	0.386	0.380	0.379
LSH+CNN	0.107	0.119	0.125	0.138	0.341	0.358	0.371	0.373

on CIFAR-10. Contrarily, DSH-GANs is able to generate meaningful and plentiful images conditioned on multi-label on the NUS-WIDE dataset, but easily lead to lack of diversity of synthetic samples conditioned on limited discrete labels on the CIFAR-10 dataset. Different from graph and DSH-GANs, our approach extracts continuous conditions through a Condition Generation module, and can well capture the distribution of triplet-wise information. The experiments on two datasets demonstrate the efficiency of our SSGAH approach.

4.5   Retrieval of Unseen Classes

To further evaluate our SSGAH approach, we additionally adopt the evaluation protocol from [23], where 75% of classes are known during the training process, and the remaining 25% classes are used to for evaluation. Specifically, the dataset is divided into four folds $train75$, $test75$, $train25$ and $test25$, where the $set75$ ($train75 + test75$) includes data of 75% classes, the $set25$ ($train25 + test25$) contains data of 25% classes, and data amount in $train$ and $test$ set are the same. Following settings in [34], we use $train75$ as training set, $test25$ as query set, and $train25 + test75$ as database set.

The specific experiment settings are as below. The $set75$ of CIFAR-10 and NUS-WIDE consist of 7 classes and 15 classes respectively, results are calculated by the average of 5 different random splits, mAP scores are calculated based on all returned images, and the non-deep methods use features extracted from $fc7$ layer of pre-trained AlexNet as inputs.

The mAP scores under the retrieval of unseen classes are shown in Table 2. As we can see, the gaps between unsupervised methods and supervised ones reduce under retrieval of unseen classes, which is because the unsupervised methods learn on the whole dataset and own better generalization performance, but the supervised methods easily overfit labeled data. SSDH achieves a good performance, which demonstrates that unlabeled data can improve the binary codes. Our SSGAH approach achieves the best result when retrieving unseen classes, which is because the generative model in our framework can capture triplet-wise information of unlabeled data, and our semi-supervised ranking loss and adversary ranking loss can make the learned binary codes not only preserve the semantic similarity of labeled data but also capture underlying relationship of data. Thus our approach achieves better generalization performance to unseen class.

Table 3. Mean Average Precision scores (mAP) under different components of our model.

Methods	CIFAR-10				NUS-WIDE			
	12bits	24bits	32bits	48bits	12bits	24bits	32bits	48bits
SSGAH	**0.819**	**0.837**	**0.847**	**0.855**	**0.835**	**0.847**	**0.859**	**0.865**
w/ssr	0.799	0.819	0.836	0.846	0.810	0.819	0.834	0.835
w/ar	0.776	0.804	0.820	0.829	0.787	0.794	0.810	0.812
$baseline$	0.744	0.771	0.782	0.789	0.759	0.780	0.794	0.803

4.6   Component Analysis

To further analyze the affect of each component in our SSGAH, we report the results of two variants of our model and a baseline method. For simplicity, we use G, D and H to represent the generative model, discriminative model and deep hashing model respectively. For the baseline method, we only train H under the supervised ranking loss $\mathcal{L}_{sr}$. For the first variant, we train the G, D and H together, but remove the semi-supervised ranking loss $\mathcal{L}_{ssr}$ from Eq. (9), and mark it as $w/\ ar$. For the second variant, we first train the G and D together under Eq. (1), and then train H under the supervised ranking loss $\mathcal{L}_{sr}$ and semi-supervised ranking loss $\mathcal{L}_{ssr}$, and mark it as w/ssr. Finally, SSGAH achieves the best performance, which demonstrates the effectiveness of our proposed approach.

As shown in Table 3, the best method is SSGAH, followed by w/ssr, w/ar and $baseline$. Firstly, w/ar improves the $baseline$ by 3.2% $\sim$ 4.0% and 0.9% $\sim$ 2.8% on CIFAR-10 and NUS-WIDE datasets, which shows that the adversary ranking loss $\mathcal{L}_{ar}$ helps for better binary codes. Secondly, w/ssr improves the $baseline$ by 4.8% $\sim$ 5.7% and 3.2% $\sim$ 5.1% on CIFAR-10 and NUS-WIDE datasets, which shows that H can capture the triplet-wise information and the semi-supervised ranking loss $\mathcal{L}_{ssr}$ can significantly improve the binary codes.

4.7   Effect of Supervision Amounts

To further analyze our proposed semi-supervised generative adversarial hashing approach, we report the results of SSGAH and $baseline$ (illustrated in Section 4.6) with different supervision amounts on the CIFAR-10 and NUS-WIDE datasets. As shown in Fig. 2, our SSGAH always outperforms the $baseline$, which demonstrates the effectiveness of our approach. What's more, the difference between the two models increases as the supervision amount decreases, which shows that our SSGAH can better utilize the unlabeled data to improve the binary codes.

4.8   Visualization of Synthetic Images

Figure 3 displays the synthetic triplets generated by our SSGAH (green) and its two variants (blue and red). As we can see, our SSGAH can generate color images with size ranging from 32×32 to 64×64. On both datasets, the synthetic images (green) are clear and meaningful, which are indistinguishable from real images. What's more, they successfully acquire the triplet-wise information, i.e. x is more similar to x^p_{syn} than to x^n_{syn}.

Besides the phenomenons above, some extra phenomenons can be observed. Firstly, the red synthetic images are noisy and meaningless and fail to constitute useful triplet, which show that vanilla generative model is hard to capture the distribution of triplet-wise information with limited labeled data. Secondly, the blue images are meaningful, and x are more similar to x^p_{syn} than to x^n_{syn}, which show that our condition generation part contributes to understanding the

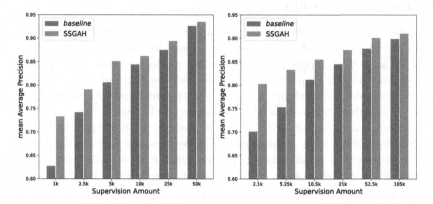

Fig. 2. Mean Average Precision (mAP) scores @48bits of SSGAH and *baseline* with different supervision amounts on the CIFAR10 (left) and NUS-WIDE (right) datasets. Note that our SSGAH always outperforms *baseline*, and the difference between the two models increase as the supervision amount decrease, both of which verify the effectiveness of our proposed approach.

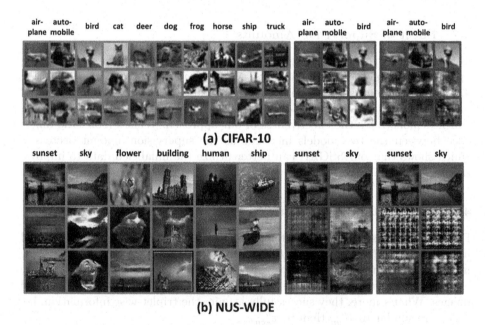

Fig. 3. Visualization of synthetic triplets on (a) CIFAR-10 and (b) NUS-WIDE datasets (better viewed in color). Images in the first row are real images x, followed by synthetic images x_{syn}^p and x_{syn}^n, which are generated by G_p and G_n respectively, thus the three images make up a synthetic triplet $(x, x_{syn}^p, x_{syn}^n)$. The green images are generated by our SSGAH, the blue images are generated by our SSGAH without the adversary ranking loss, and the red images are generated by SSGAH without adversary ranking loss and condition generation module.

triplet-wise information. Finally, compared with blue images, the green ones are not only meaningful but also realistic and clear, which verifies that the adversary learning further improves the generative model. Note that compared with synthetic images (blue) on NUSWIDE, those on CIFAR-10 are more clear and meaningful, which is because images on CIFAR-10 dataset are single-labeled and their structures are simple. Thus it's easy to capture the distribution of triplet-relation. The three phenomenons observed above verify the effectiveness of each component of our model and demonstrate that SSGAH can well capture the distribution of labeled and unlabeled data.

4.9   Conclusion

In this paper, we first propose a novel semi-supervised generative adversarial hashing (SSGAH) approach, which unifies the generative model and deep hashing model in minimax two-player game to make full use of a small amount of labeled data and lots of unlabeled data. What's more, we also propose novel semi-supervised ranking loss and adversary ranking loss to learn better binary codes that capturing semantic information of both labeled and unlabeled data. Finally, extensive experiments on two widely-used datasets demonstrate our SSGAH approach outperforms the state-of-the-art hashing mehtods.

Acknowledgments. This work was supported in part by the National Natural Science Foundation of China under Grants 61720106012, and 61533016, the Strategic Priority Research Program of Chinese Academy of Science under Grant XDBS01000000, and the Beijing Natural Science Foundation under Grant L172050.

References

1. Abadi, M. et al.: Tensorflow: Large-scale machine learning on heterogeneous distributed systems. CoRR abs/1603.04467 (2016). http://arxiv.org/abs/1603.04467
2. Chua, T.S., Tang, J., Hong, R., Li, H., Luo, Z., Zheng, Y.: Nus-wide: a real-world web image database from national university of singapore. In: Marchand-Maillet, S., Kompatsiaris, Y. (eds.) ACM International Conference on Image and Video Retrieval, p. 48. ACM (2009)
3. Dalal, N., Triggs, B.: Histograms of oriented gradients for human detection. In: Computer Vision and Pattern Recognition (CVPR), pp. 886–893. IEEE Computer Society (2005)
4. Datar, M., Immorlica, N., Indyk, P., Mirrokni, V.S.: Locality-sensitive hashing scheme based on p-stable distributions. In: Snoeyink, J., Boissonnat, J. (eds.) Proceedings of the 20th ACM Symposium on Computational Geometry, Brooklyn, New York, USA, June 8–11, 2004, pp. 253–262. ACM (2004)
5. Goodfellow, I. et al.: Generative adversarial nets. In: Ghahramani, Z., Welling, M., Cortes, C., Lawrence, N.D., Weinberger, K.Q. (eds.) Advances in Neural Information Processing Systems 27, pp. 2672–2680. Curran Associates, Inc. (2014). http://papers.nips.cc/paper/5423-generative-adversarial-nets.pdf
6. Isola, P., Zhu, J.Y., Zhou, T., Efros, A.A.: Image-to-image translation with conditional adversarial networks (2017)

7. Krizhevsky, A., Sutskever, I., Hinton, G.E.: Imagenet classification with deep convolutional neural networks. In: Bartlett, P.L., Pereira, F.C.N., Burges, C.J.C., Bottou, L., Weinberger, K.Q. (eds.) International Conference on Neural Information Processing Systems, pp. 1097–1105 (2012)

8. Kulis, B., Darrell, T.: Learning to hash with binary reconstructive embeddings. In: Bengio, Y., Schuurmans, D., Lafferty, J.D., Williams, C.K.I., Culotta, A. (eds.) Advances in Neural Information Processing Systems 22, pp. 1042–1050. Curran Associates, Inc. (2009). http://papers.nips.cc/paper/3667-learning-to-hash-with-binary-reconstructive-embeddings.pdf

9. Lai, H., Pan, Y., Liu, Y., Yan, S.: Simultaneous feature learning and hash coding with deep neural networks. In: The IEEE Conference on Computer Vision and Pattern Recognition (CVPR). IEEE Computer Society, June 2015

10. Lazebnik, S.: Iterative quantization: a procrustean approach to learning binary codes. In: IEEE Conference on Computer Vision and Pattern Recognition, pp. 817–824. IEEE Computer Society (2011)

11. Li, Q., Sun, Z., He, R., Tan, T.: Deep supervised discrete hashing. neural information processing systems, pp. 2482–2491 (2017)

12. Li, W.J., Wang, S., Kang, W.C.: Feature learning based deep supervised hashing with pairwise labels. In: Kambhampati, S. (ed.) International Joint Conference on Artificial Intelligence, pp. 1711–1717. IJCAI/AAAI Press (2016)

13. Liu, W., Wang, J., Ji, R., Jiang, Y.G.: Supervised hashing with kernels. In: Computer Vision and Pattern Recognition, pp. 2074–2081. IEEE Computer Society (2012)

14. Liu, W., Wang, J., Kumar, S., Chang, S.F.: Hashing with graphs. In: Getoor, L., Scheffer, T. (eds.) International Conference on Machine Learning, ICML 2011, Bellevue, Washington, Usa, June 28 - July, pp. 1–8. Omnipress (2011)

15. Lowe, D.G., Lowe, D.G.: Distinctive image features from scale-invariant keypoints. Int. J. Comput. Vis. **60**(2), 91–110 (2004)

16. Lcun, Y., Bottou, L., Bengio, Y., Haffner, P.: Gradient-based learning applied to document recognition. Proc. IEEE **86**(11), 2278–2324 (1998)

17. Mirza, M., Osindero, S.: Conditional generative adversarial nets. Comput. Sci., 2672–2680 (2014)

18. Norouzi, M., Fleet, D.J.: Minimal loss hashing for compact binary codes. In: Getoor, L., Scheffer, T. (eds.) International Conference on International Conference on Machine Learning, pp. 353–360. Omnipress (2011)

19. Odena, A., Olah, C., Shlens, J.: Conditional image synthesis with auxiliary classifier gans, pp. 2642–2651 (2017)

20. Oliva, A., Torralba, A.: Modeling the shape of the scene: A holistic representation of the spatial envelope. Int. J. Comput. Vis. **42**(3), 145–175 (2001)

21. Qiu, Z., Pan, Y., Yao, T., Mei, T.: Deep semantic hashing with generative adversarial networks. In: Kando, N., Sakai, T., Joho, H., Li, H., de Vries, A.P., White, R.W. (eds.) International ACM SIGIR Conference on Research and Development in Information Retrieval, pp. 225–234. ACM (2017)

22. Radford, A., Metz, L., Chintala, S.: Unsupervised representation learning with deep convolutional generative adversarial networks. Comput. Sci. (2015)

23. Sablayrolles, A., Douze, M., Usunier, N., Jegou, H.: How should we evaluate supervised hashing? In: 2017 IEEE International Conference on Acoustics, Speech and Signal Processing, ICASSP 2017, New Orleans, LA, USA, March 5–9, 2017, pp. 1732–1736. IEEE (2017)

24. Shen, F., Shen, C., Liu, W., Shen, H.T.: Supervised discrete hashing. The IEEE Conference on Computer Vision and Pattern Recognition (CVPR), pp. 37–45 (2015)
25. Wang, J., Shen, H.T., Song, J., Ji, J.: Hashing for similarity search: a survey. Comput. Sci. (2014)
26. Wang, J., Zhang, T., Song, J., Sebe, N., Shen, H.T.: A survey on learning to hash. IEEE Trans. Pattern Anal. Mach. Intell. **PP**(99), 1–1 (2017)
27. Wang, J., Kumar, S., Chang, S.F.: Semi-supervised hashing for large-scale search. IEEE Trans. Pattern Anal. Mach. Intell. **34**(12), 2393–2406 (2012)
28. Wang, J. et al.: IRGAN: A minimax game for unifying generative and discriminative information retrieval models. In: Kando, N., Sakai, T., Joho, H., Li, H., de Vries, A.P., White, R.W. (eds.) Proceedings of the 40th International ACM SIGIR Conference on Research and Development in Information Retrieval, Shinjuku, Tokyo, Japan, August 7–11, 2017, pp. 515–524. ACM (2017)
29. Weiss, Y., Torralba, A., Fergus, R.: Spectral hashing. In: Koller, D., Schuurmans, D., Bengio, Y., Bottou, L. (eds.) International Conference on Neural Information Processing Systems, pp. 1753–1760. Curran Associates, Inc. (2008)
30. Xia, R., Pan, Y., Lai, H., Liu, C., Yan, S.: Supervised hashing for image retrieval via image representation learning (2014)
31. Yan, X., Zhang, L., Li, W.J.: Semi-supervised deep hashing with a bipartite graph. In: Sierra, C. (ed.) Twenty-Sixth International Joint Conference on Artificial Intelligence, pp. 3238–3244. ijcai.org (2017)
32. Yang, H.F., Lin, K., Chen, C.S.: Supervised learning of semantics-preserving hash via deep convolutional neural networks. IEEE Trans. Pattern Anal. Mach. Intell. **PP**(99), 1–1 (2015)
33. Yi, Z., Zhang, H., Tan, P., Gong, M.: Dualgan: Unsupervised dual learning for image-to-image translation (2017)
34. Zhang, J., Peng, Y.: Ssdh: Semi-supervised deep hashing for large scale image retrieval. IEEE Trans. Circuits Syst. Video Technol. (2016)
35. Zhu, H., Long, M., Wang, J., Cao, Y.: Deep hashing network for efficient similarity retrieval. In: Schuurmans, D., Wellman, M.P. (eds.) Thirtieth AAAI Conference on Artificial Intelligence, pp. 2415–2421. AAAI Press (2016)

Person Re-identification with Deep Similarity-Guided Graph Neural Network

Yantao Shen[1], Hongsheng Li[1](✉), Shuai Yi[2], Dapeng Chen[1], and Xiaogang Wang[1]

[1] CUHK-SenseTime Joint Lab, The Chinese University of Hong Kong, Hong Kong, People's Republic of China
{ytshen,hsli,dpchen}@ee.cuhk.edu.hk
[2] SenseTime Research, Hong Kong, People's Republic of China
yishuai@sensetime.com

Abstract. The person re-identification task requires to robustly estimate visual similarities between person images. However, existing person re-identification models mostly estimate the similarities of different image pairs of probe and gallery images independently while ignores the relationship information between different probe-gallery pairs. As a result, the similarity estimation of some hard samples might not be accurate. In this paper, we propose a novel deep learning framework, named Similarity-Guided Graph Neural Network (SGGNN) to overcome such limitations. Given a probe image and several gallery images, SGGNN creates a graph to represent the pairwise relationships between probe-gallery pairs (nodes) and utilizes such relationships to update the probe-gallery relation features in an end-to-end manner. Accurate similarity estimation can be achieved by using such updated probe-gallery relation features for prediction. The input features for nodes on the graph are the relation features of different probe-gallery image pairs. The probe-gallery relation feature updating is then performed by the messages passing in SGGNN, which takes other nodes' information into account for similarity estimation. Different from conventional GNN approaches, SGGNN learns the edge weights with rich labels of gallery instance pairs directly, which provides relation fusion more precise information. The effectiveness of our proposed method is validated on three public person re-identification datasets.

Keywords: Deep learning · Person re-identification Graph Neural Networks

1 Introduction

Person re-identification is a challenging problem, which aims at finding the person images of interest in a set of images across different cameras. It plays a significant role in the intelligent surveillance systems.

V. Ferrari et al. (Eds.): ECCV 2018, LNCS 11219, pp. 508–526, 2018.
https://doi.org/10.1007/978-3-030-01267-0_30

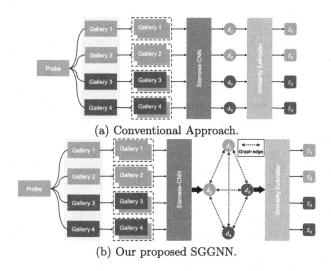

(a) Conventional Approach.

(b) Our proposed SGGNN.

Fig. 1. Illustration of our Proposed SGGNN method and conventional person re-identification approach. (a) The pipeline of conventional person re-identification approach, the pairwise relationships between different probe-gallery pairs are ignored. The similarity score of each probe-gallery pair d_i ($i = 1, 2, 3, 4$) is estimated individually. (b) Our proposed SGGNN approach, pairwise relationships between different probe-gallery pairs are involved with deeply learned message passing on a graph for more accurate similarity estimation.

To enhance the re-identification performance, most existing approaches attempt to learn discriminative features or design various metric distances for better measuring the similarities between person image pairs. In recent years, witness the success of deep learning based approaches for various tasks of computer vision [12,17,20,25,31,39,51,59,62,63,67], a large number of deep learning methods were proposed for person re-identification [37,40,64,81]. Most of these deep learning based approaches utilized Convolutional Neural Network (CNN) to learn robust and discriminative features. In the mean time, metric learning methods were also proposed [3,4,72] to generate relatively small feature distances between images of same identity and large feature distances between those of different identities.

However, most of these approaches only consider the pairwise similarity while ignore the internal similarities among the images of the whole set. For instance, when we attempt to estimate the similarity score between a probe image and a gallery image, most feature learning and metric learning approaches only consider the pairwise relationship between this single probe-gallery image pair in both training and testing stages. Other relations among different pairs of images are ignored. As a result, some hard positive or hard negative pairs are difficult to obtain proper similarity scores since only limited relationship information among samples is utilized for similarity estimation.

To overcome such limitation, we need to discover the valuable internal similarities among the image set, especially for the similarities among the gallery set. One possible solution is utilizing manifold learning [2,42], which considers the similarities of each pair of images in the set. It maps images into a manifold with more smooth local geometry. Beyond the manifold learning methods, re-ranking approaches [16,70,78] were also utilized for refining the ranking result by integrating similarities between top-ranked gallery images. However, both manifold learning and re-ranking approaches have two major limitations: (1) most manifold learning and re-ranking approaches are unsupervised, which could not fully exploit the provided training data label into the learning process. (2) These two kinds of approaches could not benefit feature learning since they are not involved in training process.

Recently, *Graph Neural Network* (GNN) [6,18,23,45] draws increasing attention due to its ability of generalizing neural networks for data with graph structures. The GNN propagates messages on a graph structure. After message traversal on the graph, node's final representations are obtained from its own as well as other node's information, and are then utilized for node classification. GNN has achieved huge success in many research fields, such as text classification [13], image classification [6,46], and human action recognition [66]. Compared with manifold learning and re-ranking, GNN incorporates graph computation into the neural networks learning, which makes the training end-to-end and benefits learning the feature representation.

In this paper, we propose a novel deep learning framework for person re-identification, named Similarity-Guided Graph Neural Network (SGGNN). SGGNN incorporates graph computation in both training and testing stages of deep networks for obtaining robust similarity estimations and discriminative feature representations. Given a mini-batch consisting of several probe images and gallery images, SGGNN will first learn initial visual features for each image (*e.g.*, global average pooled features from ResNet-50 [17].) with the pairwise relation supervisions. After that, each pair of probe-gallery images will be treated as a node on the graph, which is responsible for generating similarity score of this pair. To fully utilize pairwise relations between other pairs (nodes) of images, deeply learned messages are propagated among nodes to update and refine the pairwise relation features associated with each node. Unlike most previous GNNs' designs, in SGGNN, the weights for feature fusion are determined by similarity scores by gallery image pairs, which are directly supervised by training labels. With these similarity guided feature fusion weights, SGGNN will fully exploit the valuable label information to generate discriminative person image features and obtain robust similarity estimations for probe-gallery image pairs.

The main contribution of this paper is two-fold. (1) We propose a novel Similarity Guided Graph Neural Network (SGGNN) for person re-identification, which could be trained end-to-end. Unlike most existing methods, which utilize inter-gallery-image relations between samples in the post-processing stage, SGGNN incorporates the inter-gallery-image relations in the training stage to enhance feature learning process. As a result, more discriminative and accurate person image feature representations could be learned. (2) Different from most Graph Neural Network (GNN) approaches, SGGNN exploits the training label supervision for learning more accurate feature fusion weights for updating the nodes' features. This similarity guided manner ensures the feature fusion weights to be more precise and conduct more reasonable feature fusion. The effectiveness of our proposed method is verified by extensive experiments on three large person re-identification datasets.

2   Related Work

2.1   Person Re-identification

Person re-identification is an active research topic, which gains increasing attention from both academia and industry in recent years. The mainstream approaches for person re-identification either try to obtain discriminative and robust feature [1,7,8,10,21,28,35,54–56,58,60,61,71] for representing person image or design a proper metric distance for measuring similarity between person images [3,4,41,47,72]. For feature learning, Yi et al. [71] introduced a Siamese-CNN for person re-identification. Li et al. [28] proposed a novel filter pairing neural network, which could jointly handle feature learning, misalignment, and classification in an end-to-end manner. Ahmed et al. [1] introduced a model called Cross-Input Neighbourhood Difference CNN model, which compares image features in each patch of one input image to the other image's patch. Su et al. [60] incorporated pose information into person re-identification. The pose estimation algorithm are utilized for part extraction. Then the original global image and the transformed part images are fed into a CNN simultaneously for prediction. Shen et al. [57] utilized kronecker-product matching for person feature maps alignment. For metric learning, Paisitkriangkrai et al. [47] introduced an approach aims at learning the weights of different metric distance functions by optimizing the relative distance among triplet samples and maximizing the averaged rank-k accuracies. Bak et al. [3] proposed to learn metrics for 2D patches of person image. Yu et al. [72] introduced an unsupervised person re-ID model, which aims at learning an asymmetric metric on cross-view person images.

Besides feature learning and metric learning, manifold learning [2,42] and re-rank approaches [16,69,70,78] are also utilized for enhancing the performance of person re-identification model, Bai et al. [2] introduced Supervised Smoothed Manifold, which aims to estimating the context of other pairs of person image thus the learned relationships with between samples are smooth on the manifold. Loy et al. [42] introduced manifold ranking for revealing manifold structure by plenty of gallery images. Zhong et al. [78] utilized k-reciprocal encoding to refine the ranking list result by exploiting relationships between top rank gallery instances for a probe sample. Kodirov et al. [24] introduced graph regularised dictionary learning for person re-identification. Most of these approaches are conducted in the post-process stage and the visual features of person images could not be benefited from these post-processing approaches.

2.2 Graph for Machine Learning

In several machine learning research areas, input data could be naturally represented as graph structure, such as natural language processing [38,44], human
pose estimation [11,66,68], visual relationship detection [32], and image classification [48,50]. In [53], Scarselli *et al.* divided machine learning models into two
classes due to different application objectives on graph data structure, named
node-focused and *graph-focused* application. For *graph-focused* application, the
mapping function takes the whole graph data G as the input. One simple example for *graph-focused* application is to classify the image [48], where the image
is represented by a region adjacency graph. For *node-focused* application, the
inputs of mapping function are the nodes on the graph. Each node on the graph
will represent a sample in the dataset and the edge weights will be determined
by the relationships between samples. After the message propagation among
different nodes (samples), the mapping function will output the classification or
regression results of each node. One typical example for *node-focused* application
is graph based image segmentation [36,76], which takes pixels of image as nodes
and try to minimize the total energy function for segmentation prediction of
each pixel. Another example for *node-focused* application is object detection [5],
the input nodes are features of the proposals in a input image.

2.3 Graph Neural Network

Scarselli *et al.* [53] introduced Graph Neural Network (GNN), which is an extension for recursive neural networks and random walk models for graph structure
data. It could be applied for both graph-focused or node-focused data without
any pre or post-processing steps, which means that it can be trained end-to-
end. In recent years, extending CNN to graph data structure received increased
attention [6,13,18,23,33,45,66], Bruna *et al.* [6] proposed two constructions of
deep convolutional networks on graphs (GCN), one is based on the spectrum of
graph Laplacian, which is called spectral construction. Another is spatial construction, which extends properties of convolutional filters to general graphs.
Yan *et al.* [66] exploited spatial construction GCN for human action recognition.
Different from most existing GNN approaches, our proposed approach exploits
the training data label supervision for generating more accurate feature fusion
weights in the graph message passing.

3 Method

To evaluate the algorithms for person re-identification, the test dataset is usually
divided into two parts: a probe set and a gallery set. Given an image pair of a
probe and a gallery images, the person re-identification models aims at robustly
determining visual similarities between probe-gallery image pairs. In the previous
common settings, among a mini-batch, different image pairs of probe and gallery
images are evaluated individually, *i.e.*, the estimated similarity between a pair of

images will not be influenced by other pairs. However, the similarities between different gallery images are valuable for refining similarity estimation between the probe and gallery. Our proposed approach is proposed to better utilize such information to improve feature learning and is illustrated in Fig. 1. It takes a probe and several gallery images as inputs to create a graph with each node modeling a probe-gallery image pair. It outputs the similarity score of each probe-gallery image pair. Deeply learned messages will be propagated among nodes to update the relation features associated with each node for more accurate similarity score estimation in the end-to-end training process.

In this section, the problem formulation and node features will be discussed in Sect. 3.1. The Similarity Guided GNN (SGGNN) and deep messages propagation for person re-identification will be presented in Sect. 3.2. Finally, we will discuss the advantage of similarity guided edge weight over the conventional GNN approaches in Sect. 3.3. The implementation details will be introduced in Sect. 3.4

3.1 Graph Formulation and Node Features

In our framework, we formulate person re-identification as a *node-focused* graph application introduced in Sect. 2.2. Given a probe image and N gallery images, we construct an undirected complete graph $G(V, E)$, where $V = \{v_1, v_2, ..., v_N\}$ denotes the set of nodes. Each node represents a pair of probe-gallery images. Our goal is to estimate the similarity score for each probe-gallery image pair and therefore treat the re-identification problem as a node classification problem. Generally, the input features for any node encodes the complex relations between its corresponding probe-gallery image pair.

In this work, we adopt a simple approach for obtaining input relation features to the graph nodes, which is shown in Fig. 2(a). Given a probe image and N gallery images, each input probe-gallery image pair will be fed into a Siamese-CNN for pairwise relation feature encoding. The Siamese-CNN's structure is based on the ResNet-50 [17]. To obtain the pairwise relation features, the last global average pooled features of two images from ResNet-50 are element-wise subtracted. The pairwise feature is processed by element-wise square operation and a Batch Normalization layer [19]. The processed difference features d_i ($i = 1, 2, ..., N$) encode the deep visual relations between the probe and the i-th gallery image, and are used as the input features of the i-th node on the graph. Since our task is node-wise classification, *i.e.*, estimating the similarity score of each probe-gallery pair, a naive approach would be simply feeding each node's input feature into a linear classifier to output the similarity score without considering the pairwise relationship between different nodes. For each probe-gallery image pair in the training mini-batch, a binary cross-entropy loss function could be utilized,

$$L = -\sum_{i=1}^{N} y_i \log(f(d_i)) + (1 - y_i) \log(1 - f(d_i)), \qquad (1)$$

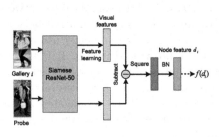

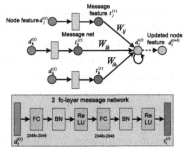

(a) Node input feature generating.   (b) Deep message passing of SGGNN.

Fig. 2. The illustration of our base model and deep message passing of SGGNN. (a) Our base model is not only utilized for calculating the probe-gallery pairs' similarity scores, but also for obtaining the gallery-gallery similarity scores, which could be utilized for deep message passing to update the relation features of probe-gallery pairs. (b) For passing more effective information, probe-gallery relation features d_i are first fed into a 2 layer message network for feature encoding. With gallery-gallery similarity scores, the probe-gallery relation feature fusion could be deduced as a message passing and feature fusion schemes, which is defined as Eq. 4.

where $f()$ denotes a linear classifier followed by a sigmoid function. y_i denotes the ground-truth label of i-th probe-gallery image pair, with 1 representing the probe and the i-th gallery images belonging to the same identity while 0 for not.

3.2   Similarity-Guided Graph Neural Network

Obviously, the naive node classification model (Eq. (1)) ignores the valuable information among different probe-gallery pairs. For exploiting such vital information, we need to establish edges E on the graph G. In our formulation, G is fully-connected and E represents the set of relationships between different probe-gallery pairs, where W_{ij} is a scalar edge weight. It represents the relation importance between node i and node j and can be calculated as,

$$W_{ij} = \begin{cases} \frac{\exp(S(g_i,g_j))}{\sum_j \exp(S(g_i,g_j))}, & i \neq j \\ 0, & i = j \end{cases}, \tag{2}$$

where g_i and g_j are the i-th and j-th gallery images. $S()$ is a pairwise similarity estimation function, that estimates the similarity score between g_i and g_j and can be modeled in the same way as the naive node (probe-gallery image pair) classification model discussed above. Note that in SGGNN, the similarity score $S(g_i,g_j)$ of gallery-gallery pair is also learned in a supervised way with person identity labels. The purpose of setting W_{ii} to 0 is to avoid self-enhancing. To enhance the initial pairwise relation features of a node with other nodes' information, we propose to propagate deeply learned messages between all connecting nodes. The node features are then updated as a weighted addition fusion of all input messages and the node's original features. The proposed relation feature fusion and updating is intuitive: using gallery-gallery similarity scores to guide the refinement of the probe-gallery relation features will make the relation features more discriminative and accurate, since the rich relation information among different pairs are involved. For instance, given one probe sample p and two gallery samples g_i, g_j. Suppose that (p, g_i) is a hard positive pair (node) while both (p, g_j) and (g_i, g_j) are relative easy positive pairs. Without any message passing among the nodes (p, g_i) and (p, g_j), the similarity score of (p, g_i) is unlikely to be high. However, if we utilize the similarity of pair (g_i, g_j) to guide the refinement of the relation features of the hard positive pair (p, g_i), the refined features of (p, g_i) will lead to a more proper similarity score. This relation feature fusion could be deduced as a message passing and feature fusion scheme.

Before message passing begins, each node first encodes a deep message for sending to other nodes that are connected to it. The nodes' input relation features d_i are fed into a message network with 2 fully-connected layers with BN and ReLU to generate deep message t_i, which is illustrated in Fig. 2(b). This process learns more suitable messages for node relation feature updating,

$$t_i = F(d_i) \quad \text{for } i = 1, 2, ..., N, \tag{3}$$

where F denotes the 2 FC-layer subnetwork for learning deep messages for propagation.

After obtaining the edge weights W_{ij} and deep message t_i from each node, the updating scheme of node relation feature d_i could be formulated as

$$d_i^{(1)} = (1 - \alpha)d_i^{(0)} + \alpha \sum_{j=1}^{N} W_{ij} t_j^{(0)} \quad \text{for } i = 1, 2, ..., N, \tag{4}$$

where $d_i^{(1)}$ denotes the i-th refined relation feature, $d_i^{(0)}$ denotes the i-th input relation feature and $t_j^{(0)}$ denotes the deep message from node j. α represents the weighting parameter that balances fusion feature and original feature.

Noted that such relation feature weighted fusion could be performed iteratively as follows,

$$d_i^{(t)} = (1 - \alpha)d_i^{(t-1)} + \alpha \sum_{j=1}^{N} W_{ij} t_j^{(t-1)} \quad \text{for } i = 1, 2, ..., N, \tag{5}$$

where t is the iteration number. The refined relation feature $d_i^{(t)}$ could substitute then relation feature d_i in Eq. (1) for loss computation and training the SGGNN. For training, Eq. (5) can be unrolled via back propagation through structure.

In practice, we found that the performance gap between iterative feature updating of multiple iterations and updating for one iteration is negligible. So we adopt Eq. (4) as our relation feature fusion in both training and testing stages. After relation feature updating, we feed the relation features of probe-gallery image pairs to a linear classifier with sigmoid function for obtaining the similarity score and trained with the same binary cross-entropy loss (Eq. (1)).

3.3 Relations to Conventional GNN

In our proposed SGGNN model, the similarities among gallery images are served as fusion weights on the graph for nodes' feature fusion and updating. These similarities are vital for refining the probe-gallery relation features. In conventional GNN [45,66] models, the feature fusion weights are usually modeled as a nonlinear function $h(d_i, d_j)$ that measures compatibility between two nodes d_i and d_j. The feature updating will be

$$d_i^{(t)} = (1 - \alpha)d_i^{(t-1)} + \alpha \sum_{j=1}^{N} h(d_i, d_j)t_j^{(t-1)} \quad \text{for } i = 1, 2, ..., N. \tag{6}$$

They lack directly label supervision and are only indirectly learned via back-propagation errors. However, in our case, such a strategy does not fully utilize the similarity ground-truth between gallery images. To overcome such limitation, we propose to use similarity scores $S(g_i, g_j)$ between gallery images g_i and g_j with directly training label supervision to serve as the node feature fusion weights in Eq. (4). Compared with conventional setting of GNN Eq. (6), these direct and rich supervisions of gallery-gallery similarity could provide feature fusion with more accurate information.

3.4 Implementation Details

Our proposed SGGNN is based on ResNet-50 [17] pretrained on ImageNet [14]. The input images are all resized to 256×128. Random flipping and random erasing [79] are utilized for data augmentation. We will first pretrain the base Siamese CNN model, we adopt an initial learning rate of 0.01 on all three datasets and reduce the learning rate by 10 times after 50 epochs. The learning rate is then fixed for another 50 training epochs. The weights of linear classifier for obtaining the gallery-gallery similarities is initialized with the weights of linear classifier we trained in the base model pretraining stage. To construct each mini-batch as a combination of a probe set and a gallery set, we randomly sample images according to their identities. First we randomly choose M identities in each mini-batch. For each identity, we randomly choose K images belonging to this identity. Among these K images of one person, we randomly choose one of them as the probe image and leave the rest of them as gallery images. As a result, a $K \times M$ sized mini-batch consists of a size K probe set and a size $K \times (M - 1)$ gallery set. In the training stage, K is set to 4 and M is set to 48, which results in a mini-batch size of 192. In the testing stage, for each probe image, we first utilize $l2$ distance between probe image feature and gallery image features by the trained ResNet-50 in our SGGNN to obtain the top-100 gallery images, then we use SGGNN for obtaining the final similarity scores. We will go though all the identities in each training epoch and Adam algorithm [22] is utilized for optimization.

We then finetune the overall SGGNN model end-to-end, the input node features for overall model are the subtracted features of base model. Note that for gallery-gallery similarity estimation $S(g_i, g_j)$, the rich labels of gallery images are also used as training supervision. we train the overall network with a learning rate of 10^{-4} for another 50 epochs and the balancing weight α is set to 0.9.

4   Experiments

4.1   Datasets and Evaluation Metrics

To validate the effectiveness of our proposed approach for person re-identification. The experiments and ablation study are conducted on three large public datasets.

CUHK03 [28] is a person re-identification dataset, which contains 14,097 images of 1,467 person captured by two cameras from the campus. We utilize its manually annotated images in this work.

Market-1501 [75] is a large-scale dataset, which contains multi-view person images for each identity. It consists of 12,936 images for training and 19,732 images for testing. The test set is divided into a gallery set that contains 16,483 images and a probe set that contains 3,249 images. There are totally 1501 identities in this dataset and all the person images are obtained by DPM detector [15].

DukeMTMC [52] is collected from campus with 8 cameras, it originally contains more than 2,000,000 manually annotated frames. There are some extensions for DukeMTMC dataset for person re-identification task. In this paper, we follow the setting of [77]. It utilizes 1404 identities, which appear in more than two cameras. The training set consists of 16,522 images with 702 identities and test set contains 19,989 images with 702 identities.

We adopt mean average precision (mAP) and CMC top-1, top-5, and top-10 accuracies as evaluation metrics. For each dataset, we just adopt the original evaluation protocol that the dataset provides. In the experiments, the query type is single query.

4.2   Comparison with State-of-the-art Methods

Results on CUHK03 Dataset. The results of our proposed method and other state-of-the-art methods are represented in Table 1. The mAP and top-1 accuracy of our proposed method are 94.3% and 95.3%, respectively. Our proposed method outperforms all the compared methods.

Quadruplet Loss [9] is modified based on triplet loss. It aims at obtaining correct orders for input pairs and pushing away negative pairs from positive pairs. Our proposed method outperforms quadruplet loss 19.8% in terms of top-1 accuracy. OIM Loss [65] maintains a look-up table. It compares distances between mini-batch samples and all the entries in the table. to learn features of person image. Our approach improves OIM Loss by 21.8% and 17.8% in terms of mAP and CMC top-1 accuracy. SpindleNet [73] considers body structure information for person re-identification. It incorporates body region features and features from different semantic levels for person re-identification. Compared with SpindleNet, our proposed method increases 6.8% for top-1 accuracy.

Table 1. mAP, top-1, top-5, and top-10 accuracies by compared methods on the CUHK03 dataset [28].

Methods	Conference	CUHK03 [28]			
		mAP	top-1	top-5	top-10
Quadruplet Loss [9]	CVPR 2017	-	75.5	95.2	99.2
OIM Loss [65]	CVPR 2017	72.5	77.5	-	-
SpindleNet [73]	CVPR 2017	-	88.5	97.8	98.6
MSCAN [26]	CVPR 2017	-	74.2	94.3	97.5
SSM [2]	CVPR 2017	-	76.6	94.6	98.0
k-reciprocal [78]	CVPR 2017	67.6	61.6	-	-
VI+LSRO [77]	ICCV 2017	87.4	84.6	97.6	98.9
SVDNet [61]	ICCV 2017	84.8	81.8	95.2	97.2
OL-MANS [80]	ICCV 2017	-	61.7	88.4	95.2
Pose Driven [60]	ICCV 2017	-	88.7	98.6	**99.6**
Part Aligned [74]	ICCV 2017	-	85.4	97.6	99.4
HydraPlus-Net [39]	ICCV 2017	-	91.8	98.4	99.1
MuDeep [49]	ICCV 2017	-	76.3	96.0	98.4
JLML [29]	IJCAI 2017	-	83.2	98.0	99.4
MC-PPMN [43]	AAAI 2018	-	86.4	98.5	**99.6**
Proposed SGGNN		**94.3**	**95.3**	**99.1**	**99.6**

MSCAN [27] stands for Multi-Scale ContextAware Network. It adopts multiple convolution kernels with different receptive fields to obtain multiple feature maps. The dilated convolution is utilized for decreasing the correlations among convolution kernels. Our proposed method gains 21.1% in terms of top-1 accuracy. SSM stands for Smoothed Supervised Manifold [2]. This approach tries to obtain the underlying manifold structure by estimating the similarity between two images in the context of other pairs of images in the post-processing stage, while the proposed SGGNN utilizes instance relation information in both training and testing stages. SGGNN outperforms SSM approach by 18.7% in terms of top-1 accuracy. k-reciprocal [78] utilized gallery-gallery similarities in the testing stage and uses a smoothed Jaccard distance for refining the ranking results. In contrast, SGGNN exploits the gallery-gallery information in the training stage for feature learning. As a result, SGGNN gains 26.7% and 33.7% increase in terms of mAP and top-1 accuracy.

Results on Market-1501 Dataset. On Market-1501 dataset, our proposed methods outperforms significantly state-of-the-art methods. SGGNN achieves mAP of 82.8% and top-1 accuracy of 92.3% on Market-1501 dataset. The results are shown in Table 2.

Table 2. mAP, top-1, top-5, and top-10 accuracies of compared methods on the Market-1501 dataset [75].

Methods	Reference	Market-1501 [75]			
		mAP	top-1	top-5	top-10
OIM Loss [65]	CVPR 2017	60.9	82.1	-	-
SpindleNet [73]	CVPR 2017	-	76.9	91.5	94.6
MSCAN [26]	CVPR 2017	53.1	76.3	-	-
SSM [2]	CVPR 2017	68.8	82.2	-	-
k-reciprocal [78]	CVPR 2017	63.6	77.1	-	-
Point 2 Set [81]	CVPR 2017	44.3	70.7	-	-
CADL [35]	CVPR 2017	47.1	73.8	-	-
VI+LSRO [77]	ICCV 2017	66.1	84.0	-	-
SVDNet [61]	ICCV 2017	62.1	82.3	92.3	95.2
OL-MANS [80]	ICCV 2017	-	60.7	-	-
Pose Driven [60]	ICCV 2017	63.4	84.1	92.7	94.9
Part Aligned [74]	ICCV 2017	63.4	81.0	92.0	94.7
HydraPlus-Net [39]	ICCV 2017	-	76.9	91.3	94.5
JLML [29]	IJCAI 2017	65.5	85.1	-	-
HA-CNN [30]	CVPR 2018	75.7	91.2	-	-
Proposed SGGNN		**82.8**	**92.3**	**96.1**	**97.4**

HydraPlus-Net [39] is proposed for better exploiting the global and local contents with multi-level feature fusion of a person image. Our proposed method outperforms HydraPlus-Net by 15.4 for top-1 accuracy. JLML [29] stands for Joint Learning of Multi-Loss. JLML learns both global and local discriminative features in different context and exploits complementary advantages jointly. Compared with JLML, our proposed method gains 17.3 and 7.2 in terms of mAP and top-1 accuracy. HA-CNN [30] attempts to learn hard region-level and soft pixel-level attention simultaneously with arbitrary person bounding boxes and person image features. The proposed SGGNN outperforms HA-CNN by 7.1% and 1.1% with respect to mAP and top-1 accuracy.

Results on DukeMTMC Dataset. In Table 3, we illustrate the performance of our proposed SGGNN and other state-of-the-art methods on DukeMTMC [52]. Our method outperforms all compared approaches. Besides approaches such as OIM Loss and SVDNet, which have been introduced previously, our method also outperforms Basel+LSRO, which integrates GAN generated data and ACRN that incorporates person of attributes for person re-identification significantly. These results illustrate the effectiveness of our proposed approach.

Table 3. mAP, top-1, top-5, and top-10 accuracies by compared methods on the DukeMTMC dataset [52].

Methods	Reference	DukeMTMC [52]			
		mAP	top-1	top-5	top-10
BoW+KISSME [75]	ICCV 2015	12.2	25.1	-	-
LOMO+XQDA [34]	CVPR 2015	17.0	30.8	-	-
ACRN [54]	CVPRW 2017	52.0	72.6	84.8	88.9
OIM Loss [65]	CVPR 2017	47.4	68.1	-	-
Basel.+LSRO [77]	ICCV 2017	47.1	67.7	-	-
SVDNet [61]	ICCV 2017	56.8	76.7	86.4	89.9
Proposed SGGNN		**68.2**	**81.1**	**88.4**	**91.2**

4.3   Ablation Study

To further investigate the validity of SGGNN, we also conduct a series of ablation studies on all three datasets. Results are shown in Table 4.

We treat the siamese CNN model that directly estimates pairwise similarities from initial node features introduced in Sect. 3.1 as the base model. We utilize the same base model and compare with other approaches that also take inter-gallery image relations in the testing stage for comparison. We conduct k-reciprocal re-ranking [78] with the image visual features learned by our base model. Compared with SGGNN approach, The mAP of k-reciprocal approach drops by 4.3%, 4.4%, 3.5% for Market-1501, CUHK03, and DukeMTMC datasets. The top-1 accuracy also drops by 0.8%, 3.1%, 1.2% respectively. Except for the visual features, base model could also provides us raw similarity scores of probe-gallery pairs and gallery-gallery pairs. A random walk [2] operation could be conducted to refine the probe-gallery similarity scores with gallery-gallery similarity scores with a closed-form equation. Compared with our method, The performance of random walk drops by 3.6%, 4.1%, and 2.2% in terms of mAP, 0.8%, 3.0%, and 0.8% in terms of top-1 accuracy. Such results illustrate the effectiveness of end-to-end training with deeply learned message passing within SGGNN. We also validate the importance of learning visual feature fusion weight with gallery-gallery similarities guidance. In Sect. 3.3, we have introduced that in the conventional GNN, the compatibility between two nodes d_i and d_j, $h(d_i, d_j)$ is calculated by a non-linear function, inner product function without direct gallery-gallery supervision. We therefore remove the directly gallery-gallery supervisions and train the model with weight fusion approach in Eq. (6), denoted by *Base Model + SGGNN w/o SG*. The performance drops by 1.6%, 1.6%, and 0.9% in terms of mAP. The top-1 accuracies drops 1.7%, 2.6%, and 0.6% compared with our SGGNN approach, which illustrates the importance of involving rich gallery-gallery labels in the training stage.

To demonstrate that our proposed model SGGNN also learns better visual features by considering all probe-gallery relations, we evaluate the re-identification performance by directly calculating the l_2 distance between different images' visual feature vectors outputted by our trained ResNet-50 model on three datasets. The results by visual features learned with base model and the conventional GNN approach are illustrated in Table 5. Visual features by our proposed SGGNN outperforms the compared base model and conventional GNN setting significantly, which demonstrates that SGGNN also learns more discriminative and robust features.

Table 4. Ablation studies on the Market-1501 [75], CUHK03 [28] and DukeMTMC [52] datasets.

Methods	Market-1501 [75]		CUHK03 [28]		DukeMTMC [52]	
	mAP	top-1	mAP	top-1	mAP	top-1
Base Model	76.4	91.2	88.9	91.1	61.8	78.8
Base Model + k-reciprocal [78]	78.5	91.5	89.9	92.2	64.7	79.9
Base Model + random walk [2]	79.2	91.5	90.2	92.3	66.0	80.3
Base Model + SGGNN w/o SG	81.2	90.6	92.7	93.6	67.3	80.5
Base Model + SGGNN	**82.8**	**92.3**	**94.3**	**95.3**	**68.2**	**81.1**

Table 5. Performances of estimating probe-gallery similarities by l_2 feature distance on the Market-1501 [75], CUHK03 [28] and DukeMTMC [52] datasets.

Model	Market-1501 [75]		CUHK03 [28]		DukeMTMC [52]	
	mAP	top-1	mAP	top-1	mAP	top-1
Base Model	74.6	90.4	87.6	91.0	60.3	77.6
Base Model + SGGNN w/o SG	75.4	90.4	87.7	91.5	61.7	78.1
Base Model + SGGNN	**76.7**	**91.5**	**88.1**	**93.6**	**64.6**	**79.1**

5   Conclusion

In this paper, we propose Similarity-Guided Graph Neural Neural to incorporate the rich gallery-gallery similarity information into training process of person re-identification. Compared with our method, most previous attempts conduct the updating of probe-gallery similarity in the post-process stage, which could not benefit the learning of visual features. For conventional Graph Neural Network setting, the rich gallery-gallery similarity labels are ignored while our approach utilized all valuable labels to ensure the weighted deep message fusion is more effective. The overall performance of our approach and ablation study illustrate the effectiveness of our proposed method.

Acknowledgements. This work is supported by SenseTime Group Limited, the General Research Fund sponsored by the Research Grants Council of Hong Kong (Nos. CUHK14213616, CUHK14206114, CUHK14205615, CUHK14203015, CUHK14239816, CUHK419412, CUHK14207814, CUHK14208417, CUHK14202217), the Hong Kong Innovation and Technology Support Program (No. ITS/121/15FX).

References

1. Ahmed, E., Jones, M., Marks, T.K.: An improved deep learning architecture for person re-identification. In: Proceedings of the IEEE Conference on Computer Vision and Pattern Recognition, pp. 3908–3916 (2015)
2. Bai, S., Bai, X., Tian, Q.: Scalable person re-identification on supervised smoothed manifold. arXiv preprint arXiv:1703.08359 (2017)
3. Bak, S., Carr, P.: Person re-identification using deformable patch metric learning. In: 2016 IEEE Winter Conference on Applications of Computer Vision (WACV), pp. 1–9. IEEE (2016)
4. Bak, S., Carr, P.: One-shot metric learning for person re-identification. In: The IEEE Conference on Computer Vision and Pattern Recognition (CVPR), July 2017
5. Bianchini, M., Maggini, M., Sarti, L., Scarselli, F.: Recursive neural networks learn to localize faces. Pattern Recogn. Lett. **26**(12), 1885–1895 (2005)
6. Bruna, J., Zaremba, W., Szlam, A., LeCun, Y.: Spectral networks and locally connected networks on graphs. arXiv preprint arXiv:1312.6203 (2013)
7. Chen, D., Li, H., Xiao, T., Yi, S., Wang, X.: Video person re-identification with competitive snippet-similarity aggregation and co-attentive snippet embedding. In: Proceedings of the IEEE Conference on Computer Vision and Pattern Recognition, pp. 1169–1178 (2018)
8. Chen, D., Xu, D., Li, H., Sebe, N., Wang, X.: Group consistent similarity learning via deep CRF for person re-identification. In: Proceedings of the IEEE Conference on Computer Vision and Pattern Recognition, pp. 8649–8658 (2018)
9. Chen, W., Chen, X., Zhang, J., Huang, K.: Beyond triplet loss: a deep quadruplet network for person re-identification. In: The IEEE Conference on Computer Vision and Pattern Recognition (CVPR), July 2017
10. Cheng, D., Gong, Y., Zhou, S., Wang, J., Zheng, N.: Person re-identification by multi-channel parts-based cnn with improved triplet loss function. In: Proceedings of the IEEE Conference on Computer Vision and Pattern Recognition, pp. 1335–1344 (2016)
11. Chu, X., Ouyang, W., Wang, X., et al.: CRF-CNN: modeling structured information in human pose estimation. In: Advances in Neural Information Processing Systems, pp. 316–324 (2016)
12. Chu, X., Yang, W., Ouyang, W., Ma, C., Yuille, A.L., Wang, X.: Multi-context attention for human pose estimation. arXiv preprint arXiv:1702.07432, 1(2) (2017)
13. Defferrard, M., Bresson, X., Vandergheynst, P.: Convolutional neural networks on graphs with fast localized spectral filtering. In: Advances in Neural Information Processing Systems, pp. 3844–3852 (2016)
14. Deng, J., Dong, W., Socher, R., Li, L.-J., Li, K., Fei-Fei, L.: Imagenet: a large-scale hierarchical image database. In: IEEE Conference on Computer Vision and Pattern Recognition, 2009. CVPR 2009, pp. 248–255. IEEE (2009)

15. Felzenszwalb, P.F., Girshick, R.B., McAllester, D., Ramanan, D.: Object detection with discriminatively trained part-based models. IEEE Trans. Pattern Anal. Mach. Intell. **32**(9), 1627–1645 (2010)
16. Garcia, J., Martinel, N., Micheloni, C., Gardel, A.: Person re-identification ranking optimisation by discriminant context information analysis. In: Proceedings of the IEEE International Conference on Computer Vision, pp. 1305–1313 (2015)
17. He, K., Zhang, X., Ren, S., Sun, J.: Deep residual learning for image recognition. In: Proceedings of the IEEE Conference on Computer Vision and Pattern Recognition, pp. 770–778 (2016)
18. Henaff, M., Bruna, J., LeCun, Y.: Deep convolutional networks on graph-structured data. arXiv preprint arXiv:1506.05163 (2015)
19. Ioffe, S., Szegedy, C.: Batch normalization: accelerating deep network training by reducing internal covariate shift. In: International Conference on Machine Learning, pp. 448–456 (2015)
20. Kang, K., et al.: Object detection in videos with tubelet proposal networks. arXiv preprint arXiv:1702.06355 (2017)
21. Karaman, S., Lisanti, G., Bagdanov, A.D., Del Bimbo, A.: Leveraging local neighborhood topology for large scale person re-identification. Pattern Recogn. **47**(12), 3767–3778 (2014)
22. Kingma, D., Ba, J.: Adam: a method for stochastic optimization. arXiv preprint arXiv:1412.6980 (2014)
23. Kipf, T.N., Welling, M.: Semi-supervised classification with graph convolutional networks. arXiv preprint arXiv:1609.02907 (2016)
24. Kodirov, Elyor, Xiang, Tao, Fu, Zhenyong, Gong, Shaogang: Person re-identification by unsupervised ℓ_1 graph learning. In: Leibe, Bastian, Matas, Jiri, Sebe, Nicu, Welling, Max (eds.) ECCV 2016. LNCS, vol. 9905, pp. 178–195. Springer, Cham (2016). https://doi.org/10.1007/978-3-319-46448-0_11
25. Krizhevsky, A., Sutskever, I., Hinton, G.E.: Imagenet classification with deep convolutional neural networks. In: Advances in Neural Information Processing Systems, pp. 1097–1105 (2012)
26. Li, D., Chen, X., Zhang, Z., Huang, K.: Learning deep context-aware features over body and latent parts for person re-identification. In: The IEEE Conference on Computer Vision and Pattern Recognition (CVPR), July 2017
27. Li, D., Chen, X., Zhang, Z., Huang, K.: Learning deep context-aware features over body and latent parts for person re-identification. In: Proceedings of the IEEE Conference on Computer Vision and Pattern Recognition, pp. 384–393 (2017)
28. Li, W., Zhao, R., Xiao, T., Wang, X.: Deepreid: deep filter pairing neural network for person re-identification. In: Proceedings of the IEEE Conference on Computer Vision and Pattern Recognition, pp. 152–159 (2014)
29. Li, W., Zhu, X., Gong, S.: Person re-identification by deep joint learning of multi-loss classification. arXiv preprint arXiv:1705.04724 (2017)
30. Li, W., Zhu, X., Gong, S.: Harmonious attention network for person re-identification. arXiv preprint arXiv:1802.08122 (2018)
31. Li, Y., Ouyang, W., Wang, X., Tang, X.: ViP-CNN: visual phrase guided convolutional neural network. In: 2017 IEEE Conference on Computer Vision and Pattern Recognition (CVPR), pp. 7244–7253. IEEE (2017)
32. Li, Y., Ouyang, W., Zhou, B., Wang, K., Wang, X.: Scene graph generation from objects, phrases and region captions. In: ICCV (2017)

33. Liang, X., Shen, X., Feng, J., Lin, L., Yan, S.: Semantic object parsing with graph LSTM. In: Leibe, B., Matas, J., Sebe, N., Welling, M. (eds.) ECCV 2016. LNCS, vol. 9905, pp. 125–143. Springer, Cham (2016). https://doi.org/10.1007/978-3-319-46448-0_8

34. Liao, S., Hu, Y., Zhu, X., Li, S.Z.: Person re-identification by local maximal occurrence representation and metric learning. In: Proceedings of the IEEE Conference on Computer Vision and Pattern Recognition, pp. 2197–2206 (2015)

35. Lin, J., Ren, L., Lu, J., Feng, J., Zhou, J.: Consistent-aware deep learning for person re-identification in a camera network. In: The IEEE Conference on Computer Vision and Pattern Recognition (CVPR), July 2017

36. Liu, F., Lin, G., Shen, C.: CRF learning with CNN features for image segmentation. Pattern Recogn. **48**(10), 2983–2992 (2015)

37. Liu, J., et al.: Multi-scale triplet CNN for person re-identification. In: Proceedings of the 2016 ACM on Multimedia Conference, pp. 192–196. ACM (2016)

38. Liu, X., Li, H., Shao, J., Chen, D., Wang, X.: Show, tell and discriminate: image captioning by self-retrieval with partially labeled data. arXiv preprint arXiv:1803.08314 (2018)

39. Liu, X., et al.: Hydraplus-net: attentive deep features for pedestrian analysis. In: The IEEE International Conference on Computer Vision (ICCV), Oct 2017

40. Liu, Y., Yan, J., Ouyang, W.: Quality aware network for set to set recognition. In: CVPR, vol. 2, p. 8 (2017)

41. Liu, Z., Wang, D., Lu, H.: Stepwise metric promotion for unsupervised video person re-identification. In: The IEEE International Conference on Computer Vision (ICCV), Oct 2017

42. Loy, C.C., Liu, C., Gong, S.: Person re-identification by manifold ranking. In: 2013 20th IEEE International Conference on Image Processing (ICIP), pp. 3567–3571. IEEE (2013)

43. Mao, C., Li, Y., Zhang, Y., Zhang, Z., Li, X.: Multi-channel pyramid person matching network for person re-identification. arXiv preprint arXiv:1803.02558 (2018)

44. Mills, M.T., Bourbakis, N.G.: Graph-based methods for natural language processing and understandinga survey and analysis. IEEE Trans. Syst. Man Cybern. Syst. **44**(1), 59–71 (2014)

45. Niepert, M., Ahmed, M., Kutzkov, K.: Learning convolutional neural networks for graphs. In: International Conference on Machine Learning, pp. 2014–2023 (2016)

46. van der Oord, A., Kalchbrenner, N., Kavukcuoglu, K.: Pixel recurrent neural networks. arXiv preprint arXiv:1601.06759 (2016)

47. Paisitkriangkrai, S., Shen, C., van den Hengel, A.: Learning to rank in person re-identification with metric ensembles. In: Proceedings of the IEEE Conference on Computer Vision and Pattern Recognition, pp. 1846–1855 (2015)

48. Pavlidis, T.: Structural Pattern Recognition, vol. 1. Springer (2013)

49. Qian, X., Fu, Y., Jiang, Y.-G., Xiang, T., Xue, X.: Multi-scale deep learning architectures for person re-identification. arXiv preprint arXiv:1709.05165 (2017)

50. Quek, A., Wang, Z., Zhang, J., Feng, D.: Structural image classification with graph neural networks. In: 2011 International Conference on Digital Image Computing Techniques and Applications (DICTA), pp. 416–421. IEEE (2011)

51. Ren, S., He, K., Girshick, R., Sun, J.: Faster R-CNN: towards real-time object detection with region proposal networks. In: Advances in Neural Information Processing Systems, pp. 91–99 (2015)

52. Ristani, E., Solera, F., Zou, R., Cucchiara, R., Tomasi, C.: Performance measures and a data set for multi-target, multi-camera tracking. In: European Conference on Computer Vision workshop on Benchmarking Multi-Target Tracking (2016)

53. Scarselli, F., Gori, M., Tsoi, A.C., Hagenbuchner, M., Monfardini, G.: The graph neural network model. IEEE Trans. Neural Netw. **20**(1), 61–80 (2009)
54. Schumann, A., Stiefelhagen, R.: Person re-identification by deep learning attribute-complementary information. In: 2017 IEEE Conference on Computer Vision and Pattern Recognition Workshops (CVPRW), pp. 1435–1443. IEEE (2017)
55. Shen, Y., Li, H., Xiao, T., Yi, S., Chen, D., Wang, X.: Deep group-shuffling random walk for person re-identification. In: Proceedings of the IEEE Conference on Computer Vision and Pattern Recognition, pp. 2265–2274 (2018)
56. Shen, Y., Xiao, T., Li, H., Yi, S., Wang, X.: Learning deep neural networks for vehicle Re-ID with visual-spatio-temporal path proposals. In: 2017 IEEE International Conference on Computer Vision (ICCV), pp. 1918–1927. IEEE (2017)
57. Shen, Y., Xiao, T., Li, H., Yi, S., Wang, X.: End-to-end deep Kronecker-product matching for person re-identification. In: Proceedings of the IEEE Conference on Computer Vision and Pattern Recognition, pp. 6886–6895 (2018)
58. Song, G., Leng, B., Liu, Y., Hetang, C., Cai, S.: Region-based quality estimation network for large-scale person re-identification. arXiv preprint arXiv:1711.08766 (2017)
59. Srivastava, N., Hinton, G.E., Krizhevsky, A., Sutskever, I., Salakhutdinov, R.: Dropout: a simple way to prevent neural networks from overfitting. J. Mach. Learn. Res. **15**(1), 1929–1958 (2014)
60. Su, C., Li, J., Zhang, S., Xing, J., Gao, W., Tian, Q.: Pose-driven deep convolutional model for person re-identification. In: The IEEE International Conference on Computer Vision (ICCV), Oct 2017
61. Sun, Y., Zheng, L., Deng, W., Wang, S.: SVDNet for pedestrian retrieval. In: The IEEE International Conference on Computer Vision (ICCV), Oct 2017
62. Wu, F., Li, S., Zhao, T., Ngan, K.N.: Model-based face reconstruction using sift flow registration and spherical harmonics. In: 2016 23rd International Conference on Pattern Recognition (ICPR), pp. 1774–1779. IEEE (2016)
63. Wu, F., Li, S., Zhao, T., Ngan, K.N.: 3D facial expression reconstruction using cascaded regression. arXiv preprint arXiv:1712.03491 (2017)
64. Xiao, T., Li, H., Ouyang, W., Wang, X.: Learning deep feature representations with domain guided dropout for person re-identification. In: Proceedings of the IEEE Conference on Computer Vision and Pattern Recognition, pp. 1249–1258 (2016)
65. Xiao, T., Li, S., Wang, B., Lin, L., Wang, X.: Joint detection and identification feature learning for person search. In: Proceedings of the CVPR (2017)
66. Yan, S., Xiong, Y., Lin, D.: Spatial temporal graph convolutional networks for skeleton-based action recognition. arXiv preprint arXiv:1801.07455 (2018)
67. Yang, W., Li, S., Ouyang, W., Li, H., Wang, X.: Learning feature pyramids for human pose estimation. In: The IEEE International Conference on Computer Vision (ICCV), vol. 2 (2017)
68. Yang, W., Ouyang, W., Li, H., Wang, X.: End-to-end learning of deformable mixture of parts and deep convolutional neural networks for human pose estimation. In: Proceedings of the IEEE Conference on Computer Vision and Pattern Recognition, pp. 3073–3082 (2016)
69. Ye, M., Liang, C., Wang, Z., Leng, Q., Chen, J.: Ranking optimization for person re-identification via similarity and dissimilarity. In: Proceedings of the 23rd ACM International Conference on Multimedia, pp. 1239–1242. ACM (2015)
70. Ye, M., et al.: Person reidentification via ranking aggregation of similarity pulling and dissimilarity pushing. IEEE Trans. Multimed. **18**(12), 2553–2566 (2016)

71. Yi, D., Lei, Z., Liao, S., Li, S.Z.: Deep metric learning for person re-identification. In: 2014 22nd International Conference on Pattern Recognition (ICPR), pp. 34–39. IEEE (2014)
72. Yu, H.-X., Wu, A., Zheng, W.-S.: Cross-view asymmetric metric learning for unsupervised person re-identification. In: The IEEE International Conference on Computer Vision (ICCV), Oct 2017
73. Zhao, H., et al.: Spindle net: person re-identification with human body region guided feature decomposition and fusion. In: Proceedings of the IEEE Conference on Computer Vision and Pattern Recognition, pp. 1077–1085 (2017)
74. Zhao, L., Li, X., Wang, J., Zhuang, Y.: Deeply-learned part-aligned representations for person re-identification. arXiv preprint arXiv:1707.07256 (2017)
75. Zheng, L., Shen, L., Tian, L., Wang, S., Wang, J., Tian, Q.: Scalable person re-identification: a benchmark. In: Proceedings of the IEEE International Conference on Computer Vision, pp. 1116–1124 (2015)
76. Zheng, S., et al.: Conditional random fields as recurrent neural networks. In: Proceedings of the IEEE International Conference on Computer Vision, pp. 1529–1537 (2015)
77. Zheng, Z., Zheng, L., Yang, Y.: Unlabeled samples generated by GAN improve the person re-identification baseline in vitro. In: Proceedings of the IEEE International Conference on Computer Vision (2017)
78. Zhong, Z., Zheng, L., Cao, D., Li, S.: Re-ranking person re-identification with k-reciprocal encoding. In: The IEEE Conference on Computer Vision and Pattern Recognition (CVPR), July 2017
79. Zhong, Z., Zheng, L., Kang, G., Li, S., Yang, Y.: Random erasing data augmentation. arXiv preprint arXiv:1708.04896 (2017)
80. Zhou, J., Yu, P., Tang, W., Wu, Y.: Efficient online local metric adaptation via negative samples for person re-identification. In: The IEEE International Conference on Computer Vision (ICCV), Oct 2017
81. Zhou, S., Wang, J., Wang, J., Gong, Y., Zheng, N.: Point to set similarity based deep feature learning for person re-identification. In: The IEEE Conference on Computer Vision and Pattern Recognition (CVPR), July 2017

Learning and Matching Multi-View Descriptors for Registration of Point Clouds

Lei Zhou[1], Siyu Zhu[1], Zixin Luo[1], Tianwei Shen[1], Runze Zhang[1(✉)], Mingmin Zhen[1], Tian Fang[2], and Long Quan[1]

[1] Hong Kong University of Science and Technology, Hong Kong, China
{lzhouai,szhu,zluoag,tshenaa,rzhangaj,mzhen,quan}@cse.ust.hk
[2] Shenzhen Zhuke Innovation Technology (Altizure), Shenzhen, China
fangtian@altizure.com

Abstract. Critical to the registration of point clouds is the establishment of a set of accurate correspondences between points in 3D space. The correspondence problem is generally addressed by the design of discriminative 3D local descriptors on the one hand, and the development of robust matching strategies on the other hand. In this work, we first propose a multi-view local descriptor, which is learned from the images of multiple views, for the description of 3D keypoints. Then, we develop a robust matching approach, aiming at rejecting outlier matches based on the efficient inference via belief propagation on the defined graphical model. We have demonstrated the boost of our approaches to registration on the public scanning and multi-view stereo datasets. The superior performance has been verified by the intensive comparisons against a variety of descriptors and matching methods.

Keywords: Point cloud registration · 3D descriptor · Robust matching

1 Introduction

Registration of point clouds integrates 3D data from different sources into a common coordinate system, serving as an essential component of many high-level applications like 3D modeling [1,2], SLAM [3] and robotic perception [4]. Critical to a registration task is the determination of correspondences between spatially localized 3D points within each cloud. To tackle the correspondence problem, on the one hand, a bunch of 3D local descriptors [5–12] have been developed to

---

Lei Zhou and Zixin Luo were summer interns, and Tianwei Shen and Runze Zhang were interns at Everest Innovation Technology (Altizure).
Siyu Zhu is with Alibaba A.I. Labs since Oct. 2017.

Electronic supplementary material The online version of this chapter (https://doi.org/10.1007/978-3-030-01267-0_31) contains supplementary material, which is available to authorized users.

ⓒ Springer Nature Switzerland AG 2018
V. Ferrari et al. (Eds.): ECCV 2018, LNCS 11219, pp. 527–544, 2018.
https://doi.org/10.1007/978-3-030-01267-0_31

facilitate the description of 3D keypoints. On the other hand, matching strategies [13–15] have also been progressing towards higher accuracy and robustness.

The exploration of 3D geometric descriptors has long been the focus of interest in point cloud registration. It involves the hand-crafted geometric descriptors [5–9] as well as the learned ones [10–12,16]. Both kinds of methods mainly rely on 3D local geometries. Meanwhile, with the significant progress of CNN-based 2D patch descriptors [17–21], more importance is attached to leveraging the 2D projections for the description of underlying 3D structures [22–25]. Particularly for the point cloud data generally co-registered with camera images [26–29], the fusion of multiple image views, which has reported success on various tasks [30–33], is expected to further improve the discriminative power of 3D local descriptors. With this motivation, we propose a multi-view descriptor, named MVDesc, for the description of 3D keypoints based on the synergy of the multi-view fusion techniques and patch descriptor learning. Rather than a replacement, the MVDesc is well complementary to existing geometric descriptors [5–12].

Given the local descriptors, the matching problem is another vital issue in point cloud registration. A set of outlier-free point matches is desired by most registration algorithms [15,34–38]. Currently, the matching strategies, *e.g.*, the nearest neighbor search, mutual best [15] and ratio test [13], basically estimate correspondences according to the similarities of local descriptors alone. Without considering the global geometric consistency, these methods are prone to spurious matches between locally-similar 3D structures. Efforts are also spent on jointly solving the outlier suppression via line process and the optimization of global registration [15]. But the spatial organizations of 3D point matches are still overlooked when identifying outliers. To address this, we develop a robust matching approach by explicitly considering the spatial consistency of point matches in 3D space. We seek to filter outlier matches based on a graphical model describing their spatial properties and provide an efficient solution via belief propagation.

The main contributions of this work can be summarized twofold. (1) We are the first to leverage the fusion of multiple image views for the description of 3D keypoints when tackling point cloud registration. (2) The proposed effective and efficient outlier filter, which is based on a graphical model and solved by belief propagation, remarkably enhances the robustness of 3D point matching.

2   Related Works

3D Local Descriptor. The representation of a 3D local structure used to rely on traditional geometric descriptors such as Spin Images [5], PFH [6], FPFH [7], SHOT [8], USC [9] and *et al.*, which are mainly produced based on the histograms over local geometric attributes. Recent studies seek to learn descriptors from different representations of local geometries, like volumetric representations of 3D patches [10], point sets [12] and depth maps [16]. The CGF [11] still leverages the traditional spherical histograms to capture the local geometry but learns to map the high-dimensional histograms to a low-dimensional space for compactness.

Rather than only using geometric properties, some existing works refer to extracting descriptors from RGB images that are commonly co-registered with point clouds as in scanning datasets [26–28] and 3D reconstruction datasets [29,39]. Registration frameworks like [22–25] use SIFT descriptors [13] as the representations of 3D keypoints based on their projections in single-view RGB images. Besides, the other state-of-the-art 2D descriptors like DeepDesc [17], L2-Net [18] and *et al.* [19–21] can easily migrate here for the description of 3D local structures.

Multi-view Fusion. The multi-view fusion technique is used to integrate information from multiple views into a single representation. It has been widely proved by the literature that the technique effectively boosts the performance of instance-level detection [30], recognition [31,32] and classification [33] compared with a single view. Su *et al.* [30] first propose a probabilistic representation of a 3D-object class model for the scenario where an object is positioned at the center of a dense viewing sphere. A more general strategy of multi-view fusion is *view pooling* [31–33,40], which aggregates the feature maps of multiple views via element-wise maximum operation.

Matching. The goal of matching for registration is to find correspondences across 3D point sets given keypoint descriptors. Almost all the registration algorithms [15,34–38] demand accurate point correspondences as input. Nearest-neighbor search, mutual best filtering [15] and ratio test [13] are effective ways of searching for potential matches based on local similarities for general matching tasks. However, as mentioned above, these strategies are prone to mismatches without considering the geometric consistency. To absorb geometric information, [41] and [42] discover matches in geometric agreement using game-theoretic scheme. Ma *et al.* [43] propose to reject outliers by enforcing consistency in local neighborhood. Zhou *et al.* [15] use a RANSAC-style tuple test to eliminate matches with inconsistent scales. Besides, the line process model [44] is applied in registration domain to account for the presence of outliers implicitly [15].

3   Multi-view Local Descriptor (MVDesc)

In this section, we propose to learn multi-view descriptors (MVDesc) for 3D keypoints which combine multi-view fusion techniques [30–33] with patch descriptor learning [17–21]. Specifically, we first propose a new view-fusion architecture to integrate feature maps across views into a single representation. Second, we build the MVDesc network for learning by putting the fusion architecture above multiple feature networks [19]. Each feature network is used to extract feature maps from the local patch of each view.

3.1   Multi-view Fusion

Currently, *view pooling* is the dominant fusion technique used to merge feature maps from different views [31–33,40]. However, as reported by the literature [32,

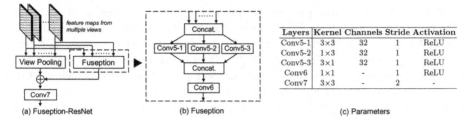

Fig. 1. An overview of proposed Fuseption-ResNet (FRN). (a) Architecture of FRN that fuses feature maps of multiple views. Backed by the view pooling branch as a shortcut connection, (b) the Fuseption branch takes charge of learning the residual mapping. (c) The parameters of the convolutional layers are listed

45, 46], the pooling operation is somewhat risky in terms of feature aggregation due to its effect of smoothing out the subtle local patterns. Inspired by ResNet [47], we propose an architecture termed *Fuseption-ResNet* which uses the view pooling as a shortcut connection and adds a sibling branch termed *Fuseption* in charge of learning the underlying residual mapping.

Fuseption. As shown in Fig. 1(b), the Fuseption is an Inception-style [48,49] architecture capped above multi-view feature maps. First, following the structure of inception modules [48,49], three lightweight cross-spatial filters with different kernel sizes, 3×3, 1×3 and 3×1, are adopted to extract different types of features. Second, the 1×1 convolution Conv6, employed above concatenated feature maps, is responsible for the merging of correlation statistics across channels and the dimension reduction as suggested by [48,50].

Fuseption-ResNet (FRN). Inspired by the effectiveness of skip connections in ResNet [47], we take view pooling as a shortcut in addition to Fuseption as shown in Fig. 1(a). As opposed to the view pooling branch which is in charge of extracting the strongest responses across views [31], the Fuseption branch is responsible for learning the underlying residual mapping. Both engaged branches reinforce each other in term of accuracy and convergence rate. On the one hand, the residual branch, Fuseption, guarantees no worse accuracy compared to just using view pooling. This is because if view pooling is optimal, the residual can be easily pulled to zeros during training. On the other hand, the shortcut branch, view pooling, greatly accelerates the convergence of learning MVDesc as illustrated in Fig. 2(a). Intuitively, since the view pooling branch has extracted the essential strongest responses across views, it is easier for the Fuseption branch to just learn the residual mapping.

3.2   Learning MVDesc

Network. The network for learning MVDesc is built by putting the proposed FRN above multiple parallel feature networks. We use the feature network from

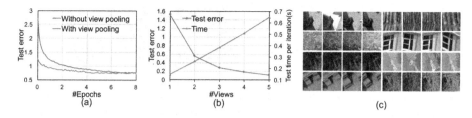

Fig. 2. (a) Test error of our MVDesc network with or without the view pooling branch. Using view pooling as a shortcut connection contributes to much faster convergence of learning. (b) Test error and forward time per iteration of MVDesc network with respect to the number of fused views. Three views are chosen as a good trade-off between accuracy and efficiency. (c) The sample multi-view patches produced by the collected SfM database for training

MatchNet [19] as the basis, in which the bottleneck layer and the metric network are removed. The feature networks of multiple views share the same parameters of corresponding convolutional layers. The channel number of Conv6 is set to be the same as that of feature maps output by a feature network. The ReLU activation [51] follows each convolutional layer except the last Conv7. A layer of L2 normalization is appended after Conv7 whose channel number can be set flexibly to adjust the dimension of descriptors. The parameters of the full network are detailed in the supplemental material.

Loss. The two-tower Siamese architecture [17,52] is adopted here for training. The formulation of the double-margin contrastive loss is used [53], *i.e.*,

$$L(\mathbf{x}_a, \mathbf{x}_b) = y \max(||\mathbf{d}_a - \mathbf{d}_b||_2 - \tau_1, 0) + (1 - y) \max(\tau_2 - ||\mathbf{d}_a - \mathbf{d}_b||_2, 0), \quad (1)$$

where $y = 1$ for positive pairs and 0 otherwise. $\mathbf{d}_a$ and $\mathbf{d}_b$ are L2-normalized MVDesc descriptors of the two sets of multi-view patches $\mathbf{x}_a$ and $\mathbf{x}_b$, output by the two towers. We set the margins $\tau_1 = 0.3, \tau_2 = 0.6$ in experiments.

View Number. Unlike [31–33] using 12 or 20 views for objects, we adopt only 3 views in our MVDesc network for the description of local keypoints, which is a good tradeoff between accuracy and efficiency as shown in Fig. 2(b).

Data Preparation. Current available patch datasets generally lack sufficient multi-view patches for training. For example, one of the largest training sets Brown [54,55] only possesses less than 25k 3D points with at least 6 views. Therefore, we prepare the training data similar to [20] based on the self-collected Structure-from-Motion (SfM) database. The database consists of 31 outdoor scenes of urban and rural areas captured by UAV and well reconstructed by a standard 3D reconstruction pipeline [1,2,56–60]. Each scene contains averagely about 900 images and 250k tracks with at least 6 projections. The multi-view patches of size 64 × 64 are cropped from the projections of each track according to SIFT scales and orientations [20], as displayed in Fig. 2(c). A positive training

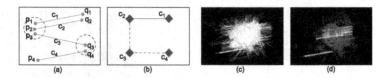

Fig. 3. (a) $c_{1\sim4}$ are four pairs of point matches. (b) The graph is defined to model the neighboring relationship between $c_{1\sim4}$. The solid/dashed lines link between compatible/incompatible neighbors. (c) 4,721 pairs of putative point matches. (d) 109 true match pairs refined by our RMBP

pair is formed by two independent sets of triple-view patches from the same track, while a negative pair from different tracks. A total number of 10 million pairs with equal ratio of positives and negatives are evenly sampled from all the 31 scenes. We turn the patches into grayscale, subtract the intensities by 128 and divide them by 160 [19].

Training. We train the network from scratch using SGD with a momentum of 0.9, a weight decay of 0.0005 and a batch size of 256. The learning rate drops by 30% after every epoch with a base of 0.0001 using exponential decay. The training is generally done within 10 epochs.

4   Robust Matching Using Belief Propagation (RMBP)

In this section, we are devoted to enhancing the accuracy and robustness of 3D point matching. Firstly, a graphical model is defined to describe the spatial organizations of point matches. Secondly, each match pair is verified by the inference from the graphical model via belief propagation. Notably, the proposed method is complementary to the existing matching algorithms [13–15,61].

4.1   Matching Model

It can be readily observed that inlier point correspondences generally hold *spatial proximity*. We illustrate it in Fig. 3(a) where $c_1 = (\mathbf{p}_1, \mathbf{q}_1)$, $c_2 = (\mathbf{p}_2, \mathbf{q}_2)$ and $c_4 = (\mathbf{p}_4, \mathbf{q}_4)$ are three pairs of inlier correspondences. For any two pairs of inlier matches, their points in each point cloud are either spatially close to each other like $\langle \mathbf{p}_1, \mathbf{p}_2 \rangle$ and $\langle \mathbf{q}_1, \mathbf{q}_2 \rangle$ or far away from each other like $\langle \mathbf{p}_2, \mathbf{p}_4 \rangle$ and $\langle \mathbf{q}_2, \mathbf{q}_4 \rangle$ at the same time. On the contrary, outlier correspondences tend to show spatial disorders. This observation implies the probabilistic dependence between neighboring point correspondences which can be modeled by a probabilistic graph.

Formally, we first define the neighborhood of point correspondences as follows. Two pairs of point correspondences $c_i = (\mathbf{p}_i, \mathbf{q}_i)$ and $c_j = (\mathbf{p}_j, \mathbf{q}_j)$ are considered as neighbors if either $\mathbf{p}_i$ and $\mathbf{p}_j$, or $\mathbf{q}_i$ and $\mathbf{q}_j$, are mutually k-nearest neighbors, *i.e.*,

$$\max(\text{rank}(\mathbf{p}_i, \mathbf{p}_j), \text{rank}(\mathbf{p}_j, \mathbf{p}_i)) < k, \tag{2}$$

$$\text{or}\quad \max(\text{rank}(\mathbf{q}_i, \mathbf{q}_j), \text{rank}(\mathbf{q}_j, \mathbf{q}_i)) < k, \tag{3}$$

where $\text{rank}(\mathbf{x}, \mathbf{y})$ denotes the rank of distance of point $\mathbf{y}$ with respect to point $\mathbf{x}$. Then, the neighboring relationship between c_i and c_j can be further divided into two categories: if Condition 2 and 3 are satisfied simultaneously, c_i and c_j are called *compatible* neighbors. They are very likely to co-exist as inlier matches. But if only one of Condition 2 or 3 is satisfied by one point pair but another pair of points in the other point cloud locate far apart from each other, *e.g.*,

$$\min(\text{rank}(\mathbf{p}_i, \mathbf{p}_j), \text{rank}(\mathbf{p}_j, \mathbf{p}_i)) > l, \qquad (4)$$

$$\text{or} \quad \min(\text{rank}(\mathbf{q}_i, \mathbf{q}_j), \text{rank}(\mathbf{q}_j, \mathbf{q}_i)) > l, \qquad (5)$$

c_i and c_j are called *incompatible* neighbors, as it is impossible for two match pairs breaching spatial proximity to be inliers simultaneously. The threshold parameter k in Condition 2 and 3 is set to a relatively small value, while the parameter l in Condition 4 and 5 is set to be larger than k by a considerable margin. These settings are intended to ensure sufficiently strict conditions on identifying compatible or incompatible neighbors for robustness.

Based on the spatial property of point matches stated above, an underlying graphical model is built to model the pairwise interactions between neighboring match pairs, as shown in Fig. 3(a) and (b). The nodes in graphical model are first defined as a set of binary variables $\mathcal{X} = \{x_i\}$ each associated with a pair of point correspondence. $x_i \in \{0, 1\}$ indicates the latent state of being an outlier or inlier, respectively. Then the undirected edges between nodes are formed based on the compatible and incompatible neighboring relationship defined above. With the purpose of rejecting outliers, the objective here is to compute the marginal of being an inlier for each point correspondence by performing inference on the defined model.

4.2 Inference by Belief Propagation

The task of computing marginals on nodes of a cyclic network is known to be NP-hard [62]. As a disciplined inference algorithm, loopy belief propagation (LBP) provides approximate yet compelling inference on arbitrary networks [63].

In the case of our graphical network with binary variables and pairwise interactions, the probabilistic distributions of all node variables are first initialized as $[0.5, 0.5]^T$ with no prior imposed. Then the iterative message update step of a standard LBP algorithm at iteration t can be written as

$$\mathbf{m}_{ij}^{t+1} = \frac{1}{Z} \mathbf{F}_{ij} \mathbf{m}_i \prod_{k \in \partial i \backslash j} \mathbf{m}_{ki}^t. \qquad (6)$$

Here, ∂i denotes the set of neighbors of node x_i and Z is the L1 norm of the incoming message for normalization. The message $\mathbf{m}_{ij}$ passed from node x_i to x_j is a two-dimensional vector, which represents the belief of x_j's probability distribution inferred by x_i. So is the constant message $\mathbf{m}_i$ passed from the observation of node x_i, which indicates the likelihood distribution of x_i given its observation measurements like descriptor similarity. The first and second components of the messages are the probabilities of being an outlier and an inlier, respectively. The product of messages is component-wise. The 2×2 matrix $\mathbf{F}_{ij}$ is the compatibility matrix of node x_i and x_j. Based on the neighboring relationship analyzed above, the compatibility matrix is supposed to favor the possibility that both nodes are inliers if they are compatible neighbors and the reverse if they are incompatible neighbors. In order to explicitly specify the bias, the compatibility matrices take two forms in the two different cases, respectively:

$$\mathbf{F}^{+} = \begin{bmatrix} 1 & 1 \\ 1 & \lambda \end{bmatrix} \quad \text{or} \quad \mathbf{F}^{-} = \begin{bmatrix} \lambda & \lambda \\ \lambda & 1 \end{bmatrix}. \tag{7}$$

The parameter λ takes a biased value greater than 1. To guarantee the convergence of LBP, Simon's condition [64] is enforced and the value of λ is thus constrained by

$$\max_{x_i \in \mathcal{X}} |\partial i| \cdot \log \lambda < 2, \tag{8}$$

in which way λ is set adaptively according to the boundary condition. The proof of the convergence's condition is detailed in the supplemental material. After convergence, the marginal distribution of node x_i is derived by

$$\mathbf{b}_i = \frac{1}{Z} \mathbf{m}_i \prod_{k \in \partial i} \mathbf{m}_{ki}, \tag{9}$$

which unifies implication from individual observations and beliefs from structured local neighborhood. After the inference, point matches with low marginals (*e.g.* < 0.5) are discarded as outliers. It greatly contributes to the matching accuracy as shown in Fig. 3(d) where 109 true match pairs are refined from 4,721 noisy putative match pairs.

Complexity Analysis. The complexity of LBP is known to be linear to the number of edges in the graph [65]. And the Condition 2 and 3 bound the degree of each node to be less than $2k$, so that the upper bound of RMBP's complexity is linear with the number of nodes.

5   Experiments

In this section, we first individually evaluate the proposed MVDesc and RMBP in Sects. 5.1 and 5.2 respectively. Then the two approaches are validated on the tasks of geometric registration in Sect. 5.3.

All the experiments, including the training and testing of neural networks, are done on a machine with a 8-core Intel i7-4770K, a 32GB memory and a NVIDIA GTX980 graphics card. In the experiments below, when we say putative matching, we mean finding the correspondences of points whose descriptors are mutually closest to each other in Euclidean space between two point sets. The matching is implemented based on OpenBLAS [66]. The traditional geometric descriptors [6–9] are produced based on PCL [67].

Table 1. The mAPs of descriptors in the three tasks of HPatches benchmark [68]. Our MVDesc holds the top place in all the three tasks

	SIFT [13]	DeepDesc [17]	L2-Net [18]	View pooling [31]	MVDesc
Patch verification	0.646	0.716	0.792	0.883	**0.921**
Image matching	0.111	0.172	0.309	0.312	**0.325**
Patch retrieval	0.269	0.357	0.414	0.456	**0.530**

5.1 Evaluation of MVDesc

The target here is to compare the description ability of the proposed MVDesc against the state-of-the-art patch descriptors [13,17,18] and geometric descriptors [6–11].

5.1.1 Comparisons with Patch Descriptors

Setup. We choose HPatches [68], one of the largest local patch benchmarks, for evaluation. It consists of 59 cases and 96,315 6-view patch sets. First, we partition each patch set into two subsets by splitting the 6-views into halves. Then, the 3-view patches are taken as input to generate descriptors. We set up the three benchmark tasks in [68] by reorganizing the 3-view patches and use the mean average precision (mAP) as measurement. For the patch verification task, we collect all the 96,315 positive pairs of 3-view patches and 100,000 random negatives. For the image matching task, we apply putative matching across the two half sets of each case after mixing 6,000 unrelated distractors into every half. For the patch retrieval task, we use the full 96,315 6-view patch sets each of which corresponds to a 3-view patch set as a query and the other 3-view set in the database. Besides, we mix 100,000 3-view patch sets from an independent image set into the database for distraction.

We make comparisons with the baseline SIFT [13] and the state-of-the-art DeepDesc [17] and L2-Net [18], for which we randomly choose a single view from the 3-view patches. To verify the advantage of our FRN over the widely-used view pooling [31–33] in multi-view fusion, we remove the Fuseption branch from our MVDesc network and train with the same data and configuration. All the descriptors have the dimensionality of 128.

Results. The statistics in Table 1 show that our MVDesc achieves the highest mAPs in all the three tasks. First, it demonstrates the advantage of our FRN over view pooling [31–33,40,69] in terms of multi-view fusion. Second, the improvement of MVDesc over DeepDesc [17] and L2-Net [18] suggests the benefits of leveraging more image views than a single one. Additionally, we illustrate in Fig. 4(a) the trade-off between the mAP of the image matching task and the dimension of our MVDesc. The mAP rises but gradually saturates with the increase of dimension.

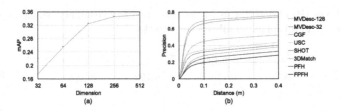

Fig. 4. (a) The trade-off of mAP versus dimension of our MVDesc on the HPatches benchmark [68]; (b) The change of matching precisions *w.r.t.* the varying threshold of point distances on the TUM dataset [28]. The 128- and 32-dimensional MVDesc rank first and second at any threshold

Table 2. Precisions and recalls of matching on the TUM dataset [28] when the threshold of points' distances equals to 0.1 meters. The average time taken to encode 1,000 descriptors is also compared. Our MVDesc hits the best in terms of precision, recall and efficiency

	CGF [11]	FPFH [7]	PFH [6]	SHOT [8]	3DMatch [10]	USC [9]	MVDesc	
Dim.	32	33	125	352	512	1980	32	128
Precision	0.447	0.194	0.244	0.322	0.278	0.342	0.664	**0.695**
Recall	0.215	0.229	0.265	0.093	0.114	0.026	0.523	**0.580**
Time (s)	7.60	1.49	14.40	0.29	2.60	0.73	**0.22**	0.23

5.1.2 Comparisons with Geometric Descriptors

Setup. Here, we perform evaluations on matching tasks of the RGB-D dataset TUM [28]. Following [11], we collect up to 3,000 pairs of overlapping point cloud fragments from 10 scenes of TUM. Each fragment is recovered from independent RGB-D sequences of 50 frames. We detect keypoints from the fragments by SIFT3D [70] and then generate geometric descriptors, including PFH [6], FPFH [7], SHOT [8], USC [9], 3DMatch [10] and CGF [11]. Our MVDesc is derived from the projected patches of keypoints in three randomly-selected camera views. For easier comparison, two dimensions, 32 and 128, of MVDesc (MVDesc-32 and MVDesc-128) are adopted. Putative matching is applied to all the fragment pairs to obtain correspondences. Following [11], we measure the performance of descriptors by the fraction of correspondences whose ground-truth distances lie below the given threshold.

Results. The precision of point matches *w.r.t.* the threshold of point distances is depicted in Fig. 4(b). The MVDesc-128 and MVDesc-32 rank first and second in precision at any threshold, outperforming the state-of-the-art works by a considerable margin. We report in Table 2 the precisions and recalls when setting the threshold to 0.1 meters and the average time of producing 1,000 descriptors. Producing geometric descriptors in general is slower than MVDesc due to the cost of computing local histograms, although the computation has been accelerated by multi-thread parallelism.

5.2   Evaluation of RMBP

Setup. To evaluate the performance of outlier rejection, we compare RMBP with RANSAC and two state-of-the-art works - Sparse Matching Game (SMG) [42] and Locality Preserving Matching (LPM) [43]. All the parameters of methods have been tuned to give the best results. We match 100 pairs of same-scale point clouds from 20 diverse indoor and outdoor scenes of TUM [28], ScanNet [65] and EPFL [39] datasets. We keep a constant number of inlier correspondences and continuously add outlier correspondences for distraction. The evaluation uses the metrics: the mean precisions and recalls of outlier rejection and inlier selection. Formally, we write $OP = \frac{\#true\ rejections}{\#rejections}$, $OR = \frac{\#true\ rejections}{\#outliers}$, $IP = \frac{\#kept\ inliers}{\#kept\ matches}$, $IR = \frac{\#kept\ inliers}{\#inliers}$. We also estimate the transformations from kept matches using RANSAC and collect the median point distance after registration.

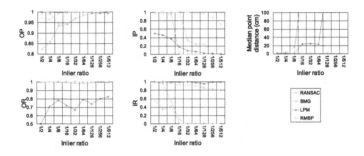

Fig. 5. The mean precisions and recalls of outlier rejection (OP, OR) and inlier selection (IP, IR), as well as median point distance after registration, *w.r.t.* the inlier ratio. RMBP performs well in all metrics and at all inlier ratios while RANSAC, SMG [42] and LPM [43] fail to give valid registrations when the inlier ratio drops below $\frac{1}{8}$, $\frac{1}{8}$ and $\frac{1}{64}$, respectively

Results. The measurements with respect to the inlier ratio are shown in Fig. 5. First, RMBP is the only method achieving high performance in all metrics and at all inlier ratios. Second, RANSAC, SMG and LPM fail to give valid registrations when the inlier ratio drops below $\frac{1}{8}$, $\frac{1}{8}$ and $\frac{1}{64}$, respectively. They obtain high OP and OR but low IP or IR when the inlier ratio is smaller than $\frac{1}{16}$, because they tend to reject almost all the matches.

5.3   Geometric Registration

In this section, we verify the practical usage of the proposed MVDesc and RMBP by the tasks of geometric registration. We operate on point cloud data obtained from two different sources: the point clouds scanned by RGB-D sensors and those reconstructed by multi-view stereo (MVS) algorithms [71].

5.3.1   Registration of Scanning Data

Setup. We use the task of loop closure as in [10,11] based on the dataset Scan-Net [72], where we check whether two overlapping sub-maps of an indoor scene can be effectively detected and registered. Similar to [10,11], we build up independent fragments of 50 sequential RGB-D frames from 6 different indoor scenes of ScanNet [72]. For each scene, we collect more than 500 fragment pairs with labeled overlap obtained from the ground truth for registration.

The commonly-used registration algorithm, putative matching plus RANSAC, is adopted in combination with various descriptors [6–11]. The proposed RMBP serves as an optional step before RANSAC. We use the same metric as [10,11], *i.e.*, the precision and recall of registration of fragment pairs. Following [10], a registration is viewed as true positive if the estimated Euclidean transformation yields more than 30% overlap between registered fragments and transformation error less then 0.2 m. We see a registration as positive if there exist more than 20 pairs of point correspondences after RANSAC.

Fig. 6. Challenging cases of loop closures from the ScanNet dataset [72]. The images in the top row indicate very limited overlap shared by the fragment pairs. Our MVDesc-32+RMBP succeeds in the registration of these cases while the top-performing geometric descriptor CGF-32 [11] fails no matter whether RMBP is employed

Table 3. The quantitative comparisons of 3D descriptors on registration of the ScanNet dataset [72]. The superscript * means the proposed RMBP is applied. The RMBP generally lifts the precisions and recalls of registration for almost all the descriptors. Our MVDesc well surpasses the state-of-the-art works in recall with comparable precision and run-time of registration

	CGF [11]	FPFH [7]	PFH [6]	SHOT [8]	3DMatch [10]	USC [9]	MVDesc	
Dim.	32	33	125	352	512	1980	32	128
Precision	0.914	0.825	0.866	0.875	0.890	0.790	0.865	0.910
Precision*	0.927	0.856	0.864	0.928	0.934	0.795	0.892	0.906
Recall	0.350	0.119	0.147	0.178	0.185	0.124	0.421	0.490
Recall*	0.419	0.272	0.338	0.198	0.145	0.157	0.482	0.513
Time (s)	0.5	0.5	0.7	1.8	2.4	8.4	0.5	0.7

Results. The precisions, recalls and the average time of registration per pair are reported in Table 3. Our MVDesc-32 and MVDesc-128 both surpass the counterparts by a significant margin in recall while with comparable precision and efficiency. Our versatile RMBP well improves the precisions for 6 out of 8 descriptors and lifts the recalls for 7 out of 8 descriptors. The sample registration results of overlap-deficient fragments are visualized in Fig. 6.

Indoor Reconstruction. The practical usage of MVDesc is additionally evaluated by indoor reconstruction of the ScanNet dataset [72]. We first build up reliable local fragments through RGB-D odometry following [73,74] and then globally register the fragments based on [15]. The RMBP is applied for outlier filtering. The FPFH [7] used in [15] is replaced by SIFT [13], CGF-32 [11] or MVDesc-32 to establish correspondences. We also test the collaboration of CGF-32 and MVDesc-32 by combining their correspondences. Our MVDesc-32 contributes to visually compelling reconstruction as shown in Fig. 7(a). And we find that MVDesc-32 functions as a solid complement to CGF-32 as shown in Fig. 7(b), especially for the scenarios with rich textures.

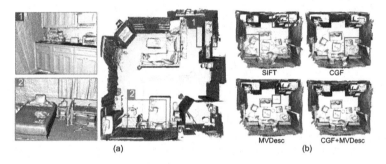

Fig. 7. (a) A complete reconstruction of an apartment from ScanNet [72] using our MVDesc-32. (b) The reconstructions using SIFT [13], CGF-32 [11] and MVDesc-32. The collaboration of MVDesc-32 and CGF-32 yields the best reconstruction as shown in the last cell of (b)

Registration of Multi-view Stereo (MVS) Data. Setup. Aside from the scanning data, we run registration on the four scenes of the MVS benchmark EPFL [39]. First, we split the cameras of each scene into two clusters in space highlighting the difference between camera views, as shown in Fig. 8. Then, the ground-truth camera poses of each cluster are utilized to independently reconstruct the dense point clouds by the MVS algorithm [71]. Next, we detect keypoints by SIFT3D [70] and generate descriptors [6–11] for each point cloud. The triple-view patches required by MVDesc-32 are obtained by projecting keypoints into 3 visible image views randomly with occlusion test by ray racing [75]. After, the correspondences between the two point clouds of each scene are obtained by putative matching and then RMBP filtering. Finally, we register the two point clouds of each scene based on FGR [15] using estimated correspondences.

Results. Our MVDesc-32 and RMBP help to achieve valid registrations for all the four scenes, whilst none of the geometric descriptors including CGF [11], 3DMatch [10], FPFH [7], PFH [6], SHOT [8] and USC [9] do, as shown in Fig. 8. It is found that the failure is mainly caused by the geometrically symmetric patterns of the four scenes. We show the correspondences between CGF-32 features [11] in Fig. 9 as an example. The putative matching has resulted in a large number of ambiguous correspondences between keypoints located at the symmetric positions. And in essence, our RMBP is incapable of resolving the ambiguity in such cases though, because the correspondences in a symmetric structure still adhere to the geometric consistency. Ultimately, the ambiguous matches lead to the horizontally-flipped registration results as shown in Fig. 8. At least in the EPFL benchmark [39], the proposed MVDesc descriptor shows superior ability of description to the geometric ones.

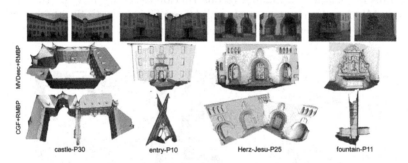

Fig. 8. Registrations of models of EPFL benchmark [39]. Given the same keypoints, our MVDesc-32+RMBP accomplishes correct registrations while CGF-32 [11]+RMBP fails due to the symmetric ambiguity of the geometry

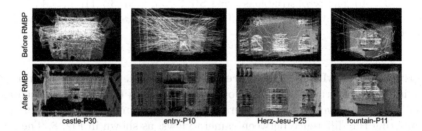

Fig. 9. Spurious correspondences of CGF features [11] before and after RMBP filtering. The two point clouds of [39] (colored in yellow and red) have been overlaid together by the ground truth transformation for visualization. Although our RMBP has eliminated most of the unorganized false matches, it is incapable of rejecting those ambiguous outliers arising from the ambiguity of the symmetric geometry

6   Conclusion

In this paper, we address the correspondence problem for the registration of point clouds. First, a multi-view descriptor, named MVDesc, has been proposed for the encoding of 3D keypoints, which strengthens the representation by applying the fusion of image views [31–33] to patch descriptor learning [17–21]. Second, a robust matching method, abbreviated as RMBP, has been developed to resolve the rejection of outlier matches by means of efficient inference through belief propagation [63] on the defined graphical matching model. Both approaches have been validated to be conductive to forming point correspondences of better quality for registration, as demonstrated by the intensive comparative evaluations and registration experiments [6–11,15,17,18,61].

Acknowledgments. This work is supported by T22-603/15N, Hong Kong ITC PSKL12EG02 and The Special Project of International Scientific and Technological Cooperation in Guangzhou Development District (No. 2017GH24).

References

1. Zhu, S. et al.: Very large-scale global sfm by distributed motion averaging. In: CVPR (2018)
2. Zhang, R. et al.: Distributed very large scale bundle adjustment by global camera consensus. In: PAMI (2018)
3. Dissanayake, M.G., Newman, P., Clark, S., Durrant-Whyte, H.F., Csorba, M.: A solution to the simultaneous localization and map building (slam) problem. IEEE Trans. Robot. Autom. **17**(3), 229–241 (2001)
4. Fraundorfer, F., Scaramuzza, D.: Visual odometry: Part ii: Matching, robustness, optimization, and applications. IEEE Robot. Autom. Mag. **19**(2), 78–90 (2012)
5. Johnson, A.E., Hebert, M.: Using spin images for efficient object recognition in cluttered 3d scenes. In: PAMI **21**(5) (1999)
6. Rusu, R.B., Blodow, N., Marton, Z.C., Beetz, M.: Aligning point cloud views using persistent feature histograms. In: IROS (2008)
7. Rusu, R.B., Blodow, N., Beetz, M.: Fast point feature histograms (fpfh) for 3d registration. In: ICRA (2009)
8. Tombari, F., Salti, S., Di Stefano, L.: Unique signatures of histograms for local surface description. In: Daniilidis, K., Maragos, P., Paragios, N. (eds.) ECCV 2010. LNCS, vol. 6313, pp. 356–369. Springer, Heidelberg (2010). https://doi.org/10.1007/978-3-642-15558-1_26
9. Tombari, F., Salti, S., Di Stefano, L.: Unique shape context for 3d data description. In: Proceedings of the ACM Workshop on 3D Object Retrieval (2010)
10. Zeng, A., Song, S., Nießner, M., Fisher, M., Xiao, J., Funkhouser, T.: 3dmatch: Learning local geometric descriptors from rgb-d reconstructions. In: CVPR (2017)
11. Khoury, M., Zhou, Q.Y., Koltun, V.: Learning compact geometric features. In: ICCV (2017)
12. Deng, H., Birdal, T., Ilic, S.: Ppfnet: Global context aware local features for robust 3d point matching. arXiv preprint (2018)
13. Lowe, D.G.: Distinctive image features from scale-invariant keypoints. IJCV **60**(2), 91–110 (2004)

14. Gold, S., Lu, C.P., Rangarajan, A., Pappu, S., Mjolsness, E.: New algorithms for 2d and 3d point matching: pose estimation and correspondence. In: Advances in Neural Information Processing Systems (1995)
15. Zhou, Q.-Y., Park, J., Koltun, V.: Fast global registration. In: Leibe, B., Matas, J., Sebe, N., Welling, M. (eds.) ECCV 2016. LNCS, vol. 9906, pp. 766–782. Springer, Cham (2016). https://doi.org/10.1007/978-3-319-46475-6_47
16. Georgakis, G., Karanam, S., Wu, Z., Ernst, J., Kosecka, J.: End-to-end learning of keypoint detector and descriptor for pose invariant 3d matching (2018)
17. Simo-Serra, E., Trulls, E., Ferraz, L., Kokkinos, I., Fua, P., Moreno-Noguer, F.: Discriminative learning of deep convolutional feature point descriptors. In: ICCV (2015)
18. Tian, B.F.Y., Wu, F.: L2-net: Deep learning of discriminative patch descriptor in euclidean space. In: CVPR (2017)
19. Han, X., Leung, T., Jia, Y., Sukthankar, R., Berg, A.C.: Matchnet: Unifying feature and metric learning for patch-based matching. In: CVPR (2015)
20. Yi, K.M., Trulls, E., Lepetit, V., Fua, P.: LIFT: learned invariant feature transform. In: Leibe, B., Matas, J., Sebe, N., Welling, M. (eds.) ECCV 2016. LNCS, vol. 9910, pp. 467–483. Springer, Cham (2016). https://doi.org/10.1007/978-3-319-46466-4_28
21. Balntas, V., Riba, E., Ponsa, D., Mikolajczyk, K.: Learning local feature descriptors with triplets and shallow convolutional neural networks. In: BMVC (2016)
22. Wu, C., Clipp, B., Li, X., Frahm, J.M., Pollefeys, M.: 3d model matching with viewpoint-invariant patches (vip). In: CVPR (2008)
23. Chu, J., Nie, C.m.: Multi-view point clouds registration and stitching based on sift feature. In: ICCRD (2011)
24. Dai, A., Nießner, M., Zollhöfer, M., Izadi, S., Theobalt, C.: Bundlefusion: Real-time globally consistent 3d reconstruction using on-the-fly surface reintegration. TO **36**(3), 24 (2017)
25. Endres, F., Hess, J., Sturm, J., Cremers, D., Burgard, W.: 3-d mapping with an rgb-d camera. IEEE Trans. Robot. **30**(1), 177–187 (2014)
26. Chang, A. et al.: Matterport3D: Learning from RGB-D data in indoor environments. In: 3DV (2017)
27. Handa, A., Whelan, T., McDonald, J., Davison, A.: A benchmark for RGB-D visual odometry, 3D reconstruction and SLAM. In: ICRA (2014)
28. Sturm, J., Engelhard, N., Endres, F., Burgard, W., Cremers, D.: A benchmark for the evaluation of rgb-d slam systems. In: IROS (2012)
29. Snavely, N., Seitz, S.M., Szeliski, R.: Photo tourism: Exploring photo collections in 3d. In: SIGGRAPH (2006)
30. Su, H., Sun, M., Fei-Fei, L., Savarese, S.: Learning a dense multi-view representation for detection, viewpoint classification and synthesis of object categories. In: ICCV (2009)
31. Su, H., Maji, S., Kalogerakis, E., Learned-Miller, E.: Multi-view convolutional neural networks for 3d shape recognition. In: ICCV (2015)
32. Wang, C., Pelillo, M., Siddiqi, K.: Dominant set clustering and pooling for multi-view 3d object recognition. In: BMVC (2017)
33. Qi, C.R., Su, H., Nießner, M., Dai, A., Yan, M., Guibas, L.J.: Volumetric and multi-view cnns for object classification on 3d data. In: CVPR (2016)
34. Besl, P.J., McKay, N.D., et al.: A method for registration of 3-d shapes. PAMI **14**(2), 239–256 (1992)
35. Pomerleau, F., Colas, F., Siegwart, R., Magnenat, S.: Comparing icp variants on real-world data sets. Autonom. Robots **34**(3) (2013)

36. Rusinkiewicz, S., Levoy, M.: Efficient variants of the ICP algorithm. In: 3DIM (2001)
37. Yang, J., Li, H., Campbell, D., Jia, Y.: Go-icp: a globally optimal solution to 3d icp point-set registration. PAMI **38**(11), 2241–2254 (2016)
38. Briales, J., Gonzalez-Jimenez, J.: Convex global 3d registration with lagrangian duality. In: CVPR (2017)
39. Strecha, C., Von Hansen, W., Van Gool, L., Fua, P., Thoennessen, U.: On benchmarking camera calibration and multi-view stereo for high resolution imagery. In: CVPR (2008)
40. Chen, X., Ma, H., Wan, J., Li, B., Xia, T.: Multi-view 3d object detection network for autonomous driving (2016)
41. Albarelli, A., Bulo, S.R., Torsello, A., Pelillo, M.: Matching as a non-cooperative game. In: ICCV (2009)
42. Rodolà, E., Albarelli, A., Bergamasco, F., Torsello, A.: A scale independent selection process for 3d object recognition in cluttered scenes. IJCV **102**(1–3) (2013)
43. Jiayi, M., Ji, Z., Hanqi, G., Junjun, J., Huabing, Z., Yuan, G.: Locality preserving matching. In: IJCAI (2017)
44. Black, M.J., Rangarajan, A.: On the unification of line processes, outlier rejection, and robust statistics with applications in early vision. IJCV **19**(1), 57–91 (1996)
45. Anastasiya, M., Dmytro, M., Filip, R., Jiri, M.: Working hard to know your neighbor's margins: Local descriptor learning loss. In: NIPS (2017)
46. Johnson, J., Alahi, A., Fei-Fei, L.: Perceptual losses for real-time style transfer and super-resolution. In: Leibe, B., Matas, J., Sebe, N., Welling, M. (eds.) ECCV 2016. LNCS, vol. 9906, pp. 694–711. Springer, Cham (2016). https://doi.org/10.1007/978-3-319-46475-6_43
47. He, K., Zhang, X., Ren, S., Sun, J.: Deep residual learning for image recognition. In: CVPR (2016)
48. Szegedy, C. et al.: Going deeper with convolutions. In: CVPR (2015)
49. Szegedy, C., Vanhoucke, V., Ioffe, S., Shlens, J., Wojna, Z.: Rethinking the inception architecture for computer vision. In: CVPR (2016)
50. Lin, M., Chen, Q., Yan, S.: Network in network (2013)
51. Xu, B., Wang, N., Chen, T., Li, M.: Empirical evaluation of rectified activations in convolutional network (2015)
52. Chopra, S., Hadsell, R., LeCun, Y.: Learning a similarity metric discriminatively, with application to face verification. In: CVPR (2005)
53. Lin, J., Morère, O., Veillard, A., Duan, L.Y., Goh, H., Chandrasekhar, V.: Deephash for image instance retrieval: getting regularization, depth and fine-tuning right. In: ICMR (2017)
54. Snavely, N., Seitz, S.M., Szeliski, R.: Modeling the world from internet photo collections. IJCV **80**(2), 189–210 (2008)
55. Goesele, M., Snavely, N., Curless, B., Hoppe, H., Seitz, S.M.: Multi-view stereo for community photo collections. In: ICCV (2007)
56. Zhou, L., Zhu, S., Shen, T., Wang, J., Fang, T., Quan, L.: Progressive large scale-invariant image matching in scale space. In: ICCV (2017)
57. Shen, T., Zhu, S., Fang, T., Zhang, R., Quan, L.: Graph-based consistent matching for structure-from-motion. In: Leibe, B., Matas, J., Sebe, N., Welling, M. (eds.) ECCV 2016. LNCS, vol. 9907, pp. 139–155. Springer, Cham (2016). https://doi.org/10.1007/978-3-319-46487-9_9
58. Zhu, S., Shen, T., Zhou, L., Zhang, R., Wang, J., Fang, T., Quan, L.: Parallel structure from motion from local increment to global averaging. arXiv preprint arXiv:1702.08601 (2017)

59. Zhang, R., Zhu, S., Fang, T., Quan, L.: Distributed very large scale bundle adjustment by global camera consensus. In: ICCV (2017)
60. Li, S., Siu, S.Y., Fang, T., Quan, L.: Efficient multi-view surface refinement with adaptive resolution control. In: Leibe, B., Matas, J., Sebe, N., Welling, M. (eds.) ECCV 2016. LNCS, vol. 9905, pp. 349–364. Springer, Cham (2016). https://doi.org/10.1007/978-3-319-46448-0_21
61. Raguram, R., Frahm, J.-M., Pollefeys, M.: A comparative analysis of RANSAC techniques leading to adaptive real-time random sample consensus. In: Forsyth, D., Torr, P., Zisserman, A. (eds.) ECCV 2008. LNCS, vol. 5303, pp. 500–513. Springer, Heidelberg (2008). https://doi.org/10.1007/978-3-540-88688-4_37
62. Cooper, G.F.: The computational complexity of probabilistic inference using bayesian belief networks. Artif. Intell. 42(2–3), 393–405 (1990)
63. Murphy, K.P., Weiss, Y., Jordan, M.I.: Loopy belief propagation for approximate inference: an empirical study. In: UAI (1999)
64. Tatikonda, S.C., Jordan, M.I.: Loopy belief propagation and gibbs measures. In: UAI (2002)
65. Yedidia, J.S., Freeman, W.T., Weiss, Y.: Understanding belief propagation and its generalizations. Exploring Artif. Intell. New millenn., 239–269 (2003)
66. Zhang, X., Wang, Q., Werner, S., Zaheer, C., Chen, S., Luo, W.: http://www.openblas.net/
67. Rusu, R.B., Cousins, S.: 3d is here: Point cloud library (pcl). In: ICRA (2011)
68. Balntas, V., Lenc, K., Vedaldi, A., Mikolajczyk, K.: Hpatches: a benchmark and evaluation of handcrafted and learned local descriptors. In: CVPR (2017)
69. Huang, H., Kalogerakis, E., Chaudhuri, S., Ceylan, D., Kim, V.G., Yumer, E.: Learning local shape descriptors from part correspondences with multiview convolutional networks. TOG 37(1), 6 (2018)
70. Flint, A., Dick, A., Van Den Hengel, A.: Thrift: Local 3d structure recognition. In: Digital Image Computing Techniques and Applications (2007)
71. Schönberger, J.L., Zheng, E., Frahm, J.-M., Pollefeys, M.: Pixelwise view selection for unstructured multi-view stereo. In: Leibe, B., Matas, J., Sebe, N., Welling, M. (eds.) ECCV 2016. LNCS, vol. 9907, pp. 501–518. Springer, Cham (2016). https://doi.org/10.1007/978-3-319-46487-9_31
72. Dai, A., Chang, A.X., Savva, M., Halber, M., Funkhouser, T., Nießner, M.: Scannet: Richly-annotated 3d reconstructions of indoor scenes. In: CVPR (2017)
73. Kerl, C., Sturm, J., Cremers, D.: Robust odometry estimation for rgb-d cameras. In: ICRA (2013)
74. Choi, S., Zhou, Q.Y., Koltun, V.: Robust reconstruction of indoor scenes. In: CVPR (2015)
75. Wald, I., Slusallek, P., Benthin, C., Wagner, M.: Interactive rendering with coherent ray tracing. Comput. Graph. Forum (2001)

Revisiting Autofocus for Smartphone Cameras

Abdullah Abuolaim$^{(\boxtimes)}$, Abhijith Punnappurath, and Michael S. Brown

Department of Electrical Engineering and Computer Science,
Lassonde School of Engineering, York University, Toronto, Canada
{abuolaim,pabhijith,mbrown}@eecs.yorku.ca

Abstract. Autofocus (AF) on smartphones is the process of determining how to move a camera's lens such that certain scene content is in focus. The underlying algorithms used by AF systems, such as contrast detection and phase differencing, are well established. However, determining a high-level objective regarding how to best focus a particular scene is less clear. This is evident in part by the fact that different smartphone cameras employ different AF criteria; for example, some attempt to keep items in the center in focus, others give priority to faces while others maximize the sharpness of the entire scene. The fact that different objectives exist raises the research question of whether there is a preferred objective. This becomes more interesting when AF is applied to videos of dynamic scenes. The work in this paper aims to revisit AF for smartphones within the context of temporal image data. As part of this effort, we describe the capture of a new 4D dataset that provides access to a full focal stack at each time point in a temporal sequence. Based on this dataset, we have developed a platform and associated application programming interface (API) that mimic real AF systems, restricting lens motion within the constraints of a dynamic environment and frame capture. Using our platform we evaluated several high-level focusing objectives and found interesting insight into what users prefer. We believe our new temporal focal stack dataset, AF platform, and initial user-study findings will be useful in advancing AF research.

Keywords: Autofocus · Focal stack · AF platform
Low-level computer vision

1 Introduction

One of the crucial steps in image capture is determining what part of the scene to focus on. In this paper, we examine this problem for smartphone cameras because smartphones now represent the dominant modality of video and image capture

Electronic supplementary material The online version of this chapter (https:// doi.org/10.1007/978-3-030-01267-0_32) contains supplementary material, which is available to authorized users.

V. Ferrari et al. (Eds.): ECCV 2018, LNCS 11219, pp. 545–559, 2018.
https://doi.org/10.1007/978-3-030-01267-0_32

performed by consumers. While manual focus is possible on smartphones–either through direct manipulation of the lens position or by clicking on regions of interest in the scene–most users rely on the camera's autofocus (AF) mechanism.

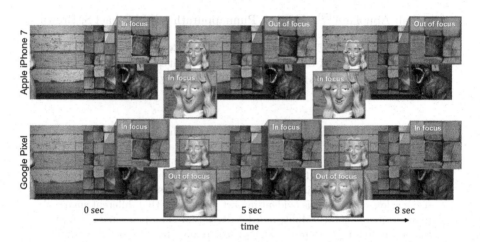

Fig. 1. An Apple iPhone 7 and Google Pixel are used to capture the same dynamic scene controlled via translating stages. At different time slots in the captured video, denoted as 0 s, 5 s, 8 s, it is clear that each phone is using a different AF objective. It is unclear which is the preferred AF objective. This is a challenging question to answer as it is very difficult to access a full (and repeatable) solution space for a given scene.

The goal of AF is straightforward. Given some high-level objective of what scene content or image region is desired to be in focus, AF systems attempt to move the lens such that these regions appear sharpest. From an optical point of view, the sharpness correlates to the desired image region lying within the len's depth of field. Smartphone cameras, as opposed to digital single-lens reflex (DSLR) and point-and-shoot cameras, are unique in this regard, since they have fixed apertures and depth of field is therefore restricted to lens position only.

The low-level algorithms used to determine image sharpness–for example, contrast detection and phase differencing–are well established. What is more challenging is using these low-level algorithms to realize high-level AF objectives for dynamic scene content in a temporal image sequence (i.e., video). This is evident from the variety of different AF criteria used by different smartphone cameras. Figure 1 shows an illustrative example. In this example, an Apple iPhone 7 and a Google Pixel have captured a scene with objects that move on a translating stage. The translating stage and controlled environment allow each camera to image the same dynamic scene content. We can see that each camera is focusing on different image regions at the same time slots in the video.

This begs the question of which of these two approaches is preferred by a user. From a research point of view, one of the major challenges when developing AF algorithms is the inability to examine the full solution space since only a fixed focal position can be captured at each time instance. While it is possible to capture a full focal stack for a static scene, it is currently not possible for a temporal image sequence in a dynamic environment. Moreover, there are additional constraints in an AF system beyond determining the right focal position given a full focal stack. For example, the lens cannot be instantaneously moved to the correct focal position; it can only advance either forward or backward within some fixed amount of time, and within this time quantum the scene content may change and the current video frame may advance. This lack of access to (1) temporal focal stack data and (2) an AF platform that holistically incorporates lens motion, scene dynamics, and frame advancement is the impetus for our work.

Contribution. The contribution of this work is a software platform for AF research and an associated 4D temporal focal stack dataset. Our AF platform allows the design, testing, and comparison of AF algorithms in a reproducible manner. Our focal stack dataset is composed of 33,000 full-frame images consisting of 10 temporal image sequences, each containing 50–90 full focal stacks. Our software platform provides an AF application programming interface (API) that mimics the real-time constraints, including lens motion timing with respect to scene motion and frame advancement. Additionally, we have performed analysis on several smartphone AF algorithms to come up with a set of representative high-level AF objectives. Using our platform and data we have implemented these algorithms to produce similar outputs found on real phones and used the results to perform a user study to see if there are any preferences. Our user study reveals that overall lens motion, and not necessarily the actual scene content in focus, is the predominant factor dictating preference. We believe our dataset and software platform will provide further opportunities for revisiting AF research.

2   Related Work

Work relating to autofocus and focal stack datasets is discussed in this section.

AF for Cameras. AF technologies have been around for several decades and a full discussion regarding existing AF methods is outside the scope of this paper. Here, we provide background to methods used in smartphone devices and that are related to our platform. The vast majority of smartphone cameras have simple optical systems with a fixed aperture that limits focus to lens motion (and not aperture adjustments). There are active AF methods that use auxiliary hardware, such as laser depth sensors; however, this paper focuses only on passive AF methods that rely on data captured from the image sensor.

There are two predominant types of passive AF: phase difference autofocus (PDAF) and contrast detection autofocus (CDAF). PDAF operates at a hardware/optics level and aims to adjust the lens position such that the phase between two light rays coming from a scene point is matched. The PDAF hardware module can be designed in two ways: (1) half sub-mirror with line sensor as used in older DSLR cameras [1,2] and (2) on-sensor dual-pixel layouts used in modern DSLR and smartphone cameras [3,4]. Compared with CDAF, PDAF methods are able to approximate the optimal lens position in a single processing step; however, PDAF alone is generally not sufficient to give an accurate focusing lens position.

CDAF is the most common approach used in DLSR and smartphone cameras. CDAF operates by applying low-level image processing algorithms (i.e., gradient magnitude analysis) to determine the sharpness of a *single* image or region of interest (ROI) in an image [5]. Because CDAF works on a single image, the camera lens needs to be moved back and forth until the image sharpness measure is maximized [6]. Many different sharpness measures have been proposed and several surveys exist that examine their performance under various conditions [7,8].

Table 1. The 10 scenes/image sequences in our AF dataset. See Sect. 3.3 for detail of the table and video/image sequence description. The final table row, discrete time points, denotes the number of full focal stacks per captured temporal image sequence

Scene	1	2	3	4	5	6	7	8	9	10
Example image										
Category	NF		FF		NF	FF	FB		NF	FF
Camera	stationary				moving	stationary		moving	stationary	
Textured background	✓	✗	✓							
Face	✗		✓		✗	✓			✗	✓
Motion switches	1				3	0	2		2	
Video length	21.6 sec				27.5 sec	29 sec	30.8 sec		39.1 sec	
Discrete time points	51				61		71		91	

Most of the recent smartphone cameras use so-called *hybrid AF* that utilizes both PDAF and CDAF. In particular, the hybrid AF performs PDAF first to move the lens to a position close to the optimal focusing position and then performs CDAF to accurately fine-tune the lens position to reach the optimal focusing position [9].

Focal Stack Datasets. Beyond various ad hoc focal stack data available online from class projects and photography enthusiasts, there are very few formal focal stack datasets available for academic research. Two notable datasets are by Mousnier et al. [10] and Li et al. [11]. The dataset in [10] provides 30 focal stacks of static scenes of images of size 1088×1088 pixels. The dataset in [11] captured 100 focal stacks of image size 1080×1080 pixels, again of static scenes. The number of images per focal stack ranges from 5 to 12. These datasets are not intended for the purpose of AF research, but instead target tangentially related topics, such as digital refocusing [12–14], depth from defocus [15,16], and depth from focal stacks [17].

In addition, the focal stacks in these datasets are synthetically generated based on the Lytro light field camera [18,19]. Unfortunately, the consumer-level

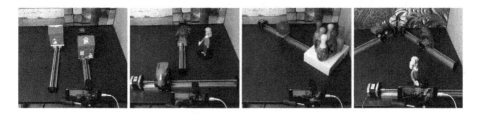

Fig. 2. A top view of our capture environment. Each shoot contains the scene components: linear stage actuators, smartphone camera, tripod, objects, and scene background.

Lytro devices do not support video capture. The new Lytro Cinema does offer video light field capture, but the cost of renting this device is prohibitively high (in the hundreds of thousands of dollars). Moreover, the Lytro Cinema is not representative of smartphones. Unlike the datasets in [10,11], our dataset provides a much larger focal stack of 50 images of size 3264 × 1836 pixels, and consists of 10 temporal image sequences with up to 90 full focal stacks per sequence.

3 AF Analysis and Dataset Capture

3.1 Capture Environment

To begin our effort, we constructed an environment that allowed scenes with different content and moving objects to be imaged in a repeatable manner. All videos and images were captured indoors using a direct current (DC) light source to avoid the flickering effect of alternating current lights [20]. To control scene motion, we used three DIY-CNC linear stage actuators that were controlled by a ST-4045-A1 motor driver and Arduino/Genuino Uno microcontroller. Each linear stage has a travel length of 410 mm and uses a stepper motor of Nema 23 24V 3A 1N.M. The three linear stage actuators can be combined together to give more degrees of freedom. We calibrated our motors to allow 106 equal steps of 3.87 mm each with a motion speed of 9.35 mm/s.

3.2 Analysis of Smartphones AF

Within this environment, we analyzed the performance of three representative consumer smartphones (Apple iPhone 7, Google Pixel, Samsung Galaxy S6) to observe their behaviour under different scenarios. The cameras are positioned such that their fields of view are as similar as possible. The frame rate for video capture is fixed at 30 frames/sec. Given the different optical systems and image formats among the cameras, there are slight differences in the field of view, but these differences are negligible in terms of their effect on the AF outcomes.

We experimented with a wide range of scene configurations, such as an object with a figurine with a human face, textured backgrounds, and various moving

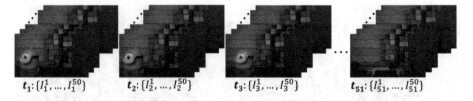

$t_1: \{I_1^1, ..., I_1^{50}\}$ $t_2: \{I_2^1, ..., I_2^{50}\}$ $t_3: \{I_3^1, ..., I_3^{50}\}$ ... $t_{51}: \{I_{51}^1, ..., I_{51}^{50}\}$

Fig. 3. Example of the temporal image sequence for scene 3. Focal stacks consist of $I_i^1, ..., I_i^{50}$ images for each time point t_i

objects. As previously illustrated in Fig. 1, we observed that the AF behaviors differ between phones. For example, in one experiment we set up a textured background and a textured object to move horizontally from left to right with respect to the camera. We observed that for the Google Pixel and Samsung Galaxy S6 Edge, the foreground object becomes in focus only when it is inside the center of the image; otherwise it is out of focus. For the same setup captured by an Apple iPhone 7, however, the foreground object is in focus most of the time regardless of its position from the center. In another experiment with a figurine with a human face, we observed that the three smartphones detected the face in a video, but only Apple iPhone 7 focused on the face region.

3.3   Scene and Image Sequence Capture

Based on our observations, we settled on 10 representative scenes that are categorized into three types: (1) scenes containing no face (NF), (2) scenes with a face in the foreground (FF), and (3) scenes with faces in the background (FB). For each of these scenes, we allowed different arrangements in terms of textured backgrounds, whether the camera moves, and how many types of objects in the scene change their directions (referred to as *motion switches*). Table 1 summarizes this information. Figure 2 shows the physical setup of several of the scenes.

For each of these 10 scenes, we captured the following data. First, each scene was imaged with the three smartphone cameras. This video capture helps to establish high-level AF objectives used on phones and determines the approximate video length needed to capture the overall scene dynamics. The duration of these videos is provided in Table 1. Due to limits on the supplemental materials, representative down-sampled versions of the videos are provided.

Next, we captured temporal focal stacks for each of these scenes. We refer to these as *image sequences* to distinguish them from the actual videos. To capture each image sequence, we replicated the video capture in a stop-motion manner. Specifically, the objects in the scene are moved in motion increments of 3.87 mm between consecutive *time points*. We used the Samsung Galaxy S6 Edge to perform the image capture using a custom Android app that fixed all camera settings (e.g., ISO, white balance, shutter speed). Our app also controlled the lens position, such that for each *time point* t_i, we captured a focal stack of 50 images where the camera lens is moved in linear steps from its minimum to

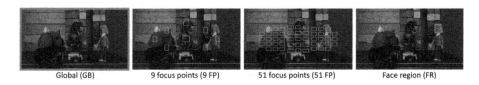

| Global (GB) | 9 focus points (9 FP) | 51 focus points (51 FP) | Face region (FR) |

Fig. 4. Our four AF objectives. The region bounded in a green box is a candidate for ROI(s).

maximum position. The last row in Table 1 shows also the number of *time points* for each captured temporal image sequence. In this paper we use the term *time point* to denote time slot in our stop-motion data. We also use the term *frame* to denote real-time video frame, either from a real video or an output produced by our AF platform.

Figure 3 shows an example of scene 2 with 50 *time points*. Each *time point* t_i in Fig. 3 has a focal stack of 50 images that are denoted as I_i^j, $j = 1, ..., 50$, where i denotes time point and j indexes the focal stack image associated to a specific lens position.

4 AF Platform and API

We begin with a short discussion on how our platform emulates PDAF and CDAF as these are the low-level algorithms of any AF system. This is followed by a discussion on the overall platform and associated API.

4.1 PDAF/CDAF Emulation

The CDAF and PDAF process can be divided into three main steps: first, determine a desired region of interest (ROI) based on the high-level AF objective; second, measure the sharpness or phase of the ROI selected; third, adjust the lens position to maximize the focus.

Based on the observed behaviour of the captured video from our three smartphone cameras on the 10 scenes, we determine four high-level AF objectives in terms of ROI as follows: (1) global ROI targeting the whole image; (2) a layout of 9 focus points with 9 ROIs; (3) a layout of 51 focus points with 51 ROIs (similar to the global ROI); (4) and a *face region* ROI where the largest region of detected faces is set as the ROI. Figure 4 shows the ROI(s) for each objective bounded in a green box.

Our AF platform provides the flexibility to manually specify the ROI; however, based on the above four objectives, we provide these as presets that the user can select. To facilitate the face region objective for our dataset, we manually labeled the face regions to avoid any face detection algorithm mistakes. Our platform allows retrieval of the labeled face region via an API call; however, when the pre-defined face region is selected, this call is automatically performed and the ROI set to the face region. Regarding the sharpness measure for the

Table 2. API calls with their parameters and return values. Each API call incurs a cost related to the number of internal clock cycles. C_{loc} current clock cycle, C_{glob} current time point, $I^j_{C_{glob}}$ current image at current C_{glob} and current lens position j, p optimal lens position, and *score* is the score of gradient energy (default or defined by user). See supplemental materials for more API details

API call	Description	Return values	Clock cycles
setScene(int sc)	Select one of the 10 scenes, sc= 0, ..., 9	null	0
setRegion(int [] reg)	Set the region either by selecting one of the predefined regions: Global (reg=[0]), 9 Focus Points (reg=[1]), 51 Focus Points (reg=[2]) or Face Region (reg=[3]), or by passing an array of size $r \times 4$ where r is the number of regions. Each region has offset (x,y), width, and height.	null	0
setSharpMeasure(int sh)	Select one of the two predefined sharpness measures: Sobel (sh=0) or Prewitt (sh=1).	null	0
setKernelSize(int ker)	Select one of the three predefined kernel sizes: 3 (ker=0), 5 (ker=1) or 7 (ker=2).	null	0
recordScript()	Start recording the subsequent API calls in a script.	null	0
endScript()	Stop recording the subsequent API calls in a script.	null	0
callPD(int ρ)	Compute phase difference and return approximate optimal lens position $p \pm \rho$.	$[C_{loc}, C_{glob}, I^j_{C_{glob}}, j, p]$	1
callCD(function fun)	Allow the user to pass custom contrast detection AF implementation as a function. Default Sobel/Prewitt with kernel size as set by user. fun is a function written in Python format.	$[C_{loc}, C_{glob}, I^j_{C_{glob}}, j, score]$	1 (if default) or defined by user
moveLensForward()	Move the lens a step forward.	$[C_{loc}, C_{glob}, I^j_{C_{glob}}, j]$	1
moveLensBackward()	Move the lens a step backward.	$[C_{loc}, C_{glob}, I^j_{C_{glob}}, j]$	1
noOp()	No operation. No lens movements. Used to increment C_{loc} in order to move in global time C_{glob}.	$[C_{loc}, C_{glob}, I^j_{C_{glob}}]$	1
getFaceRegion()	Detect face(s) and return face region(s) int face[] if exists. face[] is an array of size $m \times 4$ where m is the number of face regions. Each face region has offset (x,y), width, and height.	$[C_{loc}, C_{glob}, I^j_{C_{glob}}, face[]]$	0

CDAF, we provide two gradient based filters–namely, Sobel and Prewitt operators. Based on Loren's findings in [7], the Sobel and Prewitt filters are the most accurate among other sharpness measure methods. The size of these filters can also be controlled.

4.2   AF Platform and API Calls

Our AF API is designed to emulate AF in smartphones. The platform and API impose constraints on lens motion timing with respect to scene motion and video frame rate. As such, our API and platform have a *local* and *global* virtual clock. The local clock, denoted as C_{loc}, emulates the real-time internal clock on the smartphone, whereas the global clock, C_{glob}, emulates the real-world timing (scene dynamics).

Platform Timing. Since the Samsung Galaxy S6 was used to capture our dataset, we measured its performance to establish the mapping between the local and global clocks. Specifically, we measured how long it took the camera to respond to a scene change at a different focal positioning by sweeping the lens to this position while capturing video. To do this, we set up two objects: a textured flat background and textured flat foreground; both are parallel to the camera plane at different depth layers (one close and one far). The background object appears at the beginning of video capturing and is in focus; then, after a short delay we immediately display the foreground object closer to the camera, which causes the AF system to move the focus from background to foreground. Later, we decompose the captured video into frames and count how many frames it required to move from background to foreground. For the exact same scene scenario, we collected a full focal stack (50 images), previously discussed. To obtain how many steps the lens moved, we use the focal stack to compute at which lens positions the background and foreground objects are in focus.

Once we obtain the number of lens steps and number of frames required, we can compute from lens step to frame unit (33.33 msec). Therefore, we estimated the Samsung Galaxy S6 Edge requires 42 msec to move the lens one step (including image capturing and AF processing).

The time required for the translating stage motor to move one step (3.87 mm) is 414 msec. Recall that a single translating stage motor step in real time is equivalent to a discrete time point in our stop-motion setup. Therefore, the number of steps s allowed for the lens to move in one time point is equal to $414/42 \approx 9.86$ steps. Based on this approximate calculation, we fix s to 10 steps and we relate s to the local clock C_{loc} (one lens movement costs one clock cycle). Accordingly, the corresponding global clock C_{glob} increments every 10 clock cycles. Thus our relationship is: 10 C_{loc} advances C_{glob} by 1.

API. Our API is based on Python and provides 12 primitive calls as described in Table 2. See supplemental materials for more details.

The recordScript() and endScript() API calls are used to save the API calls and load them later for user algorithm playback purposes. These calls are also useful for capturing metadata about the performance of the algorithm–for example, lens position, API call made at each clock cycle, and ROI selected.

Our callPD(int ρ) API call is used to emulate the PDAF available on most high-end smartphone cameras. The *real* PDAF routine on a camera is able to find the approximate lens position for a desired ROI close to the optimal focal frame in the focal stack within a single processing pass of the low-level raw image. On real cameras, the PDAF result is obtained at a hardware level based on a proprietary layout of dual-pixel diodes placed on the sensor. We were not able to access this data and provided it as part of our focal stack dataset. As a result, we instead emulate the result of the phase difference by running CDAF targeted to the specified ROI on the whole focal stack at the current time-point t_i defined by the global clock C_{glob}. As mentioned previously, real camera PDAF is performed first to move the lens closer to the optimal focusing position; afterwards CDAF is typically performed to refine the lens position. To mimic this near optimality, we apply an inaccuracy tolerance ρ on the optimal focusing position obtained. This inaccuracy tolerance allows the estimated lens position to lie randomly around the optimal by $\pm[0, \rho]$ and is a parameter that can be passed to the API.

4.3 Example Implementation

Algorithm 1 provides simple pseudo-code based on our API to demonstrate how an AF algorithm based on the *global objective* for Scene 4 can be implemented.

Algorithm 1 Example of a Global ROI Objective using Optimal PDAF

1: Start API
2: `setScene(Scene4)`
3: `setRegion(Global)`
4: `recordScript()`   *//Create a script and start recording API calls*
5: **while not** *end of time points* **do**
6:     **if** *time point* t_i incremented **then**
7:         $C_{\text{loc}}, C_{\text{glob}}, I_i^j, j, p \leftarrow$ `callPD(0)`
8:     **else if** optimal lens position $p >$ current lens position j **then**
9:         $C_{\text{loc}}, C_{\text{glob}}, I_i^j, j \leftarrow$ `moveLensForward()`
10:     **else if** optimal lens position $p <$ current lens position j **then**
11:         $C_{\text{loc}}, C_{\text{glob}}, I_i^j, j \leftarrow$ `moveLensBackward()`
12:     **else if** optimal lens position $p ==$ current lens position j **then**
13:         $C_{\text{loc}}, C_{\text{glob}}, I_i^j \leftarrow$ `noOp()`
14:     **end if**
15:     $Video \leftarrow I_i^j$ *//Write the acquired image into a video*
16: **end while**
17: `endScript()`   *//Close and summarize the script(e.g., # of lens movements)*

Real Python examples and script recording and video outputs are provided in the supplemental materials. In this simple example, we set the ρ to zero, which results in `callPD()` calls returning the optimal lens position.

Based on our implementation in Algorithm 1, the time point t_i will be incremented by API every 10 clock cycles (as discussed before in Sect. 4.2). At each clock cycle API returns an image, which means we will get 10 images at each t_i. The total number of images returned by the API for a specific scene thus is equal to $10 \times n$ where n is the scene size in *time points*. To generate an output video for a scene, we write each image at each clock cycle out to a video object. Running Algorithm 1 will return metadata about the performance of the *global objective* for Scene 4. In Fig. 5 we show the lens position over local time (clock cycles) for the *global objective* (GB) in the dark blue solid line. From Fig. 5 we can analyze the lens movements over time, where the GB has fewer lens movements and less oscillation. Figure 5 also shows the lens position over time for other objectives for Scene 4.

5   User Study on AF Preference

We conducted a user study to determine if there was any particular preference for the different AF methods. As shown in Fig. 5, the AF platform gave us the opportunity to track exact lens movement for each method. Lens motion was treated as a potential factor.

Preparation. For this study we defined scene number, objective, and lens motion as our independent variables; the user preference is our dependent variable. We adopted a force-choice paired comparison approach that requires each participant in the study to choose a preferred video from a pair of videos. Both

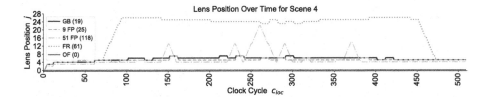

Fig. 5. This figure shows the lens position for each clock cycle for Scene 4 for each objective test. Total number of lens movements is shown in parentheses. An out-of-focus objective (OF) is included that does not move the lens over the entire sequence. For Scene 4, the 51 focus points (51 FP) objective oscillates the most. For the face region (FR) objective, the face did not enter the scene until clock cycle 70–the 9 focus points (9 FP) are applied by default when the face is not present. Global (GB) and 9 FP objectives tend to oscillate less than others with fewer lens movements.

videos in a given pair are of the same scene but have different AF objectives. We used all 10 scenes from our dataset for the study. There are six scenes with faces and four without. For the scenes with faces, there are four AF objectives–namely, global, 9 focus point, 51 focus point, and face region. The scenes without faces have only the first three AF objectives.

We generated output videos through our API and using our dataset and modifications of Algorithm 1 for each AF objective on all scenes (example video frames from Scene 1 are shown in Fig. 6). Due to limits on the supplemental materials, representative down-sampled versions of the user study videos are provided. Additionally, for each scene, we have generated an out-of-focus video, where all scene elements are out of focus. Those out-of-focus videos are generated through our API by fixing the lens to the maximum position and calling noOp() till the end-of-scene time points. However, for Scene 6, we omitted this objective because there is no lens position that makes all scene elements out-of-focus. Therefore, there are five scenes in total with five AF objectives (with the out-of-focus objective added), and another five scenes with only four AF objectives. The total number of paired comparisons is $5 \times \binom{5}{2} + 5 \times \binom{4}{2} = 80$.

Procedure. We collected 10 opinions for each video pair from 80 participants (34 females and 46 males) ranging in age from 18 to 50. Each subject was shown 10 video pairs selected in random order. We designed a simple graphical user interface that allows the user to view video pairs, one pair after the other, and easily examine the difference in AF behavior. The interface allows the participants to watch the two videos in the current pair any number of times before they make a selection and proceed to the next pair. A snapshot of our interface is provided in the supplementary material. The survey takes on average three to five minutes to complete. The experiments were carried out indoors with calibrated monitors and controlled lighting.

Outcomes. Recall our scenes are categorized as Cat. 1: scenes with no face (NF), Cat. 2: scenes with a prominent face in the foreground (FF), and Cat. 3: scenes in which the face is in the background (FB). For each category, we

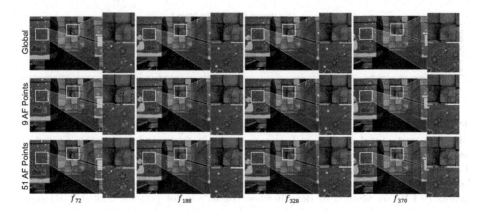

Fig. 6. Example output video frames generated by our AF platform using different objectives applied on Scene 1 over time. See supplemental materials for additional results for other scenes.

aggregated user votes into an overall score that represents user preference by counting the number of times each AF objective is preferred over any other objective. These results are presented in Figs. 7 and 8. In Fig. 7, in the first column, we show average user preference per AF objective for each category (i.e., aggregated over scenes). We can see that for NF videos, the global (GB) AF objective is the most preferred. For the FF videos, the face region (FR) AF objective is the most preferred. For the FB videos, there is no strong preference among the three objectives GB, 51 focus points (51 FP), and FR, but the most preferred is GB followed by FR. Additionally, we calculated the 95% confidence intervals for these results as represented by the error bars, which indicate the statistical significance of the results. Furthermore, the plots on the right of Fig. 7 represent the user preference per objective for individual scenes (lower plots) with a corresponding number of lens movements (upper plots with grey bars) for each of the three categories. The individual scene plots also confirm the observations from the aggregate plots for all cases except Scene 9.

To examine the correlation between user preference and the number of lens movements for each category, we plotted the user preference vs. lens movements for each category, as shown in Fig. 8. We see that there is a clear correlation between user preference and lens movements, suggesting that users tend to prefer the objectives with fewer lens movements. This is indicated by the negative correlation coefficients shown on the plots.

For the second category that contains a prominent face in the foreground, the results suggest that users prefer the face AF that locks onto the face even if more motion of the lens is required to achieve this objective. This voting pattern can be seen in the second row in Fig. 7, where the FR AF objective receives a higher percentage of votes than the GB AF, which has the least amount of lens motion. Also note that the 51 focus points (51 FP) objective has the highest amount of lens motion and is the least preferred. In the third category that contains a

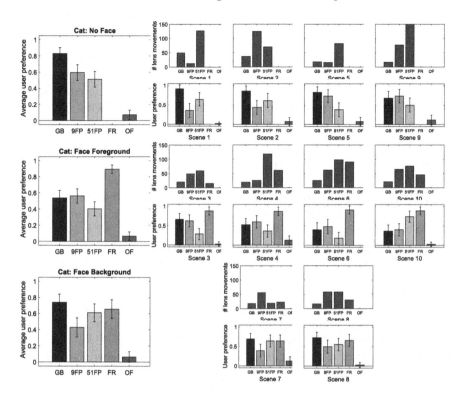

Fig. 7. User preference of AF objectives for three scene meta-categories: no face (NF), face in foreground (FF), and face in background (FB) for AF objectives: global (GB), 9 focus points (9 FP), 51 focus points (51 FP), face region (FR), and out-of-focus (OF). The left column shows the average user preference. The small plots on the right show user preference (lower plots) and lens movements (upper plots in grey) for individual scenes.

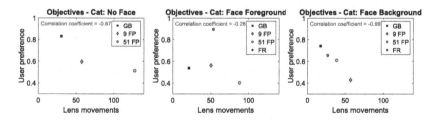

Fig. 8. The relationship between user preference and number of lens movements for AF objectives for the three scene meta-categories. Left: no face (NF). Middle: face in foreground (FF). Right: face in background (FB).

face in the background, users do not seem to have any strong preference, as seen by the near-equal distribution of votes across 51 FP, GB, and FR, all of which interestingly have roughly the same amount of lens motion (third row in Fig. 7).

It is also important to note that in agreement with our findings for the first two categories, the objective with the highest amount of lens movement, which in this case is the 9 focus points (9 FP) objective, is the least preferred.

The out-of-focus (OF) objective is preferred the least across all three categories although it has the least amount of lens motion. This agrees with the common wisdom that at least a part of the scene has to be in focus, and simply minimizing the amount of lens motion does not induce a higher preference.

6   Discussion and Summary

This paper has developed a new software platform and dataset focused on autofocus for video capture with smartphone cameras. To this end, we constructed a hardware setup that allows dynamic scenes to be accurately "replayed". Using this environment, we analyzed representative smartphone cameras' AF behaviour under 10 different scenes with various motions, backgrounds, and objects (including an object serving as a proxy for a human face). We also captured these scenes with discrete time points, producing a 4D temporal focal stack dataset for use in AF research. The overall dataset consists of 33,000 smartphone camera images and will be made publicly available. We also developed an AF platform that allows the development of AF algorithms within the content of a working camera system. API calls allow algorithms to simulate lens motion, image access, and low-level functionality, such as phase and contrast detection. This platform also restricts an AF algorithm to operate within a real camera environment, where lens motion that is directly tied to the systems clock cycle and scene motion is required to access different images in the focal stack.

From our analysis of the cameras' AF behaviour we examined four high-level AF objectives–namely, global, 9 focus points, 51 focus points, and face region. Using our AF platform, we implemented these high-level AF objectives to produce several video outputs that were used in a user study. Because our AF platform allowed accurate analysis of the underlying AF algorithms, we were able to determine that user preference is correlated higher to the overall lens motion than the actual scene objective used. For scenes with faces, focusing on the face (when sufficiently large) took priority, followed by the amount of lens motion. While these findings are somewhat intuitive (e.g., no one likes a scene with too much lens wobble), as far as we are aware, this is the first study to confirm these preferences in a controlled manner. We believe having access to our temporal focal stack dataset and AF platform will be a welcomed resource for the research community.

Acknowledgments. This study was funded in part by the Canada First Research Excellence Fund for the Vision: Science to Applications (VISTA) programme and an NSERC Discovery Grant.

References

1. Ohsawa, K.: Focus detecting device and method of operation. US Patent No. 5,530,513 (1996)
2. Inoue, D., Takahashi, H.: Focus detecting device and camera system using the same device. US Patent No. 7,577,349 (2009)
3. Śliwiński, P., Wachel, P.: A simple model for on-sensor phase-detection autofocusing algorithm. J. Comput. Commun. 1(06), 11 (2013)
4. Jang, J., Yoo, Y., Kim, J., Paik, J.: Sensor-based auto-focusing system using multi-scale feature extraction and phase correlation matching. Sensors 15(3), 5747–5762 (2015)
5. Jeon, J., Lee, J., Paik, J.: Robust focus measure for unsupervised auto-focusing based on optimum discrete cosine transform coefficients. IEEE Trans. Consum. Electron. 57(1) (2011)
6. Vuong, Q.K., Lee, J.w.: Initial direction and speed decision system for auto focus based on blur detection. In: 2013 International Conference Consumer Electronics (ICCE). IEEE (2013)
7. Shih, L.: Autofocus survey: a comparison of algorithms. In: Digital Photography III, vol. 6502, p. 65020B (2007)
8. Mir, H., Xu, P., Van Beek, P.: An extensive empirical evaluation of focus measures for digital photography. In: Digital Photography X, vol. 9023, p. 90230I (2014)
9. Nakahara, N.: Passive autofocus system for a camera. US Patent No. 7,058,294 (2006)
10. Mousnier, A., Vural, E., Guillemot, C.: Partial light field tomographic reconstruction from a fixed-camera focal stack (2015). arXiv preprint arXiv:1503.01903
11. Li, N., Ye, J., Ji, Y., Ling, H., Yu, J.: Saliency detection on light field. In: CVPR, pp. 2806–2813 (2014)
12. Baxansky, A.: Apparatus, method, and manufacture for iterative auto-focus using depth-from-defocus. US Patent No. 8,218,061 (2012)
13. Zhang, W., Cham, W.K.: Single-image refocusing and defocusing. IEEE Trans. Image Process. 21(2), 873–882 (2012)
14. Cao, Y., Fang, S., Wang, Z.: Digital multi-focusing from a single photograph taken with an uncalibrated conventional camera. IEEE Trans. Image Process. 22(9), 3703–3714 (2013)
15. Tang, H., Cohen, S., Price, B., Schiller, S., Kutulakos, K.N.: Depth from defocus in the wild. In: CVPR (2017)
16. Alexander, E., Guo, Q., Koppal, S., Gortler, S., Zickler, T.: Focal flow: measuring distance and velocity with defocus and differential motion. In: Leibe, B., Matas, J., Sebe, N., Welling, M. (eds.) ECCV 2016. LNCS, vol. 9907, pp. 667–682. Springer, Cham (2016). https://doi.org/10.1007/978-3-319-46487-9_41
17. Suwajanakorn, S., Hernandez, C., Seitz, S.M.: Depth from focus with your mobile phone. In: CVPR, pp. 3497–3506 (2015)
18. Levoy, M.: Light fields and computational imaging. Computer 39(8), 46–55 (2006)
19. Ng, R., Levoy, M., Brédif, M., Duval, G., Horowitz, M., Hanrahan, P.: Light field photography with a hand-held plenoptic camera. Comput. Sci. Tech. Rep. CSTR 2(11), 1–11 (2005)
20. Sheinin, M., Schechner, Y.Y., Kutulakos, K.N.: Computational imaging on the electric grid. In: CVPR (2017)

Deep Burst Denoising

Clément Godard[1][(✉)], Kevin Matzen[2], and Matt Uyttendaele[2]

[1] University College London, London, UK
c.godard@cs.ucl.ac.uk
[2] Facebook, Seattle, USA

Abstract. Noise is an inherent issue of low-light image capture, which is worsened on mobile devices due to their narrow apertures and small sensors. One strategy for mitigating noise in low-light situations is to increase the shutter time, allowing each photosite to integrate more light and decrease noise variance. However, there are two downsides of long exposures: (a) bright regions can exceed the sensor range, and (b) camera and scene motion will cause blur. Another way of gathering more light is to capture multiple short (thus noisy) frames in a burst and intelligently integrate the content, thus avoiding the above downsides. In this paper, we use the burst-capture strategy and implement the intelligent integration via a recurrent fully convolutional deep neural net (CNN). We build our novel, multi-frame architecture to be a simple addition to any single frame denoising model. The resulting architecture denoises all frames in a sequence of arbitrary length. We show that it achieves state of the art denoising results on our burst dataset, improving on the best published multi-frame techniques, such as VBM4D and FlexISP. Finally, we explore other applications of multi-frame image enhancement and show that our CNN architecture generalizes well to image super-resolution.

1 Introduction

Noise reduction is one of the most important problems to solve in the design of an imaging pipeline. The most straight-forward solution is to collect as much light as possible when taking a photograph. This can be addressed in camera hardware through the use of a large aperture lens, sensors with large photosites, and high quality A/D conversion. However, relative to larger standalone cameras, e.g. a DSLR, modern smartphone cameras have compromised on each of these hardware elements. This makes noise much more of a problem in smartphone capture.

Another way to collect more light is to use a longer shutter time, allowing each photosite on the sensor to integrate light over a longer period of time. This

---

C. Godard—This work was done during an internship at Facebook.

Electronic supplementary material The online version of this chapter (https://doi.org/10.1007/978-3-030-01267-0_33) contains supplementary material, which is available to authorized users.

V. Ferrari et al. (Eds.): ECCV 2018, LNCS 11219, pp. 560–577, 2018.
https://doi.org/10.1007/978-3-030-01267-0_33

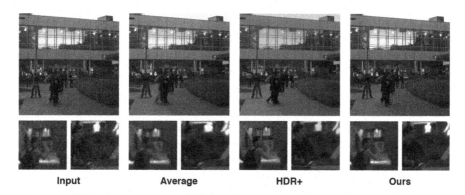

Input   **Average**   **HDR+**   **Ours**

Fig. 1. Denoising on a real raw burst from [19]. Our method is able to perform high levels of denoising on low-light bursts while maintaining details.

is commonly done by placing the camera on a tripod. The tripod is necessary as any motion of the camera will cause the collected light to blur across multiple photosites. This technique is limited though. First, any moving objects in the scene and residual camera motion will cause blur in the resulting photo. Second, the shutter time can only be set for as long as the brightest objects in the scene do not saturate the electron collecting capacity of a photosite. This means that for high dynamic range scenes, the darkest regions of the image may still exhibit significant noise while the brightest ones might staturate.

In our method we also collect light over a longer period of time, by capturing a burst of photos. Burst photography addresses many of the issues above (a) it is available on inexpensive hardware, (b) it can capture moving subjects, and (c) it is less likely to suffer from blown-out highlights. In using a burst we make the design choice of leveraging a computational process to integrate light instead of a hardware process, such as in [19,29]. In other words, we turn to computational photography.

Our computational process runs in several steps. First, the burst is stabilized by finding a homography for each frame that geometrically registers it to a common reference. Second, we employ a fully convolutional deep neural network (CNN) to denoise each frame individually. Third, we extend the CNN with a parallel recurrent network that integrates the information of all frames in the burst.

The paper presents our work as follows. In Sect. 2 we review previous single-frame and multi-frame denoising techniques. We also look at super-resolution, which can leverage multi-frame information. In Sect. 3 we describe our recurrent network in detail and discuss training. In order to compare against previous work, the network is trained on simulated Gaussian noise. We also show that our solution works well when trained on Poisson distributed noise which is typical of a real-world imaging pipeline [18]. In Sect. 4, we show significant increase in reconstruction quality on burst sequences in comparison to state of the art single-frame denoising and performance on par or better than recent state of the art multi-frame denoising methods. In addition we demonstrate that burst capture coupled with our recurrent network architecture generalizes well to super-resolution.

In summary our main contributions are:

- We introduce a recurrent architecture which is a simple yet effective extension to single-frame denoising models,
- Demonstrate that bursts provide a large improvement over the best deep learning based single-frame denoising techniques,
- Show that our model achieves performance on par with or better than recent state of the art multi-frame denoising methods, and
- Demonstrate that our recurrent architecture generalizes well by applying it to super-resolution.

2   Related Work

This work addresses a variety of inverse problems, all of which can be formulated as consisting of (1) a target "restored" image, (2) a temporally-ordered set or "burst" of images, each of which is a corrupted observation of the target image, and (3) a function mapping the burst of images to the restored target. Such tasks include denoising and super-resolution. Our goal is to craft this function, either through domain knowledge or through a data-driven approach, to solve these multi-image restoration problems.

Denoising

Data-driven single-image denoising research dates back to work that leverages block-level statistics within a single image. One of the earliest works of this nature is Non-Local Means [3], a method for taking a weighted average of blocks within an image based on similarity to a reference block. Dabov, *et al.* [9] extend this concept of block-level filtering with a novel 3D filtering formulation. This algorithm, BM3D, is the de facto method by which all other single-image methods are compared to today.

Learning-based methods have proliferated in the last few years. These methods often make use of neural networks that are purely feed-forward [1,4,15, 25,43,48,49], recurrent [44], or a hybrid of the two [7]. Methods such as Field of Experts [38] have been shown to be successful in modeling natural image statistics for tasks such as denoising and inpainting with contrastive divergence. Moreover, related tasks such as demosaicing and denoising have shown to benefit from joint formulations when posed in a learning framework [15]. The recent work of [5] applied a recurrent architecture in the context of denoising ray-traced sequenced, and finally [6] used a simple fully connected RNN for video denoising which, while failing to beat VBM4D [32,33], proved the feasibility of using RNNs for video denoising.

Multi-image variants of denoising methods exist and often focus on the best ways to align and combine images. Tico [40] returns to a block-based paradigm, but this time, blocks "within" and "across" images in a burst can be used to produce a denoised estimate. VBM3D [8] and VBM4D [32,33] provide extensions on top of the existing BM3D framework. Liu, *et al.* [29] showed how similar denoising performance in terms of PSNR could be obtained in one tenth the time of VBM3D and one one-hundredth the time of VBM4D using a novel "homography flow" alignment scheme along with a "consistent pixel" compositing operator. Systems such as FlexISP [22] and ProxImaL [21] offer end-to-end formulations of the entire image processing pipeline, including demosaicing, alignment, deblurring, etc., which can be solved jointly through efficient optimization.

We in turn also make use of a deep model and base our CNN architecture on current state of the art single-frame methods [27,36,48].

Super-Resolution

Super-resolution is the task of taking one or more images of a fixed resolution as input and producing a fused or hallucinated image of higher resolution as output.

Nasrollahi, *et al.* [35] offers a comprehensive survey of single-image super-resolution methods and Yang, *et al.* [45] offers a benchmark and evaluation of several methods. Glasner, *et al.* [16] show that single images can be super-resolved without any need of an external database or prior by exploiting block-level statistics "within" the single image. Other methods make use of sparse image statistics [46]. Borman, *et al.* offers a survey of multi-image methods [2]. Farsiu, *et al.* [13] offers a fast and robust method for solving the multi-image super-resolution problem. More recently convolutional networks have shown very good results in single image super-resolution with the works of Dong *et al.* [11] and the state of the art Ledig *et al.* [27].

Our single-frame architecture takes inspiration by recent deep super-resolution models such as [27].

2.1   Neural Architectures

It is worthwhile taking note that while image restoration approaches have often been learning-based in recent years, there's also great diversity in how those learning problems are modeled. In particular, neural network-based approaches have experienced a gradual progression in architectural sophistication over time.

In the work of Dong, *et al.* [10], a single, feed-forward CNN is used to super-resolve an input image. This is a natural design as it leveraged what was then new advancements in discriminatively-trained neural networks designed for classification and applied them to a regression task. The next step in architecture evolution was to use Recurrent Neural Networks, or RNNs, in place of the convolutional layers of the previous design. The use of one or more RNNs in a network design can both be used to increase the effective depth and thus receptive field in a single-image network [44] or to integrate observations across many frames in a multi-image network. Our work makes use of this latter principle.

While the introduction of RNNs led to network architectures with more effective depth and thus a larger receptive field with more context, the success of skip connections in classification networks [20] and segmentation networks [37,39] motivated their use in restoration networks. The work of Remez, *et al.* [36] illustrates this principle by computing additive noise predictions from each level of the network, which then sum to form the final noise prediction.

We also make use of this concept, but rather than use skip connections directly, we extract activations from each level of our network which are then fed into corresponding RNNs for integration across all frames of a burst sequence.

3   Method

In this section we first identify a number of interesting goals we would like a multi-frame architecture to meet and then describe our method and how it achieves such goals.

3.1   Goals

Our goal is to derive a method which, given a sequence of noisy images produces a denoised sequence. We identified desirable properties, that a multi-frame denoising technique should satisfy:

1. **Work for single-frame denoising.** A corollary to the first criterion is that our method should be competitive for the single-frame case.
2. **Generalize to any number of frames.** A single model should produce competitive results for any number of frames that it is given.
3. **Denoise the entire sequence.** Rather than simply denoise a single reference frame, as is the goal in most prior work, we aim to denoise the entire sequence, putting our goal closer to video denoising.
4. **Be robust to motion.** Most real-world burst capture scenarios will exhibit both camera and scene motion.
5. **Be temporally coherent.** Denoising the entire sequence requires that we do not introduce flickering in the result.
6. **Generalize to a variety of image restoration tasks.** As discussed in Sect. 2, tasks such as super-resolution can benefit from multi-frame methods, albeit, trained on different data.

In the remainder of this section we will first describe a single-frame denoising model that produces competitive results with current state of the art models. Then we will discuss how we extend this model to accommodate an arbitrary number of frames for multi-frame denoising and how it meets each of our goals.

3.2 Single Frame Denoising

We treat image denoising as a structured prediction problem, where the network is tasked with regressing a pixel-aligned denoised image $\tilde{I}_s = f_s(N, \theta_s)$ from noisy image N, given the model parameters θ_s. Following [50] we train the network by minimizing the L1 distance between the predicted output and the ground-truth target image, I.

$$E_{\text{SFD}} = |I - f_s(N, \theta_s)| \tag{1}$$

To be competitive in the single-frame denoising scenario, and to meet our 1st goal, we take inspiration from the state of the art to derive an initial network architecture. Several existing architectures [27,36,48] consist of the same base design: a fully convolutional architecture consisting of L layers with C channels each.

We follow suit and choose this simple architecture to be our single frame denoising (SFD) baseline, with $L = 8$, $C = 64$, 3×3 convolutions and ReLU [31] activation functions, except on the last layer.

3.3 Multi-frame Denoising

Following goals 1-3, our model should be competitive in the single-frame case while being able to denoise the entire input sequence. In other words, using a set of noisy images as input, forming the sequence $\{N^t\}$, we want to regress a denoised version of each noisy frame, $\tilde{I}_m^t = f_m^t(\{N^t\}, \theta_m)$, given the model parameters θ_m. Formally, our complete training objective is:

$$
\begin{aligned}
E &= \sum_t^F E_{\text{SFD}}^t + E_{\text{MFD}}^t \\
&= \sum_t^F |I^t - f_s(N^t, \theta_s)| + |I^t - f_m^t(\{N^t\}, \theta_m)|
\end{aligned}
\tag{2}
$$

A natural approach, which is already popular in the natural language and audio processing literature [47], is to process temporal data with recurrent neural network (RNN) modules [23]. RNNs operate on sequences and maintain an internal state which is combined with the input at each time step. As can be seen in Fig. 2, our model makes use of recurrent connections to aggregate activations produced by our SFD network for each frame. This satisfies our first goal as it allows for an arbitrary input sequence length.

Unlike [5,42] which use a single-track network design, we use a two track network architecture with the top track dedicated to SFD and the bottom track dedicated to fusing those results into a final prediction for MFD. This two track design decouples decoupling per-frame feature extraction from multi-frame aggregation, enabling the possibility for pre-training a network rapidly using only single-frame data. In practice, we found that this pre-training not only accelerates the learning process, but also produces significantly better results in terms

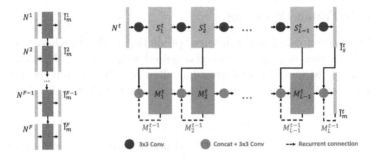

Fig. 2. Global recurrent architecture (left). Our model takes as input F noisy frames N^t and predicts F clean frames $\tilde{I}_m^t$. **Local recurrent architecture (right).** The top part of our model is a single-frame denoiser (SFD, in light blue): it takes as input a noisy image N^t and regresses a clean image $\tilde{I}_s^t$, its features S_i^t are fed to the multi-frame denoiser (MFD, in darker blue) which also makes use of recurrent connections from the previous state (dotted lines) to output a clean image $\tilde{I}_m^t$.

of PSNR than when we train the entire MFD from scratch. The core intuition is that by first learning good features for SFD, we put the network in a good state for learning how to aggregate those features across observations.

It is also important to note that the RNNs are connected in such a way as to permit the aggregation of features in several different ways. Temporal connections within the RNNs help aggregate information "across" frames, but lateral connections "within" the MFD track permit the aggregation of information at different physical scales and at different levels of abstraction.

4   Implementation and Results

We evaluate our method with the goals from Sect. 3 in mind, and examine: single-image denoising (goal 1), multi-frame denoising (goals 2–5), and multi-frame super-resolution (goal 6). In Sect. 4.5 we compare different single-frame denoising approaches, showing that quality is plateauing despite the use of deep models and that our simple single-frame denoiser is competitive with state-of-the-art. In Sect. 4.6 we show that our method significantly outperforms the reference state of the art video denoising method VBM4D [32]. Finally in Sect. 4.7 we compare our method to the state of the art burst denoising methods HDR+ [19], FlexISP [22] and ProximaL [21] on the FlexISP dataset.

4.1   Data

We trained all the networks in our evaluation using a dataset consisting of Apple Live Photos. Live Photos are burst sequences captured by Apple iPhone 6S and above[1]. This dataset is very representative as it captures what mobile phone

---

[1] https://support.apple.com/en-us/HT207310.

users often photograph, and exhibits a wide range of scenes and motions. Approximately 73k public sequences were scraped from a social media website with a resolution of 360×480. We apply a burst stabilizer to each sequence, resulting in approximately 54.5k sequences successfully stabilized. In Sect. 4.2 we describe our stabilization procedure in more detail. 50k sequences were used for training with an additional 3.5k reserved for validation and 1k reserved for testing.

4.2 Stabilization

We implemented burst sequence stabilization using OpenCV[2]. In particular, we use a Lucas-Kanade tracker [30] to find correspondences between successive frames and then a rotation-only motion model and a static focal length guess to arrive at a homography for each frame. We warp all frames of a sequence back into a reference frame's pose then crop and scale the sequence to maintain the original size and aspect ratio, but with the region of interest contained entirely within the valid regions of the warp. The stabilized sequences still exhibit some residual motion, either through moving objects or people, or through camera motion which cannot be represented by a homography. This residual motion forces the network to adapt to non static scenes. Stabilization and training on any residual motion makes our system robust to motion, achieving our 4th goal. As we show in supplementary material, stabilization improves the final results, but is not a requirement.

4.3 Training Details

We implemented the neural network from Sect. 3 using the Caffe2 framework[3]. Each model was trained using 4 Tesla M40 GPUs. As described in Sect. 3, training took place in two stages. First a single-frame model was trained. This model used a batch size of 128 and was trained for 500 epochs in approximately 5 hours. Using this single-frame model as initialization for the multi-frame (8-frame) model, we continue training with a batch size of 32 to accommodate the increased size of the multi-frame model. This second stage was trained for 125 epochs in approximately 20 h.

We used Adam [26] with a learning rate of 10^{-4} which decays to zero following a square root law. We trained on 64×64 crops with random flips. Finally, we train the multi-frame model using back-propagation through time [41].

4.4 Noise Modelling

In order to make comparison possible with previous methods, such as VBM4D, we first evaluate our architecture using additive white Gaussian noise with $\sigma = 15, 25, 50$ and 75. Additionally, to train a denoiser for real burst sequences, we implement a simulated camera processing pipeline. First real world sensor noise

---

[2] https://opencv.org/.
[3] https://caffe2.ai/.

is generated following [14]. Separate models are trained using Poisson noise, labelled a in [14], with intensity ranging from 0.001 to 0.01. We simulate a Bayer mosaic on a linearized version of our training data and add the Poisson noise to this. Next we reconstruct an RGB image using bilinear interpolation followed by conversion to sRGB and clipping. In both Gaussian and Poisson cases we add synthetic noise *before* stabilization. While it is possible to obtain a single "blind" model by training on multiple noise levels at once [49], it typically results in a small loss in accuracy. We thus follow the protocol established by [36,48] and train a separate model for each noise level, without loss of generality.

Table 1. Single frame additive white Gaussian noise denoising comparison on BSD68 (PSNR). Our baseline SFD models match BM3D at 8 layers and get close to both DnCNN and DenoiseNet at 20 layers.

	$\sigma = 15$	$\sigma = 25$	$\sigma = 50$	$\sigma = 75$
BM3D	31.10	28.57	25.62	24.20
TNRD	31.41	28.91	25.95	-
DenoiseNet [36]	31.44	29.04	26.06	24.61
DnCNN [48]	**31.73**	**29.23**	**26.23**	-
Ours single-frame 8L	31.15	28.63	25.65	24.11
Ours single-frame 20L	31.29	28.82	26.02	24.43

4.5   Single Frame Denoising

Here, we compare our baseline single frame denoiser with current state of the art methods on additive white Gaussian noise. This shows that single-frame denoising has reached a point of diminishing returns, where significant model complexity is needed improve quality by more than ∼0.2 dB.

We compare our own SFD, which is composed of 8 layers, with two 20 layer networks: DenoiseNet (2017) [36] and DnCNN (2017) [48]. For the sake of comparison, we also include a 20 layer version of our SFD. All models were trained for 2000 epochs on 8000 images from the PASCAL VOC2010 [12] using the training split from [36]. We also compare with traditional approaches, such as BM3D (2009) [9] and TNRD (2015) [7].

All models were tested on BSD68 [38], a set of 68 natural images from the Berkeley Segmentation Dataset [34]. In Table 1, we can see diminishing returns in single frame denoising PSNR over the years despite the use of deep neural networks, which confirms what Levin, *et al.* describe in [28]. We can see that our simpler SFD 20 layers model only slightly underperforms both DenoiseNet and DnCNN by ∼0.2 dB. However, as we show in the following section, the PSNR gains brought by multi-frame processing vastly outshine fractional single frame PSNR improvements.

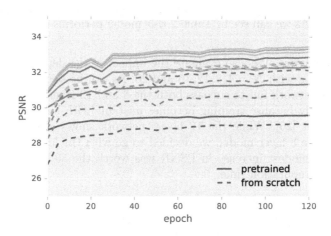

Fig. 3. Effect of pre-training on multi-frame denoising with Gaussian noise $\sigma = 50$. Each color corresponds to the average PSNR of the frames in a sequence: 1st (red), 2nd (blue), 3rd (purple) 4th (grey), 5th (yellow) and 6th (pink). As we can see the pre-trained model shows a constant lead of 0.5dB over the model trained from scratch, and reaches a stable state much quicker.

4.6 Burst Denoising

We evaluate our method on a held-out test set of Live Photos with synthetic additive white Gaussian noise added. In Table 3, we compare our architecture with single frame models as well as the multi-frame method VBM4D [32,33]. We show qualitative results with $\sigma = 50$ in Fig. 5.

Table 2. Ablation study on the Live Photos test sequences with additive white Gaussian Noise of $\sigma = 50$. All models were trained on 8 frame sequences. C2F, C4F and C8F represent **Concat** models which were trained on respectively 2, 4, and 8 concatenated frames as input. Ours *nostab* was trained and tested on the unstabilized sequences.

	C2F	C4F	C8F	Ours 4L	**Ours 8L**	Ours 12L	Ours 16L	Ours 20L	Ours *nostab*
PSNR	30.89	31.83	32.15	33.01	**33.62**	33.80	33.35	33.48	32.60

Ablation Study. We now evaluate our architecture choices, where we compare our full model, with 8 layers and trained on sequences of 8 frames with other variants.

Concat. We first compare our method with a naive multi-frame denoising approach, dubbed **Concat**, where the input consists of n concatenated frames to a single pass denoiser. We evaluated this architecture with $L = 20$ as well as

$n = 2, 4$ and 8. As we can see in Table 2 this model performs significantly worse than our model.

Number of Layers. We also evaluate the impact of the depth of the network by experimenting with $N = 4, 8, 12, 16$ and 20. As can be seen in Fig. 2, the 16 and 20 layers network fail to surpass both the 8 and 12 layers after 125 epochs of training, likely because training becomes unstable with increased depth and parameter count [20]. While the 12 layers network shows a marginal 0.18 dB increase over the 8 layer model, we decided to go with the latter as we did not think that the modest increase in PSNR was worth the 50% increase in both memory and computation time.

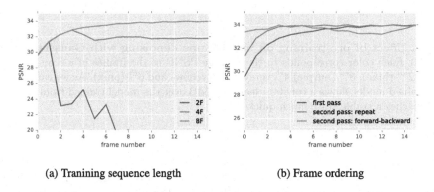

(a) Tranining sequence length   (b) Frame ordering

Fig. 4. (a) **Impact of the length F of training sequences at test time.** We test 3 models which were trained with $F = 2, 4$ and 8 on 16 frames-long test sequences. (b) **Effect of frame ordering at test time.** We can see the burn-in period on the first pass (red) as well as on the repeat pass. Feeding the sequence forward, then backward, mostly alleviates this problem.

Length of Training Sequences. Perhaps the most surprising result we encountered during training our recurrent model, was the importance of the number of frames in the training sequences. In Fig. 4a, we show that models trained on sequences of both 2 and 4 frames fail to generalize beyond their training length sequence. Only models trained with 8 frames were able to generalize to longer sequences at test time, and as we can see still denoise beyond 8 frames.

Pre-training. One of the main advantages of using a two-track network is that we can first train the SFD track independently. As just mentioned, a sequence length of 8 is required to ensure generalization to longer sequences, which makes the training of the full model much slower than training the single-frame pass. As we show in Fig. 3, pre-training makes training the MFD significantly faster.

Frame Ordering. Due to its recurrent nature, our network exhibits a period of burn-in, where the first frames are being denoised to a lesser extent than the later ones. In order to denoise an entire sequence to a high quality level, we explored different options for frame ordering. As we show in Fig. 4b, by feeding the sequence twice to the network, we are able to achieve a comparable denoising quality on all frames thus obtaining a higher average PSNR. We propose two variants, either **repeat** the sequence in the same order or reverse it the second time (named **forward-backward**). As we show in Fig. 4b, the forward-backward schedule does not suffer from burn-in and remains temporally coherenent, meeting our 5th goal. We use forward-backward for all our experiments.

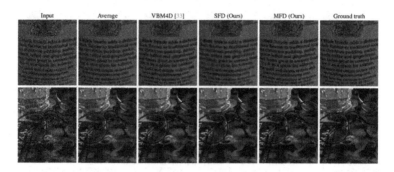

Fig. 5. Multi-frame Gaussian denoising on stabilized Live Photo test data with $\sigma = 50$. We can see that our MFD produces a significantly sharper image than both our SFD and VBM4D.

4.7   Existing Datasets

Here we evaluate our method on existing datasets, showing generization and allowing us to compare with other state-of-the-art denoising approaches. In Figs. 1 and 7 we demonstrate that our method is capable of denoising real sequences. This evaluation was performed on real noisy bursts from HDR+ [19]. Please see our supplementary material for more results.

In Fig. 6 we show the results of our method on the FlexISP dataset, comparing it with FlexISP, HDR+ and ProximaL on the FlexISP. The dataset consists of 4 noisy sequences: 2 synthetic (FLICKR DOLL and KODAK FENCE) and 2 real ones (DARKPAINTCANS and LIVINGROOM). The synthetic sequences were generated by randomly warping the input images and introducing: (for FLICKR DOLL) additive and multiplicative white Gaussian noise with $\sigma = 25.5$, and (for KODAK FENCE) additive with Gaussian noise of $\sigma = 12$ while simulating a Bayer filter. We trained a model for each synthetic scene, by replicating by replicating the corresponding noise conditions on our Live Photos dataset. To match the evaluation of previous work, we used only the first 8 frames from each sequence for denoising.

Table 3 shows that our method matches FlexISP on FLICKR DOLL and achieves a significant advantage of 0.5 dB over FlexISP KODAK FENCE. Interestingly, our method reaches a higher PSNR than FlexISP, despite showing some slight demosiacing artifacts on the fence (see in Fig. 6). This is likely due to the absence of high frequency demosaicing artifacts in our training data and would

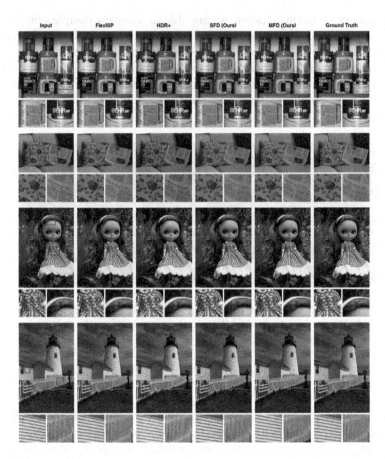

Fig. 6. Denoising results on two real and two synthetic bursts on the FlexISP dataset [22]. From top to bottom: DARKPAINTCANS, LIVINGROOM, FLICKR DOLL and KODAK FENCE. Our recurrent model is able to match the quality of FlexISP on FLICKR DOLL and beats it by 0.5 dB on KODAK FENCE.

Table 3. Multi-frame denoising comparison on Live Photo sequences (left) and the FlexISP sequences (right). Average PSNR for all frames on 1000 test 16-frames sequences with additive white Gaussian noise. **Multi-frame denoising comparison on the FlexISP images (right).** Best results are in bold. The thick line separates single frame methods and multi-frame ones.

	$\sigma = 15$	$\sigma = 25$	$\sigma = 50$	$\sigma = 75$
BM3D	35.67	32.92	29.41	27.40
DnCNN	35.84	32.93	29.13	27.06
DenoiseNet	35.91	33.17	29.56	27.49
VBM4D	36.42	33.41	29.14	26.60
Ours	**39.23**	**36.87**	**33.62**	**31.44**

	FLICKR DOLL	KODAK FENCE
BM3D	25.47	31.09
VBM3D	27.48	31.60
FlexISP	29.41	34.44
ProximaL	**30.23**	-
Ours	29.39	**34.98**

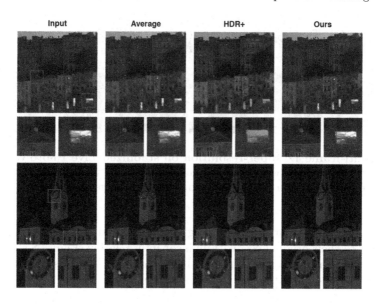

Fig. 7. Denoising results on two real bursts on the HDR+ dataset [19]. Our method produces a high level of denoising while keeping sharp details and maintaining information in highlights.

probably be fixed by generating training data following the same protocol as the test data.

Unfortunately, it is difficult to compare a thoroughly with ProximaL, as the publicly implementation does not have code for their experiments. We attempted to reimplement burst denoising using their publicly available framework, but were unable to produce stable results. As ProximaL only shows denoising results on FLICKR DOLL, this limits us to a less comprehensive comparison on only one scene, where our method falls short.

Like HDR+, we do not report quantitative results on the real scenes (DARKPAINTCANS and LIVINGROOM), as we were unable to correct for a color shift between the ground truth long exposure images and the noisy bursts. However, Fig. 6 shows that our method is able to recover a lot of details while removing the noise on these bursts.

4.8   Super Resolution

To illustrate that our approach generalizes to tasks beyond denoising, and to meet our 6th goal, we trained our model to perform 4× super-resolution, while keeping the rest of the training procedure identical to that of the denoising pipeline. That is, instead of using a burst of noisy images as input, we provide our network with a burst of low-resolution images and task it to provide us with a sharp high-resolution output. To keep the architecture the same, we do not feed low-resolution images as input to the network, but instead remove high-

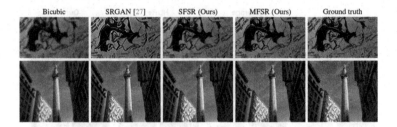

Fig. 8. Multi-frame $4\times$ **super-resolution on stabilized Live Photo test data.**
While our single frame model achieves a good upsampling, the increase in sharpness
from our multi-frame approach brings a significant quality improvement.

frequency details by first downsampling each input patch $4\times$ and then resize
them back to their original size with bilinear interpolation. Figure 8 shows how
our multi-frame model is able to recover high-frequency details, such as the crisp
contours of the lion and the railing on top of the pillar.

5   Limitations

Our single-frame architecture, based on [27,36,48], makes use of full resolution
convolutions. They are however both memory and computationally expensive,
and have a small receptive field for a given network depth. Using multiscale
architectures, such as a U-Nets [37], could help alleviate both issues, by reducing
the computational and memory load, while increasing the receptive field. While
not necessary, we trained our network on pre-stabilized sequences, we observed
a drop in accuracy on unstabilized sequences, as can be seen in Table 2, as well
as instability on longer sequences. It would be interesting to train the network to
stabilize the sequence by warping inside the network such as in [17,24]. Finally
the low resolution of our training data prevents the model from recoving high
frequency details; a higher resolution dataset would likely fix this issue.

6   Conclusion

We have presented a novel deep neural architecture to process burst of images.
We improve on a simple single frame architecture by making use of recurrent
connections and show that while single-frame models are reaching performance
limits, our recurrent architecture vastly outperforms such models for multi-frame
data. We carefully designed our method to align with the goals we stated in
Sect. 3.1. As a result, our approach achieves state-of-the-art performance in our
Live Photos dataset, and matches or beats existing multi-frame denoisers on
challenging existing real-noise datasets.

Acknowledgments. We would like to thank Sam Hasinoff and Andrew Adams for the HDR+ dataset, Jan Kautz for the FlexISP dataset and Ross Grishick for the helpful discussions. Finally huge thanks to Peter Hedman for his last minute magic.

References

1. Agostinelli, F., Anderson, M.R., Lee, H.: Adaptive multi-column deep neural networks with application to robust image denoising. In: Burges, C.J.C., Bottou, L., Welling, M., Ghahramani, Z., Weinberger, K.Q. (eds.) Advances in Neural Information Processing Systems, vol. 26, pp. 1493–1501. Curran Associates, Inc. (2013)
2. Borman, S., Stevenson, R.L.: Super-resolution from image sequences-a review. In: Proceedings of 1998 Midwest Symposium on Circuits and Systems, pp. 374–378. IEEE (1998)
3. Buades, A., Coll, B., Morel, J.M.: A non-local algorithm for image denoising. In: IEEE Computer Society Conference on Computer Vision and Pattern Recognition, CVPR 2005, vol. 2, pp. 60–65. IEEE (2005)
4. Burger, H.C., Schuler, C.J., Harmeling, S.: Image denoising: can plain neural networks compete with BM3D? In: 2012 IEEE Conference on Computer Vision and Pattern Recognition (CVPR), pp. 2392–2399. IEEE (2012)
5. Chaitanya, C.R.A., Kaplanyan, A.S., Schied, C., Salvi, M., Lefohn, A., Nowrouzezahrai, D., Aila, T.: Interactive reconstruction of monte carlo image sequences using a recurrent denoising autoencoder. ACM Trans. Graph. (TOG) **36**(4), 98 (2017)
6. Chen, X., Song, L., Yang, X.: Deep RNNs for video denoising. In: Applications of Digital Image Processing XXXIX. vol. 9971, p. 99711T. International Society for Optics and Photonics (2016)
7. Chen, Y., Pock, T.: Trainable nonlinear reaction diffusion: a flexible framework for fast and effective image restoration. IEEE Trans. Pattern Anal. Mach. Intell. **39**(6), 1256–1272 (2017)
8. Dabov, K., Foi, A., Katkovnik, V., Egiazarian, K.: Image denoising by sparse 3-D transform-domain collaborative filtering. IEEE Trans. Image Process. **16**(8), 2080–2095 (2007)
9. Dabov, K., Foi, A., Katkovnik, V., Egiazarian, K.: BM3D image denoising with shape-adaptive principal component analysis. In: SPARS 2009-Signal Processing with Adaptive Sparse Structured Representations (2009)
10. Dong, C., Loy, C.C., He, K., Tang, X.: Image super-resolution using deep convolutional networks. IEEE Trans. Pattern Anal. Mach. Intell. **38**(2), 295–307 (2016). https://doi.org/10.1109/TPAMI.2015.2439281
11. Dong, C., Loy, C.C., He, K., Tang, X.: Image super-resolution using deep convolutional networks. IEEE Trans. Pattern Anal. Mach. Intell. **38**(2), 295–307 (2016)
12. Everingham, M., Van Gool, L., Williams, C.K.I., Winn, J., Zisserman, A.: The pascal visual object classes (VOC) challenge. Int. J. Comput. Vis. **88**(2), 303–338 (2010)
13. Farsiu, S., Robinson, M.D., Elad, M., Milanfar, P.: Fast and robust multiframe super resolution. IEEE Trans. Image Process. **13**(10), 1327–1344 (2004)
14. Foi, A.: Clipped noisy images: heteroskedastic modeling and practical denoising. Signal Process. **89**(12), 2609–2629 (2009)
15. Gharbi, M., Chaurasia, G., Paris, S., Durand, F.: Deep joint demosaicking and denoising. ACM Trans. Graph. (TOG) **35**(6), 191 (2016)

16. Glasner, D., Bagon, S., Irani, M.: Super-resolution from a single image. In: ICCV (2009). http://www.wisdom.weizmann.ac.il/~vision/SingleImageSR.html
17. Godard, C., Mac Aodha, O., Brostow, G.J.: Unsupervised monocular depth estimation with left-right consistency. In: The IEEE Conference on Computer Vision and Pattern Recognition (CVPR), July 2017
18. Hasinoff, S.W., Durand, F., Freeman, W.T.: Noise-optimal capture for high dynamic range photography. In: CVPR, pp. 553–560. IEEE Computer Society (2010)
19. Hasinoff, S.W., Sharlet, D., Geiss, R., Adams, A., Barron, J.T., Kainz, F., Chen, J., Levoy, M.: Burst photography for high dynamic range and low-light imaging on mobile cameras. ACM Trans. Graph. (TOG) **35**(6), 192 (2016)
20. He, K., Zhang, X., Ren, S., Sun, J.: Deep residual learning for image recognition. In: 2016 IEEE Conference on Computer Vision and Pattern Recognition (CVPR), pp. 770–778, June 2016. https://doi.org/10.1109/CVPR.2016.90
21. Heide, F., Diamond, S., Nießner, M., Ragan-Kelley, J., Heidrich, W., Wetzstein, G.: Proximal: efficient image optimization using proximal algorithms. ACM Trans. Graph. (TOG) **35**(4), 84 (2016)
22. Heide, F., Steinberger, M., Tsai, Y.T., Rouf, M., Pajak, D., Reddy, D., Gallo, O., Liu, J., Heidrich, W., Egiazarian, K.: Flexisp: a flexible camera image processing framework. ACM Trans. Graph. (TOG) **33**(6), 231 (2014)
23. Hopfield, J.J.: Neural networks and physical systems with emergent collective computational abilities. Proc. Natl. Acad. Sci. **79**(8), 2554–2558 (1982)
24. Jaderberg, M., Simonyan, K., Zisserman, A., et al.: Spatial transformer networks. In: Advances in Neural Information Processing Systems, pp. 2017–2025 (2015)
25. Jain, V., Seung, S.: Natural image denoising with convolutional networks. In: Koller, D., Schuurmans, D., Bengio, Y., Bottou, L. (eds.) Advances in Neural Information Processing Systems, vol. 21, pp. 769–776. Curran Associates, Inc. (2009). http://papers.nips.cc/paper/3506-natural-image-denoising-with-convolutional-networks.pdf
26. Kingma, D.P., Ba, J.: Adam: a method for stochastic optimization. In: Proceedings of the 3rd International Conference on Learning Representations (ICLR) (2014)
27. Ledig, C., et al.: Photo-realistic single image super-resolution using a generative adversarial network. In: The IEEE Conference on Computer Vision and Pattern Recognition (CVPR), July 2017
28. Levin, A., Nadler, B.: Natural image denoising: optimality and inherent bounds. In: 2011 IEEE Conference on Computer Vision and Pattern Recognition (CVPR), pp. 2833–2840. IEEE (2011)
29. Liu, Z., Yuan, L., Tang, X., Uyttendaele, M., Sun, J.: Fast burst images denoising. ACM Trans. Graph. (TOG) **33**(6), 232 (2014)
30. Lucas, B.D., Kanade, T.: An iterative image registration technique with an application to stereo vision. In: Proceedings of the 7th International Joint Conference on Artificial Intelligence, IJCAI 1981, vol. 2, pp. 674–679. Morgan Kaufmann Publishers Inc., San Francisco, CA, USA (1981). http://dl.acm.org/citation.cfm?id=1623264.1623280
31. Maas, A.L., Hannun, A.Y., Ng, A.Y.: Rectifier nonlinearities improve neural network acoustic models. In: Proceedings of the ICML, vol. 30 (2013)
32. Maggioni, M., Boracchi, G., Foi, A., Egiazarian, K.: Video denoising, deblocking, and enhancement through separable 4-D nonlocal spatiotemporal transforms. IEEE Trans. Image Process. **21**(9), 3952–3966 (2012)

33. Maggioni, M., Boracchi, G., Foi, A., Egiazarian, K.O.: Video denoising using separable 4D nonlocal spatiotemporal transforms. In: Image Processing: Algorithms and Systems, p. 787003 (2011)

34. Martin, D., Fowlkes, C., Tal, D., Malik, J.: A database of human segmented natural images and its application to evaluating segmentation algorithms and measuring ecological statistics. In: Proceedings of the Eighth IEEE International Conference on Computer Vision, ICCV 2001, vol. 2, pp. 416–423. IEEE (2001)

35. Nasrollahi, K., Moeslund, T.B.: Super-resolution: a comprehensive survey. Mach. Vis. Appl. **25**(6), 1423–1468 (2014)

36. Remez, T., Litany, O., Giryes, R., Bronstein, A.M.: Deep class aware denoising. arXiv preprint arXiv:1701.01698 (2017)

37. Ronneberger, O., Fischer, P., Brox, T.: U-Net: convolutional networks for biomedical image segmentation. In: Navab, N., Hornegger, J., Wells, W.M., Frangi, A.F. (eds.) MICCAI 2015. LNCS, vol. 9351, pp. 234–241. Springer, Cham (2015). https://doi.org/10.1007/978-3-319-24574-4_28

38. Roth, S., Black, M.J.: Fields of experts: a framework for learning image priors. In: IEEE Computer Society Conference on Computer Vision and Pattern Recognition, CVPR 2005, vol. 2, pp. 860–867. IEEE (2005)

39. Shelhamer, E., Long, J., Darrell, T.: Fully convolutional networks for semantic segmentation. IEEE Trans. Pattern Anal. Mach. Intell. **39**(4), 640–651 (2017). https://doi.org/10.1109/TPAMI.2016.2572683

40. Tico, M.: Multi-frame image denoising and stabilization. In: Signal Processing Conference, 2008 16th European, pp. 1–4. IEEE (2008)

41. Werbos, P.J.: Generalization of backpropagation with application to a recurrent gas market model. Neural Netw. **1**(4), 339–356 (1988)

42. Wieschollek, P., Hirsch, M., Scholkopf, B., Lensch, H.P.A.: Learning blind motion deblurring. In: The IEEE International Conference on Computer Vision (ICCV), Oct 2017

43. Xie, J., Xu, L., Chen, E.: Image denoising and inpainting with deep neural networks. In: Pereira, F., Burges, C.J.C., Bottou, L., Weinberger, K.Q. (eds.) Advances in Neural Information Processing Systems, vol. 25, pp. 341–349. Curran Associates, Inc. (2012). http://papers.nips.cc/paper/4686-image-denoising-and-inpainting-with-deep-neural-networks.pdf

44. Xinyuan Chen, Li Song, X.Y.: Deep rnns for video denoising. In: Proceedings of the SPIE, vol. 9971, pp. 9971–9971-10 (2016). http://dx.doi.org/10.1117/12.2239260

45. Yang, Chih-Yuan, Ma, Chao, Yang, Ming-Hsuan: Single-image super-resolution: a benchmark. In: Fleet, David, Pajdla, Tomas, Schiele, Bernt, Tuytelaars, Tinne (eds.) ECCV 2014. LNCS, vol. 8692, pp. 372–386. Springer, Cham (2014). https://doi.org/10.1007/978-3-319-10593-2_25

46. Yang, J., Wright, J., Huang, T.S., Ma, Y.: Image super-resolution via sparse representation. IEEE Trans. Image Process. **19**(11), 2861–2873 (2010)

47. Yin, W., Kann, K., Yu, M., Schütze, H.: Comparative study of CNN and RNN for natural language processing. arXiv preprint arXiv:1702.01923 (2017)

48. Zhang, K., Zuo, W., Chen, Y., Meng, D., Zhang, L.: Beyond a gaussian denoiser: residual learning of deep cnn for image denoising. IEEE Trans. Image Process. **26**, 3142–3155 (2017)

49. Zhang, K., Zuo, W., Gu, S., Zhang, L.: Learning deep CNN denoiser prior for image restoration. In: The IEEE Conference on Computer Vision and Pattern Recognition (CVPR), July 2017

50. Zhao, H., Gallo, O., Frosio, I., Kautz, J.: Loss functions for image restoration with neural networks. IEEE Trans. Comput. Imaging **3**(1), 47–57 (2017)

ISNN: Impact Sound Neural Network for Audio-Visual Object Classification

Auston Sterling[1], Justin Wilson[1(✉)], Sam Lowe[1], and Ming C. Lin[1,2]

[1] Department of Computer Science, University of North Carolina at Chapel Hill,
Chapel Hill, USA
{austonst,wilson,samlowe,lin}@cs.unc.edu
[2] Department of Computer Science, University of Maryland, College Park, USA
lin@cs.umd.edu

Abstract. 3D object geometry reconstruction remains a challenge when working with transparent, occluded, or highly reflective surfaces. While recent methods classify shape features using raw audio, we present a multimodal neural network optimized for estimating an object's geometry and material. Our networks use spectrograms of recorded and synthesized object impact sounds and voxelized shape estimates to extend the capabilities of vision-based reconstruction. We evaluate our method on multiple datasets of both recorded and synthesized sounds. We further present an interactive application for real-time scene reconstruction in which a user can strike objects, producing sound that can instantly classify and segment the struck object, even if the object is transparent or visually occluded.

1 Introduction

The problem of object detection, classification, and segmentation are central to understanding complex scenes. Detection of objects is typically approached using visual cues [1,2]. Classification techniques have steadily improved, advancing our ability to accurately label an object by class given its depth image [3], voxelization [4], and/or RGB-D data [5]. Segmentation of objects from scenes provides contextual understanding of scenes [6,7]. While these state-of-the-art techniques often result in high accuracy for common scenes and environments, there is still room for improvement when accounting for different object materials, textures, lighting, and other variable conditions.

The challenges introduced by transparent and highly reflective objects remain open research areas in 3D object classification. Common vision-based approaches cannot gain information about the internal structure of objects, however audio-augmented techniques may contribute that missing information. Sound as a

---

Electronic supplementary material The online version of this chapter (https://doi.org/10.1007/978-3-030-01267-0_34) contains supplementary material, which is available to authorized users.

V. Ferrari et al. (Eds.): ECCV 2018, LNCS 11219, pp. 578–595, 2018.
https://doi.org/10.1007/978-3-030-01267-0_34

modality of input has the potential to close the audio-visual feedback loop and enhance object classification. It has been demonstrated that sound can augment visual information-gathering techniques, providing additional clues for classification of material and general shape features [8,9]. However, previous work has not focused on identifying complete object geometries. Identifying object geometry from a combined audiovisual approach expands the capabilities of scene understanding.

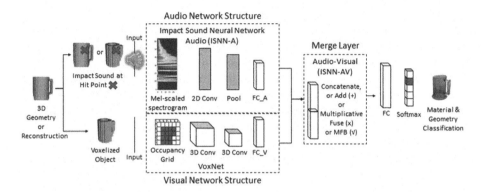

Fig. 1. Our Impact Sound Neural Network - Audio (ISNN-A) uses as input a spectrogram of sound created by a real or synthetic object being struck. Our audio-visual network (ISNN-AV) combines ISNN-A with VoxNet to produce state-of-the-art object classification accuracy.

In this paper, we consider identification of rigid objects such as tableware, tools, and furniture that are common in indoor scenes. Each object is identified by its geometry and its material. A discriminative factor for object classification is the sound that these objects produce when struck, referred to as an *impact sound*. This sound depends on a combination of the object's material composition and geometric model. Impact sounds are distinguished as object discriminators from video in that they reflect the internal structure of the object, providing clues about parts of an opaque or transparent object that cannot be seen visually. Impact sounds, therefore, complement video as an input to object recognition problems by addressing the some inherent limitations of incomplete or partial visual data.

Main Results: In this paper, we introduce an audio-only Impact Sound Neural Network (ISNN-A) and a multimodal audio-visual neural network (ISNN-AV). These networks:

– Are the first networks to show high classification accuracy of both an object's geometry and material based on its impact sound;
– Use impact sound spectrograms as input to reduce overfitting and improve accuracy and generalizability;

- Merge multimodal inputs through bilinear models, which have not been previously applied to audio-visual networks yet result in higher accuracy as demonstrated in Table 4;
- Provide state-of-the-art results on geometry classification; and
- Enable real time, interactive scene reconstruction in which users can strike objects to automatically insert the appropriate object into the scene.

2   Previous Work

3D Object Datasets. Thanks to a plethora of 3D scene and object datasets such as BigBIRD [10] and RGB-D Object Dataset [11], neural network models have been trained to label objects based on their visual representation. 3D ShapeNets [3] also provides two sets of object categories for object classification referred to as ModelNet10 and ModelNet40, which are common benchmarks for evaluation [12]. Scene-based datasets have also been built from RGB-D reconstruction scans of entire spaces, allowing for semantic data such as object and room relationships. For instance, NYU Depth Dataset [13] and SUNCG [14] enable indoor segmentation and semantic scene completion from depth images.

2.1   3D Reconstruction

Structure from Motion (SFM) [15], Multi-View Stereo (MVS) [16], and Shape from Shading [17] are all techniques to estimate shape properties of a scanned scene. Although these methods alone do not achieve a segmented representation of the objects within the scene, they serve as a foundation for many algorithms. RGB-D depth-based, active reconstruction methods can also be used to generate 3D geometrical models of static [6,18] and dynamic [19,20] scenes using commodity sensors such as the Microsoft Kinect and GPU hardware in real-time. Techniques have also been developed to overcome some limitations of vision-based reconstruction techniques [21] such as scene lighting, occlusions, clutter, and overlapping transparent objects. When limited solely to visual input, these challenges remain. Additional modalities, such as the impact sounds we explore in this paper, have the potential to address these issues.

Alternate Modalities. While image and depth-based techniques cover the majority of reconstruction use cases, edge cases have motivated research to explore alternative modalities that may procure the level of detail that vision-based techniques alone cannot. The dip transform for 3D shape reconstruction [22] uses fluid displacement of an object to obtain shape information. Time-of-Flight cameras introduce another modality to better classify materials and correct the depth of transparent objects [23]. This work uses both recorded and synthetic audio as additional modalities to complement vision-based reconstruction.

2.2   Environmental Sound Classification

Audio descriptors have been primarily explored in the context of environmental sound classification. Multiple datasets have been established for evaluating classification of various environmental sounds [24–26]. Traditional techniques use a variety of features extracted from sounds, such as Mel frequency spectral coefficients and spectral shape descriptors [27,28]. Similar approaches are used to classify an environment based on the sounds heard within it [29].

Fig. 2. We use various datasets for training and testing: (1) our RSAudio dataset with real and synthesized impact sounds from objects of varying shapes and sizes and (2) voxelized ModelNet objects. (3) Audio inputs are formatted as spectrograms.

Convolutional neural networks have also been applied to these problems, producing improved results [30,31]. Recently, some interest has been given to exploring the performance of different network structures [32,33]. Impact sounds are a specific category of environmental sounds, and in this paper we perform fine-grained object classification between perceptually similar sounds.

2.3   Object/Scene Understanding Through Sound

Sound can be used as a source of information for deeper understanding of 3D scenes and objects. Specifically considering impact sounds, sound can be used to estimate the material of objects using iterative optimization-based parameter identification techniques [34,35]. Sound has also been used to obtain information about the physical properties of objects involved in impact simulations [36]. Shape primitives were included as a part of these physical properties, but were not representative of real-world object geometries. However, it has been proven that any given impact sound may have come from one of multiple possible object geometries, and thus cannot be uniquely reconstructed [37]. Previous work has not attempted complete object reconstruction. In contrast, we constrain the outputs to known objects, making the problem tractable in this work.

Sound and video are intrinsically linked modalities for understanding the same scene, object, or event. Using visual and audio information, it is possible to predict the sound corresponding to a visual image or video [38,39]. Sound prediction from video has also been specifically explored for impact sounds [40].

Multimodal Fusion. Other works have fused audio and visual cues to better understand objects and scenes. Sparse auditory clues can supplement the ability of random fields to obtain material labels and perform segmentation [9]. Neural networks have proven valuable in fusing audio-visual input to emulate the sensory interactions of human information processing [8]. While multimodal methods have succeeded in fusing input streams to capture material and low-level shape properties to aid segmentation, they have not attempted to identify specific object geometries.

Early attempts at multimodal fusion in neural networks focused on increasing classification specificity by combining the individual classification results of separate input streams [41]. Bilinear modeling can model the multiplicative interactions of differing input types, and has been applied as a method of pooling input streams in neural networks [42,43]. Bilinear methods have been further developed to reduce complexity and increase speed, while other approaches to modeling multiplicative interactions have also been explored [44–46]. Bilinear methods have not yet been applied to merging audio-visual networks, and our ISNN-AV network is the first to do so.

3   Audio and Visual Datasets

To perform multimodal classification of object geometries, we need datasets containing appropriate multimodal information. Visual object reconstruction can provide a rough approximation of object geometry, serving as one form of input. *Impact audio produced from real or simulated object vibrations provide information about internal and occluded object structure, making for an effective second input.* Figure 2 provides examples of object geometries, while the corresponding spectrograms model the sounds that provide another input modality.

Appropriate audio can be found in some existing datasets, but the corresponding geometries are difficult to model. AudioSet contains impact sounds in its "Generic impact sounds" and "{Bell, Wood, Glass}" categories [24], while ESC-50 has specific categories including "Door knock" and "Church bells" [25]. The *Greatest Hits* sound dataset comes closest to our needs, containing impact sounds labeled according to the type of object [40]. However, many of the categories do not contain rigid objects (e.g. cloth, water, grass) or contain complex structures that cannot be represented with one geometric model of one material (e.g. a stump with roots embedded in the ground).

We want to use an impact sound as one input to identify a specific geometric model that could have created that sound. A classifier for this purpose could be trained on a large number of recorded sounds produced from struck objects. However, it is difficult and time-consuming to obtain a representative sample of real-world objects of all shapes and sizes. It is much easier to create a large dataset of synthetic sounds using geometric shapes and materials which can be applied to the objects. We now describe our methodology for generating the data used for training, as visualized in Fig. 3.

3.1   Audio Data

We create a large amount of our training data by simulating the vibrations of rigid-body objects and the sounds that they produce. Modal sound synthesis is an established method for synthesizing these sounds. We refer readers to the Supplemental Document (Sect. 1) for a mathematical overview and previous work for the full derivation of the algorithm [8,47,48]. Modal sound synthesis can be broken up into two steps: a preprocessing *modal analysis* step to process the inputs and a faster *modal synthesis* step to synthesize individual sounds.

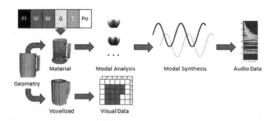

Fig. 3. We build multimodal datasets through separate processing flows. Modal sound synthesis produces spectrograms used for audio input. Voxelization as another modality provides a first estimate of shape. Incorporating audio features improves classification accuracy through understanding of how objects vibrate.

Modal Analysis. Modal analysis is a process for modeling and understanding the vibrations of objects in response to external forces. Vibrations in an object can be modeled with the wave equation [49], but in order to handle arbitrary geometries with unknown analytical solutions, it is more common to perform finite element analysis on a discretized representation of the object [47,50].

Starting with a watertight triangle mesh representation of the object's surface, the interior volume of the object is filled with a tetrahedral volumetric mesh. A finite element model can then be constructed to represent the free vibrations of the object. Damping within the object causes vibrations to decay over time; we use Rayleigh damping to model this effect.

Given this representation of a vibrating object, we are interested in determining the frequencies at which it vibrates. This can be accomplished through a generalized eigen-decomposition of the finite element matrices. Finally, the system can be decoupled into linearly separable *modes of vibration*. Each mode has a solution in the form of a damped sinusoid, each having a different frequency and rate of decay. This modal analysis step is performed once per object, and is a computationally-intensive task. The resulting modes' frequencies of vibration and damping rates are saved to be used in modal synthesis.

Modal Synthesis. Striking an object excites its modes of vibration, causing a change in pressure waves. For a simulated object, an impulse in object-space can be converted to mode impulses to determine initial amplitudes for the corresponding sinusoids. The sinusoids for the modes are then sampled through time and added to produce the final sound. This process can be repeated for different materials, geometries, and hit points to create a set of synthetic impact sounds.

3.2   Audio Augmentations

Modal sound synthesis produces the set of frequencies, damping rates, and initial amplitudes of an object's surface vibrations. However, since we are attempting to imitate real-world sounds, there are some additional auditory effects to take into account: acoustic radiance, room acoustics, background noise, and time variance.

Acoustic Radiance. Sound waves produced by the object must propagate through the air to reach a listener or microphone position. Even in an empty space, the resulting sound will change with different listener positions depending on the vibrational mode shapes; this is the acoustic radiance of the object [51]. This effect has a high computational cost for each geometric model, and since we use datasets with relatively large numbers of models, we do not include it in our simulations.

Room Acoustics. In an enclosed space, sound waves bounce off walls to produce early echo-like reflections and noisy late reverberations; this is the effect of room acoustics. We created a set of room impulse responses in rooms of different sizes and materials using a real-time sound propagation simulator, GSound [52]. Each modal sound is convolved with a randomly selected room impulse response.

Background Noise. In most real-world situations, background noise will also be present in any recording. We simulate background noise through addition of a random segment of environmental audio from the DEMAND database [53]. These noise samples come from diverse indoor and outdoor environments and contain around 1.5 h of recordings.

Time Variance. Finally, we slightly randomize the start time of each modal sound. This reflects the imperfect timing of any real-world recording process. Together, these augmentations make the synthesized sounds more accurately simulate recordings that would be taken in the real world.

3.3   Visual Data

Our visual data consists of datasets of geometric models of rigid objects, ranging from small to large and of varying complexity. Given these geometric models, we can simulate synthesized sounds for a set of possible materials. During evaluation, object classification results were tested using multiple scenarios of voxelization, scale, and material assignment (Sect. 5.2).

4   Impact Sound Neural Network (Audio and Audio-Visual)

Given the impact sounds and representation described in Sect. 3, we now examine their ability to identify materials and geometric models. We begin with an analysis of the distributions of the features themselves as proper feature selection is a key component in classifier construction.

4.1   Input Features and Analysis

Audio Features. In environmental sound classification tasks, classification accuracy can be affected by the input sound's form of representation [28,33]. A one-dimensional time series of audio samples over time can be used as features [39], but they do not capture the spectral properties of sound. A frequency dimension can be introduced to create a time-frequency representation and better represent the differentiating features of audio signals.

In this work, we use a mel-scaled spectrogram as input. Spectrograms have demonstrated high performance in CNNs for other tasks [33]. A given sound, originally represented as a waveform of audio samples over time, is first trimmed to one second in length since impact sounds are generally transient. The sound is resampled to 44.1 kHz, the Nyquist rate for the full range of audible frequencies up to 22.05 kHz. We compute the short-time Fourier transform of the sound, using a Hann window function with 2048 samples and an overlap of 25%. The result is squared to produce a canonical "spectrogram", then the frequencies are mapped into mel-scaled bins to provide appropriate weights matching the logarithmic perception of frequency. Each spectrogram is individually normalized to reduce the effects of loudness and microphone distance. To create the final input features for the classifier, we downsample the mel-spectrogram to a size of 64 frequency bins by 25 time bins.

We performed principal component analysis on a small sample of synthesized impact sounds to demonstrate the advantage of mel-spectrograms as input features for audio of this type. We used 70 models and 6 materials with a single hit per combination to synthesize a total of 420 impact sounds for this analysis. Figure 4 displays the first two principal components as mel-spectrograms, describing important distinguishing factors in our dataset. The first component identifies damping in higher frequencies, while the second component identifies specific frequency bins.

Visual Features. As in VoxNet [4], visual data serves as an input into classification models based on a 30x30x30 voxelized representation of the object geometry. We voxelize models from our real and synthetic dataset and ShapeNets ModelNet10 and ModelNet40. All objects were voxelized using the same voxel and grid size. We generated audio and visual data for our dataset and up to 200 objects (train and test) per ModelNet class.

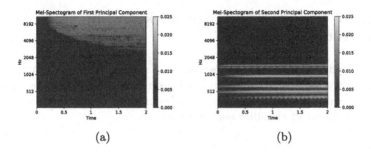

(a)   (b)

Fig. 4. The first two principal components of 420 synthesized sounds demonstrate that the key differentiating factors between sounds and models are the presence of high-frequency damping (first component) and the presence of specific frequency bins (second component).

4.2   Model Architecture

Using our audio and visual features, our approach to performing object geometry classification uses convolutional neural networks (CNNs) due to their high accuracy in a wide variety of tasks, with the specific motivation that convolutional kernels should be able to capture the recurring patterns underlying the structure of our sounds.

Audio-Only Network (ISNN-A). We first developed a network structure to perform object classification using audio only. Our audio Impact Sound Neural Network (ISNN-A) is based on optimization performed over a search space combining general network structure, such as the number of convolutional layers, and hyperparameter values. This optimization was performed using the TPE algorithm [54]. We found a single convolutional layer followed by two dense layers performs optimally on our classification tasks. This network structure utilizes a convolution kernel with increased frequency resolution to more effectively recognize spectral patterns across a range of frequencies [30]. Our generally low number of filters and narrower layer sizes aim to reduce overfitting by encouraging the learning of generalizable geometric properties.

Figure 5 shows sample activations of a convolutional layer of the ISNN-A network. Based on the PCA and modal analysis we performed, we expect that the differences between geometries primarily manifest as different sets of modal frequencies, as well as different sets of initial mode amplitudes and damping rates. These activations corroborate our expectations. In Fig. 4a, we see that damping is an important discriminating feature, which has been learned by filters (b) and (c) in Fig. 5. Similarly, the frequency patterns that we expected because of Fig. 4b can be seen in filters (a) and (d). This demonstrates that our model is learning statistically optimal kernels with high discriminatory power.

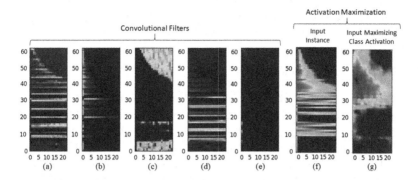

Fig. 5. Sample activations (a–e) of ISNN convolution layer. Filters identify character-istic patterns in frequencies (a) (d), damping rates (b) (c), and high-frequency noise (e). The distinguishing characteristics in these activations match the expected factors discovered in the PCA analysis in Fig. 4. An audio input spectrogram (f) and activation maximization (g) learned by the ISNN network for the toilet ModelNet10 class show correctly-learned patterns.

Multimodal Audio-Visual Network (ISNN-AV). Our audio-visual net-work, as shown in Fig. 1, consists of our audio-only network combined with a visual network based on VoxNet [4] using either a concatenation, addition, multi-plicative fusion, or bilinear pooling operation. Concatenation and addition serve as our baseline operations, in which the outputs of the first dense layers are concatenated or added before performing final classification. These operations are not ideal because they fail to emulate the interactions that occur between multiple forms of input. On the other hand, multiplicative interactions allow the input streams to modulate each other, providing a more accurate model.

We evaluate two multiplicative merging techniques to better model such interactions. Multiplicative fusion calculates element-wise products between inputs, while projecting the interactions into a lower-dimensional space to reduce dimensionality [46]. Multimodal factorized bilinear pooling takes advantage of optimizations in size and complexity, and is our final merged model [45]. This method builds on the basic idea of multiplicative fusion by performing a sequence of pooling and regularization steps after the initial element-wise multiplication.

5   Results

We now present our training and evaluation methodology along with final results. For each of the datasets, we evaluate the network architectures described in Sect. 4.2. We compare against several baselines: a K Nearest Neighbor classifier, a linear SVM trained through SGD [55], VoxNet [4], and SoundNet [39]. Our multimodal networks combined VoxNet with either ISNN-A or SoundNet8 and were merged through either concatenation (MergeCat), element-wise addition (MergeAdd), multiplicative fusion (MergeMultFuse) [46], or multimodal factor-ized bilinear pooling (MergeMFB) [45]. Training was performed using an Adam optimizer [56] and run with a batch size of 64, with remaining hyperparameters hand-tuned on a validation set before final evaluation on a test set.

5.1   RSAudio Evaluation

Our "RSAudio" dataset was constructed from real and synthesized sounds. When performing geometry classification, each geometric model is its own class; given a query sound, the network returns the geometric model that would produce the most similar sound. RSAudio combines real and synthetic sounds to increase dataset size and improve accuracy. Specific details about the recording process for the real sounds can be found in Supplemental Document (Sect. 4). The dataset is publicly available at http://gamma.cs.unc.edu/ISNN/.

Table 1. For real sounds, ISNN-A significantly outperforms all other algorithms, with an accuracy upto 92.37%. *Based on a subset of Sound-20 K.

Geometry Classification Accuracy: RSAudio and Related Work Datasets (ISNN-A Ours)

Method	Input	RSA S	RSA R	RSA Merged	Sound-20K*	Arnab A	ImageNet
Nearest Neighbor	A	**96.92%**	68.63%	97.59%	95.54%	87.50%	N/A
Linear SVM [55]	A	2.31%	2.30%	3.20%	82.07%	7.14%	N/A
SoundNet5 [39]	A	94.74%	16.10%	**97.70%**	58.81%	23.21%	N/A
SoundNet8 [39]	A	83.83%	4.24%	89.62%	71.43%	58.93%	N/A
ISNN-A	A	**96.74%**	**92.37%**	97.07%	**99.52%**	**89.29%**	N/A
Pre-trained VGG16	V	N/A	N/A	N/A	N/A	N/A	73.27%

The results for geometry classification are presented in Tables 1, 2, 3, and 4. For RSAudio synthetic (S) and real (R), ISNN-A provides competitive results with all other tested algorithms. For real sounds, where issues of recordings are most problematic, ISNN-A significantly outperforms all other algorithms, with an accuracy of 92.37%. On the merged RSAudio dataset of real and synthetic sounds, all models actually produce *higher* accuracy than on either synthetic or real alone, indicating that training on both sets improves generalizability. As an additional baseline, we classified 100 ImageNet RGB transparent object images based on the VGG16 pre-trained model and obtained 73.27% accuracy with top 5 labels and an average confidence of 46.64%. While the accuracy is not directly comparable with ModelNet and RSAudio results, it provides a preliminary suggestion that a second modality could further improve results.

5.2   ModelNet Evaluation

In Tables 2, 3, and 4, ModelNet results are categorized by input: audio (A), voxel (V), or both (AV). The "MN10" dataset consists of 119,620 total synthetic sounds: multiple sounds at different hit points for each geometry and material combination. The "o" suffix (e.g. "MN10o") indicates that only one sound per model was produced, and all models were assigned one identical material. The "s" suffix (e.g. "MN10os") indicates that each ModelNet class was assigned a realistic and normally distributed scale before synthesizing sounds. The "m" suffix (e.g. "MN10om") indicates that each ModelNet class was assigned a realistic material.

Table 2. Our audio-only ISNN-A outperforms other audio-only baselines.

Geometry Classification Accuracy: Audio Methods (ISNN-A Ours), ModelNet

Method	Input	MN10o	MN10os	MN10om	MN10osm	MN10	MN40o	MN40osm
Nearest Neighbor	A	40.73%	32.42%	62.81%	67.97%	—	26.55%	54.41%
Linear SVM	A	16.67%	7.81%	28.85%	15.63%	11.73%	3.97%	12.18%
SoundNet5	A	16.96%	10.00%	10.70%	11.00%	—	4.10%	10.95%
SoundNet8	A	10.64%	19.50%	20.74%	29.67%	—	5.73%	49.27%
ISNN-A	A	**43.35%**	**56.50%**	**68.00%**	**71.50%**	**42.90%**	**32.51%**	**65.07%**

Table 3. VoxNet [4] achieves the highest level of accuracy compared to other alternative methods for geometry classification with visual input only.

Geometry Classification Accuracy: Visual Methods (All Baselines), ModelNet

Method	Input	MN10o	MN10os	MN10om	MN10osm	MN10	MN40o	MN40osm
Nearest Neighbor	V	83.11%	72.57%	82.62%	72.96%	—	65.72%	67.23%
Linear SVM	V	74.06%	66.80%	68.65%	77.34%	35.39%	51.15%	12.06%
VoxNet [4]	V			89.47%				80.17%

By assigning a material and scale to each ModelNet10 class (MN10osm), classification performance achieved 71.50% for ISNN-A. Real-world objects within a class will tend to be made of a similar material and scale, so MN10osm is likely more reflective of performance in real-world settings where these factors provide increased potential for classification. However, for the multimodal ISNN-AV, material and scale assignments do not improve accuracy. In MN10o, larger geometric features will correspond to lower-pitched sounds (i.e. a large object will produce a deeper sound than a small object), and the multimodal fusion of those cues produces higher accuracy. However, when models are given materials and scales in MN10o{s,m,sm}, the voxel inputs remain unchanged, weakening the relationship between voxel and audio inputs. Scaling the voxel representation as well as the model used for sound synthesis may reduce this issue.

Assigning scale and material improve ModelNet40 accuracy (MN40osm) because its object classes differ more in size and material than ModelNet10. The merged audio-visual networks outperform the separate audio or visual networks in every case except for MN10os, as discussed above. Across all ModelNet10 datasets, ISNN-AV with multimodal factorized bilinear pooling produces the highest accuracy on MN10o, at 91.80%. Similarly, ModelNet40 produces optimal results using ISNN-AV with multiplicative fusion on MN40osm, at 93.24%. Entries with a "—" were not completed due to prohibitive time or memory costs when using the large MN10 dataset.

Table 4. Our merged networks produce accuracy upto 90.12% on MN10osm and upto 93.24% on MN40osm. Please visit ModelNet for more information on other methods and results.

Geometry Classification Accuracy: Audio-Visual Methods (ISNN-AV Ours), ModelNet

Method	Input	MN10o	MN10os	MN10om	MN10osm	MN10	MN40o	MN40osm
Nearest Neighbor	AV	82.91%	72.57%	83.40%	74.05%	—	65.84%	71.25%
Linear SVM	AV	80.63%	73.44%	82.50%	81.64%	36.70%	54.93%	66.15%
MergeCat (ISNN-AV)	AV	86.25%	78.50%	88.96%	88.50%	87.40%	79.93%	92.30%
MergeCat (Sound-Net8)	AV	88.14%	52.50%	72.80%	54.50%	—	79.56%	56.39%
MergeAdd (ISNN-AV)	AV	88.91%	80.00%	88.52%	86.00%	88.27%	79.40%	90.43%
MergeAdd (SoundNet8)	AV	88.58%	50.50%	72.91%	64.33%	—	79.89%	24.43%
MergeMultFuse (ISNN-AV)	AV	89.14%	84.00%	89.41%	86.24%	87.51%	81.35%	**93.24%**
MergeMultFuse (SoundNet8)	AV	83.48%	66.00%	71.79%	51.67%	—	61.44%	38.97%
MergeMFB (ISNN-AV)	AV	**91.80%**	**84.50%**	**89.97%**	**90.12%**	**89.16%**	**82.04%**	92.51%
MergeMFB (SoundNet8)	AV	88.69%	76.50%	73.02%	42.00%	—	80.90%	91.33%

5.3   Additional Evaluations

We evaluated on additional datasets such as Arnab et. al [9]. This dataset consists of audio of tabletop objects being struck, with ground-truth object labels provided. ISNN-A produces 89.29% accuracy, the highest of all evaluated algorithms. This accuracy is slightly lower than ISNN-A's accuracy on RSAudio's real sounds, likely due to the loosened constraints on the recording environment and striking methodology. The same networks were also considered for material classification, and results can be seen in Supplemental Document (Sect. 6).

We also evaluate the ability of synthetic sounds to supplement a smaller number of real sounds for training, which would reduce necessary human effort in obtaining sounds. Figure 6 shows classification accuracy on a real subset of our RSAudio dataset for ISNN-A trained on a combination of real and synthetic sounds. The training sets have identical total sizes but are created with specific percentages of real and synthetic sounds, then networks are trained on either the combined dataset or the real sounds independently. We find that the addition of synthetic sounds to the dataset improves accuracy by up to 11%. With only 30% real sounds (Point A), accuracy begins to plateau, reaching over 90% accuracy with only 60% real sounds (Point B). These indicate that synthetic audio can supplement a smaller amount of recorded audio to improve accuracy.

Augmentations in Subsect. 3.2 were designed to enhance the realism of synthetic audio for improved transfer learning from synthetic to real sounds. However, we were unable to find an instance when these augmentations significantly improved test accuracy of RSAudio real when trained on RSAudio synthetic. This indicates that *modal* components of sounds (frequencies, amplitudes) are

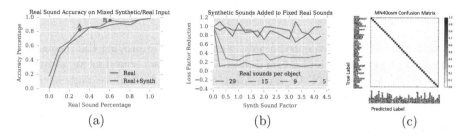

(a)   (b)   (c)

Fig. 6. Classification accuracy on a test set of real sounds using ISNN trained on a combination of real and synthetic sounds. (a) When trained on combined real and synthetic sounds (Real+Synth), classification accuracy is upto 11% higher than when trained on the real sounds alone (Real). (b) When insufficient real sounds are provided, synthetic sounds further reduce loss. (c) Our method has been able to correctly classify impact sounds with voxel data across ModelNet40 classes, as displayed by the MN40osm confusion matrix, for instance.

sufficient and most critical in object classification, and that acoustic radiance, noise, and propagation effects produce little, if any, impact on accuracy.

5.4 Application: Audio-Guided 3D Reconstruction

A primary use case of the method described in this paper is to improve reconstruction of transparent, occluded, or reflective objects. We have constructed a demo application in which our method enables real-time scene reconstruction and augmentation. We enhance open-source 3D reconstruction software [6,7] by adding an audio-based selector function. Figure 7 illustrates the application pipeline. Further details are in the Supplemental Document (Sect. 2) and demo video at http://gamma.cs.unc.edu/ISNN/.

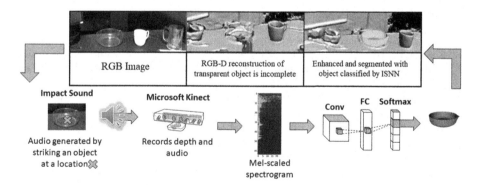

Fig. 7. A user strikes a real-world object to generate sound as an input into our ISNN network which returns material and object classification. Based on these, the real-time 3D reconstruction [6,7] is enhanced and segmented.

6 Conclusion

In this paper, we have presented a novel approach for improving the reconstruction of 3D objects using audio-visual data. Given impact sound as an additional input, ISNN-A and ISNN-AV have been optimized to achieve high accuracy on object classification tasks. The use of spectrogram representations of input reduce overfitting by directly inputting spectral information to the networks. ISNN has further shown higher performance when using a dataset with combined synthetic and real audio. Sound provides additional cues, allowing us to estimate the object's material class, provide segmentation, and enhance scene reconstruction.

Limitations and Future Work: While VoxNet serves as a strong baseline for the visual component of ISNN-AV, different visual networks in its place could identify more optimal network pairings. As with existing learning methods, VoxNet is limited to performing classifications of known geometries. However, impact sounds hold potential of identifying correct geometry, even when a model database is not provided, allowing for accurate 3D reconstructions or hole-filling.

References

1. Girshick, R., Donahue, J., Darrell, T., Malik, J.: Rich feature hierarchies for accurate object detection and semantic segmentation. In: Proceedings of the 2014 IEEE Conference on Computer Vision and Pattern Recognition, CVPR 2014, Washington, DC, USA, pp. 580–587. IEEE Computer Society (2014)
2. Ren, S., He, K., Girshick, R., Sun, J.: Faster R-CNN: towards real-time object detection with region proposal networks. In: Advances in Neural Information Processing Systems (NIPS) (2015)
3. Wu, Z., et al.: 3D ShapeNets: a deep representation for volumetric shape modeling. In: Proceedings of 28th IEEE Conference on Computer Vision and Pattern Recognition (CVPR) (2015)
4. Maturana, D., Scherer, S.: VoxNet: a 3D convolutional neural network for real-time object recognition. In: IROS (2015)
5. Socher, R., Huval, B., Bhat, B., Manning, C.D., Ng, A.Y.: Convolutional-recursive deep learning for 3D object classification. In: Conference on Neural Information Processing Systems (NIPS) (2012)
6. Golodetz, S., et al.: SemanticPaint: a framework for the interactive segmentation of 3D scenes. Technical report TVG-2015-1, Department of Engineering Science, University of Oxford, Oct 2015. Released as arXiv e-print arXiv:1510.03727
7. Valentin, J., et al.: SemanticPaint: interactive 3D labeling and learning at your fingertips. ACM Trans. Graph. **34**(5) (2015)
8. Zhang, Z., et al.: Generative modeling of audible shapes for object perception. In: The IEEE International Conference on Computer Vision (ICCV) (2017)
9. Arnab, A., et al.: Joint object-material category segmentation from audio-visual cues. In: Proceedings of the British Machine Vision Conference (BMVC) (2015)
10. Singh, A., Sha, J., Narayan, K.S., Achim, T., Abbeel, P.: BigBIRD: a large-scale 3D database of object instances. In: IEEE International Conference on Robotics and Automation (ICRA) (2014)

11. Lai, K., Bo, L., Ren, X., Fox, D.: A large-scale hierarchical multi-view RGB-D object dataset. In: IEEE International Conference on Robotics and Automation (ICRA) (2011)
12. Kanezaki, A., Matsushita, Y., Nishida, Y.: Rotationnet: learning object classification using unsupervised viewpoint estimation. CoRR abs/1603.06208 (2016)
13. Silberman, N., Hoiem, D., Kohli, P., Fergus, R.: Indoor segmentation and support inference from RGBD images. In: Fitzgibbon, A., Lazebnik, S., Perona, P., Sato, Y., Schmid, C. (eds.) ECCV 2012. LNCS, vol. 7576, pp. 746–760. Springer, Heidelberg (2012). https://doi.org/10.1007/978-3-642-33715-4_54
14. Song, S., Yu, F., Zeng, A., Chang, A.X., Savva, M., Funkhouser, T.: Semantic scene completion from a single depth image. In: Proceedings of 30th IEEE Conference on Computer Vision and Pattern Recognition (2017)
15. Westoby, M., Brasington, J., Glasser, N., Hambrey, M., Reynolds, J.: structure-from-motion photogrammetry: a low-cost, effective tool for geoscience applications. Geomorphology **179**, 300–314 (2012)
16. Seitz, S.M., Curless, B., Diebel, J., Scharstein, D., Szeliski, R.: A comparison and evaluation of multi-view stereo reconstruction algorithms. In: Proceedings of the IEEE Conference on Computer Vision and Pattern Recognition (CVPR) (2006)
17. Zhang, R., Tsai, P.S., Cryer, J.E., Shah, M.: Shape-from-shading: a survey. IEEE Trans. Pattern Anal. Mach. Intell. **21**(8), 690–706 (1999)
18. Newcombe, R.A., et al.: KinectFusion: real-time dense surface mapping and tracking. In: International Symposium on Mixed and Augmented Reality (ISMAR) (2011)
19. Newcombe, R., Fox, D., Seitz, S.: DynamicFusion: reconstruction and tracking of non-rigid scenes in real-time. In: Proceedings of 28th IEEE Conference on Computer Vision and Pattern Recognition (CVPR) (2015)
20. Dai, A., Niessner, M., Zollhofer, M., Izadi, S., Theobalt, C.: BundleFusion: real-time globally consistent 3D reconstruction using on-the-fly surface re-integration. In: SIGGRAPH (2017)
21. Lysenkov, I., Eruhimov, V., Bradski, G.: Recognition and pose estimation of rigid transparent objects with a kinect sensor. In: Robotics: Science and Systems Conference (RSS) (2013)
22. Aberman, K., et al.: Dip transform for 3D shape reconstruction. In: SIGGRAPH (2017)
23. Tanaka, K., Mukaigawa, Y., Funatomi, T., Kubo, H., Matsushita, Y., Yagi, Y.: Material classification using frequency- and depth-dependent time-of-flight distortion. In: 2017 IEEE Conference on Computer Vision and Pattern Recognition (CVPR), pp. 79–88, July 2017
24. Gemmeke, J.F., et al.: Audio set: an ontology and human-labeled dataset for audio events. In: Proceedings of the IEEE ICASSP 2017, New Orleans, LA (2017)
25. Piczak, K.J.: Esc: dataset for environmental sound classification. In: Proceedings of the 23rd ACM International Conference on Multimedia, MM 2015, New York, NY, USA, pp. 1015–1018. ACM (2015)
26. Salamon, J., Jacoby, C., Bello, J.P.: A dataset and taxonomy for urban sound research. In: Proceedings of the 22nd ACM International Conference on Multimedia, MM 2014, New York, NY, USA, pp. 1041–1044. ACM (2014)
27. Büchler, M., Allegro, S., Launer, S., Dillier, N.: Sound classification in hearing aids inspired by auditory scene analysis. EURASIP J. Adv. Signal Process. **2005**(18), 387845 (2005)
28. Cowling, M., Sitte, R.: Comparison of techniques for environmental sound recognition. Pattern Recognit. Lett. **24**(15), 2895–2907 (2003)

29. Barchiesi, D., Giannoulis, D., Stowell, D., Plumbley, M.D.: Acoustic scene classification: classifying environments from the sounds they produce. IEEE Signal Process. Mag. **32**(3), 16–34 (2015)
30. Piczak, K.J.: Environmental sound classification with convolutional neural networks. In: 2015 IEEE 25th International Workshop on Machine Learning for Signal Processing (MLSP), pp. 1–6, Sept 2015
31. Salamon, J., Bello, J.P.: Deep convolutional neural networks and data augmentation for environmental sound classification. IEEE Signal Process. Lett. **24**(3), 279–283 (2017)
32. Hershey, S., et al.: CNN architectures for large-scale audio classification. In: 2017 IEEE International Conference on Acoustics, Speech and Signal Processing (ICASSP), pp. 131–135, Mar 2017
33. Huzaifah, M.: Comparison of time-frequency representations for environmental sound classification using convolutional neural networks. CoRR abs/1706.07156 (2017)
34. Ren, Z., Yeh, H., Lin, M.C.: Example-guided physically based modal sound synthesis. ACM Trans. Graph. **32**(1), 1:1–1:16 (2013)
35. Sterling, A., Lin, M.C.: Interactive modal sound synthesis using generalized proportional damping. In: Proceedings of the 20th ACM SIGGRAPH Symposium on Interactive 3D Graphics and Games, I3D 2016, New York, NY, USA, pp. 79–86. ACM (2016)
36. Zhang, Z., Li, Q., Huang, Z., Wu, J., Tenenbaum, J., Freeman, B.: Shape and material from sound. In: Guyon, I. (eds.) Advances in Neural Information Processing Systems, vol. 30. pp. 1278–1288. Curran Associates, Inc. (2017)
37. Kac, M.: Can one hear the shape of a drum? Am. Math. Mon. **73**(4), 1–23 (1966)
38. Owens, A., Wu, J., McDermott, J.H., Freeman, W.T., Torralba, A.: Ambient sound provides supervision for visual learning. In: Leibe, B., Matas, J., Sebe, N., Welling, M. (eds.) ECCV 2016. LNCS, vol. 9905, pp. 801–816. Springer, Cham (2016). https://doi.org/10.1007/978-3-319-46448-0_48
39. Aytar, Y., Vondrick, C., Torralba, A.: Soundnet: Learning sound representations from unlabeled video. In: Advances in Neural Information Processing Systems, pp. 892–900. (2016)
40. Owens, A., Isola, P., McDermott, J., Torralba, A., Adelson, E.H., Freeman, W.T.: Visually indicated sounds. In: Proceedings of the IEEE Conference on Computer Vision and Pattern Recognition, pp. 2405–2413 (2016)
41. Simonyan, K., Zisserman, A.: Two-stream convolutional networks for action recognition in videos. In: Ghahramani, Z., Welling, M., Cortes, C., Lawrence, N.D., Weinberger, K.Q. (eds.) Advances in Neural Information Processing Systems, vol. 27, pp. 568–576. Curran Associates, Inc. (2014)
42. Tenenbaum, J.B., Freeman, W.T.: Separating style and content with bilinear models. Neural Comput. **12**(6), 1247–1283 (2000)
43. Lin, T.Y., RoyChowdhury, A., Maji, S.: Bilinear CNN models for fine-grained visual recognition. In: International Conference on Computer Vision (ICCV) (2015)
44. Gao, Y., Beijbom, O., Zhang, N., Darrell, T.: Compact bilinear pooling. In: Proceedings of the IEEE Conference on Computer Vision and Pattern Recognition, pp. 317–326 (2016)
45. Yu, Z., Yu, J., Fan, J., Tao, D.: Multi-modal factorized bilinear pooling with co-attention learning for visual question answering. In: IEEE International Conference on Computer Vision (ICCV), pp. 1839–1848 (2017)

46. Park, E., Han, X., Berg, T.L., Berg, A.C.: Combining multiple sources of knowledge in deep CNNs for action recognition. In: 2016 IEEE Winter Conference on Applications of Computer Vision (WACV), pp. 1–8. IEEE (2016)
47. O'Brien, J.F., Shen, C., Gatchalian, C.M.: Synthesizing sounds from rigid-body simulations. In: Proceedings of the 2002 ACM SIGGRAPH/Eurographics Symposium on Computer Animation, SCA 2002, New York, NY, USA, pp. 175–181. ACM (2002)
48. Raghuvanshi, N., Lin, M.C.: Interactive sound synthesis for large scale environments. In: Proceedings of the 2006 Symposium on Interactive 3D Graphics and Games, I3D 2006, New York, NY, USA, pp. 101–108. ACM (2006)
49. van den Doel, K., Pai, D.K.: The sounds of physical shapes. Presence 7, 382–395 (1996)
50. Morrison, J.D., Adrien, J.M.: Mosaic: a framework for modal synthesis. Comput. Music. J. 17(1), 45–56 (1993)
51. James, D.L., Barbič, J., Pai, D.K.: Precomputed acoustic transfer: output-sensitive, accurate sound generation for geometrically complex vibration sources. ACM Trans. Graph. (TOG) 25, 987–995 (2006)
52. Schissler, C., Manocha, D.: Gsound: interactive sound propagation for games. In: Audio Engineering Society Conference: 41st International Conference: Audio for Games, Feb 2011
53. Thiemann, J., Ito, N., Vincent, E.: The diverse environments multi-channel acoustic noise database (demand): a database of multichannel environmental noise recordings. Proc. Meet. Acoust. 19(1), 035081 (2013)
54. Bergstra, J.S., Bardenet, R., Bengio, Y., Kégl, B.: Algorithms for hyper-parameter optimization. In: Shawe-Taylor, J., Zemel, R.S., Bartlett, P.L., Pereira, F., Weinberger, K.Q. (eds.) Advances in Neural Information Processing Systems, vol. 24, pp. 2546–2554. Curran Associates, Inc. (2011)
55. Bottou, L.: Large-scale machine learning with stochastic gradient descent. In: Lechevallier, Y., Saporta, G., (eds.) Proceedings of the 19th International Conference on Computational Statistics (COMPSTAT 2010), Paris, France, pp. 177–187. Springer, Aug 2010. https://doi.org/10.1007/978-3-7908-2604-3_16
56. Kingma, D., Ba, J.: Adam: a method for stochastic optimization. In: International Conference on Learning Representations (ICLR) (2015)

StereoNet: Guided Hierarchical Refinement for Real-Time Edge-Aware Depth Prediction

Sameh Khamis$^{(\boxtimes)}$, Sean Fanello, Christoph Rhemann, Adarsh Kowdle, Julien Valentin, and Shahram Izadi

Google Inc., Mountain View, USA
sameh@google.com

Abstract. This paper presents StereoNet, the first end-to-end deep architecture for real-time stereo matching that runs at 60fps on an NVidia Titan X, producing high-quality, edge-preserved, quantization-free disparity maps. A key insight of this paper is that the network achieves a sub-pixel matching precision than is a magnitude higher than those of traditional stereo matching approaches. This allows us to achieve real-time performance by using a very low resolution cost volume that encodes all the information needed to achieve high disparity precision. Spatial precision is achieved by employing a learned edge-aware upsampling function. Our model uses a Siamese network to extract features from the left and right image. A first estimate of the disparity is computed in a very low resolution cost volume, then hierarchically the model re-introduces high-frequency details through a learned upsampling function that uses compact pixel-to-pixel refinement networks. Leveraging color input as a guide, this function is capable of producing high-quality edge-aware output. We achieve compelling results on multiple benchmarks, showing how the proposed method offers extreme flexibility at an acceptable computational budget.

Keywords: Stereo matching · Depth estimation
Edge-aware refinement · Cost volume filtering · Deep learning

1 Introduction

Stereo matching is a classical computer vision problem that is concerned with estimating depth from two slightly displaced images. Depth estimation has recently been projected to the center stage with the rising interest in virtual and augmented reality [41]. It is at the heart of many tasks from 3D reconstruction to localization and tracking [28]. Its applications span otherwise disparate research and product areas including indoor mapping and architecture, autonomous cars, and human body and face tracking.

© Springer Nature Switzerland AG 2018
V. Ferrari et al. (Eds.): ECCV 2018, LNCS 11219, pp. 596–613, 2018.
https://doi.org/10.1007/978-3-030-01267-0_35

Active depth sensors like the Microsoft Kinect provide high quality depth-maps and have not only revolutionized computer vision research [11,12,16,41, 55], but also play an important role in consumer level applications. These active depth sensors have become very popular over the recent years with the release of many other consumer devices, such as the Intel RealSense series, the structured light sensor on iPhone X, as well as time-of-flight cameras such as Kinect V2. With the rise of Augmented Reality (AR) applications on mobile devices, there is a growing need of algorithms capable of predicting precise depth under tight computational budget. With the exception of the iPhone X, all smartphones on the market can only rely on single or dual RGB streams. The release of sparse tracking and mapping tools like ARKit and ARCore impressively demonstrate coarse and sparse geometry estimation on mobile devices. However, they lack dense depth estimation and therefore cannot enable exciting AR applications such as occlusion handling or precise interaction of virtual objects with the real world. Depth estimation using a single moving camera, akin to [46], or dual cameras naturally became a requirement from the industry to scale AR to millions of users.

The state of the art in passive depth relies on stereo triangulation between two (rectified) RGB images. This has historically been dominated by CRF-based approaches. These techniques obtain very good results but are computationally slow. Inference in these models amounts to solving a generally NP-hard problem, forcing practitioners in many cases to use solvers whose runtime is in the ranges of seconds [33] or resort to approximated solutions [14,15,54,56]. Additionally, these techniques typically suffer in the presence of textureless regions, occlusions, repetitive patterns, thin-structures, and reflective surfaces. The field is slowly transitioning and since [61], it started to use deep features, mostly as unary potentials, to further advance the state of the art.

Recently, deep-architectures demonstrated a high level of accuracy at predicting depth from passive stereo data [26,29,37,42]. Despite these significant advances, the proposed methods require vast amounts of processing power and memory. For instance, [29] have 3.5 million parameters in their network and reach a throughput of about 0.95 image per second on 960×540 images, and [42] takes 0.5 s to produce a single disparity on a high end GPU.

In this paper we present StereoNet, a novel deep architecture that generated state of the art 720p depth maps at 60Hz on high end GPUs. Based on our insight that deep architectures are very good to infer matches at extremely high subpixel precision we demonstrate that a very low resolution cost volume is sufficient to achieve a depth precision that is comparable to a traditional stereo matching system that operates at full resolution. To achieve spatial precision we apply edge-aware filtering stages in a multi-scale manner to deliver a high quality output. In summary the main contributions of this work are the following:

1. We show that the subpixel matching precision of a deep architecture is an order of magnitude higher than those of "traditional" stereo approaches.

2. We demonstrate that the high subpixel precision of the network allows to achieve the depth precision of traditional stereo matching with a very low resolution cost volume resulting in an extremely efficient algorithm.
3. We show that previous work that introduced cost-volume in deep architectures was over-parameterized for the task and how this significantly help reducing the run-time and memory footprint of the system at little cost in accuracy.
4. A new hierarchical depth-refinement layer that is capable of performing high-quality up-sampling that preserves edges.
5. Finally, we demonstrate that the proposed system reaches compelling results on several benchmarks while being real-time on high end GPU architectures.

2   Related Work

Depth from stereo has been studied for a long time and we refer the interested reader to [22,49] for a survey. Correspondence search for stereo is a challenging problem and has been traditionally divided into global and local approaches. Global approaches formulate a cost function over the image that is traditionally optimized using approaches such as Belief Propagation or Graph Cuts [3,17,30, 31]. Instead, local stereo matching methods (e.g. [4]) center a support window on a pixel in the reference frame and then displace this window in the second image until the point of highest correlation is found. A major challenge for local stereo matching is to define the optimal size for the support window. On the one hand the window needs to be large to capture a sufficient amount of texture but needs to be small at the same time to avoid aggregating wrong disparity values that can lead to the well-known edge fattening effect at disparity discontinuities. To avoid this trade-off, adaptive support approaches weigh the influence of each pixel inside the support region based on e.g. its color similarity to the central pixel.

Interestingly adaptive support weight approaches were cast as cost volume filtering in [25]: a three-dimensional cost volume is constructed by computing the per-pixel matching costs at all possible disparity levels. This cost volume is then filtered with a weighted average filter. This filtering propagates local information in the spatial and depth domains producing a depth map that preserves edges across object discontinuities.

For triangulation based stereo matching system the accuracy of depth is directly linked to the precision to which the corresponding pixel in the other image can be located. Therefore, previous work strives to do matching with sub-pixel precision. The complexity of most algorithms scale linearly with the number of disparities evaluated so while one approach is to build a large cost volume with very fine grained disparity steps this is computationally in-feasible. Many algorithms therefore start with discrete matching and then refine these matches by fitting a local curve such as a parabolic fit to the cost function between the discrete disparity candidates (see e.g. [39,59]). Other works are based on continuous optimization strategies [47] or on phase correlation [48]. It was shown in [45] that under realistic conditions the bound for subpixel precision is 1/10th of a pixel while the theoretical limit under noise free conditions was found to be 10 times lower [10]. We demonstrate that this traditional wisdom does not hold true for learning-based approaches and we can achieve a subpixel precision of 1/30th of a pixel.

Recent work has progressed to using end-to-end learning for stereo matching. Various approaches combined a learned patch embedding or matching cost with global optimization approaches like semiglobal matching (SGM) for refinement [60]. [9] learn a multi-scale embedding model followed by an MRF. [61,62] learn to match image patches followed by SGM. [35] learn to match patches using a Siamese feature network and optimize globally with SGM as well. [52] uses a multi-stage approach where a highway network architecture is first used to compute the matching costs and then another network is used in postprocessing to aggregate and pool costs.

Other works attempted to solve the stereo matching problem end-to-end without postprocessing. [26,37] train end-to-end an encoder-decoder network for disparity and flow estimation achieving state-of-the-art results on existing and new benchmarks. Other end-to-end approaches used multiple refinement stages that converge to the right disparity hypotheses. [21] proposed a generic architecture for labeling problems, including depth estimation, that is trained end-to-end to predict and refine the output. [42] proposed a cascaded approach to refine predicted depth iteratively. Iterative refinement approaches, while showing good performance on various benchmarks, tend to require a considerable amount of computational resources.

More closely related to our work is [29] who used the concept of cost volume filtering but trained both the features and the filters end-to-end achieving impressive results. DeepStereo [18] used a plane-sweep volume to synthesize novel views from multi-view stereo input. Contrary to prior work, we are interested in an end-to-end learning stereo pipeline that can run in real-time, therefore we start from a very low resolution cost volume, which is then upsampled with learned, edge aware filters.

3   StereoNet Algorithm

3.1   Preliminaries

Given pairs of input images we aim to train an end-to-end disparity prediction pipeline. One approach to train such pipeline is to leverage a generic encoder-decoder network. An encoder distills the input through a series of contracting layers to a bottleneck that captures the details most relevant to the task in training, and the decoder reconstructs the output from the representation captured in the bottleneck layer through a series of expanding layers. While this approach is widely successful across various problems, including depth prediction [26,37,42], they lack several qualities we care about in stereo algorithm.

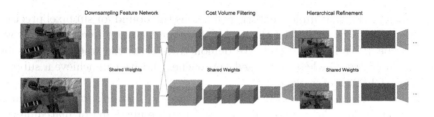

Fig. 1. Model architecture. A two stage approach is proposed: first we extract image features at a lower resolution using a Siamese network. We then build a cost volume at that resolution by matching the features along the scanlines, giving us a coarse disparity estimate. We finally refine the results hierarchically to recover small details and thin structures.

First of all, this approach does not capture any geometric intuition about the stereo matching problem. Stereo prediction is first-and-foremost a correspondence matching problem, so we aimed to design an algorithm that can be adapted without retraining to different stereo cameras with varying resolutions and baselines. Secondly, we note that similar approaches are evidently overparameterized for problems where the prediction is a pixel-to-pixel mapping that does not involve any warping of the input, and thus likely to overfit.

Our approach to stereo matching incorporates a design that leverages the problem structure and classical approaches to tackle it, akin to [29], while producing edge-preserving output using compact context-aware pixel-to-pixel refinement networks. An overview of the architecture of our model is illustrated in Fig. 1 and detailed in the following sections.

3.2   Coarse Prediction: Cost Volume Filtering

Stereo system are in general solving a correspondence problem. The problem classically boils down to forming a disparity map by finding a pixel-to-pixel match between two rectified images along their scanlines. The desire for a smooth and edge-preserving solution led to approaches like cost volume filtering [25], which explicitly model the matching problem by forming and processing a 3D volume that jointly solves across all candidate disparities at each pixel. While [25] directly used color values for the matching, we compute a feature representation at each pixel that is used for matching.

Feature Network. The first step of the pipeline finds a meaningful representation of image patches that can be accurately matched in the later stages. We recall that stereo suffer from textureless regions and traditional methods solve this issue by aggregating the cost using large windows. We replicate the same behavior in the network by making sure the features are extracted from a big receptive field. In particular, we use a feature network with shared weights between the two input images (also known as a Siamese network). We first aggressively downsample the input images using K 5×5 convolutions with a stride of 2, keeping the number of channels at 32 throughout the downsampling. In our experiments we set K to 3 or 4. We then apply 6 residual blocks [23] that employ 3×3 convolutions, batch-normalization [27], and leaky ReLu activations ($\alpha = 0.2$) [36]. Finally, this is processed using a final layer with a 3×3 convolution that does not use batch-normalization or activation. The output is a 32-dimensional feature vector at each pixel in the downsampled image. This low resolution representation is important for two reasons: (1) it has a big receptive field, useful for textureless regions. (2) It keeps the feature vectors compact.

Cost Volume. At this point, we form a cost volume at the coarse resolution by taking the difference between the feature vector of a pixel and the feature vectors of the matching candidates. We noted that asymmetric representations in general performed well, and concatenating the two vectors achieved similar results in our experiments.

At this stage, a traditional stereo method would use a winner-takes-all (WTA) approach that picks the disparity with the lowest Euclidean distance between the two feature vectors. Instead, here we let the network to learn the right metric by running multiple convolutions followed by non-linearities.

In particular, to aggregate context across the spatial domain as well as the disparity domain, we filter the cost volume with four 3D convolutions with a filter size of $3 \times 3 \times 3$, batch-normalization, and leaky ReLu activations. A final $3 \times 3 \times 3$ convolutional layer that does not use batch-normalization or activation is then applied, and the filtering layers produce a 1-dimensional output at each pixel and candidate disparity.

For an input image of size $W \times H$ and evaluating a maximum of D candidate disparities, our cost volume is of size $W/2^K \times H/2^K \times (D+1)/2^K$ for K downsampling layers. In our design of StereoNet we targeted a compact approach with a small memory footprint that can be potentially deployed to mobile platforms. Unlike [29] who form a feature representation at quarter resolution and aggregate cost volumes across multiple levels, we note that most of the time and compute is spent matching at higher resolutions, while most of the performance gain comes from matching at lower resolutions. We validate this claim in our experiments and show that the performance loss is not significant in light of the speed gain. The reason for this is that the network achieves a magnitude higher sub-pixel precision than traditional stereo matching approaches. Therefore, matching at higher resolutions is not needed.

Differentiable Arg Min. We typically would select the disparity with the minimum cost at each pixel in the filtered cost volume using arg min. For a pixel i and a cost function over disparity values $C(d)$, the selected disparity value d_i is defined as:

$$d_i = \arg \min_d C_i(d). \tag{1}$$

This however fails to learn since arg min is a non-differentiable function. We considered two differentiable variants in our approach. The first of which is soft arg min, which was originally proposed in [6] and was used in [29]. Effectively, the selected disparity is a softmax-weighted combination of all the disparity values:

$$d_i = \sum_{d=1}^{D} d \cdot \frac{\exp(-C_i(d))}{\sum_{d'} \exp(-C_i(d'))}. \tag{2}$$

The second differentiable variant is a probabilistic selection that samples from the softmax distribution over the costs:

$$d_i = d, \text{ where } d \sim \frac{\exp(-C_i(d))}{\sum_{d'} \exp(-C_i(d'))}. \tag{3}$$

Differentiating through the sampling process uses gradient estimation techniques to learn the distribution of disparities by minimizing the expected loss of the stochastic process. While this technique has roots in policy gradient approaches in reinforcement learning [57], it was recently formulated as stochastic computation graphs in [50] and applied to RANSAC-based camera localization in [5]. Additionally, the parallel between the two differentiable variants we discussed is akin to that between soft and hard attention networks [58].

Unfortunately the probabilistic approach significantly underperformed in our experiments, even with various variance reduction techniques [58]. We expect that this is because it preserves hard selections. This trait is arguably critical in many applications, but in our model it is superseded by the ability of soft arg min to regress subpixel-accurate values. This conclusion is supported by the literature on continuous action spaces in reinforcement learning [34]. The soft arg min selection was consequently faster to converge and easier to optimize, and it is what we chose to use in our experiments.

3.3 Hierarchical Refinement: Edge-Aware Upsampling

The downside to relying on coarse matching is that the resulting myopic output lacks fine details. To maintain our compact design, we approach this problem by learning an edge-preserving refinement network. We note that the network's job at this stage is to dilate or erode the disparity values to blend in high-frequency details using the color input as guide, so a compact network that learns a pixel-to-pixel mapping, similar to networks employed in recent computational photography work [7,8,20], is an appropriate approach. Specifically, we task the refinement network of only finding a residual (or a delta disparity) to add or subtract from the coarse prediction.

Our refinement network takes as input the disparity bilinearly upsampled to the output size as well as the color resized to the same dimensions. Recently deconvolutions were shown to produce checkerboard artifacts, so we opted to use bilinear upsampling and convolutions instead [40]. The concatenated color and disparity first pass through a 3×3 convolutional layer that outputs a 32-dimensional representation. This is then passed through 6 residual blocks that,

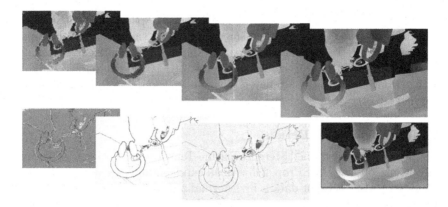

Fig. 2. Hierarchical refinement results. The result at each stage (top row), starting with the cost volume output in the top left corner, is updated with the output of the corresponding refinement network (bottom row). The refinement network output expectedly dilates and erodes around the edges using the color input as guide. The groundtruth is shown in the lower right corner. The average endpoint error at each stage for this example is: 3.27, 2.34, 1.80, and 1.26 respectively. Zoom in for details.

again, employ 3×3 convolutions, batch-normalization, and leaky ReLu activations ($\alpha = 0.2$). We use atrous convolutions in these blocks to sample from a larger context without increasing the network size [43]. We set the dilation factors for the residual blocks to 1, 2, 4, 8, 1, and 1 respectively. This output is then processed using a 3×3 convolutional layer that does not use batch-normalization or activation. The output of this network is a 1-dimensional disparity residual that is then added to the previous prediction. We apply a ReLu to the sum to constrain disparities to be positive.

In our experiments we evaluated hierarchically refining the output with a cascade of the described network, as well as applying a single refinement that upsamples the coarse output to the full resolution in one-shot. Figure 2 illustrates the output of the refinement layer at each level of the hierarchy as well as the residuals added at each level to recover the high-frequency details. The behavior of this network is reminiscent of joint bilateral upsampling [32], and indeed we believe this network is a learned edge-aware upsampling function that leverages a guide image.

3.4 Loss Function

We train StereoNet in a fully supervised manner using groundtruth-labeled stereo data. We minimize the hierarchical loss function:

$$L = \sum_k \rho(d_i^k - \hat{d}_i),\qquad(4)$$

where d_i^k is the predicted disparity at pixel i at the k-th refinement level, with $k = 0$ denoting the output pre-refinement, and $\hat{d}_i$ is the groundtruth disparity at the same pixel. The predicted disparity map is always bilinearly upsampled to match the groundtruth resolution. Finally, $\rho(.)$ is the two-parameter robust function from [2] with its parameters set as $\alpha = 1$ and $c = 2$, approximating a smoothed L1 loss.

3.5 Implementation Details

We implemented and trained StereoNet using Tensorflow [1]. All our experiments were optimized using RMSProp [24] with an exponentially-decaying learning rate initially set to 1e−3. Input data is first normalized to the range $[-1, 1]$. We use a batch size of 1 and we do not crop because of the smaller model size, unlike [29].

Our network needs around 150 k iterations to reach convergence. We found that, intuitively, training with the left and right disparity maps for an image pair at the same time significantly sped up the training time. On smaller datasets where training from scratch would be futile, we fine-tuned the pre-trained model for an additional 50 k iterations.

4 Experiments

Here, we evaluate our system on several datasets and demonstrate that we achieve high quality results at a fraction of the computational cost required by the state of the art.

4.1 Datasets and Setup

We evaluated StereoNet quantitatively and qualitatively on three datasets: Scene Flow [37], KITTI 2012 [19] and KITTI 2015 [38]. Scene Flow is a large synthetic stereo dataset suitable for deep learning models. However, the other two KITTI datasets, while more comparable to a real-world setting, are too small for full end-to-end training. We followed previous end-to-end approaches by initially training on Scene Flow and then individually fine-tuning the resulting model on the KITTI datasets [29,42]. Finally, we compare against prominent state-of-the-art methods in terms of both accuracy and runtime to show the viability of our approach in real-time scenarios.

Additionally, we performed an ablation study on the Scene Flow dataset using four variants of our model. We evaluated setting the number of downsampling convolutions K (detailed in Sect. 3.2) to 3 and 4. This controls the resolution at which the cost volume is formed. The cost volume filtering is exponentially faster with more aggressive downsampling, but comes at the expense of increasingly losing details around thin structures and small objects. The refinement layer can bring in a lot of the fine details, but if the signal is completely missing from the cost volume, it is unlikely to recover them. Additionally we evaluated using K refinement layers to hierarchically recover the details at the different scales versus using a single refinement layer to upsample the cost volume output directly to the desired final resolution.

4.2   Subpixel Precision

The precision of a depth system is usually a crucial variable when choosing the right technology for a given application. A triangulation system with a baseline b, a focal length f and a subpixel precision δ has an error ϵ which increases quadratically with the distance Z: $\epsilon = \frac{\delta Z^2}{bf}$ [53]. Competitive technologies such as Time-of-Flight do not suffer from this issue, which makes them appealing for long range applications such as room scanning and reconstruction. Despite this it has been demonstrated that multipath effects in ToF systems can distort geometry even in close-up tasks such as object scanning [13]. Long range precision remains as one of the main arguments against a stereo system and in favor of ToF.

Here we show that deep architectures are a breakthrough in terms of subpixel precision and therefore they can compete with other technologies not only for short distances but as well as in long ranges. Traditional stereo matching methods perform a discrete search and then a parabola interpolation to retrieve the accurate disparity. This methods usually leads to a subpixel precision ~ 0.25 pixels, that roughly correspond to 4.5 cm error at 3m distance for a system with a 55 cm baseline such as the Intel Realsense D415.

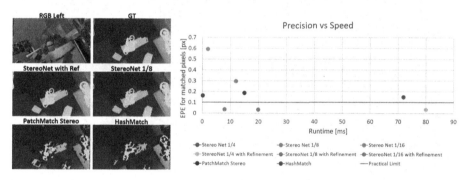

Fig. 3. Subpixel precision in stereo matching. We demonstrate that StereoNet achieves a subpixel precision of 0.03, which is one order of magnitude lower than traditional stereo approaches. The lower bound of traditional approaches was found to be 1/10th under realistic conditions (see [45]) which we indicate by the black line. Moreover, our method can run in real-time on 720p images.

To assess the precision of our method, we used the evaluation set of Scene Flow and we computed the average error only for those pixels that were correctly matched at integer locations. Results correspond to the average of over a hundred million pixels and are reported in Fig. 3. From this figure, it is important to note that: (1) the proposed method achieves a subpixel precision of **0.03** which is one order of magnitude lower than traditional stereo matching approaches such as [4,14,15]; (2) the refinement layers are performing very similarly irrespective of the resolution of the cost volume; (3) without any refinement the downsampled cost volume can still achieve a subpixel precision of 0.03 in the low resolution output. However, the error increases, almost linearly, with the downsampling factor.

Note that a subpixel precision of 0.03 means that the expected error is less than 5mm at 3m distance from the camera (Intel Realsense D415). This result makes triangulation systems very appealing and comparable with ToF technology without suffering from multi-path effects.

4.3   Quantitative Results

We now evaluate the model on standard benchmarks proving the effectiveness of the proposed methods and the different trade-offs between the resolution of the cost volume and the precision obtained.

SceneFlow. Although this data is synthetically generated, the evaluation sequences are very challenges due to the presence of occlusions, thin structures and large disparities. We evaluated our model reporting the end point error (EPE) in Table 1.

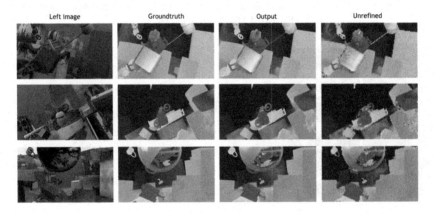

Fig. 4. Qualitative results on the FlyingThings3D test set. The proposed two-stage architecture is able to recover very fine details despite the low resolution at which we form the cost volume.

A single, unrefined model, i.e. using only the cost volume output at 1/8 of the resolution, achieves an EPE of 2.48 which is better than the full model presented in [29], which reaches an EPE of 2.51. Notice that our unrefined model is composed of 360 k parameters and runs at 12 msec at the 960 × 540 input resolution, whereas [29] uses 3.5 million parameter with a runtime of 950 msec on the same resolution. Our best, multi-scale architecture achieves the state-of-the-art error of 1.1, which is also lower than the one reported in very recent methods such as [42]. Qualitative examples can be found in Fig. 4. Notice how the method recovers very challenging fine details.

One last consideration regards the resolution of the cost volume. On one hand we proved that a coarse cost volume already carries all the information needed to retrieve a very high subpixel precision, i.e. high disparity resolution. On the

Fig. 5. Cost volume comparisons. A cost volume at 1/16 resolution has already the information required to produce high quality disparity maps. This is evident in that post refinement we recover challenging thin structures and the overall end point error (EPE) is below one pixel.

Table 1. Quantitative evaluation on SceneFlow. We achieve state of the art results compared to recent deep learning methods. We compare four variants of our model which vary in the resolution at which the cost volume is formed (8x vs 16x) and the number of refinement layers (multiple vs single).

	EPE all	EPE nocc	EPE all, unref	EPE nocc, unref
8x, multi	**1.101**	0.768	2.512	1.795
8x, single	1.532	1.058	2.486	1.784
16x, multi	1.525	1.140	3.764	2.912
16x, single	1.974	1.476	3.558	2.773
CG-Net Fast [29]	7.27	–	–	–
CG-Net Full [29]	2.51	–	–	–
CRL [42]	1.32	–	–	–

other hand, downsampling the image may lead to a loss in spatial resolution, therefore thin structures cannot be reconstructed if the output of the cost volume is very coarse. Here we demonstrate that a volume at 1/16 of the resolution is powerful enough to recover very challenging small objects. Indeed in Fig. 5, we compare the output of the three cost volumes at 1/4, 1/8, 1/16 resolutions where we also applied the refinement layers. We can observe that the fine structures that are missed in the 1/16 resolution disparity map are correctly recovered by the upsampling strategy we propose. The cost volume at 1/4 is not necessary to achieve a compelling results and this is an important finding for mobile applications. As showed in the previous subsection, even at low resolution the network achieves a subpixel precision of 1/30th pixel. However, we want to also highlight that to achieve state of the art precision on multiple benchmarks, the cost volume resolution becomes an important factor as demonstrated in Table 1.

Kitti. Kitti is a prominent stereo benchmark that was captured by driving a car equipped with cameras and a laser scanner [19]. The dataset is very challenging

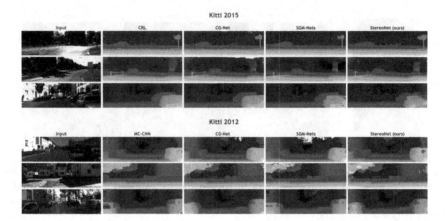

Fig. 6. Qualitative Results on Kitti 2012 and Kitti 2015. Notice how our method preserves edge and recovers details compared to the fast [51]. State of the art methods are one order of magnitude slower than the proposed approach.

Table 2. Quantitative evaluation on Kitti 2012. For StereoNet we used a model with a downsampling factor of 8 and 3 refinement levels. We report the percentage of pixels with error bigger than 2, as well as the overall EPE in both non occluded (Noc) and all the pixels (All).

	Out-Noc	Out-All	Avg-Noc	Avg-All	Runtime
StereoNet	4.91	6.02	0.8	0.9	0.015 s
CG-Net [29]	2.71	3.46	0.6	0.7	0.9 s
MC-CNN [62]	3.9	5.45	0.7	0.9	67 s
SGM-Net [51]	3.6	5.15	0.7	0.9	67 s

due to the huge variability, reflections, overexposed areas and more importantly, the lack of a big training set. Despite this, we provide the results on Kitti 2012 in Table 2. Our model uses a downsampling factor of 8 for the cost volume and 3 refinement steps. Among the top-performing methods, we compare to three significant ones. Current state of the art [29], achieves an EPE of 0.6, but it has a running time of 0.9 s per image and uses a multi-scale cost volume and several 3D deconvolutions. The earlier deep learning-based stereo matching approach of [62] takes 67 s per image and has higher error (0.9) compared to our method that runs at 0.015 s per stereo pair. The SGM-net [51] has an error comparable to ours. Although we do not reach state of the art results, we believe that the produced disparity maps are very compelling as shown in Fig. 6, bottom. We analyzed the source of errors in our model and we found that most of the wrong estimates are around reflections, which result in a wrong disparity prediction, as well as occluded regions, which do not have a correspondence in the other view. These areas cannot be explained by the data and the problem can then be formulated as an inpainting task, which our model is not trained for. State of the art [42] uses a hour-glass like architecture in their refinement step, that has been shown to be really effective for inpainting purposes [44]. This is certainly a valid solution to handle those invalid areas, however it requires significant additional computational resources. We believe that the simplicity of the proposed architecture shows important insights and it can lead the way to interesting directions to overcome the current limitations.

Similarly, we evaluated our algorithm on Kitti 2015 and report the results in Tab. 3, where similar considerations can be made. In Fig. 6 top, we show some examples from the test data.

Table 3. Quantitative evaluation on Kitti 2015. For StereoNet we used a model with a downsampling factor of 8 and 3 refinement levels. We report the percentage of pixels with error bigger than 1 in background regions (bg), foreground areas (fg), and all.

	D1-bg	D1-fg	D1-all	Runtime
StereoNet	4.30	7.45	4.83	0.015 s
CRL [42]	2.48	3.59	2.67	0.5 s
CG-Net Full [29]	2.21	6.16	2.87	0.9 s
MC-CNN [62]	2.89	8.88	3.89	67 s
SGM-Net [51]	2.66	8.64	3.66	67 s

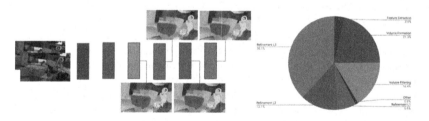

Fig. 7. Runtime analysis of StereoNet. Breakdown of the running time. Notice how most of the time is spent at the last level of refinement.

4.4 Running Time Analysis

We conclude this section with a breakdown of the running time of our algorithm. Readers interested in real-time applications would find useful to understand where the bottlenecks are. The current algorithm runs at 60fps on an NVidia Titan X and in Fig. 7 of the whole running time. Notice how feature extraction, volume formation and filtering take less than half of the whole computation (41%), and the most time consuming steps are the refinement stage: the last level of refinement done at full resolution is using 38% of the computation.

5   Discussion

We presented StereoNet, the first real-time, high quality end-to-end architecture for passive stereo matching. We started from the insight that a low resolution cost volume contains most of the information to generate high-precision disparity maps and to recover thin structures given enough training data. We demonstrated a subpixel precision of 1/30th pixel, surpassing limits published in the literature. Our refinement approach hierarchically recovers high-frequency details using the color input as guide, drawing parallels to a data-driven joint bilateral upsampling operator. The main limitation of our approach is due to the lack of supervised training data: indeed we showed that when enough examples are available, our method reaches state of the art results. To mitigate this effect, our future work involves a combination of supervised and self-supervised learning [63] to augment the training set.

References

1. Abadi, M. et al.: Tensorflow: large-scale machine learning on heterogeneous distributed systems. arXiv preprint arXiv:1603.04467 (2016)
2. Barron, J.T.: A more general robust loss function. arXiv preprint arXiv:1701.03077 (2017)
3. Besse, F., Rother, C., Fitzgibbon, A., Kautz, J.: Pmbp: Patchmatch belief propagation for correspondence field estimation. Int. J. Comput. Vis. **110**(1), 2–13 (2014)
4. Bleyer, M., Rhemann, C., Rother, C.: Patchmatch stereo-stereo matching with slanted support windows. BMVC **11**, 1–11 (2011)
5. Brachmann, E. et al.: Dsac-differentiable ransac for camera localization. In: IEEE Conference on Computer Vision and Pattern Recognition (CVPR), vol. 3 (2017)
6. Chapelle, O., Wu, M.: Gradient descent optimization of smoothed information retrieval metrics. Inf. Retr. **13**(3), 216–235 (2010)
7. Chen, Q., Koltun, V.: Photographic image synthesis with cascaded refinement networks. In: The IEEE International Conference on Computer Vision (ICCV), vol. 1 (2017)
8. Chen, Q., Xu, J., Koltun, V.: Fast image processing with fully-convolutional networks. In: IEEE International Conference on Computer Vision, vol. 9 (2017)
9. Chen, Z., Sun, X., Wang, L., Yu, Y., Huang, C.: A deep visual correspondence embedding model for stereo matching costs. In: Proceedings of the IEEE International Conference on Computer Vision, pp. 972–980 (2015)
10. Delon, J., Rougé, B.: J. Math. Imaging Vis. Small baseline stereovision, Imaging Vis (2007)
11. Dou, M. et al.: Motion2fusion: Real-time volumetric performance capture. In: SIGGRAPH Asia (2017)
12. Dou, M. et al.: Fusion4d: real-time performance capture of challenging scenes. In: SIGGRAPH (2016)
13. Fanello, S.R. et al.: Hyperdepth: learning depth from structured light without matching. In: CVPR (2016)
14. Fanello, S.R. et al: Low compute and fully parallel computer vision with hashmatch (2017)

15. Fanello, S.R. et al.: Ultrastereo: Efficient learning-based matching for active stereo systems. In: 2017 IEEE Conference on Computer Vision and Pattern Recognition (CVPR), pp. 6535–6544. IEEE (2017)
16. Fanello, S.R., Gori, I., Metta, G., Odone, F.: One-shot learning for real-time action recognition. In: Sanches, J.M., Micó, L., Cardoso, J.S. (eds.) IbPRIA 2013. LNCS, vol. 7887, pp. 31–40. Springer, Heidelberg (2013). https://doi.org/10.1007/978-3-642-38628-2_4
17. Felzenszwalb, P.F., Huttenlocher, D.P.: Efficient belief propagation for early vision. Int. J. Comput. Vis. **70**(1), 41–54 (2006)
18. Flynn, J., Neulander, I., Philbin, J., Snavely, N.: Deepstereo: learning to predict new views from the world's imagery. In: Proceedings of the IEEE Conference on Computer Vision and Pattern Recognition, pp. 5515–5524 (2016)
19. Geiger, A., Lenz, P., Urtasun, R.: Are we ready for autonomous driving? the kitti vision benchmark suite. In: 2012 IEEE Conference on Computer Vision and Pattern Recognition (CVPR), pp. 3354–3361. IEEE (2012)
20. Gharbi, M., Chen, J., Barron, J.T., Hasinoff, S.W., Durand, F.: Deep bilateral learning for real-time image enhancement. ACM Trans. Gr. (TOG) **36**(4), 118 (2017)
21. Gidaris, S., Komodakis, N.: Detect, replace, refine: deep structured prediction for pixel wise labeling. In: Proceedings of the IEEE Conference on Computer Vision and Pattern Recognition, pp. 5248–5257 (2017)
22. Hamzah, R.A., Ibrahim, H.: Literature survey on stereo vision disparity map algorithms. J. Sens. **2016** (2016)
23. He, K., Zhang, X., Ren, S., Sun, J.: Deep residual learning for image recognition. In: Proceedings of the IEEE Conference on Computer Vision and Pattern Recognition, pp. 770–778 (2016)
24. Hinton, G., Srivastava, N., Swersky, K.: Neural networks for machine learning-lecture 6a-overview of mini-batch gradient descent (2012)
25. Hosni, A., Rhemann, C., Bleyer, M., Rother, C., Gelautz, M.: Fast cost-volume filtering for visual correspondence and beyond. IEEE Trans. Pattern Anal. Mach. Intell. **35**(2), 504–511 (2013)
26. Ilg, E., Mayer, N., Saikia, T., Keuper, M., Dosovitskiy, A., Brox, T.: Flownet 2.0: evolution of optical flow estimation with deep networks. In: IEEE Conference on Computer Vision and Pattern Recognition (CVPR), vol. 2 (2017)
27. Ioffe, S., Szegedy, C.: Batch normalization: accelerating deep network training by reducing internal covariate shift. In: International Conference on Machine Learning, pp. 448–456 (2015)
28. Izadi, S. et al.: Real-time 3d reconstruction and interaction using a moving depth camera. In: UIST (2011)
29. Kendall, A. et al.: End-to-end learning of geometry and context for deep stereo regression. CoRR abs/1703.04309 (2017)
30. Klaus, A., Sormann, M., Karner, K.: Segment-based stereo matching using belief propagation and a self-adapting dissimilarity measure. In: 18th International Conference on Pattern Recognition, 2006. ICPR 2006, vol. 3, pp. 15–18. IEEE (2006)
31. Kolmogorov, V., Zabih, R.: Computing visual correspondence with occlusions using graph cuts. In: Proceedings of Eighth IEEE International Conference on Computer Vision, 2001. ICCV 2001, vol. 2, pp. 508–515. IEEE (2001)
32. Kopf, J., Cohen, M.F., Lischinski, D., Uyttendaele, M.: Joint bilateral upsampling. ACM Trans. Gr. (ToG) **26**(3), 96 (2007)
33. Krähenbühl, P., Koltun, V.: Efficient inference in fully connected crfs with gaussian edge potentials. In: NIPS (2011)

34. Lillicrap, T.P. et al.: Continuous control with deep reinforcement learning. arXiv preprint arXiv:1509.02971 (2015)
35. Geiger, A., Roser, M., Urtasun, R.: Efficient large-scale stereo matching. In: Kimmel, R., Klette, R., Sugimoto, A. (eds.) ACCV 2010. LNCS, vol. 6492, pp. 25–38. Springer, Heidelberg (2011). https://doi.org/10.1007/978-3-642-19315-6_3
36. Maas, A.L., Hannun, A.Y., Ng, A.Y.: Rectifier nonlinearities improve neural network acoustic models. In: Proceedings ICML, vol. 30, p. 3 (2013)
37. Mayer, N. et al.: A large dataset to train convolutional networks for disparity, optical flow, and scene flow estimation. In: Proceedings of the IEEE Conference on Computer Vision and Pattern Recognition, pp. 4040–4048 (2016)
38. Menze, M., Geiger, A.: Object scene flow for autonomous vehicles. In: Conference on Computer Vision and Pattern Recognition (CVPR) (2015)
39. Nehab, D., Rusinkiewicz, S., Davis, J.: Improved sub-pixel stereo correspondences through symmetric refinement. In: International Conference on Computer Vision (ICCV) (2005)
40. Odena, A., Dumoulin, V., Olah, C.: Deconvolution and checkerboard artifacts. Distill (2016). https://doi.org/10.23915/distill.00003, http://distill.pub/2016/deconv-checkerboard
41. Orts-Escolano, S. et al.: Holoportation: virtual 3d teleportation in real-time. In: UIST (2016)
42. Pang, J., Sun, W., Ren, J., Yang, C., Yan, Q.: Cascade residual learning: A two-stage convolutional neural network for stereo matching. In: International Conference on Computer Vision-Workshop on Geometry Meets Deep Learning (ICCVW 2017), vol. 3 (2017)
43. Papandreou, G., Kokkinos, I., Savalle, P.A.: Modeling local and global deformations in deep learning: Epitomic convolution, multiple instance learning, and sliding window detection. In: 2015 IEEE Conference on Computer Vision and Pattern Recognition (CVPR), pp. 390–399. IEEE (2015)
44. Park, E., Yang, J., Yumer, E., Ceylan, D., Berg, A.C.: Transformation-grounded image generation network for novel 3d view synthesis (2017)
45. Pinggera, P., Pfeiffer, D., Franke, U., Mester, R.: Know your limits: accuracy of long range stereoscopic object measurements in practice. In: Fleet, D., Pajdla, T., Schiele, B., Tuytelaars, T. (eds.) ECCV 2014. LNCS, vol. 8690, pp. 96–111. Springer, Cham (2014). https://doi.org/10.1007/978-3-319-10605-2_7
46. Pradeep, V., Rhemann, C., Izadi, S., Zach, C., Bleyer, M., Bathiche, S.: Monofusion: real-time 3d reconstruction of small scenes with a single web camera. In: ISMAR (2013)
47. Ranftl, R., Gehrig, S., Pock, T., Bischof, H.: Pushing the limits of stereo using variational stereo estimation. In: 2012 IEEE Intelligent Vehicles Symposium (2012)
48. Sanger, T.D.: Stereo disparity computation using gabor filters. Biol. Cybern. (1988)
49. Scharstein, D., Szeliski, R.: A taxonomy and evaluation of dense two-frame stereo correspondence algorithms. Int. J. Comput. Vis. **47**(1–3), 7–42 (2002)
50. Schulman, J., Heess, N., Weber, T., Abbeel, P.: Gradient estimation using stochastic computation graphs. In: Advances in Neural Information Processing Systems, pp. 3528–3536 (2015)
51. Seki, A., Pollefeys, M.: Sgm-nets: semi-global matching with neural networks. In: CVPR (2017)
52. Shaked, A., Wolf, L.: Improved stereo matching with constant highway networks and reflective confidence learning. CoRR abs/1701.00165 (2017)
53. Szeliski, R.: Computer Vision: Algorithms and Applications, 1st edn. Springer, New York Inc, New York, NY, USA (2010)

54. Tankovich, V. et al: Sos: stereo matching in o(1) with slanted support windows. In: IROS (2018)
55. Taylor, J. et al.: Articulated distance fields for ultra-fast tracking of hands interacting. In: Siggraph Asia (2017)
56. Wang, S., Fanello, S.R., Rhemann, C., Izadi, S., Kohli, P.: The global patch collider (2016)
57. Williams, R.J.: Simple statistical gradient-following algorithms for connectionist reinforcement learning. In: Reinforcement Learning, pp. 5–32. Springer (1992)
58. Xu, K. et al.: Show, attend and tell: neural image caption generation with visual attention. In: International Conference on Machine Learning, pp. 2048–2057 (2015)
59. Yang, Q., Yang, R., Davis, J., Nister, D.: Spatial-depth super resolution for range images. In: 2007 IEEE Conference on Computer Vision and Pattern Recognition (2007)
60. Zagoruyko, S., Komodakis, N.: Learning to compare image patches via convolutional neural networks. In: 2015 IEEE Conference on Computer Vision and Pattern Recognition (CVPR), pp. 4353–4361. IEEE (2015)
61. Zbontar, J., LeCun, Y.: Computing the stereo matching cost with a convolutional neural network. In: Proceedings of the IEEE Conference on Computer Vision and Pattern Recognition, pp. 1592–1599 (2015)
62. Zbontar, J., LeCun, Y.: Stereo matching by training a convolutional neural network to compare image patches. J. Mach. Learn. Res. **17**(1–32), 2 (2016)
63. Zhang, Y. et al.: Activestereonet: end-to-end self-supervised learning for active stereo systems. In: ECCV (2018)

Attention-Aware Deep Adversarial Hashing for Cross-Modal Retrieval

Xi Zhang[1,2] , Hanjiang Lai[1,2(✉)] , and Jiashi Feng[3]

[1] School of Data and Computer Science, Sun Yat-Sen University, Guangzhou, China
zhangx368@mail2.sysu.edu.cn,
laihanj3@mail.sysu.edu.cn
[2] Guangdong Key Laboratory of Big Data Analysis and Processing,
Guangzhou, China
[3] Department of Electrical and Computer Engineering, National University
of Singapore, Singapore, Singapore
elefjia@nus.edu.sg

Abstract. Due to the rapid growth of multi-modal data, hashing methods for cross-modal retrieval have received considerable attention. However, finding content similarities between different modalities of data is still challenging due to an existing heterogeneity gap. To further address this problem, we propose an adversarial hashing network with an attention mechanism to enhance the measurement of content similarities by selectively focusing on the informative parts of multi-modal data. The proposed new deep adversarial network consists of three building blocks: (1) the feature learning module to obtain the feature representations; (2) the attention module to generate an attention mask, which is used to divide the feature representations into the attended and unattended feature representations; and (3) the hashing module to learn hash functions that preserve the similarities between different modalities. In our framework, the attention and hashing modules are trained in an adversarial way: the attention module attempts to make the hashing module unable to preserve the similarities of multi-modal data w.r.t. the unattended feature representations, while the hashing module aims to preserve the similarities of multi-modal data w.r.t. the attended and unattended feature representations. Extensive evaluations on several benchmark datasets demonstrate that the proposed method brings substantial improvements over other state-of-the-art cross-modal hashing methods.

Keywords: Hashing · Adversarial learning · Attention mechanism
Cross modal retrieval

1 Introduction

Due to the rapid development of the Internet, different types of media data are also growing rapidly, e.g., texts, images, and videos. Cross-modal retrieval, which takes one type of data as the query and returns the relevant data of

V. Ferrari et al. (Eds.): ECCV 2018, LNCS 11219, pp. 614–629, 2018.
https://doi.org/10.1007/978-3-030-01267-0_36

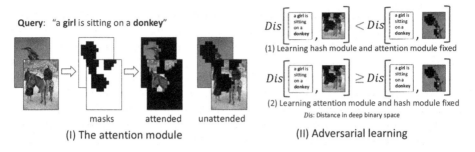

Fig. 1. Attention-aware deep adversarial hashing. To learn the attention masks, we train the attention module and the hashing module in an adversarial way (II): (1) the hashing module learns to preserve the similarities of multi-modal data, while (2) the attention module attempts to generate attention masks that make the hashing module unable to preserve the similarities of the unattended features.

another type, is increasingly receiving attention since it is a natural way to search for multi-modal data. The solution methods can be roughly divided into two categories [33]: real-valued representation learning and binary representation learning. Because of the low storage cost and fast retrieval speed of the binary representation, we only focus on cross-modal binary representation learning (i.e., hashing [17,31]) in this paper.

To date, various cross-modal hashing algorithms [3,8,15,19,36,40,41] have been proposed for embedding correlations among different modalities of data. In the cross-modal hashing procedure, feature extraction is considered the first step for representing all modalities of data, and then, these multi-modal features can be projected into a common Hamming space for future searches. Many methods [8,40] use a shallow architecture for feature extraction. For example, collective matrix factorization hashing (CMFH) [8] and semantic correlation maximization (SCM) [40] use the hand-crafted features. Recently, deep learning has also been adopted for cross-modal hashing due to its powerful ability to learn good representations of data. The representative work of deep-network-based cross-modal hashing includes deep cross-modal hashing (DCMH) [15], deep visual-semantic hashing (DVSH) [3], pairwise relationship guided deep hashing (PRDH) [36], etc.

In parallel, the computational model of "attention"' has drawn much interest due to its impressive result in various applications, e.g., image caption [34]. It is also desired for cross-modal retrieval problems. For example, as shown in Fig. 1, given a query *girl sits on donkey*, if we can locate the more informative regions in the image (e.g., the black regions), a higher degree of accuracy can be obtained. To the best of our knowledge, the attention mechanism has not been well-explored for cross-modal hashing.

In this paper, we propose an attention mechanism for cross-modal hashing. The model first decides where (i.e., which region of multi-modal data) it should attend to; then, the attended region should be favoured for retrieval. Based on this, an *attention module* is proposed to find the attended regions and a *hashing module* is to learn the similarity-preserving hash functions. In the attention module, the adaptive attention mask is generated for each data, which divides the data into attended and unattended regions. Ideally, well-learned attention masks should locate discriminative regions, which means that the unattended regions of data are uninformative and difficult to preserve the similarities. Hence, the attention module undergoes learning to make the hashing module unable to preserve the similarities of the unattended regions of data. However, the learned hash functions should preserve the similarities for both the attended (which can be viewed as easy examples) and unattended (hard examples) regions of data to enhance the robustness and performance. Thus, the hashing module undergoes learning to preserve the similarities of both the unattended and attended regions of data. Note that the attention module and the hashing module are trained in an adversarial way: the attention module attempts to find the unattended regions in which the hashing module fails to maintain the similarities, whereas the hashing module aims to preserve the similarities of the multi-modal data.

A new deep adversarial hashing for cross-modal retrieval is illustrated in Fig. 2. It consists of three major components: (1) a feature learning module that uses CNN or MLP to extract high level semantic representations for the multi-modal data; (2) an attention module that generates the adaptive attention masks and divides the feature representations into the attended and unattended feature representations; and (3) a hashing module that focuses on learning the binary codes for the multi-modal data. The adversarial retrieval loss and the cross-modal loss are proposed to obtain good attention masks and powerful hash functions.

The main contributions of our work are three-fold. First, we propose an attention-aware method for the cross-modal hashing problem. It is able to detect the informative regions of multi-modal data, which is helpful for identifying content similarities between different modalities of data. Second, we propose a deep adversarial hashing for learning effective attention masks and compact binary codes simultaneously. Third, we quantitatively evaluate the usefulness of attention in cross-modal hashing, and our method yields better performances in comparison with several state-of-the-art methods.

2 Related Work

2.1 Cross-Modal Hashing

According to the utilized information for learning the common representations, cross-modal hashing can be categorized into three groups [33]: (1) the unsupervised methods [29], (2) the pairwise-based methods [21,41] and (3) the supervised methods [4,39]. The unsupervised methods only use co-occurrence information to learn hash functions for multi-modal data. For instance, cross-view hashing (CVH) [27] extends spectral hashing from uni-modal to multi-modal scenarios. The pairwise-based methods use both the co-occurrence information and similar/dissimilar pairs to learn the hash functions. Bronstein et al. [11] proposed cross-modal similarity sensitive hashing (CMSSH), which learns the hash functions to ensure that if two samples (with different modalities) are relevant/irrelevant, their corresponding binary codes are similar/dissimilar. The supervised methods exploit label information to learn more discriminative common representation. Semantic correlation maximization (SCM) [40] uses a label vector to obtain the similarity matrix and reconstruct it through the binary codes. Xu et al. [35] proposed discrete cross-modal hashing (DCH), which directly learns discriminative binary codes with the discrete constraints. Most of these works are based on hand-crafted features.

The deep learning with neural networks has shown that this approach can effectively discover the correlations across different modalities. The deep cross-modal hashing (DCMH) [15] integrates feature learning and hash-code learning into the same framework. Cao et al. [3] proposed deep visual-semantic hashing (DVSH), which utilizes both a convolutional neural network (CNN) and long short-term memory (LSTM) to separately learn the common representations for each modality. Pairwise relationship guided deep hashing (PRDH) [36] also adopts deep CNN models to learn feature representations and hash codes simultaneously.

2.2 Generative Adversarial Network

Recently, generative adversarial networks (GANs) [10] have received a lot of attention and achieved impressive results in various applications, including image-to-image translation [42], image generation [1,23] and representation learning [22,24]. GANs have also been applied to retrieval problem. IRGAN [32] is a recently proposed method for information retrieval, in which the generative retrieval focuses on predicting relevant documents and the discriminative retrieval focuses on predicting relevancy given a query document pair. IRGAN is designed for uni-modal retrieval. While we focus on cross-modal retrieval in this paper.

Very recently, Wang et al. [28] present an adversarial cross-modal retrieval (ACMR) method to seek an effective common subspace based on adversarial learning: the modality classifier distinguishes the samples in terms of their modalities, and the feature projector generates modality-invariant representations that confuse the modality classifier. Both the ACMR and the proposed method use the adversarial learning, the main difference is that ACMR seeks to learn common subspace for the multi-modal data, while the adversarial learning in the proposed method is tailored to explicitly handle the attention-aware networks for cross-modal hashing. In addition, the ACMR falls into the category of real-valued approaches, while our method belongs to binary approaches. Further, Li et al. [18] present a self-supervised adversarial hashing (SSAH) for cross-modal retrieval.

To the best of our knowledge, the attention mechanism has not been well-explored for cross-modal hashing. The attention mechanism has been proved to be very powerful in many applications, such as image classification [2], image caption [34], image question answering [38], video action recognition [25] and

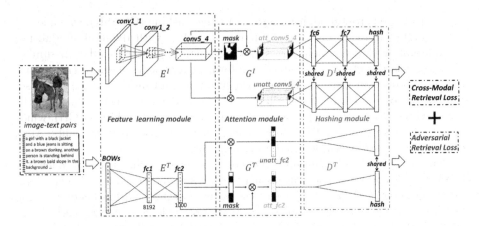

Fig. 2. Overview of our method. Above is the image modality branch, and below is the text modality branch. Each branch is divided into three parts: the feature learning module (including E^I and E^T), the attention module (G^I and G^T) and the hashing module (D^I and D^T). The feature learning module maps the input multi-modal data into the high-level feature representations. Then, the attention module learns the attention masks to divide the features representations into the attended and unattended features. Finally, the hashing module encodes all features into binary codes and learn similarity-preserving hash functions. We train the attention module and the hashing module alternately.

etc. Inspired by that, in this paper, we carefully design an attention-aware deep adversarial hashing network for cross-modal hashing.

3   Deep Adversarial Hashing for Cross-Modal Retrieval

3.1   Problem Definition

Suppose there are n training samples, each of which is represented in several modalities, e.g., audio, video, image, and text. In this paper, we only focus on two modalities: text and image. Note that our method can be easily extended to other modalities. We denote the training data as $\{I_i, T_i\}_{i=1}^n$, where I_i is the i-th image and T_i is the corresponding text description of image I_i. We also have a cross-modal similarity matrix S, where $S(i, j) = 1$ means that the i-th image and the j-th text are similar, while $S(i, j) = 0$ means that they are dissimilar. The goal of cross-modal hashing is to learn two mapping functions to transform images and texts into a common binary codes space, in which the similarities between the paired images and texts are preserved. For instance, if $S(i, j) = 1$, the Hamming distance between the generated binary codes of the i-th image and the j-th text should be small. When $S(i, j) = 0$, the Hamming distance between them should be large.

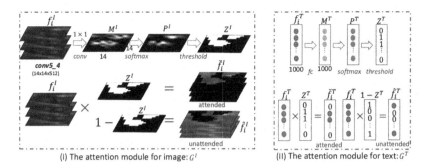

Fig. 3. The attention module. It first generates the attention masks Z^I and Z^T. Then, each feature is divided into the attended and the unattended two parts.

3.2 Network Architecture

The proposed deep adversarial hashing network contains three components: (1) the feature learning module to obtain the high-level representations of the multi-modal data; (2) the attention module to generate the attention masks, and (3) the hashing module to learn the similarity-preserving hash functions.

Feature Learning Module: E^I and E^T. For the image modality, a convolutional neural network is used to obtain the high-level representation of images. Specifically, we use VGGNet [26] to extract the image feature maps, i.e., conv5_4 in VGGNet. For representing text instances, we use a well-known bag-of-words (BOW) vector. Then, we utilize the two-layer feed-forward neural network (BOW $\rightarrow$ 8192 $\rightarrow$ 1000) to obtain the semantic text features. Let $f_i^I = E^I(I_i)$ and $f_i^T = E^T(T_i)$ denote the image feature maps and the text feature vector, respectively.

Attention Module: G^I and G^T. With the powerful image feature maps f^I and the text feature vector f^T, we first feed them into a one-layer neural network, i.e., a convolutional layer with a 1×1 kernel size for image feature maps and a fully connected layer for the text feature vector, followed by softmax and threshold functions to generate the attention distribution over the regions of the multi-modal data. Then, the attention masks are used to divide the feature representations into the attended and unattended feature representations.

More specifically, the detailed pipeline for processing the image modality is shown on the left side of Fig. 3. Suppose $f_i^I \in \mathbb{R}^{H \times W \times C}$ represents the feature maps for the i-th image, where H, W and C are the height, weight and channels, respectively. In the first step, we first use a convolutional layer to compress the feature maps f_i^I to a matrix $M_i^I = Conv(f_i^I)$, where $M_i^I \in \mathbb{R}^{H \times W}$. In the second step, the matrix M_i^I goes through a *softmax* layer, and the output is the probability matrix P_i^I. In the third step, we add a *threshold* layer to obtain the attention mask, which is defined as

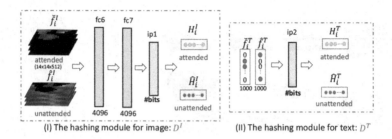

(I) The hashing module for image: D^I (II) The hashing module for text: D^T

Fig. 4. The hashing module for image modality D^I and text modality D^T.

$$Z_i^I(h, w) = \begin{cases} 1 & P_i^I(h, w) \geq \alpha \\ 0 & P_i^I(h, w) < \alpha, \end{cases} \tag{1}$$

where α is a predefined threshold. We set $\alpha = \frac{1}{H \times W}$ in our experiment. The output of the threshold layer is a binary mask. Based on the binary mask, we can calculate the attended and unattended feature maps for the i-th image by multiplying the binary mask in element-wise, which is formulated as

$$\begin{aligned} \breve{f}_i^I(h, w, c) &= Z_i^I(h, w) \times f_i^I(h, w, c), \quad \textbf{(attended)} \\ \hat{f}_i^I(h, w, c) &= \left(1 - Z_i^I(h, w)\right) \times f_i^I(h, w, c), \quad \textbf{(unattended)} \end{aligned} \tag{2}$$

for all h, w and c. For ease of representation, we denote the whole procedures as $[\breve{f}_i^I, \hat{f}_i^I] = G^I(f_i^I)$.

For the text modality, we imitate the pipeline of the image modality, which is shown on the right hand of Fig. 3:

$$\begin{aligned} M_i^T &= \text{fc}(f_i^T), \\ P_i^T &= \text{softmax}(M_i^T), \\ Z_i^T &= \text{threshold}(P_i^T), \\ \breve{f}_i^T(j) &= Z_i^T(j) \times f_i^T(j), \quad \textbf{(attended)} \\ \hat{f}_i^T(j) &= \left(1 - Z_i^T(j)\right) \times f_i^T(j), \quad \textbf{(unattended)} \end{aligned} \tag{3}$$

where fc is a fully connected layer, and $Z(j)$ is the j-th value of the vector Z. We denote $[\breve{f}_i^T, \hat{f}_i^T] = G^T(f_i^T)$ as the attended and unattended features for the i-th text.

Directly taking the derivative of the *threshold* function is incompatible with the back-propagation in training. To address this issue, we follow the idea proposed in [7], which uses the straight-through estimator to propagate the gradients of the *threshold* function.

Hashing Module: D^I and D^T. For the image modality, since we adopt VGGNet as our basic architecture, we also use the last fully connected layers, i.e., fc6 and fc7 [1]. Then, we add a fully connected layer with q dimensional features and a tanh layer that restricts the values in the range $[-1, 1]$ as shown on the left side of Fig. 4. Let the outputs of the discriminator be (1) the attended features $H_i^I = D^I(\check{f}_i^I)$ and (2) the unattended features $\hat{H}_i^I = D^I(\hat{f}_i^I)$.

For the text modality, we also add a fully connected layer and a tanh layer to encode the text features into q bits as shown on the right side of Fig. 4. The outputs are (1) the attended features $H_i^T = D^T(\check{f}_i^T)$ and (2) the unattended features $\hat{H}_i^T = D^T(\hat{f}_i^T)$.

3.3 Hashing Objectives

Our objectives contain two terms: (1) the cross-modal retrieval loss that corresponds to learning to preserve the similarities between different modalities of data and (2) the adversarial retrieval loss that corresponds to the hashing module aiming to preserve the similarities of the unattended binary codes, while the attention module tries to make the hashing module fails to maintain the similarities of the unattended binary codes.

Cross-modal Retrieval Loss. The aim of the cross-modal loss function is to keep the similarities between images and texts. The inter-modal ranking loss and the intra-modal ranking loss are used to preserve the similarities. That is, the hash codes from different modalities should preserve the semantic similarities, and the hash codes from the same modality should also preserve the semantic similarities. Hence, the cross-modal retrieval loss can be formulated as

$$\min \mathcal{F}_{T \to I} + \mathcal{F}_{I \to T} + \mathcal{F}_{I \to I} + \mathcal{F}_{T \to T}, \tag{4}$$

where the first two terms are used to preserve the semantic similarities between different modalities, and the last two terms are used to preserve the similarities in their own modality. The symbol $A \to B$ denotes the A modality is taken as the query to retrieve the relevant data of the B modality, where $A \in \{T, I\}$ and $B \in \{T, I\}$. $\mathcal{F}_{A \to B}$ is the loss function for the A modality as the query and B modality as the database, which is defined as

$$\mathcal{F}_{A \to B} = \sum_{\langle i,j,k \rangle} \max\{0, \varepsilon + ||H_i^A - H_j^B|| - ||H_i^A - H_k^B||\} \tag{5}$$
$$s.t. \quad \forall \langle i, j, k \rangle, \ S(i,j) > S(i,k),$$

where $\langle i, j, k \rangle$ is the triplet form and ε is the margin. The objective is the triplet ranking loss [16], which shows effectiveness in the retrieval problem.

---

[1] The last fully connected layer (i.e., fc8) is removed since it is for classification problems.

Adversarial Retrieval Loss. Inspired by the impressive results of the generative adversarial network, we adopt it to generate the attention distributions and learn the binary codes. Take the *text → image* as an example, which is also shown in Fig. 1. Given a query H_i^T, the hashing and the attention modules are trained in an adversarial way: (1) the hashing module preserves the semantic similarity between the query and the unattended features of the image modality, that is H_i^T is closer to $\hat{H}_j^I$ than to $\hat{H}_k^I$ when $S(i,j) > S(i,k)$; (2) the attention module tries to find the unattended regions of the images in which the hashing module fails to preserve the similarities, that is H_i^T is closer to $\hat{H}_k^I$ but not to $\hat{H}_j^I$. The objective can be defined as $\mathcal{F}_{T \to \hat{I}} = \sum_{\langle i,j,k \rangle} \max\{0, \varepsilon + ||H_i^T - \hat{H}_j^I|| - ||H_i^T - \hat{H}_k^I||\}$. The hashing module tries to minimize the objective, while the attention module tries to maximize it. The same process for the *image → text*. Thus, the loss can be expressed as

$$
\begin{aligned}
\mathcal{F}_{T \to \hat{I}} + \mathcal{F}_{I \to \hat{T}} = &\sum_{\langle i,j,k \rangle} \max\{0, \varepsilon + ||H_i^T - \hat{H}_j^I|| - ||H_i^T - \hat{H}_k^I||\} \\
&+ \sum_{\langle i,j,k \rangle} \max\{0, \varepsilon + ||H_i^I - \hat{H}_j^T|| - ||H_i^I - \hat{H}_k^T||\},
\end{aligned}
\tag{6}
$$

where $\hat{H}^T$ and $\hat{H}^I$ are the unattended features defined in Sect. 3.2. The first term corresponds to taking the text modality as the query to retrieve the unattended features of the image modality. The second term corresponds to the image modality being taken as the query to retrieve the unattended features of the text modality. G^I, G^T attempt to maximize the loss and D^I, D^T to minimize the objective:

$$
\min_{D^I, D^T} \max_{G^I, G^T} \mathcal{F}_{T \to \hat{I}} + \mathcal{F}_{I \to \hat{T}}.
\tag{7}
$$

Full Objective. Our full objective is

$$
\begin{aligned}
\mathcal{F}(E^I, E^T, G^I, G^T, D^I, D^T) = &\ \mathcal{F}_{T \to \hat{I}} + \mathcal{F}_{I \to \hat{T}} \\
&+ \mathcal{F}_{T \to I} + \mathcal{F}_{I \to T} + \mathcal{F}_{I \to I} + \mathcal{F}_{T \to T}.
\end{aligned}
$$

We train our model alternatively. The parameters in G^I and G^T are fixed, while the other parameters are trained:

$$
\min_{E^I, E^T, D^I, D^T} \mathcal{F}(E^I, E^T, G^I, G^T, D^I, D^T).
\tag{8}
$$

Then E^I, E^T, D^I, and D^T are fixed and the attention models are updated:

$$
\max_{G^I, G^T} \mathcal{F}_{T \to \hat{I}} + \mathcal{F}_{I \to \hat{T}}.
\tag{9}
$$

4   Experiments

In this section, we evaluate the performance of our proposed methods on three datasets and compare it to the performance of several stage-of-the-art algorithms.

4.1 Experimental Settings

Datasets. We choose three benchmark datasets: IAPR TC-12 [9], MIR-Flickr 25K [13] and NUS-WIDE [6].

- **IAPR TC-12** [9]: This dataset consists of 20,000 images taken from locations around the world. Each image is associated with a text caption, e.g., a sentence. The image-text pairs are annotated using 255 labels. For the text modality, each sentence is represented as a 2,912-dimensional bag-of-words vector [2].
- **MIR-Flickr 25K** [13]: This dataset contains 25,000 multi-label images downloaded from the Flickr [3] photo-sharing website. Each image is associated with several textural tags. For a fair comparison, we follow the settings in [15] to use the subset of the image-text pairs with at least 20 textual tags. For the text modality, the textural tags are represented as a 1,386-dimensional bag-of-words vector.
- **NUS-WIDE** [6]: This dataset consists of 269,648 images collected from Flickr. Each image is associated with one or multiple textural tags in 81 semantic concepts. We evaluate the performance on 195,834 image-text pairs belonging to the 21 most frequent labels, as suggested by [15]. The text is represented as a 1,000-dimensional bag-of-words vector.

We follow the settings of DCMH [15] to construct the query sets, training sets, and retrieval databases. The randomly sampled 2,000 image-text pairs are constructed as the query set for IAPR TC-12 and MIR-Flickr 25K. For the NUS-WIDE dataset, we randomly sample 2,100 image-text pairs as the query set. For all datasets, the remaining image-text pairs are used as the databases for retrieval. For all supervised methods, we also sample 10,000 pairs from the retrieval set as the training set for IAPR TC-12 and MIR-Flickr 25K, as well as 10,500 pairs from the retrieval set as the training set for NUS-WIDE.

Note that the representations of text are not the focus of this paper. Since the most related works, e.g., DCMH [15], use bag-of-words, we also use bag-of-words for a fair comparison.

Implementation details. We implement our codes based on the open source *caffe* [14] framework. In training, the networks are updated alternatively through the stochastic gradient solver, i.e., ADAM ($\alpha = 0.0002$, $\beta_1 = 0.5$). We alternate between four steps of optimizing E, D and one step of optimizing G. For the image modality, the weights of VGGNet are initialized with the pre-trained model that learns from the ImageNet dataset. For text modality, all parameters are randomly initialized with a Gaussian with mean zero and standard deviation 0.01. The batch size is 64, and the total epoch is 100. The base learning rate is 0.005, and it is changed to one-tenth of the current value after every 20 epochs. In testing, we use only the attended features of the data to construct the binary codes.

---

[2] We follow the settings of DCMH [15] for a fair comparison
[3] www.flickr.com

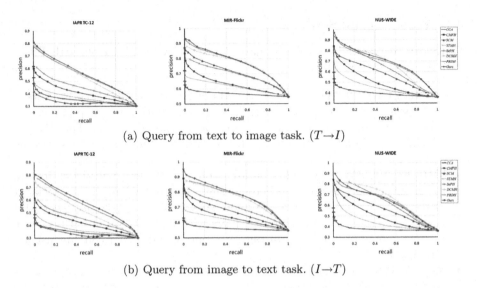

(a) Query from text to image task. $(T{\to}I)$

(b) Query from image to text task. $(I{\to}T)$

Fig. 5. Precision-recall curves on three datasets. The length of hash code is 16.

Evaluation Measures. To evaluate the performance of hashing models, we use two metrics: the mean average precision (MAP) [20] and precision-recall curves. The MAP is a standard evaluation metric for information retrieval.

4.2 Comparison with State-of-the-Art Methods

The first set of experiments is to evaluate the performance of the proposed method and compare it with the performance of several state-of-the-art algorithms [4]: CCA [12], CMFH [40], SCM [8], SMTH [30], SePH [19], DCMH [15], and PRDH [37]. The results of CCA, CMFH, SCM, STMH, SePH and DCMH are directly cited from [15] published in CVPR17 [5]. Since the experimental settings of PRDH in [37] are different from those of the proposed method, we carefully implement PRDH using the same CNN network and the same settings for a fair comparison.

The comparison results of the search accuracies on all three datasets are shown in Table 1. We can see that our method outperforms other baselines and achieves excellent performance. For example, on IAPR TC-12, the MAP of our method is 0.5439, compared to the value of 0.5135 for the second best algorithm (PRDH), on 64 bits when taking the image as the query to retrieve text. The precision-recall curves are also shown in Fig. 5. It can be seen that our method shows comparable performance to the existing baselines.

---

[4] Note that IRGAN is designed for uni-modal retrieval. ACMR is a cross-modal retrieval method that falls in the category of real-valued approaches. In this paper, we only focus on cross-modal hashing.

[5] Table 4 in http://openaccess.thecvf.com/content_cvpr_2017/papers/Jiang_Deep-Cross-Modal_Hashing_CVPR_2017_paper.pdf

Table 1. MAP of Hamming ranking w.r.t. different numbers of bits on three datasets.

Task		IAPR TC-12			MIR-Flickr 25k			NUS-WIDE		
		16 bits	32 bits	64 bits	16 bits	32 bits	64 bits	16 bits	32 bits	64 bits
Text ↓ Image	CCA	0.3493	0.3438	0.3378	0.5742	0.5713	0.5691	0.3731	0.3661	0.3613
	CMFH	0.4168	0.4212	0.4277	0.6365	0.6399	0.6429	0.5031	0.5187	0.5225
	SCM	0.3453	0.3410	0.3470	0.6939	0.7012	0.7060	0.5344	0.5412	0.5484
	STMH	0.3687	0.3897	0.4044	0.6074	0.6153	0.6217	0.4471	0.4677	0.4780
	SePH	0.4423	0.4562	0.4648	0.7216	0.7261	0.7319	0.5983	0.6025	0.6109
	DCMH	0.5185	0.5378	0.5468	0.7827	0.7900	0.7932	0.6389	0.6511	0.6571
	PRDH	0.5244	0.5434	0.5548	0.7890	0.7955	0.7964	0.6527	0.6916	0.6720
	Ours	**0.5358**	**0.5565**	**0.5648**	**0.7922**	**0.8062**	**0.8074**	**0.6789**	**0.6975**	**0.7039**
Image ↓ Text	CCA	0.3422	0.3361	0.3300	0.5719	0.5693	0.5672	0.3742	0.3667	0.3617
	CMFH	0.4189	0.4234	0.4251	0.6377	0.6418	0.6451	0.4900	0.5053	0.5097
	SCM	0.3692	0.3666	0.3802	0.6851	0.6921	0.7003	0.5409	0.5485	0.5553
	STMH	0.3775	0.4002	0.4130	0.6132	0.6219	0.6274	0.4710	0.4864	0.4942
	SePH	0.4442	0.4563	0.4639	0.7123	0.7194	0.7232	0.6037	0.6136	0.6211
	DCMH	0.4526	0.4732	0.4844	0.7410	0.7465	0.7485	0.5903	0.6031	0.6093
	PRDH	0.5003	0.4935	0.5135	0.7499	0.7546	0.7612	0.6107	**0.6302**	0.6276
	Ours	**0.5293**	**0.5283**	**0.5439**	**0.7563**	**0.7719**	**0.7720**	**0.6403**	0.6294	**0.6520**

Since the code of DVSH is not publicly available and it is difficult to re-implement the complex algorithm, we utilize the same experimental settings used in DVSH for our method. The results of DVSH are directly cited from [3] for a fair comparison. The top-500 MAP results on IAPR TC-12 are shown in Table 2. Moreover, we make a comparison with DCMH under the same settings. Please note that DVSH adopts the LSTM recurrent neural network for text representation, while DCMH and our method only use bag-of-words. From the table, we can see that our methods can achieve better performance than the baselines in most cases, even we use the weak representations of text.

Table 2. The comparison results w.r.t. the top-500 MAP on the IAPR TC-12 dataset.

Task	Methods	16 bits	32 bits	64 bits
Text →Image	DVSH	0.6037	0.6395	0.6806
	DCMH	0.6594	0.6744	0.6905
	Ours	**0.7018**	**0.6893**	**0.6941**
Image→Text	DVSH	0.5696	0.6321	**0.6964**
	DCMH	0.5780	0.6061	0.6310
	Ours	**0.6464**	**0.6373**	0.6668

We also explore the effects of small network architecture in the feature learning module for the image modality since VGGNet is a large deep network. In

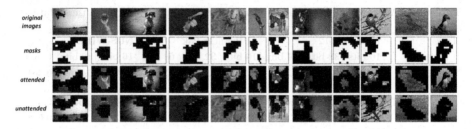

Fig. 6. Some image and mask samples. The first line represents the original images, the masks are shown in the second line, and the combinations are shown in the last two lines.

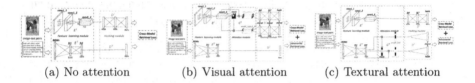

(a) No attention   (b) Visual attention   (c) Textural attention

Fig. 7. Different attention mechanisms.

Table 3. MAP on IAPR TC-12 dataset with different networks.

Task	Networks	16 bits	32 bits	64 bits
Text → Image	VGG	0.5358	0.5565	0.5648
	CNN-F	0.5267	0.5459	0.5538
Image→ Text	VGG	0.5293	0.5283	0.5439
	CNN-F	0.5211	0.5168	0.5208

this experiment, we select CNN-F [5] as the basic network for the image modality. The comparison results are shown in Table 3. We can see that VGGNet performs better than CNN-F while our method using CNN-F also achieves good performance compared to other state-of-the-art baselines.

The main reason for the good performance of our method is that we can obtain attended regions for the multi-modal data. Figure 6 shows some examples of the image modality. Note that it is difficult to visualize the text modality (the networks for the text modality are the fully connected layers instead of the CNN. The order of words in the sentence are changed after going through the fully connected layers), thus, we do not show the masks learned in the text network.

4.3   Comparison with Different Attention Mechanisms

In this section, we present an ablation study to clarify the impact of each part of the attention modules on the final performance.

To provide an intuitive comparison of our method, we compare it with the following baselines. In the first baseline, we do not use any attention mechanism as shown on the left side of Fig. 7. It is also the traditional deep cross-modal hashing. In the second baseline, we only apply the visual attention mechanism as seen in the middle of Fig. 7. Similarly, the last baseline is to explore the textural attention mechanism as shown on the right side of Fig. 7. Note that all baselines, as well as our method, use the same network. The only differences are the use of the different attention mechanisms. These comparisons can show whether the proposed attention mechanism can contribute to the accuracy.

Table 4 shows the comparison results with respect to the MAP. The results show that our proposed attention mechanism can achieve better performance than the baselines that are lacking attention mechanisms. The main reason for this is that our method can focus on the most discriminative regions of the data.

Table 4. The comparison results for different attention mechanisms.

Task	Attn.	IAPR TC-12			MIR-Flickr 25k			NUS-WIDE		
		16 bits	32 bits	64 bits	16 bits	32 bits	64 bits	16 bits	32 bits	64 bits
Text ↓ Image	No	0.5039	0.5250	0.5258	0.7758	0.7801	0.7742	0.6476	0.6824	0.6733
	Visual	0.5294	0.5474	0.5576	0.7894	0.7925	0.7906	0.6723	0.6839	0.6984
	Textual	0.5334	0.5382	0.5469	0.7885	0.7867	0.7831	0.6648	0.6851	0.6867
	Both	**0.5358**	**0.5565**	**0.5648**	**0.7922**	**0.8062**	**0.8074**	**0.6789**	**0.6975**	**0.7039**
Image ↓ Text	No	0.4903	0.5001	0.5175	0.7347	0.7482	0.7495	0.6150	0.6178	0.6311
	Visual	0.5267	0.5173	0.5285	0.7466	0.7601	0.7584	0.6314	0.6260	0.6425
	Textual	0.5279	0.5232	0.5304	0.7520	0.7673	0.7717	0.6384	0.6227	0.6459
	Both	**0.5293**	**0.5283**	**0.5439**	**0.7563**	**0.7719**	**0.7720**	**0.6403**	**0.6294**	**0.6520**

5   Conclusion

In this paper, we proposed a novel approach called deep adversarial hashing for cross-modal hashing. The proposed method contains three major components: a feature learning module, an attention module, and a hashing module. The feature learning module learns powerful representations for the multi-modal data. The attention module and the hashing module are trained in an adversarial way, in which the hashing module tries to minimize the similarity-preserving loss functions, while the attention module aims to find the unattended regions of data that maximize the retrieval loss. We performed our method on three datasets, and the experimental results demonstrate the appealing performance of our method.

Acknowledgments. This work is supported by the National Natural Science Foundation of China under Grants (61602530, U1611264, U1711262, 61472453, U1401256 and U1501252). This work is also supported by the Research Foundation of Science and Technology Plan Project in Guangdong Province (2017B030308007).

References

1. Arjovsky, M., Chintala, S., Bottou, L.: Wasserstein gan. arXiv preprint arXiv:1701.07875 (2017)
2. Ba, J., Mnih, V., Kavukcuoglu, K.: Multiple object recongnition with visual attention. In: ICLR (2015)
3. Cao, Y., Long, M., Wang, J., Yang, Q., Philip, S.Y.: Deep visual-semantic hashing for cross-modal retrieval. In: KDD, pp. 1445–1454 (2016)
4. Cao, Y., Long, M., Wang, J., Zhu, H.: Correlation autoencoder hashing for supervised cross-modal search. In: ICMR, pp. 197–204 (2016)
5. Chatfield, K., Simonyan, K., Vedaldi, A., Zisserman, A.: Return of the devil in the details: Delving deep into convolutional nets. Comput. Sci. (2014)
6. Chua, T.S., Tang, J., Hong, R., Li, H., Luo, Z., Zheng, Y.: Nus-wide: a real-world web image database from national university of singapore. In: ICIVR, p. 48 (2009)
7. Courbariaux, M., Bengio, Y.: Binarynet: training deep neural networks with weights and activations constrained to +1 or -1. abs/1602.02830 (2016)
8. Ding, G., Guo, Y., Zhou, J.: Collective matrix factorization hashing for multimodal data. In: CVPR, pp. 2075–2082 (2014)
9. Escalante, H.J.: The segmented and annotated iapr tc-12 benchmark. CVIU 114(4), 419–428 (2010)
10. Goodfellow, I. et al.: Generative adversarial nets. In: NIPS, pp. 2672–2680 (2014)
11. He, R., Zheng, W.S., Hu, B.G.: Maximum correntropy criterion for robust face recognition. TPAMI 33(8), 1561–1576 (2011)
12. Hotelling, H.: Relations Between Two Sets of Variates. Springer, New York (1992)
13. Huiskes, M.J., Lew, M.S.: The mir flickr retrieval evaluation. In: ICMIR, pp. 39–43 (2008)
14. Jia, Y. et al.: Caffe: Convolutional architecture for fast feature embedding. arXiv preprint arXiv:1408.5093 (2014)
15. Jiang, Q.Y., Li, W.: Deep cross-modal hashing. In: CVPR (2016)
16. Lai, H., Pan, Y., Liu, Y., Yan, S.: Simultaneous feature learning and hash coding with deep neural networks. In: CVPR, pp. 3270–3278 (2015)
17. Lai, H., Yan, P., Shu, X., Wei, Y., Yan, S.: Instance-aware hashing for multi-label image retrieval. TIP 25(6), 2469–2479 (2016)
18. Li, C., Deng, C., Li, N., Liu, W., Gao, X., Tao, D.: Self-supervised adversarial hashing networks for cross-modal retrieval. In: CVPR, pp. 4242–4251 (2018)
19. Lin, Z., Ding, G., Hu, M., Wang, J.: Semantics-preserving hashing for cross-view retrieval. In: CVPR, pp. 3864–3872 (2015)
20. Liu, W., Kumar, S., Kumar, S., Chang, S.F.: Discrete graph hashing. In: NIPS, pp. 3419–3427 (2014)
21. Masci, J., Bronstein, M.M., Bronstein, A.M., Schmidhuber, J.: Multimodal similarity-preserving hashing. TPAMI 36(4), 824–830 (2014)
22. Mathieu, M.F., Zhao, J.J., Zhao, J., Ramesh, A., Sprechmann, P., LeCun, Y.: Disentangling factors of variation in deep representation using adversarial training. In: NIPS, pp. 5040–5048 (2016)
23. Mirza, M., Osindero, S.: Conditional generative adversarial nets. arXiv preprint arXiv:1411.1784 (2014)
24. Radford, A., Metz, L., Chintala, S.: Unsupervised representation learning with deep convolutional generative adversarial networks. arXiv preprint arXiv:1511.06434 (2015)

25. Sharma, S., Kiros, R., Salakhutdinov, R.: Action recognition using visual attention. arXiv preprint arXiv:1511.04119 (2015)
26. Simonyan, K., Zisserman, A.: Very deep convolutional networks for large-scale image recognition. arXiv preprint arXiv:1409.1556 (2014)
27. Sun, L., Ji, S., Ye, J.: A least squares formulation for canonical correlation analysis. In: ICML, pp. 1024–1031 (2008)
28. Wang, B., Yang, Y., Xu, X., Hanjalic, A., Shen, H.T.: Adversarial cross-modal retrieval. In: ACMMM, pp. 154–162 (2017)
29. Wang, D., Cui, P., Ou, M., Zhu, W.: Learning compact hash codes for multimodal representations using orthogonal deep structure. TMM **17**(9), 1404–1416 (2015)
30. Wang, D., Gao, X., Wang, X., He, L.: Semantic topic multimodal hashing for cross-media retrieval. In: ICAI, pp. 3890–3896 (2015)
31. Wang, J., Zhang, T., Sebe, N., Shen, H.T., et al.: A survey on learning to hash. In: TPAMI (2017)
32. Wang, J. et al.: Irgan: a minimax game for unifying generative and discriminative information retrieval models. arXiv preprint arXiv:1705.10513 (2017)
33. Wang, K., Yin, Q., Wang, W., Wu, S., Wang, L.: A comprehensive survey on cross-modal retrieval. arXiv preprint arXiv:1607.06215 (2016)
34. Xu, K. et al.: Show, attend and tell: Neural image caption generation with visual attention. In: ICML, pp. 2048–2057 (2015)
35. Xu, X., Shen, F., Yang, Y., Shen, H.T., Li, X.: Learning discriminative binary codes for large-scale cross-modal retrieval. TIP **26**(5), 2494–2507 (2017)
36. Yang, E., Deng, C., Liu, W., Liu, X., Tao, D., Gao, X.: Pairwise relationship guided deep hashing for cross-modal retrieval. In: AAAI, pp. 1618–1625 (2017)
37. Yang, E., Deng, C., Liu, W., Liu, X., Tao, D., Gao, X.: Pairwise relationship guided deep hashing for cross-modal retrieval. In: AAAI (2017)
38. Yang, Z., He, X., Gao, J., Deng, L., Smola, A.: Stacked attention networks for image question answering. In: CVPR, pp. 21–29 (2016)
39. Yu, Z., Wu, F., Yang, Y., Tian, Q., Luo, J., Zhuang, Y.: Discriminative coupled dictionary hashing for fast cross-media retrieval. In: SIGIR, pp. 395–404 (2014)
40. Zhang, D., Li, W.J.: Large-scale supervised multimodal hashing with semantic correlation maximization. In: AAAI. vol. 1, p. 7 (2014)
41. Zhen, Y., Yeung, D.Y.: Co-regularized hashing for multimodal data. In: NIPS, pp. 1376–1384 (2012)
42. Zhu, J.Y., Park, T., Isola, P., Efros, A.A.: Unpaired image-to-image translation using cycle-consistent adversarial networks. arXiv preprint arXiv:1703.10593 (2017)

3DFeat-Net: Weakly Supervised Local 3D Features for Point Cloud Registration

Zi Jian Yew$^{(\boxtimes)}$ and Gim Hee Lee

Department of Computer Science, National University of Singapore,
Singapore, Singapore
{zijian.yew,gimhee.lee}@comp.nus.edu.sg

Abstract. In this paper, we propose the 3DFeat-Net which learns both 3D feature detector and descriptor for point cloud matching using weak supervision. Unlike many existing works, we do not require manual annotation of matching point clusters. Instead, we leverage on alignment and attention mechanisms to learn feature correspondences from GPS/INS tagged 3D point clouds without explicitly specifying them. We create training and benchmark outdoor Lidar datasets, and experiments show that 3DFeat-Net obtains state-of-the-art performance on these gravity-aligned datasets.

Keywords: Point cloud · Registration · Deep learning
Weak supervision

1 Introduction

3D point cloud registration plays an important role in many real-world applications such as 3D Lidar-based mapping and localization for autonomous robots, and 3D model acquisition for archaeological studies, geo-surveying and architectural inspections etc. Compared to images, point clouds exhibit less variation and can be matched under strong lighting changes, i.e. day and night, or summer and winter (Fig. 1). A two-step process is commonly used to solve the point cloud registration problem - (1) establishing 3D-3D point correspondences between the source and target point clouds, and (2) finding the optimal rigid transformation between the two point clouds that minimizes the total Euclidean distance between all point correspondences. Unfortunately, the critical step of establishing 3D-3D point correspondences is non-trivial. Even though many handcrafted 3D feature detectors [5,35] and descriptors [13,25,26,28,30] have been proposed over the years, the performance of establishing 3D-3D point correspondences remains unsatisfactory. As a result, iterative algorithms, e.g. Iterative Closest Point (ICP) [3], that circumvent the need for wide-baseline 3D-3D point correspondences with good initialization and nearest neighbors, are often used. This

Electronic supplementary material The online version of this chapter (https://doi.org/10.1007/978-3-030-01267-0_37) contains supplementary material, which is available to authorized users.

V. Ferrari et al. (Eds.): ECCV 2018, LNCS 11219, pp. 630–646, 2018.
https://doi.org/10.1007/978-3-030-01267-0_37

severely limits usage in applications such as global localization / pose estimation [16] and loop-closures [7] that require wide-baseline correspondences.

Inspired by the success of deep learning for computer vision tasks such as image-based object recognition [21], several deep learning based works that learn 3D feature descriptors for finding wide-baseline 3D-3D point matches have been proposed in the recent years. Regardless of the improvements of these deep learning based 3D descriptors over the traditional handcrafted 3D descriptors, none of them proposed a full pipeline that uses deep learning to concurrently learn both the 3D feature detector and descriptor. This is because the existing deep learning approaches are mostly based on supervised learning that requires huge amounts of hand-labeled data for training. It is impossible for anyone to manually identify and label salient 3D features from a point cloud. Hence, most existing approaches focused only on learning the 3D descriptors, while the detection of the 3D features are done with random selection [8,34]. On the other hand, it is interesting to note the availability of an abundance of GPS/INS tagged 3D point cloud based datasets collected over large environments, e.g. the Oxford RobotCar [19] and KITTI [9] datasets etc. This naturally leads us into the question: "Can we design a deep learning framework that concurrently learns the 3D feature detector and descriptor from the GPS/INS tagged 3D point clouds?"

In view of the difficulty to get datasets of accurately labeled salient 3D features for training the deep networks, we propose a *weakly supervised* deep learning framework - the 3DFeat-Net to holistically learn a 3D feature detector and descriptor from GPS/INS tagged 3D point clouds. Specifically, our 3DFeat-Net is a Siamese architecture [4] that learns to recognize whether two given 3D point clouds are taken from the same location. We leverage on the recently proposed PointNet [23,24] to enable us to directly use the 3D point cloud as input to our network. The output of our 3DFeat-Net is a set of local descriptor vectors. The network is trained by minimizing a Triplet loss [29] where the positive and "hardest" negative samples are chosen from the similarity measures between all pairs of descriptors [14] from two input point clouds. Furthermore, we add an attention layer [20] that learns importance weights that weigh the contribution of each input descriptor towards the Triplet loss. During inference, we use the output from the attention layer to determine the saliency likelihood of an input 3D point. Additionally, we take the output descriptor vector from our network as the descriptor for finding good 3D-3D correspondences. Experimental results from real-world datasets [9,19,22] validates the feasibility of our 3DFeat-Net.

Our contributions in this paper can be summarized as follows:

- Propose a *weakly supervised* network that holistically learns a 3D feature detector and descriptor using only GPS/INS tagged 3D point clouds.
- Use an attention layer [20] that allows our network to learn the saliency likelihood of an input 3D point.
- Create training and benchmark datasets from Oxford RobotCar dataset [19].

We have made our source code and dataset available online.[1]

---

[1] https://github.com/yewzijian/3DFeatNet.

Fig. 1. Left: 2D images from the Oxford dataset at different times of the day (top) or seasons of the year (bottom) give mostly wrong matches even after RANSAC. Right: 3D point cloud of the same scene remains largely the same and can be matched easily.

2   Related Work

Existing approaches of the local 3D feature detectors and descriptors are heavily influenced by the widely studied 2D local features methods [2,17], and can be broadly categorized into handcrafted [5,13,25,26,28,30,35] and learning approaches [6,8,15,27,34] - i.e. pre- and post- deep learning approaches.

Handcrafted 3D Features. Several handcrafted 3D features are proposed before the popularity of deep learning. The design of these features are largely based on the domain knowledge of 3D point clouds by the researchers. The authors of [35] and [5] detects salient keypoints which have large variations in the principal direction [35], or unique curvatures [5]. The similarity between keypoints can then be estimated using descriptors. PFH [26] and FPFH [25] consider pairwise combinations of surface normals to describe the curvature around a keypoint. Other 3D descriptors [13,30] build histograms based on the number of points falling into each spatial bin around the keypoint. A comprehensive evaluation of the common handcrafted 3D detectors and descriptors can be found in [11]. As we show in our evaluation, many of these handcrafted detectors and descriptors do not work well on real world point clouds, which can be noisy and low density.

Learned 2D Features. Some recent works have applied deep learning to learn detectors and descriptors on images for 2D-2D correspondences. LIFT [32] learns to distinguish between matching and non-matching pairs with a Siamese CNN, where the matching pairs are obtained from feature matches that survive the Structure from Motion (SfM) pipeline. TILDE [31] learns to detect keypoints that can be reliably matched over different lighting conditions. These works rely on the matches provided by handcrafted 2D features, e.g. SIFT [17], but unfortunately handcrafted 3D features are less robust and do not provide as good a starting point to learn better features. On the other hand, a recently proposed work - DELF [20] uses a weakly supervised framework to learn salient local 2D image features through an attention mechanism in a landmark classification task. This motivates our work in using an attention mechanism to identify good 3D local keypoints and descriptors for matching.

Learned 3D Features. The increasing success and popularity of deep learning has recently inspired many learned 3D features. 3DMatch [34] uses a 3D convolutional network to learn local descriptors for indoor RGB-D matching by training on matching and non-matching pairs. PPFNet [6] operates on raw points, incorporating point pair features and global context to improve the descriptor representation. Other works such as CGF [15] and LORAX [8] utilize deep learning to reduce the dimension of their handcrafted descriptors. Despite the good performance of these works, none of them learns to detect keypoints. The descriptors are either computed on all or random sampled points. On the other hand, [27] learns to detect keypoints that give good matching performance with handcrafted SHOT [28] descriptors. This provides the intuition for our work, i.e. a good keypoint is one that gives a good descriptor performance.

3   Problem Formulation

A point cloud P is represented as a set of N 3D points $\{x_i|i = 1, ..., N\}$. Each point cloud $P^{(m)}$ is cropped to a ball with fixed radius R around its centroid c_m. We assume the absolute pose of the point cloud is available during training, e.g. from GPS/INS, but is not sufficiently accurate to infer point-to-point correspondences. We define the distance between two point clouds $d(m, n)$ as the Euclidean distance between their centroids, i.e. $d(m, n) = \|c_m - c_n\|_2$.

We train our network using a set of triplets containing an anchor, positive and negative point cloud $\{P^{(anc)}, P^{(pos)}, P^{(neg)}\}$, similar to typical instance retrieval approaches [1, 10]. We define positive instances as point clouds with distance to the anchor below a threshold, $d(anc, pos) < \tau_p$. Similarly, negative instances are point clouds far away from the anchor, i.e. $d(anc, neg) > \tau_n$. The thresholds τ_p and τ_n are chosen such that positive and negative point clouds have large and small overlaps with the anchor point cloud respectively.

The objective of our network is to learn to find a set of correspondences $\{(x_1^{(m)}, x_1^{(n)}), (x_2^{(m)}, x_2^{(n)}), ..., (x_L^{(m)}, x_L^{(n)})|x_i^{(m)} \in P^{(m)}, x_j^{(n)} \in P^{(n)}\}$ between a subset of points in two point clouds $P^{(m)}$ and $P^{(n)}$. Our network learning is weakly supervised in two ways. Firstly, only model level annotations in the form of relative poses of the point clouds are provided, and we do not explicitly specify which subset of points to choose for the 3D features. Secondly, the ground truth poses are not accurate enough to infer point-to-point correspondences.

4   Our 3DFeat-Net

4.1   Network Architecture

Figure 2 shows the three-branch Siamese architecture of our 3DFeat-Net. Each branch takes an entire point cloud P as input. Point clusters $\{C_1, ..., C_K\}$ are sampled from the point cloud in a clustering layer. For each cluster C_k, an orientation θ_k and attention w_k [20] are predicted by a detector network. A descriptor network then rotates the cluster C_k to a canonical configuration using the predicted orientation θ_k and computes a descriptor $f_k \in \mathbb{R}^d$.

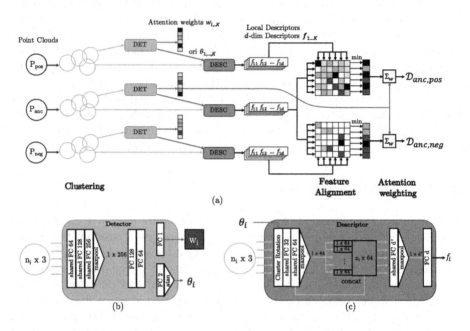

Fig. 2. (a) Network architecture of our 3DFeat-Net. The three-branch Siamese architecture uses a training tuple of an anchor, positive and negative point cloud to compute a triplet loss. (b) and (c) show detailed view of the detector and descriptor networks.

We train our network with the triplet loss to minimize the difference between the anchor and positive point clouds, while maximizing the difference between anchor and negative point clouds. To allow the loss to take individual cluster descriptors into account, we use an alignment model [14] to align each descriptor to its best match before aggregating the loss. Since not all sampled clusters have the same distinctiveness, the predicted attention w_k from the detector is used to weigh the contribution of each cluster descriptor in the training loss. These attention weights are learned on arbitrarily sampled clusters during training, and later used to detect distinctive keypoints in the point cloud during inference.

Clustering. The first stage of the network is to sample clusters from the point cloud. To this end, we use the sample and grouping layers in PointNet++ [24]. The sampling layer samples a set of points $\{x_{i_1}, x_{i_2}, \ldots, x_{i_K}\}$ from an input point cloud P. The coordinates of these sampled points and the point cloud are then passed into the grouping layer that outputs K clusters of points. Each cluster

C_k is a collection of points in a local region of a predefined radius $r_{cluster}$ around the sampled point x_{i_k}. These clusters are used as support regions to compute local descriptors, analogous to 2D image patches around detected keypoints in 2D feature matching frameworks. We use the iterative farthest point sampling scheme as in PointNet++ for sampling, but any form of sampling that can sufficiently cover the point cloud (e.g. Random Sphere Cover Set [8]) is also suitable. Such sampling schemes increases the likelihood that each sampled cluster in an anchor point cloud has a nearby cluster in the positive point cloud.

Detector. Each cluster C_k sampled by the clustering step is passed to the detector network that predicts an orientation θ_k and an attention score w_k. The attention score w_k is a positive number that indicates the saliency of the input cluster C_k. This design is inspired by typical 2D feature detectors, e.g. SIFT [17]. The predicted orientation is used to rotate the cluster to a canonical orientation, so that the final descriptor is invariant to the cluster's original orientation.

We construct our detector network using point symmetric functions defined in PointNet [23], which is defined as $f(\{x_1, ..., x_n\}) = g(h(x_1), ..., h(x_n))$, where $h(.)$ is a shared function that transforms each individual point x_i, and $g(.)$ is a symmetric function on all transformed elements. These functions are invariant to point ordering and generates fixed length features given arbitrary sized point clouds. We use a three fully connected layers (64-128-256 nodes) for the implementation of $h(.)$. The symmetric function $g(.)$ is implemented as a max-pooling followed by two fully connected layers (128-64 nodes), before branching into two 1-layer paths for orientation and attention predictions.

We only predict a single 1D rotation angle θ_i, avoiding unnecessary equivariances to retain higher discriminating power. This is reasonable since point clouds are usually aligned to the gravity direction due to the sensor setup (e.g. a Velodyne Lidar mounted upright on a car); for other cases, the gravity vector obtained from an IMU can be used to rotate the point clouds into the upright orientation. Similar to [33], we do not regress the angle directly. Instead, we regress two separate values θ_{k_1} and θ_{k_2} that denote the sine and cosine of the angle. We use a ℓ_2 normalization layer to add a constraint of $\theta_{k_1}^2 + \theta_{k_2}^2 = 1$ to ensure valid sine and cosine values. The final angle can be computed as $\theta_k = arctan2(\theta_{k_1}, \theta_{k_2})$. For the attention weights w_i's, we use the softplus activation as suggested by [20] to prevent the network from learning negative attention weights.

Descriptor. Our descriptor network takes each cluster C_k from the clustering layer and orientation θ_k from the detector network as inputs, and generates a descriptor $f_k \in \mathbb{R}^d$ for each cluster. More specifically, θ_k is first used to rotate cluster C_k into a canonical configuration, before they are passed into another point symmetric function to generate the descriptor. In practice, we find it helpful to aggregate contextual information in the computation of the descriptor. Hence, after applying max-pooling to obtain a cluster feature vector, we concatenate this cluster feature vector with the individual point features to incorporate context. We then apply a single fully connected layer with d' nodes before another max-pooling. Finally, we apply another fully connected layer and l_2 normalization to produce a final cluster descriptor $f_k \in \mathbb{R}^d$ for cluster C_k. The addition of the contextual information improves the discriminating power of the descriptor.

Feature Alignment Triplet Loss. The output from the descriptor network in the previous stage is a set of features f_i for each cluster. We use the alignment objective introduced in [14] to compare individual descriptors since the supervision is given as model-level annotations. Instead of the dot product similarity measure used in [14], we adopt the Euclidean distance measure which is more commonly used for comparing feature descriptors. Specifically, the distance between all pairs of descriptors between the two point clouds $P^{(m)}$ and $P^{(n)}$ with clusters $\mathbf{C}^{(m)}$ and $\mathbf{C}^{(n)}$ is given by:

$$\mathcal{D}_{m,n} = \sum_{C_i \in \mathbf{C}^{(m)}} \left(w_i' \cdot \min_{C_j \in \mathbf{C}^{(n)}} \| f_i - f_j \|_2 \right), \quad w_i' = \frac{w_i}{\sum_{j \in P^{(m)}} w_j}, \quad (1)$$

where w_i' is the normalized attention weight. Under this formulation, every descriptor from the first point cloud aligns to its closest descriptor in the second one. Intuitively, in a matching point cloud pair, clusters in the first point cloud should have a similar cluster in the second point cloud. For non-matching pairs, the above distance simply aligns a descriptor to one which is most similar to itself, i.e. its hardest negative. This consideration of the hardest negative descriptor in the non-matching image provides the advantage that no explicit mining for hard negatives is required. Our model trains well with randomly sampled negative point clouds. We formulate the triplet loss for each training tuple $\{P^{(anc)}, P^{(pos)}, P^{(neg)}\}$ as:

$$\mathcal{L}_{triplet} = [\mathcal{D}_{anc,pos} - \mathcal{D}_{anc,neg} + \gamma]_+, \quad (2)$$

where $[z]_+ = max(z, 0)$ denotes the hinge loss, and γ denotes the margin which is enforced between the positive and negative pairs.

4.2   Inference Pipeline

The keypoints and descriptors are computed in two separate stages during inference. In the first stage, the attention scores of all points in a given point cloud are computed. We apply non-maximal suppression over a fixed radius r_{nms} around each point, and keep the remaining M points with the highest attention weights. Furthermore, points with low attention are filtered out by rejecting those with attention $w_i < \beta * \max(w_1, w_2, ..., w_N)$. The remaining points are our detected keypoints. In the next stage, the descriptor network computes the descriptors only for these keypoints. The separation of the inference into two detector-descriptor stages is computationally and memory efficient since only the detector network needs to process all the points while the descriptor network processes only the clusters that correspond to the selected keypoints. As a result, our network can scale up to larger point clouds.

5   Evaluations and Results

5.1   Benchmark Datasets

Oxford RobotCar. We use the open-source Oxford RobotCar dataset [19] for training and evaluation. This dataset consists of a large number of traversals over the same route in central Oxford, UK, at different times over a year. The push-broom 2D scans are accumulated into 3D point clouds using the associated GPS/INS poses. For each traversal, we create a 3D point cloud with 30m radius for every 10m interval whenever good GPS/INS poses are available. Each point cloud is then downsampled using a VoxelGrid filter with a grid size of 0.2m. We split the data into two disjoint sets for training and testing. The first 35 traversals are used for training and the last 5 traversals are used for testing. We obtain a total of 21,875 training and initially 828 testing point cloud sets.

We make use of the pairwise relative poses computed from the GPS/INS poses as ground truth to evaluate the performance on the test set. However, the GPS/INS poses may contain errors in the order of several meters. To improve the fidelity of our test set, we refine these poses using ICP [3]. We set one of the test traversals as reference, and register all test point clouds within 10m to their respective point clouds in the reference. We retain matches with an estimated Root Mean Square Error (RMSE) of < 0.5 m, and perform manual visual inspection to filter out bad matches. We get 794/828 good point clouds that give us 3426 pairwise relative poses for testing (Table 1). Lastly, we randomly rotate each point cloud around the vertical axis to evaluate rotational equivariances and randomly downsample each test point cloud to 16,384 points.

Table 1. Breakdown of Oxford RobotCar data for training and testing

	# Traversals	# Point clouds	# Matched pairs
Train	35	21875	–
Test	5	828	–
Test (after registration)	5	794	3426

KITTI Dataset. We evaluate the performance of our trained network on the 11 training sequences of the KITTI Odometry dataset [9] to understand how well our trained detector and descriptor generalizes to point clouds captured in a different city using a different sensor. The KITTI dataset contains point clouds captured on a Velodyne-64 3D Lidar scaner in Karlsruhe, Germany. We sample the Lidar scans at 10m intervals to obtain 2369 point clouds, and downsample them using a VoxelGrid filter with a grid size of 0.2m. We consider the 2831 point cloud pairs that are captured within 10m range of each other. We use the provided GPS/INS pose as ground truth.

ETH Dataset. Our network is also evaluated on the "challenging dataset for point cloud registration algorithms" [22]. This dataset is captured on a ground Lidar scanner, and contains largely unstructured vegetation unlike the previous two datasets. Following [8], we accumulate point clouds captured in one season of the Gazebo and Wood scenes to build a global point cloud, and register local point clouds captured in the other season to it. We take the liberty to build the global point cloud for both scenes using the summer data since [8] did not state the season that was used. During pre-procesing, we downsample the point clouds using a VoxelGrid filter of 0.1m grid size. We choose a finer resolution because of the finer features in the vegetation in this dataset.

5.2   Experimental Setup

We train using a batch size of 6 triplets, and use the ADAM optimizer with a constant learning rate of 1e-5. We use points within a radius of $R = 20$ m from the centroid of the point cloud for training, and sample $K = 512$ clusters with a radius of $r_{cluster} = 2.0$ m. The thresholds for defining positive and negative point clouds are set to $\tau_p = 5$ m and $\tau_n = 50$ m. We randomly downsample each point cloud to 4096 points on the fly during training. We found that training with this random input dropout leads to better generalization behavior as also observed by [24]. We apply the following data augmentations during training time: random jitter to the individual points, random shifts and small rotations. Random rotations are also applied around the z-axis, i.e. upright axis in order to learn rotation equivariance. Note that our training data is already oriented in the upright direction using its GPS/INS pose.

Our network is end-to-end differentiable, but in practice, we find it sometimes hard to train. Hence, we train in two phases to improve stability. We first pretrain the network without the detector for 2 epochs, i.e. the clusters are fed directly into the descriptor network without rotation, and all clusters have equal attention weights. During this phase, we apply all data augmentations except for large 1D rotations. We use these learned weights to initialize the descriptor in the second phase, where we train the entire network and apply all the above data augmentation. Training took 34 hours on a Nvidia Geforce GTX1080Ti.

For inference, we use the following parameters for both the Oxford and KITTI odometry datasets: $r_{nms} = 0.5$ m, $\beta = 0.01$. For the ETH dataset, we use $r_{nms} = 0.3$ m, $\beta = 0.005$ to boost the number of detected keypoints in the semi-structured environments. We limit the number of keypoints M to 1024 for all cases, except for the global model in the ETH dataset which we use 2048 due to its larger size. Inference took around 0.8s for a point cloud with 16,384 points.

5.3   Baseline Algorithms

We compare our algorithm with three commonly used handcrafted 3D feature descriptors: Fast Point Feature Histograms (FPFH) [25] (33 dimensions), Spin-Image (SI) [13] (153 dimensions), and Unique Shape Context (USC) [30] (1980 dimensions). We use the implementation provided in the Point Cloud Library

(PCL) [12] for all the handcrafted descriptors. In addition, we include two recent learned 3D descriptors: Compact Geometric Features (CGF) [15] (32 dimensions) and 3DMatch [34] (512 dimensions) in our comparisons. Note that our comparisons are done using their provided weights that were pretrained on indoor datasets. This is because we are unable to train CGF and 3DMatch on the weakly supervised Oxford dataset as these networks require strong supervision. We also train a modified PointNet++ (PN++) [24] in a weakly supervised manner on a retrieval task, which we use as a baseline to show the importance of descriptor alignment in learning local descriptors. We modify PointNet++ as follows: the first set abstraction layer is replaced by our detection and description network. The second and third set abstraction layers remain unchanged. We replace the subsequent fully connected layers with fc1024-dropout-fc512 layers. During inference, we extract descriptors as the output from the first set abstraction layer. We tuned the parameters for all descriptors to the best of our ability, except in Sect. 5.4, where we used the same cluster radii for all descriptors to ensure all descriptors "see" the same information.

Since none of the above baseline feature descriptors comes with a feature detector, we use the handcrafted detector from Intrinsic Shape Signatures (ISS) [35] implemented in PCL. Following [34], we also show the performance on randomly sampled keypoints for 3DMatch.

5.4 Descriptor Matching

We first evaluate the ability of the descriptors to distinguish between different clusters using the procedure in [34]. We extract each matching cluster at randomly selected locations from two matching model pairs. Non-matching clusters are extracted from two random point clouds at locations that are at least 20m apart. We extract 30,000 pairs of 3D clusters, equally split between matches and non-matches. As in [34], our evaluation metric is the false-positive rate at 95% recall. To ensure all descriptors have access to similar amounts of information, we fixed the cluster radius $r_{cluster}$ to 2.0 m for all descriptors in this experiment.

Fig. 3 shows the performance of our descriptor at different dimensionality. We observe that there is diminishing returns above 32 dimensions, and will use a feature dimension of $d = 32$ for the rest of the experiments.

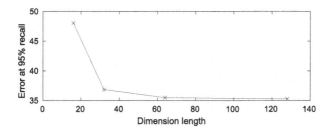

Fig. 3. Matching error at 95% recall for different descriptor dimensionality

Table 2. Descriptor matching task. Error at 95% recall. Lower is better.

	SI [13]	FPFH[25]	USC[30]	CGF [15]	3DMatch[34]	PN++[24]	**Ours**
Error (%)	68.51	54.13	91.59	69.77	38.49	50.57	**36.84**

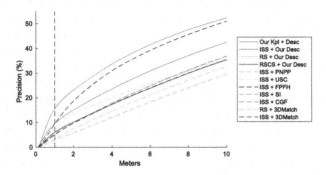

Fig. 4. Precision on the Oxford Robotcar dataset using different keypoint and descriptor combination. (Kpt = keypoints, Desc = descriptors)

Fig. 5. Left: Attention using proposed method (brighter colors indicate higher attention). Middle: Our Keypoints (red dots). Right: ISS keypoints (red dots). Colors in middle and right images indicate different heights above ground.

Table 2 compares our descriptor with the baseline algorithms. Our learned descriptor yields a lower error rate than all other descriptors despite having a similar or smaller dimension. It performs significantly better than the best hand-crafted descriptor (FPFH) which uses explicitly computed normals. The other two handcrafted descriptors (USC and SI), as well as the learned CGF consider the number of points falling in each subregion around the keypoint and could not differentiate the sparse point cloud clusters. 3DMatch performed well in differentiating randomly sampled clusters, but requiring a larger feature dimension. Lastly, the modified PointNet++ network did not learn a good descriptor in the weakly supervised setting and gives significantly higher error than our descriptor despite having the same descriptor network structure.

5.5   Keypoint Detection and Feature Description

We follow the procedure in [15] to evaluate the joint performance of keypoints and descriptors. For each keypoint descriptor in the first model of the pair, we find its nearest neighbor in the second model via exhaustive search. We then compute the distance between this nearest neighbor and its ground truth location. We obtain a precision plot, as shown in Fig. 4, by varying the distance threshold x for considering a match as correct and plotting the proportion of correct matches. We evaluate on all the baseline descriptors, and also show the performance of our descriptor with the ISS detector, random sampling of points (RS), and points obtained using Random Sphere Cover Set (RSCS) [8]. We tuned the cluster sizes for all baseline descriptors, as many of them require larger cluster sizes to work well. Nevertheless, our keypoint detector and descriptor combination still yields the best precision for all distance thresholds, and obtains a precision of 15.6% at 1m. We also note that our descriptor underperforms when used with the two random sampling methods or the generic ISS detector, indicating the importance of a dedicated feature detector.

Analysis of Keypoint Detection   Fig. 5 shows the attention weights computed by our network, as well as the retrieved keypoints. We also show the keypoints obtained using ISS for comparison. Our network learns to give higher attentions to lower regions of the walls (near the ground), and mostly ignores the ground and the cars (which are transient and not useful for matching). In comparison, ISS detects many non-distinctive keypoints on the ground and cars.

5.6   Geometric Registration

We test our keypoint detection and description algorithm on the geometric registration problem. We perform nearest neighbor matching on the computed keypoints and descriptors, and use RANSAC on these nearest neighbor matches to estimate a rigid transformation between the two point clouds. The number of RANSAC iterations is automatically adjusted based on 99% confidence but is limited to 10,000. No subsequent refinement, e.g. using ICP is performed. We evaluate the estimated pose against its ground truth using the Relative Translational Error (RTE) and Relative Rotation Error (RRE) as in [8,18]. We consider registration successful when the RTE and RRE are both below a predefined threshold of 2 m and 5°, and report the average RTE and RRE values for successful cases. We also report the average number of RANSAC iterations.

Performance on Oxford RobotCar.   Table 3 shows the performance on the Oxford dataset. We observe the following: (1) using a keypoint detector instead of random sampling improves geometric registration performance, even for 3DMatch which is designed for random keypoints, (2) our learned descriptor gives good accuracy even when used with handcrafted descriptors or random sampling, suggesting that it generalizes well to generic point clusters, (3) our

Table 3. Performance on the Oxford RobotCar dataset.

Method	RTE (m)	RRE (°)	Success rate	Avg # iter
ISS [35] + FPFH [25]	0.396 ± 0.290	1.60 ± 1.02	92.32%	7171
ISS [35] + SI [13]	0.415 ± 0.309	1.61 ± 1.12	87.45 %	9888
ISS [35] + USC [30]	0.324 ± 0.270	1.22 ± 0.95	94.02%	7084
ISS [35] + CGF [15]	0.431 ± 0.320	1.62 ± 1.10	87.36%	9628
RS + 3DMatch [34]	0.616 ± 0.407	2.02 ± 1.17	54.64%	9848
ISS [35] + 3DMatch [34]	0.494 ± 0.366	1.78 ± 1.21	69.06%	9131
ISS [35] + PN++ [24]	0.511 ± 0.391	1.88 ± 1.20	48.86%	9904
RS + Our Desc	0.435 ± 0.305	1.64 ± 1.04	90.28%	9941
RSCS [8] + Our Desc	0.386 ± 0.292	1.46 ± 1.01	92.64%	9913
ISS [35] + Our Desc	0.314 ± 0.262	1.08 ± 0.83	97.66%	7127
Our Kpt + Desc	**0.300 ± 0.255**	**1.07 ± 0.85**	**98.10%**	**2940**

detector and descriptor combination gives the highest success rates and lowest errors. This highlights the importance of designing a keypoint detector and descriptor simultaneously, and the applicability of our approach to geometric registration. Some qualitative registration results can be found in Fig. 6(a).

Performance on KITTI Dataset. We evaluate the generalization performance of our network on the KITTI odometry dataset by comparing the geometric registration performance against ISS + FPFH in Table 4. We use the same parameters as the Oxford dataset for all algorithms, and did not fine-tune our network in any way. Nevertheless, our 3DFeat-Net outperforms all other algorithms in most measures. It underperforms CGF slightly in terms of RTE, but has a significantly higher success rate and requires far fewer RANSAC iterations. We show some matching results on the KITTI dataset in Fig. 6(b).

Table 4. Performance on the KITTI odometry dataset.

Method	RTE (m)	RRE (°)	Success Rate	Avg # iter
ISS [35] + FPFH [25]	0.325 ± 0.270	1.08 ± 0.82	58.95%	7462
ISS [35] + SI [13]	0.358 ± 0.304	1.17 ± 0.94	55.92%	9219
ISS [35] + USC [30]	0.262 ± 0.275	0.83 ± 0.75	78.24%	7873
ISS [35] + CGF [15]	**0.233 ± 0.266**	0.69 ± 0.60	87.81%	7442
RS + 3DMatch [34]	0.377 ± 0.298	1.21 ± 0.84	83.96%	8674
ISS [35] + 3DMatch [34]	0.283 ± 0.272	0.79 ± 0.65	89.12%	7292
Our Kpt + Desc	0.259 ± 0.262	**0.57 ± 0.46**	**95.97%**	**3798**

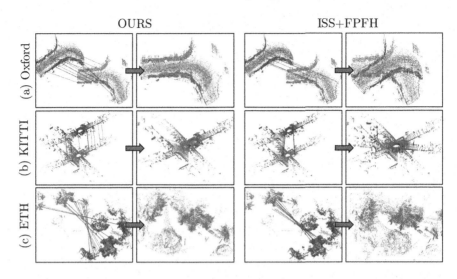

Fig. 6. Qualitative registration results, using our approach (left) and ISS + FPFH (right). We only show a random subset of matches retained after RANSAC, and exclude the ground in (c) for clarity. We also show the results using ISS + FPFH.

Table 5. Performance on the ETH dataset, the results of FPFH and LORAX are taken from [8]. The last column indicates the success rate over the entire dataset.

Method	RTE (m)	RRE (°)	Success Rate	(All)
FPFH [25]	0.44 ± 0.2	12.2 ± 4.8	67%	–
LORAX [8]	0.42 ± 0.27	2.5 ± 1.2	83%	–
ISS [35] + SI [13]	0.176 ± 0.083	1.97 ± 0.74	**100%**	93.7%
ISS [35] + USC [30]	**0.130 ± 0.056**	1.52 ± 0.30	**100%**	**100%**
ISS [35] + CGF [15]	0.157 ± 0.066	**1.47 ± 0.60**	**100%**	92.1%
RS + 3DMatch [34]	0.292 ± 0.199	4.71 ± 3.16	91.7%	33.3%
ISS [35] + 3DMatch [34]	0.401 ± 0.222	5.32 ± 3.25	**100%**	33.3%
Our Kpt + Desc	0.156 ± 0.112	1.56 ± 0.66	**100%**	95.2%

Performance on ETH Dataset. We compare our performance against LORAX [8], which evaluates on 9 models from the Gazebo dataset and 3 models from the Wood dataset. We show our performance on the best performing point clouds for each algorithm in Table 5 since it is not explicitly stated in [8] which datasets were used. Note that success rate in this experiment refers to a RTE of below 1m to be consistent to [8]. We also report the success rate over the entire dataset. Detailed results on the entire dataset can be found in the supplementary material. LORAX considers 3 best descriptor matches for each keypoint. These matches are used to compute multiple pose hypotheses which are then refined using ICP for robustness. For our algorithm and baselines, we only consider the best match, compute a single pose hypothesis and do not perform any refinement of the pose. Despite this, our approach outperforms [8] and most baseline algorithms. It only underperforms USC which uses a much larger dimension (1980D). Fig. 6(c) shows an example of a successful matching by our approach.

6   Conclusion

We proposed the 3DFeat-Net model that learns the detection and description of keypoints in Lidar point clouds in a weakly supervised fashion by making use of a triplet loss that takes into account individual descriptor similarities and the saliency of input 3D points. Experimental results showed our learned detector and descriptor compares favorably against previous handcrafted and learned ones on several outdoor gravity aligned datasets. However, we note that our network is unable to train well on overly noisy point clouds, and the use of PointNet limits the max size of the input point cloud. We also do not extract a fully rotational invariant descriptor. We leave these as future work.

References

1. Arandjelovic, R., Gronat, P., Torii, A., Pajdla, T., Sivic, J.: Netvlad: Cnn architecture for weakly supervised place recognition. In: IEEE Conference on Computer Vision and Pattern Recognition (CVPR), pp. 5297–5307 (2016). https://doi.org/10.1109/CVPR.2016.572
2. Bay, H., Tuytelaars, T., Van Gool, L.: SURF: speeded up robust features. In: Leonardis, A., Bischof, H., Pinz, A. (eds.) ECCV 2006. LNCS, vol. 3951, pp. 404–417. Springer, Heidelberg (2006). https://doi.org/10.1007/11744023_32
3. Besl, P.J., McKay, N.D.: A method for registration of 3-d shapes. IEEE Trans. Pattern Anal. Mach. Intell. (TPAMI) 14(2), 239–256 (1992). https://doi.org/10.1109/34.121791
4. Bromley, J., Guyon, I., LeCun, Y., Säckinger, E., Shah, R.: Signature verification using a "siamese" time delay neural network. In: Advances in Neural Information Processing Systems, pp. 737–744 (1994)
5. Chen, H., Bhanu, B.: 3d free-form object recognition in range images using local surface patches. In: International Conference on Pattern Recognition (ICPR), vol. 3, pp. 136–139 (2004). https://doi.org/10.1109/ICPR.2004.1334487
6. Deng, H., Birdal, T., Ilic, S.: Ppfnet: global context aware local features for robust 3d point matching. In: IEEE Conference on Computer Vision and Pattern Recognition (CVPR) (2018)
7. Dubé, R., Dugas, D., Stumm, E., Nieto, J., Siegwart, R., Cadena, C.: Segmatch: segment based loop-closure for 3d point clouds. arXiv preprint arXiv:1609.07720 (2016)
8. Elbaz, G., Avraham, T., Fischer, A.: 3d point cloud registration for localization using a deep neural network auto-encoder. In: IEEE Conference on Computer Vision and Pattern Recognition (CVPR), pp. 2472–2481 (2017). https://doi.org/10.1109/CVPR.2017.265

9. Geiger, A., Lenz, P., Urtasun, R.: Are we ready for autonomous driving? the kitti vision benchmark suite. In: IEEE Conference on Computer Vision and Pattern Recognition (CVPR), pp. 3354–3361 (2012). https://doi.org/10.1109/CVPR.2012. 6248074
10. Gordo, A., Almazán, J., Revaud, J., Larlus, D.: Deep image retrieval: learning global representations for image search. In: Leibe, B., Matas, J., Sebe, N., Welling, M. (eds.) ECCV 2016. LNCS, vol. 9910, pp. 241–257. Springer, Cham (2016). https://doi.org/10.1007/978-3-319-46466-4_15
11. Hänsch, R., Weber, T., Hellwich, O.: Comparison of 3d interest point detectors and descriptors for point cloud fusion. ISPRS Ann. Photogramm. Remote Sens. Spat. Inf. Sci. **2**(3), 57 (2014)
12. Holz, D., Ichim, A.E., Tombari, F., Rusu, R.B., Behnke, S.: Registration with the point cloud library: a modular framework for aligning in 3-d. IEEE Robot. Autom. Mag. **22**(4), 110–124 (2015). https://doi.org/10.1109/MRA.2015.2432331
13. Johnson, A.E., Hebert, M.: Using spin images for efficient object recognition in cluttered 3d scenes. IEEE Trans. Pattern Anal. Mach. Intell. (TPAMI) **21**(5), 433–449 (1999). https://doi.org/10.1109/34.765655
14. Karpathy, A., Fei-Fei, L.: Deep visual-semantic alignments for generating image descriptions. In: IEEE Conference on Computer Vision and Pattern Recognition (CVPR), pp. 3128–3137 (2015). https://doi.org/10.1109/CVPR.2015.7298932
15. Khoury, M., Zhou, Q.Y., Koltun, V.: Learning compact geometric features. In: International Conference on Computer Vision (ICCV), pp. 153–161 (2017). https://doi.org/10.1109/ICCV.2017.26
16. Lee, G.H., Li, B., Pollefeys, M., Fraundorfer, F.: Minimal solutions for the multi-camera pose estimation problem. Int. J. Robot. Res. (IJRR), 837–848 (2015). https://doi.org/10.1177/0278364914557969
17. Lowe, D.G.: Distinctive image features from scale-invariant keypoints. Int. J. Comput. Vis. **60**(2), 91–110 (2004). https://doi.org/10.1023/B:VISI.0000029664.99615. 94
18. Ma, Y., Guo, Y., Zhao, J., Lu, M., Zhang, J., Wan, J.: Fast and accurate registration of structured point clouds with small overlaps. In: IEEE Conference on Computer Vision and Pattern Recognition Workshops (CVPRW), pp. 643–651 (2016). https://doi.org/10.1109/CVPRW.2016.86
19. Maddern, W., Pascoe, G., Linegar, C., Newman, P.: 1 year, 1000 km: the oxford robotcar dataset. The Int. J. Robot. Res. (IJRR) **36**(1), 3–15 (2017). https://doi. org/10.1177/0278364916679498
20. Noh, H., Araujo, A., Sim, J., Weyand, T., Han, B.: Large-scale image retrieval with attentive deep local features. In: IEEE International Conference on Computer Vision (ICCV), pp. 3476–3485 (2017). https://doi.org/10.1109/ICCV.2017.374
21. Pavel, F.A., Wang, Z., Feng, D.D.: Reliable object recognition using sift features. In: IEEE International Workshop on Multimedia Signal Processing (MMSP), pp. 1–6 (2009). https://doi.org/10.1109/MMSP.2009.5293282
22. Pomerleau, F., Liu, M., Colas, F., Siegwart, R.: Challenging data sets for point cloud registration algorithms. Int. J. Robot. Res. (IJRR) **31**(14), 1705–1711 (2012)
23. Qi, C.R., Su, H., Mo, K., Guibas, L.J.: Pointnet: deep learning on point sets for 3d classification and segmentation. In: IEEE Conference on Computer Vision and Pattern Recognition (CVPR), pp. 77–85 (2017). https://doi.org/10.1109/CVPR. 2017.16
24. Qi, C.R., Yi, L., Su, H., Guibas, L.J.: Pointnet++: deep hierarchical feature learning on point sets in a metric space. In: Advances in Neural Information Processing Systems, pp. 5105–5114 (2017)

25. Rusu, R.B., Blodow, N., Beetz, M.: Fast point feature histograms (fpfh) for 3d registration. In: IEEE International Conference on Robotics and Automation (ICRA), pp. 3212–3217 (2009). https://doi.org/10.1109/ROBOT.2009.5152473

26. Rusu, R.B., Blodow, N., Marton, Z.C., Beetz, M.: Aligning point cloud views using persistent feature histograms. In: IEEE/RSJ International Conference on Intelligent Robots and Systems (IROS), pp. 3384–3391 (2008). https://doi.org/10.1109/IROS.2008.4650967

27. Salti, S., Tombari, F., Spezialetti, R., Stefano, L.D.: Learning a descriptor-specific 3d keypoint detector. In: IEEE International Conference on Computer Vision (ICCV), pp. 2318–2326 (2015). https://doi.org/10.1109/ICCV.2015.267

28. Salti, S., Tombari, F., Di Stefano, L.: Shot: unique signatures of histograms for surface and texture description. Comput. Vis. Image Underst. **125**, 251–264 (2014)

29. Schroff, F., Kalenichenko, D., Philbin, J.: Facenet: a unified embedding for face recognition and clustering. In: IEEE Conference on Computer Vision and Pattern recognition (CVPR), pp. 815–823 (2015). https://doi.org/10.1109/CVPR.2015.7298682

30. Tombari, F., Salti, S., Di Stefano, L.: Unique shape context for 3d data description. In: ACM Workshop on 3D Object Retrieval, pp. 57–62. 3DOR 2010, ACM (2010). https://doi.org/10.1145/1877808.1877821

31. Verdie, Y., Yi, K.M., Fua, P., Lepetit, V.: TILDE: a temporally invariant learned DEtector. In: IEEE Conference on Computer Vision and Pattern Recognition (CVPR), pp. 5279–5288 (2015). https://doi.org/10.1109/CVPR.2015.7299165

32. Yi, K.M., Trulls, E., Lepetit, V., Fua, P.: Lift: learned invariant feature transform. In: Leibe, B., Matas, J., Sebe, N., Welling, M. (eds.) European Conference on Computer Vision (ECCV), pp. 467–483. Springer International Publishing (2016). https://doi.org/10.1007/978-3-319-46466-4_28

33. Yi, K.M., Verdie, Y., Fua, P., Lepetit, V.: Learning to assign orientations to feature points. In: IEEE Conference on Computer Vision and Pattern Recognition (CVPR), pp. 107–116 (2016). https://doi.org/10.1109/CVPR.2016.19

34. Zeng, A., Song, S., Nießner, M., Fisher, M., Xiao, J., Funkhouser, T.: 3dmatch: learning local geometric descriptors from rgb-d reconstructions. In: IEEE Conference on Computer Vision and Pattern Recognition (CVPR), pp. 199–208 (2017). https://doi.org/10.1109/CVPR.2017.29

35. Zhong, Y.: Intrinsic shape signatures: a shape descriptor for 3d object recognition. In: IEEE International Conference on Computer Vision Workshops, (ICCVW), pp. 689–696 (2009). https://doi.org/10.1109/ICCVW.2009.5457637

Deep Domain Generalization via Conditional Invariant Adversarial Networks

Ya Li[1], Xinmei Tian[1]([envelope]), Mingming Gong[2,3], Yajing Liu[1], Tongliang Liu[4], Kun Zhang[2], and Dacheng Tao[4]

[1] CAS Key Laboratory of Technology in Geo-Spatial Information
Processing and Application Systems,
University of Science and Technology of China, Hefei, China
{muziyiye,lyj123}@mail.ustc.edu.cn, xinmei@ustc.edu.cn
[2] Department of Philosophy, Carnegie Mellon University, Pittsburgh, USA
gongmingnju@gmail.com, kunz1@cmu.edu
[3] Department of Biomedical Informatics, University of Pittsburgh, Pittsburgh, USA
[4] UBTECH Sydney AI Centre, SIT, FEIT, University of Sydney, Sydney, Australia
tliang.liu@gmail.com, dacheng.tao@sydney.edu.au

Abstract. Domain generalization aims to learn a classification model from multiple source domains and generalize it to unseen target domains. A critical problem in domain generalization involves learning domain-invariant representations. Let X and Y denote the features and the labels, respectively. Under the assumption that the conditional distribution $P(Y|X)$ remains unchanged across domains, earlier approaches to domain generalization learned the invariant representation $T(X)$ by minimizing the discrepancy of the marginal distribution $P(T(X))$. However, such an assumption of stable $P(Y|X)$ does not necessarily hold in practice. In addition, the representation learning function $T(X)$ is usually constrained to a simple linear transformation or shallow networks. To address the above two drawbacks, we propose an end-to-end conditional invariant deep domain generalization approach by leveraging deep neural networks for domain-invariant representation learning. The domain-invariance property is guaranteed through a conditional invariant adversarial network that can learn domain-invariant representations w.r.t. the joint distribution $P(T(X), Y)$ if the target domain data are not severely class unbalanced. We perform various experiments to demonstrate the effectiveness of the proposed method.

Keywords: Domain generalization · Adversarial networks
Domain invariant representation

© Springer Nature Switzerland AG 2018
V. Ferrari et al. (Eds.): ECCV 2018, LNCS 11219, pp. 647–663, 2018.
https://doi.org/10.1007/978-3-030-01267-0_38

1 Introduction

With the advances in deep learning in recent years, computer vision has achieved impressive success, e.g., in image classification [1,2], face recognition [3,4], and object detection [5]. The mentioned tasks rely on standard supervised learning that assumes that the training and test data follow the same distribution. However, this assumption does not hold in many real-world situations due to various changing factors, such as background noise, viewpoint changes and illumination variation. Such factors can cause biases in the collected datasets [6]. In deep learning, a common approach to eliminating data bias is through fine-tuning a pre-trained network on the target domain with a certain number of labels. However, labeling the data when moving to different new target domains is labor intensive. Domain generalization [7–16] is proposed to overcome such challenges. Given inputs and the corresponding outputs of multiple source domains, domain generalization aims to learn a domain-invariant feature representation that can generalize well to unseen target domains.

Most existing domain generalization methods learn the invariant feature transformation based on handcrafted features or features extracted from pre-trained deep learning models. Compared to handcrafted features, features extracted from pre-trained neural networks are more discriminative and descriptive. Several domain generalization methods [7–11] have demonstrated the effectiveness of features extracted from neural networks. However, the referenced methods consider the extracted features as input X and use a linear transformation or multilayer perceptrons to model the transformation $T(X)$. Such a learning strategy does not fully explore the advantages of deep neural networks. We argue that learning the invariant feature transformation directly from the original image in an end-to-end fashion will lead to better performance.

In addition, previous studies assume that the conditional distribution $P(Y|X)$ remains stable across domains and that domain-invariant learning boils down to the guarantee of invariance of the marginal distribution $P(T(X))$. If this assumption is violated, the joint distribution $P(T(X), Y)$ will not be invariant even if $P(T(X))$ is invariant after learning. According to recent results in causal learning [17,18], if the causal structure is $X \rightarrow Y$, where X is the cause and Y is the effect, $P(Y|X)$ can remain stable as $P(X)$ changes because they are "independent" of each other. However, the causal structure is often $Y \rightarrow X$ in computer vision, e.g., object classes are the causes of image features [19]. In this scenario, if $P(X)$ changes, $P(Y|X)$ often changes together with $P(X)$. Considering digital number classification as an example and denoting each rotation angle α as one domain, we obtain a different class-conditional distribution $P(X|Y, \alpha = \alpha_i)$ for each domain, i.e., the feature distribution of digital numbers depends on the rotation angle. Assuming, for simplicity, that $P(Y)$ does not change, according to the sum rule, we obtain $P(X|\alpha = \alpha_i) = \sum_{j=1}^{L} P(X|Y = j, \alpha = \alpha_i) P(Y = j)$, where L is the number of classes, and thus, the values of $P(X|\alpha = \alpha_i)$ are different across domains. Additionally, according to Bayes' rule, $P(Y|X, \alpha = \alpha_i) = P(X|Y, \alpha = \alpha_i) P(Y)/P(X|\alpha = \alpha_i)$; hence, it is very unlikely that $P(Y|X, \alpha = \alpha_i)$ are the same across domains.

In this paper, we consider the scenario whereby both $P(X)$ and $P(Y|X)$ can change across domains and address domain generalization in an end-to-end deep learning framework. This is achieved by learning a conditional invariant neural network that learns to minimize the discrepancy in $P(X|Y)$ across different domains. Inspired by generative adversarial networks [20] and recent deep domain adaptation methods [21,22], we develop an adversarial network to learn a domain-invariant representation by making the learned representations on different domains indistinguishable. The conditional invariance property is guaranteed by two adversarial losses that consider the source-domain label information overlooked by the existing methods. One aims to directly make the representations in each class indistinguishable across source domains. The other loss aims to make the representations of all classes indistinguishable across class prior-normalized source domains. The purpose of introducing class prior-based normalization is to reduce the negative effect caused by the possible class prior $P(Y)$ changes across source domains. If the prior distributions $P(Y)$ in the target domain and the pooled source domains are identical, our method can guarantee the invariance of the joint distribution $P(X, Y)$ across domains.

2   Related Work

Domain generalization has drawn substantial attention in recent years, with various approaches [7–11] having been proposed. Muandet et al. [9] proposed a domain-invariant component analysis that learns an invariant transformation by minimizing dissimilarity among domains. Ghifary et al. [8] proposed a unified framework for domain adaptation and generalization using scatter component analysis. In contrast to the above methods, Khosla et al. [7] proposed removing the dataset bias by measuring the dataset-specific model as a combination of the dataset-specific bias and a visual world model. Considering the construction ability of an autoencoder, Ghifary et al. [11] proposed a multi-task autoencoder method to learn domain-invariant features. The learned features could subsequently be used as the input to classifiers. All referenced methods are shallow domain generalization methods that need handcrafted features or features extracted from pre-trained deep learning models. Note that the multi-task autoencoder uses only one hidden layer built on the pre-learned deep features. Such pre-extracted features dramatically constrain the learning ability of the existing domain generalization methods. Our method learns the domain-invariant representation from the original images in an end-to-end deep learning framework.

In addition to the shallow architecture, the existing methods assume that $P(Y|X)$ remains invariant across domains and only aim to learn a domain-invariant feature transformation $T(X)$ to guarantee the invariance of feature distribution $P(T(X))$. Recent studies of domain adaptation have noted the importance of matching joint distributions instead of the marginal distribution. [23] and [24] suggested considering the domain adaptation problem in the generalized target shift scenario, where the causal direction is $Y \rightarrow X$. In this scenario, both the change of distribution $P(Y)$ and conditional distribution $P(X|Y)$ are considered to reduce the data bias across domains. [22,25] proposed iterative methods for matching the joint distribution by using the predicted labels from previous iterations as pseudo-labels. [26] proposed an optimal transport-based approach to matching joint distributions and obtained promising results. In contrast to the domain adaptation methods, domain generalization does not require unlabeled data from the target domains.

3 Conditional Invariant Deep Domain Generalization

3.1 Domain Generalization

Suppose the feature and label spaces are represented by $\mathcal{X}$ and $\mathcal{Y}$, respectively. A domain is represented by a joint distribution $P(X, Y)$ defined on $\mathcal{X} \times \mathcal{Y}$. To simplify notation, the m-th domain $P^m(X, Y)$ is denoted P^m, and the marginal distribution $P^m(X)$ is denoted P_X^m. In each domain, we have a sample $\mathcal{D}_m = \{(x_i^m, y_i^m)\}_{i=1}^{N^m}$ drawn from $P^m(X, Y)$, where N^m is the sample size in the m-th domain, while $(x_i^m, y_i^m) \sim P^m(X, Y)$ denotes the i-th data point in the m-th domain. Given C related source domains $\{P^1, P^2, ..., P^C\}$ and their corresponding datasets $\mathcal{D}_m = \{(x_i^m, y_i^m)\}_{i=1}^{N^m}$, where $m = \{1, 2, ..., C\}$, the goal of domain generalization is to learn a model $f : \mathcal{X} \to \mathcal{Y}$ that can well fit an unseen, yet related, target domain $P^t(X, Y)$ using all data from the source domains.

3.2 Domain Divergence

We first introduce the Jensen-Shannon divergence (JSD) that measures similarities among multiple distributions [27]. We use the marginal distribution $P(X)$ as an example to illustrate the general results in this section. The JSD among distributions $\{P^1(X), P^2(X), ..., P^C(X)\}$ is defined as the average of KL-divergences of each distribution from the average distribution:

$$JSD(P_X^1, ..., P_X^C) = \frac{1}{C} \sum_{m=1}^{C} KL(P_X^m || \bar{P}_X), \tag{1}$$

where $\bar{P}_X = \frac{1}{C} \sum_{m=1}^{C} P_X^m$ is the average (centroid) of these distributions. In [20], a two-player minimax approach is proposed for learning a generative adversarial network and is proven to be equivalent to minimizing JSD between the generative distribution and data distribution.

We extend the two-player minimax approach to multiple players and prove its equivalence to minimizing the JS divergence among multiple distributions. Denote the distributions after a feature transformation T as $\{P_T^1(T(X)), P_T^2(T(X)), ..., P_T^C(T(X))\}$, or simply as $\{P_T^1, P_T^2, ..., P_T^C\}$. Suppose that D is the learned discriminator and $D^m(T(X))$ denotes the prediction probability with discriminator D that $T(X)$ comes from the m-th domain

P_T^m, $m \in \{1, 2, \ldots, C\}$. We define the following multi-player minimax game with value function $V(T, D^1, \ldots, D^C) = \sum_{m=1}^{C} \mathbb{E}_{x \sim P^m(x)} \log D^m(T(x))$:

$$\min_{T} \max_{D^1, D^2, \ldots, D^C} V(T, D^1, \ldots, D^C),$$

$$\text{s.t.} \sum_{m=1}^{C} D^m(T(x)) = 1. \tag{2}$$

In what follows, we will show that the above minimax game reaches a global optimum at $P_T^1 = P_T^2 = \ldots = P_T^C$, i.e., the multi-player minimax game is able to learn invariant feature representations. The following proposition provides the optimal discriminator under a fixed transformation T.

Proposition 1. *Let $x' = T(x)$ for a fixed transformation T; the optimal prediction probabilities $\{D_T^1, \ldots, D_T^C\}$ of discriminator D are*

$$D_T^{m*}(x') = P_T^m(x') / \sum_{m=1}^{C} P_T^m(x'). \tag{3}$$

Proof. For a fixed T, Eq. (2) reduces to maximizing $V(T, D^1, \ldots, D^C)$ w.r.t. $\{D^1, \ldots, D^C\}$:

$$\{D_T^{1*}, \ldots, D_T^{C*}\} = \arg\max_{D^1, \ldots, D^C} \sum_{m=1}^{C} \int_{x'} P_T^m(x') log(D^m(x')) dx'$$

$$\text{s.t.} \sum_{m=1}^{C} D^m(x') = 1. \tag{4}$$

Maximizing the value function pointwise and applying Lagrange multipliers, we obtain the following problem:

$$\{D_T^{1*}, \ldots, D_T^{C*}\} = \arg\max_{D^1, \ldots, D^C} \sum_{m=1}^{C} P_T^m(x') log(D^m(x')) + \lambda(\sum_{m=1}^{C} D^m(x') - 1).$$

Setting the derivative of the above equation w.r.t. $D^m(x')$ to zero, we obtain $D_T^{m*}(x') = -\frac{P_T^m(x')}{\lambda}$. We can solve for the Lagrange multiplier λ by substituting $D_T^{m*}(x') = -\frac{P_T^m(x')}{\lambda}$ into the constraint $\sum_{m=1}^{C} D^m(x') = 1$ to obtain $\lambda = -\sum_{m=1}^{C} P_T^m(x')$. Thus, we obtain the optimal solution $D_T^{m*}(x') = \frac{P_T^m(x')}{\sum_{m=1}^{C} P_T^m(x')}$.

Theorem 1. *If $U(T)$ is the maximum value of $V(T, D^1, \ldots, D^C)$*

$$U(T) = \sum_{m=1}^{C} \mathbb{E}_{x \sim P_T^m(x')} \left[\log \frac{p_T^m(x')}{\sum_{m=1}^{C} P_T^m(x')} \right], \tag{5}$$

the global minimum of the multi-player minimax game is attained if and only if $P_T^1 = P_T^2 = \ldots = P_T^C$. At this point, $U(T)$ attains the value $-C \log C$.

Proof. If we add $C \log C$ to $U(T)$, we obtain

$$U(T) + C \log C = \sum_{m=1}^{C} \left\{ \mathbb{E}_{x \sim P_T^m(x')} \left[\log \frac{p_T^m(x')}{\sum_{m=1}^{C} P_T^m(x')} \right] + \log C \right\}$$

$$= \sum_{m=1}^{C} \mathbb{E}_{x \sim P_T^m(x')} \left[\log \frac{p_T^m(x')}{\frac{1}{C} \sum_{m=1}^{C} P_T^m(x')} \right]$$

$$= \sum_{m=1}^{C} KL \left(P_T^m(x') \middle\| \frac{1}{C} \sum_{m=1}^{C} P_T^m(x') \right). \tag{6}$$

By using the definition of the JS divergence in Eq. (1), we obtain $U(T) = -C \log C + C \cdot JSD(P_T^1, \ldots, P_T^C)$. As the Jensen-Shannon divergence among multiple distributions is always non-negative and zero iff they are equal, we have shown that $U^* = -C \log C$ is the global minimum of $U(T)$ and that the only solution is $P_T^1 = P_T^2 = \ldots = P_T^C$, i.e., the learned feature representations on all source domains are perfectly matched.

3.3   Proposed Approach

The existing methods proposed matching the marginal distribution $P(T(X))$ across domains; however, the invariance of $P(Y|T(X))$ could not be guaranteed. Our approach corrects the changes in $P(Y|X)$ by correcting the changes in $P(X|Y)$. In the ideal scenario, we expect the deep network to learn a conditional invariant feature transformation such that $P^{m=i}(T(X)|Y) = P^{m=j}(T(X)|Y) = P^t(T(X)|Y)$, where $i, j \in \{1, 2, ..., C\}$, and P^t is a single target domain. With the conditional invariant feature transformation, we can merge all source domains into a single new domain that has the joint distribution $P^{new}(T(X), Y) = P(T(X)|Y)P^{new}(Y)$. While training on the transformed and merged source domain data, we correct the possible class imbalances so that $P^{new}(Y)$ is the same for all classes. Thus, if the target domain data are class balanced, the equality of joint distributions $P(T(X), Y)$ between source domains and target domain can be guaranteed. Even if the target domain data are class unbalanced, our method can still provide reliable results if the features and labels are highly correlated, as the class prior distribution is not important to classification in this case.

The conditional invariance property is achieved by applying the minimax game to different aspects of the distributions on the source domains, resulting in the class-conditional minimax value and class prior-normalized marginal minimax value. In the following section, we will show that such two regularization terms can be easily implemented through variants of softmax loss.

Class-conditional Minimax Value. Suppose that there are L different classes in each domain, and denote by $x_{i \sim j}^m$ an example from the j-th class in the m-th domain. The class-conditional minimax value for class j can be formulated as $V_{con}(T, D_j^1, \ldots, D_j^C) = \sum_{m=1}^{C} \mathbb{E}_{x \sim P^m(x|y=j)} \log D_j^m(T(x))$, where D_j is the discriminator for the j-th image class. The multi-player minimax game is

$$\min_{T} \max_{D_j^1,\dots,D_j^C} V_{con}(T, D_j^1,\dots, D_j^C),$$

$$\text{s.t. } \sum_{m=1}^{C} D_j^m(T(x)) = 1. \tag{7}$$

The empirical minimax game value can be formulated as follows:

$$\tilde{V}_{con}(T, D_j^1,\dots, D_j^C) = \sum_{m=1}^{C} \frac{1}{N_j^m} \sum_{i=1}^{N_j^m} log D_j^m(T(x_{i\sim j}^m)), \tag{8}$$

where N_j^m denotes the number of examples in the j-th class of the m-th domain. This term computes the minimax game value among $P(X|Y)$ locally. In practice, we compute the minimax game values for all classes separately and subsequently sum such values. By optimizing the above minimax value, we can guarantee the invariance of class-conditional distributions $P(T(X)|Y = j)$ among domains.

Class Prior-Normalized Marginal Minimax Value. If the sample size is not large, overfitting can easily occur in a deep network due to a very large number of parameters. As the number of examples in certain classes is sometimes small, learning with the above class-conditional minimax value can result in overfitting. To improve learning of domain-invariant features, we propose learning a class prior-normalized marginal term that applies the minimax game value to all conditional distributions globally. Note that the marginal distribution of feature representations on the m-th domain can be formulated as

$$P^m(T(X)) = \sum_{j=1}^{L} P^m(T(X)|Y = j)P^m(Y = j). \tag{9}$$

The above equation shows that the marginal distribution $P^m(T(X)$ is determined by the conditional distribution $P^m(T(X)|Y = j)$ and the class prior distribution $P^m(Y = j)$, where $j \in \{1, 2, ..., L\}$. As shown in [23,24], we may be able to determine the conditional invariant representation $T(X)$ by matching the marginal distribution $P(T(X))$ across domains, i.e., the invariance of $P(T(X))$ may induce invariance of $P(T(X)|Y)$ if $P(Y)$ is invariant. If $P(Y)$ also changes, even with an invariant $P(T(X)|Y)$ across domains, $P(T(X))$ can still vary according to Eq. (9). In this case, minimizing the discrepancy in $P(X)$ may lead to removal of useful information, as the effect of changing $P(Y)$ is not supposed to be corrected by learning an invariant representation from X. To remove the effect caused by the changing class prior distribution $P(Y)$, we propose normalizing the class prior distribution as $P_N^m(T(X)) = \sum_{j=1}^{L} P^m(T(X)|Y = j)\frac{1}{L}$. The above class prior-normalized distribution P_N^m enforces the prior probability for each class to be the same. Consequently, the invariant class conditional distribution across domains can guarantee equality of class prior-normalized marginal distributions across domains. Suppose that $\beta^m(Y)$ is the normalized weight to ensure that $P_N^m(T(X)) = \sum_{j=1}^{L} P^m(T(X)|Y = j)P^m(Y = j)\beta^m(Y = j) =$

$\sum_{j=1}^{L} P^m(T(X)|Y = j)\frac{1}{L}$. We apply the minimax game according to the class prior-normalized marginal distribution as follows:

$$\min_{T} \max_{D^1,\dots,D^C} V_{norm}(T, D^1, \dots, D^C)$$

$$= \min_{T} \max_{D^1,\dots,D^C} \sum_{m=1}^{C} \mathbb{E}_{x \sim P_N^m(x)} \log D^m(T(x))$$

$$= \min_{T} \max_{D^1,\dots,D^C} \sum_{m=1}^{C} \mathbb{E}_{x \sim \int P^m(x|y)P^m(y)\beta^m(y)dy} \log D^m(T(x))$$

$$= \min_{T} \max_{D^1,\dots,D^C} \sum_{m=1}^{C} \int P^m(x|y)P^m(y)\beta^m(y)dy \log D^m(T(x))dx$$

$$= \min_{T} \max_{D^1,\dots,D^C} \sum_{m=1}^{C} \int P^m(x,y) \log D^m(T(x))\beta^m(y)dxdy$$

$$\text{s.t. } \sum_{m=1}^{C} D^m(T(x)) = 1. \tag{10}$$

The empirical version of a class prior-normalized minimax value is as follows:

$$\tilde{V}_{norm}(T, D^1, \dots, D^C) = \sum_{m=1}^{C} \frac{1}{N^m} \sum_{i=1}^{N^m} \log D^m(T(x_i^m))\beta^m(y_i^m), \tag{11}$$

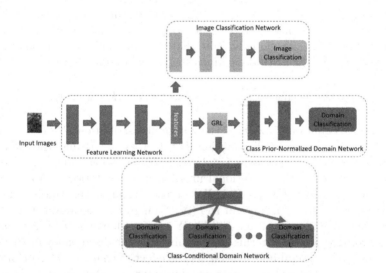

Fig. 1. The network architecture of our proposed method. It consists of four parts: feature learning network which represents the invariant feature transformation T, image classification network which classifies the images from all domains with softmax loss, class prior-normalized domain network which discriminates different domains with loss in Eq. (14), and class-conditional domain network which discriminates domains for each image class with loss in Eq. (13).

i.e., the class prior-normalized weight $\beta^m(y_i^m)$ can be viewed as a weight of the log-likelihood. And $\beta^m(y_i^m)$ can be empirically obtained as

$$\beta^m(y_i^m) = \frac{1}{L} \frac{1}{P^m(Y = y_i^m)} = \frac{N^m}{L \times N_{j=y_i^m}^m}, \tag{12}$$

where N^m denotes the total number of examples in the m-th domain and $N_{j=y_i^m}^m$ denotes the number of examples with the same label as y_i^m in the m-th domain.

4   Conditional Invariant Adversarial Network

We introduce the conditional invariant deep neural network to represent the feature transformation T and then implement the approach proposed in Sect. 3.3. The architecture is shown in Fig. 1. It contains four components: the representation learning network, the image classification network, the class-conditional domain network, and the class prior-normalized domain network. The representation learning network aims to learn a class-conditional domain-invariant feature representation, while retaining the ability to discriminate among different image classes. The two domain classification networks aim to make the features of examples from different domains indistinguishable by adversarial training. Additionally, the image classification network is used to make the learned features informative for classification. In this section, we will introduce each network and describe the process of training such networks using various loss functions.

Let x_i be an input image, $F(\cdot|\theta)$ denote a network with parameter θ, and $F(x_i|\theta)$ be the output of image x_i. To simplify notation, the feature representation learning network is denoted $F(\cdot|\theta_f)$ or $F_f(\cdot)$, the image classification network is denoted $F(\cdot|\theta_c)$ or $F_c(\cdot)$, and the class-conditional domain network for image class j is denoted $F^j(\cdot|\theta_d)$ or $F_d^j(\cdot)$. Additionally, the class prior-normalized domain network is denoted $F(\cdot|\theta_p)$ or $F_p(\cdot)$.

4.1   Class-Conditional Domain Classification Network

According to Eq. (7), we can implement the class-conditional minimax game value through a variant of softmax loss. For image class j, the class-conditional domain loss can be formulated as follows:

$$L_{con}(\theta_f, \theta_d^j) = \sum_{m=1}^{C} [\frac{1}{N_j^m} \sum_{i=1}^{N_j^m} \sum_{n=1}^{C} I[y_{i\sim j}^d = n] log P_n(F_d^j(F_f(x_{i\sim j}^m)))], \tag{13}$$

where $y_{i\sim j}^d \in \{1, 2, ..., C\}$ denotes the domain label of $x_{i\sim j}$ (i-th example in class j). $P_n(F_d^j(F_f(x_{i\sim j})))$ denotes the predicted probability that the image in j-th category belongs to the n-th domain. Note that the above loss is specifically for the j-th image class. If we have L classes, we must construct L sub-branches of the networks. Each sub-branch corresponds to one class.

4.2   Class Prior-Normalized Domain Classification Network

We introduce the class prior-normalized domain classification networks according to Eq. (11). It is also implemented using a variant of softmax loss. We obtain the prior-normalized loss as

$$L_{norm}(\theta_f, \theta_p) = \sum_{m=1}^{C} \frac{1}{N^m} [\sum_{i=1}^{N^m} \sum_{n=1}^{C} \beta^m(y_i^m) I[y_i^d = n] log P_n(F_p(F_f(x_i)))], \quad (14)$$

where y_i^m denotes the class label of the i-th image in domain m.

4.3   Learning Procedure

We combine all the above losses with the image classification loss $L_{cla}(\theta_f, \theta_c)$ used for image classification networks. Note that $L_{cla}(\theta_f, \theta_c)$ can be a standard softmax loss. The total loss can be obtained as follows:

$$R(\theta_f, \{\theta_d^j\}_{j=1}^{L}, \theta_p, \theta_c) = L_{cla}(\theta_f, \theta_c) + \lambda(\sum_{j=1}^{L} L_{con}(\theta_f, \theta_d^j) + L_{norm}(\theta_f, \theta_p))). \quad (15)$$

The learning of the above loss can be separated into two steps by determining the optimal values $(\theta_f^*, \{\theta_d^{*j}\}_{j=1}^{L}, \theta_p^*, \theta_c^*)$ as follows:

$$(\theta_f^*, \theta_c^*) = \underset{\theta_f, \theta_c}{\arg\min} R(\theta_f, \{\theta_d^j\}_{j=1}^{L}, \theta_p, \theta_c),$$

$$(\{\theta_d^{*j}\}_{j=1}^{L}, \theta_p) = \underset{\{\theta_d^j\}_{j=1}^{L}, \theta_p}{\arg\max} R(\theta_f, \{\theta_d^j\}_{j=1}^{L}, \theta_p, \theta_c). \quad (16)$$

A saddle point of the above optimization problem can be determined by performing the following gradient updates iteratively until the networks converge:

$$\theta_f^{i+1} = \theta_f^i - \gamma[\frac{\partial L_{cla}^i}{\partial \theta_f} + \lambda(\sum_{j=1}^{L} \frac{\partial L_{con}^i(\theta_f, \theta_d^j)}{\partial \theta_f} + \frac{\partial L_{norm}^i}{\partial \theta_f})],$$

$$\theta_c^{i+1} = \theta_c^i - \gamma\frac{\partial L_{cla}^i}{\partial \theta_c},$$

$$(\theta_d^j)^{i+1} = (\theta_d^j)^i + \gamma\lambda\frac{\partial L_{con}^i(\theta_f, \theta_d^j)}{\partial \theta_d^j},$$

$$\theta_p^{i+1} = \theta_p^i + \gamma\lambda\frac{\partial L_{norm}^i}{\partial \theta_p},$$

(17)

where γ is the learning rate. It is very similar to the stochastic gradient descent (SGD). The only difference is in the updating of θ_p and θ_d^j, which contain the negative gradients from two domain classification losses. Such negative gradients contribute to making the learned features similar across domains. We propose a gradient-reversal layer (GRL) to update θ_f by easily following [21]. This gradient-reversal layer does nothing and merely forwards the input to the following layer during forward propagation. However, it multiplies the gradient by -1 during the backpropagation to obtain a negative gradient from the domain classification.

5   Experiments

In this section, we conduct experiments on three domain generalization datasets to demonstrate the effectiveness of our conditional invariant deep domain generalization (CIDDG). We compare our proposed method to the following methods.

- **L-SVM** [29] is support vector machines (SVM) with a linear kernel to classify the learned feature representations.
- **Kernel Fisher discriminant analysis (KDA)** [30] is used to find a transformation of data using nonlinear kernels in all source domains.
- **Undo-bias (UB)** [7] measures the model of each task with a domain-specific weight and a globally shared weight used for domain generalization. The original UB was developed for binary domain generalization classification. We extend it to a multi-class method using a one-vs-all strategy.
- **Domain-invariant component analysis (DICA)** [9] aims at learning a domain-invariant feature representation by matching the marginal distributions across domains.

Fig. 2. Rotated MNIST dataset. Each rotation angle is viewed as one domain.

- **Scatter component analysis (SCA)** [8] is a unified framework for domain adaptation and domain generalization that also learns a domain-invariant feature transformation through marginal distributions.
- **Multi-task auto-encoder (MTAE)** [11] is a domain generalization method based on an auto-encoder to match marginal distributions across domains.
- **DeepA** refers to Deep-All, using data from all source domains to train the networks with only image classification loss.
- **DeepD** refers to Deep-Domain, using data from all source domains to train the networks with image classification loss and domain classification loss to match the marginal distribution $P(T(X))$.
- **DeepC** refers to Deep-Conditional, using data from all source domains to train networks with image classification loss and our proposed class-conditional domain classification loss in Eq. (13).
- **DeepN** refers to Deep-Normalize, using data from all source domains to train the networks with image classification loss and our proposed class prior-normalized domain classification loss in Eq. (14).
- **CIDDG** uses data from all source domains to train networks with image classification loss, class-conditional domain classification loss and class prior-normalized domain classification loss, as shown in Eq. (15).

5.1 Rotated MNIST Dataset

The rotated MNIST digits are shown in Fig. 2, which displays four different rotation angles: $0°, 30°, 60°$ and $90°$. Note that the original MNIST digits are already characterized by certain small-angle rotations. Each of the four rotation angles is viewed as one domain. Therefore, we have four domains. One domain is selected as the target domain and the other three ones are used as source domains. We repeat it four times, thus each domain is used as the target domain once. The number of training examples from each class in different domains are randomly chosen from a uniform distribution $U[80\ 160]$, to guarantee the variance of $P(Y)$ in each domain. The number of test examples is 10000 and they are obtained from the MNIST testset with corresponding rotation angles.

Table 1. Performance comparison in terms of accuracy (%) on rotated MNIST dataset.

Target	SVM	KDA	UB	DICA	SCA	MATE	DeepA	DeepD	DeepC	DeepN	CIDDG
Test0°	72.62	72.70	64.43	72.61	71.79	75.56	75.43	77.07	77.79	78.25	**78.47**
Test30°	92.17	91.95	89.60	90.72	91.85	92.84	93.44	94.16	94.11	94.71	**94.88**
Test60°	93.34	93.15	89.30	91.77	92.69	93.68	94.47	95.22	94.96	95.49	**95.64**
Test90°	77.62	72.81	69.39	72.05	73.43	78.34	79.56	82.95	80.08	83.99	**84.00**

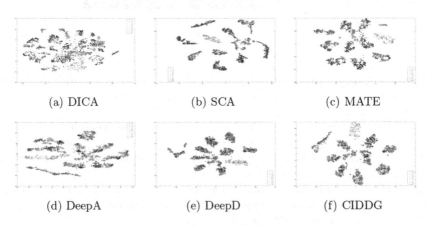

(a) DICA   (b) SCA   (c) MATE

(d) DeepA   (e) DeepD   (f) CIDDG

Fig. 3. Feature visualization of different methods on rotated MNIST dataset when the target domain is 90°. Different colors refer to different domains and the gray color denotes the target domain. Different shapes corresponds to different image classes.

The network architecture for rotated MNIST is the same as the architecture in [31]. All domain classification networks consist of three fully-connected layers $(1024 \rightarrow 1024 \rightarrow 10)$ and the GRL layer is connected to the ReLU layer after the last convolution layer. The input features for baseline methods (**SVM, KDA,**

UB, DICA, SCA, MATE) are extracted using the well-trained **DeepA** network. RBF kernel is applied to **KDA, UB, DICA** and **SCA**. Additionally, linear SVM is used to classify the learned domain-invariant features for **KDA, DICA, SCA** and **MATE**. Deep-learning-based methods, including **DeepA, DeepD, DeepC, DeepN** and **CIDDG**, use softmax layer to do the classification. The experimental results are summarized in Table 1.

Our proposed conditional-invariant adversarial network achieves the best performance when testing on different target domains. All deep-learning-based methods outperform traditional domain generalization methods. Our method can achieve better improvement on more challenging tasks, e.g. the target domain is $0°$ or $90°$, which demonstrates that our method is more robust. When the target domain is $30°$ or $60°$, the angle $30°$ or $60°$ can be interpolated from its corresponding source domains $(0°, 60°, 90°)$ or $(0°, 30°, 90°)$. It is easier to learn a generalized model when testing on an interpolation angle $(30°$ or $60°)$ than testing on an extrapolation angle $(0°$ or $90°)$.

To better understand the generalization ability of different methods, we also visualize the learned feature distribution using t-SNE [32] projection in Fig. 3. We randomly select 100 examples from each class in the target domain for visualization. In the visualization results, **DeepA** refers to original feature distribution learned by the network with just softmax loss. For **DeepA**, the feature has been learned to be discriminative but different domains are not well matched. Almost all domain generalization methods can learn better domain-invariant features. Methods like **SCA, MATE, DeepD** can well match the feature distributions of the source domains; however, the distributions of several classes in the target domain are not well matched. Note that the visualization performance of **KDA** are not promising, we do not show its visualization result considering the limited pages. For our **CIDDG**, the distributions of about two classes are not well matched. In genera, our **CIDDG** can learn more discriminative features, and better match the distributions across source domains and target domains.

5.2   VLCS Dataset

In this section, we conduct experiments on a real world image classification dataset VLCS. It consists of four different sub-datasets corresponding to four domains: PASCAL VOC2007 (V) [33], LabelMe (L) [34], Caltech-101 (C) [35] and SUN09 (S) [36]. Following the settings in previous works [7,9], we select the five shared classes (bird, car, chair, dog and person) for classification. The total image numbers in the four domains (V,L,C,S) are 3376, 2656, 1415 and 3282 respectively. We use AlexNet [1] to train all the deep learning models and extract the FC6 features as input for traditional baseline methods. All domain classification networks consist of 3 fully-connected layers $(1024 \rightarrow 1024 \rightarrow 3)$ and the GRL layer is connected to the FC6 layer. The datasets from source domains are split into two parts: 70% for training and 30% for validation, following [11,28]. The whole target domain is used for testing.

For **SVM, KDA, UB, DICA, SCA, MATE**, we first directly extract FC6 features of AlexNet from source domains and then learn domain-invariant features using these baseline domain generalization methods. Finally, linear SVM are used to train the classification model and test on target domains. For **DeepA**, we directly use all source domains to fine-tune the AlexNet and test on target domains. For **DeepD**, we use all the domains to fine-tune the AlexNet with a domain classification network to match the marginal distribution $P(X)$. **DeepC**, **DeepN** and **CIDDG** are our methods with different proposed losses. The experimental results are summarized in Table 2.

From the results, we can conclude that traditional domain generalization methods perform even worse than **DeepA** (the network just fine-tuned using all source domains). Deep domain generalization methods outperform the simply fine-tuned model **DeepA**. Additionally, our conditional-invariant domain generalization method performs better than domain generalization (**DeepD**) which matches the marginal distribution.

Table 2. Performance comparison in terms of accuracy (%) on VLCS dataset.

Target	SVM	KDA	UB	DICA	SCA	MATE	DeepA	DeepD	DeepC	DeepN	CIDDG
V	48.10	44.40	47.90	51.78	54.71	51.66	62.71	63.71	63.97	64.31	**64.38**
L	50.87	46.69	51.09	45.63	53.73	53.95	61.28	62.06	62.60	62.10	**63.06**
C	70.04	61.48	73.71	68.69	58.94	75.75	85.73	86.58	87.47	86.38	**88.83**
S	47.94	38.52	46.77	37.66	47.62	50.33	59.33	60.29	61.51	61.87	**62.10**

Table 3. Performance comparison in terms of accuracy (%) on PACS dataset.

Target	SVM	KDA	UB	DICA	SCA	MATE	DeepA	DeepD	DeepC	DeepN	CIDDG
P	55.15	59.04	55.57	55.93	59.10	58.44	77.98	80.39	**80.72**	77.45	78.65
A	41.80	47.66	42.48	47.46	50.05	45.95	57.55	60.75	62.30	59.17	**62.70**
C	52.30	53.29	48.93	57.00	58.79	51.11	67.04	68.63	69.58	67.86	**69.73**
S	47.87	48.21	46.30	40.70	50.62	49.25	58.52	60.76	64.45	60.92	**64.45**

5.3   PACS Dataset

PACS [28] consists of four sub-datasets corresponding to four different image styles, including photo (P), art-painting (A), cartoon (C) and sketch (S). Each image style can be viewed as one domain. The numbers of images in each domain are 1670, 2048, 2344, 3929 respectively. We use all the images from the source domains as train set and test on all the images from the target domain. We extract the features from FC7 layer for traditional methods and the GRL layer is also connected to FC7 layer. Other settings including the network architectures are the same as that used in VLCS dataset.

The results are shown in Table 3. Similar conclusions can be made as that in the experiments of VLCS dataset. The reason **DeepN** performs worse than **DeepC** is that PACS has larger data bias and variance of $P(Y)$. The class-conditional domain classification networks cannot learn well with just images in one specific image class and not considering the changes in $P(Y)$ across domains.

6   Conclusions

In this paper, we proposed a novel conditional-invariant deep domain generalization method. This method is superior than previous works because it matches conditional distributions by considering the changes in $P(Y)$ rather than marginal distributions, thus it can better learn domain invariant features. We prove that the distributions of multiple source domains can be perfectly matched with our proposed multi-player minimax value. Additionally, extensive experiments are conducted and the results demonstrate the effectiveness of our proposed method.

Acknowledgments. This work was supported by National Key Research and Development Program of China 2017YFB1002203, NSFC No. 61572451, and No. 61390514, Fok Ying Tung Education Foundation WF2100060004 and Youth Innovation Promotion Association CAS CX2100060016, and Australian Research Council Projects FL-170100117, DP-180103424, DP-140102164, LP-150100671.

References

1. Krizhevsky, A., Sutskever, I., Hinton, G.E.: Imagenet classification with deep convolutional neural networks. Adv. Neural Inf. Process. Syst., 1097–1105 (2012)
2. He, K., Zhang, X., Ren, S., Sun, J.: Deep residual learning for image recognition. In: Proceedings of the IEEE Conference on Computer Vision and Pattern Recognition, pp. 770–778 (2016)
3. Schroff, F., Kalenichenko, D., Philbin, J.: Facenet: a unified embedding for face recognition and clustering. In: Proceedings of the IEEE Conference on Computer Vision and Pattern Recognition, pp. 815–823 (2015)
4. Parkhi, O.M., Vedaldi, A., Zisserman, A.: Deep face recognition. BMVC **1**, 6 (2015)
5. Ren, S., He, K., Girshick, R., Sun, J.: Faster r-cnn: towards real-time object detection with region proposal networks. Adv. Neural Inf. Process. Syst., 91–99 (2015)
6. Torralba, A., Efros, A.A.: Unbiased look at dataset bias. In: 2011 IEEE Conference on Computer Vision and Pattern Recognition (CVPR), pp. 1521–1528. IEEE (2011)
7. Khosla, A., Zhou, T., Malisiewicz, T., Efros, A.A., Torralba, A.: Undoing the damage of dataset bias. In: Fitzgibbon, A., Lazebnik, S., Perona, P., Sato, Y., Schmid, C. (eds.) ECCV 2012. LNCS, vol. 7572, pp. 158–171. Springer, Heidelberg (2012). https://doi.org/10.1007/978-3-642-33718-5_12
8. Ghifary, M., Balduzzi, D., Kleijn, W.B., Zhang, M.: Scatter component analysis: a unified framework for domain adaptation and domain generalization. IEEE Trans. Pattern Anal. Mach. Intell. **39**(7), 1414–1430 (2017)
9. Muandet, K., Balduzzi, D., Schölkopf, B.: Domain generalization via invariant feature representation. In: Proceedings of the 30th International Conference on Machine Learning (ICML 2013), pp. 10–18 (2013)
10. Xu, Z., Li, W., Niu, L., Xu, D.: Exploiting low-rank structure from latent domains for domain generalization. In: Fleet, D., Pajdla, T., Schiele, B., Tuytelaars, T. (eds.) ECCV 2014. LNCS, vol. 8691, pp. 628–643. Springer, Cham (2014). https://doi.org/10.1007/978-3-319-10578-9_41

11. Ghifary, M., Bastiaan Kleijn, W., Zhang, M., Balduzzi, D.: Domain generalization for object recognition with multi-task autoencoders. In: Proceedings of the IEEE International Conference on Computer Vision, pp. 2551–2559 (2015)

12. Ding, Z., Fu, Y.: Deep domain generalization with structured low-rank constraint. IEEE Trans. Image Process. **27**(1), 304–313 (2018)

13. Zhang, K., Gong, M., Schölkopf, B.: Multi-source domain adaptation: a causal view. AAAI **I**, 3150–3157 (2015)

14. Li, Y., Gong, M., Tian, X., Liu, T., Tao, D.: Domain generalization via conditional invariant representations. AAAI **I**, 3579–3587 (2018)

15. Zhao, H., Zhang, S., Wu, G., Costeira, J.P., Moura, J.F., Gordon, G.J.: Multiple source domain adaptation with adversarial training of neural networks. arXiv preprint arXiv:1705.09684 (2017)

16. Liu, T., Tao, D., Song, M., Maybank, S.J.: Algorithm-dependent generalization bounds for multi-Task learning. IEEE Trans. Pattern Anal. Mach. Intell. **39**(2), 227–241 (2017)

17. Schölkopf, B., Janzing, D., Peters, J., Sgouritsa, E., Zhang, K., Mooij, J.: On causal and anticausal learning. arXiv preprint arXiv:1206.6471 (2012)

18. Janzing, D., Scholkopf, B.: Causal inference using the algorithmic markov condition. IEEE Trans. Inf. Theor. **56**(10), 5168–5194 (2010)

19. Lopez-Paz, D., Nishihara, R., Chintala, S., Schölkopf, B., Bottou, L.: Discovering causal signals in images. In: The IEEE Conference on Computer Vision and Pattern Recognition (CVPR 2017) (2017)

20. Goodfellow, I. et al.: Generative adversarial nets. Adv. Neural Inf. Process. Syst., 2672–2680 (2014)

21. Ganin, Y., et al.: Domain-adversarial training of neural networks. J. Mach. Learn. Res. **17**(59), 1–35 (2016)

22. Long, M., Zhu, H., Wang, J., Jordan, M.I.: Deep transfer learning with joint adaptation networks. In: Precup, D., Teh, Y.W. (eds.) Proceedings of the 34th International Conference on Machine Learning. Volume 70 of Proceedings of Machine Learning Research., International Convention Centre, Sydney, Australia, PMLR, pp. 2208–2217, 6–11 Aug 2017

23. Zhang, K., Schölkopf, B., Muandet, K., Wang, Z.: Domain adaptation under target and conditional shift. In: International Conference on Machine Learning, pp. 819–827 (2013)

24. Gong, M., Zhang, K., Liu, T., Tao, D., Glymour, C., Schölkopf, B.: Domain adaptation with conditional transferable components. In: International Conference on Machine Learning, pp. 2839–2848 (2016)

25. Long, M., Wang, J., Ding, G., Sun, J., Yu, P.S.: Transfer feature learning with joint distribution adaptation. In: Proceedings of the IEEE International Conference on Computer Vision, pp. 2200–2207 (2013)

26. Courty, N., Flamary, R., Habrard, A., Rakotomamonjy, A.: Joint distribution optimal transportation for domain adaptation. arXiv preprint arXiv:1705.08848 (2017)

27. Lin, J.: Divergence measures based on the shannon entropy. IEEE Trans. Inf. Theor. **37**(1), 145–151 (1991)

28. Li, D., Yang, Y., Song, Y.Z., Hospedales, T.M.: Deeper, broader and artier domain generalization. In: 2017 IEEE International Conference on Computer Vision (ICCV), pp. 5543–5551. IEEE (2017)

29. Fan, R.E., Chang, K.W., Hsieh, C.J., Wang, X.R., Lin, C.J.: Liblinear: a library for large linear classification. J. Mach. Learn. Res. **9**, 1871–1874 (2008)

30. Mika, S., Ratsch, G., Weston, J., Scholkopf, B., Mullers, K.R.: Fisher discriminant analysis with kernels. In: Proceedings of the 1999 IEEE Signal Processing Society Workshop Neural Networks for Signal Processing IX, 1999, pp. 41–48. IEEE (1999)
31. Srivastava, N., Hinton, G., Krizhevsky, A., Sutskever, I., Salakhutdinov, R.: Dropout: a simple way to prevent neural networks from overfitting. J. Mach. Learn. Res. **15**(1), 1929–1958 (2014)
32. Van Der Maaten, L.: Barnes-HUT-SNE. arXiv preprint arXiv:1301.3342 (2013)
33. Everingham, M., Van Gool, L., Williams, C.K., Winn, J., Zisserman, A.: The pascal visual object classes (VOC) challenge. Int. J. Comput. Vis. **88**(2), 303–338 (2010)
34. Russell, B.C., Torralba, A., Murphy, K.P., Freeman, W.T.: Labelme: a database and web-based tool for image annotation. Int. J. Comput. Vis. **77**(1), 157–173 (2008)
35. Griffin, G., Holub, A., Perona, P.: Caltech-256 object category dataset (2007)
36. Choi, M.J., Lim, J.J., Torralba, A., Willsky, A.S.: Exploiting hierarchical context on a large database of object categories. In: 2010 IEEE Conference on Computer Vision and Pattern Recognition (CVPR), pp. 129–136. IEEE (2010)

Using LIP to Gloss Over Faces in Single-Stage Face Detection Networks

Siqi Yang$^{(\boxtimes)}$, Arnold Wiliem, Shaokang Chen, and Brian C. Lovell

The University of Queensland, Brisbane, Australia
siqi.yang@uq.net.au, a.wiliem@uq.edu.au, shaokangchenuq@gmail.com,
lovell@itee.uq.edu.au

Abstract. This work shows that it is possible to fool/attack recent state-of-the-art face detectors which are based on the single-stage networks. Successfully attacking face detectors could be a serious malware vulnerability when deploying a smart surveillance system utilizing face detectors. In addition, for the privacy concern, it helps prevent faces being harvested and stored in the server. We show that existing adversarial perturbation methods are not effective to perform such an attack, especially when there are multiple faces in the inut image. This is because the adversarial perturbation specifically generated for one face may disrupt the adversarial perturbation for another face. In this paper, we call this problem the Instance Perturbation Interference (IPI) problem. This IPI problem is addressed by studying the relationship between the deep neural network receptive field and the adversarial perturbation. Besides the single-stage face detector, we find that the IPI problem also exists on the first stage of the Faster-RCNN, the commonly used two-stage object detector. As such, we propose the Localized Instance Perturbation (LIP) that confines the adversarial perturbation inside the Effective Receptive Field (ERF) of a target to perform the attack. Experimental results show the LIP method massively outperforms existing adversarial perturbation generation methods – often by a factor of 2 to 10.

Keywords: Adversarial · Interference · Effective Receptive Field
Single-stage network · Detection

1 Introduction

Deep neural networks have achieved great success in recent years on many applications [5,6,10,15,17,27,28,31,39]. However, it has been demonstrated in various works that by adding tiny, imperceptible perturbations onto the image, the network output can be changed significantly [4,11,16,19,23,25,32,35]. These perturbations are often referred to as adversarial perturbations [4]. Most prior works are primarily aimed at generating adversarial perturbations to fool neural networks for image classification tasks [4,11,16,22,23,25,32]. It is relatively

Electronic supplementary material The online version of this chapter (https://doi.org/10.1007/978-3-030-01267-0_39) contains supplementary material, which is available to authorized users.

V. Ferrari et al. (Eds.): ECCV 2018, LNCS 11219, pp. 664–681, 2018.
https://doi.org/10.1007/978-3-030-01267-0_39

easier to attack these networks as the perturbations need to change only one network decision for each image containing an instance/object of interest. This means, there is only a single target and the target is the entire image. Recently, several methods have been proposed on more challenging attacks for segmentation [2,3,19] and object detection tasks [35], where there are significantly more targets to attack within the input image.

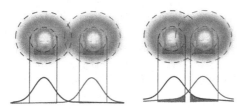

Fig. 1. An illustration of the Instance Perturbation Interference (IPI) problem. *Upper row*: two instances with their generated adversarial perturbations. The outer and inner circles indicate the Theoretical Receptive Field (TRF) and Effective Receptive Field (ERF), respectively. *Lower row*: one dimensional representation of the perturbations. IPI problem refers to the perturbation generated for one instance significantly disrupting the perturbation generated for the other instance. The disruption does not have significant effect on the left case, whereas on the right case, it will reduce the effectiveness of the attack

In the field of biometrics, Sharif *et al.* [29] showed that face recognition systems can be fooled by applying adversarial perturbations, where a detected face can be recognized as another individual. In addition, for the privacy concern, biometric data in a dataset might be utilized without the consent of the users. Therefore, Mirjalili *et al.* [20,21] developed a technique to protect the soft biometric privacy (*e.g.,* gender) without harming the accuracy of face recognition. However, in the above-mentioned methods, the faces are still captured and stored in a server. In this paper, we propose a novel way to address these privacy issues by avoiding the faces be detected completely from an image. Thus, attacking face detection is crucial for both the security and privacy concerns.

With similar goals, previous works [29,36] performed attacks on the Viola & Jones (VJ) face detector [33]. However, deep neural networks have been shown to be extremely effective in detecting faces [1,6,12,13,24,26,37,39,40], which can achieve 2 times higher detection rate than the VJ. In this work, we tackle the problem of generating effective adversarial perturbations for deep learning based face detection networks. To the best of our knowledge, this is the first study that attempts to perform such an adversarial attack on face detection networks.

Deep network based object/face detection methods can be grouped as two-stage network, *e.g.,* Faster-RCNN [28] and single-stage network [6,15,24,27,40]. In Faster-RCNN [9], a shallow region proposal network is applied to generate candidates and a deep classification network is utilized for the final decision. The Single-Stage (SS) network is similar to the region proposal network in Faster-RCNN [28] but performs both object classification and localization simultaneously. By utilizing the Single-Stage network architecture, recent detectors [6,24,40] can detect faces on various scales with a much faster running time. Due to their excellent performance, we confine this paper to attacking the most recent face detectors utilizing Single-Stage network.

We find that applying the commonly-used gradient based adversarial methods [4,23] to the state-of-the-art face detection networks has not presented satisfactory results. We point out that attacking a Single-Stage detector is challenging and the unsatisfactory performance is attributed to the Instance Perturbation Interference (IPI) problem. The IPI problem can be briefly explained as interference between the perturbation required to attack one instance and the perturbation required to attack a nearby instance. Since the recent adversarial perturbation methods [19,35] do not consider this problem, they become quite ineffective in attacking SS face detector networks.

In this work, we attribute the IPI problem to the receptive field of deep neural networks. Recent work [18] shows that the receptive field follows a 2D Gaussian distribution, where the set of input image pixels closer to an output neuron have higher impact on the neuron decision. The area where high impact pixels are concentrated is referred to as the Effective Receptive Field (ERF) [18]. As illustrated in Fig. 1, if two faces are close to each other, the perturbation generated to attack one face will reside in the ERF of another face. Prior work [34] shows that adversarial attacks might fail when the specific structure is destroyed. Thus, the residency in the ERF significantly hampers the success of attacking the other face. In other words, the IPI problem happens when the interfering perturbations disrupt the adversarial perturbations generated for the neighboring faces. This IPI problem will become more serious when multiple faces exist in close proximity and when the receptive field of the network is large. For the general two-stage object detection, Faster-RCNN [28], we find that the IPI problem also exists on its first stage network, *i.e.,* region proposal network (RPN). We believe this is the first work that describes and explains the IPI problem.

Contributions - We list our contributions as follows: (1) We describe and provide theoretical explanation of the Instance Perturbation Interference problem that makes the existing adversarial perturbation generation method fail to attack the SS face detector networks when multiple faces exist; (2) This is the first study to show that it is possible to attack deep neural network based face detector. More specifically, we propose an approach to attack Single-Stage based face detector networks. (3) To perform the attack, we propose Localised Instance Perturbation (LIP) method to generate instance based perturbations by confining the perturbations inside each instance ERF.

2   Background

2.1   Adversarial Perturbation

As mentioned, attacking a network means attempting to change the network decision on a particular target. A target t is defined as a region in the input image where the generated adversarial perturbation is added to change the network decision corresponding to this region. For example, the target t for attacking an image classification network is the entire image.

The adversarial perturbation concept was first introduced for attacking image classification networks in [4, 11, 16, 22, 23, 25, 32]. Szegedy *et al.* [32] showed that by adding imperceptible perturbations to the input images, one could make the Convolutional Neural Network (CNN) predict the wrong class label with high confidence. Goodfellow *et al.* [4] explained that the vulnerability of the neural networks to the adversarial perturbations is caused by the linear nature of the neural networks. They proposed a fast method to generate such adversarial perturbations, naming the method Fast Gradient Sign Method (FGSM) defined by: $\xi = \alpha \text{sign}(\nabla_X \ell(f(X), y^{true}))$, where α was a hyper-parameter [4]. The gradient was computed with respect to the entire input image $X \in \mathbb{R}^{w \times h}$ by back-propagation and the function sign() is the L_∞ norm. Following this, Kurakin *et al.* [11] proposed to extend FGSM by iteratively generating the adversarial perturbations. At each iteration, the values of the perturbations were clipped to control perceptibility. We denote it as I-FGSM in this work. To reduce perceptibility, Moosavi-Dezfooli *et al.* [23] proposed the method DeepFool, which iteratively adds the minimal adversarial perturbations to the images by assuming the classifier was linear at each iteration. The existence of universal perturbations for image classification was shown in [22].

More recently, adversarial examples were extended into various applications such as semantic segmentation [2, 3, 19, 35] and object detection [35]. Metzen *et al.* [19] adapted the I-FGSM described in [11] into the semantic segmentation domain, where every pixel was a target. They demonstrated that the gradients of the loss for different target pixels might point to the opposite directions. In object detection, the instances of interest are the detected objects. Thus, the targets are the detected region proposals containing the object. An approach for generating adversarial perturbations for object detection is proposed in [35]. They claimed that generating adversarial perturbations in object detection was more difficult than in the semantic segmentation task. In order to successfully attack a detected object, one needs to ensure all the region proposals associated with the object/instance are successfully attacked. For example, if only K out of R region proposals are successfully attacked, the detector can still detect the object by using the other high-confidence-score region proposals that are not successfully attacked.

We note that all of the above approaches use whole image perturbations which have the same size as the input image. This is because these perturbations are generated by calculating the gradient with respect to the entire image. Thus, a generated perturbation for one target may disrupt the perturbations generated for other targets. To contrast these methods with our work, we categorize these methods as **IM**age based **P**erturbation (IMP) methods.

2.2 Loss Function

In general, the perturbations are generated by optimizing a specific objective function. Let $\mathcal{L} = \sum_{i=1}^{T} \mathcal{L}_{t_i}$ be the loss function to optimize. The objective function is defined as follows:

$$\arg\min_{\boldsymbol{\xi}} \sum_{i=1}^{T} \mathcal{L}_{t_i}(\boldsymbol{\xi}) , \tag{1}$$

where T is the number of targets; $\mathcal{L}_{t_i}$ is the loss function for each individual target t_i; and $\boldsymbol{\xi} \in \mathbb{R}^{w \times h}$ is the adversarial perturbation which will be added into the input image $\boldsymbol{X}$.

According to the goals of adversarial attacks, the attacks can be categorized into *non-targeted adversarial attacks* [4,22,35] and *targeted adversarial attacks* [11,19]. For non-targeted adversarial attacks, the goal is to reduce the probability of truth class y^{true} of the given target t and to make the network predict any arbitrary class, whereas the goal of targeted adversarial attacks is to ensure the network predict the target class y^{target} for the target t. The objective function of the targeted attacks can be summarized into the following formula:

$$\arg\min_{\boldsymbol{\xi}} \mathcal{L}_{t_i} = \ell(f(\boldsymbol{X} + \boldsymbol{\xi}, t_i), y^{target}) - \ell(f(\boldsymbol{X} + \boldsymbol{\xi}, t_i), y^{true}), \tag{2}$$

where, $\boldsymbol{\xi}$ is the optimum adversarial perturbation; f is the network classification score matrix on the target region; and ℓ is the network loss function.

In general, the face detection problem is considered as a binary classification problem, which aims at classifying a region as face ($+1$) or non-face (-1) (*i.e.*, $y^{target} = \{+1, -1\}$). However, in order to detect faces in various scales, especially for tiny faces, recent face detectors utilizing Single-Stage networks [6,24,40] divide the face detection problem into multiple scale-specific binary classification problems, and learn their loss functions jointly. The objective function to attack such a network is defined as:

$$\arg\min_{\boldsymbol{\xi}} \quad \mathcal{L}_{t_i} = \sum_{j=1}^{S} \ell_{s_j}(f_{s_j}(\boldsymbol{X} + \boldsymbol{\xi}, t_i), y^{target}), \tag{3}$$

where, S is the number of scales; and ℓ_{s_j} is the scale-specific detector loss function. Compared to Eq. 2, the above objective is more challenging. This is because a single face can not only be detected by multiple region proposals/targets, but also by multiple scale-specific detectors. Thus, one can only successfully attack a face when the adversarial perturbation fools all the scale-specific detectors. In other words, attacking the single-stage face detection network is more challenging than the work in object detection [35].

Finally, as our main aim is to prevent faces being detected, then our objective function is formally defined as:

$$\mathcal{L} = \sum_{i=1}^{T} \mathcal{L}_{t_i} = \sum_{i=1}^{T} \sum_{j=1}^{S} \ell_{s_j}(f_{s_j}(\boldsymbol{X} + \boldsymbol{\xi}, t_i), -1). \tag{4}$$

In this work, we use the recent state-of-the-art Single-Stage face detector, HR [6], which jointly learns 25 different scale-specific detectors, *i.e.*, $S = 25$.

3   Instance Perturbations Interference

When performing an attack using the existing adversarial perturbation approaches [11,19], the Instance Perturbations Interference (IPI) problem appears when multiple faces exist in the input image. In short, the IPI problem refers to the conditions where successfully attacking one instance of interest can reduce the chance of attacking the other instances of interest. For the face detection task, the instance of interest is a face. If not addressed, the IPI problem will significantly reduce the overall attack success rate. To show the existence of the IPI problem, we perform an experiment using synthetic images. In this experiment, we apply an adaptation of the existing perturbation methods generated by minimizing Eq. 4.

3.1   Image Based Perturbation

As mentioned, we categorize the previous methods as IMage based Perturbation (IMP) as they use whole image perturbation to perform the attack. Here we adapt two of the existing methods, I-FSGM [11] and DeepFool [23], by optimizing Eq. 4. We denote them as IMP(I-FGSM) and IMP(DeepFool). In both methods, the adversarial perturbation is generated by using a gradient descent approach. At the $(n+1)$th iteration, the gradient with respect to the input image $\boldsymbol{X}$, $\nabla_{\boldsymbol{X}} \mathcal{L}(f(\boldsymbol{X}+\boldsymbol{\xi}^{(n)}),-1)$, is generated via back-propagating the network with the loss function.

For the IMP(I-FSGM) [11], we iteratively update the adversarial perturbation as follows:

$$\boldsymbol{\xi}^{(n+1)} = \text{Clip}_{\varepsilon}\{\boldsymbol{\xi}^{(n)} - \alpha \text{sign}(\nabla_{\boldsymbol{X}} \mathcal{L}(f(\boldsymbol{X}+\boldsymbol{\xi}^{(n)}),-1))\}, \tag{5}$$

where the step rate $\alpha = 1$; the epsilon ε is the maximum absolute magnitude to clip; $\boldsymbol{\xi}^{(0)} = \boldsymbol{0}$; and the loss function $\mathcal{L}$ is referred to the Eq. 4. Note that in Eq. 4, the loss function is a summation of the loss of all targets. Thus, the aggregate gradient, $\nabla_{\boldsymbol{X}} \mathcal{L}$, can be rewritten as:

$$\nabla_{\boldsymbol{X}} \mathcal{L}(f(\boldsymbol{X}+\boldsymbol{\xi}^{(n)}),-1) = \sum_{i=1}^{T}\sum_{j=1}^{S} \nabla_{\boldsymbol{X}} \ell_{s_j}(f_{s_j}(\boldsymbol{X}+\boldsymbol{\xi}^{(n)},t_i),-1). \tag{6}$$

As we assume f is a deep neural network, then the aggregate gradient $\nabla_{\boldsymbol{X}} \mathcal{L}$ can be obtained by back-propagating all of the targets at once. After obtaining the final adversarial perturbation $\boldsymbol{\xi}$, the perturbed image, $\boldsymbol{X}^{adv}$, is then generated by: $\boldsymbol{X}^{adv} = \boldsymbol{X} + \boldsymbol{\xi}$.

For the IMP(DeepFool), following [23], we configure the Eq. 5 into:

$$\boldsymbol{\xi}^{(n+1)} = \text{Clip}_{\varepsilon}\{\boldsymbol{\xi}^{(n)} - \frac{\nabla_{\boldsymbol{X}} \mathcal{L}(f(\boldsymbol{X}+\boldsymbol{\xi}^{(n)}))}{\left\|\nabla_{\boldsymbol{X}} \mathcal{L}(f(\boldsymbol{X}+\boldsymbol{\xi}^{(n)}))\right\|_2^2}\}, \tag{7}$$

where the loss function in Eq. 4 is rewritten as $\mathcal{L} = \sum_{i=1}^{T}\sum_{j=1}^{S}(f_{s_j}(\boldsymbol{X}+\boldsymbol{\xi},t_i))$.

Compare with the IMP(DeepFool), the IMP(I-FGSM) generates denser and more perceptible perturbations due to the L_{∞} norm.

3.2   Existence of the IPI Problem

To show the existence of the IPI problem, we construct a set of synthetic images by controlling the number of faces and distances between them: (1) an image containing only one face; (2) an image containing multiple faces closely located in a grid and (3) using image in (2) but increasing the distance between the faces. Examples are shown in Fig. 2. For this experiment, we use the recent state-of-the-art face detector HR-ResNet101 [6]. The synthetic images are constructed by randomly selecting 50 faces from the WIDER FACE dataset [38]. Experimental details are given in Sect. 5.2. We generate the adversarial perturbations using the IMP approaches: IMP(I-FGSM) and IMP(DeepFool).

The attack success rate is calculated as follows: $\frac{\#\text{Face removed}}{\#\text{Detected face}}$. Table 1 reports the results. For the first synthetic case where an image only contains one face, both IMP(I-FGSM) and IMP(DeepFool) are able to attack the face detector with a 100% attack success rate. The IMP method is only partially successful on the second case where the number of faces is increased to 16. The attack success rates decrease significantly to only 18.3% and 11.0% when $N = 81$. The IMP method attack success rates significantly increase when the distances between faces are increased significantly, especially for the IMP(DeepFool). It is because the IMP(DeepFool) generates sparser perturbations than the IMP(I-FGSM).

These results suggest the following: (1) IMP is effective when only a single face exists; (2) IMP is ineffective when multiple faces exist close to each other and (3) the distance between faces significantly affects the attack performance. There are two questions that arise from these results: (1) why is the attack affected by the number of faces? and (2) why does the distance between faces affect the attack success rate? We address these two questions in the next section.

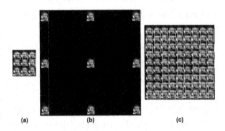

Fig. 2. Examples of synthetic images after adding adversarial perturbations from the IMage based Perturbation (IMP). The detection results of the adversarial images are shown in rectangles. Note that, as face density increases, attack success rate decreases. The IMP attack is ineffective when there are many faces in an image, as in (a) and (c). When the distance among faces is increased, the attack becomes successful as in (b)

4   Proposed Method

We first elaborate on the relationship between the Effective Receptive Field and the IPI problem. Then, the proposed Localized Instance Perturbation (LIP) method is outlined.

4.1   Effective Receptive Field (ERF)

The receptive field of a neuron in a neural network is a set of pixels in the input image that impact the neuron decision [18]. In CNNs, it has been shown in [18] that the distribution of impact within the Theoretical Receptive Field (TRF) of a neuron follows a 2D Gaussian distribution. This means most pixels that have significant impact to the neuron decision are concentrated near the neuron and the impact decays quickly away from the center of the TRF. In [18], the area where pixels still have significant impact to the neuron decision is defined as the Effective Receptive Field (ERF). The ERF only takes up a fraction of the TRF and pixels within the ERF will generate non-negligible impacts on the final outputs. We argue that understanding ERF and TRF is important for addressing the IPI problem. This is because the adversarial perturbation is aimed at changing a network decision at one or more neurons. All pixels in the input image that impact the decision must be considered.

Table 1. The IMP attack success rate (in %) on the synthetic images with respect to the number of faces and distances among faces. N is the number of faces. The IMP can achieve 100% attack success rate when there is one face per image. The attack success rate drops significantly when the number of faces is increased. With the same number of faces, the attack success rate can be increased as the distance among faces increases

(a) IMP(I-FGSM)						(b) IMP(DeepFool)					
N	1	16		81		N	1	16			81
Distance	40	40	80	160	40	Distance	40	40	60	80	40
IMP(I-FGSM)	100	34	37.5	38.9	18.3	IMP(DeepFool)	100	67.5	91.8	99.7	11.0

In this paper, we denote the Distribution of Impacts in the TRF as DI-TRF for simplicity. The DI-TRF is measured by calculating the partial derivative of the central pixel on the output layer via back-propagation. Following the notations in our paper, let us denote the central pixel as t_c, then the partial derivative of the central pixel is $\frac{\partial f(\boldsymbol{X}, t_c)}{\partial \boldsymbol{X}}$, which is the DI-TRF. According to the chain rule, we have the gradient of the target t_c [18] as: $\nabla_{\boldsymbol{X}} \mathcal{L}(f(\boldsymbol{X}, t_c), y^{target}) = \frac{\partial \mathcal{L}(f(\boldsymbol{X}, t_c), y^{target})}{\partial f(\boldsymbol{X}, t_c)} \frac{\partial f(\boldsymbol{X}, t_c)}{\partial \boldsymbol{X}}$, where the $\frac{\partial \mathcal{L}(f(\boldsymbol{X}, t_c), y^{target})}{\partial f(\boldsymbol{X}, t_c)}$ is set to 1.

Comparing the gradient of a target pixel for the adversarial perturbations in Eq. 6, the only difference with the DI-TRF is in the partial derivative of the loss function $\frac{\partial \mathcal{L}(f(\boldsymbol{X}, t_c), y^{target})}{\partial f(\boldsymbol{X}, t_c)}$, which is a scalar for one target pixel. In our work, the scalar, $\frac{\partial \mathcal{L}(f(\boldsymbol{X}, t_c), y^{target})}{\partial f(\boldsymbol{X}, t_c)}$, measures the loss between the prediction label and the target label. The logistic loss is used for the binary classification of each scale-specific detector, (i.e., the $\ell_{s_j}(f_{s_j}(\boldsymbol{X}, t_c), y^{target})$ in Eq. 4). Therefore, our adversarial perturbation for one target can be considered as a scaled distribution of the DI-TRF. Since DI-TRF follows a 2D Gaussian distribution [18], then the adversarial perturbation to change a single neuron decision is also a 2D Gaussian.

We explain the IPI problem as follows. Since an adversarial perturbation to attack a single neuron follows a 2D Gaussian, then the perturbation is mainly spread over the ERF and will have a non-zero tail outside the ERF. From the experiment, we observed that the perturbations generated to attack multiple faces in the image may interfere with other. More specifically, when these perturbations overlap with the neighboring face ERF, they may be sufficient enough to disrupt the adversarial perturbation generated to attack this neighboring face. In addition, prior work [34] shows that adversarial attacks might fail when the specific structure is destroyed. In other words, when multiple attacks are applied simultaneously, these attacks may corrupt each other, leading to a lower attack rate. We name the part of a perturbation interfering with the other perturbations for other faces as the interfering perturbation.

This also explains why the IPI is affected by the distance between faces. The closer the faces, the more chance the interfering perturbations with a larger magnitude overlap with the neighboring face ERF. When distances between faces increase, the magnitude of the interfering perturbations that overlap with the neighboring ERFs may not be strong enough to disrupt attacks for target faces.

4.2 Localized Instance Perturbation (LIP)

To address the IPI problem, we argue that the generated adversarial perturbations of one instance should be exclusively confined within the instance ERF. As such, we call our method as the Localized Instance Perturbation (LIP). The LIP comprises two main components: (1) methods to eliminate any possible interfering perturbation and (2) methods to generate the perturbation.

Eliminating the Interfering Perturbation. To eliminate the interference between perturbations, we attempt to constrain the generated perturbation for each instance individually inside the ERF. Let us consider that an image X, with $w \times h$ pixels, contains N instances $\{m_i\}_{i=1}^N$. Each instance m_i has its corresponding ERF, e_i, and we have $\{e_i\}_{i=1}^N$. For each instance, there are a set of corresponding targets represented as object proposals, $\{p_j\}_{j=1}^P$. We denote the final perturbation for the ith instance as R_{m_i} and the final combination of the perturbation of all the instances as R. Similar to the IMP method, once the final perturbation, R, has been computed, then we add the perturbation into the image $X^{adv} = X + R$.

(1) Perturbation Cropping. This step is to limit the perturbations inside the instance ERF. This is done by cropping the perturbation according to the corresponding instance ERF. Let us define a binary matrix $C_{e_i} \in \{0,1\}^{w \times h}$ as the cropping matrix for the ERF, e_i. The matrix C is defined as follows:

$$C_{e_i}(w, h) = \begin{cases} 1, & (w, h) \in e_i \\ 0, & \text{otherwise} \end{cases}, \tag{8}$$

where (w, h) is a pixel location. The cropping operation is computed by a element-wise dot product of the mask C_{e_i} and the gradient w.r.t. the input images X, is defined as:

$$R_{m_i} = C_{e_i} \cdot \nabla_X \mathcal{L}_{m_i}, \tag{9}$$

where $\mathcal{L}_{m_i}$ is the loss function of the i-th instance. $\mathcal{L}_{m_i}$ will be described in the next sub-section.

(2) Individual Instance Perturbation. It is possible to compute the perturbation of multiple instances simultaneously. However, the interfering perturbation can

still exist and may impact the attack. To that end, we propose to separately compute the perturbation for each instance, $\nabla_X \mathcal{L}_{m_i}$ before cropping. After the cropping step is applied to each instance perturbation, the final perturbation of all instances is combined via:

$$R = \sum_{i=1}^{N} C_{e_i} \cdot \nabla_X \mathcal{L}_{m_i}. \tag{10}$$

We then normalize the final perturbation, R, via: $R = \alpha \text{sign}(R)$.

Perturbation Generation. Given a set of region proposals corresponding to an instance, there are at least two methods of generating the instance perturbation R_{m_i}: (1) All proposal based generation and (2) Highest Confidence proposal based generation.

(1) All Proposal based Generation. In the first method, we utilize all the region proposals to generate the perturbation R_{m_i}. Thus, the $\mathcal{L}_{m_i}$ in Eq. 9 can be defined as a summation of the loss function of all the region proposals $\mathcal{L}_{p_j}$ belong to the instance:

$$\mathcal{L}_{m_i} = \sum_{j=1}^{P} \mathcal{L}_{p_j}. \tag{11}$$

(2) Highest Confidence Proposal based Generation. In online hard example mining [30], Shrivastava *et al.* showed the efficiency of using the hard examples to generate the gradients for updating the networks. The hard examples are the high-loss object proposals chosen by the non-maximum suppression. Non-Maximum Suppression (NMS) is similar to max-pooling, which selects the object proposal with the highest score (*i.e.,* selecting the proposal with the highest loss). Inspired by this, instead of attacking all of the object proposals corresponding to a single instance, we can use NMS to select the one with the highest loss to compute the back-propagation. Then $\mathcal{L}_{m_i}$ can be rewritten as:

$$\mathcal{L}_{m_i} = \max(\mathcal{L}_{p_j}). \tag{12}$$

5   Experiments

5.1   Implementation Details

In this section, we first describe the implementation details and then evaluate our proposed adversarial attacks on the state-of-the-art face detection datasets.

For this study, we utilize a recent state-of-the-art face detector, HR [6]. In particular, HR-ResNet101 is used. Image pyramids are utilized in HR, *i.e.,* downsampling/interpolating the input image into multiple sizes. Therefore, for every image in the pyramid, we generate corresponding adversarial examples. The detection results of the image pyramid are combined together with Non-Maximum Suppression (NMS). The chosen thresholds of NMS and classification are 0.1 and 0.5 respectively.

In order to avoid the gradient explosion when generating the perturbations, we found that by zero-padding the small input images can reduce the magnitude of the gradient. In this work, we zero pad the small images to 1000×1000 pixels. In addition, as the input images of the detection networks can have arbitrary sizes, we do not follow existing methods [19,22] that resize the input images into a canonical size.

Note that we cannot simply crop the input image to generate a successful adversarial perturbation. This is because the perturbation may be incomplete as it does not include the context information obtained from neighboring instances. An example of two non-normalized perturbations in absolute value generated with and without context is shown in supplementary materials.

For determining the perturbation cropping size, we follow the work of Luo *et al.* [18] which computes the gradient of the central proposal of an instance on the output feature map to obtain the distribution of the ERF. We average the gradients over multiple instances and determine the crop size with the definition that the ERF takes up 90% of the energy of the TRF [18]. The perturbation crop size is set to 80×80 pixels for small faces and 140×140 pixels for large faces. The maximum noise value ε is 20 and the maximum number of iterations N_0 is 40. The α is set to 1 in this work.

Perturbation Generation Methods. In our work, we compared our proposed Localized Instance Perturbation (LIP) approach with the IMage Perturbation (IMP) and Localized Perturbation (LP). The details of the perturbation generation methods evaluated are listed as follow:

(1) Localized Instance Perturbation using All proposal generation (LIP-A). The proposed LIP-A is a variant of our proposed LIP method in Sect. 4.2. As mentioned, the loss function of one instance is the summation of all proposals (refer to Eq. 11).

(2) Localized Instance Perturbation using Highest confidence proposal generation (LIP-H). The LIP-H is another variant of our proposed LIP with the loss function of Eq. 12. The loss function of one instance consists of only one loss of the highest confidence proposal.

(3) IMage Perturbation (IMP). The IMP method refers to the generation method in Sect. 3.1 which applies the perturbation without cropping it. This perturbation generation method follows the previous work [19].

(4) Localized Perturbation (LP). The LP is the localized perturbation which also crops the image perturbation. The main difference to the proposed LIP is that it computes the gradients of all the instances simultaneously before the cropping. In contrast to Eq. 10, the final perturbation is obtained by:

$$R = \bigcup_{i=1}^{N} C_{e_i} \cdot \sum_{i=1}^{N} \nabla_X \mathcal{L}_{m_i}. \tag{13}$$

where $\bigcup_{i=1}^{N} C_{e_i}$ is the union of all binary matrices. The advantage of this method is that current deep learning toolboxes can calculate the summation of the gradients of all instances, $(i.e., \sum_{i=1}^{N} \nabla_X \mathcal{L}_{m_i})$, simultaneously by back-propagating the network only once.

Benchmark Datasets. We evaluate our proposed adversarial perturbations on two recent popular face detection benchmark datasets: *(1) FDDB dataset:* [8] The FDDB dataset includes images of faces with a wide range of difficulties such as occlusions, difficult poses, low resolution and out-of-focus faces. It contains 2,845 images with a total of 5,171 faces labeled; and *(2) WIDER FACE dataset:* [38] The WIDER FACE dataset is currently the most challenging face detection benchmark dataset. It comprises 32,203 images and 393,703 annotated faces based on 61 events collected from the Internet. The images of some events, *e.g.,* parade, contain a large number of faces. According to the difficulties of the occlusions, poses, and scales, the faces are grouped into three sets: 'Easy', 'Medium' and 'Hard'.

Evaluation Metrics. The metrics for evaluating the adversarial attacks against face detection are defined as follows: *(1) Attack Success Rate:* The attack success rate is the ratio between the number of faces that are successfully attacked and the number of detected faces before the attacks; and *(2) Detection Rate:* The detection rate is the ratio between the number of detected faces and the number of faces in the images.

5.2   Evaluation on Synthetic Data

As discussed in Sect. 3, due to the IPI problem, the IMP does not perform well on the cases where (1) the number of faces per image is large; and (2) the faces are close to each other. Here, we contrast IMP with LP and LIP.

We randomly selected 50 faces from the WIDER FACE dataset [38]. These faces were first resized into a canonical size of 30×30 pixels. Each face was then duplicated and inserted into a blank image in a rectangular grid manner (*e.g.,* $3 \times 3 = 9$). The number of duplicates and the distance between the duplicates were controlled during the experiment. In total there were 50 images and the attack success rate was then averaged across 50 images. Some examples of the synthetic images are shown in Fig. 2.

The Effect of the Number of Faces. We progressively increased the number of duplication for each synthetic image from 1×1 to $9 \times 9 = 81$ duplicates. We fixed the distance between duplicates to 40 pixels. The quantitative results are shown in Fig. 3. From this figure, we can see that for the perturbation generation method I-FGSM, the IMP attack success rate significantly drops from 100% to 20% as the number of faces is increased. On the contrary, both LP and LIP-H can achieve significantly higher attack success rate than IMP. This is because both LP and LIP-H only use the generated perturbation within the corresponding instance ERF by cropping it before applying. Note that, when the number of faces is more than 36, the LP attack success rate drops from 85% ($N = 36$) to 51% ($N = 81$), whereas the LIP-H can still achieve more than 90% success rate. Since LP processes all the instances simultaneously, the accumulation of the interfering perturbations within each instance ERF will become more significant when the number of faces is increased. Similarly, for the generation method DeepFool, the LIP has demonstrated its effectiveness on addressing the IPI problem when multiple faces exist. These also suggest the existence of the IPI problem.

The Effect of Distance between Faces. In this experiment the number of faces duplication was fixed to 9. We modified the distance between face duplicates to 40, 160 and 240 pixels. It can be seen from Fig. 3b that the attack success rate for IMP increases as the distance between faces is increased. The performance of both LP and LIP-H are not affected. Similar performance is achieved on the DeepFool. More details are shown in the supplementary materials.

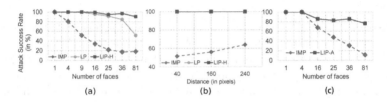

Fig. 3. The attack success rate of the I-FGSM with respect to: (a) the number of faces. The distance was fixed to 40 pixels; and (b) the distance between faces. Nine face duplicates were used. (c) The attack success rate of the DeepFool

5.3   Evaluation on Face Detection Datasets

We contrasted LIP-A and LIP-H with IMP and LP based on two existing methods: I-FSGM [11] and Deep-Fool [23]. The experiments were run on the FDDB [8] and 1,000 randomly selected images in the WIDER FACE validation set [38].

The results based on the I-FGSM, are reported in Tables 3 and 2 respectively. On the FDDB dataset (in Table 3), the face detector, HR [6], achieves 95.7% detection rate. The LP, LIP-A and LIP-H can significantly reduce the detection rate to around 5% with the attack success rate of 94.9%, 94.6% and 93.8% respectively. On the other hand, the IMP can only achieve 53.9% attack success rate (*i.e.*, significantly lower than the LP, LIP-A, LIP-H performance). This signifies

Fig. 4. Examples of the adversarial attacks on face detection network, where the perturbation generation is based on the I-FGSM. The LIP-H is successfully attack all the faces, whereas some faces are still detected when IMP is used

the importance of the perturbation cropping to eliminate the interfering perturbations. Due to the IPI problem, the interfering perturbations from the other instances will affect the adversarial attacks of the target instance. This results in the low attack success rate of the IMP. This is because to generate the perturbations, the IMP simply sums up the all perturbations including the interfering perturbations. We note that the performance of LP, LIP-A and LIP-H are on par in the FDDB dataset. This could be due to the low number of faces per image for this dataset.

Table 2. The attack success and detection rate (in %) on WIDER FACE [38]

Perturbations		None	I-FGSM				DeepFool	
			IMP	LP	LIP-A	LIP-H	IMP	LIP-A
Detection rate	easy	92.4	46.2	30.1	28.2	**26.5**	50.6	43.2
	medium	90.7	50.7	34.7	32.2	**31.1**	54.4	40.0
	hard	77.3	45.9	29.3	**23.6**	26.6	46.5	25.8
Attack success rate	easy	–	50.0	67.4	69.5	**71.3**	45.3	53.2
	medium	–	44.1	61.7	64.5	**65.7**	40.0	56.4
	hard	–	40.6	62.1	**69.5**	65.6	39.6	66.6

However, when the number of faces per image increases significantly, LIP shows its advantages. Examples can be seen in Fig. 4. This can be observed in the WIDER FACE

Table 3. The attack success and detection rates (in %) on FDDB [8]

Perturbations	None	I-FGSM			
		IMP	LP	LIP-A	LIP-H
Detection rate	95.7	44.1	4.8	5.1	5.9
Attack success rate	–	53.9	94.9	94.6	93.8

dataset (in Table 2) where LIP-A and LIP-H outperform LP by 4% points. the LIP-H can achieve attack success rates of $(69.8\%, 63.7\%, 61.4\%)$ on the (easy, medium, hard) sets, while the LP can only obtain attack success rate $(65.7\%, 59.5\%, 57.4\%)$. As the LP processes all the instances together, the interfering perturbations are accumulated within the ERF before the cropping step. Note that the interfering perturbations may have low magnitude, however, when they are accumulated due to the number of neighboring instances then disruption could be significant. These results also suggest that we do not necessarily need to attack all the region proposals as the performance of LIP-H is on par with LIP-A. Similarly, for the DeepFool based methods, the LIP has demonstrated its effectiveness on addressing the IPI problem.

5.4   Evaluation on Object Detection Dataset

To explore the existence of the IPI problem in object detection networks, we perform attacks on the pre-trained Faster-RCNN [28] (based on ResNet101 [5]) provided by the Tensorflow object detection API [7]. More specifically, we attack the 1st stage (*i.e.*, RPN) of Faster-RCNN with the goal of reducing generated proposals. We choose

Table 4. Evaluation on COCO2017 dataset [14]

Perturbations	IMP	LP
Average recall	7.9	**2.2**
Average precision	6.9	**1.9**

300 images from COCO2017 dataset [14], where the average number of objects per image is 15. The original predicted detections from the pre-trained Faster-RCNN are taken as ground truth. The results in Table 4 show that the IPI problem exists and our proposed LP method can attack more than 60% of the instances that cannot be attacked by IMP. Note that, as the RPN generates hundreds of proposals for each instance, the proposed LIP methods are not used due to the high computations.

6   Conclusions

In this paper, we presented an adversarial perturbation method to fool a recent state-of-the-art face detector utilizing the single-stage network. We described and addressed the Instance Perturbation Interference (IPI) problem which was the root cause for the failure of the existing adversarial perturbation generation methods to attack multiple faces simultaneously. We found that it was sufficient to only use the generated perturbations within an instance/face Effective Receptive Field (ERF) to perform an effective attack. In addition, it was important to exclude perturbations outside the ERF to avoid disrupting other instance perturbations. We thus proposed the Localized Instance Perturbation (LIP) approach that only confined the perturbation within the ERF. Experiments showed that the proposed LIP successfully generated perturbations for multiple faces simultaneously to fool the face detection network and outperformed existing adversarial generation methods. In the future, we plan to develop a universal perturbation generation method which can attack many faces with a general perturbation.

Acknowledgments. This work has been funded by Sullivan Nicolaides Pathology, Australia, and the Australian Research Council (ARC) Linkage Projects Grant LP160101797. Arnold Wiliem is funded by the Advance Queensland Early-Career Research Fellowship.

References

1. Chen, D., Hua, G., Wen, F., Sun, J.: Supervised transformer network for efficient face detection. In: Leibe, B., Matas, J., Sebe, N., Welling, M. (eds.) ECCV 2016. LNCS, vol. 9909, pp. 122–138. Springer, Cham (2016). https://doi.org/10.1007/978-3-319-46454-1_8

2. Cisse, M., Adi, Y., Neverova, N., Keshet, J.: Houdini: Fooling deep structured prediction models. In: Advances in Neural Information Processing Systems (NIPS) (2017)
3. Fischer, V., Kumar, M.C., Metzen, J.H., Brox, T.: Adversarial examples for semantic image segmentation. In: International Conference on Learning Representations (ICLR) Workshop (2017)
4. Goodfellow, I.J., Shlens, J., Szegedy, C.: Explaining and harnessing adversarial examples. In: International Conference on Learning Representations (ICLR) (2015)
5. He, K., Zhang, X., Ren, S., Sun, J.: Deep residual learning for image recognition. In: Computer Vision and Pattern Recognition (CVPR). IEEE (2016)
6. Hu, P., Ramanan, D.: Finding tiny faces. In: Computer Vision and Pattern Recognition (CVPR). IEEE (2017)
7. Huang, J. et al.: Speed/accuracy trade-offs for modern convolutional object detectors. In: Computer Vision and Pattern Recognition (CVPR). IEEE (2017)
8. Jain, V., Learned-Miller, E.G.: Fddb: A benchmark for face detection in unconstrained settings. UMass Amherst Technical Report (2010)
9. Jiang, H., Learned-Miller, E.: Face detection with the faster r-cnn. In: IEEE International Conference on Automatic Face & Gesture Recognition (FG). IEEE (2017)
10. Krizhevsky, A., Sutskever, I., Hinton, G.E.: Imagenet classification with deep convolutional neural networks. In: Advances in Neural Information Processing Systems (NIPS) (2012)
11. Kurakin, A., Goodfellow, I., Bengio, S.: Adversarial examples in the physical world. In: International Conference on Learning Representations (ICLR) Workshop (2017)
12. Li, H., Lin, Z., Shen, X., Brandt, J., Hua, G.: A convolutional neural network cascade for face detection. In: Computer Vision and Pattern Recognition (CVPR). IEEE (2015)
13. Li, Y., Sun, B., Wu, T., Wang, Y.: Face detection with end-to-end integration of a convnet and a 3D model. In: Leibe, B., Matas, J., Sebe, N., Welling, M. (eds.) ECCV 2016. LNCS, vol. 9907, pp. 420–436. Springer, Cham (2016). https://doi.org/10.1007/978-3-319-46487-9_26
14. Lin, T.-Y., et al.: Microsoft COCO: common objects in context. In: Fleet, D., Pajdla, T., Schiele, B., Tuytelaars, T. (eds.) ECCV 2014. LNCS, vol. 8693, pp. 740–755. Springer, Cham (2014). https://doi.org/10.1007/978-3-319-10602-1_48
15. Liu, W., Anguelov, D., Erhan, D., Szegedy, C., Reed, S., Fu, C.-Y., Berg, A.C.: SSD: single shot MultiBox detector. In: Leibe, B., Matas, J., Sebe, N., Welling, M. (eds.) ECCV 2016. LNCS, vol. 9905, pp. 21–37. Springer, Cham (2016). https://doi.org/10.1007/978-3-319-46448-0_2
16. Liu, Y., Chen, X., Liu, C., Song, D.: Delving into transferable adversarial examples and black-box attacks. In: International Conference on Learning Representations (ICLR) (2017)
17. Long, J., Shelhamer, E., Darrell, T.: Fully convolutional networks for semantic segmentation. In: Computer Vision and Pattern Recognition (CVPR). IEEE (2015)
18. Luo, W., Li, Y., Urtasun, R., Zemel, R.: Understanding the effective receptive field in deep convolutional neural networks. In: Advances in Neural Information Processing Systems (NIPS) (2016)
19. Metzen, J.H., Kumar, M.C., Brox, T., Fischer, V.: Universal adversarial perturbations against semantic image segmentation. In: International Conference on Computer Vision (ICCV). IEEE (2017)
20. Mirjalili, V., Raschka, S., Namboodiri, A., Ross, A.: Semi-adversarial networks: convolutional autoencoders for imparting privacy to face images. In: International Conference on Biometrics (ICB) (2018)

21. Mirjalili, V., Ross, A.: Soft biometric privacy: Retaining biometric utility of face images while perturbing gender. In: International Joint Conference on Biometrics (IJCB) (2017)
22. Moosavi-Dezfooli, S.M., Fawzi, A., Fawzi, O., Frossard, P.: Universal adversarial perturbations. In: Computer Vision and Pattern Recognition (CVPR). IEEE (2017)
23. Moosavi-Dezfooli, S.M., Fawzi, A., Frossard, P.: Deepfool: a simple and accurate method to fool deep neural networks. In: Computer Vision and Pattern Recognition (CVPR). IEEE (2016)
24. Najibi, M., Samangouei, P., Chellappa, R., Davis, L.: Ssh: Single stage headless face detector. In: International Conference on Computer Vision (ICCV). IEEE (2017)
25. Nguyen, A., Yosinski, J., Clune, J.: Deep neural networks are easily fooled: high confidence predictions for unrecognizable images. In: Computer Vision and Pattern Recognition (CVPR). IEEE (2015)
26. Qin, H., Yan, J., Li, X., Hu, X.: Joint training of cascaded cnn for face detection. In: Computer Vision and Pattern Recognition (CVPR). IEEE (2016)
27. Redmon, J., Divvala, S., Girshick, R., Farhadi, A.: You only look once: Unified, real-time object detection. In: Computer Vision and Pattern Recognition (CVPR). IEEE (2016)
28. Ren, S., He, K., Girshick, R., Sun, J.: Faster r-cnn: Towards real-time object detection with region proposal networks. In: Advances in Neural Information Processing Systems (NIPS) (2015)
29. Sharif, M., Bhagavatula, S., Bauer, L., Reiter, M.K.: Accessorize to a crime: real and stealthy attacks on state-of-the-art face recognition. In: Proceedings of the 2016 ACM SIGSAC Conference on Computer and Communications Security. ACM (2016)
30. Shrivastava, A., Gupta, A., Girshick, R.: Training region-based object detectors with online hard example mining. In: Computer Vision and Pattern Recognition (CVPR). IEEE (2016)
31. Simonyan, K., Zisserman, A.: Very deep convolutional networks for large-scale image recognition. In: International Conference on Learning Representations (ICLR) (2015)
32. Szegedy, C., Zaremba, W., Sutskever, I., Bruna, J., Erhan, D., Goodfellow, I., Fergus, R.: Intriguing properties of neural networks. In: International Conference on Learning Representations (ICLR) (2014)
33. Viola, P., Jones, M.: Rapid object detection using a boosted cascade of simple features. In: Computer Vision and Pattern Recognition (CVPR). IEEE (2001)
34. Xie, C., Wang, J., Zhang, Z., Ren, Z., Yuille, A.: Mitigating adversarial effects through randomization. In: International Conference on Learning Representations (ICLR) (2018)
35. Xie, C., Wang, J., Zhang, Z., Zhou, Y., Xie, L., Yuille, A.: Adversarial examples for semantic segmentation and object detection. In: International Conference on Computer Vision (ICCV). IEEE (2017)
36. Yamada, T., Gohshi, S., Echizen, I.: Privacy Visor: method for preventing face image detection by using differences in human and device sensitivity. In: De Decker, B., Dittmann, J., Kraetzer, C., Vielhauer, C. (eds.) CMS 2013. LNCS, vol. 8099, pp. 152–161. Springer, Heidelberg (2013). https://doi.org/10.1007/978-3-642-40779-6_13
37. Yang, S., Luo, P., Loy, C.C., Tang, X.: From facial parts responses to face detection: a deep learning approach. In: International Conference on Computer Vision (ICCV) (2015)

38. Yang, S., Luo, P., Loy, C.C., Tang, X.: Wider face: a face detection benchmark. In: Computer Vision and Pattern Recognition (CVPR). IEEE (2015)
39. Zhang, K., Zhang, Z., Li, Z., Qiao, Y.: Joint face detection and alignment using multitask cascaded convolutional networks. IEEE Signal Process. Lett. **23**(10), 1499–1503 (2016)
40. Zhang, S., Zhu, X., Lei, Z., Shi, H., Wang, X., Li, S.Z.: S3 fd: single shot scale-invariant face detector. In: International Conference on Computer Vision (ICCV). IEEE (2017)

HiDDeN: Hiding Data With Deep Networks

Jiren Zhu$^{(\boxtimes)}$ (ID), Russell Kaplan, Justin Johnson, and Li Fei-Fei

Computer Science Department, Stanford University, Stanford, USA
{jirenz,rjkaplan,jcjohns,feifeili}@cs.stanford.edu

Abstract. Recent work has shown that deep neural networks are highly sensitive to tiny perturbations of input images, giving rise to *adversarial examples*. Though this property is usually considered a weakness of learned models, we explore whether it can be beneficial. We find that neural networks can learn to use invisible perturbations to encode a rich amount of useful information. In fact, one can exploit this capability for the task of data hiding. We jointly train encoder and decoder networks, where given an input message and cover image, the encoder produces a visually indistinguishable encoded image, from which the decoder can recover the original message. We show that these encodings are competitive with existing data hiding algorithms, and further that they can be made robust to noise: our models learn to reconstruct hidden information in an encoded image despite the presence of Gaussian blurring, pixel-wise dropout, cropping, and JPEG compression. Even though JPEG is non-differentiable, we show that a robust model can be trained using differentiable approximations. Finally, we demonstrate that adversarial training improves the visual quality of encoded images.

Keywords: Adversarial networks · Steganography
Robust blind watermarking · Deep learning · Convolutional networks

1 Introduction

Sometimes there is more to an image than meets the eye. An image may appear normal to a casual observer, but knowledgeable recipients can extract more information. Two common settings exist for hiding information in images. In *steganography*, the goal is secret communication: a sender (Alice) encodes a message in an image such that the recipient (Bob) can decode the message, but an adversary (Eve) cannot tell whether any given image contains a message or not; Eve's task of detecting encoded images is called *steganalysis*. In *digital watermarking*,

---

J. Zhu and R. Kaplan—Equally contributed.

Electronic supplementary material The online version of this chapter (https://doi.org/10.1007/978-3-030-01267-0_40) contains supplementary material, which is available to authorized users.

© Springer Nature Switzerland AG 2018
V. Ferrari et al. (Eds.): ECCV 2018, LNCS 11219, pp. 682–697, 2018.
https://doi.org/10.1007/978-3-030-01267-0_40

the goal is to encode information robustly: Alice wishes to encode a fingerprint in an image; Eve will then somehow distort the image (by cropping, blurring, etc), and Bob should be able to detect the fingerprint in the distorted image. Digital watermarking can be used to identify image ownership: if Alice is a photographer, then by embedding digital watermarks in her images she can prove ownership of those images even if versions posted online are modified.

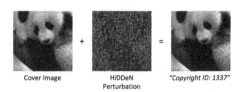

Cover Image   HiDDeN   "Copyright ID: 1337"
Perturbation

Fig. 1. Given a cover image and a binary message, the HiDDeN encoder produces a visually indistinguishable *encoded image* that contains the message, which can be recovered with high accuracy by the decoder.

Interestingly, neural networks are also capable of "detecting" information from images that are not visible to human eyes. Recent research have showed that neural networks are susceptible to *adversarial examples*: given an image and a target class, the pixels of the image can be imperceptibly modified such that it is confidently classified as the target class [1,2]. Moreover, the adversarial nature of these generated images is preserved under a variety of image transformations [3]. While the existence of adversarial examples is usually seen as a disadvantage of neural networks, it can be desirable for information hiding: if a network can be fooled with small perturbations into making incorrect class predictions, it should be possible to extract meaningful information from similar perturbations (Fig. 1).

We introduce HiDDeN, the first end-to-end trainable framework for data hiding which can be applied to both steganography and watermarking. HiDDeN uses three convolutional networks for data hiding. An *encoder* network receives a *cover image* and a message (encoded as a bit string) and outputs an *encoded image*; a *decoder* network receives the encoded image and attempts to reconstruct the message. A third network, the *adversary*, predicts whether a given image contains an encoded message; this provides an adversarial loss that improves the quality of encoded images. In many real world scenarios, images are distorted between a sender and recipient (e.g. during lossy compression). We model this by inserting optional *noise layers* between the encoder and decoder, which apply different image transformations and force the model to learn encodings that can survive noisy transmission. We model the data hiding objective by minimizing (1) the difference between the cover and encoded images, (2) the difference between the input and decoded messages, and (3) the ability of an adversary to detect encoded images.

We analyze the performance of our method by measuring *capacity*, the size of the message we can hide; *secrecy*, the degree to which encoded images can be detected by steganalysis tools (*steganalyzers*); and *robustness*, how well our encoded messages can survive image distortions of various forms. We show that our methods outperform prior work in deep-learning-based steganography, and that our methods can also produce robust blind watermarks. The networks learn to reconstruct hidden information in an encoded image despite the presence of Gaussian blurring, pixel-wise dropout, cropping, and JPEG compression. Though JPEG is not differentiable, we can reliably train networks that are robust to its perturbations using a differentiable approximation at training time.

Classical data hiding methods typically use heuristics to decide how much to modify each pixel. For example, some algorithms manipulate the least significant bits of some selected pixels [4]; others change mid-frequency components in the frequency domain [5]. These heuristics are effective in the domains for which they are designed, but they are fundamentally *static*. In contrast, HiDDeN can easily adapt to new requirements, since we directly optimize for the objectives of interest. For watermarking, one can simply retrain the model to gain robustness against a new type of noise instead of inventing a new algorithm. End-to-end learning is also advantageous in steganography, where having a diverse class of embedding functions (the same architecture, trained with different random initializations, produces very different embedding strategies) can stymie an adversary's ability to detect a hidden message.

2 Related Work

Adversarial examples. Adversarial examples were shown to disrupt classification accuracy of various networks with minimal perturbation to the original images [2]. They are typically computed by adding a small perturbation to each pixel in the direction that maximizes one output neuron [1]. Adversarial examples generated for one network can transfer to another network [6], suggesting that they come from a universal property of commonly used networks. Kurakin *et al.* showed that adversarial examples are robust against image transformations; when an adversarial example is printed and photographed, the network still misclassifies the photo [3]. Instead of injecting perturbations that lead to misclassification, we consider the possibility of transmitting useful information through adding the appropriate perturbations.

Steganography. A wide variety of steganography settings and methods have been proposed in the literature; most relevant to our work are methods for *blind image steganography*, where the message is encoded in an image and the decoder does not have access to the original cover image. Least-Significant Bit (LSB) methods modify the lowest-order bits of each image pixel depending on the bits of the secret message; several examples of LSB schemes are described in [7,8]. By design, LSB methods produce image perturbations which are not visually apparent. However, they can systematically alter the statistics of the image, leading to reliable detection [9].

Many steganography algorithms differ only in how they define a particular distortion metric to minimize during encoding. Highly Undetectable

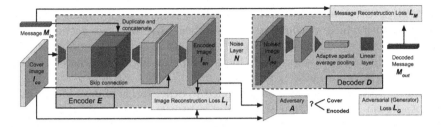

Fig. 2. Model overview. The encoder E receives the secret message M and cover image I_{co} as input and produces an encoded image I_{en}. The noise layer N distorts the encoded image, producing a noised image I_{no}. The decoder produces a predicted message from the noised image. The adversary is trained to detect if an image is encoded. The encoder and decoder are jointly trained to minimize loss $\mathcal{L}_I$ from difference between the cover and encoded image, loss $\mathcal{L}_M$ from difference between the input and predicted message and loss $\mathcal{L}_G$ from encoded image I_{en} being detected by the adversary.

Steganography (HUGO) [4] measures distortion by computing weights for local pixel neighborhoods, resulting in lower distortion costs along edges and in high-texture regions. WOW (Wavelet Obtained Weights) [10] penalizes distortion to predictable regions of the image using a bank of directional filters. S-UNIWARD [11] is similar to WOW but can be used for embedding in an arbitrary domain.

Watermarking. Watermarking is similar to steganography: both aim to encode a secret message into an image. However, while the goal of steganography is secret communication, watermarking is frequently used to prove image ownership as a form of copyright protection. As such, watermarking methods prioritize robustness over secrecy: messages should be recoverable even after the encoded image is modified or distorted. *Non-blind* methods assumes access to the unmodified cover image [12–14]; more relevant to us are *blind* methods [5] where the decoder does not assume access to the cover image. Some watermarking methods encode information in the least significant bits of image pixels [7]; however for more robust encoding many methods instead encode information in the frequency domain [5,13–15]. Other methods combine frequency-domain encoding with log-polar mapping [16] or template matching [14] to achieve robustness against spatial domain transformations.

Data Hiding with Neural Networks. Neural networks have been used for both steganography and watermarking [17]. Until recently, prior work has typically used them for one stage of a larger pipeline, such as determining watermarking strength per image region [18], or as part of the encoder [19] or the decoder [20].

In contrast, we model the entire data hiding pipeline with neural networks and train them end-to-end. Different from [18], HiDDeN is a blind method: it does not require the recipient to have access to the original image, which is more useful than non-blind methods in many practical scenarios. [20] uses gradient descent to do encoding, whereas HiDDeN hides information in a single forward pass. [21] is a recent end-to-end approach to steganography using adversarial networks, with which we compare results in Sect. 4.1. [22] train networks to hide an entire image within another image. In contrast to our work, neither of [21,22] consider encoding robustness; their focus is on steganography whereas HiDDeN can be used for watermarking as well.

Neural networks have also been applied to other forms of data hiding. Abadi and Anderson [23] show that adversarial networks can be trained for cryptography; Uchida *et al.* [24] embed watermarks into the weights of trained neural networks; Fang *et al.* [25] use LSTMs to embed secret messages into text.

3   Method

Our goal is to develop a learnable, end-to-end model for image steganography and watermarking that can be made robust to arbitrary types of image distortion. To this end, our system comprises four main components: an *encoder* E_θ, a parameterless *noise layer* N, a *decoder* D_ϕ and an *adversarial discriminator* A_γ. θ, ϕ and γ are trainable parameters. The encoder E_θ receives a *cover image* I_{co} of shape $C \times H \times W$ and a binary secret message $M_{in} \in \{0,1\}^L$ of length L and produces an *encoded image* (also called the *stego image*) I_{en} of the same shape as I_{co}. The noise layer N receives I_{co} and I_{en} as input and distorts the encoded image to produce a noised image I_{no}. The decoder D recovers a message M_{out} from I_{no}. At the same time, given an image $\tilde{I} \in \{I_{co}, I_{en}\}$, i.e. either a cover image or encoded image, the discriminator predicts $A(\tilde{I}) \in [0,1]$, the probability that $\tilde{I}$ is an encoded image.

Encoded images should look visually similar to cover images. We characterize the "similarity" with *image distortion loss*, the l_2 distance between I_{co} and I_{en}: $\mathcal{L}_I(I_{co}, I_{en}) = \|I_{co} - I_{en}\|_2^2/(CHW)$, and *adversarial loss*, the ability of the discriminator to detect an encoded image I_{en}: $\mathcal{L}_G(I_{en}) = \log(1 - A(I_{en}))$ [26]. The discriminator incurs a classification loss from its predictions $\mathcal{L}_A(I_{co}, I_{en}) = \log(1 - A(I_{co})) + \log(A(I_{en}))$. The decoded message should be the same as the encoded message. We impose a *message distortion loss* using the l_2 distance between the original and decoded messages $\mathcal{L}_M(M_{in}, M_{out}) = \|M_{in} - M_{out}\|_2^2/L$. We perform stochastic gradient descent on θ, ϕ to minimize the following loss over the distribution of input messages and images:

$$\mathbb{E}_{I_{co}, M_{in}}\left[\mathcal{L}_M(M_{in}, M_{out}) + \lambda_I \mathcal{L}_I(I_{co}, I_{en}) + \lambda_G \mathcal{L}_G(I_{en})\right] \tag{1}$$

where λ_I and λ_G control the relative weights of the losses. At the same time, we train discriminator A_γ to minimize the following loss over the same distribution:

$$\mathbb{E}_{I_{co}, M_{in}}\left[\mathcal{L}_A(I_{co}, I_{en})\right]. \tag{2}$$

Network Architecture. A diagram for our system setup is shown in Fig. 2, and details can be found in Appendix A. The **encoder** first applies convolutions to input I_{co} to form some intermediate representation. Next, we aim to incorporate the message input (of length L) in such a way that the encoder can easily learn to embed parts of it at any spatial location of the output. For this reason, we replicate the message spatially, and concatenate this "message volume" to the encoder's intermediary representation. This ensures that each convolutional filter in the next layer has access to the entire message as it convolves across each spatial location. After more convolutional layers, the encoder produces I_{en}, the encoded image. The **noise layer**, given I_{co}, I_{en}, applies noise and produces I_{no}. We do not require I_{no} to have the same dimension as I_{en}, so that we can model dimension-altering noise like cropping. The **decoder** first applies several convolutional layers to produce L feature channels in the intermediate representation. It then applies global spatial average pooling to produce a vector L of the same size of the message – the average pooling ensures that it can handle inputs of different spatial dimensions. It then applies a single linear layer to produce the predicted message. The **adversary** has a structure similar to the decoder, but it outputs a binary classification instead.

Fig. 3. Illustration of non-identity noise layers. JPEG-Mask and JPEG-Drop are differentiable approximations of the JPEG compression (see Fig. 4). **Top:** Encoded image I_{en}. **Middle:** Noised image I_{no}. **Bottom:** Magnified difference $|I_{en} - I_{no}|$. Even under heavy distortion, such as a Crop layer which retains only 3.5% of the original image, our model still learns to recover the watermark with high accuracy (see Sect. 4).

As we shall see, by varying message length L, image size C, H, W, noise layer N and weight factors λ_I and λ_G, the network setup described above can be adapted well to both steganography and watermarking. The specific choices will be discussed in their respective experiments.

Noise Layers. Our model should be able to hide images robustly against a variety of image distortions; for this reason we consider six different types of noise layers which apply different types of image distortion. Examples of all distortion types are shown in Fig. 3.

The **Identity** layer is the simplest: it leaves I_{en} unchanged. The **Dropout** and **Cropout** layers undo some of the changes made by the encoder, producing the noisy image I_{no} by combining pixels from the cover image I_{co} and the encoded image I_{en}. Both types of noise keep a percentage p of pixels from I_{en} and use the rest from I_{co}, but Dropout makes this choice independently per pixel while Cropout keeps a random square crop from I_{en}. The **Gaussian** layer blurs the encoded image I_{en} with a Gaussian kernel of width σ, and the **Crop** layer produces a random square $H' \times W'$ crop of the encoded image, where the ratio of image sizes $\frac{H' \times W'}{H \times W}$ is $p \in (0, 1)$. The **JPEG** layer applies JPEG compression to I_{en} with quality factor $Q \in (0, 100)$. Note that all non-identity noise layers have a scalar hyperparameter governing the *intensity* of the distortion: Dropout, Cropout, and Crop keep a fraction p of the pixels from I_{en}, Gaussian has a kernel width σ; and JPEG has a quality factor Q.

We experiment with an extensive family of distortions for the noise layer, N. Dropout, Crop and Cropout mainly affect the spatial domain, while Gaussian and JPEG act on the frequency domain. Granting the noise layer access to the cover image makes it more challenging as well. For an LSB algorithm, a noise layer that replaces each tampered pixel with a fixed value is analogous to a binary erasure channel, whereas a noise layer that replaces encoded pixels with original pixels acts as a binary symmetric channel. It is harder to be robust against the latter since the decoder has no information about where the tampering happens. Similarly, not only does the crop layer require the decoder to be input size agnostic, it also provides no information about where the $H' \times W'$ crop came from, further limiting the knowledge of the decoder.

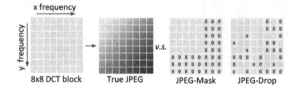

Fig. 4. JPEG compresses an image by performing a discrete cosine transform (DCT) to give an 8×8 grid of frequency components (left) which are then quantized, with higher frequency components quantized more aggressively (middle left; bright red signifies stronger quantization). The DCT transform can be implemented as a single 8 $\times$ 8 stride 8 convolution layer with 64 filters fixed to the DCT basis, but due to the quantization step, JPEG compression is not differentiable. We therefore train models using two differentiable approximations: JPEG-Mask (middle right) zeros a fixed set of high-frequency coefficients, and JPEG-Drop (right) zeros channels with higher drop probabilities for high-frequency coefficients. Models trained against either approximation perform well against true JPEG compression at test time; see Fig. 5.

"Differentiating" the JPEG compression. Although the network is trained with gradient descent, we do not need the test-time noise to be differentiable. We successfully obtain robustness against non-differentiable JPEG compression by training on differentiable approximations. JPEG compression divides the image into 8×8 regions, computes a discrete cosine transformation (DCT) within each region (essentially a change of basis in $\mathbb{R}^{64}$), then quantizes the resulting

frequency-domain coefficients to different coarseness. Thus, only perceptually relevant information is preserved [27]. The quantization step is non-differentiable, rendering JPEG compression unfit for gradient-based optimization.

Nevertheless, quantizing a value is information-theoretically equivalent to limiting the amount of information that can be transmitted through that "channel". To limit the amount of information being passed through specific frequency domain channels, we created noise layers that simulate the JPEG compression. These layers apply the DCT transformation using an 8×8 stride 8 convolution layer with each filter corresponding to a basis vector in the DCT transformation. The network activations thus represent DCT domain coefficients of the encoded image. Masking/Dropout is then applied to the DCT coefficients to limit information flow; higher frequency coefficients are more likely to be masked/dropped, see Fig. 4. The noised image I_{no} is then produced using a transpose convolution to implement the inverse DCT transform.

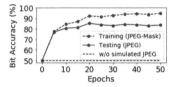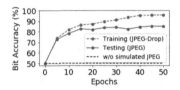

Fig. 5. Bit accuracy for models trained with JPEG-Mask (blue, zero-masking on DCT coefficients) / JPEG-Drop (red, dropout on DCT coefficients). When trained against these approximations (dashed lines), both become robust against actual JPEG compression (solid lines, quality $Q = 50$).

We call the corresponding layers **JPEG-Mask** and **JPEG-Drop**. JPEG-Mask applies a fixed masking that only keeps 25 low frequency DCT coefficients in the Y channel and 9 in the U, V channels (following JPEG, which also preserves more information in the Y channel). The other coefficients are set to zero. JPEG-Drop applies a progressive dropout on the coefficients. The coarser the quantization for a coefficient in actual JPEG compression, the more likely this coefficient is zeroed in our simulation. Both methods successfully produce models that are robust against *actual* JPEG compression, see Fig. 5.

Implementation details. All models are trained on 10,000 cover images from the COCO [28] training set, resized to experiment-specific dimensions. Evaluation is performed on a 1000 image test set unseen during training. Messages are sampled with each bit drawn uniformly at random. For gradient descent, we use Adam [29] with a learning rate of 10^{-3} and default hyperparameters. All models are trained with batch size 12. Models are trained for 200 epochs, or 400 epochs if being trained on multiple noise layers.

4   Experiments

We evaluate our model on three axes: *capacity*, the number of message bits which can be hidden per image bit; *secrecy*, the difficulty of detecting our encoded images; and *robustness*, the degree to which our method can succeed in the face of image distortions.

Metrics. We use a number of metrics to measure our performance along these axes. We measure capacity primarily with **bits per pixel** (BPP), which is the number of message bits hidden per pixel of the encoded image; this is simply $L/(HWC)$ using the notation of Sect. 3. We measure secrecy primarily with **detection rate**; we train a modern steganalyzer [30] which attempts to separate cover from stego images; its test-set accuracy is the detection rate. As a proxy to secrecy, we can also measure the image distortion between the cover and stego image using **peak signal-to-noise ratio** (PSNR); methods which distort the cover image more are likely to be more detectable. We measure robustness using **bit accuracy**, which is the number of identical bits between the input message M and the predicted message M', as we subject the model to varying image distortions between the encoder and decoder during testing.

Many of these metrics compete against each other. Models which have higher capacity typically sacrifice secrecy, since hiding more information in images naturally leads to larger image distortions; models that are very robust to noise typically sacrifice capacity or secrecy, since the message must be encoded in the image redundantly. In some sense, steganography and watermarking are at two ends of a spectrum of problems prioritizing these different axes; steganography stresses secrecy while watermarking emphasizes robustness. Since HiDDeN encompasses a whole family of data hiding algorithms, we can flexibly train models emphasizing different axes by the varying message length L, using different noise layers, and so on.

4.1   Steganography: Capacity and Secrecy

We train our model to encode binary messages of length $L = 52$ in grayscale images of size 16×16, giving our trained model a capacity of $52/(16 \times 16) \approx 0.203$ BPP. For larger images, we use a longer message to preserve encoding capacity. Our model encodes an L-bit chunk of the message on each 16×16 patch of the image. Steganography typically assumes noiseless transmission, so we set N to be the identity layer. We first compare with traditional methods [4,10,11] in Fig. 6 and then with a neural-network-based approach [21] in Fig. 7.

Image quality We compare with three recent steganography methods: HUGO [4], WOW [10], and S-UNIWARD [11]. Each is configured with a capacity of 0.2 BPP to closely match our model. We test all methods on 512×512 cover images from the BOSS dataset [31], which is a common testbed for steganography algorithms. Since our model was trained on COCO, this showcases its generality to new data. Fig. 6 shows example cover and stego images from our method and from HUGO (other classical baselines give results indistinguishable from

HUGO). Both HUGO and our method generate encoded images which are visually indistinguishable from the cover image.

Capacity. Our model closely matches the baselines on BPP (0.203 vs 0.200). One disadvantage of neural networks in steganography is the possibility for the decoder network to make mistakes. As shown in Fig. 6, our method reconstructs the message accurately but not perfectly, having an error rate of $< 10^{-5}$. One can use error correcting codes if higher accuracy is desired.

Secrecy. We measure secrecy by training the steganalyzer ATS [30] to distinguish between cover and stego images for all methods; results are shown in Fig. 6. Following the recommendation of the authors for best performance [30], we provide ATS with small datasets for each algorithm: 250 cover and 250 stego images.

ATS generates an eponymous *artificial training set* from this unlabeled test set by repeatedly applying the steganography algorithm to the data, then uses this artificial training set to train a supervised classifier. Finally, the trained classifier is evaluated on its ability to recognize stego images in the test set.

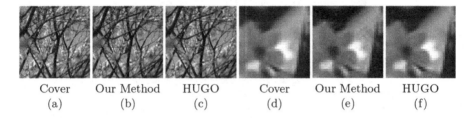

| Cover | Our Method | HUGO | Cover | Our Method | HUGO |
| (a) | (b) | (c) | (d) | (e) | (f) |

Fig. 6. Top: Capacity and secrecy of HiDDeN versus classical steganography methods. With comparable capacity to baselines as measured by bits per pixel and bit accuracy, our method is undetectable (50%, no better than chance) by ATS under the assumption that an adversary has access to the algorithm but not the trained model weights. **Bottom**: Example of 512×512 encoded images. (a) Cover, (b) encoded by our method, (c) encoded by HUGO [4]. (d), (e), (f) are 32×32 crops of (a), (b), (c).

For our model we evaluate two threat scenarios. We first train one encoder-decoder pair and evaluate ATS assuming it has access to the learned model directly. In this setting (model weights known), ATS achieves a detection accuracy of 98%, showing the susceptibility of our model to statistical analysis when the precise weights are known. In the second threat scenario, we consider the case where the attacker knows HiDDeN is being used (and furthermore, knows the precise architecture, hyperparameters and dataset) but does not have access to the trained model itself (which is not exactly reproducible without the random seed used to initialize the parameters). To test this scenario, we train five identical HiDDeN models with different seeds and provide these models to ATS for building its artificial training set. Finally, we train a sixth model with a new random initialization for evaluation. When we test ATS on this sixth model (Ours – different model), it achieves a detection accuracy of 50%, no better than random guessing. In comparison, ATS achieves detection accuracies of 70% for HUGO and 68% for WOW and S-UNIWARD. This result shows that image distortion patterns produced by each trained model are unique, which makes our approach undetectable by ATS without access to the trained model directly. This hints at an advantage of learned steganography models: unlike static classical algorithms, they can employ a diverse set of encoding strategies.

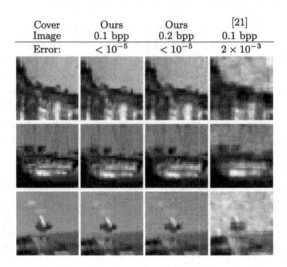

Fig. 7. Comparison of our encoding method against [21]. We encode twice as many bits in images of the same size, while having smaller decoding error and better encoded image quality.

Against other neural network based methods. Compared to [21] which uses a fully connected network to generate encoded images, our method uses convolutional networks, greatly improving encoded image quality. Figure 7 compares our results with [21]; at double their bit rate we achieve lower error and generate images much closer to the cover image.

4.2   Watermarking: Robustness

Digital watermarking prioritizes robustness over capacity and secrecy; it hides only a small message in the image, but that information should remain even after significant distortions are applied to the encoded image. By varying the type of image distortion applied at training time, we show that our model can learn robustness to a variety of different image distortions.

We train our model on YUV color images of size $C \times H \times W = 3 \times 128 \times 128$ with message length $L = 30$ and weight factors $\lambda_I = 0.7$ and $\lambda_G = 0.001$. A model is trained on the identity noise layer as reference. Six models are trained using different noise layers N at training time: Dropout ($p = 0.3$), Cropout

	Digimarc	Identity	Dropout	Cropout	Crop	Gaussian	JPEG-mask	JPEG-drop	Combined
PSNR(Y)	62.12	44.63	42.52	47.24	35.20	40.55	30.09	28.79	33.55
PSNR(U)	38.23	45.44	38.52	40.97	33.31	41.96	35.33	32.51	38.92
PSNR(V)	52.06	46.90	41.05	41.88	35.86	42.88	36.27	33.42	39.38

		Trained with Adversary			No Adversary
Cover	Digimarc	Crop	Gaussian	Combined	Combined

Fig. 8. Image distortions for watermarking algorithms. **Top:** Mean PSNR between cover and encoded images for Digimarc and our model trained with different noise layers. **Bottom:** A cover image and encoded images from both Digimarc and our model trained with Crop, Gaussian, and Combined noise layers. **Bottom Right:** An encoded image from a model trained with combined noise but without an adversary. Adversarial training significantly improves the visual quality of the encoded images.

($p = 0.3$), Crop ($p = 0.035$), Gaussian ($\sigma = 2.0$), JPEG-mask and JPEG-drop. We call these types of noise-resistant models *specialized models* as they are trained to be robust against a particular kind of noise. We additionally train a noise-resistant *combined* model by using a different noise layer for each mini-batch during training. See the supplementary materials for details.

Baseline. To the best of our knowledge, there are no open source implementations of recent methods for digital watermarking. As a baseline we compare to Digimarc [32], a closed source commercial package for digital watermarking. Since Digimarc is closed source, there are certain limitations when comparing HiDDeN against it, especially for comparing transmission accuracy. Detailed analysis and comparison methodology are provided in the appendix.

Qualitative Results. Figure 8 shows qualitative examples of 128×128 images encoded with each of our trained models, as well as a 128×128 image encoded with Digimarc. For each image we report the PSNR between the cover image I_{co} and the encoded image I_{en}. We see that encoded images from our models are visually indistinguishable from the cover image, and that we can train a single model (Combined) that is simultaneously robust to all types of noise without sacrificing image quality.

Adversary. Figure 8 also compares generated images of two models, one trained with the adversary and the other trained without the adversary. Both models are trained on the combined noise layer and tuned individually. The model trained with l_2 loss alone has visible artifacts, as shown in the rightmost image of Fig. 8. The model trained against an adversarial discriminator produces images with no visible artifacts (Fig. 8, second image from the right).

Robustness. The intensity of an image distortion can be controlled with a scalar: keep percentage p for Dropout, Cropout, and Crop, kernel width σ for Gaussian, and quality Q for JPEG compression. Figure 9 shows the bit accuracy of models when they are tested on various noise layers. For each tested noise layer, we evaluate the model trained with the identity noise layer, i.e. no noise (blue), the model trained on the same noise layer (orange), and the model trained on combined noise layers (green). Bit accuracies are measured on 1000 images unseen during training. Figure 10 reports bit accuracy as a function of test time distortion intensity.

The model trained without noise unsurprisingly performs poorly when tested against different noise layers, and fails completely (50% bit accuracy, no better than chance) when tested on Crop and JPEG. Since this model enjoyed lossless transmission between the encoder and decoder during training, it has no incentive to learn robustness to any type of image distortion.

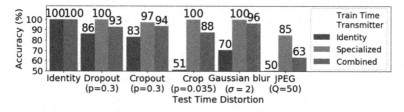

Fig. 9. Robustness of our models against different test time distortions. Each cluster uses a different test time distortion. Identity (blue) is trained with no image distortion; Specialized (orange) is trained on the same type of distortion used during testing; Combined (green) is trained on all types of distortions.

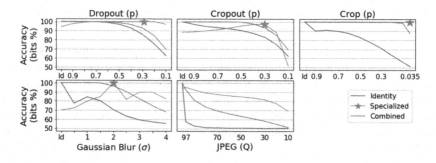

Fig. 10. Bit accuracy under various distortions and intensities. Stars denote the noise intensity used during training. The specialized JPEG model is trained on the differentiable approximation JPEG-Mask, and the plot shows performance on actual JPEG.

However, the high bit accuracies of the Specialized models (orange bars) in Fig. 9 demonstrate that models *can* learn robustness to many different types of image distortion when these distortions are introduced into the training process.

This remains true even when the distortion is non-differentiable: Models trained without noise have 50% bit accuracy when tested against true JPEG compression, but this improves to 85% when trained with simulated JPEG noise.

Finally, we see that in most cases the Combined model, which is trained on all types of noise, is competitive with specialized models despite its increased generality. For example, it achieves 94% accuracy against Cropout, close to the 97% accuracy of the specialized model.

Comparison with Digimarc. Digimarc is closed source, and it only reports success or failure for decoding a fixed-size watermark. It provides no information about its bit error rate, which makes comparing it with HiDDeN difficult.

To ensure a fair comparison, we first estimate the capacity of Digimarc, and then apply an error correcting code that matches HiDDeN's bit rate with Digimarc. This also allows us to converts bit accuracy to decode success rate since a few errors can be corrected (see Appendix B for full methodology). From this analysis, we consider $\geq 95\%$ bit accuracy for our model to be comparable to a successful Digimarc decoding, and $\leq 90\%$ bit accuracy to be a failed decoding.

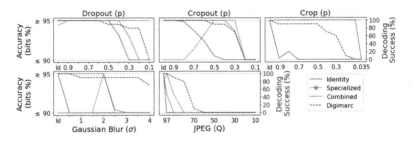

Fig. 11. Model performance under different distortions and intensities. We compare the model trained with no noise (blue), models specialized to a particular distortion (orange), and a Combined model trained on all distortion types (green). We also show Digimarc's decoding success rate for 256×256 images (purple). The two axes are scaled to translate bit accuracy into full reconstruction rate. See Appendix B for detail.

We report the comparison in Fig. 11, with the y-axis clipped according to our analysis. For spatial domain noise, our model exceeds the performance of Digimarc at high noise intensities. Against Dropout ($p = 0.1$), our specialized model has bit accuracy $\geq 95\%$, yet Digimarc fails completely. Against Crop ($p = 0.1$), both the specialized and combined models have bit accuracy $\geq 95\%$, but Digimarc cannot reconstruct any of the ten watermarks tested. For frequency domain noise, our model performs worse than Digimarc. This is likely due to the fact that we baked no assumptions about frequency domain transformations into the architecture, whereas watermarking tools commonly work directly in the frequency domain.

5   Conclusion

We have developed a framework for data hiding in images which is trained end-to-end using neural networks. Compared to classical data hiding methods, ours allows flexibly trading off between capacity, secrecy, and robustness to different types of noise by varying parameters or noise layers at training-time. Compared to deep learning methods for steganography, we demonstrate improved quantitative and qualitative performance. For robust watermarking, HiDDeN is to our knowledge the first end-to-end method using neural networks. Ultimately, end-to-end methods like HiDDeN have a fundamental advantage in robust data-hiding: new distortions can be incorporated directly into the training procedure, with no need to design new, specialized algorithms. In future work, we hope to see improvements in message capacity, robustness to more diverse types of image distortions – such as geometric transforms, contrast change, and other lossy compression schemes – and procedures for data hiding in other input domains, such as audio and video.

Acknowledgements. Our work is supported by an ONR MURI grant. We would like to thank Ehsan Adeli, Rishi Bedi, Jim Fan, Kuan Fang, Adithya Ganesh, Agrim Gupta, De-An Huang, Ranjay Krishna, Damian Mrowca, Ben Zhang and anonymous reviewers for their feedback on our work.

References

1. Goodfellow, I.J., Shlens, J., Szegedy, C.: Explaining and harnessing adversarial examples. In: ICLR (2015)
2. Szegedy, C. et al.: Intriguing properties of neural networks. In: ICLR (2014)
3. Kurakin, A., Goodfellow, I., Bengio, S.: Adversarial examples in the physical world. In: ICLR Workshop (2017)
4. Pevný, T., Filler, T., Bas, P.: Using high-dimensional image models to perform highly undetectable steganography. In: Böhme, R., Fong, P.W.L., Safavi-Naini, R. (eds.) IH 2010. LNCS, vol. 6387, pp. 161–177. Springer, Heidelberg (2010). https://doi.org/10.1007/978-3-642-16435-4_13
5. Bi, N., Sun, Q., Huang, D., Yang, Z., Huang, J.: Robust image watermarking based on multiband wavelets and empirical mode decomposition. IEEE Trans. Image Process. 16(8), 1956–66 (2007)
6. Papernot, N., McDaniel, P., Goodfellow, I., Jha, S., Celik, Z.B., Swami, A.: Practical black-box attacks against machine learning. In: Proceedings of the 2017 ACM on Asia Conference on Computer and Communications Security, pp. 506–519. ACM (2017)
7. Van Schyndel, R.G., Tirkel, A.Z., Osborne, C.F.: A digital watermark. In: IEEE Converence on Image Processing, 1994, IEEE (1994)
8. Wolfgang, R.B., Delp, E.J.: A watermark for digital images. In: Proceedings of International Conference on Image Processing, 1996, vol. 3, pp. 219–222. IEEE (1996)
9. Qin, J., Xiang, X., Wang, M.X.: A review on detection of LSB matching steganography. Inf. Technol. J. 9(8), 1725–1738 (2010)

10. Holub, V., Fridrich, J.: Designing steganographic distortion using directional filters. In: 2012 IEEE International Workshop on Information Forensics and Security (WIFS), pp. 234–239, December 2012
11. Holub, V., Fridrich, J., Denemark, T.: Universal distortion function for steganography in an arbitrary domain. EURASIP J. Inf. Secur. **2014**(1), 1 (2014)
12. Cox, I.J., Kilian, J., Leighton, F.T., Shamoon, T.: Secure spread spectrum watermarking for multimedia. IEEE Trans. Iimage Process. **6**(12), 1673–1687 (1997)
13. Hsieh, M.S., Tseng, D.C., Huang, Y.H.: Hiding digital watermarks using multiresolution wavelet transform. IEEE Trans. Ind. Electron. **48**(5), 875–882 (2001)
14. Pereira, S., Pun, T.: Robust template matching for affine resistant image watermarks. IEEE Trans. Image Process. **9**(6), 1123–1129 (2000)
15. Potdar, V., Han, S., Chang, E.: A survey of digital image watermarking techniques. In: 3rd IEEE International Conference on Industrial Informatics (INDIN 2005), pp. 709–716. IEEE (2005)
16. Zheng, D., Zhao, J., El Saddik, A.: Rst-invariant digital image watermarking based on log-polar mapping and phase correlation. IEEE Trans. Circuits Syst. Video Technol. (2003)
17. Isac, B., Santhi, V.: A study on digital image and video watermarking schemes using neural networks. Int. J. Comput. Appl. **12**(9), 1–6 (2011)
18. Jin, C., Wang, S.: Applications of a neural network to estimate watermark embedding strength. In: Workshop on Image Analysis for Multimedia Interactive Services, IEEE (2007)
19. Kandi, H., Mishra, D., Gorthi, S.R.S.: Exploring the learning capabilities of convolutional neural networks for robust image watermarking. Comput. Secur. (2017)
20. Mun, S.M., Nam, S.H., Jang, H.U., Kim, D., Lee, H.K.: A robust blind watermarking using convolutional neural network. arXiv preprint arXiv:1704.03248 (2017)
21. Hayes, J., Danezis, G.: Generating steganographic images via adversarial training. In: NIPS (2017)
22. Baluja, S.: Hiding images in plain sight: deep steganography. In: NIPS (2017)
23. Abadi, M., Andersen, D.G.: Learning to protect communications with adversarial neural cryptography. arXiv preprint arXiv:1610.06918 (2016)
24. Uchida, Y., Nagai, Y., Sakazawa, S., Satoh, S.: Embedding watermarks into deep neural networks. In: International Conference on Multimedia Retrieval (2017)
25. Fang, T., Jaggi, M., Argyraki, K.: Generating steganographic text with LSTMs. In: ACL Student Research Workshop 2017. Number EPFL-CONF-229881 (2017)
26. Goodfellow, I. et al.: Generative adversarial nets. In: NIPS (2014)
27. Wallace, G.K.: The jpeg still picture compression standard. IEEE Trans. Consum. Electron. **38**(1), xviii–xxxiv (1992)
28. Lin, T.-Y., et al.: Microsoft COCO: common objects in context. In: Fleet, D., Pajdla, T., Schiele, B., Tuytelaars, T. (eds.) ECCV 2014. LNCS, vol. 8693, pp. 740–755. Springer, Cham (2014). https://doi.org/10.1007/978-3-319-10602-1_48
29. Kingma, D., Ba, J.: Adam: a method for stochastic optimization. In: ICLR (2015)
30. Lerch-Hostalot, D., Megas, D.: Unsupervised steganalysis based on artificial training sets. Eng. Appl. Artif. Intell. **50**, 45–59 (2016)
31. Bas, P., Filler, T., Pevný, T.: "Break Our Steganographic System": the ins and outs of organizing BOSS. In: Filler, T., Pevný, T., Craver, S., Ker, A. (eds.) IH 2011. LNCS, vol. 6958, pp. 59–70. Springer, Heidelberg (2011). https://doi.org/10.1007/978-3-642-24178-9_5
32. Digimarc: Digimarc. https://www.digimarc.com/home

Multimodal Dual Attention Memory for Video Story Question Answering

Kyung-Min Kim[1], Seong-Ho Choi[2], Jin-Hwa Kim[3],
and Byoung-Tak Zhang[2,4(✉)]

[1] Clova AI Research, NAVER Corp, Seongnam 13561, South Korea
kmkim@bi.snu.ac.kr
[2] Computer Science and Engineering, Seoul National University,
Seoul 08826, South Korea
{shchoi,btzhang}@bi.snu.ac.kr
[3] SK T-Brain, Seoul 04539, South Korea
jhkim@bi.snu.ac.kr
[4] Surromind Robotics, Seoul 08826, South Korea

Abstract. We propose a video story question-answering (QA) architecture, Multimodal Dual Attention Memory (MDAM). The key idea is to use a dual attention mechanism with late fusion. MDAM uses self-attention to learn the latent concepts in scene frames and captions. Given a question, MDAM uses the second attention over these latent concepts. Multimodal fusion is performed after the dual attention processes (late fusion). Using this processing pipeline, MDAM learns to infer a high-level vision-language joint representation from an abstraction of the full video content. We evaluate MDAM on PororoQA and MovieQA datasets which have large-scale QA annotations on cartoon videos and movies, respectively. For both datasets, MDAM achieves new state-of-the-art results with significant margins compared to the runner-up models. We confirm the best performance of the dual attention mechanism combined with late fusion by ablation studies. We also perform qualitative analysis by visualizing the inference mechanisms of MDAM.

Keywords: Video story QA · Visual QA · Attention mechanism
Multimodal learning · Deep learning

1 Introduction

Question-answering (QA) on a video story based on multimodal content input is an emerging topic in artificial intelligence. In recent years, multimodal deep learning studies have been successfully improving QA performance for still

K.-M. Kim—Work carried out at Seoul National University and Surromind Robotics
J.-H. Kim—Work carried out at Seoul National University.

V. Ferrari et al. (Eds.): ECCV 2018, LNCS 11219, pp. 698–713, 2018.
https://doi.org/10.1007/978-3-030-01267-0_41

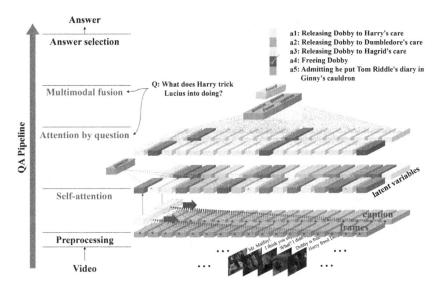

Fig. 1. The system architecture of Multimodal Dual Attention Memory (MDAM). (1) At the self-attention step, MDAM learns the latent variables of frames and captions based on the full video content. (2) For a given question, MDAM attend to the latent variables to remove unnecessary information. (3) At the multimodal fusion step, the question, caption, and frame information are fused using residual learning. During the whole inference process, multimodal fusion occurs only once.

images [1,3,10,23] and video along with supporting content like subtitles, scripts, plot synopses, *etc.* [9,12,16,24]. Please note that video story QA is more challenging than image QA for the following two reasons.

First, video story QA involves multimodal content aligned on time-series. The model must learn the joint representations among at least two multimodal contents and given questions, and those joint representations must consider dynamic patterns over the time-series. Therefore, the use of multimodal fusion methods such as concatenation [8,15] or Multimodal Bilinear Pooling [3,11,16] along with time axis might be prohibitively expensive and have the risk of over-fitting.

Second, video story QA requires to extract high-level meanings from the multimodal contents, *i.e.*, scene frames and captions segmented based on the consistency of story. However, scene frames and captions in a video are redundant, highly-complex, and sometimes ambiguous information for the task, although humans can easily reason and infer based on the understanding of the video storyline in an abstract-level. It implies that humans can successfully extract the latent variables related to the multimodal content, which are used by the process of reasoning and inference. These latent variables are conditioned on a given question to give a correct answer. However, the previous work on video story QA has focused on the understanding of raw scene frames and captions without modeling on the latent variable [9,12,16,24].

Here, we propose a novel model for video story QA task, Multimodal Dual Attention Memory (MDAM), which uses ResNet [6], GloVe [18], positional encoding [4], and casing features [19] to represent scene frames and captions of a video. Then, using multi-head attention networks [22], self-attention calculates the latent variables for the scene frames and captions. For a given question, the MDAM attends to the subset of the latent variables to compress scene frame and caption information to each single representation. After that, multimodal fusion occurs only once during the entire QA process, using the multimodal residual learning used in image QA [10]. This learning pipeline consists of five submodules, preprocessing, self-attention, attention by question, multimodal fusion, and answer selection, which is learned end-to-end, supervised by given annotations. Figure 1 shows the proposed model at an abstract level.

We evaluate our model on the large-scale video story QA datasets, MovieQA [20] and PororoQA [12]. The experimental results demonstrate two hypotheses of our model that (1) maximize QA related information through the dual attention process considering high-level video contents, and (2) multimodal fusion should be applied after high-level latent information is captured by our early process.

The main contributions of this paper are as follow: (1) we propose a novel video story QA architecture with two hypotheses for video understanding; dual attention and late multimodal fusion, (2) we achieve the state-of-the-art results on both PororoQA and MovieQA datasets, and our model is ranked at the first entry in the *MovieQA Challenge* at the time of submission.

2   Related Works

2.1   Video Story QA Datasets

MovieQA aims to provide a movie dataset with high semantic diversity [20]. The dataset consists of 408 movies and 14,944 multiple choices QAs. The dataset includes the stories of various genres such as action, fantasy, and drama; hence a QA model must be able to handle a variety of stories. The tasks of MovieQA can be divided into a text story QA mode (8,482 QA pairs) and a video story QA mode (6,462 QA pairs). The *MovieQA Challenge* provides the evaluation server for test split so that participants can evaluate the performance of their models from this server.

Unlike MovieQA, PororoQA focuses on a coherent storyline [12]. Since the videos are from a cartoon series, they provide more structured and simpler storylines. The dataset contains 27,328 scene descriptions and 8,834 multiple choices QA pairs with 171 videos of the children's cartoon video series, *Pororo*.

2.2   Video Story QA Models

Deep Embedded Memory Networks (DEMN) [12] replaces videos with generated text by combining scene descriptions and captions represented in a common linear embedding space. To solve QA tasks, DEMN evaluates all question-story sentence-answer triplets with the supervision of question and story sentence.

Read Write Memory Networks (RWMN) [16] fuse individual captions with the corresponding frames using Compact Bilinear Pooling [3] and store them in memory slots. Given the fact that each memory slot is not an independent entity, multi-layer convolutional neural networks are used to represent temporally adjacent slots. Our model provides a better solution to capture the latent variables of scene frames and captions through our dual attention mechanism for the full memory slots compared to the convolutional approach. Note that our multimodal fusion is applied to the latent variables instead of the early fusion in this work for high-level reasoning process.

ST-VQA applies attention mechanism on both spatial and temporal features of the videos [9]. Unlike our proposed model, these attentions are only given to scene frames since the input of ST-VQA is short video clips such as GIFs without captions. ST-VQA concatenates C3D [21] and residual network features extracted from every interval of a video clip to obtain the spatial features. The model then calculates the temporal features of the intervals by feeding the spatial features into an LSTM. Given a question, attention mechanism is applied to both spatial and temporal features.

3   Multimodal Dual Attention Memory

Our goal is to build a video QA model that maximizes information needed for QA through attention mechanisms and fuses the multimodal information at a high-level of abstraction. We tackle this problem by introducing the two attention layers, which leverage the multi-head attention functions [22], followed by the residual learning of multimodal fusion.

Figure 2 shows the overall architecture of our proposed model - Multimodal Dual Attention Memory(MDAM) for video story QA. The MDAM consists of five modules. (1) The first module is the preprocessing module. All input including frames and captions of a given video is converted to the tensor formats. (2) In the self-attention module, the MDAM learns to obtain latent variables of the preprocessed frames and captions based on the whole video content. This process mimics a human who watches the full content of a video and then understands the story by recalling the frames and captions himself using the episodic buffer [2]. (3) In the attention by question module, the MDAM learns to give attention scores to find the relevant latent variables for a given question. It can be regarded as a cognitive process of finding points that contain answer information based on the understood story. (4) These attentively refined frames and captions, and a question are fused using the residual function in the multimodal fusion module. (5) Finally, the answer selection module selects the correct answer by producing confidence score values over the five candidate answer sentences.

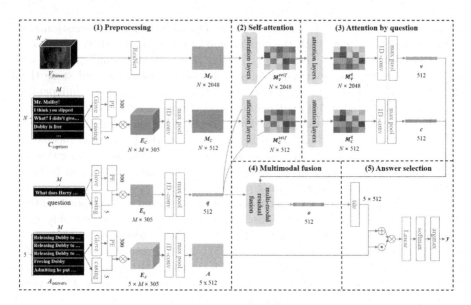

Fig. 2. Five steps in our processing pipeline of Multimodal Dual Attention Memory for the video story QA task. (1) All given inputs are embedded as tensors and stored into long-term memory (Sect. 3.1). (2) The frame tensor M_V^{self} and caption tensor M_C^{self} have latent variables of the frames and captions through the self-attention mechanism (Sect. 3.2 and Fig. 3). (3) By using attention once again but with a question, the frames and captions are abstracted by the rank-1 tensors v and c (Sect. 3.3 and Fig. 3). (4) The fused representation o is calculated using residual learning fusion (Sect. 3.4 and Fig. 4). (5) Finally, the correct answer sentence is selected with element-wise operations followed by the softmax classifier (Sect. 3.5).

3.1   Preprocessing

The input of the model is composed of (1) a sequence of frames V_{frames} and (2) a sequence of captions $C_{captions}$ of a video clip $I_{clip} = \{ V_{frames}, C_{captions} \}$, (3) a question, and (4) a set of five candidate answer sentences $A_{answers} = (a_1, \ldots, a_5)$. V_{frames} and $C_{captions}$ consist of N multiple frames and captions, $V_{frames} = (v_1, \ldots, v_N)$, $C_{captions} = (c_1, \ldots, c_N)$, where c_i is a i-th dialogue caption of the I_{clip}, and v_i is an image frame sampled at the midpoint between the start and end times of the caption c_i. The value of the story length N is fixed differently depending on the dataset used in this work. If the number of captions in the video is less than N, zero padding is added. In Sect. 4.2, we will report the values of the hyperparameters.

The main purpose of the preprocessing module is to transform the raw input as tensor formats, $M_V \in \mathbb{R}^{N \times 2048}$, $M_C \in \mathbb{R}^{N \times 512}$, $q \in \mathbb{R}^{512}$, $A \in \mathbb{R}^{5 \times 512}$, respectively, and store these in long-term memory, *e.g.*, RAM.

Linguistic Inputs. We first convert $C_{captions}$, question, $A_{answers}$ as word-level tensor representations, $E_C \in \mathbb{R}^{N \times M \times 305}$, $E_q \in \mathbb{R}^{M \times 305}$, $E_A \in \mathbb{R}^{5 \times M \times 305}$, respectively. M is the fixed value denoting the maximum number of words in a sentence. Like the story length N, the value of M depends on the dataset. For a sentence with less than M words, zero padding is added. To represent each word of the inputs, we concatenate 300-D GloVe [18] with positional encoding [4], and 5-D casing features.

GloVe and Positional Encoding. Each word in the sentences is mapped to a GloVe embedding followed by positional encoding.

$$e_i = g_i + p_i \in \mathbb{R}^{300} \tag{1}$$

where g_i is GloVe embedding, and p_i is the learnable embedding vector of the position index i. e_i is an output embedding.

Casing Features. As is used in the existing NLP studies [19], we add the following 5-D flag for each word representation. (1) A capitalization flag. This flag assigns the label True if at least one character of a word is upper-cased. (2) A numeric flag that assigns the label True if at least one character is numeric. (3) A personal pronouns flag that captures whether the word is a personal pronoun, *e.g.*, she, he, they. (4) A unigram flag and (5) A bigram flag that indicate whether there is a unigram/bigram match between question and captions or question and candidate answer sentences. The casing feature is mapped to a five-dimensional zero-one vector.

To obtain 512-D sentence-level tensor representations, we apply the shared 1-D convolution layers consisting of filters with varying window sizes $w_{conv}^{e_1} \in \mathbb{R}^{M \times 1 \times 1 \times 128}$, $w_{conv}^{e_2} \in \mathbb{R}^{M \times 2 \times 1 \times 128}$, $w_{conv}^{e_3} \in \mathbb{R}^{M \times 3 \times 1 \times 128}$, $w_{conv}^{e_4} \in \mathbb{R}^{M \times 4 \times 1 \times 128}$ and max pooling operations to the word-level tensor representations, $\boldsymbol{E}_C$, $\boldsymbol{E}_q$, $\boldsymbol{E}_A$ [13].

$$\boldsymbol{M}_C[i] = \max(\text{ReLU}(\text{conv}(\boldsymbol{E}_C[i,:,:], [w_{conv}^{e_1}, w_{conv}^{e_2}, w_{conv}^{e_3}, w_{conv}^{e_4}]))) \tag{2}$$

$$\boldsymbol{q} = \max(\text{ReLU}(\text{conv}(\boldsymbol{E}_q, [w_{conv}^{e_1}, w_{conv}^{e_2}, w_{conv}^{e_3}, w_{conv}^{e_4}]))) \tag{3}$$

$$\boldsymbol{A}[j] = \max(\text{ReLU}(\text{conv}(\boldsymbol{E}_A[j,:,:], [w_{conv}^{e_1}, w_{conv}^{e_2}, w_{conv}^{e_3}, w_{conv}^{e_4}]))) \tag{4}$$

where conv (input, filters) means the convolution layer, ReLU is the elementwise ReLU activation [17]. Finally, the output tensors for the captions, question, answer sentences are $\boldsymbol{M}_C \in \mathbb{R}^{N \times 512}$, $\boldsymbol{q} \in \mathbb{R}^{512}$, $\boldsymbol{A} \in \mathbb{R}^{5 \times 512}$, respectively, and they are stored into long-term memory.

Visual Inputs. The 2048-D sized activation output of 152-layer residual networks [6] is used to represent V_{frame} as $\boldsymbol{M}_V \in \mathbb{R}^{N \times 2048}$. It is stored in long-term memory.

3.2   Self-attention

This module imports the frame tensor $\boldsymbol{M}_V \in \mathbb{R}^{N \times 2048}$, and caption tensor $\boldsymbol{M}_C \in \mathbb{R}^{N \times 512}$ from the long-term memory as input. The output is the tensors

$M_V^{self} \in \mathbb{R}^{N \times 2048}$ and $M_C^{self} \in \mathbb{R}^{N \times 512}$ that have latent values of the input by using attention layers [22]. The module provides separate attention to frames and captions.

Figure 3(a) shows the process of the attention layers consisting of L_{attn} identical layers [22]. Each layer has two sub-layers; (1) multi-head self-attention networks and (2) point-wise fully connected feed forward networks. There are a residual connection and layer normalization between each sub-layer. The L_{attn} layers use different learning parameters for each layer.

Multi-head Self-attention Networks. In this sub-layer, each frame and caption can attend to all frames and captions including itself to obtain a latent variable. It is achieved by selecting one pivot from the frames or captions and updating it using the attention mechanism. Figure 3(b) illustrates the detailed process. There are a pivot $p \in \mathbb{R}^{d_k}$ and key set $K \in \mathbb{R}^{N \times d_k}$. K is the output of the previous layer or the input embedding, $i.e.$, M_V, M_C, for the first layer. Each row vector of K is a key whose latent variable is to be computed. d_k is the dimension of the key, $i.e.$, 512 or 2048. The pivot p is selected from one of the N keys of K.

First, the networks project the pivot p and N keys to d_{proj} dimensions h times, with different, learnable projection matrices. Then, for each projection, the weighted average using the scores obtained from the dot product-based attention by pivot p aggregates N keys.

$$head_i = \text{average}(\text{DotProdAttn}(pW_i^p, KW_i^K))) \in \mathbb{R}^{d_{proj}} \tag{5}$$

$$\text{where DotProdAttn}(x, Y) = \text{softmax}(xY^T / \sqrt{d_{proj}})Y \tag{6}$$

h outputs are concatenated and projected once again to become the updated key value $\tilde{K}[j, :]$ if the pivot p is $K[j, :]$.

$$\tilde{K}[j, :] = (head_1 \otimes \cdots \otimes head_h)W_o \in \mathbb{R}^{d_k} \tag{7}$$

where $\otimes$ denotes concatenation, and $W_o \in \mathbb{R}^{h d_{proj} \times d_k}$ is a projection matrix. The networks change a pivot p from $K[1, :]$ to $K[N, :]$ and repeat the Eqs. (5)–(7) to obtain the updated key set $\tilde{K}$.

In this work, we use $h = 8$, $d_{proj} = 64$. In Sect. 4.3, we will report the model performances according to the various L_{attn} values.

Feed Forward Networks. Fully-connected feed forward networks apply two linear transformations and a ReLU activation function separately and identically for every point of the input.

$$\text{FFN}(x) = \text{ReLU}(xW_1 + b_1)W_2 + b_2 \tag{8}$$

where x is a point of the input. The dimension size of input and output is d_k, and the inner-layer has a dimension size of $2d_k$.

3.3 Attention by Question

This module takes the final output tensors, M_V^{self}, M_C^{self}, of the self-attention module and again calculates the attention scores separately, by using the question. Attention information is aggregated using the 1-D convolutional neural networks to produce the output, $v \in \mathbb{R}^{512}$ and $c \in \mathbb{R}^{512}$, for the frames and captions, respectively.

Multi-head Attention Networks. Like the self-attention module of Sect. 3.2, this module uses the attention layers consisting of L_{attn} identical layers illustrated in Fig. 3(a) [22]. However, the attention layers differ from that of the self-attention module in that they have the multi-head attention networks inside.

Figure 3(c) shows the multi-head attention networks. The networks calculate the updated key set $\tilde{K}$ by applying attention to the key set K as in Eqs. (5)–(7), but there are three differences when calculating Eqs. (5) and (7). (1) The networks use the question tensor q as a pivot by reading from the long-term memory. (2) The networks calculate the attention output values without average, i.e., $head_i = \text{DotProdAttn}(...) \in \mathbb{R}^{N \times d_{proj}}$. (3) The output of the Eq. (7) becomes $\tilde{K} \in \mathbb{R}^{N \times d_k}$ which is not a specific point of $\tilde{K}$.

We denote the final output of the attention layers as $M_V^q \in \mathbb{R}^{N \times 2048}$ and $M_C^q \in \mathbb{R}^{N \times 512}$. Then, these are seperately aggregated using the 1-D convolutional neural networks and max pooling operation to get the outputs $v \in \mathbb{R}^{512}$ and $c \in \mathbb{R}^{512}$.

$$v = \max(\text{ReLU}(\text{conv}(M_V^q, [w_{conv}^{v1}, w_{conv}^{v2}, w_{conv}^{v3}, w_{conv}^{v4}]))) \tag{9}$$

$$c = \max(\text{ReLU}(\text{conv}(M_C^q, [w_{conv}^{c1}, w_{conv}^{c2}, w_{conv}^{c3}, w_{conv}^{c4}]))) \tag{10}$$

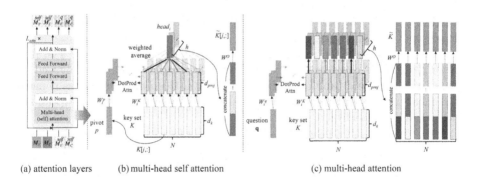

(a) attention layers   (b) multi-head self attention   (c) multi-head attention

Fig. 3. (a) Illustration of the attention layers consisting of L_{attn} identical layers. The self-attention module uses the multi-head self-attention networks while the attention by question module uses the multi-head attention networks. (b) The multi-head self-attention networks select a pivot p from the key set K to obtain the updated key set $\tilde{K}$. (c) The multi-head attention networks use the question q as a pivot to obtain the updated key set $\tilde{K}$.

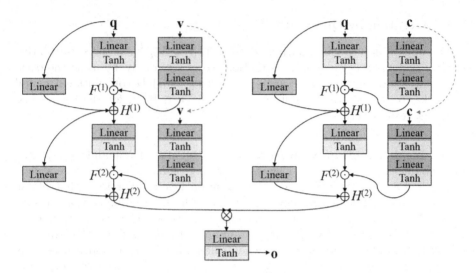

Fig. 4. A schematic diagram of the multimodal fusion module with the two deep residual blocks. The final output o is the concatenation of the outputs from the two residual blocks, $H^{(2)}$(question q - frame v) and $H^{(2)}$(question q - caption c), followed by a linear projection and *tanh* activation.

where $w_{conv}^{v_i} \in \mathbb{R}^{2048 \times i \times 1 \times 128}$ denote 1-D convolution filters of length i for M_V^q, and $w_{conv}^{c_i} \in \mathbb{R}^{512 \times i \times 1 \times 128}$ denote 1-D convolution filters of length i for M_C^q.

3.4 Multimodal Fusion

During the entire QA process, multimodal fusion occurs only once in this module. The module fuses the refined frames $v \in \mathbb{R}^{512}$, and captions $c \in \mathbb{R}^{512}$, with the question $q \in \mathbb{R}^{512}$ to output a single representation $o \in \mathbb{R}^{512}$. We borrow the idea of multimodal residual learning [10].

Figure 4 illustrates an example of our multimodal fusion module. The final output, o, is the concatenation of the two deep residual blocks, followed by linear projection and tanh activation. Each of the deep residual blocks consists of element-wise multiplication of question q and frames v, or q and captions c, with residual connection.

$$o = \sigma(W_o(H^{(L_m)}(q, v) \otimes H^{(L_m)}(q, c))) \qquad (11)$$

$$\text{where } H^{(L_m)}(q, x) = q \prod_{l=1}^{L_m} W_q^{(l)} + \sum_{l=1}^{L_m} \{F^{(l)}(H^{(l-1)}, x) \prod_{n=l+1}^{M} W_q^{(n)}\} \qquad (12)$$

$$F^{(l)}(H, x) = \sigma(HW_H^{(l)}) \odot \sigma(\sigma(xW_1^{(l)})W_2^{(l)}) \qquad (13)$$

where L_m is the depth of the learning blocks. We use various values for L_m in this work. $\otimes$ is the concatenation operation, σ is the element-wise *tanh* activation, and $\odot$ is the element-wise multiplication. $H^{(L_m)}(q, v)$ and $H^{(L_m)}(q, c)$ use different learning parameters.

3.5   Answer Selection

This module learns to select the correct answer sentence using the basic element-wise calculation between the output of multimodal fusion module, $o \in \mathbb{R}^{512}$, and the answer sentence tensor, $A \in \mathbb{R}^{5 \times 512}$, which is read from the long-term memory, followed by the softmax classifier.

$$O_A = (o_{tile} \odot A) \otimes (o_{tile} \oplus A) \tag{14}$$
$$z = \mathrm{softmax}(O_A W + b) \tag{15}$$

where $o_{tile} \in \mathbb{R}^{5 \times 512}$ is the tiled tensor of o. $\oplus$ is the element-wise addition. $z \in \mathbb{R}^5$ is the confidence score vector over the five candidate answer sentences. Finally, we predict the answer y with the highest score value, $y = argmax_{i \in [1,5]}(z_i)$.

4   Experimental Results

4.1   Dataset

The MovieQA dataset for the video QA mode consists of 140 movies with 6,462 QA pairs [20]. Each question is coupled with a set of five possible answers; one correct and four incorrect answers. A QA model should choose a correct answer for a given question only using provided video clips and subtitles. The average length of a video clip is 202 s. If there are multiple video clips given in one question, we link them together into a single video clip. The number of QA pairs in train/val/test are 4318/886/1258, respectively.

The PororoQA dataset has 171 episodes with 8,834 QA pairs [12]. Like MovieQA, each question has one correct answer sentence and four incorrect answer sentences. One episode consists of a video clip of 431 s average length. For experiments, we split all 171 episodes into train(103 ep.)/val(34 ep.)/test(34 ep.) sets. The number of QA pairs in train/val/test are 5521/1955/1437, respectively. Unlike the MovieQA, the PororoQA has supporting fact labels that indicate which of the frames and captions of the video clip contain correct answer information, and description set. However, because our model does not use any supporting fact label or description, we do not use them in the experiment.

4.2   Experimental Setup

Pretrained Parameters. In the preprocessing module, *ResNet-152* [6] pre-trained with *ImageNet* is used to encode the raw visual input, V_{frame}. GloVe [18] pre-trained with *Gigaword 5* and *Wikipedia 2014* consisting of 6B tokens is used to encode the raw linguistic input, $C_{captions}$, question, and $A_{answers}$.

Hyperparameters. For MovieQA, we limit the number of sentences per video clip to 40, *i.e.*, $N = 40$, and the number of words per sentence to 60, *i.e.*, $M = 60$. For PororoQA, we use $N = 20$ and $M = 100$. These are the maximum lengths of the sentences and words in each dataset. Sentences or words below the given length are padded with zero values. We prevent the zero padding from participating in the error in the learning process.

The learnable parameters are initialized using the Xavier method [5] except for the pretrained models. The batch size is 16, and the number of epochs is fixed to 160. Adam [14] is used for optimization, and dropouts [7] are used for regularization.

For learning rate and loss function, we empirically found that good parameters can be obtained by pre-training the model with the cross-entropy loss between the ground-truth one-hot vector z_{gt} and prediction z at a learning rate of 0.01 and then learning it again with the categorical hinge loss at a learning rate of 0.0001 from the best point.

We train 20 different models and ensemble them using bayesian optimization.

Baselines. To compare the performance of each component, we conduct the ablation experiments with the following five model variants. (1) MDAM-MulFusion: model using element-wise multiplication instead of the residual learning function in the multimodal fusion module (self-attention is used). (2) MDAM-FrameOnly: model using only scene frames. (3) MDAM-CaptOnly: model using only captions. (4) MDAM-EarlyFusion: model that moves the position of the multimodal fusion module forward in the QA pipeline; thus the information flow goes through the following steps (i) preprocessing, (ii) multimodal fusion, (iii) self-attention, (iv) attention by question, (v) answer selection. The fusions of frames and captions occur N times by fusing M_V and M_C. (5) MDAM-NoSelfAttn: model without the self-attention module. Furthermore, we measure the performance comparisons between our MDAM and other state-of-the-art models.

4.3   Quantitative Results

MovieQA. We report the experimental results of our model for validation and test sets. We conduct the ablation experiments using the validation set to set the hyper-parameters of our models. Based on these results, we participated in the *MovieQA Challenge*. At the time of submission of the paper, our MDAM has recorded the highest accuracy of 41.41%

Ablation Experiments Fig. 5 shows the results of the ablation experiments. Due to the small size of the MovieQA data set, the overall performance pattern shows a tendency to decrease as the depth of the attention layers L_{attn} and the depth of the learning blocks in the multimodal fusion module L_m increase. Comparing the performance results by module, the models, in which multimodal fusions occur early in the QA pipeline (MDAM-EarlyFusion), shows little performance difference with the models, which use only sub-part of the video input (MDAM-FrameOnly, MDAM-CaptOnly). In addition, even if multimodal fusion occurs

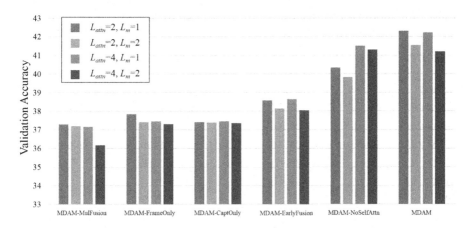

Fig. 5. The results of the model variants on the validation set of MovieQA. L_{attn} denotes the number of layers in the attention networks. L_m denotes the depth of the learning blocks in the multimodal fusion module.

late, the performance is degraded where a simple element-wise multiplication is used as the fusion method (MDAM-MulFusion). Finally, the MDAM with self-attention through the full video content performs the best among our variant models. These results imply the validity of our hypotheses of the model that (1) maximize the QA related information through the dual attention module and (2) fuse the multimodal information at a high-level of abstraction.

MovieQA Challenge The *MovieQA Challenge* provides a separate evaluation server for the test set so that participants can evaluate the performance of their models using the server. The evaluation is limited to once for every 72 h.

Table 1 shows the performance comparison with the other models released on the *MovieQA Challenge* leaderboard. Our MDAM ($L_{attn} = 2$, $L_m = 1$) achieves 41.41% and shows the performance gain of 2.38% compared to the runner-up model, Layered Memory Network, which achieves 39.03%.

PororoQA. In Table 2, we present the experimental results of our MDAM for the PororoQA dataset. The comparative models are the five MDAM variants and the existing baseline methods (BoW V+Q, W2V V+Q, LSTM V+Q) which do not use the descriptions and supporting fact labels like ours [12]. As a result, MDAM achieves a state-of-the art performance (48.9%), marginally beating the existing methods. Furthermore, we observe that the two hypotheses of MDAM are valid in PororoQA. The self-attention module helps MDAM achieve better performance (48.9% for MDAM vs. 47.3% for MDAM-NoSelfAttn), and multimodal fusion with high-level latent information by our module performs better than early fusion baseline (46.1% for MDAM-EarlyFusion). All MDAM variants use $L_{attn} = 2$ and $L_m = 1$.

Table 1. Performance comparison with other models proposed in the *MovieQA Challenge* leaderboard of the video QA section.

Method	Test
LSTM+CNN	23.45
Simple MLP	24.09
LSTM+discriminative CNN	24.32
DEMN [12]	29.97
MuSM	34.74
RWMN [16]	36.25
Local Avg. pooling networks	38.16
Layered Memory Networks	39.03
MDAM (ours)	**41.41**

Table 2. Performance comparison between other models proposed in [12] and MDAM variants on the test set of PororoQA.

Method	Test
LSTM+CNN	23.45
Simple MLP	24.09
LSTM+discriminative CNN	24.32
DEMN [12]	29.97
MuSM	34.74
RWMN [16]	36.25
Local Avg. pooling networks	38.16
Layered Memory Networks	39.03
MDAM (ours)	**41.41**

4.4 Qualitative Results

In this section, we visually analyze the inference mechanism of MDAM. Figure 6 shows the selected qualitative results of MDAM and MDAM without self-attention (MDAM-NoSelfAttn) for MovieQA.

Figure 6(a)–(c) show the successful examples of MDAM. Given a question, MDAM solves the QA task correctly by attending to frames and captions containing answer-related information, which is performed by the attention by question module. Note that the model attends to frames and captions separately. It allows the model to focus on single modality one-by-one in the self-attention and attention by question modules for scene frames and captions in parallel.

Figure 6(d) shows a challenging example of the MovieQA dataset. The given video clip persists similar scenes with a long narrative by the character. These inputs make our MDAM to be challenging to select keyframes and corresponding captions which contain the information related to the given question, *i.e.* time interval and the location of the watch.

5 Concluding Remarks

We proposed a video story QA architecture, MDAM. The fundamental idea of MDAM is to provide the dual attention structure that captures a high-level abstraction of the full video content by learning the latent variables of the video input, *i.e.*, frames and captions, then, late multimodal fusion is applied to get a joint representation. We empirically demonstrated that our architectural choice is valid by showing the state-of-the-art performance on MovieQA and PrororQA datasets. Exploring various alternative models in our ablation studies, we conjecture the following two points: (1) The position of multimodal fusion in our

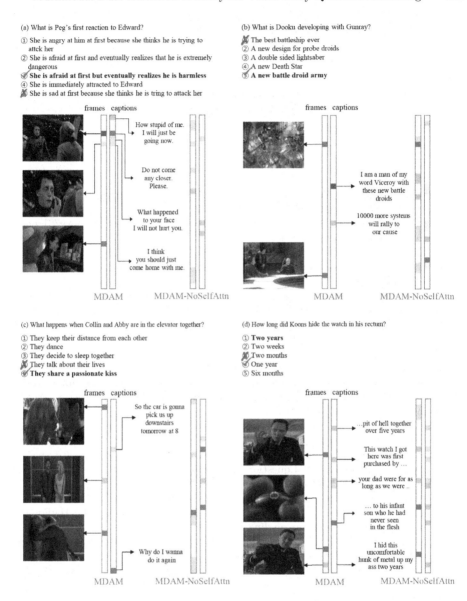

Fig. 6. Qualitative results for the MovieQA of MDAM with and without the self-attention module (MDAM and MDAM-NoSelfAttn, respectively). The successful cases are (a), (b), and (c), and the failure case is (d). Bold sentences are ground-truth answers. Green check symbols indicate the predictions of MDAM. Red cross symbols indicate the predictions of MDAM-NoSelfAttn. In each case, we show that which scene frames and captions are attended by the model for a given question.

QA pipeline is important to increase the performance. We learned that the early fusion models are easy to overfit, and the training loss fluctuates during a training phase due to many fusions occurred on time domain. On the other hand, the late fusion model were faster in convergence, leading to better performance results. (2) For a given question, it is useful to attend to video content after self-attention. Because questions and scene frames are different modalities, *i.e.*, language and vision, attending to a subset of the frames using a question tends to get a poor result if two hidden representations are not sufficiently aligned. Our self-attention module relieved this problem by calculating latent variables of frames and captions.

References

1. Agrawal, A., Lu, J., Antol, S., Mitchell, M., Zitnick, C.L., Batra, D., Parikh, D.: Vqa: Visual question answering. In: ICCV (2015)
2. Baddeley, A.: The episodic buffer: a new component of working memory? Trends Cogn. Sci. **4**(11), 417–423 (2000)
3. Fukui, A., Park, D.H., Yang, D., Rohrbach, A., Darrell, T., Rohrbach, M.: Multimodal compact bilinear pooling for visual question answering and visual grounding. In: EMNLP (2016)
4. Gehring, J., Auli, M., Grangier, D., Yarats, D., Dauphin, Y.N.: Convolutional sequence to sequence learning. Arxiv eprint arXiv:1705.03122 (2017)
5. Glorot, X., Bengio, Y.: Understanding the difficulty of training deep feedforward neural networks. In: AISTATS (2010)
6. He, K., Zhang, X., Ren, S., Sun, J.: Deep residual learning for image recognition. In: CVPR (2016)
7. Hinton, G.E., Srivastava, N., Krizhevsky, A., Sutskever, I., Salakhutdinov, R.R.: Improving neural networks by preventing co-adaptation of feature detectors. ArXiv eprint arXiv:1207.0580 (2012)
8. Jabri, A., Joulin, A., van der Maaten, L.: Revisiting visual question answering baselines. In: ECCV (2016)
9. Jang, Y.S., Song, Y., Yu, Y.J., Kim, Y.J., Kim, G.H.: Tgif-qa: Toward spatio-temporal reasoning in visual question answering. In: CVPR (2017)
10. Kim, J.H., Lee, S.W., Kwak, D.H., Heo, M.O., Kim, J.H., Ha, J.W., Zhang, B.T.: Multimodal residual learning for visual qa. In: NIPS (2016)
11. Kim, J.H., On, K.W., Lim, W.S., Kim, J.H., Ha, J.W., Zhang, B.T.: Hadamard product for low-rank bilinear pooling. In: ICLR (2017)
12. Kim, K.M., Heo, M.O., Choi, S.H., Zhang, B.T.: Deep story video story qa by deep embedded memory networks. In: IJCAI (2017)
13. Kim, Y.: Convolutional neural networks for sentence classification. In: EMNLP (2014)
14. Kingma, D.P., Ba, J.: Adam: a method for stochastic optimization. In: ICLR (2015)
15. Lu, J., Yang, J., Batra, D., Parikh, D.: Hierarchical question-image co-attention for visual question answering. In: NIPS (2016)
16. Na, S.I., Lee, S.H., Kim, J.S., Kim, G.H.: A read-write memory network for movie story understanding. In: ICCV (2017)
17. Nair, V., Hinton, G.E.: Rectified linear units improve restricted boltzmann machines. In: ICML (2010)
18. Pennington, J., Socher, R., Manning, C.D.: Glove: global vectors for word representation. In: EMNLP (2014)
19. Reimers, N., Gurevych, I.: Optimal hyperparameters for deep lstm-networks for sequence labeling tasks. In: EMNLP (2017)

20. Tapaswi, M., Zhu, Y., Stiefelhagen, R., Torralba, A., Urtasun, R., Fidler, S.: Movieqa: Understanding stories in movies through question-answering. In: CVPR (2016)
21. Tran, D., Bourdev, L.D., Fergus, R., Torresani, L., Paluri, M.: Learning spatiotemporal features with 3d convolutional networks. In: ICCV (2015)
22. Vaswani, A., Shazeer, N., Parmar, N., Uszkoreit, J., Jones, L., Gomez, A.N., Kaiser, L., Polosukhin, I.: Attention is all you need. In: NIPS (2017)
23. Xu, H., Saenko, K.: Ask, attend and answer: exploring question guided spatial attention for visual question answering. In: ECCV (2016)
24. Zeng, K.H., Chen, T.H., Chuang, C.Y., Liao, Y.H., Niebles, J.C., Sun, M.: Leveraging video descriptions to learn video question answering. In: AAAI (2017)

Deep Variational Metric Learning

Xudong Lin, Yueqi Duan, Qiyuan Dong, Jiwen Lu$^{(\boxtimes)}$, and Jie Zhou

Tsinghua University, Beijing 100084, China
stein6@163.com, {duanyq14,dqy15}@mails.tsinghua.edu.cn,
{lujiwen,jzhou}@tsinghua.edu.cn

Abstract. Deep metric learning has been extensively explored recently, which trains a deep neural network to produce discriminative embedding features. Most existing methods usually enforce the model to be indiscriminating to intra-class variance, which makes the model over-fitting to the training set to minimize loss functions on these specific changes and leads to low generalization power on unseen classes. However, these methods ignore a fact that in the central latent space, the distribution of variance within classes is actually independent on classes. In this paper, we propose a deep variational metric learning (DVML) framework to explicitly model the intra-class variance and disentangle the intra-class invariance, namely, the class centers. With the learned distribution of intra-class variance, we can simultaneously generate discriminative samples to improve robustness. Our method is applicable to most of existing metric learning algorithms, and extensive experiments on three benchmark datasets including CUB-200-2011, Cars196 and Stanford Online Products show that our DVML significantly boosts the performance of currently popular deep metric learning methods.

Keywords: Metric learning · Variational auto-encoder
Discriminative samples generating

1 Introduction

Metric learning aims to learn a mapping with covariant relationship of distance. A good metric produces embeddings where samples from the same class have small distances and samples from different classes have large distances. Recent supervised metric learning methods uncover the potential of deep convolutional neural networks as the nonlinear mapping function through designing sampling algorithms [8,10,18,21,24,34,37,40] or modifying loss functions [3,7,18,23,33, 36,37]. These methods usually share the same motivation of better maximizing

Electronic supplementary material The online version of this chapter (https://doi.org/10.1007/978-3-030-01267-0_42) contains supplementary material, which is available to authorized users.

© Springer Nature Switzerland AG 2018
V. Ferrari et al. (Eds.): ECCV 2018, LNCS 11219, pp. 714–729, 2018.
https://doi.org/10.1007/978-3-030-01267-0_42

inter-class distance and minimize intra-class distance. Behind this motivation, there is actually a basic assumption that every sample from the same class shares the same embedding feature. However, is this assumption really accurate?

In this paper, we provide a negative answer. Indeed, there are intra-class variances, such as pose, view point, illumination, etc., and a robust model should be able to handle these variances. However given a limited training set, deep models will easily be over-fitting if we force it to be indiscriminating to these intra-class variances. For example, in image classification, if the illumination of the object region varies too much among different samples, the model would probably be trained to ignore these important parts but to classify the training samples from their backgrounds. This leads to poor generalization ability. Therefore this assumption is ideal but not practical.

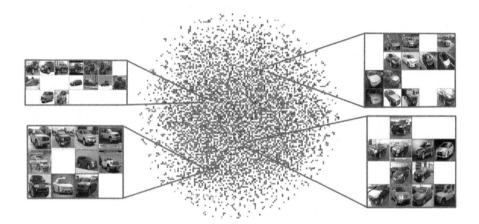

Fig. 1. Our insight: in the central latent space, the distribution of intra-class variance is independent on classes. This is the visualization of central latent space of features learned with the N-pair loss [23] using Barnes-Hut t-SNE [30] on the Cars196 test set. The color of the bounding box for each image represents the class label. Here we construct central latent space through subtracting samples' class centers from their features. We assumed and verified that similar change of original images, like the same pose change or the same view-point change, affects their features in a similar way. (Best viewed when zoomed in.)

Our insight is that the distribution of intra-class variance is actually independent on classes. It is obvious that for each class, the possible intra-class variances are from exactly the same set. As presented in Fig. 1, a similar pose change in samples from different classes leads to a cluster in the central latent space. Furthermore, if we know the distribution of intra-class variance, then we can generate potential hard samples from easy samples by adding intra-class variance to it. Therefore we can confidently propose our modified assumptions: Embedding features of samples from the same class consist of two parts;

One represents the intra-class invariance, and the other represents the intra-class variance which obeys the identical distribution among different classes.

In this paper, we propose a deep variational metric learning (DVML) framework following this assumption. Utilizing variational inference, we can force the conditional distribution of intra-class variance, given a certain image sample, to be isotropic multivariate Gaussian. Moreover, we can utilize most of the current metric learning algorithms to train the intra-class invariance. To be specific, the training procedure of DVML is simultaneously constrained by the following four loss functions: (1) the KL divergence between learned distribution and isotropic multivariate Gaussian; (2) the reconstruction loss of original images and images generated by the decoder; (3) the metric learning loss of learned intra-class invariance; (4) the metric learning loss of the combination of sampled intra-class variance and learned intra-class invariance. The first two losses ensure that the intra-class variance shares the same distribution and does contain sample-specific information of each image sample. The third ensures that the intra-class invariance represents a good class center for each class, and the fourth ensures a robust boundary among classes.

To the best of our knowledge, this is the first work that utilizes variational inference to disentangle intra-class variance and leverages the distribution to generate discriminative samples to improve robustness. It is noticeable that our framework is also applicable to hard negative mining methods. Additionally, experimental results on three benchmark datasets including CUB-200-2011, Cars196 and Stanford Online Products, show that DVML[1] significantly boosts the performance of existing deep metric learning algorithms.

2   Related Work

Great progress has been made about metric learning [6,9,10,15,35,39,41] recently. In the conventional metric learning algorithms, our goal is to learn a linear Mahalanobis distance to measure the similarities of samples [1,5,19,20,36]. Some of the previous works [32,38] also tried to formulate metric learning as a variational inference problem, while focusing on the distribution of pairwise distance. There are also attempts on combining latent variables and metric learning [26], while in this work latent variables are the features of patches cropped from images.

Recently, metric learning with deep neural networks has been densely explored. There are mainly two subjects: sampling methods and loss functions. By sampling methods [8,10,18,21,24,34,37,40], we aim to mine samples which improve robustness. For example, Wu et al. [37] proposed a distance weighted sampling method. By loss functions [3,7,18,23,33,36,37], we aim to fully use the data in a mini-batch to learn a discriminative boundary among classes. For example, Song et al. [23] presented a N-pair loss which takes advantage of the whole training batch. There are also works about synthesized negative samples. In [16], they generated a proxy for each class which represents the tight upper

---

[1] Code is coming soon on https://github.com/XudongLinthu.

bound of the class. However, this is different from our generating hard samples simultaneously in the training procedure, which better uncover the potential of easy negative samples. Inspired by the central limit theorem and recent works [2,12,14,29], we begin to think about the invariance among classes.

In [4], they also model intra-class variance with an isotropic Gaussian, while it is based on the assumption that each class shares the same prior probability and covariance, which is aimed to tackle the imbalance among samples in long-tailed datasets. The core distinction is that we disentangle intra-class variance and class centers. In [4], they only learn the conditional probability of belonging to a certain class given the input image. Instead, DVML is the combination of a discriminative model and a generative model, where the former outputs class centers and the latter fits intra-class variance. Our DVML is able to boost current metric learning methods by disentangling intra-class variance and class centers, and generating potentially hard and positive samples.

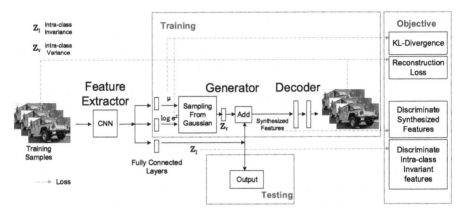

Fig. 2. Our proposed DVML framework. Taking the output of a backbone feature extractor as input, the following layers consist of two parts. The upper part is to model intra-class variance, and it only works in the training procedure. The third fully connected layers following the feature extractor is used to learn intra-class invariant features $\mathbf{z}_I$, namely, the class centers, which is also the output of our model. The generator takes as inputs the class centers $\mathbf{z}_I$ and the features sampled from the learned distribution $\mathcal{N}(\mathbf{z}_V; \boldsymbol{\mu}^{(i)}, \boldsymbol{\sigma}^{2(i)}\mathbf{I})$, and then outputs element-wise sum of them as synthesized discriminative samples. In order to reduce computation cost, we reconstruct the 1024-dimension features, which are the output of the backbone feature extractor, instead of the whole images. (Best viewed when zoomed in.)

3 Proposed Approach

In the conventional metric learning methods, intra-class variance and class centers are entangled, which brings two limitations to further improvement of metric learning algorithms:

- Given a limited dataset with a large range of variance within classes, current metric learning methods are easily over-fitting and lose discriminative power on unseen classes;
- Without disentangling intra-class variance and class centers, current methods learn a metric by exploring the boundary among classes, which means numerous easy negative samples contribute little to the training procedure.

We explored a way beyond these two limitations, with the proposed deep variational metric learning (DVML) framework. In this section, we first review current deep metric learning methods, and introduce the variational inference for intra-class variance distribution. After explaining discriminative sample generation, we give the whole picture of deep variational metric learning. In the end, we introduce the implementation details.

3.1 Preliminaries

Most of recently popular deep metric learning algorithms optimize an appropriate objective function L to get the parameters of a deep neural network F.

$$\phi_F = \arg\min_{\phi_F} L_m(\phi_F; \mathbf{X}, F), \tag{1}$$

Here $\mathbf{X}$ represents the whole training set. In the training procedure, we usually construct mini-batches of training data, X_b. Based on different ways of constructing mini-batches, various types of objective functions are designed. There are mainly three types of methods to construct mini-batches: pair-based, triplet-based, and batch-based.

In pair-based mini-batch construction, a mini-batch consists of pairs of positive and negative samples, $\mathbf{x}_p$ and $\mathbf{x}_n$. In triplet-based mini-batch construction, a mini-batch consists of triplets. In a triplet, there are three samples, the negative $\mathbf{x}_n$, the positive $\mathbf{x}_p$, and the anchor $\mathbf{x}_a$. The positive and the anchor have the same class label, and the negative is from other classes. In batch-based mini-batch construction, we know each sample's class information. Many hard negative mining algorithms are also batch-based, for they usually have to leverage class information to mine hard pairs or triplets within a mini-batch.

With these mini-batch construction methods, most of current objective functions aim to enforce the negative samples to be away from positive ones. We utilized the following loss as our baseline methods.

Triplet-based, Triplet [18,36]:

$$L_m = \sum_{i=1}^{N} \max\left(\alpha + D(\mathbf{z}_{(a)}^{(i)}, \mathbf{z}_{(p)}^{(i)})^2 - D(\mathbf{z}_{(a)}^{(i)}, \mathbf{z}_{(n)}^{(i)})^2, 0\right), \tag{2}$$

where $\mathbf{z}_{(p)}^{(i)} = F(\mathbf{x}_{(p)}^{(i)})$, $\mathbf{z}_{(a)}^{(i)} = F(\mathbf{x}_{(a)}^{(i)})$, and $\mathbf{z}_{(n)}^{(i)} = F(\mathbf{x}_{(n)}^{(i)})$. Here $\mathbf{x}_{(p)}^{(i)}$, $\mathbf{x}_{(n)}^{(i)}$, $\mathbf{x}_{(a)}^{(i)}$ denote the positive, the negative, and the anchor samples. N is the number of triplets. $D(\mathbf{z}_{(p)}^{(i)}, \mathbf{z}_{(n)}^{(i)})$ is the distance between features embedded from image samples.

Batch-based, N-pair [23]:

$$L_m = \frac{1}{N} \sum_{i=1}^{N} \log\left(1 + \sum_{j \neq i} \exp\left(\mathbf{z}^{(i)T}\mathbf{z}_+^{(j)} - \mathbf{z}^{(i)T}\mathbf{z}_+^{(i)}\right)\right), \tag{3}$$

where $\mathbf{z}_i = F(\mathbf{x}^{(i)})$, and the batch consists of $\mathbf{x}$ and $\mathbf{x}_+$. Here $\mathbf{x}^{(i)}$ and $\mathbf{x}_+^{(j)}$ are from the same class, only when $i = j$.

Batch-based, Triplet$_2$ with Distance Weighted Sampling [37]:

$$L_m = \sum_{i=1}^{N} \max\left(\alpha + D(\mathbf{z}_{(a)}^{(i)}, \mathbf{z}_{(p)}^{(i)}) - D(\mathbf{z}_{(a)}^{(i)}, \mathbf{z}_{(n)}^{(i)}), 0\right), \tag{4}$$

where $\mathbf{z}_{(a)}^{(i)}$'s, $\mathbf{z}_{(p)}^{(i)}$'s and $\mathbf{z}_{(n)}^{(i)}$'s original image samples are determined by distance weighted sampling over a mini-batch. According to [37], this loss performed better than aforementioned triplet loss.

3.2 Variational Inference for Intra-Class Variance

With our insight that the distribution of intra-class variance is inter-class invariant, we can disentangle intra-class variance and intra-class invariance. Therefore our model can more explicitly learn appropriate class centers, and has the nature of robustness toward a large range of intra-class variance.

As it is hard to directly represent intra-class variance without extra annotations about pose, view point, illumination, etc., we refer to the setting of generative models. It is natural to believe that from the sum of good intra-class variance and class centers, we can reconstruct the original image.

To be specific, given $\mathbf{X} = (\mathbf{x}^{(1)}, \cdots, \mathbf{x}^{(n)})$ as the dataset, consisting of N i.i.d images from M classes, we assume the data are generated by a random process, involving an unobserved continuous random variable $\mathbf{z} = \mathbf{z}_V + \mathbf{z}_{I_k}$, which is actually the embedding features of given samples. The process consists of three steps: (1) a value $\mathbf{z}_V^{(i)}$ is generated from some conditional distribution $\mathbf{p}_\theta^*(\mathbf{z})$, which is intra-class variance of sample i from class k; (2) $\mathbf{z}_{I_k}^{(i)}$ is the intra-class invariance of sample i from class k, and $\mathbf{z}^{(i)}$ equals the sum of $\mathbf{z}_V^{(i)}$ and $\mathbf{z}_{I_k}^{(i)}$; (3) an image $\mathbf{x}^{(i)}$ is generated from some conditional distribution $\mathbf{p}_\theta^*(\mathbf{x}|\mathbf{z})$.

Here, we assume that the prior $\mathbf{p}_\theta^*(\mathbf{z})$ and the the likelihood $\mathbf{p}_\theta^*(\mathbf{x}|\mathbf{z})$ is generated from some parametric families of distributions $\mathbf{p}_\theta(\mathbf{z})$ and $\mathbf{p}_\theta(\mathbf{x}|\mathbf{z})$. As we simultaneously learn the intra-class variance and intra-class invariance, so here for sample i from class k, its $\mathbf{z}_{I_k}^{(i)}$ is deterministic. Therefore all the distributions related $\mathbf{z}$ could be taken as the distribution related to $\mathbf{z}_V$. Using Monte Carlo estimator similar to VAE [12], we can get the approximated loss for the modeling of intra-class variance,

$$L(\theta, \phi; \mathbf{x}^{(i)}) \approx -D_{KL}(q_\phi(\mathbf{z}_V|\mathbf{x}^{(i)}) \| p_\theta(\mathbf{z}_V)) + \frac{1}{L}\sum_{l=1}^{L} \log p_\theta(\mathbf{x}^{(i)}|\mathbf{z}_V^{(i,l)}). \tag{5}$$

Here we let the prior distribution of $\mathbf{z}_V$ is the centered isotropic multivariate Gaussian $\mathbf{p}_\theta(\mathbf{z}_V) = \mathcal{N}(\mathbf{z}_V; \mathbf{0}, \mathbf{I})$. For the approximation posterior, we let it be a multivariate Gaussian with a diagonal covariance.

$$\log q_\phi(\mathbf{z}_V | \mathbf{x}^{(i)}) = \mathcal{N}(\mathbf{z}_V; \boldsymbol{\mu}^{(i)}, \boldsymbol{\sigma}^{2(1)}\mathbf{I}). \tag{6}$$

We use the outputs of fully-connected layers, to approximate the mean and s.d. of the posterior, $\boldsymbol{\mu}^{(i)}$ and $\boldsymbol{\sigma}^{(i)}$. With the reparameterization trick, we can finally get the first two terms of our objective.

$$\mathcal{L}(\theta, \phi; \mathbf{X}_b) \approx \frac{1}{2B} \sum_{i=1}^{B} \sum_{j=1}^{J} (1 + \log((\sigma_j^{(i)})^2) - (\mu_j^{(i)})^2 - (\sigma_j^{(i)})^2)$$
$$+ \frac{1}{TB} \sum_{i=1}^{B} \sum_{t=1}^{L} \log p_\theta(\mathbf{x}^{(i)} | \mathbf{z}^{(i,t)})$$
$$\triangleq L_1 + L_2, \tag{7}$$

where T is the number of generating iterations and B is the batch-size of the mini-batch. L_1 enforces the distribution of intra-class variance to be isotropic centered Gaussian, and L_2 ensures the intra-class variance preserve sample-specific information. Derivation details are in the supplementary materials.

Furthermore, for simplicity, in the training procedure, we utilize L-2 distance instead of original maximum likelihood estimation to handle the decoding term $p_\theta(\mathbf{x}^{(i)} | \mathbf{z}^{(i,t)})$, which gives us a simplified term:

$$L_1 = \frac{1}{2B} \sum_{i=1}^{B} \sum_{j=1}^{J} (1 + \log((\sigma_j^{(i)})^2) - (\mu_j^{(i)})^2 - (\sigma_j^{(i)})^2), \tag{8}$$

$$L_2 = \frac{1}{TB} \sum_{i=1}^{B} \sum_{t=1}^{T} ||\mathbf{x}^{(i)} - \hat{\mathbf{x}}^{(i,t)}||_2. \tag{9}$$

$\mathbf{x}^{(i)}$ represents original image samples, and $\hat{\mathbf{x}}^{(i,t)}$ is the fake sample synthesized from the sum of intra-class invariance features and intra-class variance features sampled from the distribution $\mathcal{N}(\mathbf{z}_V; \boldsymbol{\mu}^{(i)}, \boldsymbol{\sigma}^{2(i)}\mathbf{I})$.

3.3 Discriminative Sample Generation

As we addressed previously, most of current metric learning algorithms cannot uncover the full potential of easy samples. However, with the learned distribution of intra-class variance, we can generate potential hard samples from easy negative samples by adding the embedding features of easy samples with an biased term sampled from the distribution of intra-class variance.

Since we have learned an approximated conditional distribution of the intra-class variance, $\mathcal{N}(\mathbf{z}_V; \boldsymbol{\mu}^{(i)}, \boldsymbol{\sigma}^{2(1)}\mathbf{I})$, an idea is naturally raised: we can also draw samples from this distribution to construct synthesized embedding features, and take them as the inputs of metric learning loss functions.

$$L_3 = L_m(\hat{\mathbf{z}}), \qquad (10)$$

where $\hat{\mathbf{z}} = \mathbf{z}_{I_k} + \hat{\mathbf{z}}_V$, and $\hat{\mathbf{z}}_V$ is sampled intra-class variance features. By $\mathbf{z}_{I_k}$, we want to stress that different classes have different intra-class variance, yet we do not compute class centers over classes.

Remembering that the distribution of intra-class variance is independent on classes, we confidently conclude that these synthesized embedding features contain a larger range of intra-class variance than original samples, and training with them will bring us a more robust model. Here is a simple example. In class A, the original samples only contain view point changes, and in class B, the original samples only contain illumination changes. Different from current models trained with only their original samples, our model is also robust to an unseen class which contains both view point changes and illumination changes.

Table 1. Comparisons of clustering and retrieval performance (%) on the Cars196 dataset

Method	NMI	F_1	R@1	R@2	R@4	R@8
Triplet [18,36]	56.2	21.3	58.5	68.8	77.1	84.2
DVML+Triplet	**61.1**	**28.2**	**64.3**	**73.7**	**79.2**	**85.1**
N-pair [23]	62.9	31.9	72.3	79.9	86.8	90.9
DVML+N-pair	**66.0**	**34.6**	**80.4**	**85.8**	**91.8**	**95.1**
Contrastive [7]	44.8	11.2	35.8	47.5	59.7	71.5
Lifted [25]	60.0	27.9	70.0	79.5	86.8	92.0
Angular [33]	61.2	30.8	70.1	80.2	86.7	91.6
Triplet$_2$+DWS [37]	65.4	34.3	78.9	85.6	91.0	94.7
DVML+Triplet$_2$+DWS	**67.6**	**36.8**	**82.0**	**88.4**	**93.3**	**96.3**
HDC [40]	–	–	73.7	83.2	89.5	93.8
Proxy-NCA [16]	64.9	–	73.2	82.4	86.4	88.7

3.4 Deep Variational Metric Learning

Finally we have the whole picture of our proposed DVML framework. Besides aforementioned three terms of loss functions, our final objective also contains a constraint term of intra-class invariance:

$$L_4 = L_m(\mathbf{z}_I), \qquad (11)$$

where $\mathbf{z}_I$ is the intra-class invariance features and also the output of our model in testing. This term enforces the intra-class invariance, namely the class centers, to be discriminative. It is noticeable that here we do not calculate class centers. We call them class centers for we have disentangled this part from the intra-class variance. Therefore our method is applicable to most of current deep metric learning algorithms.

The final objective function is:

$$L = \lambda_1 L_1 + \lambda_2 L_2 + \lambda_3 L_3 + \lambda_4 L_4. \tag{12}$$

By simply applying sampling methods to both original features and synthesized features, or replace L_m with custom loss functions, we can combine our method with most of current metric learning approaches.

Here we want to highlight our contributions. First, to the best of our knowledge, this is the first work to disentangle intra-class variance and intra-class invariance, which makes it possible to explicitly learn appropriate class centers by simultaneously minimizing L_4. Second, different from previous hard negative mining methods which ignore numerous easy negative samples, with the learned distribution of intra-class variance, we generate discriminative samples which contains the possible intra-class variance over the whole training set. It is obvious that our discriminative sample generation is entirely different from conventional data augmentation methods. We simultaneously generate latent variables, namely, the embedding features, in the training procedure. More importantly, our synthesized samples have the variance of the whole training set.

Table 2. Comparisons of clustering and retrieval performance (%) on the Stanford Online Products dataset

Method	NMI	F_1	R@1	R@10	R@100
Triplet [18,36]	86.5	20.2	54.9	71.5	85.2
DVML+Triplet	**89.0**	**31.1**	**66.5**	**82.3**	**91.8**
N-pair [23]	87.9	27.1	66.4	82.9	92.1
DVML+N-pair	**90.2**	**37.1**	**70.0**	**85.1**	**93.7**
Contrastive [7]	83.5	10.4	37.4	52.7	69.4
Lifted [25]	88.4	30.6	65.2	81.3	91.7
Angular [33]	87.7	26.4	66.8	82.8	92.0
Triplet$_2$+DWS [37]	89.0	31.1	66.8	82.0	91.0
DVML+Triplet$_2$+DWS	**90.8**	**37.2**	**70.2**	**85.2**	**93.8**
HDC [40]	-	-	69.5	84.4	92.8
Proxy-NCA [16]	-	-	73.7	-	-

3.5 Implementation Details

We implement all the compared baseline methods and our methods on Chainer [28], with the GoogLeNet [27] pre-trained on ILSVRC2012 [17] as the backbone for a fair comparison. Following standard pre-processing of data, we first normalize the images into 256×256, and then we perform random crop and horizontal mirroring for data augmentation. We add three parallel fully-connected layers after the average pooling layer of GoogLeNet, with same output dimension which is the required embedding size. Two of them are used to approximate μ and $\log \sigma^2$. The other's output is the intra-class variance. For the reconstruction part, due to the high cost of image reconstruction, we use the output features of GoogLeNet's last average pooling layer as the reconstruction target. We use two fully-connected layers with output dimension 512 and 1024 respectively as the decoder network, where tanh is used as the activation function. We randomly initialize all the added fully-connected layers.

There are two phases in the training procedure. In the first phase, we cut off the back-propagation of the gradients from the decoder network for the stability of the embedding part. We empirically set $\lambda_1 = 1, \lambda_2 = 1, \lambda_3 = 0.1,$ and $\lambda_4 = 1$. In the second phase, we release the constraint and empirically set $\lambda_1 = 0.8, \lambda_2 = 1, \lambda_3 = 0.2,$ and $\lambda_4 = 0.8$. As the experimental study in [25] showed that the embedding size does not largely affect the performance, we follow [33] and fix the embedding size to 512 in all the experiments. We set the batch size as 128 for the pair-based and batch-based input and 120 for the triplet input. For the iterations of discriminative sample generation, we set $T = 20$ throughout the experiments. To optimize the objective, we take Adam [11] as the optimizer and set the training rate to be 0.0001.

Table 3. Comparisons of clustering and retrieval performance (%) on the CUB-200-2011 dataset

Mehtod	NMI	F_1	R@1	R@2	R@4	R@8
Triplet [18,36]	52.7	19.8	39.8	51.9	63.7	74.5
DVML+Triplet	**55.5**	**25.0**	**43.7**	**56.0**	**67.8**	**76.9**
N-pair [23]	60.1	27.1	50.6	63.1	73.8	82.2
DVML+N-pair	**61.1**	**28.5**	**52.5**	**64.9**	**75.3**	**84.1**
Contrastive [7]	43.8	11.0	32.8	44.1	55.2	69.4
Lifted [25]	56.8	22.9	47.8	60.1	71.4	81.9
Angular [33]	58.3	27.8	50.6	64.1	74.1	83.2
Triplet$_2$+DWS [37]	58.0	24.8	49.8	61.6	73.2	83.6
DVML+Triplet$_2$+DWS	**61.4**	**28.8**	**52.7**	**65.1**	**75.5**	**84.3**
HDC [40]	-	-	53.6	65.7	77.0	85.6
Proxy-NCA [16]	59.5	–	49.2	61.9	67.9	72.4

Table 4. Average p-value and relative deviation (%) on three datasets

Train	Cars196	CUB-200-2011	Products
Triplet p-value	76.00 ± 1.25	76.87 ± 1.42	83.87 ± 8.24
Triplet	79.99	86.14	73.10
DVML+Triplet	**40.75**	**44.50**	**44.48**
Test	Cars196	CUB-200-2011	Products
Triplet p-value	74.87 ± 2.29	77.01 ± 1.19	83.75 ± 8.12
Triplet	97.98	105.80	73.46
DVML+Triplet	**57.08**	**57.56**	**46.94**

4   Experiments

To demonstrate the effectiveness of our DVML, we conduct experiments on three widely-used datasets for both retrieval and clustering tasks.

4.1   Settings

We follow [24,25,33] to split the training and testing set in a zero-shot manner for all the datasets.

- The CUB-200-2011 dataset [31] contains 11,788 images from 200 bird species. We take the first 100 classes with 5,864 images for training, and the rest 100 classes with 5,924 images for testing.
- The Cars196 dataset [13] contains 16,185 images of 196 car types. We take the first 98 classes with 8,054 images for training, and the rest 98 classes with 8,131 images for testing.
- The Stanford Online Products dataset [25] contains 120,053 images of 22,634 products. We take the first 11,318 classes with 59,551 images for training, and the rest 11,316 classes with 60,502 images for testing.

In the retrieval task, we calculate the percentage of test samples that have at least one sample from the same class in R nearest neighbors. In the clustering task, we report the NMI [25] score and F_1 [25] score. For NMI, the input is a set of clusters $\Omega = \{\omega_1, \cdots, \omega_K\}$ and the ground truth classes $\mathbb{C} = \{c_1, \cdots, c_K\}$. ω_i indicates the samples that are assigned to the ith cluster, and c_j is the set of samples with the ground truth label j. NMI is the ratio of mutual information and the mean entropy of clusters and the ground truth: $\text{NMI}(\Omega, \mathbb{C}) = \frac{2I(\Omega;\mathbb{C})}{(H(\Omega)+H(\mathbb{C}))}$. F_1 score is defined as the harmonic mean of precision and recall: $F_1 = \frac{2PR}{P+R}$.

4.2   Compared Methods

We apply our deep variational metric learning framework to three aforementioned baseline methods. They are Triplet loss [36], N-pair loss [23], and Triplet$_2$

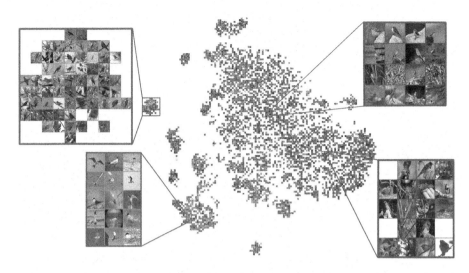

Fig. 3. Visualization of the proposed DVML+N-pair with Barnes-Hut t-SNE [30] on the CUB-200-2011 test set. The color of the bounding box for each image represents the label. (Best viewed when zoomed in.)

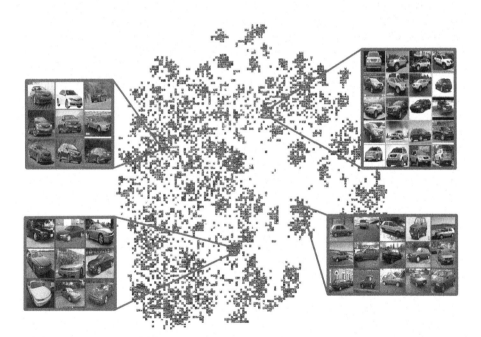

Fig. 4. Visualization of the proposed DVML+N-pair with Barnes-Hut t-SNE [30] on the Cars196 test set. The color of the bounding box for each image represents the label. (Best viewed when zoomed in.)

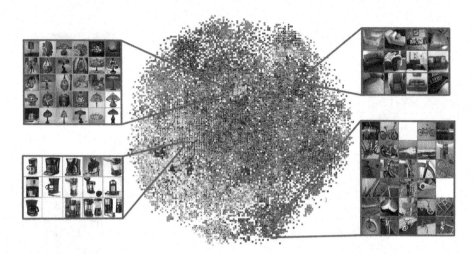

Fig. 5. Visualization of the proposed DVML+N-pair with Barnes-Hut t-SNE [30] on the Stanford Online Products test set. The color of the bounding box for each image represents the label. (Best viewed when zoomed in.)

loss with Distance Weighted Sampling [37]. We compare the performance of baseline methods before and after using our DVML framework to demonstrate the effectiveness of our proposed framework. We also compare DVML with other widely used or state-of-the-art methods, where there are two categories: designing sampling algorithms and modifying loss functions. For loss functions, we compare our methods with the widely-used Contrastive loss [7], the Lifted-Structure loss [25], and the state-of-the-art Angular loss [33]. For sampling methods, we take the state-of-the-art methods including HDC [40] and an upper bound generating method Proxy-NCA [16]. We report the most relevant results according to their original papers. Except them, we re-implement all the compared methods. In the re-implementation, we observe some differences from the reported results in original papers, but this does not affect the fairness of comparison.

4.3   Quantitative Results

Tables 1, 2, and 3 present the experimental results of our DVML and all compared methods on the Cars196, Stanford Online Product, and CUB-200-2011 datasets respectively.

From the comparison with baseline method, we notice that our proposed DVML significantly improved the performance of baseline methods. It is surprising that our proposed DVML significantly improves the performance of N-pair loss which has already gained success on the Cars196 and Stanford Online Products datasets, which further proves the limitation we stress before does exist. In the CUB-200-2011, our proposed DVML's effectiveness is relatively less significant than the other two datasets. We suppose that it is due to the different nature of datasets. In Cars196 and Stanford Online Products, the difficulty lies in a large range of intra-class variance, while in CUB-200-2011, the difficulty lies in localizing discriminative fine-grained regions.

In the comparison with other methods, we observe that on the Cars196 dataset, our **DVML+Triplet$_2$+DWS** achieves better performance than the previous state-of-the-art. In the other two datasets, our DVML also achieves comparable performance. It is noticeable that we take both sampling algorithms and modified loss functions as baselines and compete with the state-of-the-art in both of the categories, which further shows the effectiveness of our DVML.

To further verify our assumption, we first apply Kolmogorov-Smirnov test [22] to the central features learned with Triplet loss [18,36] and measure the p-value. The results in Table 4 show that central features of classes in every dataset probably obey the isotropic Gaussian and their distributions are probably similar because the deviation of p-value over classes is small. We also measure the average relative deviation of features with and without DVML, and the result suggests that our DVML does remove intra-class variance from output features and helps to explicitly learn class centers.

4.4 Qualitative Results

Using a well-known visualization method t-SNE [30], we first visualize the central latent space of features learned with the N-pair loss [23] to illustrate our insight in Fig. 1.

Figures 3, 4, and 5 show the visualization of DVML+N-pair on the CUB-200-2011, Cars196 and Stanford Online Products datasets. The figures are best viewed when zoomed in. The color of the bounding box on each samples' images represent their class label. Following [25,33], we enlarge certain regions to highlight the discriminability of learned features. The visualization explicitly show that our proposed DVML learns a good metric which well preserves the distance relationships among classes, given a large range of intra-class variance.

5 Conclusion

In this paper, we have presented a novel applicable framework: deep variational metric learning (DVML). We assume and illustrate that the distribution of intra-class variance is invariant among classes. To the best of our knowledge, this is the first work to disentangle intra-class variance via variational inference, and the first to leverage the intra-class variance's distribution to generate discriminative samples. We stress that with our DVML, current metric learning algorithms could be significantly improved. Furthermore, there are many future works, including image generating given certain classes, and utilizing those generated images to further improve robustness of metric learning models.

Acknowledgement. This work was supported in part by the National Key Research and Development Program of China under Grant 2017YFA0700802, in part by the

National Natural Science Foundation of China under Grant 61672306, Grant U1713214, Grant 61572271, and in part by the Shenzhen Fundamental Research Fund (Subject Arrangement) under Grant JCYJ20170412170602564.

References

1. Davis, J.V., Kulis, B., Jain, P., Sra, S., Dhillon, I.S.: Information-theoretic metric learning. In: ICML, pp. 209–216 (2007)
2. Duan, Y., Wang, Z., Lu, J., Lin, X., Zhou, J.: Graphbit: bitwise interaction mining via deep reinforcement learning. In: The IEEE Conference on Computer Vision and Pattern Recognition (CVPR), June 2018
3. Duan, Y., Zheng, W., Lin, X., Lu, J., Zhou, J.: Deep adversarial metric learning. In: The IEEE Conference on Computer Vision and Pattern Recognition (CVPR), June 2018
4. Fragoso, V., Ramanan, D.: Bayesian embeddings for long-tailed datasets (2018)
5. Globerson, A., Roweis, S.T.: Metric learning by collapsing classes. In: NIPS, pp. 451–458 (2006)
6. Guillaumin, M., Verbeek, J., Schmid, C.: Is that you? Metric learning approaches for face identification. In: CVPR, pp. 498–505 (2009)
7. Hadsell, R., Chopra, S., LeCun, Y.: Dimensionality reduction by learning an invariant mapping. In: CVPR, pp. 1735–1742 (2006)
8. Harwood, B., Carneiro, G., Reid, I., Drummond, T.: Smart mining for deep metric learning. In: ICCV, pp. 2821–2829 (2017)
9. Hu, J., Lu, J., Tan, Y.P.: Deep metric learning for visual tracking. TCSVT **26**(11), 2056–2068 (2016)
10. Hu, J., Lu, J., Tan, Y.P.: Discriminative deep metric learning for face and kinship verification. TIP **26**(9), 4269–4282 (2017)
11. Kingma, D.P., Ba, J.: Adam: a method for stochastic optimization. arXiv preprint arXiv:1412.6980 (2014)
12. Kingma, D.P., Welling, M.: Auto-encoding variational bayes. arXiv preprint arXiv:1312.6114 (2013)
13. Krause, J., Stark, M., Deng, J., Feifei, L.: 3d object representations for fine-grained categorization. In: ICCVW (2013)
14. Larsen, A.B.L., Sønderby, S.K., Larochelle, H., Winther, O.: Autoencoding beyond pixels using a learned similarity metric. arXiv preprint arXiv:1512.09300 (2015)
15. Liu, Z., Wang, D., Lu, H.: Stepwise metric promotion for unsupervised video person re-identification. In: ICCV, pp. 2429–2438 (2017)
16. Movshovitz-Attias, Y., Toshev, A., Leung, T.K., Ioffe, S., Singh, S.: No fuss distance metric learning using proxies. In: ICCV, pp. 360–368 (2017)
17. Russakovsky, O., Deng, J., Su, H., Krause, J., Satheesh, S., Ma, S., Huang, Z., Karpathy, A., Khosla, A., Bernstein, M., Berg, A.C., Fei-Fei, L.: ImageNet large scale visual recognition challenge. Int. J. Comput. Vis. (IJCV) **115**(3), 211–252 (2015). https://doi.org/10.1007/s11263-015-0816-y
18. Schroff, F., Kalenichenko, D., Philbin, J.: Facenet: a unified embedding for face recognition and clustering. In: CVPR, pp. 815–823 (2015)
19. Schultz, M., Joachims, T.: Learning a distance metric from relative comparisons. In: NIPS, pp. 41–48 (2004)
20. Shalev-Shwartz, S., Singer, Y., Ng, A.Y.: Online and batch learning of pseudo-metrics. In: ICML (2004)

21. Shrivastava, A., Gupta, A., Girshick, R.: Training region-based object detectors with online hard example mining. In: CVPR, pp. 761–769 (2016)
22. Smirnov, N.: Table for estimating the goodness of fit of empirical distributions. Ann. Math. Statist. **19**(2), 279–281 (1948). https://doi.org/10.1214/aoms/1177730256
23. Sohn, K.: Improved deep metric learning with multi-class n-pair loss objective. In: NIPS, pp. 1849–1857 (2016)
24. Song, H.O., Jegelka, S., Rathod, V., Murphy, K.: Deep metric learning via facility location. In: CVPR, pp. 5382–5390 (2017)
25. Song, H.O., Xiang, Y., Jegelka, S., Savarese, S.: Deep metric learning via lifted structured feature embedding. In: CVPR, pp. 4004–4012 (2016)
26. Sun, C., Wang, D., Lu, H.: Person re-identification via distance metric learning with latent variables. IEEE Trans. Image Process. **26**(1), 23–34 (2017)
27. Szegedy, C., Liu, W., Jia, Y., Sermanet, P., Reed, S.E., Anguelov, D., Erhan, D., Vanhoucke, V., Rabinovich, A.: Going deeper with convolutions. In: CVPR, pp. 1–9 (2015)
28. Tokui, S., Oono, K., Hido, S., Clayton, J.: Chainer: a next-generation open source framework for deep learning. In: Proceedings of Workshop on Machine Learning Systems (LearningSys) in The Twenty-ninth Annual Conference on Neural Information Processing Systems (NIPS) (2015). http://learningsys.org/papers/LearningSys_2015_paper_33.pdf
29. Tolstikhin, I., Bousquet, O., Gelly, S., Schoelkopf, B.: Wasserstein auto-encoders. arXiv preprint arXiv:1711.01558 (2017)
30. Van Der Maaten, L.: Accelerating t-SNE using tree-based algorithms. JMLR **15**(1), 3221–3245 (2014)
31. Wah, C., Branson, S., Welinder, P., Perona, P., Belongie, S.J.: The Caltech-UCSD Birds-200-2011 dataset. Technical Report CNS-TR-2011-001, California Institute of Technology (2011)
32. Wang, D., Tan, X.: Robust distance metric learning via Bayesian inference. IEEE Trans. Image Process. **27**(3), 1542–1553 (2018)
33. Wang, J., Zhou, F., Wen, S., Liu, X., Lin, Y.: Deep metric learning with angular loss. In: ICCV, pp. 2593–2601 (2017)
34. Wang, X., Gupta, A.: Unsupervised learning of visual representations using videos. In: ICCV, pp. 2794–2802 (2015)
35. Wang, X., Hua, G., Han, T.X.: Discriminative tracking by metric learning. In: ECCV, pp. 200–214 (2010)
36. Weinberger, K.Q., Saul, L.K.: Distance metric learning for large margin nearest neighbor classification. JMLR **10**(Feb), 207–244 (2009)
37. Wu, C.Y., Manmatha, R., Smola, A.J., Krähenbühl, P.: Sampling matters in deep embedding learning. arXiv preprint arXiv:1706.07567 (2017)
38. Yang, L., Jin, R., Sukthankar, R.: Bayesian active distance metric learning. arXiv preprint arXiv:1206.5283 (2012)
39. Yu, H.X., Wu, A., Zheng, W.S.: Cross-view asymmetric metric learning for unsupervised person re-identification. In: ICCV, pp. 994–1002 (2017)
40. Yuan, Y., Yang, K., Zhang, C.: Hard-aware deeply cascaded embedding. In: ICCV, pp. 814–823 (2017)
41. Zhou, J., Yu, P., Tang, W., Wu, Y.: Efficient online local metric adaptation via negative samples for person re-identification. In: ICCV, pp. 2420–2428 (2017)

HGMR: Hierarchical Gaussian Mixtures for Adaptive 3D Registration

Benjamin Eckart[(✉)], Kihwan Kim, and Jan Kautz

NVIDIA Research, Santa Clara, CA, USA
beckart@nvidia.com

Abstract. Point cloud registration sits at the core of many important and challenging 3D perception problems including autonomous navigation, SLAM, object/scene recognition, and augmented reality. In this paper, we present a new registration algorithm that is able to achieve state-of-the-art speed and accuracy through its use of a Hierarchical Gaussian Mixture representation. Our method, Hierarchical Gaussian Mixture Registration (HGMR), constructs a top-down multi-scale representation of point cloud data by recursively running many small-scale data likelihood segmentations in parallel on a GPU. We leverage the resulting representation using a novel optimization criterion that adaptively finds the best scale to perform data association between spatial subsets of point cloud data. Compared to previous Iterative Closest Point and GMM-based techniques, our tree-based point association algorithm performs data association in logarithmic-time while dynamically adjusting the level of detail to best match the complexity and spatial distribution characteristics of local scene geometry. In addition, unlike other GMM methods that restrict covariances to be isotropic, our new PCA-based optimization criterion well-approximates the true MLE solution even when fully anisotropic Gaussian covariances are used. Efficient data association, multi-scale adaptability, and a robust MLE approximation produce an algorithm that is up to an order of magnitude both faster and more accurate than current state-of-the-art on a wide variety of 3D datasets captured from LiDAR to structured light.

1 Introduction

Point cloud registration is the task of aligning two or more point clouds by estimating the relative transformation between them, and it has been an essential part of many computer vision algorithms such as 3D object matching [8], localization and mapping [30], dense 3D reconstruction of a scene [29], and object pose estimation [31].

Recently point set registration methods [38] have been gaining more importance due to the growing commercial interest of virtual and mixed reality [25], commercial robotics, and autonomous driving applications [17,23]. In most of these applications, massive amounts of 3D point cloud data (PCD) are directly captured from various active sensors (i.e., LiDAR and depth cameras) but at different times under different poses or local coordinate systems. The task of point

© Springer Nature Switzerland AG 2018
V. Ferrari et al. (Eds.): ECCV 2018, LNCS 11219, pp. 730–746, 2018.
https://doi.org/10.1007/978-3-030-01267-0_43

cloud registration is then to try to find a common coordinate system, which is done by estimating some type of geometric similarity in the point data that can be recovered through optimization over a set of spatial transformations.

One of the oldest and most widely used registration algorithms, Iterative Closest Point (ICP) [1,3], is based on an iterative matching process where point proximity establishes candidate point pair sets. Given a set of point pairs, the rigid transformation that minimizes the sum of squared point pair distances can be calculated efficiently in closed form. ICP and its dozens of variants [34] often fail to produce correct results in many common but challenging scenarios, where the presence of noise, uneven point density, occlusions, or when large pose displacements can cause a large proportion of points to be without valid matches.

Compared to traditional ICP-based approaches, much research has been done on the use of statistical models for registration, which in principle can provide better estimates for outlier rejection, convergence, and geometric matching [15, 27,39]. In particular, many statistical methods have been designed around the Expectation Maximization (EM) algorithm [7] as it has been shown that EM generalizes the ICP algorithm under a few basic assumptions [16,35]. Many statistical registration techniques have explicitly utilized this paradigm to deliver better robustness and accuracy [6,13,16,18], but these algorithms tend to be much slower than ICP and often offer only marginal improvement in all but a few specific circumstances. As a result, ICP-based methods are still heavily used in practice for many real-world applications.

Our proposed method falls into the category of GMM-based statistical registration algorithms. We tackle the typical shortcomings of these methods, slow speeds and lack of generality, by adopting an efficient hierarchical construction for the creation of an adaptive multi-scale point matching process. *Efficiency:* The search over multiple scales as a recursive tree-based search produces a highly performant logarithmic-time algorithm that quickly and adaptively finds the most appropriate level of geometric detail with which to match points. *Generality:* By using a data-driven point matching procedure over multiple scales, our proposed algorithm can automatically adapt to many different types of scenes, particularly with real-world data where widely varying sampling sparsity and scene complexity are common. Finally, we introduce a novel Mahalanobis distance approximation resembling ICP's point-to-plane distance minimization metric, which more faithfully approximates the true MLE solution under general anisotropic covariances than previous methods.

2   Related Work

Our method builds on previous work in GMM-based methods for registration such as GMM-Reg [19,21], JRMPC [13], and MLMD [9], while also leveraging recent results using hierarchical GMMs for point cloud modeling [10]. By adopting a GMM-based paradigm, we gain robustness in situations of large pose displacement, optimal solutions in the form of maximum likelihood estimates, and

Table 1. A Comparison of Registration Methods. *Multiply Linked:* Many-to-one or many-to-many correspondences, *Anisotropic:* General shape alignment using unrestricted covariance structures, *Multi-Scale:* Registration at multiple levels of granularity, *Data Transform:* Underlying data structure or transform, *Association Complexity:* Complexity of data association problem over all N points (E Step in the case of EM-based methods), *Optimization Complexity:* Size of the optimization problem (M Step in the case of EM-based methods). Assuming both point clouds size N, number of voxels/grid points V, and number of mixture components J.

Method		Mult. link	Anisotropic	Multi-scale	Data trans	Assoc. complex	Opt. complex.
ICP [1]	1992				–	N^2	N
SoftAssign [15]	1998	✓		✓a	–	N^2	N^2
EM-ICP [16]	2002	✓		✓	kd-tree	$N \log N$	N^2
LM-ICP [14]	2003				grid approx.	N	N
KC [40]	2004	✓			grid approx.	N	V
TrICP [4]	2005				voxels	$\frac{N^2}{V}$	N
FICP [32]	2007				kd-tree	$N \log N$	N
G-ICP [35]	2009		✓		kd-tree	$N \log N$	N
CPD [27]	2010	✓			FGT	N	N^2
ECMPR [18]	2011	✓	✓		FGT	N	N
GMMReg [20]	2011	✓		✓a	FGT	N	N^2
NDT-P2D [37]	2012	✓	✓	✓	voxels+kd-tree	$N \log V$	N
NDT-D2D [37]	2012	✓	✓	✓	voxels+kd-tree	$V \log V$	V
REM-Seg [11]	2013	✓	✓	✓a	GMM	NJ	N
MLMD [9]	2015	✓	✓		GMM	NJ	J
SVR [2]	2015	✓		✓a	GMMb	$N^2 \sim N^3$	J
JRMPC [12]	2017	✓			GMM	NJ	J
HGMR	–	✓	✓	✓	GMM-Tree	$N \log J$	$\log J \sim J$

a Implicitly multi-scale via annealing,
b Conversion to GMM via SVM

an ability to more easily leverage point-level parallelism on GPUs. By augmenting the GMM into a hierarchy, we can efficiently compress empty space, achieve logarithmic-time matching, and perform robust multi-scale data analysis.

The earliest statistical methods placed an isotropic covariance around every point in the first set of points and then registered the second set of points to it under an MLE framework (MPM [6], EM-ICP [16], CPD [27,28]). More modern statistical approaches utilize a generative model framework, where a GMM is usually constructed from the points explicitly and registration is solved in an MLE sense using an EM or ECM [26] algorithm (REM-Seg [11], ECMPR [18], JRMPC [13], MLMD [9]), though some utilize a max correlation or L_2 distance approach (Kernel Correlation [40], GMM-Reg [19,21], SVR [2], NDT-D2D [36]). Since a statistical framework for point cloud registration tends to be more heavyweight than ICP, techniques such as decimation (EM-ICP [16]), voxelization (NDT methods [36,37]), or Support Vector Machines (SVR [2]) have been used to create smaller or more efficient models, while others have relied on computational tricks such as the Fast Gauss Transform (CPD [27], ECMPR [18]), or have devised ways to exploit point-level parallelism and GPU-computation for increased computational tractability and speed (MLMD [9], parallelized EM-ICP [39]).

In contrast to these statistical model-based approaches, modern robust variants of point-to-plane ICP (e.g. Trimmed ICP [5], Fractional ICP [32]) are often much faster and sometimes perform nearly as well, especially under real-world conditions [33]. See Table 1 for a detailed comparison of key registration algorithms utilizing the ICP and GMM paradigms. Our proposed method offers favorable complexity over both classes of algorithms due to its novel use of a GMM-Tree structure, without needing to resort to discretization strategies like the NDT-based methods.

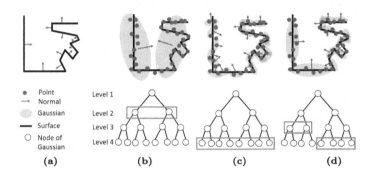

Fig. 1. Multi-Scale Representation using a Hierarchy of Gaussian Mixtures: Top-row shows identical geometries (black lines) and associated points (blue circles), which are represented by different levels of Gaussian models (green contour for 1 σ.) (a) (Top) Ideal Normals (red arrows) on the surfaces, (b) Too coarse (only two Gaussians in Level 2): poor segmentation leads to incorrect normals, which will degrade accuracy when registering points to model, (c) Too fine (using finest level of Gaussian models): over-segmentation leads to erroneous normals as sample noise overtakes real facet geometry (d) Adaptive multi-scale (Mixture of level 3 and level 4 models): point-to-model association can be much more robust when fidelity adaptively changes according to data distribution so that facets can be well-modeled given differing spatial frequencies and sampling densities.

3   Registration as Expectation Maximization

The Expectation Maximization (EM) algorithm forms the theoretical foundation for most modern statistical approaches to registration and also generalizes ICP under certain basic assumptions. EM is commonly employed for MLE optimization in the case where directly maximizing the data likelihood for the sought after variable is intractable, but maximizing the expected joint data likelihood conditioned on a set of latent variables is tractable. For the registration case, the sought after variable is the transformation T between point clouds and the latent variables are the point-model associations.

The problem is set up as follows: Given point clouds $\mathcal{Z}_1$ and $\mathcal{Z}_2$, we would like to maximize the data probability of $\mathcal{Z}_2$ under a set of transformations T with respect to a probability model $\boldsymbol{\Theta}_{\mathcal{Z}_1}$ derived from the first point cloud $\mathcal{Z}_1$.

$$\hat{T} = \underset{T}{\operatorname{argmax}}\, p(T(\mathcal{Z}_2)|\hat{\boldsymbol{\Theta}}_{\mathcal{Z}_1}) \tag{1}$$

That is, the most likely estimate of the transformation $\hat{T}$ is the estimate that maximizes the probability that the samples of the transformed point cloud $T(\mathcal{Z}_2)$ came from some probabilistic representation of spatial likelihood (parameterized by $\hat{\boldsymbol{\Theta}}$) derived from the spatial distribution of the first point cloud $\mathcal{Z}_1$. The most common form for parametrizing this probability distribution is through a Gaussian Mixture Model (GMM), whose data probability is defined as a convex combination of J Gaussians weighted by the J-component vector $\boldsymbol{\pi}$,

$$p(z|\boldsymbol{\Theta}_{\mathcal{Z}_1}) = \sum_{j=1}^{J} \pi_j \mathcal{N}(z|\boldsymbol{\Theta}_j) \tag{2}$$

The derivation of the probability model $\boldsymbol{\Theta}_{\mathcal{Z}_1}$ may be as simple as statically setting an isotropic covariance around each point in $\mathcal{Z}_1$ (e.g. EM-ICP [16]), or as complicated as framing the search for $\boldsymbol{\Theta}_{\mathcal{Z}_1}$ as a completely separate optimization problem (e.g. SVR [2], MLMD [9]). Regardless of how the model is constructed, however, EM provides an iterative procedure to solve for T through the introduction of a set of latent correspondence variables $\mathcal{C} = \{c_{ij}\}$ that dictate how points $\mathbf{z}_i \in \mathcal{Z}_2$ probabilistically associate to the J subcomponents $\boldsymbol{\Theta}_j$ of the model $\boldsymbol{\Theta}_{\mathcal{Z}_1}$. Intuitively, we can view EM as a statistical generalization of ICP: The E Step estimates data associations, replacing ICP's matching step, while the M Step maximizes the expected likelihood conditioned on these data associations, replacing ICP's distance minimization step over matched pairs.

In the E Step, we use Bayes' rule to calculate expectations over the correspondences. For a particular point $\mathbf{z}_i$, its expected correspondence to $\boldsymbol{\Theta}_j$ ($E[c_{ij}]$) can be calculated as follows,

$$E[c_{ij} = 1] = \frac{\pi_j \mathcal{N}(\mathbf{z}_i|\boldsymbol{\Theta}_j)}{\sum_{k=1}^{J} \pi_k \mathcal{N}(\mathbf{z}_i|\boldsymbol{\Theta}_k)} \tag{3}$$

Generally speaking, larger model sizes (larger J) produce more accurate registration results since larger models have more representational fidelity. However, large models produce very slow registration algorithms: Given N points in $\mathcal{Z}_2$, Eq. 3 must be calculated $N \times J$ times for each subsequent M Step. For methods that utilize models of size $J \approx O(N)$ (e.g. EM-ICP [16], CPD [27], GMM-Reg [21]), this causes a data association complexity of $O(N^2)$ and thus these algorithms have problems scaling beyond small point cloud sizes.

To combat this scaling problem, our approach builds from recent advances in fast statistical point cloud modeling via hierarchical generative models [10]. In this approach, point cloud data is modeled via a GMM-Tree, which is built in a top-down recursive fashion from small-sized Gaussian Mixtures. This GPU-based approach can produce high-fidelity GMM-Trees in real-time, but given that they were originally designed to optimize reconstructive fidelity and for dynamic occupancy map generation, it is not obvious how to adapt these models for use in a registration setting. That is, we must derive a way to associate new data to the model and then use the associations to drive an optimization over T. As such, we can use their model construction algorithm in order to construct $\Theta_{\mathcal{Z}_1}$ from Z_1 (see [10] for details), but we must derive a separate and new EM algorithm to use these GMM-Tree models for registration.

4 Hierarchical Gaussian Mixture Mahalanobis Estimation

In this section, we review our proposed approach for hierarchical GMM-based registration under a new EM framework. In Sect. 4.1 we discuss our new E Step for probabilistic data association that utilizes the GMM-Tree representation for point clouds, and in Sect. 4.2 we introduce a new optimization criterion to approximate the MLE T for rigid transformations.

4.1 E Step: Adaptive Tree Search

Our proposed E Step uses a recursive search procedure to perform probabilistic data association in logarithmic time. We also introduce an early stopping heuristic in order to select the most appropriate scale at which to associate data to the hierarchical model.

The GMM-Tree representation from [10] forms a top-down hierarchy of 8-component GMM nodes, with each individual Gaussian component in a node having its own 8-component GMM child. Thus, a particular node in the GMM-Tree functions in two ways: first, as a probabilistic partition of the data and second, as a statistical description of the data within a partition. We exploit both of these properties in our proposed E Step by using the partitioning information to produce an efficient search algorithm and by using the local data distributions as a scale selection heuristic.

Logarithmic Search Each level in the GMM-Tree forms a statistical segmentation at finer levels of granularity and detail. Crucially, the expectation of a point $\mathbf{z}_i$ to a particular Gaussian component Θ_j is exactly the sum of the expectations of that point to its child GMM. Thus, if we query a parent node's point-model expectation and it falls under a threshold, we can effectively *prune* away all its children's expectations, thus avoiding calculating all $N \times J$ probabilistic associations. Refer to Algorithm 1 for details. In our implementation, we only traverse down the maximum likelihood path at each step. By utilizing the hierarchy in this way, we can recursively search through the tree in logarithmic time ($O(\log J)$) to calculate a point's expectation. This is opposed to previous registration algorithms using traditional GMM's, where a linear search much be performed over all mixture components ($O(J)$) in order to match data to the model.

Algorithm 1 E Step for Registration

1: **procedure** E_STEP_ADAPTIVE($\mathcal{Z}_2$, $\boldsymbol{\Theta}_{\mathcal{Z}_1}$)
2:    **for** $\mathbf{z}_i \in \mathcal{Z}_2$ **in parallel do**
3:       searchID $\leftarrow -1$, $\gamma \leftarrow \{0,0,0,0,0,0,0,0\}$
4:       **for** $l = 0$ to $L - 1$ **do** // L is max tree level
5:          $\mathcal{G} \leftarrow$ Children(searchID) // Children(-1) $\overset{\text{def}}{=} \{0..7\}$
6:          **for** $j \in \mathcal{G}$ **do** // for each child in subtree
7:             $\gamma[j] \propto \pi_j \mathcal{N}(\mathbf{z}_i | \boldsymbol{\Theta}_j)$ // calculate data-model expectation
8:          **end for**
9:          searchID $\leftarrow \text{argmax}_{j \in \mathcal{G}} \gamma[j]$ // Update with most likely association
10:          **if** Complexity($\boldsymbol{\Theta}[\text{searchID}]$)) $\leq \lambda_c$ **then**
11:             **break** // early stopping heuristic to prune clusters too simple
12:          **end if**
13:       **end for**
14:       // Accumulate 0th, 1st, 2nd moments $\{M_j^0, M_j^1, M_j^2\}$ for next M_Step
15:       $\{M_j^0, M_j^1, M_j^2\} \leftarrow$ Accumulate($M_j^0, M_j^1, M_j^2, \gamma[\text{searchID}]$, $\mathbf{z}_i$)
16:    **end for**
17:    **return** $\{M_j^0, M_j^1, M_j^2\}$
18: **end procedure**

Multiscale Adaptivity. Real-world point clouds often exhibit large spatial discrepancies in sampling sparsity and geometric complexity, and so different parts of the scene may benefit from being represented at different scales when performing point-scene association. Refer to Fig. 1 for an overview of this concept. Under a single scale, the point cloud modeling and matching process might succumb to noise or sampling inadequacies if the given modeling fidelity is not appropriate to the local data distribution.

To take advantage of the GMM-Tree multiscale representation and prevent overfitting, we make a check for the current mixture component's geometric complexity and stop early if this condition is not met. This complexity check acts as a heuristic for proper scale selection. We implement our complexity function (Complexity($\cdot$) in Algorithm 1, L10) as $\frac{\lambda_3}{\lambda_1 + \lambda_2 + \lambda_3}$ for each covariance where $\lambda_1 \geq \lambda_2 \geq \lambda_3$ are its associated eigenvalues. We experimentally set our adaptive threshold, $\lambda_C = 0.01$ for all experiments. This means we terminate the search at a particular scale if the current cluster associated to the point becomes too planar: when 1% or less of its variance occurs along its normal direction. Experimentally, we have found that if we recurse further, we will likely start to chase noise.

Figure 2 shows a graphical depiction of what our adaptive threshold looks like in practice. The Gaussian mixture components break down the point cloud data at a static tree level of 2 ($J = 64$) and 3 ($J = 512$) as compared to an adaptive model that is split into different recursion levels according to a complexity threshold $\lambda_C = 0.01$. The points are color coded according to their expected cluster ownership. Note that the adaptive model has components of both levels of the GMM hierarchy according how smooth or complex the facet

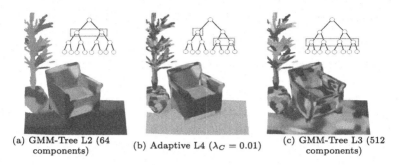

(a) GMM-Tree L2 (64 components)   (b) Adaptive L4 ($\lambda_C = 0.01$)   (c) GMM-Tree L3 (512 components)

Fig. 2. Scale Selection using a GMM-Tree To show qualitatively how scale selection works, we first build a model over a crop (couch, plant, and floor) of the Stanford Scene Lounge dataset [42]. We then associate random colors to each mixture component and color each point according to its data-model expectation. (a) shows this coloring given a static recursion level of 2 in the GMM-Tree, while (c) shows this coloring for a static recursion level of 3. We contrast this with (b), which shows our adaptively scale-selected model containing components at varying levels of recursion depending on the local properties of the mixture components. The scale selection process provides our Mahalanobis estimator (Sect. 4.2) robust component normals, preventing the use of over-fitted or under-fitted mixture components and resulting in a more accurate registration result.

geometry is. The ability to adapt to changing levels of complexity allows our M Step to always use a robustly modeled piece of geometry (cf. Fig. 1).

4.2 M Step: Mahalanobis Estimation

In this section, we will derive a new M Step for finding the optimal transformation T between a point set $\mathcal{Z}_2$ and an arbitrary GMM $\hat{\boldsymbol{\Theta}}_{\mathcal{Z}_1}$ representing point set $\mathcal{Z}_1$.

First, given N points $\mathbf{z}_i$ and J clusters $\boldsymbol{\Theta}_j \in \hat{\boldsymbol{\Theta}}_{\mathcal{Z}_1}$, we introduce a $N \times J$ set of point-cluster correspondences $\mathcal{C} = \{c_{ij}\}$, so that the full joint probability becomes

$$\ln p(T(\mathcal{Z}), \mathcal{C}|\boldsymbol{\Theta}) = \sum_{i=1}^{N} \sum_{j=1}^{J} c_{ij}\{\ln \pi_j + \ln \mathcal{N}(T(\mathbf{z}_i)|\boldsymbol{\Theta}_j)\} \qquad (4)$$

We iterate between E and M Steps. On the E Step, we calculate $\gamma_{ij} \overset{\text{def}}{=} E[c_{ij}]$ under the current posterior. On the M Step, we maximize the expected data log likelihood with respect to T while keeping all γ_{ij} fixed,

$$\hat{T} = \underset{T}{\operatorname{argmax}} E_{p(\mathcal{C}|T(\mathcal{Z}), \boldsymbol{\Theta})}[\ln p(T(\mathcal{Z}), \mathcal{C}|\boldsymbol{\Theta})] \qquad (5)$$

$$= \arg\min_{T} \sum_{ij} \gamma_{ij}(T(\mathbf{z}_i) - \boldsymbol{\mu}_j)^T \boldsymbol{\Sigma}_j^{-1}(T(\mathbf{z}_i) - \boldsymbol{\mu}_j) \qquad (6)$$

From this construction, we see that the most likely transformation T between point sets is the one that minimizes the weighted sum of squared Mahalanobis distances between points of $\mathcal{Z}_2$ and individual clusters of $\Theta_{\mathcal{Z}_1}$, with weights determined by calculating expected correspondences given the current best guess for $\hat{T}$.

As shown mathematically in previous work [9,13,16,18], if we restrict T solely to the set of all rigid transformations ($T \in SE(3)$) we can further reduce the double sum over both points and clusters into a single sum over clusters. This leaves us with a simplified MLE optimization criterion over weighted moments,

$$\hat{T} = \arg\min_T \sum_j M_j^0 \left(T\left(\frac{M_j^1}{M_j^0}\right) - \boldsymbol{\mu}_j \right)^T \boldsymbol{\Sigma}_j^{-1} \left(T\left(\frac{M_j^1}{M_j^0}\right) - \boldsymbol{\mu}_j \right) \quad (7)$$

where $M_j^0 = \sum_i \gamma_{ij}$ and $M_j^1 = \sum_i \gamma_{ij} \mathbf{z}_i$.

One can interpret the Mahalanobis distance as a generalization of point-to-point distance where the coordinate system has undergone some affine transformation. In the case of GMM-based registration, each affine transformation is determined by the covariance, or shape, of the cluster to which points are being registered. For example, clusters that are mostly planar in shape (two similar eigenvalues and one near zero) will tend to aggressively pull points toward it along its normal direction while permitting free movement in the plane. This observation should match one's intuition: given that we have chosen a probabilistic model that accurately estimates local geometry, an MLE framework will utilize this information to pull like geometry together as a type of probabilistic shape matching. By using fully anisotropic covariances, arbitrarily oriented point-to-geometry relations can be modeled. Previous algorithms in the literature, however, have yet to fully leverage this general MLE construction. Simplifications are made either by (1) placing *a priori* restrictions on the complexity of the Gaussian covariance structure (e.g. isotropic only [13] or a single global bandwidth term [16]), or by (2) using approximations to the MLE criterion that remove or degrade this information [9]. The reasons behind both model simplification and MLE approximation are the same: Eq. 7 has no closed form solution. However, we will show how simply reinterpreting the Mahalanobis distance calculation can lead to a highly accurate and novel method for registration.

We first rewrite the inner Mahalanobis distance inside the MLE criterion of Eq. 7 by decomposing each covariance $\boldsymbol{\Sigma}_j$ into its associated eigenvalues λ and eigenvectors $\boldsymbol{n}$, thereby producing the following equivalence,

$$\left\| T\left(\frac{M_j^1}{M_j^0}\right) - \boldsymbol{\mu}_j \right\|_{\boldsymbol{\Sigma}_j}^2 = \sum_{l=1}^3 \frac{1}{\lambda_l} \left(\boldsymbol{n}_l^T \left(T\left(\frac{M_j^1}{M_j^0}\right) - \boldsymbol{\mu}_j \right) \right)^2 \quad (8)$$

Thus, we can reinterpret each cluster's Mahalanobis distance term inside the MLE criterion as a weighted sum of three separate point-to-plane distances. The weights are inversely determined by the eigenvalues, with their associated eigenvectors constituting each plane's normal vector. Going back to the example of a nearly planar Gaussian, its covariance will have two large eigenvalues and one near-zero eigenvalue, with the property that the eigenvectors associated with the larger eigenvalues will lie in the plane and the eigenvector associated with the smallest eigenvalue will point in the direction of its normal vector. Since the weights are inversely related to the eigenvalues, we can easily see that the MLE criterion will mostly disregard any point-to-μ_j distance inside its plane (that is, along the two dominant PCA axes) and instead disproportionately focus on minimizing out-of-plane distances by pulling nearby points along the normal to the plane.

We can see that by plugging in this equivalence back into Eq. 7, we arrive at the following MLE criterion,

$$\hat{T} = \arg\min_T \sum_{j=1}^{J} \sum_{l=1}^{3} \frac{M_j^0}{\lambda_{j_l}} \left(n_{j_l}^T \left(T \left(\frac{M_j^1}{M_j^0} \right) - \mu_j \right) \right)^2 \tag{9}$$

where the set of $n_{j_l}, l = 1..3$ represent the three eigenvectors for the jth Gaussian (anisotropic) covariance, and λ_{j_l} the associated eigenvalues.

We have transformed the optimization from the minimization of a weighted sum of J squared Mahalanobis distances to an equivalent minimization of a weighted sum of $3J$ squared point-to-plane distances. In doing so, we arrive at a form that can be leveraged by any number of minimization techniques previously developed for point-to-plane ICP [3]. Note that unlike traditional point-to-plane methods, which usually involve the computationally difficult task of finding planar approximations over local neighborhoods at every point and sometimes also for multiple scales [22, 41], the normals in Eq. 9 are found through a very small number of 3×3 eigendecompositions (typically $J \leq 1000$ for even complex geometric models) over the model covariances, with appropriate scales chosen through our proposed recursive search over the covariances in the GMM-Tree (Sect. 4.1).

We solve Eq. 9 using the linear least squares technique described by Low [24] for point-to-plane ICP optimization, which we adapt into a weighted form. The only approximation required is a linearization of R using the small-angle assumption.

5   Speed Vs Accuracy

For every registration algorithm, there is an inherent trade-off between accuracy and speed. To explore how different registration algorithms perform under various accuracy/speed trade-offs, we have designed a synthetic experiment using the Stanford Bunny. We take 100 random 6DoF transformations of the bunny and then run each algorithm over the same group of random point subsets of increasing cardinality. Our method of obtaining a random transformation is to sample each axis of rotation uniformly from $[-15, 15]$ degrees and each translation uniformly from $[-0.05, 0.05]$ (roughly half the extent of the bunny). We can then plot speed vs accuracy as a scatter plot in order to see how changing the point cloud size (a proxy for model complexity) affects the speed vs accuracy tradeoff.

The algorithms and code used in the following experiments were either provided directly by the authors (JRMPC, ECMPR, NDT-D2D, NDT-P2D, SVR, GMMReg), taken from popular open source libraries (libpointmatcher for TrICP-pt2pt, TrICP-pt2pl, FICP), or are open source re-implementations of the original algorithms with various performance optimizations (EM-ICP-GPU, SoftAssign-GPU, ICP-OpenMP, CPD-C++). Links to the sources can be found in our project page. Parameters were set for all algorithms according to what was recommended by the authors and/or by the software. All our experiments were run on Intel Core i7-5920K and NVIDIA Titan X.

In order to test how each design decision affects the performance of the proposed algorithm, we test against three variants:

Adaptive Ln: The full algorithm proposed in this paper: Hierarchical Gaussian Mixture Registration (HGMR). Adaptive multi-scale data association using a GMM-Tree that was constructed up to a max recursion level of n.

GMM-Tree Ln: Here we use the same GMM-Tree representation for logarithmic time data association, but without multi-scale adaptivity ($\lambda_c = 0$). The tree is constructed up to a max recursion level of n. By comparing *GMM-Tree* to *Adaptive*, we can see the benefits of stopping our recursive search according to data complexity.

GMM J=n: This variant forgoes a GMM-Tree representation and uses a simple, fixed complexity, single-level GMM with n mixture components. Similar to other fixed complexity GMM-based registration approaches (e.g. [9,13,16,21]), both recursive data-association and adaptive complexity cannot be used. However, it is still GPU-optimized and uses the new MLE optimization. Comparing this approach to the tree-based representations (*GMM-Tree* and *Adaptive*) shows how the tree-based data representation affects registration performance.

Figure 3(a) shows each algorithm's speed vs accuracy trade-off by plotting registration error vs time elapsed. The lower left corner is best (both fast and accurate). One can quickly see how different classes of algorithms clearly dominate each other on the speed/accuracy continuum. For additional clarity, Fig. 3(b) explicitly plots the time scaling of each registration method as a function of point cloud size. For both timing and accuracy, one can see that, roughly speaking, our adaptive tree formulation performs the best, followed by our non-adaptive tree formulation, followed by our non-adaptive non-tree formulation, then ICP-based variants, and then finally previous GMM-based variants (black > cyan > red > blue > green).

It should be noted that even though our proposed algorithms (black, cyan, and red) tend to dominate the lower left corner of Fig. 3(a), certain robust point-to-plane ICP methods sometimes produce more accurate results, albeit at much slower speeds. See for example in Fig. 3 that some point-to-plane ICP results were less than $10^{-2\circ}$ angular error and near 1 second convergence time. We estimate that this timing gap might be decreased given a good GPU-optimized

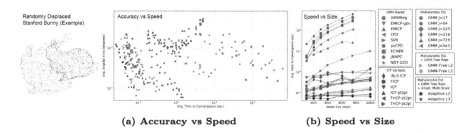

(a) Accuracy vs Speed   **(b) Speed vs Size**

Fig. 3. Each data point represents a particular algorithm's average speed and accuracy when registering together randomly transformed Stanford Bunnies. We produce multiple points for each algorithm at different speed/accuracy levels by applying the methods multiple times to different sized point clouds. The lower left corner shows the fastest and most accurate algorithms for a particular model size. Our proposed algorithms (black, cyan, and red) tend to dominate the bottom left corner, though robust point-to-plane ICP methods sometimes produce more accurate results, albeit at much slower speeds (e.g. Trimmed ICP).

robust planar ICP implementation, though it is unclear if the neighborhood-based planar approximation scheme used by these algorithms could benefit from GPU parallelization as much as our proposed Expectation Maximization approach, which is designed to be almost completely data parallel at the point level. However, if computation time is not a constraint for a given application (e.g. offline approaches), we would recommend trying both types of algorithms (our model-based approach vs a robust planar ICP-based approach) to see which provides the best accuracy.

For completeness, we repeated the test with two frames of real-world Lidar data, randomly transformed and varyingly subsampled as before in order to obtain our set of speed/accuracy pairs. The results are shown in Fig. 4. As in Fig. 3(a), the bottom left corner is most desirable (both fast and accurate), our methods shown in red, teal, and black. Given that the bunny and LiDAR scans have very different sampling properties, a similar outcome for all three tests shows that the relative performance of the proposed approach isn't dependent on evenly sampled point clouds.

6   Evaluation on Real-World Data

Lounge Dataset. In this test, we calculate the frame-to-frame accuracy on the Stanford Lounge dataset, which consists of range data produced by moving a handheld Kinect around an indoor environment [42]. We register together every 5th frame for the first 400 frames, each downsampled to 5000 points. To measure the resulting error, we calculate the average Euler angle deviation from ground truth. Refer to Table 2(a) for error and timing. All our experiments were run on Intel Core i7-5920K and NVIDIA Titan X. We chose to focus on rotation error since this was where the largest discrepancies were found among algorithms. The

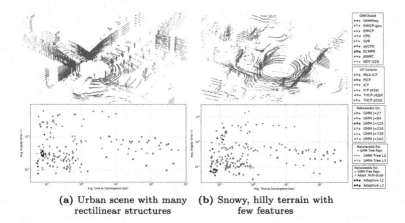

(a) Urban scene with many   **(b)** Snowy, hilly terrain with
rectilinear structures   few features

Fig. 4. Speed vs accuracy tests for two types of real-world LiDAR frames with very different sampling properties from the Stanford Bunny. In general, similar results are obtained as in Fig. 3.

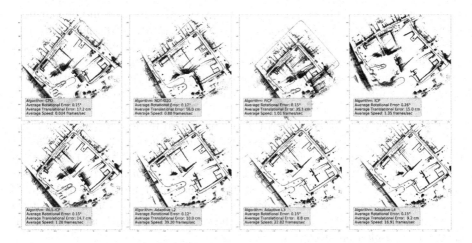

Fig. 5. Frame-to-Frame Registration with Outdoor LiDAR Dataset: Ground truth path shown in **red**, calculated path shown in **blue**. Each frame of LiDAR data represents a single sweep. We register successive frames together and concatenate the transformation in order to plot the results in a single coordinate system. Note that drift is expected over such long distances as we perform no loop closures. The first two examples in top row are from GMM-Based methods, next three results are from modern ICP variants, the last three results show our proposed adaptive GMM-Tree methods at three different max recursion levels. For our methods, the timing results include the time to build the GMM model. GMM-Based methods generally perform slowly. ICP-based methods fared better in our testing, though our proposed methods show an order of magnitude improvement in speed while beating or competing with other state-of-the-art in accuracy.

Table 2. Comparison of Registration Methods for the Lounge and LiDAR Datasets Timing results for both datasets include the time to build the GMM-Tree. Errors are frame-to-frame averages. Speed given is in average frames per second that the data could be processed (note that the sensor outputs data frames at 30 Hz for the Lounge data and roughly 10 Hz for the LiDAR data).

Method	Ang. Error (°)	Speed (fps)	Method	Ang. Error (°)	Trans. Error (cm)	Speed (fps)
CPD	2.11	0.18	CPD	0.15	17.2	0.004
GMMReg	3.02	.04	GMMReg	0.73	102.1	0.22
NDT-D2D	14.25	11.76	NDT-D2D	0.17	16.0	0.88
FICP	1.44	4.9	FICP	0.15	35.1	1.01
ICP	7.29	2.58	ICP	0.26	15.0	1.35
IRLS-ICP	2.29	7.1	IRLS-ICP	0.15	14.7	1.28
EMICP	10.47	1.44	EMICP	0.99	103.1	2.05
SVR	2.67	0.35	SVR	0.21	39.1	0.27
ECMPR	2.21	0.059	ECMPR	0.31	24.1	0.21
JRMPC	8.27	0.042	JRMPC	0.60	73.1	0.05
TrICP-pt2pl	0.54	8.4	TrICP-pt2pl	0.15	43.2	1.74
TrICP-pt2pt	1.26	5.5	TrICP-pt2pt	0.21	66.2	1.75
ICP-pt2pl	2.24	7.6	ICP-pt2pl	0.27	7.5	1.48
GMM-Tree L2	**0.77**	**31.3**	**GMM-Tree L2**	**0.11**	**12.5**	**39.34**
GMM-Tree L3	**0.48**	**20.4**	**GMM-Tree L3**	**0.18**	**23.9**	**21.41**
GMM-Tree L4	**0.56**	**14.2**	**GMM-Tree L4**	**0.20**	**29.5**	**15.00**
Adaptive L2	**0.76**	**29.6**	**Adaptive L2**	**0.12**	**10.0**	**39.20**
Adaptive L3	**0.46**	**19.8**	**Adaptive L3**	**0.15**	**8.8**	**22.82**
Adaptive L4	**0.37**	**14.5**	**Adaptive L4**	**0.15**	**9.2**	**16.91**
(a) Lounge Dataset			**(b) LiDAR Dataset**			

best performing algorithm we tested against, Trimmed ICP with point-to-plane distance error minimization, had an average Euler angle error of 0.54 degrees and took on average 119 ms to converge. Our best algorithm, the adaptive algorithm to a max depth of 3, had an average Euler angle error of 0.46 degrees and took on average less than half the time (50.5 ms) to converge. The accuracy of our proposed methods is comparable with the best ICP variants, but at roughly twice the speed.

Velodyne LiDAR Dataset. We performed frame-to-frame registration on an outdoor LiDAR dataset using a Velodyne (VLP-16) LiDAR and overlaid the results in a common global frame. See Fig. 5 for a qualitative depiction of the result. Table 2(b) summarizes the quantitative results from Fig. 5 in an easier to read table format. In Fig. 5, the ground truth path is shown in red, and the calculated path is shown in blue. Since there is no loop closures, the error is expected to compound and cause drift over time. However, despite the compounding error, the bottom right three diagrams of Fig. 5 (and correspondingly, the bottom three line items of Table 2(b)) show that the proposed methods can be used for fairly long distances (city blocks), without the need for any odometry (e.g. INS or GPS) or loop closures. Given that this sensor outputs sweeps at roughly 10 Hz, our methods achieve faster than real-time speeds (17–39 Hz), while the state-of-the-art ICP methods are an order of magnitude slower (≈1 fps). Also, note that our times include the time to build the model (the GMM-Tree), which could be utilized for other concurrent applications besides registration.

7 Conclusion

We propose a registration algorithm using a Hierarchical Gaussian Mixture to efficiently perform point-to-model association. Data association as recursive tree search results in orders of magnitude speed-up relative to traditional GMM-based approaches that linearly perform these associations. In addition, we leverage the model's multi-scale anisotropic representation using a new approximation scheme that reduces the MLE optimization criteria to a weighted point-to-plane measure. We test our proposed methods against state-of-the-art and find that our approach is often an order of magnitude faster while achieving similar or greater accuracy.

References

1. Besl, P., McKay, H.: A method for registration of 3-D shapes. IEEE Trans. Pattern Anal. Mach. Intell. **14**(2), 239–256 (1992). https://doi.org/10.1109/34.121791
2. Campbell, D., Petersson, L.: An adaptive data representation for robust point-set registration and merging. In: Proceedings of the IEEE International Conference on Computer Vision, pp. 4292–4300 (2015)
3. Chen, Y., Medioni, G.: Object modelling by registration of multiple range images. Image Vis. Comput. **10**(3), 145–155 (1992). Range Image Understanding
4. Chetverikov, D., Stepanov, D., Krsek, P.: Robust Euclidean alignment of 3D point sets: the trimmed iterative closest point algorithm. Image Vis. Comput. **23**(3), 299–309 (2005)
5. Chetverikov, D., Svirko, D., Stepanov, D., Krsek, P.: The trimmed iterative closest point algorithm. In: 2002 Proceedings of the 16th International Conference on Pattern Recognition, vol. 3, pp. 545–548. IEEE (2002)
6. Chui, H., Rangarajan, A.: A feature registration framework using mixture models. In: IEEE Workshop on Mathematical Methods in Biomedical Image Analysis, pp. 190–197 (2000)
7. Dempster, A., Laird, N., Rubin, D.: Maximum likelihood from incomplete data via the EM algorithm. J. R. Stat. Soc. 1–38 (1977)
8. Drost, B., Ulrich, M., Navab, N., Ilic, S.: Model globally, match locally: efficient and robust 3D object recognition. In: 2010 IEEE Conference on CVPR, pp. 998–1005 (2010)
9. Eckart, B., Kim, K., Troccoli, A., Kelly, A., Kautz, J.: Mlmd: maximum likelihood mixture decoupling for fast and accurate point cloud registration. In: IEEE International Conference on 3D Vision. IEEE (2015)
10. Eckart, B., Kim, K., Troccoli, A., Kelly, A., Kautz, J.: Accelerated generative models for 3D point cloud data. In: CVPR. IEEE (2016)
11. Eckart, B., Kelly, A.: REM-Seg: a robust EM algorithm for parallel segmentation and registration of point clouds. In: IEEE Conference on Intelligent Robots and Systems, pp. 4355–4362 (2013)
12. Evangelidis, G.D., Horaud, R.: Joint alignment of multiple point sets with batch and incremental expectation-maximization. IEEE Trans. Pattern Anal. Mach. Intell. (2017)
13. Evangelidis, G.D., Kounades-Bastian, D., Horaud, R., Psarakis, E.Z.: A generative model for the joint registration of multiple point sets. In: Fleet, D., Pajdla, T., Schiele, B., Tuytelaars, T. (eds.) ECCV 2014. LNCS, vol. 8695, pp. 109–122. Springer, Cham (2014). https://doi.org/10.1007/978-3-319-10584-0_8

14. Fitzgibbon, A.W.: Robust registration of 2D and 3D point sets. Image Vis. Comput. **21**(13), 1145–1153 (2003)
15. Gold, S., Rangarajan, A., Lu, C., Pappu, S., Mjolsness, E.: New algorithms for 2D and 3D point matching: pose estimation and correspondence. Pattern Recognit. **31**(8), 1019–1031 (1998)
16. Granger, S., Pennec, X.: Multi-scale EM-ICP: a fast and robust approach for surface registration. In: Heyden, A., Sparr, G., Nielsen, M., Johansen, P. (eds.) ECCV 2002. LNCS, vol. 2353, pp. 418–432. Springer, Heidelberg (2002). https://doi.org/10.1007/3-540-47979-1_28
17. Hahnel, D., Thrun, S., Burgard, W.: An extension of the ICP algorithm for modeling nonrigid objects with mobile robots. In: Proceedings of the 18th International Joint Conference on Artificial Intelligence, IJCAI 2003, pp. 915–920 (2003)
18. Horaud, R., Forbes, F., Yguel, M., Dewaele, G., Zhang, J.: Rigid and articulated point registration with expectation conditional maximization. IEEE Trans. Pattern Anal. Mach. Intell. **33**(3), 587–602 (2011). http://doi.ieeecomputersociety.org/10.1109/TPAMI.2010.94
19. Jian, B., Vemuri, B.C.: A robust algorithm for point set registration using mixture of Gaussians. In: IEEE International Conference on Computer Vision, pp. 1246–1251 (2005)
20. Jian, B., Vemuri, B.C.: Robust point set registration using gaussian mixture models. IEEE Trans. Pattern Anal. Mach. Intell. **33**(8), 1633–1645 (2011)
21. Jian, B., Vemuri, B.C.: Robust point set registration using Gaussian mixture models. IEEE Trans. Pattern Anal. Mach. Intell. **33**(8), 1633–1645 (2011). http://gmmreg.googlecode.com
22. Lalonde, J., Unnikrishnan, R., Vandapel, N., Hebert, M.: Scale selection for classification of Point-Sampled 3-D surfaces. In: Fifth International Conference on 3-D Digital Imaging and Modeling (3DIM 2005), pp. 285–292. Ottawa, ON, Canada (2005). https://doi.org/10.1109/3DIM.2005.71, http://ieeexplore.ieee.org/lpdocs/epic03/wrapper.htm?arnumber=1443257
23. Levinson, J., et al.: Towards fully autonomous driving: systems and algorithms. In: Intelligent Vehicles Symposium, pp. 163–168. IEEE (2011)
24. Low, K.L.: Linear least-squares optimization for point-to-plane ICP surface registration, Chapel Hill, University of North Carolina (2004)
25. Mehta, S.U., Kim, K., Pajak, D., Pulli, K., Kautz, J., Ramamoorthi, R.: Filtering environment illumination for interactive physically-based rendering in mixed reality. In: Eurographics Symposium on Rendering (2015)
26. Meng, X.L., Rubin, D.B.: Maximum likelihood estimation via the ECM algorithm: a general framework. Biometrika **80**(2), 267–278 (1993)
27. Myronenko, A., Song, X.: Point set registration: coherent point drift. IEEE Trans. Pattern Anal. Mach. Intell. **32**(12), 2262–2275 (2010)
28. Myronenko, A., Song, X., Carreira-Perpinán, M.A.: Non-rigid point set registration: coherent point drift. In: Advances in Neural Information Processing Systems, pp. 1009–1016 (2006)
29. Newcombe, R.A., et al.: Kinectfusion: real-time dense surface mapping and tracking. In: IEEE ISMAR, pp. 127–136. IEEE (2011)
30. Nüchter, A., Lingemann, K., Hertzberg, J., Surmann, H.: 6d SLAM—3D mapping outdoor environments: research articles. J. Field Robot. **24**(8–9), 699–722 (2007)
31. Park, I.K., Germann, M., Breitenstein, M.D., Pfister, H.: Fast and automatic object pose estimation for range images on the GPU. Mach. Vis. Appl. **21**, 749–766 (2010)

32. Phillips, J.M., Liu, R., Tomasi, C.: Outlier robust ICP for minimizing fractional RMSD. In: 2007 Sixth International Conference on 3-D Digital Imaging and Modeling, 3DIM 2007, pp. 427–434. IEEE (2007)

33. Pomerleau, F., Colas, F., Siegwart, R., Magnenat, S.: Comparing ICP variants on real-world data sets. Auton. Robot. **34**(3), 133–148 (2013)

34. Rusinkiewicz, S., Levoy, M.: Efficient variants of the ICP algorithm. In: International Conference on 3-D Digital Imaging and Modeling, pp. 145–152 (2001)

35. Segal, A., Haehnel, D., Thrun, S.: Generalized ICP. Robot. Sci. Syst. **2**(4) (2009)

36. Stoyanov, T., Magnusson, M., Lilienthal, A.J.: Point set registration through minimization of the L2 distance between 3D-NDT models. In: IEEE International Conference on Robotics and Automation, pp. 5196–5201 (2012)

37. Stoyanov, T.D., Magnusson, M., Andreasson, H., Lilienthal, A.: Fast and accurate scan registration through minimization of the distance between compact 3D NDT representations. Int. J. Robot. Res. (2012)

38. Tam, G.K., Cheng, Z.Q., Lai, Y.K., Langbein, F., Liu, Y., Marshall, A.D., Martin, R., Sun, X., Rosin, P.: Registration of 3D point clouds and meshes: a survey from rigid to nonrigid. IEEE Trans. Vis. Comput. Graph. **19**(7), 1199–1217 (2013)

39. Tamaki, T., Abe, M., Raytchev, B., Kaneda, K.: Softassign and EM-ICP on GPU. In: IEEE International Conference on Networking and Computing, pp. 179–183 (2010)

40. Tsin, Y., Kanade, T.: A correlation-based approach to robust point set registration. In: Pajdla, T., Matas, J. (eds.) ECCV 2004. LNCS, vol. 3023, pp. 558–569. Springer, Heidelberg (2004). https://doi.org/10.1007/978-3-540-24672-5_44

41. Unnikrishnan, R., Lalonde, J., Vandapel, N., Hebert, M.: Scale selection for the analysis of point-sampled curves. In: International Symposium on 3D Data Processing Visualization and Transmission, vol. 0, pp. 1026–1033. IEEE Computer Society, Los Alamitos (2006). http://doi.ieeecomputersociety.org/10.1109/3DPVT.2006.123

42. Zhou, Q.Y., Koltun, V.: Dense scene reconstruction with points of interest. ACM Trans. Graph. **32**(4), 112 (2013)

Bi-Real Net: Enhancing the Performance of 1-Bit CNNs with Improved Representational Capability and Advanced Training Algorithm

Zechun Liu[1], Baoyuan Wu[2], Wenhan Luo[2], Xin Yang[3(✉)], Wei Liu[2], and Kwang-Ting Cheng[1]

[1] Hong Kong University of Science and Technology, Hong Kong, China
zliubq@connect.ust.hk, timcheng@ust.hk
[2] Tencent AI Lab, Beijing, China
wubaoyuan1987@gmail.com, whluo.china@gmail.com, wliu@ee.columbia.edu
[3] Huazhong University of Science and Technology, Wuhan, China
xinyang2014@hust.edu.cn

Abstract. In this work, we study the 1-bit convolutional neural networks (CNNs), of which both the weights and activations are binary. While being efficient, the classification accuracy of the current 1-bit CNNs is much worse compared to their counterpart real-valued CNN models on the large-scale dataset, like ImageNet. To minimize the performance gap between the 1-bit and real-valued CNN models, we propose a novel model, dubbed Bi-Real net, which connects the real activations (after the 1-bit convolution and/or BatchNorm layer, before the sign function) to activations of the consecutive block, through an identity shortcut. Consequently, compared to the standard 1-bit CNN, the representational capability of the Bi-Real net is significantly enhanced and the additional cost on computation is negligible. Moreover, we develop a specific training algorithm including three technical novelties for 1-bit CNNs. Firstly, we derive a tight approximation to the derivative of the non-differentiable sign function with respect to activation. Secondly, we propose a magnitude-aware gradient with respect to the weight for updating the weight parameters. Thirdly, we pre-train the real-valued CNN model with a clip function, rather than the ReLU function, to better initialize the Bi-Real net. Experiments on ImageNet show that the Bi-Real net with the proposed training algorithm achieves 56.4% and 62.2% top-1 accuracy with 18 layers and 34 layers, respectively. Compared to the state-of-the-arts (*e.g.*, XNOR Net), Bi-Real net achieves up to 10% higher top-1 accuracy with more memory saving and lower computational cost.

© Springer Nature Switzerland AG 2018
V. Ferrari et al. (Eds.): ECCV 2018, LNCS 11219, pp. 747–763, 2018.
https://doi.org/10.1007/978-3-030-01267-0_44

1 Introduction

Deep Convolutional Neural Networks (CNNs) have achieved substantial advances in a wide range of vision tasks, such as object detection and recognition [3,5,12,20,23,25], depth perception [2,16], visual relation detection [29,30], face tracking and alignment [24,27,28,32,34], object tracking [17], etc. However, the superior performance of CNNs usually requires powerful hardware with abundant computing and memory resources. For example, high-end Graphics Processing Units (GPUs). Meanwhile, there are growing demands to run vision tasks, such as augmented reality and intelligent navigation, on mobile hand-held devices and small drones. Most mobile devices are not equipped with a powerful GPU neither an adequate amount of memory to run and store the expensive CNN model. Consequently, the high demand for computation and memory becomes the bottleneck of deploying the powerful CNNs on most mobile devices. In general, there are three major approaches to alleviate this limitation. The first is to reduce the number of weights, such as Sparse CNN [15]. The second is to quantize the weights (e.g., QNN [8] and DoReFa Net [33]). The third is to quantize both weights and activations, with the extreme case of both weights and activations being binary.

In this work, we study the extreme case of the third approach, i.e., the binary CNNs. It is also called 1-bit CNNs, as each weight parameter and activation can be represented by 1-bit. As demonstrated in [19], up to 32× memory saving and 58× speedup on CPUs have been achieved for a 1-bit convolution layer, in which the computationally heavy matrix multiplication operations become light-weighted bitwise XNOR operations and bit-count operations. The current binarization method achieves comparable accuracy to real-valued networks on small datasets (e.g., CIFAR-10 and MNIST). However on the large-scale datasets (e.g., ImageNet), the binarization method based on AlexNet in [7] encounters severe accuracy degradation, i.e., from 56.6% to 27.9% [19]. It reveals that the capability of conventional 1-bit CNNs is not sufficient to cover great diversity in large-scale datasets like ImageNet. Another binary network called XNOR-Net [19] was proposed to enhance the performance of 1-bit CNNs, by utilizing the absolute mean of weights and activations.

The objective of this study is to further improve 1-bit CNNs, as we believe its potential has not been fully explored. One important observation is that during the inference process, 1-bit convolution layer generates integer outputs, due to the bit-count operations. The integer outputs will become real values if there is a BatchNorm [10] layer. But these real-valued activations are then binarized to −1 or +1 through the consecutive sign function, as shown in Fig. 1(a). Obviously, compared to binary activations, these integers or real activations contain more information, which is lost in the conventional 1-bit CNNs [7]. Inspired by this observation, we propose to keep these real activations via adding a simple yet effective shortcut, dubbed Bi-Real net. As shown in Fig. 1(b), the shortcut connects the real activations to an addition operator with the real-valued activations of the next block. By doing so, the representational capability of the proposed model is much higher than that of the original 1-bit CNNs, with only a negligible computational cost incurred by the extra element-wise addition and without any additional memory cost.

Moreover, we further propose a novel training algorithm for 1-bit CNNs including three technical novelties:

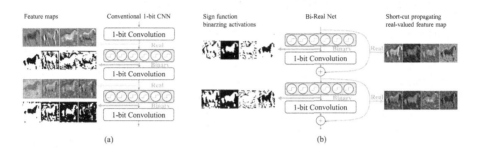

(a)   (b)

Fig. 1. Network with intermediate feature visualization, yellow lines denote value propagated inside the path being real while blue lines denote binary values. (a) 1-bit CNN without shortcut (b) proposed Bi-Real net with shortcut propagating the real-valued features.

- **Approximation to the derivative of the sign function with respect to activations.** As the sign function binarizing the activation is non-differentiable, we propose to approximate its derivative by a piecewise linear function in the backward pass, derived from the piecewise polynomial function that is a second-order approximation of the sign function. In contrast, the approximated derivative using a step function (*i.e.*, $1_{|x|<1}$) proposed in [7] is derived from the clip function (*i.e.*, clip(-1, x, 1)), which is also an approximation to the sign function. We show that the piecewise polynomial function is a closer approximation to the sign function than the clip function. Hence, its derivative is more effective than the derivative of the clip function.
- **Magnitude-aware gradient with respect to weights.** As the gradient of loss with respect to the binary weight is not large enough to change the sign of the binary weight, the binary weight cannot be directly updated using the standard gradient descent algorithm. In BinaryNet [7], the real-valued weight is first updated using gradient descent, and the new binary weight is then obtained through taking the sign of the updated real weight. However, we find that the gradient with respect to the real weight is only related to the sign of the current real weight, while independent of its magnitude. To derive a more effective gradient, we propose to use a magnitude-aware sign function during training, then the gradient with respect to the real weight depends on both the sign and the magnitude of the current real weight. After convergence, the binary weight (*i.e.*, -1 or $+1$) is obtained through the sign function of the final real weight for inference.

- **Initialization.** As a highly non-convex optimization problem, the training of 1-bit CNNs is likely to be sensitive to initialization. In [17], the 1-bit CNN model is initialized using the real-valued CNN model with the ReLU function pre-trained on ImageNet. We propose to replace ReLU by the clip function in pre-training, as the activation of the clip function is closer to the binary activation than that of ReLU.

Experiments on ImageNet show that the above three ideas are useful to train 1-bit CNNs, including both Bi-Real net and other network structures. Specifically, their respective contributions to the improvements of top-1 accuracy are up to 12%, 23% and 13% for a 18-layer Bi-Real net. With the dedicatedly-designed shortcut and the proposed optimization techniques, our Bi-Real net, with only binary weights and activations inside each 1-bit convolution layer, achieves 56.4% and 62.2% top-1 accuracy with 18-layer and 34-layer structures, respectively, with up to 16.0× memory saving and 19.0× computational cost reduction compared to the full-precision CNN. Comparing to the state-of-the-art model (*e.g.*, XNOR-Net), Bi-Real net achieves 10% higher top-1 accuracy on the 18-layer network.

2   Related Work

Reducing the Number of Parameters. Several methods have been proposed to compress neural networks by reducing the number of parameters and neural connections. For instance, He et al. [5] proposed a bottleneck structure which consists of three convolution layers of filter size 1×1, 3×3 and 1×1 with a shortcut connection as a preliminary building block to reduce the number of parameters and to speed up training. In SqueezeNet [9], some 3×3 convolutions are replaced with 1×1 convolutions, resulting in a 50× reduction in the number of parameters. FitNets [21] imitates the soft output of a large teacher network using a thin and deep student network, and in turn yields 10.4× fewer parameters and similar accuracy to a large teacher network on the CIFAR-10 dataset. In Sparse CNN [15], a sparse matrix multiplication operation is employed to zero out more than 90% of parameters to accelerate the learning process. Motivated by the Sparse CNN, Han et al. proposed Deep Compression [4] which employs connection pruning, quantization with retraining and Huffman coding to reduce the number of neural connections, thus, in turn, reduces the memory usage.

Parameter Quantization. The previous study [13] demonstrated that real-valued deep neural networks such as AlexNet [12], GoogLeNet [25] and VGG-16 [23] only encounter marginal accuracy degradation when quantizing 32-bit parameters to 8-bit. In Incremental Network Quantization, Zhou et al. [31] quantize the parameter incrementally and show that it is even possible to further reduce the weight precision to 2–5 bits with slightly higher accuracy than a full-precision network on the ImageNet dataset. In BinaryConnect [1], Courbariaux et al. employ 1-bit precision weights (1 and −1) while maintaining sufficiently high accuracy on the MNIST, CIFAR10 and SVHN datasets.

Quantizing weights properly can achieve considerable memory savings with little accuracy degradation. However, acceleration via weight quantization is limited due to the real-valued activations (*i.e.*, the input to convolution layers).

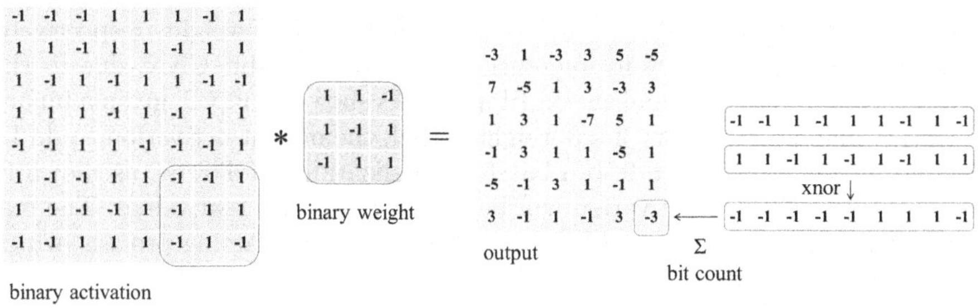

Fig. 2. The mechanism of xnor operation and bit-counting inside the 1-bit CNNs presented in [19].

Several recent studies have been conducted to explore new network structures and/or training techniques for quantizing both weights and activations while minimizing accuracy degradation. Successful attempts include DoReFa-Net [33] and QNN [8], which explore neural networks trained with 1-bit weights and 2-bit activations, and the accuracy drops by 6.1% and 4.9% respectively on the ImageNet dataset compared to the real-valued AlexNet. Additionally, BinaryNet [7] uses only 1-bit weights and 1-bit activations in a neural network and achieves comparable accuracy as full-precision neural networks on the MNIST and CIFAR-10 datasets. In XNOR-Net [19], Rastegari et al. further improve BinaryNet by multiplying the absolute mean of the weight filter and activation with the 1-bit weight and activation to improve the accuracy. ABC-Net [14] proposes to enhance the accuracy by using more weight bases and activation bases. The results of these studies are encouraging, but admittedly, due to the loss of precision in weights and activations, the number of filters in the network (thus the algorithm complexity) grows in order to maintain high accuracy, which offsets the memory saving and speedup of binarizing the network.

In this study, we aim to design 1-bit CNNs aided with a real-valued shortcut to compensate for the accuracy loss of binarization. Optimization strategies for overcoming the gradient dismatch problem and discrete optimization difficulties in 1-bit CNNs, along with a customized initialization method, are proposed to fully explore the potential of 1-bit CNNs with its limited resolution.

3   Methodology

3.1   Standard 1-Bit CNNs and Its Representational Capability

1-bit convolutional neural networks (CNNs) refer to the CNN models with binary weight parameters and binary activations in intermediate convolution layers.

Specifically, the binary activation and weight are obtained through a sign function,

$$a_b = \text{Sign}(a_r) = \begin{cases} -1 \text{ if } a_r < 0 \\ +1 \text{ otherwise} \end{cases}, \qquad w_b = \text{Sign}(w_r) = \begin{cases} -1 \text{ if } w_r < 0 \\ +1 \text{ otherwise} \end{cases}, \quad (1)$$

where a_r and w_r indicate the real activation and the real weight, respectively. a_r exists in both training and inference process of the 1-bit CNN, due to the convolution and batch normalization (if used). As shown in Fig. 2, given a binary activation map and a binary 3×3 weight kernel, the output activation could be any odd integer from -9 to 9. If a batch normalization is followed, as shown in Fig. 3, then the integer activation will be transformed into real values. The real weight will be used to update the binary weights in the training process, which will be introduced later.

Compared to the real-valued CNN model with the 32-bit weight parameter, the 1-bit CNNs obtains up to 32× memory saving. Moreover, as the activation is also binary, then the convolution operation could be implemented by the bitwise XNOR operation and a bit-count operation [19]. One simple example of the bitwise operation is shown in Fig. 2. In contrast, the convolution operation in real-valued CNNs is implemented by the expensive real value multiplication. Consequently, the 1-bit CNNs could obtain up to 64× computation saving.

However, it has been demonstrated in [7] that the classification performance of the 1-bit CNNs is much worse than that of the real-valued CNN models on large-scale datasets like ImageNet. We believe that the poor performance of 1-bit CNNs is caused by its low representational capacity. We denote $\mathbb{R}(\mathbf{x})$ as the representational capability of $\mathbf{x}$, $i.e.$, the number of all possible configurations of $\mathbf{x}$, where $\mathbf{x}$ could be a scalar, vector, matrix or tensor. For example, the representational capability of 32 channels of a binary 14×14 feature map $\mathbf{A}$ is $\mathbb{R}(\mathbf{A}) = 2^{14 \times 14 \times 32} = 2^{6272}$. Given a $3 \times 3 \times 32$ binary weight kernel $\mathbf{W}$, each entry of $\mathbf{A} \otimes \mathbf{W}$ ($i.e.$, the bitwise convolution output) can choose the even values from (-288 to 288), as shown in Fig. 3. Thus, $\mathbb{R}(\mathbf{A} \otimes \mathbf{W}) = 289^{6272}$. Note that since the BatchNorm layer is a unique mapping, it will not increase the number of different choices but scale the (-288,288) to a particular value. If adding the 1-bit convolution layer behind the output, each entry in the feature map is binarized, and the representational capability shrinks to 2^{6272} again.

3.2   Bi-Real Net Model and Its Representational Capability

We propose to preserve the real activations before the sign function to increase the representational capability of the 1-bit CNN, through a simple shortcut. Specifically, as shown in Fig. 3(b), one block indicates the structure that "Sign → 1-bit convolution → batch normalization → addition operator". The shortcut connects the input activations to the sign function in the current block to the output activations after the batch normalization in the same block, and these two activations are added through an addition operator, and then the combined activations are inputted to the sign function in the next block. The representational capability of each entry in the added activations is 289^2. Consequently,

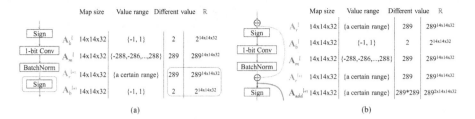

	Map size	Value range	Different value	R
$\mathbf{A}_b^l$	14x14x32	{-1, 1}	2	$2^{14x14x32}$
$\mathbf{A}_m^l$	14x14x32	{-288,-286,...,288}	289	$289^{14x14x32}$
$\mathbf{A}_r^{l+1}$	14x14x32	{a certain range}	289	$289^{14x14x32}$
$\mathbf{A}_b^{l+1}$	14x14x32	{-1, 1}	2	$2^{14x14x32}$

(a)

	Map size	Value range	Different value	R
$\mathbf{A}_r^l$	14x14x32	{a certain range}	289	$289^{14x14x32}$
$\mathbf{A}_b^l$	14x14x32	{-1, 1}	2	$2^{14x14x32}$
$\mathbf{A}_m^l$	14x14x32	{-288,-286,...,288}	289	$289^{14x14x32}$
$\mathbf{A}_r^l$	14x14x32	{a certain range}	289	$289^{14x14x32}$
$\mathbf{A}_{add}^{l+1}$	14x14x32	{a certain range}	289*289	$289^{2x14x14x32}$

(b)

Fig. 3. The representational capability ($\mathbb{R}$) of each layer in (a) 1-bit CNNs without shortcut (b) 1-bit CNNs with shortcut. $\mathbf{A}_b^l$ indicates the output of the Sign function; $\mathbf{A}_m^l$ denotes the output of the 1-bit convolution layer; $\mathbf{A}_r^{l+1}$ represents the output of the BatchNorm layer; The superscript l indicates the block index.

the representational capability of each block in the 1-bit CNN with the above shortcut becomes $(289^2)^{6272}$. As both real and binary activations are kept, we call the proposed model as Bi-Real net.

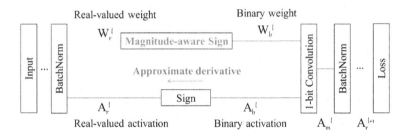

Fig. 4. A graphical illustration of the training process of the 1-bit CNNs, with A being the activation, W being the weight, and the superscript l denoting the lth block consisting with Sign, 1-bit Convolution, and BatchNorm. The subscript r denotes real value, b denotes binary value, and m denotes the intermediate output before the BatchNorm layer.

The representational capability of each block in the 1-bit CNN is significantly enhanced due to the simple identity shortcut. The only additional cost of computation is the addition operation of two real activations, as these real activations already exist in the standard 1-bit CNN (*i.e.*, without shortcuts). Moreover, as the activations are computed on the fly, no additional memory is needed.

3.3 Training Bi-real Net

As both activations and weight parameters are binary, the continuous optimization method, *i.e.*, the stochastic gradient descent(SGD), cannot be directly adopted to train the 1-bit CNN. There are two major challenges. One is how to compute the gradient of the sign function on activations, which is non-differentiable. The other is that the gradient of the loss with respect to the binary weight is too small to change the weight's sign. The authors of [7] proposed to adjust the standard SGD algorithm to approximately train the 1-bit

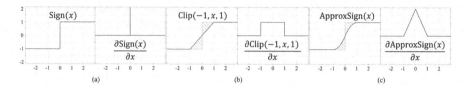

Fig. 5. (a) Sign function and its derivative, (b) Clip function and its derivative for approximating the derivative of the sign function, proposed in [7], (c) Proposed differentiable piecewise polynomial function and its triangle-shaped derivative for approximating the derivative of the sign function in gradients computation.

CNN. Specifically, the gradient of the sign function on activations is approximated by the gradient of the piecewise linear function, as shown in Fig. 5(b). To tackle the second challenge, the method proposed in [7] updates the real-valued weights by the gradient computed with regard to the binary weight and obtains the binary weight by taking the sign of the real weights. As the identity shortcut will not add difficulty for training, the training algorithm proposed in [7] can also be adopted to train the Bi-Real net model. However, we propose a novel training algorithm to tackle the above two major challenges, which is more suitable for the Bi-Real net model as well as other 1-bit CNNs. Besides, we also propose a novel initialization method.

We present a graphical illustration of the training of Bi-Real net in Fig. 4. The identity shortcut is omitted in the graph for clarity, as it will not change the main part of the training algorithm.

Approximation to the Derivative of the Sign Function with Respect to Activations. As shown in Fig. 5(a), the derivative of the sign function is an impulse function, which cannot be utilized in training.

$$\frac{\partial \mathcal{L}}{\partial \mathbf{A}_r^{l,t}} = \frac{\partial \mathcal{L}}{\partial \mathbf{A}_b^{l,t}} \frac{\partial \mathbf{A}_b^{l,t}}{\partial \mathbf{A}_r^{l,t}} = \frac{\partial \mathcal{L}}{\partial \mathbf{A}_b^{l,t}} \frac{\partial Sign(\mathbf{A}_r^{l,t})}{\partial \mathbf{A}_r^{l,t}} \approx \frac{\partial \mathcal{L}}{\partial \mathbf{A}_r^{l,t}} \frac{\partial F(\mathbf{A}_r^{l,t})}{\partial \mathbf{A}_r^{l,t}}, \qquad (2)$$

where $F(\mathbf{A}_r^{l,t})$ is a differentiable approximation of the non-differentiable $Sign(\mathbf{A}_r^{l,t})$. In [7], $F(\mathbf{A}_r^{l,t})$ is set as the clip function, leading to the derivative as a step-function (see Fig. 5(b)). In this work, we utilize a piecewise polynomial function (see Fig. 5(c)) as the approximation function, as Eq. (3) left.

$$F(a_r) = \begin{cases} -1 & \text{if } a_r < -1 \\ 2a_r + a_r^2 & \&\text{if } -1 \leqslant a_r < 0 \\ 2a_r - a_r^2 & \text{if } 0 \leqslant a_r < 1 \\ 1 & \text{otherwise} \end{cases},$$

$$\frac{\partial F(a_r)}{\partial a_r} = \begin{cases} 2 + 2a_r & \&\text{if } -1 \leqslant a_r < 0 \\ 2 - 2a_r & \text{if } 0 \leqslant a_r < 1 \\ 0 & \text{otherwise} \end{cases}, \qquad (3)$$

As shown Fig. 5, the shaded areas with blue slashes can reflect the difference between the sign function and its approximation. The shaded area corresponding to the clip function is 1, while that corresponding to Eq. (3) left is $\frac{2}{3}$. We conclude that Eq. (3) left is a closer approximation to the sign function than the clip function. Consequently, the derivative of Eq. (3) left is formulated as Eq. (3) right, which is a piecewise linear function.

Magnitude-aware gradient with respect to weights. Here we present how to update the binary weight parameter in the lth block, *i.e.*, $\mathbf{W}_b^l \in \{-1, +1\}$. For clarity, we assume that there is only one weight kernel, *i.e.*, $\mathbf{W}_b^l$ is a matrix.

The standard gradient descent algorithm cannot be directly applied as the gradient is not large enough to change the binary weights. To tackle this problem, the method of [7] introduced a real weight $\mathbf{W}_r^l$ and a sign function during training. Hence the binary weight parameter can be seen as the output to the sign function, *i.e.*, $\mathbf{W}_b^l = Sign(\mathbf{W}_r^l)$, as shown in the upper sub-figure in Fig. 4. Consequently, $\mathbf{W}_r^l$ is updated using gradient descent in the backward pass, as follows

$$\mathbf{W}_r^{l,t+1} = \mathbf{W}_r^{l,t} - \eta \frac{\partial \mathcal{L}}{\partial \mathbf{W}_r^{l,t}} = \mathbf{W}_r^{l,t} - \eta \frac{\partial \mathcal{L}}{\partial \mathbf{W}_b^{l,t}} \frac{\partial \mathbf{W}_b^{l,t}}{\partial \mathbf{W}_r^{l,t}}. \tag{4}$$

Note that $\frac{\partial \mathbf{W}_b^{l,t}}{\partial \mathbf{W}_r^{l,t}}$ indicates the element-wise derivative. In [7], $\frac{\partial \mathbf{W}_b^{l,t}(i,j)}{\partial \mathbf{W}_r^{l,t}(i,j)}$ is set to 1 if $\mathbf{W}_r^{l,t}(i,j) \in [-1, 1]$, otherwise 0. The derivative $\frac{\partial \mathcal{L}}{\partial \mathbf{W}_b^{l,t}}$ is derived from the chain rule, as follows

$$\frac{\partial \mathcal{L}}{\partial \mathbf{W}_b^{l,t}} = \frac{\partial \mathcal{L}}{\partial \mathbf{A}_r^{l+1,t}} \frac{\partial \mathbf{A}_r^{l+1,t}}{\partial \mathbf{A}_m^{l,t}} \frac{\partial \mathbf{A}_m^{l,t}}{\partial \mathbf{W}_b^{l,t}} = \frac{\partial \mathcal{L}}{\partial \mathbf{A}_r^{l+1,t}} \theta^{l,t} \mathbf{A}_b^l, \tag{5}$$

where $\theta^{l,t} = \frac{\partial \mathbf{A}_r^{l+1,t}}{\partial \mathbf{A}_m^{l,t}}$ denotes the derivative of the BatchNorm layer (see Fig. 4) and has a negative correlation to $\mathbf{W}_b^{l,t}$. As $\mathbf{W}_b^{l,t} \in \{-1, +1\}$, the gradient $\frac{\partial \mathcal{L}}{\partial \mathbf{W}_r^{l,t}}$ is only related to the sign of $\mathbf{W}_r^{l,t}$, while is independent of its magnitude.

Based on this observation, we propose to replace the above sign function by a magnitude-aware function, as follows:

$$\overline{\mathbf{W}}_b^{l,t} = \frac{\| \mathbf{W}_r^{l,t} \|_{1,1}}{|\mathbf{W}_r^{l,t}|} Sign(\mathbf{W}_r^{l,t}), \tag{6}$$

where $|\mathbf{W}_r^{l,t}|$ denotes the number of entries in $\mathbf{W}_r^{l,t}$. Consequently, the update of $\mathbf{W}_r^l$ becomes

$$\mathbf{W}_r^{l,t+1} = \mathbf{W}_r^{l,t} - \eta \frac{\partial \mathcal{L}}{\partial \overline{\mathbf{W}}_b^{l,t}} \frac{\partial \overline{\mathbf{W}}_b^{l,t}}{\partial \mathbf{W}_r^{l,t}} = \mathbf{W}_r^{l,t} - \eta \frac{\partial \mathcal{L}}{\partial \mathbf{A}_r^{l+1,t}} \overline{\theta}^{l,t} \mathbf{A}_b^l \frac{\partial \overline{\mathbf{W}}_b^{l,t}}{\partial \mathbf{W}_r^{l,t}}, \tag{7}$$

where $\frac{\partial \overline{\mathbf{W}}_b^{l,t}}{\partial \mathbf{W}_r^{l,t}} \approx \frac{\|\mathbf{W}_r^{l,t}\|_{1,1}}{|\mathbf{W}_r^{l,t}|} \cdot \frac{\partial Sign(\mathbf{W}_r^{l,t})}{\partial \mathbf{W}_r^{l,t}} \approx \frac{\|\mathbf{W}_r^{l,t}\|_{1,1}}{|\mathbf{W}_r^{l,t}|} \cdot \mathbf{1}_{|\mathbf{W}_r^{l,t}|<1}$ and $\overline{\theta}^{l,t}$ is associated with the magnitude of $\mathbf{W}_r^{l,t}$. Thus, the gradient $\frac{\partial \mathcal{L}}{\partial \mathbf{W}_r^{l,t}}$ is related to both the sign and magnitude of $\mathbf{W}_r^{l,t}$. After training for convergence, we still use $Sign(\mathbf{W}_r^l)$ to obtain the binary weight $\mathbf{W}_b^l$ (*i.e.*, -1 or +1), and use θ^l to absorb $\frac{\|\mathbf{W}_r^l\|_{1,1}}{|\mathbf{W}_r^l|}$ and to associate with the magnitude of $\mathbf{W}_b^l$ used for inference.

Initialization. In [14], the initial weights of the 1-bit CNNs are derived from the corresponding real-valued CNN model pre-trained on ImageNet. However, the activation of ReLU is non-negative, while that of Sign is -1 or $+1$. Due to this difference, the real CNNs with ReLU may not provide a suitable initial point for training the 1-bit CNNs. Instead, we propose to replace ReLU with clip(-1, x, 1) to pre-train the real-valued CNN model, as the activation of the clip function is closer to the sign function than ReLU. The efficacy of this new initialization will be evaluated in experiments.

4   Experiments

In this section, we firstly introduce the dataset for experiments and implementation details in Sect. 4.1. Then we conduct ablation study in Sect. 4.2 to investigate the effectiveness of the proposed techniques. This part is followed by comparing our Bi-Real net with other state-of-the-art binary networks regarding accuracy in Sect. 4.3. Section 4.4 reports memory usage and computation cost in comparison with other networks.

4.1   Dataset and Implementation Details

The experiments are carried out on the ILSVRC12 ImageNet classification dataset [22]. ImageNet is a large-scale dataset with 1000 classes and 1.2 million training images and 50k validation images. Compared to other datasets like CIFAR-10 [11] or MNIST [18], ImageNet is more challenging due to its large scale and great diversity. The study on this dataset will validate the superiority of the proposed Bi-Real network structure and the effectiveness of three training methods for 1-bit CNNs. In our comparison, we report both the top-1 and top-5 accuracies.

For each image in the ImageNet dataset, the smaller dimension of the image is rescaled to 256 while keeping the aspect ratio intact. For *training*, a random crop of size 224 × 224 is selected. Note that, in contrast to XNOR-Net and the full-precision ResNet, we do not use the operation of random resize, which might improve the performance further. For *inference*, we employ the 224 × 224 center crop from images.

Training: We train two instances of the Bi-Real net, including an *18-layer Bi-Real net* and a *34-layer Bi-Real net*. The training of them consists of two steps: training the 1-bit convolution layer and retraining the BatchNorm. In the first step, the weights in the 1-bit convolution layer are binarized to the sign of real-valued weights multiplying the absolute mean of each kernel. We use the SGD solver with the momentum of 0.9 and set the weight-decay to 0, which means we no longer encourage the weights to be close to 0. For the 18-layer Bi-Real net, we run the training algorithm for 20 epochs with a batch size of 128. The learning rate starts from 0.01 and is decayed twice by multiplying 0.1 at the $10th$ and the $15th$ epoch. For the 34-layer Bi-Real net, the training process includes 40 epochs and the batch size is set to 1024. The learning rate starts from 0.08 and is multiplied by 0.1 at the $20th$ and the $30th$ epoch, respectively. In the second step, we constrain the weights to -1 and 1, and set the learning rate in all convolution layers to 0 and retrain the BatchNorm layer for 1 epoch to absorb the scaling factor.

Inference: we use the trained model with binary weights and binary activations in the 1-bit convolution layers for inference.

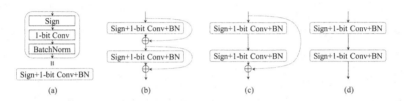

Fig. 6. Three different networks differ in the shortcut design of connecting the blocks shown in (a) conjoint layers of Sign, 1-bit Convolution, and the BatchNorm. (b) Bi-Real net with shortcut bypassing every block (c) Res-Net with shortcut bypassing two blocks, which corresponds to the ReLU-only pre-activation proposed in [6] and (d) Plain-Net without the shortcut. These three structures shown in (b), (c) and (d) have the same number of weights.

4.2   Ablation Study

Three building blocks. The shortcut in our Bi-Real net transfers real-valued representation without additional memory cost, which plays an important role in improving its capability. To verify its importance, we implemented a Plain-Net structure without shortcut as shown in Fig. 6(d) for comparison. At the same time, as our network structure employs the same number of weight filters and layers as the standard ResNet, we also make a comparison with the standard ResNet shown in Fig. 6(c). For a fair comparison, we adopt the ReLU-only pre-activation ResNet structure in [6], which differs from Bi-Real net only in the structure of two layers per block instead of one layer per block. The layer order and shortcut design in Fig. 6(c) are also applicable for 1-bit CNN. The comparison can justify the benefit of implementing our Bi-Real net by specifically replacing the 2-conv-layer-per-block Res-Net structure with two 1-conv-layer-per-block Bi-Real structure.

As discussed in Sect. 3, we proposed to overcome the optimization challenges induced by discrete weights and activations by (1) approximation to the derivative of the sign function with respect to activations, (2) magnitude-aware gradient with respect to weights and (3) clip initialization. To study how these proposals benefit the 1-bit CNNs individually and collectively, we train the 18-layer structure and the 34-layer structure with a combination of these techniques on the ImageNet dataset. Thus we derive $2 \times 3 \times 2 \times 2 \times 2 = 48$ pairs of values of top-1 and top-5 accuracy, which are presented in Table 1.

Based on Table 1, we can evaluate each technique's individual contribution and collective contribution of each unique combination of these techniques towards the final accuracy.

(1) Comparing the $4^{th} - 7^{th}$ columns with the $8^{th} - 9^{th}$ columns, both the proposed Bi-Real net and the binarized standard ResNet outperform their plain counterparts with a significant margin, which validates the effectiveness of short-cut and the disadvantage of directly concatenating the 1-bit convolution layers. As Plain-18 has a thin and deep structure, which has the same weight filters but no shortcut, binarizing it results in very limited network representational capacity in the last convolution layer, and thus can hardly achieve good accuracy.

(2) Comparing the $4^{th} - 5^{th}$ and $6^{th} - 7^{th}$ columns, the 18-layer Bi-Real net structure improves the accuracy of the binarized standard ResNet-18 by about 18%. This validates the conjecture that the Bi-Real net structure with more shortcuts further enhances the network capacity compared to the standard ResNet structure. Replacing the 2-conv-layer-per-block structure employed in Res-Net with two 1-conv-layer-per-block structure, adopted by Bi-Real net, could even benefit a real-valued network.

(3) All proposed techniques for initialization, weight update and activation backward improve the accuracy at various degrees. For the 18-layer Bi-Real net structure, the improvement from the weight (about 23%, by comparing the 2nd and 4th rows) is greater than the improvement from the activation (about 12%, by comparing the 2nd and 4th rows) and the improvement from replacing ReLU with Clip for initialization (about 13%, by comparing the 2nd and 7th rows). These three proposed training mechanisms are independent and can function collaboratively towards enhancing the final accuracy.

(4) The proposed training methods can improve the final accuracy for all three networks in comparison with the original training method, which implies these proposed three training methods are universally suitable for various networks.

(5) The two implemented Bi-Real nets (*i.e.* the 18-layer and 34-layer structures) together with the proposed training methods, achieve approximately 83% and 89% of the accuracy level of their corresponding full-precision networks, but with a huge amount of speedup and computation cost saving.

In short, the shortcut enhances the network representational capability, and the proposed training methods help the network to approach the accuracy upper bound.

4.3   Accuracy Comparison with State-of-The-Art

While the ablation study demonstrates the effectiveness of our 1-layer-per-block structure and the proposed techniques for optimal training, it is also necessary to compare with other state-of-the-art methods to evaluate Bi-Real net's overall

Table 1. Top-1 and top-5 accuracies (in percentage) of different combinations of the three proposed techniques on three different network structures, Bi-Real net, ResNet and Plain Net, shown in Fig. 6.

Initialization	Weight update	Activation backward	Bi-Real-18		Res-18		Plain-18		Bi-Real-34		Res-34		Plain-34	
			top-1	top-5	top-1	top-5	top-1	top-5	top-1	top-5	top-1	top-5	top-1	top-5
ReLU	Original	Original	32.9	56.7	27.8	50.5	3.3	9.5	53.1	76.9	27.5	49.9	1.4	4.8
		Proposed	36.8	60.8	32.2	56.0	4.7	13.7	58.0	81.0	33.9	57.9	1.6	5.3
	Proposed	Original	40.5	65.1	33.9	58.1	4.3	12.2	59.9	82.0	33.6	57.9	1.8	6.1
		Proposed	47.5	71.9	41.6	66.4	8.5	21.5	61.4	83.3	47.5	72.0	2.1	6.8
	Real-valued net		68.5	88.3	67.8	87.8	67.5	87.5	70.4	89.3	69.1	88.3	66.8	86.8
Clip	Original	Original	37.4	62.4	32.8	56.7	3.2	9.4	55.9	79.1	35.0	59.2	2.2	6.9
		Proposed	38.1	62.7	34.3	58.4	4.9	14.3	58.1	81.0	38.2	62.6	2.3	7.5
	Proposed	Original	53.6	77.5	42.4	67.3	6.7	17.1	60.8	82.9	43.9	68.7	2.5	7.9
		Proposed	**56.4**	**79.5**	45.7	70.3	12.1	27.7	**62.2**	**83.9**	49.0	73.6	2.6	8.3
	Real-valued net		68.0	88.1	67.5	87.6	64.2	85.3	69.7	89.1	67.9	87.8	57.1	79.9
Full-precision original ResNet [5]			69.3	89.2							73.3	91.3		

Table 2. This table compares both the top-1 and top-5 accuracies of our Bi-real net with other state-of-the-art binarization methods: BinaryNet [7] , XNOR-Net [19], ABC-Net [14] on both the Res-18 and Res-34 [5]. The Bi-Real net outperforms other methods by a considerable margin.

		Bi-Real net	BinaryNet	ABC-Net	XNOR-Net	Full-precision
18-layer	Top-1	56.4%	42.2%	42.7%	51.2%	69.3%
	Top-5	79.5%	67.1%	67.6%	73.2%	89.2%
34-layer	Top-1	62.2%	–	52.4%	–	73.3%
	Top-5	83.9%	–	76.5%	–	91.3%

performance. To this end, we carry out a comparative study with three methods: BinaryNet [7], XNOR-Net [19] and ABC-Net [14]. These three networks are representative methods of binarizing both weights and activations for CNNs and achieve the state-of-the-art results. Note that, for a fair comparison, our Bi-Real net contains the same amount of weight filters as the corresponding ResNet that these methods attempt to binarize, differing only in the shortcut design.

Table 2 shows the results. The results of the three networks are quoted directly from the corresponding references, except that the result of BinaryNet is quoted from ABC-Net [14]. The comparison clearly indicates that the proposed Bi-Real net outperforms the three networks by a considerable margin in terms of both the top-1 and top-5 accuracies. Specifically, the 18-layer Bi-Real net outperforms its 18-layer counterparts BinaryNet and ABC-Net with relative 33% advantage, and achieves a roughly 10% relative improvement over the XNOR-Net. Similar improvements can be observed for 34-layer Bi-Real net. In short, our Bi-Real net is more competitive than the state-of-the-art binary networks.

4.4   Efficiency and Memory Usage Analysis

In this section, we analyze the saving of memory usage and speedup in computation of Bi-Real net by comparing with the XNOR-Net [19] and the full-precision network individually.

The memory usage is computed as the summation of 32 bit times the number of real-valued parameters and 1 bit times the number of binary parameters in the network. For efficiency comparison, we use FLOPs to measure the total real-valued multiplication computation in the Bi-Real net, following the calculation method in [5]. As the bitwise XNOR operation and bit-counting can be performed in a parallel of 64 by the current generation of CPUs, the FLOPs is calculated as the amount of real-valued floating point multiplication plus 1/64 of the amount of 1-bit multiplication.

We follow the suggestion in XNOR-Net [19], to keep the weights and activations in the first convolution and the last fully-connected layers to be real-valued. We also adopt the same real-valued 1x1 convolution in Type B short-cut [5] as implemented in XNOR-Net. Note that this 1x1 convolution is for the transition between two stages of ResNet and thus all information should be preserved. As

Table 3. Memory usage and FLOPs calculation in Bi-Real net.

		Memory usage	Memory saving	FLOPs	Speedup
18-layer	Bi-Real net	33.6 Mbit	11.14 ×	1.63×10^8	11.06 ×
	XNOR-Net	33.7 Mbit	11.10 ×	1.67×10^8	10.86 ×
	Full-precision Res-Net	374.1 Mbit	–	1.81×10^9	–
34-layer	Bi-Real net	43.7 Mbit	15.97 ×	1.93×10^8	18.99 ×
	XNOR-Net	43.9 Mbit	15.88 ×	1.98×10^8	18.47 ×
	Full-precision Res-Net	697.3 Mbit	–	3.66×10^9	–

the number of weights in those three kinds of layers accounts for only a very small proportion of the total number of weights, the limited memory saving for binarizing them does not justify the performance degradation caused by the information loss.

For both the 18-layer and the 34-layer networks, the proposed Bi-Real net reduces the memory usage by 11.1 times and 16.0 times individually, and achieves computation reduction of about 11.1 times and 19.0 times, in comparison with the full-precision network. Without using real-valued weights and activations for scaling binary ones during inference time, our Bi-Real net requires fewer FLOPs and uses less memory than XNOR-Net and is also much easier to implement.

5   Conclusion

In this work, we have proposed a novel 1-bit CNN model, dubbed Bi-Real net. Compared with the standard 1-bit CNNs, Bi-Real net utilizes a simple short-cut to significantly enhance the representational capability. Further, an advanced training algorithm is specifically designed for training 1-bit CNNs (including Bi-Real net), including a tighter approximation of the derivative of the sign function with respect the activation, the magnitude-aware gradient with respect to the weight, as well as a novel initialization. Extensive experimental results demonstrate that the proposed Bi-Real net and the novel training algorithm show superiority over the state-of-the-art methods. In future, we will explore other advanced integer programming algorithms (*e.g.*, Lp-Box ADMM [26]) to train Bi-Real Net.

References

1. Courbariaux, M., Bengio, Y., David, J.P.: Binaryconnect: training deep neural networks with binary weights during propagations. In: Advances in Neural Information Processing Systems, pp. 3123–3131 (2015)
2. Garg, Ravi, B.G., Vijay Kumar, Carneiro, Gustavo, Reid, Ian: Unsupervised CNN for single view depth estimation: geometry to the rescue. In: Leibe, Bastian, Matas, Jiri, Sebe, Nicu, Welling, Max (eds.) ECCV 2016. LNCS, vol. 9912, pp. 740–756. Springer, Cham (2016). https://doi.org/10.1007/978-3-319-46484-8_45

3. Girshick, R., Donahue, J., Darrell, T., Malik, J.: Rich feature hierarchies for accurate object detection and semantic segmentation. In: Proceedings of the IEEE Conference on Computer Vision and Pattern Recognition, pp. 580–587 (2014)

4. Han, S., Mao, H., Dally, W.J.: Deep compression: compressing deep neural networks with pruning, trained quantization and Huffman coding. arXiv preprint arXiv:1510.00149 (2015)

5. He, K., Zhang, X., Ren, S., Sun, J.: Deep residual learning for image recognition. In: Proceedings of the IEEE Conference on Computer Vision and Pattern Recognition, pp. 770–778 (2016)

6. He, Kaiming, Zhang, Xiangyu, Ren, Shaoqing, Sun, Jian: Identity mappings in deep residual networks. In: Leibe, Bastian, Matas, Jiri, Sebe, Nicu, Welling, Max (eds.) ECCV 2016. LNCS, vol. 9908, pp. 630–645. Springer, Cham (2016). https://doi.org/10.1007/978-3-319-46493-0_38

7. Hubara, I., Courbariaux, M., Soudry, D., El-Yaniv, R., Bengio, Y.: Binarized neural networks. In: Lee, D.D., Sugiyama, M., Luxburg, U.V., Guyon, I., Garnett, R. (eds.) Advances in Neural Information Processing Systems, vol. 29, pp. 4107–4115. Curran Associates, Inc. (2016). http://papers.nips.cc/paper/6573-binarized-neural-networks.pdf

8. Hubara, I., Courbariaux, M., Soudry, D., El-Yaniv, R., Bengio, Y.: Quantized neural networks: training neural networks with low precision weights and activations (2016)

9. Iandola, F.N., Han, S., Moskewicz, M.W., Ashraf, K., Dally, W.J., Keutzer, K.: Squeezenet: alexnet-level accuracy with $50\times$ fewer parameters and <0.5 mb model size. arXiv preprint arXiv:1602.07360 (2016)

10. Ioffe, S., Szegedy, C.: Batch normalization: accelerating deep network training by reducing internal covariate shift. arXiv preprint arXiv:1502.03167 (2015)

11. Krizhevsky, A., Hinton, G.: Learning multiple layers of features from tiny images. Technical report, Citeseer (2009)

12. Krizhevsky, A., Sutskever, I., Hinton, G.E.: Imagenet classification with deep convolutional neural networks. In: Advances in Neural Information Processing Systems, pp. 1097–1105 (2012)

13. Lai, L., Suda, N., Chandra, V.: Deep convolutional neural network inference with floating-point weights and fixed-point activations. arXiv preprint arXiv:1703.03073 (2017)

14. Lin, X., Zhao, C., Pan, W.: Towards accurate binary convolutional neural network. In: Advances in Neural Information Processing Systems, pp. 345–353 (2017)

15. Liu, B., Wang, M., Foroosh, H., Tappen, M., Pensky, M.: Sparse convolutional neural networks. In: Proceedings of the IEEE Conference on Computer Vision and Pattern Recognition, pp. 806–814 (2015)

16. Liu, F., Shen, C., Lin, G., Reid, I.D.: Learning depth from single monocular images using deep convolutional neural fields. IEEE Trans. Pattern Anal. Mach. Intell. **38**(10), 2024–2039 (2016)

17. Luo, W., Sun, P., Zhong, F., Liu, W., Zhang, T., Wang, Y.: End-to-end active object tracking via reinforcement learning. ICML (2018)

18. Netzer, Y., Wang, T., Coates, A., Bissacco, A., Wu, B., Ng, A.Y.: Reading digits in natural images with unsupervised feature learning. In: NIPS Workshop on Deep Learning and Unsupervised Feature Learning, vol. 2011, p. 5 (2011)

19. Rastegari, Mohammad, Ordonez, Vicente, Redmon, Joseph, Farhadi, Ali: XNOR-Net: imagenet classification using binary convolutional neural networks. In: Leibe, Bastian, Matas, Jiri, Sebe, Nicu, Welling, Max (eds.) ECCV 2016. LNCS, vol. 9908, pp. 525–542. Springer, Cham (2016). https://doi.org/10.1007/978-3-319-46493-0_32

20. Ren, S., He, K., Girshick, R., Sun, J.: Faster r-cnn: towards real-time object detection with region proposal networks. In: Advances in Neural Information Processing Systems, pp. 91–99 (2015)

21. Romero, A., Ballas, N., Kahou, S.E., Chassang, A., Gatta, C., Bengio, Y.: Fitnets: hints for thin deep nets. arXiv preprint arXiv:1412.6550 (2014)

22. Russakovsky, O., Deng, J., Su, H., Krause, J., Satheesh, S., Ma, S., Huang, Z., Karpathy, A., Khosla, A., Bernstein, M.: Imagenet large scale visual recognition challenge. Int. J. Comput. Vis. **115**(3), 211–252 (2015)

23. Simonyan, K., Zisserman, A.: Very deep convolutional networks for large-scale image recognition. arXiv preprint arXiv:1409.1556 (2014)

24. Sun, Y., Wang, X., Tang, X.: Deep convolutional network cascade for facial point detection. In: Proceedings of the IEEE Conference on Computer Vision and Pattern Recognition, pp. 3476–3483 (2013)

25. Szegedy, C., et al.: Going deeper with convolutions. In: Proceedings of the IEEE Conference on Computer Vision and Pattern Recognition, pp. 1–9 (2015)

26. Wu, B., Ghanem, B.: lp-box ADMM: a versatile framework for integer programming. IEEE Trans. Pattern Anal. Mach. Intell. (2018)

27. Wu, B., Hu, B.G., Ji, Q.: A coupled hidden Markov random field model for simultaneous face clustering and tracking in videos. Pattern Recognit. **64**, 361–373 (2017)

28. Wu, B., Lyu, S., Hu, B.G., Ji, Q.: Simultaneous clustering and tracklet linking for multi-face tracking in videos. In: Proceedings of the IEEE International Conference on Computer Vision, pp. 2856–2863 (2013)

29. Zhang, H., Kyaw, Z., Chang, S.F., Chua, T.S.: Visual translation embedding network for visual relation detection. In: CVPR, vol. 1, p. 5 (2017)

30. Zhang, H., Kyaw, Z., Yu, J., Chang, S.F.: Ppr-fcn: weakly supervised visual relation detection via parallel pairwise r-fcn. arXiv preprint arXiv:1708.01956 (2017)

31. Zhou, A., Yao, A., Guo, Y., Xu, L., Chen, Y.: Incremental network quantization: towards lossless cnns with low-precision weights. arXiv preprint arXiv:1702.03044 (2017)

32. Zhou, E., Fan, H., Cao, Z., Jiang, Y., Yin, Q.: Extensive facial landmark localization with coarse-to-fine convolutional network cascade. In: Proceedings of the IEEE International Conference on Computer Vision Workshops, pp. 386–391 (2013)

33. Zhou, S., Wu, Y., Ni, Z., Zhou, X., Wen, H., Zou, Y.: Dorefa-net: training low bitwidth convolutional neural networks with low bitwidth gradients. arXiv preprint arXiv:1606.06160 (2016)

34. Zhu, X., Lei, Z., Liu, X., Shi, H., Li, S.Z.: Face alignment across large poses: a 3d solution. In: Proceedings of the IEEE Conference on Computer Vision and Pattern Recognition, pp. 146–155 (2016)

Orthogonal Deep Features Decomposition for Age-Invariant Face Recognition

Yitong Wang[ID], Dihong Gong[ID], Zheng Zhou[ID], Xing Ji[ID], Hao Wang[ID], Zhifeng Li[✉][ID], Wei Liu[✉][ID], and Tong Zhang[ID]

Tencent AI Lab, Beijing, China
{yitongwang,encorezhou,denisji,hawelwang,michaelzfli}@tencent.com,
gongdihong@gmail.com, wl2223@columbia.edu, tongzhang@tongzhang-ml.org

Abstract. As facial appearance is subject to significant intra-class variations caused by the aging process over time, age-invariant face recognition (AIFR) remains a major challenge in face recognition community. To reduce the intra-class discrepancy caused by the aging, in this paper we propose a novel approach (namely, Orthogonal Embedding CNNs, or OE-CNNs) to learn the age-invariant deep face features. Specifically, we decompose deep face features into two orthogonal components to represent age-related and identity-related features. As a result, identity-related features that are robust to aging are then used for AIFR. Besides, for complementing the existing cross-age datasets and advancing the research in this field, we construct a brand-new large-scale Cross-Age Face dataset (CAF). Extensive experiments conducted on the three public domain face aging datasets (MORPH Album 2, CACD-VS and FG-NET) have shown the effectiveness of the proposed approach and the value of the constructed CAF dataset on AIFR. Benchmarking our algorithm on one of the most popular general face recognition (GFR) dataset LFW additionally demonstrates the comparable generalization performance on GFR.

Keywords: Age-invariant face recognition
Convolutional neural networks · Cross-age face dataset

1 Introduction

As one of the most important topics in computer vision and pattern recognition, face recognition has attracted much attention from both academic and industry for decades [2,4,18,19,23,37,40,44]. With the evolution of deep learning, the performance of general face recognition (GFR) has been significantly improved in recent years, even higher than humans' abilities [24,32–35,39,43]. As a major challenge in face recognition, age-invariant face recognition (AIFR) is extremely valuable on various application scenarios, such as looking for lost children after decades, matching face images in different ages, etc. In contrast to GFR, AIFR involves more diversity with the significant intra-class variations caused by the

© Springer Nature Switzerland AG 2018
V. Ferrari et al. (Eds.): ECCV 2018, LNCS 11219, pp. 764–779, 2018.
https://doi.org/10.1007/978-3-030-01267-0_45

aging process and thus is more challenging. It is very often that the inter-class variation is much smaller than the intra-class variation in the presence of age variation, as illustrated in Fig. 1a. Figure 1b also exhibits the difficulty of AIFR where the same identity greatly varies in appearance with the aging process.

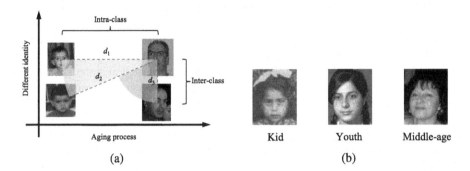

Fig. 1. The major challenge of AIFR: the intrinsic large intra-class variations in the aging process. (a) An example where intra-class distance is larger than inter-class distance. (b) The cross-age images for one subject in the FG-NET [1].

Recent AIFR researches primarily concentrate on two technical schemes: generative scheme and discriminative scheme. The generative scheme models the AIFR by synthesizing faces to one or more fixed age category then performs recognition with the artificial face representations [9,16,28]. Benefited from the advancement of the deep generative model, the generative scheme becomes more promising on AIFR as well [3,8,46]. However, the generative scheme still remains several significant shortcomings. Firstly, generative scheme usually separates the recognition process into two steps. Hence it is not easy for the generative models to optimize recognition performance in an end-to-end manner. Secondly, generation models are often unstable so the synthesizing face images will introduce additional noises, which may result in negative effects on the recognition process. Moreover, constructing an accurate, parametric generation model is fairly difficult since the aging process of humans' face is easily impacted by many latent factors such as social environments, diet, etc.

The discriminative scheme aims at constructing the sophisticated discriminative model to solve the problem of AIFR. Related works on discriminative model include [5–7,10,11,17,20–22]. By combining the deep learning algorithm, the discriminative scheme has achieved substantial improvement on AIFR. For example, Wen et al. [42] extended the HFA method [10] to a deep CNN model called latent factor guided convolutional neural networks (LF-CNNs), which achieved the state-of-the-art recognition accuracy in this field. Zheng et al. [47] also used the linear combination of jointly-learned deep features to represent identity and age information, which is similar to the HFA based deep CNN model.

In this paper, we aim at designing a new deep learning approach to effectively learn age-invariant components from features mixed with age-related information. The key idea of our approach is to decompose face features into age-related and identity-related components, where the identity-related component is age-invariant and suitable for AIFR. More specifically, inspired by a recent state-of-the-art deep learning GFR system with A-Softmax loss [24] where features of different identities are discriminated by different angles, we decompose face features in the spherical coordinate system which consists of radial coordinate r and angular coordinates $\phi_1, \ldots, \phi_n$. Then the identity-related components are represented with angular coordinates, and the age-related information is encoded with radial coordinate. Features separated by the two mutually orthogonal coordinate systems are then trained jointly with different supervision signals. Identity-related features are trained as a multi-class classification task supervised by identity labels with the A-Softmax loss, and age-related features are trained as a regression task supervised by age labels. As such, we extract age-invariant features from angular coordinates by separating age-related components with radial coordinates. Since face features are decomposed into mutually orthogonal coordinate systems, we name our approach as orthogonal embedding CNNs (OE-CNNs). A related work Decoupled Network also discussed how to decouple the CNN with orthogonal geometry in details. Nevertheless, this work merely studies the generalization of networks rather than specifically modeling the age into decomposed features in the AIFR application scenario. We verify the effectiveness of OE-CNNs with extensive experiments on three face aging datasets (MORPH Album2 [30], CACD-VS [5] and FG-NET [1]) and one GFR dataset (LFW [12]), and achieve the state-of-the-art performances.

The major contributions of this paper are summarized as follows:

1. We propose a new approach called OE-CNNs to tackle the problem on how to jointly model the age-related features and identity-related features in a deep CNN model. Based on the proposed model, age-invariant deep features can be effectively obtained for improved AIFR performance.
2. We introduce a new large-scale Cross-Age Face dataset, named CAF, to help advance the research in this field. This dataset contains more than 313,986 images from 4,668 identities. The face data in CAF has been manually cleaned in order to be noise-free.
3. We demonstrate the effectiveness of our proposed approach with several extensive experiments over three face aging datasets (MORPH Album2 [30], CACD-VS [5] and FG-NET [1]) and one GFR dataset (LFW [12]). The experimental results have shown the superior performance of the proposed approach over the state-of-the-art either on AIFR or GFR.

2   Proposed Approach

2.1   Orthogonal Deep Features Decomposition

Two certain difficulties involved in AIFR include the considerable variations of the identical individual in different age categories (intra-class variations) caused by aging process (such as shape changes, texture changes, etc.), and

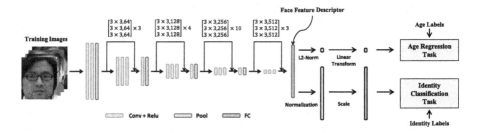

Fig. 2. The proposed ResNet-Like CNN architecture.

the inevitable mixture of unrelated components in the deep features extracted from a general deep CNN model. Large intra-class variation usually leads to erroneous identification on a pair of faces from the same individual at different ages. The mixed features (age features and identity features) potentially reduce the robustness of recognizing cross-age faces. To address this, we propose a new approach called orthogonal embedding CNNs. Below we first walk through the problem of deep AIFR in detail.

Given an observed Fully-Connected (FC) feature x extracted from the deep CNN model, we decompose it into two components (vectors). One is identity-related component x_{id} and the other is age-related component x_{age}. Thus, after removing x_{age} from x, we can obtain x_{id} that is supposed to be age-invariant. Recent works [10,42,47] use a linear combination to model x_{age} and x_{id} as the solution. In this paper, we propose a new approach to model x_{age} and x_{id} in an orthogonal manner with deep convolutional neural networks. Inspired by A-Softmax [24], where features of different identities are discriminated by different angles, we decompose feature x in spherical coordinate system $x_{sphere} = \{r; \phi_1, \phi_2, ..., \phi_n\}$. The angular components $\{\phi_1, \phi_2, ..., \phi_n\}$ represent identity-related information, and the rest radial component r is used to encode age-related information. Formally, $x \in R^n$ is decomposed under x_{sphere} as

$$x = x_{age} \cdot x_{id}, \tag{1}$$

where $x_{age} = ||x||_2$, and $x_{id} = \{\frac{x_1}{||x||_2}, \frac{x_2}{||x||_2}, ..., \frac{x_n}{||x||_2}\}$, with $||x_{id}||_2 = 1$. Here $||.||_2$ represents for L_2 norm, and x_n is the n-th component of x. For convenience, we will use n_x to represent for $||x||_2$ and $\tilde{x}$ for $\frac{x}{||x||_2}$.

2.2 Multi-task Learning

According to Eq. 1, feature x output from the last FC layer is decomposed into x_{age} and x_{id}. In this part, we describe a multi-task based learning algorithm to jointly learn these features. An overview of the proposed CNN model is illustrated in Fig. 2.

Learning Age-Related Component. In order to dig out the intrinsic clues of age information, we utilize an age estimation task to learn the relationship between the component x_{age} (n_x) and the ground truth of age. For simplicity, linear regression is adopted to the age estimation task, and the regression loss can be formulated as follows:

$$L_{age} = \frac{1}{2M} \sum_{i=1}^{M} ||f(n_{x_i}) - z_i||_2^2 \tag{2}$$

where n_{x_i} is the L_2 norm of the i-th embedding feature x_i, z_i is the corresponding i-th age label. $f(x)$ is a mapping function aimed to associate n_{x_i} and z_i. Since the L_2 norm n_{x_i} is a scalar, we use linear polynomial $f(x) = k \cdot x + b$ as the mapping function. We also explored other more complicated functions such as non-linear multi-layer perceptron network, but they did not perform as well as a simple linear transformation. We believe this is because a more complicated model overfits the underlying feature which is one-dimensional here.

Learning Identity-Related Component. When performing face verification or identification, $\tilde{x}$ is the only part which participates in the final similarity measure. Thus, the identity-related component x_{id} should be as discriminative as possible. Following the recent state-of-the-art GFR algorithm A-Softmax [24], we use a similar loss function to increase classification margin between different training persons in angular space:

$$L_{id} = \frac{1}{M} \sum_{i=1}^{M} -\log\left(\frac{e^{s \cdot \psi(\theta_{y_i,i})}}{e^{s \cdot \psi(\theta_{y_i,i})} + \sum_{j \neq y_i} e^{s \cdot \cos(\theta_{j,i})}}\right) \tag{3}$$

in which $\psi(.)$ is defined as $\psi(\theta_{y_i,i}) = (-1)^k \cos(m\theta_{y_i,i}) - 2k$, $\theta_{y_i,i}$ is the angle between the i-th feature $\tilde{x}_i$ and label y_i's weight vector, $\theta_{y_i,i} \in [\frac{k\pi}{m}, \frac{(k+1)\pi}{m}]$, and $k \in [0, m-1]$. $m \geq 1$ is an integer hyper-parameter that controls the size of angular margin, and $s > 0$ is an adjustable scale factor introduced to compensate the learning of Softmax. From the geometric perspective, Eq. 3 adds a constraint which guarantees the angle of the feature x with its corresponding weight vector should less than $\frac{1}{m}$ of the angle between the feature x and any other weight vectors. Consequently, the margin between two arbitrary classes can be increased. Compared with the original A-Softmax, Eq. 3 replaces L_2 norm of $\tilde{x}$ with an adjustable scalar factor s. In our model, according to Eq. 1, $||\tilde{x}||_2$ is always equal to 1. Thus, it is necessary to introduce an extra free variable to compensate for the loss of L_2 norm.

Overall, the two losses are combined to a multi-task loss for jointly optimizing, as below:

$$L = L_{id} + \lambda L_{age} \tag{4}$$

where λ is a scalar hyper-parameter to balance the two losses. Equation 4 is used to guide the learning of our CNN model in the training phase. In the testing phase, only the identity-related component x_{id} is used for the AIFR task.

2.3   Discussion

Compared with HFA Based AIFR Methods. The HFA based AIFR methods [10,11,42] suggest modeling the identity-related component and age-related

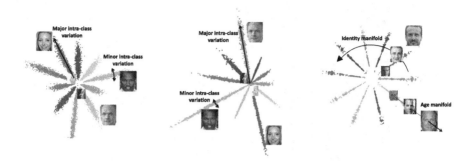

Fig. 3. Visualization of deep features learned with Softmax (Left), A-Softmax (Middle) and the proposed algorithm (Right). It is noteworthy that only 10 individuals are used to train CNN models, and the output dimension is set to 2. Colors are used to distinguish identities, and placement of face images is based on the corresponding features.

component of features by the simple linear combination. Specifically, given a feature x, the HFA based methods decompose the x as $x = m + Ux_{age} + Vx_{id} + \varepsilon$, where m is the mean feature regarding identity-related component, ε is the additional noise and U, V are the transformation matrices for identity-related component x_{id} and age-related component x_{age} respectively. The major advancements of the proposed approach over the HFA based methods are described in the following aspects: Firstly, the proposed approach revises the decomposition of x in the HFA based methods to the multiplication of hidden components x_{id} and x_{age}, which is more intuitive and concise to model the unrelated components with less extra hyper-parameters. Secondly, we explicitly project the identity features on a hypersphere to match the cosine similarity measurement for effectively combining the improvement strategies based on the Softmax loss and the margin of decision boundaries. Thirdly, the HFA based methods have to iteratively run the EM algorithm in contrast to our approach which jointly trains the network in the desirable end-to-end manner of feature learning. For the foregoing reasons, our method is more recommendable to be embedded into CNN framework for the purpose of learning age-invariant features, as supported by our experimental results.

Compared with SphereFace. SphereFace [24] introduces A-Softmax loss to learn the angular margin between identities for GFR. Though we train the identity-related component with a loss function similar to A-Softmax, the proposed algorithm takes advantage of the age information to explicitly train age-related component with an additional age regression task (Eq. 2). To intuitively investigate the impact by introducing such additional age regression task, we construct a toy example to compare features learned by Softmax, A-Softmax and our proposed algorithm. Specifically, we train CNN models with 10 individuals and set the output dimension of feature x as 2. For simplicity we let $f(x) = x$ (see Eq. 2) in this case. Figure 3 is the visualization for training

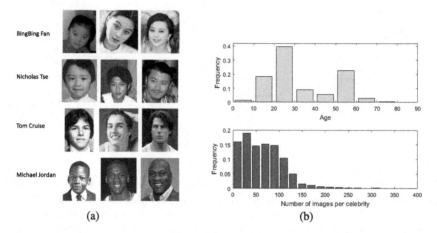

(a)   (b)

Fig. 4. Overview of the CAF dataset. (a) Example images of CAF. Note that since our images are collected from Internet, CAF not only varies in ages but also in poses, races, etc. (b) The distribution of CAF. Top: The distribution of the number of different ages. Bottom: The distribution of the number of different identities.

features. Based on this example, we conclude that: (1) features of different persons are discriminated mostly by angles, which intuitively justifies our decomposition design; (2) both A-Softmax and the proposed algorithm have noticeably larger classification margins than Softmax, as a result of the A-Softmax loss; (3) most importantly, for our model age of a person is reflected in radial direction (e.g. larger L_2 norms for older faces), while the other two models do not have this property. We believe this property further constrains the training problem, which reduces the risk of over-fitting and consequently leads to superior performance for AIFR.

Generalization of Our Approach. One of the noticeable highlights of the proposed algorithm is its generalization capability. Intuitively, our method is specifically designed to fit cross-age training data. However, the experimental results surprisingly unfold the excellent performance of the proposed method even trained with general training data (as shown in Sect. 4.4). Furthermore, as the objective of the algorithm is to generate identity-related features, the proposed algorithm is not only suitable for AIFR but also for GFR. Finally, The age component can be easily generalized to any other common component such as pose, illumination, emotion, etc.

3   Large-Scale Cross-Age Face Dataset (CAF)

In order to further motivate the development of AIFR and enrich the capability of the current model, a dataset with a large age gap is urgently needed. Besides, the dataset size should be large enough to avoid overfitting. To this end, we collect a new dataset with a large number of cross-age celebrities' faces, named large-scale Cross-Age Face dataset (CAF).

3.1 Dataset Collection

To build the cross-age celebrity dataset, it is inevitable to collect celebrity's name to form a list. The collected names in the list come from multiple sources such as IMDB, Forbes celebrity list, child actors name list from Wikipedia, etc. This guarantees the comparatively large age gap in the later data collection. Next, we iteratively search the name in the list by the Google Search Engine. Each searching term has been thresholded to a certain number, that is, we keep the name in the list if the number of responses exceeds a certain threshold, which ensures the sufficient number of data for each celebrity. Moreover, to the best of our knowledge, the current public cross-age datasets have very limited Asian individuals. For the purpose of increasing the diversity of our cross-age dataset, we collect a large number of Asian celebrities. After filtering the name list, we download the face images on several commercial image search engine (such as Google, Baidu) querying by the celebrity's name companied with several keywords like *yearbook, past and now, childhood, young, from young to old*, etc., to obtain the face images with different age categories. The data cleaning is performed thereafter. Specifically, we apply face detection algorithm MTCNN [14] to filter the images without any faces, then manually wipe off the near-duplicates and false face images (faces do not belong to that celebrity). Finally, we delete some of the images that have a large proportion in a certain age category to keep the age distribution more balanced.

Table 1. Comparison over cross-age datasets.

Dataset	CAF	IMDB-WIKI [31]	CACD [5]	MORPH [30]	AgeDB [26]	FG-NET [1]
# Images	313K	523K	163K	78K	16K	1K
# Subjects	4,668	20,284	2,000	20,000	568	82
Noise-free	Yes	No	Yes	Yes	Yes	Yes

3.2 Dataset Statistics

Following the above labeling and cleaning process, we construct a cross-age face dataset which totally includes about 313,986 face images from 4,668 identities. Each identity has approximately 80 face images. All of these images have been carefully and manually annotated. Example images of the dataset are shown in Fig. 4a. Considering the lack of exact age information, we utilize the public pre-trained age estimation model DEX [31] to predict the rough age label for each face image. Figure 4b shows the distribution histogram of CAF. One can observe our data are well-distributed in every possible age category. Table 1 fairly compares our dataset with existing released cross-age datasets. It is clear that except IMDB-WIKI [31], we have the comparatively largest scale in terms of the number of pictures and the number of individuals. Furthermore, as IMDB-WIKI is collected by automatically online crawling, some of the downloaded data might be redundant and noise-severe. Superior to IMDB-WIKI, CAF has minimized the noise data by manually annotating.

4   Experiments

For a direct and fair comparison to the existing work in this field, we evaluate our approach on existing public-domain cross-age face benchmark datasets MORPH Album 2 [30], CACD-VS [5] and FG-NET [1]. We also evaluate our algorithm on LFW [12] for verifying the generalization performance on GFR.

4.1   Implementation Details

The training set is composed of two parts: a cross-age face dataset and a general face dataset (without cross-age face data). The cross-age face dataset that we use is the collected CAF dataset introduced in Sect. 3 while the general face dataset consists of three public face datasets: CASIA-WebFace [45], VGG Face [29] and celebrity+ [25]. The same identities appeared in different datasets are carefully merged together. Since our testing dataset contains MORPH, CACD-VS, FG-NET, and LFW, we have excluded these data from the training set. Finally, our training set contains 1,765,828 images with 19,976 identities in total, which includes 313,986 cross-age face images with 4,668 identities and 1,451,842 general face images with 17609 identities respectively. In addition, the age label predicted from the public pre-trained age estimation model DEX [31] is treated as the regression target of Euclidean loss. Prior to training stage, we perform the same pre-processing on both training set and testing set: Using MTCNN [14] to detect the face and facial key points in images, then applying similarity transformation to crop the face patch to 112×96 pixels according to the 5 facial key points (two eyes, nose and two mouth corners), finally normalizing the cropped face patch by subtracting 127.5 then divided by 128. The proposed loss in Eq. 3 serves as the supervisory signal of identity classification. In terms of the age branch, we use Euclidean loss function to guide the network to learn the age label. The hyper-parameters m, s mentioned in Eqs. 3 and 4 are set to 4, 32 according to the recommendations of [24,38]. For the factor λ, we empirically selected an optimal value 0.01 to balance the two losses. All models are trained with Caffe [13] framework and optimized with stochastic gradient descent (SGD) algorithm. Training batch size is set to 512 and the number of iterations is set to 21 epochs. The initial learning rate is set to 0.05 and the training process adaptively decreases the learning rate 3 times when the loss becomes stable (roughly at the 9-th, 15-th and 18-th epoch).

4.2   Experiments on the MORPH Album 2 Dataset

Following [10,11,17,42], in this study we use an extended version of MORPH Album 2 dataset [30] for performance evaluation. It has 78,000 face images of

20,000 identities in total. The data has been split into training and testing set. The training set contains 10,000 identities. The rest of 10,000 identities belong to testing set where each identity has 2 photos with a large age gap. The testing data have been divided into gallery set and probe set. We follow the testing procedure given by [10] to evaluate the performance of our algorithm. We set up several schemes for comparison including: (1) **Softmax:** the CNN-baseline model trained by the original Softmax loss, (2) **A-Softmax:** the CNN-baseline model guided by the A-Softmax loss, (3) **OE-CNNs:** the proposed approach, and (4) other recently proposed top-performing AIFR algorithm in the literatures.

Firstly, we compare the proposed approach to baseline algorithms that are most related to the proposed algorithm to demonstrate its effectiveness. Table 2 compares the rank 1 identification rates testing on 10,000 subjects of Morph Album 2 over Softmax, A-Softmax, and OE-CNNs, with and without CAF dataset. As shown in the table, The proposed **OE-CNNs** significantly outperforms both Softmax and A-Softmax under both settings. Specifically, though we've used similar loss function with A-Softmax for training the identity-related features, **OE-CNNs** noticeably improves the performance of A-Softmax, which confirms the effectiveness of our features decomposition method for AIFR. Note that, all compared networks have the same base network (from input to FC layer). When comparing performances trained with and without CAF dataset, we can see that with CAF the identification rate improves consistently for all systems, which confirms that the CAF dataset is valuable to AIFR research.

Secondly, for ensuring a fair comparison with other methods, we neglect the CAF dataset and conduct an experiment with the same training data as related work [42] has used. Specifically, WebFace [45], celebrity+ [25] and CACD [5] form the training set to train a CNN base model. The trained model is later fine-tuned with Morph training data. Table 3 depicts our result compared with other methods. There are conventionally two evaluation schemes on Morph benchmark: testing on 10,000 subjects or 3,000 subjects. For fairly comparing against other methods, we evaluate the proposed OE-CNN approach on both schemes. As can be seen in Table 3, the OE-CNN approach shows its capability by substantially outperforming all other methods in both two evaluation schemes. Particularly, our method surpasses the LF-CNN model by 1.0% and AE-CNN model by 0.5%, which is an outstanding improvement on the accuracy level above 98%.

4.3   Experiments on the CACD-VS Dataset

CACD dataset comprises comprehensively 163,446 images from 2,000 distinct celebrities. The age ranges from 10 to 62 years old. This dataset collects the celebrity's images with the effect of various illumination condition, different poses and makeup, which can effectively reflect the robustness of the AIFR algorithm. CACD-VS is a subset of CACD which is picked from CACD to composes 2,000 pairs of positive sample and 2,000 pairs of negative samples, and 4,000 pairs of samples in total. We follow the pipeline of [5] to calculate the similarity score of all sample pairs and the ROC curves and its corresponding AUC. We take 9 folds from 10 folds that have already been separated officially to compute threshold

Table 2. Performance comparisons of different baselines on Morph Album 2.

Training dataset	Method	Rank-1 identification rates
Public datasets	Softmax	94.84%
Public datasets	A-Softmax	96.27%
Public datasets	**OE-CNNs**	**97.46%**
Public datasets + CAF	Softmax	95.49%
Public datasets + CAF	A-Softmax	96.59%
Public datasets + CAF	**OE-CNNs**	**98.57%**

Table 3. Performance comparisons of different approaches on Morph Album 2.

Method	#Test subjects	Rank-1 identification rates
HFA [10]	10,000	91.14%
CARC [5]	10,000	92.80%
MEFA [11]	10,000	93.80%
MEFA+SIFT+MLBP [11]	10,000	94.59%
LPS+HFA [17]	10,000	94.87%
LF-CNNs [42]	10,000	97.51%
OE-CNNs	10,000	**98.55%**
GSM [21]	3,000	94.40%
AE-CNNs [47]	3,000	98.13%
OE-CNNs	3,000	**98.67%**

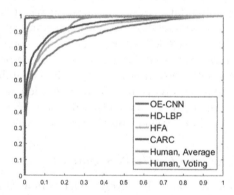

Fig. 5. ROC comparisons of different approaches on CACD-VS.

references and use this threshold to evaluate on the rest of 1 fold. By repeating this procedure 10 times, we finally calculate the average accuracy as another measure.

Table 4. Performance comparisons of different approaches on CACD-VS.

Method	Acc	AUC
High-dimensional LBP [7]	81.6%	88.8%
HFA [10]	84.4%	91.7%
CARC [5]	87.6%	94.2%
LF-CNNs [42]	98.5%	99.3%
Human, Average [6]	85.7%	94.6%
Human, Voting [6]	94.2%	99.0%
Softmax	98.4%	99.4%
A-Softmax	98.7%	99.5%
OE-CNNs	**99.2%**	**99.5%**

The results of all the baselines are shown in Table 4 and Fig. 5. As illustrated, the proposed OE-CNN approach significantly outperforms all the other baselines. Furthermore, our approach also surpasses the human-level performance, which demonstrates the effectiveness of our proposed age-invariant deep features.

4.4   Experiments on the FG-NET Dataset

The FG-NET dataset consists of 1,002 pictures from 82 different identities, each identity has multiple face images with huge variability in the age covering from child to elder. Following the evaluation protocols of Megaface challenge 1 (MF1) [15] and Megaface challenge 2 (MF2) [27] we employ the 1 million images from Flickr as the distractor set. Particularly, under the small protocol of MF1, we reduce our training data to 0.5 million images from 12,073 identities in the training phase. The cross-age face images in FG-NET servers as the probe set in which a probe image is compared against each image from distractor set. We evaluate the rank-1 performance of the presented algorithm under the protocols of MF1 and MF2, as shown in Tables 5 and 6, respectively.

Under the small protocol of MF1, the proposed method not only obtains a significant performance improvement over Softmax and A-Softmax baseline but also surpasses the existing methods (including a specific age-invariant method TNVP [8]) by a clear margin. Under the protocol of MF2, all the algorithms need to be trained using the same training dataset (which does not involve the cross-age training data) provided by MF2 organizer. It is encouraging to see that our algorithm also outperforms all other methods with a large margin, which strongly proves the effectiveness of our algorithm on AIFR.

4.5   Experiments on the LFW Dataset

LFW is a very famous benchmark for general face recognition. The dataset has 13,233 face images from 5,749 subjects acquiring from the arbitrary environment.

Table 5. Performance comparisons of different approaches under the protocols of MF1 [15] on FG-NET.

Method	Protocol	Rank-1 identification rates
FUDAN-CS_SDS [41]	Small	25.56%
SphereFace [24]	Small	47.55%
TNVP [8]	Small	47.72%
Softmax	Small	35.11%
A-Softmax	Small	46.77%
OE-CNNs (single-patch)	Small	52.67%
OE-CNNs (3-patch ensemble)	Small	**58.21%**

Table 6. Performance comparisons of different approaches under the protocol of MF2 [27] on FG-NET.

Method	Protocol	Rank-1 identification rates
GRCCV	Large	21.04%
NEC	Large	29.29%
3DiVi	Large	35.79%
GT-CMU-SYSU	Large	38.21%
OE-CNNs (single-patch)	Large	**53.26%**

Table 7. Performance comparisons of different approaches on LFW.

Method		Images	Networks	Acc
General approaches	DeepFace [36]	4M	3	97.35%
	FaceNet [32]	200M	1	99.65%
	DeepID2+ [35]	–	25	99.47%
	Center loss [43]	0.7M	1	99.28%
	SphereFace [24]	0.5M	1	99.42%
Cross-age approaches	LF-CNNs [42]	0.7M	1	99.10%
	OE-CNNs	0.5M	1	**99.35%**
	OE-CNNs	1.7M	1	**99.47%**

We experiment our algorithm on LFW following the official unrestricted with labeled outside data protocol. We test our model on 6,000 face pairs. The training data are disjoint from the testing data. Table 7 exhibits our results. One can see that the proposed OE-CNN approach achieves comparable performance without any ensemble trick to the state-of-the-art approaches, which demonstrates the excellent generalization ability of the proposed approach. Additionally, after we expand the training dataset to 1.7M (including CAF dataset), the performance of OE-CNNs further improves to 99.47%, which also proves that our CAF dataset is not only valuable for AIFR but also helpful for GFR.

5 Conclusion

AIFR is a remained challenging computer vision task on account of the aging process of the human. Inspired by pioneering work and the observation of hidden components, this paper proposes a novel approach which separates deep face feature into the orthogonal age-related component and identity-related component to improve AIFR. The highly discriminative age-invariant features can be consequently extracted from a multi-task deep CNN model based on the proposed approach. Furthermore, we build a large cross-age celebrity dataset named CAF that is both noise-free and vast in the number of images. As a part of training data, CAF greatly boosts the performance of the models for AIFR. Extensive evaluations of several face aging datasets have been done to show the effectiveness of our orthogonal embedding CNN (OE-CNN) approach. More studies on how to incorporate the generative scheme and improve the discriminative scheme will be explored in our future work to benefit the AIFR community.

References

1. FG-NET Aging Database. http://www.fgnet.rsunit.com/
2. Ahonen, T., Hadid, A., Pietikainen, M.: Face description with local binary patterns: application to face recognition. IEEE Trans. Pattern Anal. Mach. Intell. (T-PAMI) (2006)
3. Antipov, G., Baccouche, M., Dugelay, J.L.: Face Aging With Conditional Generative Adversarial Networks. In: IEEE International Conference on Image Processing (ICIP) (2017)
4. Belhumeur, P., Hespanha, J.P., Kriegman, D.: Eigenfaces vs. fisherfaces: recognition using class specific linear projection. IEEE Trans. Pattern Anal. Mach. Intell. (T-PAMI) (1997)
5. Chen, B.C., Chen, C.S., Hsu, W.H.: Cross-age reference coding for age-invariant face recognition and retrieval. In: European Conference on Computer Vision (ECCV) (2014)
6. Chen, B.C., Chen, C.S., Hsu, W.H.: Face recognition and retrieval using cross-age reference coding with cross-age celebrity dataset. IEEE Trans. Multimed. **17**(6), 804–815 (2015)
7. Chen, D., Cao, X., Wen, F., Sun, J.: Blessing of dimensionality: high-dimensional feature and its efficient compression for face verification. In: IEEE Conference on Computer Vision and Pattern Recognition (CVPR), pp. 3025–3032 (2013)
8. Duong, C.N., Quach, K.G., Luu, K., Savvides, M., et al.: Temporal non-volume preserving approach to facial age-progression and age-invariant face recognition. In: IEEE Conference on Computer Vision and Pattern Recognition (CVPR) (2017)
9. Geng, X., Zhou, Z.H., Smith-Miles, K.: Automatic age estimation based on facial aging patterns. IEEE Trans. Pattern Anal. Mach. Intell. (TPAMI) (2007)
10. Gong, D., Li, Z., Lin, D., Liu, J., Tang, X.: Hidden factor analysis for age invariant face recognition. In: International Conference on Computer Vision (ICCV) (2013)

11. Gong, D., Li, Z., Tao, D., Liu, J., Li, X.: A maximum entropy feature descriptor for age invariant face recognition. In: IEEE Conference on Computer Vision and Pattern Recognition (CVPR), pp. 5289–5297 (2015)

12. Huang, G.B., Ramesh, M., Berg, T., Learned-Miller, E.: Labeled faces in the wild: a database for studying face recognition in unconstrained environments. Technical Report 07–49, University of Massachusetts, Amherst (2007)

13. Jia, Y., Shelhamer, E., Donahue, J., Karayev, S., Long, J., Girshick, R., Guadarrama, S., Darrell, T.: Caffe: convolutional architecture for fast feature embedding. In: Proceedings of the 2016 ACM on Multimedia Conference (ACM MM) (2014)

14. Zhang, K., Zhang, Z., Li, Z., Qiao, Y.: Joint face detection and alignment using multi-task cascaded convolutional networks. Signal Process. Lett. **23**(10), 1499–1503 (2016)

15. Kemelmacher-Shlizerman, I., Seitz, S.M., Miller, D., Brossard, E.: The megaface benchmark: 1 million faces for recognition at scale. In: IEEE Conference on Computer Vision and Pattern Recognition (CVPR) (2016)

16. Lanitis, A., Taylor, C.J., Cootes, T.F.: Toward automatic simulation of aging effects on face images. IEEE Trans. Pattern Anal. Mach. Intell. (TPAMI) (2002)

17. Li, Z., Gong, D., Li, X., Tao, D.: Aging face recognition: a hierarchical learning model based on local patterns selection. IEEE Trans. Image Process. (TIP) **25**(5), 2146–2154 (2016)

18. Li, Z., Lin, D., Tang, X.: Nonparametric discriminant analysis for face recognition. IEEE Trans. Pattern Anal. Mach. Intell. (T-PAMI) **31**, 755–761 (2009)

19. Li, Z., Liu, W., Lin, D., Tang, X.: Nonparametric subspace analysis for face recognition. In: Conference on Computer Vision and Pattern Recognition (CVPR) (2005)

20. Li, Z., Park, U., Jain, A.K.: A discriminative model for age invariant face recognition. IEEE Trans. Inf. Forensics Secur. (TIFS) (2011)

21. Lin, L., Wang, G., Zuo, W., Feng, X., Zhang, L.: Cross-domain visual matching via generalized similarity measure and feature learning. IEEE Trans. Pattern Anal. Mach. Intell. (TPAMI) **39**(6), 1089–1102 (2017)

22. Ling, H., Soatto, S., Ramanathan, N., Jacobs, D.W.: Face verification across age progression using discriminative methods. IEEE Trans. Inf. Forensics Secur. (TIFS) (2010)

23. Liu, W., Li, Z., Tang, X.: Spatio-temporal embedding for statistical face recognition from video. In: Leonardis, A., Bischof, H., Pinz, A. (eds.) European Conference on Computer Vision (ECCV) (2006)

24. Liu, W., Wen, Y., Yu, Z., Li, M., Raj, B., Song, L.: SphereFace: deep hypersphere embedding for face recognition. In: IEEE Conference on Computer Vision and Pattern Recognition (CVPR) (2017)

25. Liu, Z., Luo, P., Wang, X., Tang, X.: Deep learning face attributes in the wild. In: International Conference on Computer Vision (ICCV) (2015)

26. Moschoglou, S., Papaioannou, A., Sagonas, C., Deng, J., Kotsia, I., Zafeiriou, S.: Agedb: the first manually collected in-the-wild age database. In: IEEE Conference on Computer Vision and Pattern Recognition Workshops (CVPRW) (2017)

27. Nech, A., Kemelmacher-Shlizerman, I.: Level playing field for million scale face recognition. In: IEEE Conference on Computer Vision and Pattern Recognition (CVPR) (2017)

28. Park, U., Tong, Y., Jain, A.K.: Age-invariant face recognition. IEEE Trans. Pattern Anal. Mach. Intell. (TPAMI) (2010)

29. Parkhi, O.M., Vedaldi, A., Zisserman, A.: Deep face recognition. In: British Machine Vision Conference (BMVC) (2015)

30. Ricanek, K., Tesafaye, T.: Morph: a longitudinal image database of normal adult age-progression. In: International Conference on Automatic Face and Gesture Recognition (2006)

31. Rothe, R., Timofte, R., Gool, L.V.: Dex: deep expectation of apparent age from a single image. In: International Conference on Computer Vision Workshops (ICCVW), December 2015

32. Schroff, F., Kalenichenko, D., Philbin, J.: Facenet: a unified embedding for face recognition and clustering. In: IEEE Conference on Computer Vision and Pattern Recognition (CVPR) (2015)

33. Sun, Y., Chen, Y., Wang, X., Tang, X.: Deep learning face representation by joint identification-verification. In: Advances in Neural Information Processing Systems (NIPS) (2014)

34. Sun, Y., Liang, D., Wang, X., Tang, X.: Deepid3: face recognition with very deep neural networks. arXiv preprint arXiv:1502.00873 (2015)

35. Sun, Y., Wang, X., Tang, X.: Deeply learned face representations are sparse, selective, and robust. In: IEEE Conference on Computer Vision and Pattern Recognition (CVPR) (2015)

36. Taigman, Y., Yang, M., Ranzato, M., Wolf, L.: Deepface: closing the gap to human-level performance in face verification. In: IEEE Conference on Computer Vision and Pattern Recognition (CVPR) (2014)

37. Turk, M.A., Pentland, A.P.: Face recognition using eigenfaces. In: Conference on Computer Vision and Pattern Recognition (CVPR) (1991)

38. Wang, F., Xiang, X., Cheng, J., Yuille, A.L.: NormFace: L_2 hypersphere embedding for face verification. In: Proceedings of the 2017 ACM on Multimedia Conference (ACM MM) (2017)

39. Wang, H., Wang, Y., Zhou, Z., Ji, X., Li, Z., Gong, D., Zhou, J., Liu, W.: Cosface: large margin cosine loss for deep face recognition. In: Conference on Computer Vision and Pattern Recognition (CVPR) (2018)

40. Wang, X., Tang, X.: A unified framework for subspace face recognition. IEEE Trans. Pattern Anal. Mach. Intell. (TPAMI) (2004)

41. Wang, Z., He, K., Fu, Y., Feng, R., Jiang, Y.G., Xue, X.: Multi-task deep neural network for joint face recognition and facial attribute prediction. In: Proceedings of the 2017 ACM on International Conference on Multimedia Retrieval (ICMR) (2017)

42. Wen, Y., Li, Z., Qiao, Y.: Latent factor guided convolutional neural networks for age-invariant face recognition. In: IEEE Conference on Computer Vision and Pattern Recognition (CVPR) (2016)

43. Wen, Y., Zhang, K., Li, Z., Qiao, Y.: A discriminative feature learning approach for deep face recognition. In: European Conference on Computer Vision (ECCV), pp. 499–515 (2016)

44. Xiong, Y., Liu, W., Zhao, D., Tang, X.: Face recognition via archetype hull ranking. In: International Conference on Computer Vision (ICCV) (2013)

45. Yi, D., Lei, Z., Liao, S., Li, S.Z.: Learning face representation from scratch. arXiv preprint arXiv:1411.7923 (2014)

46. Zhang, Z., Song, Y., Qi, H.: Age progression/regression by conditional adversarial autoencoder. In: IEEE Conference on Computer Vision and Pattern Recognition (CVPR) (2017)

47. Zheng, T., Deng, W., Hu, J.: Age estimation guided convolutional neural network for age-invariant face recognition. In: IEEE Conference on Computer Vision and Pattern Recognition Workshops (CVPRW) (2017)

Broadcasting Convolutional Network for Visual Relational Reasoning

Simyung Chang[1,2], John Yang[1], SeongUk Park[1], and Nojun Kwak[1(✉)]

[1] Seoul National University, Seoul, South Korea
{yjohn,swpark0703,nojunk}@snu.ac.kr
[2] Samsung Electronics, Suwon, South Korea
timelighter@snu.ac.kr

Abstract. In this paper, we propose the *Broadcasting Convolutional Network* (BCN) that extracts key object features from the global field of an entire input image and recognizes their relationship with local features. BCN is a simple network module that collects effective spatial features, embeds location information and broadcasts them to the entire feature maps. We further introduce the *Multi-Relational Network* (multiRN) that improves the existing Relation Network (RN) by utilizing the BCN module. In pixel-based relation reasoning problems, with the help of BCN, multiRN extends the concept of 'pairwise relations' in conventional RNs to 'multiwise relations' by relating each object with multiple objects at once. This yields in $\mathcal{O}(n)$ complexity for n objects, which is a vast computational gain from RNs that take $\mathcal{O}(n^2)$. Through experiments, multiRN has achieved a state-of-the-art performance on CLEVR dataset, which proves the usability of BCN on relation reasoning problems.

Keywords: Visual relational reasoning · BCN · Broadcast · CLEVR Multi-RN · Visuo-spatial features

1 Introduction

A complete cognizance of a visual scene is achieved by relational reasonings of a set of detected entities in an attempt to discover the underlying structure [18]. Reasoning comparative relationships allows artificial intelligence to infer semantic similarities or transitive orders among objects in scenes with various perspectives and scales [5]. While the core of relational reasoning instrumentally depends on spatial learning [3,28], the relational networks (RNs) [27,29] have fostered the performance vastly on related tasks based on their spatial grid features. However, the number of objects in conventional RNs upsurges as their

Electronic supplementary material The online version of this chapter (https://doi.org/10.1007/978-3-030-01267-0_46) contains supplementary material, which is available to authorized users.

method assumes that each grid represents an object at the corresponding position within the scene regardless of the existence of an object at a grid position. Moreover, the computational cost increases quadratically as RNs are based on pairwise computation of objects' relations for relational reasoning.

This computational burden is inevitable for visual reasoning problems if conventional architectures of convolutional neural networks (CNNs) [21] are used. Although, CNNs have allowed success in many computer vision problems [6,7,9,12,19,24], yet they still suffer from difficulties in generalization over geometric variations of scenes. This is mainly due to the receptive fields that are mapped with convolution filters at fixed areas, which derives CNNs to disregard spatial locations in the process of searching for optimal features. Either bigger size of filters that embrace multiple input entities or repetitive usage of smaller filters in deeper networks are typically used to learn spatial relationships. CNNs, however, still show limited performances for large deformations of inputs as long as the receptive fields of convolution or pooling filters stay local and small-sized [13,14,23,25].

In order to learn relationships among objects, the correlation of objects needs to be defined along with the segregation of non-object features. And, CNNs' structural loss of spatial information also needs to be overcome to handle dynamic variations of object sizes and locations. We are motivated to solve such issues through globally extending receptive fields of object features and efficiently learning correlations among objects in an end-to-end manner. To this end, we propose a modular technique named *Broadcasting Convolutional Network* (BCN) that can be applied in any CNNs to enable learning spatial features with absolute positional information, broadcasting the features and analyzing visual relations among given objects. This technique not only overcomes the limitations of conventional narrow-sighted convolution operations by extending the receptive fields ideally to the global manner, but also allows to define a novel neural network called the *Multi-relational Network* (multiRN) that outperforms on the relational reasoning tasks in terms of both performance and computational efficiency. The proposed multiRN achieves the state-of-the-art performance on the CLEVR dataset which is the representative dataset for relational reasoning.

The paper is organized as follows. In Sects. 2 and 3, the proposed BCN and multiRN are explained in detail. In Sect. 4, the novelty of our work is described by comparing the methods with the related works. Section 5 shows experimental results and finally, Sect. 6 concludes the paper.

2   Broadcasting Convolutional Network

In this section, we first describe the overall architecture of BCN with details of our implementations and their purposes. The proposed BCN is depicted in Fig. 1 which mainly consists of three components: (1) coordinate channel embedding (CCE), (2) encoding visual features with objective spatial information and (3) broadcasting globally max-pooled features through expansions.

The BCN is applied after each pixel of the feature maps acquires proper sizes of receptive fields through basic convolutions. The module makes feature

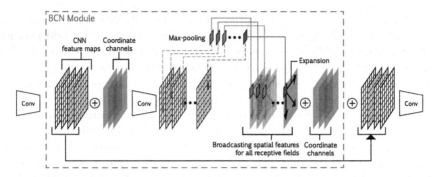

Fig. 1. Broadcasting Convolutional Network Modules. Feature maps acquired from previous convolution layers are concatenated with coordinate planes during CCE phase. Then, additional light-weight convolution layer(s) (*e.g.* two layers of 1×1 convolution with ReLU activation) is(are) applied. An $1 \times 1 \times n$ vector is generated by max-pooling from each filter channel of the n resultant feature maps. The vector is then expanded to emulate the size of the original feature maps, and merged with the original feature maps as an input to the next layer of convolution.

maps that represent the coordinate information and concatenates them with the original CNN feature maps. Then, rather simple convolution operations (*e.g.* a few layers of 1×1 convolution with ReLU activation) are applied, which is followed by a global max-pooling stage. Let us say that a feature map in the shape of $h \times w \times n$ is generated from the previous convolution operations, where n is the number of filters and h and w represent height and width of the feature maps produced, respectively. In this sense, a maximum element can be extracted from each filter so that an $1 \times 1 \times n$ vector is generated. The feature vector is then expanded to emulate the same size of the original feature maps, and then merged with the original feature maps to be convolutionally mapped together.

Our intention of such structure concentrates on reusing the relationship among current positional features and broadcasting them for global comparisons during further convolution operations. Concatenating extracted features with the original feature maps, further convolution filters are able to correlate the objective visuospatial features (convolved features with CCE) and the relative visuospatial features (broadcasting features).

The whole structure of BCN can be succinctly described in an equation as:

$$\mathcal{BCN}(F) = [\mathcal{E}(\max([F, C] * k), h, w), C], \tag{1}$$

where $[\cdot, \cdot]$ refers to the concatenation of feature maps. Here, $F \in \mathbb{R}^{h \times w \times n'}$ is the input feature map for the broadcast convolution module, $C \in \mathbb{R}^{h \times w \times n_c}$ is n_c coordinate planes, $*k$ represents a few layers of convolutional operations whose structure is defined in k (*e.g.* two layers of 1×1 convolution with ReLU activation). Assuming that n is the number of filters in the last layer of successive convolution operations $*k$, the max-pooling operation is taken for each of n output feature maps such that it results in an $1 \times 1 \times n$ vector. $\mathcal{E}$ denotes an

Fig. 2. An example of coordinate planes, c_x, c_y and c_r, for feature maps with 2:1 aspect ratio of width to height. The brighter, the higher value.

expansion operation which copies its input vector to the entire $h \times w$ positions. The proposed BCN outputs a broadcast feature map $B \in \mathbb{R}^{h \times w \times (n+n_c)}$ which is concatenated with the original feature maps F and fed to the next layer as shown in Fig. 1.

The convolution layer(s) right after the CCE phase can be one or multiple, however the major purpose of its(their) presence is to generate abstract representations based on locations. This allows the further convolutional mappings in the later process to infer relative positions among features with the implanted information on the objective positions. In this paper, we have implemented two or three layers of 1×1 convolution after CCE for all experiments to make each pixel in feature maps being convolved depth-wise with undissolved coordinate information. Additionally, the number of feature maps has kept fairly small so that the coordinate planes can be adequately reflected to the outputs after convolution operations. Yet, the number of coordinate planes can apparently be adjusted if needed. This simple setting allows a large improvement on efficiency of extracting and utilizing spatial features in CNNs without much additional computation.

Since CNNs have performed generalization by taking advantage of sharing convolutional kernels in all input locations, their consequential structures are difficult to conserve spatial information throughout the layers. One of the intuitive ways to reflect location information to filtered outputs is to embed unique coordinates into the inputs. In our method, the feature location information is implanted in original feature maps as additional channels. This specific decision comes from the motivation to assign objective positional components to each feature during convolutions before the max-pooling phase, and to establish relative location for the comparison against other spatial features when broadcasting. This furthers the productivity of coordinate embedded visual features and allows additional convolutional mappings to reflect the feature positions when generating higher level features.

Three different coordinate planes are defined as in Fig. 2 and used in this paper; one for the x-axis, c_x, another for the y-axis, c_y and the last one for the radial distance from the center, c_r. Similar to the conventional coordinate feature embedding approaches [22,26,29,32], these planes with the normalized coordinates reduce initial learning bias and provide additional feature location information. Since inputs of our module may not necessarily have the shape of a square, elements of each plane are normalized according to the aspect ratio of inputs. As it can be seen in Fig. 2, the Cartesian coordinates c_x and c_y tend to be

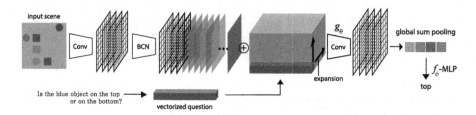

Fig. 3. Multi-Relational Networks. For visual relational reasoning problems, input scenes are fed into ordinary convolutional layers and a BCN module. Since the outputs of BCNs connote visuospatial features of multiple objects, they can be merged with the original features and the expanded question tensor for further convolution operations, g_θ. Then, global sum poolings are operated on feature maps produced, and the outcomes are integrated to answer questions.

zero towards the center. This prevents features from being initially biased near bottom right-side which occurs if coordinates near top left start from zero as used in usual computer graphics. Also, when inputs with different aspect ratios are given, initial values in CCE are scaled to cope with the different aspect ratio.

3   Multi-relational Network

Visuospatial tasks necessitate recognition of relevant features from the spatial organization of stimuli and selection of stimulus that matches one or more of these identified features [3,28]. Algorithms such as relation networks (RNs) [27, 29] have introduced solutions for relational reasoning problems including CLEVR dataset [16] based on their spatial grid features – the dataset is explained in a more detailed manner later in this paper. Utilizing BCN, RNs can be greatly improved in both performance and computational efficiency.

In [29], an RN module for a set of n objects, $O = \{o_1, \cdots, o_n\}$, is introduced, which consists of two functions f_ϕ and g_θ such that:

$$\mathcal{RN}(O) = f_\phi(\sum_i \sum_j g_\theta(o_i, o_j)), \tag{2}$$

where f_ϕ represents multi-layer perceptron (MLP) operations on the visuospatial relation features that have been generated by another MLP operation g_θ from all pairwise combinations of objects. The 'relations' are the outputs of $\mathcal{O}(n^2)$ time of computations from g_θ. Earlier in this paper, we have explained how BCN allows multiple spatial features to be represented in one dimensional vector. With the help of BCN described in (1), original RN in (2) can be revised into Multi-Relational Networks (multiRN) as follows:

$$multi\mathcal{RN}(O) = f_\phi(\sum_i g_\theta(o_i, \mathcal{BCN}(O))). \tag{3}$$

Since $\mathcal{BCN}(O)$ connotes multi-location features for multiple objects, each object feature can be paired with multiple object location features, fed into g_θ and computed in $\mathcal{O}(n)$. This allows not only exponential gain in computation complexity but also relational comparison with multiple objects at once. The outputs of g_θ should, in our context, be redefined as 'multiple relations', and can be trained end-to-end to convey information about how much of certain object feature at particular location should be reflected for visual relational reasoning.

Furthermore, the number of objects, n, in pixel-based relational reasoning problems is defined by $n = h \times w$ where h, w are height and width of resultant 3-dimensional tensors from previous convolution layers. Such trait allows us to replace the MLP operation for g_θ in RNs with 1×1 convolution after channel concatenations of BCN outputs as shown in Fig. 3. The non-pixel-based objects such as questions in visual question and answering (VQA) problems can be additionally concatenated in channels. The final form of our multi-relational network is:

$$multiRN(O) = f_\phi(\sum_i g_\theta(o_i, \mathcal{BCN}(O), question). \tag{4}$$

In practice, *questions* are expanded for channel embedding, and the final tensor is fed into g_θ-convolution operations to achieve 'multiple relations'.

4   Related Works

Our motif has two aspects: 1. extracting and condensing dynamic spatial features and 2. globally projecting them to previous feature maps which largely widen the receptive fields just as demanded in multi-scale reasonings and full resolution dense relational predictions.

Many previous computer vision related researches have used pooling techniques for extracting meaningful spatial features [4]. Spatial pyramid pooling [8] uses manual control over pooling scales and regional features are extracted from variations of hand-engineered pooling scopes. This issue has been developed in [15] where a large set of various pooling bins are initiated and the algorithm learns to select sparse subset of them. These works take hand-crafted pooling regions that cannot be learned end-to-end.

ROI pooling structure [4,5] is similar to our method's in a way of executing pooling methods in channel-wise. Each channel represents feature maps from starting stride point to last, and thus may possess objective spatial features. However, with conventional ROI pooling methods, each feature map does not reflect any relations among feature maps.

While effective receptive field size is previously known to increase linearly with the number of convolutional layers [25], the works in [5] have found that it actually increases with square root of the number of layers which is a much slower rate. This finding further leads to a logical doubt that deep CNNs may not have large enough receptive field size even at top layers. This phenomenon is prominent in fully convolutional networks (FCNs) with a large input image. To overcome the issue, large enough receptive field size is not the only aspect that is essential but the learning of its flexibility depending upon situations, which explains why atrous convolution methods are used widely.

Deformable convolutional neural networks (Deformable ConvNet) [5] is engaged with deformable convolutions that learn the applicable filters with adaptive receptive fields. Their convolution filters are chained with offset parameters which represent the mapping of the original receptive fields to unique and irregularly dispersed receptive fields from each spatial location. The offset parameters are optimized along with the convolutional filters during back-propagation. However, Deformable ConvNets require extra computation upon original CNNs, and their feature map sampling method in a local manner hinders themselves from having complete spatial support. They, as their primitive motivation, further emphasize the importance of adaptive receptive learning in the needs of effectively computing large enough receptive fields at top layers.

Other atrous convolution usages include increasing the receptive field size by sampling from dilated sparse regions [11]. This allows to retain the same computational complexity as previous CNNs' while increasing receptive field sizes, and thus is widely used in semantic segmentation problems [1,24,33]. If depth conditions are excluded, the method is still doubted on utilizing enough size of receptive fields. Our model handles extracted convolutional features by projecting them to global receptive fields, intending to convolve the features from various spatial locations with the original features.

A dominant approach used in the visual relational reasoning domain is the Relation Network module (RN) [29]. As mentioned in Sect. 3, RN learns the relations among objectified features of CNN through pairwise combinations, computations of which increase quadratically with the number of the objects while multiRN gains a comparable improvement on computation efficiency through manipulation of 'multiple relations' induced by the BCN module. A FiLM module [26], as another method for relational reasoning problems, conditions features before activation functions in a similar way as done in LSTM gates [10] and SENET's feature excitations [12]. Such attempt of learning visual feature conditionings for reasoning largely differs from our method of extracting and broadcasting key object features to the entire receptive fields. Also, compared to their suggested model that incorporates multiple residual blocks and large GRUs and MLPs, a multiRN model requires much smaller networks to achieve similar performances.

5   Experiments

The proposed method is tested in several experiments and compared with other similar methods to verify the effectiveness of BCN and MultiRN. The purposes of the experiments are to investigate the followings:

(1) the capability of BCN in representation power of features, (2) the effectiveness of MultiRN on visual reasoning problems, (3) feasible extensions of receptive fields caused by BCN and practical expressions of multiple objects in

multiRN as specified in Sect. 3, and (4) variations of coordinate embeddings in visual features and their performances.

5.1 Tasks

We have experimented our methods on four datasets, Scaled-MNIST, STL-10, Sort-of-CLEVR with pixels, and CLEVR with pixels, for different purposes.

Scaled-MNIST dataset is our own remodeled version of original MNIST dataset [20] to verify that the BCN can effectively handle positional information while globally extending the receptive field. Locating the original MNIST of size 28×28 to 128×128 image space, we randomly scale the width irregularly ranging from 28 to 105 pixels and the aspect ratio from 1:0.8 to 1:1.2. All digits are positioned randomly within the new image space, preserving its complete form. Along with the class labels, another label is added for the locations of center points for each digit in order to evaluate localization performances of the models.

STL-10 [2] is used to evaluate the capability of BCN for natural image classification problems. It is a set of natural image with ten class labels each of which has 500 training images and 800 test images. There are also unlabeled images within the dataset, but we do not use them because experiments on them are irrelevant to our intentions. The data consists of images sized in 96×96 with higher resolution than those of CIFAR-10 but less number of training images.

CLEVR with pixels [16] is one of the visual QA datasets which is a challenging problem set requiring high-level relational reasonings. The dataset contains images of 3-D rendered objects and corresponding questions asking about several attributes of the objects. We have experimented only on the pixel version of the CLEVR dataset whose images are represented in 2-D pixel-wise.

Sort-of-CLEVR with pixels [29] is our main experiment for multiRN. Sort-of-CLEVR is a more simplified version of CLEVR, which is a set of images combined with caption dataset for relation and non-relation reasonings. Each image contains six of differently colored 2-D geometric shapes, and corresponding 20 questions; 10 for relational and 10 for non-relational reasonings. Questions in this dataset are already vectorized, and thus the experiments are independent from any additional vector embedding models, which allows more reasonable comparison based on the results.

5.2 Evaluation of BCN

For all experiments, BCN uses multiple convolution layers with different size of 1×1 kernels and ReLUs for non-linearity. The number of filters in m convolution layers for a BCN is written in the form of $[S_1, \cdots, S_m]$ in each experiment.

Scaled-MNIST: As a baseline model, we have stacked three to five of convolutional layers with 24 of 3×3 kernels, stride size of 2 and padding size of 1 for

Table 1. The model with BCN has the highest classification accuracy and the lowest localization error on the Scaled-MNIST data. Skip-connection denotes using the shape of 1×1 convolution layers for BCN. This can be viewed just the same as skip-connection [30]

Model	Classification Acc.	Localization Err.	#Params	Runtime[1]
Baseline	84.4%	0.151	11.2 K	4.5 ms
Baseline(depth 4)	94.9%	0.149	16.5 K	5.1 ms
Baseline(depth 5)	96.4%	0.089	21.9 K	5.5 ms
Baseline(depth 5, 2× filters)	97.2%	0.077	85.2 K	8.5 ms
Base + Deformable Conv [5]	90.8%	0.087	32.0 K	16.7 ms
Base + Dilated Conv [33]	91.0%	0.152	11.2 K	4.7 ms
Base + CCE	84.8%	0.088	11.9 K	4.6 ms
Base + Skip-connection	87.0%	0.151	29.0 K	8.4 ms
Base + CCE + Skip-connection	87.9%	0.071	29.2 K	8.41 ms
Base + BCN w/ average pooling	92.7%	0.064	29.2 K	8.42 ms
Base + BCN	**97.5%**	**0.023**	29.2 K	8.42 ms

each edge, followed by a ReLU activation function and a batch normalization, depending on the comparison target. With the same baseline model (a 3-layered CNN), experiments of deformable convolutions and dilated convolutions are also done. The deformable convolution filters are applied to all three layers, and the dilated convolution filters are applied in the second layer of the baseline model with 2×2 dilation. A BCN with an output channel length of $[64, 64, 128]$ is applied once in between the second and third layers. After applying the BCN, the number of feature maps increases, so in order to match the input dimension of the third layer, 1×1 convolutions are operated for dimension reduction to 24. This setting is purposefully designed to compare performance of a simpler model with BCN against that of baseline model with more depths and kinds of convolution on the given data. Also, the network structure of expanding channels from 24 to 128 is intended for having more channels when globally max-pooling spatial features to preserve enough visual context information for broadcasting.

Table 1 shows[1] the performance enhancement of our method on both classification and localization results on the Scaled-MNIST dataset. Considering the baseline model achieves 97.8% classification accuracy in our experiment on the original MNIST, its performance of the Scaled-MNIST clearly implies its structurally inherent limitation as the size of the required receptive field increases while making the model deeper to extend the receptive field yields a better result as shown in the table. Even if we increase the receptive field by deepening the convolution net with up to five layers, it can be seen that our method with a shallower depth of three layers reaches a higher performance. The model with BCN even shows better performance than the 5-layer baseline model with twice

---

[1] All runtimes are the training time measured on Nvidia Titan X (Pascal) GPU and 8 core CPU(i7-6700K) per 100 samples.

Table 2. Results on STL-10. All models are trained from scratch without any external dataset

Model	Accuracy	#Params	Runtime[1]
Tho17-2 Single [31]	75.76%	1.46 M	–
Tho17-2 Ensemble [31]	78.66%	1.46 M	–
Baseline	68.75%	114 K	18.1 ms
Baseline + Skip-connection	69.79%	192.7 K	18.2 ms
Baseline + BCN	**72.18%**	193.2 K	18.2 ms
Resnet18	76.27%	11.2M	102.2 ms
Resnet18 + BCN	**77.00%**	11.46 M	105.5 ms

the number of filters by 0.3% for classification and three times less error for localization.

Furthermore, the significance of the broadcasting phase can be well analyzed from the results. While embedding additional coordinate information reduces the localization error and the skip-connection alone improves the classification performance, compared to the model using both, the model with BCN improves the classification accuracy by 9.6% and reduces the localization error by 0.48. Besides from aspects of CCE and the skip-connection technique, concatenation of expanded max-pooled features of BCN allows the network to globally broaden receptive fields and directly learn visually relational features. And the result of the BCN using average-pooling instead of max-pooling shows a significant performance decline, which indicates that average-pooling is not a suitable method considering that the purpose of max-pooling is to extract key features.

The goal of deformable convolutions is similar to ours in many ways, and the implementation has also led to desirable results, getting better scores on both classification and localization. The model with dilated convolutions has also resulted in an impressive improvement on classification accuracy while conserving the same parameter numbers and computation speed as those of the baseline. Nonetheless, the performance of BCN model outperforms both models. In addition, BCN shows relatively high robustness against deformations compared to other methods, and the experimental results are included in the supplementary material.

STL-10: For a baseline model for the STL-10 dataset, four layers of convolutions with 64 of 3×3 kernels with the stride size of 2 and the padding size of 1 for each edge are applied. A ReLU activation function and a batch normalizing operation follow after each convolution layer. A BCN module of size [128, 128, 256] is applied in between the third and the fourth convolution layers. After applying the BCN module, the number of feature maps increases, so in order to match the input dimension of the fourth layer, an 1×1 convolution layer is used for dimension reduction to 64. We, in addition, have applied the same size of BCN to a Resnet18 model [9]. The BCN module within the Resnet18 model is applied between the third and the fourth residual blocks. Then, 256 of 1×1 convolution filters are used to reduce number of feature maps, and the entire model is trained end-to-end from scratch.

We compare our model against the baseline model in Table 2 to evaluate the performance of BCN for a natural image classification problem. Because BCN extends the receptive field size to whole image grids, it allows 3.4% of performance enhancement. Also, this is an even better result than the model using the same convolution layers of BCN as a Skip-connection. The additional experiment where BCN is applied within the Resnet18 model shows that our approach sets a new state-of-the-art performance in STL-10 experiment on a single network basis with 77.0% accuracy, which is 1.24% higher than the single model of Tho17-2 [31].

Table 3. Results on Sort-of-CLEVR. RN* is the reproduced result with same model of [29] on a single GPU. RN† is a model of which the network structure is set the same as multiRN except that pairwise comparison for a fair comparison. CNN_h denotes the CNN that has 1 stride for fourth convolution layer instead of 2 stride to handle more objects

Model	Relational	Non-relational	#Params	Runtime[1]
CNN+RN [29]	94%↑	94%↑	19.5 M	-
CNN+RN*	91.0%	99.6%	19.5M	575.8 ms
CNN+RN†	89.9%	99.8%	365K	23.5 ms
CNN_h+RN†	96.5%	99.9%	365K	315.6 ms
CNN+MLP	74.2%	65.0%	239 K	6.2 ms
CNN+CCE+MLP	72.9%	64.5%	258 K	6.2 ms
CNN+multiRN w/o BCN	88.7%	99.3%	224 K	7.5 ms
CNN+multiRN	92.9%	99.9%	345 K	8.3 ms
CNN_h+multiRN	**96.7%**	**99.9%**	345 K	9.9 ms

5.3   Pixel-Based Relational Reasoning Problem

Model: For relational reasoning experiments, we construct our multiRN model based on the RN model that is used for the CLEVR dataset out of two models reported in [29] which consists of one trained for the Sort-of-CLEVR dataset and a shallower model for the CLEVR. Four convolution layers with 24 of 3×3 kernels, followed by ReLU activations and batch normalizations, are used for the CNN part. MultiRN consists of a BCN of size [128, 128, 256], two convolution layers with 256 1×1 kernels for g_θ, and two MLP layers of 256 units for f_ϕ. Also, to verify that multiRNs use computation resource efficiently, we change the fourth convolution layer's stride from 2 to 1 in the CNN_h, which quadruples the number of objects that the following network has to handle. MultiRN, for the CLEVR task, uses LSTM of 128 hidden unit of 2 layers for natural language question processing.

Sort-of-CLEVR: Results of Table 3 suggest that using our version of RN (multiRN) is better than the RN with similar structure at reasoning relations by 3%, which is the main job of Sort-of-CLEVR task, despite of comparably less computational cost. Compared to both RN and multiRN, CNN+MLP model performs far poorly. Even embedding coordinate information into the same model worsens the performance, supposedly, due to overfitting. This implies that the performance enhancement of RN and multiRN is not simply caused by the addition of coordinate maps. For a further ablation study, the BCN module is removed along with the coordinate encoding function, while having g_θ and f_ϕ remained in order to generate the 'CNN+multiRN w/o BCN' model. This model lacks information of correlations among multiple objects, and thus performs 4.2% lower than the CNN+multiRN model. To check the efficiency when the number of object inputs upsurges for the multiRN to manage, we reduce the stride of the last layer of the preceding CNN from 2 to 1, denoting as CNN_h. Since the computation complexity of multiRN is $\mathcal{O}(n)$, which is a strong advantage over RNs with $\mathcal{O}(n^2)$ for n number of objects, the multiRN's computation cost is only quadrupled (25 to 100) for CNN_h while RN takes 16 times greater computation loads (625 to 10000). Both RN and multiRN with CNN_h have achieved impressive performance gain with increase in the number of feature objects, but there is a large difference in computational efficiency.

Table 4. Results on CLEVR from Pixel. RN* is the result when we reproduce the same model as the paper [29] on a single GPU. ‡ denotes the result of changing the size of an input image from 128×128 to 224×224, which is the same as FiLM [26]

Model	Overall	Count	Exist	Compare numbers	Query attribute	Compare attribute
Human [17]	92.6	86.7	96.6	86.5	95.0	96.0
Q-type baseline [17]	41.8	34.6	50.2	51.0	36.0	51.3
LSTM [17]	46.8	41.7	61.1	69.8	36.8	51.8
CNN+LSTM [17]	52.3	43.7	65.2	67.1	49.3	53.0
CNN+LSTM+SA [17]	68.5	52.2	71.1	73.5	85.3	52.3
CNN+LSTM+RN [29]	95.5	90.1	97.8	93.6	97.9	97.1
CNN+LSTM+RN*	90.9	86.7	97.4	90.0	90.2	93.5
CNN+GRU+FiLM with ResNet-101 [26]	**97.7**	94.3	99.1	96.8	99.1	99.1
CNN+GRU+FiLM from raw pixels [26]	97.6	94.3	**99.3**	93.4	**99.3**	**99.3**
CNN+LSTM+ multiRN	92.3	85.2	96.5	93.6	95.1	92.9
CNN$_h$+LSTM+ multiRN	97.2	94.1	98.9	**98.3**	98.6	97.6
CNN$_h$+LSTM+ multiRN‡	**97.7**	**94.9**	99.2	97.2	98.7	98.3

CLEVR: An experiment has been done on a more challenging relational reasoning problem to test the performance of multiRN compared to existing methods.

The model is replicated having internal RN module replaced with multiRN to create 'CNN+LSTM+MultiRN'. The structure of multiRN model is the same as it was used for Sort-of-CLEVR dataset, and question vectors are generated from an LSTM model which is also implemented in the original RN module.

The results of the comparative experiments on CLEVR are shown in Table 4. The RN*, our reproduced version of the relational network from [29], has not been able to achieve the same performance as in the paper due to lack of original version's details of hyper-parameters and additional network control factors. However, since the input convolutional feature maps and question vectors are generated with the same CNN+LSTM settings, reasonable comparisons can still be made among the candidate methods. For this problem, our implementation using multiRN performs 1.4% better than RN*, and multiRN with CNN_h achieves even far better performance enhancement of 6.3%. This is an impressive result considering that the same CNN+LSTM+RN model architecture is used as in RN* and allows 95.5% of performance whilst both of multiRN and multiRN with CNN_h require a much smaller amount of computation. We have not been able to proceed an experiment with the CNN_h+LSTM+RN model because of the out-of-memory problem when dealing with an increased number of objects. Furthermore, our model achieves 97.7% of test accuracy by changing the size of an input image to 224×224 which is the same as it is in FiLM [26]. For the best of our knowledge, this score is the state-of-the-art performance on CLEVR with raw pixels, and is compatible with FiLM using ResNet-101 [9] pre-trained on ImageNet [6].

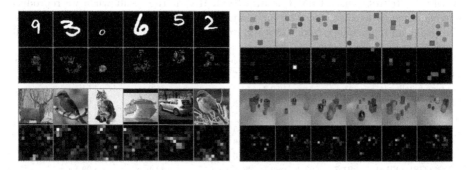

Fig. 4. Activation map shows how much information is broadcasted at each location. From top to bottom are Scaled-MNIST and STL-10 on the left, Sort-of-CLEVR and CLEVR on the right. More activation maps are included in the supplementary material.

5.4 Can BCN Extend the Receptive Field Globally and Represent Multiple Objects?

For better understanding of our model, visualization of activation maps for different images of each experiment is provided in Fig. 4. Activation maps are acquired by unsampling the global max-pooling layer, and simply masking the pixel as 1

Table 5. Results on coordinate embedding methods. Our method outperforms conventional coordinate methods in both Scaled-MNIST and Sort-of-CLEVR

	Scaled-MNIST		Sort-of-CLEVR	
Method	Accuracy	Localization err.	Relational acc.	Non-relational acc.
No Coordinate channels	92.5%	0.151	91.4%	91.8%
X, Y Coordinates with top-left zero	96.9%	0.029	92.6%	99.9%
X, Y Coordinates with zero-centered	97.5%	0.025	96.1%	99.9%
X, Y Coordinates with zero-centered + Radial distance	97.5%	0.023	96.7%	99.9%

from where it was chosen. The number of masks is the same as the number of 1×1 convolution filters, and summing them through feature dimension outputs of the activation map. In activation maps for Scaled-MNIST, we can intuitively find that the activation map corresponds well with each digit's location in the original image. The Scaled-MNIST dataset may have too many zero inputs for a network to easily respond to spatial features, but activation maps in STL-10 apparently show that BCN makes abstractions of features well even in natural images. Notably, we could observe that activation maps tend to draw features from important locations, such as edges, faces, legs and so on. As this information is broadcast to all locations, the receptive field expands globally. For Sort-of-CLEVR task and CLEVR task, we can obviously see that BCN is well trained to make abstractions of multiple objects in their image. This means that the 'multiple relations' of multiRN described in Sect. 3 is established through BCN. Note that since activation maps only represent the maxpooled features, it does not have to include all objects by themselves. Output convolution features that are inputted to the BCN module, which will be further combined with BCN output, also contain features of objects.

5.5 Study on Coordinate Embedding Methods

Our demonstration on the effects of coordinate channels is shown in Table 5. The result without coordinate channels has far less score compared to the result with the coordinate channels embedded. The model of coordinates with zero-centered shows a significantly higher relational accuracy than the model of conventional coordinates with top-left zero for Sort-of-CLEVR, but it is slightly worse than that of three planes with extra radial distance plane included. Figure 5 shows the absolute values of the output from the convolution kernel with randomly initialized weights passing through the coordinate channels. As shown, a coordinate system with a conventional top-left of zero is deflected diagonally, but a coordinate system with zero center is deflected to the outside. On the other hand, by adding coordinate channels with radial distances, it can be seen that most of the deflection can be removed while providing additional coordinate information. Furthermore, although we have expected better feature representation and localization performance by concatenating an additional coordinate plane and reducing initial weight bias, the performance gain has only occurred in the localization aspect. This evidently implies that convolution operations are inherently biased towards the center with Gaussian distribution [25], and thus the additional coordinate plane have not been a critical catalyst.

Fig. 5. The outputs of coordinate planes through the convolution kernel. Left: X, Y coordinates with top-left zero. Center: X, Y coordinates with zero-centered. Right: X, Y coordinates with zero-centered and additional Radial channel. The right has the least deflection.

6   Conclusion

We have shown that utilizing Broadcasting Convolutional Network (BCN) allows conventional CNNs to effectively collect and represent spatial information with efficient extension of receptive fields, which results in remarkable performance on localization problems. With BCN's ability of representing compounded spatial features in all receptive fields, we have proposed Multi-Relational Networks that greatly improve RN [29] in terms of computational gains while achieving a state-of-the-art performance in pixel-based relation reasoning problems.

In future works, we intend to study whether BCN can be applied to other domains such as object detection or semantic segmentation. And we need to study applying multiRN to various problems that require visual relational reasoning.

Acknowledgement. This work was supported by Next-Generation Information Computing Development Program through the National Research Foundation of Korea (2017M3C4A7077582).

References

1. Chen, L.C., Papandreou, G., Kokkinos, I., Murphy, K., Yuille, A.L.: Deeplab: semantic image segmentation with deep convolutional nets, atrous convolution, and fully connected CRFs. arXiv preprint arXiv:1606.00915 (2016)

2. Coates, A., Ng, A., Lee, H.: An analysis of single-layer networks in unsupervised feature learning. In: Proceedings of the Fourteenth International Conference on Artificial Intelligence and Statistics, pp. 215–223 (2011)
3. Crone, E.A., Wendelken, C., Van Leijenhorst, L., Honomichl, R.D., Christoff, K., Bunge, S.A.: Neurocognitive development of relational reasoning. Dev. Sci. **12**(1), 55–66 (2009)
4. Dai, J., Li, Y., He, K., Sun, J.: R-fcn: object detection via region-based fully convolutional networks. In: Advances in Neural Information Processing Systems, pp. 379–387 (2016)
5. Dai, J., Qi, H., Xiong, Y., Li, Y., Zhang, G., Hu, H., Wei, Y.: Deformable convolutional networks. arXiv preprint arXiv:1703.06211 (2017)
6. Deng, J., Dong, W., Socher, R., Li, L.J., Li, K., Fei-Fei, L.: ImageNet: a large-scale hierarchical image database. In: CVPR 2009 (2009)
7. Girshick, R., Donahue, J., Darrell, T., Malik, J.: Rich feature hierarchies for accurate object detection and semantic segmentation. In: Proceedings of the IEEE Conference on Computer Vision and Pattern Recognition, pp. 580–587 (2014)
8. He, Kaiming, Zhang, Xiangyu, Ren, Shaoqing, Sun, Jian: Spatial pyramid pooling in deep convolutional networks for visual recognition. In: Fleet, David, Pajdla, Tomas, Schiele, Bernt, Tuytelaars, Tinne (eds.) ECCV 2014. LNCS, vol. 8691, pp. 346–361. Springer, Cham (2014). https://doi.org/10.1007/978-3-319-10578-9_23
9. He, K., Zhang, X., Ren, S., Sun, J.: Deep residual learning for image recognition. In: Proceedings of the IEEE Conference on Computer Vision and Pattern Recognition, pp. 770–778 (2016)
10. Hochreiter, S., Schmidhuber, J.: Long short-term memory. Neural Comput. **9**(8), 1735–1780 (1997)
11. Holschneider, M., Kronland-Martinet, R., Morlet, J., Tchamitchian, P.: A real-time algorithm for signal analysis with the help of the wavelet transform. In: Wavelets, pp. 286–297. Springer, Heidelberg (1990)
12. Hu, J., Shen, L., Sun, G.: Squeeze-and-excitation networks. arXiv preprint arXiv:1709.01507 (2017)
13. Jaderberg, M., Simonyan, K., Zisserman, A., et al.: Spatial transformer networks. In: Advances in Neural Information Processing Systems, pp. 2017–2025 (2015)
14. Jeon, Y., Kim, J.: Active convolution: learning the shape of convolution for image classification. arXiv preprint arXiv:1703.09076 (2017)
15. Jia, Y., Huang, C., Darrell, T.: Beyond spatial pyramids: receptive field learning for pooled image features. In: 2012 IEEE Conference on Computer Vision and Pattern Recognition (CVPR), pp. 3370–3377. IEEE (2012)
16. Johnson, J., Hariharan, B., van der Maaten, L., Fei-Fei, L., Zitnick, C.L., Girshick, R.: Clevr: a diagnostic dataset for compositional language and elementary visual reasoning. arXiv preprint arXiv:1612.06890 (2016)
17. Johnson, J., et al.: Inferring and executing programs for visual reasoning. arXiv preprint arXiv:1705.03633 (2017)
18. Kemp, C., Tenenbaum, J.B.: The discovery of structural form. Proc. Natl. Acad. Sci. **105**(31), 10687–10692 (2008)
19. Krizhevsky, A., Sutskever, I., Hinton, G.E.: Imagenet classification with deep convolutional neural networks. In: Advances in Neural Information Processing Systems, pp. 1097–1105 (2012)
20. LeCun, Y.: The MNIST database of handwritten digits (1998). http://yann.lecun.com/exdb/mnist/
21. LeCun, Y., Bengio, Y.: Convolutional networks for images, speech, and time series. Handb. Brain Theory Neural Netw. **3361**(10), 1995 (1995)

22. Liang, X., Wei, Y., Shen, X., Yang, J., Lin, L., Yan, S.: Proposal-free network for instance-level object segmentation. arXiv preprint arXiv:1509.02636 (2015)

23. Logan, G.D., Sadler, D.D.: A computational analysis of the apprehension of spatial relations (1996)

24. Long, J., Shelhamer, E., Darrell, T.: Fully convolutional networks for semantic segmentation. In: Proceedings of the IEEE Conference on Computer Vision and Pattern Recognition, pp. 3431–3440 (2015)

25. Luo, W., Li, Y., Urtasun, R., Zemel, R.: Understanding the effective receptive field in deep convolutional neural networks. In: Advances in Neural Information Processing Systems, pp. 4898–4906 (2016)

26. Perez, E., Strub, F., De Vries, H., Dumoulin, V., Courville, A.: Film: visual reasoning with a general conditioning layer. arXiv preprint arXiv:1709.07871 (2017)

27. Raposo, D., Santoro, A., Barrett, D., Pascanu, R., Lillicrap, T., Battaglia, P.: Discovering objects and their relations from entangled scene representations. arXiv preprint arXiv:1702.05068 (2017)

28. Raven, J.C.: Standardization of progressive matrices, 1938. Psychol. Psychother. Theory, Res. Pract. **19**(1), 137–150 (1941)

29. Santoro, A., et al.: A simple neural network module for relational reasoning. arXiv preprint arXiv:1706.01427 (2017)

30. Srivastava, R.K., Greff, K., Schmidhuber, J.: Training very deep networks. In: Advances in Neural Information Processing Systems, pp. 2377–2385 (2015)

31. Thoma, M.: Analysis and optimization of convolutional neural network architectures. arXiv preprint arXiv:1707.09725 (2017)

32. Tian, Y., Zhu, Y.: Better computer go player with neural network and long-term prediction. arXiv preprint arXiv:1511.06410 (2015)

33. Yu, F., Koltun, V.: Multi-scale context aggregation by dilated convolutions. arXiv preprint arXiv:1511.07122 (2015)

Improving Spatiotemporal Self-supervision by Deep Reinforcement Learning

Uta Büchler$^{(\boxtimes)}$, Biagio Brattoli$^{(\boxtimes)}$, and Björn Ommer

Heidelberg University, HCI/IWR, Heidelberg, Germany
{uta.buechler,biagio.brattoli,bjoern.ommer}@iwr.uni-heidelberg.de

Abstract. Self-supervised learning of convolutional neural networks can harness large amounts of cheap unlabeled data to train powerful feature representations. As surrogate task, we jointly address ordering of visual data in the spatial and temporal domain. The permutations of training samples, which are at the core of self-supervision by ordering, have so far been sampled randomly from a fixed preselected set. Based on deep reinforcement learning we propose a sampling policy that adapts to the state of the network, which is being trained. Therefore, new permutations are sampled according to their expected utility for updating the convolutional feature representation. Experimental evaluation on unsupervised and transfer learning tasks demonstrates competitive performance on standard benchmarks for image and video classification and nearest neighbor retrieval.

Keywords: Deep reinforcement learning · Self-supervision · Shuffling
Action recognition · Image understanding

1 Introduction

Convolutional neural networks (CNNs) have demonstrated to learn powerful visual representations from large amounts of tediously labeled training data [23]. However, since visual data is cheap to acquire but costly to label, there has recently been great interest in learning compelling features from unlabeled data. Without any annotations, self-supervision based on surrogate tasks, for which the target value can be obtained automatically, is commonly pursued [2,8,9,16,17,26,27,29–31,33,34,38,44]. In colorization [26], for instance, the color information is stripped from an image and serves as the target value,

Electronic supplementary material The online version of this chapter (https://doi.org/10.1007/978-3-030-01267-0_47) contains supplementary material, which is available to authorized users.

© Springer Nature Switzerland AG 2018
V. Ferrari et al. (Eds.): ECCV 2018, LNCS 11219, pp. 797–814, 2018.
https://doi.org/10.1007/978-3-030-01267-0_47

which has to be recovered. Various surrogate tasks have been proposed, including predicting a sequence of basic motions [29], counting parts within regions [34] or embedding images into text topic spaces [38].

The key competence of visual understanding is to recognize structure in visual data. Thus, breaking the order of visual patterns and training a network to recover the structure provides a rich training signal. This general framework of permuting the input data and learning a feature representation, from which the inverse permutation (and thus the correct order) can be inferred, is a widely applicable strategy. It has been pursued on still images [8–10, 33, 35] by employing spatial shuffling of images (especially permuting jigsaws) and in videos [5, 16, 27, 31] by utilizing temporally shuffled sequences. Since spatial and temporal shuffling are both ordering tasks, which only differ in the ordering dimension, they should be addressed jointly.

We observe that there has been unused potential in self-supervision based on ordering: Previous work [5, 16, 27, 33, 35] has *randomly* selected the permutations used for training the CNN. However, can we not find permutations that are of higher utility for improving a CNN representation than the random set? For instance, given a 3×3 jigsaw grid, shuffling two neighboring image patches, two patches in faraway corners, or shuffling all patches simultaneously will learn structure of different granularity. Thus diverse permutations will affect the CNN in a different way. Moreover the effect of the permutations on the CNN changes during training since the state of the network evolves. During learning we can examine the previous errors the network has made when recovering order and then identify a set of best suited permutations. Therefore, wrapped around the standard back-propagation training of the CNN, we have a reinforcement learning algorithm that acts by proposing permutations for the CNN training. To learn the function for proposing permutations we simultaneously train a policy and self-supervised network by utilizing the improvement over time of the CNN network as a reward signal.

2   Related Work

We first present previous work on self-supervised learning using one task or a combination of surrogate approaches. Then we introduce curriculum learning procedures and discuss meta-learning for deep neural network.

Self-supervised Representation Learning: In self-supervision, the feature representation is learned indirectly by solving a surrogate task. For that matter, visual data like images [8–10, 17, 26, 40, 49, 52, 55] or videos [5, 16, 27, 29, 31, 39, 51, 52] are utilized as source of information, but also text [38] or audio [37]. In contrast to the majority of recent self-supervised learning approaches, Doersch et al. [10] and Wang et al. [52] combine surrogate tasks to train a multi-task network. Doersch et al. choose 4 surrogate tasks and evaluate a naive and a mediated combination of those. Wang et al. besides a naive multi-task combination of these self-supervision tasks, use the learned features to build a graph of semantically similar objects, which is then used to train a triplet loss. Since they combine heterogeneous tasks, both methods use an additional technique on top of the self-supervised training to exploit the full potential of their approach. Our model combines two directly related ordering tasks, which are complementary without the need of additional adjustment approaches.

Curriculum Learning: In 2009 Bengio et al. [3] proposed curriculum learning (CL) to enhance the learning process by gradually increasing the complexity of the task during training. CL has been utilized by different deep learning methods [6,18,47] with the limitation that the complexity of samples and their scheduling during training typically has to be established a priori. Kumar et al. [25] define the sample complexity from the perspective of the classifier, but still manually define the scheduling. In contrast, our policy dynamically selects the permutations based on the current state of the network.

Meta-learning for Deep Neural Networks: Recently, methods have proposed ways to improve upon the classical training of neural networks by, for example, automatizing the selection of hyper-parameters [1,7,15,36,41,56]. Andrychowicz et al. [1] train a recurrent neural network acting as an optimizer which makes informative decisions based on the state of the network. Fan et al. [15] propose a system to improve the final performance of the network using a reinforcement learning approach which schedules training samples during learning. Opitz et al. [36] use the gradient of the last layer for selecting uncorrelated samples to improve performance. Similar to [1,15,36] we propose a method which affects the training of a network to push towards better performances. In contrast to these supervised methods, where the image labels are fixed, our policy has substantial control on the training of the main network since it can directly alter the input data by proposing permutations.

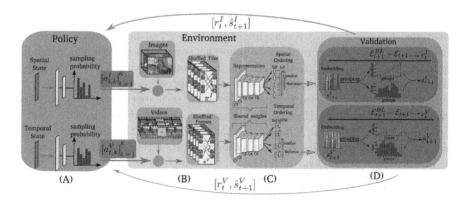

Fig. 1. (A) Deep RL of a policy for sampling permutations. (B) Permuting training images/videos by the proposed actions of (A) to provide self-supervision for our network architecture (C). (D) Evaluating the update network (C) on validation data to receive reward and state.

3   Approach

Now we present a method for training two self-supervised tasks simultaneously to learn a general and meaningful feature representation. We then present a deep reinforcement learning approach to learn a policy that proposes best suited permutations at a given stage during training.

3.1   Self-supervised Spatiotemporal Representation Learning

Subsequently, we learn a CNN feature representation (CaffeNet [21] architecture up to pool5) for images and individual frames of a video using spatiotemporal self-supervision (see Fig. 1C). Training starts from scratch with a randomly initialized network. To obtain training samples for the spatial ordering task, we divide images into a $m \times m$ regular grid of tiles as suggested by [33] (Fig. 1B top). For temporal ordering of u frames from a video sequence(Fig. 1B bottom), shuffling is performed on frame level and with augmentation (detailed in Sect. 4.1). Note that we do not require an object-of-interest detection, as for example done in [27,31] by using motion (optical flow), since our approach randomly samples the frames from a video.

For the following part of this section, we are going to talk about a sample x in general, referring to a sequence of frames (temporal task) or a partitioned image (spatial task). Let $x = (x_1, x_2, \dots)$ be the sample that is to be shuffled by permuting its parts by some index permutation $\psi_i = (\psi_{i,1}, \psi_{i,2}, \cdots)$,

$$\psi_i(x) := \left(x_{\psi_{i,1}}, x_{\psi_{i,2}}, \dots \right). \tag{1}$$

The set of all possible permutations $\Psi^\star$ contains $u!$ or $(m \cdot m)!$ elements. If, for example, $u = 8$ the total number of possible permutations equals $8! = 40320$. For practical reasons, a pre-processing step reduces the set of all possible permutations, following [33], by sampling a set $\Psi \subset \Psi^\star$ of maximally diverse permutations $\psi_i \in \Psi$. We iteratively include the permutation with the maximum Hamming distance $d(\bullet, \bullet)$ to the already chosen ones. Both self-supervised tasks have their own set of permutations. For simplicity, we are going to explain our approach based on a general Ψ without referring to a specific task. To solve the ordering task of undoing the shuffling based on the pool5 features we want to learn (Fig. 1(C)), we need a classifier that can identify the permutation. The classifier architecture begins with an fc6 layer. For spatial ordering, the fc6 output of all tiles is stacked in an fc7 layer; for temporal ordering the fc6 output of the frames is combined in a recurrent neural network implemented as LSTM [19] (see Fig. 1(C) and Sect. 4.1 for implementation details). The output of fc7 or the LSTM is then processed by a final fully connected classification layer. This last fc layer estimates the permutation ψ_i applied to the input sample and is trained using cross-entropy loss. The output activation $\varphi_i, i \in \{1, \dots |\Psi|\}$ of the classifier corresponds to the permutation $\psi_i \in \Psi$ and indicates how certain the network is that the permutation applied to the input x is ψ_i. The network is trained in parallel with two batches, one of spatially permuted tiles and one of temporally shuffled frames. Back-propagation then provides two gradients, one from the spatial and one from the temporal task, which back-propagate through the entire network down to conv1.

The question is now, which permutation to apply to which training sample.

3.2 Finding an Optimal Permutation Strategy by Reinforcement Learning

In previous works [5,16,27,31,33], for each training sample one permutation is randomly selected from a large set of candidate permutations $\psi_i \in \Psi$. Selecting the data permutation independent from the input data is beneficial as it avoids overfitting to the training data (permutations triggered only by specific samples). However, permutations should be selected conditioned on the state of the network that is being trained to sample new permutations according to their utility for learning the CNN representation.

A Markov Decision Process for Proposing Permutations: We need to learn a function that proposes permutations conditioned on the network state and independent from samples x to avoid overfitting. Knowingly, the state of the network cannot be represented directly by the network weights, as the dimensionality would be too high for learning to be feasible. To capture the network state at time step t in a compact state vector s, we measure performance of the network on a set of validation samples $x \in X_{val}$. Each x is permuted by some $\psi_i \in \Psi$. A forward pass through the network then leads to activations φ_i and a softmax activation of the network,

$$y_i^\star = \frac{exp(\varphi_i)}{\sum_k exp(\varphi_k)}. \tag{2}$$

Given all the samples, the output of the softmax function indicates how good a permutation ψ_i can already be reconstructed and which ones are hard to recover (low $y_i^\star$). Thus, it reflects the complexity of a permutation from the view point of the network and $y_i^\star$ can be utilized to capture the network state s. To be precise, we measure the network's confidence regarding its classification using the ratio of correct class l vs. second highest prediction p (or highest if the true label l is not classified correctly):

$$y_l(x) = \frac{y_l^\star(x) + 1}{y_p^\star(x) + 1}, \tag{3}$$

where $x \in X_{val}$ and adding 1 to have $0.5 \leq y_l \leq 2$, so that $y_l > 1$ indicates a correct classification. The state s is then defined as

$$s = \begin{bmatrix} y_1(x_1) & \cdots & y_1(x_{|X_{val}|}) \\ \vdots & & \vdots \\ y_{|\Psi|}(x_1) & \cdots & y_{|\Psi|}(x_{|X_{val}|}), \end{bmatrix} \tag{4}$$

where one row contains the softmax ratios of a permutation ψ_i applied to all samples $x \in X_{val}$ (see Fig. 1(D)). Using a validation set for determining the state has the advantage of obtaining the utility for all permutations ψ_i and not only for the ones applied in the previous training phase. Moreover, it guarantees the comparability between validations applied at different time points independently by the policy. The action $a = (x, \psi_i) \in A = X \times \Psi$ of training the network by applying a permutation ψ_i to a random training sample x changes the state s (in practice we sample an entire mini-batch of tuples for one training iteration rather than only one). Training changes the network state s at time point t into s' according to some transition probability $T(s'|s, a)$. To evaluate the chosen action a we need a reward signal r_t given the revised state s'. The challenge is now to find *the action* which maximizes the expected reward

$$R(s, a) = \mathbb{E}[r_t | s_t = s, a], \tag{5}$$

given the present state of the network. The underlying problem of finding suitable permutations and training the network can be formulated as a Markov Decision Process (MDP) [48], a 5-tuple $< S, A, T, R, \gamma >$, where S is a set of states s_t, A is a set of actions a_t, $T(s'|s, a)$ the transition probability, $R(a, s)$ the reward and $\gamma \in [0, 1]$ is the discount which scales future rewards against present ones.

Defining a Policy: As a reward r_t we need a score which measures the impact the chosen permutations have had on the overall performance in the previous training phase. For that, the error

$$\mathcal{E} := 1 - \frac{1}{|\Psi| \cdot |X_{val}|} \sum_{l=1}^{|\Psi|} \sum_{x \in X_{val}} \delta_{l, \underset{p=\{1,\dots,|\Psi|\}}{\operatorname{argmax}} y_p^\star(x)} \tag{6}$$

with δ the Kronecker delta, can be used to assess the influence of a permutation. To make the reward more informative, we compare this value against a baseline (BL), which results from simply extrapolating the error of previous iterations, i.e. $\mathcal{E}_{t+1}^{BL} = 2\mathcal{E}_t - \mathcal{E}_{t-1}$. We then seek an action that improves upon this baseline. Thus, the reward r_t obtained at time point $t + 1$ (we use the index t for r at time step $t + 1$ to indicate the connection to a_t) is defined as

$$r_t := \mathcal{E}_{t+1}^{BL} - \mathcal{E}_{t+1}. \tag{7}$$

We determine the error using the same validation set as already employed for obtaining the state. In this way no additional computational effort is required.

Given the earlier defined state s of the network and the actions A we seek to learn a policy function

$$\pi(a|s, \theta) = P(a_t = a | s_t = s, \theta_t = \theta), \tag{8}$$

that, given the θ parameters of the policy, proposes an action $a = (x, \psi_i)$ for a randomly sampled training data point x based on the state s, where $\pi(a|s, \theta)$ is the probability of applying action $a \in A$ at time point t given the state s.

The parameters θ can be learned by maximizing the reward signal r. It has been proven that a neural network is capable of learning a powerful approximation of π [32,45,48]. However, the objective function (maximizing the reward) is not differentiable. In this case, Reinforcement Learning (RL) [48] has now become a standard approach for learning π in this particular case.

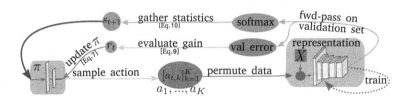

Fig. 2. Training procedure of π. The policy proposes actions $[a_{t,k}]_{k=1}^{K}$ to permute the data X, used for training the unsupervised network. The improvement of the network is then used as reward r to update the policy.

Policy Gradient: There are two main approaches for attacking deep RL problems: Q-Learning and Policy Gradient. We require a policy which models action probabilities to prevent the policy from converging to a small subset of permutations. Thus, we utilize a Policy Gradient (PG) algorithm which learns a stochastic policy and additionally guarantees convergence (at least to a local optimum) as opposed to Q-Learning. The objective of a PG algorithm is to maximize the expected cumulative reward (Eq. 5) by iteratively updating the policy weights through back-propagation. One update at time point $t + 1$ with learning rate α is given by

$$\theta_{t+1} = \theta_t + \alpha \left(\sum_{t' \geq t} \gamma^{t'-t} r_{t'} \right) \nabla \log \pi(a|s,\theta), \tag{9}$$

Action Space: The complexity of deep RL increases significantly with the number of actions. Asking the policy to permute a sample x given the full space Ψ leads to a large action space. Thus, we dynamically group the permutations into $|C|$ groups based on the state of the spatiotemporal network. The permutations which are equally difficult or equally easy to classify are grouped at time point t and this grouping changes over time according to the state of the network. We utilize the state s (Eq. 4) as input to the grouping approach, where one row s_i represents the embedding of permutation ψ_i. A policy then proposes one group $c_j \in C$ of permutations and randomly selects one instance $\psi_i \in c_j$ of the group. Then a training data point x is randomly sampled and shuffled by ψ_i. This constitutes an action $a = (x, \psi_i)$. Rather than directly proposing individual permutations ψ_i, this strategy only proposes a set of related permutations c_j. Since $|C| << |\Psi|$, the effective dimensionality of actions is significantly reduced and learning a policy becomes feasible.

Network State: To obtain a more concise representation $\hat{s} = [\hat{s}_j]_{j=1}^{|C|}$ of the state of the spatiotemporal network (the input to the policy), we aggregate the characteristics of all permutations within a group c_j. Since the actions are directly linked to the groups, the features should contain the statistics of c_j based on the state of the network. Therefore we utilize per group (i) the number of permutations belonging to c_j and (ii) the median of the softmax ratios (Eq. 3) over the (ψ_i, x) pairs with $\psi_i \in c_j$ and $x \in X_{val}$

$$\hat{s} = [|c_j|, median([s_i]_{\psi_i \in c_j})]_{j=1}^{|C|}. \tag{10}$$

The median over the softmax ratios reflects how well the spatiotemporal network can classify the set of permutations which are grouped together. Including the size $|c_j|$ of the groups helps the policy to avoid the selection of very small groups which could lead to overfitting of the self-supervised network on certain permutations. The proposed $\hat{s}$ have proven to be an effective and efficient representation of the state. Including global features, as for example the iteration or learning rate utilized in previous work [14,15], does not help in our scenario. It rather increases the complexity of the state and hinders policy learning. Figure 1(D) depicts the validation process, including the calculation of state $\hat{s}$ and the reward r.

Training Algorithm: We train the self-supervised network and the policy simultaneously, where the training can be divided in two phases: the self-supervised training and the policy update (see Fig. 2 and Algorithm 1 in section A of the Supplementary Material). The total training runs for T steps. Between two steps t and $t+1$ solely the self-supervised network is trained (π is fixed) using SGD for several iterations using the permutations proposed by π. Then, $\hat{s}$ is updated using the validation procedure explained above. At each time step t an episode (one update of π) is performed. During episode t, the policy proposes a batch of K actions $[a_t]_{k=1}^K$, based on the updated state $\hat{s}_t$, which are utilized to train the self-supervised network for a small amount of iterations. At the end of the episode, another validation is applied to determine the reward r_t for updating π (Eq. 9). The two phases alternate each other until the end of the training.

Computational Extra Costs during Training: With respect to the basic self-supervised training, the extra cost for training the policy derives only from the total number of episodes × the time needed for performing an episode. If the number of SGD iterations between two policy updates t and $t+1$ is significantly higher than the steps within an episode, the computational extra costs for training the policy is small in comparison to the basic training. Fortunately, sparse policy updates are, in our scenario, possible since the policy network improves significantly faster than the self-supervised network. We observed a computational extra cost of ~40% based on the optimal parameters. Previous work, [14,56] which utilize deep RL for meta-learning, need to repeat the full training of the network several times to learn the policy, thus being several times slower.

4   Experiments

In this section, we provide additional details regarding the self-supervised training of our approach which we evaluate quantitatively and qualitatively using nearest neighbor search. Then, we validate the transferability of our trained feature representation on a variety of contrasting vision tasks, including image classification, object detection, object segmentation and action recognition (Sect. 4.2). We then perform an ablation study to analyze the gain of the proposed reinforcement learning policy and of combining both self-supervision tasks.

4.1   Self-supervised Training

We first describe all implementation details, including the network architecture and the preprocessing of the training data. We then utilize two different datasets for the evaluation of the feature representation trained only with self-supervision.

Implementation Details: Our shared basic model of the spatiotemporal network up to pool5 has the same architecture as CaffeNet [21] with batch normalization [20] between the conv layers. To train the policy we use the Policy Gradient algorithm REINFORCE (with moving average subtraction for variance reduction) and add the entropy of the policy to the objective function which improves the exploration and therefore prevents overfitting (proposed by [53]). The policy network contains 2 FC layers, where the hidden layer has 16 dimensions. We use K-means clustering for grouping the permutations in 10 groups. The validation set contains 100 ($|X_{val}| = 100$) samples and is randomly sampled from the training set (and then excluded for training). The still images utilized for the spatial task are chosen from the training set of the Imagenet dataset [43]. For training our model with the temporal task, we utilize the frames from split1 of the human action dataset UCF-101 [46]. We use 1000 initial permutations for both tasks ($|\Psi| = 1000$). Further technical details can be found in the supplementary material, section B.

Nearest Neighbor Search: To evaluate unsupervised representation learning, which has no labels provided, nearest neighbor search is the method of choice. For that, we utilize two different datasets: split1 of the human action dataset UCF-101 and the Pascal VOC 2007 dataset. UCF-101 contains 101 different action classes and over 13k clips. We extract 10 frames per video for computing the nearest neighbor. The Pascal VOC 2007 dataset consists of 9,963 images, containing 24,640 annotated objects which are divided in 20 classes. Based on the default split, 50% of the images belong to the training/validation set and 50% to the testing set. We use the provided bounding boxes of the dataset to extract the individual objects, whereas patches with less than 10k pixels are discarded. We use the model trained with our self-supervised approach to extract the pool5 features of the training and testing set and the images have an input size of 227×227. Then, for every test sample we compute the Top$k$ nearest neighbors in the training set by using cosine distance. A test sample is considered as correctly

Table 1. Quantitative evaluation of our self-supervised trained feature representation using nearest neighbor search on split1 of UCF-101 and Pascal VOC 2007 dataset. Distance measure is cosine distance of pool5 features. For UCF101, 10 frames per video are extracted. Images of the test set are used as queries and the images of the training set as the retrieval targets. We report mean accuracies [%] over all chosen test frames. If the class of a test sample appears within the top$k$ it is considered correctly predicted. We compare the results gained by (i) a random initialization, (ii) a spatial approach [33], (iii) a temporal method [27], and (iv) our model. For extracting the features based on the weights of (ii) and (iii) we utilize their published models

Methods	UCF101					Pascal				
	Top1	Top5	Top10	Top20	Top50	Top1	Top5	Top10	Top20	Top50
Random	18.8	25.7	30.0	35.0	43.3	17.6	61.6	75.5	85.5	94.2
Jigsaw [33]	19.7	28.5	33.5	40.0	49.4	39.2	71.6	82.2	89.5	96.0
OPN [27]	19.9	28.7	34.0	40.6	51.6	33.2	67.1	78.5	87.0	94.6
Ours	**25.7**	**36.2**	**42.2**	**49.2**	**59.5**	**54.3**	**73.0**	**83.0**	**89.9**	**96.2**

predicted if its class can be found within the Top$k$ nearest neighbors. The final accuracy is then determined by computing the mean over all testing samples. Table 1 shows the accuracy for $k = 1, 5, 10, 20, 50$ computed on UCF-101 and Pascal VOC 2007, respectively. It can be seen, that our model achieves the highest accuracy for all k, meaning that our method produces more informative features for object/video classification. Note, that especially the accuracy of Top1 is much higher in comparison to the other approaches.

We additionally evaluate our features qualitatively by depicting the Top5 nearest neighbors in the training set given a query image from the test set (see Fig. 3). We compare our results with [27,33], a random initialization, and a network with supervised training using the Imagenet dataset.

4.2   Transfer Capabilities of the Self-supervised Representation

Subsequently, we evaluate how well our self-trained representation can transfer to different tasks and also to other datasets. For the following experiments we initialize all networks with our trained model up to conv5 and fine-tune on the specific task using standard evaluation procedures.

Imagenet [43]: The Imagenet benchmark consists of ~1.3M images divided in 1000 objects category. The unsupervised features are tested by training a classifier on top of the frozen conv layers. Two experiments are proposed, one introduced by [54] using a linear classifier, and one using a two layer neural network proposed by [33]. Table 2 shows that our features obtain more than 2% over the best model with a comparable architecture, and almost 4% in the linear task. The modified CaffeNet introduced by [17] is not directly comparable to our model since it has 60% more parameters due to larger conv layers (groups parameter of the caffe framework [21]).

Query   Imagenet   Ours   OPN   Jigsaw   Random

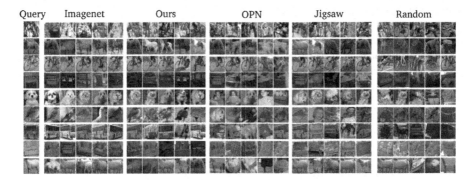

Fig. 3. Unsupervised evaluation of the feature representation by nearest neighbor search on the VOC07 dataset. For every test sample we show the Top5 nearest neighbors from the training set (Top1 to Top5 from left to right) using the cosine distance of the pool5 features. We compare the models from (i) supervised training with the Imagenet classification task, (ii) our spatiotemporal approach, (iii) OPN as a temporal approach [27], (iv) Jigsaw as a spatial method [33] and (v) a random initialization.

Table 2. Test accuracy [%] of the Imagenet classification task. A Linear [54] and Non-linear [33] classifier are trained over the frozen features (pool5) of the methods shown in the left column. (*: indicates our implementation of the model, +: indicates bigger architecture due to missing groups in the conv layers)

Method	Non-linear	Linear
Imagenet	59.7	50.5
Random	12.0	14.1
RotNet+ [17]	43.8	36.5
Videos [51]	29.8	–
OPN* [27]	29.6	–
Context [9]	30.4	29.6
Colorization [54]	35.2	30.3
BiGan [11]	34.8	28.0
Split-Brain [55]	–	32.8
NAT [4]	36.0	–
Jigsaw [33]	34.6	27.1
Ours	**38.2**	**36.5**

Action Recognition: For evaluating our unsupervised pre-trained network on the action recognition task we use the three splits of two different human action datasets: UCF-101 [46] with 101 different action classes and over 13k clips and HMDB-51 [24] with 51 classes and around 7k clips. The supervised training is performed using single frames as input, whereas the network is trained and tested on every split separately. If not mentioned otherwise, all classification

Table 3. Transferability of features learned using self-supervision to action recognition. The network is initialized until conv5 with the approach shown in the left column and fine-tuned on UCF-101 and HMDB-51. Accuracies [%] are reported for each approach. '*': Jigsaw (Noroozi et al. [33]) do not provide results for this task, we replicate their results using our PyTorch implementation

Method	UCF-101	HMDB-51
Random	47.8	16.3
Imagenet	67.7	28.0
Shuffle&Learn [31]	50.2	18.1
VGAN [49]	52.1	–
Luo et. al [29]	53.0	–
OPN [27]	56.3	22.1
Jigsaw* [33]	51.5	22.5
Ours	**58.6**	**25.0**

accuracies presented in this paragraph are computed by taking the mean over the three splits of the corresponding dataset. For training and testing we utilize the PyTorch implementation[1] provided by Wang et al. [50] for augmenting the data and for the finetuning and evaluation step, but network architecture and hyperparameters are retained from our model. Table 3 shows that we outperform the state-of-the-art by 2.3% on UCF-101 and 2.9% on HMDB-51. During our self-supervised training our network has never seen videos from the HMDB-51 dataset, showing that our model can transfer nicely to another dataset.

Pascal VOC: We evaluate the transferability of the unsupervised features by fine-tuning on three different tasks: multi-class object classification and object detection on Pascal VOC 2007 [12], and object segmentation on Pascal VOC 2012 [13]. In order to be comparable to previous work, we fine-tuned the model without batch normalization, using the standard CaffeNet with groups in conv2, conv4 and conv5. Previous methods using deeper networks, such as [10,52], are omitted from Table 4. For object classification we fine-tune our model on the dataset using the procedure described in [22]. We do not require the pre-processing and initialization method described in [22] for any of the shown experiments. For object detection we train Fast RCNN [42] following the experimental protocol described in [42]. We use FCN [28] to fine-tune our features on the segmentation task. The results in Table 4 show that we significantly improve upon the other approaches. Our method outperforms even [17] in object classification and segmentation, which uses batch normalization also during fine-tuning and uses a larger network due to the group parameter in the conv layers.

---

[1] https://github.com/yjxiong/temporal-segment-networks.

Table 4. Evaluating the transferability of representations learned using self-supervision to three tasks on Pascal VOC. We initialize the network until conv5 with the method shown in the left column and fine-tune for (i) multi-label image classification [22], (ii) object detection using Fast R-CNN [42] and (iii) image segmentation [28]. (i) and (ii) are evaluated on PASCAL VOC'07, (iii) on PASCAL VOC'12. For (i) and (ii) we show the mean average precision (mAP), for (iii) the mean intersection over union (mIoU). The fine-tuning has been performed using the standard CaffeNet, without batch normalization and groups 2 for conv [2,4,5]. ('+': significantly larger conv layers)

Method	Classification [12]	Detection [12]	Segmentation [13]
Imagenet	78.2	56.8	48.0
Random	53.3	43.4	19.8
RotNet [17]+	73.0	54.4	39.1
OPN [27]	63.8	46.9	–
Color17 [26]	65.9	–	38.4
Counting [34]	67.7	51.4	36.6
PermNet [8]	69.4	49.5	37.9
Jigsaw [33]	67.6	**53.2**	37.6
Ours	**74.2**	52.8	**42.8**

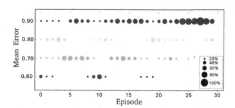

Fig. 4. Permutations chosen by the policy in each training episode. For legibility, ψ_i are grouped by validation error into four groups. The policy, updated after every episode, learns to sample hard permutations more often in later iterations

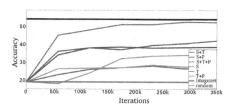

Fig. 5. The test accuracy from Top1 nearest neighbor search evaluation on VOC07 is used for comparing different ablations of our architecture during training. The curves show a faster improvement of the features when the policy (P) is used

4.3 Ablation Study

In this section, we compare the performances of the combined spatiotemporal (S+T) model with the single tasks (S,T) and show the improvements achieved by training the networks with the permutations proposed by the policy (P).

Table 5. We compare the different models on the multi-object classification task using the Pascal VOC07 and on the action recognition task using UCF-101. (S): **Spatial** task, (T): **Temporal** task, (S+T):**Spatial** and **Temporal** task simultaneously, (S+P): **Spatial** task + **Policy**, (S+T): **Temporal** task + **Policy**, (S&T): first solely **Spatial** task, followed by solely **Temporal** task, (S+T+P):all approaches simultaneously

Method	S	S+P	T	T+P	S& T	S+T	S+T+P
Pascal	67.6	71.3	64.1	65.9	69.8	72.0	**74.2**
UCF-101	51.5	54.6	52.8	55.7	54.2	57.3	**58.6**

Unsupervised Feature Evaluation: In Fig. 5 the models are evaluated on the Pascal VOC object classification task without any further fine-tuning by extracting pool5 features and computing cosine similarities for nearest neighbor search as described in Sect. 4.1. This unsupervised evaluation shows how well the unsupervised features can generalize to a primary task, such as object classification. Figure 5 illustrates that the combined spatiotemporal model (S+T) clearly outperforms the networks trained on only one task (by 7% on the spatial and 14% on the temporal model). Furthermore, the combined network shows a faster improvement, which may be explained by the regularization effect that the temporal has on the spatial task and vice-versa. Figure 5 also shows, that each of the three models has a substantial gain when the CNN is trained using the policy. Our final model, composed of the spatiotemporal task with policy (S+T+P), reaches almost the supervised features threshold ("imagenet" line in Fig. 5).

Supervised Fine-Tuning: In Table 5, a supervised evaluation has been performed starting from the self-supervised features. Each model is fine-tuned on the multi-class object classification task on Pascal VOC 2007 and on video classification using UCF-101. The results are consistent throughout the unsupervised evaluation, showing that the features of the spatiotemporal model (S+T) outperform both single-task models and the methods with RL policy (S+P and T+P) improve over the baseline models. The combination of the two tasks has been performed in parallel (S+T) and in a serial manner (S&T) by initializing the temporal task using the features trained on the spatial task. Training the permutation tasks in parallel provides a big gain over the serial version, showing that the two tasks benefit from each other and should be trained together.

Policy Learning: Fig. 4 shows the permutations chosen by the policy while it is trained at different episodes (x-axis). The aim of this experiment is to analyze the learning behavior of the policy. For this reason we initialize the policy network randomly and the CNN model from an intermediate checkpoint (average validation error 72.3%). Per episode, the permutations are divided in four complexities (based on the validation error) and the relative count of permutations selected by the policy is shown per complexity. Initially the policy selects the permutations uniformly in the first three episodes, but then learns to sample with higher frequency from the hard permutations (with high error; top red) and less from the easy permutations (bottom purple), without overfitting to a specific complexity but mixing the hard classes with intermediate ones.

Figure 6 depicts the spatial validation error over the whole training process of the spatiotemporal network with and without the policy. The results are consistent with the unsupervised evaluation, showing a faster improvement when training with the permutations proposed by the policy than with random permutations. Note that (B) in Fig. 6 shows a uniform improvement over all permutations, whereas (A) demonstrates the selection process of the policy with a non-uniform decrease in error.

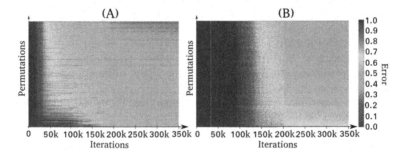

Fig. 6. Error over time of the spatial task, computed using the validation set and sorted by the average error. Each row shows how the error for one permutation evolves over time. (A): with Policy, (B): without policy

5   Conclusion

We have brought together the two directly related self-supervision tasks of spatial and temporal ordering. To sample data permutations, which are at the core of any surrogate ordering task, we have proposed a policy based on RL requiring relatively small computational extra cost during training in comparison to the basic training. Therefore, the sampling policy adapts to the state of the network that is being trained. As a result, permutations are sampled according to their expected utility for improving representation learning. In experiments on diverse tasks ranging from image classification and segmentation to action recognition in videos, our adaptive policy for spatiotemporal permutations has shown favorable results compared[2] to the state-of-the-art.

---

[2] This work has been supported in part by DFG grant OM81/1-1, the Heidelberg Academy of Science, and an Nvidia hardware donation.

References

1. Andrychowicz, M., et al.: Learning to learn by gradient descent by gradient descent. In: Advances in Neural Information Processing Systems, pp. 3981–3989 (2016)
2. Bautista, M.A., Sanakoyeu, A., Ommer, B.: Deep unsupervised similarity learning using partially ordered sets. In: Proceedings of IEEE Computer Vision and Pattern Recognition (2017)
3. Bengio, Y., Louradour, J., Collobert, R., Weston, J.: Curriculum learning. In: Proceedings of the 26th Annual International Conference on Machine Learning, pp. 41–48. ACM (2009)
4. Bojanowski, P., Joulin, A.: Unsupervised learning by predicting noise (2017). arXiv preprint arXiv:1704.05310
5. Brattoli, B., Büchler, U., Wahl, A.S., Schwab, M.E., Ommer, B.: Lstm self-supervision for detailed behavior analysis. In: IEEE Conference on Computer Vision and Pattern Recognition (CVPR) (2017)
6. Chang, H.S., Learned-Miller, E., McCallum, A.: Active bias: training more accurate neural networks by emphasizing high variance samples. In: Advances in Neural Information Processing Systems, pp. 1003–1013 (2017)
7. Chen, Y., et al.: Learning to learn without gradient descent by gradient descent. In: International Conference on Machine Learning, pp. 748–756 (2017)
8. Cruz, R.S., Fernando, B., Cherian, A., Gould, S.: Deeppermnet: visual permutation learning. In: CVPR (2017)
9. Doersch, C., Gupta, A., Efros, A.A.: Unsupervised visual representation learning by context prediction. In: Proceedings of the IEEE International Conference on Computer Vision, pp. 1422–1430 (2015)
10. Doersch, C., Zisserman, A.: Multi-task self-supervised visual learning (2017). arXiv preprint arXiv:1708.07860
11. Donahue, J., Krähenbühl, P., Darrell, T.: Adversarial feature learning (2016). arXiv preprint arXiv:1605.09782
12. Everingham, M., Van Gool, L., Williams, C.K.I., Winn, J., Zisserman, A.: The PASCAL visual object classes challenge 2007 (VOC2007) Results. http://www.pascal-network.org/challenges/VOC/voc2007/workshop/index.html
13. Everingham, M., Van Gool, L., Williams, C.K.I., Winn, J., Zisserman, A.: The PASCAL visual object classes challenge 2012 (VOC2012) results. http://www.pascal-network.org/challenges/VOC/voc2012/workshop/index.html
14. Fan, Y., Tian, F., Qin, T., Li, X.Y., Liu, T.Y.: Learning to teach. In: International Conference on Learning Representations (2018). https://openreview.net/forum?id=HJewuJWCZ
15. Fan, Y., Tian, F., Qin, T., Liu, T.Y.: Neural data filter for bootstrapping stochastic gradient descent (2016)
16. Fernando, B., Bilen, H., Gavves, E., Gould, S.: Self-supervised video representation learning with odd-one-out networks. In: IEEE Conference on Computer Vision and Pattern Recognition (CVPR) (2017). http://arxiv.org/abs/1611.06646
17. Gidaris, S., Singh, P., Komodakis, N.: Unsupervised representation learning by predicting image rotations. In: International Conference on Learning Representations (2018). https://openreview.net/forum?id=S1v4N2l0-
18. Graves, A., Bellemare, M.G., Menick, J., Munos, R., Kavukcuoglu, K.: Automated curriculum learning for neural networks (2017). arXiv preprint arXiv:1704.03003
19. Hochreiter, S., Schmidhuber, J.: Long short-term memory. Neural Comput. 9(8), 1735–1780 (1997)

20. Ioffe, S., Szegedy, C.: Batch normalization: accelerating deep network training by reducing internal covariate shift (2015). arXiv preprint arXiv:1502.03167
21. Jia, Y., et al.: Caffe: convolutional architecture for fast feature embedding. In: Proceedings of the 22nd ACM International Conference on Multimedia, pp. 675–678. ACM (2014)
22. Krähenbühl, P., Doersch, C., Donahue, J., Darrell, T.: Data-dependent initializations of convolutional neural networks (2015). arXiv preprint arXiv:1511.06856
23. Krizhevsky, A., Sutskever, I., Hinton, G.E.: Imagenet classification with deep convolutional neural networks. In: Advances in Neural Information Processing Systems, pp. 1097–1105 (2012)
24. Kuehne, H., Jhuang, H., Garrote, E., Poggio, T., Serre, T.: HMDB: a large video database for human motion recognition. In: Proceedings of the International Conference on Computer Vision (ICCV) (2011)
25. Kumar, M.P., Packer, B., Koller, D.: Self-paced learning for latent variable models. In: Advances in Neural Information Processing Systems, pp. 1189–1197 (2010)
26. Larsson, G., Maire, M., Shakhnarovich, G.: Colorization as a proxy task for visual understanding (2017). arXiv preprint arXiv:1703.04044
27. Lee, H.Y., Huang, J.B., Singh, M.K., Yang, M.H.: Unsupervised representation learning by sorting sequences. In: IEEE International Conference on Computer Vision (ICCV) (2017)
28. Long, J., Shelhamer, E., Darrell, T.: Fully convolutional networks for semantic segmentation. In: Proceedings of the IEEE Conference on Computer Vision and Pattern Recognition, pp. 3431–3440 (2015)
29. Luo, Z., Peng, B., Huang, D.A., Alahi, A., Fei-Fei, L.: Unsupervised learning of long-term motion dynamics for videos. In: IEEE Conference on Computer Vision and Pattern Recognition (CVPR) (2017)
30. Milbich, T., Bautista, M., Sutter, E., Ommer, B.: Unsupervised video understanding by reconciliation of posture similarities. In: Proceedings of the IEEE International Conference on Computer Vision (2017)
31. Misra, I., Zitnick, C.L., Hebert, M.: Unsupervised learning using sequential verification for action recognition (2016)
32. Mnih, V., Kavukcuoglu, K., Silver, D., Rusu, A.A., Veness, J., Bellemare, M.G., Graves, A., Riedmiller, M., Fidjeland, A.K., Ostrovski, G., et al.: Human-level control through deep reinforcement learning. Nature 518(7540), 529 (2015)
33. Noroozi, M., Favaro, P.: Unsupervised learning of visual representations by solving jigsaw puzzles. In: IEEE European Conference on Computer Vision (ECCV) (2016)
34. Noroozi, M., Pirsiavash, H., Favaro, P.: Representation learning by learning to count (2017). arXiv preprint arXiv:1708.06734
35. Noroozi, M., Vinjimoor, A., Favaro, P., Pirsiavash, H.: Boosting self-supervised learning via knowledge transfer. In: The IEEE Conference on Computer Vision and Pattern Recognition (CVPR), June 2018
36. Noroozi, M., Favaro, P.: Unsupervised learning of visual representations by solving Jigsaw puzzles. In: Leibe, B., Matas, J., Sebe, N., Welling, M. (eds.) ECCV 2016. LNCS, vol. 9910, pp. 69–84. Springer, Cham (2016). https://doi.org/10.1007/978-3-319-46466-4_5
37. Owens, A., Wu, J., McDermott, J.H., Freeman, W.T., Torralba, A.: Ambient sound provides supervision for visual learning. In: Leibe, B., Matas, J., Sebe, N., Welling, M. (eds.) ECCV 2016. LNCS, vol. 9905, pp. 801–816. Springer, Cham (2016). https://doi.org/10.1007/978-3-319-46448-0_48

38. Patel, Y., Gomez, L., Rusiñol, M., Jawahar, C., Karatzas, D.: Self-supervised learning of visual features through embedding images into text topic spaces. In: IEEE Conference on Computer Vision and Pattern Recognition (CVPR) (2017)
39. Pathak, D., Girshick, R., Dollár, P., Darrell, T., Hariharan, B.: Learning features by watching objects move. In: IEEE Conference on Computer Vision and Pattern Recognition (CVPR) (2017)
40. Pathak, D., Krahenbuhl, P., Donahue, J., Darrell, T., Efros, A.A.: Context encoders: feature learning by inpainting. In: Proceedings of the IEEE Conference on Computer Vision and Pattern Recognition, pp. 2536–2544 (2016)
41. Ravi, S., Larochelle, H.: Optimization as a model for few-shot learning (2016)
42. Ren, S., He, K., Girshick, R., Sun, J.: Faster R-CNN: Towards real-time object detection with region proposal networks. In: Advances in Neural Information Processing Systems, pp. 91–99 (2015)
43. Russakovsky, O., et al.: ImageNet large scale visual recognition challenge. Int. J. Comput. Vis. (IJCV) **115**(3), 211–252 (2015). https://doi.org/10.1007/s11263-015-0816-y
44. Sanakoyeu, A., Bautista, M.A., Ommer, B.: Deep unsupervised learning of visual similarities. Pattern Recognit. **78**, 331–343 (2018)
45. Silver, D., Huang, A., Maddison, C.J., Guez, A., Sifre, L., Van Den Driessche, G., Schrittwieser, J., Antonoglou, I., Panneershelvam, V., Lanctot, M.: Mastering the game of go with deep neural networks and tree search. Nature **529**(7587), 484–489 (2016)
46. Soomro, K., Zamir, A.R., Shah, M.: Ucf101: a dataset of 101 human actions classes from videos in the wild (2012). arXiv preprint arXiv:1212.0402
47. Sümer, Ö., Dencker, T., Ommer, B.: Self-supervised learning of pose embeddings from spatiotemporal relations in videos. In: 2017 IEEE International Conference on Computer Vision (ICCV), pp. 4308–4317. IEEE (2017)
48. Sutton, R.S., Barto, A.G.: Reinforcement Learning: An Introduction, vol. 1. MIT press, Cambridge (1998)
49. Vondrick, C., Pirsiavash, H., Torralba, A.: Generating videos with scene dynamics. In: Conference on Neural Information Processing Systems (NIPS) (2016)
50. Wang, L., et al.: Temporal segment networks: towards good practices for deep action recognition. In: IEEE European Conference on Computer Vision (ECCV) (2016)
51. Wang, X., Gupta, A.: Unsupervised learning of visual representations using videos. In: Proceedings of the IEEE International Conference on Computer Vision, pp. 2794–2802 (2015)
52. Wang, X., He, K., Gupta, A.: Transitive invariance for self-supervised visual representation learning. In: IEEE International Conference on Computer Vision (ICCV) (2017)
53. Williams, R.J., Peng, J.: Function optimization using connectionist reinforcement learning algorithms. Connect. Sci. **3**(3), 241–268 (1991)
54. Zhang, R., Isola, P., Efros, A.A.: Colorful image colorization. In: Leibe, B., Matas, J., Sebe, N., Welling, M. (eds.) ECCV 2016. LNCS, vol. 9907, pp. 649–666. Springer, Cham (2016). https://doi.org/10.1007/978-3-319-46487-9_40
55. Zhang, R., Isola, P., Efros, A.A.: Split-brain autoencoders: unsupervised learning by cross-channel prediction (2016). arXiv preprint arXiv:1611.09842
56. Zoph, B., Le, Q.V.: Neural architecture search with reinforcement learning (2016). arXiv preprint arXiv:1611.01578

Learning to Look around Objects for Top-View Representations of Outdoor Scenes

Samuel Schulter[1]($\boxtimes$), Menghua Zhai[2], Nathan Jacobs[2],
and Manmohan Chandraker[1,3]

[1] NEC-Laboratories, Cupertino, CA 95014, USA
samuel@nec-labs.com
[2] University of Kentucky, Lexington, KY 40506, USA
[3] University of California San Diego, La Jolla, CA 92093, USA

Abstract. Given a single RGB image of a complex outdoor road scene in the perspective view, we address the novel problem of estimating an occlusion-reasoned semantic scene layout in the top-view. This challenging problem not only requires an accurate understanding of both the 3D geometry and the semantics of the visible scene, but also of occluded areas. We propose a convolutional neural network that learns to predict occluded portions of the scene layout by looking around foreground objects like cars or pedestrians. But instead of hallucinating RGB values, we show that directly predicting the semantics and depths in the occluded areas enables a better transformation into the top-view. We further show that this initial top-view representation can be significantly enhanced by learning priors and rules about typical road layouts from simulated or, if available, map data. Crucially, training our model does not require costly or subjective human annotations for occluded areas or the top-view, but rather uses readily available annotations for standard semantic segmentation in the perspective view. We extensively evaluate and analyze our approach on the KITTI and Cityscapes data sets.

Keywords: 3D scene understanding · Occlusion reasoning
Semantic top-view representations

1 Introduction

Visual completion is a crucial ability for an intelligent agent to navigate and interact with the three-dimensional (3D) world. Several tasks such as driving in urban scenes, or a robot grasping objects on a cluttered desk, require innate

---

S. Schulter and M. Zhai—equal contribution.

Electronic supplementary material The online version of this chapter (https:// doi.org/10.1007/978-3-030-01267-0_48) contains supplementary material, which is available to authorized users.

reasoning about unseen regions. A top-view or bird's eye view (BEV) representation[1] of the scene where occlusion relationships have been resolved is useful in such situations [11]. It is a compact description of agents and scene elements with semantically and geometrically consistent relationships, which is intuitive for human visualization and precise for autonomous decisions.

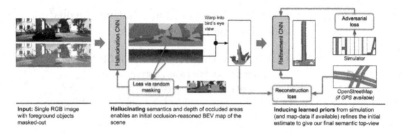

Fig. 1. Given a single RGB image of a typical street scene (left), our approach creates an **occlusion-reasoned semantic map of the scene layout in the bird's eye view**. We present a CNN that can hallucinate depth and semantics in areas occluded by foreground objects (marked in red and obtained via standard semantic segmentation), which gives an initial but noisy and incomplete estimate of the scene layout (middle). To fill in unobserved areas in the top-view, we further propose a refinement-CNN that induces learning strong priors from simulated and OpenStreetMap data (right), which comes at no additional annotation costs.

In this work, we derive such top-view representations through a novel framework that simultaneously reasons about geometry and semantics from just *a single RGB image*, which we illustrate in the particularly challenging scenario of outdoor road scenes. The focus of this work lies in the estimation of the scene layout, although foreground objects can be placed on top using existing 3D localization methods [24,38]. Our learning-based approach estimates a geometrically and semantically consistent spatial layout even in regions hidden behind foreground objects, like cars or pedestrians, without requiring human annotation for occluded pixels or the top-view itself. Note that human supervision for such occlusion-reasoned top-view maps is likely to be subjective and of course, expensive to procure. Instead, we derive supervisory signals from readily available annotations for semantic segmentation in the perspective view, a depth sensor or stereo (for visible areas) and a knowledge corpus of typical road scenes via simulations and OpenStreetMap data. Figure 1 provides an illustration.

Specifically, in Sect. 3.1, we propose a novel CNN that takes as input an image with occluded regions (corresponding to foreground objects) masked out, and estimates the segmentation labels and depth values over the entire image, essentially *hallucinating distances and semantics in the occluded regions*. In contrast to standard image in-painting approaches, we operate in the semantic and depth spaces rather than the RGB image space. Section 3.1 shows how to train this CNN without additional human annotations for occluded regions. The

---

[1] We use the terms "top-view" and "bird's eye view" interchangeably.

hallucinated depth map is then used to map the hallucinated semantic segmentation of each pixel into the bird's eye view, see Sect. 3.2.

This initial prediction can be incomplete and erroneous, for instance, since BEV pixels far away from the camera can be unobserved due to limited image resolution or due to imperfect depth estimation. Thus, Sect. 3.3 proposes a refinement and completion neural network to leverage easily obtained training data from *simulations that encode general priors and rules* about road scene layouts. Since there is no correspondence between actual images and simulated data, we employ an *adversarial loss* for teaching our CNN a generative aspect about typical layouts. When GPS is available for training images, we also show how *map data provides an additional training signal* for our models. We demonstrate this using OpenStreetMap (OSM) [19]. Maps provide rough correspondence with RGB images through the GPS location, but it can be noisy and lacks information on scene scale, besides mislabels in the map itself. We handle these issues by *learning a warping function* that aligns OSM data with image evidence using a variant of spatial transformer network [13]. Note that a single RGB image is used at test time, with simulations or OSM limited to training.

In Sect. 4, we evaluate our proposed semantic BEV synthesis on the KITTI [8] and Cityscapes [4] datasets. For a quantitative evaluation, we manually annotate validation images with the scene layout in both the perspective and the top-view, which is a time-consuming and error-prone process but again highlights the benefit of our method that resorts only to readily available annotations. Since, to the best of our knowledge, no prior work exists solving this problem in a similar setup to allow a fair comparison, we comprehensively evaluate with several baselines to study the role of each module. Our experiments consider roads and sidewalks for layout estimation, with cars and persons as occluding foreground objects, although extensions to other semantic classes are straightforward in future work. While not our focus, we visualize a simple application in Sect. 4.3 to include foreground objects such as cars and pedestrians in our representation. We observe qualitatively meaningful top-view estimates, which also obtain low errors on our annotated test set.

2   Related Work

General scene understanding is one of the fundamental goals of computer vision and many approaches exist that tackle this problem from different directions.

Indoor: Recent works like [2,16,26] have shown great progress by leveraging strong priors about indoor environments obtained from large-scale data sets. While these approaches can rely on strong assumptions like a Manhattan world layout, our work focuses on less constrained outdoor driving scenarios.

Outdoor: Scene understanding for outdoor scenes has received a lot of interest in recent years [5,10,27,30,37], especially due to applications like driver assistance systems or autonomous driving. Wang et al. [29] propose a conditional random field that infers 3D object locations, semantic segmentation as well as a depth reconstruction of the scene from a single geo-tagged image, which also enables the use of OSM data. At test time, their approach requires as input accurate GPS and map information. In contrast, we require only the RGB image at test time. Seff and Xiao [21] leverage OpenStreetMap (OSM) data to predict several road layout attributes from a single image, like the distance to an intersection, drivable directions, heading angle, etc.While we also leverage OSM for training our models and make predictions only from a single RGB image, we infer a full semantic map in the top view instead of a discrete set of attributes.

Top-View Representations: Sengupta et al. [22] derive a top-view representation by relating semantic segmentation in perspective images to a ground plane with a homography. However, this is a simplifying (flat-world) assumption where non-flat objects will produce artifacts in the ground plane, like shadows or cones. To alleviate these artifacts, they aggregate semantics over multiple frames. However, removing all artifacts would require viewing objects from many different angles. In contrast, our approach enables reasoning about occlusion from just a single image, which is enabled by automatically learned and context-dependent priors about the world. Geiger et al. [7] represent road scenes with a complex model in the bird's eye view. However, input to the model comes from multiple sources (vehicle tracklets, vanishing points, scene flow, etc.) and inference requires MCMC, while our approach efficiently computes the BEV representation from just a single image. Moreover, their hand-crafted parametric model might not account for all possible scene layouts, whereas our approach is nonparametric and thus more flexible. Máttyus et al. [18] combine perspective and top-view images to estimate road layouts and Zhai et al. [34] predict the semantic layouts of top-view images by learning the transformation between the perspective and the top-view. Gupta et al. [11] demonstrate the suitability of a BEV representation for mapping and planning, even though it is not explicitly learned.

Occlusion Reasoning: Most recent works in this area focus on occlusions of foreground objects and use complex hand-crafted models [5,30,37,38]. In contrast, we estimate the layout of a scene occluded by foreground objects. Guo and Hoiem [10] employ a scene parsing approach that retrieves existing shapes from training data based on visible pixels. Our approach learns to hallucinate occluded areas and does not rely on an existing and fixed set of polygons from training data. Liu et al. [17] also hallucinate the semantics and depth of regions occluded by foreground objects. However, (i) their approach relies on a handcrafted graphical model while ours is learning-based and (ii) they assume sparse depth from a laser scanner as input, while we estimate depth from a single RGB image (the sparse depth maps are actually ground truth for training our models).

3   Generating Bird's Eye View Representations

We now present our approach for transforming a single RGB image in the perspective view into an occlusion-reasoned semantic representation in the bird's eye view, see Fig. 1. We take as input an image $I \in \mathbb{R}^{h \times w \times 3}$ with spatial dimension

h and w and a semantic segmentation $S^{\text{fg}} \in \mathbb{R}^{h \times w \times C}$ of the *visible* scene, where C is the number of categories. Note that any semantic segmentation method can be used and we rely on the recently proposed pyramid scene parsing (PSP) network [35]. S^{fg} provides the location of foreground objects that occlude the scene. In this work, we consider foreground objects like cars or pedestrians as occluders but other definitions are possible as well.

To reason about these occlusions, we define a masked image I^M, where pixels of foreground objects have been removed. In Sect. 3.1, we propose a CNN that takes I^M as input and hallucinates the depth as well as the semantics of the entire image, including occluded pixels. The occlusion-reasoned depth map D^{bg} allows us to map the occlusion-reasoned semantic segmentation S^{bg} into 3D and then into the bird's eye view (BEV), see Sect. 3.2.

While this initial BEV map B^{init} is already better than mapping the non-occlusion reasoned semantic map S^{fg} into 3D, there can still be unobserved or erroneous pixels. In Sect. 3.3, we thus propose a CNN that learns priors from simulated data to further improve our representation. If a GPS signal is available, OpenStreetMap (OSM) data can be additionally included as supervisory signal.

3.1   Learning to see Around Foreground Objects

An important step towards an occlusion-reasoned representation of the scene is to infer the semantics and the geometry behind foreground objects.

Masking: Given the semantic segmentation S^{fg}, we define the mask of foreground pixels as $M \in \mathbb{R}^{h \times w}$, where a pixel in the mask M_{ij} is 1 if and only if the segmentation at that pixel S_{ij}^{fg} belongs to any of the foreground classes. Otherwise, the pixel in the mask is 0. In order to inform the CNN about which pixels have to be in-painted, we apply the mask on the input RGB image and define each pixel in the masked input I^M as

$$I_{ij}^M = \begin{cases} \bar{m}, & \text{if } M_{ij} = 1 \\ I_{ij}, & \text{otherwise}, \end{cases}$$

where $\bar{m}$ is the mean RGB value of the color range, such that after normalization the input to the CNN is zero for those pixels. Given I^M, we extract a feature representation by applying ResNet-50 [12]. Similar to recent semantic segmentation literature [35], we use a larger stride in convolutions and dilation [32] to increase the feature map resolution from $\frac{h}{32} \times \frac{w}{32}$ to $\frac{h}{8} \times \frac{w}{8}$.

In addition to masking the input image, we explicitly provide the mask as input to the CNN for two reasons: (i) While the value m becomes 0 after centering the input of the CNN, other visible pixels might still share the same value and confuse the training of the CNN. (ii) An explicit mask input allows encoding more information like the category of the occluded pixel. We thus define another mask $M^{\text{cls}} \in \mathbb{R}^{h \times w \times C^{\text{fg}}}$, where C^{fg} is the number of foreground classes and each channel corresponds to one of them. We encode M^{cls} with a small CNN and fuse the resulting feature with the one from the masked image, see Fig. 2a.

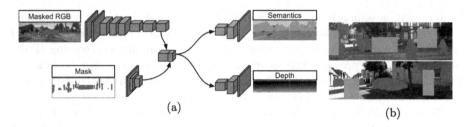

Fig. 2. (a) The *inpainting CNN* first encodes a masked image and the mask itself. The extracted features are concatenated and two decoders predict semantics and depth for visible and occluded pixels. **(b)** To train the inpainting CNN we ignore foreground objects as no ground truth is available (red) but we *artificially add masks (green)* over background regions where full annotation is already available

Hallucination: We then put two decoders on the fused feature representation of I^M and M^{cls} for predicting semantic segmentation and the depthmap of the occlusion-free scene. For semantic segmentation, we again use the PSP module [35], which is particularly useful for in-painting where contextual information is crucial. For depth prediction, we follow [15] in defining the network architecture. Both decoders are followed by a bilinear upsampling layer to provide the output at the same resolution as the input, see Fig. 2a. While traditional in-painting methods fill missing pixels with RGB values, note that we directly go from an RGB image to the in-painted semantics and the geometry of the scene, which has two benefits: (1) The computational costs are smaller as we avoid the (in our case) unnecessary detour in the RGB space. (2) The task of in-painting in the RGB space is presumably harder than in-painting semantics and depth as there is no need for predicting any texture or color.

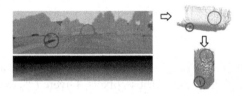

Fig. 3. The process of mapping the semantic segmentation with corresponding depth first into a 3D point cloud and then into the bird's eye view. The red and blue circles illustrate corresponding locations in all views.

Training: We train the proposed CNN in a supervised way. However, as mentioned before, it would be very costly to annotate the semantics and particularly the geometry behind foreground objects. We thus resort to an alternative that only requires standard semantic segmentation and depth ground truth. Because our desired ground truth is unknown for real foreground objects in the masked input image I^M, we do not infer any loss at those pixels. However, we augment

I^M with additional randomly sampled masks, but for which we still have ground truth, see Fig. 2b. In this way, we can teach our CNN to hallucinate occluded areas of the input image without acquiring costly human annotations. Note that an alternative to masking regions in the input image is to paste real foreground objects into the scene. However, this strategy requires separate instances of foreground objects cropped at the semantic boundaries and a good understanding of the scene geometry for generating a realistic looking training image.

3.2   Mapping into the Bird's Eye View

Given the depth map D^{bg} and the intrinsic camera parameters $\mathbf{K}$, we can map each coordinate of the perspective view into the 3D space. We drop the z-coordinate (height axis) for each 3D point and assign x and y coordinates to the closest integer, which gives us a mapping into bird's eye view representation. We use this mapping to transfer the class probability distribution of each pixel in the perspective view, i.e., S^{bg}, into the bird's eye view, which we denote $B^{\mathrm{init}} \in \mathbb{R}^{k \times l \times C^{\mathrm{bg}}}$, where C^{bg} is the number of background classes and k and l are the spatial dimensions. Throughout the paper, we use $k = 128$ and $l = 64$ pixels that we relate to 60×30 meters in the point cloud. For all points that are mapped to the same pixel in the top view, we average the corresponding class distribution. Figure 3 illustrates the geometric transformation.

Note that B^{init} is our first occlusion-reasoned semantic representation in the bird's eye view. However, B^{init} also has several remaining issues. Some pixels in B^{init} will not be assigned any class probability, especially those far from the camera due to image foreshortening in the perspective view. Imperfect depth prediction is also an issue because it may assign a well classified pixel in the perspective view a wrong depth value, which puts the point into a wrong location in top-view. This can lead to unnatural arrangements of semantic classes in B^{init}.

3.3   Refinement with a Knowledge Corpus

To remedy the above mentioned issues, we propose a refinement CNN that takes B^{init} and predicts the final output $B^{\mathrm{final}} \in \mathbb{R}^{k \times l \times C^{\mathrm{bg}}}$, which has the same dimensions as B^{init}. The refinement CNN has an encoder-decoder structure with a fully-connected bottleneck layer, see Fig. 4b. The main difficulty in training the refinement CNN is the lack of semantic ground truth data in the bird's eye view, which is very hard and costly to annotate. In the following we present two sources of supervisory signals that are easy to acquire.

Simulation: The first source of information we leverage is a simulator that renders the semantics of typical road scenes in the bird's eye view. The simulator models roads with different types of intersections, lanes and sidewalks, see Fig. 4a for some examples. Note that it is easy to create such a simulator as we do not need to model texture, occlusions or any perspective distortions in the scene. A simple generative model about road topology, number of lanes, radius for curved roads, etc.is enough. Since there is no correspondence with the real training data, we rely on an adversarial loss [1] between predictions of the refinement CNN B^{final} and data from the simulator B^{sim}

$$\mathcal{L}^{\text{sim}} = \sum_{i=1}^{m} d\left(B_i^{\text{final}}; \Theta_{\text{discr}}\right) - \sum_{i=1}^{m} d\left(B_i^{\text{sim}}; \Theta_{\text{discr}}\right) ,$$

where m is the batch size and $d\left(.; \Theta_{\text{discr}}\right)$ is the discriminator function with parameters Θ_{discr}. Note that $d\left(.; \Theta_{\text{discr}}\right)$ needs to be a K-Lipschitz function [1], which is enforced by gradient clipping on the parameters Θ_{discr} during training. While any other variant of adversarial loss is possible, we found [1] to provide the most stable training. The adversarial loss injects prior information about typical road scene layouts and remedies errors of B^{init} like unobserved pixels or unnatural shapes of objects due to depth or semantic prediction errors.

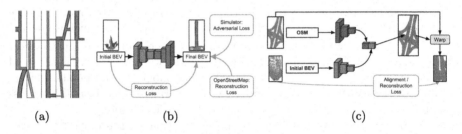

(a)   (b)   (c)

Fig. 4. (a) Simulated road shapes in the top-view. (b) The refinement-CNN is an encoder-decoder network receiving three supervisory signals: self-reconstruction with the input, adversarial loss from simulated data, and reconstruction loss with aligned OpenStreetMap (OSM) data. (c) The alignment CNN takes as input the initial BEV map and a crop of OSM data (via noisy GPS and yaw estimate given). The CNN predicts a warp for the OSM map and is trained to minimize the reconstruction loss with the initial BEV map.

Since $\mathcal{L}^{\text{sim}}$ operates without any correspondence, the refinement network needs additional regularization to not deviate too much from the actual input, i.e., B^{init}. We add a reconstruction loss between B^{init} and B^{final} to define the final loss as $\mathcal{L} = \mathcal{L}^{\text{sim}} + \lambda \cdot \mathcal{L}^{\text{reconst}}$ with

$$\mathcal{L}^{\text{reconst}} = \frac{\|(B^{\text{init}} - B^{\text{final}}) \odot \mathbf{M}\|^2}{\sum_{ij} \mathbf{M}} ,$$

where $\odot$ is an element-wise multiplication and $\mathbf{M} \in \mathbb{R}^{k \times l}$ is a mask of 0's for unobserved pixels in B^{init} and 1's otherwise.

OpenStreetMap Data: Driving imagery often comes with a GPS signal and an estimate of the driving direction, which enables the use of OpenStreetMap (OSM) data as another source of supervisory signal for the refinement CNN. The most simple approach is to render the OSM data for the given location and angle, B^{osm}, and define a reconstruction loss with B^{final} as $\mathcal{L}^{\text{OSM}} = \|B^{\text{final}} - B^{\text{osm}}\|^2$.

This loss can be included into the final loss $\mathcal{L}$ in addition to or instead of $\mathcal{L}^{\mathrm{reconst}}$. In any case, $\mathcal{L}^{\mathrm{OSM}}$ ignores noise in the GPS and the direction estimate as well as imperfect renderings due to annotation noise and missing information in OSM.

We therefore propose to align the initial OSM map B^{osm} with the semantics and geometry observed in the actual RGB image with a warping function $\hat{B}^{\mathrm{osm}} = w\left(B^{\mathrm{osm}}; \theta\right)$ parameterized by θ. We use a composition of a similarity transformation implemented as a parametric spatial transformer (handling translation, rotation, and scale; denoted "Box") and a non-parametric warp implemented as bilinear sampling (handling non-linear misalignments due to OSM rendering; denoted "Flow") [13], see Fig. 5. We minimize the masked reconstruction between $\hat{B}^{\mathrm{osm}}$ and the initial BEV map B^{init},

$$\theta^* = \arg\min_\theta \frac{\left\|\left(B^{\mathrm{init}} - w\left(B^{\mathrm{osm}}; \theta\right)\right) \odot \mathbf{M}\right\|^2}{\sum_{ij}\mathbf{M}} + \lambda_2 \Gamma(w\left(B^{\mathrm{osm}}; \theta\right)) + \lambda_3 \|\theta\|_2^2 \,,$$

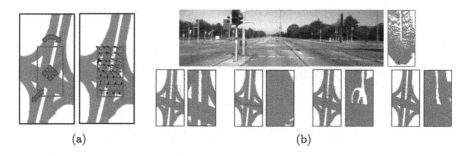

(a)   (b)

Fig. 5. (a) We use a composition of similarity transform (left, "box") and a non-parametric warp (right, "flow") to align noisy OSM with image evidence. **(b, top)** Input image and the corresponding B^{init}. **(b, bottom)** Resulting warping grid overlaid on the OSM map and the warping result for 4 different warping functions, respectively: "box", "flow", "box+flow", "box+flow (with regularization)". Note the importance of composing the transformations and the induced regularization.

where $w\left(.; \theta\right)$ is differentiable [13], and $\Gamma(.)$ is a low-pass filter similar to [28, 36], and $\|.\|_2^2$ the squared ℓ_2-norm, both acting as regularizing functions. The hyper-parameters λ_2 and λ_3 are manually set.

To minimize the alignment error the first choice is non-linear optimization, e.g., LBFG-S [3]. However, we found this to produce satisfactory results only for parts of the data, while a significant portion would require hand-tuning of several hyper-parameters. This is mostly due to noise in the initial BEV map B^{init} as well as the rendering B^{osm}. An alternative, which proved to be more stable and easy to realize, is to learn a function that predicts the warping parameters, which has the benefit that the predictive function can implicitly leverage other examples of $(B^{\mathrm{init}}, B^{\mathrm{osm}})$ pairs in the training corpus. We thus train a CNN that takes B^{init} and B^{osm} as inputs and predicts the warping parameters θ by minimizing the alignment error. Also, we can either train this CNN separately or jointly with the refinement CNN, thus providing different training signals for the refinement module. We evaluate these options in Sect. 4.2. Figure 4c illustrates the process of aligning the OSM data.

4   Experiments

Our quantitative and qualitative evaluation focuses on occlusion reasoning via hallucination in the perspective view (Sect. 4.1) and scene completion via the refinement network in the bird's eye view (Sect. 4.2).

Datasets: Creating the proposed BEV representation requires data for learning the parameters of the modules described above. Importantly, the only supervisory signal that we need is semantic segmentation (human annotation) and depth (LiDAR or stereo), although not both are required for the same input image. Both KITTI [8] and Cityscapes [4] fulfill our requirements. Both data sets come with a GPS signal and a yaw estimate of the driving direction, which allows us to additionally leverage OSM data during training.

Fig. 6. Qualitative example of our hallucination CNN: Semantics and depth without (left) and with (right) hallucination.

Table 1. Hallucination results for two general in-painting strategies and different mask encodings

Method	Random-boxes		Human-gt	
	Hidden		Visible	Hidden
	IoU	ARD	IoU	IoU
RGB-inpaint	**68.83**	.1428	79.25	55.79
Direct	64.63	**.1413**	**81.12**	**60.06**
RGB-only	63.07	.1440	79.71	60.77
+ mask	63.47	**.1435**	80.14	60.24
+ cls-encode	**64.79**	.1453	**80.63**	**61.06**

The KITTI [8] data set contains many sequences of typical driving scenarios and contains accurate GPS location and driving direction as well as a 3D point cloud from a laser scanner. However, annotation for semantic segmentation is scarce. We create two versions of the data set based on segmentation annotation: *KITTI-Ros* consists of 31 sequences (14201 frames) for training, where 100 of them have semantic annotation, and of 9 sequences (4368) for validation, where 46 images are annotated for segmentation. The segmentation ground truth comes from [20]. *KITTI-RAW* consists of 31 sequences (16273 frames) for training and 9 sequences (2296 frames) for validation. 1074 images from the training set and 233 images from the validation set have ground truth annotations for semantic segmentation, which we collected on our own.

The *Cityscapes* data set [4] contains 2975 training and 500 validation images, all of which are fully annotated for semantic segmentation and are provided as stereo image pairs. For ease of implementation, we rely on a strong stereo method [33] to serve as our training signal for depth, although unsupervised methods exists for direct training from stereo images [6,9]. GPS location and heading are also provided, although accuracy is lower compared to KITTI.

Validation Data for Occlusion-Reasoning: For a quantitative evaluation of occlusion reasoning in the perspective view as well as in the bird's eye view, we manually annotated all validation image of the three data sets that also have semantic segmentation ground truth. We asked annotators to draw the scene layout by hand for the categories "road" and "sidewalk". Other pixels are annotated as "background".

Implementation Details: We train our in-painting models with a batch size of 2 for 80k iterations with ADAM [14]. The initial learning rate is 0.0002, which is decreased by a factor of 10 for the last 20k iterations. The refinement network is trained with a batch size of 64 for 80k iterations and a learning rate of 0.0001.

4.1 Occlusion Reasoning by Hallucination

Here we analyze our hallucination CNN proposed in Sect. 3.1, which targets at in-painting the semantics and depth of areas occluded by foreground objects. To the best of our knowledge, there is no prior art that can serve as a *fair* comparison point. Although [17] addresses the same task, their approach assumes sparse depth information as input, which serves as ground truth in our approach. Nevertheless, we have created fair baselines that justify our design choices.

Evaluation Protocol: We split our evaluation protocol into two parts. First, we follow [17] by randomly masking out background regions in the input and evaluate the predictions of the hallucination CNNs (random-boxes). For this case, note that evaluation can be done for all semantic classes and depth. While this is the only possible evaluation without human annotation for occluded areas, the sampling process may not resemble objects realistically. Thus, we also evaluate with our newly acquired annotations (human-gt) for the categories "road" and "sidewalk", which was not done in [17]. We measure mean IoU for segmentation and absolute relative distance (ARD) for depth estimation as in [15].

Semantics and Depth Space Versus RGB Space: We compare our hallucination CNN with a baseline that takes the traditional approach of in-painting and operates in the RGB pixel space. This baseline consists of two CNNs, one for in-painting in the RGB space and one for semantic and depth prediction. For a fair comparison, we equip both CNNs with the same ResNet-50 feature extractor. For RGB-space in-painting, we use the same decoder structure as for depth prediction but with 3 output channels and train it with the random mask sampling strategy. The second CNN has the exact same architecture as our hallucination CNN and is trained without masking inputs but instead uses the already in-painted RGB images. From Table 1 we can see that the proposed direct hallucination network outperforms in-painting in the RGB space for depth prediction and segmentation with the human-provided ground truth while it trails for segmentation of all categories with random boxes. The reason for the inferior performance might be missing context information that is available to the baseline by the RGB-space supervision. However, note that the proposed architecture is twice as efficient, since in-painting and prediction of semantics and depth are obtained in the same forward pass. Qualitative examples of our direct hallucination CNN are given in Fig. 6.

Mask-Encoding: We also analyze different variants of how to encode the foreground mask as input to the proposed hallucination CNN. Table 1 demonstrates the beneficial impact of explicitly encoding the foreground mask ("+mask") in addition to masking the RGB image ("RGB-only"), as well as providing the class information of the foreground objects inside the mask ("+cls-encode").

4.2   Refining the BEV Representation

We now evaluate the refinement model described in Sect. 3.3 on all three data sets with the acquired annotations in the bird's eye view. The evaluation metric again is mean IOU for the categories "road" and "sidewalk". We compare four models: (1) The initial BEV map, without refinement. (2) A refinement heuristic, where missing semantic information at pixel (i, j) is filled with the semantics of the closest pixels in y-direction towards the camera. (3) The proposed refinement module with simulated data and the self-reconstruction loss.

Table 2. (a) Results on the KITTI-RAW data set showing the impact of the refinement module with simulated and OSM data compared to B^{init} and a simple refinement heuristic. We also show the impact of hallucination and depth prediction. (b) Results for KITTI-Ros and Cityscapes

	(a)				(b)			

Setting (KITTI-RAW)	Road	Sidewalk	Mean	Dataset	Setting	Road	Sidewalk	Mean
BEV-init	58.13	29.33	43.73	KITTI-	BEV-init	56.93	40.71	48.82
Refine-heuristic	67.93	30.12	49.02	Ros	Refine-heuristic	69.59	41.31	55.45
Simulation	66.98	29.73	48.36		Simulation	62.96	43.19	53.08
Simulation+OSM	**68.89**	**30.35**	**49.62**		Simulation+OSM	**71.82**	**44.77**	**58.29**
no halluc.	51.85	24.76	38.31	City-	BEV-init	51.40	17.47	34.43
no halluc. (refine)	65.67	25.91	45.79	scapes	Refine-heuristic	52.06	17.22	34.64
no depth pred.	44.54	8.61	26.58		Simulation	52.89	17.89	35.39
no depth pred. (refine)	46.11	7.73	26.92		Simulation+OSM	**56.46**	**19.60**	**38.03**

Table 3. An ablation study of the proposed BEV-refinement module. We analyze different types of warping functions and OSM alignment optimization strategies

Experiment	Setting	Road	Sidewalk	Mean
Warping-method	Box	64.77	30.51	47.64
	Flow	66.03	**30.74**	48.39
	Box+Flow	**68.89**	30.35	**49.62**
Warp-optimization	LBFGS	22.31	29.24	25.78
	CNN	63.91	29.19	46.55
	CNN-joint	**68.89**	**30.35**	**49.62**

(4) The refinement module with the additional OSM-reconstruction loss. Table 2 clearly shows that the combination of simulated and aligned OSM data provides the best supervisory signal for the refinement module on all three data sets. Interestingly, the refinement heuristic is a strong competitor but this is probably because evaluation is limited to only "road" and "sidewalk", where simple rules are often correct. This heuristic will likely fail for classes like "vegetation" and "building". Importantly, all refinement strategies improve upon the initial BEV map. Because no fair comparison point to prior art is available to us, we further analyze two alternative baselines on the KITTI-RAW data set.

Importance of Hallucination: We train a refinement module that takes as input BEV maps that omit the hallucination step ("No halluc."). To create this BEV map, we train a joint segmentation and depth prediction network (same architecture as for hallucination) with standard foreground annotation and map the semantics of background classes into the BEV map as described in Sect. 3.2. Table 2 shows that avoiding the hallucination step hurts the performance. Note that the proposed refinement CNN recovers most errors for roads, while the relative performance drop for sidewalks is larger. We believe this is due to long stretches of non-occluded roads in the KITTI data set. Sidewalks, on the other hand, are typically more occluded due to parked cars and pedestrians.

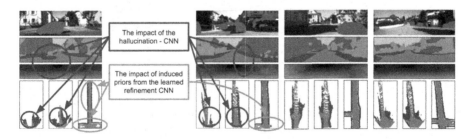

Fig. 7. Examples of our BEV representation. Each one shows the masked RGB input, the hallucinated semantics and depth, as well as three BEV maps, which are (from left to right), The BEV map without hallucination, with hallucination, and after refinement.

Importance of Depth Prediction: We train a CNN that takes as input the RGB image in the perspective view and directly predicts the BEV map, without depth prediction ("No depth pred."). The CNN extracts basic features with ResNet-50 [12], applies strided convolutions for further down-sampling, a fully-connected layer resembling a transformation from 2D to 3D, and transposed convolutions for up-sampling into the BEV dimensions. To create a training signal for this network, we map ground truth segmentation with the ground truth depth data (LiDAR) into the bird's eye view. On top of the output of this CNN, we still apply the proposed refinement module for a fair comparison. The importance of depth prediction becomes clearly evident from Table 2. In this case, not even the refinement-CNN is able to recover. While there can be better architectures for directly predicting a semantic BEV map from the perspective view than our baseline, it is important to note that depth is an intermediary that clearly eases the task by enabling the use of known geometric transformations.

Warping OSM Data: In Table 3, we compare different warping functions and optimization strategies for aligning the OSM data, as described in Sect. 3.3. Our results show that the composition of "Box" (translation, scale and rotation) and "Flow" (displacement field) is superior to individual warps. We can also see that the proposed alignment CNN trained jointly with the refinement module provides the best training signal from OSM data. As already mentioned in Sect. 3.3, LBFG-S alignment failed for around 30% of the training data, which explains the superiority of the proposed CNN for predicting warping parameters.

Qualitative Results: Figure 7 demonstrates the beneficial impact of both the hallucination and refinement modules with several qualitative examples. In the first three cases, we can observe the learned priors of the hallucination CNN that correctly handles largely occluded areas, which is evident from both the hallucinated semantics and the difference in the first two illustrated BEV maps (before and after hallucination). Other examples illustrate how the refinement CNN completes unobserved areas and even completes whole side roads and intersections.

Fig. 8. Two examples of a BEV map including foreground objects, like cars here. For each example, we also shows the input image, the semantic segmentation and the predicted depth map.

4.3   Incorporating Foreground Objects into the BEV Map

Finally, we show how foreground objects like cars or pedestrians can be handled in the proposed framework. Since it is not the main focus of this paper, we use a simple baseline to lift 2D bounding boxes of cars into the BEV map. Importantly, we demonstrate that our refinement module is able to handle foreground objects as well. First we leverage the 3D ground truth annotations of the KITTI data set and estimate the mean dimensions of a 3D bounding box. Then, for a given 2D bounding box in the perspective view, we use the estimated depth map to compute the 3D point of the bottom center of the bounding box, which is then used to translate our prior 3D bounding box in the BEV map. The refinement network takes the initial BEV map that now includes foreground objects. We extend the simulator to render objects as rectangles in the top-view and employ a self-reconstruction loss since OSM cannot provide such information. Figure 8 gives two examples of the obtained BEV-map with foreground objects for illustrative purpose. A full quantitative evaluation for localization accuracy and consistency with background requires significant extensions to be studied in our future work.

5   Conclusion

Our work addresses a complex problem in 3D scene understanding, namely, occlusion-reasoned semantic representation of outdoor scenes in the top-view, using just a single RGB image in the perspective view. This requires solving the canonical challenge of hallucinating semantics and geometry in areas occluded by foreground objects, for which we propose a CNN trained using only standard annotations in the perspective image. Further, we show that adversarial and warping-based refinement allow leveraging simulation and map data as valuable supervisory signals to learn prior knowledge. Quantitative and qualitative evaluations on the KITTI and Cityscapes datasets show attractive results compared to several baselines. While we have shown the feasibility of solving this problem using a single image, incorporating temporal information might be a promising extension for further gains. We finally note that with the use of indoor data sets like [23,25], along with simulators [31] and floor plans [16], a similar framework may be derived for indoor scenes, which will be the subject of our future work.

Acknowledgments. This material is based upon work supported by the National Science Foundation under Grant No. (IIS-1553116). The work was part of M. Zhai's internship at NEC Labs America, in Cupertino.

References

1. Arjovsky, M., Chintala, S., Bottou, L.: Wasserstein generative adversarial networks. In: ICML (2017)
2. Armeni, I., et al.: 3D semantic parsing of large-scale indoor spaces. In: CVPR (2016)

3. Byrd, R.H., Lu, P., Nocedal, J., Zhu, C.: A limited memory algorithm for bound constrained optimization. SIAM J. Sci. Comput. **16**(5), 1190–1208 (1995)
4. Cordts, M., et al.: The cityscapes dataset for semantic urban scene understanding. In: CVPR (2016)
5. Dhiman, V., Tran, Q.H., Corso, J.J., Chandraker, M.: A continuous occlusion model for road scene understanding. In: CVPR (2016)
6. Garg, R., BG, V.K., Carneiro, G., Reid, I.: Unsupervised CNN for single view depth estimation: geometry to the rescue. In: Leibe, B., Matas, J., Sebe, N., Welling, M. (eds.) ECCV 2016. LNCS, vol. 9912, pp. 740–756. Springer, Cham (2016). https://doi.org/10.1007/978-3-319-46484-8_45
7. Geiger, A., Lauer, M., Wojek, C., Stiller, C., Urtasun, R.: 3D traffic scene understanding from movable platforms. In: PAMI (2014)
8. Geiger, A., Lenz, P., Stiller, C., Urtasun, R.: Vision meets Robotics: the KITTI Dataset. Int. J. Robot. Res. (IJRR) (2013)
9. Godard, C., Aodha, O.M., Brostow, G.J.: Unsupervised monocular depth estimation with left-right consistency. In: CVPR (2017)
10. Guo, R., Hoiem, D.: Beyond the line of sight: labeling the underlying surfaces. In: Fitzgibbon, A., Lazebnik, S., Perona, P., Sato, Y., Schmid, C. (eds.) ECCV 2012. LNCS, vol. 7576, pp. 761–774. Springer, Heidelberg (2012). https://doi.org/10.1007/978-3-642-33715-4_55
11. Gupta, S., Davidson, J., Levine, S., Sukthankar, R., Malik, J.: Cognitive mapping and planning for visual navigation. In: CVPR (2017)
12. He, K., Zhang, X., Ren, S., Sun, J.: Deep residual learning for image recognition. In: CVPR (2016)
13. Jaderberg, M., Simonyan, K., Zisserman, A., Kavukcuoglu, K.: Spatial transformer networks. In: NIPS (2015)
14. Kingma, D.P., Ba, J.: Adam: a method for stochastic optimization. In: ICLR (2015)
15. Laina, I., Christian Rupprecht, V.B., Tombari, F., Navab, N.: Deeper depth prediction with fully convolutional residual networks. In: 3DV (2016)
16. Liu, C., Schwing, A.G., Kundu, K., Urtasun, R., Fidler, S.: Rent3D: floor-plan priors for monocular layout estimation. In: CVPR (2015)
17. Liu, M., He, X., Salzmann, M.: Building scene models by completing and hallucinating depth and semantics. In: Leibe, B., Matas, J., Sebe, N., Welling, M. (eds.) ECCV 2016. LNCS, vol. 9910, pp. 258–274. Springer, Cham (2016). https://doi.org/10.1007/978-3-319-46466-4_16
18. Máttyus, G., Wang, S., Fidler, S., Urtasun, R.: HD maps: fine-grained road segmentation by parsing ground and aerial images. In: CVPR (2016)
19. OpenStreetMap contributors: Planet dump. Retrieved from https://planet.osm.org, https://www.openstreetmap.org (2017)
20. Ros, G., Ramos, S., Granados, M., Bakhtiary, A., Vazquez, D., Lopez, A.M.: Vision-based offline-online perception paradigm for autonomous driving. In: WACV (2015)
21. Seff, A., Xiao, J.: Learning from maps: visual common sense for autonomous driving arXiv:1611.08583 (2016)
22. Sengupta, S., Sturgess, P., Ladický, L., Torr, P.H.S.: Automatic dense visual semantic mapping from street-level imagery. In: IROS (2012)
23. Silberman, N., Hoiem, D., Kohli, P., Fergus, R.: Indoor segmentation and support inference from RGBD images. In: Fitzgibbon, A., Lazebnik, S., Perona, P., Sato, Y., Schmid, C. (eds.) ECCV 2012. LNCS, vol. 7576, pp. 746–760. Springer, Heidelberg (2012). https://doi.org/10.1007/978-3-642-33715-4_54
24. Song, S., Chandraker, M.: Robust scale estimation in real-time monocular SFM for autonomous driving. In: CVPR (2014)

25. Song, S., Lichtenberg, S.P., Xiao, J.: SUN RGB-D: a RGB-D scene understanding benchmark suite. In: CVPR (2015)
26. Song, S., Yu, F., Zeng, A., Chang, A.X., Savva, M., Funkhouser, T.: Semantic scene completion from a single depth image. In: CVPR (2017)
27. Sturgess, P., Alahari, K., Ladický, L., Torr, P.H.S.: Combining appearance and structure from motion features for road scene understanding. In: BMVC (2009)
28. Vijayanarasimhan, S., Ricco, S., Schmid, C., Sukthankar, R., Fragkiadaki, K.: SfM-net: learning of structure and motion from video. CoRR abs/1704.07804 (2017)
29. Wang, S., Fidler, S., Urtasun, R.: Holistic 3D scene understanding from a single geo-tagged image. In: CVPR (2015)
30. Wojek, C., Walk, S., Roth, S., Schindler, K., Schiele, B.: Monocular visual scene understanding: understanding multi-object traffic scenes. PAMI **36**, 882–897 (2013)
31. Wu, Y., Wu, Y., Gkioxari, G., Tian, Y.: Building generalizable agents with a realistic and rich 3D environment. CoRR abs/1801.02209 (2018)
32. Yu, F., Koltun, V.: Multi-scale context aggregation by dilated convolutions. In: ICLR (2016)
33. Zbontar, J., LeCun, Y.: Stereo matching by training a convolutional neural network to compare image patches. JMLR **17**, 1–32 (2016)
34. Zhai, M., Bessinger, Z., Workman, S., Jacobs, N.: Predicting ground-level scene layout from aerial imagery. In: CVPR (2017)
35. Zhao, H., Shi, J., Qi, X., Wang, X., Jia, J.: Pyramid scene parsing network. In: CVPR (2017)
36. Zhou, T., Brown, M., Snavely, N., Lowe, D.G.: Unsupervised learning of depth and ego-motion from video. In: CVPR (2017)
37. Zia, M.Z., Stark, M., Schindler, K.: Explicit occlusion modeling for 3D object class representations. In: CVPR (2013)
38. Zia, M.Z., Stark, M., Schindler, K.: Towards Scene Understanding with Detailed 3D Object Representations (2015)

Hierarchical Metric Learning and Matching for 2D and 3D Geometric Correspondences

Mohammed E. Fathy[1], Quoc-Huy Tran[2(✉)], M. Zeeshan Zia[3], Paul Vernaza[2], and Manmohan Chandraker[2,4]

[1] Google Cloud AI, New York, USA
[2] NEC Laboratories America, Inc., Princeton, USA
qhtran@nec.labs.com
[3] Microsoft Hololens, London, UK
[4] University of California, San Diego, US

Abstract. Interest point descriptors have fueled progress on almost every problem in computer vision. Recent advances in deep neural networks have enabled task-specific learned descriptors that outperform hand-crafted descriptors on many problems. We demonstrate that commonly used metric learning approaches do not optimally leverage the feature hierarchies learned in a Convolutional Neural Network (CNN), especially when applied to the task of geometric feature matching. While a metric loss applied to the deepest layer of a CNN, is often expected to yield ideal features irrespective of the task, in fact the growing receptive field as well as striding effects cause shallower features to be better at high precision matching tasks. We leverage this insight together with explicit supervision at multiple levels of the feature hierarchy for better regularization, to learn more effective descriptors in the context of geometric matching tasks. Further, we propose to use activation maps at different layers of a CNN, as an effective and principled replacement for the multi-resolution image pyramids often used for matching tasks. We propose concrete CNN architectures employing these ideas, and evaluate them on multiple datasets for 2D and 3D geometric matching as well as optical flow, demonstrating state-of-the-art results and generalization across datasets.

Keywords: Hierarchical metric learning · Hierarchical matching Geometric correspondences · Dense correspondences

---

Part of this work was done during M. E. Fathy's internship at NEC Labs America. Code and models will be made available at http://www.nec-labs.com/~mas/HiLM/.

Electronic supplementary material The online version of this chapter (https://doi.org/10.1007/978-3-030-01267-0_49) contains supplementary material, which is available to authorized users.

© Springer Nature Switzerland AG 2018
V. Ferrari et al. (Eds.): ECCV 2018, LNCS 11219, pp. 832–850, 2018.
https://doi.org/10.1007/978-3-030-01267-0_49

1   Introduction

The advent of repeatable high curvature point detectors [24,37,40] heralded a revolution in computer vision that shifted the emphasis of the field from holistic object models and direct matching of image patches [67], to highly discriminative hand-crafted descriptors. These descriptors made a mark on a wide array of problems in computer vision, with pipelines created to solve tasks such as optical flow [9], object detection [18], 3D reconstruction [51] and action recognition [55].

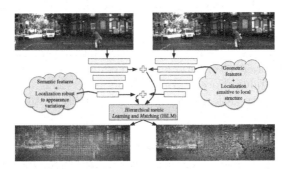

Fig. 1. Our hierarchical metric learning retains the best properties of various levels of abstraction in CNN feature representations. For geometric matching, we combine the robustness of deep layers that imbibe greater invariance, with the localization sensitivity of shallow layers. This allows learning better features, as well as a better correspondence search strategy that progressively exploits features from higher recall (robustness) to higher precision (spatial discrimination).

The current decade is witnessing as wide-ranging a revolution, brought about by the widespread use of deep neural networks. Yet there exist computer vision pipelines that, thanks to extensive engineering efforts, have proven impervious to end-to-end learned solutions. Despite some recent efforts [8,28,54], deep learning solutions do not yet outperform or achieve similar generality as state-of-the-art methods on problems such as structure from motion (SfM) [56] and object pose estimation [44]. Indeed, we see a consensus emerging that some of the systems employing interest point detectors and descriptors are here to stay, but it might instead be advantageous to leverage deep learning for their individual components.

Recently, a few convolutional neural network (CNN) architectures [16,58, 61,65] have been proposed with the aim of learning strong geometric feature descriptors for matching images, and have yielded mixed results [6,49]. We posit that the ability of CNNs to learn representation hierarchies, which has made them so valuable for many visual recognition tasks, becomes a hurdle when it comes to low-level geometric feature learning, unless specific design choices are made in training and inference to exploit that hierarchy. This paper presents such strategies for the problem of *dense geometric correspondence*.

Most recent works employ various metric learning losses and extract feature descriptors from the deepest layers [16,58,61,65], with the expectation that the loss would yield good features right before the location of the loss layer. On the contrary, several studies [64,68] suggest that deeper layers respond to high-level abstract concepts and are by design invariant to local transformations in the input image. However, shallower layers are found to be more sensitive to local structure, which is not exploited by most deep-learning based approaches for geometric correspondence that use only deeper layers. To address this, we propose a novel *hierarchical metric learning* approach that combines the best characteristics of various levels of feature hierarchies, to simultaneously achieve robustness and localization sensitivity. Our framework is widely applicable, which we demonstrate through improved matching for interest points in both 2D and 3D data modalities, on KITTI Flow [42] and 3DMatch [65] datasets, respectively.

Further, we leverage recent studies that highlight the importance of carefully marshaling the training process: (i) by deeply supervising [31,33] intermediate feature layers to learn task-relevant features, and (ii) on-the-fly hard negative mining [16] that forces each iteration of training to achieve more. Finally, we exploit the intermediate activation maps generated within the CNN itself as a proxy for image pyramids traditionally used to enable coarse-to-fine matching [17]. Thus, at test time, we employ a *hierarchical matching* framework, using deeper features to perform coarse matching that benefits from greater context and higher-level visual concepts, followed by a fine grained matching step that involves searching for shallower features. Figure 1 illustrates our proposed approach.

In summary, our contributions include:

- We demonstrate that while in theory metric learning should produce good features irrespective of the layer the loss is applied to, in fact shallower features are superior for high-precision geometric matching tasks, whereas deeper features help obtain greater recall.
- We leverage deep supervision [31,33] for feature descriptor learning, while employing hard negative mining at multiple layers.
- We propose a CNN-driven scheme for coarse-to-fine hierarchical matching, as an effective and principled replacement for conventional pyramid approaches.
- We experimentally validate our ideas by comparing against state-of-the-art geometric matching approaches and feature fusion baselines, as well as perform an ablative analysis of our proposed solution. We evaluate for the tasks of 2D and 3D interest point matching and refinement, as well as optical flow, demonstrating state-of-the-art results and generalization ability.

We review literature in Sect. 2 and introduce our framework in Sect. 3. We discuss experimental results in Sect. 4, concluding the paper in Sect. 5.

2   Related Work

With the use of deep neural networks, many new ideas have emerged both pertaining to learned feature descriptors and directly learning networks for low-level vision tasks in an end-to-end fashion, which we review next.

Hand-Crafted Descriptors. SIFT [40], SURF [7], BRISK [32] were designed to complement high curvature point detectors, with [40] even proposing its own algorithm for such a detector. In fact, despite the interest in learned methods, they are still the state-of-the-art for precision [6,49], even if they are less effective in achieving high recall rates.

Learned Descriptors. While early work [36,39,59] leveraged intermediate activation maps of a CNN trained with an arbitrary loss for keypoint matching, most recent methods rely on an explicit metric loss [16,22,60,61,63,65,66] to learn descriptors. The hidden assumption behind using contrastive or triplet loss at the final layer of a CNN is that this explicit loss will cause the relevant features to emerge at the top of the feature hierarchy. But it has also been observed that early layers of the CNN are the ones that learn local geometric features [64]. Thus, many of these works show superior performance to handcrafted descriptors on semantic matching tasks but often lag behind on geometric matching.

Matching in 2D. LIFT [61] is a moderately deep architecture for end-to-end interest point detection and matching, which uses features at a single level of hierarchy and does not perform dense matching. Universal Correspondence Network (UCN) [16] combines a fully convolutional network in a Siamese setup, with a spatial transformer module [26] and contrastive loss [15] for dense correspondence, to achieve state-of-the-art on semantic matching tasks but not on geometric matching. Like them, we use GPU to speed up k-nearest neighbour for on-the-fly hard negative mining, albeit across multiple feature learning layers. Recently, AutoScaler [58] explicitly applies a learned feature extractor on multiple scales of the input image. While this takes care of the issue that a deep layer may have an unnecessarily large receptive field when learning on the basis of contrastive loss, we argue that it is more elegant for the CNN to "look at the image" at multiple scales, rather than separately process multiple scales.

Matching in 3D. Descriptors for matching in 3D voxel grid representations are learned by 3DMatch [65], employing a Siamese 3D CNN setup on a $30 \times 30 \times 30 \, \text{cm}^3$ voxel grid with a contrastive loss. It performs self-supervised learning by utilizing RGB-D scene reconstructions to obtain ground truth correspondence labels for training, outperforming a state-of-the-art hand-crafted descriptor [48]. Thus, 3DMatch provides an additional testbed to validate our ideas, where we report positive results from incorporating our hierarchical metric learning and matching into the approach.

Learned Optical Flow. Recent works achieve state-of-the-art results on optical flow by training CNNs in an end-to-end fashion [20,25], followed by Conditional Random Field (CRF) inference [45] to capture detailed boundaries. We also demonstrate the efficacy of our matching on optical flow benchmarks. However, we do not use heavily engineered or end-to-end learning for minimizing flow metrics, rather we show that our matches along with an off-the-shelf interpolant [45] already yield strong results.

Deep Supervision. Recent works [31,33,34] suggest that providing explicit supervision to intermediate layers of a CNN can yield higher performance on unseen data, by regularizing the training process. However, to the best of our knowledge, the idea has neither been tested on the task of keypoint matching nor had the learned intermediate features been evaluated. We do both in our work.

Image Pyramids and Hierarchical Fusion. Downsampling pyramids have been a steady fixture of computer vision for exploiting information across multiple scales [41]. Recently, many techniques have been developed for fusing features from different layers within a CNN and producing output at high resolution, *e.g.* semantic segmentation [12,23,43,46], depth estimation [21], and optical flow [20,25]. Inspired by [17] for image alignment, we argue that the growing receptive field in deep CNN layers [64] provides a natural way to parse an image at multiple scales. Thus, in our hierarchical matching scheme, we employ features extracted from a deeper layer with greater receptive field and higher-level semantic notions [68] for coarsely locating the corresponding point, followed by shallower features for precise localization. We show gains in correspondence estimation by using our approach over prior feature fusion methods, *e.g.* [23,43].

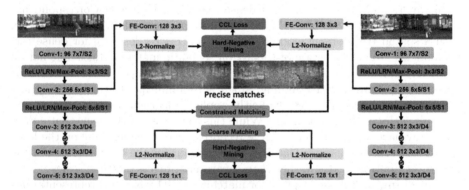

Fig. 2. One instantiation of our proposed ideas. Note that the hard negative mining and CCL losses (red blocks) are relevant for training, and matching (blue blocks) for testing. Convolutional blocks (green) in the left and right Siamese branches share weights. 'S' and 'D' denote striding and dilation offsets.

3 Method

In the following, we first identify the general principles behind our framework, then propose concrete neural network architectures that realize them. In this section, we limit our discussion to models for 2D images. We detail and validate our ideas on the 3DMatch [65] architecture in Sect. 4.3.

3.1 Hierarchical Metric Learning

We follow the standard CNN-based metric learning setup proposed as the Siamese architecture [15]. This involves two Fully Convolutional Networks (FCN) [38] with tied weights, parsing two images of the same scene. We extract features out of the intermediate convolutional layer activation maps at the locations corresponding to the training points, and after normalization obtain their Euclidean distance. At training time, separate contrastive losses are applied to multiple levels in the feature hierarchy to encourage the network to learn embedding functions that minimizes the distance between the descriptors of matching points, while maximizing the distance between unmatched points.

Correspondence Contrastive Loss (CCL). We borrow the correspondence contrastive loss formulation introduced in [16], and adapted from [15]. Here, $\phi_l^I(x)$ represents the feature extracted from the l-th feature level of the reference image I at a pixel location x; similarly, $\phi_l^{I'}(x')$ represents the feature extracted from the l-th feature level of the target image I' at a pixel location x'. Let $\mathcal{D}$ represent a dataset of triplets (x, x', y), where x is a location in the reference image I, x' is a location in the target image I', and $y \in \{0, 1\}$ is 1 if and only if (x, x') are a match. Let m be a margin parameter and c be a window size. We define:

$$\hat{\phi}_l^I(x) := \frac{\phi_l^I(x)}{\|\phi_l^I(x)\|_2}, \qquad d_l(x, x') := \|\hat{\phi}_l^I(x) - \hat{\phi}_l^{I'}(x')\|_2. \tag{1}$$

Then, our training loss, $\mathcal{L}$, sums CCL losses over multiple levels l:

$$\mathcal{L} := \sum_{l=1}^{L} \sum_{(x, x', y) \in \mathcal{D}} y \cdot d_l^2(x, x') + (1 - y) \cdot (\max(0, m - d_l(x, x')))^2. \tag{2}$$

Deep Supervision. Our rationale in applying CCL losses at multiple levels of the feature hierarchy is twofold. Recent studies [31,33] indicate that deep supervision contributes to improved regularization, by encouraging the network early on to learn task-relevant features. Secondly, both deep and shallow layers can be supervised for matching simultaneously within one network.

Hard Negative Mining. Since our training data includes only positive correspondences, we actively search for hard negative matches "on-the-fly" to speed up training and to leverage the latest instance of network weights. We adopt the approach of UCN [16], but in contrast to it, our hard negative mining happens independently for each of the feature levels being supervised.

Network Architectures. We visualize one specific instantiation of the above ideas in Fig. 2, adapting the VGG-M [11] architecture for the task. We retain the first 5 convolutional layers, initializing them with weights pre-trained for ImageNet classification [47]. We use ideas from semantic segmentation literature [12,62] to increase the resolution of the intermediate activation maps by (a) eliminating down-sampling in the second convolutional and pooling layers (setting their stride value to 1, down from 2) (b) increasing the pooling window size for the second layer from 3×3 to 5×5 and (c) dilating [62] the subsequent convolutional layers (*conv3*, *conv4* and *conv5*) to retain their pretrained receptive fields.

At training, the network is provided with a pair of images and a set of point correspondences. The network is replicated in a Siamese scheme [15] during training (with shared weights) where each sub-network processes one image from the pair; and thus after each feed-forward pass, we have 4 feature maps: 2 shallow ones and 2 deep ones, respectively from the second and fifth convolutional layers (*conv2*, *conv5*). We apply supervision after these same layers (*conv2*, *conv5*).

We also experiment with a GoogLeNet [52] baseline as employed in UCN [16]. Specifically, we augment the network with a 1×1 convolutional layer and L2 normalization following the fourth convolutional block (*inception_4a/output*) for learning deep features, as in UCN. In addition, for learning shallow features, we augment the network with a 3×3 convolutional layer right after the second convolutional layer (*conv2/3 × 3*), followed by L2 normalization, but before the corresponding non-linear ReLU squashing function. We extract the shallow and deep feature maps based on the normalized outputs after the second convolutional layer *conv2/3 × 3* and the *inception_4a/output* layers respectively. We provide the detailed architecture of our GoogLeNet variant as supplementary material.

Network Training. We implement our system in Caffe [27] and use ADAM [29] to train our network for 50 K iterations using a base learning rate of 10^{-3} on a P6000 GPU. Pre-trained layers are fine-tuned with a learning rate multiplier of 0.1 whereas the weights of the newly-added feature-extraction layers are randomly initialized using Xavier's method. We use a weight decay parameter of 10^{-4} and L2 weight regularization. During training, each batch consists of three randomly chosen image pairs and we randomly choose 1K positive correspondences from each pair. It takes the VGG-M variant of our system around 43 hours to train whereas it takes 30 hours to train our GoogLeNet-based variant.

3.2   Hierarchical Matching

We adapt and train our networks as described in the previous section, optimizing network weights for matching using features extracted from different layers. Yet, we find that features from different depths offer complementary capabilities as predicted by earlier works [64,68] and confirmed by our empirical evaluation in Sect. 4. Specifically, features extracted from shallower layers obtain superior matching accuracies for smaller distance thresholds (precision), whereas those from deeper layers provide better accuracies for larger distance thresholds (recall). Such coarse-to-fine matching has been well-known in computer vision [41], however recent work highlights how employing CNN feature hierarchies for the task (at least in the context of image alignment [17]) is more robust.

To establish correspondences, we compare the deep and shallow features of the input images I and I' as follows. Assuming the shallow feature coordinates p_s and the deep feature coordinates p_d in the reference image I are related by $p_d = p_s * 1/f$ with a scaling factor f, we first use the deep feature descriptor

$\phi_d^I(p_d)$ in the reference image I to find the point p_d' in the target image I' with $\phi_d^{I'}(p_d')$ closest to $\phi_d^I(p_d)$ with nearest neighbor search.[1] Next, we refine the location of p_d' by searching within a circle of a radius of 32 pixels around $p_s' = p_d' * f$ (assuming input images have the same size, thus, $f' = f$) to find the point $\hat{p}_s'$ whose shallow feature descriptor $\phi_s^{I'}(\hat{p}_s')$ is closest to $\phi_s^I(p_s)$, forming a correspondence $(p_s, \hat{p}_s')$.

Our proposed hierarchical matching is implemented on CUDA and run on a P6000 GPU, requiring an average of 8.41 seconds to densely extract features and compute correspondences for a pair of input images of size 1242×376.

4   Experiments

In this section, we first benchmark our proposed method for 2D correspondence estimation against standard metric learning and matching approaches, feature fusion, as well as state-of-the-art learned and hand-crafted methods for extracting correspondences. Next, we show how our method for correspondence estimation can be applied for optical flow and compare it against recent optical flow methods. Finally, we incorporate our ideas in a state-of-the-art 3D fully convolutional network [65] and show improved performance. In the following, we denote our method as *HiLM*, which is short for *Hi*erarchical metric *L*earning and *M*atching.

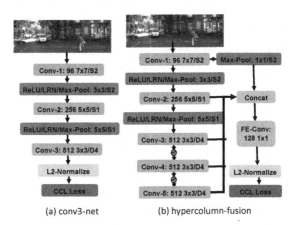

(a) conv3-net   (b) hypercolumn-fusion

Fig. 3. One Siamese branch of two for baseline architectures in our evaluation. The *conv3-net* (a) is obtained by truncating all layers after VGG-M *conv3* in Fig. 2 and adding a convolutional layer, L2 normalization and CCL loss. Other *convi-net* baselines are obtained similarly. The 1×1 max pooling layer after *conv1* in the *hypercolumn-fusion* baseline (b) is added to down sample the *conv1* feature map for valid concatenation with other feature maps. '*S*' and '*D*' denote striding and dilation offsets.

---

[1] If p_d is fractional, we use bilinear interpolation to compute $\phi_d^I(p_d)$.

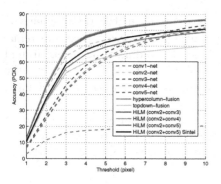 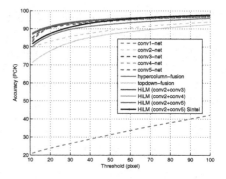

(a) Accuracy over small thresholds   **(b)** Accuracy over large thresholds

Fig. 4. Accuracy of different CNN-based methods for 2D correspondence estimation on KITTI Flow 2015.

4.1   2D Correspondence Experiments

We empirically evaluate our ideas against different approaches for dense correspondence estimation. We first consider metric learning and matching approaches based on feature sets extracted from a single convolutional layer[2], where we separately train five networks, based on the VGG-M baseline in Fig. 2. Each one of the five networks has a different depth and we refer to the i-th network by *convi-net* to indicate that the network is truncated at the i-th convolutional layer (*convi*), for $i \in 1, 2, ..., 5$. We train a *convi-net* network by adding a convolutional layer, L2 normalization, and CCL loss after the output of the last layer (*convi*). Figure 3 (a) shows one branch of the *conv3-net* baseline as an example.

In addition, we also compare our method against two alternatives for fusing features from different layers inspired by ideas from semantic segmentation [23,43]. One is *hypercolumn-fusion* – Fig. 3 (b), where feature sets from all layers (first through fifth) are concatenated for every interest point and a set of 1x1 convolution kernels are trained to fuse features before L2 normalization and CCL loss. Instead of upsampling deeper feature maps as in [23], we extract deep features at higher resolution by setting the stride of multiple convolutional/pooling layers to 1 while dilating the subsequent convolutions appropriately as shown in Fig. 3. Another approach we consider is *topdown-fusion*, where refinement modules similar to [43] are used to refine the top-level *conv5* features gradually down the network by combining with lower-level features till *conv2* (please see supplementary material for details).

We evaluate on KITTI Flow 2015 [42] where all networks are trained on 80% of the image pairs and the remaining 20% are used for evaluation. For a fair comparison, we use the same train-test split for all methods and train each with

---

[2] LIFT [61] is not designed for dense matching and hence not included in our experiments. Note that LIFT also uses features from only a single convolutional layer.

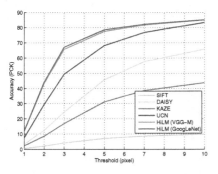 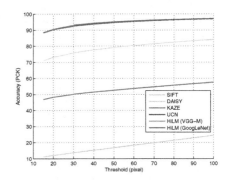

(a) Accuracy over small thresholds   **(b)** Accuracy over large thresholds

Fig. 5. Accuracy of CNN-based and hand-crafted methods for 2D correspondence estimation on KITTI Flow 2015.

1K correspondences per image pair and for 50K iterations. During testing, we use the correspondences $\{(x_i, x_i')\}$ in each image pair (obtained using all non-occluded ground truth flows) for evaluation. Specifically, each method predicts a point $\hat{x}_i'$ in the target image that matches the point x_i from the reference image $\forall i$.

Evaluation Metric. Following prior works [16,39,58], we use Percentage of Correct Keypoints (PCK) as our evaluation metric. Given a pixel threshold θ, the PCK measures the percentage of predicted points $\hat{x}_i'$ that are within θ pixels from the ground truth corresponding point x_i' (and so are considered as correct matches up to θ pixels).

Single-Layer and Feature Fusion Descriptors. We plot PCK curves obtained for all methods under consideration in Fig. 4 where we split the graph into sub-graphs based on the pixel threshold range. These plots reveal that, for smaller thresholds, shallower features (*e.g. conv2-net* with 73.89% @ 5 pixels) provide higher PCK than deeper ones (*e.g. conv5-net* with 61.78% @ 5 pixels), with the exception of *conv1-net* which performs worst. Contrarily, deeper features have better performance for higher thresholds (*e.g. conv5-net* with 87.57% versus *conv2-net* with 81.36% @ 15 pixels). This suggests that, for best performance, one would need to utilize the shallower as well as deeper features produced by the network rather than just the output of the last layer.

The plot also indicates that while baseline approaches for fusing features improve the PCK for smaller thresholds (*e.g. hypercolumn-fusion* with 69.41% versus *conv5-net* with 61.78% @ 5 pixels), they do not perform on par with the simple *conv2*-based features (*e.g. conv2-net* with 73.89% @ 5 pixels).

Different variants of our full approach achieve the highest PCK for smaller thresholds (*e.g.* HiLM (*conv2+conv4*) with 80.17% @ 5 pixels), without losing accuracy for higher thresholds. In fact, our method is able to outperform the *conv2* features (*e.g. conv2-net* with 73.89% @ 5 pixels) although it uses them for refining the rough correspondences estimated by the deeper layers. This is explained by the relative invariance of deeper features to local structure, which helps to avoid matching patches that have similar local appearance but rather belong to different objects.

Generalization. We also perform experiments on cross-domain generalization ability. Specifically, we train HiLM (*conv2+conv5*) on MPI Sintel [10] and evaluate it on KITTI Flow 2015 as the previous experiment, plotting the result in Fig. 4 (black curve). As expected the Sintel model is subpar compared to the same model trained on KITTI (72.37% vs. 79.11% @ 5 pixels), however it outperforms both *hypercolumn-fusion* (69.41%) and *topdown-fusion* (63.14%) trained on KITTI, across all PCK thresholds. Similar generalization results are obtained when cross-training with HPatches [6] (please see supplementary material for details).

Hand-Crafted Descriptors. We also compare the performance of (a) our HiLM (*conv2+conv5*, VGG-M), (b) a variant of our method based on GoogLeNet/ UCN (described in Sect. 3), (c) the original UCN [16], and (d) the following hand-crafted descriptors: SIFT [40], KAZE [2], DAISY [53]. We use the same KITTI Flow 2015 evaluation set utilized in the previous experiment. To evaluate hand-crafted approaches, we use them to compute the descriptors at test pixels in the reference image (for which ground truth correspondences are available) and match the resulting descriptors against the descriptors computed on the target image over a grid of 4 pixel spacing in both directions.

Figure 5 compares the resulting PCKs and shows that our HiLM (VGG-M) outperforms UCN [16] for smaller thresholds (*e.g.* HiLM (VGG-M) with 43.26% versus UCN with 29.38% @ 2 pixels). That difference in performance is not the result of baseline shift since our GoogLeNet variant (same baseline network as UCN) has similar or slightly better performance compared to our VGG-M variant. The graph also indicates the relatively higher invariance of CNN-based descriptors to local structure that allows them to obtain a higher percentage of roughly-localized correspondences (*e.g.* UCN with 83.42%, HiLM (VGG-M) with 85.08%, and HiLM (GoogLeNet) with 85.18%, all at 10 pixel threshold).

Fig. 6. Optical flow pipeline. (a) Input image. (b) Initial HiLM matches. (c) Filtered matches after consistency checks and motion constraints. (d) After interpolation using EpicFlow [45].

Table 1. Quantitative results on KITTI Flow 2015. Following KITTI convention: '*Fl-bl*', '*Fl-fg*', and '*Fl-all*' represent the outlier percentage on background pixels, foreground pixels and all pixels respectively. The methods are ranked by their '*Fl-all*' errors. **Bold** numbers represent best results, while <u>underlined</u> numbers are second best ones. Note that FlowNet2 [25] optimizes flow metric directly, while SDF [4] and SOF [50] require semantic knowledge.

Method	Fl-bg	Fl-fg	Fl-all
FlowNet2 [25]	*10.75%*	**8.75%**	**10.41%**
SDF [4]	**8.61%**	26.69%	*11.62%*
SOF [50]	14.63%	27.73%	16.81%
CNN-HPM [5]	18.33%	24.96%	19.44%
HiLM (Ours)	23.73%	*21.79%*	23.41%
SPM-BP [35]	24.06%	24.97%	24.21%
FullFlow [13]	23.09%	30.11%	24.26%
AutoScaler [58]	21.85%	31.62%	25.64%
EpicFlow [45]	25.81%	33.56%	27.10%
DeepFlow2 [59]	27.96%	35.28%	29.18%
PatchCollider [57]	30.60%	33.09%	31.01%

4.2 Optical Flow Experiments

In this section, we demonstrate the application of our geometric correspondences for obtaining optical flows. We emphasize that the objective here is not to outperform methods that have been extensively engineered [4,25,50] for optical flows, including minimizing flow metric (end-point error) directly, *e.g.* FlowNet2 [25]. Yet, we consider it useful to garner insights from flow benchmarks since the tasks (*i.e.* geometric correspondence and optical flow) are conceptually similar.

Network Architecture. For dense optical flow estimation, we leverage GoogLeNet [52] as our backbone architecture. However, at test time, we modify the trained network to obtain dense per-pixel correspondences. To this end: (i) we set the stride to 1 in the first convolutional and pooling layers (*conv1* and *pool1*), (ii) we set the kernel size of the first pooling layer (*pool1*) to 5 instead of 3, (iii) we set the dilation offset of the second convolutional layer (*conv2*) to 4, and (iv) we set the stride of the second pooling layer (*pool2*) to 4. These changes allow us to obtain our shallow feature maps at the same resolution as the input images ($W \times H$) and the deep feature maps at $W/4 \times H/4$, and to obtain dense per-pixel correspondences faster and with significantly fewer requirements on the GPU memory as compared to an approach that would process the feature maps at full resolution through all layers of the network.

Procedure. We first extract and match feature descriptors for every pixel in the input images using our proposed method. These initial matches are usually contaminated by outliers or incorrect matches. Therefore, we follow the protocol of AutoScaler [58] for outlier removal. In particular, we enforce local motion constraints using a window of $[-240, 240] \times [-240, 240]$ and perform forward-backward consistency checks with a threshold of 0 pixel. These filtered matches are then fed to EpicFlow [45] interpolation for producing the final optical flow output. Figure 6 illustrates an example of this procedure.

Fig. 7. Qualitative results on KITTI Flow 2015. First row: input images. Second row: DeepFlow2 [59]. Third row: EpicFlow [45]. Forth row: SPM-BP [35]. Fifth row: HiLM. Red colors mean high errors while blue colors mean low errors.

Quantitative Evaluation. We tabulate our quantitative evaluation results on KITTI Flow 2015 in Table 1. As mentioned earlier, our objective is not necessarily to obtain the best optical flow performance, rather we wish to emphasize that we are able to provide high-quality interest point matches. In fact, many recent works [4,50] focus on embedding rich domain priors at the level of explicit object classes into their models, which allows them to make good guesses when data is missing (*e.g.* due to occlusions, truncations, homogenous surfaces). Yet, we are able to outperform several methods in our comparisons except [25] for foreground pixels (*i.e.* by *Fl-fg*, HiLM with 21.79% versus other methods with 24.96–35.28%, excluding [25] with 8.75%). As expected, we do not get as good matches in regions of the image where relatively less structure is present (*e.g.* background), and for such regions methods [4,50] employing strong prior models have significant advantages. However, even on background regions, we are able to either beat or perform on par with most of our competitors (*i.e.* by *Fl-bg*, 23.73% versus 18.33–30.60%), including machinery proposed for optical flows such as [13,45,59]. Overall, we outperform 6 state-of-the-art methods evaluated in Table 1 (*i.e.* by *Fl-all*), including the multi-scale correspondence approach of [58].

Qualitative Evaluation. We plot some qualitative results in Fig. 7, to contrast DeepFlow2 [59], EpicFlow [45], and SPM-BP [35] against our method. As expected from the earlier discussion, we observe superior results for our method on the image regions belonging to the vehicles, because of strong local structures, whereas for instance in first column (fourth row) SPM-BP [35] entirely fails on the blue car. We observe errors in the estimates of our method largely in regions which are occluded (surroundings of other cars) or truncated (lower portion of the images), where the competing methods also have high errors.

4.3   3D Correspondence Experiments

To demonstrate the generality of our contributions to different data modalities, we now consider an extension of our proposed method in Sect. 3 to 3D correspondence estimation. In the following, we first present the details of our network architecture and then discuss the results of our quantitative evaluation.

Network Architecture. We use 3DMatch [65] as our baseline architecture. We insert two $3 \times 3 \times 3$ convolutional layers (stride of 2 each) and one $5 \times 5 \times 5$ pooling layer (stride of 1) after the second convolutional layer of 3DMatch to obtain a 512-dimensional vector, which serves as the shallow feature descriptor. Our deep feature descriptor is computed after the eighth convolutional layer in the same manner as 3DMatch. Our hierarchical metric learning scheme again employs two CCL losses (Sect. 3.1) for learning shallow and deep feature descriptors simultaneously. We disable hard negative mining in this experiment to enable a fair comparison with 3DMatch. Our network is implemented in Marvin [1] and trained with stochastic gradient descent using a base learning rate of 10^{-3} for 137 K iterations on a TITAN XP GPU. We use pre-trained weights provided by 3DMatch to initialize the common layers in our network, which have a learning rate multiplier of 0.1, whereas the weights of the newly added layers are initialized using Xavier's method and have a learning rate multiplier of 1.0. We generate correspondence data for training using the same procedure as 3DMatch.

Protocol. 3DMatch evelutes classification accuracy of putative correspondences, using fixed keypoint locations and binary labels. Since our method enables refinement with shallow features and hence shifts hypothesized correspondence location in space, we define a protocol suitable to measure refinement performance. We employ PCK as our evaluation metric, similar to 2D experiments. We generate test data consisting of 10 K ground truth correspondences using the procedure of 3DMatch. We use a region of $30 \times 30 \times 30 \, \mathrm{cm}^3$ centered on the reference keypoint (in the reference "image") following [65] to compute the reference descriptor. This is matched against putative keypoints in a $60 \times 60 \times 60 \, \mathrm{cm}^3$ region (in the target "image"), to refine this coarse prior estimate[3]. Specifically, we divide this region into subvolumes of $30 \times 30 \times 30 \, \mathrm{cm}^3$ and employ our hierarchical matching approach to exhaustively search[4] for the subvolume whose descriptor is most similar to the reference descriptor. In particular, once the coarse matching using deeper feature descriptors yields an approximate

---

[3] In fact, the ground truth keypoint correspondence lies at the center of this region, but this knowledge is not available to the method in any way.

[4] We use a sampling gap of 3 cm along all three dimensions in searching for subvolumes to reduce computational costs.

location in the $60 \times 60 \times 60 \, \text{cm}^3$ region, we constrain the refinement by shallow feature descriptors to a search radius of 15 cm around the approximate location returned from the coarse matching.

Quantitative Evaluation. We compare our complete framework, namely, HiLM (*conv2+conv8*) against variants which are trained with hierarchical metric loss but rely either on deep or shallow features for matching (HiL (*conv8*) and HiL (*conv2*), respectively), and 3DMatch which use only deep features. Figure 8 shows the PCK curves of all competing methods computed over 10K test correspondences generated by the procedure of 3DMatch. From the results, our shallow features trained with hierarchical metric learning are able to outperform their deep counterparts for most PCK thresholds (*e.g.* HiL (*conv2*) with 21.50% versus HiL (*conv8*) with 20.78% @ 9 cm). By utilizing both deep and shallow features, our complete framework achieves higher PCK numbers than its variants and outperforms 3DMatch across all PCK thresholds (*e.g.* HiLM (*conv2+conv8*) with 24.36% versus 3DMatch with 22.04% @ 9 cm).

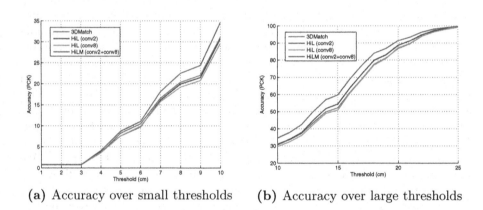

(a) Accuracy over small thresholds   (b) Accuracy over large thresholds

Fig. 8. Accuracy of different CNN-based methods for 3D correspondence estimation.

5   Conclusion and Future Work

We draw inspiration from recent studies [64,68] as well as conventional intuitions about CNN architectures to enhance learned representations for dense 2D and 3D geometric matching. Convolutional network architectures naturally learn hierarchies of features, thus, a contrastive loss applied at a deep layer will return features that are less sensitive to local image structure. We propose to remedy this by employing features at multiple levels of the feature hierarchy for interest point description. Further, we leverage recent ideas in deep supervision to explicitly obtain task-relevant features at intermediate layers. Finally, we exploit the receptive field growth for increasing layer depths as a proxy to replace conventional coarse-to-fine image pyramid approaches for matching. We thoroughly evaluate these ideas realized as concrete network architectures, on challenging benchmark datasets. Our evaluation on the task of explicit keypoint matching outperforms hand-crafted descriptors, a state-of-the-art descriptor learning approach [16], as well as various ablative baselines including hypercolumn-fusion and topdown-fusion. Further, an evaluation for optical flow computation outperforms several competing methods even without extensive engineering or leveraging higher-level semantic scene understanding. Finally, augmenting a recent 3D descriptor learning framework [65] with our ideas yields performance improvements, hinting at wider applicability. Our future work will explore applications of our correspondences, such as flexible ground modeling [3, 19, 30] and geometric registration [14, 65].

References

1. Marvin: a minimalist GPU-only N-dimensional ConvNet framework. http:// marvin.is. Last accessed 2015 Nov 10
2. Alcantarilla, P.F., Bartoli, A., Davison, A.J.: KAZE features. In: Fitzgibbon, A., Lazebnik, S., Perona, P., Sato, Y., Schmid, C. (eds.) ECCV 2012. LNCS, vol. 7577, pp. 214–227. Springer, Heidelberg (2012). https://doi.org/10.1007/978-3-642-33783-3_16
3. Ansari, J.A., Sharma, S., Majumdar, A., Murthy, J.K., Krishna, K.M.: The earth ain't Flat: monocular reconstruction of vehicles on steep and graded roads from a moving camera. In: ArXiv (2018)
4. Bai, M., Luo, W., Kundu, K., Urtasun, R.: Exploiting semantic information and deep matching for optical flow. In: Leibe, B., Matas, J., Sebe, N., Welling, M. (eds.) ECCV 2016. LNCS, vol. 9910, pp. 154–170. Springer, Cham (2016). https://doi.org/10.1007/978-3-319-46466-4_10
5. Bailer, C., Varanasi, K., Stricker, D.: CNN-based patch matching for optical flow with thresholded hinge embedding loss. In: CVPR (2017)
6. Balntas, V., Lenc, K., Vedaldi, A., Mikolajczyk, K.: HPatches: a benchmark and evaluation of handcrafted and learned local descriptors. In: CVPR (2017)
7. Bay, H., Tuytelaars, T., Van Gool, L.: SURF: speeded up robust features. In: Leonardis, A., Bischof, H., Pinz, A. (eds.) ECCV 2006. LNCS, vol. 3951, pp. 404–417. Springer, Heidelberg (2006). https://doi.org/10.1007/11744023_32
8. Brachmann, E., Krull, A., Nowozin, S., Shotton, J., Frank Michel, S.G., Rother, C.: DSAC - differentiable RANSAC for camera localization. In: CVPR (2017)
9. Brox, T., Malik, J.: Large displacement optical flow: descriptor matching in variational motion estimation. PAMI 33(3), 500–513 (2011)
10. Butler, D.J., Wulff, J., Stanley, G.B., Black, M.J.: A naturalistic open source movie for optical flow evaluation. In: Fitzgibbon, A., Lazebnik, S., Perona, P., Sato, Y., Schmid, C. (eds.) ECCV 2012. LNCS, vol. 7577, pp. 611–625. Springer, Heidelberg (2012). https://doi.org/10.1007/978-3-642-33783-3_44
11. Chatfield, K., Simonyan, K., Vedaldi, A., Zisserman, A.: Return of the devil in the details: delving deep into convolutional nets. In: BMVC (2014)
12. Chen, L.C., Papandreou, G., Kokkinos, I., Murphy, K., Yuille, A.L.: DeepLab: semantic image segmentation with deep convolutional nets, atrous convolution, and fully connected CRFs. PAMI (2017)
13. Chen, Q., Koltun, V.: Full flow: optical flow estimation by global optimization over regular grids. In: CVPR (2016)

14. Choi, S., Zhou, Q.Y., Koltun, V.: Robust reconstruction of indoor scenes. In: CVPR (2015)
15. Chopra, S., Hadsell, R., LeCun, Y.: Learning a similarity metric discriminatively, with application to face verification. In: CVPR (2005)
16. Choy, C.B., Gwak, J., Savarese, S., Chandraker, M.: Universal correspondence network. In: NIPS (2016)
17. Czarnowski, J., Leutenegger, S., Davison, A.J.: Semantic texture for robust dense tracking. In: ICCVW (2017)
18. Dalal, N., Triggs, B.: Histogram of oriented gradients for human detection. In: CVPR (2005)
19. Dhiman, V., Tran, Q.H., Corso, J.J., Chandraker, M.: A Continuous occlusion model for road scene understanding. In: CVPR (2016)
20. Dosovitskiy, A., et al.: FlowNet: learning optical flow with convolutional networks. In: ICCV (2015)
21. Eigen, D., Puhrsch, C., Fergus, R.: Depth map prediction from a single image using a multi-scale deep network. In: NIPS (2014)
22. Gadot, D., Wolf, L.: PatchBatch: a batch augmented loss for optical flow. In: CVPR (2016)
23. Hariharan, B., Arbeláez, P., Girshick, R., Malik, J.: Hypercolumns for object segmentation and fine-grained localization. In: CVPR (2015)
24. Harris, C., Stephens, M.: A combined corner and edge detector. In: Proceedings of the Alvey Vision Conference (AVC) (1988)
25. Ilg, E., Mayer, N., Saikia, T., Keuper, M., Dosovitskiy, A., Brox, T.: FlowNet 2.0: evolution of optical flow estimation with deep networks. In: CVPR (2017)
26. Jaderberg, M., Simonyan, K., Zisserman, A., Kavukcuoglu, K.: Spatial transformer networks. In: NIPS (2015)
27. Jia, Y., et al.: Caffe: convolutional architecture for fast feature embedding. In: ACM Multimedia (2014)
28. Kendall, A., Grimes, M., Cipolla, R.: PoseNet: a convolutional network for real-time 6-DOF camera relocalization. In: ICCV (2015)
29. Kingma, D., Ba, J.: Adam: a method for stochastic optimization. ICLR (2014)
30. Lee, B., Daniilidis, K., Lee, D.D.: Online self-supervised monocular visual odometry for ground vehicles. In: ICRA (2015)
31. Lee, C.Y., Xie, S., Gallagher, P., Zhang, Z., Tu, Z.: Deeply-supervised nets. AISTATS (2015)
32. Leutenegger, S., Chli, M., Siegwart, R.Y.: BRISK: binary robust invariant scalable keypoints. In: ICCV (2011)
33. Li, C., Zia, M.Z., Tran, Q.H., Yu, X., Hager, G.D., Chandraker, M.: Deep supervision with shape concepts for occlusion-aware 3D object parsing. In: CVPR (2017)
34. Li, C., Zia, M.Z., Tran, Q.H., Yu, X., Hager, G.D., Chandraker, M.: Deep supervision with intermediate concepts. In: ArXiv (2018)
35. Li, Y., Min, D., Brown, M.S., Do, M.N., Lu, J.: SPM-BP: Sped-up patchmatch belief propagation for continuous MRFs. In: ICCV (2015)
36. Lin, K., Lu, J., Chen, C.S., Zhou, J.: Learning compact binary descriptors with unsupervised deep neural networks. In: CVPR (2016)
37. Lindeberg, T.: Feature detection with automatic scale selection. IJCV 30(2), 79–116 (1998)
38. Long, J., Shelhamer, E., Darrell, T.: Fully convolutional networks for semantic segmentation. In: CVPR (2015)
39. Long, J.L., Zhang, N., Darrel, T.: Do convnets learn correspondence? In: NIPS (2014)

40. Lowe, D.G.: Distinctive image features from scale-invariant keypoints. IJCV **60**(2), 91–110 (2004)
41. Lucas, B.D., Kanade, T.: Optical navigation by the method of differences. In: IJCAI (1985)
42. Menze, M., Geiger, A.: Object scene flow for autonomous vehicles. In: CVPR (2015)
43. Pinheiro, P.O., Lin, T.-Y., Collobert, R., Dollár, P.: Learning to refine object segments. In: Leibe, B., Matas, J., Sebe, N., Welling, M. (eds.) ECCV 2016. LNCS, vol. 9905, pp. 75–91. Springer, Cham (2016). https://doi.org/10.1007/978-3-319-46448-0_5
44. Rad, M., Lepetit, V.: BB8: a scalable, accurate, robust to partial occlusion method for predicting the 3D poses of challenging objects without using depth. In: ICCV (2017)
45. Revaud, J., Weinzaepfel, P., Harchaoui, Z., Schmid, C.: EpicFlow: edge-preserving interpolation of correspondences for optical flow. In: CVPR (2015)
46. Ronneberger, O., Fischer, P., Brox, T.: U-Net: convolutional networks for biomedical image segmentation. In: Navab, N., Hornegger, J., Wells, W.M., Frangi, A.F. (eds.) MICCAI 2015. LNCS, vol. 9351, pp. 234–241. Springer, Cham (2015). https://doi.org/10.1007/978-3-319-24574-4_28
47. Russakovsky, O., Deng, J., Su, H., Krause, J., Satheesh, S., Ma, S., Huang, Z., Karpathy, A., Khosla, A., Bernstein, M., Berg, A.C., Fei-Fei, L.: Imagenet large scale visual recognition challenge. IJCV **115**(3), 211–252 (2015)
48. Rusu, R.B., Blodow, N., Beetz, M.: Fast point feature histograms (FPFH) for 3D registration. In: ICRA (2009)
49. Schönberger, J.L., Hardmeier, H., Sattler, T., Pollefeys, M.: Comparative evaluation of hand-crafted and learned local features. In: CVPR (2017)
50. Sevilla-Lara, L., Sun, D., Jampani, V., Black, M.J.: Optical flow with semantic segmentation and localized layers. In: CVPR (2016)
51. Snavely, N., Seitz, S.M., Szeliski, R.: Photo tourism: exploring photo collections in 3D. TOG **25**(3), 835–846 (2006)
52. Szegedy, C., et al.: Going deeper with convolutions. In: CVPR (2015)
53. Tola, E., Lepetit, V., Fua, P.: DAISY: an efficient dense descriptor applied to wide-baseline stereo. PAMI **32**(5), 815–830 (2010)
54. Vijayanarasimhan, S., Ricco, S., Schmid, C., Sukthankar, R., Fragkiadaki, K.: SfM-Net: learning of structure and motion from video. In: ArXiv (2017)
55. Wang, H., Kläser, A., Schmid, C., Liu, C.L.: Action recognition by dense trajectories. In: CVPR (2011)
56. Wang, S., Clark, R., Wen, H., Trigoni, N.: DeepVO: towards end-to-end visual odometry with deep recurrent convolutional neural networks. In: ICRA (2017)
57. Wang, S., Fanello, S., Rhemann, C., Izadi, S., Kohli, P.: The global patch collider. In: CVPR (2016)
58. Wang, S., Luo, L., Zhang, N., Li, J.: AutoScaler: scale-attention networks for visual correspondence. In: BMVC (2017)
59. Weinzaepfel, P., Revaud, J., Harchaoui, Z., Schmid, C.: DeepFlow: large displacement optical flow with deep matching. In: ICCV (2013)
60. Yang, T.Y., Hsu, J.H., Lin, Y.Y., Chuang, Y.Y.: DeepCD: learning deep complementary descriptors for patch representations. In: ICCV (2017)
61. Yi, K.M., Trulls, E., Lepetit, V., Fua, P.: LIFT: learned invariant feature transform. In: Leibe, B., Matas, J., Sebe, N., Welling, M. (eds.) ECCV 2016. LNCS, vol. 9910, pp. 467–483. Springer, Cham (2016). https://doi.org/10.1007/978-3-319-46466-4_28

62. Yu, F., Koltun, V.: Multi-scale context aggregation by dilated convolutions. In: ICLR (2016)
63. Zbontar, J., LeCun, Y.: Stereo matching by training a convolutional neural network to compare image patches. J. Mach. Learn. Res. (JMLR) **17**, 1–32 (2016)
64. Zeiler, M.D., Fergus, R.: Visualizing and understanding convolutional networks. In: Fleet, D., Pajdla, T., Schiele, B., Tuytelaars, T. (eds.) ECCV 2014. LNCS, vol. 8689, pp. 818–833. Springer, Cham (2014). https://doi.org/10.1007/978-3-319-10590-1_53
65. Zeng, A., Song, S., Nießner, M., Fisher, M., Xiao, J., Funkhouser, T.: 3DMatch: learning local geometric descriptors from RGB-D reconstructions. In: CVPR (2017)
66. Zhang, X., Yu, F.X., Kumar, S., Chang, S.F.: Learning spread-out local feature descriptors. In: ICCV (2017)
67. Zhang, Z., Deriche, R., Faugeras, O., Luong, Q.T.: A robust technique for matching two uncalibrated images through the recovery of the unknown epipolar geometry. Artif. Intell. **78**, 87–119 (1995)
68. Zhou, B., Khosla, A., Lapedriza, A., Oliva, A., Torralba, A.: Object detectors emerge in deep scene CNNs. In: ICLR (2015)

Deep Component Analysis via Alternating Direction Neural Networks

Calvin Murdock$^{(\boxtimes)}$, Ming-Fang Chang, and Simon Lucey

Carnegie Mellon University, Pittsburgh, USA
{cmurdock,mingfanc,slucey}@cs.cmu.edu

Abstract. Despite a lack of theoretical understanding, deep neural networks have achieved unparalleled performance in a wide range of applications. On the other hand, shallow representation learning with component analysis is associated with rich intuition and theory, but smaller capacity often limits its usefulness. To bridge this gap, we introduce Deep Component Analysis (DeepCA), an expressive multilayer model formulation that enforces hierarchical structure through constraints on latent variables in each layer. For inference, we propose a differentiable optimization algorithm implemented using recurrent Alternating Direction Neural Networks (ADNNs) that enable parameter learning using standard backpropagation. By interpreting feed-forward networks as single-iteration approximations of inference in our model, we provide both a novel perspective for understanding them and a practical technique for constraining predictions with prior knowledge. Experimentally, we demonstrate performance improvements on a variety of tasks, including single-image depth prediction with sparse output constraints.

Keywords: Component analysis · Deep learning · Constraints

1 Introduction

Deep convolutional neural networks have achieved remarkable success in the field of computer vision. While far from new [24], the increasing availability of extremely large, labeled datasets along with modern advances in computation with specialized hardware have resulted in state-of-the-art performance in many problems, including essentially all visual learning tasks. Examples include image classification [19], object detection [20], and semantic segmentation [10]. Despite a rich history of practical and theoretical insights about these problems, modern deep learning techniques typically rely on task-agnostic models and poorly-understood heuristics. However, recent work [6,28,43] has shown that specialized architectures incorporating classical domain knowledge can increase parameter efficiency, relax training data requirements, and improve performance.

Prior to the advent of modern deep learning, optimization-based methods like component analysis and sparse coding dominated the field of representation

© Springer Nature Switzerland AG 2018
V. Ferrari et al. (Eds.): ECCV 2018, LNCS 11219, pp. 851–867, 2018.
https://doi.org/10.1007/978-3-030-01267-0_50

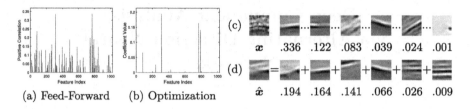

(a) Feed-Forward   (b) Optimization

Fig. 1. An example of the "explaining away" conditional dependence provided by optimization-based inference. Sparse representations constructed by feed-forward non-negative soft thresholding (a) have many more non-zero elements due to redundancy and spurious activations (c). On the other hand, sparse representations found by ℓ_1-penalized, nonnegative least-squares optimization (b) yield a more parsimonious set of components (d) that optimally reconstruct approximations of the data.

learning. These techniques use structured matrix factorization to decompose data into linear combinations of shared components. Latent representations are inferred by minimizing reconstruction error subject to constraints that enforce properties like uniqueness and interpretability. Importantly, unlike feed-forward alternatives that construct representations in closed-form via independent feature detectors, this iterative optimization-based approach naturally introduces conditional dependence between features in order to best explain data, a useful phenomenon commonly referred to as "explaining away" within the context of graphical models [4]. An example of this effect is shown in Fig. 1, which compares sparse representations constructed using feed-forward soft thresholding with those given by optimization-based inference with an ℓ_1 penalty. While many components in an overcomplete set of features may have high-correlation with an image, constrained optimization introduces competition between components resulting in more parsimonious representations.

Component analysis methods are also often guided by intuitive goals of incorporating prior knowledge into learned representations. For example, statistical independence allows for the separation of signals into distinct generative sources [22], non-negativity leads to parts-based decompositions of objects [25], and sparsity gives rise to locality and frequency selectivity [35]. Due to the difficulty of enforcing intuitive constraints like these with feed-forward computations, deep learning architectures are instead often motivated by distantly-related biological systems [39] or poorly-understand internal mechanisms such as covariate shift [21] and gradient flow [17]. Furthermore, while a theoretical understanding of deep learning is fundamentally lacking [47], even non-convex formulations of matrix factorization are often associated with guarantees of convergence [2], generalization [29], uniqueness [13], and even global optimality [16].

In order to unify the intuitive and theoretical insights of component analysis with the practical advances made possible through deep learning, we introduce the framework of Deep Component Analysis (DeepCA). This novel model formulation can be interpreted as a multilayer extension of traditional component analysis in which multiple layers are learned jointly with intuitive constraints

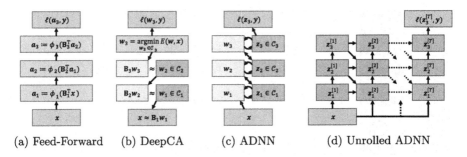

(a) Feed-Forward   (b) DeepCA   (c) ADNN   (d) Unrolled ADNN

Fig. 2. A comparison between feed-forward neural networks and the proposed deep component analysis (DeepCA) model. Standard deep networks construct learned representations as feed-forward compositions of nonlinear functions (a). DeepCA instead treats them as unknown latent variables to be inferred by constrained optimization (b). To accomplish this, we propose a differentiable inference algorithm that can be expressed as an Alternating Direction Neural Network (ADNN) (c), a recurrent generalization of feed-forward networks that can be unrolled to a fixed number of iterations for learning via backpropagation (d).

intended to encode structure and prior knowledge. DeepCA can also be motivated from the perspective of deep neural networks by relaxing the implicit assumption that the input to a layer is constrained to be the output of the previous layer, as shown in Eq. 1 below. In a feed-forward network (left), the output of layer j, denoted $\boldsymbol{a}_j$, is given in closed-form as a nonlinear function of $\boldsymbol{a}_{j-1}$. DeepCA (right) instead takes a generative approach in which the latent variables $\boldsymbol{w}_j$ associated with layer j are *inferred* to optimally reconstruct $\boldsymbol{w}_{j-1}$ as a linear combination of learned components subject to some constraints $\mathcal{C}_j$.

$$\text{Feed-Forward: } \boldsymbol{a}_j = \phi(\mathbf{B}_j^{\mathsf{T}} \boldsymbol{a}_{j-1}) \implies \text{DeepCA: } \mathbf{B}_j \boldsymbol{w}_j \approx \boldsymbol{w}_{j-1} \text{ s.t. } \boldsymbol{w}_j \in \mathcal{C}_j \quad (1)$$

From this perspective, intermediate network "activations" cannot be found in closed-form but instead require explicitly solving an optimization problem. While a variety of different techniques could be used for performing this inference, we propose the Alternating Direction Method of Multipliers (ADMM) [5]. Importantly, we demonstrate that after proper initialization, a single iteration of this algorithm is equivalent to a pass through an associated feed-forward neural network with nonlinear activation functions interpreted as proximal operators corresponding to penalties or constraints on the coefficients. The full inference procedure can thus be implemented using Alternating Direction Neural Networks (ADNN), recurrent generalizations of feed-forward networks that allow for parameter learning using backpropagation. A comparison between standard neural networks and DeepCA is shown in Fig. 2. Experimentally, we demonstrate that recurrent passes through convolutional neural networks enable better sparsity control resulting in consistent performance improvements in both supervised and unsupervised tasks without introducing any additional parameters.

More importantly, DeepCA also allows for other constraints that would be impossible to effectively enforce with a single feed-forward pass through a net-

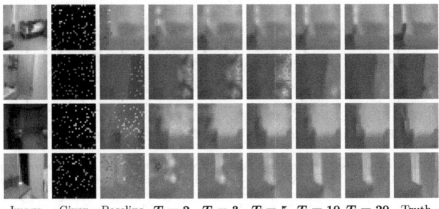

Image   Given   Baseline $T = 2$ $T = 3$ $T = 5$ $T = 10$ $T = 20$ Truth

Fig. 3. A demonstration of DeepCA applied to single-image depth prediction using images concatenated with sparse sets of known depth values as input. Baseline feed-forward networks are not guaranteed to produce outputs that are consistent with the given depth values. In comparison, ADNNs with an increasing number of iterations ($T > 1$) learn to satisfy the sparse output constraints, resolving ambiguities for more accurate predictions without unrealistic discontinuities.

work. As an example, we consider the task of single-image depth prediction, a difficult problem due to the absence of three-dimensional information such as scale and perspective. In many practical scenarios, however, sparse sets of known depth outputs are available for resolving these ambiguities to improve accuracy. This prior knowledge can come from additional sensor modalities like LIDAR or from other 3D reconstruction algorithms that provide sparse depths around textured image regions. Feed-forward networks have been proposed for this problem by concatenating known depth values as an additional input channel [30]. However, while this provides useful context, predictions are not guaranteed to be consistent with the given outputs leading to unrealistic discontinuities. In comparison, DeepCA enforces the constraints by treating predictions as unknown latent variables. Some examples of how this behavior can resolve ambiguities are shown in Fig. 3 where ADNNs with additional iterations learn to propagate information from the given depth values to produce more accurate predictions.

In addition to practical advantages, our model also provides a novel perspective for conceptualizing deep learning techniques. Specifically, rectified linear unit (ReLU) activation functions [14], which are ubiquitous among many state-of-the-art models in a variety of applications, are equivalent to ℓ_1-penalized, sparse projections onto non-negativity constraints. Alongside the interpretation of feed-forward networks as single-iteration approximations of reconstruction objective functions, this suggests new insights towards better understanding the effectiveness of deep neural networks from the perspective of sparse approximation theory.

2   Background and Related Work

In order to motivate our approach, we first provide some background on matrix factorization, component analysis, and deep neural networks.

Component analysis is a common approach for shallow representation learning that approximately decomposes data $\boldsymbol{x} \in \mathbb{R}^d$ into linear combinations of learned components in $\mathbf{B} \in \mathbb{R}^{d \times k}$. This is typically accomplished by minimizing reconstruction error subject to constraints $\mathcal{C}$ on the coefficients that serve to resolve ambiguity or incorporate prior knowledge such as low-rank structure or sparsity. Some examples include Principal Component Analysis (PCA) [44] for dimensionality reduction and sparse dictionary learning [2] which accommodates overcomplete representations by enforcing sparsity.

While the problem of learning both the components and coefficients is typically non-convex, its structure naturally suggests simple alternating minimization strategies that are often guaranteed to converge [45]. However, these techniques typically require careful initialization in order to avoid poor local minima. This differs from backpropagation with stochastic gradient descent wherein random initializations are often sufficient. Alternatively, we consider a nested optimization problem that separates learning from inference:

$$\arg\min_{\mathbf{B}} \sum_{i=1}^{n} \tfrac{1}{2} \|\boldsymbol{x}^{(i)} - \mathbf{B}\boldsymbol{f}(\boldsymbol{x}^{(i)})\|_2^2 \quad \text{s.t.} \ \ \boldsymbol{f}(\boldsymbol{x}) = \arg\min_{w \in \mathcal{C}} \tfrac{1}{2} \|\boldsymbol{x} - \mathbf{B}\boldsymbol{w}\|_2^2 \quad (2)$$

Here, the inference function $\boldsymbol{f} : \mathbb{R}^d \to \mathbb{R}^k$ is a potentially nonlinear transformation that maps data to their corresponding representations by solving an optimization problem with fixed parameters. For unconstrained PCA with orthogonal components, this inference problem has a simple closed-form solution given by the linear transformation $\boldsymbol{f}^{\mathrm{PCA}}(\boldsymbol{x}) = \mathbf{B}^{\mathsf{T}}\boldsymbol{x}$. Substituting this into Eq. 2 results in a linear autoencoder with one hidden layer and tied weights, which has the same unique global minimum but can be trained by backpropagation [1].

With general constraints, inference typically cannot be accomplished in closed form but must instead rely on an iterative optimization algorithm. However, if this algorithm is composed as a finite sequence of differentiable transformations, then the model parameters can still be learned in the same way by backpropagating gradients through the steps of the inference algorithm. We extend this idea by representing an algorithm for inference in our DeepCA model as a recurrent neural network unrolled to a fixed number of iterations.

Recently, deep neural networks have emerged as the preferred alternative to component analysis for representation learning of visual data. Their ability to jointly learn multiple layers of abstraction has been shown to allow for encoding increasingly complex features such as textures and object parts [26]. Unlike with component analysis, inference is given in closed-form by design. Specifically, a representation is constructed by passing an image $\boldsymbol{x}$ through the composition of alternating linear transformations with parameters $\mathbf{B}_j$ and $\boldsymbol{b}_j$ and fixed nonlinear activation functions ϕ_j for layers $j = 1, \ldots, l$ as follows:

$$\boldsymbol{f}^{\mathrm{DNN}}(\boldsymbol{x}) = \phi_l\big(\mathbf{B}_l^{\mathsf{T}} \cdots \phi_2(\mathbf{B}_2^{\mathsf{T}}(\phi_1(\mathbf{B}_1^{\mathsf{T}}\boldsymbol{x} - \boldsymbol{b}_1) - \boldsymbol{b}_2) \cdots - \boldsymbol{b}_l\big) \quad (3)$$

Instead of considering the forward pass of a neural network as an arbitrary nonlinear function, we interpret it as a method for approximate inference in an unsupervised generative model. This follows from previous work which has shown it to be equivalent to bottom-up inference in a probabilistic graphical model [38] or approximate inference in a multi-layer convolutional sparse coding model [36,40]. However, these approaches have limited practical applicability due to their reliance on careful hyperparameter selection and specialized optimization algorithms. While ADMM has been proposed as a gradient-free alternative to backpropagation for parameter learning [42], we use it only for inference which allows for simpler learning using backpropagation with arbitrary loss functions.

Aside from ADNNs, recurrent feedback has been proposed in other models to improve performance by iteratively refining predictions, especially for applications such as human pose estimation or image segmentation where outputs have complex correlation patterns [3,7,27]. While some methods also implement feedback by directly unrolling iterative algorithms, they are often geared towards specific applications such as graphical model inference [11,18], solving under-determined inverse problems [12,15,41], or image alignment [28]. Similar to [46], DeepCA provides a more general mechanism for low-level feedback in arbitrary neural networks, but it is motivated by the more interpretable goal of minimizing reconstruction error subject to constraints on network activations.

3   Deep Component Analysis

Deep Component Analysis generalizes the shallow inference objective function in Eq. 2 by introducing additional layers $j = 1, \ldots, l$ with parameters $\mathbf{B}_j \in \mathbb{R}^{p_{j-1} \times p_j}$. Optimal DeepCA inference can then be accomplished by solving:

$$f^*(x) = \underset{\{w_j\}}{\arg\min} \sum_{j=1}^{l} \tfrac{1}{2} \|w_{j-1} - \mathbf{B}_j w_j\|_2^2 + \Phi_j(w_j) \quad \text{s.t. } w_0 = x \qquad (4)$$

Instead of constraint sets $\mathcal{C}_j$, we use penalty functions $\Phi_j : \mathbb{R}^{p_j} \to \mathbb{R}$ to enable more general priors. Note that hard constraints can still be represented by indicator functions $I(w_j \in \mathcal{C}_j)$ that equal zero if $w_j \in \mathcal{C}_j$ and infinity otherwise. While we use pre-multiplication with a weight matrix $\mathbf{B}_j$ to simplify notation, our method also supports any linear transformation by replacing transposed weight matrix multiplication with its corresponding adjoint operator. For example, the adjoint of convolution is transposed convolution, a popular approach to upsampling in convolutional networks [34].

If the penalty functions are convex, this problem is also convex and can be solved using standard optimization methods. While this appears to differ substantially from inference in deep neural networks, we later show that it can be seen as a generalization of the feed-forward inference function in Eq. 3. In the remainder of this section, we justify the use of penalty functions in lieu of explicit nonlinear activation functions by drawing connections between non-negative ℓ_1 regularization and ReLU activation functions. We then propose a general algorithm for solving Eq. 4 for the unknown coefficients and formalize the relationship between DeepCA and traditional deep neural networks, which enables parameter learning via backpropagation.

3.1 From Activation Functions to Constraints

Before introducing our inference algorithm, we first discuss the connection between penalties and their nonlinear proximal operators, which forms the basis of the close relationship between DeepCA and traditional neural networks. Ubiquitous within the field of convex optimization, proximal algorithms [37] are methods for solving nonsmooth optimization problems. Essentially, these techniques work by breaking a problem down into a sequence of smaller problems that can often be solved in closed-form by proximal operators $\phi : \mathbb{R}^d \to \mathbb{R}^d$ associated with penalty functions $\Phi : \mathbb{R}^d \to \mathbb{R}$ given by the solution to the following optimization problem, which generalizes projection onto a constraint set:

$$\phi(\boldsymbol{w}) = \arg\min_{\boldsymbol{w}'} \tfrac{1}{2} \left\| \boldsymbol{w} - \boldsymbol{w}' \right\|_2^2 + \Phi(\boldsymbol{w}') \tag{5}$$

Within the framework of DeepCA, we interpret nonlinear activation functions in deep networks as proximal operators associated with convex penalties on latent coefficients in each layer. While this connection cannot be used to generalize all nonlinearities, many can naturally be interpreted as proximal operators. For example, the sparsemax activation function is a projection onto the probability simplex [31]. Similarly, the ReLU activation function is a projection onto the nonnegative orthant. When used with a negative bias $\boldsymbol{b}$, it is equivalent to nonnegative soft-thresholding $\mathcal{S}_{\boldsymbol{b}}^+$, the proximal operator associated with nonnegative ℓ_1 regularization:

$$\Phi^{\ell_1^+}(\boldsymbol{w}) = I(\boldsymbol{w} \geq 0) + \textstyle\sum_p b_p |w_p| \quad \implies \quad \phi^{\ell_1^+}(\boldsymbol{w}) = \mathcal{S}_{\boldsymbol{b}}^+(\boldsymbol{w}) = \mathrm{ReLU}(\boldsymbol{w} - \boldsymbol{b}) \tag{6}$$

While this equivalence has been noted previously as a means to theoretically analyze convolutional neural networks [36], DeepCA supports optimizing the bias $\boldsymbol{b}$ as an ℓ_1 penalty hyperparameter via backpropagation for adaptive regularization, which results in better control of representation sparsity.

In addition to standard activation functions, DeepCA also allows for enforcing additional constraints that encode prior knowledge if their corresponding proximal operators can be computed efficiently. For our example of single-image depth prediction with a sparse set of known outputs $\boldsymbol{y}$ provided as prior knowledge, the penalty function on the final output $\boldsymbol{w}_l$ is $\Phi_l(\boldsymbol{w}_l) = I(\mathbf{S}\boldsymbol{w}_l = \boldsymbol{y})$ where the selector matrix $\mathbf{S}$ extracts the indices corresponding to the known outputs in $\boldsymbol{y}$. The associated proximal operator ϕ_l projects onto this constraint set by simply correcting the outputs that disagree with the known constraints. Note that this would not be an effective output nonlinearity in a feed-forward network because, while the constraints would be technically satisfied, there is nothing to enforce that they be consistent with neighboring predictions leading to unrealistic discontinuities. In contrast, DeepCA inference minimizes the reconstruction error at each layer subject to these constraints by taking multiple iterations through the network.

3.2   Inference by the Alternating Direction Method of Multipliers

With the model parameters fixed, we solve our DeepCA inference problem using the Alternating Direction Method of Multipliers (ADMM), a general optimization technique that has been successfully used in a wide variety of applications [5]. To derive the algorithm applied to our problem, we first modify our objective function by introducing auxiliary variables z_j that we constrain to be equal to the unknown coefficients w_j, as shown in Eq. 7 below.

$$\underset{\{w_j, z_j\}}{\arg\min} \sum_{j=1}^{l} \tfrac{1}{2} \|z_{j-1} - \mathbf{B}_j w_j\|_2^2 + \varPhi_j(z_j) \quad \text{s.t. } w_0 = x, \forall j : w_j = z_j \qquad (7)$$

From this, we construct the augmented Lagrangian $\mathcal{L}_\rho$ with dual variables $\boldsymbol{\lambda}$ and a quadratic penalty hyperparameter $\rho = 1$:

$$\mathcal{L}_\rho = \sum_{j=1}^{l} \tfrac{1}{2} \|z_{j-1} - \mathbf{B}_j w_j\|_2^2 + \varPhi_j(z_j) + \boldsymbol{\lambda}_j^{\mathsf{T}}(w_j - z_j) + \tfrac{\rho}{2} \|w_j - z_j\|_2^2 \qquad (8)$$

The ADMM algorithm then proceeds by iteratively minimizing $\mathcal{L}_\rho$ with respect to each set of variables with the others fixed, breaking our full inference problem into smaller pieces that can each be solved in closed form. Due to the decoupling of layers in our DeepCA model, the latent activations can be updated incrementally by stepping through each layer in succession, resulting in faster convergence and computations that mirror the computational structure of deep neural networks. With only one layer, our objective function is separable and so this algorithm reduces to the classical two-block ADMM, which has extensive convergence guarantees [5]. For multiple layers, however, our problem becomes non-separable and so this algorithm can be seen as an instance of cyclical multi-block ADMM with quadratic coupling terms. While our experiments have shown this approach to be effective in our applications, theoretical analysis of its convergence properties is still an active area of research [9].

A single iteration of our algorithm proceeds by taking the following steps for all layers $j = 1, \ldots, l$ in succession:

(1.) First, w_j is updated by minimizing the Lagrangian after fixing the associated auxiliary variable z_j from the previous iteration along with that of the previous layer z_{j-1} from the current iteration:

$$\begin{aligned} w_j^{[t+1]} &:= \underset{w_j}{\arg\min}\, \mathcal{L}_\rho(w_j, z_{j-1}^{[t+1]}, z_j^{[t]}, \boldsymbol{\lambda}_j^{[t]}) \\ &= \left(\mathbf{B}_j^{\mathsf{T}}\mathbf{B}_j + \rho\mathbf{I}\right)^{-1} \left(\mathbf{B}_j^{\mathsf{T}} z_{j-1}^{[t+1]} + \rho z_j^{[t]} - \boldsymbol{\lambda}_j^{[t]}\right) \end{aligned} \qquad (9)$$

This is an unconstrained linear least squares problem, so it's solution is given by solving a linear system of equations.

(2.) Next, z_j is updated by fixing the newly updated w_j along with the next layer's coefficients w_{j+1} from the previous iteration:

$$z_j^{[t+1]} := \arg\min_{z_j} \mathcal{L}_\rho(w_j^{[t+1]}, w_{j+1}^{[t]}, z_j, \lambda_j^{[t]}) \tag{10}$$

$$= \phi_j\left(\tfrac{1}{\rho+1}\mathbf{B}_{j+1} w_{j+1}^{[t]} + \tfrac{\rho}{\rho+1}(w_j^{[t+1]} + \tfrac{1}{\rho}\lambda_j^{[t]})\right)$$

$$z_l^{[t+1]} := \phi_j\left(w_j^{[t+1]} + \tfrac{1}{\rho}\lambda_j^{[t]}\right)$$

This is the proximal minimization problem from Eq. 5, so its solution is given in closed form via the proximal operator ϕ_j associated with the penalty function Φ_j. Note that for $j \neq l$, its argument is a convex combination of the current coefficients w_j and feedback that enforces consistency with the next layer.

(3.) Finally, the dual variables λ_j are updated with the constraint violations scaled by the penalty parameter ρ.

$$\lambda_j^{[t+1]} := \lambda_j^{[t]} + \rho(w_j^{[t+1]} - z_j^{[t+1]}) \tag{11}$$

This process is then repeated until convergence. Though not available as a closed-form expression, in the next section we demonstrate how this algorithm can be posed as a recurrent generalization of a feed-forward neural network.

4   Alternating Direction Neural Networks

Our inference algorithm essentially follows the same pattern as a deep neural network: for each layer, a learned linear transformation is applied to the previous output followed by a fixed nonlinear function. Building upon this observation, we implement it using a recurrent network with standard layers, thus allowing the model parameters to be learned using backpropagation.

Recall that the w_j update in Eq. 9 requires solving a linear system of equations. While differentiable, this introduces additional computational complexity not present in standard neural networks. To overcome this, we implicitly assume that the parameters in over-complete layers are Parseval tight frames, i.e. so that $\mathbf{B}_j\mathbf{B}_j^\mathsf{T} = \mathbf{I}$. This property is theoretically advantageous in the field of sparse approximation [8] and has been used as a constraint to encourage robustness in deep neural networks [32]. However, in our experiments we found that it was unnecessary to explicitly enforce this assumption during training; with appropriate learning rates, backpropagating through our inference algorithm was enough to ensure that repeated iterations did not result in diverging sequences of variable updates. Thus, under this assumption, we can simplify the update in Eq. 9 using the Woodbury matrix identity as follows:

$$w_j^{[t+1]} := \tilde{z}_j^{[t]} + \tfrac{1}{\rho+1}\mathbf{B}_j^\mathsf{T}(z_{j-1}^{[t+1]} - \mathbf{B}_j\tilde{z}_j^{[t]}), \quad \tilde{z}_j^{[t]} := z_j^{[t]} - \tfrac{1}{\rho}\lambda_j^{[t]} \tag{12}$$

As this only involves simple linear transformations, our ADMM algorithm for solving the optimization problem in our inference function f^* can be expressed as

Algorithm 1: Feed-Forward

Input: x, $\{\mathbf{B}_j, b_j\}$
Output: $\{w_j\}$, $\{z_j\}$
Initialize: $z_0 = x$
for $j = 1, \ldots, l$ **do**
$\quad$ Pre-activation:
$\quad$ $w_j := \mathbf{B}_j^\mathsf{T} z_{j-1}$
$\quad$ Activation:
$\quad$ $z_j := \phi_j(w_j - b_j)$
end

Algorithm 2: Alternating Direction Neural Network

Input: x, $\{\mathbf{B}_j, b_j\}$
Output: $\{w_j^{[T]}\}$, $\{z_j^{[T]}\}$
Initialize: $\{\boldsymbol{\lambda}_j^{[0]}\} = 0$, $\{w_j^{[1]}, z_j^{[1]}\}$ from Alg. 1
for $t = 1, \ldots, T - 1$ **do**
$\quad$ **for** $j = 1, \ldots, l$ **do**
$\quad\quad$ Dual: Update $\boldsymbol{\lambda}_j^{[t]}$ (Eq. 11)
$\quad\quad$ Pre-activation: Update $w_j^{[t+1]}$ (Eq. 12)
$\quad\quad$ Activation: Update $z_j^{[t+1]}$ (Eq. 10)
$\quad$ **end**
end

a recurrent neural network that repeatedly iterates until convergence. In practice, however, we unroll the network to a fixed number of iterations T for an approximation of optimal inference so that $f^{[T]}(x) \approx f^*(x)$. Our full algorithm is summarized in Algorithms 1 and 2.

4.1 Generalization of Feed-Forward Networks

Given proper initialization of the variables, a single iteration of this algorithm is identical to a single pass through a feed-forward network. Specifically, if we let $\boldsymbol{\lambda}_j^{[0]} = 0$ and $z_j^{[0]} = \mathbf{B}_j^\mathsf{T} z_{j-1}^{[1]}$, where we again denote $z_0^{[1]} = x$, then $w_j^{[1]}$ is equivalent to the pre-activation of a neural network layer:

$$w_j^{[1]} := \mathbf{B}_j^\mathsf{T} z_{j-1}^{[1]} + \tfrac{1}{\rho+1} \mathbf{B}_j^\mathsf{T} \big(z_{j-1}^{[1]} - \mathbf{B}_j(\mathbf{B}_j^\mathsf{T} z_{j-1}^{[1]}) \big) = \mathbf{B}_j^\mathsf{T} z_{j-1}^{[1]} \qquad (13)$$

Similarly, if we initialize $w_{j+1}^{[0]} = \mathbf{B}_{j+1}^\mathsf{T} w_j^{[1]}$, then $z_j^{[1]}$ is equivalent to the corresponding nonlinear activation using the proximal operator ϕ_j:

$$z_j^{[1]} := \phi_j\big(\tfrac{1}{\rho+1} \mathbf{B}_{j+1}(\mathbf{B}_{j+1}^\mathsf{T} w_j^{[1]}) + \tfrac{\rho}{\rho+1} w_j^{[1]} \big) = \phi_j\big(w_j^{[1]} \big) \qquad (14)$$

Thus, one iteration of our inference algorithm is equivalent to the standard feed-forward neural network given in Eq. 3, i.e. $f^{[1]}(x) = f^{\mathrm{DNN}}(x)$, where nonlinear activation functions are interpreted as proximal operators corresponding to the penalties of our DeepCA model. Additional iterations through the network lead to more accurate inference approximations while explicitly satisfying constraints on the latent variables.

4.2 Learning by Backpropagation

With DeepCA inference approximated by differentiable ADNNs, the model parameters can be learned in the same way as standard feed-forward networks. Extending the nested component analysis optimization problem from Eq. 2, the

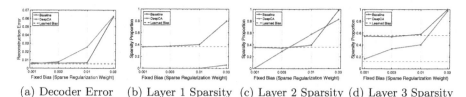

(a) Decoder Error   (b) Layer 1 Sparsity   (c) Layer 2 Sparsity   (d) Layer 3 Sparsity

Fig. 4. A demonstration of the effects of fixed (solid lines) and learnable (dotted lines) bias parameters on the reconstruction error (a) and activation sparsity (b–d) comparing feed forward networks (blue) with DeepCA (red). All models consist of three layers each with 512 components. Due to the conditional dependence provided by recurrent feedback, DeepCA learns to better control the sparsity level in order improve reconstruction error. As ℓ_1 regularization weights, the biases converge towards zero resulting in denser activations and higher network capacity for reconstruction.

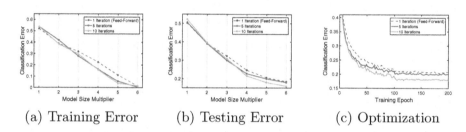

(a) Training Error   (b) Testing Error   (c) Optimization

Fig. 5. The effect of increasing model size on training (a) and testing (b) classification error, demonstrating consistently improved performance of ADNNs over feed-forward networks, especially in larger models. The base model consists of two 3×3, 2-strided convolutional layers followed by one fully-connected layer with 4, 8, and 16 components respectively. Also shown are is the classification error throughout training (c).

inference function $f^{[T]}$ can be used as a generalization of feed-forward network inference $f^{[1]}$ for backpropagation with arbitrary loss functions L that encourage the output to be consistent with provided supervision $y^{(i)}$, as shown in Eq. 15 below. Here, only the latent coefficients $f_l^{[T]}(x^{(i)})$ from the last layer are shown in the loss function, but other intermediate outputs $j \neq l$ could also be included.

$$\underset{\{\mathbf{B}_j, b_j\}}{\arg\min} \sum_{i=1}^n L\big(f_l^{[T]}(x^{(i)}), y^{(i)}\big) \tag{15}$$

From an agnostic perspective, an ADNN can thus be seen as an end-to-end deep network architecture with a particular sequence of linear and nonlinear transformations and tied weights. More iterations ($T > 1$) result in networks with greater effective depth, potentially allowing for the representation of more complex nonlinearities. However, because the network architecture was derived from an algorithm for inference in our DeepCA model instead of arbitrary compositions of parameterized transformations, the greater depth requires no additional

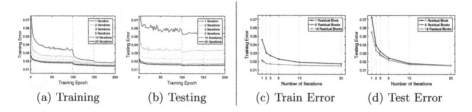

Fig. 6. Quantitative results demonstrating the improved generalization performance of ADNN inference. The training (a) and testing (b) reconstruction errors throughout optimization show that more iterations $(T > 1)$ substantially reduce convergence time and give much lower error on held-out test data. With a sufficiently large number of iterations, even lower-capacity models with encoders consisting of fewer residual blocks all achieve nearly the same level of performance with small discrepancies between training (c) and testing (d) errors.

parameters and serves the very specific purpose of satisfying constraints on the latent variables while enforcing consistency with the model parameters.

5   Experimental Results

In this section, we demonstrate some practical advantages of more accurate inference approximations in our DeepCA model using recurrent ADNNs over feed-forward networks. Even without additional prior knowledge, standard convolutional networks with ReLU activation functions still benefit from additional recurrent iterations as demonstrated by consistent improvements in both supervised and unsupervised tasks on the CIFAR-10 dataset [23]. Specifically, for an unsupervised autoencoder with an ℓ_2 reconstruction loss, Fig. 4 shows that the additional iterations of ADNNs allow for better sparsity control, resulting in higher network capacity through denser activations and lower reconstruction error. This suggests that recurrent feedback allows ADNNs to learn richer representation spaces by explicitly penalizing activation sparsity. For supervised classification with a cross-entropy loss, ADNNs also see improved accuracy as shown in Fig. 5, particularly for larger models with more parameters per layer. Because we treat layer biases as learned hyperparameters that modulate the relative weight of ℓ_1 activation penalties, this improvement could again be attributed to this adaptive sparsity encouraging more discriminative representations across semantic categories.

While these experiments emphasize the importance of sparsity in deep networks and justify our DeepCA model formulation, the effectiveness of feed-forward soft thresholding as an approximation of explicit ℓ_1 regularization limits the amount of additional capacity that can be achieved with more iterations. As such, ADNNs provide much greater performance gains when prior knowledge is available in the form of constraints that *cannot* be effectively approximated by feed-forward nonlinearities. This is exemplified by our application of output-constrained single-image depth prediction where simple feed-forward correction

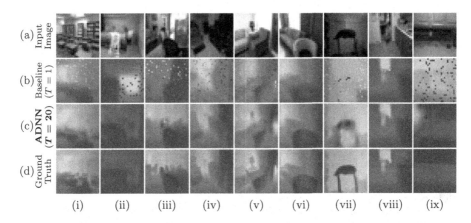

Fig. 7. Qualitative depth prediction results given a single image (a) and a sparse set of known depth values as input. Outputs of the baseline feed-forward model (b) are inconsistent with the constraints as evidenced by unrealistic discontinuities. An ADNN with $T = 20$ iterations (c) learns to enforce the constraints, resolving ambiguities for more detailed predictions that better agree with ground truth depth maps (d). Depending on the difficulty, additional iterations may have little effect on the output (viii) or be insufficient to consistently integrate the known constraint values (ix).

of the known depth values results in inconsistent discontinuities. We demonstrate this with the NYU-Depth V2 dataset [33], from which we sample 60k training images and 500 testing images from held-out scenes. To enable clearer visualization, we resize the images to 28×28 and then randomly sample 10% of the ground truth depth values to simulate known measurements. Following [30], our model architecture uses a ResNet encoder for feature extraction of the image concatenated with the known depth values as an additional input channel. This is followed by an ADNN decoder composed of three transposed convolution upsampling layers with biased ReLU nonlinearites in the first two layers and a constraint correction proximal operator in the last layer. Fig. 6 shows the mean absolute prediction errors of this model with increasing numbers of iterations and different encoder sizes. While all models have similar prediction error on training data, ADNNs with more iterations achieve significantly improved generalization performance, reducing the test error of the feed-forward baseline by over 72% from 0.054 to 0.015 with 20 iterations even with low-capacity encoders. Qualitative visualizations in Fig. 7 show that these improvements result from consistent constraint satisfaction that serves to resolve depth ambiguities.

In Fig. 8, we also show qualitative and quantitative results on the full-sized images, an easier problem due to reduced ambiguities provided by higher-resolution details. While feed-forward models have achieved good performance given sufficient model capacity [30], they generalize poorly due to globally-biased prediction errors causing disagreement with the known measurements. By explicitly enforcing agreement with the sparse output constraints, ADNNs reduce out-

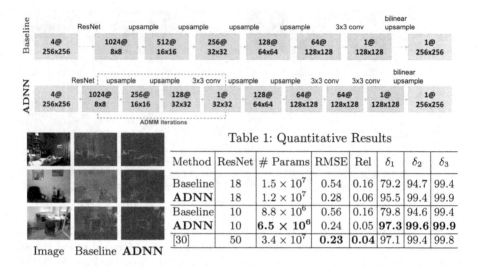

Table 1: Quantitative Results

Method	ResNet	# Params	RMSE	Rel	δ_1	δ_2	δ_3
Baseline	18	1.5×10^7	0.54	0.16	79.2	94.7	99.4
ADNN	18	1.2×10^7	0.28	0.06	95.5	99.4	99.9
Baseline	10	8.8×10^6	0.56	0.16	79.8	94.6	99.4
ADNN	10	$\mathbf{6.5 \times 10^6}$	0.24	0.05	**97.3**	**99.6**	**99.9**
[30]	50	3.4×10^7	**0.23**	**0.04**	97.1	99.4	99.8

Image   Baseline   **ADNN**

Fig. 8. Results on full-sized images from the NYU-Depth V2 dataset, comparing the feed-forward baseline and ADNN (with 10 iterations) architectures shown on top. On the left, example absolute error maps are visualized with lighter colors corresponding to higher errors and gray points indicating the locations of 200 randomly sampled measurements. On the right, quantitative metrics (following [30]) demonstrate the effect of changing the ResNet encoder size on prediction performance. Despite having far fewer learnable parameters, ADNNs perform comparably to a state-of-the-art feed-forward model due to explicit enforcement of the sparse output constraints.

liers and give improved test performance that is comparable with feed-forward networks requiring significantly more learnable parameters.

6   Conclusion

DeepCA is a novel deep model formulation that extends shallow component analysis techniques to increase representational capacity. Unlike feed-forward networks, intermediate network activations are interpreted as latent variables to be inferred using an iterative constrained optimization algorithm implemented as a recurrent ADNN. This allows for learning with arbitrary loss functions and provides a tool for consistently integrating prior knowledge in the form of constraints or regularization penalties. Due to its close relationship to feed-forward networks, which are equivalent to one iteration of this algorithm with proximal operators replacing nonlinear activation functions, DeepCA also provides a novel perspective from which to interpret deep learning, suggesting possible new directions for the analysis and design of network architectures from the perspective of sparse approximation theory.

References

1. Baldi, P., Hornik, K.: Neural networks and principal component analysis: learning from examples without local minima. Neural Netw. **2**(1), 53–58 (1989)
2. Bao, C., Ji, H., Quan, Y., Shen, Z.: Dictionary learning for sparse coding: algorithms and convergence analysis. Pattern Anal. Mach. Intell. (PAMI) **38**(7), 1356–1369 (2016)
3. Belagiannis, V., Zisserman, A.: Recurrent human pose estimation. In: International Conference on Automatic Face & Gesture Recognition (FG) (2017)
4. Bengio, Y., Courville, A., Vincent, P.: Representation learning: a review and new perspectives. Pattern Anal. Mach. Intell. (PAMI) **35**(8), 1798–1828 (2013)
5. Boyd, S., Parikh, N., Chu, E., Peleato, B., Eckstein, J.: Distributed optimization and statistical learning via the alternating direction method of multipliers. Found. Trends® Mach. Learn. **3**(1) (2011)
6. Brachmann, E., et al.: DSAC-differentiable RANSAC for camera localization. In: Conference on Computer Vision and Pattern Recognition (CVPR) (2017)
7. Carreira, J., Agrawal, P., Fragkiadaki, K., Malik, J.: Human pose estimation with iterative error feedback. In: Conference on Computer Vision and Pattern Recognition (CVPR) (2016)
8. Casazza, P.G., Kutyniok, G.: Finite Frames: Theory and Applications. Springer (2012)
9. Chen, C., Li, M., Liu, X., Ye, Y.: Extended ADMM and BCD for nonseparable convex minimization models with quadratic coupling terms: convergence analysis and insights. Math. Program. (2017)
10. Chen, L.C., Papandreou, G., Kokkinos, I., Murphy, K., Yuille, A.L.: DeepLab: semantic image segmentation with deep convolutional nets, atrous convolution, and fully connected CRFs. Pattern Anal. Mach. Intell. (PAMI) **PP**(99) (2017)
11. Chen, L.C., Schwing, A., Yuille, A., Urtasun, R.: Learning deep structured models. In: International Conference on Machine Learning (ICML) (2015)
12. Diamond, S., Sitzmann, V., Heide, F., Wetzstein, G.: Unrolled optimization with deep priors. arXiv preprint arXiv:1705.08041 (2017)
13. Gillis, N.: Sparse and unique nonnegative matrix factorization through data preprocessing. J. Mach. Learn. Res. (JMLR) **13**(November), 3349–3386 (2012)
14. Glorot, X., Bordes, A., Bengio, Y.: Deep sparse rectifier neural networks. In: International Conference on Artificial Intelligence and Statistics (AISTATS) (2011)
15. Gregor, K., LeCun, Y.: Learning fast approximations of sparse coding. In: International Conference on Machine Learning (ICML) (2010)
16. Haeffele, B., Young, E., Vidal, R.: Structured low-rank matrix factorization: Optimality, algorithm, and applications to image processing. In: International Conference on Machine Learning (ICML) (2014)
17. He, K., Zhang, X., Ren, S., Sun, J.: Identity mappings in deep residual networks. In: Leibe, B., Matas, J., Sebe, N., Welling, M. (eds.) ECCV 2016. LNCS, vol. 9908, pp. 630–645. Springer, Cham (2016). https://doi.org/10.1007/978-3-319-46493-0_38
18. Hu, P., Ramanan, D.: Bottom-up and top-down reasoning with hierarchical rectified gaussians. In: Conference on Computer Vision and Pattern Recognition (CVPR) (2016)
19. Huang, G., Liu, Z., Weinberger, K.Q., van der Maaten, L.: Densely connected convolutional networks. In: Conference on Computer Vision and Pattern Recognition (CVPR) (2017)

20. Huang, J., et al.: Speed/accuracy trade-offs for modern convolutional object detectors. In: Conference on Computer Vision and Pattern Recognition (CVPR) (2017)
21. Ioffe, S., Szegedy, C.: Batch normalization: Accelerating deep network training by reducing internal covariate shift. In: International Conference on Machine Learning (ICML), pp. 448–456 (2015)
22. Jutten, C., Herault, J.: Blind separation of sources, part I: an adaptive algorithm based on neuromimetic architecture. Signal Process. **24**(1), 1–10 (1991)
23. Krizhevsky, A., Hinton, G.: Learning multiple layers of features from tiny images. Technical report, University of Toronto (2009)
24. LeCun, Y., Bottou, L., Bengio, Y., Haffner, P.: Gradient-based learning applied to document recognition. Proc. IEEE **86**(11), 2278–2324 (1998)
25. Lee, D.D., Seung, H.S.: Learning the parts of objects by non-negative matrix factorization. Nature **401**(6755), 788–791 (1999)
26. Lee, H., Grosse, R., Ranganath, R., Ng, A.Y.: Convolutional deep belief networks for scalable unsupervised learning of hierarchical representations. In: International Conference on Machine Learning (ICML) (2009)
27. Li, K., Hariharan, B., Malik, J.: Iterative instance segmentation. In: Conference on Computer Vision and Pattern Recognition (CVPR) (2016)
28. Lin, C.H., Lucey, S.: Inverse compositional spatial transformer networks. In: Conference on Computer Vision and Pattern Recognition (CVPR) (2017)
29. Liu, T., Tao, D., Xu, D.: Dimensionality-dependent generalization bounds for k-dimensional coding schemes. Neural Comput. (2016)
30. Ma, F., Karaman, S.: Sparse-to-dense: depth prediction from sparse depth samples and a single image. In: International Conference on Robotics and Automation (ICRA) (2018)
31. Martins, A., Astudillo, R.: From softmax to sparsemax: a sparse model of attention and multi-label classification. In: International Conference on Machine Learning (ICML) (2016)
32. Moustapha, C., Piotr, B., Edouard, G., Yann, D., Nicolas, U.: Parseval networks: improving robustness to adversarial examples. arXiv preprint arXiv:1704.08847 (2017)
33. Silberman, N., Hoiem, D., Kohli, P., Fergus, R.: Indoor segmentation and support inference from RGBD images. In: Fitzgibbon, A., Lazebnik, S., Perona, P., Sato, Y., Schmid, C. (eds.) ECCV 2012. LNCS, vol. 7576, pp. 746–760. Springer, Heidelberg (2012). https://doi.org/10.1007/978-3-642-33715-4_54
34. Noh, H., Hong, S., Han, B.: Learning deconvolution network for semantic segmentation. In: International Conference on Computer Vision (ICCV) (2015)
35. Olshausen, B.A., et al.: Emergence of simple-cell receptive field properties by learning a sparse code for natural images. Nature **381**(6583), 607–609 (1996)
36. Papyan, V., Romano, Y., Elad, M.: Convolutional neural networks analyzed via convolutional sparse coding. J. Mach. Learn. Res. (JMLR) **18**(83) (2017)
37. Parikh, N., Boyd, S., et al.: Proximal algorithms. Found. Trends® Optim. **1**(3) (2014)
38. Patel, A.B., Nguyen, M.T., Baraniuk, R.: A probabilistic framework for deep learning. In: Advances in Neural Information Processing Systems (NIPS) (2016)
39. Simonyan, K., Zisserman, A.: Two-stream convolutional networks for action recognition in videos. In: Advances in Neural Information Processing Systems (NIPS) (2014)
40. Sulam, J., Papyan, V., Romano, Y., Elad, M.: Multi-layer convolutional sparse modeling: pursuit and dictionary learning. arXiv preprint arXiv:1708.08705 (2017)

41. Sun, J., Li, H., Xu, Z., et al.: Deep ADMM-net for compressive sensing MRI. In: Advances in Neural Information Processing Systems (NIPS) (2016)
42. Taylor, G., Burmeister, R., Xu, Z., Singh, B., Patel, A., Goldstein, T.: Training neural networks without gradients: A scalable ADMM approach. In: International Conference on Machine Learning (ICML) (2016)
43. Tulsiani, S., Zhou, T., Efros, A.A., Malik, J.: Multi-view supervision for single-view reconstruction via differentiable ray consistency. In: Conference on Computer Vision and Pattern Recognition (CVPR) (2017)
44. Wold, S., Esbensen, K., Geladi, P.: Principal component analysis. Chemom. Intell. Lab. Syst. **2**(1–3), 37–52 (1987)
45. Xu, Y., Yin, W.: A block coordinate descent method for regularized multiconvex optimization with applications to nonnegative tensor factorization and completion. SIAM J. Imaging Sci. **6**(3), 1758–1789 (2013)
46. Zamir, A.R., Wu, T.L., Sun, L., Shen, W., Malik, J., Savarese, S.: Feedback networks. In: Advances in Neural Information Processing Systems (NIPS) (2017)
47. Zhang, C., Bengio, S., Hardt, M., Recht, B., Vinyals, O.: Understanding deep learning requires rethinking generalization. In: International Conference on Learning Representations (ICLR) (2017)

ADVISE: Symbolism and External Knowledge for Decoding Advertisements

Keren Ye[✉] and Adriana Kovashka

University of Pittsburgh, Pittsburgh, PA 15260, USA
{yekeren,kovashka}@cs.pitt.edu

Abstract. In order to convey the most content in their limited space, advertisements embed references to outside knowledge via symbolism. For example, a motorcycle stands for adventure (a positive property the ad wants associated with the product being sold), and a gun stands for danger (a negative property to dissuade viewers from undesirable behaviors). We show how to use symbolic references to better understand the meaning of an ad. We further show how anchoring ad understanding in general-purpose object recognition and image captioning improves results. We formulate the ad understanding task as matching the ad image to human-generated statements that describe the action that the ad prompts, and the rationale it provides for taking this action. Our proposed method outperforms the state of the art on this task, and on an alternative formulation of question-answering on ads. We show additional applications of our learned representations for matching ads to slogans, and clustering ads according to their topic, without extra training.

Keywords: Advertisements · Symbolism · Question answering
External knowledge · Vision and language · Representation learning

1 Introduction

Advertisements are a powerful tool for affecting human behavior. Product ads convince us to make large purchases, e.g. for cars and home appliances, or small but recurrent purchases, e.g. for laundry detergent. Public service announcements (PSAs) encourage socially beneficial behaviors, e.g. combating domestic violence or driving safely. To stand out from the rest, ads have to be both eye-catching and memorable [71], while also conveying the information that the ad designer wants to impart. All this must be done in a limited space (one image) and time (however many seconds the viewer spends looking at the ad).

Electronic supplementary material The online version of this chapter (https:// doi.org/10.1007/978-3-030-01267-0_51) contains supplementary material, which is available to authorized users.

ⓒ Springer Nature Switzerland AG 2018
V. Ferrari et al. (Eds.): ECCV 2018, LNCS 11219, pp. 868–886, 2018.
https://doi.org/10.1007/978-3-030-01267-0_51

How can ads get the most "bang for their buck"? One technique is to make references to knowledge viewers already have, e.g. cultural knowledge, associations, and *symbolic mappings* humans have learned [34,35,54,57]. These symbolic references might come from literature (e.g. a snake symbolizes evil or danger), movies (a motorcycle symbolizes adventure or coolness), common sense (a flexed arm symbolizes strength), or pop culture (Usain Bolt symbolizes speed).

In this paper, we describe how to use symbolic mappings to predict the messages of advertisements. On one hand, we model how components of the ad image serve as visual anchors to concepts outside the image, using annotations in the Ads Dataset of [22]. On the other hand, we use knowledge sources external to the main task, such as object detection models, to better relate ad images to their corresponding messages. Both of these are forms of using outside knowledge, and they both boil down to learning links between objects and symbolic concepts. We use each type of knowledge in two ways, as a constraint or as an additive component for the learned image representation.

Fig. 1. Our key idea: Use symbolic associations shown in yellow (a gun symbolizes danger; a motorcycle symbolizes coolness) and recognized objects shown in red, to learn an image-text space where each ad maps to the correct statement that describes the message of the ad. The symbol "cool" brings images B and C closer together in the learned space, and further from image A and its associated symbol "danger." At test time (shown in orange), we use the learned image-text space to retrieve a matching statement for test image D. At test time, the symbol labels are *not* provided.

We focus on the following multiple-choice task, implemented via ranking: Given an image and several statements, the system must identify the correct statement to pair with the ad. For example, for test image D in Fig. 1, the system might predict the right statement is "Buy this drink because it's exciting." Our method learns a joint image-text embedding that associates ads with their corresponding messages. The method has three components: (1) an image embedding which takes into account individual regions in the image, (2) constraints on the learned space from symbol labels and object predictions, and (3) an additive expansion of the image representation using a symbol distribution. These three components are shown in Fig. 1, and all of them rely on external knowledge in the form of symbols and object predictions. Note that we can recognize the symbolic association to danger in Fig. 1 via two channels: either a direct classifier that learns to link certain visuals to the "danger" concept, or learning associations between actual *objects* in the image which can be recognized by object detection methods (e.g. "gun"), and symbolic concepts. We call our method ADVISE: **AD**s **VI**sual **S**emantic **E**mbedding.

We primarily focus on public service announcements, rather than product (commercial) ads. PSAs tend to be more conceptual and challenging, often involving multiple steps of reasoning. Quantitatively, 59% of the product ads in the dataset of [22] are straightforward, i.e. would be nearly solved with traditional recognition advancements. In contrast, only 33% of PSAs use straightforward strategies, while the remaining 67% use challenging non-literal rhetoric. Our method outperforms several recent baselines, including prior visual-semantic embeddings [10,11] and methods for understanding ads [22].

In addition to showing how to use external knowledge to solve ad-understanding, we demonstrate how recent advances in object recognition help with this task. While [22] evaluates basic techniques, it does not employ recent advances like region proposals [14,16,38,50] or attention [7,12,39,45,47,49,56, 67,69,70,75].

To summarize, our contributions are as follows:

- We show how to effectively use symbolism to better understand ads.
- We show how to make use of noisy caption predictions to bridge the gap between the abstract task of predicting the message of an ad, and more accessible information such as the objects present in the image. Detected objects are mapped to symbols via a domain-specific knowledge base.
- We improve the state of the art in understanding ads by 21%.
- We show for "abstract" PSAs, conceptual knowledge helps more, while for product ads, general-purpose object recognition techniques are more helpful.

The remainder of the paper is organized as follows. We overview related work in Sect. 2. In Sect. 3.1, we describe our ranking task, and in Sect. 3.2, we describe standard triplet embedding on ads. In Sect. 3.3, we discuss the representation of an image as a combination of region representations, weighed by their importance via an attention model. In Sect. 3.4, we describe how we use external knowledge to constrain the learned space. In Sect. 3.5, we develop an optional additive refinement of the image representation. In Sect. 4, we compare our method to the state of the art, and conduct ablation studies. We conclude in Sect. 5.

2 Related Work

Advertisements and Multimedia. The most related work to ours is [22] which proposes the problem of decoding ads, formulated as answering the question "*Why* should I [action]?" where [action] is what the ad suggests the viewer should do, e.g. buy a car or help prevent domestic violence. The dataset contains 64,832 image ads. Annotations include the topic (product or subject) of the ad, sentiments and actions the ad prompts, rationales provided for why the action should be done, symbolic mappings (referred to as signifier-signified, e.g.

motorcycle-adventure), etc. Considering the media domain more broadly, [26] analyze in what light a photograph portrays a politician, and [27] examine how the facial features of a candidate determine the outcome of an election. This work only applies to images of people. Also related is work in parsing infographics, charts and comics [4,23,29]. In contrast to these, our interest is analyzing the *implicit* arguments ads were created to make.

Vision, Language and Image-Text Embeddings. Recently there is great interest in joint vision-language tasks, e.g. captioning [2,8,9,13,25,28,32,47,55,61–63, 68,70,73], visual question answering [3,19,24,41,56,59,60,64,66,69,72,76,77], and cross-domain retrieval [5,6,36,74]. These often rely on learned image-text embeddings. [11,30] use triplet loss where an image and its corresponding human-provided caption should be closer in the space than pairs that do not match. [10] propose a bi-directional network to maximize correlation between matching images and text, akin to CCA [18]. None of these consider images with implicit persuasive intent, as we do. We compare against [10,11] in Sect. 4.

External Knowledge for Vision-Language Tasks. [24,60,64,66,77] examine the use of knowledge bases and perform explicit reasoning for answering visual questions. [62] use external sources to diversify their image captioning model. [43] learn to compose object classifiers by relating semantic and visual similarity. [15,42] use knowledge graphs or hierarchies to aid in object recognition. These works all use mappings that are objectively/scientifically grounded, i.e. lion is a type of cat. In contrast, we use cultural associations that arose in the media/literature and are internalized by humans, e.g. motorcycles are associated with adventure.

Region Proposals and Attention. Region proposals [14,16,38,50] guide an object detector to regions likely to contain objects. Attention [7,12,39,45,47,49,56,67, 69,70,75] focuses prediction tasks on regions likely to be relevant. We show that for our task, the attended-to regions must be those likely to be visual anchors for symbolic references.

3 Approach

We learn an embedding space where we can evaluate the similarity between ad images and ad messages. We use symbols and external knowledge in three ways: by representing the image as a weighted average of its regions that are likely to make symbolic references (Sect. 3.3), by enforcing that images with the same symbol labels or detected objects are close (Sect. 3.4), and by enhancing the image representation via an attention-masked symbol distribution (Sect. 3.5). In Sect. 4 we demonstrate the utility of each component.

3.1 Task and Dataset

In [22], the authors tackled answering the question "Q: Why should I [action]?" with "A: [one-word reason]." An example question-answer pair is "Q: Why should I speak up about domestic violence? A: bad." In other words, question-answering is formulated as a classification task. The ground-truth one-word answers in [22]'s evaluation are picked from human-provided full-sentence answers, also available in the dataset. However, using a single word is insufficient to capture the rhetoric of complex ads. On one hand, summarizing the full sentence using only one word is too challenging, for example, for the question "Q: Why should I buy authentic Adidas shoes?", the ground-truth answer "feet" used in [22] cannot convey both the meaning of "protect" and "feet" while the full-sentence answer "Because it will protect my feet" does capture both. On the other hand, picking one word as the answer may be misleading and imprecise, for example, for the "Q: Why should I buy the Triple Double Crunchwrap?", picking "short" from the sentence "Because it looks tasty and is only available for a short time" is problematic. Thus, while we show that we outperform prior art on the original question-answering task of [22], we focus on an alternative formulation.

We ask the system to pick which *action-reason statement* is most appropriate for the image. We retrieve statements in the format: "I should [action] because [reason]." e.g. "I should speak up about domestic violence because *being quiet is as bad as committing violence yourself.*" For each image, we use three related statements (i.e. statements provided by humans for this image) and randomly sample 47 unrelated statements (written for *other* images). The system must rank these 50 statements based on their similarity to the image.

This ranking task is akin to multiple-choice question-answering, which was also used in prior VQA works [3,59], but unlike these, we do not take the question as input. Similarly, in image captioning, [11,28] look for the most suitable image description from a much larger candidates pool.

3.2 Basic Image-Text Triplet Embedding

We first directly learn an embedding that optimizes for the ranking task. We require that the distance between an image and its corresponding statement should be smaller than the distance between that image and any other statement, or between other images and that statement. In other words, we minimize:

$$L(\boldsymbol{v}, \boldsymbol{t}; \boldsymbol{\theta}) = \sum_{i=1}^{K} \Big[\underbrace{\sum_{j \in N_{vt}(i)} \big[\|\boldsymbol{v}_i - \boldsymbol{t}_i\|_2^2 - \|\boldsymbol{v}_i - \boldsymbol{t}_j\|_2^2 + \beta\big]_+}_{\text{image as anchor, rank statements}}$$
$$+ \underbrace{\sum_{j \in N_{tv}(i)} \big[\|\boldsymbol{t}_i - \boldsymbol{v}_i\|_2^2 - \|\boldsymbol{t}_i - \boldsymbol{v}_j\|_2^2 + \beta\big]_+}_{\text{statement as anchor, rank images}} \Big] \tag{1}$$

where K is the batch size; β is the margin of triplet loss; $\boldsymbol{v}$ and $\boldsymbol{t}$ are the visual and textual embeddings we are learning, respectively; $\boldsymbol{v}_i$, $\boldsymbol{t}_i$ correspond to the same ad; $N_{vt}(i)$ is the negative statement set for the i-th image, and $N_{tv}(i)$ is the negative image set for the i-th statement, defined in Eq. 2. These two negative sample sets involve the most challenging k' examples within the size-K batch. A natural explanation of Eq. 2 is that it seeks to find a subset $A \subseteq \{1, ..., K\}$ which involves the k' most confusing examples.

$$N_{vt}(i) = \underset{\substack{A \subseteq \{1,...,K\}, \\ |A|=k'}}{\arg\min} \sum_{\substack{j \in A, \\ i \neq j}} \|v_i - t_j\|_2^2, \quad N_{tv}(i) = \underset{\substack{A \subseteq \{1,...,K\}, \\ |A|=k'}}{\arg\min} \sum_{\substack{j \in A, \\ i \neq j}} \|t_i - v_j\|_2^2 \quad (2)$$

Image Embedding. We extract the image's Inception-v4 CNN feature (1536-D) using [58], then use a fully-connected layer with parameter $w \in \mathbb{R}^{200 \times 1536}$ to project it to the 200-D joint embedding space:

$$v = w \cdot CNN(x) \quad (3)$$

Text Embedding. We use mean-pooling to aggregate word embedding vectors into 200-D text embedding t and use GloVe [48] to initialize the embedding matrix. There are two reasons for us to choose mean-pooling: (1) comparable performance to the LSTM[1], and (2) better interpretability. By using mean-pooling, image and words are projected to the same feature space, allowing us to assign word-level semantics to an image, or even to image regions. In contrast, LSTMs encode meaning of nearby words which is undesirable for interpretability.

Hard Negative Mining. Different ads might convey similar arguments, so the sampled negative may be a viable positive. For example, for a car ad with associated statement "I should buy the car because it's fast", a hard negative "I should drive the car because of its speed" may also be proper. Using the k' most challenging examples in the size-K batch (Eq. 2) is our trade-off between using all and using only the most challenging example, inspired by [11,17,53,65]. Our experiment (in supp) shows this trade-off is better than either extreme.

3.3   Image Embedding Using Symbol Regions

Since ads are carefully designed, they may involve complex narratives with several distinct components, i.e. several regions in the ad might need to be interpreted individually first to decode the full ad's meaning. Thus, we represent an image as a collection of its constituent regions, using an attention module to aggregate all the representations from different regions.

Importantly, the chosen regions should be those likely to serve as visual anchors for symbolic references (such as the motorcycle or shades in Fig. 1, rather than the bottles). Thus we consider all the 13,938 images, which are annotated as containing symbols, each with up to five bounding box annotations. Our intuition is that ads draw the viewer's attention in a particular way, and the symbol bounding boxes, without symbol labels, can be used to approximate

---

[1] Non-weighted/weighted mean-pooling of word embeddings achieved 2.45/2.47 rank. The last hidden layer of an LSTM achieved 2.74 rank, while non-weighted/weighted averaging of the hidden layers achieved 2.43/2.46, respectively. Lower is better.

this. More specifically, we use the SSD object detection model [38] implemented by [20], pre-train it on the COCO [37] dataset, and fine-tune it with the symbol bounding box annotations [22]. We show in Sect. 4.3 that this fine-tuning is crucial, i.e. general-purpose regions such as COCO boxes produce inferior results.

We use bottom-up attention [1,31,60] to aggregate the information from symbolic regions (see Fig. 2). More specifically, we use the Inception-v4 model [58] to extract the 1536-D CNN features for all symbol proposals. Then, for each CNN feature $x_i, i \in \{1, \ldots, M\}$ (we set $M = 10$, i.e., 10 proposals per image), a fully-connected layer is applied to project it to: (1) a 200-D embedding vector v_i (Eq. 4, $w \in \mathbb{R}^{200 \times 1536}$), and (2) a confidence score a_i saying how much the region should contribute to the final representation (Eq. 5, $w_a \in \mathbb{R}^{1 \times 1536}$). The final image representation z is a weighted sum of these region-based vectors (Eq. 6).

$$v_i = w \cdot CNN(x_i) \tag{4}$$

$$a_i = w_a \cdot CNN(x_i), \quad \alpha = softmax(a) \tag{5}$$

$$z = \sum_{i=1}^{M} \alpha_i v_i \tag{6}$$

The loss used to learn the image-text embedding is the same as in Eq. 1, but defined using the region-based image representation z instead of v: $L(z, t; \theta)$.

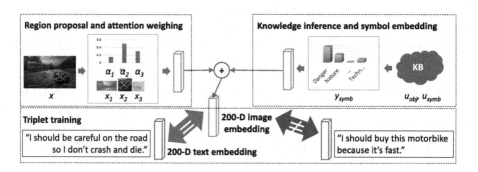

Fig. 2. Our image embedding model with knowledge branch. In the main branch (top left), multiple image symbolic anchors are proposed. Attention weighting is applied, and the image is represented as a weighted combination of the regions. The knowledge branch (top right) predicts the existence of symbols, maps these to 200-D, and adds them to the image embedding. We then perform triplet training to learn such an embedding space that keeps images close to their matching action-reason statements.

3.4 Constraints Via Symbols and Captions

We next exploit the symbol labels which are part of [22]. Symbols are abstract words such as "freedom" and "happiness" that provide additional information humans sense from the ads. We add additional constraints to the loss terms such that two images/statements that were annotated with the same symbol are closer in the learned space than images/statements annotated with different symbols. In the *extra* loss term (Eq. 7), s is the 200-D embedding of a symbol word; z is the 200-D region-based image representation defined in Eq. 6; and $N_{sz}(i)$ and $N_{st}(i)$ are the negative image/statement sets of the i-th symbol in the batch, defined similar to Eq. 2.

$$
L_{sym}(\boldsymbol{s}, \boldsymbol{z}, \boldsymbol{t}; \boldsymbol{\theta}) = \sum_{i=1}^{K} \Big[\underbrace{\sum_{j \in N_{sz}(i)} \big[\|\boldsymbol{s}_i - \boldsymbol{z}_i\|_2^2 - \|\boldsymbol{s}_i - \boldsymbol{z}_j\|_2^2 + \beta \big]_+}_{\text{symbol as anchor, rank images}}
$$

$$
+ \underbrace{\sum_{j \in N_{st}(i)} \big[\|\boldsymbol{s}_i - \boldsymbol{t}_i\|_2^2 - \|\boldsymbol{s}_i - \boldsymbol{t}_j\|_2^2 + \beta \big]_+}_{\text{symbol as anchor, rank statements}} \Big]
$$

(7)

Much like symbols, the objects found in an image are quite telling of the message of the ad. For example, environment ads often feature animals, safe driving ads feature cars, beauty ads feature faces, drink ads feature bottles, etc. However, since the Ads Dataset contains insufficient data to properly model object categories, we use DenseCap [25] to bridge the objects defined in Visual Genome [33] to the ads reasoning statements. More specifically, we use the DenseCap model to generate image captions and treat these as pre-fetched knowledge. For example, the caption "woman wearing a black dress" provides extra information about the objects in the image: "woman" and "black dress". We create additional constraints: If two images/statements have similar DenseCap predicted captions, they should be closer than images/statements with different captions. The *extra* loss term is defined similar to Eq. 7 using c for the caption representations.

In our setting, word embedding weights are not shared among the three vocabularies (ads statement, symbols, and DenseCap predictions). Our consideration is that the meaning of the same surface words may vary in these domains thus they need to have different embeddings. We weigh the symbol-based and object-based constraints by 0.1 since they in isolation do not tell the full story of the ad. We found that it is not sufficient to use *any* type of label as constraint in the domain of interest (see supp): using symbols as constraints gives greater benefit than the topic (product) labels in [22]'s dataset, and this point is not discussed in the general proxy learning literature [44].

3.5 Additive External Knowledge

In this section, we describe how to make use of external knowledge that is adaptively added, to compensate for inadequacies of the image embedding. This external knowledge can take the form of a mapping between physical objects and implicit concepts, or a classifier mapping pixels to concepts. Given a challenging ad, a human might look for visual cues and check if they remind him/her of concepts (e.g. "danger", "beauty", "nature") seen in other ads. Our model interprets ads in the same way: based on an external knowledge base, it *infers* the abstract symbols. In contrast to Sect. 3.4 which uses the *annotated* symbols at training time, here we use a *predicted* symbol distribution at both training and test time as a secondary image representation. Fig. 2 (top right) shows the general idea of the external knowledge branch. Note our model only uses external knowledge to compensate its own lack of knowledge (since we train the knowledge branch after the convergence of the visual semantic embedding branch), and it assigns small weights for uninformative knowledge.

We propose two ways to additively expand the image representation with external knowledge, and describe *two ways of setting y_{symb} in Eq. 8*. Both ways are a form of knowledge base (KB) mapping physical evidence to concepts.

KB Symbols. The first way is to directly train classifiers to link certain visuals to symbolic concepts. We learn a multilabel classifier u_{symb} to obtain a symbol distribution $y_{symb} = sigmoid(u_{symb} \cdot x)$. We learn a weight α_j^{symb} for each of $j \in \{1, \ldots, C = 53\}$ symbols from the Ads Dataset, denoting whether a particular symbol is helpful for the statement matching task.

KB Objects. The second method is to learn associations between surface words for detected objects and abstract concepts. For example, what type of ad might I see a "car" in? What about a "rock" or "animal"? We first construct a knowledge base associating object words to symbol words. We compute the similarity in the learned image-text embedding space between symbol words and DenseCap words, then create a mapping rule ("[object] implies [symbol]") for each symbol and its five most similar DenseCap words. This results in a $53 \times V$ matrix u_{obj}, where V is the size of DenseCap's vocabulary. Each row contains five entries of 1 denoting the mapping rule, and $V - 5$ entries of 0. Examples of learned mappings are shown in Table 3. For a given image, we use [25] to predict the three most probable words in the DenseCap vocabulary, and put the results in a multi-hot $y_{obj} \in \mathbb{R}^{V \times 1}$ vector. We then matrix-multiply to accumulate evidence for the presence of all symbols using the detected objects: $y_{symb} = u_{obj} \cdot y_{obj}$. We associate a weight α_{jl}^{symb} with each rule in the KB.

For both methods, we first use the attention weights α^{symb} as a mask, then project the 53-D symbol distribution y_{symb} into 200-D, and add it to the image embedding. This additive branch is most helpful when the information it contains is not already contained in the main image embedding branch. We found this happens when the discovered symbols are rare.

3.6   ADVISE: Our Final Model

Our final **AD**s **VI**sual **S**emantic **E**mbedding loss combines the losses from Sects. 3.2, 3.3, 3.4, and 3.5:

$$L_{final}(z, t, s, c; \theta) = L(z + y_{symb}, t; \theta) +$$
$$0.1 \, L_{sym}(s, z + y_{symb}, t; \theta) + 0.1 \, L_{obj}(c, z + y_{symb}, t; \theta) \tag{8}$$

4   Experimental Validation

We evaluate to what extent our proposed method is able to match an ad to its intended message (see Sect. 3.1). We present the baselines against which we compare (Sect. 4.1), our metrics (Sect. 4.2), quantitative results on our main ranking task (Sect. 4.3), results on QA as classification (Sect. 4.4) and on three additional tasks (Sect. 4.5). Please see the supplementary file for implementation details, in-depth quantitative results, and qualitative results.

4.1 Baselines

We compare our ADVISE method (Sect. 3.6) to the following approaches from recent literature. All methods are trained on the Ads Dataset [22], using a train/val/test split of 60%/20%/20%, resulting in around 39,000 images and more than 111,000 associated statements for training.

- HUSSAIN-RANKING adapts [22], the only prior method for decoding the message of ads. This method also uses symbol information, but in a less effective manner. The original method combines image, symbol, and question features, and trains for the 1000-way classification task. To adapt it, we pointwise-add the image features (Inception-v4 as for our method) and symbol features (distribution over 53 predicted symbols), and embed them in 200-D using Eq. 1 (using hard negative mining), setting v to the image-symbol feature. We tried four other ways (described in supp) of adapting [22] to ranking, but they performed worse.
- VSE++ [11] (follow-up to [30]) uses the same method as Sect. 3.2. It is representative of one major group of recent image-text embeddings using triplet-like losses [28,40,46,51].
- VSE, which is like VSE++ but without hard negative mining, for a more fair comparison to the next baseline.
- 2-WAY NETS uses our implementation of [10] (published code only demoed the network on MNIST) and is representative of a second type of image-text embeddings using reconstruction losses [10,21].

4.2 Metrics

We compute two metrics: Rank, which is the averaged ranking value of the highest-ranked true matching statement (highest possible rank is 1, which means first place), and Recall@3, which denotes the number of correct statements ranked in the Top-3. We expect a good model to have low Rank and high Recall scores. We use five random splits of the dataset into train/val/test sets, and show mean results and standard error over a total of 62,468 test cases (removing statements that do not follow the template "I should [action] because [reason].").

4.3 Results on the Main Ranking Task

We show the improvement that our method produces over state of the art methods, in Table 1. We show the better of the two alternative methods from Sect. 3.5, namely KB-SYMBOLS. Since public service announcements (e.g. domestic violence or anti-bullying campaigns) typically use different strategies and sentiments

Table 1. Our main result. We show two methods that do not use hard negative mining, and three that do. Our method greatly outperforms three recent methods in retrieving matching statements for each ad. All methods are trained on the Ads Dataset of [22]. The best method is shown in **bold**, and the second-best in *italics*.

Method	Rank (Lower ↓ is better)		Recall@3 (Higher ↑ is better)	
	PSA	Product	PSA	Product
2-WAY NETS	4.836 (± 0.090)	4.170 (± 0.023)	0.923 (± 0.016)	1.212 (± 0.004)
VSE	4.155 (± 0.091)	3.202 (± 0.019)	1.146 (± 0.017)	1.447 (± 0.004)
VSE++	4.139 (± 0.094)	3.110 (± 0.019)	1.197 (± 0.017)	1.510 (± 0.004)
HUSSAIN-RANKING	*3.854* (± 0.088)	*3.093* (± 0.019)	*1.258* (± 0.017)	*1.515* (± 0.004)
ADVISE (ours)	**3.013** (± 0.075)	**2.469** (± 0.015)	**1.509** (± 0.017)	**1.725** (± 0.004)

than product ads (e.g. ads for cars or coffee), we separately show the result for PSAs and products. We observe that our method greatly outperforms the prior relevant research. PSAs in general appear harder than product ads (see Sect. 1).

Compared to 2-WAY NETS [10], VSE which does *not* use hard negative mining is stronger by a large margin (14–23% for rank, and 19–24% for recall). VSE++ produces more accurate results than both 2-WAY NETS and VSE, but is outperformed by HUSSAIN-RANKING and our ADVISE. Our method is the strongest overall. It improves upon VSE++ [11] by 20–27% for rank, and 14–26% for recall. Compared to the strongest baseline, HUSSAIN-RANKING [22], our method is 20–21% stronger in terms of rank, and 13-19% stronger in recall. Fig. 3 shows a qualitative result contrasting the best methods.

We also conduct ablation studies to verify the benefit of each component of our method. We show the BASE TRIPLET embedding (Sect. 3.2) similar to VSE++; a GENERIC REGION embedding using image regions learned using [38] trained on the COCO [37] detection dataset; SYMBOL REGION embedding and ATTENTION (Sect. 3.3); adding SYMBOL/OBJECT constraints (Sect. 3.4); and including additive knowledge (Sect. 3.5) using either KB OBJECTS or KB SYMBOLS.

The results are shown in Table 2 (left for PSAs, right for products). We also show percent improvement of each new component, computed with respect to the previous row, except for KB OBJECTS and KB SYMBOLS, whose improvement is computed with respect to the third-to-last row, i.e. the method on which both KB methods are based. The largest increase in performance comes from focusing on individual regions within the image. This makes sense because ads are carefully designed and multiple elements work together to convey the message. We see that these regions must be learned as visual anchors to symbolic concepts (SYMBOL REGION vs GENERIC REGION) to further increase performance.

Beyond this, the story that the results tell differs between PSAs and products. Symbol/object constraints and additive branches are more helpful for the challenging, abstract PSAs that are the focus of our work. For PSAs, the additive inclusion of external information helps more when we directly predict the symbols (KB SYMBOLS), but also when we first extract objects and map these to

Table 2. (Left) Ablation study on PSAs. All external knowledge components except attention improve over basic triplet embedding. (Right) Ablation on products. General-purpose recognition approaches, e.g. regions and attention, produce the main boost.

Method	PSA				Product			
	Rank ↓	Rec@3 ↑	% improvement		Rank ↓	Rec@3 ↑	% improvement	
			Rank	Rec@3			Rank	Rec@3
BASE TRIPLET	4.139	1.197			3.110	1.510		
GENERIC REGION	3.444	1.375	17	15	2.650	1.670	15	11
SYMBOL REGION	3.174	1.442	8	5	2.539	1.697	4	2
+ ATTENTION	3.258	1.428	−3	−1	2.488	1.726	2	2
+ SYMBOL/OBJECT	3.149	1.466	3	3	2.469	1.727	1	<1
+ KB OBJECTS	3.108	1.482	1	1	2.471	1.725	<1	<1
+ KB SYMBOLS	3.013	1.509	4	3	2.469	1.725	<1	<1

VSE++: "I should try this makeup because its fun."

Hussain-ranking: "I should stop smoking because it destroys your looks."

ADVISE (ours): "I should be careful to how I treat Earth because when the water leaves we die."

VSE++: "I should wear Nivea because it leaves no traces."

Hussain-ranking: "I should be eating these because it has fresh ingredients."

ADVISE (ours): "I should buy GeoPack paper because their cutlery is eco-friendly."

Fig. 3. Our ADVISE method compared to the two stronger baselines. On the left, VSE++ incorrectly guessed this is a makeup ad, likely because often faces appear in makeup ads. HUSSAIN-RANKING correctly determined this is a PSA, but only our method was able to predict the topic, namely water/environment preservation. On the right, both HUSSAIN-RANKING and our method recognized the concepts of fresh-ness/naturalness, but our method picked a more specific statement.

symbols (KB OBJECTS). Note that KB SYMBOLS required 64,131 symbol labels. In contrast, KB OBJECTS relies on mappings between object and symbol words, which can be obtained more efficiently. While we obtain them as object-symbol similarities in our learned space, they could also be obtained from a purely textual, ad-specific resource. Thus, KB OBJECTS would generalize better to a new domain of ads (e.g. a different culture) where the data from [22] does not apply.

In Table 3, we show the object-symbol knowledge base that KB OBJECTS (Sect. 3.5) uses. We show "synonyms" across three vocabularies: the 53 symbol words from [22], the 27,999 words from the action/reason statements, and the 823 words from captions predicted for ads. We compute the nearest neighbors for each word in the learned space. This can be used as a "dictionary": If I see a given object, what should I predict the message of the ad is, or if I want to make a point, what objects should I use? In triplet ID 1, we see to allude to "comfort," one might use a soft sofa. From ID 2, if the statement contains "driving," perhaps this is a safe driving ad, where visuals allude to safety and injury, and contain cars and windshields. We observe the different role of "ketchup" (ID 3) vs "tomato" (ID 4): the former symbolizes flavor, and the latter health.

Table 3. Discovered synonyms between symbol, action/reason, and DenseCap words.

ID	Symbol	Statement	DenseCap
1	*comfort*	couch, sofa, soft	pillow, bed, blanket
2	safety, danger, injury	*driving*	car, windshield, van
3	delicious, hot, food	*ketchup*	beer, pepper, sauce
4	food, healthy, hunger	salads, food, salad	*tomato*

In Fig. 4, we show the learned association between the individual words and symbolic regions. By learning from the ads image and statement pairs, our ADVISE model propagates words in the statement to the regions in the image thus associates each label-agnostic region proposal with semantically meaningful words. At training time, we have neither box-level nor word-level annotations.

Fig. 4. Application for ads image retrieval (see details in supp). We extract the CNN feature of each image region (Eq. 4), then use the word embeddings of "abuse/abused" and "mascara" to retrieve the most similar image regions (denoted using green boxes).

4.4 Results on Question-Answering as Classification

For additional comparison to [22], we evaluate our method on the question-answering task formulated as 1000-way single-word answer classification (Sect. 3.1). We now directly optimize for this classification task, but add our symbol-based region proposals, symbol/object constraints, and additive knowledge-based image representation. Our implementation of the method of Hussain et al. [22] pointwise-adds Inception-v4 image features and the symbol distribution, and obtains 10.03% top-1 accuracy on PSAs, and 11.89% accuracy on product ads (or 11.69% average across ads regardless of type, which is dominated by product ads, and is close to the 11.96% reported in [22]). Representing the image with a weighted summation of generic regions produced 10.42% accuracy for PSAs, and 12.45% for products (a 4% and 5% improvement, respectively). Using our method resulted in 10.94% accuracy for PSAs, and 12.64%

for products (a 9% and 6% improvement over [22], respectively). Note that a method known to work well for many recognition tasks, i.e. region proposals, leads to very small improvement in the case of QA classification for ads, so it is unlikely that any particular method would lead to a large improvement on this task. This is why we believe the ranking task we evaluate in Sect. 4.3 is more meaningful.

Table 4. Other tasks our learned image-text embedding helps with. We show rank for the first two (lower is better) and homogeneity [52] for the third (higher is better).

Method	Hard statements ($\downarrow$ better)	Slogans ($\downarrow$ better)	Clustering ($\uparrow$ better)
HUSSAIN-RANKING	5.595 ($\pm$ 0.027)	4.082 ($\pm$ 0.090)	0.291 ($\pm$ 0.002)
VSE++	5.635 ($\pm$ 0.027)	4.102 ($\pm$ 0.091)	0.292 ($\pm$ 0.002)
ADVISE (ours)	**4.827** ($\pm$ 0.025)	**3.331** ($\pm$ 0.077)	**0.355** ($\pm$ 0.001)

4.5 Results on Additional Tasks

In Table 4, we demonstrate the versatility of our learned embedding, compared to the stronger two baselines from Table 1. None of the methods were retrained, i.e. we simply used the pre-trained embedding evaluated on statement ranking. First, we show a harder statement retrieval task: all statements that are to be ranked are from the same topic (e.g. all statements are about car safety or about beauty products). The second task uses creative captions that MTurk workers were asked to write for 2,000 ads in [22]. We rank these slogans, using an image as the query, and report the rank of the correct slogan. Finally, we check how well an embedding clusters ad images with respect to a ground-truth clustering defined by the topics of the ads.

5 Conclusion

We presented a method for matching image advertisements to statements which describe the idea of the ad. Our method uses external knowledge in the form of symbols and predicted objects in two ways, as constraints for a joint image-text embedding space, and as an additive component for the image representation. We also verify the effect of state-of-the-art object recognition techniques in the form of region proposals and attention. Our method outperforms existing image-text embedding techniques [10,11] and a previous ad-understanding technique [22] by a large margin. Our region embedding relying on visual symbolic anchors greatly improves upon traditional embeddings. For PSAs, regularizing with external info provides further benefit. In the future, we will investigate other external resources for decoding ads, such as predictions about the memorability or human attention over ads, and textual resources for additional mappings between physical and abstract content. We will use our object-symbol mappings to analyze the visual variability the same object category exhibits when used for different ad topics.

Acknowledgments. This material is based upon work supported by the National Science Foundation under Grant Number 1566270. This research was also supported by an NVIDIA hardware grant. Any opinions, findings, and conclusions or recommendations expressed in this material are those of the author(s) and do not necessarily reflect the views of the National Science Foundation. We thank the anonymous reviewers for their feedback and encouragement.

References

1. Anderson, P., et al.: Bottom-up and top-down attention for image captioning and visual question answering. In: The IEEE Conference on Computer Vision and Pattern Recognition (CVPR), June 2018
2. Anne Hendricks, L., Venugopalan, S., Rohrbach, M., Mooney, R., Saenko, K., Darrell, T.: Deep compositional captioning: describing novel object categories without paired training data. In: The IEEE Conference on Computer Vision and Pattern Recognition (CVPR), June 2016
3. Antol, S., et al.: VQA: visual question answering. In: The IEEE International Conference on Computer Vision (ICCV), Dec 2015
4. Bylinskii, Z., et al.: Understanding infographics through textual and visual tag prediction. arXiv preprint arXiv:1709.09215 (2017)
5. Cao, Y., Long, M., Wang, J., Liu, S.: Deep visual-semantic quantization for efficient image retrieval. In: CVPR (2017)
6. Chen, K., Bui, T., Fang, C., Wang, Z., Nevatia, R.: AMC: attention guided multimodal correlation learning for image search. In: The IEEE Conference on Computer Vision and Pattern Recognition (CVPR), July 2017
7. Chen, L.C., Yang, Y., Wang, J., Xu, W., Yuille, A.L.: Attention to scale: Scale-aware semantic image segmentation. In: Computer Vision and Pattern Recognition (CVPR). IEEE (2016)
8. Chen, T.H., Liao, Y.H., Chuang, C.Y., Hsu, W.T., Fu, J., Sun, M.: Show, adapt and tell: adversarial training of cross-domain image captioner. In: The IEEE International Conference on Computer Vision (ICCV), Oct 2017
9. Donahue, J., et al.: Long-term recurrent convolutional networks for visual recognition and description. In: The IEEE Conference on Computer Vision and Pattern Recognition (CVPR), June 2015
10. Eisenschtat, A., Wolf, L.: Linking image and text with 2-way nets. In: CVPR (2017)
11. Faghri, F., Fleet, D.J., Kiros, J.R., Fidler, S.: VSE++: improved visual-semantic embeddings. arXiv preprint arXiv:1707.05612 (2017)
12. Fu, J., Zheng, H., Mei, T.: Look closer to see better: recurrent attention convolutional neural network for fine-grained image recognition. In: IEEE Conference on Computer Vision and Pattern Recognition (CVPR) (2017)
13. Gan, C., Gan, Z., He, X., Gao, J., Deng, L.: Stylenet: generating attractive visual captions with styles. In: The IEEE Conference on Computer Vision and Pattern Recognition (CVPR), July 2017
14. Girshick, R., Donahue, J., Darrell, T., Malik, J.: Rich feature hierarchies for accurate object detection and semantic segmentation. In: Proceedings of the IEEE conference on computer vision and pattern recognition, pp. 580–587 (2014)
15. Goo, W., Kim, J., Kim, G., Hwang, S.J.: Taxonomy-regularized semantic deep convolutional neural networks. In: Leibe, B., Matas, J., Sebe, N., Welling, M. (eds.) ECCV 2016. LNCS, vol. 9906, pp. 86–101. Springer, Cham (2016). https://doi.org/10.1007/978-3-319-46475-6_6

16. He, K., Gkioxari, G., Dollar, P., Girshick, R.: Mask R-CNN. In: The IEEE International Conference on Computer Vision (ICCV), Oct 2017
17. Hermans, A., Beyer, L., Leibe, B.: In defense of the triplet loss for person re-identification. arXiv preprint arXiv:1703.07737 (2017)
18. Hotelling, H.: Relations between two sets of variates. Biometrika **28**(3/4), 321–377 (1936)
19. Hu, R., Andreas, J., Rohrbach, M., Darrell, T., Saenko, K.: Learning to reason: end-to-end module networks for visual question answering. In: The IEEE International Conference on Computer Vision (ICCV), Oct 2017
20. Huang, J., et al.: Speed/accuracy trade-offs for modern convolutional object detectors. In: The IEEE Conference on Computer Vision and Pattern Recognition (CVPR), July 2017
21. Hubert Tsai, Y.H., Huang, L.K., Salakhutdinov, R.: Learning robust visual-semantic embeddings. In: The IEEE International Conference on Computer Vision (ICCV), Oct 2017
22. Hussain, Z., et al.: Automatic understanding of image and video advertisements. In: The IEEE Conference on Computer Vision and Pattern Recognition (CVPR), July 2017
23. Iyyer, M., et al.: The amazing mysteries of the gutter: drawing inferences between panels in comic book narratives. In: The IEEE Conference on Computer Vision and Pattern Recognition (CVPR), July 2017
24. Johnson, J., et al.: Inferring and executing programs for visual reasoning. In: ICCV (2017)
25. Johnson, J., Karpathy, A., Fei-Fei, L.: Densecap: fully convolutional localization networks for dense captioning. In: The IEEE Conference on Computer Vision and Pattern Recognition (CVPR), June 2016
26. Joo, J., Li, W., Steen, F.F., Zhu, S.C.: Visual persuasion: Inferring communicative intents of images. In: Proceedings of the IEEE Conference on Computer Vision and Pattern Recognition (CVPR) (2014)
27. Joo, J., Steen, F.F., Zhu, S.C.: Automated facial trait judgment and election outcome prediction: social dimensions of face. In: Proceedings of the IEEE International Conference on Computer Vision, pp. 3712–3720 (2015)
28. Karpathy, A., Fei-Fei, L.: Deep visual-semantic alignments for generating image descriptions. In: The IEEE Conference on Computer Vision and Pattern Recognition (CVPR), June 2015
29. Kembhavi, A., Salvato, M., Kolve, E., Seo, M., Hajishirzi, H., Farhadi, A.: A diagram is worth a dozen images. In: Leibe, B., Matas, J., Sebe, N., Welling, M. (eds.) ECCV 2016. LNCS, vol. 9908, pp. 235–251. Springer, Cham (2016). https://doi.org/10.1007/978-3-319-46493-0_15
30. Kiros, R., Salakhutdinov, R., Zemel, R.S.: Unifying visual-semantic embeddings with multimodal neural language models. In: TACL (2015)
31. Krause, J., Johnson, J., Krishna, R., Fei-Fei, L.: A hierarchical approach for generating descriptive image paragraphs. In: The IEEE Conference on Computer Vision and Pattern Recognition (CVPR), July 2017
32. Krishna, R., Hata, K., Ren, F., Fei-Fei, L., Carlos Niebles, J.: Dense-captioning events in videos. In: The IEEE International Conference on Computer Vision (ICCV), Oct 2017
33. Krishna, R., Zhu, Y., Groth, O., Johnson, J., Hata, K., Kravitz, J., Chen, S., Kalantidis, Y., Li, L.J., Shamma, D.A.: Visual genome: connecting language and vision using crowdsourced dense image annotations. Int. J. Comput. Vis. **123**(1), 32–73 (2017)

34. Leigh, J.H., Gabel, T.G.: Symbolic interactionism: its effects on consumer behaviour and implications for marketing strategy. J. Serv. Mark. **6**(3), 5–16 (1992)

35. Levy, S.J.: Symbols for sale. Harv. Bus. Rev. **37**(4), 117–124 (1959)

36. Li, X., Hu, D., Lu, X.: Image2song: song retrieval via bridging image content and lyric words. In: The IEEE International Conference on Computer Vision (ICCV), Oct 2017

37. Lin, T.Y., et al.: Microsoft COCO: common objects in context. In: Fleet, D., Pajdla, T., Schiele, B., Tuytelaars, T. (eds.) ECCV 2014. LNCS, vol. 8693, pp. 740–755. Springer, Cham (2014). https://doi.org/10.1007/978-3-319-10602-1_48

38. Liu, W., et al.: SSD: single shot multibox detector. In: Leibe, B., Matas, J., Sebe, N., Welling, M. (eds.) ECCV 2016. LNCS, vol. 9905, pp. 21–37. Springer, Cham (2016). https://doi.org/10.1007/978-3-319-46448-0_2

39. Lu, J., Xiong, C., Parikh, D., Socher, R.: Knowing when to look: adaptive attention via a visual sentinel for image captioning. In: CVPR (2017)

40. Mai, L., Jin, H., Lin, Z., Fang, C., Brandt, J., Liu, F.: Spatial-semantic image search by visual feature synthesis. In: The IEEE Conference on Computer Vision and Pattern Recognition (CVPR), July 2017

41. Malinowski, M., Rohrbach, M., Fritz, M.: Ask your neurons: a neural-based approach to answering questions about images. In: The IEEE International Conference on Computer Vision (ICCV), Dec 2015

42. Marino, K., Salakhutdinov, R., Gupta, A.: The more you know: using knowledge graphs for image classification. In: The IEEE Conference on Computer Vision and Pattern Recognition (CVPR), July 2017

43. Misra, I., Gupta, A., Hebert, M.: From red wine to red tomato: composition with context. In: The IEEE Conference on Computer Vision and Pattern Recognition (CVPR), July 2017

44. Movshovitz-Attias, Y., Toshev, A., Leung, T.K., Ioffe, S., Singh, S.: No fuss distance metric learning using proxies. In: ICCV (2017)

45. Nam, H., Ha, J.W., Kim, J.: Dual attention networks for multimodal reasoning and matching. In: CVPR (2017)

46. Niu, Z., Zhou, M., Wang, L., Gao, X., Hua, G.: Hierarchical multimodal LSTM for dense visual-semantic embedding. In: The IEEE International Conference on Computer Vision (ICCV), Oct 2017

47. Pedersoli, M., Lucas, T., Schmid, C., Verbeek, J.: Areas of attention for image captioning. In: The IEEE International Conference on Computer Vision (ICCV), Oct 2017

48. Pennington, J., Socher, R., Manning, C.: Glove: global vectors for word representation. In: Proceedings of the 2014 Conference on Empirical Methods in Natural Language Processing (EMNLP), pp. 1532–1543 (2014)

49. Ren, M., Zemel, R.S.: End-to-end instance segmentation with recurrent attention. In: The IEEE Conference on Computer Vision and Pattern Recognition (CVPR), July 2017

50. Ren, S., He, K., Girshick, R., Sun, J.: Faster R-CNN: towards real-time object detection with region proposal networks. In: Advances in Neural Information Processing Systems, pp. 91–99 (2015)

51. Ren, Z., Jin, H., Lin, Z., Fang, C., Yuille, A.: Joint image-text representation by gaussian visual-semantic embedding. In: Proceedings of the 2016 ACM on Multimedia Conference, pp. 207–211. ACM (2016)

52. Rosenberg, A., Hirschberg, J.: V-measure: a conditional entropy-based external cluster evaluation measure. In: EMNLP-CoNLL, vol. 7, pp. 410–420 (2007)

53. Schroff, F., Kalenichenko, D., Philbin, J.: Facenet: A unified embedding for face recognition and clustering. In: Proceedings of the IEEE Conference on Computer Vision and Pattern Recognition (CVPR), pp. 815–823 (2015)
54. Scott, L.M.: Images in advertising: the need for a theory of visual rhetoric. J. Consum. Res. **21**(2), 252–273 (1994)
55. Shetty, R., Rohrbach, M., Anne Hendricks, L., Fritz, M., Schiele, B.: Speaking the same language: matching machine to human captions by adversarial training. In: The IEEE International Conference on Computer Vision (ICCV), Oct 2017
56. Shih, K.J., Singh, S., Hoiem, D.: Where to look: focus regions for visual question answering. In: Computer Vision and Pattern Recognition (CVPR). IEEE (2016)
57. Spears, N.E., Mowen, J.C., Chakraborty, G.: Symbolic role of animals in print advertising: content analysis and conceptual development. J. Bus. Res. **37**(2), 87–95 (1996)
58. Szegedy, C., Ioffe, S., Vanhoucke, V., Alemi, A.A.: Inception-v4, inception-resnet and the impact of residual connections on learning. In: AAAI (2017). https://arxiv.org/abs/1602.07261
59. Tapaswi, M., Zhu, Y., Stiefelhagen, R., Torralba, A., Urtasun, R., Fidler, S.: Movieqa: understanding stories in movies through question-answering. In: The IEEE Conference on Computer Vision and Pattern Recognition (CVPR), June 2016
60. Teney, D., Anderson, P., He, X., van den Hengel, A.: Tips and tricks for visual question answering: learnings from the 2017 challenge. In: The IEEE Conference on Computer Vision and Pattern Recognition (CVPR), June 2018
61. Vedantam, R., Bengio, S., Murphy, K., Parikh, D., Chechik, G.: Context-aware captions from context-agnostic supervision. In: The IEEE Conference on Computer Vision and Pattern Recognition (CVPR), July 2017
62. Venugopalan, S., Anne Hendricks, L., Rohrbach, M., Mooney, R., Darrell, T., Saenko, K.: Captioning images with diverse objects. In: The IEEE Conference on Computer Vision and Pattern Recognition (CVPR), July 2017
63. Vinyals, O., Toshev, A., Bengio, S., Erhan, D.: Show and tell: a neural image caption generator. In: Proceedings of the IEEE Conference on Computer Vision and Pattern Recognition, pp. 3156–3164 (2015)
64. Wang, P., Wu, Q., Shen, C., Dick, A., van den Hengel, A.: FVQA: fact-based visual question answering. IEEE Trans. Pattern Anal. Mach. Intell. (2017)
65. Wu, C.Y., Manmatha, R., Smola, A.J., Krahenbuhl, P.: Sampling matters in deep embedding learning. In: The IEEE International Conference on Computer Vision (ICCV), Oct 2017
66. Wu, Q., Wang, P., Shen, C., Dick, A., van den Hengel, A.: Ask me anything: free-form visual question answering based on knowledge from external sources. In: The IEEE Conference on Computer Vision and Pattern Recognition (CVPR), June 2016
67. Xu, H., Saenko, K.: Ask, attend and answer: exploring question-guided spatial attention for visual question answering. In: Leibe, B., Matas, J., Sebe, N., Welling, M. (eds.) ECCV 2016. LNCS, vol. 9911, pp. 451–466. Springer, Cham (2016). https://doi.org/10.1007/978-3-319-46478-7_28
68. Yang, L., Tang, K., Yang, J., Li, L.J.: Dense captioning with joint inference and visual context. In: The IEEE Conference on Computer Vision and Pattern Recognition (CVPR), July 2017
69. Yang, Z., He, X., Gao, J., Deng, L., Smola, A.: Stacked attention networks for image question answering. In: Computer Vision and Pattern Recognition (CVPR). IEEE (2016)

70. You, Q., Jin, H., Wang, Z., Fang, C., Luo, J.: Image captioning with semantic attention. In: The IEEE Conference on Computer Vision and Pattern Recognition (CVPR), June 2016
71. Young, C.E.: The Advertising Research Handbook. Ideas in Flight (2005)
72. Yu, L., Park, E., Berg, A.C., Berg, T.L.: Visual madlibs: fill in the blank description generation and question answering. In: The IEEE International Conference on Computer Vision (ICCV), Dec 2015
73. Yu, Y., Choi, J., Kim, Y., Yoo, K., Lee, S.H., Kim, G.: Supervising neural attention models for video captioning by human gaze data. In: The IEEE Conference on Computer Vision and Pattern Recognition (CVPR), July 2017
74. Yu, Y., Ko, H., Choi, J., Kim, G.: End-to-end concept word detection for video captioning, retrieval, and question answering. In: The IEEE Conference on Computer Vision and Pattern Recognition (CVPR), July 2017
75. Zheng, H., Fu, J., Mei, T., Luo, J.: Learning multi-attention convolutional neural network for fine-grained image recognition. In: The IEEE International Conference on Computer Vision (ICCV), Oct 2017
76. Zhu, Y., Groth, O., Bernstein, M., Fei-Fei, L.: Visual7w: grounded question answering in images. In: The IEEE Conference on Computer Vision and Pattern Recognition (CVPR), June 2016
77. Zhu, Y., Lim, J.J., Fei-Fei, L.: Knowledge acquisition for visual question answering via iterative querying. In: The IEEE Conference on Computer Vision and Pattern Recognition (CVPR), July 2017

Author Index

Printed in the United States
By Bookmasters